with Microsoft®

Office 2010

Volume 1

**Shelley Gaskin, Robert L. Ferrett,
Alicia Vargas, and Carolyn McLellan**

Prentice Hall
Boston Columbus Indianapolis New York San Francisco Upper Saddle River
Amsterdam Cape Town Dubai London Madrid Milan Munich Paris Montreal Toronto
Delhi Mexico City Sao Paulo Sydney Hong Kong Seoul Singapore Taipei Tokyo

Associate VP/Executive Acquisitions Editor, Print:
   Stephanie Wall
Editorial Project Manager: Laura Burgess
Editor in Chief: Michael Payne
Product Development Manager: Eileen Bien Calabro
Development Editor: Ginny Munroe
Editorial Assistant: Nicole Sam
Director of Marketing: Kate Valentine
Marketing Manager: Tori Olson Alves
Marketing Coordinator: Susan Osterlitz
Marketing Assistant: Darshika Vyas
Senior Managing Editor: Cynthia Zonneveld
Associate Managing Editor: Camille Trentacoste
Production Project Manager: Mike Lackey
Operations Director: Alexis Heydt
Operations Specialist: Natacha Moore

Senior Art Director: Jonathan Boylan
Cover Photo: © Ben Durrant
Text and Cover Designer: Blair Brown
Manager, Cover Visual Research & Permissions:
   Karen Sanatar
Manager, Rights and Permissions: Zina Arabia
AVP/Director of Online Programs, Media: Richard Keaveny
AVP/Director of Product Development, Media: Lisa Strite
Media Project Manager, Editorial: Alana Coles
Media Project Manager, Production: John Cassar
Full-Service Project Management: PreMediaGlobal
Composition: PreMediaGlobal
Printer/Binder: Quad/Graphics Taunton
Cover Printer: Lehigh-Phoenix Color
Text Font: Bookman Light

Credits and acknowledgments borrowed from other sources and reproduced, with permission, in this textbook appear on appropriate page within text. Photos appearing in Word chapters 1 and 2 supplied by Robert Ferrett and used with permission. Photos appearing in PowerPoint chapters 1 and 3 supplied by Alicia Vargas and used with permission.

Microsoft® and Windows® are registered trademarks of the Microsoft Corporation in the U.S.A. and other countries. Screen shots and icons reprinted with permission from the Microsoft Corporation. This book is not sponsored or endorsed by or affiliated with the Microsoft Corporation.

Library of Congress Cataloging-in-Publication Data
Go! with Microsoft Office 2010 / Shelley Gaskin ... [et al.].
     p. cm.
  "Volume 1."
  Includes index.
  ISBN-13: 978-0-13-245446-9
  ISBN-10: 0-13-245446-7
  1. Microsoft Office. 2. Business—Computer programs. I. Gaskin, Shelley.
  HF5548.4.M525G6254 2011
  005.5—dc22

                                    2010019636

10 9 8 7 6 5 4 3

Prentice Hall
is an imprint of

www.pearsonhighered.com

ISBN 10: 0-13-245446-7
ISBN 13: 978-0-13-245446-9

Brief Contents

Contents

Word

Chapter 1 Creating Documents with Microsoft Word 2010 49

Chapter 3 Analyzing Data with Pie Charts, Line Charts, and What-If Analysis Tools 353

Access

Chapter 1 Getting Started with Access Databases 417

Chapter 2   Sort and Query a Database 483

Chapter 3   Forms, Filters, and Reports 551

Business Running Case 1: Access Chapters 1–3 617

PowerPoint

Chapter 1 Getting Started with PowerPoint 621

GO! System Contributors

We thank the following people for their hard work and support in making the *GO!* System all that it is!

Instructor Resource Authors

Adickes, Erich	Parkland College	Holland, Susan	Southeast Community College-Nebraska
Baray, Carrie	Ivy Tech Community College		
Clausen, Jane	Western Iowa Tech Community College	Landenberger, Toni	Southeast Community College-Nebraska
Crossley, Connie	Cincinnati State Technical and Community College	McMahon, Richard	University of Houston—Downtown
		Miller, Sandra	Wenatchee Valley College
Emrich, Stefanie	Metropolitan Community College of Omaha, Nebraska	Niebur, Katherine	Dakota County Technical College
		Nowakowski, Anthony	Buffalo State
Faix, Dennis	Harrisburg Area Community College	Pierce, Tonya	Ivy Tech Community College
Hadden, Karen	Western Iowa Tech Community College	Roselli, Diane	Harrisburg Area Community College
		St. John, Steve	Tulsa Community College
Hammerle, Patricia	Indiana University/Purdue University at Indianapolis	Sterr, Jody	Blackhawk Technical College
		Thompson, Joyce	Lehigh Carbon Community College
Hines, James	Tidewater Community College	Tucker, William	Austin Community College

Technical Editors

Matthew Bisi	Barbara Edington	Joyce Nielsen	Jan Snyder
Mary Corcoran	Sarah Evans	Janet Pickard	Mara Zebest
Lori Damanti	Adam Layne	Sean Portnoy	

Student Reviewers

Albinda, Sarah Evangeline	Phoenix College	Innis, Tim	Tulsa Community College
Allen, John	Asheville-Buncombe Tech Community College	Jarboe, Aaron	Central Washington University
		Key, Penny	Greenville Technical College
Alexander, Steven	St. Johns River Community College	Klein, Colleen	Northern Michigan University
Alexander, Melissa	Tulsa Community College	Lloyd, Kasey	Ivy Tech Bloomington
Bolz, Stephanie	Northern Michigan University	Moeller, Jeffrey	Northern Michigan University
Berner, Ashley	Central Washington University	Mullen, Sharita	Tidewater Community College
Boomer, Michelle	Northern Michigan University	Nelson, Cody	Texas Tech University
Busse, Brennan	Northern Michigan University	Nicholson, Regina	Athens Tech College
Butkey, Maura	Central Washington University	Niehaus, Kristina	Northern Michigan University
Cates, Concita	Phoenix College	Nisa, Zaibun	Santa Rosa Community College
Charles, Marvin	Harrisburg Area Community College	Nunez, Nohelia	Santa Rosa Community College
		Oak, Samantha	Central Washington University
Christensen, Kaylie	Northern Michigan University	Oberly, Sara	Harrisburg Area Community College Lancaster
Clark, Glen D. III	Harrisburg Area Community College		
		Oertii, Monica	Central Washington University
Cobble, Jan N.	Greenville Technical College	Palenshus, Juliet	Central Washington University
Connally, Brianna	Central Washington University	Pohl, Amanda	Northern Michigan University
Davis, Brandon	Northern Michigan University	Presnell, Randy	Central Washington University
Davis, Christen	Central Washington University	Reed, Kailee	Texas Tech University
De Jesus Garcia, Maria	Phoenix College	Ritner, April	Northern Michigan University
Den Boer, Lance	Central Washington University	Roberts, Corey	Tulsa Community College
Dix, Jessica	Central Washington University	Rodgers, Spencer	Texas Tech University
Moeller, Jeffrey	Northern Michigan University	Rodriguez, Flavia	Northwestern State University
Downs, Elizabeth	Central Washington University	Rogers, A.	Tidewater Community College
Elser, Julie	Harrisburg Area Community College	Rossi, Jessica Ann	Central Washington University
		Rothbauer, Taylor	Trident Technical College
Erickson, Mike	Ball State University	Rozelle, Lauren	Texas Tech University
Frye, Alicia	Phoenix College	Schmadeke, Kimberly	Kirkwood Community College
Gadomski, Amanda	Northern Michigan University	Shafapay, Natasha	Central Washington University
Gassert, Jennifer	Harrisburg Area Community College	Shanahan, Megan	Northern Michigan University
		Sullivan, Alexandra Nicole	Greenville Technical College
Gross, Mary Jo	Kirkwood Community College	Teska, Erika	Hawaii Pacific University
Gyselinck, Craig	Central Washington University	Torrenti, Natalie	Harrisburg Area Community College
Harrison, Margo	Central Washington University		
Hatt, Patrick	Harrisburg Area Community College	Traub, Amy	Northern Michigan University
Heacox, Kate	Central Washington University	Underwood, Katie	Central Washington University
Hedgman, Shaina	Tidewater College	Walters, Kim	Central Washington University
Hill, Cheretta	Northwestern State University	Warren, Jennifer L.	Greenville Technical College
Hochstedler, Bethany	Harrisburg Area Community College Lancaster	Wilson, Kelsie	Central Washington University
		Wilson, Amanda	Green River Community College
Homer, Jean	Greenville Technical College	Wylie, Jimmy	Texas Tech University

Series Reviewers

Abraham, Reni	Houston Community College	Cannon, Kim	Greenville Technical College
Addison, Paul	Ivy Tech Community College	Carreon, Cleda	Indiana University—Purdue University, Indianapolis
Agatston, Ann	Agatston Consulting Technical College	Carriker, Sandra	North Shore Community College
Akuna, Valeria, Ph.D.	Estrella Mountain Community College	Casey, Patricia	Trident Technical College
		Cates, Wally	Central New Mexico Community College
Alexander, Melody	Ball Sate University		
Alejandro, Manuel	Southwest Texas Junior College	Chaffin, Catherine	Shawnee State University
Alger, David	Tidewater Community College Chesapeake Campus	Chauvin, Marg	Palm Beach Community College, Boca Raton
Allen, Jackie	Rowan-Cabarrus Community College	Challa, Chandrashekar	Virginia State University
		Chamlou, Afsaneh	NOVA Alexandria
Ali, Farha	Lander University	Chapman, Pam	Wabaunsee Community College
Amici, Penny	Harrisburg Area Community College	Christensen, Dan	Iowa Western Community College
Anderson, Patty A.	Lake City Community College	Clay, Betty	Southeastern Oklahoma State University
Andrews, Wilma	Virginia Commonwealth College, Nebraska University		
Anik, Mazhar	Tiffin University	Collins, Linda D.	Mesa Community College
Armstrong, Gary	Shippensburg University	Cone, Bill	Northern Arizona University
Arnold, Linda L.	Harrisburg Area Community College	Conroy-Link, Janet	Holy Family College
		Conway, Ronald	Bowling Green State University
Ashby, Tom	Oklahoma City Community College	Cornforth, Carol G.	WVNCC
		Cosgrove, Janet	Northwestern CT Community
Atkins, Bonnie	Delaware Technical Community College	Courtney, Kevin	Hillsborough Community College
		Coverdale, John	Riverside Community College
Aukland, Cherie	Thomas Nelson Community College	Cox, Rollie	Madison Area Technical College
		Crawford, Hiram	Olive Harvey College
Bachand, LaDonna	Santa Rosa Community College	Crawford, Sonia	Central New Mexico Community College
Bagui, Sikha	University of West Florida		
Beecroft, Anita	Kwantlen University College	Crawford, Thomasina	Miami-Dade College, Kendall Campus
Bell, Paula	Lock Haven College		
Belton, Linda	Springfield Tech. Community College	Credico, Grace	Lethbridge Community College
		Crenshaw, Richard	Miami Dade Community College, North
Bennett, Judith	Sam Houston State University		
Bhatia, Sai	Riverside Community College	Crespo, Beverly	Mt. San Antonio College
Bishop, Frances	DeVry Institute—Alpharetta (ATL)	Crooks, Steven	Texas Tech University
Blaszkiewicz, Holly	Ivy Tech Community College/Region 1	Crossley, Connie	Cincinnati State Technical Community College
Boito, Nancy	HACC Central Pennsylvania's Community College	Curik, Mary	Central New Mexico Community College
Borger-Boglin, Grietje L.	San Antonio College/Northeast Lakeview College	De Arazoza, Ralph	Miami Dade Community College
		Danno, John	DeVry University/Keller Graduate School
Branigan, Dave	DeVry University		
Bray, Patricia	Allegany College of Maryland	Davis, Phillip	Del Mar College
Britt, Brenda K.	Fayetteville Technical Community College	Davis, Richard	Trinity Valley Community College
		Davis, Sandra	Baker College of Allen Park
Brotherton, Cathy	Riverside Community College	Dees, Stephanie D.	Wharton County Junior College
Brown, Judy	Western Illinois University	DeHerrera, Laurie	Pikes Peak Community College
Buehler, Lesley	Ohlone College	Delk, Dr. K. Kay	Seminole Community College
Buell, C	Central Oregon Community College	Denton, Bree	Texas Tech University
		Dix, Jeanette	Ivy Tech Community College
Burns, Christine	Central New Mexico Community College	Dooly, Veronica P.	Asheville-Buncombe Technical Community College
Byars, Pat	Brookhaven College	Doroshow, Mike	Eastfield College
Byrd, Julie	Ivy Tech Community College	Douglas, Gretchen	SUNYCortland
Byrd, Lynn	Delta State University, Cleveland, Mississippi	Dove, Carol	Community College of Allegheny
		Dozier, Susan	Tidewater Community College, Virginia Beach Campus
Cacace, Richard N.	Pensacola Junior College		
Cadenhead, Charles	Brookhaven College	Driskel, Loretta	Niagara Community College
Calhoun, Ric	Gordon College	Duckwiler, Carol	Wabaunsee Community College
Cameron, Eric	Passaic Community College	Duhon, David	Baker College
Canine, Jill	Ivy Tech Community College of Indiana	Duncan, Mimi	University of Missouri-St. Louis
		Duthie, Judy	Green River Community College
Cannamore, Madie	Kennedy King	Duvall, Annette	Central New Mexico Community College

Ecklund, Paula — Duke University
Eilers, Albert — Cincinnati State Technical and Community College
Eng, Bernice — Brookdale Community College
Epperson, Arlin — Columbia College
Evans, Billie — Vance-Granville Community College
Evans, Jean — Brevard Community College
Feuerbach, Lisa — Ivy Tech East Chicago
Finley, Jean — ABTCC
Fisher, Fred — Florida State University
Foster, Nancy — Baker College
Foster-Shriver, Penny L. — Anne Arundel Community College
Foster-Turpen, Linda — CNM
Foszcz, Russ — McHenry County College
Fry, Susan — Boise State University
Fustos, Janos — Metro State
Gallup, Jeanette — Blinn College
Gelb, Janet — Grossmont College
Gentry, Barb — Parkland College
Gerace, Karin — St. Angela Merici School
Gerace, Tom — Tulane University
Ghajar, Homa — Oklahoma State University
Gifford, Steve — Northwest Iowa Community College
Glazer, Ellen — Broward Community College
Gordon, Robert — Hofstra University
Gramlich, Steven — Pasco-Hernando Community College
Graviett, Nancy M. — St. Charles Community College, St. Peters, Missouri
Greene, Rich — Community College of Allegheny County
Gregoryk, Kerry — Virginia Commonwealth State
Griggs, Debra — Bellevue Community College
Grimm, Carol — Palm Beach Community College
Guthrie, Rose — Fox Valley Technical College
Hahn, Norm — Thomas Nelson Community College
Haley-Hunter, Deb — Bluefield State College
Hall, Linnea — Northwest Mississippi Community College
Hammerschlag, Dr. Bill — Brookhaven College
Hansen, Michelle — Davenport University
Hayden, Nancy — Indiana University—Purdue University, Indianapolis
Hayes, Theresa — Broward Community College
Headrick, Betsy — Chattanooga State
Helfand, Terri — Chaffey College
Helms, Liz — Columbus State Community College
Hernandez, Leticia — TCI College of Technology
Hibbert, Marilyn — Salt Lake Community College
Hinds, Cheryl — Norfolk State University
Hines, James — Tidewater Community College
Hoffman, Joan — Milwaukee Area Technical College
Hogan, Pat — Cape Fear Community College
Holland, Susan — Southeast Community College
Holliday, Mardi — Community College of Philadelphia
Hollingsworth, Mary Carole — Georgia Perimeter College
Hopson, Bonnie — Athens Technical College
Horvath, Carrie — Albertus Magnus College
Horwitz, Steve — Community College of Philadelphia

Hotta, Barbara — Leeward Community College
Howard, Bunny — St. Johns River Community
Howard, Chris — DeVry University
Huckabay, Jamie — Austin Community College
Hudgins, Susan — East Central University
Hulett, Michelle J. — Missouri State University
Humphrey, John — Asheville Buncombe Technical Community College
Hunt, Darla A. — Morehead State University, Morehead, Kentucky
Hunt, Laura — Tulsa Community College
Ivey, Joan M. — Lanier Technical College
Jacob, Sherry — Jefferson Community College
Jacobs, Duane — Salt Lake Community College
Jauken, Barb — Southeastern Community
Jerry, Gina — Santa Monica College
Johnson, Deborah S. — Edison State College
Johnson, Kathy — Wright College
Johnson, Mary — Kingwood College
Johnson, Mary — Mt. San Antonio College
Jones, Stacey — Benedict College
Jones, Warren — University of Alabama, Birmingham
Jordan, Cheryl — San Juan College
Kapoor, Bhushan — California State University, Fullerton
Kasai, Susumu — Salt Lake Community College
Kates, Hazel — Miami Dade Community College, Kendall
Keen, Debby — University of Kentucky
Keeter, Sandy — Seminole Community College
Kern-Blystone, Dorothy Jean — Bowling Green State
Kerwin, Annette — College of DuPage
Keskin, Ilknur — The University of South Dakota
Kinney, Mark B. — Baker College
Kirk, Colleen — Mercy College
Kisling, Eric — East Carolina University
Kleckner, Michelle — Elon University
Kliston, Linda — Broward Community College, North Campus
Knuth, Toni — Baker College of Auburn Hills
Kochis, Dennis — Suffolk County Community College
Kominek, Kurt — Northeast State Technical Community College
Kramer, Ed — Northern Virginia Community College
Kretz, Daniel — Fox Valley Technical College
Laird, Jeff — Northeast State Community College
Lamoureaux, Jackie — Central New Mexico Community College
Lange, David — Grand Valley State
LaPointe, Deb — Central New Mexico Community College
Larsen, Jacqueline Anne — A-B Tech
Larson, Donna — Louisville Technical Institute
Laspina, Kathy — Vance-Granville Community College
Le Grand, Dr. Kate — Broward Community College
Lenhart, Sheryl — Terra Community College
Leonard, Yvonne — Coastal Carolina Community College
Letavec, Chris — University of Cincinnati
Lewis, Daphne L, Ed.D. — Wayland Baptist University
Lewis, Julie — Baker College-Allen Park
Liefert, Jane — Everett Community College

Lindaman, Linda	Black Hawk Community College
Lindberg, Martha	Minnesota State University
Lightner, Renee	Broward Community College
Lindberg, Martha	Minnesota State University
Linge, Richard	Arizona Western College
Logan, Mary G.	Delgado Community College
Loizeaux, Barbara	Westchester Community College
Lombardi, John	South University
Lopez, Don	Clovis-State Center Community College District
Lopez, Lisa	Spartanburg Community College
Lord, Alexandria	Asheville Buncombe Tech
Lovering, LeAnne	Augusta Technical College
Lowe, Rita	Harold Washington College
Low, Willy Hui	Joliet Junior College
Lucas, Vickie	Broward Community College
Luna, Debbie	El Paso Community College
Luoma, Jean	Davenport University
Luse, Steven P.	Horry Georgetown Technical College
Lynam, Linda	Central Missouri State University
Lyon, Lynne	Durham College
Lyon, Pat Rajski	Tomball College
Macarty, Matthew	University of New Hampshire
MacKinnon, Ruth	Georgia Southern University
Macon, Lisa	Valencia Community College, West Campus
Machuca, Wayne	College of the Sequoias
Mack, Sherri	Butler County Community College
Madison, Dana	Clarion University
Maguire, Trish	Eastern New Mexico University
Malkan, Rajiv	Montgomery College
Manning, David	Northern Kentucky University
Marcus, Jacquie	Niagara Community College
Marghitu, Daniela	Auburn University
Marks, Suzanne	Bellevue Community College
Marquez, Juanita	El Centro College
Marquez, Juan	Mesa Community College
Martin, Carol	Harrisburg Area Community College
Martin, Paul C.	Harrisburg Area Community College
Martyn, Margie	Baldwin-Wallace College
Marucco, Toni	Lincoln Land Community College
Mason, Lynn	Lubbock Christian University
Matutis, Audrone	Houston Community College
Matkin, Marie	University of Lethbridge
Maurel, Trina	Odessa College
May, Karen	Blinn College
McCain, Evelynn	Boise State University
McCannon, Melinda	Gordon College
McCarthy, Marguerite	Northwestern Business College
McCaskill, Matt L.	Brevard Community College
McClellan, Carolyn	Tidewater Community College
McClure, Darlean	College of Sequoias
McCrory, Sue A.	Missouri State University
McCue, Stacy	Harrisburg Area Community College
McEntire-Orbach, Teresa	Middlesex County College
McKinley, Lee	Georgia Perimeter College
McLeod, Todd	Fresno City College
McManus, Illyana	Grossmont College
McPherson, Dori	Schoolcraft College
Meck, Kari	HACC
Meiklejohn, Nancy	Pikes Peak Community College
Menking, Rick	Hardin-Simmons University
Meredith, Mary	University of Louisiana at Lafayette
Mermelstein, Lisa	Baruch College
Metos, Linda	Salt Lake Community College
Meurer, Daniel	University of Cincinnati
Meyer, Colleen	Cincinnati State Technical and Community College
Meyer, Marian	Central New Mexico Community College
Miller, Cindy	Ivy Tech Community College, Lafayette, Indiana
Mills, Robert E.	Tidewater Community College, Portsmouth Campus
Mitchell, Susan	Davenport University
Mohle, Dennis	Fresno Community College
Molki, Saeed	South Texas College
Monk, Ellen	University of Delaware
Moore, Rodney	Holland College
Morris, Mike	Southeastern Oklahoma State University
Morris, Nancy	Hudson Valley Community College
Moseler, Dan	Harrisburg Area Community College
Nabors, Brent	Reedley College, Clovis Center
Nadas, Erika	Wright College
Nadelman, Cindi	New England College
Nademlynsky, Lisa	Johnson & Wales University
Nagengast, Joseph	Florida Career College
Nason, Scott	Rowan Cabarrus Community College
Ncube, Cathy	University of West Florida
Newsome, Eloise	Northern Virginia Community College Woodbridge
Nicholls, Doreen	Mohawk Valley Community College
Nicholson, John R.	Johnson County Community College
Nielson, Phil	Salt Lake Community College
Nunan, Karen L.	Northeast State Technical Community College
O'Neal, Lois Ann	Rogers State University
Odegard, Teri	Edmonds Community College
Ogle, Gregory	North Community College
Orr, Dr. Claudia	Northern Michigan University South
Orsburn, Glen	Fox Valley Technical College
Otieno, Derek	DeVry University
Otton, Diana Hill	Chesapeake College
Oxendale, Lucia	West Virginia Institute of Technology
Paiano, Frank	Southwestern College
Pannell, Dr. Elizabeth	Collin College
Patrick, Tanya	Clackamas Community College
Paul, Anindya	Daytona State College
Peairs, Deb	Clark State Community College
Perez, Kimberly	Tidewater Community College
Porter, Joyce	Weber State University
Prince, Lisa	Missouri State University-Springfield Campus
Proietti, Kathleen	Northern Essex Community College
Puopolo, Mike	Bunker Hill Community College
Pusins, Delores	HCCC
Putnam, Darlene	Thomas Nelson Community College

Raghuraman, Ram	Joliet Junior College	Sullivan, Denise	Westchester Community College
Rani, Chigurupati	BMCC/CUNY	Sullivan, Joseph	Joliet Junior College
Reasoner, Ted Allen	Indiana University—Purdue	Swart, John	Louisiana Tech University
Reeves, Karen	High Point University	Szurek, Joseph	University of Pittsburgh at Greensburg
Remillard, Debbie	New Hampshire Technical Institute		
Rhue, Shelly	DeVry University	Taff, Ann	Tulsa Community College
Richards, Karen	Maplewoods Community College	Taggart, James	Atlantic Cape Community College
Richardson, Mary	Albany Technical College	Tarver, Mary Beth	Northwestern State University
Rodgers, Gwen	Southern Nazarene University	Taylor, Michael	Seattle Central Community College
Rodie, Karla	Pikes Peak Community College	Terrell, Robert L.	Carson-Newman College
Roselli, Diane Maie	Harrisburg Area Community College	Terry, Dariel	Northern Virginia Community College
Ross, Dianne	University of Louisiana in Lafayette		
Rousseau, Mary	Broward Community College, South	Thangiah, Sam	Slippery Rock University
Rovetto, Ann	Horry-Georgetown Technical College	Thayer, Paul	Austin Community College
Rusin, Iwona	Baker College	Thompson, Joyce	Lehigh Carbon Community College
Sahabi, Ahmad	Baker College of Clinton Township	Thompson-Sellers, Ingrid	Georgia Perimeter College
Samson, Dolly	Hawaii Pacific University	Tomasi, Erik	Baruch College
Sams, Todd	University of Cincinnati	Toreson, Karen	Shoreline Community College
Sandoval, Everett	Reedley College	Townsend, Cynthia	Baker College
Santiago, Diana	Central New Mexico Community College	Trifiletti, John J.	Florida Community College at Jacksonville
Sardone, Nancy	Seton Hall University	Trivedi, Charulata	Quinsigamond Community College, Woodbridge
Scafide, Jean	Mississippi Gulf Coast Community College		
		Tucker, William	Austin Community College
Scheeren, Judy	Westmoreland County Community College	Turgeon, Cheryl	Asnuntuck Community College
		Turpen, Linda	Central New Mexico Community College
Scheiwe, Adolph	Joliet Junior College		
Schneider, Sol	Sam Houston State University	Upshaw, Susan	Del Mar College
Schweitzer, John	Central New Mexico Community College	Unruh, Angela	Central Washington University
		Vanderhoof, Dr. Glenna	Missouri State University-Springfield Campus
Scroggins, Michael	Southwest Missouri State University		
Sedlacek, Brenda	Tidewater Community College	Vargas, Tony	El Paso Community College
Sell, Kelly	Anne Arundel Community College	Vicars, Mitzi	Hampton University
Sever, Suzanne	Northwest Arkansas Community College	Villarreal, Kathleen	Fresno
		Vitrano, Mary Ellen	Palm Beach Community College
Sewell, John	Florida Career College	Vlaich-Lee, Michelle	Greenville Technical College
Sheridan, Rick	California State University-Chico	Volker, Bonita	Tidewater Community College
Silvers, Pamela	Asheville Buncombe Tech	Waddell, Karen	Butler Community College
Sindt, Robert G.	Johnson County Community College	Wahila, Lori (Mindy)	Tompkins Cortland Community College
Singer, Noah	Tulsa Community College		
Singer, Steven A.	University of Hawai'i, Kapi'olani Community College	Wallace, Melissa	Lanier Technical College
		Walters, Gary B.	Central New Mexico Community College
Sinha, Atin	Albany State University		
Skolnick, Martin	Florida Atlantic University	Waswick, Kim	Southeast Community College, Nebraska
Smith, Kristi	Allegany College of Maryland		
Smith, Patrick	Marshall Community and Technical College	Wavle, Sharon M.	Tompkins Cortland Community College
		Webb, Nancy	City College of San Francisco
Smith, Stella A.	Georgia Gwinnett College	Webb, Rebecca	Northwest Arkansas Community College
Smith, T. Michael	Austin Community College		
Smith, Tammy	Tompkins Cortland Community Collge	Weber, Sandy	Gateway Technical College
		Weissman, Jonathan	Finger Lakes Community College
Smolenski, Bob	Delaware County Community College	Wells, Barbara E.	Central Carolina Technical College
		Wells, Lorna	Salt Lake Community College
Smolenski, Robert	Delaware Community College	Welsh, Jean	Lansing Community College Nebraska
Southwell, Donald	Delta College		
Spangler, Candice	Columbus State	White, Bruce	Quinnipiac University
Spangler, Candice	Columbus State Community College	Willer, Ann	Solano Community College
Stark, Diane	Phoenix College	Williams, Mark	Lane Community College
Stedham, Vicki	St. Petersburg College, Clearwater	Williams, Ronald D.	Central Piedmont Community College
Stefanelli, Greg	Carroll Community College		
Steiner, Ester	New Mexico State University	Wilms, Dr. G. Jan	Union University
Stenlund, Neal	Northern Virginia Community College, Alexandria	Wilson, Kit	Red River College
		Wilson, MaryLou	Piedmont Technical College
St. John, Steve	Tulsa Community College	Wilson, Roger	Fairmont State University
Sterling, Janet	Houston Community College	Wimberly, Leanne	International Academy of Design and Technology
Stoughton, Catherine	Laramie County Community College		
Sullivan, Angela	Joliet Junior College		

Winters, Floyd — Manatee Community College
Worthington, Paula — Northern Virginia Community College
Wright, Darrell — Shelton State Community College
Wright, Julie — Baker College
Yauney, Annette — Herkimer County Community College

Yip, Thomas — Passaic Community College
Zavala, Ben — Webster Tech
Zaboski, Maureen — University of Scranton
Zlotow, Mary Ann — College of DuPage
Zudeck, Steve — Broward Community College, North
Zullo, Matthew D. — Wake Technical Community College

About the Authors

Shelley Gaskin, Series Editor, is a professor in the Business and Computer Technology Division at Pasadena City College in Pasadena, California. She holds a bachelor's degree in Business Administration from Robert Morris College (Pennsylvania), a master's degree in Business from Northern Illinois University, and a doctorate in Adult and Community Education from Ball State University. Before joining Pasadena City College, she spent 12 years in the computer industry where she was a systems analyst, sales representative, and Director of Customer Education with Unisys Corporation. She also worked for Ernst & Young on the development of large systems applications for their clients. She has written and developed training materials for custom systems applications in both the public and private sector, and has written and edited numerous computer application textbooks.

This book is dedicated to my students, who inspire me every day.

Robert L. Ferrett recently retired as the Director of the Center for Instructional Computing at Eastern Michigan University, where he provided computer training and support to faculty. He has authored or co-authored more than 70 books on Access, PowerPoint, Excel, Publisher, WordPerfect, Windows, Word, OpenOffice, and Computer Fundamentals. He has been designing, developing, and delivering computer workshops for more than three decades. Before writing for the *GO! Series*, Bob was a series editor for the Learn Series. He has a bachelor's degree in Psychology, a master's degree in Geography, and a master's degree in Interdisciplinary Technology from Eastern Michigan University. His doctoral studies were in Instructional Technology at Wayne State University.

I'd like to dedicate this book to my wife Mary Jane, whose constant support has been so important all these years.

Alicia Vargas is a faculty member in Business Information Technology at Pasadena City College. She holds a master's and a bachelor's degree in business education from California State University, Los Angeles, and has authored several textbooks and training manuals on Microsoft Word, Microsoft Excel, and Microsoft PowerPoint.

This book is dedicated with all my love to my husband Vic, who makes everything possible; and to my children Victor, Phil, and Emmy, who are an unending source of inspiration and who make everything worthwhile.

Carolyn McLellan is the Dean of the Division of Information Technology and Business at Tidewater Community College in Virginia Beach, Virginia. She has a master's degree in Secondary Education from Regent University and a bachelor's degree in Business Education from Old Dominion University. She taught for Norfolk Public Schools for 17 years in Business Education and served as a faculty member at Tidewater Community College for eight years teaching networking, where she developed over 23 new courses and earned the Microsoft Certified Trainer and Microsoft Certified System Engineer industry certifications. In addition to teaching, Carolyn loves to play volleyball, boogie board at the beach, bicycle, crochet, cook, and read.

This book is dedicated to my daughters, Megan and Mandy, who have my eternal love; to my mother, Jean, who always believes in me and encouraged me to become a teacher; to my sister Debbie, who was my first student and who inspires me with her strength in overcoming hardships; to my niece Jenna, for her bravery, composure, and beauty; to my grandsons, Damon and Jordan, who bring me happiness and a renewed joie de vie; and to the students and IT faculty at Tidewater Community College.

Teach the Course You Want in Less Time

A Microsoft® Office textbook designed for student success!

- **Project-Based** – Students learn by creating projects that they will use in the real world.

- **Microsoft Procedural Syntax** – Steps are written to put students in the right place at the right time.

- **Teachable Moment** – Expository text is woven into the steps—at the moment students need to know it—not chunked together in a block of text that will go unread.

- **Sequential Pagination** – Students have actual page numbers instead of confusing letters and abbreviations.

Student Outcomes and Learning Objectives – Objectives are clustered around projects that result in student outcomes.

Project Activities – A project summary stated clearly and quickly.

Project Files – Clearly shows students which files are needed for the project and the names they will use to save their documents.

Scenario – Each chapter opens with a story that sets the stage for the projects the student will create.

Project Results – Shows students how their final outcome will appear.

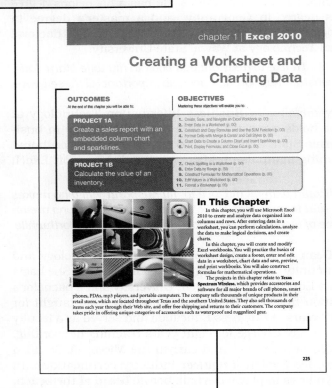

Objective 1 | Create, Save, and Navigate an Excel Workbook

On startup, Excel displays a new blank *workbook*—the Excel document that stores your data—which contains one or more pages called a *worksheet*. A worksheet—or *spreadsheet*—is stored in a workbook, and is formatted as a pattern of uniformly spaced horizontal rows and vertical columns. The intersection of a column and a row forms a box referred to as *a cell*.

Activity 1.01 | Starting Excel and Naming and Saving a Workbook

1 **Start** Excel. In the lower right corner of the window, if necessary, click the Normal button, and then to the right, locate the zoom—magnification—level.

Your zoom level should be 100%, although some figures in this textbook may be shown at a higher zoom level.

Another Way
Use the keyboard shortcut [F12] to display the Save As dialog box.

2 In the upper left corner of your screen, click the **File tab** to display *Backstage* view, click **Save As**, and then in the **Save As** dialog box, navigate to the location where you will store your workbooks for this chapter.

3 In your storage location, create a new folder named **Excel Chapter 1** Open the new folder to display its folder window, and then in the **File name** box, notice that *Book1* displays as the default file name.

4 In the **File name** box, click *Book1* to select it, and then using your own name, type **Lastname_Firstname_1A_Quarterly_Sales** being sure to include the underscore (Shift) + [-] instead of spaces between words. Compare your screen with Figure 1.2.

Figure 1.2

Path to your new Excel Chapter 1 folder in address bar

File name with your name and underscores between words

Save button

Project 1A: Sales Report with Embedded Column Chart and Sparklines | Excel **227**

---

6 In the vertical scroll bar, click the **down scroll arrow** one time to move **Row 1** out of view.

A *row* is a horizontal group of cells. Beginning with number 1, a unique number identifies each row—this is the *row heading*, located at the left side of the worksheet. A single worksheet has 1,048,576 rows.

7 In the lower left corner, click the **Sheet1 tab**.

The first worksheet in the workbook becomes the active worksheet. By default, new workbooks contain three worksheets. When you save a workbook, the worksheets are contained within it and do not have separate file names.

8 Use the skills you just practiced to scroll horizontally to display **column A**, and if necessary, **row 1**.

Objective 2 | Enter Data in a Worksheet

Cell content, which is anything you type in a cell, can be one of two things: either a *constant value*—referred to simply as a *value*—or a *formula*. A formula is an equation that performs mathematical calculations on values in your worksheet. The most commonly used values are *text values* and *number values*, but a value can also include a date or a time of day.

Activity 1.03 | Entering Text and Using AutoComplete

A text value, also referred to as a *label*, usually provides information about number values in other worksheet cells. For example, a title such as First Quarter Accessory Sales gives the reader an indication that the data in the worksheet relates to information about sales of accessories during the three-month period January through March.

1 Click the **Sheet1 tab** to make it the active sheet. Point to and then click the cell at the intersection of **column A** and **row 1** to make it the *active cell*—the cell is outlined in black and ready to accept data.

The intersecting column letter and row number form the *cell reference*—also called the *cell address*. When a cell is active, its column letter and row number are highlighted. The cell reference of the selected cell, A1, displays in the Name Box.

2 With cell **A1** as the active cell, type the worksheet title **Texas Spectrum Wireless** and then press Enter. Compare your screen with Figure 1.7.

Text or numbers in a cell are referred to as *data*. You must confirm the data you type in a cell by pressing Enter or by some other keyboard movement, such as pressing Tab or an arrow key. Pressing Enter moves the selection to the cell below.

230 Excel

End-of-Chapter

Content-Based Assessments – Assessments with defined solutions.

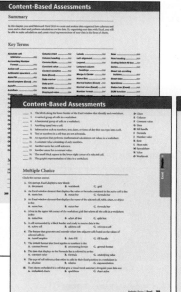

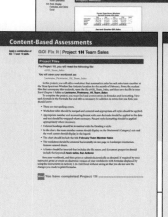

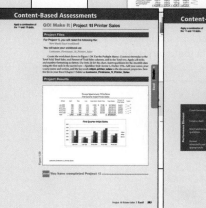

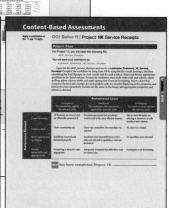

End-of-Chapter

Outcomes-Based Assessments – Assessments with open-ended solutions.

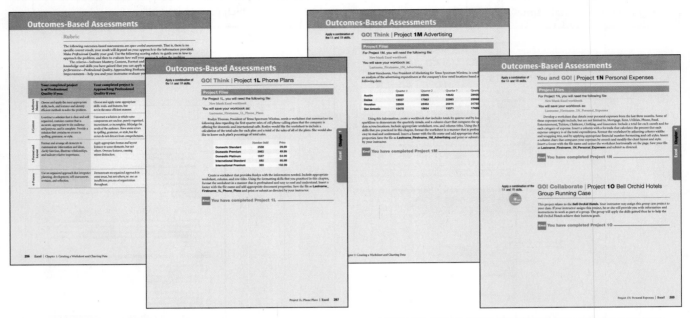

Task-Specific Rubric – A matrix specific to the **GO! Solve It** projects that states the criteria and standards for grading these defined-solution projects.

Outcomes Rubric – A matrix specific to the **GO! Think** projects that states the criteria and standards for grading these open-ended assessments.

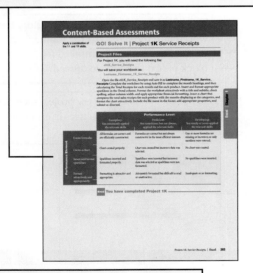

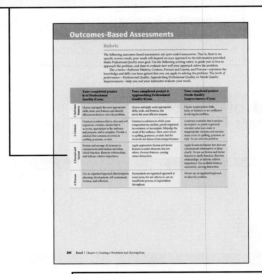

Student CD – All student data files readily available on a CD that comes with the book.

Student Videos – A visual and audio walk-through of every A and B project in the book (see sample images on following page).

  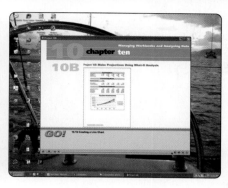

Student Videos! – Each chapter comes with two videos that include audio, demonstrating the objectives and activities taught in the chapter.

All Instructor materials available on the IRCD

Instructor Materials

Annotated Instructor Edition - An instructor tool includes a full copy of the student textbook annotated with teaching tips, discussion topics, and other useful pieces for teaching each chapter.

Assignment Sheets – Lists all the assignments for the chapter. Just add in the course information, due dates, and points. Providing these to students ensures they will know what is due and when.

Scripted Lectures – Classroom lectures prepared for you.

Annotated Solution Files – Coupled with the assignment tags, these create a grading and scoring system that makes grading so much easier for you.

PowerPoint Lectures – PowerPoint presentations for each chapter.

Scoring Rubrics – Can be used either by students to check their work or by you as a quick check-off for the items that need to be corrected.

Syllabus Templates - For 8-week, 12-week, and 16-week courses.

Test Bank – Includes a variety of test questions for each chapter.

Companion Website – Online content such as the Online Study Guide, Glossary, and Student Data Files are all at **www.pearsonhighered.com/go**.

Using the Common Features of Microsoft Office 2010

OUTCOMES
At the end of this chapter you will be able to:

PROJECT 1A
Create, save, and print a Microsoft Office 2010 file.

OBJECTIVES
Mastering these objectives will enable you to:

1. Use Windows Explorer to Locate Files and Folders (p. 3)
2. Locate and Start a Microsoft Office 2010 Program (p. 6)
3. Enter and Edit Text in an Office 2010 Program (p. 9)
4. Perform Commands from a Dialog Box (p. 11)
5. Create a Folder, Save a File, and Close a Program (p. 13)
6. Add Document Properties and Print a File (p. 18)

PROJECT 1B
Use the Ribbon and dialog boxes to perform common commands in a Microsoft Office 2010 file.

7. Open an Existing File and Save It with a New Name (p. 22)
8. Explore Options for an Application (p. 25)
9. Perform Commands from the Ribbon (p. 26)
10. Apply Formatting in Office Programs (p. 32)
11. Use the Microsoft Office 2010 Help System (p. 43)
12. Compress Files (p. 44)

olly/Shutterstock

In This Chapter

In this chapter, you will use Windows Explorer to navigate the Windows folder structure, create a folder, and save files in Microsoft Office 2010 programs. You will also practice using the features of Microsoft Office 2010 that are common across the major programs that comprise the Microsoft Office 2010 suite. These common features include creating, saving, and printing files.

Common features also include the new Paste Preview and Microsoft Office Backstage view. You will apply formatting, perform commands, and compress files. You will see that creating professional-quality documents is easy and quick in Microsoft Office 2010, and that finding your way around is fast and efficient.

The projects in this chapter relate to **Oceana Palm Grill**, which is a chain of 25 casual, full-service restaurants based in Austin, Texas. The Oceana Palm Grill owners plan an aggressive expansion program. To expand by 15 additional restaurants in North Carolina and Florida by 2018, the company must attract new investors, develop new menus, and recruit new employees, all while adhering to the company's quality guidelines and maintaining its reputation for excellent service. To succeed, the company plans to build on its past success and maintain its quality elements.

Project 1A PowerPoint File

myitlab
Project 1A Training

Project Activities

In Activities 1.01 through 1.06, you will create a PowerPoint file, save it in a folder that you create by using Windows Explorer, and then print the file or submit it electronically as directed by your instructor. Your completed PowerPoint slide will look similar to Figure 1.1.

Project Files

For Project 1A, you will need the following file:

New blank PowerPoint presentation

You will save your file as:

Lastname_Firstname_1A_Menu_Plan

Project Results

<figure>

Oceana Palm Grill Menu Plan

Prepared by Firstname Lastname
For Laura Hernandez

</figure>

Figure 1.1
Project 1A Menu Plan

Objective 1 | Use Windows Explorer to Locate Files and Folders

A *file* is a collection of information stored on a computer under a single name, for example, a Word document or a PowerPoint presentation. Every file is stored in a *folder*—a container in which you store files—or a *subfolder*, which is a folder within a folder. Your Windows operating system stores and organizes your files and folders, which is a primary task of an operating system.

You *navigate*—explore within the organizing structure of Windows—to create, save, and find your files and folders by using the *Windows Explorer* program. Windows Explorer displays the files and folders on your computer, and is at work anytime you are viewing the contents of files and folders in a *window*. A window is a rectangular area on a computer screen in which programs and content appear; a window can be moved, resized, minimized, or closed.

Activity 1.01 | Using Windows Explorer to Locate Files and Folders

1 Turn on your computer and display the Windows *desktop*—the opening screen in Windows that simulates your work area.

> **Note | Comparing Your Screen with the Figures in This Textbook**
>
> Your screen will match the figures shown in this textbook if you set your screen resolution to 1024 × 768. At other resolutions, your screen will closely resemble, but not match, the figures shown. To view your screen's resolution, on the Windows 7 desktop, right-click in a blank area, and then click Screen resolution. In Windows Vista, right-click a blank area, click Personalize, and then click Display Settings. In Windows XP, right-click the desktop, click Properties, and then click the Settings tab.

2 In your CD/DVD tray, insert the **Student CD** that accompanies this textbook. Wait a few moments for an **AutoPlay** window to display. Compare your screen with Figure 1.2.

> *AutoPlay* is a Windows feature that lets you choose which program to use to start different kinds of media, such as music CDs, or CDs and DVDs containing photos; it displays when you plug in or insert media or storage devices.

> **Note | If You Do Not Have the Student CD**
>
> If you do not have the Student CD, consult the inside back flap of this textbook for instructions on how to download the files from the Pearson Web site.

Figure 1.2

AutoPlay window

Close button

Windows desktop (yours may vary in color and arrangement)

3 In the upper right corner of the **AutoPlay** window, move your mouse over—*point* to—the **Close** button ▣, and then *click*—press the left button on your mouse pointing device one time.

4 On the left side of the **Windows taskbar**, click the **Start** button 🔵 to display the **Start menu**. Compare your screen with Figure 1.3.

The *Windows taskbar* is the area along the lower edge of the desktop that contains the *Start button* and an area to display buttons for open programs. The Start button displays the *Start menu*, which provides a list of choices and is the main gateway to your computer's programs, folders, and settings.

Figure 1.3

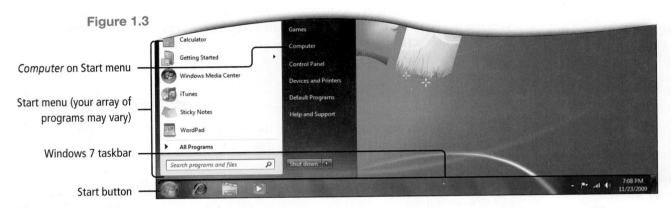

Computer on Start menu

Start menu (your array of programs may vary)

Windows 7 taskbar

Start button

5 On the right side of the **Start menu**, click **Computer** to see the disk drives and other hardware connected to your computer. Compare your screen with Figure 1.4, and then take a moment to study the table in Figure 1.5.

The *folder window* for *Computer* displays. A folder window displays the contents of the current folder, *library*, or device, and contains helpful parts so that you can navigate within Windows.

In Windows 7, a library is a collection of items, such as files and folders, assembled from *various locations*; the locations might be on your computer, an external hard drive, removable media, or someone else's computer.

The difference between a folder and a library is that a library can include files stored in *different locations*—any disk drive, folder, or other place that you can store files and folders.

Figure 1.4

Back and Forward

Address bar

File list

Navigation pane

Folder window toolbar

Views button

Search box

Preview pane button

Details pane

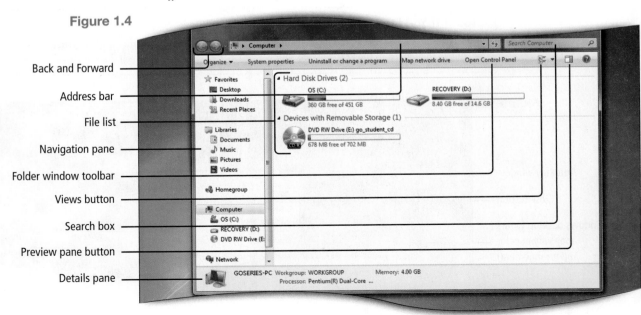

Window Part	Use to:
Address bar	Navigate to a different folder or library, or go back to a previous one.
Back and Forward buttons	Navigate to other folders or libraries you have already opened without closing the current window. These buttons work in conjunction with the address bar; that is, after you use the address bar to change folders, you can use the Back button to return to the previous folder.
Details pane	Display the most common file properties—information about a file, such as the author, the date you last changed the file, and any descriptive *tags*, which are custom file properties that you create to help find and organize your files.
File list	Display the contents of the current folder or library. In Computer, the file list displays the disk drives.
Folder window for *Computer*	Display the contents of the current folder, library, or device. The Folder window contains helpful features so that you can navigate within Windows.
Folder window toolbar	Perform common tasks, such as changing the view of your files and folders or burning files to a CD. The buttons available change to display only relevant tasks.
Navigation pane	Navigate to, open, and display favorites, libraries, folders, saved searches, and an expandable list of drives.
Preview pane button	Display (if you have chosen to open this pane) the contents of most files without opening them in a program. To open the preview pane, click the Preview pane button on the toolbar to turn it on and off.
Search box	Look for an item in the current folder or library by typing a word or phrase in the search box.
Views button	Choose how to view the contents of the current location.

Figure 1.5

6 On the toolbar of the **Computer** folder window, click the **Views button arrow** 📇 ▾— the small arrow to the right of the Views button—to display a list of views that you can apply to the file list. If necessary, on the list, click **Tiles**.

> The Views button is a *split button*; clicking the main part of the button performs a *command* and clicking the arrow opens a menu or list. A command is an instruction to a computer program that causes an action to be carried out.

> When you open a folder or a library, you can change how the files display in the file list. For example, you might prefer to see large or small *icons*—pictures that represent a program, a file, a folder, or some other object—or an arrangement that lets you see various types of information about each file. Each time you click the Views button, the window changes, cycling through several views—additional view options are available by clicking the Views button arrow.

Another Way
Point to the CD/DVD drive, right-click, and then click Open.

7 In the **file list**, under **Devices with Removable Storage**, point to your **CD/DVD Drive**, and then *double-click*—click the left mouse button two times in rapid succession—to display the list of folders on the CD. Compare your screen with Figure 1.6.

> When double-clicking, keep your hand steady between clicks; this is more important than the speed of the two clicks.

Figure 1.6

Views button indicates
Details view

List of folders on the
CD in Details view

Views button arrow

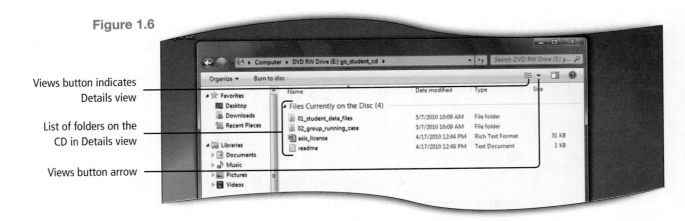

8 In the **file list**, point to the folder **01_student_data_files** and double-click to display the list of subfolders in the folder. Double-click to open the folder **01_common_features**. Compare your screen with Figure 1.7.

The Student Resource CD includes files that you will use to complete the projects in this textbook. If you prefer, you can also copy the **01_student_data_files** folder to a location on your computer's hard drive or to a removable device such as a *USB flash drive*, which is a small storage device that plugs into a computer USB port. Your instructor might direct you to other locations where these files are located; for example, on your learning management system.

Figure 1.7

Address bar displays
sequence of folders

One folder in the
01_common_features
folder

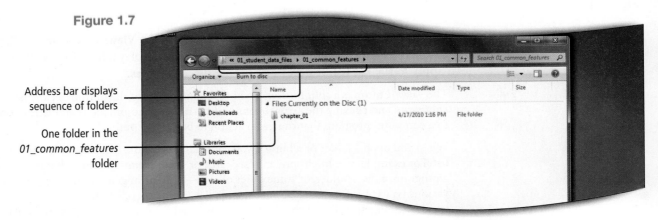

9 In the upper right corner of the **Computer** window, click the **Close** button to redisplay your desktop.

Objective 2 | Locate and Start a Microsoft Office 2010 Program

Microsoft Office 2010 includes programs, servers, and services for individuals, small organizations, and large enterprises. A *program*, also referred to as an *application*, is a set of instructions used by a computer to perform a task, such as word processing or accounting.

Activity 1.02 | Locating and Starting a Microsoft Office 2010 Program

1 On the **Windows taskbar**, click the **Start** button to display the **Start** menu.

2 From the displayed **Start** menu, locate the group of **Microsoft Office 2010** programs on your computer—the Office program icons from which you can start the program may be located on your Start menu, in a Microsoft Office folder on the **All Programs** list, on your desktop, or any combination of these locations; the location will vary depending on how your computer is configured.

All Programs is an area of the Start menu that displays all the available programs on your computer system.

3 Examine Figure 1.8, and notice the programs that are included in the Microsoft Office Professional Plus 2010 group of programs. (Your group of programs may vary.)

Microsoft Word is a word processing program, with which you create and share documents by using its writing tools.

Microsoft Excel is a spreadsheet program, with which you calculate and analyze numbers and create charts.

Microsoft Access is a database program, with which you can collect, track, and report data.

Microsoft PowerPoint is a presentation program, with which you can communicate information with high-impact graphics and video.

Additional popular Office programs include *Microsoft Outlook* to manage e-mail and organizational activities, *Microsoft Publisher* to create desktop publishing documents such as brochures, and *Microsoft OneNote* to manage notes that you make at meetings or in classes and to share notes with others on the Web.

The Professional Plus version of Office 2010 also includes *Microsoft SharePoint Workspace* to share information with others in a team environment and *Microsoft InfoPath Designer and Filler* to create forms and gather data.

Figure 1.8

All Programs menu

Microsoft Office folder

Programs in Microsoft Office (your list may vary)

4 Click to open the program **Microsoft PowerPoint 2010**. Compare your screen with Figure 1.9, and then take a moment to study the description of these screen elements in the table in Figure 1.10.

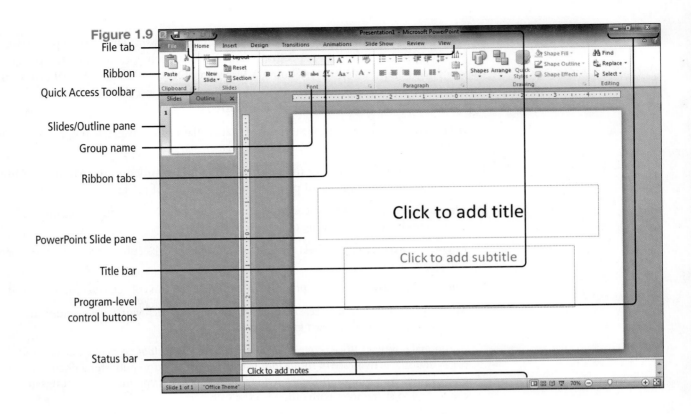

Figure 1.9

- File tab
- Ribbon
- Quick Access Toolbar
- Slides/Outline pane
- Group name
- Ribbon tabs
- PowerPoint Slide pane
- Title bar
- Program-level control buttons
- Status bar

Screen Element	Description
File tab	Displays Microsoft Office Backstage view, which is a centralized space for all of your file management tasks such as opening, saving, printing, publishing, or sharing a file—all the things you can do *with* a file.
Group names	Indicate the name of the groups of related commands on the displayed tab.
PowerPoint Slide pane	Displays a large image of the active slide in the PowerPoint program.
Program-level control buttons	Minimizes, restores, or closes the program window.
Quick Access Toolbar	Displays buttons to perform frequently used commands and resources with a single click. The default commands include Save, Undo, and Redo. You can add and delete buttons to customize the Quick Access Toolbar for your convenience.
Ribbon	Displays a group of task-oriented tabs that contain the commands, styles, and resources you need to work in an Office 2010 program. The look of your Ribbon depends on your screen resolution. A high resolution will display more individual items and button names on the Ribbon.
Ribbon tabs	Display the names of the task-oriented tabs relevant to the open program.
Slides/Outline pane	Displays either thumbnails of the slides in a PowerPoint presentation (Slides tab) or the outline of the presentation's content (Outline tab). In each Office 2010 program, different panes display in different ways to assist you.
Status bar	Displays file information on the left and View and Zoom on the right.
Title bar	Displays the name of the file and the name of the program. The program window control buttons—Minimize, Maximize/Restore Down, and Close—are grouped on the right side of the title bar.

Figure 1.10

Objective 3 | Enter and Edit Text in an Office 2010 Program

All of the programs in Office 2010 require some typed text. Your keyboard is still the primary method of entering information into your computer. Techniques to *edit*—make changes to—text are similar among all of the Office 2010 programs.

Activity 1.03 | Entering and Editing Text in an Office 2010 Program

1 In the middle of the PowerPoint Slide pane, point to the text *Click to add title* to display the ⌐I⌐ pointer, and then click one time.

> The *insertion point*—a blinking vertical line that indicates where text or graphics will be inserted—displays.

> In Office 2010 programs, the mouse *pointer*—any symbol that displays on your screen in response to moving your mouse device—displays in different shapes depending on the task you are performing and the area of the screen to which you are pointing.

2 Type **Oceana Grille Info** and notice how the insertion point moves to the right as you type. Point slightly to the right of the letter *e* in *Grille* and click to place the insertion point there. Compare your screen with Figure 1.11.

Figure 1.11

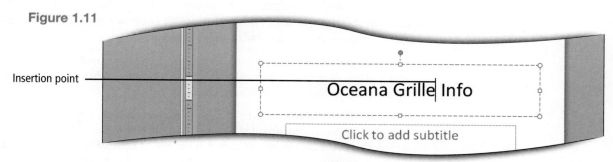

Insertion point

Oceana Grille|Info

Click to add subtitle

3 On your keyboard, locate and press the ⌐Backspace⌐ key to delete the letter *e*.

> Pressing ⌐Backspace⌐ removes a character to the left of the insertion point.

4 Point slightly to the left of the *I* in *Info* and click one time to place the insertion point there. Type **Menu** and then press ⌐Spacebar⌐ one time. Compare your screen with Figure 1.12.

> By *default*, when you type text in an Office program, existing text moves to the right to make space for new typing. Default refers to the current selection or setting that is automatically used by a program unless you specify otherwise.

Figure 1.12

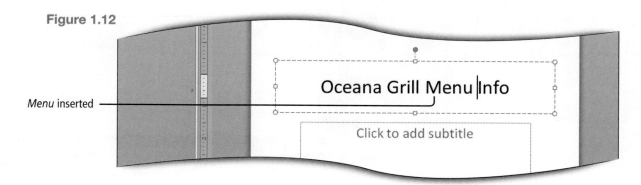

Menu inserted

Oceana Grill Menu |Info

Click to add subtitle

5 Press Del four times to delete *Info* and then type **Plan**

> Pressing Del removes—deletes—a character to the right of the insertion point.

6 With your insertion point blinking after the word *Plan*, on your keyboard, hold down the Ctrl key. While holding down Ctrl, press ← three times to move the insertion point to the beginning of the word *Grill*.

> This is a **keyboard shortcut**—a key or combination of keys that performs a task that would otherwise require a mouse. This keyboard shortcut moves the insertion point to the beginning of the previous word.
>
> A keyboard shortcut is commonly indicated as Ctrl + ← (or some other combination of keys) to indicate that you hold down the first key while pressing the second key. A keyboard shortcut can also include three keys, in which case you hold down the first two and then press the third. For example, Ctrl + Shift + ← selects one word to the left.

7 With the insertion point blinking at the beginning of the word *Grill*, type **Palm** and press Spacebar.

8 Click anywhere in the text *Click to add subtitle*. With the insertion point blinking, type the following and include the spelling error: **Prepered by Annabel Dunham**

9 With your mouse, point slightly to the left of the *A* in *Annabel*, hold down the left mouse button, and then **drag**—hold down the left mouse button while moving your mouse—to the right to select the text *Annabel Dunham*, and then release the mouse button. Compare your screen with Figure 1.13.

> The **Mini toolbar** displays commands that are commonly used with the selected object, which places common commands close to your pointer. When you move the pointer away from the Mini toolbar, it fades from view.
>
> To **select** refers to highlighting, by dragging with your mouse, areas of text or data or graphics so that the selection can be edited, formatted, copied, or moved. The action of dragging includes releasing the left mouse button at the end of the area you want to select. The Office programs recognize a selected area as one unit, to which you can make changes. Selecting text may require some practice. If you are not satisfied with your result, click anywhere outside of the selection, and then begin again.

Figure 1.13

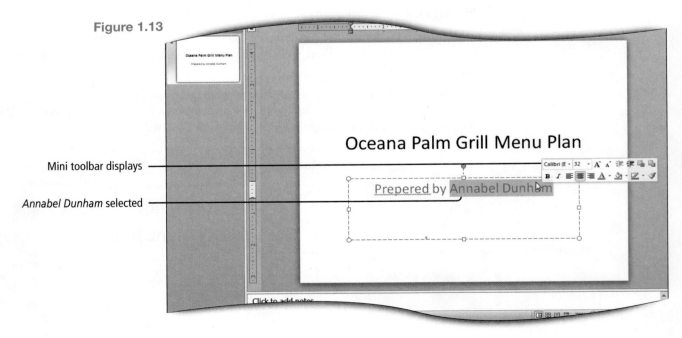

Mini toolbar displays

Annabel Dunham selected

Oceana Palm Grill Menu Plan

Prepered by Annabel Dunham

10 With the text *Annabel Dunham* selected, type your own firstname and lastname.

In any Windows-based program, such as the Microsoft Office 2010 programs, selected text is deleted and then replaced when you begin to type new text. You will save time by developing good techniques to select and then edit or replace selected text, which is easier than pressing the [Del] key numerous times to delete text that you do not want.

11 Notice that the misspelled word *Prepered* displays with a wavy red underline; additionally, all or part of your name might display with a wavy red underline.

Office 2010 has a dictionary of words against which all entered text is checked. In Word and PowerPoint, words that are *not* in the dictionary display a wavy red line, indicating a possible misspelled word or a proper name or an unusual word—none of which are in the Office 2010 dictionary.

In Excel and Access, you can initiate a check of the spelling, but wavy red underlines do not display.

12 Point to *Prepered* and then **right-click**—click your right mouse button one time.

The Mini toolbar and a **shortcut menu** display. A shortcut menu displays commands and options relevant to the selected text or object—known as **context-sensitive commands** because they relate to the item you right-clicked.

Here, the shortcut menu displays commands related to the misspelled word. You can click the suggested correct spelling *Prepared*, click Ignore All to ignore the misspelling, add the word to the Office dictionary, or click Spelling to display a **dialog box**. A dialog box is a small window that contains options for completing a task. Whenever you see a command followed by an **ellipsis** (…), which is a set of three dots indicating incompleteness, clicking the command will always display a dialog box.

13 On the displayed shortcut menu, click **Prepared** to correct the misspelled word. If necessary, point to any parts of your name that display a wavy red underline, right-click, and then on the shortcut menu, click Ignore All so that Office will no longer mark your name with a wavy underline in this file.

More Knowledge | Adding to the Office Dictionary

The main dictionary contains the most common words, but does not include all proper names, technical terms, or acronyms. You can add words, acronyms, and proper names to the Office dictionary by clicking Add to Dictionary when they are flagged, and you might want to do so for your own name and other proper names and terms that you type often.

Objective 4 | Perform Commands from a Dialog Box

In a dialog box, you make decisions about an individual object or topic. A dialog box also offers a way to adjust a number of settings at one time.

Activity 1.04 | Performing Commands from a Dialog Box

1 Point anywhere in the blank area above the title *Oceana Palm Grill Menu Plan* to display the ▯ pointer.

2 Right-click to display a shortcut menu. Notice the command *Format Background* followed by an ellipsis (…). Compare your screen with Figure 1.14.

> Recall that a command followed by an ellipsis indicates that a dialog box will display if you click the command.

Figure 1.14

Shortcut menu

Ellipsis following command

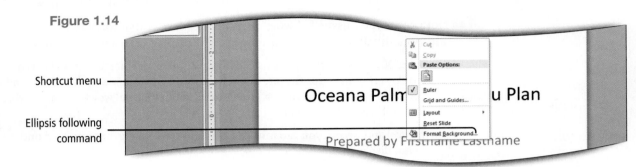

3 Click **Format Background** to display the **Format Background** dialog box, and then compare your screen with Figure 1.15.

Figure 1.15

Fill selected

Format Background dialog box

Options related to the background fill

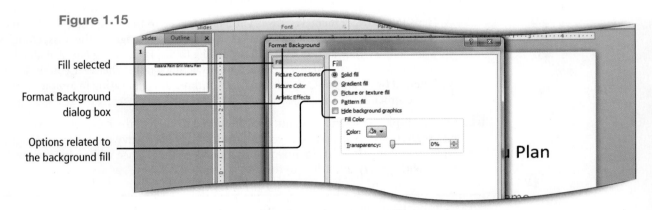

4 On the left, if necessary, click **Fill** to display the **Fill** options.

> *Fill* is the inside color of an object. Here, the dialog box displays the option group names on the left; some dialog boxes provide a set of tabs across the top from which you can display different sets of options.

5 On the right, under **Fill**, click the **Gradient fill** option button.

> The dialog box displays additional settings related to the gradient fill option. An *option button* is a round button that enables you to make one choice among two or more options. In a gradient fill, one color fades into another.

6 Click the **Preset colors arrow**—the arrow in the box to the right of the text *Preset colors*—and then in the gallery, in the second row, point to the fifth fill color to display the ScreenTip *Fog*.

> A *gallery* is an Office feature that displays a list of potential results. A *ScreenTip* displays useful information about mouse actions, such as pointing to screen elements or dragging.

7 Click **Fog**, and then notice that the fill color is applied to your slide. Click the **Type arrow**, and then click **Rectangular** to change the pattern of the fill color. Compare your screen with Figure 1.16.

Figure 1.16

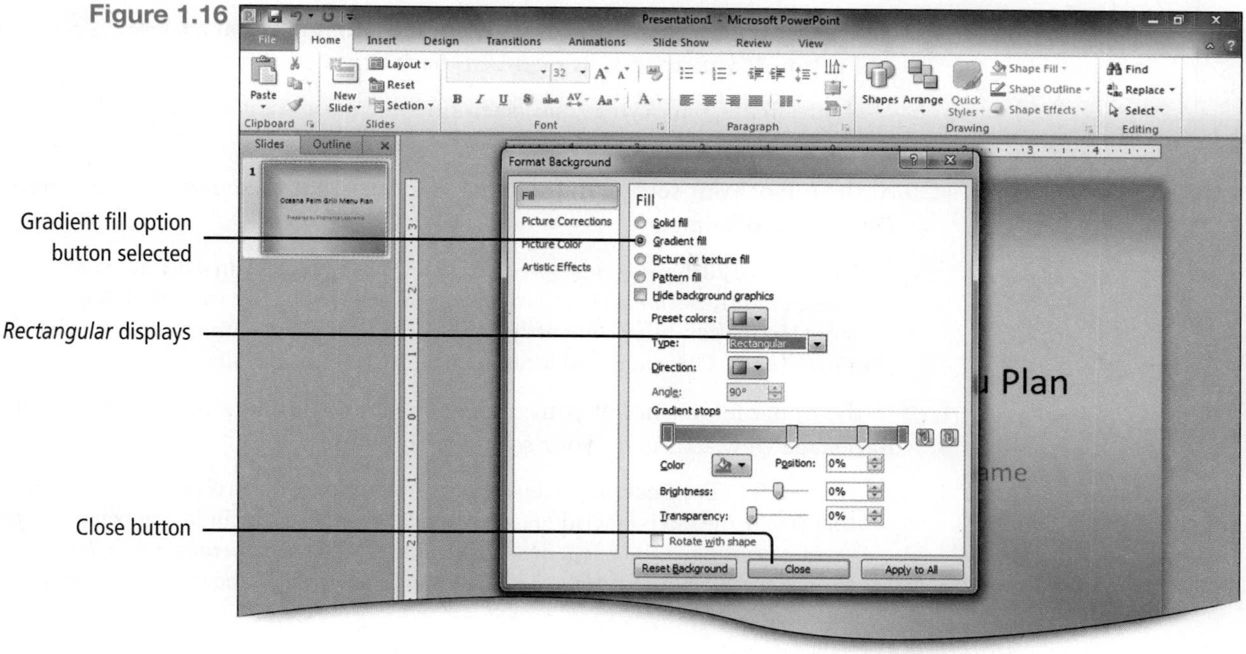

Gradient fill option button selected

Rectangular displays

Close button

8 At the bottom of the dialog box, click **Close**.

As you progress in your study of Microsoft Office, you will practice using many dialog boxes and applying dramatic effects such as this to your Word documents, Excel spreadsheets, Access databases, and PowerPoint slides.

Objective 5 | Create a Folder, Save a File, and Close a Program

A *location* is any disk drive, folder, or other place in which you can store files and folders. Where you store your files depends on how and where you use your data. For example, for your classes, you might decide to store primarily on a removable USB flash drive so that you can carry your files to different locations and access your files on different computers.

If you do most of your work on a single computer, for example your home desktop system or your laptop computer that you take with you to school or work, store your files in one of the Libraries—Documents, Music, Pictures, or Videos—provided by your Windows operating system.

Although the Windows operating system helps you to create and maintain a logical folder structure, take the time to name your files and folders in a consistent manner.

Activity 1.05 | Creating a Folder, Saving a File, and Closing a Program

A PowerPoint presentation is an example of a file. Office 2010 programs use a common dialog box provided by the Windows operating system to assist you in saving files. In this activity, you will create a folder on a USB flash drive in which to store files. If you prefer to store on your hard drive, you can use similar steps to store files in your My Documents folder in your Documents library.

1 Insert a USB flash drive into your computer, and if necessary, **Close** ⬜ the **AutoPlay** dialog box. If you are not using a USB flash drive, go to Step 2.

> As the first step in saving a file, determine where you want to save the file, and if necessary, insert a storage device.

2 At the top of your screen, in the title bar, notice that *Presentation1 – Microsoft PowerPoint* displays.

> Most Office 2010 programs open with a new unsaved file with a default name—*Presentation1*, *Document1*, and so on. As you create your file, your work is temporarily stored in the computer's memory until you initiate a Save command, at which time you must choose a file name and location in which to save your file.

3 In the upper left corner of your screen, click the **File tab** to display **Microsoft Office Backstage** view. Compare your screen with Figure 1.17.

> Microsoft Office **Backstage view** is a centralized space for tasks related to *file* management; that is why the tab is labeled *File*. File management tasks include, for example, opening, saving, printing, publishing, or sharing a file. The **Backstage tabs**—*Info*, *Recent*, *New*, *Print*, *Save & Send*, and *Help*—display along the left side. The tabs group file-related tasks together.

> Above the Backstage tabs, **Quick Commands**—*Save*, *Save As*, *Open*, and *Close*—display for quick access to these commands. When you click any of these commands, Backstage view closes and either a dialog box displays or the active file closes.

> Here, the **Info tab** displays information—*info*—about the current file. In the center panel, various file management tasks are available in groups. For example, if you click the Protect Presentation button, a list of options that you can set for this file that relate to who can open or edit the presentation displays.

> On the Info tab, in the right panel, you can also examine the **document properties**. Document properties, also known as **metadata**, are details about a file that describe or identify it, such as the title, author name, subject, and keywords that identify the document's topic or contents. On the Info page, a thumbnail image of the current file displays in the upper right corner, which you can click to close Backstage view and return to the document.

More Knowledge | Deciding Where to Store Your Files

Where should you store your files? In the libraries created by Windows 7 (Documents, Pictures, and so on)? On a removable device like a flash drive or external hard drive? In Windows 7, it is easy to find your files, especially if you use the libraries. Regardless of where you save a file, Windows 7 will make it easy to find the file again, even if you are not certain where it might be.

In Windows 7, storing all of your files within a library makes sense. If you perform most of your work on your desktop system or your laptop that travels with you, you can store your files in the libraries created by Windows 7 for your user account—Documents, Pictures, Music, and so on. Within these libraries, you can create folders and subfolders to organize your data. These libraries are a good choice for storing your files because:

- From the Windows Explorer button on the taskbar, your libraries are always just one click away.
- The libraries are designed for their contents; for example, the Pictures folder displays small images of your digital photos.
- You can add new locations to a library; for example, an external hard drive, or a network drive. Locations added to a library behave just like they are on your hard drive.
- Other users of your computer cannot access your libraries.
- The libraries are the default location for opening and saving files within an application, so you will find that you can open and save files with fewer navigation clicks.

Figure 1.17

Save command
Information about the file you are working on
Info tab selected
Backstage tabs, Info tab active
Groups
Indicates unsaved file with default name
Document Properties
Screen thumbnail

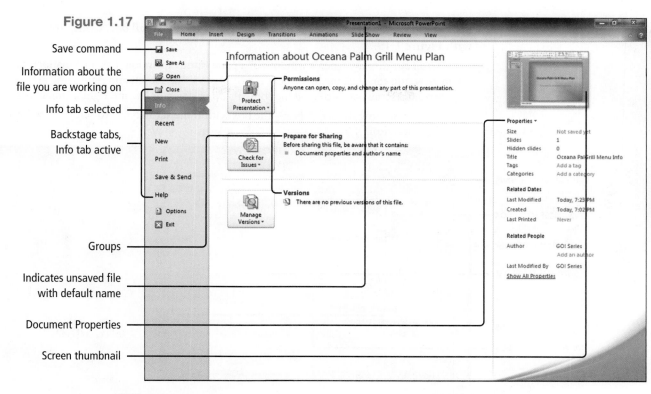

4 Above the **Backstage tabs**, click **Save** to display the **Save As** dialog box.

Backstage view closes and the Save As dialog box, which includes a folder window and an area at the bottom to name the file and set the file type, displays.

When you are saving something for the first time, for example a new PowerPoint presentation, the Save and Save As commands are identical. That is, the Save As dialog box will display if you click Save or if you click Save As.

Note | Saving Your File

After you have named a file and saved it in your desired location, the Save command saves any changes you make to the file without displaying any dialog box. The Save As command will display the Save As dialog box and let you name and save a new file based on the current one—in a location that you choose. After you name and save the new document, the original document closes, and the new document—based on the original one—displays.

---

5 In the **Save As** dialog box, on the left, locate the **navigation pane**; compare your screen with Figure 1.18.

By default, the Save command opens the Documents library unless your default file location has been changed.

Figure 1.18

Save As dialog box
Address bar
Default save location
Navigation pane
File list (yours will vary)
File name box
Save as type defaults to *PowerPoint Presentation*

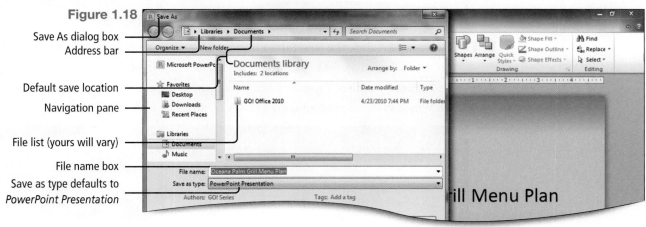

6 On the right side of the **navigation pane**, point to the **scroll bar**. Compare your screen with Figure 1.19.

> A *scroll bar* displays when a window, or a pane within a window, has information that is not in view. You can click the up or down scroll arrows—or the left and right scroll arrows in a horizontal scroll bar—to scroll the contents up or down or left and right in small increments.
>
> You can also drag the *scroll box*—the box within the scroll bar—to scroll the window in either direction.

Figure 1.19

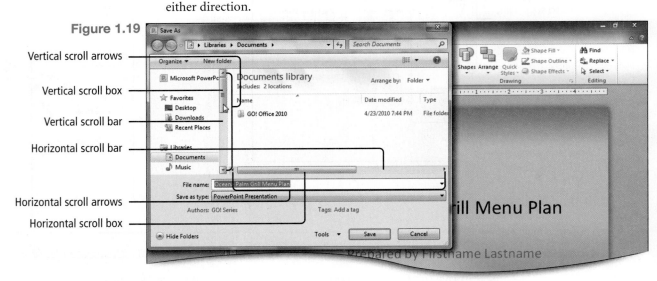

Vertical scroll arrows
Vertical scroll box
Vertical scroll bar
Horizontal scroll bar
Horizontal scroll arrows
Horizontal scroll box

7 Click the **down scroll arrow** as necessary so that you can view the lower portion of the **navigation pane**, and then click the icon for your USB flash drive. Compare your screen with Figure 1.20. (If you prefer to store on your computer's hard drive instead of a USB flash drive, in the navigation pane, click Documents.)

Figure 1.20

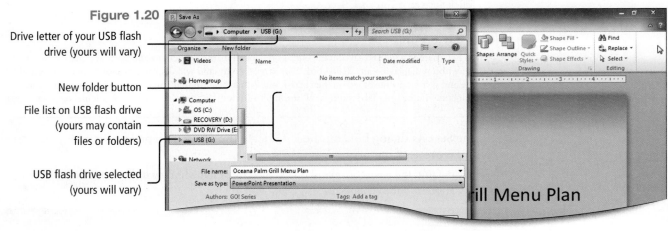

Drive letter of your USB flash drive (yours will vary)
New folder button
File list on USB flash drive (yours may contain files or folders)
USB flash drive selected (yours will vary)

8 On the toolbar, click the **New folder** button.

> In the file list, a new folder is created, and the text *New folder* is selected.

9 Type **Common Features Chapter 1** and press Enter. Compare your screen with Figure 1.21.

> In Windows-based programs, the Enter key confirms an action.

Figure 1.21

New folder

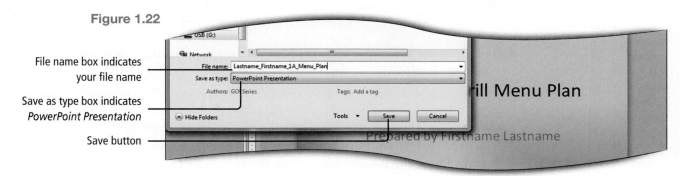

10 In the **file list**, double-click the name of your new folder to open it and display its name in the **address bar**.

11 In the lower portion of the dialog box, click in the **File name** box to select the existing text. Notice that Office inserts the text at the beginning of the presentation as a suggested file name.

12 On your keyboard, locate the ⏢ key. Notice that the Shift of this key produces the underscore character. With the text still selected, type **Lastname_Firstname_1A_ Menu_Plan** Compare your screen with Figure 1.22.

> You can use spaces in file names, however some individuals prefer not to use spaces. Some programs, especially when transferring files over the Internet, may not work well with spaces in file names. In general, however, unless you encounter a problem, it is OK to use spaces. In this textbook, underscores are used instead of spaces in file names.

Figure 1.22

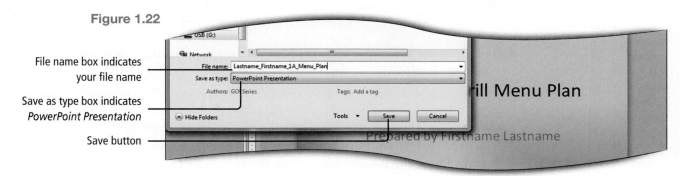

File name box indicates your file name

Save as type box indicates *PowerPoint Presentation*

Save button

13 In the lower right corner, click **Save**; or press Enter. See Figure 1.23.

> Your new file name displays in the title bar, indicating that the file has been saved to a location that you have specified.

Figure 1.23

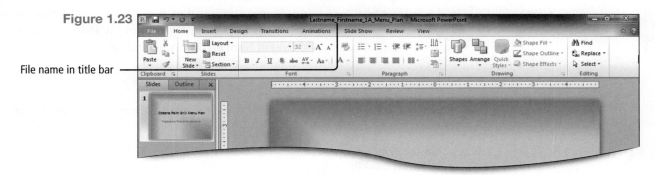

File name in title bar

14 In the text that begins *Prepared by*, click to position the insertion point at the end of your name, and then press Enter to move to a new line. Type **For Laura Hernandez**

15 Click the **File tab** to display **Backstage** view. At the top of the center panel, notice that the path where your file is stored displays. Above the Backstage tabs, click **Close** to close the file. In the message box, click **Save** to save the changes you made and close the file. Leave PowerPoint open.

> PowerPoint displays a message asking if you want to save the changes you have made. Because you have made additional changes to the file since your last Save operation, an Office program will always prompt you to save so that you do not lose any new data.

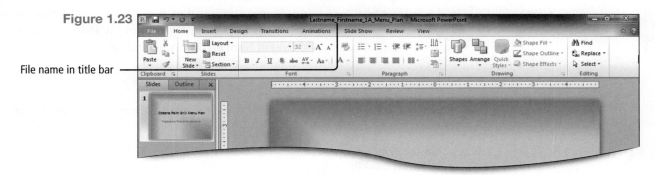

Objective 6 | Add Document Properties and Print a File

The process of printing a file is similar in all of the Office applications. There are differences in the types of options you can select. For example, in PowerPoint, you have the option of printing the full slide, with each slide printing on a full sheet of paper, or of printing handouts with small pictures of slides on a page.

Activity 1.06 | Adding Document Properties and Printing a File

> **Alert! | Are You Printing or Submitting Your Files Electronically?**
>
> If you are submitting your files electronically only, or have no printer attached, you can still complete this activity. Complete Steps 1-9, and then submit your file electronically as directed by your instructor.

1 In the upper left corner, click the **File tab** to display **Backstage** view. Notice that the **Recent tab** displays.

Because no file was open in PowerPoint, Office applies predictive logic to determine that your most likely action will be to open a PowerPoint presentation that you worked on recently. Thus, the Recent tab displays a list of PowerPoint presentations that were recently open on your system.

2 At the top of the **Recent Presentations** list, click your **Lastname_Firstname_1A_ Menu_Plan** file to open it.

3 Click the **File tab** to redisplay **Backstage** view. On the right, under the screen thumbnail, click **Properties**, and then click **Show Document Panel**. In the **Author** box, delete the existing text, and then type your firstname and lastname. Notice that in PowerPoint, some variation of the slide title is automatically inserted in the Title box. In the **Subject** box, type your Course name and section number. In the **Keywords** box, type **menu plan** and then in the upper right corner of the **Document Properties** panel, click the **Close the Document Information Panel** button ⊠ .

Adding properties to your documents will make them easier to search for in systems such as Microsoft SharePoint.

> **Another Way**
>
> Press Ctrl + P or Ctrl + F2 to display the Print tab in Backstage view.

4 Redisplay **Backstage** view, and then click the **Print tab**. Compare your screen with Figure 1.24.

On the Print tab in Backstage view, in the center panel, three groups of printing-related tasks display—Print, Printer, and Settings. In the right panel, the *Print Preview* displays, which is a view of a document as it will appear on the paper when you print it.

At the bottom of the Print Preview area, on the left, the number of pages and arrows with which you can move among the pages in Print Preview display. On the right, *Zoom* settings enable you to shrink or enlarge the Print Preview. Zoom is the action of increasing or decreasing the viewing area of the screen.

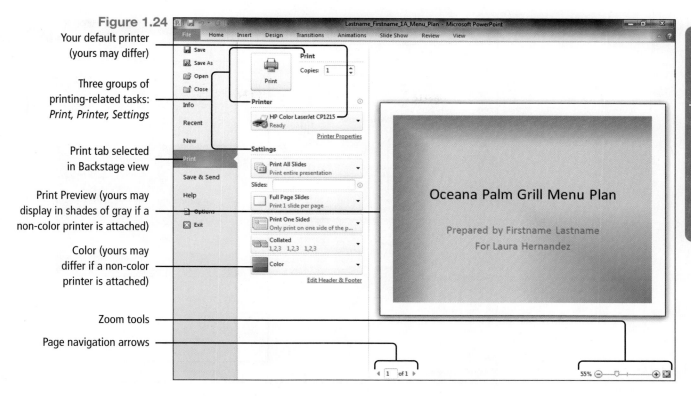

Figure 1.24

Your default printer (yours may differ)

Three groups of printing-related tasks: *Print, Printer, Settings*

Print tab selected in Backstage view

Print Preview (yours may display in shades of gray if a non-color printer is attached)

Color (yours may differ if a non-color printer is attached)

Zoom tools

Page navigation arrows

5 Locate the **Settings group**, and notice that the default setting is to **Print All Slides** and to print **Full Page Slides**—each slide on a full sheet of paper.

6 Point to **Full Page Slides**, notice that the button glows orange, and then click the button to display a gallery of print arrangements. Compare your screen with Figure 1.25.

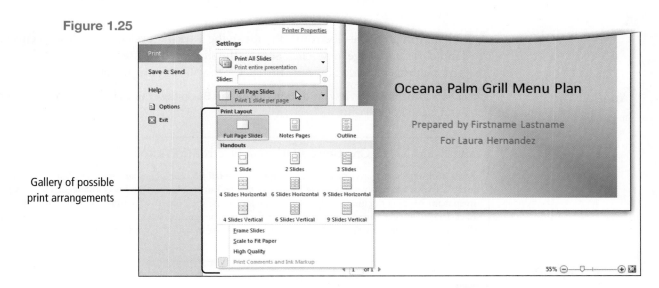

Figure 1.25

Gallery of possible print arrangements

7 In the displayed gallery, under **Handouts**, click **1 Slide**, and then compare your screen with Figure 1.26.

The Print Preview changes to show how your slide will print on the paper in this arrangement.

Figure 1.26

Handouts selected

Print Preview displays
the 1 slide printed as
handouts setting

8 To submit your file electronically, skip this step and move to Step 9. To print your slide, be sure your system is connected to a printer, and then in the **Print group**, click the **Print** button. On the Quick Access Toolbar, click **Save** 🖫 , and then move to Step 10.

> The handout will print on your default printer—on a black and white printer, the colors will print in shades of gray. Backstage view closes and your file redisplays in the PowerPoint window.

9 To submit your file electronically, above the **Backstage tabs**, click **Close** to close the file and close **Backstage** view, click **Save** in the displayed message, and then follow the instructions provided by your instructor to submit your file electronically.

Another Way

In the upper right corner of your PowerPoint window, click the red Close button.

10 Display **Backstage** view, and then below the **Backstage tabs**, click **Exit** to close your file and close PowerPoint.

More Knowledge | Creating a PDF as an Electronic Printout

From Backstage view, you can save an Office file as a *PDF file*. *Portable Document Format* (PDF) creates an image of your file that preserves the look of your file, but that cannot be easily changed. This is a popular format for sending documents electronically, because the document will display on most computers. From Backstage view, click Save & Send, and then in the File Types group, click Create PDF/XPS Document. Then in the third panel, click the Create PDF/XPS button, navigate to your chapter folder, and then in the lower right corner, click Publish.

End **You have completed Project 1A** ————————————

Project 1B Word File

Project Activities

In Activities 1.07 through 1.16, you will open, edit, save, and then compress a Word file. Your completed document will look similar to Figure 1.27.

Project Files

For Project 1B, you will need the following file:

cf01B_Cheese_Promotion

You will save your Word document as:

Lastname_Firstname_1B_Cheese_Promotion

Project Results

Memo

TO: Laura Mabry Hernandez, General Manager

FROM: Donna Jackson, Executive Chef

DATE: December 17, 2014

SUBJECT: Cheese Specials on Tuesdays

To increase restaurant traffic between 4:00 p.m. and 6:00 p.m., I am proposing a trial cheese event in one of the restaurants, probably Orlando. I would like to try a weekly event on Tuesday evenings where the focus is on a good selection of cheese.

I envision two possibilities: a selection of cheese plates or a cheese bar—or both. The cheeses would have to be matched with compatible fruit and bread or crackers. They could be used as appetizers, or for desserts, as is common in Europe. The cheese plates should be varied and diverse, using a mixture of hard and soft, sharp and mild, unusual and familiar.

I am excited about this new promotion. If done properly, I think it could increase restaurant traffic in the hours when individuals want to relax with a small snack instead of a heavy dinner.

The promotion will require that our employees become familiar with the types and characteristics of both foreign and domestic cheeses. Let's meet to discuss the details and the training requirements, and to create a flyer that begins something like this:

Oceana Palm Grill Tuesday Cheese Tastings

Lastname_Firstname_1B_Cheese_Promotion

Figure 1.27
Project 1B Cheese Promotion

Objective 7 | Open an Existing File and Save It with a New Name

In any Office program, use the Open command to display the *Open dialog box*, from which you can navigate to and then open an existing file that was created in that same program.

The Open dialog box, along with the Save and Save As dialog boxes, are referred to as *common dialog boxes*. These dialog boxes, which are provided by the Windows programming interface, display in all of the Office programs in the same manner. Thus, the Open, Save, and Save As dialog boxes will all look and perform the same in each Office program.

Activity 1.07 | Opening an Existing File and Saving it with a New Name

In this activity, you will display the Open dialog box, open an existing Word document, and then save it in your storage location with a new name.

1 Determine the location of the student data files that accompany this textbook, and be sure you can access these files.

> For example:
>
> If you are accessing the files from the Student CD that came with this textbook, insert the CD now.
>
> If you copied the files from the Student CD or from the Pearson Web site to a USB flash drive that you are using for this course, insert the flash drive in your computer now.
>
> If you copied the files to the hard drive of your computer, for example in your Documents library, be sure you can locate the files on the hard drive.

2 Determine the location of your **Common Features Chapter 1** folder you created in Activity 1.05, in which you will store your work from this chapter, and then be sure you can access that folder.

> For example:
>
> If you created your chapter folder on a USB flash drive, insert the flash drive in your computer now. This can be the same flash drive where you have stored the student data files; just be sure to use the chapter folder you created.
>
> If you created your chapter folder in the Documents library on your computer, be sure you can locate the folder. Otherwise, create a new folder at the computer at which you are working, or on a USB flash drive.

3 Using the technique you practiced in Activity 1.02, locate and then start the **Microsoft Word 2010** program on your system.

Another Way

In the Word (or other program) window, press Ctrl + F12 to display the Open dialog box.

4 On the Ribbon, click the **File tab** to display **Backstage** view, and then click **Open** to display the **Open** dialog box.

5 In the **navigation pane** on the left, use the scroll bar to scroll as necessary, and then click the location of your student data files to display the location's contents in the **file list**. Compare your screen with Figure 1.28.

> For example:
>
> If you are accessing the files from the Student CD that came with your book, under Computer, click the CD/DVD.
>
> If you are accessing the files from a USB flash drive, under Computer, click the flash drive name.
>
> If you are accessing the files from the Documents library of your computer, under Libraries, click Documents.

Figure 1.28

Open dialog box

Scroll bar in navigation pane

Navigation pane

CD/DVD selected (or location of your student files)

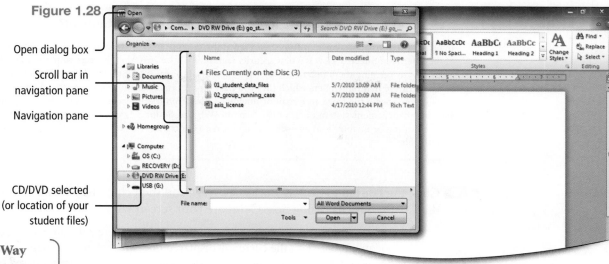

Another Way
Point to a folder name, right-click, and then from the shortcut menu, click Open.

▸ **6** Point to the folder **01_student_data_files** and double-click to open the folder. Point to the subfolder **01_common_features**, double-click, and then compare your screen with Figure 1.29.

Figure 1.29

File list displays the contents of the *01_common_features* folder

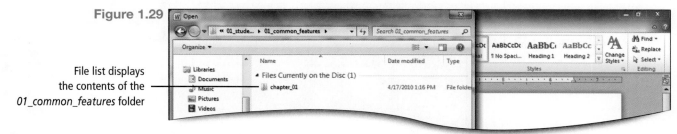

Another Way
Click one time to select the file, and then press Enter or click the Open button in the lower right corner of the dialog box.

▸ **7** In the **file list**, point to the **chapter_01** subfolder and double-click to open it. In the **file list**, point to Word file **cf01B_Cheese_Promotion** and then double-click to open and display the file in the Word window. On the Ribbon, on the **Home tab**, in the **Paragraph group**, if necessary, click the **Show/Hide** button ¶ so that it is active—glowing orange. Compare your screen with Figure 1.30.

On the title bar at the top of the screen, the file name displays. If you opened the document from the Student CD, (*Read-Only*) will display. If you opened the document from another source to which the files were copied, (*Read-Only*) might not display. ***Read-Only*** is a property assigned to a file that prevents the file from being modified or deleted; it indicates that you cannot save any changes to the displayed document unless you first save it with a new name.

Figure 1.30

File name displays in the title bar (*Read-only* will display if opened from the CD)

Show/Hide button active

Word document displays in the Word window

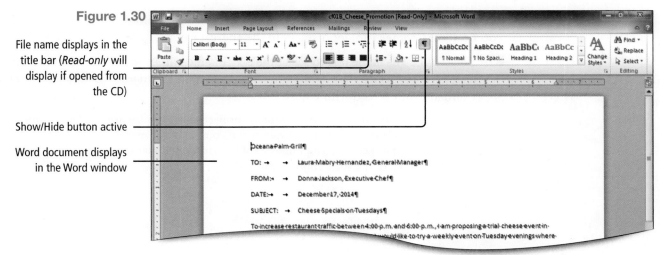

Alert! | Do You See a Message to Enable Editing or Enable Content?

In Office 2010, some files open in *Protected View* if the file appears to be from a potentially risky location, such as the Internet. Protected View is a new security feature in Office 2010 that protects your computer from malicious files by opening them in a restricted environment until you enable them. *Trusted Documents* is another security feature that remembers which files you have already enabled. You might encounter these security features if you open a file from an e-mail or download files from the Internet; for example, from your college's learning management system or from the Pearson Web site. So long as you trust the source of the file, click Enable Editing or Enable Content—depending on the type of file you receive—and then go ahead and work with the file.

Another Way

Press F12 to display the Save As dialog box.

8 Click the **File tab** to display **Backstage** view, and then click the **Save As** command to display the **Save As** dialog box. Compare your screen with Figure 1.31.

> The Save As command displays the Save As dialog box where you can name and save a *new* document based on the currently displayed document. After you name and save the new document, the original document closes, and the new document—based on the original one—displays.

Figure 1.31

Save As dialog box

Navigation pane

Current file name selected

Default type is *Word Document*

9 In the **navigation pane**, click the location in which you are storing your projects for this chapter—the location where you created your **Common Features Chapter 1** folder; for example, your USB flash drive or the Documents library.

10 In the **file list**, double-click the necessary folders and subfolders until your **Common Features Chapter 1** folder displays in the **address bar**.

11 Click in the **File name** box to select the existing file name, or drag to select the existing text, and then using your own name, type **Lastname_Firstname_1B_Cheese_Promotion** Compare your screen with Figure 1.32.

> As you type, the file name from your 1A project might display briefly. Because your 1A project file is stored in this location and you began the new file name with the same text, Office predicts that you might want the same or similar file name. As you type new characters, the suggestion is removed.

24   Office | Chapter 1: Using the Common Features of Microsoft Office 2010

Figure 1.32

Your folder name in address bar

File name box displays your new file name

Save button

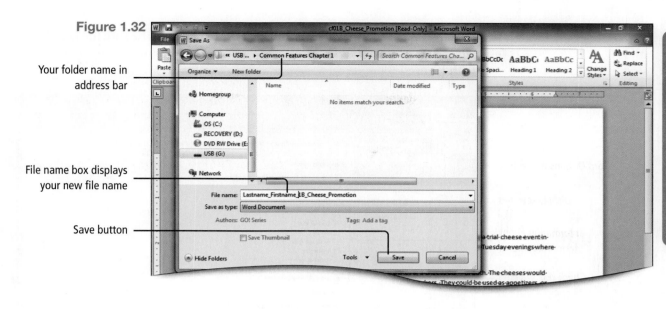

12 In the lower right corner of the **Save As** dialog box, click **Save**; or press Enter. Compare your screen with Figure 1.33.

> The original document closes, and your new document, based on the original, displays with the name in the title bar.

Figure 1.33

New document name in title bar

Insertion point at beginning of document

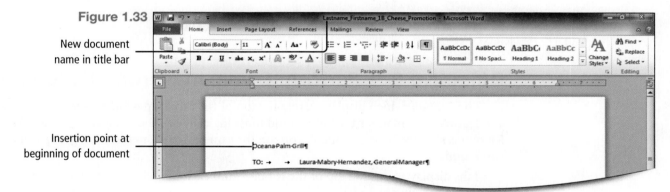

Objective 8 | Explore Options for an Application

Within each Office application, you can open an *Options dialog box* where you can select program settings and other options and preferences. For example, you can set preferences for viewing and editing files.

Activity 1.08 | Viewing Application Options

1 Click the **File tab** to display **Backstage** view. Under the **Help tab**, click **Options**.

2 In the displayed **Word Options** dialog box, on the left, click **Display**, and then on the right, locate the information under **Always show these formatting marks on the screen**.

> When you press Enter, Spacebar, or Tab on your keyboard, characters display to represent these keystrokes. These screen characters do not print, and are referred to as *formatting marks* or *nonprinting characters*.

3 Under **Always show these formatting marks on the screen**, be sure the last check box, **Show all formatting marks**, is selected—select it if necessary. Compare your screen with Figure 1.34.

Figure 1.34

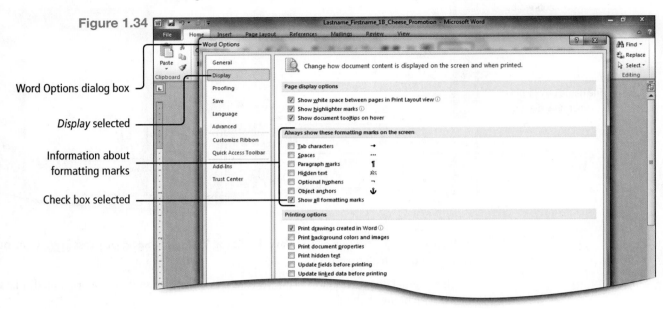

Word Options dialog box

Display selected

Information about formatting marks

Check box selected

4 In the lower right corner of the dialog box, click **OK**.

Objective 9 | Perform Commands from the Ribbon

The **Ribbon**, which displays across the top of the program window, groups commands and features in a manner that you would most logically use them. Each Office program's Ribbon is slightly different, but all contain the same three elements: **tabs**, **groups**, and **commands**.

Tabs display across the top of the Ribbon, and each tab relates to a type of activity; for example, laying out a page. Groups are sets of related commands for specific tasks. Commands—instructions to computer programs—are arranged in groups, and might display as a button, a menu, or a box in which you type information.

You can also minimize the Ribbon so only the tab names display. In the minimized Ribbon view, when you click a tab the Ribbon expands to show the groups and commands, and then when you click a command, the Ribbon returns to its minimized view. Most Office users, however, prefer to leave the complete Ribbon in view at all times.

Activity 1.09 | Performing Commands from the Ribbon

1 Take a moment to examine the document on your screen.

This document is a memo from the Executive Chef to the General Manager regarding a new restaurant promotion.

2 On the Ribbon, click the **View tab**. In the **Show group**, if necessary, click to place a check mark in the **Ruler** check box, and then compare your screen with Figure 1.35.

> When working in Word, display the rulers so that you can see how margin settings affect your document and how text aligns. Additionally, if you set a tab stop or an indent, its location is visible on the ruler.

Figure 1.35
Quick Access Toolbar
Ruler selected
Button to minimize Ribbon
Rulers

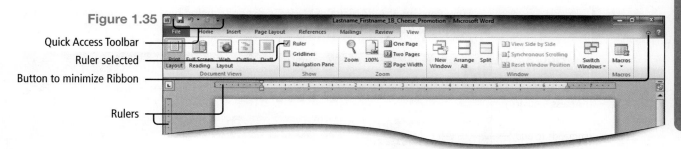

3 On the Ribbon, click the **Home tab**. In the **Paragraph group**, if necessary, click the **Show/Hide** button ¶ so that it glows orange and formatting marks display in your document. Point to the button to display information about the button, and then compare your screen with Figure 1.36.

> When the Show/Hide button is active—glowing orange—formatting marks display. Because formatting marks guide your eye in a document—like a map and road signs guide you along a highway—these marks will display throughout this instruction. Many expert Word users keep these marks displayed while creating documents.

Figure 1.36
Show/Hide button glows orange
Paragraph group
ScreenTip for Show/Hide button
Paragraph mark
Tab mark

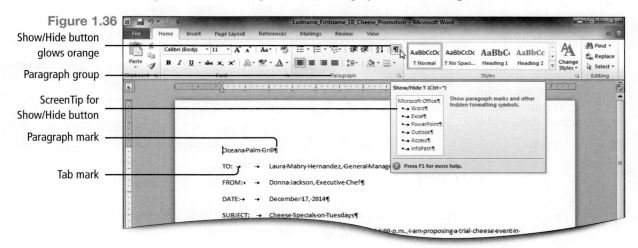

4 In the upper left corner of your screen, above the Ribbon, locate the **Quick Access Toolbar**.

> The **Quick Access Toolbar** contains commands that you use frequently. By default, only the commands Save, Undo, and Redo display, but you can add and delete commands to suit your needs. Possibly the computer at which you are working already has additional commands added to the Quick Access Toolbar.

5 At the end of the Quick Access Toolbar, click the **Customize Quick Access Toolbar** button ▾.

6 Compare your screen with Figure 1.37.

> A list of commands that Office users commonly add to their Quick Access Toolbar displays, including *Open*, *E-mail*, and *Print Preview and Print*. Commands already on the Quick Access Toolbar display a check mark. Commands that you add to the Quick Access Toolbar are always just one click away.

> Here you can also display the More Commands dialog box, from which you can select any command from any tab to add to the Quick Access Toolbar.

Figure 1.37

Customize Quick Access Toolbar

Popular commands to add

Existing commands checked

Displays *More Commands* dialog box

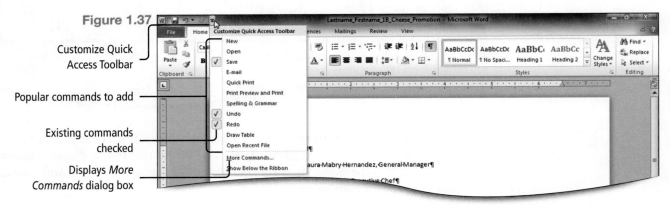

Another Way

Right-click any command on the Ribbon, and then on the shortcut menu, click Add to Quick Access Toolbar.

7 On the displayed list, click **Print Preview and Print**, and then notice that the icon is added to the **Quick Access Toolbar**. Compare your screen with Figure 1.38.

> The icon that represents the Print Preview command displays on the Quick Access Toolbar. Because this is a command that you will use frequently while building Office documents, you might decide to have this command remain on your Quick Access Toolbar.

Figure 1.38

Icon for Print Preview command added to Quick Access Toolbar

8 In the first line of the document, be sure your insertion point is blinking to the left of the *O* in *Oceana*. Press Enter one time to insert a blank paragraph, and then click to the left of the new paragraph mark (¶) in the new line.

> The ***paragraph symbol*** is a formatting mark that displays each time you press Enter.

9 On the Ribbon, click the **Insert tab**. In the **Illustrations group**, point to the **Clip Art** button to display its ScreenTip.

> Many buttons on the Ribbon have this type of ***enhanced ScreenTip***, which displays more descriptive text than a normal ScreenTip.

10 Click the **Clip Art** button.

> The Clip Art ***task pane*** displays. A task pane is a window within a Microsoft Office application that enables you to enter options for completing a command.

11 In the **Clip Art** task pane, click in the **Search for** box, delete any existing text, and then type **cheese grapes** Under **Results should be:**, click the arrow at the right, if necessary click to *clear* the check mark for **All media types** so that no check boxes are selected, and then click the check box for **Illustrations**. Compare your screen with Figure 1.39.

Figure 1.39

Search term

Blank paragraph

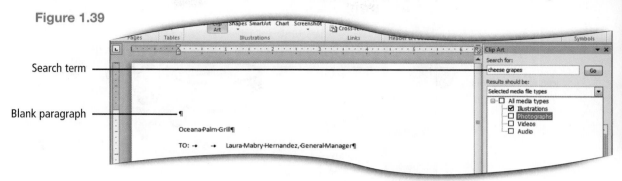

12 Click the **Results should be arrow** again to close the list, and then if necessary, click to place a check mark in the **Include Office.com content** check box.

> By selecting this check box, the search for clip art images will include those from Microsoft's online collections of clip art at www.office.com.

13 At the top of the **Clip Art** task pane, click **Go**. Wait a moment for clips to display, and then locate the clip indicated in Figure 1.40.

Figure 1.40

Check box selected

Locate this image

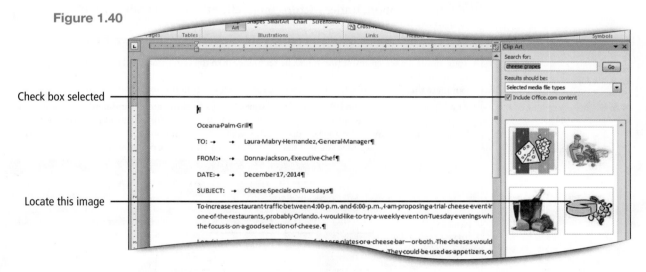

14 Click the image indicated in Figure 1.40 one time to insert it at the insertion point, and then in the upper right corner of the **Clip Art** task pane, click the **Close** [X] button.

> **Alert! | If You Cannot Locate the Image**
>
> If the image shown in Figure 1.40 is unavailable, select a different cheese image that is appropriate.

15 With the image selected—surrounded by a border—on the Ribbon, click the **Home tab**, and then in the **Paragraph group**, click the **Center** button [≡]. Click anywhere outside of the bordered picture to *deselect*—cancel the selection. Compare your screen with Figure 1.41.

Figure 1.41

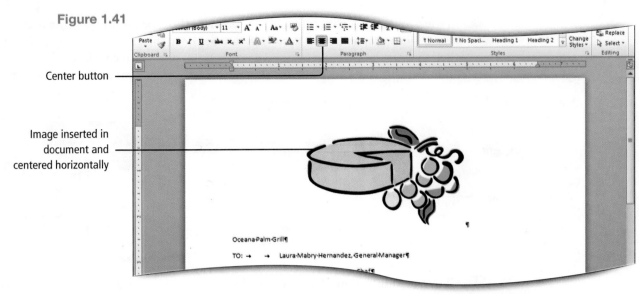

Center button

Image inserted in
document and
centered horizontally

Oceana·Palm·Grill¶

TO: → → Laura·Mabry·Hernandez, General·Manager¶

16 Point to the inserted clip art image, and then watch the last tab of the Ribbon as you click the image one time to select it.

> The *Picture Tools* display and an additional tab—the *Format* tab—is added to the Ribbon. The Ribbon adapts to your work and will display additional tabs—referred to as ***contextual tabs***—when you need them.

17 On the Ribbon, under **Picture Tools**, click the **Format tab**.

Alert! | The Size of Groups on the Ribbon Varies with Screen Resolution

Your monitor's screen resolution might be set higher than the resolution used to capture the figures in this book. In Figure 1.42 below, the resolution is set to 1024 × 768, which is used for all of the figures in this book. Compare that with Figure 1.43 below, where the screen resolution is set to 1280 × 1024.

At a higher resolution, the Ribbon expands some groups to show more commands than are available with a single click, such as those in the Picture Styles group. Or, the group expands to add descriptive text to some buttons, such as those in the Arrange group. Regardless of your screen resolution, all Office commands are available to you. In higher resolutions, you will have a more robust view of the commands.

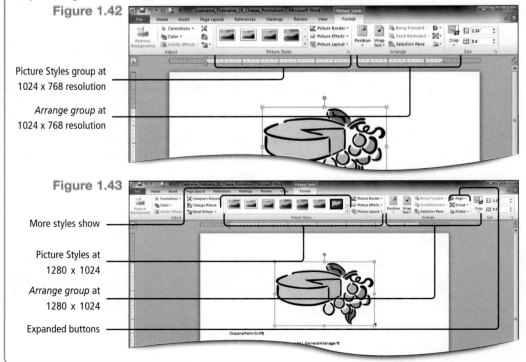

Figure 1.42

Picture Styles group at
1024 x 768 resolution

Arrange group at
1024 x 768 resolution

Figure 1.43

More styles show

Picture Styles at
1280 x 1024

Arrange group at
1280 x 1024

Expanded buttons

18 In the **Picture Styles group**, point to the first style to display the ScreenTip *Simple Frame, White*, and notice that the image displays with a white frame.

19 Watch the image as you point to the second picture style, and then to the third, and then to the fourth.

This is *Live Preview*, a technology that shows the result of applying an editing or formatting change as you point to possible results—*before* you actually apply it.

20 In the **Picture Styles group**, click the fourth style—**Drop Shadow Rectangle**—and then click anywhere outside of the image to deselect it. Notice that the Picture Tools no longer display on the Ribbon. Compare your screen with Figure 1.44.

Contextual tabs display only when you need them.

Figure 1.44

Picture Tools no longer display on the Ribbon

Drop Shadow Rectangle picture style applied to image

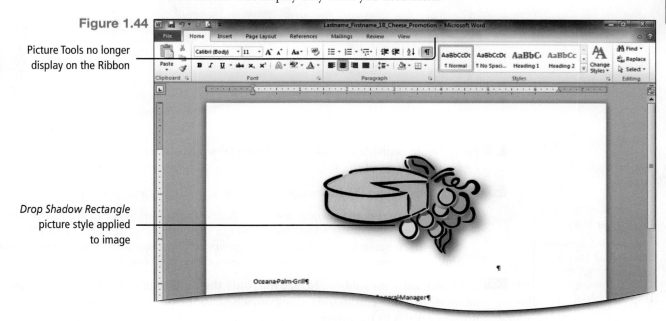

21 In the upper left corner of your screen, on the Quick Access Toolbar, click the **Save** button to save the changes you have made.

Activity 1.10 | Minimizing and Using the Keyboard to Control the Ribbon

Instead of a mouse, some individuals prefer to navigate the Ribbon by using keys on the keyboard. You can activate keyboard control of the Ribbon by pressing the Alt key. You can also minimize the Ribbon to maximize your available screen space.

1 On your keyboard, press the Alt key, and then on the Ribbon, notice that small labels display. Press N to activate the commands on the **Insert tab**, and then compare your screen with Figure 1.45.

Each label represents a *KeyTip*—an indication of the key that you can press to activate the command. For example, on the Insert tab, you can press F to activate the Clip Art task pane.

Figure 1.45

KeyTips indicate that keyboard control of the Ribbon is active

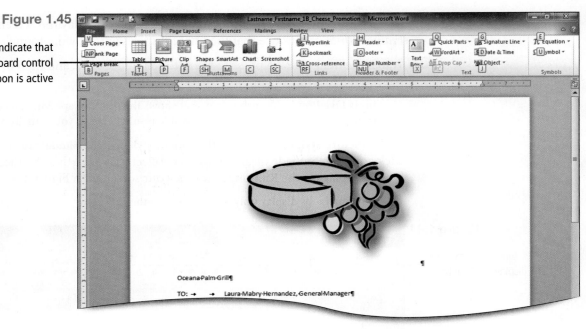

2 Press Esc to redisplay the KeyTips for the tabs. Then, press Alt again to turn off keyboard control of the Ribbon.

3 Point to any tab on the Ribbon and right-click to display a shortcut menu.

Here you can choose to display the Quick Access Toolbar below the Ribbon or minimize the Ribbon to maximize screen space. You can also customize the Ribbon by adding, removing, renaming, or reordering tabs, groups, and commands on the Ribbon, although this is not recommended until you become an expert Office user.

> **Another Way**
>
> Double-click the active tab; or, click the Minimize the Ribbon button at the right end of the Ribbon.

4 Click **Minimize the Ribbon**. Notice that only the Ribbon tabs display. Click the **Home tab** to display the commands. Click anywhere in the document, and notice that the Ribbon reverts to its minimized view.

> **Another Way**
>
> Double-click any tab to redisplay the full Ribbon.

5 Right-click any Ribbon tab, and then click **Minimize the Ribbon** again to turn the minimize feature off.

Most expert Office users prefer to have the full Ribbon display at all times.

6 Point to any tab on the Ribbon, and then on your mouse device, roll the mouse wheel. Notice that different tabs become active as your roll the mouse wheel.

You can make a tab active by using this technique, instead of clicking the tab.

Objective 10 | Apply Formatting in Office Programs

Formatting is the process of establishing the overall appearance of text, graphics, and pages in an Office file—for example, in a Word document.

Activity 1.11 | Formatting and Viewing Pages

In this activity, you will practice common formatting techniques used in Office applications.

1 On the Ribbon, click the **Insert tab**, and then in the **Header & Footer group**, click the **Footer** button.

Another Way

On the Design tab, in the Insert group, click Quick Parts, click Field, and then under Field names, click FileName.

2 At the top of the displayed gallery, under **Built-In**, click **Blank**. At the bottom of your document, with *Type text* highlighted in blue, using your own name type the file name of this document **Lastname_Firstname_1B_Cheese_Promotion** and then compare your screen with Figure 1.46.

Header & Footer Tools are added to the Ribbon. A *footer* is a reserved area for text or graphics that displays at the bottom of each page in a document. Likewise, a *header* is a reserved area for text or graphics that displays at the top of each page in a document. When the footer (or header) area is active, the document area is inactive (dimmed).

Figure 1.46

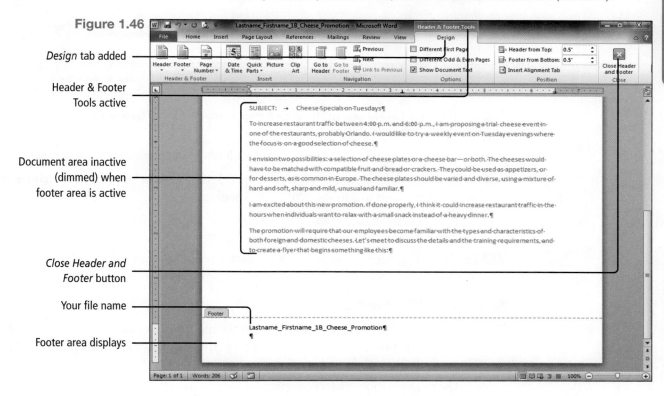

Design tab added

Header & Footer Tools active

Document area inactive (dimmed) when footer area is active

Close Header and Footer button

Your file name

Footer area displays

3 On the Ribbon, on the **Design tab**, in the **Close group**, click the **Close Header and Footer** button.

4 On the Ribbon, click the **Page Layout tab**. In the **Page Setup group**, click the **Orientation** button, and notice that two orientations display—*Portrait* and *Landscape*. Click **Landscape**.

In *portrait orientation*, the paper is taller than it is wide. In *landscape orientation*, the paper is wider than it is tall.

5 In the lower right corner of the screen, locate the **Zoom control** buttons.

To *zoom* means to increase or decrease the viewing area. You can zoom in to look closely at a section of a document, and then zoom out to see an entire page on the screen. You can also zoom to view multiple pages on the screen.

6 Drag the **Zoom slider** to the left until you have zoomed to approximately *60%*. Compare your screen with Figure 1.47.

Figure 1.47

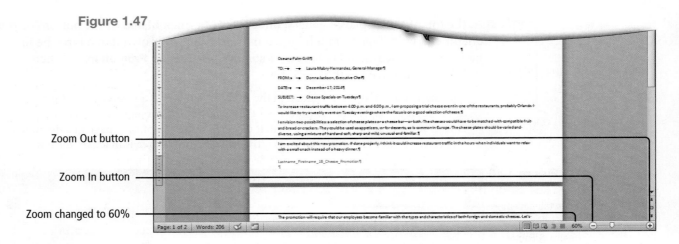

Zoom Out button

Zoom In button

Zoom changed to 60%

7 On the **Page Layout tab**, in the **Page Setup group**, click the **Orientation** button, and then click **Portrait**.

> Portrait orientation is commonly used for business documents such as letters and memos.

8 In the lower right corner of your screen, click the **Zoom In** button ⊕ as many times as necessary to return to the **100%** zoom setting.

> Use the zoom feature to adjust the view of your document for editing and for your viewing comfort.

9 On the Quick Access Toolbar, click the **Save** button 🖫 to save the changes you have made to your document.

Activity 1.12 | Formatting Text

1 To the left of *Oceana Palm Grill*, point in the margin area to display the 🖈 pointer and click one time to select the entire paragraph. Compare your screen with Figure 1.48.

> Use this technique to select complete paragraphs from the margin area. Additionally, with this technique you can drag downward to select multiple-line paragraphs—which is faster and more efficient than dragging through text.

Figure 1.48

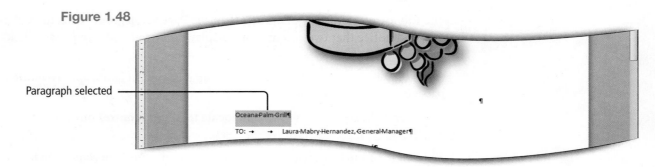

Paragraph selected

2 On the Ribbon, click the **Home tab**, and then in the **Paragraph group**, click the **Center** button ☰ to center the paragraph.

> *Alignment* refers to the placement of paragraph text relative to the left and right margins. *Center alignment* refers to text that is centered horizontally between the left and right margins. You can also align text at the left margin, which is the default alignment for text in Word, or at the right margin.

3 On the **Home tab**, in the **Font group**, click the **Font button arrow** [Calibri (Body) ▾]. At the top of the list, point to **Cambria**, and as you do so, notice that the selected text previews in the Cambria font.

> A *font* is a set of characters with the same design and shape. The default font in a Word document is Calibri, which is a *sans serif* font—a font design with no lines or extensions on the ends of characters.
>
> The Cambria font is a *serif* font—a font design that includes small line extensions on the ends of the letters to guide the eye in reading from left to right.
>
> The list of fonts displays as a gallery showing potential results. For example, in the Font gallery, you can see the actual design and format of each font as it would look if applied to text.

4 Point to several other fonts and observe the effect on the selected text. Then, at the top of the **Font** gallery, under **Theme Fonts**, click **Cambria**.

> A *theme* is a predesigned set of colors, fonts, lines, and fill effects that look good together and that can be applied to your entire document or to specific items.
>
> A theme combines two sets of fonts—one for text and one for headings. In the default Office theme, Cambria is the suggested font for headings.

5 With the paragraph *Oceana Palm Grill* still selected, on the **Home tab**, in the **Font group**, click the **Font Size button arrow** [11 ▾], point to **36**, and then notice how Live Preview displays the text in the font size to which you are pointing. Compare your screen with Figure 1.49.

Figure 1.49

Font Size button

Font button

Font Size list

Pointing to 36 pt font size

Oceana Palm Grill centered, Cambria font applied

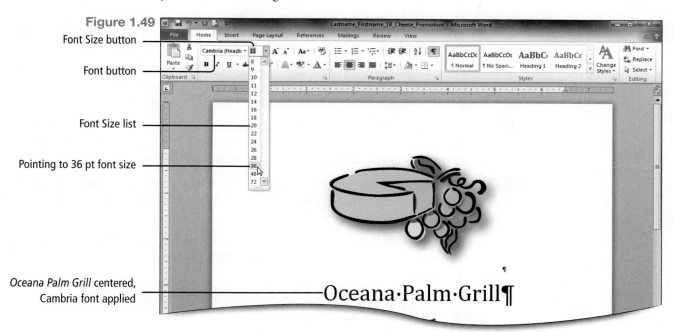

6 On the displayed list of font sizes, click **20**.

> Fonts are measured in *points*, with one point equal to 1/72 of an inch. A higher point size indicates a larger font size. Headings and titles are often formatted by using a larger font size. The word *point* is abbreviated as *pt*.

7 With *Oceana Palm Grill* still selected, on the **Home tab**, in the **Font group**, click the **Font Color button arrow** [A ▾]. Under **Theme Colors**, in the seventh column, click the last color—**Olive Green, Accent 3, Darker 50%**. Click anywhere to deselect the text.

8 To the left of *TO:*, point in the left margin area to display the 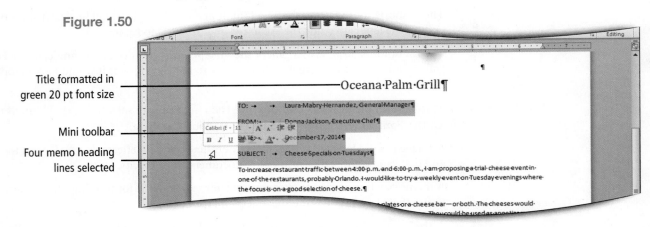 pointer, hold down the left mouse button, and then drag down to select the four memo headings. Compare your screen with Figure 1.50.

> Use this technique to select complete paragraphs from the margin area—dragging downward to select multiple-line paragraphs—which is faster and more efficient than dragging through text.

Figure 1.50

Title formatted in green 20 pt font size

Mini toolbar

Four memo heading lines selected

9 With the four paragraphs selected, on the Mini toolbar, click the **Font Color** button ，which now displays a dark green bar instead of a red bar.

> The font color button retains its most recently used color—Olive Green, Accent 3, Darker 50%. As you progress in your study of Microsoft Office, you will use other buttons that behave in this manner; that is, they retain their most recently used format.

> The purpose of the Mini toolbar is to place commonly used commands close to text or objects that you select. By selecting a command on the Mini toolbar, you reduce the distance that you must move your mouse to access a command.

10 Click anywhere in the paragraph that begins *To increase*, and then *triple-click*—click the left mouse button three times—to select the entire paragraph. If the entire paragraph is not selected, click in the paragraph and begin again.

11 With the entire paragraph selected, on the Mini toolbar, click the **Font Color button arrow** ，and then under **Theme Colors**, in the sixth column, click the first color—**Red, Accent 2**.

> It is convenient to have commonly used commands display on the Mini toolbar so that you do not have to move your mouse to the top of the screen to access the command from the Ribbon.

12 Select the text *TO:* and then on the displayed Mini toolbar, click the **Bold** button and the **Italic** button .

> *Font styles* include bold, italic, and underline. Font styles emphasize text and are a visual cue to draw the reader's eye to important text.

13 On the displayed Mini toolbar, click the **Italic** button again to turn off the Italic formatting. Notice that the Italic button no longer glows orange.

> A button that behaves in this manner is referred to as a *toggle button*, which means it can be turned on by clicking it once, and then turned off by clicking it again.

14 With *TO:* still selected, on the Mini toolbar, click the **Format Painter** button . Then, move your mouse under the word *Laura*, and notice the mouse pointer. Compare your screen with Figure 1.51.

> You can use the ***Format Painter*** to copy the formatting of specific text or of a paragraph and then apply it in other locations in your document.

> The pointer takes the shape of a paintbrush, and contains the formatting information from the paragraph where the insertion point is positioned. Information about the Format Painter and how to turn it off displays in the status bar.

Figure 1.51

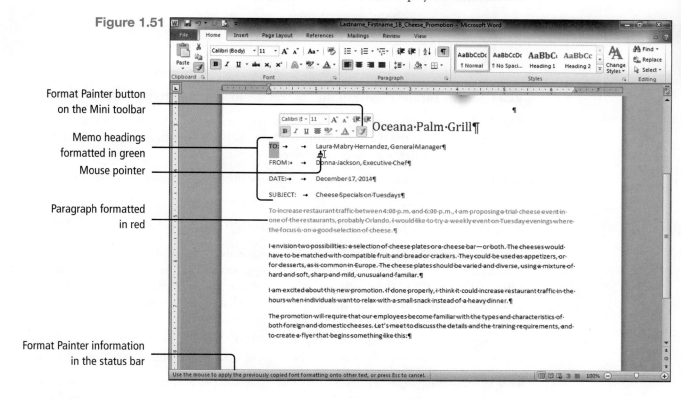

Format Painter button on the Mini toolbar

Memo headings formatted in green

Mouse pointer

Paragraph formatted in red

Format Painter information in the status bar

15 With the pointer, drag to select the text *FROM:* and notice that the Bold formatting is applied. Then, point to the selected text *FROM:* and on the Mini toolbar, *double-click* the **Format Painter** button .

16 Select the text *DATE:* to copy the Bold formatting, and notice that the pointer retains the shape.

> When you *double-click* the Format Painter button, the Format Painter feature remains active until you either click the Format Painter button again, or press Esc to cancel it—as indicated on the status bar.

17 With Format Painter still active, select the text *SUBJECT:*, and then on the Ribbon, on the **Home tab**, in the **Clipboard group**, notice that the **Format Painter** button is glowing orange, indicating that it is active. Compare your screen with Figure 1.52.

Figure 1.52

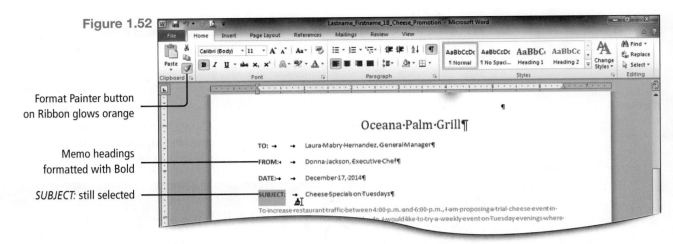

Format Painter button
on Ribbon glows orange

Memo headings
formatted with Bold

SUBJECT: still selected

18 Click the **Format Painter** button on the Ribbon to turn the command off.

19 In the paragraph that begins *To increase*, triple-click again to select the entire paragraph. On the displayed Mini toolbar, click the **Bold** button B and the **Italic** button I. Click anywhere to deselect.

20 On the Quick Access Toolbar, click the **Save** button to save the changes you have made to your document.

Activity 1.13 | Using the Office Clipboard to Cut, Copy, and Paste

The **Office Clipboard** is a temporary storage area that holds text or graphics that you select and then cut or copy. When you **copy** text or graphics, a copy is placed on the Office Clipboard and the original text or graphic remains in place. When you **cut** text or graphics, a copy is placed on the Office Clipboard, and the original text or graphic is removed—cut—from the document.

After cutting or copying, the contents of the Office Clipboard are available for you to **paste**—insert—in a new location in the current document, or into another Office file.

1 Hold down Ctrl and press Home to move to the beginning of your document, and then take a moment to study the table in Figure 1.53, which describes similar keyboard shortcuts with which you can navigate quickly in a document.

To Move	Press
To the beginning of a document	Ctrl + Home
To the end of a document	Ctrl + End
To the beginning of a line	Home
To the end of a line	End
To the beginning of the previous word	Ctrl + ←
To the beginning of the next word	Ctrl + →
To the beginning of the current word (if insertion point is in the middle of a word)	Ctrl + ←
To the beginning of a paragraph	Ctrl + ↑
To the beginning of the next paragraph	Ctrl + ↓
To the beginning of the current paragraph (if insertion point is in the middle of a paragraph)	Ctrl + ↑
Up one screen	PgUp
Down one screen	PageDown

Figure 1.53

Another Way

Right-click the selection, and then click Copy on the shortcut menu; or, use the keyboard shortcut Ctrl + C.

2 To the left of *Oceana Palm Grill*, point in the left margin area to display the pointer, and then click one time to select the entire paragraph. On the **Home tab**, in the **Clipboard group**, click the **Copy** button.

Because anything that you select and then copy—or cut—is placed on the Office Clipboard, the Copy command and the Cut command display in the Clipboard group of commands on the Ribbon.

There is no visible indication that your copied selection has been placed on the Office Clipboard.

3 On the **Home tab**, in the **Clipboard group**, to the right of the group name *Clipboard*, click the **Dialog Box Launcher** button, and then compare your screen with Figure 1.54.

The Clipboard task pane displays with your copied text. In any Ribbon group, the **Dialog Box Launcher** displays either a dialog box or a task pane related to the group of commands.

It is not necessary to display the Office Clipboard in this manner, although sometimes it is useful to do so. The Office Clipboard can hold 24 items.

Figure 1.54

Copy button

Dialog Box Launcher in Clipboard group

Clipboard task pane displays

Selected text on the Office Clipboard

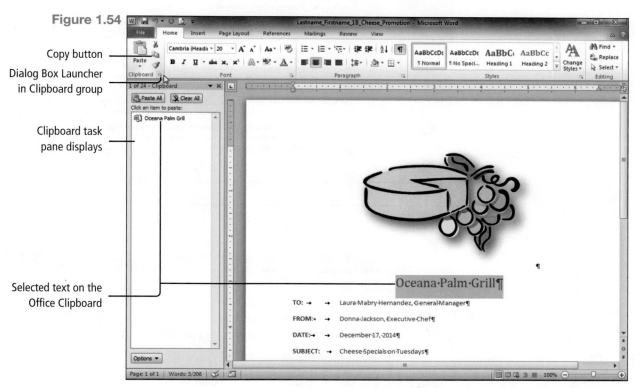

4 In the upper right corner of the **Clipboard** task pane, click the **Close** button.

Another Way

Right-click, on the shortcut menu under Paste Options, click the desired option button.

5 Press Ctrl + End to move to the end of your document. Press Enter one time to create a new blank paragraph. On the **Home tab**, in the **Clipboard group**, point to the **Paste** button, and then click the *upper* portion of this split button.

The Paste command pastes the most recently copied item on the Office Clipboard at the insertion point location. If you click the lower portion of the Paste button, a gallery of Paste Options displays.

6 Click the **Paste Options** button 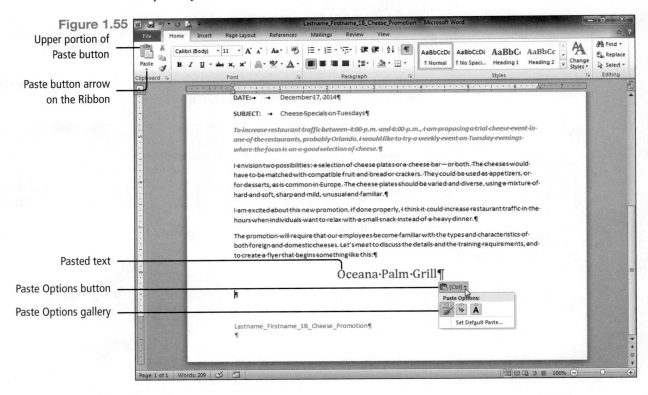 that displays below the pasted text as shown in Figure 1.55.

> Here you can view and apply various formatting options for pasting your copied or cut text. Typically you will click Paste on the Ribbon and paste the item in its original format. If you want some other format for the pasted item, you can do so from the *Paste Options gallery*.

> The Paste Options gallery provides a Live Preview of the various options for changing the format of the pasted item with a single click. The Paste Options gallery is available in three places: on the Ribbon by clicking the lower portion of the Paste button—the Paste button arrow; from the Paste Options button that displays below the pasted item following the paste operation; or, on the shortcut menu if you right-click the pasted item.

Figure 1.55
Upper portion of Paste button
Paste button arrow on the Ribbon
Pasted text
Paste Options button
Paste Options gallery

7 In the displayed **Paste Options** gallery, *point* to each option to see the Live Preview of the format that would be applied if you clicked the button.

> The contents of the Paste Options gallery are contextual; that is, they change based on what you copied and where you are pasting.

8 Press (Esc) to close the gallery; the button will remain displayed until you take some other screen action.

Another Way

On the Home tab, in the Clipboard group, click the Cut button; or, use the keyboard shortcut (Ctrl) + (X).

9 Press (Ctrl) + (Home) to move to the top of the document, and then click the **cheese image** one time to select it. While pointing to the selected image, right-click, and then on the shortcut menu, click **Cut**.

> Recall that the Cut command cuts—removes—the selection from the document and places it on the Office Clipboard.

10 Press [Del] one time to remove the blank paragraph from the top of the document, and then press [Ctrl] + [End] to move to the end of the document.

11 With the insertion point blinking in the blank paragraph at the end of the document, right-click, and notice that the **Paste Options** gallery displays on the shortcut menu. Compare your screen with Figure 1.56.

Figure 1.56

Paste Options on shortcut menu

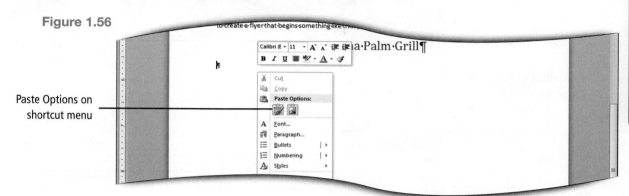

12 On the shortcut menu, under **Paste Options**, click the first button—**Keep Source Formatting** .

13 Click the picture to select it. On the **Home tab**, in the **Paragraph group**, click the **Center** button .

14 Above the cheese picture, click to position the insertion point at the end of the word *Grill*, press [Spacebar] one time, and then type **Tuesday Cheese Tastings** Compare your screen with Figure 1.57.

Figure 1.57

Heading

Picture inserted and centered

Activity 1.14 | Viewing Print Preview and Printing a Word Document

1 Press [Ctrl] + [Home] to move to the top of your document. Select the text *Oceana Palm Grill*, and then replace the selected text by typing **Memo**

2 Display **Backstage** view, on the right, click **Properties**, and then click **Show Document Panel**. Replace the existing author name with your first and last name. In the **Subject** box, type your course name and section number, and then in the **Keywords** box, type **cheese promotion** and then **Close** × the **Document Information Panel**.

Another Way

Press Ctrl + F2 to display Print Preview.

3 On the Quick Access Toolbar, click **Save** 🔲 to save the changes you have made to your document.

4 On the Quick Access Toolbar, click the **Print Preview** button 🔍 that you added. Compare your screen with Figure 1.58.

Figure 1.58

Memo typed

If no printer is attached to your system, OneNote is the default printer

Print tab active in Backstage view

Print Preview (if you have a non-color printer as your default printer, the preview may display in shades of gray)

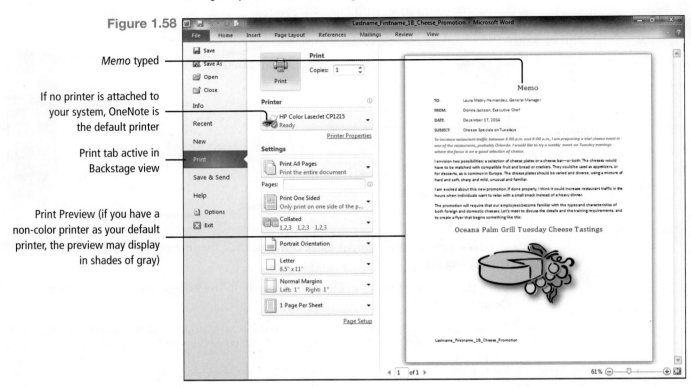

5 Examine the **Print Preview**. Under **Settings**, notice that in **Backstage** view, several of the same commands that are available on the Page Layout tab of the Ribbon also display.

For convenience, common adjustments to Page Layout display here, so that you can make last-minute adjustments without closing Backstage view.

6 If you need to make any corrections, click the Home tab to return to the document and make any necessary changes.

It is good practice to examine the Print Preview before printing or submitting your work electronically. Then, make any necessary corrections, re-save, and redisplay Print Preview.

7 If you are directed to do so, click Print to print the document; or, above the Info tab, click Close, and then submit your file electronically according to the directions provided by your instructor.

If you click the Print button, Backstage view closes and the Word window redisplays.

8 On the Quick Access Toolbar, point to the **Print Preview icon** 🔍 you placed there, right-click, and then click **Remove from Quick Access Toolbar**.

If you are working on your own computer and you want to do so, you can leave the icon on the toolbar; in a lab setting, you should return the software to its original settings.

9 At the right end of the title bar, click the program **Close** button ⊠ .

10 If a message displays asking if you want the text on the Clipboard to be available after you quit Word, click **No**.

> This message most often displays if you have copied some type of image to the Clipboard. If you click Yes, the items on the Clipboard will remain for you to use.

Objective 11 | Use the Microsoft Office 2010 Help System

Within each Office program, the Help feature provides information about all of the program's features and displays step-by-step instructions for performing many tasks.

Activity 1.15 | Using the Microsoft Office 2010 Help System in Excel

In this activity, you will use the Microsoft Help feature to find information about formatting numbers in Excel.

> **Another Way**
> Press F1 to display Help.

1 **Start** the **Microsoft Excel 2010** program. In the upper right corner of your screen, click the **Microsoft Excel Help** button ❓.

2 In the **Excel Help** window, click in the white box in upper left corner, type **formatting numbers** and then click **Search** or press Enter.

3 On the list of results, click **Display numbers as currency**. Compare your screen with Figure 1.59.

Figure 1.59

Excel Help window
Search term
Print button
Search button

Help information

Excel Help button

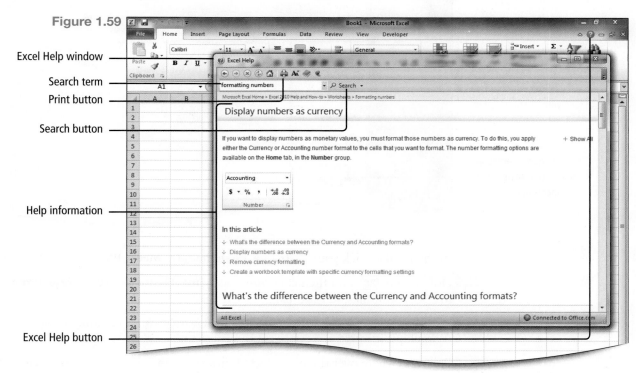

4 If you want to do so, on the toolbar at the top of the **Excel Help** window, click the Print 🖨 button to print a copy of this information for your reference.

5 On the title bar of the Excel Help window, click the **Close** button ⊠. On the right side of the Microsoft Excel title bar, click the **Close** button ⊠ to close Excel.

Objective 12 | Compress Files

A *compressed file* is a file that has been reduced in size. Compressed files take up less storage space and can be transferred to other computers faster than uncompressed files. You can also combine a group of files into one compressed folder, which makes it easier to share a group of files.

Activity 1.16 | Compressing Files

In this activity, you will combine the two files you created in this chapter into one compressed file.

1 On the Windows taskbar, click the **Start** button ⊕, and then on the right, click **Computer**.

2 On the left, in the **navigation pane**, click the location of your two files from this chapter—your USB flash drive or other location—and display the folder window for your **Common Features Chapter 1** folder. Compare your screen with Figure 1.60.

Figure 1.60

Address bar displays path

Your chapter files in file list (your name displays)

Folder window for your chapter folder

Location selected in navigation pane (your location may vary)

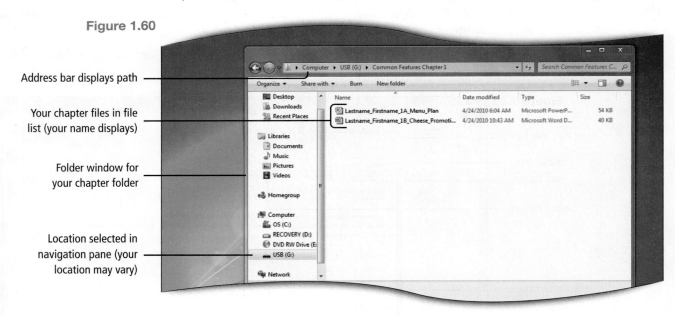

3 In the **file list**, click your **Lastname_Firstname_1A_Menu_Plan** file one time to select it.

4 Hold down Ctrl, and then click your **Lastname_Firstname_1B_Cheese_Promotion** file to select both files. Release Ctrl.

In any Windows-based program, holding down Ctrl while selecting enables you to select multiple items.

5 Point anywhere over the two selected files and right-click. On the shortcut menu, point to **Send to**, and then compare your screen with Figure 1.61.

Figure 1.61

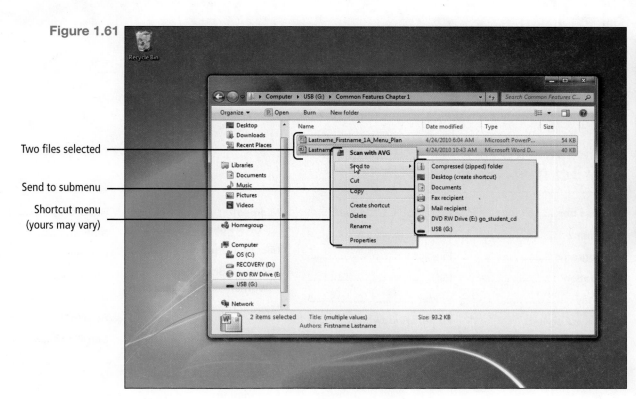

Two files selected

Send to submenu

Shortcut menu
(yours may vary)

6 On the shortcut submenu, click **Compressed (zipped) folder**.

Windows creates a compressed folder containing a *copy* of each of the selected files. The
folder name is the name of the file or folder to which you were pointing, and is selected—
highlighted in blue—so that you can rename it.

7 Using your own name, type **Lastname_Firstname_Common_Features_Ch1** and
press [Enter].

The compressed folder is now ready to attach to an e-mail or share in some other
electronic format.

8 **Close** [X] the folder window. If directed to do so by your instructor, submit your
compressed folder electronically.

More Knowledge | Extracting Compressed Files

Extract means to decompress, or pull out, files from a compressed form. When you extract a file, an uncompressed copy is placed in the folder that you specify. The original file remains in the compressed folder.

End **You have completed Project 1B** ————————————————

Content-Based Assessments

Summary

In this chapter, you used Windows Explorer to navigate the Windows file structure. You also used features that are common across the Microsoft Office 2010 programs.

Key Terms

Content-Based Assessments

Matching

Match each term in the second column with its correct definition in the first column by writing the letter of the term on the blank line in front of the correct definition.

_____ 1. A collection of information stored on a computer under a single name.

_____ 2. A container in which you store files.

_____ 3. A folder within a folder.

_____ 4. The program that displays the files and folders on your computer.

_____ 5. The Windows menu that is the main gateway to your computer.

_____ 6. In Windows 7, a window that displays the contents of the current folder, library, or device, and contains helpful parts so that you can navigate.

_____ 7. In Windows, a collection of items, such as files and folders, assembled from various locations that might be on your computer.

_____ 8. The bar at the top of a folder window with which you can navigate to a different folder or library, or go back to a previous one.

_____ 9. An instruction to a computer program that carries out an action.

_____ 10. Small pictures that represent a program, a file, a folder, or an object.

_____ 11. A set of instructions that a computer uses to perform a specific task.

_____ 12. A spreadsheet program used to calculate numbers and create charts.

_____ 13. The user interface that groups commands on tabs at the top of the program window.

_____ 14. A bar at the top of the program window displaying the current file and program name.

_____ 15. One or more keys pressed to perform a task that would otherwise require a mouse.

A Address bar

B Command

C File

D Folder

E Folder window

F Icons

G Keyboard shortcut

H Library

I Microsoft Excel

J Program

K Ribbon

L Start menu

M Subfolder

N Title bar

O Windows Explorer

Multiple Choice

Circle the correct answer.

1. A small toolbar with frequently used commands that displays when selecting text or objects is the:
   A. Quick Access Toolbar   **B.** Mini toolbar   **C.** Document toolbar

2. In Office 2010, a centralized space for file management tasks is:
   A. a task pane   **B.** a dialog box   **C.** Backstage view

3. The commands Save, Save As, Open, and Close in Backstage view are located:
   A. above the Backstage tabs   **B.** below the Backstage tabs   **C.** under the screen thumbnail

4. The tab in Backstage view that displays information about the current file is the:
   A. Recent tab   **B.** Info tab   **C.** Options tab

5. Details about a file, including the title, author name, subject, and keywords are known as:
   A. document properties   **B.** formatting marks   **C.** KeyTips

6. An Office feature that displays a list of potential results is:
   A. Live Preview   **B.** a contextual tab   **C.** a gallery

7. A type of formatting emphasis applied to text such as bold, italic, and underline, is called:

    A. a font style   **B.** a KeyTip   **C.** a tag

8. A technology showing the result of applying formatting as you point to possible results is called:

    A. Live Preview   **B.** Backstage view   **C.** gallery view

9. A temporary storage area that holds text or graphics that you select and then cut or copy is the:

    A. paste options gallery   **B.** ribbon   **C.** Office clipboard

10. A file that has been reduced in size is:

    A. a compressed file   **B.** an extracted file   **C.** a PDF file

Creating Documents with Microsoft Word 2010

OUTCOMES

At the end of this chapter you will be able to:

PROJECT 1A
Create a flyer with a picture.

PROJECT 1B
Format text, paragraphs, and documents.

OBJECTIVES

Mastering these objectives will enable you to:

1. Create a New Document and Insert Text (p. 51)
2. Insert and Format Graphics (p. 53)
3. Insert and Modify Text Boxes and Shapes (p. 58)
4. Preview and Print a Document (p. 62)

5. Change Document and Paragraph Layout (p. 67)
6. Create and Modify Lists (p. 73)
7. Set and Modify Tab Stops (p. 78)
8. Insert a SmartArt Graphic (p. 80)

Joy Brown/Shutterstock

In This Chapter

In this chapter, you will use Microsoft Word, which is one of the most common programs found on computers and one that almost everyone has a reason to use. You will use many of the new tools found in Word 2010. When you learn word processing, you are also learning skills and techniques that you need to work efficiently on a computer. You can use Microsoft Word to perform basic word processing tasks such as writing a memo, a report, or a letter. You can also use Word to complete complex word processing tasks, such as creating sophisticated tables, embedding graphics, writing blogs, creating publications, and inserting links into other documents and the Internet. Word is a program that you can learn gradually, and then add more advanced skills one at a time.

The projects in this chapter relate to **Laurel College**. The college offers this diverse geographic area a wide range of academic and career programs, including associate degrees, certificate programs, and non-credit continuing education and personal development courses. The college makes positive contributions to the community through cultural and athletic programs and partnerships with businesses and nonprofit organizations. The college also provides industry-specific training programs for local businesses through its growing Economic Development Center.

Project 1A Flyer

myitlab
Project 1A Training

Project Activities

In Activities 1.01 through 1.12, you will create a flyer announcing a new rock climbing class offered by the Physical Education Department at Laurel College. Your completed document will look similar to Figure 1.1.

Project Files

For Project 1A, you will need the following files:

New blank Word document
w01A_Fitness_Flyer
w01A_Rock_Climber

You will save your document as:

Lastname_Firstname_1A_Fitness_Flyer

Project Results

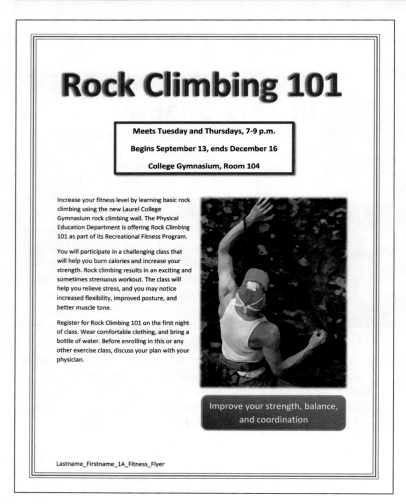

Figure 1.1
Project 1A Fitness Flyer

Objective 1 | Create a New Document and Insert Text

When you create a new document, you can type all of the text, or you can type some of the text and then insert additional text from another source.

Activity 1.01 | Starting a New Word Document and Inserting Text

1 **Start** Word and display a new blank document. On the **Home tab**, in the **Paragraph group**, if necessary click the Show/Hide button ⁋ so that it is active (glows orange) to display the formatting marks. If the rulers do not display, click the View tab, and then in the Show group, select the Ruler check box.

2 Type **Rock Climbing 101** and then press Enter two times. As you type the following text, press the Spacebar only one time at the end of a sentence: **Increase your fitness level by learning basic rock climbing using the new Laurel College Gymnasium rock climbing wall. The Physical Education Department is offering Rock Climbing 101 as part of its Recreational Fitness Program.**

As you type, the insertion point moves to the right, and when it approaches the right margin, Word determines whether the next word in the line will fit within the established right margin. If the word does not fit, Word moves the entire word down to the next line. This feature is called *wordwrap* and means that you press Enter *only* when you reach the end of a paragraph—it is not necessary to press Enter at the end of each line of text.

Note | Spacing Between Sentences

Although you might have learned to add two spaces following end-of-sentence punctuation, the common practice now is to space only one time at the end of a sentence.

---

3 Press Enter one time. Take a moment to study the table in Figure 1.2 to become familiar with the default document settings in Microsoft Word, and then compare your screen with Figure 1.3.

When you press Enter, Spacebar, or Tab on your keyboard, characters display in your document to represent these keystrokes. These characters do not print and are referred to as *formatting marks* or *nonprinting characters*. These marks will display throughout this instruction.

Default Document Settings in a New Word Document	
Setting	**Default format**
Font and font size	The default font is Calibri and the default font size is 11.
Margins	The default left, right, top, and bottom page margins are 1 inch.
Line spacing	The default line spacing is 1.15, which provides slightly more space between lines than single spacing does—an extra 1/6 of a line added between lines than single spacing.
Paragraph spacing	The default spacing after a paragraph is 10 points, which is slightly less than the height of one blank line of text.
View	The default view is Print Layout view, which displays the page borders and displays the document as it will appear when printed.

Figure 1.2

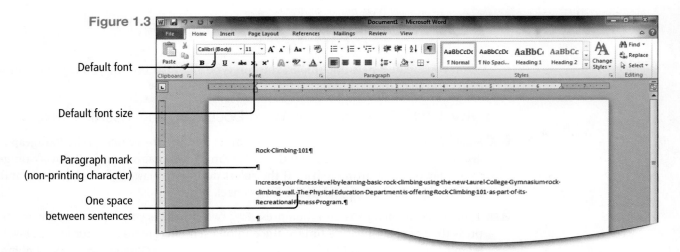

Figure 1.3

Default font

Default font size

Paragraph mark
(non-printing character)

One space
between sentences

4 On the Ribbon, click the **Insert tab**. In the **Text group**, click the **Object button arrow**, and then click **Text from File**.

> **Alert! | Does the Object Dialog Box Display?**
>
> If the Object dialog box displays, you probably clicked the Object *button* instead of the Object *button arrow*. Close the Object dialog box, and then in the Text group, click the Object button arrow, as shown in Figure 1.4. Click *Text from File*, and then continue with Step 5.

Another Way

Open the file, copy the required text, close the file, and then paste the text into the current document.

5 In the **Insert File** dialog box, navigate to the student files that accompany this textbook, locate and select **w01A_Fitness_Flyer**, and then click **Insert**. Compare your screen with Figure 1.4.

A *copy* of the text from the w01A_Fitness_Flyer file displays at the insertion point location; the text is not removed from the original file.

Figure 1.4

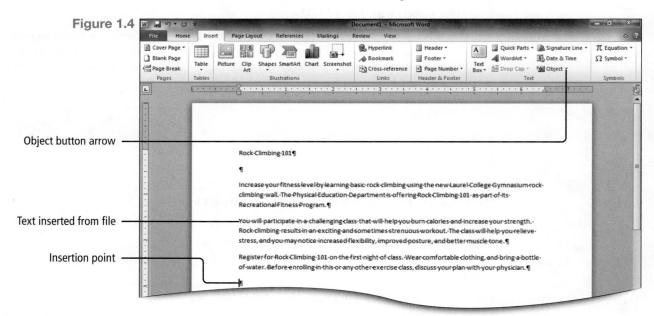

Object button arrow

Text inserted from file

Insertion point

6 On the **Quick Access Toolbar**, click the **Save** button. In the **Save As** dialog box, navigate to the location where you are saving your files for this chapter, and then create and open a new folder named **Word Chapter 1** In the **File name** box, replace the existing text with **Lastname_Firstname_1A_Fitness_Flyer** and then click **Save**.

Objective 2 | Insert and Format Graphics

To add visual interest to a document, insert **graphics**. Graphics include pictures, clip art, charts, and **drawing objects**—shapes, diagrams, lines, and so on. For additional visual interest, you can convert text to an attractive graphic format; add, resize, move, and format pictures; and add an attractive page border.

Activity 1.02 | Formatting Text Using Text Effects

Text effects are decorative formats, such as shadowed or mirrored text, text glow, 3-D effects, and colors that make text stand out.

1 Including the paragraph mark, select the first paragraph of text—*Rock Climbing 101*. On the **Home tab**, in the **Font group**, click the **Text Effects** button Ⓐ▾.

2 In the displayed **Text Effects** gallery, in the first row, point to the second effect to display the ScreenTip *Fill - None, Outline - Accent 2* and then click this effect.

3 With the text still selected, in the **Font group**, click in the **Font Size** box 11 ▾ to select the existing font size. Type **60** and then press Enter.

> When you want to change the font size of selected text to a size that does not display in the Font Size list, type the number in the Font Size button box and press Enter to confirm the new font size.

4 With the text still selected, in the **Paragraph group**, click the **Center** button ≣ to center the text. Compare your screen with Figure 1.5.

Figure 1.5

Text Effects button

Center button glowing orange indicates centering applied

Text effects applied to title (title selected)

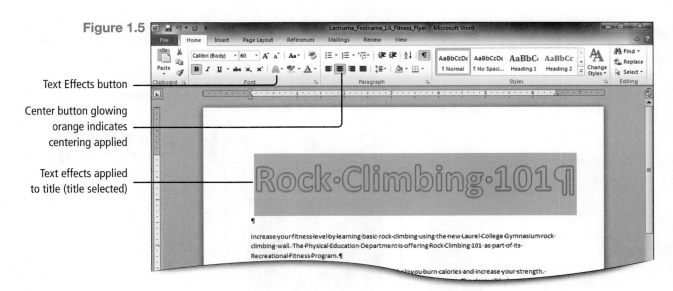

5 With the text still selected, in the **Font group**, click the **Text Effects** button Ⓐ▾. Point to **Shadow**, and then under **Outer**, in the second row, click the third style—**Offset Left**.

6 With the text still selected, in the **Font group**, click the **Font Color button arrow** Ⓐ▾. Under **Theme Colors**, in the fourth column, click the first color—**Dark Blue, Text 2**.

7 Click anywhere in the document to deselect the text, and then compare your screen with Figure 1.6.

Figure 1.6

Title color changed and shadow added

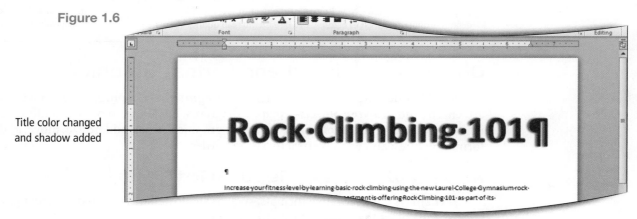

8 **Save** 🖫 your document.

Activity 1.03 | Inserting and Resizing Pictures

1 In the paragraph that begins *Increase your fitness*, click to position the insertion point at the beginning of the paragraph.

2 On the **Insert tab**, in the **Illustrations group**, click the **Picture** button. In the **Insert Picture** dialog box, navigate to your student data files, locate and click **w01A_Rock_Climber**, and then click **Insert**.

Word inserts the picture as an ***inline object***; that is, the picture is positioned directly in the text at the insertion point, just like a character in a sentence. Sizing handles surround the picture indicating it is selected.

3 If necessary, scroll to view the entire picture. Notice the round and square sizing handles around the border of the selected picture, as shown in Figure 1.7.

The round corner sizing handles resize the graphic proportionally. The square sizing handles resize a graphic vertically or horizontally only; however, sizing with these will distort the graphic. A green rotate handle, with which you can rotate the graphic to any angle, displays above the top center sizing handle.

Figure 1.7

Center sizing handle

Rotate handle

Corner sizing handles

4 At the lower right corner of the picture, point to the round sizing handle until the ⤢ pointer displays. Drag upward and to the left until the bottom of the graphic is aligned at approximately **4 inches on the vertical ruler**. Compare your screen with Figure 1.8. Notice that the graphic is proportionally resized.

Figure 1.8

Picture resized

4-inch mark on the vertical ruler

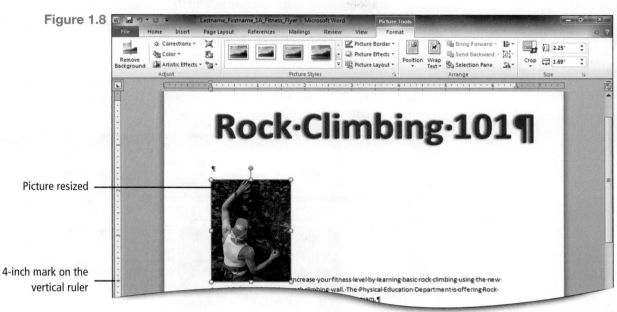

Another Way

Click the Undo button to undo the change.

5 On the **Format tab**, in the **Adjust group**, click the **Reset Picture button arrow** 🖼, and then click **Reset Picture & Size**.

6 In the **Size group**, click the **Shape Height spin box up arrow** 📏 1.5" as necessary to change the height of the picture to **4.5"**. Scroll down to view the entire picture on your screen, compare your screen with Figure 1.9, and then **Save** 💾 your document.

When you use the Height and Width *spin boxes* to change the size of a graphic, the graphic will always resize proportionally; that is, the width adjusts as you change the height and vice versa.

Figure 1.9

Picture height increased to 4.5 inches

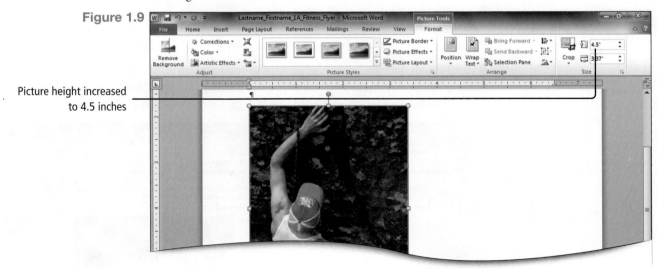

Activity 1.04 | Wrapping Text Around a Picture

Graphics inserted as inline objects are treated like characters in a sentence, which can result in unattractive spacing. You can change an inline object to a *floating object*—a graphic that can be moved independently of the surrounding text characters.

1 Be sure the picture is selected—you know it is selected if the sizing handles display.

2 On the **Format tab**, in the **Arrange group**, click the **Wrap Text** button to display a gallery of text wrapping arrangements.

Text wrapping refers to the manner in which text displays around an object.

3 From the gallery, click **Square** to wrap the text around the graphic, and then notice the *anchor* symbol to the left of the first line of the paragraph. Compare your screen with Figure 1.10.

Select square text wrapping when you want to wrap the text to the left or right of the image. When you apply text wrapping, the object is always associated with—anchored to—a specific paragraph.

Figure 1.10

Wrap Text button

Anchor symbol

Text wrapped around picture

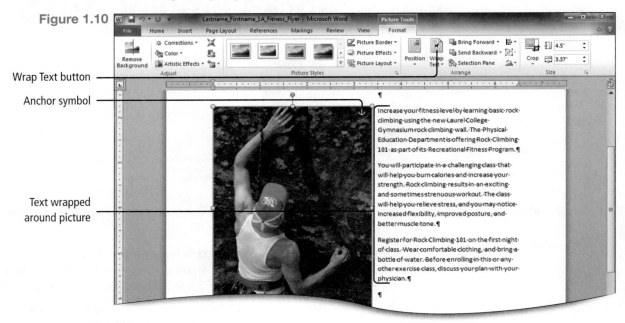

4 **Save** your document.

Activity 1.05 | Moving a Picture

1 Point to the rock climber picture to display the pointer.

2 Hold down Shift and drag the picture to the right until the right edge of the picture aligns at approximately **6.5 inches on the horizontal ruler**. Notice that the picture moves in a straight line when you hold down Shift. Compare your screen with Figure 1.11.

Figure 1.11

Right edge aligned with right margin

Top edge aligned with top of paragraph

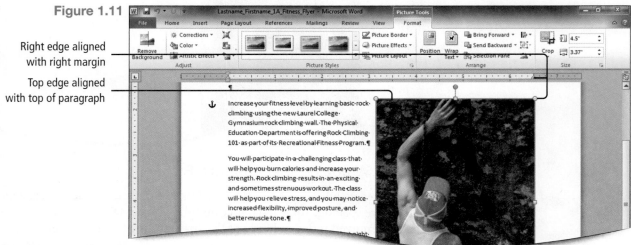

3 If necessary, press any of the arrow keys on your keyboard to *nudge*—move in small increments—the picture in any direction so that the text wraps to match Figure 1.11. **Save** 🖫 your document.

Activity 1.06 | Applying Picture Styles and Artistic Effects

Picture styles include shapes, shadows, frames, borders, and other special effects with which you can stylize an image. *Artistic effects* are formats that make pictures look more like sketches or paintings.

1 Be sure the rock climber picture is selected. On the **Format tab**, in the **Picture Styles group**, click the **Picture Effects** button. Point to **Soft Edges**, and then click **5 Point**.

The Soft Edges feature fades the edges of the picture. The number of points you choose determines how far the fade goes inward from the edges of the picture.

2 On the **Format tab**, in the **Adjust group**, click the **Artistic Effects** button. In the first row of the gallery, point to, but do not click, the third effect—**Pencil Grayscale**.

Live Preview displays the picture with the *Pencil Grayscale* effect added.

3 In the second row of the gallery, click the third effect—**Paint Brush**. Notice that the picture looks like a painting, rather than a photograph, as shown in Figure 1.12. **Save** 🖫 your document.

Figure 1.12

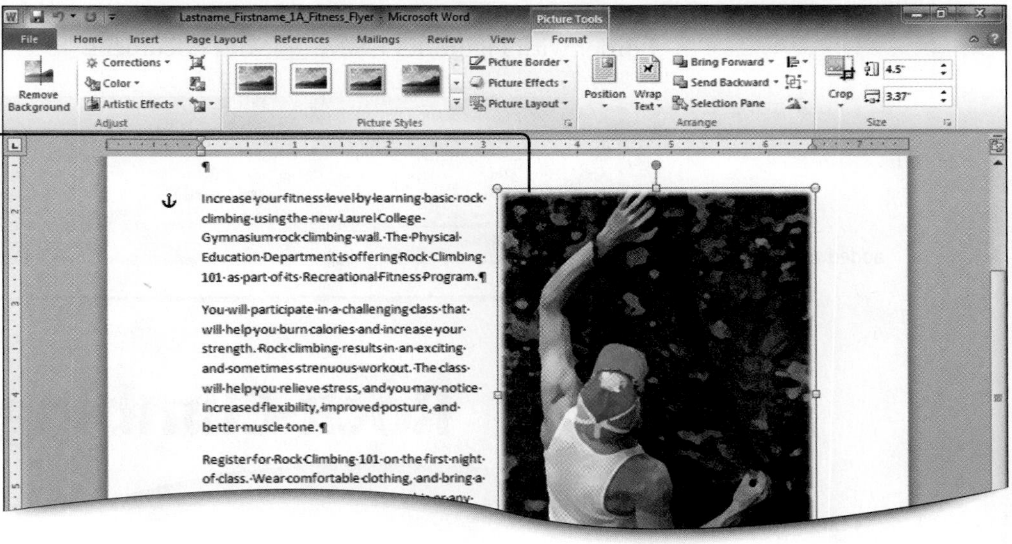

Paint Brush artistic effect applied to picture

Activity 1.07 | Adding a Page Border

Page borders frame a page and help to focus the information on the page.

1 Click anywhere outside the picture to deselect it. On the **Page Layout tab**, in the **Page Background group**, click the **Page Borders** button.

2 In the **Borders and Shading** dialog box, under **Setting**, click **Box**. Under **Style**, scroll down the list about a third of the way and click the heavy top line with the thin bottom line—check the **Preview** area to be sure the heavier line is the nearest to the edges of the page.

3 Click the **Color arrow**, and then in the fourth column, click the first color—**Dark Blue, Text 2**.

4 Under **Apply to**, be sure *Whole document* is selected, and then compare your screen with Figure 1.13.

Figure 1.13

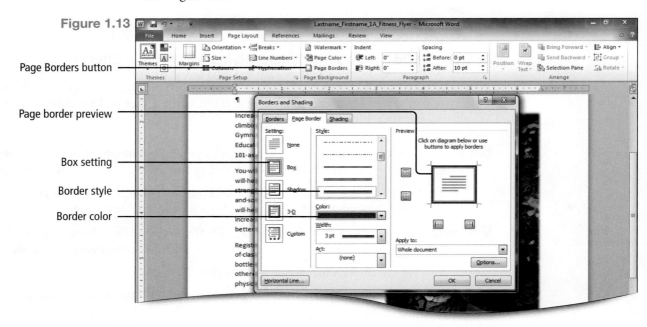

Page Borders button

Page border preview

Box setting

Border style

Border color

5 At the bottom of the **Borders and Shading** dialog box, click **OK**.

6 Press Ctrl + Home to move to the top of the document, and then compare your page border with Figure 1.14. **Save** 🖫 your document.

Figure 1.14

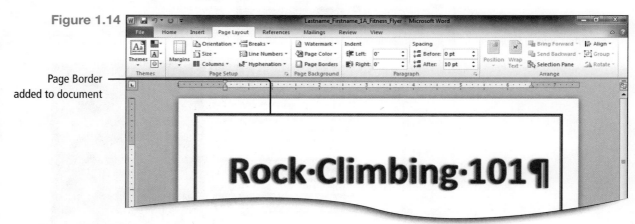

Page Border
added to document

Objective 3 | Insert and Modify Text Boxes and Shapes

Word provides predefined *shapes* and *text boxes* that you can add to your documents. A shape is an object such as a line, arrow, box, callout, or banner. A text box is a movable, resizable container for text or graphics. Use these objects to add visual interest to your document.

Activity 1.08 | Inserting a Shape

1 Press ↓ one time to move to the blank paragraph below the title. Press Enter four times to make space for a text box, and notice that the picture anchored to the paragraph moves with the text.

2 Press Ctrl + End to move to the bottom of the document, and notice that your insertion point is positioned in the empty paragraph at the end of the document.

3 Click the **Insert tab**, and then in the **Illustrations group**, click the **Shapes** button to display the gallery. Compare your screen with Figure 1.15.

Figure 1.15

Shapes button

Rounded Rectangle shape

Shapes gallery

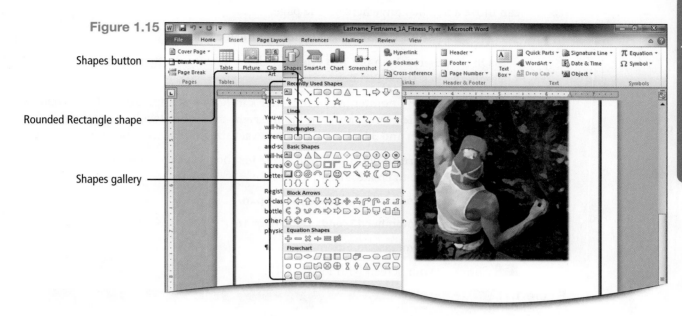

4 Under **Rectangles**, click the second shape—**Rounded Rectangle**, and then move your pointer. Notice that the ⊞ pointer displays.

5 Position the ⊞ pointer just under the lower left corner of the picture, and then drag down approximately **1 inch** and to the right edge of the picture.

6 Point to the shape and right-click, and then from the shortcut menu, click **Add Text**.

7 With the insertion point blinking inside the shape, point inside the shape and right-click, and then on the Mini toolbar, change the **Font Size** to **16**, and be sure **Center** ≡ alignment is selected.

8 Click inside the shape again, and then type **Improve your strength, balance, and coordination** If necessary, use the lower middle sizing handle to enlarge the shape to view your text. Compare your screen with Figure 1.16. **Save** 🖫 your document.

Figure 1.16

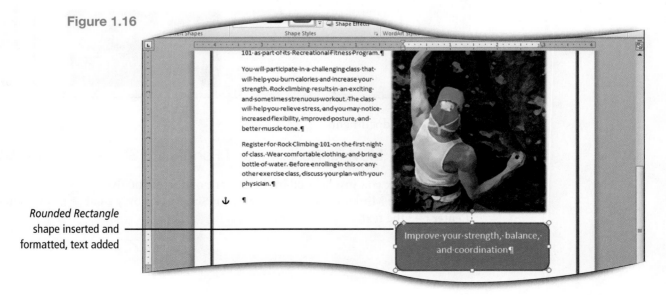

Rounded Rectangle shape inserted and formatted, text added

Activity 1.09 | Inserting a Text Box

A text box is useful to differentiate portions of text from other text on the page. You can move a text box anywhere on the page.

1 Press (Ctrl) + (Home) to move to the top of the document.

2 On the **Insert tab**, in the **Text group**, click the **Text Box** button. At the bottom of the gallery, click **Draw Text Box**.

3 Position the ⊞ pointer below the letter *k* in *Rock*—at approximately **1.5 inches on the vertical ruler**. Drag down and to the right to create a text box approximately **1.5 inches** high and **3 inches** wide—the exact size and location need not be precise.

4 With the insertion point blinking in the text box, type the following, pressing (Enter) after each line to create a new paragraph:

> **Meets Tuesdays and Thursdays, 7-9 p.m.**
>
> **Begins September 13, ends December 16**
>
> **College Gymnasium, Room 104**

5 Compare your screen with Figure 1.17.

Figure 1.17

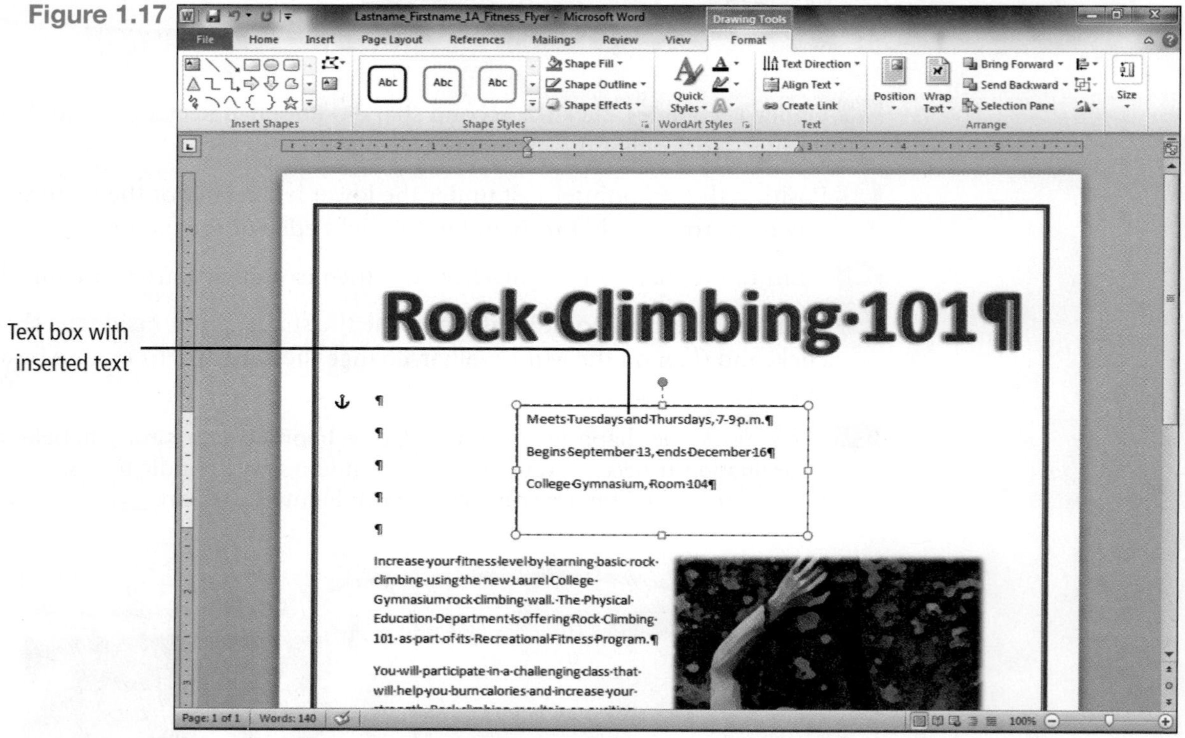

Text box with inserted text

6 **Save** 🖫 your document.

Activity 1.10 | Moving, Resizing, and Formatting Shapes and Text Boxes

1 In the text box you just created in the upper portion of the flyer, select all of the text. From the Mini toolbar, change the **Font Size** to **14**, apply **Bold** 🅱, and then **Center** ≣ the text.

2 On the **Format tab**, in the **Size group**, if necessary, click the **Size** button. Click the **Shape Height spin arrows** as necessary to set the height of the text box to **1.2″**. Click the **Shape Width spin arrows** as necessary to set the width of the text box to **4″**.

3 In the **Shape Styles group**, click the **Shape Effects** button. Point to **Shadow**, and then under **Outer**, in the first row, click the first style—**Offset Diagonal Bottom Right**.

4 In the **Shape Styles group**, click the **Shape Outline button arrow**. In the fourth column, click the first color—**Dark Blue, Text 2** to change the color of the text box border.

5 Click the **Shape Outline button arrow** again, point to **Weight**, and then click **3 pt**.

6 Click anywhere in the document to deselect the text box. Notice that with the text box deselected, you can see all the measurements on the horizontal ruler.

7 Click anywhere in the text box and point to the text box border to display the pointer. By dragging, visually center the text box vertically and horizontally in the space below the *Rock Climbing 101* title. Then, if necessary, press any of the arrow keys on your keyboard to nudge the text box in precise increments to match Figure 1.18.

Figure 1.18

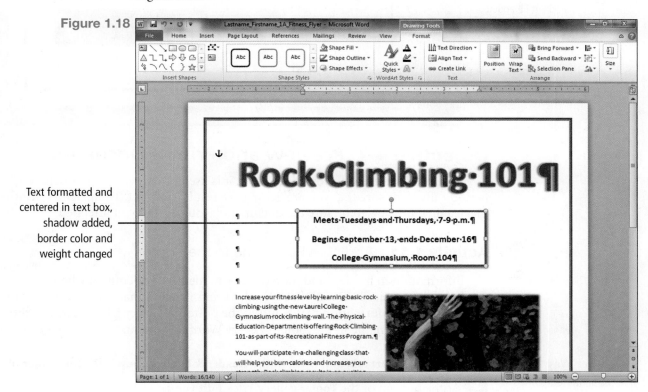

Text formatted and centered in text box, shadow added, border color and weight changed

8 Press Ctrl + End to move to the bottom of the document. Click on the border of the rounded rectangular shape to select it.

9 On the **Format tab**, in the **Size group**, if necessary, click the **Size** button. Click the **Shape Height spin arrows** as necessary to change the height of the shape to **0.8″**.

10 In the **Shape Styles group**, click the **Shape Fill button arrow**, and then at the bottom of the gallery, point to **Gradient**. Under **Dark Variations**, in the third row click the first gradient—**Linear Diagonal - Bottom Left to Top Right**.

11 In the **Shape Styles group**, click the **Shape Outline button arrow**. In the sixth column, click the first color—**Red, Accent 2**.

12 Click the **Shape Outline button arrow** again, point to **Weight**, and then click **1 1/2 pt**. Click anywhere in the document to deselect the shape. Compare your screen with Figure 1.19, and then **Save** 🖫 your document.

Figure 1.19

Gradient fill added, shape outline formatted

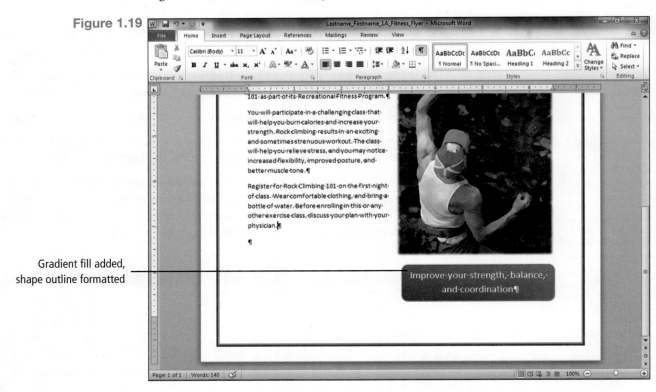

Objective 4 | Preview and Print a Document

While you are creating your document, it is useful to preview your document periodically to be sure that you are getting the result you want. Then, before printing, make a final preview to be sure the document layout is what you intended.

Activity 1.11 | Adding a File Name to the Footer

Information in headers and footers helps to identify a document when it is printed or displayed electronically. Recall that a header is information that prints at the top of every page; a footer is information that prints at the bottom of every page. In this textbook, you will insert the file name in the footer of every Word document.

> **Another Way**
>
> At the bottom edge of the page, right-click; from the shortcut menu, click Edit Footer.

1 Click the **Insert tab**, and then, in the **Header & Footer group**, click the **Footer** button.

2 At the bottom of the **Footer** gallery, click **Edit Footer**.

The footer area displays with the insertion point blinking at the left edge, and on the Ribbon, the Header & Footer Tools display and add the Design tab.

3 On the **Design tab**, in the **Insert group**, click the **Quick Parts** button, and then click **Field**. In the **Field** dialog box, under **Field names**, use the vertical scroll bar to examine the items that you can insert in a header or footer.

A *field* is a placeholder that displays preset content such as the current date, the file name, a page number, or other stored information.

4 In the **Field names** list, scroll as necessary to locate and then click **FileName**. Compare your screen with Figure 1.20.

Figure 1.20

Quick Parts button

Field dialog box

FileName field

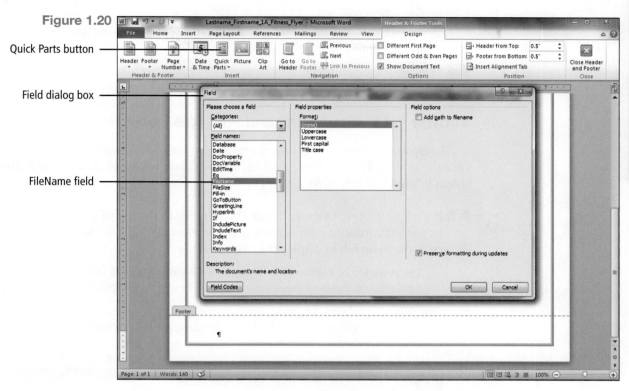

5 In the lower right corner of the **Field** dialog box, click **OK**, and then compare your screen with Figure 1.21.

Figure 1.21

Document text and image dimmed when footer is open

File name in footer

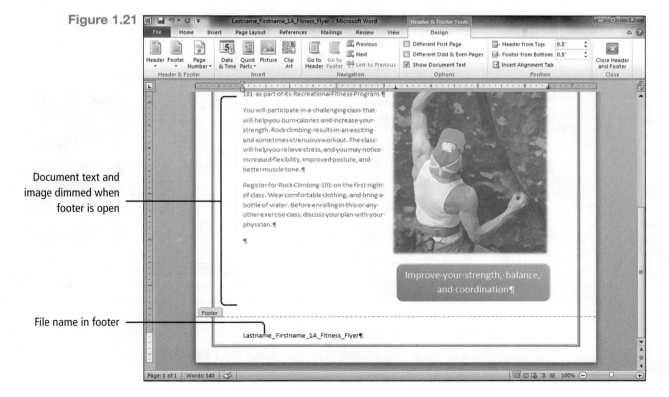

Another Way

Double-click anywhere
in the document to
close the footer area.

6 On the **Design tab**, at the far right in the **Close group**, click the **Close Header and Footer** button.

When the body of the document is active, the footer text is dimmed—displays in gray. Conversely, when the footer area is active, the footer text is not dimmed; instead, the document text is dimmed.

7 Save 🖫 your document.

Activity 1.12 | Previewing and Printing a Document

To ensure that you are getting the result you want, it is useful to periodically preview your document. Then, before printing, make a final preview to be sure the document layout is what you intended.

Another Way

Press Ctrl + F2 to
display Print Preview.

1 Press Ctrl + Home to move the insertion point to the top of the document. In the upper left corner of your screen, click the **File tab** to display **Backstage** view, and then click the **Print tab** to display the **Print Preview**.

The Print tab in Backstage view displays the tools you need to select your settings. On the right, Print Preview displays your document exactly as it will print; the formatting marks do not display.

2 In the lower right corner of the **Print Preview**, notice the zoom buttons that display. Compare your screen with Figure 1.22.

Figure 1.22

Print tab

Print Preview of document

Zoom buttons

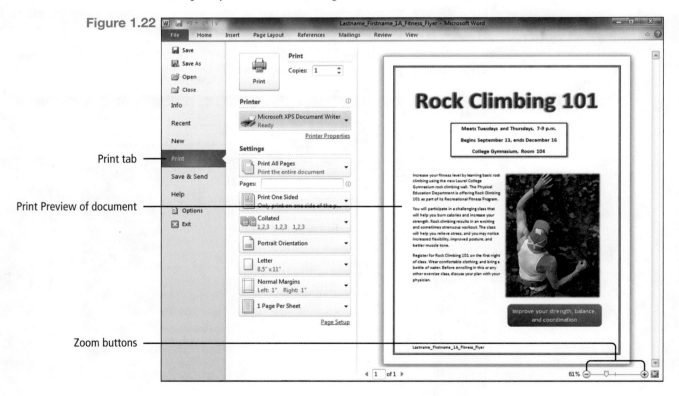

3 Click the **Zoom In** button ⊕ to view the document at full size, and notice that a larger preview is easier to read. Click the **Zoom Out** button ⊖ to view the entire page.

4 Click the **Info tab**. On the right, under the screen thumbnail, click **Properties**, and then click **Show Document Panel**.

Here you can adjust the document properties.

5 In the **Author** box, delete any text and then type your firstname and lastname. In the **Subject** box type your course name and section number, and in the **Keywords** box type **fitness, rock climbing Close** ⊠ the Document Panel.

6 **Save** 🖫 your document. To print, display **Backstage** view, and then on the **navigation bar**, click **Print**. In the **Settings** group, be sure the correct printer is selected, and then in the **Print group**, click the **Print** button. Or, submit your document electronically as directed by your instructor.

7 In **Backstage** view, click **Exit** to close the document and exit Word.

End You have completed Project 1A ———————————

Project 1B Information Handout

myitlab
Project 1B Training

Project Activities

In Activities 1.13 through 1.23, you will format and add lists to an information handout that describes student activities at Laurel College. Your completed document will look similar to Figure 1.23.

Project Files

For Project 1B, you will need the following file:

w01B_Student_Activities

You will save your document as:

Lastname_Firstname_1B_Student_Activities

Project Results

Every spring, students vote for the President, Vice President, Treasurer, Secretary, and Student Trustee for the following year. Executive Officers work with the college administration to manage campus activities and to make changes to policies and procedures. For example, the Student Trustee is a ... h consists of elected members from the ... college budget, and employee hiring. ... the Board to vote for a proposal to ... ocations in Laurelton and outlying areas.

... lubs and academic organizations vote for ... on information and applications on the ... mpus and in the student newspaper.

... f interests, including academic, political, ... currently in existence at Laurel College. A ... oin a club, you may enjoy being a member ... or you may decide to take a leadership role

... fice in the Campus Center, Room CC208, or ... d complete the form online. Clubs accept ... e following are the first meeting dates and

... October 8, 2:00 p.m., Room CC214
... ctober 5, 5:00 p.m., Computer Café
... 7, 3:00 p.m., Field House, Room 2A
... October 6, 2:00 p.m., Room CC212
... 6, 4:00 p.m., Math Tutoring Lab, L35
... October 8, 3:00 p.m., Room CC214
... 4, 5:30 p.m., Photo Lab, Foster Hall
...........October 8, 5:00 p.m., Room L24
... October 7, 4:30 p.m., Room CC214
... October 4, 3:00 p.m., Little Theater

... listed here, are great, but your goals are ... ing a degree or certificate. Maybe you want ... ou leave Laurel College. Whatever your ... ur education, work experience, and ... lly ones in which you had a leadership role,

Associated Students of Laurel College

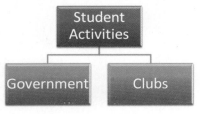

Get Involved in Student Activities

Your experience at Laurel College will be richer and more memorable if you get involved in activities that take you beyond the classroom. You will have the opportunity to meet other students, faculty, and staff members and will participate in organizations that make valuable contributions to your college and to the community.

Consider becoming involved in student government or joining a club. You might take part in activities such as these:

- ✓ Volunteering to help with a blood drive
- ✓ Traveling to a foreign country to learn about other cultures
- ✓ Volunteering to assist at graduation
- ✓ Helping to organize a community picnic
- ✓ Planning and implementing advertising for a student event
- ✓ Meeting with members of the state legislature to discuss issues that affect college students—for example, tuition costs and financial aid

Student Government

As a registered student, you are eligible to attend meetings of the Executive Officers of the Associated Students of Laurel College. At the meetings, you will have the opportunity to learn about college issues that affect students. At the conclusion of each meeting, the Officers invite students to voice their opinions. Eventually, you might decide to run for an office yourself. Running for office is a three-step process:

1. Pick up petitions at the Student Government office.
2. Obtain 100 signatures from current students.
3. Turn in petitions and start campaigning.

Lastname_Firstname_1B_Student_Activities

Figure 1.23
Project 1B Student Activities

Objective 5 | Change Document and Paragraph Layout

Document layout includes *margins*—the space between the text and the top, bottom, left, and right edges of the paper. Paragraph layout includes line spacing, indents, and tabs. In Word, the information about paragraph formats is stored in the paragraph mark at the end of a paragraph. When you press the Enter, the new paragraph mark contains the formatting of the previous paragraph, unless you take steps to change it.

Activity 1.13 | Setting Margins

1 **Start** Word. From **Backstage** view, display the **Open** dialog box. From your student files, locate and open the document **w01B_Student_Activities**. On the **Home tab**, in the **Paragraph group**, be sure the **Show/Hide** button ¶ is active—glows orange—so that you can view the formatting marks.

2 From **Backstage** view, display the **Save As** dialog box. Navigate to your **Word Chapter 1** folder, and then **Save** the document as **Lastname_Firstname_1B_Student_Activities**

3 Click the **Page Layout tab**. In the **Page Setup group**, click the **Margins** button, and then take a moment to study the buttons in the Margins gallery.

The top button displays the most recent custom margin settings, while the other buttons display commonly used margin settings.

4 At the bottom of the **Margins** gallery, click **Custom Margins**.

5 In the **Page Setup** dialog box, press Tab as necessary to select the value in the **Left** box, and then, with *1.25"* selected, type **1**

This action will change the left margin to 1 inch on all pages of the document. You do not need to type the inch (") mark.

6 Press Tab to select the margin in the **Right** box, and then type **1** At the bottom of the dialog box, notice that the new margins will apply to the **Whole document**. Compare your screen with Figure 1.24.

Figure 1.24

Margins button

Left and Right margins changed

Changes applied to entire document

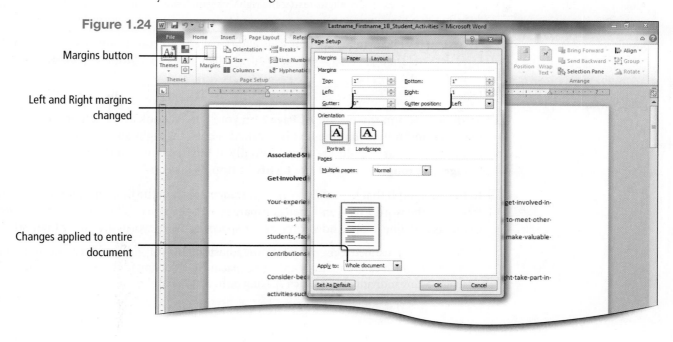

Another Way

Click the View tab, and then in the Show group, select the Ruler check box.

7 Click **OK** to apply the new margins and close the dialog box. If the ruler below the Ribbon is not displayed, at the top of the vertical scroll bar, click the View Ruler button [icon].

8 Scroll to view the bottom of **Page 1** and the top of **Page 2**. Notice that the page edges display, and the page number and total number of pages display on the left side of the status bar.

9 Near the bottom edge of **Page 1**, point anywhere in the margin area, right-click, and then click **Edit Footer** to display the footer area.

10 On the **Design tab**, in the **Insert group**, click the **Quick Parts** button, and then click **Field**. In the **Field** dialog box, under **Field names**, locate and click **FileName**, and then click **OK**.

11 Double-click anywhere in the document to close the footer area, and then **Save** [icon] your document.

Activity 1.14 | Aligning Text

Alignment refers to the placement of paragraph text relative to the left and right margins. Most paragraph text uses *left alignment*—aligned at the left margin, leaving the right margin uneven. Three other types of paragraph alignment are: *center alignment*—centered between the left and right margins; *right alignment*—aligned at the right margin with an uneven left margin; and *justified alignment*—text aligned evenly at both the left and right margins. See the table in Figure 1.25.

Paragraph Alignment Options

Alignment	Button	Description and Example
Align Text Left	[icon]	Align Text Left is the default paragraph alignment in Word. Text in the paragraph aligns at the left margin, and the right margin is uneven.
Center	[icon]	Center alignment aligns text in the paragraph so that it is centered between the left and right margins.
Align Text Right	[icon]	Align Text Right aligns text at the right margin. Using Align Text Right, the left margin, which is normally even, is uneven.
Justify	[icon]	The Justify alignment option adds additional space between words so that both the left and right margins are even. Justify is often used when formatting newspaper-style columns.

Figure 1.25

1 Scroll to position the middle of **Page 2** on your screen, look at the left and right margins, and notice that the text is justified—both the right and left margins of multiple-line paragraphs are aligned evenly at the margins. On the **Home tab**, in the **Paragraph group**, notice that the **Justify** button [icon] is active.

2 In the paragraph that begins *Every spring, students vote*, in the first line, look at the space following the word *Every*, and then compare it with the space following the word *Trustee* in the second line. Notice how some of the spaces between words are larger than others.

To achieve a justified right margin, Word adjusts the size of spaces between words in this manner, which can result in unattractive spacing in a document that spans the width of a page. Many individuals find such spacing difficult to read.

Another Way

On the Home tab, in the Editing group, click the Select button, and then click Select All.

3 Press [Ctrl] + [A] to select all of the text in the document, and then on the **Home tab**, in the **Paragraph group**, click the **Align Text Left** button ▤.

4 Press [Ctrl] + [Home]. At the top of the document, in the left margin area, point to the left of the first paragraph—*Associated Students of Laurel College*—until the 🔊 pointer displays, and then click one time to select the paragraph. On the Mini toolbar, change the **Font Size** to **26**.

> Use this technique to select entire lines of text.

5 Point to the left of the first paragraph—*Associated Students of Laurel College*—to display the 🔊 pointer again, and then drag down to select the first two paragraphs, which form the title and subtitle of the document.

6 On the Mini toolbar, click the **Center** button ▤ to center the title and subtitle between the left and right margins, and then compare your screen with Figure 1.26.

Figure 1.26

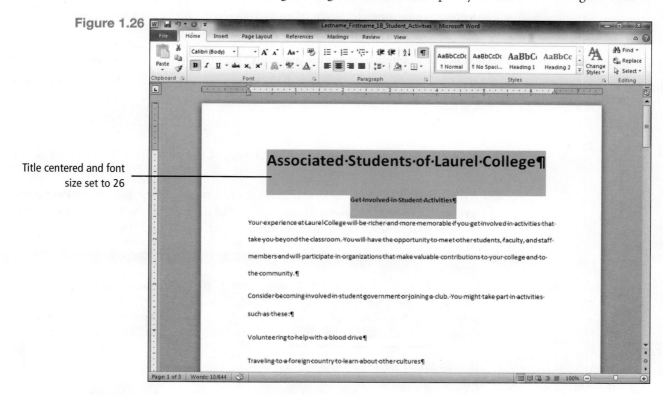

Title centered and font size set to 26

7 Scroll down to view the bottom of **Page 1**, and then locate the first bold subheading—*Student Government*. Point to the left of the paragraph to display the 🔊 pointer, and then click one time.

8 With *Student Government* selected, use your mouse wheel or the vertical scroll bar to bring the lower portion of **Page 2** into view. Locate the subheading *Clubs*. Move the pointer to the left of the paragraph to display the 🔊 pointer, hold down [Ctrl], and then click one time.

> Two subheadings are selected; in Windows-based programs, you can hold down [Ctrl] to select multiple items.

9 On the Mini toolbar, click the **Center** button ▤ to center both subheadings, and then click **Save** 🖬.

Activity 1.15 | Changing Line Spacing

Line spacing is the distance between lines of text in a paragraph. Three of the most commonly used line spacing options are shown in the table in Figure 1.27.

Line Spacing Options	
Alignment	**Description, Example, and Information**
Single spacing	**This text in this example uses single spacing.** Single spacing was once the most commonly used spacing in business documents. Now, because so many documents are read on a computer screen rather than on paper, single spacing is becoming less popular.
Multiple 1.15 spacing	**This text in this example uses multiple 1.15 spacing.** The default line spacing in Microsoft Word 2010 is 1.15, which is equivalent to single spacing with an extra 1/6 line added between lines to make the text easier to read on a computer screen. Many individuals now prefer this spacing, even on paper, because the lines of text appear less crowded.
Double spacing	**This text in this example uses double spacing.** College research papers and draft documents that need space for notes are commonly double-spaced; there is space for a full line of text between each document line.

Figure 1.27

1 Press [Ctrl] + [Home] to move to the beginning of the document. Press [Ctrl] + [A] to select all of the text in the document.

2 With all of the text in the document selected, on the **Home tab**, in the **Paragraph group**, click the **Line Spacing** button, and notice that the text in the document is double spaced—**2.0** is checked. Compare your screen with Figure 1.28.

Figure 1.28

Document text double-spaced

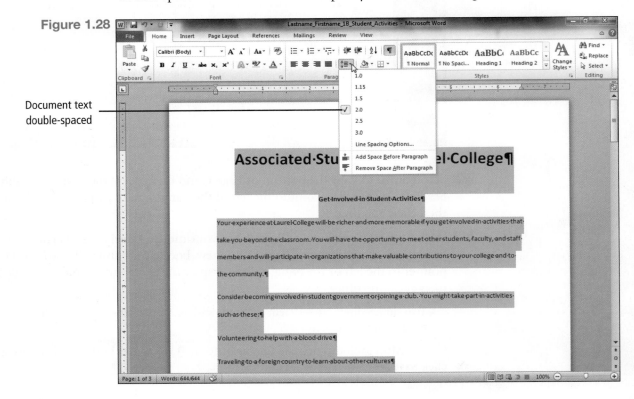

3 On the **Line Spacing** menu, click the *second* setting—**1.15**—and then click anywhere in the document. Compare your screen with Figure 1.29, and then **Save** 💾 your document.

> Double spacing is most commonly used in research papers and rough draft documents. Recall that 1.15 is the default line spacing for new Word documents. Line spacing of 1.15 has slightly more space between the lines than single spacing. On a computer screen, spacing of 1.15 is easier to read than single spacing. Because a large percentage of Word documents are read on a computer screen, 1.15 is the default spacing for a new Word document.

Figure 1.29

Line spacing changed to 1.15

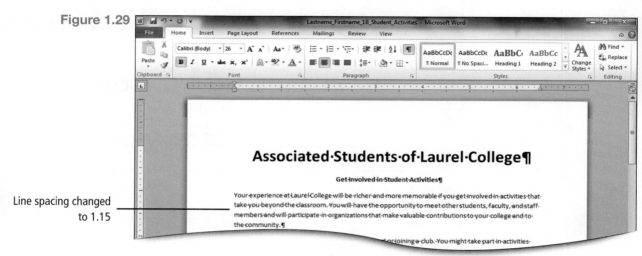

Activity 1.16 | Indenting Text and Adding Space After Paragraphs

Common techniques to distinguish paragraphs include adding space after each paragraph, indenting the first line of each paragraph, or both.

1 Below the title and subtitle of the document, click anywhere in the paragraph that begins *Your experience.*

2 On the **Home tab**, in the **Paragraph group**, click the **Dialog Box Launcher** 🔲.

3 In the **Paragraph** dialog box, on the **Indents and Spacing tab**, under **Indentation**, click the **Special arrow**, and then click **First line** to indent the first line by 0.5″, which is the default indent setting. Compare your screen with Figure 1.30.

Figure 1.30

First line indent applied

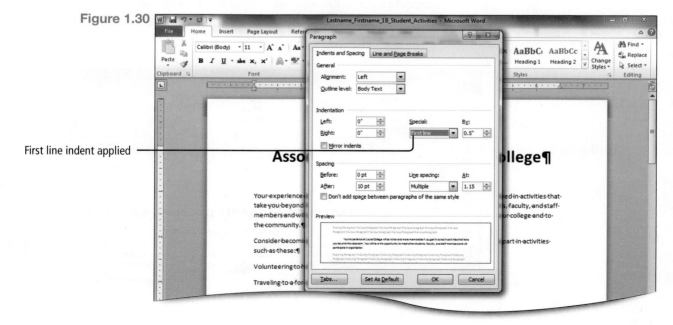

4 Click **OK**, and then click anywhere in the next paragraph, which begins *Consider becoming*. On the ruler under the Ribbon, drag the **First Line Indent** button ⬙ to **0.5 inches on the horizontal ruler**, and then compare your screen with Figure 1.31.

Figure 1.31

First line Indent button

First lines indented

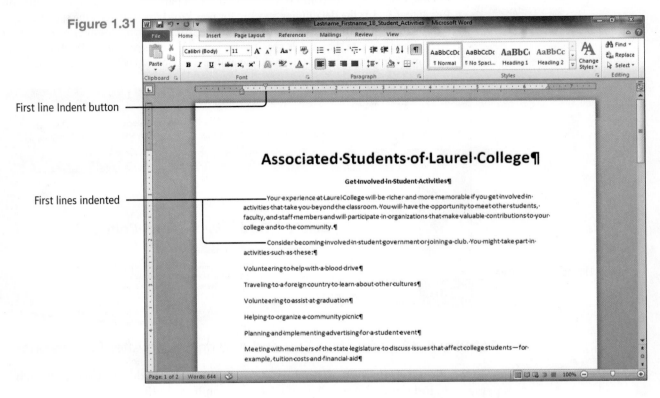

➔

Another Way

On either the Home tab or the Page Layout tab, display the Paragraph dialog box from the Paragraph group, and then under Spacing, click the spin box arrows as necessary.

5 By using either of the techniques you just practiced, or by using the Format Painter, apply a first line indent of **0.5"** in the paragraph that begins *As a registered* to match the indent of the remaining paragraphs in the document.

6 Press [Ctrl] + [A] to select all of the text in the document. Click the **Page Layout tab**, and then in the **Paragraph group**, under **Spacing**, click the **After spin box down arrow** one time to change the value to **6 pt**.

> To change the value in the box, you can also select the existing number, type a new number, and then press [Enter]. This document will use 6 pt spacing after paragraphs.

7 Press [Ctrl] + [Home], and then compare your screen with Figure 1.32.

Figure 1.32

Spacing After set to 6 pt

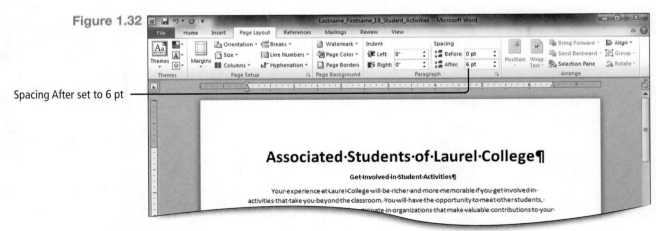

8 Scroll to view the lower portion of **Page 1**. Select the subheading *Student Government*, including the paragraph mark following it, hold down ⌃Ctrl, and then select the subheading *Clubs*.

9 With both subheadings selected, in the **Paragraph group**, under **Spacing**, click the **Before up spin box arrow** two times to set the **Spacing Before** to **12 pt**. Compare your screen with Figure 1.33, and then **Save** 🖫 your document.

This action increases the amount of space above each of the two subheadings, which will make them easy to distinguish in the document. The formatting is applied only to the two selected paragraphs.

Figure 1.33
Spacing before set to 12 pt.

12-point spacing before paragraphs

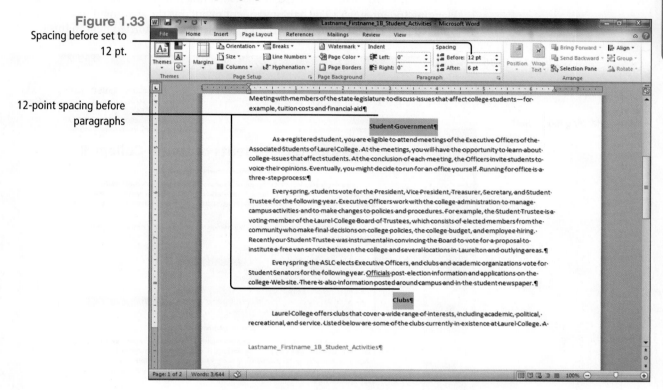

Objective 6 | Create and Modify Lists

To display a list of information, you can choose a **bulleted list**, which uses **bullets**—text symbols such as small circles or check marks—to introduce each item in a list. You can also choose a **numbered list**, which uses consecutive numbers or letters to introduce each item in a list.

Use a bulleted list if the items in the list can be introduced in any order; use a numbered list for items that have definite steps, a sequence of actions, or are in chronological order.

Activity 1.17 | Creating a Bulleted List

1 In the upper portion of **Page 1**, locate the paragraph that begins *Volunteering to help*, and then point to this paragraph from the left margin area to display the 🔌 pointer. Drag down to select this paragraph and the next five paragraphs.

2 On the **Home tab**, in the **Paragraph group**, click the **Bullets** button ▤⁻ to change the selected text to a bulleted list.

> The spacing between each of the bulleted points changes to the spacing between lines in a paragraph—in this instance, 1.15 line spacing. The spacing after the last item in the list is the same as the spacing after each paragraph—in this instance, 6 pt. Each bulleted item is automatically indented.

3 On the ruler, point to the **First Line Indent** button ▽ and read the ScreenTip, and then point to the **Hanging Indent** button △. Compare your screen with Figure 1.34.

> By default, Word formats bulleted items with a first line indent of 0.25″ and adds a Hanging Indent at 0.5″. The hanging indent maintains the alignment of text when a bulleted item is more than one line, for example, the last bulleted item in this list.

Figure 1.34

Hanging Indent button on ruler

Bulleted list

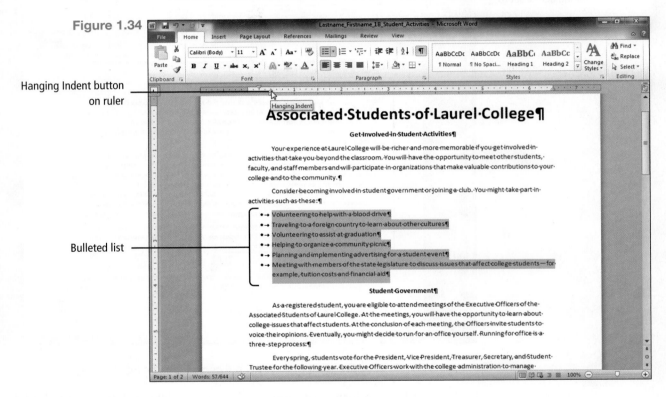

4 Scroll down to view **Page 2**. By using the 🔊 pointer from the left margin area, select all of the paragraphs that indicate the club names and meeting dates, beginning with *Chess Club* and ending with *Theater Club*.

5 In the **Paragraph group**, click the **Bullets** button ▤⁻, and then **Save** 🖫 your document.

Activity 1.18 | Creating a Numbered List

1 Scroll to view **Page 1**, and then under the subheading *Student Government*, in the paragraph that begins *As a registered student*, click to position the insertion point at the *end* of the paragraph following the colon. Press Enter to create a blank paragraph.

2 Notice that the paragraph is indented, because the First Line Indent from the previous paragraph carried over to the new paragraph.

3 To change the indent formatting for this paragraph, on the ruler, drag the **First Line Indent** button ⬇ to the left so that it is positioned directly above the lower button. Compare your screen with Figure 1.35.

Figure 1.35

First Line Indent button

Paragraph with no first line indent

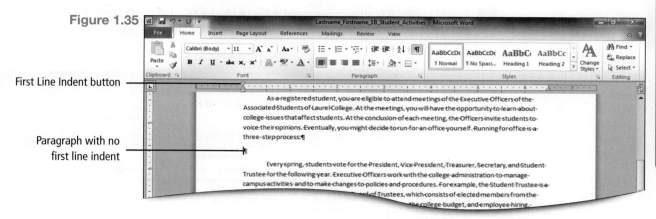

4 Being sure to include the period, type **1.** and press Spacebar.

Word determines that this paragraph is the first item in a numbered list and formats the new paragraph accordingly, indenting the list in the same manner as the bulleted list. The space after the number changes to a tab, and the AutoCorrect Options button displays to the left of the list item. The tab is indicated by a right arrow formatting mark.

Alert! | Activating Automatic Numbered Lists

If a numbered list does not begin automatically, display Backstage view, and then click the Options tab. On the left side of the Word Options dialog box, click Proofing. Under AutoCorrect options, click the AutoCorrect Options button. In the AutoCorrect dialog box, click the AutoFormat As You Type tab. Under *Apply as you type*, select the *Automatic numbered lists* check box, and then click OK two times to close both dialog boxes.

---

5 Click the **AutoCorrect Options** button 🕉 ▾, and then compare your screen with Figure 1.36.

From the displayed list, you can remove the automatic formatting here, or stop using the automatic numbered lists option in this document. You also have the option to open the AutoCorrect dialog box to *Control AutoFormat Options*.

Figure 1.36

AutoCorrect Options button

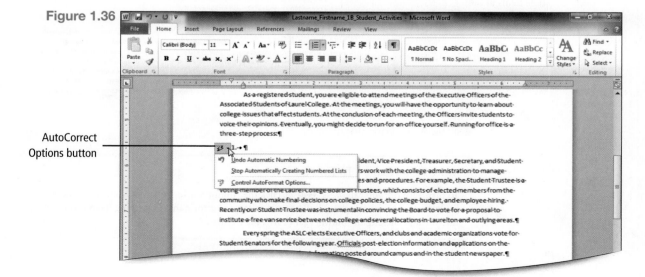

6 Click the **AutoCorrect Options** button again to close the menu without selecting any of the commands. Type **Pick up petitions at the Student Government office.** and press Enter. Notice that the second number and a tab are added to the next line.

7 Type **Obtain 100 signatures from current students.** and press Enter. Type **Turn in petitions and start campaigning.** and press Enter. Compare your screen with Figure 1.37.

Figure 1.37

Numbered list

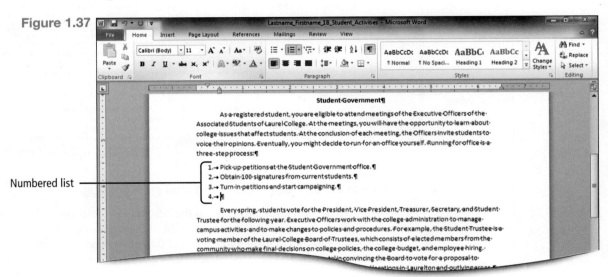

8 Press ←Bksp to turn off the list numbering. Then, press ←Bksp three more times to remove the blank paragraph. Compare your screen with Figure 1.38.

Figure 1.38

Three items in the list, item 4 deleted

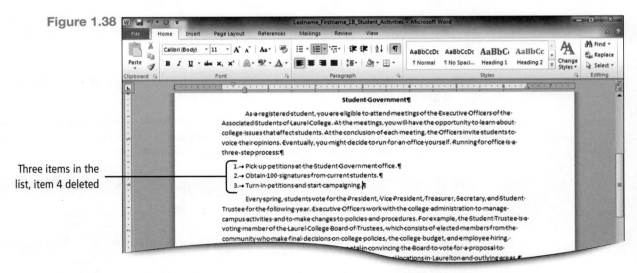

9 **Save** 💾 your document.

More Knowledge | To End a List

To turn a list off, you can press ←Bksp, click the Numbering or Bullets button, or press Enter a second time. Both list buttons—Numbering and Bullets—act as *toggle buttons*; that is, clicking the button one time turns the feature on, and clicking the button again turns the feature off.

Activity 1.19 | Customizing Bullets

1 Press [Ctrl] + [End] to move to the end of the document, and then scroll up as necessary to display the bulleted list containing the list of clubs.

2 Point to the left of the first list item to display the ▨ pointer, and then drag down to select all the clubs in the list—the bullet symbols are not highlighted.

3 Point to the selected list and right-click. From the shortcut menu, point to **Bullets**, and then compare your screen with Figure 1.39.

Figure 1.39

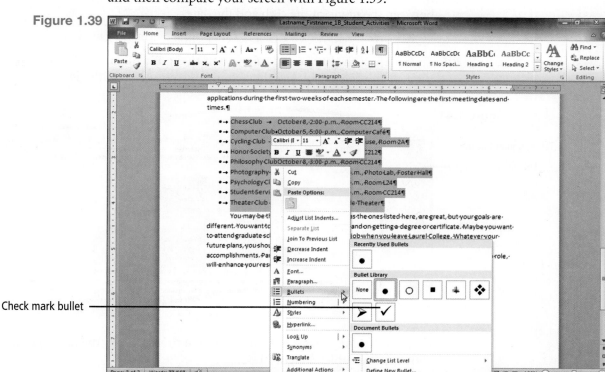

Check mark bullet

4 Under **Bullet Library**, click the **check mark** symbol. If the check mark is not available, choose another bullet symbol.

Another Way

On the Home tab, in the Clipboard group, click the Format Painter button.

5 With the bulleted list still selected, right-click over the list, and then on the Mini toolbar, click the **Format Painter** button ▨.

6 Use the vertical scroll bar or your mouse wheel to scroll to view **Page 1**. Move the pointer to the left of the first item in the bulleted list to display the ▨ pointer, and then drag down to select all of the items in the list and to apply the format of the second bulleted list to this list. Compare your screen with Figure 1.40, and then **Save** ▨ your document.

Figure 1.40

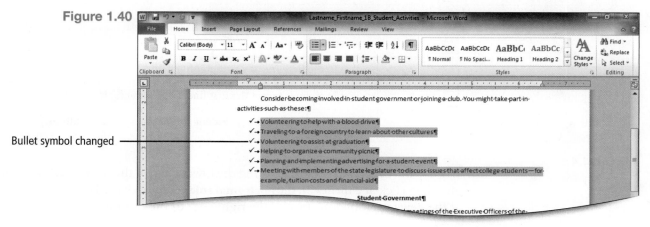

Bullet symbol changed

Objective 7 | Set and Modify Tab Stops

Tab stops mark specific locations on a line of text. Use tab stops to indent and align text, and use the Tab key to move to tab stops.

Activity 1.20 | Setting Tab Stops

1 Scroll to view the middle of **Page 2**, and then by using the [pointer] pointer at the left of the first item, select all of the items in the bulleted list. Notice that there is a tab mark between the name of the club and the date.

> The arrow that indicates a tab is a nonprinting formatting mark.

2 To the left of the horizontal ruler, point to the **Tab Alignment** button [L] to display the *Left Tab* ScreenTip, and then compare your screen with Figure 1.41.

Figure 1.41

Tab Alignment button

Left Tab ScreenTip

Tab mark

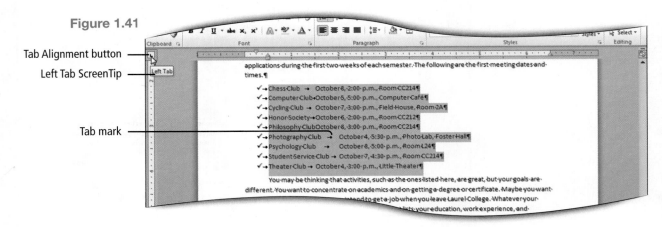

3 Click the **Tab Alignment** button [L] several times to view the tab alignment options shown in the table in Figure 1.42.

Tab Alignment Options

Type	Tab Alignment Button Displays This Marker	Description
Left	[L]	Text is left aligned at the tab stop and extends to the right.
Center	[⊥]	Text is centered around the tab stop.
Right	[⅃]	Text is right aligned at the tab stop and extends to the left.
Decimal	[⊥.]	The decimal point aligns at the tab stop.
Bar	[|]	A vertical bar displays at the tab stop.
First Line Indent	[▽]	Text in the first line of a paragraph indents.
Hanging Indent	[△]	Text in all lines except the first line in the paragraph indents.
Left Indent	[⊔]	Moves both the First Line Indent and Hanging Indent buttons.

Figure 1.42

4 Display the **Left Tab** button [L]. Along the lower edge of the horizontal ruler, point to and then click at **3 inches on the horizontal ruler**. Notice that all of the dates left align at the new tab stop location, and the right edge of the column is uneven.

5 Compare your screen with Figure 1.43, and then **Save** 🔲 your document.

Figure 1.43

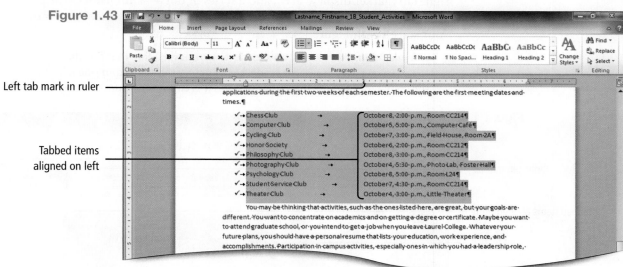

Left tab mark in ruler

Tabbed items aligned on left

Activity 1.21 | Modifying Tab Stops

Tab stops are a form of paragraph formatting, and thus, the information about tab stops is stored in the paragraph mark in the paragraphs to which they were applied.

1 With the bulleted list still selected, on the ruler, point to the new tab marker, and then when the *Left Tab* ScreenTip displays, drag the tab marker to **3.5 inches on the horizontal ruler**.

In all of the selected lines, the text at the tab stop left aligns at 3.5 inches.

> **Another Way**
>
> On the Home tab, in the Paragraph group, click the Dialog Box Launcher. At the bottom of the Paragraph dialog box, click the Tabs button.

2 On the ruler, point to the tab marker to display the ScreenTip, and then double-click to display the **Tabs** dialog box.

3 In the **Tabs** dialog box, under **Tab stop position**, if necessary select *3.5″* and then type **6**

4 Under **Alignment**, click the **Right** option button. Under **Leader**, click the **2** option button. Near the bottom of the **Tabs** dialog box, click **Set**.

Because the Right tab will be used to align the items in the list, the tab stop at 3.5″ is no longer necessary.

5 In the **Tabs** dialog box, in the **Tab stop position** box, click **3.5″** to select this tab stop, and then in the lower portion of the **Tabs** dialog box, click the **Clear** button to delete this tab stop, which is no longer necessary. Compare your screen with Figure 1.44.

Figure 1.44

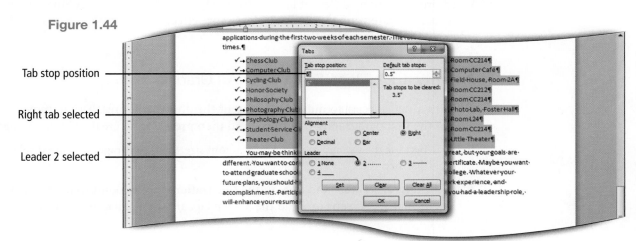

Tab stop position

Right tab selected

Leader 2 selected

6 Click **OK**. On the ruler, notice that the left tab marker at *3.5″* no longer displays, a right tab marker displays at *6″*, and a series of dots—a **dot leader**—displays between the columns of the list. Notice also that the right edge of the column is even. Compare your screen with Figure 1.45.

A **leader character** creates a solid, dotted, or dashed line that fills the space to the left of a tab character and draws the reader's eyes across the page from one item to the next. When the character used for the leader is a dot, it is commonly referred to as a dot leader.

Figure 1.45

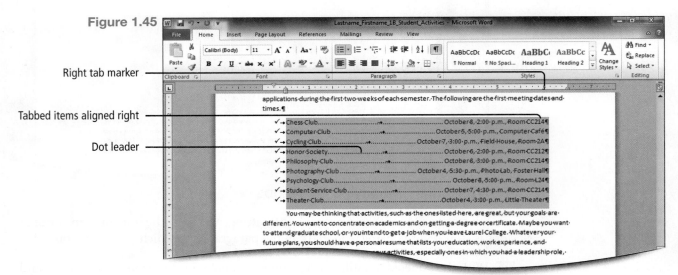

Right tab marker

Tabbed items aligned right

Dot leader

7 In the bulleted list that uses dot leaders, locate the *Honor Society* item, and then click to position the insertion point at the end of that line. Press Enter to create a new blank bullet item.

8 Type **Math Club** and press Tab. Notice that a dot leader fills the space to the tab marker location.

9 Type **October 6, 4:00 p.m., Math Tutoring Lab, L35** and notice that the text moves to the left to maintain the right alignment of the tab stop.

10 **Save** 💾 your document.

Objective 8 | Insert a SmartArt Graphic

SmartArt graphics are designer-quality visual representations of information, and Word provides many different layouts from which you can choose. A SmartArt graphic can communicate your messages or ideas more effectively than plain text and adds visual interest to a document or Web page.

Activity 1.22 | Inserting a SmartArt Graphic

1 Press Ctrl + Home to move to the top of the document. Press End to move to the end of the first paragraph—the title—and then press Enter to create a blank paragraph.

Because the paragraph above is 26 pt font size, the new paragraph mark displays in that size.

2 Click the **Insert tab**, and then in the **Illustrations group**, point to the **SmartArt** button to display its ScreenTip. Read the ScreenTip, and then click the button.

3 In the center portion of the **Choose a SmartArt Graphic** dialog box, scroll down and examine the numerous types of SmartArt graphics available.

4 On the left, click **Hierarchy**, and then in the first row, click the first graphic— **Organization Chart**.

At the right of the dialog box, a preview and description of the graphic displays.

5 Compare your screen with Figure 1.46.

Figure 1.46

SmartArt button

Preview of selected
SmartArt

Hierarchy category

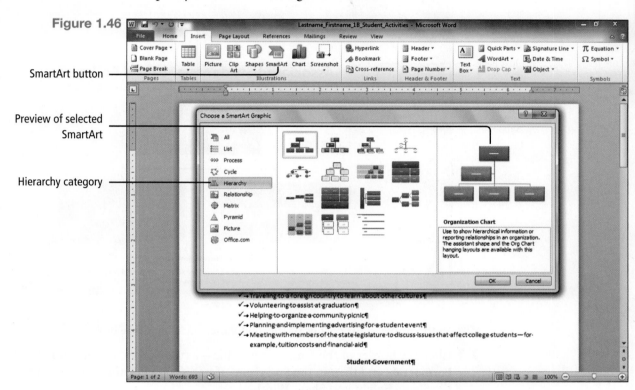

6 Click **OK**. If the pane indicating *Type your text here* does not display on the left side of the graphic, on the Design tab, in the Create Graphic group, click the Text Pane button. **Save** 🖫 your document.

The SmartArt graphic displays at the insertion point location and consists of two parts— the graphic itself, and the Text Pane. On the Ribbon, the SmartArt Tools add the Design tab and the Format tab. You can type directly into the graphics, or type in the Text Pane. By typing in the Text Pane, you might find it easier to organize your layout.

Activity 1.23 | Modifying a SmartArt Graphic

1 In the SmartArt graphic, in the second row, click the border of the *[Text]* box to display a *solid* border and sizing handles, and then press ⌈Del⌉. Repeat this procedure in the bottom row to delete the middle *[Text]* box.

Another Way

Close the Text Pane and
type the text directly in
the SmartArt boxes.

2 In the **Text Pane**, click in the top bulleted point, and then type **Student Activities** Notice that the first bulleted point aligns further to the left than the other points.

The ***top-level points*** are the main points in a SmartArt graphic. ***Subpoints*** are indented second-level bullet points.

3 Press ↓. Type **Government** and then press ↓ again. Type **Clubs** and then compare your screen with Figure 1.47.

Figure 1.47

SmartArt graphic ——

Text Pane ——

Top-level point ——

Subpoints ——

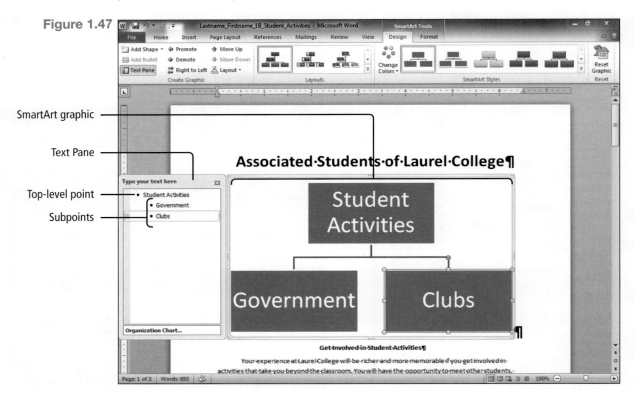

4 In the upper right corner of the **Text Pane**, click the **Close** button.

5 Click the border of the SmartArt graphic—a pale border surrounds it. Click the **Format tab**, and then in the **Size group**, if necessary click the **Size** button to display the **Shape Height** and **Shape Width** boxes.

6 Set the **Height** to **2.5″** and the **Width** to **4.2″**, and then compare your screen with Figure 1.48.

Figure 1.48

Size button ——

Height and Width set ——

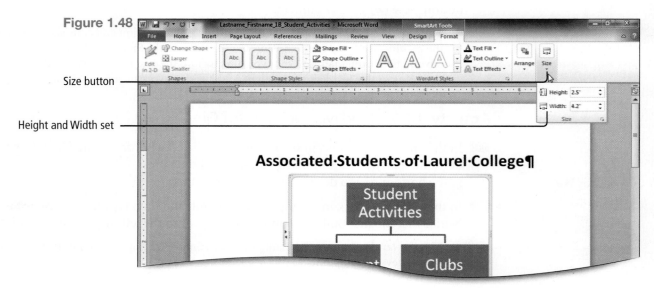

7 With the SmartArt graphic still selected, click the **Design tab**, and then in the **SmartArt Styles group**, click the **Change Colors** button. Under **Colorful**, click the second style—**Colorful Range - Accent Colors 2 to 3**.

8 On the **Design tab**, in the **SmartArt Styles group**, click the **More** button . Under **3-D**, click the first style—**Polished**. Compare your screen with Figure 1.49.

Figure 1.49

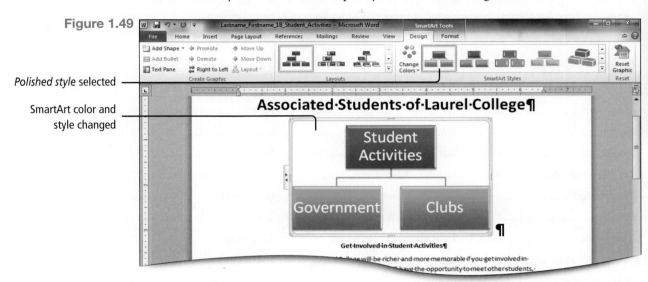

Polished style selected

SmartArt color and style changed

9 Click outside of the graphic to deselect it. Display **Backstage** view. On the right, under the screen thumbnail, click **Properties**, and then click **Show Document Panel**. In the **Author** box, delete any text and then type your firstname and lastname. In the **Subject** box, type your course name and section number, and in the **Keywords** box type **Student Activities, Associated Students Close** the Document Panel and **Save** your document.

10 Display **Backstage** view, and then click **Print** to display **Print Preview**. At the bottom of the preview, click the **Next Page** and **Previous Page** buttons to move between pages. If necessary, return to the document and make any necessary changes.

11 As directed by your instructor, print your document or submit it electronically. **Close** Word.

More Knowledge | Changing the Bullet Level in a SmartArt Graphic

To increase or decrease the level of an item, on the Design tab, in the Create Graphic group, click either the Promote or the Demote button.

End **You have completed Project 1B**

Content-Based Assessments

Summary

In this chapter, you created and formatted documents using Microsoft Word 2010. You inserted and formatted graphics, created and formatted bulleted and numbered lists, and created and formatted text boxes. You also created lists using tab stops with dot leaders, and created and modified a SmartArt graphic.

Key Terms

Alignment 68

Anchor.............................56

Artistic effects 57

Bar tab stop 78

Bulleted list....................73

Bullets 73

Center alignment 68

Center tab stop 78

Decimal tab stop 78

Dot leader 80

Drawing objects..............53

Field................................62

Floating object 55

Formatting marks............51

Graphics 53

Inline object 54

Justified alignment..........68

Leader characters 80

Left alignment.................68

Left tab stop 78

Line spacing 70

Margins 67

Nonprinting
    characters...................51

Nudge 57

Numbered list 73

Picture styles 57

Right alignment 68

Right tab stop.................78

Shapes 58

SmartArt 80

Spin box 55

Subpoints 81

Tab stop...........................78

Text box...........................58

Text effects 53

Text wrapping 56

Toggle button 76

Top-level points 81

Wordwrap 51

Matching

Match each term in the second column with its correct definition in the first column by writing the letter of the term on the blank line in front of the correct definition.

_____ 1. Formats that make pictures look more like sketches or paintings.

_____ 2. A small box with an upward- and downward-pointing arrow that enables you to move rapidly through a set of values by clicking.

_____ 3. Small circles in the corners of a selected graphic with which you can resize the graphic proportionally.

_____ 4. The manner in which text displays around an object.

_____ 5. An object or graphic that can be moved independently of the surrounding text.

_____ 6. The process of using the arrow keys to move an object in small precise increments.

_____ 7. An object or graphic inserted in a document that acts like a character in a sentence.

_____ 8. Frames, shapes, shadows, borders, and other special effects that can be added to an image to create an overall visual style for the image.

_____ 9. Predefined drawing objects, such as stars, banners, arrows, and callouts, included with Microsoft Office, and that can be inserted into documents.

A Artistic effects

B Bullets

C Floating object

D Inline object

E Justified alignment

F Left alignment

G Line spacing

H Nudge

I Picture styles

J Shapes

K Sizing handles

L SmartArt

M Spin box

N Tab stop

O Text wrapping

_____ 10. A commonly used alignment of text in which text is aligned at the left margin, leaving the right margin uneven.

_____ 11. An alignment of text in which the text is evenly aligned on both the left and right margins.

_____ 12. The distance between lines of text in a paragraph.

_____ 13. Text symbols such as small circles or check marks that introduce items in a list.

_____ 14. A mark on the ruler that indicates the location where the insertion point will be placed when you press the Tab key.

_____ 15. A designer-quality graphic used to create a visual representation of information.

Multiple Choice

Circle the correct answer.

1. Characters that display on the screen to show the location of paragraphs, tabs, and spaces, but that do not print, are called:
   A. text effects
   B. bullets
   C. formatting marks

2. The placement of paragraph text relative to the left and right margins is referred to as:
   A. alignment
   B. spacing
   C. indents

3. The symbol that indicates to which paragraph an image is attached is:
   A. a small arrow
   B. an anchor
   C. a paragraph mark

4. A movable, resizable container for text or graphics is a:
   A. text box
   B. dialog box
   C. SmartArt graphic

5. A banner is an example of a predefined:
   A. paragraph
   B. format
   C. shape

6. A placeholder that displays preset content, such as the current date, the file name, a page number, or other stored information is:
   A. a leader
   B. a field
   C. a tab

7. The space between the text and the top, bottom, left, and right edges of the paper are referred to as:
   A. alignment
   B. margins
   C. spacing

8. A group of items in which items are displayed in order to indicate definite steps, a sequence of actions, or chronological order is a:
   A. numbered list
   B. bulleted list
   C. outline list

9. A series of dots following a tab that serve to guide the reader's eye is a:
   A. leader
   B. field
   C. shape

10. Tab stops are a form of:
    A. line formatting
    B. document formatting
    C. paragraph formatting

Skills Review | Project **1C** Welcome Week

In the following Skills Review, you will create and edit a flyer for the Laurel College New Student
Welcome Week. Your completed document will look similar to Figure 1.50.

Project Files

For Project 1C, you will need the following files:

New blank Word document
w01C_Welcome_Text
w01C_Welcome_Picture

You will save your document as:

Lastname_Firstname_1C_Welcome_Week

Project Results

Figure 1.50

(Project 1C Welcome Week continues on the next page)

Content-Based Assessments

1 **Start** Word and display a new blank document. On the **Home tab**, in the **Paragraph group**, be sure the **Show/Hide ¶** button is active so that you can view formatting marks. In the **Quick Access Toolbar**, click the **Save** button, navigate to your **Word Chapter 1** folder, and then **Save** the document as **Lastname_Firstname_1C_Welcome_Week**

a. Type **Welcome Week** and then press Enter two times.

b. Type **The Laurel College Student Government Association is sponsoring a week of special activities for new students. This is your opportunity to meet the people and learn about the programs that will help you succeed at Laurel College.**

c. Press Enter one time. Click the **Insert tab**. In the **Text group**, click the **Object button arrow**, and then click **Text from File**. Navigate to your student files, select the file **w01C_Welcome_Text**, and then at the bottom of the **Insert File** dialog box, click **Insert**. **Save** your document.

2 At the top of the document, in the left margin area, point to the left of the first paragraph—*Welcome Week*—until the pointer displays, and then click one time to select the paragraph. On the **Home tab**, in the **Font group**, click the **Text Effects** button. In the displayed **Text Effects** gallery, in the first row, click the fourth effect—**Fill - White, Outline - Accent 1**.

a. With the text still selected, in the **Font group**, click the **Font Size button arrow**, and then click **72**. In the **Paragraph group**, click the **Center** button.

b. With the text still selected, in the **Font group**, click the **Text Effects** button. Point to **Shadow**, and then under **Outer**, in the first row click the third style—**Offset Diagonal Bottom Left**. In the **Font group**, click the **Font Color button arrow**. Under **Theme Colors**, in the fourth column, click the first color—**Dark Blue, Text 2**.

c. In the paragraph that begins *The Laurel College*, click to position the insertion point at the beginning of the paragraph. On the **Insert tab**, in the **Illustrations group**, click the **Picture** button. From your student data files, **Insert** the file **w01C_Welcome_Picture**. On the **Format tab**, in the **Size group**, click the **Shape Height down spin arrow** as necessary to change the height of the picture to **2″**.

d. With the picture still selected, on the **Format tab**, in the **Arrange group**, click the **Wrap Text** button. From the **Wrap Text** gallery, click **Square**.

e. Hold down Shift and point anywhere in the picture to display the pointer. Drag the picture to align the right edge of the picture just to the left of the right margin.

f. On the **Format tab**, in the **Picture Styles group**, click the **Picture Effects** button. Point to **Glow**, and then under **Glow Variations**, in the third row, click the first style—**Blue, 11 pt glow, Accent color 1**. Nudge as necessary to match the picture position shown in Figure 1.50.

g. Click anywhere to deselect the picture. Click the **Page Layout tab**, and then in the **Page Background group**, click the **Page Borders** button. In the **Borders and Shading** dialog box, under **Setting**, click **Box**. Under **Style**, scroll down the list. About two-thirds down the list, click the style with a thin top and bottom line and a slightly thicker middle line.

h. Click the **Color arrow**, and then under **Theme Colors**, in the fourth column, click the first color—**Dark Blue, Text 2**. Click **OK**, and then **Save** your document.

3 Press Ctrl + End to move to the bottom of the document. On the **Insert tab**, in the **Text group**, click the **Text Box** button. At the bottom of the **Text Box** gallery, click **Draw Text Box**.

a. At the bottom of the document, position the pointer in an open area near the left margin, and then drag down and to the right to create a text box approximately **2.5 inches** high and **5.5 inches** wide; you need not be precise.

b. With the insertion point positioned in the text box, type the following:

Welcome Week Highlights

Tuesday: Campus tour and meeting with administrators

Wednesday: Open house in all academic departments

Thursday: Club meetings to recruit members

Friday: Student Government-hosted barbecue

(Project 1C Welcome Week continues on the next page)

c. In the text box, select all of the text. On the Mini toolbar, click the **Font Size button arrow**, and then click **14**. Click the **Bold** button, and then click the **Center** button.

d. On the **Format tab**, in the **Size group**, if necessary click the **Size** button. Click the **Shape Height spin arrows** as necessary to change the height of the text box to **2.5″**. Click the **Shape Width button up spin arrow** as necessary to widen the text box to **5.5″**.

e. In the **Shape Styles group**, click the **Shape Effects** button. Point to **Shadow**, and then under **Outer**, in the second row, click the second style—**Offset Center**. In the **Shape Styles group**, click the **Shape Outline button arrow**. Under **Theme Colors**, in the fourth column, click the first color—**Dark Blue, Text 2**.

f. If necessary, click anywhere inside the text box. Point to the text box border to display the ⟦↖⟧ pointer. Drag the text box to align the left edge at approximately **0.5 inches on the horizontal ruler** and to align the top edge at approximately **5.5 inches on the vertical ruler**. You may have to click outside the text box several times to see the exact location on the rulers.

g. On the **Insert tab**, in the **Illustrations group**, click the **Shapes** button. Under **Basic Shapes**, in the first row, click the seventh shape—**Diamond**.

h. Position the ⟦＋⟧ pointer slightly under the text box and at approximately **2 inches on the horizontal ruler**. Drag down approximately **1 inch** and to the right approximately **2 inches**. On the **Format tab**, in the **Size group**, adjust the **Shape Height** to **0.9″** and the **Shape Width** to **2″**.

i. Right-click the new shape, and then click **Add Text**. Type **Enjoy!** and then select the text you typed. On the Mini toolbar, click the **Font Size button arrow**,

and then click **20**. Click the **Bold** button, and then if necessary, click the **Center** button.

j. On the **Format tab**, in the **Shape Styles group**, click the **Shape Fill button arrow**, and then under **Theme Colors**, in the fourth column, click the first color—**Dark Blue, Text 2**.

k. Point to the shape border until the ⟦↖⟧ pointer displays, and then position the shape with its widest points aligned with the lower edge of the text box and approximately centered. As necessary, move the shape in small increments by pressing the arrow keys on your keyboard. Refer to Figure 1.50 for approximate placement. **Save** your document.

4 Click the **Insert tab**, and then, in the **Header & Footer group**, click the **Footer** button. At the bottom of the **Footer** gallery, click **Edit Footer**.

a. On the **Design tab**, in the **Insert group**, click the **Quick Parts** button, and then click **Field**. In the **Field names** list, scroll as necessary to locate and click **FileName**. Click **OK**, and then double-click anywhere in the document.

b. Press ⟦Ctrl⟧ + ⟦Home⟧ to move the insertion point to the beginning of the document. Display **Backstage** view. On the right, under the screen thumbnail, click **Properties**, and then click **Show Document Panel**. In the **Author** box, delete any text and then type your firstname and lastname. In the **Subject** box, type your course name and section number, and in the **Keywords** box type **Welcome Week**

c. **Close** the Document Panel. In **Backstage** view, click the **Print tab** to display the **Print Preview**. If necessary, return to the document to make any corrections or adjustments.

d. **Save** your document, print or submit electronically as directed by your instructor, and then **Close** Word.

End You have completed Project 1C

Content-Based Assessments

Apply 1B skills from these Objectives:

5 Change Document and Paragraph Layout

6 Create and Modify Lists

7 Set and Modify Tab Stops

8 Insert a SmartArt Graphic

Skills Review | Project **1D** Constitution

In the following Skills Review, you will edit the constitution of the Associated Students of Laurel College. Your completed document will look similar to Figure 1.51.

Project Files

For Project 1D, you will need the following file:

w01D_Constitution

You will save your document as:

Lastname_Firstname_1D_Constitution

Project Results

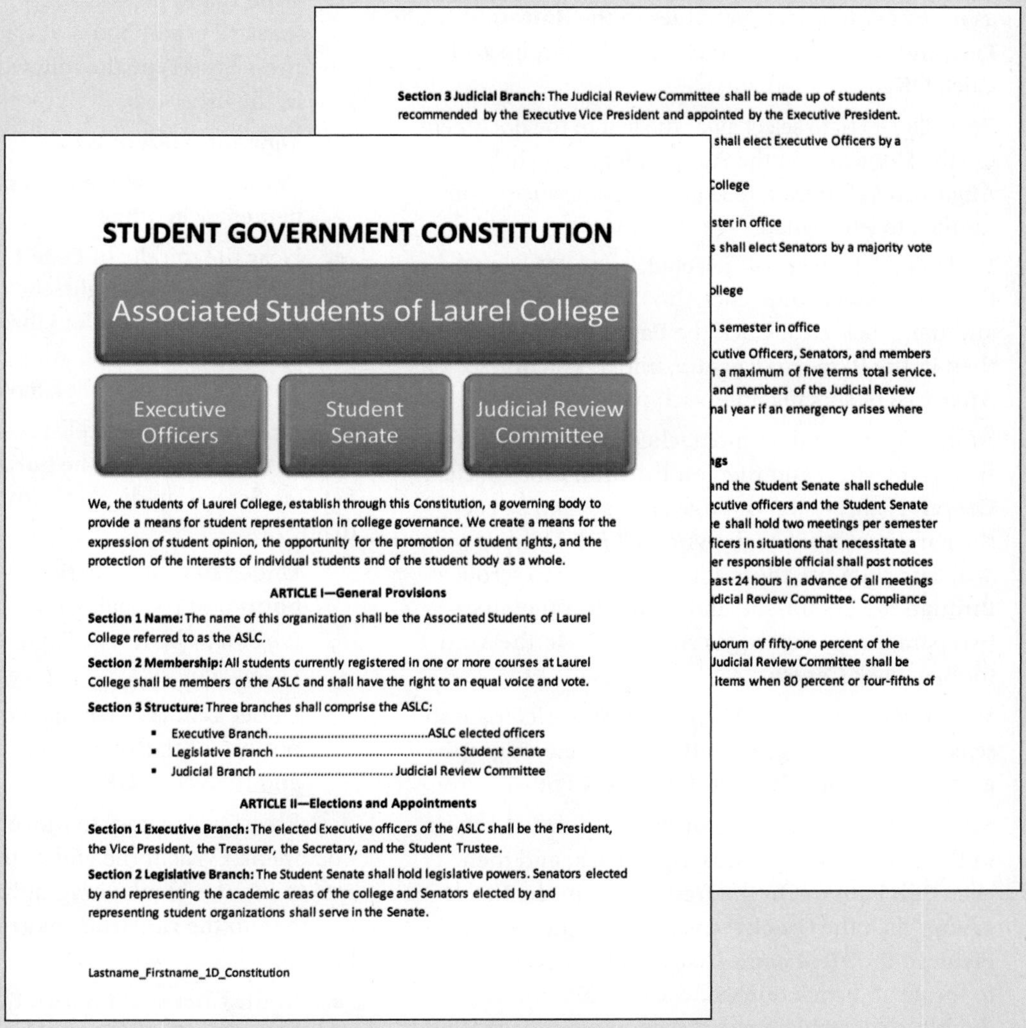

Figure 1.51

(Project 1D Constitution continues on the next page)

Skills Review | Project **1D** Constitution (continued)

1 **Start** Word. From your student files, locate and open the document **w01D_Constitution**. Display **Backstage** view, click **Save As**, and then navigate to your **Word Chapter 1** folder. **Save** the document as **Lastname_Firstname_1D_Constitution**

a. On the **Home tab**, in the **Paragraph group**, be sure the **Show/Hide** button is active so you can view formatting marks. Click the **Page Layout tab**. In the **Page Setup group**, click the **Margins** button, and then at the bottom of the **Margins** gallery, at the bottom of the list, click **Custom Margins**. In the **Page Setup** dialog box, in the **Top** box, type **1** Press Tab as necessary to select the values in the **Bottom**, **Left**, and **Right** boxes and change all margins to **1**. Click **OK**.

b. Press Ctrl + A to select all of the text in the document. On the **Home tab**, in the **Paragraph group**, click the **Align Text Left** button to change the alignment from justified to left aligned.

c. With all of the text still selected, on the **Home tab**, in the **Paragraph group**, click the **Line Spacing** button, and then click **1.15**. Click the **Page Layout tab**, and then in the **Paragraph group**, under **Spacing**, set **After** to **6 pt** spacing after each paragraph.

d. At the top of the document, click anywhere in the title, right-click, and then on the Mini toolbar, click **Center**. Near the top of **Page 1**, locate and select the paragraph that begins *ARTICLE 1*. Hold down Ctrl, and then use the vertical scroll bar to scroll through the document, and then select the other two paragraphs that begin *ARTICLE*. On the Mini toolbar, click **Center**.

e. With the three subheadings that begin *ARTICLE* still selected, on the **Page Layout tab**, in the **Paragraph group**, under **Spacing**, set **Before** to **12 pt**.

f. Scroll to view the bottom of **Page 1**, point anywhere in the bottom margin area, right-click, and then click **Edit Footer**. On the **Design tab**, in the **Insert group**, click the **Quick Parts** button, and then click **Field**. In the **Field names** list, scroll as necessary to locate and click **FileName**. Click **OK**, and then double-click anywhere in the document to exit the footer area.

2 Near the middle of **Page 1**, *above* the *ARTICLE II* subheading, locate the paragraph that begins *Executive Branch*, and then move the pointer into the left margin

area to display the pointer. Drag down to select this paragraph and the next two paragraphs. On the **Home tab**, in the **Paragraph group**, click the **Bullets** button.

a. Scroll to view the bottom of **Page 1**, and then locate the paragraph that begins *Completion of at least*. Select that paragraph and the next two paragraphs. On the **Home tab**, in the **Paragraph group**, click the **Numbering** button.

b. Locate the paragraph that begins *Section 4 Elections*. Click to position the insertion point at the *end* of that paragraph after the colon, and then press Enter.

c. Type **1.** and press Spacebar. Type **Completion of at least 12 credit hours at Laurel College** and then press Enter. Type the following text for items 2 and 3 in the list:

Minimum GPA of 2.75

Enrollment in at least six credit hours each semester in office

d. Near the middle of **Page 1**, select the three items in the bulleted list, right-click the list, and then point to **Bullets**. Under **Bullet Library**, click the **black square** symbol. If the black square is not available, choose another bullet symbol. **Save** your document.

3 Be sure the bulleted list is still selected. Point to the left tab marker at **2″ on the horizontal ruler**. When the *Left Tab* ScreenTip displays, double-click to open the **Tabs** dialog box.

a. Under **Tab stop position**, with *2″* selected, at the bottom of the dialog box, click **Clear** to delete this tab stop. Then, type **5.5** in the **Tab stop position** box.

b. Under **Alignment**, click the **Right** option button. Under **Leader**, click the **2** option button. At the bottom of the **Tabs** dialog box, click the **Set** button, and then click **OK**.

4 Press Ctrl + Home to move to the top of the document. Click at the end of the title, and then press Enter to insert a blank paragraph. Click the **Insert tab**, and then in the **Illustrations group**, click the **SmartArt** button.

a. In the **Choose a SmartArt Graphic** dialog box, on the left, click **Hierarchy**, and in the second row, click the fourth style—**Table Hierarchy**. At the bottom of the **Choose a SmartArt Graphic** dialog box, click **OK**. If necessary, on the Design tab, in the Create Graphic group, activate the Text Pane button.

(Project 1D Constitution continues on the next page)

b. In the SmartArt graphic, in the second row, click the border of the first *[Text]* box, and then press Del. Press Del again to delete a second *[Text]* box. In the **Text Pane**, under **Type your text here** box, click in the last bulleted point. On the **Design tab**, in the **Create Graphic group**, click the **Promote** button to move the list item up one level.

c. In the **Text Pane**, click in the top bulleted point, type **Associated Students of Laurel College** and then press ↓. Type the following in the three remaining boxes:

Executive Officers

Student Senate

Judicial Review Committee

d. In the upper right corner of the **Text Pane**, click the **Close** button. Be sure the graphic is selected—a pale border surrounds the entire graphic, and then click the outside border one time. Click the **Format tab**, and then in the **Size group**, if necessary click the **Size** button. By clicking the spin box arrows, change the **Shape Height** to **2.6"** and the **Shape Width** to **6.5"**.

e. With the SmartArt graphic still selected, on the **Design tab**, in the **SmartArt Styles group**, click the **Change Colors** button. Scroll down, and then under **Accent 5**, click the second style—**Colored Fill - Accent 5**.

f. On the **Design tab**, in the **SmartArt Styles group**, click the **More** button. Under **3-D**, click the second style—**Inset**. Click anywhere in the document to deselect the graphic. Press Ctrl + Home to move the insertion point to the beginning of the document.

g. Display **Backstage** view, on the right, under the screen thumbnail, click **Properties**, and then click **Show Document Panel**. In the **Author** box, type your firstname and lastname. In the **Subject** box type your course name and section number, and in the **Keywords** box type **student constitution**

h. **Close** the Document Panel. Click **Save**. Display **Backstage** view and click the **Print tab**. Examine the **Print Preview**. Print or submit electronically as directed. **Close** Word.

End You have completed Project 1D ————————————

Apply **1A** skills from
these Objectives:

1 Create a New
Document and
Insert Text

2 Insert and Format
Graphics

3 Insert and Modify
Text Boxes and
Shapes

4 Preview and Print a
Document

Mastering Word | Project **1E** Retreat

In the following Mastering Word project, you will create a flyer announcing a retreat for the Associated Students of Laurel College Board. Your completed document will look similar to Figure 1.52.

Project Files

For Project 1E, you will need the following files:

New blank Word document
w01E_Retreat_Text
w01E_Retreat_Picture

You will save your document as:

Lastname_Firstname_1E_Retreat

Project Results

Figure 1.52

(Project 1E Retreat continues on the next page)

Content-Based Assessments

Mastering Word | Project **1E** Retreat (continued)

1 **Start** Word and display a new blank document. **Save** the document in your **Word Chapter 1** folder as **Lastname_Firstname_1E_Retreat** and then add the file name to the footer. Be sure the formatting marks and rulers display.

2 Type **ASLC Board Retreat** and press Enter two times. Type **College President Diane Gilmore is pleased to announce a retreat for the Board of the Associated Students of Laurel College.** Press Enter one time. **Insert** the file **w01E_Retreat_Text**.

3 Select the title *ASLC Board Retreat*. On the **Home tab**, in the **Font group**, display the **Text Effects** gallery, and then in the third row, apply the first effect—**Fill - White, Gradient Outline - Accent 1**. Change the **Font Size** to **56** pt. Apply a **Shadow** text effect using the first effect under **Outer—Offset Diagonal Bottom Right**. Change the **Font Color** to **Olive Green, Accent 3, Darker 25%**—in the seventh column, the fifth color.

4 Click to position the insertion point at the beginning of the paragraph that begins *College President*, and then from your student files, **Insert** the picture **w01E_Retreat_Picture**. Change the **Shape Height** of the picture to **2″**, and then set the **Wrap Text** to **Square**. Move the picture so that the right edge aligns with the right margin, and the top edge aligns with the top edge of the text that begins *College President*. Apply a **Film Grain Artistic Effect**—the third effect in the third row. From **Picture Effects**, add a **5 Point Soft Edge**.

5 Scroll to view the lower portion of the page. **Insert** a **Text Box** beginning at the left margin and at approximately **7 inches on the vertical ruler** that is approximately 1″ high and 4.5″ wide. Then, in the **Size group**, make the measurements exact by setting the **Height** to **1″** and the **Width** to **4.6″**. Type the following text in the text box:

> **Prize drawings at lunch include concert tickets, college football jerseys, coffee mugs, and restaurant gift cards.**

6 Select the text in the text box. Change the **Font Size** to **16** pt, apply **Bold**, and **Center** the text. Add a **Shape Fill** to the text box using the theme color **Olive Green, Accent 3, Lighter 40%**. Then apply a **Gradient** fill using the **Linear Right** gradient. Change the **Shape Outline** color to **White, Background 1**. Drag the text box as necessary to center it horizontally between the left and right margins, and vertically between the last line of text and the footer.

7 Display the **Document Panel**. Type your firstname and lastname in the **Author** box, your course name and section number in the **Subject** box, and then in the **Keywords** box type **retreat, ASLC**

8 **Close** the Document Panel. **Save** and preview your document, make any necessary adjustments, and then print your document or submit it electronically as directed. **Close** Word.

End **You have completed Project 1E** ————————————————————

Content-Based Assessments

Apply **1B** skills from these Objectives:

5 Change Document and Paragraph Layout

6 Create and Modify Lists

7 Set and Modify Tab Stops

8 Insert a SmartArt Graphic

Mastering Word | Project **1F** Cycling Trip

In the following Mastering Word project, you will create an informational handout about a planned trip by the Laurel College Cycling Club. Your completed document will look similar to Figure 1.53.

Project Files

For Project 1F, you will need the following file:

w01F_Cycling_Trip

You will save your document as:

Lastname_Firstname_1F_Cycling_Trip

Project Results

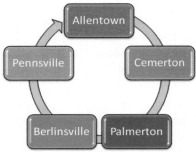

Figure 1.53

(Project 1F Cycling Trip continues on the next page)

Content-Based Assessments

Mastering Word | Project **1F** Cycling Trip (continued)

1 **Start** Word. From your student files open the document **w01F_Cycling_Trip**. **Save** the document in your **Word Chapter 1** folder as **Lastname_Firstname_1F_Cycling_Trip** Add the file name to the footer. Display formatting marks.

2 Display the **Page Setup** dialog box. Set the **Top** margin to **1.25"** and the other three margins to **1"**. Select all of the text in the document, including the title. Add **6 pt** spacing after all paragraphs. Change the **Line Spacing** to **1.15**. Change the alignment to **Align Text Left**. **Center** the document title—*Cycling Club Trip*.

3 Locate the paragraph that begins *Bicycle in good*. Select that paragraph and the three paragraphs that follow it. Create a bulleted list from the selected text. Use the shortcut menu to display bullet options, and change the bullet character to a **check mark** or another symbol if the check mark is unavailable.

4 Position the insertion point in the blank paragraph at the end of the document. Add a **Right** tab stop at **3.5"**. Display the **Tabs** dialog box and add a dot leader. **Set** the tab stop, and then add and **Set** another **Right** tab stop with a dot leader at **6.5"**.

5 Type the text shown in **Table 1**, pressing ⟨Tab⟩ between columns and ⟨Enter⟩ at the end of each line. Refer to Figure 1.53.

6 Select the first two lines in the tabbed list and change the **Space After** to **0 pt**. Near the top of the document, position the insertion point in the blank line below the title. Display the **Choose a SmartArt Graphic** dialog box, select the **Cycle** category, and then in the second row, select the first style—**Continuous Cycle**.

7 Display the **Text Pane**. Add the following cities in this order: **Allentown** and **Cemerton** and **Palmerton** and **Berlinsville** and **Pennsville**

8 **Close** the Text Pane. Click the SmartArt border. On the **Format tab**, set the **Shape Width** of the SmartArt graphic to **6.5"** and the **Shape Height** to **3"**. On the **Design tab**, from the **SmartArt Styles** gallery, apply the **Cartoon 3-D** style, and change the colors to the first color under **Colorful—Colorful – Accent Colors**.

9 Display the **Document Panel**, type your firstname and lastname in the **Author** box, your course name and section number in the **Subject** box, and then in the **Keywords** box type **cycling, cycling club**

10 **Close** the Document Panel. **Save** your document. Preview your document, check for and make any adjustments, and then print your document or submit it electronically as directed. **Close** Word.

Table 1

Thursday, October 7	3:00 p.m.	Field House Room B
Thursday, November 11	7:30 p.m.	Student Activities Center L-7
Thursday, December 9	5:00 p.m.	Little Theater

- - - ▶ (Return to Step 6)

End **You have completed Project 1F** ——————————————————————

Apply a combination of
1A and **1B** skills:

1. Create a New Document and Insert Text

2. Insert and Format Graphics

3. Insert and Modify Text Boxes and Shapes

4. Preview and Print a Document

5. Change Document and Paragraph Layout

6. Create and Modify Lists

7. Set and Modify Tab Stops

8. Insert a SmartArt Graphic

Mastering Word | Project **1G** Web Sites

In the following Mastering Word project, you will edit guidelines for club Web sites at Laurel College. Your completed document will look similar to Figure 1.54.

Project Files

For Project 1G, you will need the following files:

New blank Word document
w01G_Chess_Club_Picture
w01G_Web_Sites_Text

You will save your document as:

Lastname_Firstname_1G_Web_Sites

Project Results

Figure 1.54

(Project 1G Web Sites continues on the next page)

Content-Based Assessments

Mastering Word | Project **1G** Web Sites (continued)

1 **Start** Word and display a new blank document. Display formatting marks and rulers. **Save** the document in your **Word Chapter 1** folder as **Lastname_Firstname_1G_Web_Sites** Add the file name to the footer.

Type **Club Web Sites** and then press [Enter]. Select the title you just typed. From the **Text Effects** gallery, in the fourth row, apply the second effect—**Gradient Fill - Orange, Accent 6, Inner Shadow**, change the **Font Size** to **72** pt, and **Center** the title.

2 Click in the blank line below the title. Locate and insert the file **w01G_Web_Sites_Text**. *Except* for the document title, select all of the document text. **Align Text Left**, change the **Line Spacing** to **1.15**, and change the **Spacing After** to **6 pt**. Locate and **Center** the document subtitle that begins *Published by*.

3 In the middle of **Page 1**, under the subheading *Be sure that*, select the six paragraphs down to, but not including, the *General information* subheading. Format the selected text as a bulleted list. Near the bottom of **Page 1** and the top of **Page 2**, under the *Web Site Design Guidelines* subheading, select all of the paragraphs to the end of the document—not including the blank paragraph mark—and create another bulleted list.

4 Under the subheading that begins *General information*, select the six paragraphs and apply **Numbering** to create a numbered list.

Near the top of the document, position the insertion point to the left of the paragraph that begins The Web site. **Insert** the picture **w01G_Chess_Club_Picture**. Set the **Wrap Text** to **Square**. Decrease the picture **Width** to **2.7"**. From the **Picture Effects** gallery, apply the **Soft Edges** effect using **5 Point**.

5 Press [Ctrl] + [End] to move to the blank line at the end of the document. Type **For assistance, Student Computing Services hours are:** and then press [Enter]. Set a **Left** tab stop at **1.5"**. Display the **Tabs** dialog box. At **5"** add a **Right** tab stop with a **dot leader** and click **Set**. Click **OK** to close the dialog box, press [Tab] to begin, and then type the following information; be sure to press [Tab] to

begin each line and press [Tab] between the days and the times and press [Enter] at the end of each line:

Monday–Thursday	8 a.m. to 10 p.m.
Friday	8 a.m. to 5 p.m.
Saturday	8 a.m. to 12 noon

6 At the top of **Page 2**, position the insertion point to the left of the subheading *Web Site Design Guidelines*. Press [Enter] one time, and then click in the blank paragraph you just created. **Insert** a **SmartArt** graphic, and then from the **Process** group, select the **Basic Chevron Process**—in the fourth row, the third graphic. Click the border of the graphic, and then on the **Format tab**, set the **Shape Height** of the graphic to **1"** and the **Shape Width** of the graphic to **6.5"**. From the **Design tab**, display the **Text Pane**, and then type **Club** and **Web Site** and **New Members Close** the **Text Pane**. Change style to **3-D Inset** and the colors to **Colored Fill – Accent 6**, which is in the last set of colors.

7 At the bottom of **Page 2**, **Insert** a **Text Box** and set the height to **0.7"** and the width to **5"**. In the text box, type: **The Student Computing Services office is located in the Cedar Building, Room 114, call (215) 555-0932.**

Select the text in the text box. From the Mini toolbar, change the **Font Size** to **16** pt, apply **Bold**, and **Center** the text. Change the **Shape Fill** to **Orange, Accent 6, Darker 25%**. From the **Shape Effects** gallery, apply a **Circle Bevel**. By using the pointer, visually center the text box horizontally between the left and right margins and vertically between the tabbed list and the footer.

8 As the document properties, type your firstname and lastname in the **Author** box, your course name and section number in the **Subject** box, and then in the **Keywords** box type **Web sites, guidelines, Student Computing Services Save** your document, examine the Print Preview, check for and make any adjustments, and then print your document or submit it electronically as directed. **Close** Word.

End You have completed Project 1G ————————————

Content-Based Assessments

Apply a combination of the **1A** and **1B** skills.

GO! Fix It | Project **1H** Guidelines

Project Files

For Project 1H, you will need the following file:

w01H_Guidelines

You will save your document as:

Lastname_Firstname_1H_Guidelines

From the student files that accompany this textbook, locate and open the file w01H_More_Guidelines, and then save the file in your Word Chapter 1 folder as **Lastname_Firstname_1H_Guidelines**

This document contains errors that you must find and correct. Read and examine the document, and then edit to correct any errors that you find and to improve the overall document format. Types of errors could include, but are not restricted to:

- Wasted space due to text not wrapping around pictures
- Inconsistent line spacing in paragraphs
- Inconsistent spacing between paragraphs
- Inconsistent paragraph indents
- Inconsistent indenting of lists
- Titles that do not extend across the page
- Text boxes that are too small
- Tabbed lists with wide spaces that do not contain leaders
- Spaces between paragraphs created using empty paragraphs rather than space after paragraphs

Things you should know to complete this project:

- Displaying formatting marks will assist in locating spacing errors.
- There are no errors in the fonts, although the title font size is too small.
- The final flyer should fit on one page.

Save your document and add the file name to the footer. In the Document Panel, type your firstname and lastname in the Author box and your course name and section number in the Subject box. In the Keywords box type **Web site guidelines** and then save your document and submit as directed.

End You have completed Project 1H ————————————————————

Content-Based Assessments

Apply a combination of the **1A** and **1B** skills.

GO! Make It | Project **1I** Flyer

Project Files

For Project 1I, you will need the following files:

    w01I_Team_Building   w01I_Park_Picture

You will save your document as:

    Lastname_Firstname_1I_Team_Building

From the student files that accompany this textbook, locate and open the file w01I_Team_Building, and then save the file in your chapter folder as **Lastname_Firstname_1I_Team_Building**

Use the skills you have practiced, create the document shown in Figure 1.55. The title uses Gradient Fill – Blue, Accent 1, 48 pt. The SmartArt graphic uses the Radial Cycle with an Intense Effect style, is 3″ high and 6.5″ wide, has the Colorful Range – Accent Colors 2 to 3 applied. The w01I_Park_Picture picture has a 2.5 pt soft edge, and is 2.5″ wide. The page border uses Dark Blue, Text 2.

Add the file name to the footer; in the Document Panel, add your name and course information and the Keywords **team building**; save your document; and then submit as directed.

Project Results

Figure 1.55

End You have completed Project 1I

Content-Based Assessments

GO! Solve It | Project 1J Food Drive

Project Files

For Project 1J, you will need the following file:

New blank Word document
w01J_Food_Drive

You will save your document as:

Lastname_Firstname_1J_Food_Drive

Create a new document and save it in your Word Chapter 1 folder as **Lastname_Firstname_1J_Food_Drive** Use the following information to create a flyer that includes a title that uses Text Effects, introductory text, two lists of an appropriate type, one text box, and a picture with appropriate formatting and text wrapping. Use your own picture or w01J_Food_Drive.

This Thanksgiving, the Associated Students of Laurel College is sponsoring a food drive for the local community. All college clubs are invited to participate. Results will be adjusted for club membership by measuring the results in pounds of food per member. Three kinds of food are acceptable: canned goods, non-perishable dry goods, and boxed or canned dry drink mixes, such as coffee, tea, or lemonade.

To participate, a club must follow this procedure: fill out a competition form, collect the goods, and then turn the food in on November 13. The address and telephone number for the ASLC is the Cedar Building, Room 222, Laurelton, PA 19100, (215) 555-0902.

Add the file name to the footer. To the Properties area, add your name, your course name and section number, and the keywords **food drive, clubs**

Performance Criteria	Performance Level		
	Exemplary: You consistently applied the relevant skills	Proficient: You sometimes, but not always, applied the relevant skills	Developing: You rarely or never applied the relevant skills
Create and format lists	Both lists use the proper list type and are formatted correctly.	One of the lists is formatted correctly.	Neither of the lists are formatted correctly.
Insert and format a picture	The picture is inserted and positioned correctly, and text is wrapped around the picture.	The picture is inserted but not formatted properly.	No picture is inserted.
Insert a text box	A text box with appropriate information is inserted and formatted.	A text box is adequately formatted but is difficult to read or unattractive.	No text box is inserted.
Insert introductory text	Introductory text explains the reason for the flyer, with no spelling or grammar errors.	Some introductory text is included, but does not contain sufficient information and/or includes spelling or grammar errors.	No introductory text, or insufficient introductory text.
Insert title using Text Effects	Text Effects title inserted and centered on the page.	Text Effects title is inserted, but not centered or formatted attractively on the page.	No Text Effects title is included.

End You have completed Project 1J

Content-Based Assessments

Apply a combination of the 1A and 1B skills..

GO! Solve It | Project **1K** Fitness Services

Project Files

For Project 1K, you will need the following files:

New blank Word document
w01K_Volleyball

You will save your document as:

Lastname_Firstname_1K_Fitness_Services

Create a new file and save it as **Lastname_Firstname_1K_Fitness Services** Use the following information to create a flyer that includes introductory text, a SmartArt graphic, a title that uses Text Effects, and a picture that has an artistic effect applied and uses text wrapping. Use your own picture or w01K_Volleyball.

The Associated Students of Laurel College sponsors fitness activities. These take place both on campus and off campus. The activities fall into two categories: Fitness Services and Intramural Sports. Fitness Services are noncompetitive activities, with the most popular being Kickboxing, Jogging, and Aerobics. The most popular Intramural Sports activities—which include competitive team and club sports—are Field Hockey, Volleyball, and Basketball.

Add the file name to the footer, and add your name, your course name and section number, and the keywords **fitness, sports** to the Properties area.

		Performance Level	
	Exemplary: You consistently applied the relevant skills	**Proficient:** You sometimes, but not always, applied the relevant skills	**Developing:** You rarely or never applied the relevant skills
Insert title using Text Effects	Text Effects title inserted and centered on the page.	Text Effects title is inserted, but not centered on the page.	No Text Effects title is included.
Insert introductory text	Introductory text explains the reason for the flyer, with no spelling or grammar errors.	Some introductory text is included, but does not sufficiently explain the topic and/or includes spelling or grammar errors.	No or insufficient introductory text is included.
Insert and format a picture	The picture is inserted and positioned correctly, an artistic effect is applied, and text is wrapped around the picture.	The picture is inserted but not formatted properly.	No picture is inserted in the document.
Insert and format SmartArt	The SmartArt graphic displays both categories of fitness activities and examples of each type.	The SmartArt graphic does not display fitness activities by category.	No SmartArt graphic inserted.

Performance Criteria

End You have completed Project 1K

Outcomes-Based Assessments

Rubric

The following outcomes-based assessments are *open-ended assessments*. That is, there is no specific correct result; your result will depend on your approach to the information provided. Make *Professional Quality* your goal. Use the following scoring rubric to guide you in *how* to approach the problem and then to evaluate *how well* your approach solves the problem.

The *criteria*—Software Mastery, Content, Format and Layout, and Process—represent the knowledge and skills you have gained that you can apply to solving the problem. The *levels of performance*—Professional Quality, Approaching Professional Quality, or Needs Quality Improvements—help you and your instructor evaluate your result.

	Your completed project is of Professional Quality if you:	Your completed project is Approaching Professional Quality if you:	Your completed project Needs Quality Improvements if you:
1-Software Mastery	Choose and apply the most appropriate skills, tools, and features and identify efficient methods to solve the problem.	Choose and apply some appropriate skills, tools, and features, but not in the most efficient manner.	Choose inappropriate skills, tools, or features, or are inefficient in solving the problem.
2-Content	Construct a solution that is clear and well organized, contains content that is accurate, appropriate to the audience and purpose, and is complete. Provide a solution that contains no errors in spelling, grammar, or style.	Construct a solution in which some components are unclear, poorly organized, inconsistent, or incomplete. Misjudge the needs of the audience. Have some errors in spelling, grammar, or style, but the errors do not detract from comprehension.	Construct a solution that is unclear, incomplete, or poorly organized; contains some inaccurate or inappropriate content; and contains many errors in spelling, grammar, or style. Do not solve the problem.
3-Format and Layout	Format and arrange all elements to communicate information and ideas, clarify function, illustrate relationships, and indicate relative importance.	Apply appropriate format and layout features to some elements, but not others. Overuses features, causing minor distraction.	Apply format and layout that does not communicate information or ideas clearly. Do not use format and layout features to clarify function, illustrate relationships, or indicate relative importance. Use available features excessively, causing distraction.
4-Process	Use an organized approach that integrates planning, development, self-assessment, revision, and reflection.	Demonstrate an organized approach in some areas, but not others; or, uses an insufficient process of organization throughout.	Do not use an organized approach to solve the problem.

Outcomes-Based Assessments

Apply a combination of the **1A** and **1B** skills..

GO! Think | Project **1L** Academic Services

Project Files

For Project 1L, you will need the following file:

New blank Word document

You will save your document as:

Lastname_Firstname_1L_Academic_Services

The Services Coordinator of the Associated Students of Laurel College needs to create a flyer to inform students of academic services available at the ASLC office. Referrals are available for medical, legal, and counseling services, as well as tutoring and volunteer organizations. Among the services offered at the ASLC office are free printing (up to 250 pages per semester), help with minor legal issues, housing information, bicycle repair, minor computer repair, and help placing students with volunteer organizations.

Create a flyer with basic information about the services provided. Be sure the flyer is easy to read and understand and has an attractive design. If you need more information about student services available at other colleges, search the Web for **student government** and add whatever services you think might be (or should be) available at your college. Add appropriate information to the Document Panel. Save the document as **Lastname_Firstname_1L_Academic_Services** and submit it as directed.

End You have completed Project 1L ———————————————

Apply a combination of the **1A** and **1B** skills.

GO! Think | Project **1M** Campus Bookstore

Project Files

For Project 1M, you will need the following files:

New blank Word document
w01L_Campus_Bookstore

You will save your document as:

Lastname_Firstname_1M_Campus_Bookstore

The manager of the Laurel College Bookstore needs to create a flyer that can be handed out by the ASLC to students during Welcome Week. The bookstore gives students attending Welcome Week a discount of 20% on special items such as sweatshirts and other college-related clothing, coffee mugs, calendars, and similar items. Door prizes will also be awarded. The bookstore is open Monday and Thursday from 8 a.m. to 10 p.m., Tuesday and Wednesday from 8 a.m. to 8 p.m., and Friday from 8 a.m. to 5 p.m.

Using your own campus bookstore as an example, create a flyer that gives general information about the bookstore, provides one or more lists of items that are on sale, displays the picture w01M_ Campus_Bookstore, and has a highlighted area that gives the store hours.

Add appropriate information to the Document Panel. Save the document as **Lastname_Firstname_1M_Campus_Bookstore** and submit it as directed.

End You have completed Project 1M ———————————————

Outcomes-Based Assessments

Apply a combination of the **1A** and **1B** skills.

You and GO! | Project **1N** Family Flyer

Project Files

For Project 1N, you will need the following file:

New blank Word document

You will save your document as

Lastname_Firstname_1N_Family_Flyer

In this project, you will create a one-page flyer that you can send to your family. Include any information that may interest your family members, such as work-related news, school events, vacation plans, and the activities and accomplishments of you, your spouse, your friends, or other family members. Choose any writing style that suits you—chatty, newsy, entertaining, or humorous.

To complete the assignment, be sure to include a title, at least one list, a picture, and either a SmartArt graphic or a text box or shape. Before you submit the flyer, be sure to check it for grammar and spelling errors, and also be sure to format the document in an attractive manner, using the skills you practiced in this chapter.

Save the file as **Lastname_Firstname_1N_Family_Flyer** Add the file name to the footer, and add your name, your course name and section number, and the keywords **flyer** and **family** to the Properties area. Submit your file as directed.

End **You have completed Project 1N** ——————————

Apply a combination of the **1A** and **1B** skills.

GO! Collaborate | Project **1O** Bell Orchid Hotels Group Running Case

This project relates to the **Bell Orchid Hotels**. Your instructor may assign this group case project to your class. If your instructor assigns this project, he or she will provide you with information and instructions to work as part of a group. The group will apply the skills gained thus far to help the Bell Orchid Hotels achieve their business goals.

End **You have completed Project 1O** ——————————

Using Tables and Templates to Create Resumes and Cover Letters

OUTCOMES
At the end of this chapter you will be able to:

OBJECTIVES
Mastering these objectives will enable you to:

PROJECT 2A
Create a resume by using a Word table.

1. Create a Table (p. 107)
2. Add Text to a Table (p. 108)
3. Format a Table (p. 111)

PROJECT 2B
Create a cover letter and resume by using a template.

4. Create a New Document from an Existing Document (p. 120)
5. Change and Reorganize Text (p. 123)
6. Use the Proofing Options (p. 130)
7. Create a Document Using a Template (p. 134)

James Thew/Shutterstock

In This Chapter

Tables are useful for organizing and presenting data. Because a table is so easy to use, many individuals prefer to arrange tabular information in a Word table rather than setting a series of tabs. Use a table when you want to present rows and columns of information or to create a structure for a document such as a resume.

When using Word to write business or personal letters, use a commonly approved letter format. You will make a good impression on prospective employers if you use a standard business letter style when you are writing a cover letter for a resume. You can create a resume using one of the Microsoft resume templates included with Microsoft Office or available online.

The projects in this chapter relate to **Madison Staffing Services**. Many companies prefer to hire employees through a staffing service, so that both the employer and the employee can determine if the match is a good fit. Madison Staffing Services takes care of the details of recruiting, testing, hiring, and paying the employee. At the end of the employment assignment, neither the employer nor the employee is required to make a permanent commitment. Many individuals find full-time jobs with an employer for whom they initially worked through a staffing agency.

Project 2A Resume

Project Activities

In Activities 2.01 through 2.09, you will create a table to use as the structure for a resume for one of Madison Staffing Services' clients. Your completed document will look similar to Figure 2.1.

Project Files

For Project 2A, you will need the following file:

w02A_Experience

You will save your document as:

Lastname_Firstname_2A_Resume

Project Results

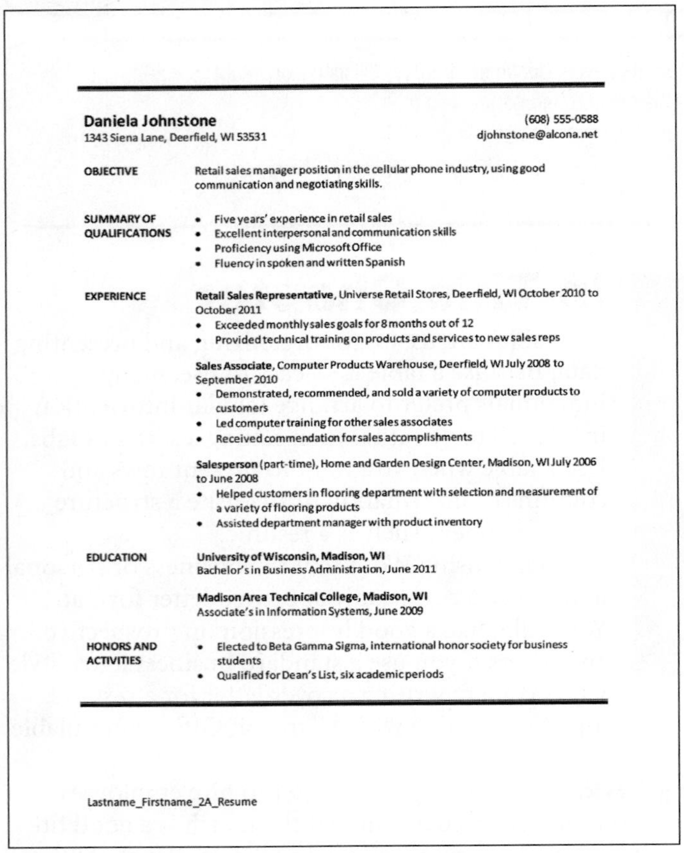

Daniela Johnstone
1343 Siena Lane, Deerfield, WI 53531

(608) 555-0588
djohnstone@alcona.net

OBJECTIVE — Retail sales manager position in the cellular phone industry, using good communication and negotiating skills.

SUMMARY OF QUALIFICATIONS
- Five years' experience in retail sales
- Excellent interpersonal and communication skills
- Proficiency using Microsoft Office
- Fluency in spoken and written Spanish

EXPERIENCE — **Retail Sales Representative**, Universe Retail Stores, Deerfield, WI October 2010 to October 2011
- Exceeded monthly sales goals for 8 months out of 12
- Provided technical training on products and services to new sales reps

Sales Associate, Computer Products Warehouse, Deerfield, WI July 2008 to September 2010
- Demonstrated, recommended, and sold a variety of computer products to customers
- Led computer training for other sales associates
- Received commendation for sales accomplishments

Salesperson (part-time), Home and Garden Design Center, Madison, WI July 2006 to June 2008
- Helped customers in flooring department with selection and measurement of a variety of flooring products
- Assisted department manager with product inventory

EDUCATION — **University of Wisconsin, Madison, WI**
Bachelor's in Business Administration, June 2011

Madison Area Technical College, Madison, WI
Associate's in Information Systems, June 2009

HONORS AND ACTIVITIES
- Elected to Beta Gamma Sigma, international honor society for business students
- Qualified for Dean's List, six academic periods

Lastname_Firstname_2A_Resume

Figure 2.1
Project 2A Resume

Objective 1 | Create a Table

A ***table*** is an arrangement of information organized into rows and columns. The intersection of a row and a column in a table creates a box called a ***cell*** into which you can type. Tables are useful to present information in a logical and orderly manner.

Activity 2.01 | Creating a Table

1 Start **Word**, and in the new blank document, display formatting marks and rulers.

2 Click the **File tab**, and then in **Backstage** view, click **Save As**. In the **Save As** dialog box, navigate to the location where you are storing your projects for this chapter. Create a new folder named **Word Chapter 2**

3 **Save** the file in the **Word Chapter 2** folder as **Lastname_Firstname_2A_Resume**

4 Scroll to the end of the document, right-click near the bottom of the page, and then click **Edit Footer**. On the **Design tab**, in the **Insert group**, click the **Quick Parts** button, and then click **Field**.

5 Under **Field names**, scroll down, click **FileName**, and then click **OK. Close** the footer area.

6 On the **Insert tab**, in the **Tables group**, click the **Table** button. In the **Table** grid, in the fourth row, point to the second square, and notice that the cells display in orange and *2 × 4 Table* displays at the top of the grid. Compare your screen with Figure 2.2.

Figure 2.2

Table button
Table size
Pointer indicates table size
Preview of table

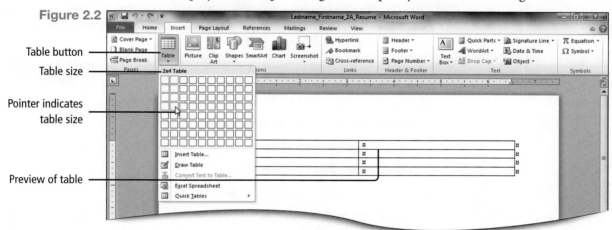

7 Click one time to create the table. Notice that formatting marks in each cell indicate the end of the contents of each cell and the mark to the right of each *row* indicates the row end. **Save** your document, and then compare your screen with Figure 2.3.

A table with four rows and two columns displays at the insertion point location, and the insertion point displays in the upper left cell. The table fills the width of the page, from the left margin to the right margin. On the Ribbon, Table Tools display and add two tabs—*Design* and *Layout*. Borders display around each cell in the table.

Figure 2.3

Table Tools
Indicates the end of a row
Indicates the end of cell contents

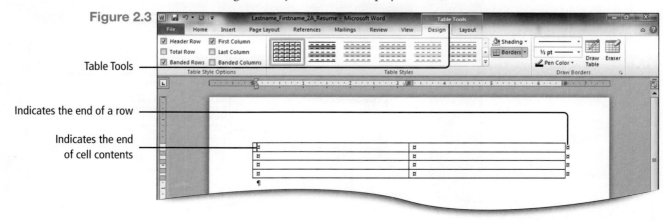

Objective 2 | Add Text to a Table

In a Word table, each cell behaves similarly to a document. For example, as you type in a cell, when you reach the right border of the cell, wordwrap moves the text to the next line. When you press [Enter], the insertion point moves down to a new paragraph in the same cell. You can also insert text from another document into a table cell.

Activity 2.02 | Adding Text to a Table

There are numerous acceptable formats for resumes, many of which can be found in Business Communications textbooks. The layout used in this project is suitable for a recent college graduate and places topics in the left column and details in the right column.

1 Scroll up to view the top of the document. With the insertion point blinking in the first cell in the first row, type **OBJECTIVE** and then press [Tab].

Pressing [Tab] moves the insertion point to the next cell in the row, or, if the insertion point is already in the last cell in the row, pressing [Tab] moves the insertion point to the first cell in the following row.

2 Type **Retail sales manager position in the cellular phone industry, using good communication and negotiating skills.** Notice that the text wraps in the cell and the height of the row adjusts to fit the text.

3 Press [Tab] to move to the first cell in the second row. Type **SUMMARY OF QUALIFICATIONS** and then press [Tab]. Type the following, pressing [Enter] at the end of each line *except* the last line:

Five years' experience in retail sales

Excellent interpersonal and communication skills

Proficiency using Microsoft Office

Fluency in spoken and written Spanish

The default font and font size in a table are the same as for a document—Calibri 11 pt. The default line spacing in a table is single spacing with no space before or after paragraphs, which differs from the defaults for a document.

4 **Save** 🖫 your document, and then compare your screen with Figure 2.4.

Figure 2.4

Text typed in cells

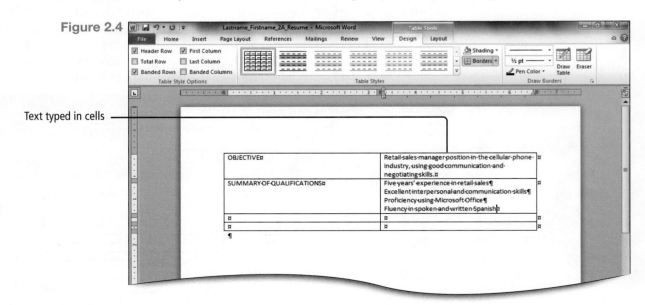

Activity 2.03 | Inserting Existing Text into a Table Cell

1 Press Tab to move to the first cell in the third row. Type **EXPERIENCE** and then press Tab.

2 Type the following, pressing Enter after each line:

> **Retail Sales Representative, Universe Retail Stores, Deerfield, WI October 2010 to October 2011**
>
> **Exceeded monthly sales goals for 8 months out of 12**
>
> **Provided technical training on products and services to new sales reps**

3 Be sure your insertion point is positioned in the second column to the left of the cell marker below *sales reps*. Compare your screen with Figure 2.5.

Figure 2.5

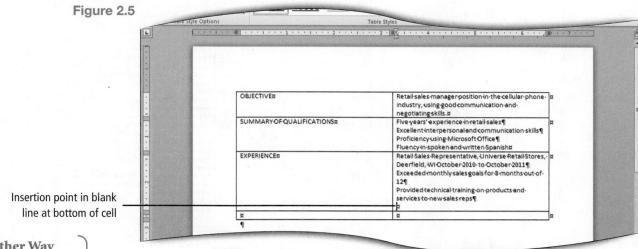

Insertion point in blank line at bottom of cell

> **Another Way**
>
> Open the second document and select the text you want. Copy the text, and then paste at the desired location.

4 On the **Insert tab**, in the **Text group**, click the **Object button arrow**, and then click **Text from File**. Navigate to your student files, select **w02A_Experience**, and then click **Insert**.

5 Press Backspace one time to remove the blank line at the end of the inserted text, and then compare your screen with Figure 2.6.

Figure 2.6

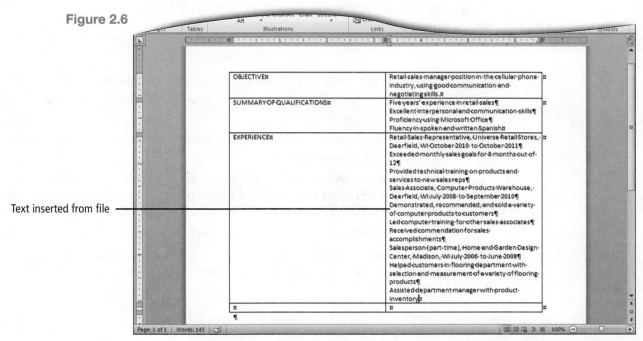

Text inserted from file

6 Press `Tab` to move to the first cell in the fourth row. Type **EDUCATION** and then press `Tab`.

7 Type the following, pressing `Enter` at the end of each item *except* the last one:

University of Wisconsin, Madison, WI

Bachelor's in Business Administration, June 2011

Madison Area Technical College, Madison, WI

Associate's in Information Systems, June 2009

8 Compare your screen with Figure 2.7.

Figure 2.7

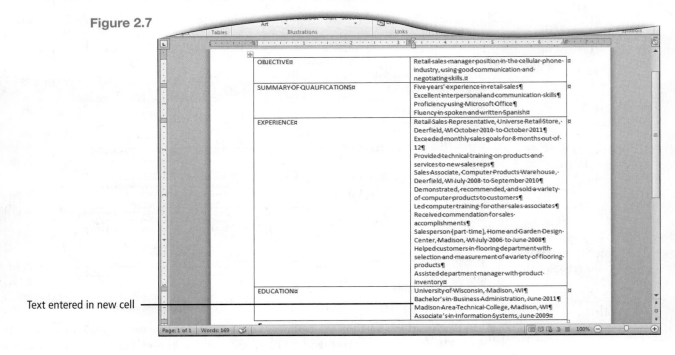

Text entered in new cell

9 **Save** 💾 your document.

Activity 2.04 | Creating Bulleted Lists in a Table

1 Scroll to view the top of your document, and then in the cell to the right of *SUMMARY OF QUALIFICATIONS*, select all of the text.

2 On the **Home tab**, in the **Paragraph group**, click the **Bullets** button ⊞▾.

The selected text displays as a bulleted list. Using a bulleted list in this manner makes each qualification more distinctive.

3 In the **Paragraph group**, click the **Decrease Indent** button 📊 one time to align the bullets at the left edge of the cell.

4 In the **Clipboard group**, double-click the **Format Painter** button. In the cell to the right of *EXPERIENCE*, select the second and third paragraphs—beginning *Exceeded* and *Provided*—to create the same style of bulleted list as you did in the previous step.

When you double-click the Format Painter button, it remains active until you turn it off.

5 In the same cell, under *Sales Associate*, select the three paragraphs that begin *Demonstrated* and *Led* and *Received* to create another bulleted list aligned at the left edge of the cell.

6 With the Format Painter pointer still active, in the same cell, select the paragraphs that begin *Helped* and *Assisted* to create the same type of bulleted list.

7 Press [Esc] to turn off the Format Painter. Click anywhere in the table to deselect the text, and then compare your screen with Figure 2.8.

Figure 2.8

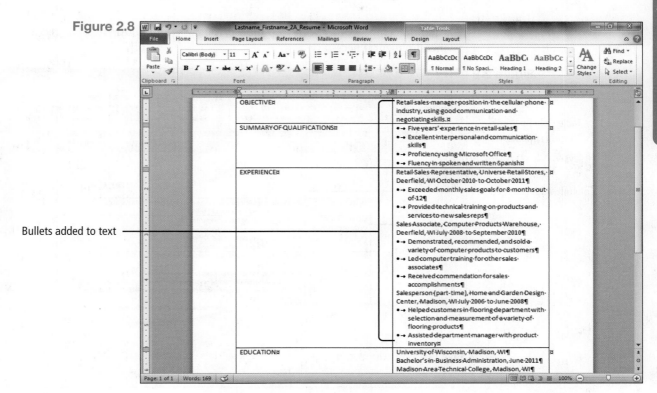

Bullets added to text

8 Save 🖫 your document.

Objective 3 | Format a Table

Use Word's formatting tools to make your tables attractive and easy to read. Types of formatting you can add to a table include changing the row height and the column width, removing or adding borders, increasing or decreasing the paragraph or line spacing, or enhancing the text.

Activity 2.05 | Changing the Width of Table Columns

When you create a table, all of the columns are of equal width. In this activity, you will change the width of the columns.

1 In any row, point to the vertical border between the two columns to display the ⊶ pointer.

2 Drag the column border to the left to approximately **1.25 inches on the horizontal ruler**.

3 Scroll to the top of the document. Notice that in the second row, the text *SUMMARY OF QUALIFICATIONS* wraps to two lines to accommodate the new column width.

4 If necessary, in the left column, click in any cell. On the Ribbon, under **Table Tools**, click the **Layout tab**.

5 In the **Cell Size group**, click the **Table Column Width button spin arrows** ⊞ 1.37" ↕ as necessary to change the width of the first column to **1.4"**. Compare your screen with Figure 2.9.

> After dragging a border with your mouse, use the Width button to set a precise measurement if necessary.

Figure 2.9

Table Column Width button spin arrows

Column width changed

Text wraps in cell

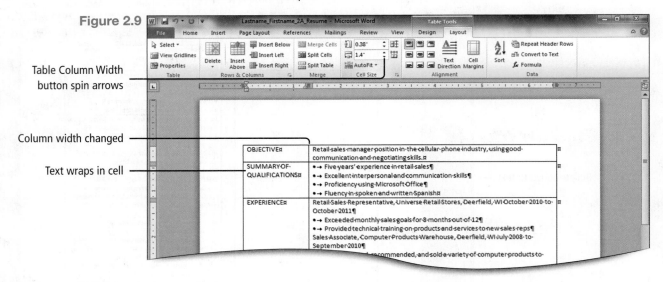

6 Save 🖫 your document.

More Knowledge | Changing Column Widths

You will typically get the best results if you change the column widths starting at the left side of the table, especially in tables with three or more columns. Word can also calculate the best column widths for you. To do this, select the table. Then, on the Layout tab, in the Cell Size group, click the AutoFit button and click AutoFit Contents.

Activity 2.06 | Adding Rows to a Table

You can add rows or columns anywhere in a table.

1 Scroll to view the lower portion of the table. In the last row of the table, click anywhere in the *second* cell that contains the educational information, and then press Tab.

> A new row displays at the bottom of the table. When the insertion point is in the last cell in the bottom row of a table, you can add a row by pressing the Tab key; the insertion point will display in the first cell of the new row.

2 Type **HONORS AND ACTIVITIES** and then press Tab.

3 Type the following, pressing Enter after the first item but not the second item:

Elected to Beta Gamma Sigma, international honor society for business students

Qualified for Dean's List, six academic periods

4 Select the text you typed in the last cell of the bottom row. On the **Home tab**, in the **Paragraph group**, click the **Bullets** button ⊟▾, and then click the **Decrease Indent** button ⬅ one time to align the bullets at the left edge of the cell.

5 Scroll up to view the entire table, click anywhere in the table to deselect the text, and then compare your screen with Figure 2.10.

Figure 2.10

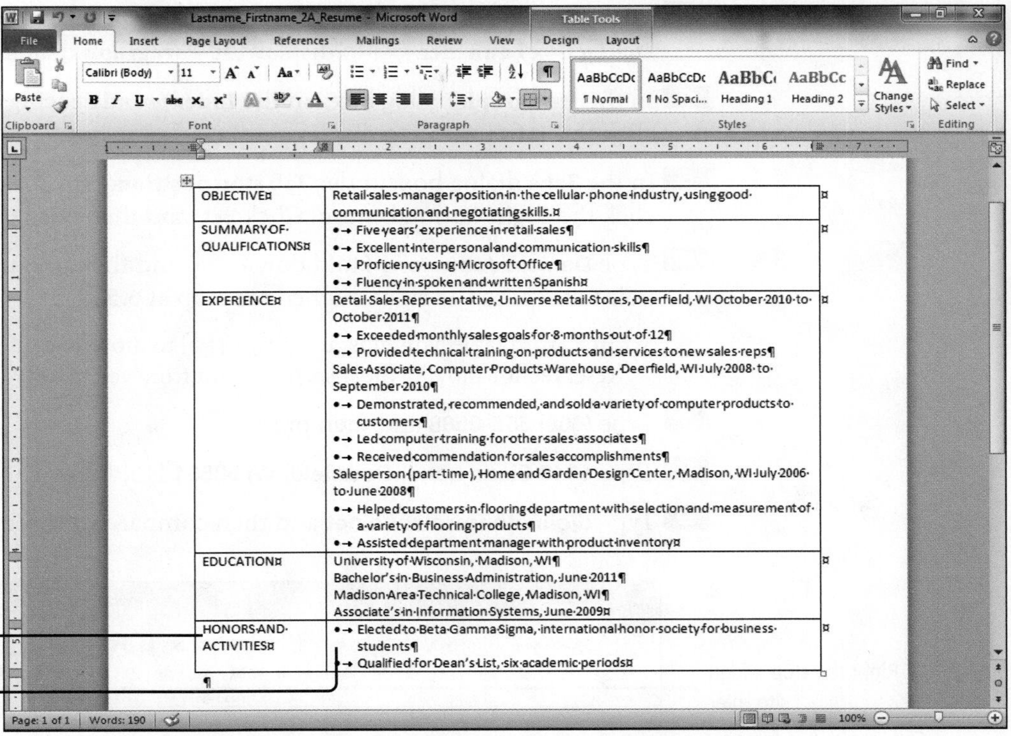

Row added to table

Bullets added to text

6 Click anywhere in the top row of the table.

Another Way

Right-click in the top row, point to Insert, and then click Insert Rows Above.

7 On the **Layout tab**, in the **Rows & Columns group**, click the **Insert Above** button. Compare your screen with Figure 2.11.

A new row displays above the row that contained the insertion point, and the new row is selected.

Figure 2.11

Row inserted at top of table

8 Save 🖫 your document.

Activity 2.07 | Merging Cells

The title of a table typically spans all of the columns. In this activity, you will merge cells so that you can position the personal information across both columns.

1 Be sure the two cells in the top row are selected; if necessary, drag across both cells to select them.

Another Way

Right-click the selected row and click Merge Cells on the shortcut menu.

2 On the **Layout tab**, in the **Merge group**, click the **Merge Cells** button.

> The cell border between the two cells no longer displays.

3 With the merged cell still selected, on the **Home tab**, in the **Paragraph group**, click the **Dialog Box Launcher** to display the **Paragraph** dialog box.

4 In the **Paragraph** dialog box, on the **Indents and Spacing tab**, in the lower left corner, click the **Tabs** button to display the **Tabs** dialog box.

5 In the **Tabs** dialog box, under **Tab stop position**, type **6.5** and then under **Alignment**, click the **Right** option button. Click **Set**, and then click **OK** to close the dialog box.

6 Type **Daniela Johnstone** Hold down Ctrl and then press Tab. Notice that the insertion point moves to the right-aligned tab stop at 6.5″.

> In a Word table, you must use Ctrl + Tab to move to a tab stop, because pressing Tab is reserved for moving the insertion point from cell to cell.

7 Type **(608) 555-0588** and then press Enter.

8 Type **1343 Siena Lane, Deerfield, WI 53531** Hold down Ctrl and then press Tab.

9 Type **djohnstone@alcona.net** and then compare your screen with Figure 2.12.

Figure 2.12

Right tab stop added to ruler

Cells merged in top row

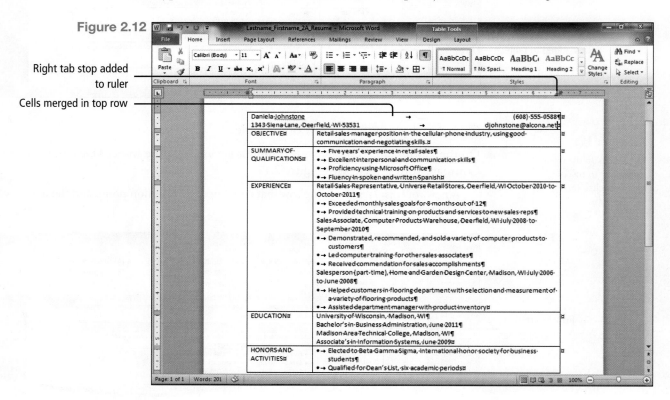

10 **Save** your document.

Activity 2.08 | Formatting Text in Cells

1 In the first row of the table, select the name *Daniela Johnstone*, and then on the Mini toolbar, apply **Bold** and change the **Font Size** to **16**.

2 Under *Daniela Johnstone*, click anywhere in the second line of text, which contains the address and e-mail address.

3 On the **Page Layout tab**, in the **Paragraph group**, click the **Spacing After up spin arrow** three times to add **18 pt** spacing between the first row of the table and the second row. Compare your screen with Figure 2.13.

These actions separate the personal information from the body of the resume and adds focus to the applicant's name.

Figure 2.13

Text formatted

18 pt space added after paragraph

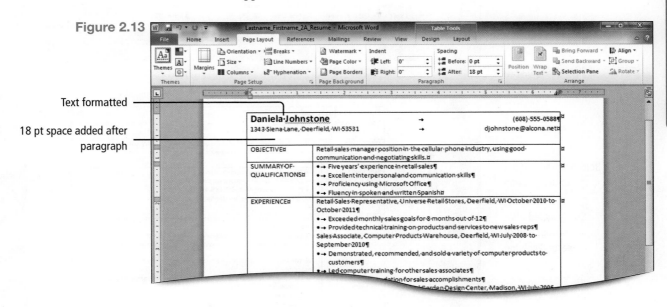

4 Using the technique you just practiced, in the second column, click in the last paragraph of every cell and add **18 pt Spacing After** the last paragraph of all rows including the last row; a border will be added to the bottom of the table, and spacing will be needed between the last row and the border.

5 In the second row, point to the word *OBJECTIVE*, hold down the left mouse button, and then drag downward in the first column only to select all the headings in uppercase letters. On the Mini toolbar, click the **Bold** button **B**.

Note | Selecting Only One Column

When you drag downward to select the first column, a fast mouse might also begin to select the second column when you reach the bottom. If this happens, drag upward slightly to deselect the second column and select only the first column.

---

6 In the cell to the right of *EXPERIENCE*, without selecting the following comma, select *Retail Sales Representative* and then on the Mini toolbar, click the **Bold** button **B**.

7 In the same cell, apply **Bold B** to the other job titles—*Sales Associate* and *Salesperson*—but do not bold *(part time)*.

8 In the cell to the right of *EDUCATION*, apply **Bold B** to *University of Wisconsin, Madison, WI* and *Madison Area Technical College, Madison, WI*.

9 In the same cell, click anywhere in the line beginning *Bachelor's*. On the **Page Layout tab**, in the **Paragraph group**, click the **Spacing After up spin arrow** two times to add **12 pt** spacing after the paragraph.

10 In the cell to the right of *EXPERIENCE*, under *Retail Sales Representative*, click anywhere in the second bulleted item, and then add **12 pt Spacing After** the item.

11 In the same cell, repeat this process for the last bulleted item under *Sales Associate*.

12 Scroll to the top of the screen, and then compare your screen with Figure 2.14.

Figure 2.14

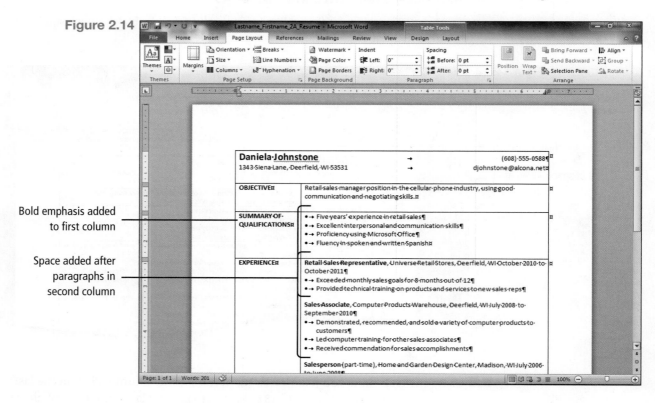

Bold emphasis added to first column

Space added after paragraphs in second column

13 Save 🖫 your document.

Activity 2.09 | Changing the Table Borders

When you create a table, all of the cells have black borders. Most resumes do not display any cell borders. A border at the top and bottom of the resume, however, is attractive and adds a professional look to the document.

1 If necessary, press Ctrl + Home to move the insertion point to the top of the table, and then point slightly outside of the upper left corner of the table to display the **table move handle** ⊞.

2 With the 🔗 pointer, click one time to select the entire table, and notice that the row markers at the end of each row are also selected.

Shaded row markers indicate that the entire row is selected.

3 Click the **Design tab**. In the **Table Styles group**, click the **Borders button arrow**, and then click **No Border**.

The black borders no longer display; instead, depending on your setup, either no borders—the default setting—or nonprinting blue dashed borders display.

4 Click the **File tab** to display **Backstage** view, and then click the **Print tab** to preview the table. Notice that no borders display in the preview, as shown in Figure 2.15.

Figure 2.15

Document preview

All table borders removed

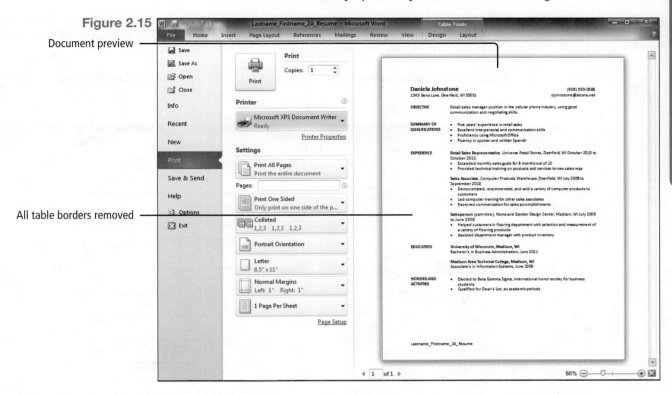

Another Way

Right-click the selected table, click Borders and Shading, and then click the Borders tab.

5 Click the **Design tab**; be sure the table is still selected. In the **Table Styles group**, click the **Borders button arrow**, and then at the bottom of the **Borders** gallery, click **Borders and Shading**.

6 Under **Setting**, click the **Custom** button. Under **Style**, scroll down about a third of the way and click the style with the thick upper line and the thin lower line.

Another Way

Click the top border button, which is one of the buttons that surround the Preview.

7 In the **Preview** box at the right, point to the *top* border of the small preview and click one time.

8 Under **Style**, click the style with the thin upper line and the thick lower line, and then in the **Preview** box, click the *bottom* border of the preview. Compare your screen with Figure 2.16.

Figure 2.16

Borders applied to table

Borders display in Preview

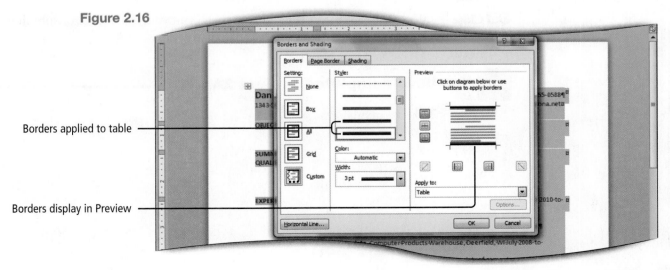

9 Click **OK**, click anywhere to cancel the selection, and then notice that there is only a small amount of space between the upper border and the first line of text.

10 Click anywhere in the text *Daniela Johnstone*, and then on the **Page Layout tab**, in the **Paragraph group**, click the **Spacing Before up spin arrow** as necessary to add **18 pt** spacing before the first paragraph.

11 Display **Backstage** view. Click the **Print tab** to preview the table. Compare your screen with Figure 2.17.

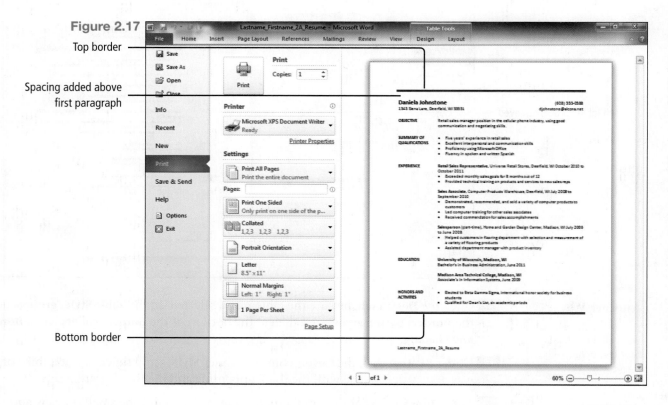

Figure 2.17

Top border

Spacing added above first paragraph

Bottom border

12 In **Backstage** view, click the **Info tab**. On the right, under the document thumbnail, click **Properties**, and then click **Show Document Panel**. In the **Author** box, delete any text and then type your firstname and lastname. In the **Subject** box, type your course name and section number, and in the **Keywords** box type **resume, Word table**

13 **Close** ✕ the **Document Panel**. **Save** 🖫 and then print your document, or submit it electronically, as directed by your instructor. **Exit** Word.

End **You have completed Project 2A**

Project 2B Cover Letter and Resume

myitlab
Project 2B Training

Project Activities

In Activities 2.10 through 2.22, you will create a letterhead, and then use the letterhead to create a cover letter. You will also create a short resume using a Microsoft template and save it as a Web page. Your completed documents will look similar to Figure 2.18.

Project Files

For Project 2B, you will need the following file:

w02B_Cover_Letter_Text

You will save your documents as:

Lastname_Firstname_2B_Letterhead
Lastname_Firstname_2B_Cover_Letter
Lastname_Firstname_2B_Brief_Resume
Lastname_Firstname_2B_HTML_Resume

Project Results

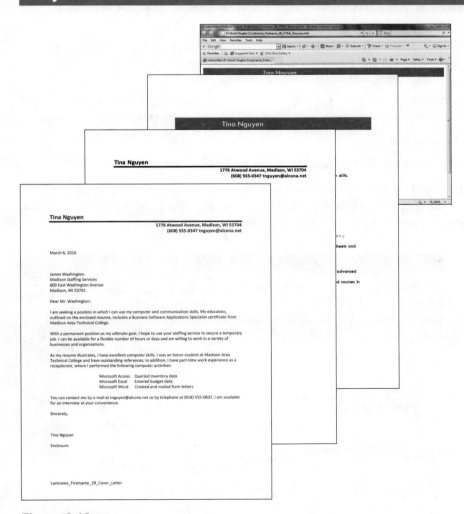

Figure 2.18
Project 2B Cover Letter and Resume

Objective 4 | Create a New Document from an Existing Document

A **template** is an *existing* document that you use as a starting point for a *new* document. The template document opens a copy of itself, unnamed, and then you use the structure—and possibly some content, such as headings—as the starting point for a new document.

All documents are based on a template. When you create a new blank document, it is based on Word's **Normal template**, which serves as the starting point for all new Word documents.

Activity 2.10 | Creating a Letterhead

A **letterhead** is the personal or company information that displays at the top of a letter, and which commonly includes a name, address, and contact information. The term also refers to a piece of paper imprinted with such information at the top.

1 **Start** Word, and in the new blank document, be sure that formatting marks and rulers display.

2 On the **Home tab**, in the **Styles group**, click the **More** button ☑. In the displayed gallery, click the **No Spacing** button.

> Recall that the default spacing for a new Word document is 10 points of blank space following a paragraph and line spacing of 1.15. The **No Spacing style** inserts *no* extra space following a paragraph and uses single spacing.

> By using the No Spacing style, you will be able to follow the prescribed format of a letter, which Business Communications texts commonly describe in terms of single spacing.

3 Type **Tina Nguyen** and then press Enter.

4 Type **1776 Atwood Avenue, Madison, WI 53704** and then press Enter.

5 Type **(608) 555-0347 tnguyen@alcona.net** and then press Enter. If the e-mail address changes to blue text, right-click the e-mail address, and then from the shortcut menu, click **Remove Hyperlink**. Compare your screen with Figure 2.19.

Figure 2.19

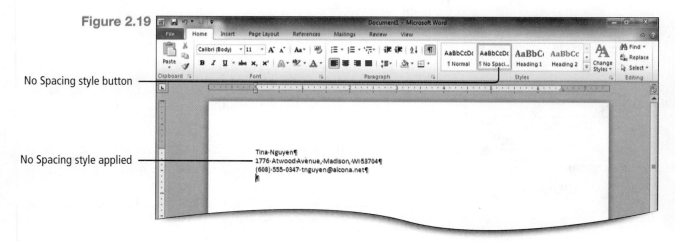

No Spacing style button

No Spacing style applied

Tina·Nguyen¶
1776·Atwood·Avenue,·Madison,·WI·53704¶
(608)·555-0347·tnguyen@alcona.net¶

6 Select the first paragraph—*Tina Nguyen*—and then on the Mini toolbar, apply **Bold** **B** and change the **Font Size** to **16**.

7 Select the second and third paragraphs. On the Mini toolbar, apply **Bold** $\boxed{B}$ and change the **Font Size** to **12**.

8 With the two paragraphs still selected, on the **Home tab**, in the **Paragraph group**, click the **Align Text Right** button $\boxed{\equiv}$.

9 Click anywhere in the first paragraph—*Tina Nguyen*. In the **Paragraph group**, click the **Borders button arrow** $\boxed{\boxplus \cdot}$, and then at the bottom, click **Borders and Shading**.

10 In the **Borders and Shading** dialog box, under **Style**, be sure the first style—a single solid line—is selected.

11 Click the **Width arrow**, and then click **3 pt**. To the right, under **Preview**, click the bottom border of the diagram. Under **Apply to**, be sure *Paragraph* displays. Compare your screen with Figure 2.20.

Figure 2.20

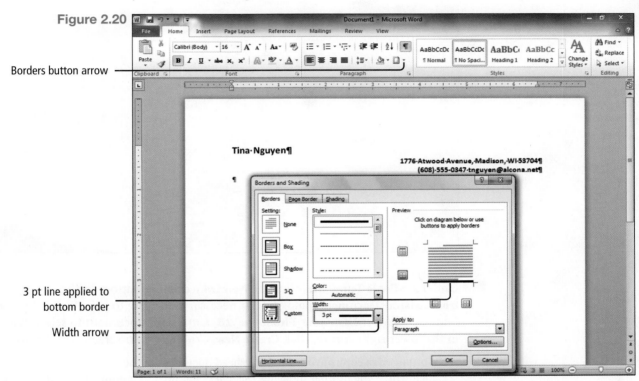

Borders button arrow

3 pt line applied to bottom border

Width arrow

12 Click **OK** to display a 3 pt line below *Tina Nguyen*, which extends from the left margin to the right margin.

13 Display **Save As** dialog box, **Save** the document in your **Word Chapter 2** folder as **Lastname_Firstname_2B_Letterhead** and then add the file name to the footer.

14 Display **Backstage** view, click the **Info tab**, and then on the right, under the document thumbnail, click **Properties**. Click **Show Document Panel**. In the **Author** box, delete any text and then type your firstname and lastname. In the **Subject** box, type your course name and section number, and in the **Keywords** box type **personal letterhead**

15 **Close** $\boxed{\times}$ the **Document Panel**.

16 **Save** $\boxed{\blacksquare}$ your document. Display **Backstage** view, and then click **Close** to close the document but leave Word open. Hold this file until you complete this project.

Activity 2.11 | Creating a Document from an Existing Document

To use an existing document as the starting point for a new document, Word provides the *New from existing* command.

1 Click the **File tab** to display **Backstage** view, and then click **New** to display the new document options. Compare your screen with Figure 2.21.

> Here you can create a new document in a variety of ways, including from an existing document.

Figure 2.21

New from Existing template

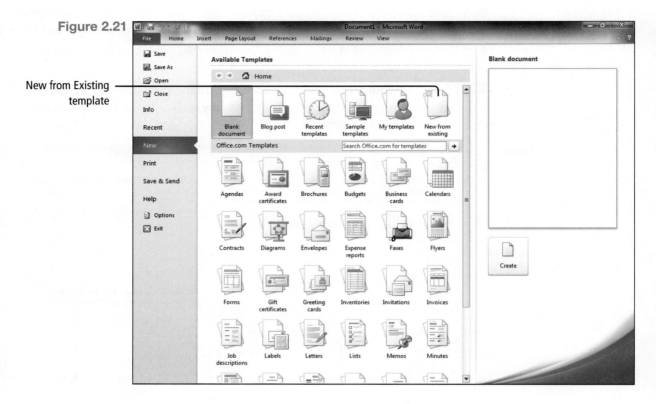

2 Under **Available Templates**, click the **New from existing** button. In the displayed **New from Existing Document** dialog box, if necessary, navigate to your **Word Chapter 2** folder, click your **Lastname_Firstname_2B_Letterhead** document to select it, and then in the lower right corner, click **Create New**. Compare your screen with Figure 2.22.

> Word opens a copy of your 2B_Letterhead document in the form of a new Word document—the title bar indicates *Document* followed by a number. You are not opening the original document, and changes that you make to this new document will not affect the contents of your 2B_Letterhead document.

Figure 2.22

Document opens unnamed

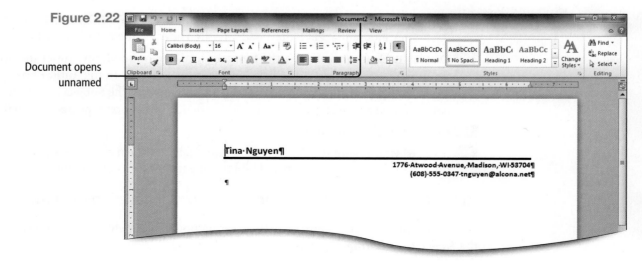

3 Display the **Save As** dialog box, and then navigate to your **Word Chapter 2** folder. **Save** the file as **Lastname_Firstname_2B_Cover_Letter**

> The personal information that you typed in the 2B_Letterhead Document Panel remains in the new document.

4 Scroll down to view the footer area, and notice that a footer displays.

> The footer displays because it was included in the document that you saved as a template. The *FileName* field does not automatically update to the new file name.

5 Point to the footer and right-click, and then click **Edit Footer**. Point to the highlighted footer text, right-click, and then from the shortcut menu, click **Update Field**. At the far right end of the Ribbon, click the **Close Header and Footer** button.

6 **Save** 🖫 your document.

More Knowledge | **Creating a Template File**

You can also identify an original document so that your Windows operating system always knows that you want to create a new unnamed copy. To do so, save your document as a template file instead of a document. Word will then attach the dotx extension to the file, instead of the docx extension that is applied for a document, and will store the template file in a special location with other templates. Then, you can open the template from the New Document dialog box by clicking *My templates*.

Objective 5 | Change and Reorganize Text

Business letters follow a standard format and contain the following parts: the current date, referred to as the *date line*; the name and address of the person receiving the letter, referred to as the *inside address*; a greeting, referred to as the *salutation*; the text of the letter, usually referred to as the *body* of the letter; a closing line, referred to as the *complimentary closing*; and the *writer's identification*, which includes the name or job title (or both) of the writer, and which is also referred to as the *writer's signature block*.

Some letters also include the initials of the person who prepared the letter, an optional *subject line* that describes the purpose of the letter, or a list of *enclosures*—documents included with the letter.

Activity 2.12 | Recording AutoCorrect Entries

You can correct commonly misspelled words automatically by using Word's *AutoCorrect* feature. Commonly misspelled words—such as *teh* instead of *the*—are corrected using a built-in list that is installed with Office. If you have words that you frequently misspell, you can add them to the list for automatic correction.

1 Click the **File tab** to display **Backstage** view. On the **Help tab**, click **Options** to display the **Word Options** dialog box.

2 On the left side of the **Word Options** dialog box, click **Proofing**, and then under **AutoCorrect options**, click the **AutoCorrect Options** button.

3 In the **AutoCorrect** dialog box, click the **AutoCorrect tab**. Under **Replace**, type **resumee** and under **With**, type **resume**

If another student has already added this AutoCorrect entry, a Replace button will display.

4 Click **Add**. If the entry already exists, click Replace instead, and then click Yes.

5 In the **AutoCorrect** dialog box, under **Replace**, type **computr** and under **With**, type **computer** and then compare your screen with Figure 2.23.

Figure 2.23

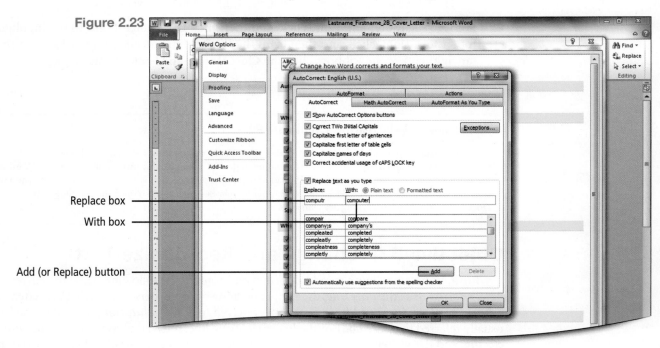

Replace box

With box

Add (or Replace) button

6 Click **Add** (or Replace) and then click **OK** two times to close the dialog boxes.

Activity 2.13 | Creating a Cover Letter

There are a variety of accepted letter formats that you will see in reference manuals and Business Communication texts. The one used in this chapter is a block style cover letter taken from *Business Communication Today*.

1 Press [Ctrl] + [End] to move the insertion point to the blank line below the letterhead. Press [Enter] three times, and then type **March 16, 2016** to create the dateline.

Most Business Communication texts recommend that the dateline be positioned at least 0.5 inch (3 blank lines) below the letterhead; or, position the dateline approximately 2 inches from the top edge of the paper.

2 Press [Enter] four times, which leaves three blank lines. Type the following inside address on four lines, but do not press [Enter] following the last line:

James Washington

Madison Staffing Services

600 East Washington Avenue

Madison, WI 53701

The recommended space between the dateline and inside address varies slightly among Business Communication texts and office reference manuals. However, all indicate that the space can be from one to 10 blank lines depending on the length of your letter.

3 Press [Enter] two times to leave one blank line. Compare your screen with Figure 2.24.

Figure 2.24

Three blank lines between letterhead and dateline

Dateline

Three blank lines between dateline and inside address

Inside address

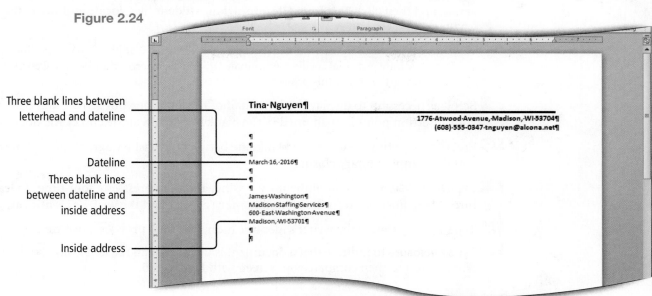

4 Type the salutation **Dear Mr. Washington:** and then press [Enter] two times.

Always leave one blank line above and below the salutation.

5 Type, exactly as shown, the following opening paragraph that includes an intentional word usage error: **I am seeking a position in witch I can use my** and press [Spacebar]. Type, exactly as shown, **computr** and then watch *computr* as you press [Spacebar].

The AutoCorrect feature recognizes the misspelled word, and then changes *computr* to *computer* when you press [Spacebar], [Enter], or a punctuation mark.

6 Type the following, including the misspelled last word: **and communication skills. My education, outlined on the enclosed resumee** and then type **,** (a comma). Notice that when you type the comma, AutoCorrect replaces *resumee* with *resume*.

7 Press [Spacebar]. Complete the paragraph by typing **includes a Business Software Applications Specialist certificate from MATC.** Compare your screen with Figure 2.25.

Figure 2.25

Paragraphs are single spaced

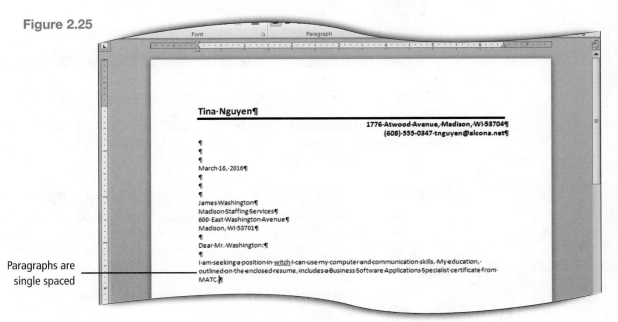

8 Press [Enter] two times. On the **Insert tab**, in the **Text group**, click the **Object button arrow**, and then click **Text from File**. From your student files, locate and **Insert** the file **w02B_Cover_Letter_Text**.

Some of the words in the cover letter text display red, green, or blue wavy underlines. These indicate potential spelling, grammar, or word usage errors, and you will correct them before the end of this project.

9 Scroll as necessary to display the lower half of the letter on your screen, and be sure your insertion point is positioned in the blank paragraph at the end of the document.

10 Press [Enter] one time to leave one blank line between the last paragraph of the letter and the complimentary closing.

11 Type **Sincerely,** as the complimentary closing, and then press [Enter] four times to leave three blank lines between the complimentary closing and the writer's identification.

12 Type **Tina Nguyen** as the writer's identification, and then press [Enter] two times.

13 Type **Enclosure** to indicate that a document is included with the letter. **Save** 🖫 your document, and then compare your screen with Figure 2.26.

Figure 2.26

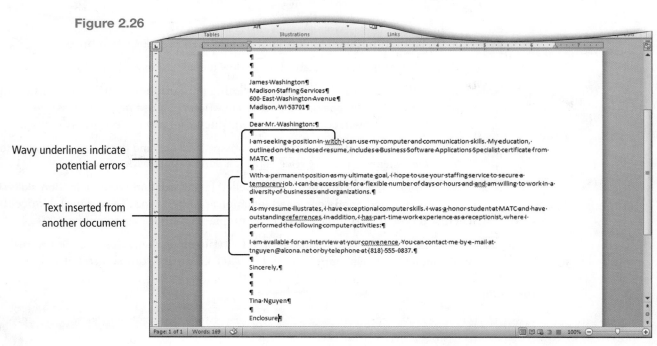

Wavy underlines indicate potential errors

Text inserted from another document

Activity 2.14 | Finding and Replacing Text

Use the Find command to locate text in a document quickly. Use the Find and Replace command to make the same change, or to make more than one change at a time, in a document.

1 Press [Ctrl] + [Home] to position the insertion point at the beginning of the document.

Because a find operation—or a find and replace operation—begins from the location of the insertion point and proceeds to the end of the document, it is good practice to position the insertion point at the beginning of the document before initiating the command.

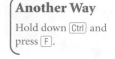
Another Way
Hold down [Ctrl] and press [F].

2 On the **Home tab**, in the **Editing group**, click the **Find** button.

The Navigation Pane displays on the left side of the screen, with a search box at the top of the pane.

3 In the search box, type **ac** If necessary, scroll down slightly in your document to view the entire body text of the letter, and then compare your screen with Figure 2.27.

> In the document, the search letters *ac* are selected and highlighted in yellow for all three words that contain the letters *ac* together. In the Navigation Pane, the three instances are shown in context—*ac* displays in bold.

Figure 2.27

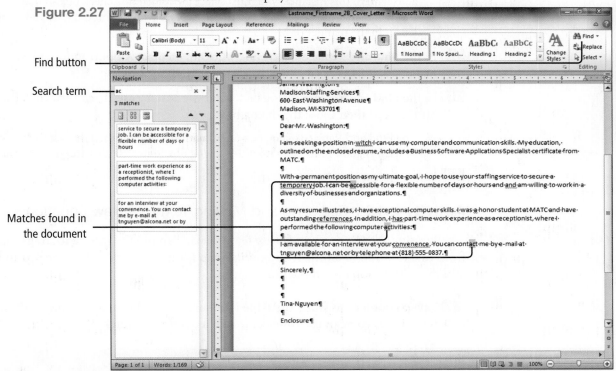

Find button

Search term

Matches found in the document

4 In the search box, complete the word **accessible**.

> One match for the search term displays in context in the Navigation Pane and is highlighted in the document.

5 In the document, point to the yellow highlighted word *accessible*, double-click, and then type **available** to replace the word. Notice that the list of results is now empty.

6 **Close** ☒ the **Navigation Pane**, and then on the **Home tab**, in the **Editing group**, click the **Replace** button.

7 In the **Find and Replace** dialog box, in the **Find what** box, replace the existing text by typing **MATC** In the **Replace with** box, type **Madison Area Technical College** and then compare your screen with Figure 2.28

Figure 2.28

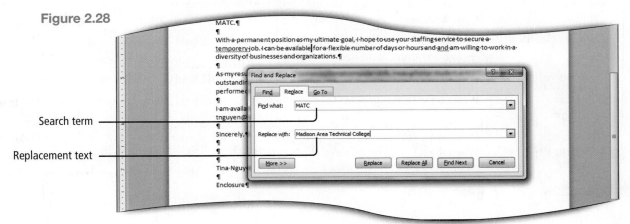

Search term

Replacement text

8 In the lower left corner of the dialog box, click the **More** button to expand the dialog box, and then under **Search Options**, select the **Match case** check box.

> The acronym *MATC* appears in the document two times. In a formal letter, the reader may not know what the acronym means, so you should include the full text instead of an acronym. In this instance, you must select the *Match case* check box so that the replaced text will match the case you typed in the Replace with box, and *not* display in all uppercase letters in the manner of *MATC*.

9 In the **Find and Replace** dialog box, click the **Replace All** button to replace both instances of *MATC*. Click **OK** to close the message box.

10 In the **Find and Replace** dialog box, clear the **Match case** check box, click the **Less** button, and then **Close** the dialog box.

> The Find and Replace dialog box opens with the settings used the last time it was open. Thus, it is good practice to reset this dialog box to its default settings each time you use it.

11 **Save** 🖫 your document.

Activity 2.15 | Selecting and Moving Text to a New Location

By using Word's ***drag-and-drop*** feature, you can use the mouse to drag selected text from one location to another. Drag-and-drop is most effective when the text to be moved and the destination are on the same screen.

1 Take a moment to study the table in Figure 2.29 to become familiar with the techniques you can use to select text in a document quickly.

Selecting Text in a Document

To Select	Do This
A portion of text	Click to position the insertion point at the beginning of the text you want to select, hold down Shift, and then click at the end of the text you want to select. Alternatively, hold down the left mouse button and drag from the beginning to the end of the text you want to select.
A word	Double-click the word.
A sentence	Hold down Ctrl and click anywhere in the sentence.
A paragraph	Triple-click anywhere in the paragraph; or, move the pointer to the left of the line, into the margin area. When the 🔏 pointer displays, double-click.
A line	Move the pointer to the left of the line. When the 🔏 pointer displays, click one time.
One character at a time	Position the insertion point to the left of the first character, hold down Shift, and press ← or → as many times as desired.
A string of words	Position the insertion point to the left of the first word, hold down Shift and Ctrl, and then press ← or → as many times as desired.
Consecutive lines	Position the insertion point to the left of the first word, hold down Shift and press ↑ or ↓.
Consecutive paragraphs	Position the insertion point to the left of the first word, hold down Shift and Ctrl and press ↑ or ↓.
The entire document	Hold down Ctrl and press A. Alternatively, move the pointer to the left of any line in the document. When the 🔏 pointer displays, triple-click.

Figure 2.29

2 Be sure you can view the entire body of the letter on your screen. In the paragraph that begins *With a permanent position*, in the second line, locate and double-click *days*.

3 Point to the selected word to display the ⬚ pointer.

4 Drag to the right until the dotted vertical line that floats next to the pointer is positioned to the right of the word *hours* in the same line, as shown in Figure 2.30.

Figure 2.30

Word will be dragged to new location

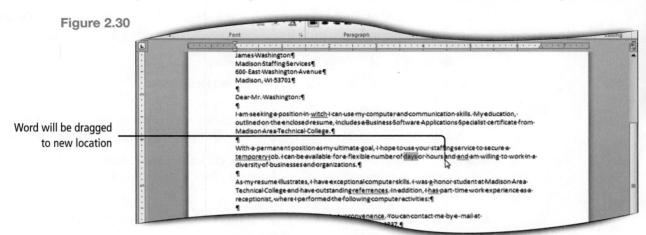

5 Release the mouse button to move the text. Select the word *hours* and drag it to the left of the word *or*—the previous location of the word *days*. Click anywhere in the document to deselect the text.

6 Examine the text that you moved, and add or remove spaces as necessary.

7 Hold down `Ctrl`, and then in the paragraph that begins *I am available*, click anywhere in the first sentence to select the entire sentence.

8 Drag the selected sentence to the end of the paragraph by positioning the small vertical line that floats with the pointer to the left of the paragraph mark. Compare your screen with Figure 2.31.

Figure 2.31

Sentence moved to end of paragraph

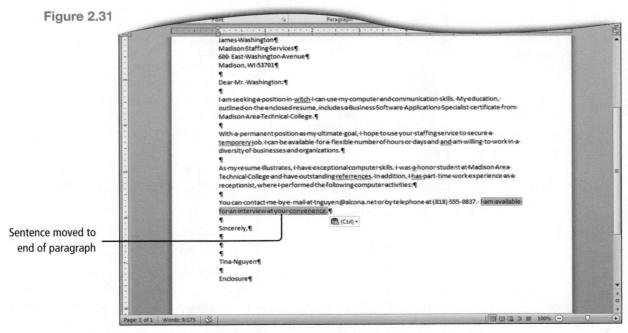

9 **Save** 🖫 your document.

Activity 2.16 | Inserting and Formatting a Table in a Document

1 Locate the paragraph that begins *As my resume*, and then click to position the insertion point in the blank line below that paragraph. Press Enter one time.

2 On the **Insert tab**, in the **Tables group**, click the **Table** button. In the **Table** grid, in the third row, click the second square to insert a 2 × 3 table.

3 In the first cell of the table, type **Microsoft Access** and then press Tab. Type **Queried inventory data** and then press Tab. Complete the table using the following information:

| Microsoft Excel | Entered budget data |
| Microsoft Word | Created and mailed form letters |

4 Point slightly outside of the upper left corner of the table to display the **table move handle** button ⊞. With the ⟲ pointer, click one time to select the entire table.

5 On the **Layout tab**, in the **Cell Size group**, click the **AutoFit** button, and then click **AutoFit Contents** to have Word choose the best column widths for the two columns based on the text you entered.

6 On the **Home tab**, in the **Paragraph group**, click the **Center** button ≡ to center the table between the left and right margins.

7 On the **Design tab**, in the **Table Styles group**, click the **Borders button arrow**, and then click **No Border**. Click anywhere to cancel the selection of the table, and then compare your screen with Figure 2.32.

A light dashed line may display in place of the original table borders if your default settings have been changed.

Figure 2.32

Table inserted in letter ⟶

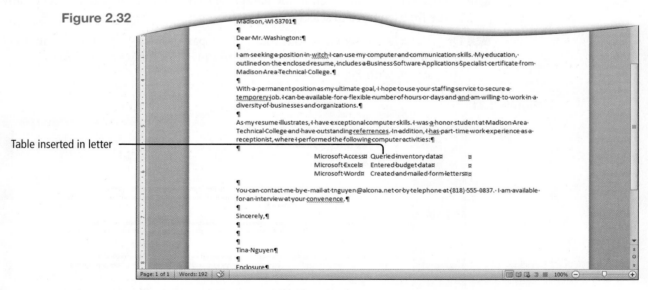

8 **Save** 🖫 your document.

Objective 6 | Use the Proofing Options

Word compares your typing to words in the Office dictionary and compares your phrases and punctuation to a list of grammar rules. This automatic proofing is set by default. Words that are not in the dictionary are marked with a wavy red underline. Phrases and punctuation that differ from the grammar rules are marked with a wavy green underline.

Word also compares commonly misused words with a set of word usage rules, and marks misused words with a wavy blue underline; for example the misuse of *their*, *there*, and *they're*. However, Word will not flag the word *sign* as misspelled even though you intended to type *sing a song* rather than *sign a song*, because both are words contained within Word's dictionary. Your own knowledge and proofreading skills are still required, even when using a sophisticated Word processing program like Word.

Activity 2.17 | Checking Spelling and Grammar Errors

There are two ways to respond to spelling and grammar errors flagged by Word. You can right-click a flagged word or phrase, and then from the shortcut menu choose a correction or action. Or, you can initiate the Spelling and Grammar command to display the Spelling and Grammar dialog box, which provides more options than the shortcut menus.

Alert! | Spelling and Grammar Checking

If you do not see any wavy red, green, or blue lines under words, the automatic spelling and/or grammar checking has been turned off on your system. To activate the spelling and grammar checking, display Backstage view, on the Help tab, click Options, click Proofing, and then under *When correcting spelling in Microsoft Office programs*, select the first four check boxes. Under *When correcting spelling and grammar in Word*, select the first four check boxes, and then click the Writing Style arrow and click Grammar Only. Under *Exceptions for*, clear both check boxes. To display the flagged spelling and grammar errors, click the Recheck Document button, and then close the dialog box.

---

1 Position the body of the letter on your screen, and then examine the text to locate green, red, and blue wavy underlines. Compare your screen with Figure 2.33.

A list of grammar rules applied by a computer program like Word can never be exact, and a computer dictionary cannot contain all known words and proper names. Thus, you will need to check any words flagged by Word with wavy underlines, and you will also need to proofread for content errors.

Figure 2.33

Blue wavy underline indicates potential word usage problem

Red wavy underline indicates potential spelling problem

Green wavy underline indicates potential grammar problem

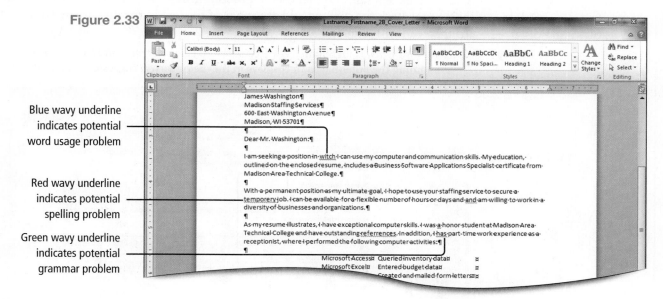

2 In the lower left corner of your screen, in the status bar, locate and point to the ⬚ icon to display the ScreenTip *Proofing errors were found. Click to correct.*

If this button displays, you know there are potential errors identified in the document.

3 In the paragraph that begins *With a permanent*, locate the word *temporery* with the wavy red underline. Point to the word and right-click to display the shortcut menu, and then compare your screen with Figure 2.34.

Figure 2.34

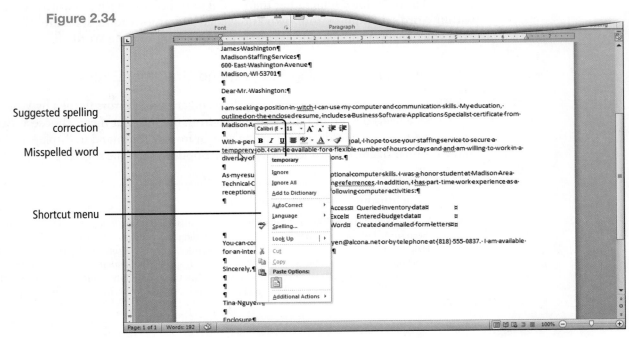

Suggested spelling correction

Misspelled word

Shortcut menu

4 On the shortcut menu, click **temporary** to correct the spelling error.

5 In the next line, locate the word *and* that displays with a wavy red underline, point to word and right-click, and then from the shortcut menu, click **Delete Repeated Word** to delete the duplicate word.

Another Way

Press [F7] to start the Spelling & Grammar command.

6 Press [Ctrl] + [Home] to move the insertion point to the beginning of the document. Click the **Review tab**, and then in the **Proofing group**, click the **Spelling & Grammar** button to check the spelling and grammar of the text in the document. Compare your screen with Figure 2.35.

The word *witch* is highlighted—a *Possible Word Choice Error*—and the sentence containing the potential error displays in the dialog box. A suggested change also displays.

Figure 2.35

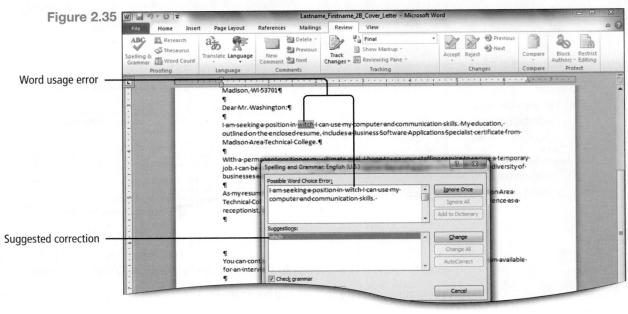

Word usage error

Suggested correction

7 In the **Spelling and Grammar** dialog box, click the **Change** button to change to the correct usage *which*.

The next marked word—a possible spelling error—displays.

8 Click the **Change** button to change *references* to *references*. Notice that the next error is a possible grammar error.

9 Click the **Change** button to change *a* to *an*. Continue the spelling and grammar check and change *has* to *have* and correct the spelling of *convenence*.

10 When Word indicates *The spelling and grammar check is complete*, click **OK**.

11 Save 🖫 your document.

Activity 2.18 | Using the Thesaurus

A ***thesaurus*** is a research tool that lists ***synonyms***—words that have the same or similar meaning to the word you selected.

1 Scroll so that you can view the body of the letter. In the paragraph that begins *With a permanent*, at the end of the second line, locate and right-click the word *diversity*.

2 On the shortcut menu, point to **Synonyms**, and then compare your screen with Figure 2.36.

A list of synonyms displays; the list will vary in length depending on the selected word.

Figure 2.36

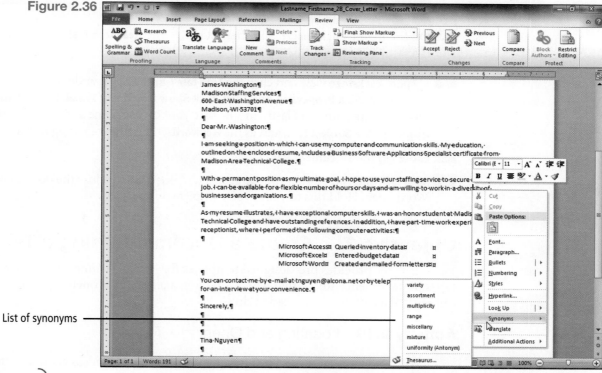

List of synonyms

Another Way

Click the word, and then on the Review tab, in the Proofing group, click the Thesaurus button.

3 From the list of synonyms, click **variety** to replace *diversity* with *variety*.

4 In the paragraph that begins *As my resume*, point to the word *exceptional*, right-click, point to **Synonyms**, and then at the bottom of the shortcut menu, click **Thesaurus** to display the **Research** task pane.

5 In the **Research** task pane, under **Thesaurus**, point to the non-bold word *excellent*, and then click the **arrow**. Compare your screen with Figure 2.37.

Figure 2.37

Synonym

Selected word

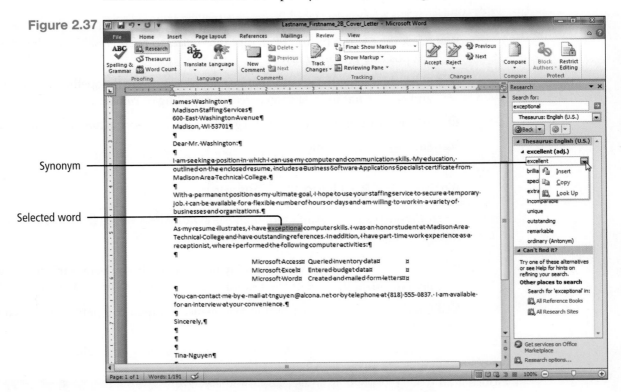

6 On the menu, click **Insert**, and then **Close** ☒ the **Research** task pane.

excellent replaces the word *exceptional*.

7 Display **Backstage** view and click the **Info tab**. On the right, under the document thumbnail, click **Properties**, and then click **Show Document Panel**. In the **Author** box, type your firstname and lastname. Be sure your course name and section number display in the **Subject** box, and as the **Keywords**, replace any existing text with **cover letter**

8 Close ☒ the **Document Panel**.

9 Save 🖫, and then display **Backstage** view. Click **Close** to close the document but leave Word open. Hold this file until you complete this project.

Objective 7 | Create a Document Using a Template

Microsoft provides pre-designed templates for letters, resumes, invoices, and other types of documents. Recall that when you open a template, it opens unnamed so that you can reuse it as often as you need to do so.

Activity 2.19 | Locating and Opening a Template

If you need to create a short resume quickly, or if you need ideas about how to format your resume, Microsoft Word provides pre-designed resume templates. Some templates are available on your computer; many more are available online. After opening a template, you can add text as indicated, modify the layout and design, and add or remove resume elements.

1 Close any open documents, and then from **Backstage** view, click **New**.

2 Under **Available Templates**, click **Sample templates**.

3 Under **Available Templates**, scroll toward the bottom of the window, and then click **Median Resume**. Notice that a preview of the *Median Resume* template displays on the right. Compare your screen with Figure 2.38.

Figure 2.38

Preview of template

Selected template

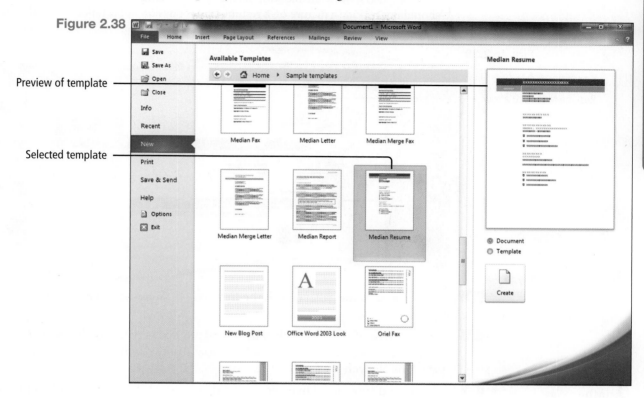

4 In the lower right corner, click the **Create** button.

The template opens a copy of itself in the form of a new Word document—the title bar indicates *Document* followed by a number. Recall that you are not opening the template itself, and that changes you make to this new document will not affect the contents of the template file.

5 Display the **Save As** dialog box. **Save** the document in your **Word Chapter 2** folder as **Lastname_Firstname_2B_Brief_Resume** and then add the file name to the footer— called the *First Page Footer* in this template.

6 **Save** your document.

Activity 2.20 | Replacing Template Placeholder Text

After you save the template file as a Word document, you can begin to substitute your own information in the indicated locations. You can also remove unneeded resume elements that are included with the template.

1 Click on the picture, and notice that a Picture Tool tab is added to the Ribbon.

2 Click the **Layout tab**, and then in the **Table group**, click the **View Gridlines** button to display non-printing table borders.

This template consists of two Word tables, and the name in the first row of the upper table displays either the user name or the text *[Type your name]* in square brackets.

3 At the top of the upper table, click the **Resume Name tab arrow**, and then compare your screen with Figure 2.39.

> There are two styles available with the Median template—with or without a photo. You should not include a picture on a resume unless physical appearance is directly related to the job for which you are applying—for example, for a job as an actor or a model.

Figure 2.39

Resume Name tab arrow ——

Two styles available ——

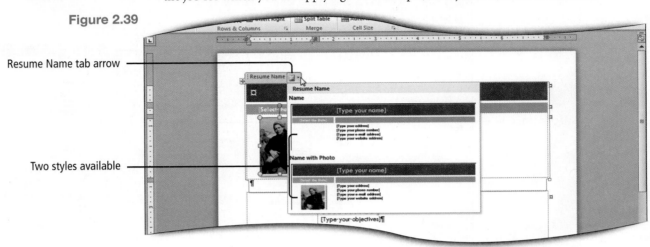

4 In the **Resume Name** gallery, click the first style—**Name**—to switch to the style with no picture.

5 In the first row of the table, select the displayed text—typically the name of your computer as indicated in your Windows operating system—and replace the text by typing **Tina Nguyen**

Another Way

Select the entire row, right-click, and then from the shortcut menu, click Delete Rows.

6 In the second row, click anywhere in the date control *[Select the Date]*. On the Ribbon, click the **Layout tab**. In the **Rows & Columns group**, click the **Delete** button, and then click **Delete Rows**.

> Text surrounded by brackets is called a ***content control***. There are several different types of content controls, including date, picture, and ***text controls***. Most of the controls in this template are text controls. Because resumes do not typically include a date, you can delete this row.

7 Click anywhere in the content control *[Type your address]*. Compare your screen with Figure 2.40.

> For the name and address at the top of the document, all of the text controls are grouped together. Each control has ***placeholder text***, text that indicates the type of information to be entered. The name in the first row may also be a content control with placeholder text.

Figure 2.40

Placeholder text replaced ——

Date removed ——

Picture removed ——

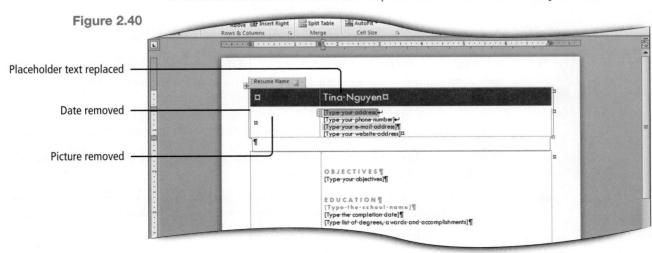

8 Complete the personal information by using the following information:

[Type your address]	**1776 Atwood Avenue, Madison, WI 53704**
[Type your phone number]	**(608) 555-0347**
[Type your e-mail address]	**tnguyen@alcona.net**
[Type your website address]	(leave this blank)

9 In the lower table, click in the *[Type your objectives]* control, and then type **To obtain a position using my computer and communications skills.**

10 Complete the **Education** section by using the following information:

[Type the school name]	**Madison Area Technical College**
[Type the completion date]	**June 2015**
[Type list of degrees, awards and accomplishments] *(type three separate lines)*	**Business Computing Specialist certificate** **Dean's List, four semesters** **President, Community Service Club**

11 Complete the **Experience** section by using the following information:

[Type the job title]	**Office Assistant (part-time)**
[Type the company name]	**The Robinson Company**
[Type the start date]	**September 2014**
[Type the end date]	**present**
[Type list of job responsibilities]	**Data entry and report generation using company spreadsheets and databases.**

12 Click in the *[Type list of skills]* control, type **Proficiency using Word, Excel, and Access (completed advanced courses in Microsoft Office programs)** and then press Enter.

13 As the second bulleted point, type **Excellent written and verbal communications (completed courses in Business Communications, PowerPoint, and Speech)** and then compare your screen with Figure 2.41. **Save** your document.

Figure 2.41

Placeholder text replaced ————

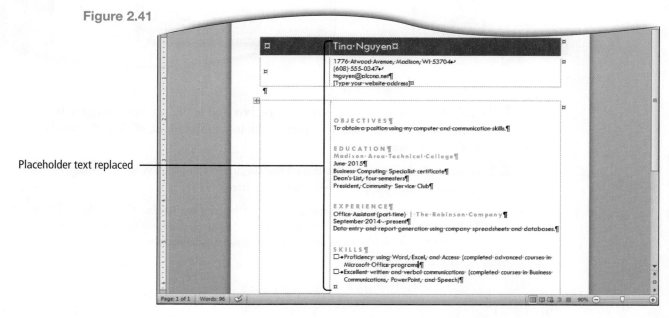

Activity 2.21 │ Removing Template Controls and Formatting the Resume

1 Near the top of the document, point to the text control that you did not use—*[Type your website address]*. Right-click the control, and then from the shortcut menu, click **Remove Content Control**. Press Backspace as necessary to position the insertion point at the end of the e-mail address. Select the three lines with the address, phone, and e-mail information. On the Mini toolbar, notice that the text size is *11.5*. Click the **Font Size button arrow**, and then click **12**.

2 Click anywhere in lower table—the table with the *Objectives* row at the top—and then point to the upper left corner of the active table to display the **move table handle**. Click one time to select the lower table.

3 On the Mini toolbar, change the **Font Size** to **12** to match the table above.

4 Click anywhere to cancel the selection. On the **Page Layout tab**, in the **Page Setup group**, click the **Margins** button, and then click **Custom Margins**. Change the **Top** margin to **1.5** and the **Left** and **Right** margins to **1** to make this short resume better fill the page. Compare your screen with Figure 2.42.

Figure 2.42

New margins

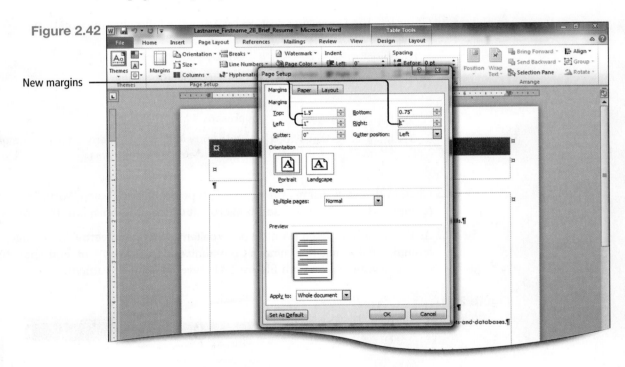

5 Click **OK** to close the **Page Setup** dialog box and apply the new margins. If the name at the top of the document changes back to a placeholder, click the control and type **Tina Nguyen**

6 Right-click the name at the top of the document—*Tina Nguyen*—and then from the shortcut menu, click **Remove Content Control**.

This action will leave the name but remove the control. Remove the control if the Document Properties will have an author other than the name in this control. If you do *not* remove the content control, when you add document properties, the name will change to the name you type in the Author box.

7 Press ⌈Ctrl⌉ + ⌈F2⌉ to display the Print Preview in **Backstage** view. Click the **Info tab**. On the right, under the document thumbnail, click **Properties**, and then click **Show Document Panel**. In the **Author** box, delete any text and then type your firstname and lastname. In the **Subject** box, type your course name and section number, and in the **Keywords** box, type **short resume, template**

8 **Close** ☒ the **Document Panel**. **Save** 🖫 your document, and then hold this file until you complete this project. Leave the resume displayed on your screen.

Activity 2.22 | Saving a Resume as a Web Page

You can save your resume as a Web page. This enables you to post the Web page on your own Web site or on Web space provided by your college. It also enables you to send the resume as an e-mail attachment that can be opened using any Web browser.

1 With your **2B_Brief_Resume** still open on your screen, click **Save** 🖫 to be sure the current version of the document is saved.

2 Display the **Save As** dialog box. In the lower portion of the **Save As** dialog box, click the **Save as type arrow**, and then click **Single File Web Page**.

A *Single File Web Page* is a document saved using the *Hypertext Markup Language (HTML)*. HTML is the language used to format documents that can be opened using a Web browser such as Internet Explorer.

3 In the **Save As** dialog box, in the **File name** box, type **Lastname_Firstname_2B_HTML_ Resume** Click **Save**, and then click **Yes** if a message box displays. Notice that the Web page displays in Word.

4 Display **Backstage** view. On the right, click **Properties**, and then click **Advanced Properties**. In the **Properties** dialog box, on the **Summary tab**, in the **Subject** box, be sure your course name and section number display. In the **Author** box, be sure your first and last names display. In the **Keywords** box, replace the existing text with **HTML** Click **OK**, and then click the **Home tab**. **Save** 🖫 the document; print or submit electronically as directed.

5 **Exit** Word. From the **Start** menu ⊕, click **Computer**. Navigate to your **Word Chapter 2** folder, and then double-click your **Lastname_Firstname_2B_HTML_Resume** file to open the resume in your Web browser. Compare your screen with Figure 2.43.

Figure 2.43

Resume displayed in a Web browser

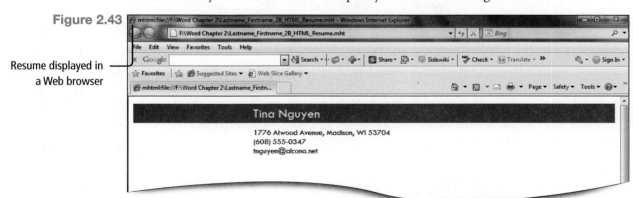

6 **Close** ☒ your Web browser. As directed by your instructor, print or submit electronically the four files from this project—2B_Letterhead, 2B_Cover_Letter, 2B_Brief_Resume, and 2B_HTML_Resume.

End **You have completed Project 2B** ————————————————————

Content-Based Assessments

Summary

In this chapter, you created a table, and then used the table to create a resume. You created a letterhead template, and then created a document using a copy of the letterhead template. You created a cover letter for the resume, moved text, corrected spelling and grammar, and used the built-in thesaurus. Finally, you created a short resume using a template, and also saved the resume as a Web page.

Key Terms

Matching

Match each term in the second column with its correct definition in the first column by writing the letter of the term on the blank line in front of the correct definition.

_____ 1. An arrangement of information organized into rows and columns.

_____ 2. The box at the intersection of a row and column in a table.

_____ 3. A document structure that opens a copy of itself, opens unnamed, and is used as the starting point for another document.

_____ 4. The template that serves as a basis for all new Word documents.

_____ 5. The personal or company information that displays at the top of a letter.

_____ 6. The Word style that inserts no extra space following a paragraph and uses single spacing.

_____ 7. The first line in a business letter that contains the current date and that is positioned just below the letterhead if a letterhead is used.

_____ 8. The name and address of the person receiving a letter and positioned below the date line.

_____ 9. The greeting line of a letter.

_____ 10. A parting farewell in a letter.

_____ 11. The name and title of the author of a letter, placed near the bottom of the letter under the complimentary closing.

_____ 12. The optional line following the inside address in a business letter that states the purpose of the letter.

A AutoCorrect

B Cell

C Complimentary closing

D Date line

E Drag and drop

F Enclosures

G Inside address

H Letterhead

I No Spacing

J Normal template

K Salutation

L Subject line

M Table

N Template

O Writer's identification

_____ 13. Additional documents included with a business letter.

_____ 14. A Word feature that corrects common spelling errors as you type, for example changing _teh_ to _the_.

_____ 15. A technique by which you can move, by dragging, selected text from one location in a document to another.

Multiple Choice

Circle the correct answer.

1. When you create a table, the width of all of cells in the table is:
   A. equal   B. proportional   C. 1 inch

2. To indicate words that might be misspelled because they are not in Word's dictionary, Word flags text with:
   A. blue wavy underlines   B. green wavy underlines   C. red wavy underlines

3. To indicate possible grammar errors, Word flags text with:
   A. blue wavy underlines   B. green wavy underlines   C. red wavy underlines

4. To indicate possible errors in word usage, Word flags text with:
   A. blue wavy underlines   B. green wavy underlines   C. red wavy underlines

5. A research tool that provides a list of words with similar meanings is:
   A. a thesaurus   B. a dictionary   C. an encyclopedia

6. A word with the same or similar meaning as another word is:
   A. an acronym   B. a search term   C. a synonym

7. In a template, an area indicated by placeholder text into which you can add text, pictures, dates, or lists is a:
   A. text control   B. content control   C. quick control

8. A document saved in HTML, which can be opened using a Web browser, is a:
   A. Web page   B. template   C. resume

9. Using drag-and-drop to move text is most useful when both the text and the destination are on the same:
   A. document   B. section   C. screen

10. To locate specific text in a document quickly, use the:
    A. Find command   B. Replace command   C. Locate command

Content-Based Assessments

Apply **2A** skills from these Objectives:

1 Create a Table
2 Add Text to a Table
3 Format a Table

Skills Review | Project **2C** Student Resume

In the following Skills Review, you will use a table to create a resume for Joshua Green. Your completed resume will look similar to Figure 2.44.

Project Files

For Project 2C, you will need the following files:

New blank Word document
w02C_Skills
w02C_Experience

You will save your document as:

Lastname_Firstname_2C_Student_Resume

Project Results

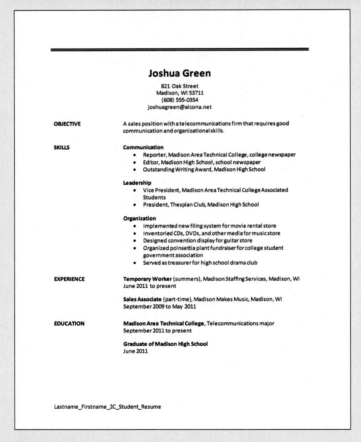

Figure 2.44

(Project 2C Student Resume continues on the next page)

Skills Review | Project **2C** Student Resume (continued)

1 **Start** Word. In the new blank document, be sure that formatting marks and rulers display. **Save** the document in your **Word Chapter 2** folder as **Lastname_Firstname_2C_Student_Resume**

a. Add the file name to the footer, and then close the footer area. Click the **Insert tab**, and then in the **Tables group**, click the **Table** button. In the **Table** grid, in the fourth row, click the second square to insert a **2 × 4** table.

b. In the first cell of the table, type **Joshua Green** and then press Enter. Type the following text, pressing Enter after each line *except* the last line:

821 Oak Street

Madison, WI 53711

(608) 555-0354

joshuagreen@alcona.net

c. Press ↓ to move to the first cell in the second row. Type **SKILLS** and then press ↓ to move to the first cell in the third row.

d. Type **EXPERIENCE** and then press ↓. Type **EDUCATION**

e. In the first cell, if the e-mail address displays in blue, right-click the e-mail address, and then from the shortcut menu, click **Remove Hyperlink**. **Save** your document

2 Click in the cell to the right of *SKILLS*, and then type the following, pressing Enter after each item:

Communication
Reporter, Madison Area Technical College, college newspaper
Editor, Madison High School, school newspaper
Outstanding Writing Award, Madison High School

a. With the insertion point in the new line at the end of the cell, click the **Insert tab**. In the **Text group**, click the **Object button arrow**, and then click **Text from File**.

b. Navigate to your student files, select **w02C_Skills**, and then click **Insert**. Press Backspace one time to remove the blank line.

c. Click in the cell to the right of *EXPERIENCE*, and then insert the file **w02C_Experience**. Press Backspace one time to remove the blank line.

d. Click in the cell to the right of *EDUCATION*, and then type the following, pressing Enter after all *except* the last item:

Madison Area Technical College, Telecommunications major

September 2011 to present

Graduate of Madison High School

June 2011

3 Click anywhere in the top row of the table. Click the **Layout tab**, and then in the **Rows & Columns group**, click the **Insert Below** button. Type **OBJECTIVE** and then press Tab.

a. Type **A sales position with a telecommunications firm that requires good communication and organizational skills.**

b. In any row, point to the vertical border between the two columns to display the ⊣⊢ pointer. Drag the column border to the left to approximately **1.75 inches on the horizontal ruler**.

c. Click anywhere in the left column. Click the **Layout tab**. In the **Cell Size group**, in the **Table Column Width** box, if necessary, type **1.75** and press Enter.

d. In the first row of the document, drag across both cells to select them. On the **Layout tab**, in the **Merge group**, click the **Merge Cells** button. Right-click the selected cell, and then from the Mini toolbar, click the **Center** button.

e. In the top row, select the first paragraph of text— *Joshua Green*. From the Mini toolbar, increase the **Font Size** to **20** and apply **Bold**.

f. In the second row, point to the word *OBJECTIVE*, hold down the left mouse button, and then drag down to select the row headings in uppercase letters. On the Mini toolbar, click the **Bold** button. **Save** your document.

4 Click in the cell to the right of *OBJECTIVE*. On the **Page Layout tab**, in the **Paragraph group**, click the **Spacing After up spin arrow** three times to change the spacing to **18 pt**.

a. In the cell to the right of *SKILLS*, apply **Bold** to the words *Communication*, *Leadership*, and *Organization*. Then, under each bold heading in the cell, select the lines of text, and create a bulleted list.

b. In the first two bulleted lists, click in the last bullet item, and then on the **Page Layout tab**, in the **Paragraph group**, set the **Spacing After** to **12 pt**.

(Project 2C Student Resume continues on the next page)

c. In the last bulleted list, click in the last bullet item, and then set the **Spacing After** to **18 pt**.

d. In the cell to the right of *EXPERIENCE*, apply **Bold** to *Temporary Worker* and *Sales Associate*. Click in the line *June 2011 to present* and apply **Spacing After** of **12 pt**. Click in the line *September 2009 to May 2011* and apply **Spacing After** of **18 pt**.

e. In the cell to the right of *EDUCATION*, apply **Bold** to *Madison Area Technical College* and *Graduate of Madison High School*.

f. In the same cell, click in the line *September 2011 to present* and apply **Spacing After** of **12 pt**.

g. In the first row, click in the last line—*joshuagreen@alcona.net*—and then change the **Spacing After** to **18 pt**. Click in the first line—*Joshua Green*—and set the **Spacing Before** to **30 pt** and the **Spacing After** to **6 pt**.

5 Point to the upper left corner of the table, and then click the displayed **table move handle** button ⊞ to select the entire table. On the **Design tab**, in the **Table Styles group**, click the **Borders button arrow**, and then click **No Border**.

a. On the **Design tab**, in the **Table Styles group**, click the **Borders button arrow** again, and then at the bottom of the gallery, click **Borders and Shading**. In the **Borders and Shading** dialog box, under **Setting**, click **Custom**. Under **Style**, scroll down slightly, and then click the style with two equal lines.

b. Click the **Width arrow**, and then click **1 1/2 pt**. Under **Preview**, click the top border of the preview box, and then click **OK**.

c. Click the **File tab** to display **Backstage** view, and then click the **Print tab** to display the Print Preview.

d. Click the **Info tab**. On the right side, under the document thumbnail, click **Properties**, and then click **Show Document Panel**.

e. In the **Author** box, delete any text and then type your firstname and lastname. In the **Subject** box, type your course name and section number, and in the **Keywords** box type **resume, table**

f. **Close** the **Document Panel**. **Save** 🖫 and then, as directed by your instructor, print your document or submit it electronically. **Exit** Word.

End **You have completed Project 2C** ————————————————————

Content-Based Assessments

Apply 2B skills from these Objectives:

- **4** Create a New Document from an Existing Document
- **5** Change and Reorganize Text
- **6** Use the Proofing Options
- **7** Create a Document Using a Template

Skills Review | Project **2D** Ross Letter

In the following Skills Review, you will create a letterhead, and then create a new document from the letterhead to create a resume cover letter. You will also create a short resume using a Microsoft template and save it as a Web page. Your completed documents will look similar to Figure 2.45.

Project Files

For Project 2D, you will need the following files:

> New blank Word document
> w02D_Letter_Text
> Equity Resume Template from Word's installed templates

You will save your documents as:

> Lastname_Firstname_2D_Ross_Letterhead
> Lastname_Firstname_2D_Ross_Letter
> Lastname_Firstname_2D_Resume
> Lastname_Firstname_2D_Web_Resume

Project Results

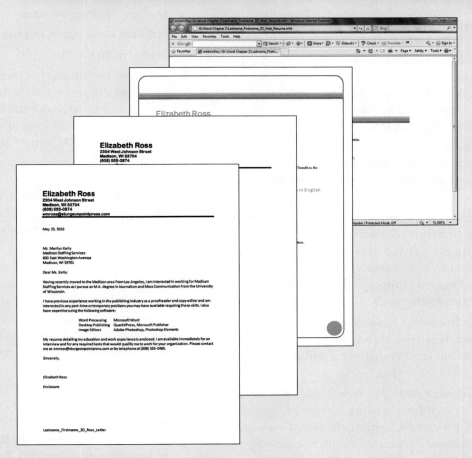

Figure 2.45

(Project 2D Ross Letter continues on the next page)

1 **Start** Word. In the new blank document, be sure that formatting marks and rulers display. On the **Home tab**, in the **Styles group**, click the **No Spacing** button.

a. Type **Elizabeth Ross** and then press Enter. Type **2304 West Johnson Street** and press Enter. Type **Madison, WI 53704** and then press Enter.

b. Type **(608) 555-0874** and then press Enter. Type **emross@sturgeonpointpress.com** and then press Enter three times. If the e-mail address changes to blue text, right-click the e-mail address, and then click Remove Hyperlink.

c. Select all five lines of the personal information, but do not select the blank paragraphs. From the Mini toolbar, change the **Font** to **Arial Rounded MT Bold**. Select the first paragraph—*Elizabeth Ross*—and then on the Mini toolbar, apply **Bold** and change the **Font Size** to **20**.

d. Click anywhere in the fifth line of text—the e-mail address. On the **Home tab**, in the **Paragraph group**, click the **Borders button arrow**, and then click **Borders and Shading**. Under **Style**, click the first style—a single solid line. Click the **Width arrow**, and then click **3 pt**. In the **Preview** area, click the bottom border, and then click **OK**.

e. Display **Backstage** view, and then click **Save As**. Save the document in your **Word Chapter 2** folder as **Lastname_Firstname_2D_Ross_Letterhead**

f. Add the file name to the footer, and then close the footer area. Display **Backstage** view, click **Properties**, and then click **Show Document Panel**. In the **Author** box, delete any text and then type your firstname and lastname. In the **Subject** box, type your course name and section number, and in the **Keywords** box, type **personal letterhead**

g. **Close** the **Document Panel**. **Save** your document. From **Backstage** view, click **Close** to close the document but leave Word open. Hold this file until you complete the project.

2 From **Backstage** view, click **New**. Under **Available Templates**, click **New from existing**. Navigate to your **Word Chapter 2** folder, click your **Lastname_Firstname_ 2D_Ross_Letterhead** document, and then in the lower right corner, click **Create New**. From **Backstage** view, click **Save As**. Navigate to your **Word Chapter 2** folder, and **Save** the file as **Lastname_Firstname_2D_Ross_Letter**

Double-click the footer, right-click the file name, and then click **Update Field**. Close the footer area.

a. From **Backstage** view, display the **Word Options** dialog box. In the **Word Options** list, click **Proofing**, and then under **AutoCorrect options**, click the **AutoCorrect Options** button.

b. In the **AutoCorrect** dialog box, click the **AutoCorrect tab**. Under **Replace**, type **expereince** and under **With**, type **experience** Click **Add**. If the entry already exists, click Replace instead, and then click Yes. Click **OK** two times to close the dialog boxes.

c. Press Ctrl + End, type **May 25, 2016** and then press Enter four times. Type the following inside address using four lines:

Ms. Marilyn Kelly

Madison Staffing Services

600 East Washington Avenue

Madison, WI 53701

d. Press Enter two times, type **Dear Ms. Kelly:** and then press Enter two times. On the **Insert tab**, in the **Text group**, click the **Object button arrow**, and then click **Text from File**. From your student files, locate and insert the file **w02D_Letter_Text**.

e. Scroll to view the lower portion of the page, and be sure your insertion point is in the empty paragraph mark at the end. Press Enter, type **Sincerely,** and then press Enter four times. Type **Elizabeth Ross** and press Enter two times. Type **Enclosure** and then **Save** your document.

f. Near the bottom of the document, locate the paragraph that begins *I am available* and click to position the insertion point at the beginning of the paragraph. Type **My resume detailing my education and work** Press Spacebar and then type the misspelled word **expereince** Press Spacebar and notice that AutoCorrect corrects the misspelling. Type **is enclosed.** and then press Spacebar.

g. Press Ctrl + Home. On the **Home tab**, in the **Editing group**, click the **Replace** button. In the **Find what** box, type **association** In the **Replace with** box, type **organization** and then click **Replace All**. Click **OK** to close the message box, and then **Close** the **Find and Replace** dialog box.

(Project 2D Ross Letter continues on the next page)

Skills Review | Project **2D** Ross Letter (continued)

h. In the paragraph that begins *I have previous*, double-click *experience*. Point to the selected word to display the ⬚ pointer, and then drag the word to the left of *working*. Adjust spacing as necessary.

i. Below the paragraph that begins *I have previous*, position the insertion point in the second blank line. On the **Insert tab**, in the **Tables group**, click the **Table** button. In the **Table** grid, in the third row, click the second square to insert a 2 × 3 table. Type the following information in the table:

Word Processing	Microsoft Word
Desktop Publishing	QuarkXPress, Microsoft Publisher
Image Editors	Adobe Photoshop, Photoshop Elements

j. Point outside of the upper left corner and click the **table move handle** button to select the entire table. On the **Layout tab**, in the **Cell Size group**, click the **AutoFit** button, and then click **AutoFit Contents**. On the **Home tab**, in the **Paragraph group**, click the **Center** button. On the **Design tab**, in the **Table Styles group**, click the **Borders button arrow**, and then click **No Border**. **Save** your document.

3 If you do not see any wavy red and green lines under words, refer to the Alert in Activity 2.17 to enable the default settings for automatic proofing.

a. In the paragraph that begins *Having lately*, in the second line, locate and right-click the phrase *an M.A. degrees*, and then from the shortcut menu, click *an M.A. degree*. In the same paragraph, locate and right-click *Journlism*. From the shortcut menu, click *Journalism*.

b. Press Ctrl + Home. On the **Review tab**, in the **Proofing group**, click the **Spelling & Grammar** button. In the **Spelling and Grammar** dialog box, click the **Change** button to change *are* to *am*. For the misspelled word *expertis*, under **Suggestions**, be sure *expertise* is selected, and then click **Change**.

c. Change *qualifie* to *qualify*, and then click **OK** to close the message box.

d. Near the top of the document, in the paragraph that begins *Having lately*, right-click *lately*. In the shortcut menu, point to **Synonyms**, and then click *recently*. In the same line, right-

click *region*, and replace it with the synonym *area*.

e. Display **Backstage** view, click **Properties**, and then click **Show Document Panel**. Type your firstname and lastname as the **Author** and your course number and section as the **Subject**. In the **Keywords** box, replace any existing text with **cover letter Close** the **Document Panel**. **Save** your document. From **Backstage** view, **Close** the document but leave Word open. Hold this file until you complete the project.

4 Display **Backstage** view, and then click **New**. Under **Available Templates**, click **Sample templates**. Locate and click **Equity Resume**. In the lower right corner, click **Create**.

a. **Save** the document in your **Word Chapter 2** folder as **Lastname_Firstname_2D_Resume** and then add the file name to the footer—called *First Page Footer* in this template. At the top of the resume, select the text in the first control, which displays the name of the computer at which you are working. Replace this text by typing **Elizabeth Ross** Right-click the name, and then from the shortcut menu, click **Remove Content Control**.

b. Click the *[Type your phone number]* control, and then type **(608) 555-0874** Click the *[Type your address]* control, type **2304 West Johnson Street** and press Enter. Type **Madison, WI 53703**

c. Click the *[Type your e-mail address]* control, and then type **emross@sturgeonpointpress.com** Right-click the *[Type your website]* control, and then from the shortcut menu, click **Remove Content Control**. Press Backspace to remove the *website* line.

d. Click the *[Type the objectives]* control, and then type **A copy editing or proofreading position where my editing and advanced computer skills will be of benefit to the organization.**

e. Under *Education*, click the *[Type the completion date]* control, and then type **University of Wisconsin-Milwaukee, May 2015** Click the *[Type the degree]* control, and then type **Bachelor of Arts in English** For the *[Type list of accomplishments]* bulleted list, type:

Dean's list, six terms

Harriet McArthur Creative Writing Award

(Project 2D Ross Letter continues on the next page)

Assistant Editor of college newspaper

3.8 GPA

f. Under *Experience*, enter the text shown in **Table 1** below.

g. Click the *[Type list of skills]* control and type **Word** Press Enter, and then type two additional bullet points with **QuarkXPress** and **Adobe Photoshop**

h. Display **Backstage** view, click **Properties**, and then click **Show Document Panel**. Type your firstname and lastname as the **Author**. In the **Subject** box, type your course and section number. In the **Keywords** box, **resume, template Close** the **Document Panel**.

i. **Save** your document.

j. Display **Backstage** view, click **Save As**, and then in the **Save as type** box, click **Single File Web Page**. Navigate to your **Word Chapter 2** folder. In the **File name** box,

type **Lastname_Firstname_2D_Web_Resume** Click **Save**.

k. Display **Backstage** view, click **Properties**, and then click **Advanced Properties**. In the **Properties** dialog box, be sure your name displays in the *Author* box, and then in the **Keywords** box, add **HTML** to the list of keywords. Click **OK** and **Save** your document.

l. **Exit** Word. From the **Start** menu, click **Computer** (or My Computer). Navigate to your **Word Chapter 2** folder, and then double-click your **2D_Web_Resume** file to open the resume in your Web browser. **Close** the Web browser. As directed by your instructor, print or submit electronically the four files that are the results of this project—2D_Ross_Letterhead, 2D_Ross_Letter, 2D_Resume, and 2D_Web_Resume.

Table 1

[Type the start date]	**May 2012**
[Type the end date]	**Present-**
[Type the job title]	**Senior Copy Editor**
[Type the company name]	**Sturgeon Point Press**
[Type the company address]	**Milwaukee, WI**
[Type job responsibilities]	**Produced final edited copy of books, technical manuals, and pamphlets; supervised three copy editors.**

(**Return to Step 4-g**)

End **You have completed Project 2D**

Apply 2A skills from these Objectives:

1. Create a Table
2. Add Text to a Table
3. Format a Table

Mastering Word | Project **2E** Job Listings

In the following Mastering Word project, you will create an announcement for new job postings at Madison Staffing Services. Your completed document will look similar to Figure 2.46.

Project Files

For Project 2E, you will need the following files:

New blank Word document
w02E_New_Jobs

You will save your document as:

Lastname_Firstname_2E_Job_Listings

Project Results

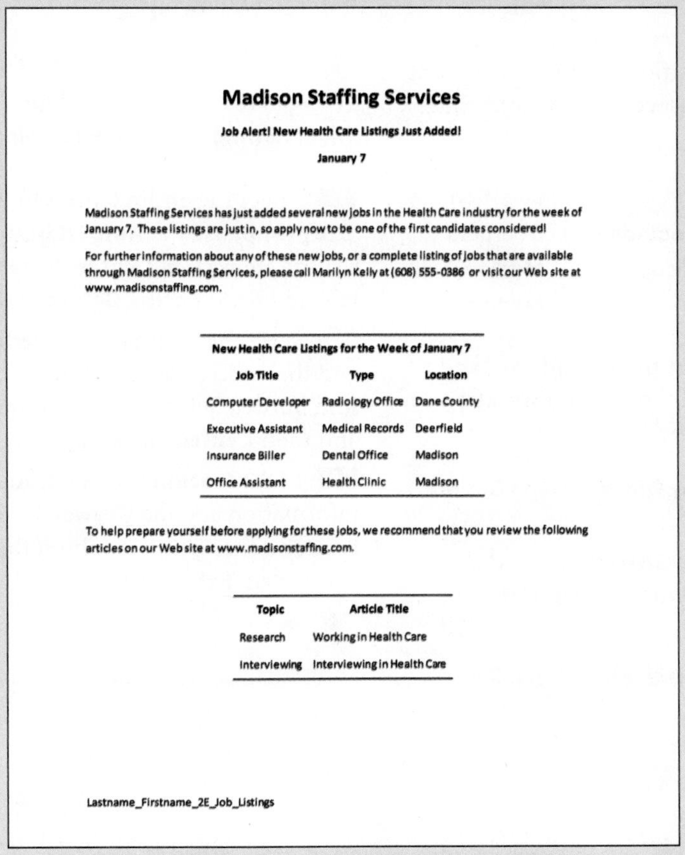

Madison Staffing Services

Job Alert! New Health Care Listings Just Added!

January 7

Madison Staffing Services has just added several new jobs in the Health Care industry for the week of January 7. These listings are just in, so apply now to be one of the first candidates considered!

For further information about any of these new jobs, or a complete listing of jobs that are available through Madison Staffing Services, please call Marilyn Kelly at (608) 555-0386 or visit our Web site at www.madisonstaffing.com.

New Health Care Listings for the Week of January 7		
Job Title	**Type**	**Location**
Computer Developer	Radiology Office	Dane County
Executive Assistant	Medical Records	Deerfield
Insurance Biller	Dental Office	Madison
Office Assistant	Health Clinic	Madison

To help prepare yourself before applying for these jobs, we recommend that you review the following articles on our Web site at www.madisonstaffing.com.

Topic	**Article Title**
Research	Working in Health Care
Interviewing	Interviewing in Health Care

Lastname_Firstname_2E_Job_Listings

Figure 2.46

(Project 2E Job Listings continues on the next page)

Mastering Word | Project **2E** Job Listings (continued)

1 **Start** Word and display a new blank document; display formatting marks and rulers. **Save** the document in your **Word Chapter 2** folder as **Lastname_Firstname_ 2E_Job_Listings** and then add the file name to the footer.

2 Type **Madison Staffing Services** and press Enter. Type **Job Alert! New Health Care Listings Just Added!** and press Enter. Type **January 7** and press Enter two times. **Insert** the file **w02E_New_Jobs**.

3 At the top of the document, select and **Center** the three title lines. Select the title *Madison Staffing Services* and change the **Font Size** to **20** pt and apply **Bold**. Apply **Bold** to the second and third title lines. Locate the paragraph that begins *For further information*, and then below that paragraph, click to position the insertion point in the second blank paragraph. **Insert** a **3 × 4** table. Enter the following:

Job Title	Type	Location
Executive Assistant	Medical Records	Deerfield
Insurance Biller	Dental Office	Madison
Office Assistant	Health Clinic	Madison

4 In the table, click anywhere in the second row, and then insert a row above. Add the following information so that the job titles remain in alphabetic order:

Computer Developer	Radiology Office	Dane County

5 Select the entire table. On the **Layout tab**, in the **Cell Size group**, use the **AutoFit** button to **AutoFit**

Contents. With the table still selected, **Center** the table. With the table still selected, on the **Page Layout tab**, add **6 pt Spacing Before** and **6 pt Spacing After**.

6 With the table still selected, remove all table borders, and then add a **Custom 1 pt** solid line top border and bottom border. Select all three cells in the first row, apply **Bold**, and then **Center** the text. Click anywhere in the first row, and then insert a new row above. Merge the three cells in the new top row, and then type **New Health Care Listings for the Week of January 7** Notice that the new row keeps the formatting of the row from which it was created.

7 At the bottom of the document, **Insert** a **2 × 3** table. Enter the following:

Topic	Article Title
Research	Working in Health Care
Interviewing	Interviewing in Health Care

8 Select the entire table. On the **Layout tab**, in the **Cell Size group**, use the **AutoFit** button to **AutoFit Contents**. On the **Home tab**, **Center** the table. On the **Page Layout tab**, add **6 pt Spacing Before** and **6 pt Spacing After**.

9 With the table still selected, remove all table borders, and then add a **Custom 1 pt** solid line top border and bottom border. Select the cells in the first row, apply **Bold**, and then **Center** the text.

10 In the **Document Panel**, add your name and course information and the **Keywords new listings, health care Save** and then print or submit the document electronically as directed. **Exit** Word.

End **You have completed Project 2E**

Content-Based Assessments

Apply 2B skills from these Objectives:

- **4** Create a New Document from an Existing Document
- **5** Change and Reorganize Text
- **6** Use the Proofing Options
- **7** Create a Document Using a Template

Mastering Word | Project **2F** Job Tips

In the following Mastering Word project, you will create a fax and a memo that includes job tips for Madison Staffing Services employees. Your completed documents will look similar to Figure 2.47.

Project Files

For Project 2F, you will need the following files:

> w02F_Memo_Heading
> w02F_Memo_Text
> Origin Fax template from Word's installed templates

You will save your documents as:

> Lastname_Firstname_2F_Job_Tips
> Lastname_Firstname_2F_Fax

Project Results

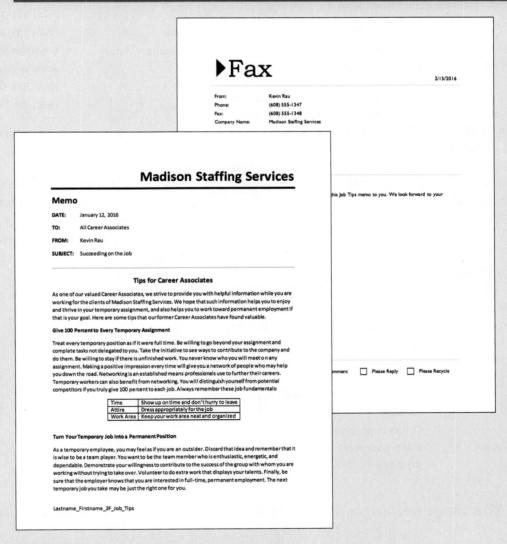

Figure 2.47

(Project 2F Job Tips continues on the next page)

Content-Based Assessments

1 **Start** Word; display rulers and formatting marks. In **Backstage** view, create a **New** document using the **New from existing** template. In the **New from Existing Document** dialog box, navigate to your student files, click **w02F_Memo_Heading**, and then click **Create New**.

2 Display the **Document Panel**, add your name and course information and the **Keywords memo, associates**

3 **Save** the document in your **Word Chapter 2** folder as **Lastname_Firstname_2F_Job_Tips** Add the file name to the footer.

4 At the top of your document, in the *DATE* paragraph, click to the right of the tab formatting mark, and then type **January 12, 2016** Use a similar technique to add the following information:

TO:	All Career Associates
FROM:	Kevin Rau
SUBJECT:	Succeeding on the Job

5 Position the insertion point in the blank paragraph below the memo heading. **Insert** the file **w02F_Memo_Text** and press Backspace to remove the blank line at the end of the selected text.

6 Select and **Center** the title *Tips for Career Associates*. By using either the **Spelling and Grammar** dialog box, or by right-clicking selected words, correct all spelling, grammar, and word usage errors.

7 In the first line of the paragraph that begins *Treat every*, locate and right-click *provisional*. Use the shortcut menu to change the word to the synonym *temporary*. In the second line of the same paragraph, change *donate* to the synonym *contribute*.

8 At the end of the paragraph that begins *Treat every temporary*, create a blank paragraph. **Insert** at **2 × 3** table, and then type the following information:

Time	Show up on time and don't hurry to leave
Attire	Dress appropriately for the job
Work Area	Keep your work area neat and organized

9 Select the entire table. **AutoFit Contents** and **Center** the table. Display **Backstage** view and preview the document. **Save** and **Close** the document but leave Word open. Hold this file until you complete this project.

10 From **Sample templates**, create a document based on the **Origin Fax** template. Save the document in your **Word Chapter 2** folder as **Lastname_Firstname_2F_Fax** and then add the file name to the footer—called the *First Page Footer* in this template.

11 Click the *Pick a date* placeholder, type **2/15/2016** and then type the following for the remaining controls:

From:	Kevin Rau
Phone:	(608) 555-1347
Fax:	(608) 555-1348
Company Name:	Madison Staffing Services
To:	Jane Westerfield
Phone:	(608) 555-0034
Fax:	(608) 555-0035

12 Locate and right-click *Kevin Rau*; remove the content control. Delete the lower *Company Name* text and remove the control to its right. In the *Type comments* control, type **Jane: I know you are on leave, so I thought I would fax this Job Tips memo to you. We look forward to your return.**

13 In the **Document Panel**, add your name and course information and the **Keywords job tips, fax Save** the document.

14 As directed by your instructor, print or submit electronically the two files that are the results of this project. **Exit** Word.

End You have completed Project 2F ———————————

Apply **2A** and **2B** skills from these Objectives:

1. Create a Table
2. Add Text to a Table
3. Format a Table
4. Create a New Document from an Existing Document
5. Change and Reorganize Text
6. Use the Proofing Options
7. Create a Document Using a Template

Mastering Word | Project **2G** Job Letter

In the following Mastering Word project, you will create a new document from an existing document, format a table, and then create a fax cover using a template. Your completed documents will look similar to Figure 2.48.

Project Files

For Project 2G, you will need the following files:

> w02G_Letter_Text
> w02G_Letterhead
> w02G_Resume
> Equity Fax template from Word's installed templates

You will save your documents as:

> Lastname_Firstname_2G_Job_Letter
> Lastname_Firstname_2G_Resume
> Lastname_Firstname_2G_Fax

Project Results

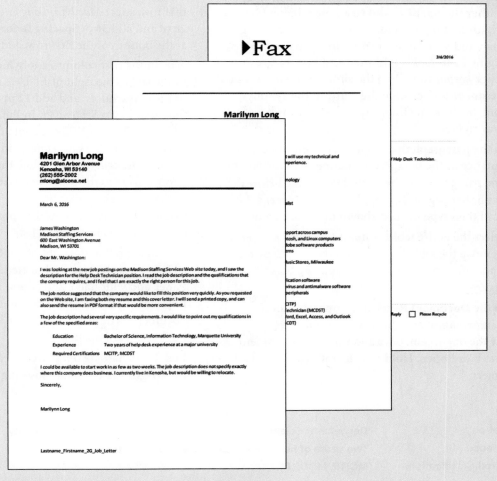

Figure 2.48

(Project 2G Job Letter continues on the next page)

1 **Start** Word and display rulers and formatting marks. By using the **New from existing** template, create a document from the file **w02G_Letterhead**. **Save** the document in your **Word Chapter 2** folder as **Lastname_Firstname_2G_Job_Letter** Add the file name to the footer. Move to the end of the document, and then on the **Home tab**, apply the **No Spacing** style. Type **March 6, 2016** and then press Enter four times. Type the following:

> **James Washington**
> **Madison Staffing Services**
> **600 East Washington Avenue**
> **Madison, WI 53701**

2 Press Enter two times, type **Dear Mr. Washington:** and press Enter two times. **Insert** the text from the file **w02G_Letter_Text** and remove the blank line at the bottom of the selected text.

3 Move to the top of the document, and then by using either the **Spelling and Grammar** dialog box, or by right-clicking selected words, correct spelling, grammar, and word usage errors. In the paragraph that begins *I was looking*, in the third line, locate and right-click *corporation*. Use the shortcut menu to open the **Thesaurus** and change the word to the synonym *company*. In the same line, change *correct* to the synonym *right*.

4 In the paragraph that begins *I currently*, select the first sentence of the paragraph and drag it to the end of the same paragraph. In the second blank line below the paragraph that begins *The job description*, **Insert** a **2 × 3** table, and then type the text shown in **Table 1** below.

5 Select the entire table. **AutoFit Contents**, **Center** the table, remove the table borders, and then add **3 pt** spacing before and after by typing **3** in the **Spacing** boxes and pressing Enter.

6 In the **Document Panel**, add your name and course information and the **Keywords job letter** Preview the document. **Save** and **Close** the document but leave Word open. Hold the file until you complete this project.

7 From your student files, open **w02G_Resume**. **Save** the document in your **Word Chapter 2** folder as **Lastname_Firstname_2G_Resume** Add the file name to the footer.

8 **Insert** a new second row in the table. In the first cell of the new row, type **OBJECTIVE** and then press Tab. Type **To obtain a Help Desk Technician position that will use my technical and communication skills and computer support experience.** In the same cell, add **12 pt Spacing After**.

9 Select the entire table. On the **Layout tab**, **AutoFit Contents**. Remove the table borders, and then display the **Borders and Shading** dialog box. With the table selected, create a **Custom** single solid line **1 1/2 pt** top border.

10 In the first row of the table, select both cells and then **Merge Cells**. **Center** the five lines and apply **Bold**. In the first row, select *Marilynn Long* and change the **Font Size** to **20 pt** and add **36 pt Spacing Before**. In the e-mail address at the bottom of the first row, add **24 pt Spacing After**.

11 In the first column, apply **Bold** to the four headings. In the cell to the right of *EDUCATION*, **Bold** the names of the two schools, and add **12 pt Spacing After** the two lines that begin *September*. In the cell to the right of *RELEVANT EXPERIENCE*, bold the names of the two jobs—*IT Help Desk Specialist* and *Computer Technician*. In the same cell, below the line that begins *January 2014*, apply bullets to the four lines that comprise the job duties. Create a similar bulleted list for the duties as a Computer Technician. Add **12 pt Spacing After** to the last line of each of the bulleted lists.

12 In the cell to the right of *CERTIFICATIONS*, select all four lines and create a bulleted list. In the **Document Panel**, add your name and course information and the **Keywords help desk resume** and then submit your document as directed. **Save** and **Close** the document but leave Word open.

13 From **Sample templates**, create a document based on the **Origin Fax** template. **Save** the document in your **Word**

Table 1

Education	Bachelor of Science, Information Technology, Marquette University
Experience	Two years of help desk experience at a major university
Required Certifications	MCITP, MCDST

(**Return to Step 5**)

(Project 2G Job Letter continues on the next page)

Mastering Word | Project 2G Job Letter (continued)

Chapter 2 folder as **Lastname_Firstname_2G_Fax** and then add the file name to the footer—called a *First Page Footer* in this template.

14 Type the text shown in **Table 2** for the content controls.

15 Locate and right-click *Marilynn Long*; remove the content control. In the **Document Panel**, add your name and course information and the **Keywords fax cover page** As directed by your instructor, print or submit electronically the three files from this project. **Exit** Word.

Table 2

Pick a date	**3/6/2016**
From:	**Marilynn Long**
Phone:	**(608) 555-0967**
Fax:	**(608) 555-0966**
Company Name:	Remove this content control and row heading
To:	**James Washington, Recruiter**
Phone:	**(608) 555-0034**
Fax:	**(608) 555-0035**
Company Name	**Madison Staffing Services**
Comments:	**Two pages to follow that include my resume and a cover letter for the position of Help Desk Technician.**

(**Return to Step 15**)

End **You have completed Project 2G**

Content-Based Assessments

GO! Fix It | Project **2H** New Jobs

In this project, you will construct a solution by applying any combination of the skills you practiced from the Objectives in Projects 2A and 2B.

Project Files

For Project 2H, you will need the following file:

w02H_New_Jobs

You will save your document as:

Lastname_Firstname_2H_New_Jobs

From the student files that accompany this textbook, locate and open the file w02H_New_Jobs, and then save the file in your Word Chapter 2 folder as **Lastname_Firstname_2H_New_Jobs**

This document contains errors that you must find and correct. Read and examine the document, and then edit to correct the errors that you find and to improve the overall document format. Types of errors could include, but are not restricted to:

- Spelling errors
- Grammar errors
- Word choice errors
- Duplicate words
- Unattractive table column widths
- Title not merged across the top row of the table
- Inconsistent spacing before and after paragraphs in the table

Things you should know to complete this project:

- Viewing the document in Print Preview will help identify some of the problems
- The Spelling and Grammar checker will be useful
- Adjust the column widths *before* merging the title

Save your document and add the file name to the footer. In the Document Panel, type your firstname and lastname in the Author box and your course name and section number in the Subject box. In the Keywords box type **job listings** and then save your document and submit as directed.

End You have completed Project 2H _____

Content-Based Assessments

Apply a combination of the **2A** and **2B** skills.

GO! Make It | Project **2I** Training

Project Files

For Project 2I, you will need the following file:

New blank Word document

You will save your document as:

Lastname_Firstname_2I_Training

Start Word, and then save the file in your Word Chapter 2 folder as **Lastname_Firstname_ 2I_Training**

Use the skills you practiced in this chapter to create the table shown in Figure 2.49. The first row font is Cambria 16 pt, the remainder is Cambria 14 pt. The spacing after the first row is 36 pt, the spacing at the bottom of the rows is 12 pt.

Add the file name to the footer; in the Document Panel, add your name and course information and the Keywords **online training** Save your document, and then submit as directed.

Project Results

Figure 2.49

Selected Training Programs Available Online

Software	Program Title
Microsoft Word	• Create your first Word document I • Getting started with Word 2010 • Use the Navigation Pane to search and move around in your document • Create your first Word document II
Microsoft Excel	• Get to know Excel 2010: Create your first workbook • Charts I: How to create a chart in Excel • Get to know Excel 2010: Enter formulas • Sort data in a range or table

Lastname_Firstname_2I_Training

End You have completed Project 2I

Content-Based Assessments

GO! Solve It | Project 2J Job Postings

Project Files

For Project 2J, you will need the following files:

> New blank Word document
> w02J_Job_Postings

You will save your documents as:

> Lastname_Firstname_2J_Letterhead
> Lastname_Firstname_2J_Job_Postings

Print the w02J_Job_Postings document, and use the information to complete this project. Create a new company letterhead and save it in your Word Chapter 2 folder as **Lastname_Firstname_2J_Letterhead** Add the file name to the footer. Add your name, your course name and section number, and the keyword **letterhead** to the Properties area.

Create a new document based on the existing document you just created. The new document will be a list of new jobs posted by Madison Staffing Services. The job posting should include the letterhead, introductory text, and a table that includes the information about the new jobs that are currently available. The job list should be in table format. Use either two or three columns, and label the columns appropriately. Format the table, the table borders, and the text in an attractive, readable manner.

Save the document as **Lastname_Firstname_2J_Job_Postings** Add the file name to the footer, and add your name, your course name and section number, and the keywords **new jobs** to the Properties area. Submit your two files as directed.

	Performance Level		
	Exemplary: You consistently applied the relevant skills	**Proficient:** You sometimes, but not always, applied the relevant skills	**Developing:** You rarely or never applied the relevant skills
Create and format a letterhead template	The text in the letterhead is appropriately formatted, the company name stands out, and the spacing between paragraphs is attractive.	The letterhead is complete, but the line spacing or text formatting is not appropriate for a letterhead.	The spacing and formatting is not appropriate for a letterhead.
Insert a table	The inserted table has the appropriate number of columns and rows to display the information.	The table is not structured to effectively display the information.	No table is inserted in the document.
Format the table structure	Table column widths fit the information, extra space is added between the rows, and borders are attractively formatted.	The column widths do not reflect the amount of information in the column, and the spacing between the cells is insufficient.	Table displays only default column widths and spacing.
Format the text in the table	Important text is highlighted and formatted appropriately, making the text easy to read and interpret.	Some text formatting is added, but the formatting does not highlight the important information.	No text formatting is included.

Performance Element (label on left side of table)

End You have completed Project 2J

Content-Based Assessments

Apply a combination of the 2A and 2B skills.

GO! Solve It | Project 2K Agenda

Project Files

For Project 2K, you will need the following file:

> Agenda template from Word's Online templates

You will save your document as:

> Lastname_Firstname_2K_Agenda

Create a new document based on an agenda template—such as the *Formal meeting agenda* template—from the Agenda templates at Microsoft Office Online. Save the agenda as **Lastname_Firstname_2K_Agenda** Use the following information to prepare an agenda for a Madison Staffing Services meeting.

The meeting will be chaired by Marilyn Kelly and will be the monthly meeting of the company administrators—Kevin Rau, Marilyn Kelly, Andre Randolph, Susan Nguyen, and Charles James. The meeting will be held on March 15, 2016, at 3:00 p.m. The old business (open issues) include 1) expanding services into the printing and food service industries; 2) recruitment at the UW-Madison and MATC campuses; and 3) the addition of a part-time trainer. The new business will include 1) recruitment at the University of Wisconsin, Milwaukee; 2) rental of office space in or around Milwaukee; 3) purchase of new computers for the training room; and 4) renewal of snow removal service contract.

Add the file name to the footer, and add your name, your course name and section number, and the keywords **agenda, monthly administrative meeting** to the Properties area. Submit as directed.

	Performance Level		
	Exemplary: You consistently applied the relevant skills	**Proficient:** You sometimes, but not always, applied the relevant skills	**Developing:** You rarely or never applied the relevant skills
Select an agenda template	Agenda template is appropriate for the information provided for the meeting.	Agenda template is used, but does not fit the information provided.	No template is used for the agenda.
Add appropriate information to the template	All information is inserted in the appropriate places. All unused controls are removed.	All information is included, but not in the appropriate places, and not all of the unused controls are removed.	Information is missing and unused placeholders are not removed.
Format template information	All text in the template is properly aligned and formatted.	All text is included, but alignment or formatting is inconsistent.	No additional formatting has been added.

(Performance Element)

End You have completed Project 2K

Outcomes-Based Assessments

Rubric

The following outcomes-based assessments are *open-ended assessments*. That is, there is no specific correct result; your result will depend on your approach to the information provided. Make *Professional Quality* your goal. Use the following scoring rubric to guide you in *how* to approach the problem and then to evaluate *how well* your approach solves the problem.

The *criteria*—Software Mastery, Content, Format and Layout, and Process—represent the knowledge and skills you have gained that you can apply to solving the problem. The *levels of performance*—Professional Quality, Approaching Professional Quality, or Needs Quality Improvements—help you and your instructor evaluate your result.

	Your completed project is of Professional Quality if you:	Your completed project is Approaching Professional Quality if you:	Your completed project Needs Quality Improvements if you:
1-Software Mastery	Choose and apply the most appropriate skills, tools, and features and identify efficient methods to solve the problem.	Choose and apply some appropriate skills, tools, and features, but not in the most efficient manner.	Choose inappropriate skills, tools, or features, or are inefficient in solving the problem.
2-Content	Construct a solution that is clear and well organized, contains content that is accurate, appropriate to the audience and purpose, and is complete. Provide a solution that contains no errors in spelling, grammar, or style.	Construct a solution in which some components are unclear, poorly organized, inconsistent, or incomplete. Misjudge the needs of the audience. Have some errors in spelling, grammar, or style, but the errors do not detract from comprehension.	Construct a solution that is unclear, incomplete, or poorly organized; contains some inaccurate or inappropriate content; and contains many errors in spelling, grammar, or style. Do not solve the problem.
3-Format and Layout	Format and arrange all elements to communicate information and ideas, clarify function, illustrate relationships, and indicate relative importance.	Apply appropriate format and layout features to some elements, but not others. Overuse features, causing minor distraction.	Apply format and layout that does not communicate information or ideas clearly. Do not use format and layout features to clarify function, illustrate relationships, or indicate relative importance. Use available features excessively, causing distraction.
4-Process	Use an organized approach that integrates planning, development, self-assessment, revision, and reflection.	Demonstrate an organized approach in some areas, but not others; or, use an insufficient process of organization throughout.	Do not use an organized approach to solve the problem.

Outcomes-Based Assessments

Apply a combination of the 2A and 2B skills.

GO! Think | Project **2L** Workshops

Project Files

For Project 2L, you will need the following files:

New blank Word document
w02L_Workshop_Information

You will save your document as:

Lastname_Firstname_2L_Workshops

Madison Staffing Services offers a series of workshops for its employee-clients. Any temporary employee who is available during the workshop hours can attend the workshops and there is no fee. Currently, the company offers three-session workshops covering Excel and Word, a two-session workshop covering Business Communication, and a one-session workshop covering *Creating a Resume*.

Print the w02L_Workshop_Information file and use the information to complete this project. Create an announcement with a title, an introductory paragraph, and a table listing the workshops and the topics covered in each workshop. Use the file w02L_Workshop_Information for help with the topics covered in each workshop. Format the table cells appropriately. Add an appropriate footer and information to the Document Panel. Save the document as **Lastname_Firstname_2L_ Workshops** and submit it as directed.

End You have completed Project 2L ——————————————

Apply a combination of the 2A and 2B skills.

GO! Think | Project **2M** Planner

Project Files

For Project 2M, you will need the following files:

Weekly appointment sheet template from Word's Online templates
w02M_Workshop_Information

You will save your document as:

Lastname_Firstname_2M_Planner

To keep track of workshops provided to employees, the trainer fills out a weekly schedule. Each workshop lasts two hours. Print the w02M_Workshop_Information file and use part or all of the information to complete this project.

Create a new document using a template, for example the *Weekly appointment sheet* template found in the Planners category in the online template list. Create a template for a week, and include the first part of each workshop series, along with the Creating a Resume workshop. Customize the template as necessary to include *Room* and *Workshop* titles for each day of the week. The computer skills workshops are held in the Lab, the others are held in Room 104. The trainer always schedules the hour before each workshop for preparation. Fill out the workshop schedule and use your choice of formatting to indicate that the workshops cover a two-hour period. Add appropriate information to the Document Panel. Save the document as **Lastname_Firstname_2M_Planner** and submit it as directed.

End You have completed Project 2M ——————————————

Outcomes-Based Assessments

Apply a combination of the 2A and 2B skills.

You and GO! | Project **2N** Personal Resume

Project Files

For Project 2N, you will need the following file:

New blank Word document

You will save your documents as

Lastname_Firstname_2N_Personal_Resume
Lastname_Firstname_2N_Cover_Letter

Locate and print the information for a job for which you would like to apply, and then create your own personal resume using a table and a cover letter. Include any information that is appropriate, including your objective for a specific job, your experience, skills, education, honors, or awards. Create your own letterhead and cover letter, using the cover letter you created in Project 2B as a guide.

To complete the assignment, be sure to format the text appropriately, resize the table columns in the resume to best display the information, and check both documents for spelling and grammar errors.

Save the resume as **Lastname_Firstname_2N_Personal_Resume** and the cover letter as **Lastname_Firstname_2N_Personal_Cover_Letter** Add the file name to the footer, and add your name, your course name and section number, and the keywords **my resume** and **cover letter** to the Properties area. Submit your file as directed.

End **You have completed Project 2N** ⸺⸺⸺⸺⸺⸺

Apply a combination of the 2A and 2B skills.

GO! Collaborate | Project **2O** Bell Orchid Hotels Group Running Case

Your instructor may assign this group case project to your class. If your instructor assigns this project, he or she will provide you with information and instructions to work as part of a group. The group will apply the skills gained thus far to help the Bell Orchid Hotel Group achieve its business goals.

End **You have completed Project 2O** ⸺⸺⸺⸺⸺⸺

Creating Research Papers, Newsletters, and Merged Mailing Labels

OUTCOMES
At the end of this chapter you will be able to:

OBJECTIVES
Mastering these objectives will enable you to:

PROJECT 3A
Create a research paper that includes citations and a bibliography.

1. Create a Research Paper (p. 165)
2. Insert Footnotes in a Research Paper (p. 167)
3. Create Citations and a Bibliography in a Research Paper (p. 172)

PROJECT 3B
Create a multiple-column newsletter and merged mailing labels.

4. Format a Multiple-Column Newsletter (p. 181)
5. Use Special Character and Paragraph Formatting (p. 186)
6. Create Mailing Labels Using Mail Merge (p. 189)

Shutterstock

In This Chapter

Microsoft Word provides many tools for creating complex documents. For example, Word has tools that enable you to create a research paper that includes citations, footnotes, and a bibliography. You can also create multiple-column newsletters, format the nameplate at the top of the newsletter, use special character formatting to create distinctive title text, and add borders and shading to paragraphs to highlight important information.

In this chapter, you will edit and format a research paper, create a two-column newsletter, and then create a set of mailing labels to mail the newsletter to multiple recipients.

The projects in this chapter relate to **Memphis Primary Materials** located in the Memphis area. In addition to collecting common recyclable materials, the company collects and recycles computers, monitors, copiers and fax machines, cell phones, wood pallets, and compostable materials. The company's name comes from the process of capturing the "primary materials" of used items for reuse. Memphis Primary Materials ensures that its clients comply with all state and local regulations. They also provide training to clients on the process and benefits of recycling.

Project 3A Research Paper

Project Activities

In Activities 3.01 through 3.07, you will edit and format a research paper that contains an overview of recycling activities in which businesses can engage. This paper was created by Elizabeth Freeman, a student intern working for Memphis Primary Metals, and will be included in a customer information packet. Your completed document will look similar to Figure 3.1.

Project Files

For Project 3A, you will need the following file:

w03A_Green_Business

You will save your document as:

Lastname_Firstname_3A_Green_Business

Project Results

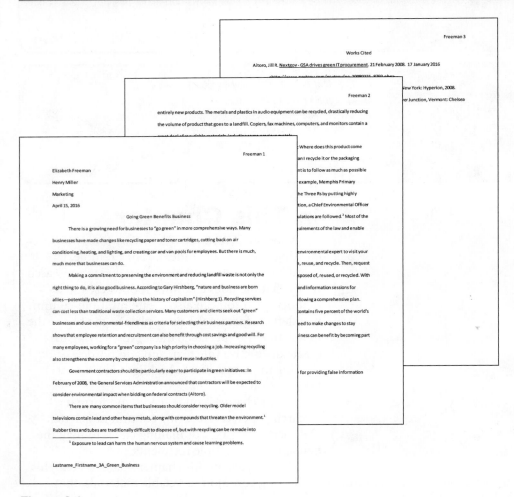

Figure 3.1
Project 3A Green Business

Objective 1 | Create a Research Paper

When you write a research paper or a report for college or business, follow a format prescribed by one of the standard *style guides*—a manual that contains standards for the design and writing of documents. The two most commonly used styles for research papers are those created by the *Modern Language Association (MLA)* and the *American Psychological Association (APA)*; there are several others.

Activity 3.01 | Formatting Text and Page Numbers in a Research Paper

When formatting the text for your research paper, refer to the standards for the style guide that you have chosen. In this activity, you will create a research paper using the MLA style. The MLA style uses 1-inch margins, a 0.5″ first line indent, and double spacing throughout the body of the document, with no extra space above or below paragraphs.

1 **Start** Word. From your student files, locate and open the document **w03A_Green_Business**. If necessary, display the formatting marks and rulers. In the location where you are storing your projects for this chapter, create a new folder named **Word Chapter 3** and then save the file in the folder as **Lastname_Firstname_3A_Green_Business**

2 Press Ctrl + A to select the entire document. On the **Home tab**, in the **Paragraph group**, click the **Line and Paragraph Spacing** button, and then change the line spacing to **2.0**. On the **Page Layout tab**, in the **Paragraph group**, change the **Spacing After** to **0 pt**.

3 Press Ctrl + Home to deselect and move to the top of the document. Press Enter one time to create a blank line at the top of the document, and then click to position the insertion point in the blank line. Type **Elizabeth Freeman** and press Enter.

4 Type **Henry Miller** and press Enter. Type **Marketing** and press Enter. Type **April 15, 2016** and press Enter. Type **Going Green Benefits Business** Right-click anywhere in the line you just typed, and then on the Mini toolbar, click the **Center** button. Compare your screen with Figure 3.2.

Figure 3.2

Title centered

Text double-spaced

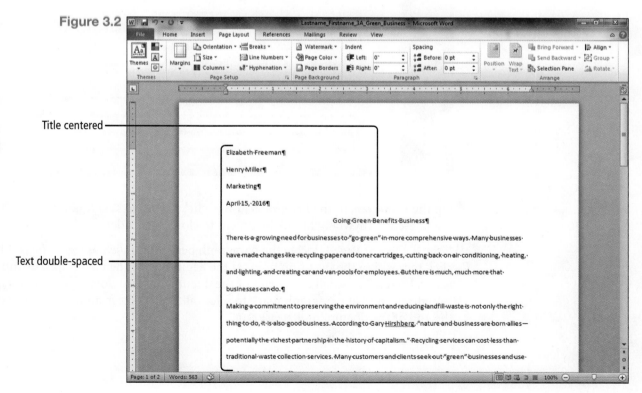

5 At the top of the **Page 1**, point anywhere in the white top margin area, right-click, and then click **Edit Header**. In the header area, type **Freeman** and then press Spacebar.

> Recall that the text you insert into a header or footer displays on every page of a document. Within a header or footer, you can insert many different types of information; for example, automatic page numbers, the date, the time, the file name, or pictures.

6 On the **Design tab**, in the **Header & Footer group**, click the **Page Number** button, and then point to **Current Position**. In the displayed gallery, under **Simple**, click **Plain Number**. Compare your screen with Figure 3.3.

> Word will automatically number the pages using this number format.

Figure 3.3

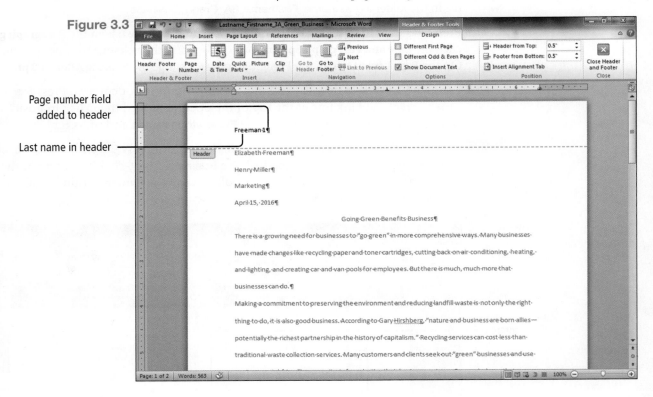

Page number field added to header

Last name in header

7 On the **Home tab**, in the **Paragraph group**, click the **Align Text Right** button ≡. Double-click anywhere in the document to close the header area.

8 Near the top of **Page 1**, locate the paragraph beginning *There is a growing*, and then click to position the insertion point at the beginning of the paragraph. By moving the vertical scroll bar, scroll to the end of the document, hold down Shift, and then click to right of the last paragraph mark to select all of the text from the insertion point to the end of the document. Release Shift.

9 With the text selected, on the ruler, point to the **First Line Indent** button 🔻, and then drag the button to **0.5" on the horizontal ruler**. Compare your screen with Figure 3.4.

> The MLA style uses 0.5-inch indents at the beginning of the first line of every paragraph. Indenting—moving the beginning of the first line of a paragraph to the right or left of the rest of the paragraph—provides visual cues to the reader to help divide the document text and make it easier to read.

Figure 3.4

First Line Indent button moved to 0.5" on the ruler

First line indented 0.5 inch

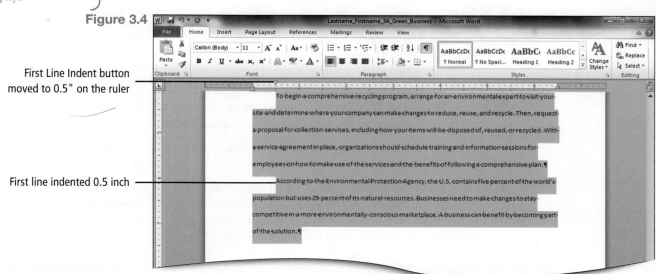

10 Click anywhere to deselect the text. Scroll to view the bottom of **Page 1**, point anywhere in the bottom white margin area, right-click, and then click **Edit Footer**. On the **Design tab**, in the **Insert group**, click the **Quick Parts** button, and then click **Field**. In the **Field** dialog box, under **Field names**, locate and click **FileName**, and then click **OK**.

> The file name in the footer is *not* part of the research report format, but it is included in projects in this textbook so that you and your instructor can identify your work.

11 Double-click anywhere in the document to close the Footer area, and then **Save** 💾 your document.

More Knowledge | Suppressing the Page Number on the First Page

Some style guidelines require that the page number and other header and footer information on the first page be hidden from view—*suppressed*. To hide the information contained in the header and footer areas on Page 1 of a document, double-click in the header or footer area. Then, on the Design tab, in the Options group, select the Different First Page check box.

Objective 2 | Insert Footnotes in a Research Paper

Reports and research papers typically include information that you find in other sources, and these must be credited. Within report text, numbers mark the location of *notes*—information that expands on the topic being discussed but that does not fit well in the document text. The numbers refer to *footnotes*—notes placed at the bottom of the page containing the note, or to *endnotes*—notes placed at the end of a document or chapter.

Activity 3.02 | Inserting Footnotes

Footnotes can be added as you type the document or after the document is complete. Word renumbers the footnotes automatically, so footnotes do not need to be entered in order, and if one footnote is removed, the remaining footnotes renumber automatically.

1 Scroll to view the top of **Page 2**. Locate the paragraph that begins *Consumers and businesses*. In the seventh line of text, toward the end of the line, click to position the insertion point to the right of the period after *followed*.

2 On the **References tab**, in the **Footnotes group**, click the **Insert Footnote** button.

> Word creates space for a footnote in the footnote area at the bottom of the page and adds a footnote number to the text at the insertion point location. Footnote *1* displays in the footnote area, and the insertion point moves to the right of the number. A short black line is added just above the footnote area. You do not need to type the footnote number.

3 Type **Tennessee, for example, imposes penalties of up to $10,000 for providing false information regarding the recycling of hazardous waste.**

> This is an explanatory footnote; the footnote provides additional information that does not fit well in the body of the report.

4 Click the **Home tab**, and then in the **Font group**, notice that the font size of the footer is *10 pt*. In the **Paragraph group**, click the **Line and Paragraph Spacing** button, and notice that the line spacing is *1.0*—single-spaced—even though the font size of the document text is 11 pt and the text is double-spaced, as shown in Figure 3.5.

Figure 3.5

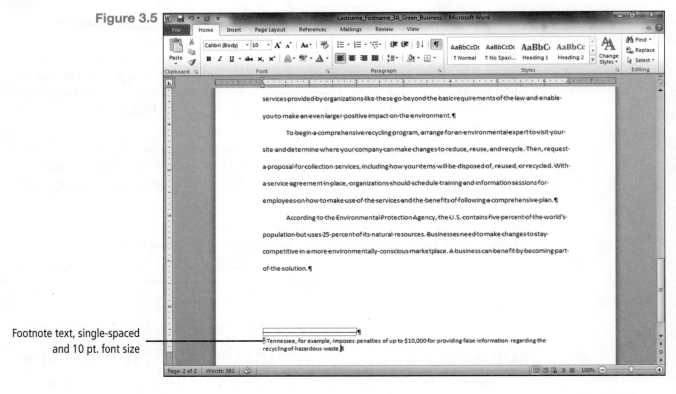

Footnote text, single-spaced and 10 pt. font size

5 Scroll to view the bottom of **Page 1**, and then locate the paragraph that begins *There are many common*. At the end of the second line of text, click to position the insertion point to the right of the period following *environment*.

6 On the **References tab**, in the **Footnotes group**, click the **Insert Footnote** button. Type **Exposure to lead can harm the human nervous system and cause learning problems.** Notice that the footnote you just added becomes the new footnote *1*, as shown in Figure 3.6.

> The first footnote is renumbered as footnote *2*.

Figure 3.6

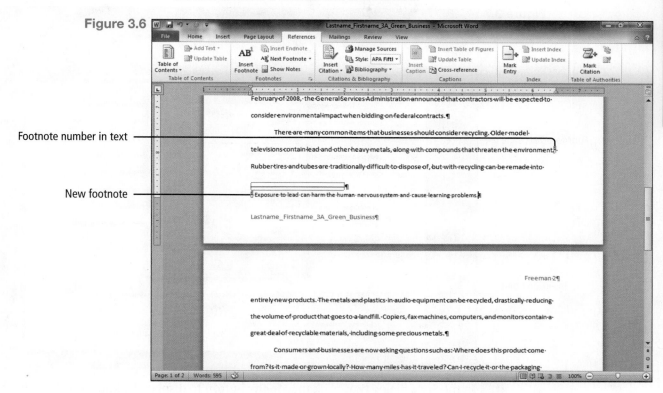

Footnote number in text

New footnote

7 **Save** your document.

More Knowledge | Using Symbols Rather Than Numbers for Notes

Instead of using numbers to designate footnotes, you can use standard footnote symbols. The seven traditional symbols, available from the Footnote and Endnote dialog box, in order, are * (asterisk), † (dagger), ‡ (double dagger), § (section mark), || (parallels), ¶ (paragraph mark), and # (number or pound sign). This sequence can be continuous (this is the default setting), or can begin anew with each page.

Activity 3.03 | Modifying a Footnote Style

Microsoft Word contains built-in paragraph formats called ***styles***—groups of formatting commands, such as font, font size, font color, paragraph alignment, and line spacing—which can be applied to a paragraph with one command.

The default style for footnote text is a single-spaced paragraph that uses a 10-point Calibri font and no paragraph indents. MLA style specifies double-spaced text in all areas of a research paper—including footnotes. According to the MLA style, first lines of footnotes must also be indented 0.5 inch and use the same font size as the report text.

1 Scroll to view the bottom of **Page 2**. Point anywhere in the footnote text and right-click, and then from the shortcut menu, click **Style**. Compare your screen with Figure 3.7.

The Style dialog box displays, listing the styles currently in use in the document, in addition to some of the word processing elements that come with special built-in styles. Because you right-clicked on the footnote text, the selected style is the Footnote Text style.

Figure 3.7

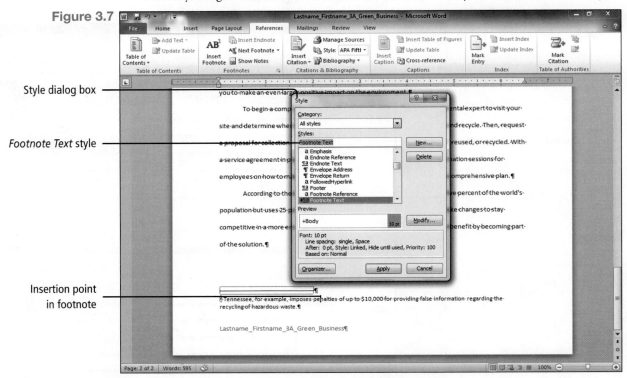

Style dialog box

Footnote Text style

Insertion point in footnote

2 In the **Style** dialog box, click the **Modify** button to display the **Modify Style** dialog box.

3 In the **Modify Style** dialog box, locate the small **Formatting** toolbar in the center of the dialog box, click the **Font Size button arrow**, click **11**, and then compare your screen with Figure 3.8.

Figure 3.8

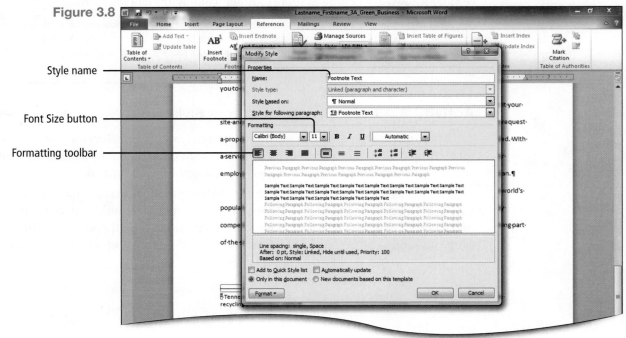

Style name

Font Size button

Formatting toolbar

4 In the lower left corner of the dialog box, click the **Format** button, and then click **Paragraph**. In the **Paragraph** dialog box, under **Indentation**, click the **Special arrow**, and then click **First line**.

5 Under **Spacing**, click the **Line spacing** button arrow, and then click **Double**. Compare your dialog box with Figure 3.9.

Figure 3.9

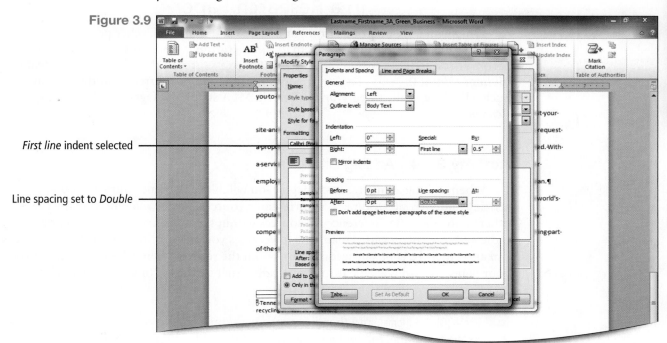

First line indent selected

Line spacing set to *Double*

6 Click **OK** to close the **Paragraph** dialog box, click **OK** to close the **Modify Style** dialog box, and then click **Apply** to apply the new style. Notice that when you click Apply, the Style dialog box closes. Compare your screen with Figure 3.10.

Your inserted footnotes are formatted with the new Footnote Text paragraph style; any new footnotes that you insert will also use this format.

Figure 3.10

First line indented

Footnote text double-spaced

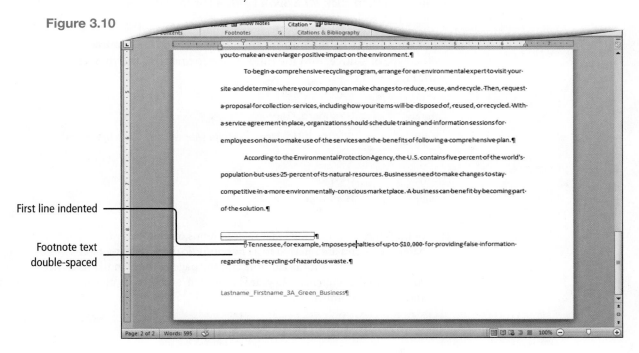

7 Scroll to view the bottom of **Page 1** to confirm that the new format was also applied to the first footnote, and then **Save** 🖫 your document.

Objective 3 | Create Citations and a Bibliography in a Research Paper

When you use quotations from, or detailed summaries of, other people's work, you must specify the source of the information. A ***citation*** is a note inserted into the text of a report or research paper that refers the reader to a source in the bibliography. Create a ***bibliography*** at the end of a document to list the sources referred to in the document. Such a list is typically titled ***Works Cited*** (in MLA style), *Bibliography*, *Sources*, or *References*.

Activity 3.04 | Adding Citations

When writing a long research paper, you will likely reference numerous books, articles, and Web sites. Some of your research sources may be referenced many times, others only one time. References to sources within the text of your research paper are indicated in an *abbreviated* manner. However, as you enter a citation for the first time, you can also enter the *complete* information about the source. Then, when you have finished your paper, you will be able to automatically generate the list of sources that must be included at the end of your research paper.

1 Press [Ctrl] + [Home], and then locate the paragraph that begins *Making a commitment*. In the third line, following the word *capitalism*, click to position the insertion point to the right of the quotation mark.

> The citation in the document points to the full source information in the bibliography, which typically includes the name of the author, the full title of the work, the year of publication, and other publication information.

2 On the **References tab**, in the **Citations & Bibliography group**, click the **Style button arrow**, and then click **MLA Sixth Edition** (or the latest edition) to insert a reference using MLA style.

3 Click the **Insert Citation** button, and then click **Add New Source**. Be sure *Book* is selected as the **Type of Source**. Add the following information, and then compare your screen with Figure 3.11:

Author:	**Hirshberg, Gary**
Title:	**Stirring it Up: How to Make Money and Save the World**
Year:	**2008**
City:	**New York**
Publisher:	**Hyperion**

> In the MLA style, citations that refer to items on the *Works Cited* page are placed in parentheses and are referred to as ***parenthetical references***—references that include the last name of the author or authors and the page number in the referenced source, which you add to the reference. No year is indicated, and there is no comma between the name and the page number.

Figure 3.11

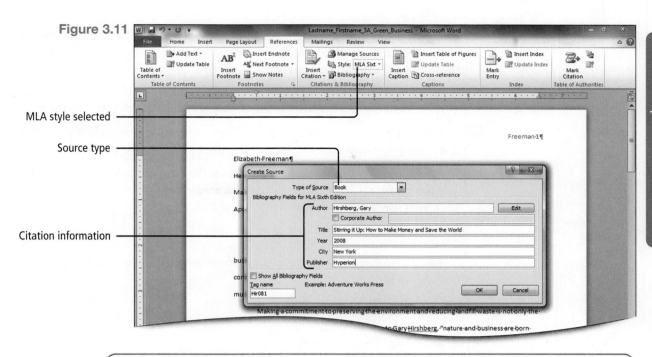

MLA style selected

Source type

Citation information

> **Note** | Citing Corporate Authors
>
> If the author of a document is identified as the name of an organization only, select the Corporate Author check box and type the name of the organization in the Corporate Author box.

4 Click **OK** to insert the citation. In the paragraph, point to *(Hirshberg)* and click one time to select the citation.

5 In the lower right corner of the box that surrounds the reference, point to the small arrow to display the ScreenTip *Citation Options*. Click this **Citation Options arrow**, and then from the list of options, click **Edit Citation**.

6 In the **Edit Citation** dialog box, under **Add**, in the **Pages** box, type **1** to indicate that you are citing from page 1 of this source. Compare your screen with Figure 3.12.

Figure 3.12

Page number

Parenthetical reference

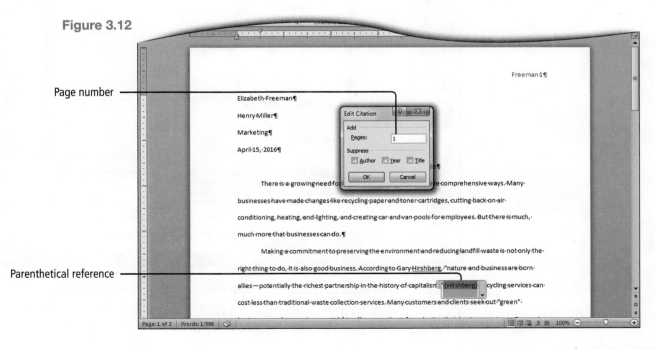

7 Click **OK** to display the page number of the citation. Click outside of the citation box to deselect it. Then type a period to the right of the citation, and delete the period to the left of the quotation mark.

> In the MLA style, if the reference occurs at the end of a sentence, the parenthetical reference always displays to the left of the punctuation mark that ends the sentence.

8 In the next paragraph, which begins *Government contractors*, click to position the insertion point at the end of the paragraph, but before the period.

9 In the **Citations & Bibliography group**, click the **Insert Citation** button, and then click **Add New Source**. Click the **Type of Source arrow**, scroll down as necessary, and then click **Web site**. Add the following information:

Author:	**Aitoro, Jill R.**
Name of Web Page:	**Nextgov - GSA drives green IT procurement**
Year:	**2008**
Month:	**February**
Day:	**21**
Year Accessed:	**2016**
Month Accessed:	**January**
Day Accessed:	**17**
URL:	**http://www.nextgov.com/nextgov/ng_20080221_8792.php**

10 Compare your screen with Figure 3.13, and then click **OK** to close the **Create Source** dialog box and add the citation.

> A parenthetical reference is added. Because the cited Web page has no page numbers, only the author name is used in the parenthetical reference.

Figure 3.13

Web site citation

Insertion point indicates location of parenthetical reference

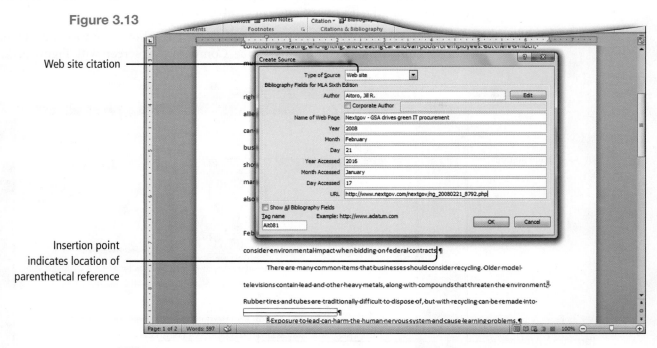

11 Near the top of **Page 2**, in the paragraph that begins *Consumers and businesses*, in the third line, click to position the insertion point following the word *toxic* to the left of the question mark.

12 In the **Citations & Bibliography group**, click the **Insert Citation** button, and then click **Add New Source**. Click the **Type of Source arrow**, if necessary scroll to the top of the list, click **Book**, and then add the following information:

Author:	**Scott, Nicky**
Title:	**Reduce, Reuse, Recycle: An Easy Household Guide**
Year:	**2007**
City:	**White River Junction, Vermont**
Publisher:	**Chelsea Green Publishing**

13 Click **OK**. Click the inserted citation to select it, click the **Citation Options arrow**, and then click **Edit Citation**.

14 In the **Edit Citation** dialog box, under **Add**, in the **Pages** box, type **7** to indicate that you are citing from page 7 of this source. Click **OK**.

15 On the **References tab**, in the **Citations & Bibliography group**, click the **Manage Sources** button. In the **Source Manager** dialog box, under **Current List**, click the third source and then compare your screen with Figure 3.14.

The Source Manager dialog box displays. Other citations on your computer display in the Master List box. The citations for the current document display in the Current List box. Word maintains the Master List so that if you use the same sources regularly, you can copy sources from your Master List to the current document. A preview of the selected bibliography entry also displays at the bottom of the dialog box.

Figure 3.14

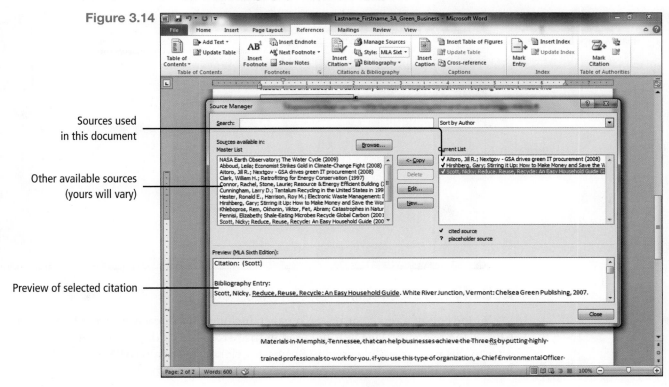

Sources used in this document

Other available sources (yours will vary)

Preview of selected citation

16 At the bottom of the **Source Manager** dialog box, click **Close**. Click anywhere in the document to deselect the parenthetical reference, and then **Save** your document.

Activity 3.05 | Inserting Page Breaks

In this activity you will insert a manual page break so that you can begin your bibliography on a new page.

1 Press `Ctrl` + `End` to move the insertion point to the end of the document. Notice that the insertion point displays at the end of the final paragraph, but above the footnote—the footnote is always associated with the page that contains the citation.

2 Press `Ctrl` + `Enter` to insert a manual page break.

> A *manual page break* forces a page to end at the insertion point location, and then places any subsequent text at the top of the next page. Recall that the new paragraph retains the formatting of the previous paragraph, so the first line is indented.

3 On the ruler, point to the **First Line Indent** button ▽, and then drag the **First Line Indent** button to the left to **0 inches on the horizontal ruler**.

4 Scroll as necessary to position the bottom of **Page 2** and the top of **Page 3** on your screen.

5 Compare your screen with Figure 3.15, and then **Save** 🖫 your document.

> A *page break indicator*, which shows where a manual page break was inserted, displays at the bottom of the Page 2, and the footnote remains on the page that contains the citation, even though it displays below the page break indicator.

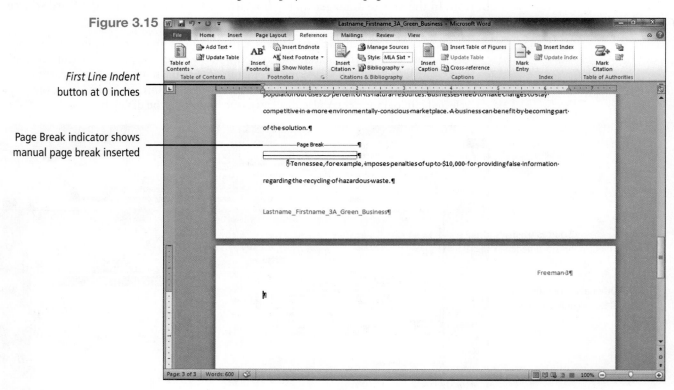

Figure 3.15

First Line Indent button at 0 inches

Page Break indicator shows manual page break inserted

Activity 3.06 | Creating a Reference Page

At the end of a report or research paper, include a list of each source referenced. *Works Cited* is the reference page heading used in the MLA style guidelines. Other styles may refer to this page as a *Bibliography* (Business Style) or *References* (APA Style). This information is always displayed on a separate page.

1 With the insertion point blinking in the first line of **Page 3**, type **Works Cited** and then press `Enter`. On the **References tab**, in the **Citations & Bibliography group**, in the **Style** box, be sure *MLA* displays.

2 In the **Citations & Bibliography group**, click the **Bibliography** button, and then near the bottom of the list, click **Insert Bibliography**.

3 Scroll as necessary to view the entire list of three references, and then click anywhere in the inserted text.

> The bibliography entries that you created display as a field, which is indicated by the gray shading when you click in the text. The field links to the Source Manager for the citations. The references display alphabetically by the author's last name.

4 In the bibliography, point to the left of the first entry—beginning *Aitoro, Jill*—to display the ⚐ pointer. Drag down to select all three references.

> **Another Way**
>
> Display the Paragraph dialog box. Under Spacing, click the Line spacing arrow, and then click Double. Under Spacing, in the After box, type **0**.

5 On the **Home tab**, in the **Paragraph group**, change the **Line spacing** to **2.0**, and then on the **Page Layout tab**, in the **Paragraph group**, change the **Spacing After** to **0 pt**.

> The entries display according to MLA guidelines; the text is double-spaced, the extra space between paragraphs is removed, and each entry uses a *hanging indent*—the first line of each entry extends 0.5 inch to the left of the remaining lines of the entry.

6 At the top of **Page 3**, right-click the *Works Cited* title, and then click the **Center** button ▤. Compare your screen with Figure 3.16, and then **Save** 🖫 your document.

> In MLA style, the *Works Cited* title is centered.

Figure 3.16

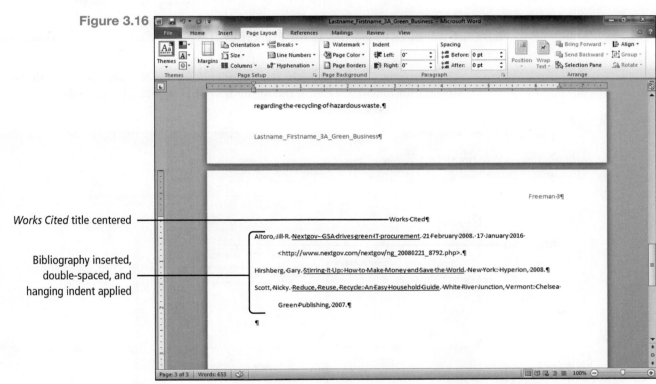

Works Cited title centered

Bibliography inserted, double-spaced, and hanging indent applied

Activity 3.07 | Managing Document Properties

Recall that document property information is stored in the Document Panel. An additional group of property categories is also available.

1 Display **Backstage** view. On the right, under the document thumbnail, click **Properties**, and then click **Show Document Panel** to display the **Document Panel**.

2 Type your name and course information, and then add the keywords **green business, research paper**

3 In the upper left corner of the **Document Panel**, click the **Document Properties** button, and then compare your screen with Figure 3.17.

Figure 3.17

Document Panel

Document Properties button

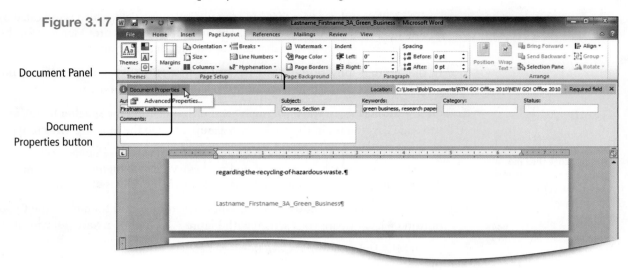

4 Click **Advanced Properties**. In the **Properties** dialog box, click the **Statistics tab**, and then compare your screen with Figure 3.18.

The document statistics show the number of revisions made to the document, the last time the document was edited, and the number of paragraphs, lines, words, and characters in the document.

Figure 3.18

Statistics tab

Document statistics (yours may vary)

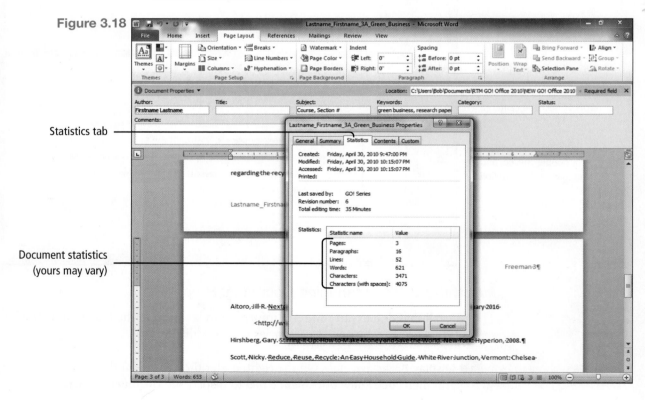

5 In the **Properties** dialog box, click the **Summary tab**. Notice that not all of the categories are filled in, and also notice that there are categories on this tab that are not found in the Document Panel.

Some of the boxes may contain information from your computer system.

6 In the **Properties** dialog box, click in the **Title** box and type **Going Green Benefits Business**

7 Click in the **Manager** box and type **Henry Miller**

8 In the **Company** box, select and delete any existing text, and then type **Memphis Primary Materials**

9 Click in the **Category** box and type **Marketing Documents**

10 Click in the **Comments** box and type **Draft copy of a research report that will be included in the marketing materials packet**

> Additional information categories are available by clicking the Custom tab.

11 Compare your screen with Figure 3.19, and then at the bottom of the **Properties** dialog box, click **OK**.

Figure 3.19

Summary tab

Properties not available on Document Information Panel

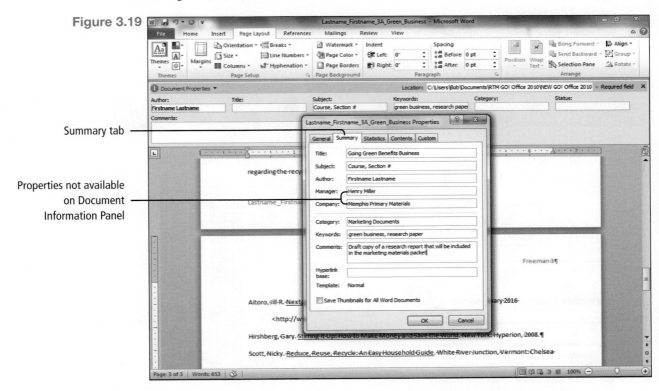

12 **Close** ☒ the **Document Panel**. Press Ctrl + F2, and then examine the three pages of your document in **Print Preview**. Redisplay your document.
If necessary, make any corrections or adjustments.

13 **Save** 💾 your document, and then print or submit electronically as directed by your instructor. **Exit** Word.

End You have completed Project 3A _____

Project 3B Newsletter with Mailing Labels

myitlab
Project 3B Training

Project Activities

In Activities 3.08 through 3.17, you will edit a newsletter that Memphis Primary Materials sends to its list of customers and subscribers. Your completed documents will look similar to Figure 3.20.

Project Files

For Project 3B, you will need the following files:

New blank Word document
w03B_Memphis_Newsletter
w03B_Addresses

You will save your documents as:

Lastname_Firstname_3B_Memphis_Newsletter
Lastname_Firstname_3B_Mailing_Labels
Lastname_Firstname_3B_Addresses

Project Results

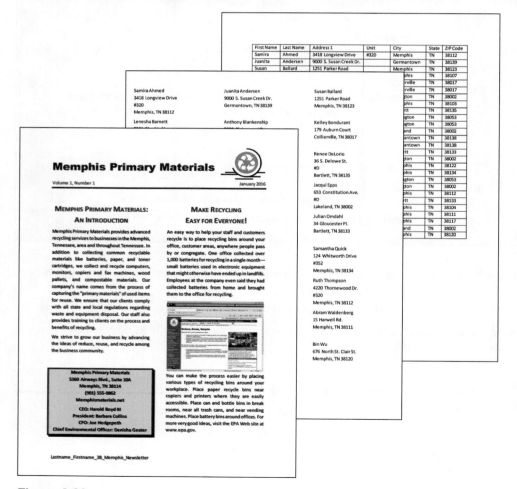

Figure 3.20
Project 3B Memphis Newsletter

Objective 4 | Format a Multiple-Column Newsletter

All newspapers and most magazines and newsletters use multiple columns for articles because text in narrower columns is easier to read than text that stretches across a page. Word has a tool with which you can change a single column of text into two or more columns, and then format the columns. If a column does not end where you want it to, you can end the column at a location of your choice by inserting a ***manual column break***.

Activity 3.08 | Changing One Column of Text to Two Columns

Newsletters are usually two or three columns wide. When using 8.5 × 11-inch paper in portrait orientation, avoid creating four or more columns because they are so narrow that word spacing looks awkward, often resulting in one long word on a line by itself.

1 **Start** Word. From your student files, locate and open the document **w03B_Memphis_ Newsletter**. If necessary, display the formatting marks and rulers. **Save** the file in your **Word Chapter 3** folder as **Lastname_Firstname_3B_Memphis_Newsletter** and then add the file name to the footer.

2 Select the first paragraph of text—*Memphis Primary Materials*. From the Mini toolbar, change the **Font** to **Arial Black** and the **Font Size** to **24**.

3 Select the first two paragraphs—the title and the Volume information and date. From the Mini toolbar, click the **Font Color button arrow** [A ▾], and then under **Theme Colors**, in the fifth column, click the last color—**Blue, Accent 1, Darker 50%**.

4 With the text still selected, on the **Home tab**, in the **Paragraph group**, click the **Borders button arrow**, and then at the bottom, click **Borders and Shading**.

5 In the **Borders and Shading** dialog box, on the **Borders tab**, click the **Color arrow**, and then under **Theme Colors**, in the fifth column, click the last color—**Blue, Accent 1, Darker 50%**.

Another Way

In the Preview area, click the Bottom Border button.

6 Click the **Width arrow**, and then click **3 pt**. In the **Preview** box at the right, point to the *bottom* border of the small preview and click one time. Compare your screen with Figure 3.21.

Figure 3.21

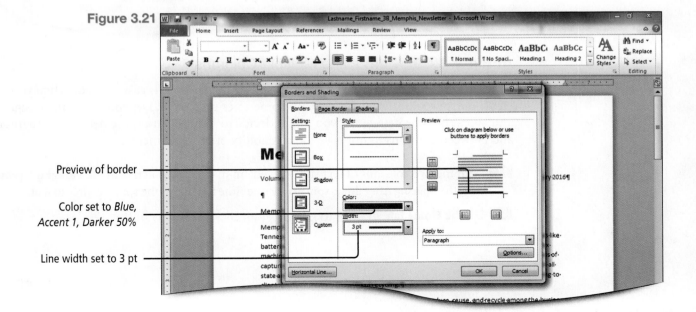

Preview of border

Color set to *Blue, Accent 1, Darker 50%*

Line width set to 3 pt

7 In the **Borders and Shading** dialog box, click **OK**.

The line visually defines the newsletter *nameplate*—the banner on the front page of a newsletter that identifies the publication.

8 Below the nameplate, beginning with the paragraph *Memphis Primary Materials: An Introduction*, select all of the text to the end of the document, which extends to two pages.

9 On the **Page Layout tab**, in the **Page Setup group**, click the **Columns** button. From the **Columns** gallery, click **Two**.

10 Scroll up to view the top of **Page 1**, and then compare your screen with Figure 3.22, and then **Save** 💾 the document.

Word divides the text into two columns, and inserts a ***section break*** below the nameplate, dividing the one-column section of the document from the two-column section of the document. A ***section*** is a portion of a document that can be formatted differently from the rest of the document. A section break marks the end of one section and the beginning of another section. Do not be concerned if your columns do not break at the same line as shown in the figure.

Figure 3.22

Section break inserted

Text displays in two columns

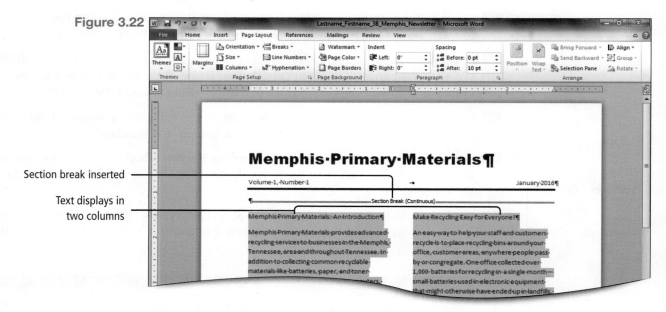

Activity 3.09 | Formatting Multiple Columns

The uneven right margin of a single page-width column is easy to read. When you create narrow columns, justified text is sometimes preferable. Depending on the design and layout of your newsletter, you might decide to reduce extra space between paragraphs and between columns to improve the readability of the document.

1 With the two columns of text still selected, on the **Page Layout tab**, in the **Paragraph group**, click the **Spacing After down spin arrow** one time to change the spacing after to **6 pt**.

2 On the **Home tab**, in the **Paragraph group**, click the **Justify** button 🔲.

3 Click anywhere in the document to deselect the text, and then compare your screen with Figure 3.23. **Save** 🖫 the document.

Figure 3.23

Column text justified

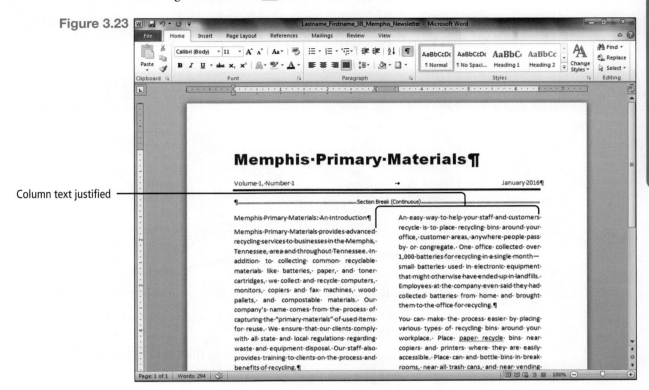

More Knowledge | Justifying Column Text

Although many magazines and newspapers still justify text in columns, there are a variety of opinions about whether to justify the columns, or to use left alignment and leave the right edge uneven. Justified text tends to look more formal and cleaner, but in a word processing document, it also results in uneven spacing between words. It is the opinion of some authorities that justified text is more difficult to read, especially in a page-width document. Let the overall look and feel of your newsletter be your guide.

Activity 3.10 | Inserting a Column Break

1 Scroll down to view the lower portion of the page. In the first column, locate the company address that begins with the paragraph *Memphis Primary Materials*, and then select that paragraph and the three following paragraphs, ending with the telephone number.

2 On the **Page Layout tab**, in the **Paragraph group**, click the **Spacing After down spin arrow** one time to change the spacing after to **0 pt**.

3 Select the three paragraphs that begin with *CEO* and end with *CFO*, and then in the **Paragraph group**, change the **Spacing After** to **0 pt**.

4 Near the bottom of the first column, click to position the insertion point at the beginning of the line that begins *Make Recycling*.

5 On the **Page Layout tab**, in the **Page Setup group**, click the **Breaks** button to display the gallery of Page Breaks and Section Breaks. Compare your screen with Figure 3.24.

Figure 3.24

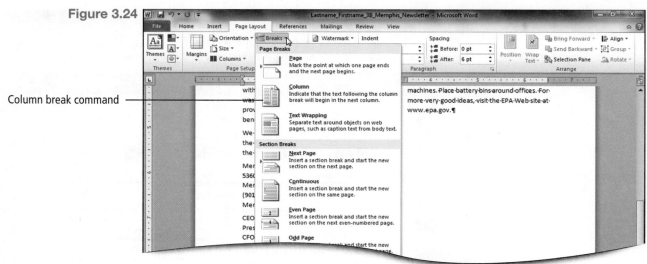

Column break command

6 Under **Page Breaks**, click **Column**. Scroll to view the bottom of the first column.

A column break displays at the insertion point; text to the right of the insertion point moves to the top of the next column.

7 Compare your screen with Figure 3.25, and then **Save** 🖫 the document.

A *column break indicator*—a dotted line containing the words *Column Break*—displays at the bottom of the column.

Figure 3.25

Manual column break inserted

Activity 3.11 | Inserting a Clip Art Image

Clip art images—predefined graphics included with Microsoft Office or downloaded from the Web—can make your document visually appealing and more interesting.

1 Press [Ctrl] + [Home]. On the **Insert tab**, in the **Illustrations group**, click the **Clip Art** button to display the **Clip Art** task pane on the right of your screen.

2 In the **Clip Art** task pane, click in the **Search for** box, and then replace any existing text with **environmental awareness** so that Word can search for images that contain the keywords *environmental* and *awareness*.

3 In the **Clip Art** task pane, click the **Results should be arrow**. Be sure the **Illustrations** check box is selected, and then click as necessary to clear the *Photographs*, *Videos*, and *Audio* check boxes. Click the **Results should be** arrow again to collapse the list. Be sure the **Include Office.com content** check box is selected.

4 In the **Clip Art** task pane, click the **Go** button. Locate the image of the three white arrows in a blue circle. Click on the image to insert it, and then compare your screen with Figure 3.26.

> Recall that when you insert a graphic, it is inserted as an inline object; that is, it is treated as a character in a line of text. Here, the inserted clip art becomes the first character in the nameplate.

Figure 3.26

Clip Art task pane

Search term

Selected image

Image inserted in document

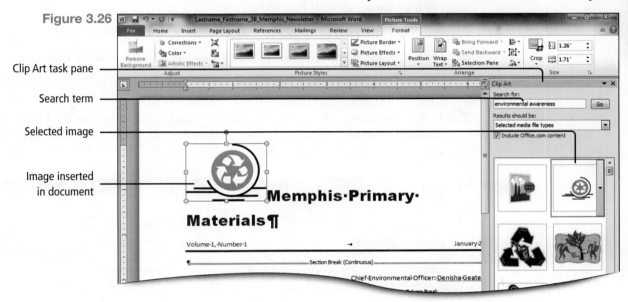

5 **Close** ☒ the **Clip Art** task pane. With the image still selected, on the **Format tab**, in the **Size group**, click in the **Shape Height** box, type **1** and then press Enter. In the **Arrange group**, click the **Wrap Text** button, and then click **Square**.

6 Point to the image to display the 🔁 pointer, and then drag the image to the right so that the bottom edge aligns slightly above *January 2016*, and the right side aligns with the right margin. Recall that you can press the arrow keys as necessary to move the image in small, precise increments.

7 Compare your screen with Figure 3.27, and then **Save** 💾 the document.

Figure 3.27

Image resized

Text wrapping applied to image

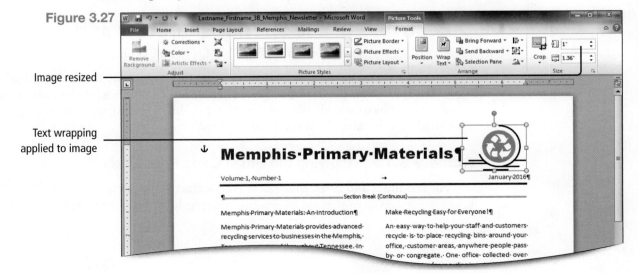

Activity 3.12 | Inserting a Screenshot

A ***screenshot*** is an image of an active window on your computer that you can paste into a document. Screenshots are especially useful when you want to insert an image of a Web site into a document you are creating in Word. You can insert a screenshot of any open window on your computer.

1 In the second column, click to position the insertion point at the beginning of the paragraph that begins *You can make*. Open your Internet browser, and then in the address bar type **www.epa.gov/osw/conserve/rrr** and press Enter. Maximize [■] the browser window, if necessary.

2 From the taskbar, redisplay your **3B_Memphis_Newletter** document.

3 On the **Insert tab**, in the **Illustrations group**, click the **Screenshot** button.

All of your open windows display in the Available Windows gallery and are available to paste into the document.

4 In the **Screenshot** gallery, click the browser window that contains the EPA site to insert the screenshot at the insertion point, and notice that the image resizes to fit between the column margins. Compare your screen with Figure 3.28. **Save** [■] the document.

Figure 3.28

Screenshot inserted in document

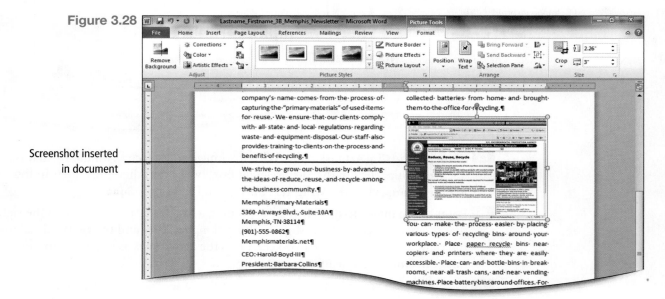

Objective 5 | Use Special Character and Paragraph Formatting

Special text and paragraph formatting is useful to emphasize text, and it makes your newsletter look more professional. For example, you can place a border around one or more paragraphs or add shading to a paragraph. When adding shading, use light colors; dark shading can make the text difficult to read.

Activity 3.13 | Applying the Small Caps Font Effect

For headlines and titles, ***small caps*** is an attractive font effect. The effect changes lowercase letters to uppercase letters, but with the height of lowercase letters.

1. At the top of the first column, select the paragraph *Memphis Primary Materials: An Introduction* including the paragraph mark.

2. Right-click the selected text, and then from the shortcut menu, click **Font**. In the **Font** dialog box, click the **Font color arrow**, and then under **Theme Colors**, in the fifth column, click the last color—**Blue, Accent 1, Darker 50%**.

3. Under **Font style**, click **Bold**. Under **Size**, click **18**. Under **Effects**, select the **Small caps** check box. Compare your screen with Figure 3.29.

> The Font dialog box provides more options than are available on the Ribbon and enables you to make several changes at the same time. In the Preview box, the text displays with the selected formatting options applied.

Figure 3.29

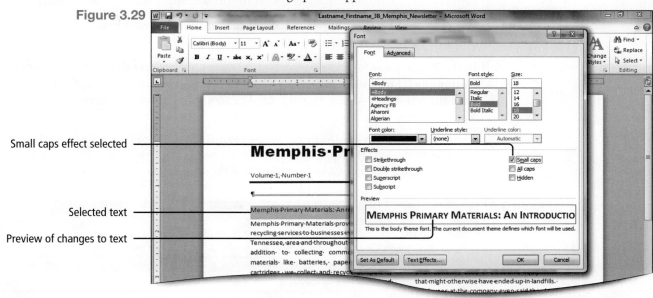

Small caps effect selected

Selected text

Preview of changes to text

4. Click **OK**. Right-click the selected text, and then on the Mini toolbar, click **Center**.

5. With the text still selected, right-click, and then on the Mini toolbar, click the **Format Painter** button. Then, with the pointer, at the top of the second column, select the paragraph *Make Recycling Easy for Everyone!* to apply the same formats. Notice that the column title wraps placing a single word on the second line.

6. Position the insertion point to the right of the word *Recycling*, and then press Del to remove the space. Hold down Shift and then press Enter.

> Holding down Shift while pressing Enter inserts a ***manual line break***, which moves the text to the right of the insertion point to a new line while keeping the text in the same paragraph. A ***line break indicator***, in the shape of a bent arrow, indicates that a manual line break was inserted.

7. Compare your screen with Figure 3.30, and then **Save** the document.

Figure 3.30

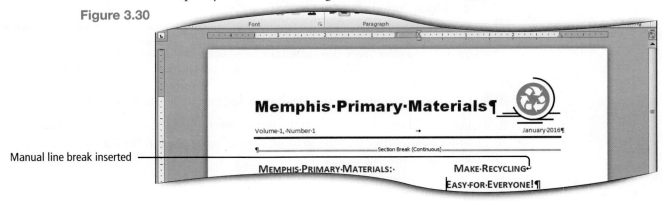

Manual line break inserted

Activity 3.14 | Adding a Border and Shading to a Paragraph

Paragraph borders provide strong visual cues to the reader. Paragraph shading can be used with or without borders. When used with a border, light shading can be very effective in drawing the reader's eye to the text.

1 In the first column, in the paragraph that begins *We strive to grow*, click to position the insertion point at the end of the paragraph, and then press Enter one time.

2 At the bottom of the column, select the nine lines of company information, beginning with *Memphis Primary Materials* and ending with the paragraph that begins *Chief Environmental*. On the Mini toolbar, apply **Bold** **B** and **Center** ≡.

3 With the text still selected, on the **Home tab**, in the **Paragraph group**, click the **Borders button arrow** ⊞▼, and then click **Borders and Shading**.

4 In the **Borders and Shading** dialog box, be sure the **Borders tab** is selected. Under **Setting**, click **Shadow**. If necessary, click the **Color arrow**, and then in the fifth column, click the last color—**Blue, Accent 1, Darker 50%**. Click the **Width arrow**, and then click **3 pt**. Compare your screen with Figure 3.31.

In the lower right portion of the Borders and Shading dialog box, the *Apply to* box displays *Paragraph*. The *Apply to* box directs where the border will be applied—in this instance, the border will be applied only to the selected paragraphs.

Figure 3.31

Preview of paragraph border

Shadow border selected

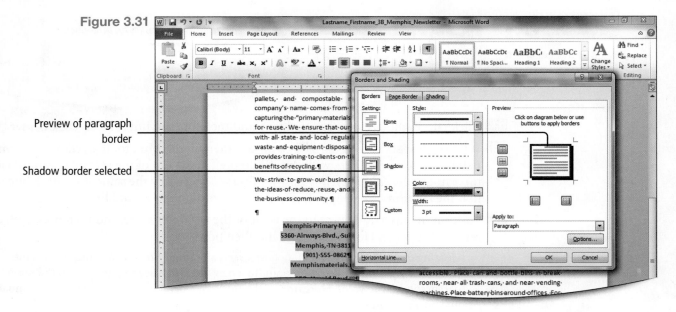

Note | Adding Simple Borders to Text

You can add simple borders from the Borders button gallery, located in the Paragraph group. This button offers less control over the border appearance, however, because the line thickness and color applied will match whatever was last used on this computer. The Borders and Shading dialog box enables you to make your own custom selections.

---

5 At the top of the **Borders and Shading** dialog box, click the **Shading tab**.

6 Click the **Fill arrow**, and then in the fifth column, click the second color—**Blue, Accent 1, Lighter 80%**. Notice that the shading change is reflected in the Preview area on the right side of the dialog box.

7 At the bottom of the **Borders and Shading** dialog box, click **OK**. Click anywhere in the document to deselect the text, and then compare your screen with Figure 3.32.

Figure 3.32

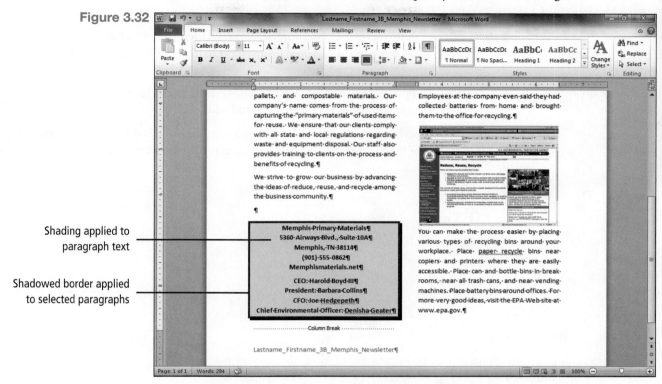

Shading applied to paragraph text

Shadowed border applied to selected paragraphs

8 From **Backstage** view, display the **Document Panel**.

9 In the **Author** box, delete any text and then type your firstname and lastname. In the **Subject** box, type your course name and section number, and in the **Keywords** box, type **newsletter, January Close** ☒ the **Document Panel**.

10 Press Ctrl + F2 to view the **Print Preview. Close** the preview, make any necessary corrections, and then click **Save** 🖫. **Exit** Word; hold this file until you complete this Project.

Objective 6 | Create Mailing Labels Using Mail Merge

Word's *mail merge* feature joins a *main document* and a *data source* to create customized letters or labels. The main document contains the text or formatting that remains constant. For labels, the main document contains the formatting for a specific label size. The data source contains information including the names and addresses of the individuals for whom the labels are being created. Names and addresses in a data source might come from a Word table, an Excel spreadsheet, or an Access database.

The easiest way to perform a mail merge is to use the Mail Merge Wizard, which asks you questions and, based on your answers, walks you step by step through the mail merge process.

Activity 3.15 | Opening the Mail Merge Wizard Template

In this activity, you will open the data source for the mail merge, which is a Word table containing names and addresses.

1 **Start** Word and display a new blank document. Display formatting marks and rulers. **Save** the document in your **Word Chapter 3** folder as **Lastname_Firstname_3B_Mailing_Labels**

2 With your new document open on the screen, **Open** the file **w03B_Addresses**. **Save** the address file in your **Word Chapter 3** folder as **Lastname_Firstname_3B_Addresses** and then add the file name to the footer.

> This document contains a table of addresses. The first row contains the column names. The remaining rows contain the names and addresses.

3 Click to position the insertion point in the last cell in the table, and then press Tab to create a new row. Enter the following information, and then compare your table with Figure 3.33:

First Name	**John**
Last Name	**Wisniewski**
Address 1	**1226 Snow Road**
Address 2	**#234**
City	**Lakeland**
State	**TN**
ZIP Code	**38002**

Figure 3.33

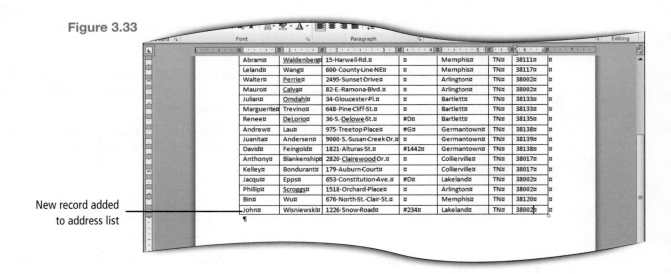

New record added to address list

4 **Save** , and then **Close** the table of addresses. Be sure your blank **Lastname_Firstname_3B_Mailing_Labels** document displays.

5 Click the **Mailings tab**. In the **Start Mail Merge group**, click the **Start Mail Merge** button, and then click **Step by Step Mail Merge Wizard** to display the **Mail Merge** task pane.

6 Under **Select document type**, click the **Labels** option button. At the bottom of the task pane, click **Next: Starting document** to display Step 2 of 6 of the Mail Merge Wizard.

7 Under **Select starting document**, be sure **Change document layout** is selected, and then under **Change document layout**, click **Label options**.

8 In the **Label Options** dialog box, under **Printer information**, click the **Tray arrow**, and then click **Default tray (Automatically Select)**—the exact wording may vary depending on your printer, but select the *Default* or *Automatic* option—to print the labels on regular paper rather than manually inserting labels in the printer.

9 Under **Label information**, click the **Label vendors arrow**, and then click **Avery US Letter**. Under **Product number**, scroll about halfway down the list, and then click **5160 Easy Peel Address Labels**. Compare your screen with Figure 3.34.

> The Avery 5160 address label is a commonly used label. The precut sheets contain three columns of 10 labels each—for a total of 30 labels per sheet.

Figure 3.34

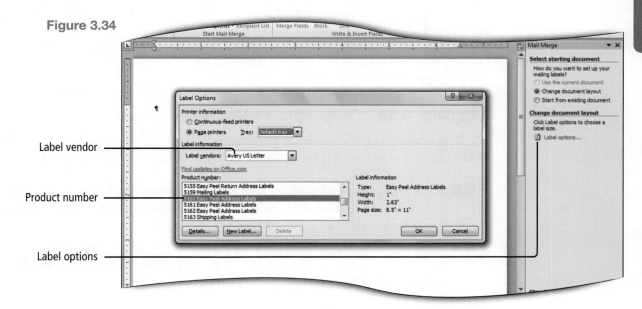

Label vendor

Product number

Label options

10 At the bottom of the **Label Options** dialog box, click **OK**. If a message box displays, click OK to set up the labels. At the bottom of the task pane, click **Next: Select recipients**.

> The label page is set up with three columns and ten rows. The label borders may or may not display on your screen, depending on your settings. Here in Step 3 of the Mail Merge Wizard, you must identify the recipients—the data source. For your recipient data source, you can choose to use an existing list—for example, a list of names and addresses that you have in an Access database, an Excel worksheet, a Word table, or your Outlook contacts list. If you do not have an existing data source, you can type a new list at this point in the wizard.

11 If gridlines do not display, click the **Layout tab**. In the **Table group**, click the **View Gridlines** button, and then notice that each label is outlined with a dashed line. If you cannot see the right and left edges of the page, in the status bar, click the **Zoom Out** button as necessary to see the right and left edges of the label sheet on your screen.

12 Under **Select recipients**, be sure the **Use an existing list** option button is selected. Under **Use an existing list**, click **Browse**.

13 Navigate to your **Word Chapter 3** folder, select your **Lastname_Firstname_3B_ Addresses** file, and then click **Open** to display the **Mail Merge Recipients** dialog box.

> In the Mail Merge Recipients dialog box, the column headings are formed from the text in the first row of your Word table of addresses. Each row of information that contains data for one person is referred to as a *record*. The column headings—for example, *Last_Name* and *First_Name*—are referred to as *fields*. An underscore replaces the spaces between words in the field name headings.

14 Compare your screen with Figure 3.35.

Figure 3.35

Mail Merge Recipients dialog box

Gridlines indicate label borders

Path containing your file name

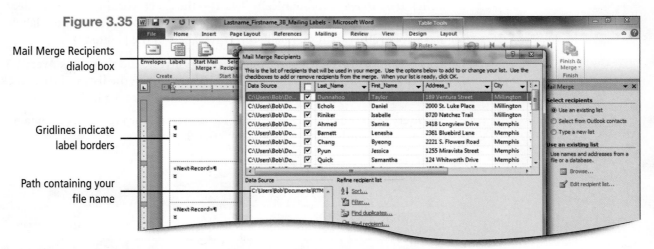

Activity 3.16 | Completing the Mail Merge Wizard

You can add or edit names and addresses while completing the Mail Merge Wizard. You can also match your column names with preset names used in Mail Merge.

1 In the lower left portion of the **Mail Merge Recipients** dialog box, in the **Data Source** box, click the path that contains your file name. Then, at the bottom of the **Mail Merge Recipients** dialog box, click **Edit**.

2 In the upper right corner of the **Data Form** dialog box, click **Add New**. In the blank record, type the following, pressing Tab to move from field to field, and then compare your **Data Form** dialog box with Figure 3.36.

First_Name	**Susan**
Last_Name	**Ballard**
Address_1	**1251 Parker Road**
Unit:	
City	**Memphis**
State	**TN**
ZIP_Code	**38123**

Figure 3.36

New record

Edit button

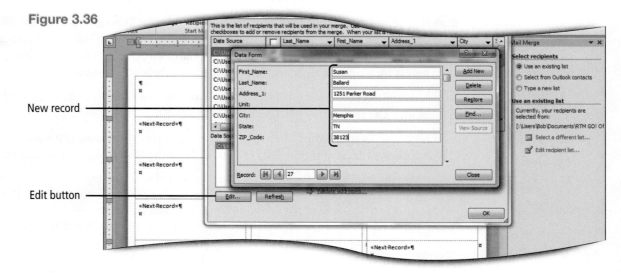

3 In the lower right corner of the **Data Form** dialog box, click **Close**. Scroll to the end of the recipient list to confirm that the record for *Susan Ballard* that you just added is in the list. At the bottom of the **Mail Merge Recipients** dialog box, click **OK**.

4 At the bottom of the **Mail Merge** task pane, click **Next: Arrange your labels**.

5 Under **Arrange your labels**, click **Address block**. In the **Insert Address Block** dialog box, under **Specify address elements**, examine the various formats for names. If necessary, under *Insert recipient's name in this format*, select the *Joshua Randall Jr.* format. Compare your dialog box with Figure 3.37.

Figure 3.37

Format selected

Preview of address block

Match Fields button

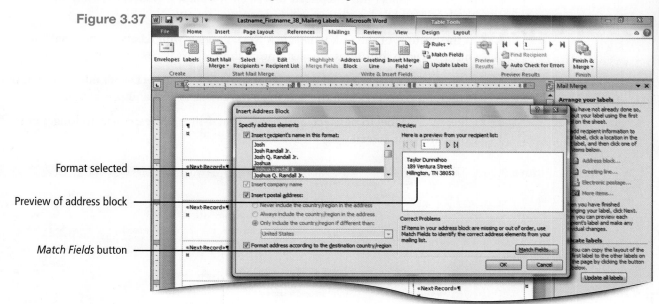

6 In the lower right corner of the **Insert Address Block** dialog box, click **Match Fields**.

If your field names are descriptive, the Mail Merge program will identify them correctly, as is the case with most of the information in the *Required for Address Block* section. However, the Address 2 field is unmatched—in the source file, this column is named *Unit*.

7 Scroll down and examine the dialog box, and then compare your screen with Figure 3.38.

Figure 3.38

Address 2 unmatched

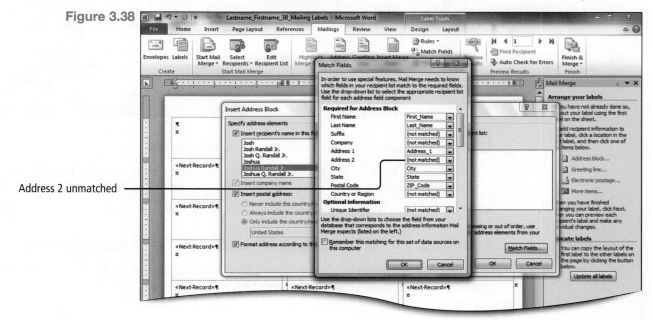

8 Click the **Address 2 arrow**, and then from the list of available fields, click **Unit** to match the Mail Merge field with the field in your data source.

9 At the bottom of the **Match Fields** dialog box, click **OK**. At the bottom of the **Insert Address Block** dialog box, click **OK**.

Word inserts the Address block in the first label space surrounded by double angle brackets. The *AddressBlock* field name displays, which represents the address block you saw in the Preview area of the Insert Address Block dialog box.

10 In the task pane, under **Replicate labels**, click **Update all labels** to insert an address block in each label space for each subsequent record.

11 At the bottom of the task pane, click **Next: Preview your labels**. Notice that for addresses with four lines, the last line of the address is cut off.

12 Press Ctrl + A to select all of the label text, click the **Page Layout tab**, and then in the **Paragraph group**, click in the **Spacing Before** box. Type **3** and press Enter.

13 Click in any label to deselect, and notice that 4-line addresses are no longer cut off. Compare your screen with Figure 3.39.

Figure 3.39

Preview of mailing labels

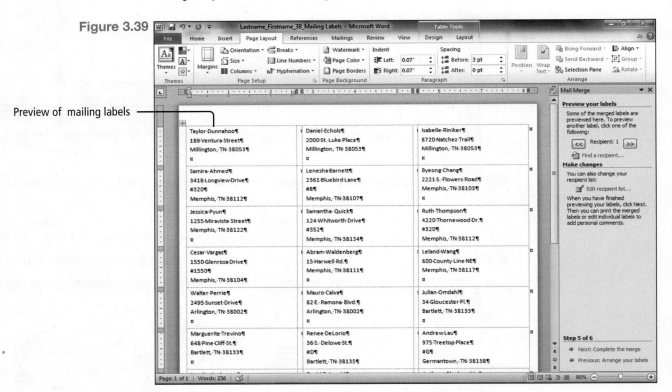

14 At the bottom of the task pane, click **Next: Complete the merge**.

Step 6 of the Mail Merge task pane displays. At this point you can print or edit your labels, although this is done more easily in the document window.

15 **Save** your labels, and then **Close** the **Mail Merge** task pane.

Activity 3.17 | Previewing and Printing the Mail Merge Document

If you discover that you need to make further changes to your labels, you can still make them even though the Mail Merge task pane is closed.

1 Add the file name to the footer, close the footer area, and then move to the top of Page 2. Click anywhere in the empty table row, click the **Layout tab**, in the **Rows & Columns group**, click the **Delete** button, and then click **Delete Rows**.

Adding footer text to a label sheet replaces the last row of labels on a page with the footer text, and moves the last row of labels to the top of the next page. In this instance, a blank second page is created, which you can delete by deleting the blank row.

2 Press $\boxed{Ctrl}$ + $\boxed{F2}$ to display the **Print Preview**. Notice that the labels do not display in alphabetical order.

3 Click the **Mailings tab**, and then in the **Start Mail Merge group**, click the **Edit Recipient List** button to display the list of names and addresses.

4 In the **Mail Merge Recipients** dialog box, click the **Last_Name** field heading, and notice that the names are sorted alphabetically by the recipient's last name.

Mailing labels are often sorted by either last name or by ZIP Code.

5 Click the **Last_Name** field heading again, and notice that the last names are sorted in descending order. Click the **Last_Name** field one more time to return to ascending order, and then click **OK**. Press $\boxed{Ctrl}$ + $\boxed{Home}$, and then compare your screen with Figure 3.40.

Figure 3.40

Labels in alphabetical order

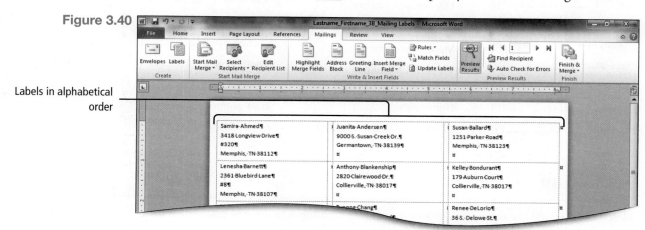

6 From **Backstage** view, display the **Document Panel**. In the **Author** box, delete any text and then type your firstname and lastname. In the **Subject** box, type your course name and section number, and in the **Keywords** box type **newsletter mailing labels** **Close** ☒ the **Document Panel**.

7 Click **Save** 🔲. Display **Backstage** view, and then click the **Print tab**. Examine the **Print Preview** on the right side of the window.

8 As directed by your instructor, print or submit electronically.

If you print, the labels will print on whatever paper is in the printer; unless you have preformatted labels available, the labels will print on a sheet of paper. Printing the labels on plain paper enables you to proofread the labels before you print them on more expensive label sheets.

9 **Close** the document, click **Yes** to save the data source, and then if necessary, click **Save** to save the labels.

10 In addition to your labels and address document, print or submit your **3B_Memphis_ Newsletter** document as directed. **Exit** Word.

End You have completed Project 3B

Content-Based Assessments

Summary

In this chapter, you created a research paper using the MLA style. You added a header, footnotes, citations, and a bibliography, and changed the footnote style. You created a newsletter that used multiple columns. You added a column break, a page break, and a manual line break. You added special font effects, and added a border and shading to a paragraph. Finally, you used the Mail Merge Wizard to create a set of mailing labels for the newsletter.

Key Terms

Matching

Match each term in the second column with its correct definition in the first column by writing the letter of the term on the blank line in front of the correct definition.

_____ 1. A manual that contains standards for the design and writing of documents.

_____ 2. One of two commonly used style guides for formatting research papers.

_____ 3. An image of an active window on your computer that you can paste into a document.

_____ 4. In a research paper, information that expands on the topic, but that does not fit well in the document text.

_____ 5. In a research paper, a note placed at the bottom of the page.

_____ 6. In a research paper, a note placed at the end of a document or chapter.

_____ 7. A list of cited works in a report or research paper, also referred to as *Works Cited*, *Sources*, or *References*, depending upon the report style.

_____ 8. In the MLA style, a list of cited works placed at the end of a research paper or report.

_____ 9. A group of formatting commands, such as font, font size, font color, paragraph alignment, and line spacing that can be applied to a paragraph with one command.

_____ 10. A note, inserted into the text of a research paper that refers the reader to a source in the bibliography.

_____ 11. In the MLA style, a citation that refers to items on the *Works Cited* page, and which is placed in parentheses; the citation includes the last name of the author or authors, and the page number in the referenced source.

A American Psychological Association (APA)

B Bibliography

C Citation

D Endnote

E Footnote

F Hanging indent

G Manual column break

H Manual page break

I Note

J Page break indicator

K Parenthetical reference

L Screenshot

M Style

N Style guide

O Works Cited

Content-Based Assessments

_____ 12. The action of forcing a page to end and placing subsequent text at the top of the next page.

_____ 13. A dotted line with the text *Page Break* that indicates where a manual page break was inserted.

_____ 14. An indent style in which the first line of a paragraph extends to the left of the remaining lines, and that is commonly used for bibliographic entries.

_____ 15. An artificial end to a column to balance columns or to provide space for the insertion of other objects.

Multiple Choice

Circle the correct answer.

1. Column text that is aligned to both the left and right margins is referred to as:
   A. centered
   B. justified
   C. indented

2. The banner on the front page of a newsletter that identifies the publication is the:
   A. heading
   B. nameplate
   C. title

3. A portion of a document that can be formatted differently from the rest of the document is a:
   A. tabbed list
   B. paragraph
   C. section

4. A font effect, commonly used in titles, that changes lowercase text into uppercase letters using a reduced font size is:
   A. Small Caps
   B. Level 2 Head
   C. Bevel

5. To end a line before the normal end of the line, without creating a new paragraph, hold down the Shift key while pressing the:
   A. Enter key
   B. Ctrl key
   C. Alt key

6. The nonprinting symbol that displays where a manual line break is inserted is the:
   A. short arrow
   B. bent arrow
   C. anchor

7. In mail merge, the document that contains the text or formatting that remains constant is the:
   A. data source
   B. mailing list
   C. main document

8. In mail merge, the list of variable information, such as names and addresses, that is merged with a main document to create customized form letters or labels is the:
   A. data source
   B. mailing list
   C. main document

9. In mail merge, a row of information that contains data for one person is a:
   A. record
   B. field
   C. label

10. To perform a mail merge using Word's step-by-step guided process, use the:
    A. Mail Merge Template
    B. Mail Merge Management Source
    C. Mail Merge Wizard

Content-Based Assessments

Apply **3A** skills from these Objectives:

1. Create a Research Paper
2. Insert Footnotes in a Research Paper
3. Create Citations and a Bibliography in a Research Paper

Skills Review | Project **3C** Recycling Report

In the following Skills Review, you will format and edit a research paper for Memphis Primary Materials. The research topic is recycling in the natural environment. Your completed document will look similar to Figure 3.41.

Project Files

For Project 3C, you will need the following file:

w03C_Recycling_Report

You will save your document as:

Lastname_Firstname_3C_Recycling_Report

Project Results

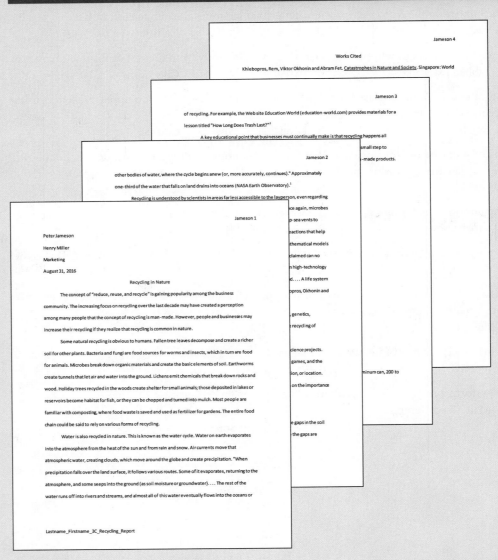

Figure 3.41

(Project 3C Recycling Report continues on the next page)

Content-Based Assessments

Skills Review | Project 3C Recycling Report (continued)

1 **Start** Word. From your student files, locate and open the document **w03C_Recycling_Report**. Display the formatting marks and rulers. **Save** the file in your **Word Chapter 3** folder as **Lastname_Firstname_3C_Recycling_Report**

a. Press Ctrl + A. On the **Home tab**, in the **Paragraph group**, click the **Line spacing** button, and then change the line spacing to **2.0**. On the **Page Layout tab**, in the **Paragraph group**, change the **Spacing After** to **0 pt**.

b. Press Ctrl + Home, press Enter to create a blank line at the top of the document, and then click to position the insertion point in the blank line. Type **Peter Jameson** and then press Enter. Type **Henry Miller** and then press Enter. Type **Marketing** and then press Enter. Type **August 31, 2016** and then press Enter.

c. Type **Recycling in Nature** and then right-click anywhere in the title you just typed. From the Mini toolbar, **Center** the title.

d. Near the top of **Page 1**, locate the paragraph beginning *The concept of*, and then click to position the insertion point at the beginning of the paragraph. Scroll to the end of the document, hold down Shift, and then click to the right of the last paragraph mark to select all of the text from the insertion point to the end of the document. On the horizontal ruler, drag the **First Line Indent** button to **0.5″**.

e. On **Page 1**, point to the top margin area and right-click. Click **Edit Header**. In the header area, type **Jameson** and then press Spacebar.

f. On the **Design tab**, in the **Header & Footer group**, click the **Page Number** button, and then point to **Current Position**. In the displayed gallery, under **Simple**, click **Plain Number**. On the **Home tab**, in the **Paragraph group**, click the **Align Text Right** button.

g. Click the **Design tab**, and then in the **Navigation group**, click the **Go to Footer** button. In the **Insert group**, click the **Quick Parts** button, and then click **Field**. In the **Field** dialog box, under **Field names**, locate and click **FileName**, and then click **OK**.

h. Double-click anywhere outside the footer area. **Save** your document.

2 Scroll to view the top of **Page 2**, locate the paragraph that ends *drains into oceans*, and then click to position the

insertion point to the right of the period following *oceans*. On the **References tab**, in the **Footnotes group**, click the **Insert Footnote** button.

a. Type **Groundwater is found in two layers of the soil, the "zone of aeration," where gaps in the soil are filled with both air and water, and, further down, the "zone of saturation," where the gaps are completely filled with water.**

b. In the lower half of **Page 2**, locate the paragraph that begins *School students*. Click to position the insertion point at the end of the paragraph and insert a footnote.

c. As the footnote text, type **A wool sock will last one year in a landfill; a soup can, 80 to 100 years; an aluminum can, 200 to 500 years; and plastic rings from a six–pack of cans, 450 years. Save** your document.

d. At the bottom of **Page 2**, right-click anywhere in either footnote. From the shortcut menu, click **Style**. In the **Style** dialog box, click the **Modify** button. In the **Modify Style** dialog box, locate the small Formatting toolbar in the center of the dialog box, click the **Font Size button arrow**, and then click **11**.

e. In the lower left corner of the dialog box, click the **Format** button, and then click **Paragraph**. In the **Paragraph** dialog box, under **Indentation**, click the **Special arrow**, and then click **First line**. Under **Spacing**, click the **Line spacing button arrow**, and then click **Double**.

f. Click **OK** to close the **Paragraph** dialog box, click **OK** to close the **Modify Style** dialog box, and then click **Apply** to apply the new style. Notice that the second footnote moves to **Page 3**. **Save** your document.

3 Scroll to view the top of **Page 2**, and then locate the footnote marker at the end of the second line of text. Click to position the insertion point to the left of the period at the end of the paragraph.

a. On the **References tab**, in the **Citations & Bibliography group**, click the **Style button arrow**, and then click **MLA** to insert a reference using MLA style. Click the **Insert Citation** button, and then click **Add New Source**. Click the **Type of Source arrow**,

(Project 3C Recycling Report continues on the next page)

and then click **Web site**. Select the **Corporate Author** check box, and then add the following information (type the URL on one line):

Corporate Author:	**NASA Earth Observatory**
Name of Web Page:	**The Water Cycle**
Year:	**2009**
Month:	**March**
Day:	**3**
Year Accessed:	**2016**
Month Accessed:	**May**
Day Accessed:	**24**
URL:	**http://earthobservatory.nasa.gov/ Features/Water/water_2.php**

b. Click **OK** to insert the citation. In the next paragraph, which begins *Recycling is understood,* in the fifth line, click to position the insertion point to the right of the quotation mark. In the **Citations & Bibliography group**, click the **Insert Citation** button, and then click **Add New Source**. Click the **Type of Source arrow**, click **Journal Article**, and then add the following information (type the Title on one line):

Author:	**Pennisi, Elizabeth**
Title:	**Shale-Eating Microbes Recycle Global Carbon**
Journal Name:	**Science**
Year:	**2001**
Pages:	**1043**

c. Click **OK**. In the text, click to select the citation, click the **Citation Options arrow**, and then click **Edit Citation**. In the **Edit Citation** dialog box, under **Add**, in the **Pages** box, type **1043** and then click **OK**. Add a period to the right of the citation and delete the period to the left of the quotation mark.

d. In the same paragraph, position the insertion point at the end of the paragraph. In the **Citations & Bibliography group**, click the **Insert Citation** button, and then click **Add New Source**. Click the **Type of**

Source arrow, click **Book**, and then add the following information (type the Author information on one line):

Author:	**Khlebopros, Rem; Okhonin, Viktor; Fet, Abram**
Title:	**Catastrophes in Nature and Society**
Year:	**2007**
City:	**Singapore**
Publisher:	**World Scientific Publishing Company**

e. Click **OK**. Click to select the citation, click the **Citation Options arrow**, and then click **Edit Citation**. In the **Edit Citation** dialog box, under **Add**, in the **Pages** box, type **111** Click **OK**. Add a period to the right of the citation and delete the period to the left of the quotation mark.

f. Press Ctrl + End to move the insertion point to the end of the document. Press Ctrl + Enter to insert a manual page break. On the ruler, drag the **First Line Indent** button to the left to **0 inches on the horizontal ruler**.

g. Type **Works Cited** and then press Enter. On the **References tab**, in the **Citations & Bibliography group**, be sure **MLA** displays in the **Style** box. In the **Citations & Bibliography group**, click the **Bibliography** button, and then click **Insert Bibliography**.

h. In the bibliography, move the pointer to the left of the first entry—beginning *Khlebopros*—to display the ⬚ pointer. Drag down to select all three references. On the **Home tab**, in the **Paragraph group**, set the **Line spacing** to **2.0**. On the **Page Layout tab**, set the **Spacing After** to **0 pt**.

i. Right-click the *Works Cited* title, and then from the Mini toolbar, click the **Center** button. **Save** your document.

4 From **Backstage** view, display the **Document Panel**, type your name and course information, and then add the keywords **recycling, nature, research paper** In the upper left corner of the panel, click the **Document Properties** button, and then click **Advanced Properties**.

(Project 3C Recycling Report continues on the next page)

Content-Based Assessments

a. In the **Properties** dialog box, click the **Summary tab**. In the **Properties** dialog box, fill in the following information:

Title:	**Recycling in Nature**
Manager:	**Henry Miller**
Company:	**Memphis Primary Materials**
Comments:	**Draft of a new white paper research report on recycling**

b. At the bottom of the **Properties** dialog box, click **OK**. **Close** the **Document Panel**. **Save** your document. View the Print Preview, and then print or submit electronically as directed by your instructor. **Exit** Word.

End **You have completed Project 3C** _____

Content-Based Assessments

Apply **3B** skills from these Objectives:

- 4 Format a Multiple-Column Newsletter
- 5 Use Special Character and Paragraph Formatting
- 6 Create Mailing Labels Using Mail Merge

Skills Review | Project **3D** Company Newsletter

In the following Skills Review, you will format a newsletter for Memphis Primary Materials, and then create a set of mailing labels for the newsletter. Your completed documents will look similar to Figure 3.42.

Project Files

For Project 3D, you will need the following files:

New blank Word document
w03D_Company_Newsletter
w03D_Addresses

You will save your documents as:

Lastname_Firstname_3D_Company_Newsletter
Lastname_Firstname_3D_Addresses
Lastname_Firstname_3D_Labels

Project Results

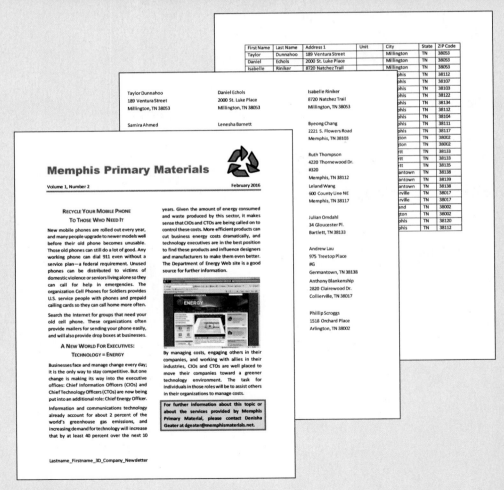

Figure 3.42

(Project 3D Company Newsletter continues on the next page)

Content-Based Assessments

Skills Review | Project **3D** Company Newsletter (continued)

1 **Start** Word. From your student files, open the document **w03D_Company_Newsletter**. **Save** the file in your **Word Chapter 3** folder as **Lastname_Firstname_3D_ Company_Newsletter** and then add the file name to the footer.

a. Select the first paragraph of text—*Memphis Primary Materials*. From the Mini toolbar, change the **Font** to **Arial Black** and the **Font Size** to **24**. Select the title you just formatted. Click the **Font Color button arrow**, and then under **Theme Colors**, in the seventh column, click the fifth color—**Olive Green, Accent 3, Darker 25%**.

b. Select the second paragraph. On the **Home tab**, in the **Paragraph group**, click the **Borders button arrow**, and then click **Borders and Shading**. In the **Borders and Shading** dialog box, click the **Color arrow**, and then under **Theme Colors**, in the seventh column, click the fifth color—**Olive Green, Accent 3, Darker 25%**. Click the **Width arrow**, and then click **3 pt**. In the **Preview** area, click the *bottom* border of the Preview and then click **OK**.

c. Below the nameplate, locate the paragraph that begins *Recycle Your Mobile*, and then select all of the text from that point to the end of the document. On the **Page Layout tab**, in the **Page Setup group**, click the **Columns** button, and then click **Two**.

d. With the text still selected, in the **Paragraph group**, set **Spacing After** to **6 pt**. On the **Home tab**, in the **Paragraph group**, click the **Justify** button. Click anywhere in the document to deselect the text, and then **Save** the newsletter.

e. Press [Ctrl] + [Home]. On the **Insert tab**, in the **Illustrations group**, click the **Clip Art** button. In the **Clip Art** task pane, click in the **Search for** box, and then type **conservation**

f. In the **Clip Art** task pane, click the **Results should be arrow**, and be sure that only the **Illustrations** check box is selected. Be sure the **Include Office.com content** check box is selected, and then click **Go**. Locate the image of three green arrows, as shown in Figure 3.42, and then click on the image.

g. On the **Format tab**, in the **Size group**, click in the **Shape Height** box, type **1** and then press [Enter]. In the **Arrange group**, click the **Wrap Text** button, and then click **Square**. **Close** the Clip Art task pane, and then drag the image to the location shown in Figure 3.42.

h. In the second column, position the insertion point at the beginning of the paragraph that begins *By managing costs*. Open your Web browser. In the address bar, type **www.energy.gov** and then press [Enter]. Maximize the browser window. Use the taskbar to return to your Word document.

i. On the **Insert tab**, in the **Illustrations group**, click the **Screenshot** button. In the gallery, click the DOE screenshot to insert it. **Close** your Web browser, and then **Save** your document.

2 At the top of the first column, select the paragraph that begins *Recycle Your Mobile*. Be sure to include the paragraph mark. Right-click the selected text, and then click **Font**. In the **Font** dialog box, click the **Font color arrow**, and then under **Theme Colors**, in the seventh column, click the last color—**Olive Green, Accent 3, Darker 50%**. Under **Font style**, click **Bold**. Under **Size**, click **14**. Under **Effects**, select the **Small caps** check box.

a. In the **Font** dialog box, click **OK**. Right-click the selected text, and then click the **Center** button. In the title you just formatted, click to position the insertion point to the right of *Phone*, and then press [Del] to remove the space. Hold down [Shift], and then press [Enter] to insert a manual line break.

b. Select and right-click the title you just formatted, and then on the Mini toolbar, click the **Format Painter** button. Near the middle of the first column, select the paragraph that begins *A New World* to apply the same formatting.

c. At the bottom of the second column, in the paragraph that begins *For further*, select the entire paragraph. On the Mini toolbar, apply **Bold**.

d. With the text still selected, on the **Home tab**, in the **Paragraph group**, click the **Borders button arrow**, and then click **Borders and Shading**. In the **Borders and Shading** dialog box, be sure the **Borders tab** is selected. Under **Setting**, click **Box**. Click the **Width arrow**, and then click **3 pt**. If necessary, click the **Color arrow**, and then in the seventh column, click the fifth color—**Olive Green, Accent 3, Darker 25%**.

e. At the top of the **Borders and Shading** dialog box, click the **Shading tab**. Click the **Fill arrow**, and then in the seventh column, click the second color—**Olive Green, Accent 3, Lighter 80%**. At the bottom of the **Borders and Shading** dialog box, click **OK**. Click anywhere in the document to deselect the text.

(Project 3D Company Newsletter continues on the next page)

f. Near the bottom of the first column, in the paragraph that begins *Information and communications*, click to position the insertion point at the beginning of the sixth line. On the **Page Layout tab**, in the **Page Setup group**, click the **Breaks** button. Under **Page Breaks**, click **Column**.

g. From **Backstage** view, display the **Document Panel**, type your name and course information. Add the keywords **newsletter, energy** and then **Close** the **Document Panel**. **Save** the document, view the Print Preview, and then **Exit** Word. Hold this file until you complete this project.

3 **Start** Word and display a new blank document. Display formatting marks and rulers. **Save** the document in your **Word Chapter 3** folder as **Lastname_Firstname_3D_Labels Open** the file **w03D_Addresses Save** the address file in your **Word Chapter 3** folder as **Lastname_Firstname_3D_Addresses** and then add the file name to the footer.

a. Click to position the insertion point in the last cell in the table, and then press [Tab] to create a new row. Enter the following new record:

First Name	Eldon
Last Name	Aarons
Address 1	5354 Thornewood Dr.
Unit	#2B
City	Memphis
State	TN
ZIP Code	38112

b. **Save**, and then **Close** the table of addresses; be sure your blank **Lastname_Firstname_3D_Labels** document displays. Click the **Mailings tab**. In the **Start Mail Merge group**, click the **Start Mail Merge** button, and then click **Step by Step Mail Merge Wizard**. Under **Select document type**, click the **Labels** option button.

c. At the bottom of the task pane, click **Next: Starting document**. Under **Select starting document**, be sure **Change document layout** is selected, and then under **Change document layout**, click **Label options**.

d. In the **Label Options** dialog box, under **Printer information**, click the **Tray arrow**, and then click **Default tray (Automatically Select)**.

e. Under **Label information**, click the **Label vendors arrow**, and then click **Avery US Letter**. Under **Product number**, scroll about halfway down the list, and then click **5160**. At the bottom of the **Label Options** dialog box, click **OK**. At the bottom of the task pane, click **Next: Select recipients**.

f. Under **Select recipients**, be sure the **Use an existing list** option button is selected. Under **Use an existing list**, click **Browse**. Navigate to your **Word Chapter 3** folder, select your **Lastname_Firstname_3D_Addresses** file, and then click **Open**. At the bottom of the **Mail Merge Recipients** dialog box, click **OK**, and then in the **Mail Merge** task pane, click **Next: Arrange your labels**.

g. Under **Arrange your labels**, click **Address block**. If necessary, in the **Insert Address Block** dialog box, under **Insert recipient's name in this format**, select the **Joshua Randall Jr.** format.

h. Click **Match Fields**. Click the **Address 2 arrow**, and then click **Unit**. Click **OK** two times.

i. In the task pane, under **Replicate labels**, click **Update all labels**. Click **Next: Preview your labels**. Press [Ctrl] + [A] to select all of the label text, and then on the **Page Layout tab**, click in the **Spacing Before** box, type **4** and press [Enter] to ensure that the four-line addresses will fit on the labels. **Save** your labels, and then **Close** the **Mail Merge** task pane.

4 Add the file name to the footer, and then close the footer area. Click in the bottom empty row of the table, click the **Layout tab**, in the **Rows & Columns group**, click **Delete**, and then click **Delete Rows**. From **Backstage** view, display the **Document Panel**, type your name and course information, and then add the keywords **newsletter mailing labels Close** the **Document Panel**.

a. Print or submit electronically your 3D_Company_Newsletter, 3D_Addresses, and 3D_Labels documents.

b. **Close** the document, click **Save** to save the labels, and then **Exit** Word.

End **You have completed Project 3D**

Content-Based Assessments

Apply **3A** skills from these Objectives:

1. Create a Research Paper
2. Insert Footnotes in a Research Paper
3. Create Citations and a Bibliography in a Research Paper

Mastering Word | Project **3E** Hazards

In the following Mastering Word project, you will edit and format a research paper for Memphis Primary Materials, the topic of which is hazardous materials in electronic waste. Your completed document will look similar to Figure 3.43.

Project Files

For Project 3E, you will need the following file:

w03E_Hazards

You will save your document as:

Lastname_Firstname_3E_Hazards

Project Results

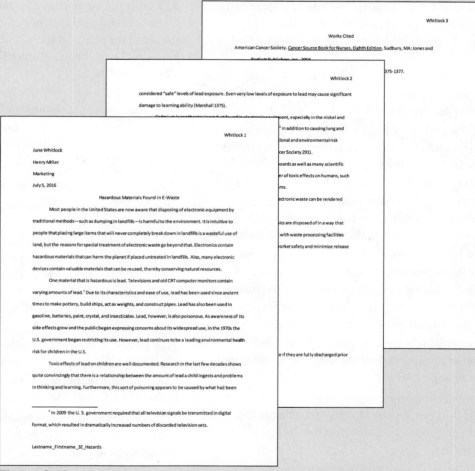

Figure 3.43

(Project 3E Hazards continues on the next page)

Content-Based Assessments

Mastering Word | Project **3E** Hazards (continued)

1 **Start** Word. From your student files open the document **w03E_Hazards**. **Save** the document in your **Word Chapter 3** folder as **Lastname_Firstname_3E_ Hazards** Display the header area, type **Whitlock** and then press Spacebar. Display the **Page Number gallery**, and then in the **Current Position**, add the **Plain Number** style. Apply **Align Text Right** formatting to the header. Add the file name to the footer.

2 Return to the beginning of the document, press Enter to insert a blank line, click in the blank line, type **June Whitlock** and then press Enter. Type **Henry Miller** and press Enter. Type **Marketing** and press Enter. Type **July 5, 2016**

3 Select all of the text in the document. Change the **Line Spacing** to **2.0**, and change the **Spacing After** to **0 pt**. Deselect the text, right-click anywhere in the title *Hazardous Materials Found in E-Waste*, and then **Center** the title.

Starting with the paragraph that begins *Most people*, select the text from that point to the end of the document, and then set the **First Line Indent** to **0.5"**.

4 Near the middle of **Page 1**, in the paragraph that begins *One material*, in the second line, click to position the insertion point to the right of the period following *lead*, and then add the following footnote:

> **In 2009 the U.S. government required that all television signals be transmitted in digital format, which resulted in dramatically increased numbers of discarded television sets.**

On **Page 2**, in the paragraph that begins *Cadmium is another*, in the second line, click to position the insertion point to the right of the period following *devices*, and then add the following footnote:

> **Newer lithium batteries are not considered hazardous waste if they are fully discharged prior to disposal.**

5 Right-click anywhere in the footnote, modify the **Style** to set the **Font Size** to **11**, and then change the **Format** of paragraphs to add a **First line** indent and use double-spacing.

Near the bottom of **Page 1**, locate the paragraph that begins *Toxic effects*, and then click position the insertion

point to the left of the period at the end of the paragraph, which displays at the top of **Page 2**. In the **MLA** format, add the following **Journal Article** citation (type the Title on one line):

Author:	Marshall, Eliot
Title:	EPA May Allow More Lead in Gasoline
Journal Name:	Science
Year:	1982
Pages:	1375–1377

6 Near the top of **Page 2**, locate the paragraph that begins *Cadmium*, and then click to position the insertion point to the left of the period at the end of the paragraph. Add the following **Book** citation, using a **Corporate Author** (type the Title on one line):

Corporate Author:	American Cancer Society
Title:	Cancer Source Book for Nurses, Eighth Edition
Year:	2004
City:	Sudbury, MA
Publisher:	Jones and Bartlett Publishers, Inc.

Select the *Marshall* citation and add the page number **1375** At the end of the next paragraph, select the *American Cancer Society* citation and add the page number **291**

7 Move to the end of the document, and then insert a manual page break to create a new page. Change the **First Line Indent** to **0"**. Add a **Works Cited** title, and then **Insert Bibliography**. Select the two references, apply **Double** line spacing, and then remove spacing after the paragraphs. **Center** the *Works Cited* title.

Display the **Document Panel** and add your name and course information and the keywords **hazardous materials Save** your document. Display the Print Preview, make any necessary adjustments, and then print or submit electronically as directed. **Exit** Word.

End **You have completed Project 3E** ⸺⸺⸺⸺⸺⸺

Content-Based Assessments

Apply 3B skills from these Objectives:

- **4** Format a Multiple-Column Newsletter
- **5** Use Special Character and Paragraph Formatting
- **6** Create Mailing Labels Using Mail Merge

Mastering Word | Project **3F** Spring Newsletter

In the following Mastering Word project, you will format a newsletter for Memphis Primary Materials, and then create a set of mailing labels for the newsletter. Your completed documents will look similar to Figure 3.44.

Project Files

For Project 3F, you will need the following files:

New blank Word document
w03F_Spring_Newsletter
w03F_Addresses

You will save your documents as:

Lastname_Firstname_3F_Spring_Newsletter
Lastname_Firstname_3F_Labels

Project Results

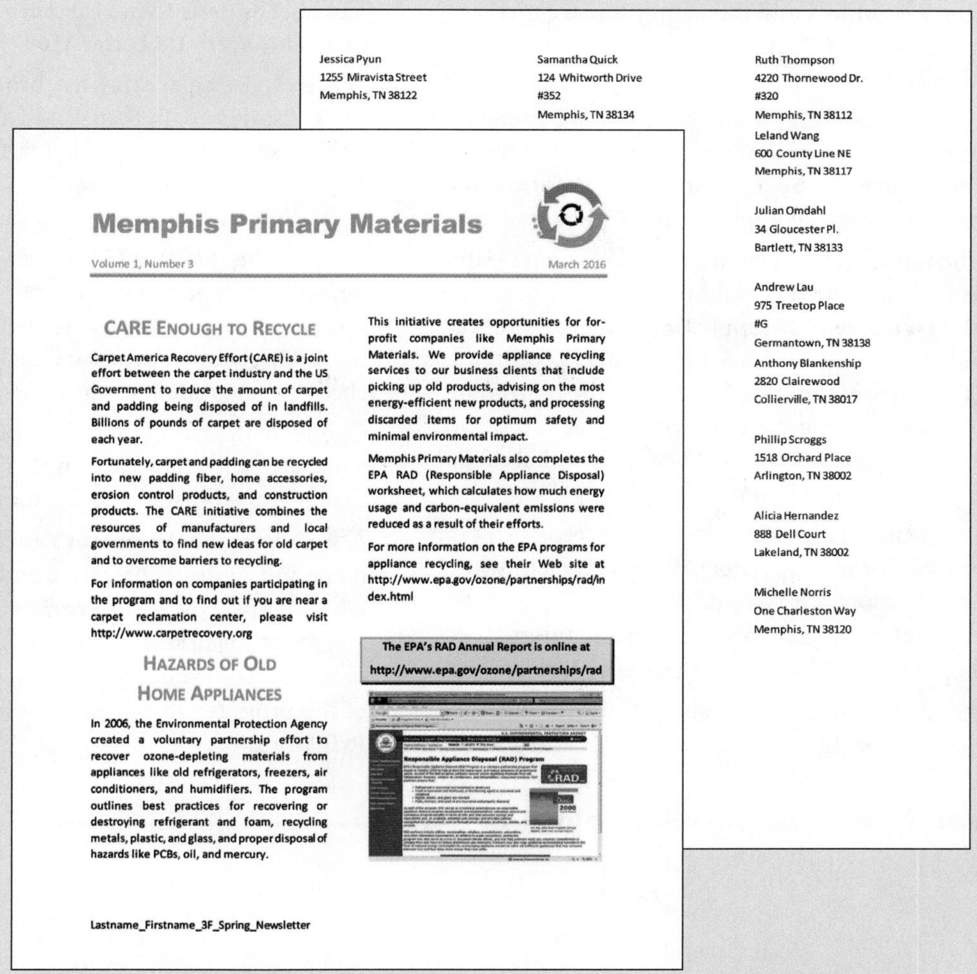

Jessica Pyun
1255 Miravista Street
Memphis, TN 38122

Samantha Quick
124 Whitworth Drive
#352
Memphis, TN 38134

Ruth Thompson
4220 Thornewood Dr.
#320
Memphis, TN 38112

Leland Wang
600 County Line NE
Memphis, TN 38117

Julian Omdahl
34 Gloucester Pl.
Bartlett, TN 38133

Andrew Lau
975 Treetop Place
#G
Germantown, TN 38138

Anthony Blankenship
2820 Clairewood
Collierville, TN 38017

Phillip Scroggs
1518 Orchard Place
Arlington, TN 38002

Alicia Hernandez
888 Dell Court
Lakeland, TN 38002

Michelle Norris
One Charleston Way
Memphis, TN 38120

Memphis Primary Materials

Volume 1, Number 3

March 2016

CARE ENOUGH TO RECYCLE

Carpet America Recovery Effort (CARE) is a joint effort between the carpet industry and the US Government to reduce the amount of carpet and padding being disposed of in landfills. Billions of pounds of carpet are disposed of each year.

Fortunately, carpet and padding can be recycled into new padding fiber, home accessories, erosion control products, and construction products. The CARE initiative combines the resources of manufacturers and local governments to find new ideas for old carpet and to overcome barriers to recycling.

For information on companies participating in the program and to find out if you are near a carpet reclamation center, please visit http://www.carpetrecovery.org

HAZARDS OF OLD HOME APPLIANCES

In 2006, the Environmental Protection Agency created a voluntary partnership effort to recover ozone-depleting materials from appliances like old refrigerators, freezers, air conditioners, and humidifiers. The program outlines best practices for recovering or destroying refrigerant and foam, recycling metals, plastic, and glass, and proper disposal of hazards like PCBs, oil, and mercury.

This initiative creates opportunities for for-profit companies like Memphis Primary Materials. We provide appliance recycling services to our business clients that include picking up old products, advising on the most energy-efficient new products, and processing discarded items for optimum safety and minimal environmental impact.

Memphis Primary Materials also completes the EPA RAD (Responsible Appliance Disposal) worksheet, which calculates how much energy usage and carbon-equivalent emissions were reduced as a result of their efforts.

For more information on the EPA programs for appliance recycling, see their Web site at http://www.epa.gov/ozone/partnerships/rad/index.html

The EPA's RAD Annual Report is online at http://www.epa.gov/ozone/partnerships/rad

Lastname_Firstname_3F_Spring_Newsletter

Figure 3.44

(Project 3F Spring Newsletter continues on the next page)

Content-Based Assessments

1 **Start** Word. Open **w03F_Spring_Newsletter**, and then save it in your **Word Chapter 3** folder as **Lastname_ Firstname_3F_Spring_Newsletter** Add the file name to the footer. Display the rulers and formatting marks.

Select the first line of text—*Memphis Primary Materials*. Change the **Font** to **Arial Black**, the **Font Size** to **24**, and the **Font Color** to **Orange, Accent 6, Darker 25%**.

Select the second line of text—the date and volume. Change the **Font Color** to **Orange, Accent 6, Darker 25%**. Display the **Borders and Shading** dialog box, and then add an **Orange, Accent 6, Darker 25%, 3 pt** line below the selected text.

2 Click at the beginning of the newsletter title. Display the **Clip Art** task pane, search for **recycle earth** and then insert the image of the orange and tan recycle arrows. Change the **Height** to **1** and then apply **Square** text wrapping. Close the **Clip Art** task pane. Drag the image to the location shown in Figure 3.44.

Starting with the paragraph that begins *CARE enough*, select all of the text from that point to the end of the document. Change the **Spacing After** to **6 pt**, format the text in two columns, and apply the **Justify** alignment.

3 At the top of the first column, select the paragraph *CARE Enough to Recycle*. From the **Font** dialog box, change the **Font Size** to **20**, apply **Bold**, add the **Small caps** effect, and change the **Font color** to **Orange, Accent 6, Darker 25%**. **Center** the paragraph. Near the bottom of the same column, apply the same formatting to the paragraph that begins *Hazards of Old*. Add a manual line break between *Old* and *Home*.

Move to the blank line at the bottom of the second column. Open your Web browser and open the **www.epa.gov/ ozone/partnerships/rad/** Web site. Maximize the browser window and return to your Word document. Insert a **Screenshot** of the EPA Web page. **Close** your Web browser.

4 Select the two lines of text above the inserted screenshot. **Center** the text and apply **Bold**. Add a **Shadow**

border, change the **Color** to **Tan, Background 2, Darker 25%**, the **Width** to **1 1/2 pt**, and then on the **Shading tab** of the dialog box, apply a **Fill** of **Tan, Background 2** shading—in the third column, the first color.

Display the **Document Panel** and add your name, course information, and the **Keywords Spring newsletter** Display the **Print Preview**, return to your document and make any necessary corrections, and then **Save** and **Close** the document. Hold this document until you complete the project.

5 Display a **New** blank document. **Save** the document in your **Word Chapter 3** folder as **Lastname_Firstname_ 3F_Labels** On the **Mailings tab**, start the **Step by Step Mail Merge Wizard.**

In **Step 1**, select **Labels** as the document type. In **Step 2**, set **Label options** to use the **Auto default** tray (yours may vary) and **Avery US Letter 5160**.

In **Step 3**, use an existing list, browse to select **w03F_Addresses**. In **Step 4**, add an **Address block** to the labels, use the *Joshua Randall Jr.* format, and then **Match Fields** by matching *Address 2* to *Unit*.

Update all labels and **Preview**. Select all of the label text, and then on the **Page Layout tab**, click in the **Spacing Before** box, type **4** and press Enter to ensure that the four-line addresses will fit on the labels. On the **Layout tab**, in the **Table group**, if necessary click **View Gridlines** to check the alignment of the labels.

Complete the merge, and then **Close** the **Mail Merge** task pane. Delete the last two empty rows of the table, and then add the file name to the footer.

6 Display the **Document Panel**, and then add your name and course information and the keywords **mailing labels** Display the **Print Preview**, return to your document and make any necessary corrections, and then **Save**. Print or submit electronically your two files that are the results of this project—3F_Spring_Newsletter and 3F_Labels. **Exit** Word.

End **You have completed Project 3F**

Word | Chapter 3

Mastering Word | Project **3G** Economics

In the following Mastering Word project, you will edit and format a newsletter and a research paper for Memphis Primary Materials on the topic of environmental economics. Your completed documents will look similar to Figure 3.45.

Project Files

For Project 3G, you will need the following files:

New blank Word document
w03G_Economics
w03G_Addresses
w03G_April_Newsletter

You will save your documents as:

Lastname_Firstname_3G_Economics
Lastname_Firstname_3G_April_Newsletter
Lastname_Firstname_3G_Labels

Project Results

Figure 3.45

(Project 3G Economics continues on the next page)

Mastering Word | Project **3G** Economics (continued)

1 **Start** Word. Open the document **w03G_April_Newsletter**, and then save the document in your **Word Chapter 3** folder as **Lastname_Firstname_3G_April_Newsletter** Add the file name to the footer. Starting with the paragraph that begins *Research on Environmental Economics*, select all of the text from that point to the end of the document—the document text extends to two pages. Set the **Spacing After** to **6 pt**, format the selected text as two columns, and set the alignment to **Justify**.

2 Near the bottom of the first column, in the paragraph that begins *Maine has already*, click to position the insertion point to the left of the sixth line, which begins *pollutants would*. Insert a column break. At the top of the first column, select the paragraph *Research on Environmental Economics*.

Display the **Font** dialog box, set the **Font Size** to **14**, apply **Bold**, set the **Font color** to **Dark Blue, Text 2**, and then add the **Small caps** effect. **Center** the paragraph. Use the Format Painter to copy the formatting and then apply the same formatting to the paragraph *The Hard Costs of Pollution* located near the bottom of the first column and to *Environmental Economics Conference* in the second column.

3 At the bottom of the second column, select the last two paragraphs of text. From the **Borders and Shading** dialog box, apply a **1 1/2 pt**, **Shadow** border using the **Dark Blue, Text 2** color, and then on the **Shading tab**, apply a **Fill** of **Dark Blue, Text 2, Lighter 80%**.

In the second column, click to position the insertion point at the beginning of the paragraph that begins *Memphis Primary Materials is a cosponsor*. Display the **Clip Art** task pane. Search for **conference** and limit your search to **Illustrations**. **Insert** the image shown in Figure 3.45, apply **Top and Bottom** text wrapping, decrease the **Height** of the image to **1″**, and position the image as shown. **Close** the Clip Art task pane.

Display the **Document Panel** and add your name and course information and the **Keywords April newsletter Save** and then **Close** the document. Hold this file until you complete this project.

4 From your student files, open the document **w03G_Economics**, and then save it in your **Word Chapter 3** folder as **Lastname_Firstname_3G_Economics** Display the header area, type **Jaworski** and then press ⟨Spacebar⟩. In the **Header & Footer group**, add a **Plain Number** from the

Current Position gallery. Apply **Align Text Right** formatting to the header. Move to the footer area and add the file name to the footer.

Select all of the text in the document. Change the **Line Spacing** to **2.0**, and change the **Spacing After** to **0**. Near the top of the document, **Center** the title *Environmental Economics and Business*. Beginning with the text below the centered title, select the text from that point to the end of the document, and then set a **First Line Indent** at **0.5″**.

5 At the bottom of **Page 1**, in the paragraph that begins *Environmental economics also*, in the second line, click to position the insertion point to the right of the comma following *Protocol*, and then insert the following footnote:

> **The Kyoto Protocol is an international agreement under the UN Framework Convention on Climate Change that went into effect in 2005.**

In the next paragraph, which begins *In the United States*, in the second line, position the insertion point to the right of the period following *Economics*, and then insert the following footnote:

> **The NCEE offers a centralized source of technical expertise to the EPA, as well as other federal agencies, Congress, universities, and other organizations.**

Right-click in the footnote, and then modify the style to set the **Font Size** to **11** and the format of the paragraph to include a **First line** indent and double-spacing. **Save** your document.

6 Near the bottom of **Page 1**, in the paragraph that begins *Environmental economists*, position the insertion point to the left of the period at the end of the paragraph. Using **MLA** format, add the following **Article in a Periodical** citation (type the Title on one line):

Author:	Abboud, Leila
Title:	Economist Strikes Gold in Climate-Change Fight
Periodical Title:	The Wall Street Journal
Year:	2008
Month:	March
Day:	13

(Project 3G Economics continues on the next page)

Select the *Abboud* citation and add the page number **A1** Near the middle of **Page 2**, in the paragraph that begins *In the United States*, click to position the insertion point to the left of the period at the end of the paragraph. Add the following **Book** citation in **MLA** format (type the Title on one line):

Author:	**Tietenberg, Tom; Folmer, Henk, Editors**
Title:	**The International Yearbook of Environmental Resource Economics, 2006/2007**
Year:	**2006**
City:	**Northampton, MA**
Publisher:	**Edward Elgar Publishers**

7 Select the *Tietenberg* citation and add the page number **1** Insert a manual page break at the end of the document. On the new **Page 3**, on the ruler, set the **First Line Indent** to **0″**. Type **Works Cited** and then press Enter.

On the **References tab**, in the **Citations & Bibliography group**, be sure *MLA* displays in the **Style** box. Insert the bibliography. Select the inserted references, set the **Line Spacing** to **2.0**, and then set **Spacing After** to **0 pt**. **Center** the *Works Cited* title.

Display the **Document Panel** and add your name and course information and the **Keywords environmental**

economics Display the **Print Preview** to check your document, make any necessary adjustments, **Save**, and then **Close** the document. Hold this file until you complete this project.

8 Display a **New** blank document. **Save** the document in your **Word Chapter 3** folder as **Lastname_Firstname_3G_Labels** On the **Mailings tab**, start the **Step by Step Mail Merge Wizard**. In **Step 1**, select **Labels** as the document type. In **Step 2**, set **Label options** to use the **Auto default** tray (yours may vary) and **Avery US Letter 5160**. If you cannot see the gridlines, on the **Layout tab**, in the **Table group**, click **View Gridlines**. In **Step 3**, use an existing list, browse to select **w03G_Addresses**, and then click **OK**.

In **Step 4**, add an **Address block** to the labels, use the *Joshua Randall Jr.* format, and then **Match Fields** by matching *Address 2* to *Unit*. **Update all labels** and then **Preview**. Select all of the label text, and then on the **Page Layout tab**, click in the **Spacing Before** box, type **4** and press Enter. Complete the merge, and then **Close** the **Mail Merge** task pane. Delete the last two empty rows of the table, and then add the file name to the footer, which adds an additional page.

Display the **Document Panel**, and then add your name, course information, and the keywords **mailing labels** Click **Save**. Print or submit electronically your three files that are the results of this project—3G_Economics, 3G_April_Newsletter, and 3G_Labels. **Exit** Word.

End You have completed Project 3G

GO! Fix It | Project **3H** Metals Report

Project Files

For Project 3H, you will need the following file:

w03H_Metals_Report

You will save your document as:

Lastname_Firstname_3H_Metals_Report

From the student files that accompany this textbook, locate and open the file w03H_Metals_Report, and then save the file in your Word Chapter 3 folder as **Lastname_Firstname_3H_Metals_Report**

This document contains errors that you must find and correct. Read and examine the document, and then edit to correct any errors that you find and to improve the overall document format. Types of errors could include, but are not restricted to:

- Formatting does not match MLA style guidelines that you practiced in the chapter
- Incorrect header format
- Incorrect spacing between paragraphs
- Incorrect paragraph indents
- Incorrect line spacing
- Incorrect footnote format
- Incorrectly formatted reference page

Things you should know to complete this project:

- Displaying formatting marks will assist in locating spacing errors.
- There are no errors in the parenthetical references in the document.
- There are no errors in the information in the footnotes or bibliographical references.

Save your document and add the file name to the footer. In the Document Panel, add your name, course information, and the keywords **valuable metals, recycling** Save your document and submit as directed.

End You have completed Project 3H ———————————————

Content-Based Assessments

Apply a combination of the **3A** and **3B** skills.

GO! Make It | Project **3I** Green Newsletter

Project Files

For Project 3I, you will need the following files:

New blank Word document   w03I_Kids
w03I_Competition

You will save your document as:

Lastname_Firstname_3I_Green_Newsletter

Start with a new Word document, and then save the file in your chapter folder as **Lastname_Firstname_3I_Green_Newsletter** Create the document shown in Figure 3.46. Create a nameplate, and then insert the files w03I_Competition and w03I_Kids. The title is Arial Black, 24 pt, Dark Blue, Text 2. Other titles and borders are Dark Blue, Text 2. The two titles in the columns are Calibri, 16 pt. The clip art image can be found by using the search term **recycle** and the screenshot can be found at the Web address in the last line of the newsletter.

Add the file name to the footer; in the Document Panel, add your name and course information and the Keywords **green, campuses, kids** Save your document and submit as directed.

Project Results

Memphis Primary Materials

Volume 1, Number 4   April 2016

THE COMPETITIVE SPIRIT OF GREEN

One way to increase people's willingness to reuse and recycle is to invoke their spirit of competition—and prizes do not hurt either. College campuses are proving this by participating in the America's Greenest Campus competition.

America's Greenest Campus is a nationwide contest, with the goal of reducing the carbon footprint of entire campus populations across the country.

Partnering with Smart Power and the U.S. Department of Energy, the winning campus will receive a donation of $10,000. As of February 2009, the University of Maryland has reduced its CO2 emissions by 2% and George Mason University by 3%.

Students, faculty, and staff are encouraged to recycle, turn off lights, reduce heating and air conditioning, and engage in many other small and large changes that can help the environment. Treehugger.com calls the contest, "the NCAA of sustainability."

Another college competition for environmentalism is RecycleMania. Designed to encourage colleges and universities to reduce waste, the competition collects reports on recycling and trash over a 10-week period. This competition thinks of colleges of community universities as small cities that consume large amounts of resources and generate a lot of solid waste. Participating campuses are ranked by categories such as "least amount of waste per capita." Weekly results are distributed to the

participants so they can benchmark against their competition and step up their efforts.

With growing awareness of the need to reduce, reuse, and recycle among students, expect some competition if you are part of a campus community!

CLEANUP IS FOR KIDS

Cleaning up the planet isn't just for college students. Younger students often have a desire to get involved with environmental activities, and there is no shortage of resources.

Start at the website of the Environmental Protection Agency. They provide resources like Cleanup for Kids, a Web site of the National Oceanic and Atmospheric Administration (NOAA), which makes the hazards of oil spills real through science demonstrations. The brochure, *Environmental Protection Begins With You*, outlines examples of community volunteer projects in which students can participate.

Learn more at the EPA website:
http://www.epa.gov/highschool/waste.htm

Lastname_Firstname_3I_Green_Newsletter

Figure 3.46

 End **You have completed Project 3I**

Content-Based Assessments

GO! Solve It | Project 3J Municipal Newsletter

Project Files

For Project 3J, you will need the following file:

New blank Word document

You will save your document as:

Lastname_Firstname_3J_Municipal_Newsletter

Memphis Primary Materials writes an informational newsletter for customers. Create a new document and save it in your Word Chapter 3 folder as **Lastname_Firstname_3J_Municipal_Newsletter** Use the following information to create a newsletter that includes a nameplate, multiple columns, at least two articles with article titles formatted so that they stand out, at least one clip art image, one screenshot, and one paragraph that includes a border and shading.

This issue (Volume 1, Number 6—June 2016) will focus on municipal solid waste—the waste generated by householders and small businesses. This category of waste does not include hazardous, industrial, or construction waste. The articles you write can be on any topic regarding municipal waste, and might include an introduction to the topic and a discussion of recycling in the U.S. or in the Memphis community. You will need to research this topic on the Web. A good place to start is www.epa.gov, which has many articles on solid municipal waste, and also provides links to further articles on the topic. You might also consider doing a Web search for the term **municipal solid waste recycling**

Add the file name to the footer. To the Document Panel, add your name, your course name and section number, and the keywords **municipal solid waste recycling**

Performance Level			
	Exemplary: You consistently applied the relevant skills	**Proficient:** You sometimes, but not always, applied the relevant skills	**Developing:** You rarely or never applied the relevant skills
Create and format nameplate	The nameplate includes both the company name and the date and volume information, and is formatted attractively.	One or more of the nameplate elements are done correctly, but other items are either omitted or not formatted properly.	The newsletter does not include a nameplate.
Insert at least two articles in multiple-column format	The newsletter contains at least two articles, displayed in multiple columns that are well written and are free of grammar and spelling errors.	The newsletter contains only one article, or the text is not divided into two columns, or there are spelling and grammar errors in the text.	The newsletter contains only one article, the article is not divided into multiple columns, and there are spelling and grammar errors.
Insert and format at least one clip art image	An appropriate clip art image is included. The image is sized and positioned appropriately.	A clip art image is inserted, but is either inappropriate, or is formatted or positioned poorly.	No clip art image is included.
Border and shading added to a paragraph	One or more paragraphs display an attractive border with shading that enables the reader to read the text.	A border or shading is displayed, but not both; or, the shading is too dark to enable the reader to easily read the text.	No border or shading is added to a paragraph.
Insert a screenshot	A screenshot is inserted in one of the columns; the screenshot is related to the content of the article.	A screenshot is inserted in the document, but does not relate to the content of the article.	No screenshot is inserted.

Performance Element

End You have completed Project 3J

Content-Based Assessments

Apply a combination of the **3A** and **3B** skills.

GO! Solve It | Project **3K** Paper Report

Project Files

For Project 3K, you will need the following file:

> New blank Word document

You will save your document as:

> Lastname_Firstname_3K_Paper_Report

Create a new file and save it as **Lastname_Firstname_3K_Paper_Report** Use the following information to create a report written in the MLA format. The report should include at least two footnotes, at least two citations, and should include a *Works Cited* page.

Memphis Primary Materials writes and distributes informational reports on topics of interest to the people of Memphis. This report will be written by Sarah Stanger for the head of Marketing, Henry Miller. Information reports are provided as a public service of the company, and are distributed free of charge.

The topic of the report is recycling and reuse of paper and paper products. The report should contain an introduction, and then details about how much paper is used, what it is used for, the increase of paper recycling over time, and how paper products can be recycled or reused. A good place to start is www.epa.gov, which has many articles on paper use and recycling, and also provides links to further articles on the topic. You might also consider doing a Web search for the terms **paper recycling**

Add the file name to the footer, and add your name, your course name and section number, and the keywords **paper products, recycling** to the Document Panel.

		Performance Level		
		Exemplary: You consistently applied the relevant skills	**Proficient:** You sometimes, but not always, applied the relevant skills	**Developing:** You rarely or never applied the relevant skills
Performance Element	Format the header and heading	The last name and page number are right-aligned in the header, and the report has a four-line heading and a centered title.	The header and heading are included, but are not formatted according to MLA style guidelines.	The header or heading is missing or incomplete.
	Format the body of the report	The report is double-spaced, with no space after paragraphs. The first lines of paragraphs are indented 0.5″.	Some, but not all, of the report formatting is correct.	The majority of the formatting does not follow MLA guidelines.
	Footnotes are included and formatted correctly	Two or more footnotes are included, and the footnote text is 11 pt, double-spaced, and the first line of each footnote is indented.	The correct number of footnotes is included, but the footnotes are not formatted properly.	No footnotes are included.
	Citations and bibliography are included and formatted according to MLA guidelines	At least two citations are included in parenthetical references, with page numbers where appropriate, and the sources are included in a properly formatted Works Cited page.	Only one citation is included, or the citations and sources are not formatted correctly.	No citations or Works Cited page are included.

End You have completed Project 3K

Outcomes-Based Assessments

Rubric

The following outcomes-based assessments are *open-ended assessments*. That is, there is no specific correct result; your result will depend on your approach to the information provided. Make *Professional Quality* your goal. Use the following scoring rubric to guide you in *how* to approach the problem, and then to evaluate *how well* your approach solves the problem.

The *criteria*—Software Mastery, Content, Format and Layout, and Process—represent the knowledge and skills you have gained that you can apply to solving the problem. The *levels of performance*—Professional Quality, Approaching Professional Quality, or Needs Quality Improvements—help you and your instructor evaluate your result.

	Your completed project is of Professional Quality if you:	Your completed project is Approaching Professional Quality if you:	Your completed project Needs Quality Improvements if you:
1-Software Mastery	Choose and apply the most appropriate skills, tools, and features and identify efficient methods to solve the problem.	Choose and apply some appropriate skills, tools, and features, but not in the most efficient manner.	Choose inappropriate skills, tools, or features, or are inefficient in solving the problem.
2-Content	Construct a solution that is clear and well organized, contains content that is accurate, appropriate to the audience and purpose, and is complete. Provide a solution that contains no errors in spelling, grammar, or style.	Construct a solution in which some components are unclear, poorly organized, inconsistent, or incomplete. Misjudge the needs of the audience. Have some errors in spelling, grammar, or style, but the errors do not detract from comprehension.	Construct a solution that is unclear, incomplete, or poorly organized; contains some inaccurate or inappropriate content; and contains many errors in spelling, grammar, or style. Do not solve the problem.
3-Format and Layout	Format and arrange all elements to communicate information and ideas, clarify function, illustrate relationships, and indicate relative importance.	Apply appropriate format and layout features to some elements, but not others. Overuse features, causing minor distraction.	Apply format and layout that does not communicate information or ideas clearly. Do not use format and layout features to clarify function, illustrate relationships, or indicate relative importance. Use available features excessively, causing distraction.
4-Process	Use an organized approach that integrates planning, development, self-assessment, revision, and reflection.	Demonstrate an organized approach in some areas, but not others; or, use an insufficient process of organization throughout.	Do not use an organized approach to solve the problem.

Outcomes-Based Assessments

Apply a combination of
the 3A and 3B skills.

GO! Think | Project 3L Jobs Newsletter

Project Files

For Project 3L, you will need the following file:

New blank Word document

You will save your document as:

Lastname_Firstname_3L_Jobs_Newsletter

The marketing manager of Memphis Primary Materials needs to create the next issue of the company's monthly newsletter (Volume 1, Number 7—July 2016), which will focus on "green jobs." Green jobs are jobs associated with environmentally friendly companies or are positions with firms that manufacture, sell, or install energy-saving or resource-saving products.

Use the following information to create a newsletter that includes a nameplate, multiple columns, at least two articles with article titles formatted so that they stand out, at least one clip art image, one screenshot, and one paragraph that includes a border and shading.

The articles you write can be on any topic regarding green jobs, and might include an introduction to the topic, information about a recent (or future) green job conference, and a discussion of green jobs in the United States. You will need to research this topic on the Web. A good place to start is www.epa.gov. You might also consider doing a Web search for the terms **green jobs** or **green jobs conference**

Add the file name to the footer. Add appropriate information to the Document Panel. Save the document as **Lastname_Firstname_3L_Jobs_Newsletter** and submit it as directed.

End You have completed Project 3L ——————————————

Apply a combination of
the 3A and 3B skills.

GO! Think | Project 3M Construction Report

Project Files

For Project 3M, you will need the following file:

New blank Word document

You will save your document as:

Lastname_Firstname_3M_Construction_Report

As part of the ongoing research provided on environment topics by the staff of Memphis Primary Materials, the Marketing Director, Henry Miller, has asked a summer intern, James Bodine, to create a report on recycling and reuse in the construction and demolition of buildings.

Create a new file and save it as **Lastname_Firstname_3M_Construction_Report** Use the following information to create a report written in the MLA format. The report should include at least two footnotes, at least two citations, and should include a *Works Cited* page.

The report should contain an introduction, and then details about, for example, how much construction material can be salvaged from existing buildings, how these materials can be reused in future buildings, and how materials can be saved and recycled on new building projects. A good place to start is www.epa.gov, which has a number of articles on recycling and reuse of materials during construction and demolition. You might also consider doing a Web search for the terms **construction recycling** or **demolition recycling** or **construction and demolition**

Add the file name to the footer. Add appropriate information to the Document Panel and submit it as directed.

End You have completed Project 3M ——————————————

Outcomes-Based Assessments

Apply a combination of the **3B** skills.

You and GO! | Project **3N** College Newsletter

Project Files

For Project 3N, you will need the following file:

New blank Word document

You will save your document as

Lastname_Firstname_3N_College_Newsletter

In this project, you will create a one-page newsletter. The newsletter should include at least one article describing your college and one article about an academic or athletic program at your college.

Be sure to include a nameplate, at least two articles, at least one clip art or screenshot image, and a bordered paragraph or paragraphs. Before you submit the newsletter, be sure to check it for grammar and spelling errors, and also be sure to format the newsletter in an attractive manner by using the skills you practiced in this chapter.

Save the file as **Lastname_Firstname_3N_College_Newsletter** Add the file name to the footer, and add your name, your course name and section number, and the keywords **newsletter** and **college** to the Document Panel. Save and submit your file as directed.

 You have completed Project 3N ⎯⎯⎯⎯⎯⎯⎯⎯⎯⎯⎯⎯

Apply a combination of the **3A** and **3B** skills.

GO! Collaborate | Project **3O** Bell Orchid Hotels Group Running Case

Your instructor may assign this group case project to your class. If your instructor assigns this project, he or she will provide you with information and instructions to work as part of a group. The group will apply the skills gained thus far to help the Bell Orchid Hotel Group achieve its business goals.

 You have completed Project 3O ⎯⎯⎯⎯⎯⎯⎯⎯⎯⎯⎯⎯

Business Running Case

Razvan CHIRNOAGA/Shutterstock

This project relates to **Front Range Action Sports**, which is one of the country's largest retailers of sports gear and outdoor recreation merchandise. The company has large retail stores in Colorado, Washington, Oregon, California, and New Mexico, in addition to a growing online business. Major merchandise categories include fishing, camping, rock climbing, winter sports, action sports, water sports, team sports, racquet sports, fitness, golf, apparel, and footwear.

In this project, you will apply skills you practiced from the Objectives in Word Chapters 1-3. You will assist Irene Shviktar, the Vice President of Marketing, to edit and create documents for a National Sales Meeting that will precede a Winter Sports Expo sponsored by Front Range Action Sports. The first document is a cover letter from the vice president to the company president. The letter will accompany a packet of materials for the meeting and the expo, which includes a brief resume for the guest speaker, a flyer that will announce the expo, a newsletter for employees, a research paper on the history and development of skis, and a set of name tags for a group of employees attending the national sales meeting. Your completed documents will look similar to Figure 1.1.

Project Files

For Project BRC1, you will need the following files:

> New blank Word document
> wBRC1_Cover_Letter_Text
> wBRC1_Newsletter
> wBRC1_Career_Text
> wBRC1_Ski_Research
> wBRC1_Addresses
> wBRC1_Flyer_Text
> wBRC1_Downhill_Racing
> wBRC1_Powder_Skiing

You will save your documents as:

> Lastname_Firstname_BRC1_Cover_Letter
> Lastname_Firstname_BRC1_Newsletter
> Lastname_Firstname_BRC1_Resume
> Lastname_Firstname_BRC1_Ski_Research
> Lastname_Firstname_BRC1_Name_Tags
> Lastname_Firstname_BRC1_Flyer

Project Results

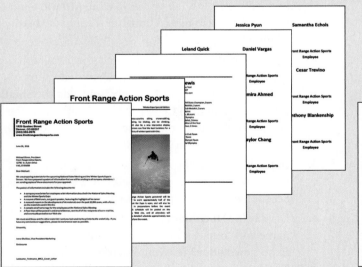

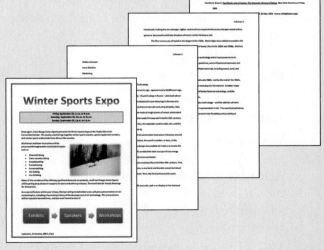

Figure 1.1

Business Running Case

Front Range Action Sports

1 **Start** Word and display a new document. Display rulers and formatting marks. In the location where you are storing your projects, create a new folder named **Front Range Action Sports** or navigate to this folder if you have already created it. **Save** the new document as **Lastname_Firstname_BRC1_Cover_Letter** Add the file name to the footer. Apply the **No Spacing** style to the document, and then type the following to form a letterhead:

> **Front Range Action Sports**
>
> **1926 Quebec Street**
>
> **Denver, CO 80207**
>
> **(303) 555-0970**
>
> **www.frontrangeactionsports.com**

a. Press Enter to create a blank line below the letterhead. If the Web address changes to blue, right-click the address, and then from the shortcut menu, remove the hyperlink.

b. Select the letterhead text, but not the blank line. Change the **Font** to **Arial Rounded MT Bold**. Select the first line, and increase the **Font Size** to **28 pt** Change the **Font Size** of the remaining four lines to **12 pt**. Select all five lines of the letterhead, display the **Borders and Shading** dialog box, and then create a **6 pt**, **Black** border on the left side of the selected text.

c. Enter the following information using business letter format:

> **June 26, 2016**
>
> **Michael Dixon, President**
>
> **Front Range Action Sports**
>
> **12756 St. Aubin Drive**
>
> **Vail, CO 81658**

d. Press Enter two times. With the insertion point in the second blank line below the inside address, **Insert** the text from the file **wBRC1_Cover_Letter_Text**, and then remove the blank line at the bottom of the selected text.

e. Move to the top of the document, and then by using either the **Spelling and Grammar** dialog box, or by right-clicking selected words, correct the *three* spelling, grammar, and word usage errors. Ignore proper names. In the paragraph that begins *If you have any*, select the first sentence and move it to the end of the paragraph.

f. In the middle of the document, select the five paragraphs beginning with *A company newsletter*, and create a bulleted list. In the fourth bullet, select the text *national sales meeting*, and then on the **Home tab**, in the **Font group**, click the **Change Case** button [Aa▾], and then click **Capitalize Each Word**.

g. Display the **Document Panel**, add your name, course information, and the **Keywords expo, national sales meeting** View your document in **Print Preview,** make any necessary adjustments, **Save** and **Close** your document, and then hold this file until you complete the project.

2 From your student files, open **wBRC1_Newsletter**, and then **Save** it in your **Front Range Action Sports** folder as **Lastname_Firstname_BRC1_Newsletter** Add the file name to the footer.

a. Select the first paragraph of text—*Front Range Action Sports*. Change the **Font** to **Arial Rounded MT Bold**, the **Font Size** to **36**, and **Center** the text. Select the second paragraph of text, display the **Borders and Shading** dialog box, and then add a **Black**, **3 pt** line below the selected text.

b. Starting with the paragraph that begins *National Sales*, select all of the text from that point to the end of the document. Change the **Spacing After** to **6 pt**, format the text in two columns, and apply the **Justify** alignment.

c. At the top of the first column, select the paragraph *National Sales Meeting*. From the **Font** dialog box, change the **Font Size** to **20**, apply **Bold**, add the **Small caps** effect, and then **Center** the paragraph. Near the bottom of the same column, apply the same formatting to the paragraph *Winter Sports Expo*.

d. In the blank line above the last paragraph of the newsletter, **Insert** the picture **wBRC1_Powder_Skiing**. Set the **Width** of the picture to **3"**.

e. Display the **Document Panel**, and then add your name and course information and the **Keywords Expo newsletter** View your document in **Print Preview,** make any necessary adjustments, **Save** and **Close** your document, and then hold this file until you complete the project.

3 Display a new blank document and **Save** it in your **Front Range Action Sports** folder as **Lastname_Firstname_BRC1_Resume** Add the file name to the footer. **Insert** a **2 × 3** table.

(Business Running Case: Front Range Action Sports continues on the next page)

Business Running Case

Front Range Action Sports (continued)

a. In the first cell of the table, type on four lines:

Robert Lewis

1227 Aspen Lake Trail

Vail, CO 81657

www.boblewisskis.com

b. In the second row, in the first cell, type **CAREER HIGHLIGHTS** In the cell to the immediate right, **Insert** the text from the file **wBRC1_Career_Text**, and then press Backspace to remove the blank line at the bottom of the inserted text.

c. In the third row, in the first cell, type **EDUCATION** In the cell to the right, type Mr. Lewis' educational information as follows:

University of Colorado

Ph.D. in Psychology

University of Colorado

M.S. in Psychology

University of Minnesota

B.S. in Psychology

d. Insert a new row at the bottom of the table. In the first cell of the new row, type **CONSULTANT** and then in the cell to the right, type the following:

U.S. Junior Ski Team

U.S. National Ski Team

Special Olympics

e. Apply **Bold** to the headings *CAREER HIGHLIGHTS*, *EDUCATION*, and *CONSULTANT*. Drag the vertical border between the two columns to approximately **1.5 inches on the horizontal ruler**.

f. In the first row, **Merge** the two cells, and then **Center** the text. Select *Robert Lewis*, increase the font size to **24 pt**, apply **Bold**, and then add **12 pt** spacing **Before** the text. If necessary, remove the hyperlink from the Web address. Select the Web address and add **18 pt** spacing after the text.

g. Create a bulleted list for the items below *SKIING* and below *COACHING*. In the cells to the right of *EDUCATION* and *CONSULTANT*, add **12 pt** spacing **After** the last item in each cell. Add **12 pt** spacing **After** *Ph.D. in Psychology* and *M.S. in Psychology*. Apply **Bold** to the three paragraphs that begin *University*.

h. Select the table, and then remove all borders. From the **Borders and Shading** dialog box, add a **3 pt** border to the top and bottom of the table. Change the top

margin to **1.5"**. To the **Document Panel**, add your name, course information, and the **Keywords Robert Lewis resume** View your document in **Print Preview,** make any necessary adjustments, **Save** and then **Close** your document. Hold this file until you complete the project.

4 From your student files, open the document **wBRC1_Ski_Research**. **Save** the document in your **Front Range Action Sports** folder as **Lastname_Firstname_BRC1_Ski_Research** Display the header area, type **Johnson** and then press Spacebar. Display the **Page Number gallery**, and then in the **Current Position**, add the **Plain Number** style. Apply **Align Text Right** formatting to the header. Add the file name to the footer.

a. In the blank line at the beginning of the document, type **Walter Johnson** and then press Enter. Type **Irene Shviktar** and press Enter. Type **Marketing** and press Enter. Type **June 5, 2016**

b. Select all of the text in the document. Change the **Line Spacing** to **2.0**, and then change the **Spacing After** to **0 pt**. Click anywhere in the title that begins *The Evolution* and then **Center** the title.

c. Beginning with the paragraph that begins *The use of skis*, select the text from that point to the end of the document. Indent the first line of each selected paragraph to **0.5"**.

d. Near the top of **Page 1**, in the paragraph that begins *The use of skis*, in the third line, position the insertion point to the right of the period following *wood*, and then insert the following footnote:

The oldest known ski and pole is more than 4,000 years old, and is on display in the National Ski Hall of Fame and Museum in Ishpeming, Michigan.

e. Select the footnote text, change the **Font Size** to **11 pt**, add a **First Line Indent** of **0.5"**, and set **Line spacing** to **2.0"**.

f. In the paragraph that begins *The use of skis*, position the insertion point to the left of the period at the end of the paragraph. Using the **MLA** format, insert the following **Book** citation:

Author: **Huntford, Roland**

Title: **Two Planks and a Passion: The Dramatic History of Skiing**

Year: **2008**

City: **New York**

Publisher: **Continuum Press**

(Business Running Case: Front Range Action Sports continues on the next page)

Front Range Action Sports (continued)

g. In the text, select the *Huntford* citation and insert the page numbers **4-6** Position the insertion point to the left of the period at the end of the document. Add the following **Web site** citation:

Author:	**Lund, Morten; Masia, Seth**
Name of Web Page:	**A Short History of Skis**
Year Accessed:	**2016**
Month Accessed:	**May**
Day Accessed:	**25**
URL:	**www.skiinghistory.org**

h. At the end of the document, insert a manual page break to create a new page. Change the **First Line Indent** to **0"**. Add a **Works Cited** title, display the **Bibliography** gallery, and then at the bottom of the gallery, click **Insert Bibliography**. Select the two references, remove the space after the paragraphs, and change the line spacing to **2.0. Center** the *Works Cited* title.

i. Press [Ctrl] + [A] to move to the top of the document, and then on the **Review tab**, in the **Proofing group**, click **Spelling & Grammar**. Ignore proper names, change *polyethelene* to *polyethylene*, and correct the subject-verb agreement between *have* and *has* in the last paragraph. Display the **Document Panel** and add your name and course information and the **Keywords ski history, ski research** View your document in **Print Preview** and make any necessary adjustments. **Save** and **Close** your document, and hold this file until you complete the project.

5 Display a **New** blank document. Start the **Step by Step Mail Merge Wizard** and select **Labels** as the document type. In **Step 2**, set **Label options** to use the **Auto default** tray (yours may vary) and **Avery US Letter 74541 Clip Style Name Badges**. In **Step 3**, **Use an existing list**, browse to select **wBRC1_Addresses**, click **Open**, and then click **OK**. This is a Name Badge label, and the steps differ slightly from the steps for creating mailing labels.

a. In **Step 4**, on the Ribbon, in the **Write & Insert Fields group**, click the **Insert Merge Field button arrow**, click **First_Name** field, press [Spacebar], and then repeat for the **Last_Name** field. Press [Enter] six times.

b. Type **Front Range Action Sports** and press [Enter]. Type **Employee** Select the first line of the label—

<<First_Name>> <<Last_Name>>. Change the **Font Size** to **24**, apply **Bold**, and then **Center** the text. Select the last two lines of text, change the **Font Size** to **18**, apply **Bold**, and then **Center** the text. In the **Mail Merge** task pane, click **Update all labels**, and then move to step 5—**Preview your labels**.

c. **Complete the merge**. On the **Mailings tab**, in the **Finish group**, click the **Finish & Merge** button, and then click **Edit Individual Documents**. Merge **All** of the records. **Save** the resulting document in your **Front Range Action Sports** folder as **Lastname_Firstname_BRC1_Name_Tags** and then if necessary, close the Mail Merge task pane. Add the file name to the footer. Preview the labels in **Print Preview** and make any necessary adjustments.

d. Display the **Document Panel**, and then add your name and course information and the **Keywords name tags, expo Save** and close your label document. **Close** the original document without saving. Hold this file until you complete the project.

6 From your student files, open **wBRC1_Flyer_Text**, and then **Save** it in your **Front Range Action Sports** folder as **Lastname_Firstname_BRC1_Flyer** Add the file name to the footer.

a. Select the title *Winter Sports Expo*, and apply a **Gradient Fill - Blue, Accent 1 Text Effect**—in the third row, the fourth effect. Increase the **Font Size** to **56** point, and then **Center** the title. Select the two paragraphs below the title that begin *Friday* and *Saturday*, and then change the **Spacing After** to **0**. Select the three paragraphs below the title—the three days and times—and then **Center** and apply **Bold**.

b. With the three paragraphs still selected, display the **Borders and Shading** dialog box. Apply a **Box** border using theme color **Blue, Accent 1** and a **3 pt** border, and add **Shading** using theme color **Blue, Accent 1, Lighter 80%**. Apply a **Page Border** using the **Box** setting, and the theme color **Blue, Accent 1** with a **Weight** of **6 pt**.

c. Format the seven sport topics—beginning with *Downhill skiing*—as a bulleted list, and then click anywhere to deselect the bulleted list. **Insert** the picture **wBRC1_Downhill_Racing**. Change the **Width** of the picture to **3.5"**, and then set **Wrap Text** to **Square**. Move the picture so that the right edge

(Business Running Case: Front Range Action Sports continues on the next page)

Front Range Action Sports (continued)

aligns with the right margin, and the top edge aligns with the top edge of the text that begins *Workshops and how-to*. Apply a **Picture Effect** using the **Soft Edge** of **10 point**.

d. Move to the end of the document and press Enter two times. Display the **Choose a SmartArt Graphic** dialog box, select **Process**, and then choose the first style—**Basic Process**. Click the border of the SmartArt graphic to deselect the first box. On the **Format tab**, set the **Width** of the SmartArt graphic to **6.5"** and the **Height** to **1"**; or, drag the SmartArt graphic sizing handles to change the width to **6.5"** and the height to **1"**.

In the three boxes, add the following text in this order: **Exhibits** and **Speakers** and **Workshops** On the **Design tab**, apply the **3-D Polished** style. Click anywhere outside of the SmartArt to deselect it. Display your document in **Print Preview** and make any necessary adjustments.

e. Display the **Document Panel** and add your name and course information and the **Keywords expo, flyer Save** and **Close** the document. Submit the six files that you created in this project—the cover letter, newsletter, resume, research paper, name tag labels, and flyer—as directed by your instructor. **Exit** Word.

End **You have completed Business Running Case 1** ────────────

Creating a Worksheet and Charting Data

OUTCOMES

At the end of this chapter you will be able to:

OBJECTIVES

Mastering these objectives will enable you to:

PROJECT 1A
Create a sales report with an embedded column chart and sparklines.

1. Create, Save, and Navigate an Excel Workbook (p. 227)
2. Enter Data in a Worksheet (p. 230)
3. Construct and Copy Formulas and Use the SUM Function (p. 236)
4. Format Cells with Merge & Center and Cell Styles (p. 240)
5. Chart Data to Create a Column Chart and Insert Sparklines (p. 242)
6. Print, Display Formulas, and Close Excel (p. 247)

PROJECT 1B
Calculate the value of an inventory.

7. Check Spelling in a Worksheet (p. 253)
8. Enter Data by Range (p. 255)
9. Construct Formulas for Mathematical Operations (p. 256)
10. Edit Values in a Worksheet (p. 261)
11. Format a Worksheet (p. 262)

Shutterstock

In This Chapter

In this chapter, you will use Microsoft Excel 2010 to create and analyze data organized into columns and rows. After entering data in a worksheet, you can perform calculations, analyze the data to make logical decisions, and create charts.

In this chapter, you will create and modify Excel workbooks. You will practice the basics of worksheet design, create a footer, enter and edit data in a worksheet, chart data, and then save, preview, and print workbooks. You will also construct formulas for mathematical operations.

The projects in this chapter relate to **Texas Spectrum Wireless**, which provides accessories and software for all major brands of cell phones, smart phones, PDAs, mp3 players, and portable computers. The company sells thousands of unique products in their retail stores, which are located throughout Texas and the southern United States. They also sell thousands of items each year through their Web site, and offer free shipping and returns to their customers. The company takes pride in offering unique categories of accessories such as waterproof and ruggedized gear.

Project 1A Sales Report with Embedded Column Chart and Sparklines

Project Activities

In Activities 1.01 through 1.16, you will create an Excel worksheet for Roslyn Thomas, the President of Texas Spectrum Wireless. The worksheet displays the first quarter sales of wireless accessories for the current year, and includes a chart to visually represent the data. Your completed worksheet will look similar to Figure 1.1.

Project Files

For Project 1A, you will need the following file:

New blank Excel workbook

You will save your workbook as:

Lastname_Firstname_1A_Quarterly_Sales

Project Results

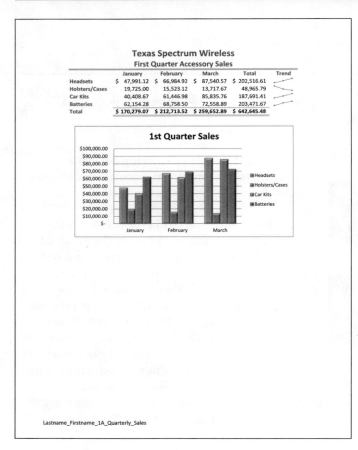

Figure 1.1
Project 1A Quarterly Sales

Objective 1 | Create, Save, and Navigate an Excel Workbook

On startup, Excel displays a new blank ***workbook***—the Excel document that stores your data—which contains one or more pages called a ***worksheet***. A worksheet—or ***spreadsheet***—is stored in a workbook, and is formatted as a pattern of uniformly spaced horizontal rows and vertical columns. The intersection of a column and a row forms a box referred to as a ***cell***.

Activity 1.01 | Starting Excel and Naming and Saving a Workbook

1 **Start** Excel. In the lower right corner of the window, if necessary, click the Normal button ▦, and then to the right, locate the zoom—magnification—level.

> Your zoom level should be 100%, although some figures in this textbook may be shown at a higher zoom level.

Another Way
Use the keyboard shortcut F12 to display the Save As dialog box.

2 In the upper left corner of your screen, click the **File tab** to display **Backstage** view, click **Save As**, and then in the **Save As** dialog box, navigate to the location where you will store your workbooks for this chapter.

3 In your storage location, create a new folder named **Excel Chapter 1** Open the new folder to display its folder window, and then in the **File name** box, notice that *Book1* displays as the default file name.

4 In the **File name** box, click *Book1* to select it, and then using your own name, type **Lastname_Firstname_1A_Quarterly_Sales** being sure to include the underscore (Shift + -) instead of spaces between words. Compare your screen with Figure 1.2.

Figure 1.2

Path to your new *Excel Chapter 1* folder in address bar (yours may vary)

File name with your name and underscores between words

Save button

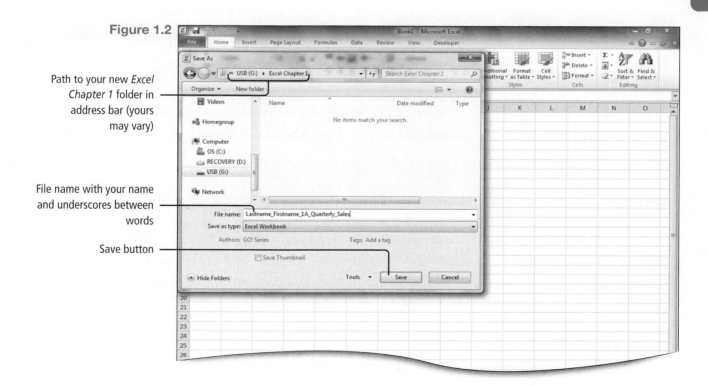

5 Click **Save**. Compare your screen with Figure 1.3, and then take a moment to study the Excel window parts in the table in Figure 1.4.

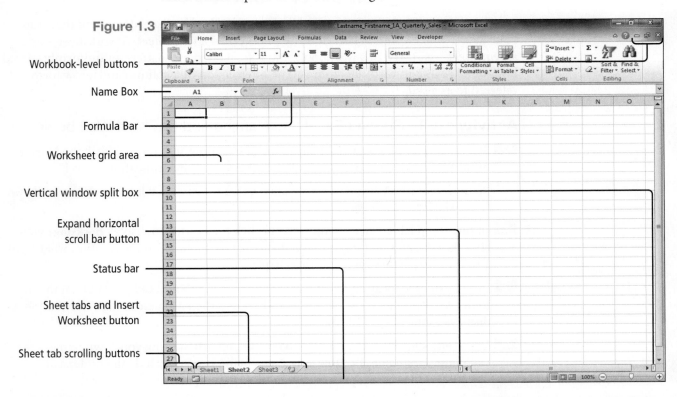

Figure 1.3

Workbook-level buttons
Name Box
Formula Bar
Worksheet grid area
Vertical window split box
Expand horizontal scroll bar button
Status bar
Sheet tabs and Insert Worksheet button
Sheet tab scrolling buttons

Parts of the Excel Window

Screen Part	Description
Expand horizontal scroll bar button	Increases the width of the horizontal scroll bar.
Formula Bar	Displays the value or formula contained in the active cell; also permits entry or editing.
Sheet tabs and Insert Worksheet button	Identify the worksheets in a workbook and inserts an additional worksheet.
Name Box	Displays the name of the selected cell, table, chart, or object.
Sheet tab scrolling buttons	Display sheet tabs that are not in view when there are numerous sheet tabs.
Status bar	Displays the current cell mode, page number, worksheet information, view and zoom buttons, and for numerical data, common calculations such as Sum and Average.
Vertical window split box	Splits the worksheet into two vertical views of the same worksheet.
Workbook-level buttons	Minimize, close, or restore the previous size of the displayed workbook.
Worksheet grid area	Displays the columns and rows that intersect to form the worksheet's cells.

Figure 1.4

Activity 1.02 | Navigating a Worksheet and a Workbook

1 Take a moment to study Figure 1.5 and the table in Figure 1.6 to become familiar with the Excel workbook window.

Figure 1.5

Expand Formula Bar button
Lettered column headings
Select All box
Numbered row headings
Excel pointer
Horizontal window split box

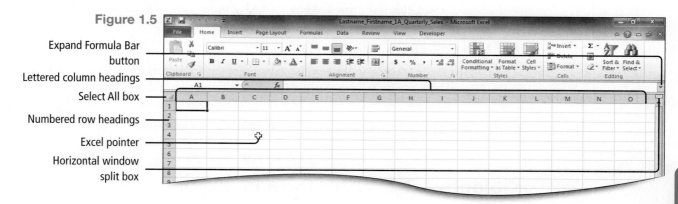

Excel Workbook Window Elements

Workbook Window Element	Description
Excel pointer	Displays the pointer in Excel.
Expand Formula Bar button	Increases the height of the Formula Bar to display lengthy cell content.
Horizontal window split box	Splits the worksheet into two horizontal views of the same worksheet.
Lettered column headings	Indicate the column letter.
Numbered row headings	Indicate the row number.
Select All box	Selects all the cells in a worksheet.

Figure 1.6

2 In the lower right corner of the screen, in the horizontal scroll bar, click the **right scroll arrow** one time to shift **column A** out of view.

A *column* is a vertical group of cells in a worksheet. Beginning with the first letter of the alphabet, *A*, a unique letter identifies each column—this is called the *column heading*. Clicking one of the horizontal scroll bar arrows shifts the window either left or right one column at a time.

3 Point to the **right scroll arrow**, and then hold down the left mouse button until the columns begin to scroll rapidly to the right; release the mouse button when you begin to see pairs of letters as the column headings.

4 Slowly drag the horizontal scroll box to the left, and notice that just above the scroll box, ScreenTips with the column letters display as you drag. Drag the horizontal scroll box left or right—or click the left or right scroll arrow—as necessary to position **column Z** near the center of your screen.

Column headings after column Z use two letters starting with AA, AB, and so on through ZZ. After that, columns begin with three letters beginning with AAA. This pattern provides 16,384 columns. The last column is XFD.

5 In the lower left portion of your screen, click the **Sheet2 tab**.

The second worksheet displays and is the active sheet. Column A displays at the left.

6 In the vertical scroll bar, click the **down scroll arrow** one time to move **Row 1** out of view.

> A *row* is a horizontal group of cells. Beginning with number 1, a unique number identifies each row—this is the *row heading*, located at the left side of the worksheet. A single worksheet has 1,048,576 rows.

7 In the lower left corner, click the **Sheet1 tab**.

> The first worksheet in the workbook becomes the active worksheet. By default, new workbooks contain three worksheets. When you save a workbook, the worksheets are contained within it and do not have separate file names.

8 Use the skills you just practiced to scroll horizontally to display **column A**, and if necessary, **row 1**.

Objective 2 | Enter Data in a Worksheet

Cell content, which is anything you type in a cell, can be one of two things: either a *constant value*—referred to simply as a *value*—or a *formula*. A formula is an equation that performs mathematical calculations on values in your worksheet. The most commonly used values are *text values* and *number values*, but a value can also include a date or a time of day.

Activity 1.03 | Entering Text and Using AutoComplete

A text value, also referred to as a *label*, usually provides information about number values in other worksheet cells. For example, a title such as First Quarter Accessory Sales gives the reader an indication that the data in the worksheet relates to information about sales of accessories during the three-month period January through March.

1 Click the **Sheet1 tab** to make it the active sheet. Point to and then click the cell at the intersection of **column A** and **row 1** to make it the *active cell*—the cell is outlined in black and ready to accept data.

> The intersecting column letter and row number form the *cell reference*—also called the *cell address*. When a cell is active, its column letter and row number are highlighted. The cell reference of the selected cell, *A1*, displays in the Name Box.

2 With cell **A1** as the active cell, type the worksheet title **Texas Spectrum Wireless** and then press Enter. Compare your screen with Figure 1.7.

> Text or numbers in a cell are referred to as *data*. You must confirm the data you type in a cell by pressing Enter or by some other keyboard movement, such as pressing Tab or an arrow key. Pressing Enter moves the selection to the cell below.

Figure 1.7

Name Box displays active cell—A2

Column heading and row heading of the active cell highlighted

Worksheet title entered

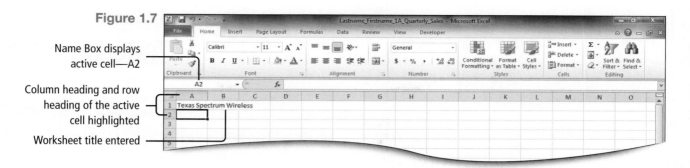

3 In cell **A1**, notice that the text does not fit; the text spills over and displays in cells **B1** and **C1** to the right.

If text is too long for a cell and cells to the right are empty, the text will display. If the cells to the right contain other data, only the text that will fit in the cell displays.

4 In cell **A2**, type the worksheet subtitle **First Quarter Accessory Sales** and then press Enter. Compare your screen with Figure 1.8.

Figure 1.8

Name Box displays *A3* (cell reference of active cell)

Column heading and row heading of selected cell highlighted

Worksheet subtitle typed

Excel pointer

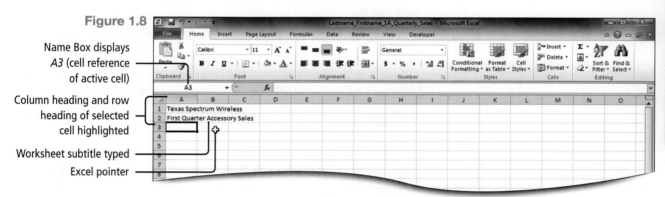

5 Press Enter again to make cell **A4** the active cell. In cell **A4**, type **Headsets** which will form the first row title, and then press Enter.

The text characters that you typed align at the left edge of the cell—referred to as *left alignment*—and cell A5 becomes the active cell. Left alignment is the default for text values.

6 In cell **A5**, type **H** and notice the text from the previous cell displays.

If the first characters you type in a cell match an existing entry in the column, Excel fills in the remaining characters for you. This feature, called *AutoComplete*, assists only with alphabetic values.

Another Way

Use the keyboard shortcut Ctrl + S to Save changes to your workbook.

7 Continue typing the remainder of the row title **olsters/Cases** and press Enter.

The AutoComplete suggestion is removed when the entry you are typing differs from the previous value.

8 In cell **A6**, type **Car Kits** and press Enter. In cell **A7**, type **Batteries** and press Enter. In cell **A8**, type **Total** and press Enter. On the Quick Access Toolbar, click **Save** 🖫.

Excel | Chapter 1

Activity 1.04 | Using Auto Fill and Keyboard Shortcuts

1 Click cell **B3**. Type **J** and notice that when you begin to type in a cell, on the **Formula Bar**, the **Cancel** and **Enter** buttons become active, as shown in Figure 1.9.

Figure 1.9

Cancel and Enter buttons

Row titles entered

Excel pointer when entering text in a cell

2 Continue to type **anuary** On the **Formula Bar**, notice that values you type in a cell also display there. Then, on the **Formula Bar**, click the **Enter** button ✔ to confirm the entry and keep cell **B3** active.

3 With cell **B3** active, locate the small black square in the lower right corner of the selected cell.

> You can drag this ***fill handle***—the small black square in the lower right corner of a selected cell—to adjacent cells to fill the cells with values based on the first cell.

4 Point to the **fill handle** until the ➕ pointer displays, hold down the left mouse button, drag to the right to cell **D3**, and as you drag, notice the ScreenTips *February* and *March*. Release the mouse button.

5 Under the text that you just filled, click the **Auto Fill Options** button 🖫▾ that displays, and then compare your screen with Figure 1.10.

> ***Auto Fill*** generates and extends a ***series*** of values into adjacent cells based on the value of other cells. A series is a group of things that come one after another in succession; for example, *January, February, March.*

> The Auto Fill Options button displays options to fill the data; options vary depending on the content and program from which you are filling, and the format of the data you are filling.

> *Fill Series* is selected, indicating the action that was taken. Because the options are related to the current task, the button is referred to as being ***context sensitive***.

Figure 1.10

January, February, March display in cells B3, C3, and D3

Fill handle

Auto Fill Options list

Auto Fill Options button

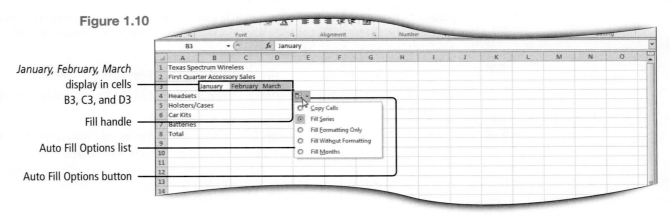

6 Click in any cell to cancel the display of the Auto Fill Options list.

> The list no longer displays; the button will display until you perform some other screen action.

7 Press `Ctrl` + `Home`, which is the keyboard shortcut to make cell **A1** active.

8 On the Quick Access Toolbar, click **Save** 🖫 to save the changes you have made to your workbook, and then take a moment to study the table in Figure 1.11 to become familiar with additional keyboard shortcuts with which you can navigate the Excel worksheet.

Keyboard Shortcuts to Navigate the Excel Window

To Move the Location of the Active Cell:	Press:
Up, down, right, or left one cell	`↑`, `↓`, `→`, `←`
Down one cell	`Enter`
Up one cell	`Shift` + `Enter`
Up one full screen	`Page Up`
Down one full screen	`PageDown`
To column A of the current row	`Home`
To the last cell in the last column of the active area (the rectangle formed by all the rows and columns in a worksheet that contain entries)	`Ctrl` + `End`
To cell A1	`Ctrl` + `Home`
Right one cell	`Tab`
Left one cell	`Shift` + `Tab`

Figure 1.11

Excel | Chapter 1

Activity 1.05 | Aligning Text and Adjusting the Size of Columns

1 In the **column heading area**, point to the vertical line between **column A** and **column B** to display the ⬌ pointer, press and hold down the left mouse button, and then compare your screen with Figure 1.12.

A ScreenTip displays information about the width of the column. The default width of a column is 64 *pixels*. A pixel, short for *picture element*, is a point of light measured in dots per square inch. Sixty-four pixels equal 8.43 characters, which is the average number of digits that will fit in a cell using the default font. The default font in Excel is Calibri and the default font size is 11.

Figure 1.12

Column heading area —

Mouse pointer —

ScreenTip —

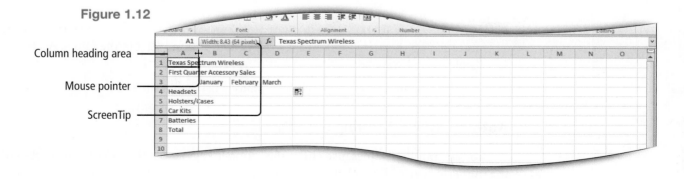

2 Drag to the right, and when the number of pixels indicated in the ScreenTip reaches **100 pixels**, release the mouse button. If you are not satisfied with your result, click Undo 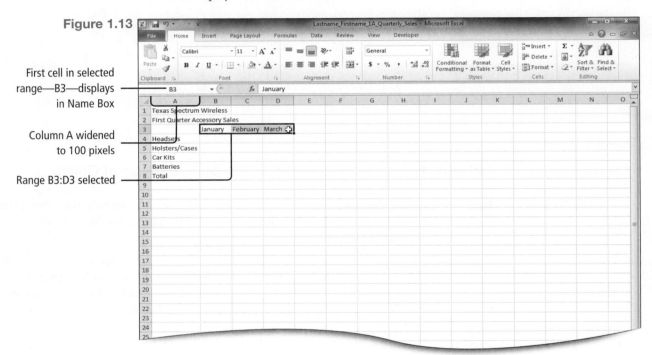 on the Quick Access Toolbar and begin again.

> This width accommodates the longest row title in cells A4 through A8—*Holsters/Cases*. The worksheet title and subtitle in cells A1 and A2 span more than one column and still do not fit in column A.

3 Point to cell **B3** and then drag across to select cells **B3**, **C3**, and **D3**. Compare your screen with Figure 1.13; if you are not satisfied with your result, click anywhere and begin again.

> The three cells, B3 through D3, are selected and form a ***range***—two or more cells on a worksheet that are adjacent (next to each other) or nonadjacent (not next to each other). This range of cells is referred to as *B3:D3*. When you see a colon (:) between two cell references, the range includes all the cells between the two cell references.

> A range of cells that is selected in this manner is indicated by a dark border, and Excel treats the range as a single unit so you can make the same changes to more than one cell at a time. The selected cells in the range are highlighted except for the first cell in the range, which displays in the Name Box.

Figure 1.13

First cell in selected range—B3—displays in Name Box

Column A widened to 100 pixels

Range B3:D3 selected

4 With the range **B3:D3** selected, point anywhere over the selected range, right-click, and then on the Mini toolbar, click the **Center** button. On the Quick Access Toolbar, click **Save**.

> The column titles *January*, *February*, *March* align in the center of each cell.

Activity 1.06 | Entering Numbers

To type number values, use either the number keys across the top of your keyboard or the numeric keypad if you have one—laptop computers may not have a numeric keypad.

1 Under *January*, click cell **B4**, type **47991.12** and then on the **Formula Bar**, click the **Enter** button ✓ to maintain cell **B4** as the active cell. Compare your screen with Figure 1.14.

By default, *number* values align at the right edge of the cell. The default ***number format***—a specific way in which Excel displays numbers—is the ***general format***. In the default general format, whatever you type in the cell will display, with the exception of trailing zeros to the right of a decimal point. For example, in the number 237.50 the *0* following the *5* is a trailing zero.

Data that displays in a cell is the ***displayed value***. Data that displays in the Formula Bar is the ***underlying value***. The number of digits or characters that display in a cell—the displayed value—depends on the width of the column. Calculations on numbers will always be based on the underlying value, not the displayed value.

Figure 1.14

Underlying value in the Formula Bar

Displayed value in the cell

General indicated as the Number format

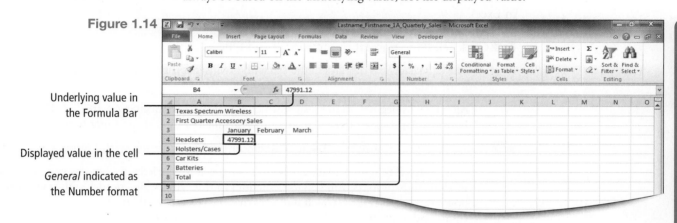

2 Press [Tab] to make cell **C4** active. Then, enter the remaining sales numbers as shown by using the following technique: Press [Tab] to confirm your entry and move across the row, and then press [Enter] at the end of a row to move to the next row.

	January	February	March
Headsets	47991.12	**66984.92**	**87540.57**
Holsters/Cases	**19725**	**15523.12**	**13717.67**
Car Kits	**40408.67**	**61446.98**	**85835.76**
Batteries	**62154.28**	**68758.50**	**72558.89**

3 Compare the numbers you entered with Figure 1.15 and then **Save** 🖫 your workbook.

In the default general format, trailing zeros to the right of a decimal point will not display. For example, when you type *68758.50*, the cell displays 68758.5 instead.

Figure 1.15

Values entered for each category in each month

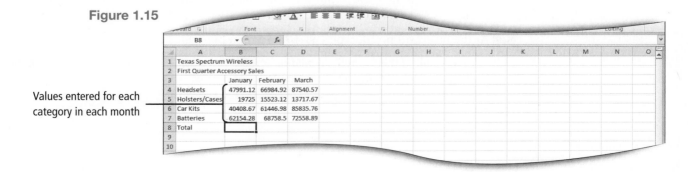

Objective 3 | Construct and Copy Formulas and Use the SUM Function

A cell contains either a constant value (text or numbers) or a formula. A formula is an equation that performs mathematical calculations on values in other cells, and then places the result in the cell containing the formula. You can create formulas or use a *function*—a prewritten formula that looks at one or more values, performs an operation, and then returns a value.

Activity 1.07 | Constructing a Formula and Using the SUM Function

In this activity, you will practice three different ways to sum a group of numbers in Excel.

1 Click cell **B8** to make it the active cell and type **=**

The equal sign (=) displays in the cell with the insertion point blinking, ready to accept more data.

All formulas begin with the = sign, which signals Excel to begin a calculation. The Formula Bar displays the = sign, and the Formula Bar Cancel and Enter buttons display.

2 At the insertion point, type **b4** and then compare your screen with Figure 1.16.

A list of Excel functions that begin with the letter *B* may briefly display—as you progress in your study of Excel, you will use functions of this type. A blue border with small corner boxes surrounds cell B4, which indicates that the cell is part of an active formula. The color used in the box matches the color of the cell reference in the formula.

Figure 1.16

Cell B4 outlined in blue to show it is part of an active formula

Cell B8 displays the beginning of the formula, with *b4* in blue to match outlined cell

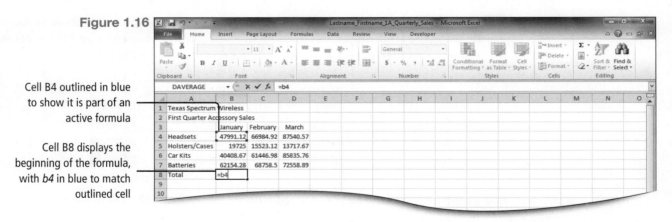

3 At the insertion point, type **+** and then type **b5**

A border of another color surrounds cell B5, and the color matches the color of the cell reference in the active formula. When typing cell references, it is not necessary to use uppercase letters.

4 At the insertion point, type **+b6+b7** and then press Enter.

The result of the formula calculation—*170279.1*—displays in the cell. Recall that in the default General format, trailing zeros do not display.

5 Click cell **B8** again, look at the **Formula Bar**, and then compare your screen with Figure 1.17.

> The formula adds the values in cells B4 through B7, and the result displays in cell B8. In this manner, you can construct a formula by typing. Although cell B8 displays the *result* of the formula, the formula itself displays in the Formula Bar. This is referred to as the *underlying formula*.

> Always view the Formula Bar to be sure of the exact content of a cell—*a displayed number may actually be a formula.*

Figure 1.17

Formula displays in Formula Bar

Total of values in cells B4:B7 displays in cell B8

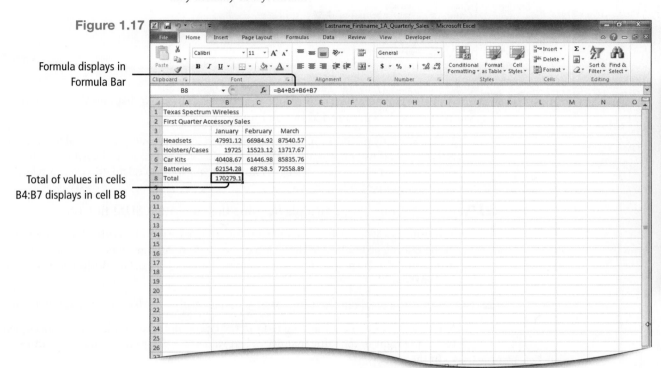

6 Click cell **C8** and type **=** to signal the beginning of a formula. Then, point to cell **C4** and click one time.

> The reference to the cell C4 is added to the active formula. A moving border surrounds the referenced cell, and the border color and the color of the cell reference in the formula are color coded to match.

7 At the insertion point, type **+** and then click cell **C5**. Repeat this process to complete the formula to add cells **C4** through **C7**, and then press Enter.

> The result of the formula calculation—*212713.5*—displays in the cell. This method of constructing a formula is the *point and click method*.

Another Way

Use the keyboard shortcut Alt + = ; or, on the Formulas tab, in the Function Library group, click the AutoSum button.

8 Click cell **D8**. On the **Home tab**, in the **Editing group**, click the **Sum** button Σ, and then compare your screen with Figure 1.18.

> *SUM* is an Excel function—a prewritten formula. A moving border surrounds the range D4:D7 and *=SUM(D4:D7)* displays in cell D8.

> The = sign signals the beginning of a formula, *SUM* indicates the type of calculation that will take place (addition), and *(D4:D7)* indicates the range of cells on which the sum calculation will be performed. A ScreenTip provides additional information about the action.

Figure 1.18

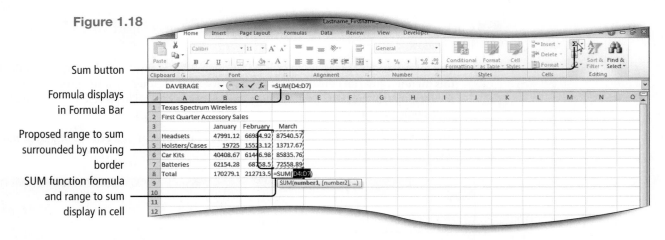

Sum button

Formula displays in Formula Bar

Proposed range to sum surrounded by moving border

SUM function formula and range to sum display in cell

9 Look at the **Formula Bar**, and notice that the formula also displays there. Then, look again at the cells surrounded by the moving border.

> When you activate the Sum function, Excel first looks *above* the active cell for a range of cells to sum. If no range is above the active cell, Excel will look to the *left* for a range of cells to sum. If the proposed range is not what you want to calculate, you can select a different group of cells.

10 Press Enter to construct a formula by using the prewritten SUM function.

> Your total is *259652.9*. Because the Sum function is frequently used, it has its own button in the Editing group on the Home tab of the Ribbon. A larger version of the button also displays on the Formulas tab in the Function Library group. This button is also referred to as *AutoSum*.

11 Notice that the totals in the range **B8:D8** display only *one* decimal place. Click **Save** 💾.

> Number values that are too long to fit in the cell do *not* spill over into the unoccupied cell to the right in the same manner as text values. Rather, Excel rounds the number to fit the space.

> *Rounding* is a procedure that determines which digit at the right of the number will be the last digit displayed and then increases it by one if the next digit to its right is 5, 6, 7, 8, or 9.

Activity 1.08 | Copying a Formula by Using the Fill Handle

You have practiced three ways to create a formula—by typing, by using the point-and-click technique, and by using a Function button from the Ribbon. You can also copy formulas. When you copy a formula from one cell to another, Excel adjusts the cell references to fit the new location of the formula.

1 Click cell **E3**, type **Total** and then press Enter.

> The text in cell E3 is centered because the centered format continues from the adjacent cell.

2 With cell **E4** as the active cell, hold down Alt, and then press =. Compare your screen with Figure 1.19.

> Alt + = is the keyboard shortcut for the Sum function. Recall that Excel first looks above the selected cell for a proposed range of cells to sum, and if no data is detected, Excel looks to the left and proposes a range of cells to sum.

Figure 1.19

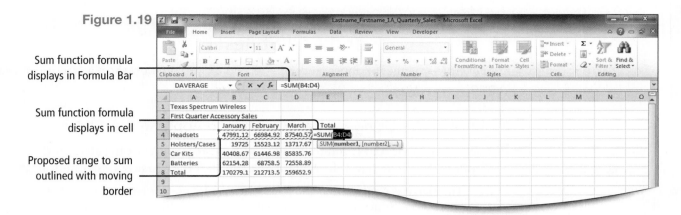

Sum function formula displays in Formula Bar

Sum function formula displays in cell

Proposed range to sum outlined with moving border

---

3 On the **Formula Bar**, click the **Enter** button ☑ to display the result and keep cell **E4** active.

> The total dollar amount of *Headsets* sold in the quarter is *202516.6*. In cells E5:E8, you can see that you need a formula similar to the one in E4, but formulas that refer to the cells in row 5, row 6, and so on.

4 With cell **E4** active, point to the fill handle in the lower right corner of the cell until the ⊞ pointer displays. Then, drag down through cell **E8**; if you are not satisfied with your result, on the Quick Access Toolbar, click Undo 🔄 and begin again. Compare your screen with Figure 1.20.

Figure 1.20

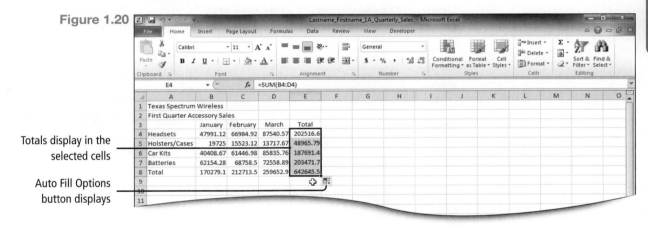

Totals display in the selected cells

Auto Fill Options button displays

---

5 Click cell **E5**, look at the **Formula Bar**, and notice the formula *=SUM(B5:D5)*. Click cell **E6**, look at the **Formula Bar**, and then notice the formula *=SUM(B6:D6)*.

> In each row, Excel copied the formula but adjusted the cell references *relative to* the row number. This is called a *relative cell reference*—a cell reference based on the relative position of the cell that contains the formula and the cells referred to.

> The calculation is the same, but it is performed on the cells in that particular row. Use this method to insert numerous formulas into spreadsheets quickly.

6 Click cell **F3,** type **Trend** and then press Enter. **Save** 💾 your workbook.

Objective 4 | Format Cells with Merge & Center and Cell Styles

Format—change the appearance of—cells to make your worksheet attractive and easy to read.

Activity 1.09 | Using Merge & Center and Applying Cell Styles

Another Way

Select the range, right-click over the selection, and then on the Mini toolbar, click the Merge & Center button.

1 Select the range **A1:F1**, and then in the **Alignment group**, click the **Merge & Center** button 🖼. Then, select the range **A2:F2** and click the **Merge & Center** button 🖼.

The *Merge & Center* command joins selected cells into one larger cell and centers the contents in the new cell; individual cells in the range B1:F1 and B2:F2 can no longer be selected—they are merged into cell A1 and A2 respectively.

2 Click cell **A1**. In the **Styles group**, click the **Cell Styles** button, and then compare your screen with Figure 1.21.

A *cell style* is a defined set of formatting characteristics, such as font, font size, font color, cell borders, and cell shading.

Figure 1.21

Cell Styles button
Cell A1 merged and centered
Cell A2 merged and centered
Cell Styles gallery

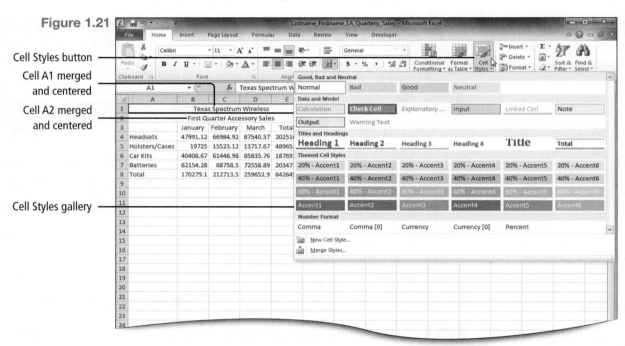

3 In the displayed gallery, under **Titles and Headings**, click **Title** and notice that the row height adjusts to accommodate this larger font size.

4 Click cell **A2**, display the **Cell Styles** gallery, and then under **Titles and Headings**, click **Heading 1**.

Use cell styles to maintain a consistent look in a worksheet and across worksheets in a workbook.

5 Select the range **B3:F3**, hold down ⌈Ctrl⌋, and then select the range **A4:A8** to select the column titles and the row titles.

Use this technique to select two or more ranges that are nonadjacent—not next to each other.

6 Display the **Cell Styles** gallery, click **Heading 4** to apply this cell style to the column titles and row titles, and then **Save** 🖫 your workbook.

Another Way

In the Name Box type b4:e4,b8:e8 and then press Enter.

Activity 1.10 | Formatting Financial Numbers

1 Select the range **B4:E4**, hold down Ctrl, and then select the range **B8:E8**.

This range is referred to as *b4:e4,b8:e8* with a comma separating the references to the two nonadjacent ranges.

Another Way

Display the Cell Styles gallery, and under Number Format, click Currency.

2 On the **Home tab**, in the **Number group**, click the **Accounting Number Format** button $ ·. Compare your screen with Figure 1.22.

The ***Accounting Number Format*** applies a thousand comma separator where appropriate, inserts a fixed U.S. dollar sign aligned at the left edge of the cell, applies two decimal places, and leaves a small amount of space at the right edge of the cell to accommodate a parenthesis when negative numbers are present. Excel widens the columns to accommodate the formatted numbers.

Figure 1.22

Accounting Number Format button

Nonadjacent ranges selected with Accounting Number Format applied

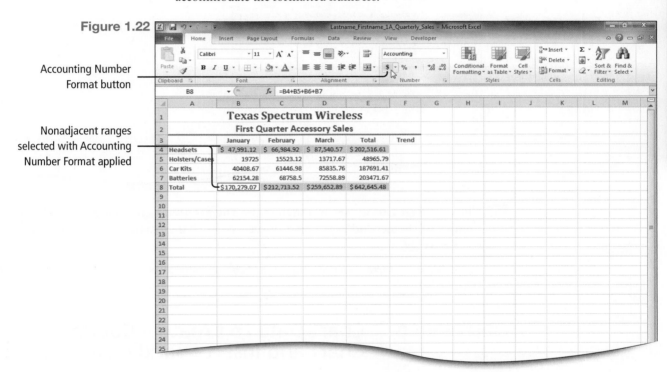

3 Select the range **B5:E7**, and then in the **Number group**, click the **Comma Style** button ·.

The ***Comma Style*** inserts thousand comma separators where appropriate and applies two decimal places. Comma Style also leaves space at the right to accommodate a parenthesis when negative numbers are present.

When preparing worksheets with financial information, the first row of dollar amounts and the total row of dollar amounts are formatted in the Accounting Number Format; that is, with thousand comma separators, dollar signs, two decimal places, and space at the right to accommodate a parenthesis for negative numbers, if any. Rows that are *not* the first row or the total row should be formatted with the Comma Style.

4 Select the range **B8:E8**. From the **Styles group**, display the **Cell Styles** gallery, and then under **Titles and Headings**, click **Total**. Click any blank cell to cancel the selection, and then compare your screen with Figure 1.23.

> This is a common way to apply borders to financial information. The single border indicates that calculations were performed on the numbers above, and the double border indicates that the information is complete. Sometimes financial documents do not display values with cents; rather, the values are rounded up. You can do this by selecting the cells, and then clicking the Decrease Decimal button two times.

Figure 1.23

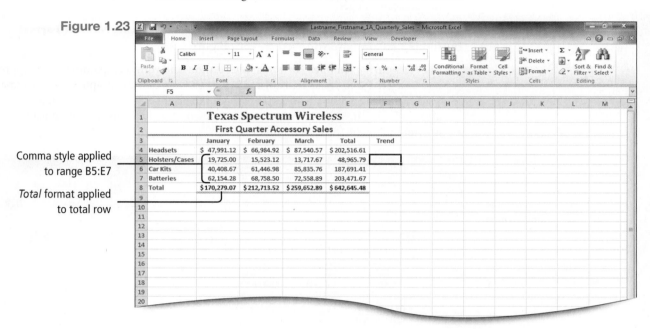

Comma style applied to range B5:E7

Total format applied to total row

5 Click the **Page Layout tab**, and then in the **Themes group**, click **Themes**. Click the **Composite** theme, and notice that the cell styles change to match the new theme. Click **Save** 🖫 .

> Recall that a theme is a predefined set of colors, fonts, lines, and fill effects that look good together.

Objective 5 | Chart Data to Create a Column Chart and Insert Sparklines

A *chart* is a graphic representation of data in a worksheet. Data presented as a chart is easier to understand than a table of numbers. *Sparklines* are tiny charts embedded in a cell and give a visual trend summary alongside your data. A sparkline makes a pattern more obvious to the eye.

Activity 1.11 | Charting Data in a Column Chart

In this activity, you will create a *column chart* showing the monthly sales of accessories by category during the first quarter. A column chart is useful for illustrating comparisons among related numbers. The chart will enable the company president, Rosalyn Thomas, to see a pattern of overall monthly sales.

1 Select the range **A3:D7**. Click the **Insert tab**, and then in the **Charts group**, click **Column** to display a gallery of Column chart types.

> When charting data, typically you should *not* include totals—include only the data you want to compare. By using different *chart types*, you can display data in a way that is meaningful to the reader—common examples are column charts, pie charts, and line charts.

2 On the gallery of column chart types, under **2-D Column**, point to the first chart to display the ScreenTip *Clustered Column*, and then click to select it. Compare your screen with Figure 1.24.

> A column chart displays in the worksheet, and the charted data is bordered by colored lines. Because the chart object is selected—surrounded by a border and displaying sizing handles—contextual tools named *Chart Tools* display and add contextual tabs next to the standard tabs on the Ribbon.

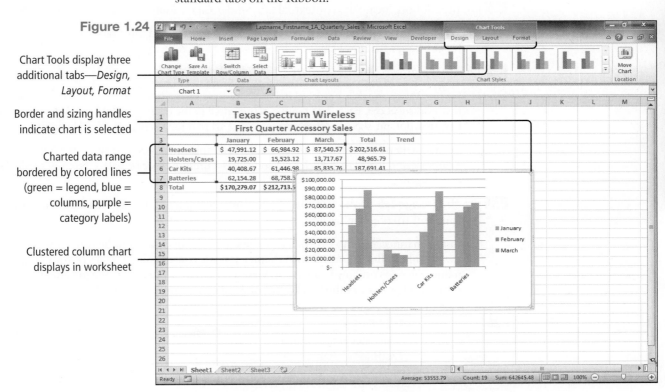

Figure 1.24

Chart Tools display three additional tabs—*Design, Layout, Format*

Border and sizing handles indicate chart is selected

Charted data range bordered by colored lines (green = legend, blue = columns, purple = category labels)

Clustered column chart displays in worksheet

3 Point to the top border of the chart to display the pointer, and then drag the upper left corner of the chart just inside the upper left corner of cell **A10**, approximately as shown in Figure 1.25.

> Based on the data you selected in your worksheet, Excel constructs a column chart and adds *category labels*—the labels that display along the bottom of the chart to identify the category of data. This area is referred to as the *category axis* or the *x-axis*. Excel uses the row titles as the category names.

> On the left, Excel includes a numerical scale on which the charted data is based; this is the *value axis* or the *y-axis*. On the right, a *legend*, which identifies the patterns or colors that are assigned to the categories in the chart, displays.

Figure 1.25

New chart location

Columns represent
blue bordered cells

Category axis, also called
x-axis, represents purple-
bordered cells

Category labels

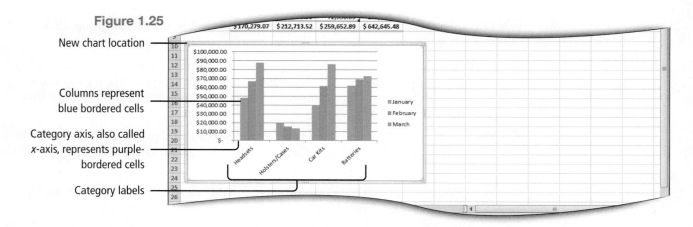

4 On the Ribbon, locate the contextual tabs under **Chart Tools—Design**, **Layout**, and **Format**.

When a chart is selected, Chart Tools become available and three tabs provide commands for working with the chart.

5 Locate the group of cells bordered in blue.

Each of the twelve cells bordered in blue is referred to as a ***data point***—a value that originates in a worksheet cell. Each data point is represented in the chart by a ***data marker***—a column, bar, area, dot, pie slice, or other symbol in a chart that represents a single data point.

Related data points form a ***data series***; for example, there is a data series for *January*, for *February*, and for *March*. Each data series has a unique color or pattern represented in the chart legend.

6 On the **Design tab** of the Ribbon, in the **Data group**, click the **Switch Row/Column** button, and then compare your chart with Figure 1.26.

In this manner, you can easily change the categories of data from the row titles, which is the default, to the column titles. Whether you use row or column titles as your category names depends on how you want to view your charted data. Here, the president wants to see monthly sales and the breakdown of product categories within each month.

Figure 1.26

Each value in selected
range is a data point

Value axis (y-axis) based
on total quarterly sales

Data series switched to
row names (accessory
types) as defined
in legend

Categories switched to
column names (months)

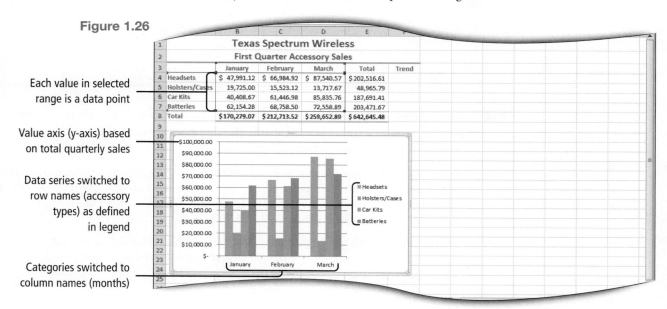

7 On the **Design tab**, in the **Chart Layouts group**, locate and click the **More** button ⏷. Compare your screen with Figure 1.27.

In the *Chart Layouts gallery*, you can select a predesigned *chart layout*—a combination of chart elements, which can include a title, legend, labels for the columns, and the table of charted cells.

Figure 1.27

Chart Layouts gallery

More buttons in Chart Styles group

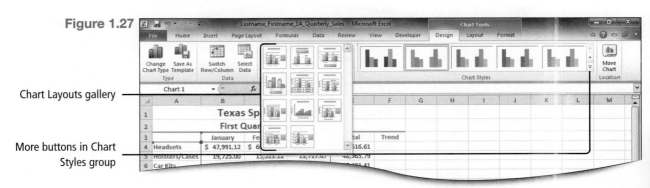

8 Click several different layouts to see the effect on your chart, and then using the ScreenTips as your guide, locate and click **Layout 1**.

9 In the chart, click anywhere in the text *Chart Title* to select the title box, watch the **Formula Bar** as you type **1st Quarter Sales** and then press Enter to display the new chart title.

10 Click in a white area just slightly *inside* the chart border to deselect the chart title. On the **Design tab**, in the **Chart Styles group**, click the **More** button ⏷. Compare your screen with Figure 1.28.

The *Chart Styles gallery* displays an array of pre-defined *chart styles*—the overall visual look of the chart in terms of its colors, backgrounds, and graphic effects such as flat or beveled columns.

Figure 1.28

Chart Styles gallery

Title added to chart

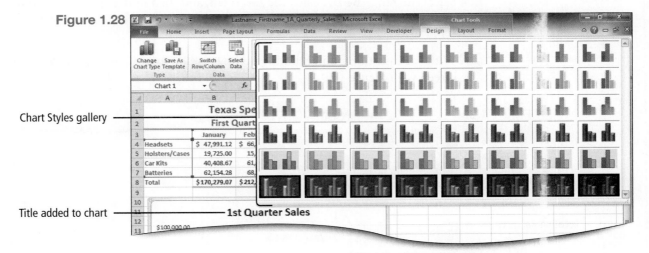

11 Using the ScreenTips as your guide, locate and click **Style 26**.

This style uses a white background, formats the columns with theme colors, and applies a beveled effect. With this clear visual representation of the data, the president can see the sales of all product categories in each month, and can see that the sale of headsets and car kits has risen quite markedly during the quarter.

12 Click any cell to deselect the chart, and notice that the *Chart Tools* no longer display in the Ribbon. Click **Save** 💾, and then compare your screen with Figure 1.29.

> Contextual tabs display when an object is selected, and then are removed from view when the object is deselected.

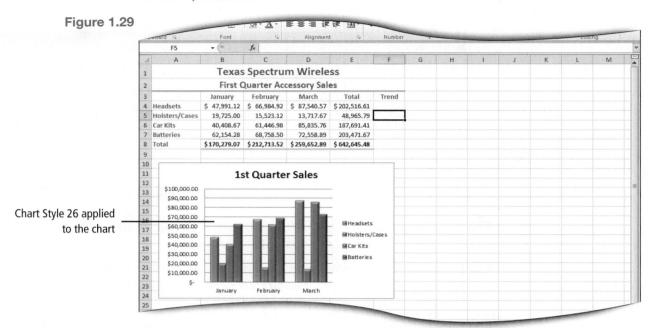

Figure 1.29

Chart Style 26 applied to the chart

Activity 1.12 | Creating and Formatting Sparklines

By creating sparklines, you provide a context for your numbers. Your readers will be able to see the relationship between a sparkline and its underlying data quickly.

Another Way

In the worksheet, select the range F4:F7 to insert it into the Location Range box.

1 Select the range **B4:D7**. Click the **Insert tab**, and then in the **Sparklines group**, click **Line**. In the displayed **Create Sparklines** dialog box, notice that the selected range *B4:D7* displays.

2 With the insertion point blinking in the **Location Range** box, type **f4:f7** Compare your screen with Figure 1.30.

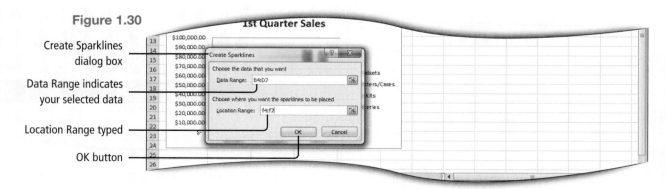

Figure 1.30

Create Sparklines dialog box

Data Range indicates your selected data

Location Range typed

OK button

3 Click **OK** to insert the trend lines in the range F4:F7, and then on the **Design tab**, in the **Show group**, click the **Markers** check box to select it.

> Alongside each row of data, the sparkline provides a quick visual trend summary for sales of each accessory item over the three-month period. For example, you can see instantly that of the four items, only Holsters/Cases had declining sales for the period.

4 In the **Style group**, click the **More** button ⊡. In the second row, click the fourth style—**Sparkline Style Accent 4, Darker 25%**. Click cell **A1** to deselect the range. Click **Save** 🖫. Compare your screen with Figure 1.31.

> Use markers, colors, and styles in this manner to further enhance your sparklines.

Figure 1.31

Sparklines inserted
and formatted

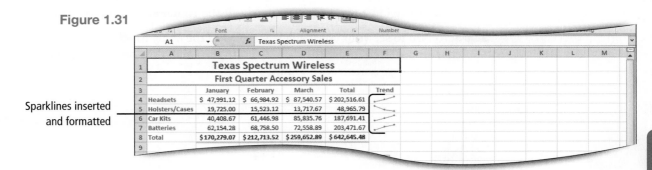

Excel | Chapter 1

Objective 6 | Print, Display Formulas, and Close Excel

Use *Page Layout view* and the commands on the Page Layout tab to prepare for printing.

Activity 1.13 | Changing Views, Creating a Footer, and Using Print Preview

For each Excel project in this textbook, you will create a footer containing your name and the project name.

1 Be sure the chart is *not* selected. Click the **Insert tab**, and then in the **Text group**, click the **Header & Footer** button to switch to Page Layout view and open the **Header area**. Compare your screen with Figure 1.32.

> In Page Layout view, you can see the edges of the paper of multiple pages, the margins, and the rulers. You can also insert a header or footer by typing in the areas indicated and use the Header & Footer Tools.

Figure 1.32

Go to Footer button

Rulers

Header area with three
sections open; center
section selected

Margin

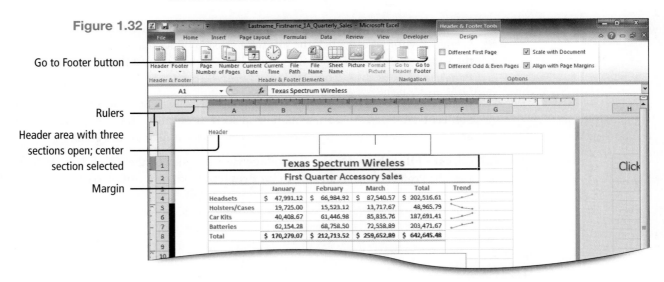

2 On the **Design tab**, in the **Navigation group**, click **Go to Footer** to open the **Footer area**, and then click just above the word *Footer* to place the insertion point in the **left section** of the **Footer area**.

3 In the **Header & Footer Elements group**, click the **File Name** button to add the name of your file to the footer—&*[File]* displays in the left section of the **Footer area**. Then, click in a cell just above the footer to exit the **Footer area** and view your file name.

4 Scroll up to see your chart, click a corner of the chart to select it, and then see if the chart is centered under the data. *Point* to the small dots on the right edge of the chart; compare your screen with Figure 1.33.

Figure 1.33

Horizontal resize pointer

Border indicates
chart is selected

5 Drag the ⟷ pointer to the right so that the right border of the chart is just inside the right border of **column F**. Be sure the left and right borders of the chart are just slightly **inside** the left border of **column A** and the right border of **column F**—adjust as necessary.

6 Click any cell to deselect the chart. Click the **Page Layout tab**, in the **Page Setup group**, click the **Margins** button, and then at the bottom of the **Margins** gallery, click **Custom Margins**. In the **Page Setup** dialog box, under **Center on page**, select the **Horizontally** check box.

> This action will center the data and chart horizontally on the page, as shown in the Preview area.

7 In the lower right corner of the **Page Setup** dialog box, click **OK**. In the upper left corner of your screen, click the **File tab** to display **Backstage** view. On the **Info tab**, on the right under the screen thumbnail, click **Properties**, and then click **Show Document Panel**.

8 In the **Author** box, replace the existing text with your firstname and lastname. In the **Subject** box, type your course name and section number. In the **Keywords** box type **accessory sales** and then **Close** ☒ the **Document Information Panel**.

Another Way
Press Ctrl + F2 to view the Print Preview.

9 Click the **File tab** to redisplay **Backstage** view, and then on the left, click the **Print tab** to view the Print commands and the **Print Preview**. Compare your screen with Figure 1.34.

Figure 1.34

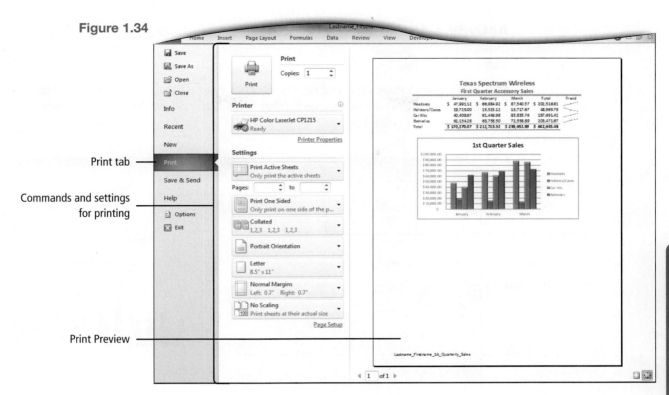

Print tab

Commands and settings for printing

Print Preview

10 Note any adjustments that need to be made, and then on the Ribbon, click the **Home tab** to close Backstage view and return to the worksheet. In the lower right corner of your screen, click the **Normal** button 🎛 to return to the Normal view, and then press Ctrl + Home to return to cell **A1**.

> The **Normal view** maximizes the number of cells visible on your screen and keeps the column letters and row numbers closer. The vertical dotted line between columns indicates that as currently arranged, only the columns to the left of the dotted line will print on the first page. The exact position of the vertical line may depend on your default printer setting.

11 Make any necessary adjustments, and then **Save** 🖫 your workbook.

Activity 1.14 | Deleting Unused Sheets in a Workbook

A new Excel workbook contains three blank worksheets. It is not necessary to delete unused sheets, but doing so saves storage space and removes any doubt that additional information is in the workbook.

1 At the bottom of your worksheet, click the **Sheet2 tab** to display the second worksheet in the workbook and make it active.

Another Way

On the Home tab, in the Cells group, click the Delete button arrow, and then click Delete Sheet.

2 Hold down Ctrl, and then click the **Sheet3 tab**. Release Ctrl, and then with both sheets selected (the tab background is white), point to either of the selected sheet tabs, right-click, and then on the shortcut menu, click **Delete**.

> Excel deletes the two unused sheets from your workbook. If you attempt to delete a worksheet with data, Excel will display a warning and permit you to cancel the deletion. **Sheet tabs** are labels along the lower border of the Excel window that identify each worksheet.

Activity 1.15 | Printing a Worksheet

1 Click **Save** 🖫.

2 Display **Backstage** view and on the left click the Print tab. Under **Print**, be sure **Copies** indicates *1*. Under **Settings**, verify that *Print Active Sheets* displays. Compare your screen with Figure 1.35.

Figure 1.35

Copies indicates *1*

Print Active Sheets

Print Preview

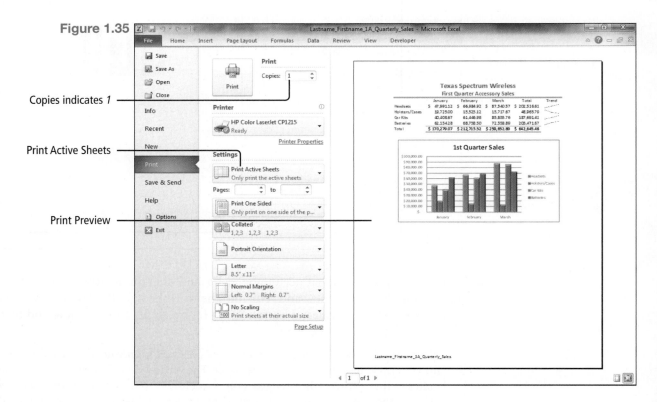

3 To print on paper, be sure that a printer is available to your system, and then in the **Print group**, click the **Print** button. To create an electronic printout, on the Backstage tabs, click the **Save & Send tab**, under **File Types** click **Create PDF/XPS Document**, and then on the right, click **Create PDF/XPS**. In the **Publish as PDF or XPS** dialog box, navigate to your storage location, and then click the **Publish** button to create the PDF file. Close the Adobe window.

Activity 1.16 | Displaying, Printing, and Hiding Formulas

When you type a formula in a cell, the cell displays the *results* of the formula calculation. Recall that this value is called the displayed value. You can view and print the underlying formulas in the cells. When you do so, a formula often takes more horizontal space to display than the result of the calculation.

1 If necessary, redisplay your worksheet. Because you will make some temporary changes to your workbook, on the Quick Access Toolbar, click **Save** 🖫 to be sure your work is saved up to this point.

> **Another Way**
>
> Hold down Ctrl, and then press ` (usually located below Esc).

2 On the **Formulas tab**, in the **Formula Auditing group**, click the **Show Formulas** button. Then, in the **column heading area**, point to the **column A** heading to display the ↓ pointer, hold down the left mouse button, and then drag to the right to select columns **A:F**. Compare your screen with Figure 1.36.

Figure 1.36

Dotted line shows page break

Underlying formulas displayed

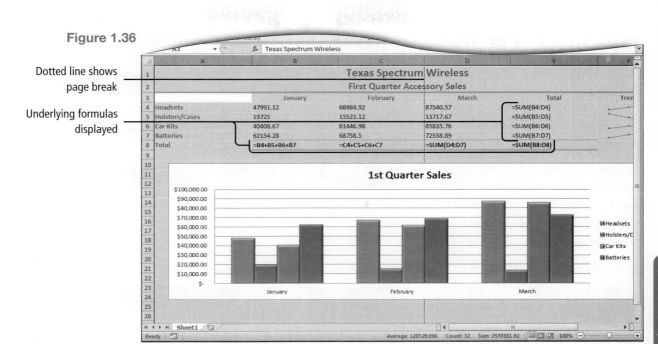

Note | Turning the Display of Formulas On and Off

The Show Formulas button is a toggle button. Clicking it once turns the display of formulas on—the button will glow orange. Clicking the button again turns the display of formulas off.

3 Point to the column heading boundary between any two of the selected columns to display the ⟷ pointer, and then double-click to AutoFit the selected columns.

AutoFit adjusts the width of a column to fit the cell content of the *widest* cell in the column.

Another Way

In the Scale to Fit group, click the Dialog Box Launcher button to display the Page tab of the Page Setup dialog box. Then, under Scaling, click the Fit to option button.

4 On the **Page Layout tab**, in the **Page Setup group**, click **Orientation**, and then click **Landscape**. In the **Scale to Fit** group, click the **Width arrow**, and then click **1 page** to scale the data to fit onto one page.

Scaling shrinks the width (or height) of the printed worksheet to fit a maximum number of pages, and is convenient for printing formulas. Although it is not always the case, formulas frequently take up more space than the actual data.

Another Way

In the Page Setup group, click the Dialog Box Launcher button to display the Page tab of the Page Setup dialog box. Then, under Orientation, click the Landscape option button.

5 In the **Page Setup group**, click the **Dialog Box Launcher** button 🔲. In the **Page Setup** dialog box, click the **Margins tab**, and then under **Center on page**, if necessary, click to select the **Horizontally** check box.

6 Click **OK** to close the dialog box. Check to be sure your chart is centered below the data and the left and right edges are slightly inside column A and column F—drag a chart edge and then deselect the chart if necessary. Display the **Print Preview**, and then submit your worksheet with formulas displayed, either printed or electronically, as directed by your instructor.

7 Click the **File tab** to display **Backstage** view, click **Close**, and when prompted, click **Don't Save** so that you do *not* save the changes you made—displaying formulas, changing column widths and orientation, and scaling—to print your formulas.

8 In the upper right corner of your screen, click the **Close** button 🗙 to exit Excel.

End You have completed Project 1A ———————————

Project 1B Inventory Valuation

myitlab
Project 1B Training

Project Activities

In Activities 1.17 through 1.24, you will create a workbook for Josette Lovrick, Operations Manager, which calculates the retail value of an inventory of car convenience products. Your completed worksheet will look similar to Figure 1.37.

Project Files

For Project 1B, you will need the following file:

New blank Excel workbook

You will save your workbook as:

Lastname_Firstname_1B_Car_Products

Project Results

Texas Spectrum Wireless
Car Products Inventory Valuation
As of December 31

	Warehouse Location	Quantity In Stock	Retail Price	Total Retail Value	Percent of Total Retail Value
Antenna Signal Booster	Dallas	1,126	$ 19.99	$ 22,508.74	8.27%
Car Power Port Adapter	Dallas	3,546	19.49	69,111.54	25.39%
Repeater Antenna	Houston	1,035	39.99	41,389.65	15.21%
SIM Card Reader and Writer	Houston	2,875	16.90	48,587.50	17.85%
Sticky Dash Pad	Houston	3,254	11.99	39,015.46	14.33%
Window Mount GPS Holder	Dallas	2,458	20.99	51,593.42	18.95%
Total Retail Value for All Products				$ 272,206.31	

Lastname_Firstname_1B_Car_Products

Figure 1.37
Project 1B Car Products

Objective 7 | Check Spelling in a Worksheet

In Excel, the spelling checker performs similarly to the other Microsoft Office programs.

Activity 1.17 | Checking Spelling in a Worksheet

1 **Start** Excel and display a new blank workbook. In cell **A1**, type **Texas Spectrum Wireless** and press Enter. In cell **A2**, type **Car Products Inventory** and press Enter.

2 On the Ribbon, click the **File tab** to display **Backstage** view, click **Save As**, and then in the **Save As** dialog box, navigate to your **Excel Chapter 1** folder. As the **File name**, type **Lastname_Firstname_1B_Car_Products** and then click **Save**.

3 Press Tab to move to cell **B3**, type **Quantity** and press Tab. In cell **C3**, type **Average Cost** and press Tab. In cell **D3**, type **Retail Price** and press Tab.

4 Click cell **C3**, and then look at the **Formula Bar**. Notice that in the cell, the displayed value is cut off; however, in the **Formula Bar**, the entire text value—the underlying value—displays. Compare your screen with Figure 1.38.

> Text that is too long to fit in a cell spills over to cells on the right only if they are empty. If the cell to the right contains data, the text in the cell to the left is truncated. The entire value continues to exist, but is not completely visible.

Figure 1.38

Entire contents of C3 display in Formula Bar

Cell C3 active, text cut off

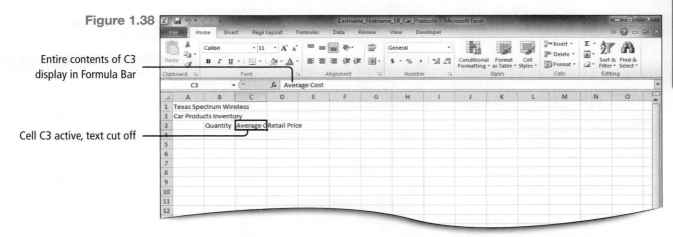

5 Click cell **E3**, type **Total Retail Value** and press Tab. In cell **F3**, type **Percent of Total Retail Value** and press Enter.

6 Click cell **A4**. *Without* correcting the spelling error, type **Antena Signal Booster** Press Enter. In the range **A5:A10**, type the remaining row titles shown below. Then compare your screen with Figure 1.39.

> **Car Power Port Adapter**
>
> **Repeater Antenna**
>
> **SIM Card Reader and Writer**
>
> **Sticky Dash Pad**
>
> **Window Mount GPS Holder**
>
> **Total Retail Value for All Products**

Figure 1.39

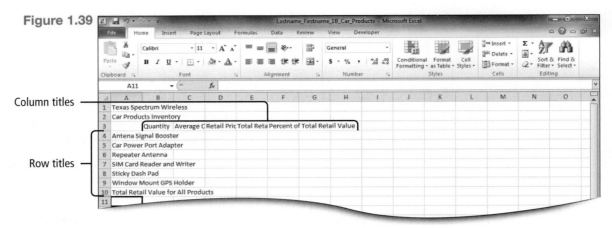

Column titles

Row titles

7 In the **column heading area**, point to the right boundary of **column A** to display the ⟨+⟩ pointer, and then drag to the right to widen **column A** to **215** pixels.

8 Select the range **A1:F1**, **Merge & Center** 🔲 the text, and then from the **Cell Styles** gallery, apply the **Title** style.

9 Select the range **A2:F2**, **Merge & Center** 🔲 the text, and then from the **Cell Styles** gallery, apply the **Heading 1** style. Press ⌃Ctrl + ⌂Home to move to the top of your worksheet.

Another Way

Press F7, which is the keyboard shortcut for the Spelling command.

10 With cell **A1** as the active cell, click the **Review tab**, and then in the **Proofing group**, click the **Spelling** button. Compare your screen with Figure 1.40.

Figure 1.40

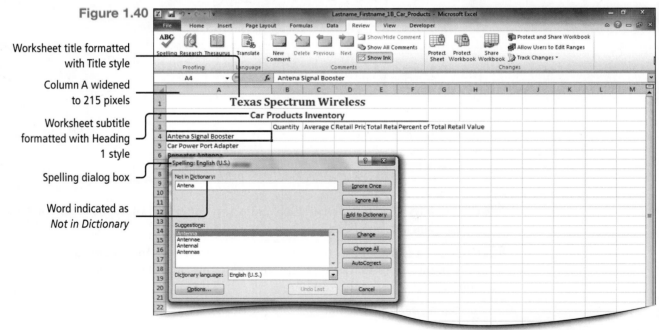

Worksheet title formatted with Title style

Column A widened to 215 pixels

Worksheet subtitle formatted with Heading 1 style

Spelling dialog box

Word indicated as *Not in Dictionary*

Alert! | Does a Message Display Asking if You Want to Continue Checking at the Beginning of the Sheet?

If a message displays asking if you want to continue checking at the beginning of the sheet, click Yes. The Spelling command begins its checking process with the currently selected cell and moves to the right and down. Thus, if your active cell was a cell after A4, this message may display.

11 In the **Spelling** dialog box, under **Not in Dictionary**, notice the word *Antena*.

The spelling tool does not have this word in its dictionary. Under *Suggestions*, Excel provides a list of suggested spellings.

12 Under **Suggestions**, click **Antenna**, and then click the **Change** button.

Antena, a typing error, is changed to *Antenna*. A message box displays *The spelling check is complete for the entire sheet*—unless you have additional unrecognized words. Because the spelling check begins its checking process starting with the currently selected cell, it is good practice to return to cell A1 before starting the Spelling command.

13 Correct any other errors you may have made. When the message displays, *The spelling check is complete for the entire sheet*, click **OK**. **Save** 🔲 your workbook.

Objective 8 | Enter Data by Range

You can enter data by first selecting a range of cells. This is a time-saving technique, especially if you use the numeric keypad to enter the numbers.

Activity 1.18 | Entering Data by Range

1 Select the range **B4:D9**, type **1126** and then press Enter.

The value displays in cell B4, and cell B5 becomes the active cell.

2 With cell **B5** active in the range, and pressing Enter after each entry, type the following, and then compare your screen with Figure 1.41:

4226
1035
2875
3254
2458

After you enter the last value and press Enter, the active cell moves to the top of the next column within the selected range. Although it is not required to enter data in this manner, you can see that selecting the range before you enter data saves time because it confines the movement of the active cell to the selected range.

Figure 1.41

Cell C4 active

Range B4:D9 selected

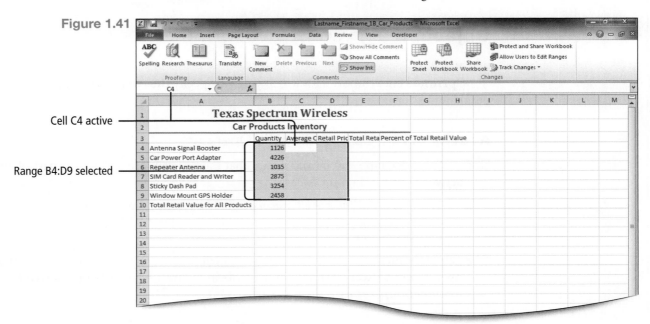

3 With the selected range still active, from the following table, beginning in cell **C4** and pressing Enter after each entry, enter the data for the **Average Cost** column and then the **Retail Price** column. If you prefer, deselect the range to enter the values—typing in a selected range is optional.

Average Cost	Retail Price
9.75	19.99
9.25	19.49
16.90	39.99
9.55	16.90
4.20	12.99
10.45	20.99

Recall that the default number format for cells is the *General* number format, in which numbers display exactly as you type them and trailing zeros do not display, even if you type them.

4 Click any blank cell, and then compare your screen with Figure 1.42. Correct any errors you may have made while entering data, and then click **Save** 💾.

Figure 1.42

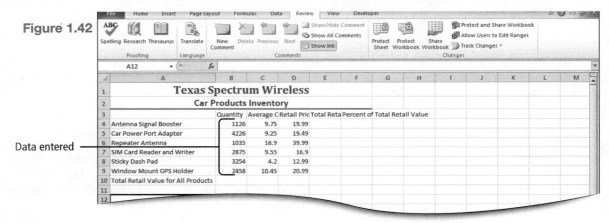

Data entered

Objective 9 | Construct Formulas for Mathematical Operations

Operators are symbols with which you can specify the type of calculation you want to perform in a formula.

Activity 1.19 | Using Arithmetic Operators

1 Click cell **E4**, type **=b4*d4** and notice that the two cells are outlined as part of an active formula. Then press Enter.

The *Total Retail Value* of all *Antenna Signal Booster* items in inventory—*22508.74*—equals the *Quantity* (1,126) times the *Retail Price* (selling price) of 19.99. In Excel, the asterisk (*) indicates multiplication.

2 Take a moment to study the symbols you will use to perform basic mathematical operations in Excel, as shown in the table in Figure 1.43, which are referred to as *arithmetic operators*.

Symbols Used in Excel for Arithmetic Operators

Operator Symbol	Operation
+	Addition
-	Subtraction (also negation)
*	Multiplication
/	Division
%	Percent
^	Exponentiation

Figure 1.43

3 Click cell **E4**.

> You can see that in cells E5:E9, you need a formula similar to the one in E4, but one that refers to the cells in row 5, row 6, and so forth. Recall that you can copy formulas and the cell references will change *relative* to the row number.

4 With cell **E4** selected, position your pointer over the fill handle in the lower right corner of the cell until the + pointer displays. Then, drag down through cell **E9** to copy the formula.

Another Way

Select the range, display the Cell Styles gallery, and then under Number Format, click Comma [0].

5 Select the range **B4:B9**, and then on the **Home tab**, in the **Number group**, click the **Comma Style** button. Then, in the **Number group**, click the **Decrease Decimal** button two times to remove the decimal places from these values.

> Comma Style formats a number with two decimal places; because these are whole numbers referring to quantities, no decimal places are necessary.

6 Select the range **E4:E9**, and then at the bottom of your screen, in the status bar, notice the displayed values for **Average**, **Count**, and **Sum**—*48118.91833, 6* and *288713.51*.

> When you select numerical data, three calculations display in the status bar by default—Average, Count, and Sum. Here, Excel indicates that if you averaged the selected values, the result would be *48118.91833*, there are 6 cells in the selection that contain values, and that if you added the values the result would be 288713.51.

7 Click cell **E10**, in the **Editing group**, click the **Sum** button Σ, notice that Excel selects a range to sum, and then press Enter to display the total *288713.5*.

8 Select the range **C5:E9** and apply the **Comma Style**; notice that Excel widens **column E**.

9 Select the range **C4:E4**, hold down Ctrl, and then click cell **E10**. Release Ctrl and then apply the **Accounting Number Format** $. Notice that Excel widens the columns as necessary.

10 Click cell **E10**, and then from the **Cell Styles** gallery, apply the **Total** style. Click any blank cell, and then compare your screen with Figure 1.44.

Figure 1.44

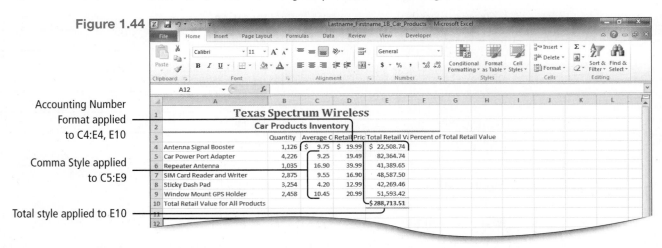

Accounting Number Format applied to C4:E4, E10

Comma Style applied to C5:E9

Total style applied to E10

11 **Save** your workbook.

> **More Knowledge | Multiple Status Bar Calculations**
>
> You can display a total of six calculations on the status bar. To add additional calculations—Minimum, Maximum, and Numerical Count (the number of selected cells that contain a number value)—right-click on the status bar, and then click the additional calculations that you want to display.

Activity 1.20 | Copying Formulas Containing Absolute Cell References

In a formula, a relative cell reference refers to a cell by its position *in relation to* the cell that contains the formula. An ***absolute cell reference***, on the other hand, refers to a cell by its *fixed* position in the worksheet, for example, the total in cell E10.

A relative cell reference automatically adjusts when a formula is copied. In some calculations, you do *not* want the cell reference to adjust; rather, you want the cell reference to remain the same when the formula is copied.

1 Click cell **F4**, type = and then click cell **E4**. Type / and then click cell **E10**.

The formula *=E4/E10* indicates that the value in cell E4 will be *divided* by the value in cell E10. Why? Because Ms. Lovrick wants to know the percentage by which each product's Total Retail Value makes up the Total Retail Value for All Products.

Arithmetically, the percentage is computed by dividing the *Total Retail Value* for each product by the *Total Retail Value for All Products*. The result will be a percentage expressed as a decimal.

2 Press Enter. Click cell **F4** and notice that the formula displays in the **Formula Bar**. Then, point to cell **F4** and double-click.

The formula, with the two referenced cells displayed in color and bordered with the same color, displays in the cell. This feature, called the ***range finder***, is useful for verifying formulas because it visually indicates which workbook cells are included in a formula calculation.

3 Press [Enter] to redisplay the result of the calculation in the cell, and notice that approximately 8% of the total retail value of the inventory is made up of Antenna Signal Boosters.

4 Click cell **F4** again, and then drag the fill handle down through cell **F9**. Compare your screen with Figure 1.45.

> Each cell displays an error message—*#DIV/0!* and a green triangle in the upper left corner of each cell indicates that Excel detects an error.
>
> Like a grammar checker, Excel uses rules to check for formula errors and flags errors in this manner. Additionally, the Auto Fill Options button displays, from which you can select formatting options for the copied cells.

Figure 1.45

Auto Fill Options button

Cells F5:F9 display error message and green triangles

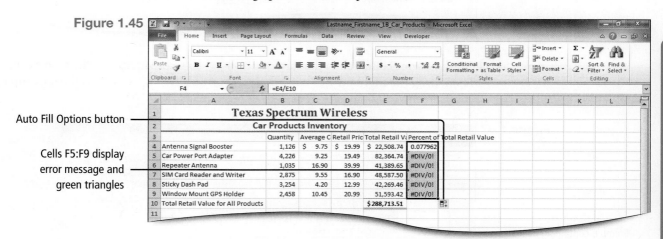

5 Click cell **F5**, and to the left of the cell, point to the **Error Checking** button ⬦ to display its ScreenTip—*The formula or function used is dividing by zero or empty cells.*

> In this manner, Excel suggests the cause of an error.

6 Look at the **Formula Bar** and examine the formula.

> The formula is *=E5/E11*. The cell reference to E5 is correct, but the cell reference following the division operator (/) is *E11*, and E11 is an *empty* cell.

7 Click cell **F6**, point to the **Error Checking** button ⬦, and in the **Formula Bar** examine the formula.

> Because the cell references are relative, Excel builds the formulas by increasing the row number for each equation. But in this calculation, the divisor must always be the value in cell E10—the *Total Retail Value for All Products*.

8 Point to cell **F4**, and then double-click to place the insertion point within the cell.

Another Way

Edit the formula so that it indicates *=E4/$E$10*

9 Within the cell, use the arrow keys as necessary to position the insertion point to the left of *E10*, and then press [F4]. Compare your screen with Figure 1.46.

> Dollar signs ($) display, which changes the reference to cell E10 to an absolute cell reference. The use of the dollar sign to denote an absolute reference is not related in any way to whether or not the values you are working with are currency values. It is simply the symbol that Excel uses to denote an absolute cell reference.

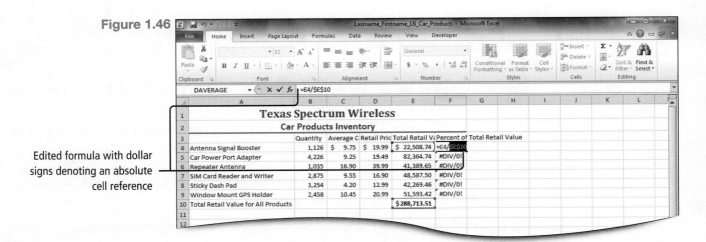

Figure 1.46

Edited formula with dollar signs denoting an absolute cell reference

10 On the **Formula Bar**, click the **Enter** button ✔ so that **F4** remains the active cell. Then, drag the fill handle to copy the new formula down through cell **F9**. Compare your screen with Figure 1.47.

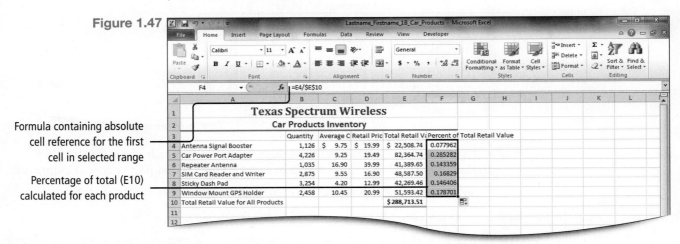

Figure 1.47

Formula containing absolute cell reference for the first cell in selected range

Percentage of total (E10) calculated for each product

11 Click cell **F5**, examine the formula in the **Formula Bar**, and then examine the formulas for cells **F6**, **F7**, **F8**, and **F9**.

For each formula, the cell reference for the *Total Retail Value* of each product changed relative to its row; however, the value used as the divisor—*Total Retail Value for All Products* in cell F10—remained absolute. Thus, using either relative or absolute cell references, it is easy to duplicate formulas without typing them.

12 **Save** 🖫 your workbook.

More Knowledge | Calculate a Percentage if You Know the Total and the Amount

Using the equation *amount/total = percentage*, you can calculate the percentage by which a part makes up a total—with the percentage formatted as a decimal. For example, if on a test you score 42 points correctly out of 50, your percentage of correct answers is 42/50 = 0.84 or 84%.

Objective 10 | Edit Values in a Worksheet

Excel performs calculations on numbers; that is why you use Excel. If you make changes to the numbers, Excel automatically *re*-calculates. This is one of the most powerful and valuable features of Excel.

Activity 1.21 | Editing Values in a Worksheet

You can edit text and number values directly within a cell or on the Formula Bar.

1 In cell **E10**, notice the column total *$288,713.51*. Then, click cell **B5**, and to change its value type **3546** Watch cell **E5** and press Enter.

> Excel formulas *re-calculate* if you change the value in a cell that is referenced in a formula. It is not necessary to delete the old value in a cell; selecting the cell and typing a new value replaces the old value with your new typing.

> The *Total Retail Value* of all *Car Power Port Adapters* items recalculates to *69,111.54* and the total in cell E10 recalculates to *$275,460.31*. Additionally, all of the percentages in column F recalculate.

2 Point to cell **D8**, and then double-click to place the insertion point within the cell. Use the arrow keys to move the insertion point to left or right of *2*, and use either Del or Backspace to delete *2* and then type **1** so that the new Retail Price is *11.99*.

3 Watch cell **E8** and **E10** as you press Enter, and then notice the recalculation of the formulas in those two cells.

> Excel recalculates the value in cell E8 to *39,015.46* and the value in cell E10 to *$272,206.31*. Additionally, all of the percentages in column F recalculate because the *Total Retail Value for All Products* recalculated.

4 Point to cell **A2** so that the ⊕ pointer is positioned slightly to the right of the word *Inventory*, and then double-click to place the insertion point in the cell. Edit the text to add the word **Valuation** pressing Spacebar as necessary, and then press Enter.

5 Click cell **B3**, and then in the **Formula Bar**, click to place the insertion point after the letter *y*. Press Spacebar one time, type **In Stock** and then on the **Formula Bar**, click the **Enter** button ✔. Click **Save** 🖫, and then compare your screen with Figure 1.48.

> Recall that if text is too long to fit in the cell and the cell to the right contains data, the text is truncated—cut off—but the entire value still exists as the underlying value.

Figure 1.48

In Stock added to column title

Valuation added to subtitle

New value in cell B5

New value in cell D8

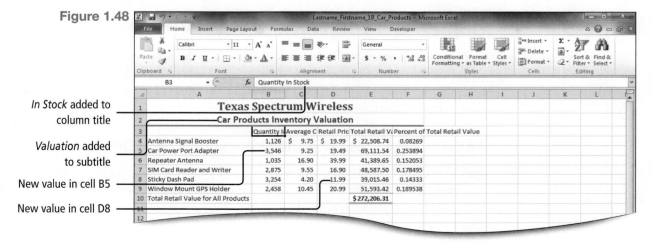

Activity 1.22 | Formatting Cells with the Percent Style

A percentage is part of a whole expressed in hundredths. For example, 75 cents is the same as 75 percent of one dollar. The Percent Style button formats the selected cell as a percentage rounded to the nearest hundredth.

1 Click cell **F4**, and then in the **Number group**, click the **Percent Style** button ⟦%⟧.

Your result is 8%, which is *0.08269* rounded to the nearest hundredth and expressed as a percentage. Percent Style displays the value of a cell as a percentage.

2 Select the range **F4:F9**, right-click over the selection, and then on the Mini toolbar, click the **Percent Style** button ⟦%⟧, click the **Increase Decimal** button ⟦.00⟧ two times, and then click the **Center** ⟦≡⟧ button.

Percent Style may not offer a percentage precise enough to analyze important financial information—adding additional decimal places to a percentage makes data more precise.

3 Click any cell to cancel the selection, **Save** ⟦💾⟧ your workbook, and then compare your screen with Figure 1.49.

Figure 1.49

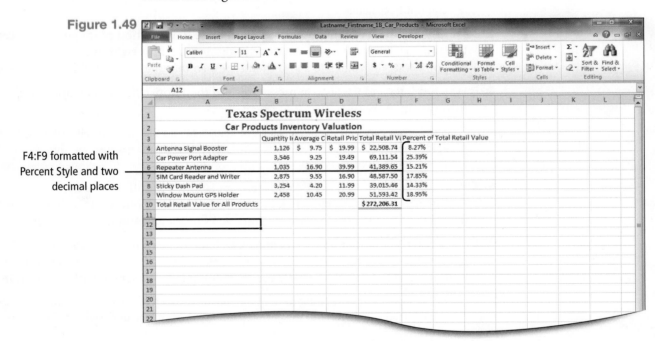

F4:F9 formatted with Percent Style and two decimal places

Objective 11 | Format a Worksheet

Formatting refers to the process of specifying the appearance of cells and the overall layout of your worksheet. Formatting is accomplished through various commands on the Ribbon, for example, applying Cell Styles, and also from shortcut menus, keyboard shortcuts, and the Format Cells dialog box.

Activity 1.23 | Inserting and Deleting Rows and Columns

1 In the **row heading area** on the left side of your screen, point to the row heading for **row 3** to display the ⟦→⟧ pointer, and then right-click to simultaneously select the row and display a shortcut menu.

Another Way

Select the row, on the Home tab, in the Cells group, click the Insert button arrow, and then click Insert Sheet Rows. Or, select the row and click the Insert button— the default setting of the button inserts a new sheet row above the selected row.

2 On the displayed shortcut menu, click **Insert** to insert a new **row 3**.

The rows below the new row 3 move down one row, and the Insert Options button displays. By default, the new row uses the formatting of the row *above*.

3 Click cell **E11**. On the **Formula Bar**, notice that the range changed to sum the new range **E5:E10**. Compare your screen with Figure 1.50.

If you move formulas by inserting additional rows or columns in your worksheet, Excel automatically adjusts the formulas. Excel adjusted all of the formulas in the worksheet that were affected by inserting this new row.

Figure 1.50

Formula Bar displays the formula in E11

New row 3 inserted

Insert Options button

Cell E11 selected

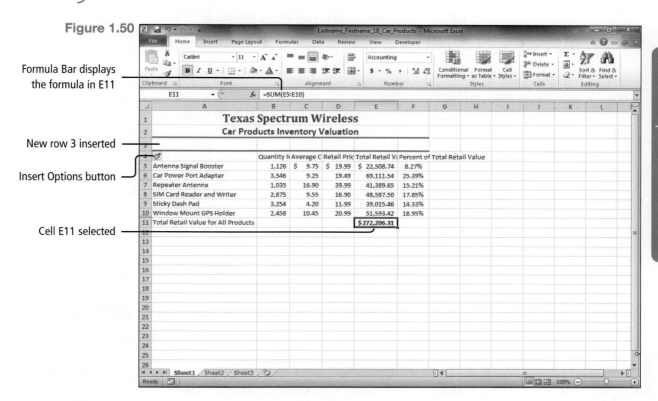

4 Click cell **A3**, type **As of December 31** and then on the **Formula Bar**, click the **Enter** button ✓ to maintain **A3** as the active cell. **Merge & Center** ▦ the text across the range **A3:F3**, and then apply the **Heading 2** cell style.

Another Way

Select the column, on the Home tab, in the Cells group, click the Insert button arrow, and then click Insert Sheet Columns. Or, select the column and click the Insert button—the default setting of the button inserts a new sheet column to the right of the selected column.

5 In the **column heading area**, point to **column B** to display the ↓ pointer, right-click, and then click **Insert**.

By default, the new column uses the formatting of the column to the *left*.

6 Click cell **B4**, type **Warehouse Location** and then press Enter.

7 In cell **B5**, type **Dallas** and then type **Dallas** again in cells **B6** and **B10**. Use AutoComplete to speed your typing by pressing Enter as soon as the AutoComplete suggestion displays. In cells **B7**, **B8**, and **B9**, type **Houston**

8 In the **column heading area**, point to **column D**, right-click, and then click **Delete**.

The remaining columns shift to the left, and Excel adjusts all the formulas in the worksheet accordingly. You can use a similar technique to delete a row in a worksheet.

9 Compare your screen with Figure 1.51, and then **Save** 💾 your workbook.

Figure 1.51

Text entered and formatted in cell A3

New column B with warehouse locations added

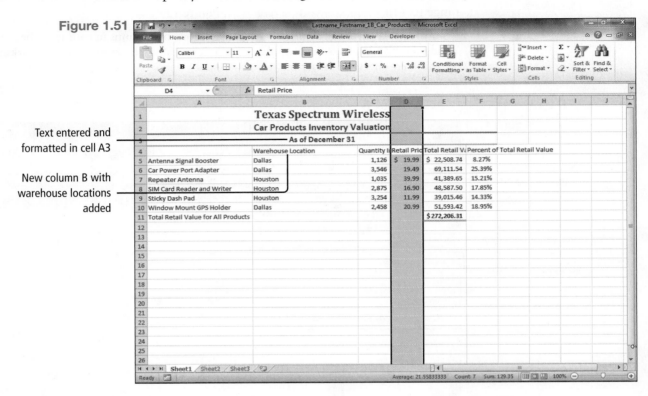

Activity 1.24 | Adjusting Column Widths and Wrapping Text

Use the Wrap Text command to display the contents of a cell on multiple lines.

1 In the **column heading area**, point to the **column B** heading to display the ⬇ pointer, and then drag to the right to select **columns B:F**.

2 With the columns selected, in the **column heading area**, point to the right boundary of any of the selected columns to display the ➕ pointer, and then drag to set the width to **90 pixels**.

Use this technique to format multiple columns or rows simultaneously.

3 Select the range **B4:F4** that comprises the column headings, and then on the **Home tab**, in the **Alignment group**, click the **Wrap Text** button 📋. Notice that the row height adjusts.

4 With the range **B4:F4** still selected, in the **Alignment group**, click the **Center** button ▤ and the **Middle Align** button ▤. With the range **B4:F4** still selected, apply the **Heading 4** cell style.

The Middle Align command aligns text so that it is centered between the top and bottom of the cell.

5 Select the range **B5:B10**, right-click, and then on the shortcut menu, click the **Center** button ▤. Click cell **A11**, and then from the **Cell Styles** gallery, under **Themed Cell Styles**, click **40% - Accent1**. Click any blank cell, and then compare your screen with Figure 1.52.

Figure 1.52

Width of columns B:F set to 90 pixels

Column headings wrapped and formatted

Warehouse locations centered

Accent applied to cell A11

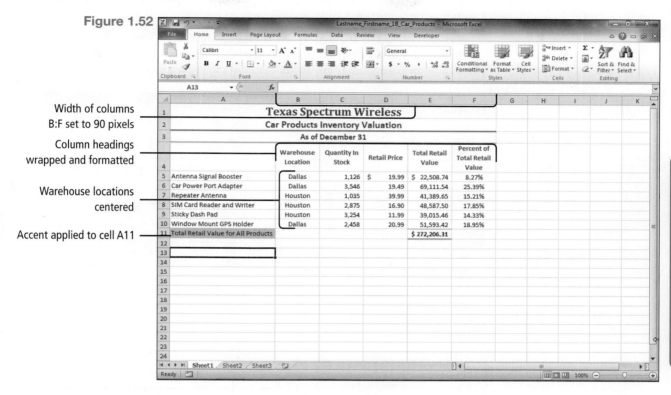

6 Click the **Insert tab**, and then in the **Text group**, click **Header & Footer** to switch to Page Layout view and open the **Header area**.

7 In the **Navigation group**, click the **Go to Footer** button to move to the bottom of the page and open the **Footer area**, and then click just above the word *Footer* to place the insertion point in the **left section** of the **Footer area**.

8 In the **Header & Footer Elements group**, click the **File Name** button to add the name of your file to the footer—&*[File]* displays in the left section of the **Footer area**. Then, click in a cell above the footer to exit the **Footer area** and view your file name.

9 Click the **Page Layout tab**, in the **Page Setup group**, click the **Margins** button, and then at the bottom of the **Margins gallery**, click **Custom Margins**. In the **Page Setup** dialog box, under **Center on page**, select the **Horizontally** check box; click **OK**.

10 In the upper left corner of your screen, click **File** to display **Backstage** view. On the **Info tab**, on the right under the screen thumbnail, click **Properties**, and then click **Show Document Panel**.

11 In the **Author** box, replace the existing text with your firstname and lastname. In the **Subject** box, type your course name and section number. In the **Keywords** box, type **car products, inventory** and then **Close** ✕ the **Document Information Panel**.

12 Press `Ctrl` + `F2` to view the **Print Preview**. At the bottom of the **Print Preview**, click the **Next Page** button ▶, and notice that as currently formatted, the worksheet occupies two pages.

13 In the center panel, under **Settings**, click **Portrait Orientation**, and then click **Landscape Orientation**. Compare your screen with Figure 1.53.

> You can change the orientation on the Page Layout tab, or here, in the Print Preview. Because it is in the Print Preview that you will often see adjustments that need to be made, commonly used settings display on the Print tab in Backstage view.

Figure 1.53

Worksheet displays in landscape orientation

Worksheet displayed in Print Preview

Landscape Orientation selected

Footer with your name

Worksheet occupies one page

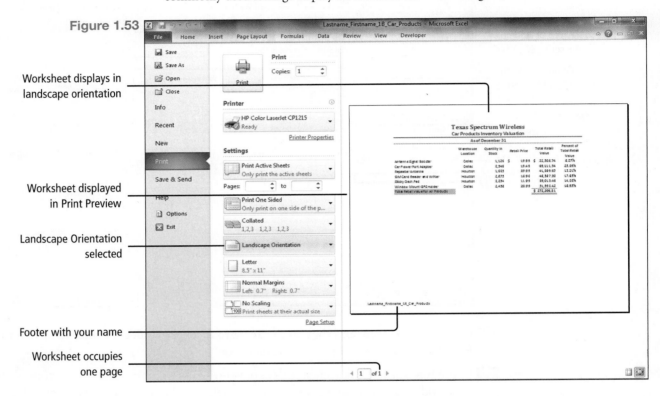

14 Note any additional adjustments or corrections that need to be made, and then on the Ribbon, click **Home** to redisplay your worksheet. In the lower right corner of your screen, on the right side of the status bar, click the **Normal** button 🔲 to return to the Normal view, and then press `Ctrl` + `Home` to return to cell **A1**.

15 Make any necessary corrections. Then, at the bottom of your worksheet, click the **Sheet2 tab** to make it the active worksheet. Hold down `Ctrl`, and then click the **Sheet3 tab**. Release `Ctrl`, and then with both sheets selected (tab background is white), point to either of the selected sheet tabs, right-click, and click **Delete** to delete the unused sheets in the workbook.

16 **Save** 🖫 your workbook.

17 Print or submit your worksheet electronically as directed by your instructor. If required by your instructor, print or create an electronic version of your worksheet with formulas displayed using the instructions in Activity 1.16 in Project 1A.

18 Close your workbook and close Excel.

End **You have completed Project 1B** ————————————————

Content-Based Assessments

Summary

In this chapter, you used Microsoft Excel 2010 to create and analyze data organized into columns and rows and to chart and perform calculations on the data. By organizing your data with Excel, you will be able to make calculations and create visual representations of your data in the form of charts.

Key Terms

Matching

Match each term in the second column with its correct definition in the first column by writing the letter of the term on the blank line in front of the correct definition.

_____ 1. An Excel file that contains one or more worksheets.

_____ 2. Another name for a worksheet.

_____ 3. The intersection of a column and a row.

A Cell

B Cell address

C Cell content

Content-Based Assessments

_____ 4. The labels along the lower border of the Excel window that identify each worksheet.

_____ 5. A vertical group of cells in a worksheet.

_____ 6. A horizontal group of cells in a worksheet.

_____ 7. Anything typed into a cell.

_____ 8. Information such as numbers, text, dates, or times of day that you type into a cell.

_____ 9. Text or numbers in a cell that are not a formula.

_____ 10. An equation that performs mathematical calculations on values in a worksheet.

_____ 11. A constant value consisting of only numbers.

_____ 12. Another name for a cell reference.

_____ 13. Another name for a constant value.

_____ 14. The small black square in the lower right corner of a selected cell.

_____ 15. The graphic representation of data in a worksheet.

D Chart
E Column
F Constant value
G Data
H Fill handle
I Formula
J Number value
K Row
L Sheet tabs
M Spreadsheet
N Value
O Workbook

Multiple Choice

Circle the correct answer.

1. On startup, Excel displays a new blank:
   A. document   **B.** workbook   **C.** grid

2. An Excel window element that displays the value or formula contained in the active cell is the:
   A. name box   **B.** status bar   **C.** formula bar

3. An Excel window element that displays the name of the selected cell, table, chart, or object is the:
   A. name box   **B.** status bar   **C.** formula bar

4. A box in the upper left corner of the worksheet grid that selects all the cells in a worksheet is the:
   A. name box   **B.** select all box   **C.** split box

5. A cell surrounded by a black border and ready to receive data is the:
   A. active cell   **B.** address cell   **C.** reference cell

6. The feature that generates and extends values into adjacent cells based on the values of selected cells is:
   A. AutoComplete   **B.** Auto Fill   **C.** fill handle

7. The default format that Excel applies to numbers is the:
   A. comma format   **B.** accounting format   **C.** general format

8. The data that displays in the Formula Bar is referred to as the:
   A. constant value   **B.** formula   **C.** underlying value

9. The type of cell reference that refers to cells by their fixed position in a worksheet is:
   A. absolute   **B.** relative   **C.** exponentiation

10. Tiny charts embedded in a cell that give a visual trend summary alongside your data are:
    A. embedded charts   **B.** sparklines   **C.** chart styles

Apply **1A** skills from these Objectives:

1. Create, Save, and Navigate an Excel Workbook
2. Enter Data in a Worksheet
3. Construct and Copy Formulas and Use the Sum Function
4. Format Cells with Merge & Center and Cell Styles
5. Chart Data to Create a Column Chart and Insert Sparklines
6. Print, Display Formulas, and Close Excel

Skills Review | Project **1C** GPS Sales

In the following Skills Review, you will create a new Excel worksheet with a chart that summarizes the first quarter sales of GPS (Global Positioning System) navigation devices. Your completed worksheet will look similar to Figure 1.54.

Project Files

For Project 1C, you will need the following file:

New blank Excel workbook

You will save your workbook as:

Lastname_Firstname_1C_GPS_Sales

Project Results

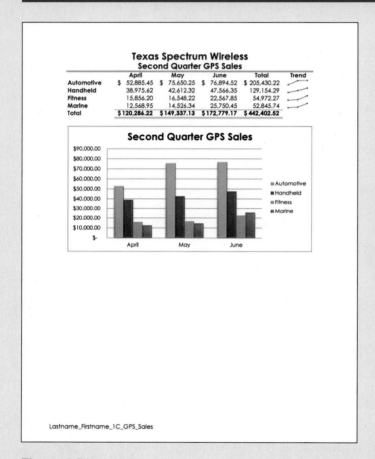

Figure 1.54

(Project 1C GPS Sales continues on the next page)

Content-Based Assessments

Skills Review | Project **1C** GPS Sales (continued)

1 **Start** Excel. Click the **File tab** to display **Backstage** view, click **Save As**, and then in the **Save As** dialog box, navigate to your **Excel Chapter 1** folder. In the **File name** box, using your own name, type **Lastname_Firstname_1C_GPS_Sales** and then press Enter.

a. With cell **A1** as the active cell, type the worksheet title **Texas Spectrum Wireless** and then press Enter. In cell **A2**, type the worksheet subtitle **Second Quarter GPS Sales** and then press Enter.

b. Click in cell **A4**, type **Automotive** and then press Enter. In cell **A5**, type **Handheld** and then press Enter. In cell **A6**, type **Fitness** and then press Enter. In cell **A7**, type **Marine** and then press Enter. In cell **A8**, type **Total** and then press Enter.

c. Click cell **B3**. Type **April** and then in the **Formula Bar**, click the **Enter** button to keep cell **B3** the active cell. With **B3** as the active cell, point to the fill handle in the lower right corner of the selected cell, drag to the right to cell **D3**, and then release the mouse button to enter the text *May* and *June*.

d. Press Ctrl + Home, to make cell **A1** the active cell. In the **column heading area**, point to the vertical line between **column A** and **column B** to display the ⟷ pointer, hold down the left mouse button and drag to the right to increase the column width to **100 pixels**.

e. Point to cell **B3**, and then drag across to select cells **B3** and **C3** and **D3**.With the range **B3:D3** selected, point anywhere over the selected range, right-click, and then on the Mini toolbar, click the **Center** button.

f. Click cell **B4**, type **52885.45** and press Tab to make cell **C4** active. Enter the remaining values, as shown in **Table 1**, pressing Tab to move across the rows and Enter to move down the columns.

2 Click cell **B8** to make it the active cell and type **=**

a. At the insertion point, type **b4** and then type **+** Type **b5** and then type **+b6+b7** Press Enter. Your result is *120286.2*.

b. Click in cell **C8**. Type **=** and then click cell **C4**. Type **+** and then click cell **C5**. Repeat this process to complete the formula to add cells **C4** through **C7**, and then press Enter. Your result is *149337.1*.

c. Click cell **D8**. On the **Home tab**, in the **Editing group**, click the **Sum** button, and then press Enter to construct a formula by using the SUM function. Your result is *172779.2*. You can use any of these methods to add values; the Sum button is the most efficient.

d. In cell **E3** type **Total** and press Enter. With cell **E4** as the active cell, hold down Alt, and then press =. On the **Formula Bar**, click the **Enter** button to display the result and keep cell **E4** active.

e. With cell **E4** active, point to the fill handle in the lower right corner of the cell. Drag down through cell **E8**, and then release the mouse button to copy the formula with relative cell references down to sum each row.

3 Click cell **F3**. Type **Trend** and then press Enter.

a. Select the range **A1:F1**, and then on the **Home tab**, in the **Alignment group**, click the **Merge & Center** button. Select the range **A2:F2**, and then click the **Merge & Center** button.

b. Click cell **A1**. In the **Styles group**, click the **Cell Styles** button. Under **Titles and Headings**, click **Title**. Click cell **A2**, display the **Cell Styles** gallery, and then click **Heading 1**.

c. Select the range **B3:F3**, hold down Ctrl, and then select the range **A4:A8**. From the **Cell Styles** gallery, click **Heading 4** to apply this cell style to the column and row titles.

d. Select the range **B4:E4**, hold down Ctrl, and then select the range **B8:E8**. On the **Home tab**, in the **Number group**, click the **Accounting Number Format** button. Select the range **B5:E7**, and then in the **Number group**, click the **Comma Style** button. Select the range **B8:E8**. From the **Styles group**, display the **Cell Styles** gallery, and then under **Titles and Headings**, click **Total**.

Table 1

	April	May	June
Automotive	52885.45	75650.25	76894.52
Handheld	38975.62	42612.32	47566.35
Fitness	15856.20	16548.22	22567.85
Marine	12568.95	14526.34	25750.45

- - - → (Return to Step 2)

(Project 1C GPS Sales continues on the next page)

Content-Based Assessments

Skills Review | Project **1C** GPS Sales (continued)

e. On the Ribbon, click the **Page Layout tab**, and then from the **Themes group**, click the **Themes** button to display the **Themes** gallery. Click the **Austin** theme.

4 Select the range **A3:D7**. Click the **Insert tab**, and then in the **Charts group**, click **Column**. From the gallery of column chart types, under **2-D Column**, click the first chart—**Clustered Column**.

a. On the Quick Access Toolbar, click the **Save** button to be sure that you have saved your work up to this point. Point to the top border of the chart to display the ![pointer] pointer, and then drag to position the chart inside the upper left corner of cell **A10**.

b. On the **Design tab**, in the **Data group**, click the **Switch Row/Column** button so that the months display on the Horizontal (Category) axis and the types of GPS equipment display in the legend.

c. On the **Design tab**, in the **Chart Layouts group**, click the first layout—**Layout 1**.

d. In the chart, click anywhere in the text *Chart Title* to select the text box. Type **Second Quarter GPS Sales** and then press Enter.

e. Click anywhere in the chart so that the chart title text box is not selected. On the **Design tab**, in the **Chart Styles group**, click the **More** button. Using the ScreenTips as your guide, locate and click **Style 18**.

f. Point to the lower right corner of the chart to display the ![pointer] pointer, and then drag down and to the right so that the lower right border of the chart is positioned just inside the lower right corner of cell **F26**.

5 Select the range **B4:D7**. Click the **Insert tab**, and then in the **Sparklines group**, click **Line**. In the **Create Sparklines** dialog box, in the **Location Range** box, type **f4:f7** and then click **OK** to insert the sparklines.

a. On the **Design tab**, in the **Show group**, select the **Markers** check box to display markers in the sparklines.

b. On the **Design tab**, in the **Style group**, click the **More** button, and then in the second row, click the fourth style—**Sparkline Style Accent 4, Darker 25%**.

6 On the **Insert tab**, in the **Text group**, click **Header & Footer** to switch to **Page Layout** view and open the **Header** area.

a. In the **Navigation group**, click the **Go to Footer** button to open the Footer area. Click just above the word *Footer* to place the insertion point in the **left section** of the Footer.

b. In the **Header & Footer Elements group**, click the **File Name** button, and then click in a cell just above the footer to exit the Footer area.

7 On the right side of the status bar, click the **Normal** button to return to Normal view, and then press Ctrl + Home to make cell **A1** active.

a. Click the **File tab**, and then on the right, click **Properties**. Click **Show Document Panel**, and then in the **Author** box, delete any text and type your firstname and lastname. In the **Subject** box, type your course name and section number, and in the **Keywords** box, type **GPS sales Close** the Document Information Panel.

b. At the bottom of your worksheet, click the **Sheet2** tab. Hold down Ctrl, and then click the **Sheet3** tab. With both sheets selected, point to either of the selected sheet tabs, right-click, and then click **Delete** to delete the sheets.

c. Click the **Page Layout tab**. In the **Page Setup group**, click the **Margins** button, and then at the bottom of the **Margins** gallery, click **Custom Margins**. In the **Page Setup** dialog box, under **Center on page**, select the **Horizontally** check box.

d. In the lower right corner of the **Page Setup** dialog box, click **OK**. On the **File tab**, click **Print** to view the **Print Preview**. Click the **Home tab** to return to Normal view and if necessary, make any necessary corrections and resize and move your chart so that it is centered under the worksheet.

e. On the Quick Access Toolbar, click the **Save** button to be sure that you have saved your work up to this point.

f. Print or submit your workbook electronically as directed by your instructor. If required by your instructor, print or create an electronic version of your worksheets with formulas displayed by using the instructions in Activity 1.16. **Exit** Excel without saving so that you do not save the changes you made to print formulas.

End You have completed Project 1C ————————————

Content-Based Assessments

Apply **1B** skills from these Objectives:

7 Check Spelling in a Worksheet

8 Enter Data by Range

9 Construct Formulas for Mathematical Operations

10 Edit Values in a Worksheet

11 Format a Worksheet

Skills Review | Project **1D** Charger Inventory

In the following Skills Review, you will create a worksheet that summarizes the inventory of cell phone chargers. Your completed worksheet will look similar to Figure 1.55.

Project Files

For Project 1D, you will need the following file:

New blank Excel workbook

You will save your workbook as:

Lastname_Firstname_1D_Charger_Inventory

Project Results

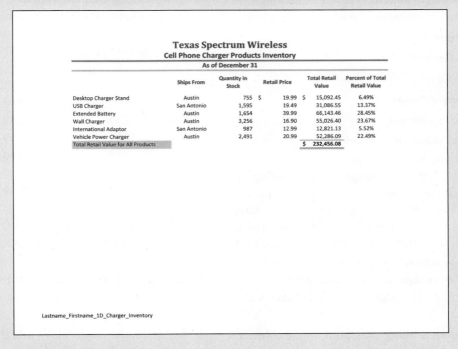

Texas Spectrum Wireless
Cell Phone Charger Products Inventory

	Ships From	Quantity in Stock	Retail Price	Total Retail Value	Percent of Total Retail Value
As of December 31					
Desktop Charger Stand	Austin	755	$ 19.99	$ 15,092.45	6.49%
USB Charger	San Antonio	1,595	19.49	31,086.55	13.37%
Extended Battery	Austin	1,654	39.99	66,143.46	28.45%
Wall Charger	Austin	3,256	16.90	55,026.40	23.67%
International Adaptor	San Antonio	987	12.99	12,821.13	5.52%
Vehicle Power Charger	Austin	2,491	20.99	52,286.09	22.49%
Total Retail Value for All Products				$ 232,456.08	

Lastname_Firstname_1D_Charger_Inventory

Figure 1.55

(Project 1D Charger Inventory continues on the next page)

Skills Review | Project **1D** Charger Inventory (continued)

1 **Start** Excel and display a new blank workbook. **Save** the workbook in your **Excel Chapter 1** folder, as **Lastname_Firstname_1D_Charger_Inventory** In cell **A1** type **Texas Spectrum Wireless** and in cell **A2** type **Cell Phone Charger Products Inventory**

a. Click cell **B3**, type **Quantity in Stock** and press `Tab`. In cell **C3** type **Average Cost** and press `Tab`. In cell **D3**, type **Retail Price** and press `Tab`. In cell **E3**, type **Total Retail Value** and press `Tab`. In cell **F3** type **Percent of Total Retail Value** and press `Enter`.

b. Click cell **A4**, type **Desktop Charger Stand** and press `Enter`. In the range **A5:A10**, type the remaining row titles as shown, including the misspelled words.

   USB Charger

   Extended Battery

   Wall Charger

   International Adaptor

   Vehicle Powr Charger

   Total Retail Value for All Products

c. Press `Ctrl` + `Home` to move to the top of your worksheet. On the **Review tab**, in the **Proofing group**, click the **Spelling** button. Correct *Powr* to **Power** and any other spelling errors you may have made, and then when the message displays, *The spelling check is complete for the entire sheet*, click **OK**.

d. In the **column heading area**, point to the right boundary of **column A** to display the ⊞ pointer, and then drag to the right to widen **column A** to **225** pixels.

e. In the **column heading area**, point to the **column B** heading to display the ⬇ pointer, and then drag to the right to select **columns B:F**. With the columns selected, in the **column heading area**, point to the right boundary of any of the selected columns, and then drag to the right to set the width to **100 pixels**.

f. Select the range **A1:F1**. On the **Home tab**, in the **Alignment group**, click the **Merge & Center** button, and then from the **Cell Styles** gallery, apply the **Title** style. Select the range **A2:F2**. **Merge & Center** the text across the selection, and then from the **Cell Styles** gallery, apply the **Heading 1** style.

2 Select the empty range **B4:D9**. With cell B4 active in the range, type **755** and then press `Enter`.

a. With cell **B5** active in the range, and pressing `Enter` after each entry, type the following data in the *Quantity in Stock* column:

   1595

   2654

   3256

   987

   2491

b. With the selected range still active, from the following table, beginning in cell **C4** and pressing `Enter` after each entry, enter the following data for the **Average Cost** column and then the **Retail Price** column. If you prefer, type without selecting the range first; recall that this is optional.

Average Cost	Retail Price
9.75	19.99
9.25	19.49
16.90	39.99
9.55	16.90
14.20	12.99
10.45	20.99

3 In cell **E4**, type **=b4*d4** and then press `Enter` to construct a formula that calculates the *Total Retail Value* of the *Desktop Charger Stands* (Quantity × Retail Price).

a. Click cell **E4**, position your pointer over the fill handle, and then drag down through cell **E9** to copy the formula.

b. Select the range **B4:B9**, and then on the **Home tab**, in the **Number group**, click the **Comma Style** button. Then, in the **Number group**, click the **Decrease Decimal** button two times to remove the decimal places from these non-currency values.

c. Click cell **E10**, in the **Editing group**, click the **Sum** button, and then press `Enter` to calculate the *Total Retail Value for All Products*. Your result is *272446.1*.

d. Select the range **C5:E9** and apply the **Comma Style**. Select the range **C4:E4**, hold down `Ctrl`, and then click cell **E10**. With the nonadjacent cells selected, apply the **Accounting Number Format**. Click cell **E10**, and then from the **Cell Styles** gallery, apply the **Total** style.

(Project 1D Charger Inventory continues on the next page)

Content-Based Assessments

e. Click cell **F4**, type = and then click cell **E4**. Type **/** and then click cell **E10**. Press F4 to make the reference to cell *E10* absolute, and then on the **Formula Bar**, click the **Enter** button so that **F4** remains the active cell. Drag the fill handle to copy the formula down through cell **F9**.

f. Point to cell **B6**, and then double-click to place the insertion point within the cell. Use the arrow keys to move the insertion point to left or right of *2*, and use either Del or Backspace to delete 2, and then type **1** and press Enter so that the new *Quantity in Stock* is *1654*. Notice the recalculations in the worksheet.

4 Select the range **F4:F9**, right-click over the selection, and then on the Mini toolbar, click the **Percent Style** button. Click the **Increase Decimal** button two times, and then **Center** the selection.

a. In the **row heading area** on the left side of your screen, point to **row 3** to display the ➡ pointer, and then right-click to simultaneously select the row and display a shortcut menu. On the displayed shortcut menu, click **Insert** to insert a new **row 3**.

b. Click cell **A3**, type **As of December 31** and then on the **Formula Bar**, click the **Enter** button to keep cell **A3** as the active cell. **Merge & Center** the text across the range **A3:F3**, and then apply the **Heading 2** cell style.

5 In the **column heading area**, point to **column B**. When the ⬇ pointer displays, right-click, and then click **Insert** to insert a new column.

a. Click cell **B4**, and type **Ships From** and press Enter. In cell **B5**, type **Austin** and then press Enter. In cell **B6,** type **San Antonio** and then press Enter

b. Using AutoComplete to speed your typing by pressing Enter as soon as the AutoComplete suggestion displays, in cells **B7**, **B8**, and **B10** type **Austin** and in cell **B9** type **San Antonio**

c. In the **column heading area**, point to the right boundary of **column B**, and then drag to the left and set the width to **90 pixels**. From the **column heading area**, point to **column D**, right-click, and then click **Delete**.

d. Select the range **B4:F4**, and then on the **Home tab**, in the **Alignment group**, click the **Wrap Text** button, the **Center** button, and the **Middle Align** button. With the range still selected, apply the **Heading 4** cell style.

e. Select the range **B5:B10**, right-click, and then click the **Center** button. Click cell **A11**, and then from the **Cell Styles** gallery, under **Themed Cell Styles**, click **40% - Accent1**.

6 On the **Insert tab**, in the **Text group**, click **Header & Footer**. In the **Navigation group**, click the **Go To Footer** button, and then click just above the word *Footer*. In the **Header & Footer Elements group**, click the **File Name** button to add the name of your file to the footer. Click in a cell just above the footer to exit the **Footer area**, and then return the worksheet to **Normal** view.

a. Press Ctrl + Home to move the insertion point to cell **A1**. On the **Page Layout tab**, in the **Page Setup group**, click **Orientation**, and then click **Landscape**.

b. In the **Page Setup group**, click the **Margins** button, and then at the bottom of the **Margins gallery**, click **Custom Margins**. In the **Page Setup** dialog box, under **Center on page**, select the **Horizontally** check box, and then click **OK**.

c. Click the **File tab** to display **Backstage** view, and then on the right, click **Properties**. Click **Show Document Panel**, and then in the **Author** box, delete any text and type your firstname and lastname. In the **Subject** box type your course name and section number, in the **Keywords** box type **cell phone chargers** and then **Close** the **Document Information Panel**.

d. Select **Sheet2** and **Sheet3**, and then **Delete** both sheets.

e. **Save** your file and then print or submit your workbook electronically as directed by your instructor. If required by your instructor, print or create an electronic version of your worksheet with formulas displayed by using the instructions in Activity 1.16. **Exit** Excel without saving so that you do not save the changes you made to print formulas.

End **You have completed Project 1D**

Content-Based Assessments

Apply 1A skills from these Objectives:

1. Create, Save, and Navigate an Excel Workbook
2. Enter Data in a Worksheet
3. Construct and Copy Formulas and Use the SUM Function
4. Format Cells with Merge & Center and Cell Styles
5. Chart Data to Create a Column Chart and Insert Sparklines
6. Print, Display Formulas, and Close Excel

Mastering Excel | Project **1E** Hard Drives

In the following Mastering Excel project, you will create a worksheet comparing the sales of different types of external hard drives sold in the second quarter. Your completed worksheet will look similar to Figure 1.56.

Project Files

For Project 1E, you will need the following file:

New blank Excel workbook

You will save your workbook as:

Lastname_Firstname_1E_Hard_Drives

Project Results

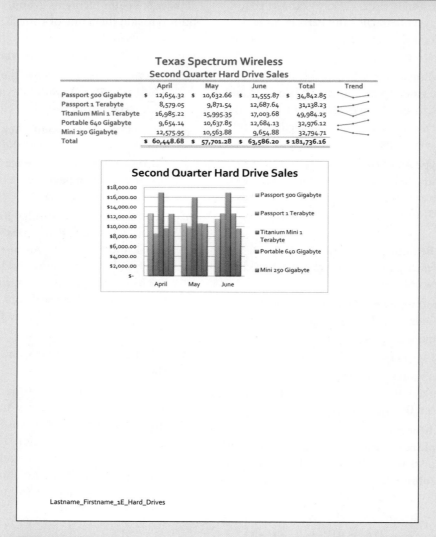

Figure 1.56

(Project 1E Hard Drives continues on the next page)

Mastering Excel | Project **1E** Hard Drives (continued)

1 **Start** Excel. In cell **A1**, type **Texas Spectrum Wireless** and in cell **A2**, type **Second Quarter Hard Drive Sales** Change the **Theme** to **Module**, and then **Save** the workbook in your **Excel Chapter 1** folder as **Lastname_Firstname_1E_Hard_Drives**

2 In cell **B3**, type **April** and then use the fill handle to enter the months *May* and *June* in the range **C3:D3**. In cell **E3**, type **Total** and in cell **F3**, type **Trend**

3 **Center** the column titles in the range **B3:F3**. **Merge & Center** the title across the range **A1:F1**, and apply the **Title** cell style. **Merge & Center** the subtitle across the range **A2:F2**, and apply the **Heading 1** cell style.

4 Widen **column A** to **170 pixels**, and then in the range **A4:A9**, type the following row titles:

> Passport 500 Gigabyte
>
> Passport 1 Terabyte
>
> Titanium Mini 1 Terabyte
>
> Portable 640 Gigabyte
>
> Mini 250 Gigabyte
>
> Total

5 Widen columns **B:F** to **100 pixels**, and then in the range **B4:D8**, enter the monthly sales figures for each type of hard drive, as shown in **Table 1** at the bottom of the page.

6 In cell **B9**, **Sum** the *April* hard drive sales, and then copy the formula across to cells **C9:D9**. In cell **E4**, **Sum** the *Passport 500 Gigabyte sales*, and then copy the formula down to cells **E5:E9**.

7 Apply the **Heading 4** cell style to the row titles and the column titles. Apply the **Total** cell style to the totals in the range **B9:E9**. Apply the **Accounting Number Format**

to the first row of sales figures and to the total row. Apply the **Comma Style** to the remaining sales figures.

8 To compare the monthly sales of each product visually, select the range that represents the sales figures for the three months, including the month names, and for each product name—do not include any totals in the range. With this data selected, **Insert** a **2-D Clustered Column** chart. Switch the Row/Column data so that the months display on the category axis and the types of hard drives display in the legend.

9 Position the upper left corner of the chart in the approximate center of cell **A11** so that the chart is visually centered below the worksheet, as shown in Figure 1.56. Apply **Chart Style 26**, and then modify the **Chart Layout** by applying **Layout 1**. Change the **Chart Title** to **Second Quarter Hard Drive Sales**

10 In the range **F4:F8**, insert **Line** sparklines that compare the monthly data. Do not include the totals. Show the sparkline **Markers** and apply **Sparkline Style Accent 2, Darker 50%**—in the first row, the second style.

11 Insert a **Footer** with the **File Name** in the **left section**, and then return the worksheet to **Normal** view. Display the **Document Panel**, add your name, your course name and section, and the keywords **hard drives, sales** Delete the unused sheets, and then center the worksheet **Horizontally** on the page. Check your worksheet by previewing it in **Print Preview**, and then make any necessary corrections.

12 **Save** your workbook, and then print or submit electronically as directed. If required by your instructor, print or create an electronic version of your worksheets with formulas displayed by using the instructions in Activity 1.16. **Exit** Excel without saving so that you do not save the changes you made to print formulas.

Table 1

	April	May	June
Passport 500 Gigabyte	12654.32	10632.66	11555.87
Passport 1 Terabyte	8579.05	9871.54	12687.64
Titanium Mini 1 Terabyte	16985.22	15995.35	17003.68
Portable 640 Gigabyte	9654.14	10637.85	12684.13
Mini 250 Gigabyte	12575.95	10563.88	9654.88

(Return to Step 6)

End **You have completed Project 1E** ——————————————

Content-Based Assessments

Apply **1B** skills from these Objectives:

■7 Check Spelling in a Worksheet

■8 Enter Data by Range

■9 Construct Formulas for Mathematical Operations

■10 Edit Values in a Worksheet

■11 Format a Worksheet

Mastering Excel | Project **1F** Camera Accessories

In the following Mastering Excel project, you will create a worksheet that summarizes the sale of digital camera accessories. Your completed worksheet will look similar to Figure 1.57.

Project Files

For Project 1F, you will need the following file:

New blank Excel workbook

You will save your workbook as:

Lastname_Firstname_1F_Camera_Accessories

Project Results

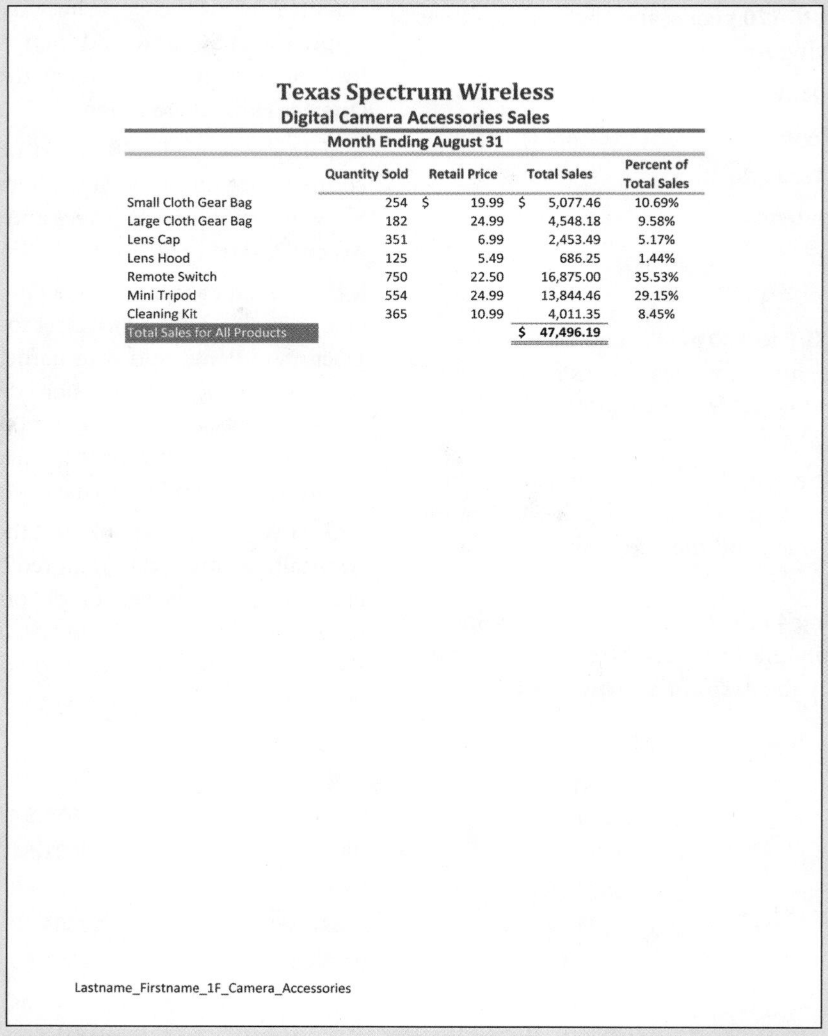

Texas Spectrum Wireless
Digital Camera Accessories Sales

	Month Ending August 31			
	Quantity Sold	Retail Price	Total Sales	Percent of Total Sales
Small Cloth Gear Bag	254	$ 19.99	$ 5,077.46	10.69%
Large Cloth Gear Bag	182	24.99	4,548.18	9.58%
Lens Cap	351	6.99	2,453.49	5.17%
Lens Hood	125	5.49	686.25	1.44%
Remote Switch	750	22.50	16,875.00	35.53%
Mini Tripod	554	24.99	13,844.46	29.15%
Cleaning Kit	365	10.99	4,011.35	8.45%
Total Sales for All Products			$ 47,496.19	

Lastname_Firstname_1F_Camera_Accessories

Figure 1.57

(Project 1F Camera Accessories continues on the next page)

Content-Based Assessments

Mastering Excel | Project **1F** Camera Accessories (continued)

1 **Start** Excel and display a new blank workbook. **Save** the workbook in your **Excel Chapter 1** folder as **Lastname_Firstname_1F_Camera_Accessories** In cell **A1**, type **Texas Spectrum Wireless** In cell **A2**, type **Digital Camera Accessories Sales** and then **Merge & Center** the title and the subtitle across **columns A:F**. Apply the **Title** and **Heading 1** cell styles respectively.

2 Beginning in cell **B3**, type the following column titles: **Product Number** and **Quantity Sold** and **Retail Price** and **Total Sales** and **Percent of Total Sales**

3 Beginning in cell **A4**, type the following row titles, including misspelled words:

> **Small Cloth Gear Bag**
>
> **Large Cloth Gear Bag**
>
> **Lens Cap**
>
> **Lens Hood**
>
> **Remote Switch**
>
> **Mini Tripod**
>
> **Cleening Kit**
>
> **Total Sales for All Products**

4 Make cell **A1** the active cell, and then check spelling in your worksheet. Correct *Cleening* to **Cleaning**, and make any other necessary corrections. Widen **column A** to **180 pixels** and **columns B:F** to **90 pixels**.

5 In the range **B4:D10**, type the data shown in **Table 1** at the bottom of the page.

6 In cell **E4**, construct a formula to calculate the *Total Sales* of the *Small Cloth Gear Bags* by multiplying the *Quantity Sold* times the *Retail Price*. Copy the formula down for the remaining products. In cell **E11**, use the **SUM** function to calculate the *Total Sales for All Products*, and then apply the **Total** cell style to the cell.

7 Using absolute cell references as necessary so that you can copy the formula, in cell **F4**, construct a formula to calculate the *Percent of Total Sales* for the first product by dividing the *Total Sales* of the *Small Cloth Gear Bags* by the *Total Sales for All Products*. Copy the formula down for the remaining products. To the computed percentages, apply **Percent Style** with two decimal places, and then **Center** the percentages.

8 Apply the **Comma Style** with no decimal places to the *Quantity Sold* figures. To cells **D4**, **E4**, and **E11** apply the **Accounting Number Format**. To the range **D5:E10**, apply the **Comma Style**.

9 Change the *Retail Price* of the *Mini Tripod* to **24.99** and the *Quantity Sold* of the *Remote Switch* to **750** Delete **column B**, and then **Insert** a new **row 3**. In cell **A3**, type **Month Ending August 31** and then **Merge & Center** the text across the range **A3:E3**. Apply the **Heading 2** cell style. To cell **A12**, apply the **Accent1** cell style. Select the four column titles, apply **Wrap Text**, **Middle Align**, and **Center** formatting, and then apply the **Heading 3** cell style.

10 Insert a **Footer** with the **File Name** in the **left section**, and then return to **Normal** view. Display the **Document Panel**, add your name, your course name and section, and the keywords **digital camera accessories, sales**

11 Delete the unused sheets, and then center the worksheet **Horizontally** on the page. Preview the worksheet in **Print Preview**, and make any necessary corrections.

12 **Save** your workbook, and then print or submit electronically as directed. If required by your instructor, print or create an electronic version of your worksheets with formulas displayed by using the instructions in Activity 1.16. **Exit** Excel without saving so that you do not save the changes you made to print formulas.

Table 1

	Product Number	Quantity Sold	Retail Price
Small Cloth Gear Bag	CGB-3	254	19.99
Large Cloth Gear Bag	CGB-8	182	24.99
Lens Cap	LC-2	351	6.99
Lens Hood	LH-4	125	5.49
Remote Switch	RS-5	677	22.50
Mini Tripod	MTP-6	554	29.99
Cleaning Kit	CK-8	365	10.99

- - - ► (Return to Step 6)

End You have completed Project 1F

Content-Based Assessments

Apply **1A** and **1B** skills from these Objectives:

1 Create, Save, and Navigate an Excel Workbook

2 Enter Data in a Worksheet

3 Construct and Copy Formulas and Use the SUM Function

4 Format Cells with Merge & Center and Cell Styles

5 Chart Data to Create a Column Chart and Insert Sparklines

6 Print, Display Formulas, and Close Excel

7 Check Spelling in a Worksheet

8 Enter Data by Range

9 Construct Formulas for Mathematical Operations

10 Edit Values in a Worksheet

11 Format a Worksheet

Mastering Excel | Project **1G** Sales Comparison

In the following Mastering Excel project, you will create a new worksheet that compares annual laptop sales by store location. Your completed worksheet will look similar to Figure 1.58.

Project Files

For Project 1G, you will need the following file:

New blank Excel workbook

You will save your workbook as:

Lastname_Firstname_1G_Sales_Comparison

Project Results

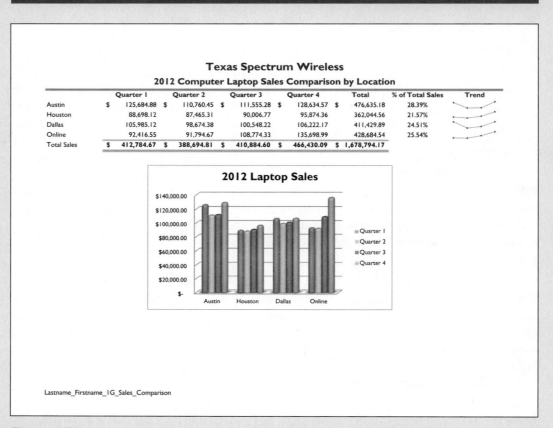

Figure 1.58

(Project 1G Sales Comparison continues on the next page)

Mastering Excel | Project **1G** Sales Comparison (continued)

1 **Start** Excel. In a new blank workbook, as the worksheet title, in cell **A1**, type **Texas Spectrum Wireless** As the worksheet subtitle, in cell **A2**, type **2012 Computer Laptop Sales Comparison by Location** and then **Save** the workbook in your **Excel Chapter 1** folder as **Lastname_Firstname_1G_Sales_Comparison**

2 In cell **B3**, type **Quarter 1** and then use the fill handle to enter *Quarter 2*, *Quarter 3*, and *Quarter 4* in the range **C3:E3**. In cell **F3**, type **Total** In cell **G3**, type **% of Total Sales** In cell **H3**, type **Trend**

3 In the range **A4:A7**, type the following row titles: **Austin** and **Houston** and **Online** and **Total Sales**

4 Widen columns **A:H** to **115 pixels**. Merge & Center the title across the range **A1:H1**, and then apply the **Title** cell style. **Merge & Center** the subtitle across the range **A2:H2**, and then apply the **Heading 1** cell style. Select the seven column titles, apply **Center** formatting, and then apply the **Heading 4** cell style.

5 In the range **B4:E6**, enter the sales values for each Quarter as shown in **Table 1** at the bottom of the page.

6 **Sum** the *Quarter 1* sales, and then copy the formula across for the remaining Quarters. **Sum** the sales for the *Austin* location, and then copy the formula down through cell **F7**. Apply the **Accounting Number Format** to the first row of sales figures and to the total row, and the **Comma Style** to the remaining sales figures. Format the totals in **row 7** with the **Total** cell style.

7 **Insert** a new **row 6** with the row title **Dallas** and the following sales figures for each quarter: **105985.12** and **98674.38** and **100548.22** and **106222.17** Copy the formula in cell **F5** down to cell **F6** to sum the new row.

8 Using absolute cell references as necessary so that you can copy the formula, in cell **G4** construct a formula to calculate the *Percent of Total Sales* for the first location by dividing the *Total* for the *Austin* location by the *Total Sales* for all Quarters. Copy the formula down for the remaining locations. To the computed percentages, apply

Percent Style with two decimal places, and then **Center** the percentages.

9 Insert **Line** sparklines in the range **H4:H7** that compare the quarterly data. Do not include the totals. Show the sparkline **Markers** and apply the second style in the second row—**Sparkline Style Accent 2, Darker 25%**.

10 **Save** your workbook. To compare the quarterly sales of each location visually, select the range that represents the sales figures for the four quarters, including the quarter names and each location—do not include any totals in the range. With this data selected, **Insert** a **Column, Clustered Cylinder** chart.

11 Switch the row/column data so that the locations display on the category axis. Position the top edge of the chart in **row 10** and visually center it below the worksheet data. Apply **Chart Style 26**, and then modify the **Chart Layout** by applying **Layout 1**. Change the **Chart Title** to **2012 Laptop Sales**

12 Deselect the chart. Change the **Orientation** to **Landscape**, center the worksheet **Horizontally** on the page, and then change the **Theme** to **Solstice**. Scale the worksheet so that the **Width** fits to **1 page**. Insert a **Footer** with the **File Name** in the **left section**. Return the worksheet to **Normal** view and make **A1** the active cell so that you can view the top of your worksheet.

13 Display the **Document Panel**, add your name, your course name and section, and the keywords **laptops, sales** Delete the unused sheets, preview your worksheet in **Print Preview**, and then make any necessary corrections.

14 **Save** your workbook, and then print or submit electronically as directed. If required by your instructor, print or create an electronic version of your worksheets with formulas displayed by using the instructions in Activity 1.16. **Exit** Excel without saving so that you do not save the changes you made to print formulas.

Table 1

	Quarter 1	Quarter 2	Quarter 3	Quarter 4
Austin	125684.88	110760.45	111555.28	128634.57
Houston	88698.12	87465.31	90006.77	95874.36
Online	92416.55	91794.67	108774.33	135698.99

- - - ▶ (Return to Step 6)

End **You have completed Project 1G** ————————

Content-Based Assessments

Apply a combination of the 1A and 1B skills.

GO! Fix It | Project **1H** Team Sales

Project Files

For Project 1H, you will need the following file:

e01H_Team_Sales

You will save your workbook as:

Lastname_Firstname_1H_Team_Sales

In this project, you will edit a worksheet that summarizes sales by each sales team member at the Texas Spectrum Wireless San Antonio location for the month of February. From the student files that accompany this textbook, open the file e01H_Team_Sales, and then save the file in your Excel Chapter 1 folder as **Lastname_Firstname_1H_Team_Sales**

To complete the project, you must find and correct errors in formulas and formatting. View each formula in the Formula Bar and edit as necessary. In addition to errors that you find, you should know:

- There are two spelling errors.
- Worksheet titles should be merged and centered and appropriate cell styles should be applied.
- Appropriate number and accounting format with zero decimals should be applied to the data and text should be wrapped where necessary. Percent style formatting should be applied appropriately where necessary.
- Column headings should be formatted with the Heading 4 style.
- In the chart, the team member names should display on the Horizontal (Category) axis and the week names should display in the legend.
- The chart should include the title **February Team Member Sales**
- The worksheet should be centered horizontally on one page in Landscape orientation. Remove unused sheets.
- A footer should be inserted that includes the file name, and document properties should include the keywords **team sales, San Antonio**

Save your workbook, and then print or submit electronically as directed. If required by your instructor, print or create an electronic version of your worksheets with formulas displayed by using the instructions in Activity 1.16. Exit Excel without saving so that you do not save the changes you made to print formulas.

End **You have completed Project 1H** ⎯⎯⎯⎯⎯⎯⎯⎯⎯⎯⎯

Content-Based Assessments

Apply a combination of the **1A** and **1B** skills.

GO! Make It | Project 1I Printer Sales

Project Files

For Project 1I, you will need the following file:

New blank Excel workbook

You will save your workbook as:

Lastname_Firstname_1I_Printer_Sales

Create the worksheet shown in Figure 1.59. Use the Pushpin theme and change the Orientation to Landscape. Construct formulas in the Total Sold, Total Sales, and Percent of Total Sales columns, and in the Total row. Apply cell styles and number formatting as shown. Use Style 26 for the chart. Insert sparklines for the monthly data using the first style in the second row—Sparkline Style Accent 1, Darker 25%. Add your name, your course name and section, and the keywords **inkjet, printer, sales** to the document properties. Save the file in your Excel Chapter 1 folder as **Lastname_Firstname_1I_Printer_Sales**

Project Results

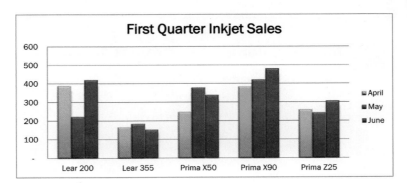

Texas Spectrum Wireless
First Quarter Inkjet Printer Sales

Model	April	May	June	Total Sold	Retail Price	Total Sales	Percent of Total Sales	Trend
Lear 200	390	224	421	1,035	$ 79.99	$ 82,789.65	8.50%	
Lear 355	168	186	153	507	169.99	86,184.93	8.85%	
Prima X50	250	379	339	968	199.99	193,590.32	19.88%	
Prima X90	386	423	482	1,291	249.99	322,737.09	33.15%	
Prima Z25	261	244	307	812	354.99	288,251.88	29.61%	
Total	1,455	1,456	1,702	4,613		$ 973,553.87		

Lastname_Firstname_1I_Printer_Sales

Figure 1.59

 You have completed Project 1I

Content-Based Assessments

GO! Solve It | Project **1J** Warranty Sales

Project Files

For Project 1J, you will need the following file:

e01J_Warranty_Sales

You will save your workbook as:

Lastname_Firstname_1J_Warranty_Sales

Open the file e01J_Warranty_Sales and save it as **Lastname_Firstname_1J_Warranty_Sales** Complete the worksheet by using Auto Fill to enter the Quarter headings, and then calculating *Total Sold*, *Total Sales*, *Total For All Products*, and *Percent of Total Sales*. Format the worksheet attractively, and apply appropriate financial formatting. Insert a chart that compares the total number of warranties sold for each item across Quarters, and format the chart to display the information appropriately. Include the file name in the footer, add appropriate document properties, and submit as directed.

		Performance Level		
		Exemplary: You consistently applied the relevant skills	**Proficient:** You sometimes, but not always, applied the relevant skills	**Developing:** You rarely or never applied the relevant skills
Performance Element	Create formulas	All formulas are correct and are efficiently constructed.	Formulas are correct but not always constructed in the most efficient manner.	One or more formulas are missing or incorrect; or only numbers were entered.
	Create a chart	Chart created properly.	Chart was created but incorrect data was selected.	No chart was created.
	Format attractively and appropriately	Formatting is attractive and appropriate.	Adequately formatted but difficult to read or unattractive.	Inadequate or no formatting.

End You have completed Project 1J

Content-Based Assessments

GO! Solve It | Project **1K** Service Receipts

Project Files

For Project 1K, you will need the following file:

    e01K_Service_Receipts

You will save your workbook as:

    Lastname_Firstname_1K_Service_Receipts

Open the file e01K_Service_Receipts and save it as **Lastname_Firstname_1K_Service_ Receipts** Complete the worksheet by using Auto Fill to complete the month headings, and then calculating the Total Receipts for each month and for each product. Insert and format appropriate sparklines in the Trend column. Format the worksheet attractively with a title and subtitle, check spelling, adjust column width, and apply appropriate financial formatting. Insert a chart that compares the total sales receipts for each product with the months displaying as the categories, and format the chart attractively. Include the file name in the footer, add appropriate properties, and submit as directed.

Performance Element	Performance Level		
	Exemplary: You consistently applied the relevant skills	Proficient: You sometimes, but not always, applied the relevant skills	Developing: You rarely or never applied the relevant skills
Create formulas	All formulas are correct and are efficiently constructed.	Formulas are correct but not always constructed in the most efficient manner.	One or more formulas are missing or incorrect; or only numbers were entered.
Create a chart	Chart created properly.	Chart was created but incorrect data was selected.	No chart was created.
Insert and format sparklines	Sparklines inserted and formatted properly.	Sparklines were inserted but incorrect data was selected or sparklines were not formatted.	No sparklines were inserted.
Format attractively and appropriately	Formatting is attractive and appropriate.	Adequately formatted but difficult to read or unattractive.	Inadequate or no formatting.

End You have completed Project 1K

Outcomes-Based Assessments

Rubric

The following outcomes-based assessments are *open-ended assessments*. That is, there is no specific correct result; your result will depend on your approach to the information provided. Make *Professional Quality* your goal. Use the following scoring rubric to guide you in *how to* approach the problem, and then to evaluate *how well* your approach solves the problem.

The *criteria*—Software Mastery, Content, Format and Layout, and Process—represent the knowledge and skills you have gained that you can apply to solving the problem. The *levels of performance*—Professional Quality, Approaching Professional Quality, or Needs Quality Improvements—help you and your instructor evaluate your result.

	Your completed project is of Professional Quality if you:	Your completed project is Approaching Professional Quality if you:	Your completed project Needs Quality Improvements if you:
1-Software Mastery	Choose and apply the most appropriate skills, tools, and features and identify efficient methods to solve the problem.	Choose and apply some appropriate skills, tools, and features, but not in the most efficient manner.	Choose inappropriate skills, tools, or features, or are inefficient in solving the problem.
2-Content	Construct a solution that is clear and well organized, contains content that is accurate, appropriate to the audience and purpose, and is complete. Provide a solution that contains no errors in spelling, grammar, or style.	Construct a solution in which some components are unclear, poorly organized, inconsistent, or incomplete. Misjudge the needs of the audience. Have some errors in spelling, grammar, or style, but the errors do not detract from comprehension.	Construct a solution that is unclear, incomplete, or poorly organized; contains some inaccurate or inappropriate content; and contains many errors in spelling, grammar, or style. Do not solve the problem.
3-Format and Layout	Format and arrange all elements to communicate information and ideas, clarify function, illustrate relationships, and indicate relative importance.	Apply appropriate format and layout features to some elements, but not others. Overuse features, causing minor distraction.	Apply format and layout that does not communicate information or ideas clearly. Do not use format and layout features to clarify function, illustrate relationships, or indicate relative importance. Use available features excessively, causing distraction.
4-Process	Use an organized approach that integrates planning, development, self-assessment, revision, and reflection.	Demonstrate an organized approach in some areas, but not others; or, use an insufficient process of organization throughout.	Do not use an organized approach to solve the problem.

Apply a combination of the 1A and 1B skills.

GO! Think | Project 1L Phone Plans

Project Files

For Project 1L, you will need the following file:

New blank Excel workbook

You will save your workbook as:

Lastname_Firstname_1L_Phone_Plans

Roslyn Thomas, President of Texas Spectrum Wireless, needs a worksheet that summarizes the following data regarding the first quarter sales of cell phone calling plans that the company is offering for domestic and international calls. Roslyn would like the worksheet to include a calculation of the total sales for each plan and a total of the sales of all of the plans. She would also like to know each plan's percentage of total sales.

	Number Sold	Price
Domestic Standard	2556	29.99
Domestic Premium	3982	49.99
Domestic Platinum	1647	64.99
International Standard	582	85.99
International Premium	365	102.99

Create a worksheet that provides Roslyn with the information needed. Include appropriate worksheet, column, and row titles. Using the formatting skills that you practiced in this chapter, format the worksheet in a manner that is professional and easy to read and understand. Insert a footer with the file name and add appropriate document properties. Save the file as **Lastname_Firstname_1L_Phone_Plans** and print or submit as directed by your instructor.

End You have completed Project 1L

Apply a combination of the 1A and 1B skills.

GO! Think | Project 1M Advertising

Project Files

For Project 1M, you will need the following file:

New blank Excel workbook

You will save your workbook as:

Lastname_Firstname_1M_Advertising

Eliott Verschoren, Vice President of Marketing for Texas Spectrum Wireless, is conducting an analysis of the advertising expenditures at the company's four retail locations based on the following data:

	Quarter 1	Quarter 2	Quarter 3	Quarter 4
Austin	22860	25905	18642	28405
Dallas	18557	17963	22883	25998
Houston	32609	28462	25915	31755
San Antonio	12475	15624	13371	17429

Using this information, create a workbook that includes totals by quarter and by location, sparklines to demonstrate the quarterly trends, and a column chart that compares the quarterly data across locations. Include appropriate worksheet, row, and column titles. Using the formatting skills that you practiced in this chapter, format the worksheet in a manner that is professional and easy to read and understand. Insert a footer with the file name and add appropriate document properties. Save the file as **Lastname_Firstname_1M_Advertising** and print or submit as directed by your instructor.

End You have completed Project 1M ——————————————————

Outcomes-Based Assessments

Apply a combination of the **1A** and **1B** skills.

You and GO! | Project **1N** Personal Expenses

Project Files

For Project 1N, you will need the following file:

New blank Excel workbook

You will save your workbook as:

Lastname_Firstname_1N_Personal_Expenses

Develop a worksheet that details your personal expenses from the last three months. Some of these expenses might include, but are not limited to, Mortgage, Rent, Utilities, Phone, Food, Entertainment, Tuition, Childcare, Clothing, and Insurance. Include a total for each month and for each category of expense. Insert a column with a formula that calculates the percent that each expense category is of the total expenditures. Format the worksheet by adjusting column widths and wrapping text, and by applying appropriate financial number formatting and cell styles. Insert a column chart that compares your expenses by month and modify the chart layout and style. Insert a footer with the file name and center the worksheet horizontally on the page. Save your file as **Lastname_Firstname_1N_Personal_Expenses** and submit as directed.

 End You have completed Project 1N ————

Apply a combination of the **1A** and **1B** skills.

GO! Collaborate | Project **1O** Bell Orchid Hotels Group Running Case

This project relates to the **Bell Orchid Hotels**. Your instructor may assign this group case project to your class. If your instructor assigns this project, he or she will provide you with information and instructions to work as part of a group. The group will apply the skills gained thus far to help the Bell Orchid Hotels achieve their business goals.

 End You have completed Project 1O ————

Using Functions, Creating Tables, and Managing Large Workbooks

OUTCOMES

At the end of this chapter you will be able to:

OBJECTIVES

Mastering these objectives will enable you to:

PROJECT 2A

Analyze inventory by applying statistical and logical calculations to data and by sorting and filtering data.

1. Use the SUM, AVERAGE, MEDIAN, MIN, and MAX Functions (p. 293)
2. Move Data, Resolve Error Messages, and Rotate Text (p. 297)
3. Use COUNTIF and IF Functions and Apply Conditional Formatting (p. 299)
4. Use Date & Time Functions and Freeze Panes (p. 304)
5. Create, Sort, and Filter an Excel Table (p. 306)
6. Format and Print a Large Worksheet (p. 309)

PROJECT 2B

Summarize the data on multiple worksheets.

7. Navigate a Workbook and Rename Worksheets (p. 314)
8. Enter Dates, Clear Contents, and Clear Formats (p. 315)
9. Copy and Paste by Using the Paste Options Gallery (p. 319)
10. Edit and Format Multiple Worksheets at the Same Time (p. 320)
11. Create a Summary Sheet with Column Sparklines (p. 326)
12. Format and Print Multiple Worksheets in a Workbook (p. 330)

Shutterstock

In This Chapter

In this chapter, you will use the Statistical functions to calculate the average of a group of numbers, and use other Logical and Date & Time functions. You will use the counting functions and apply conditional formatting to make data easy to visualize. In this chapter, you will also create a table and analyze the table's data by sorting and filtering the data. You will summarize a workbook that contains multiple worksheets.

The projects in this chapter relate to **Laurales Herbs and Spices**. After ten years as an Executive Chef, Laura Morales started her own business, which offers quality products for cooking, eating, and entertaining in retail stores and online. In addition to herbs and spices, there is a wide variety of condiments, confections, jams, sauces, oils, and vinegars. Later this year, Laura will add a line of tools, cookbooks, and gift baskets. The company name is a combination of Laura's first and last names, and also the name of an order of plants related to cinnamon.

Project 2A Inventory Status Report

Project Activities

In Activities 2.01 through 2.15, you will edit a worksheet for Laura Morales, President, detailing the current inventory of flavor products at the Oakland production facility. Your completed worksheet will look similar to Figure 2.1.

Project Files

For Project 2A, you will need the following file:

e02A_Flavor_Inventory

You will save your workbook as:

Lastname_Firstname_2A_Flavor_Inventory

Project Results

Oakland Facility: Inventory Status of Flavor Products
As of June 30

Flavor Statistics

Total Items in Stock	11,015
Average Price	$ 8.72
Median Price	$ 7.85
Lowest Price	$ 2.55
Highest Price	$ 31.95

Seasoning Types: 20
Extract Types: 8 (2,190 total items in stock)

Quantity in Stock	Item #	Product Name	Retail Price	Size	Packaging	Category	Stock Level
228	13189	Pepper, Florida	8.75	8 oz.	Jar	Seasoning	OK
110	13558	French Four Spice	6.56	2 oz.	Foil Packet	Seasoning	Order
135	15688	Pepper, Lemon	6.25	4 oz.	Jar	Seasoning	OK
95	16555	Tuscan Sunset	4.55	2 oz.	Foil Packet	Seasoning	Order
125	21683	Galena Street Rub	3.95	4 oz.	Jar	Rub	OK
135	22189	Northwoods Fire	9.85	16 oz.	Foil Packet	Seasoning	OK
143	23677	Marjoram	7.89	8 oz.	Foil Packet	Herb	OK
146	23688	Curry Powder, Hot	9.99	8 oz.	Jar	Spice	OK
234	24896	Butcher's Pepper	5.29	4 oz.	Foil Packet	Rub	OK
135	25678	Curry Powder, Sweet	9.99	8 oz.	Jar	Spice	OK
254	25844	Herbes De Provence	10.25	4 oz.	Foil Packet	Herb	OK
165	26787	Creole Dip Seasoning	8.75	8 oz.	Foil Packet	Seasoning	OK
156	32544	Mint, Spearmint	10.29	8 oz.	Foil Packet	Herb	OK
156	34266	Basil, French	10.19	8 oz.	Foil Packet	Herb	OK
188	34793	Onion Salt	3.55	2 oz.	Jar	Seasoning	OK
266	34878	Ginger, Cracked	7.89	8 oz.	Foil Packet	Spice	OK
177	34982	Jerk, Chicken and Fish	5.45	4 oz.	Foil Packet	Seasoning	OK
245	35677	Jerk, Pork	9.85	8 oz.	Foil Packet	Seasoning	OK
245	35690	Jerk, Jamaican	7.99	8 oz.	Jar	Rub	OK
145	35988	Basil, California	11.95	8 oz.	Foil Packet	Herb	OK
167	36820	Mint, Peppermint	10.39	8 oz.	Foil Packet	Herb	OK
248	37803	Chili Powder, Hot	3.39	2 oz.	Jar	Seasoning	OK
188	37845	Coffee	17.29	8 oz.	Bottle	Extract	OK
150	38675	Paprika, Hungarian Sweet	2.99	4 oz.	Jar	Seasoning	OK
168	38700	Chili Powder, Mild	3.39	2 oz.	Jar	Seasoning	OK
45	38744	Bicentennial Beef	4.49	4 oz.	Jar	Rub	Order
133	39704	Paprika, Californian	5.79	8 oz.	Jar	Seasoning	OK
165	42599	Ginger, Crystallized	9.85	8 oz.	Foil Packet	Spice	OK

Lastname_Firstname_2A_Flavor_Inventory

Quantity in Stock	Item #	Product Name	Retail Price	Size	Packaging	Category	Stock Level
425	43153	Cinnamon, Chinese	4.09	2 oz.	Foil Packet	Spice	OK
95	43625	Orange Peel	8.19	4 oz.	Tin	Seasoning	Order
211	43633	Peppermint	5.65	4 oz.	Bottle	Extract	OK
244	43813	Marjoram	4.45	4 oz.	Jar	Herb	OK
168	44482	Garlic Powder	5.89	6 oz.	Jar	Seasoning	OK
75	44587	Tandoori	16.85	8 oz.	Foil Packet	Spice	Order
235	44589	Garlic, Californian Flakes	11.25	2 oz.	Jar	Seasoning	OK
160	44879	Ginger	7.95	8 oz.	Jar	Spice	OK
165	45265	Pickling Spice	6.49	2 oz.	Jar	Spice	OK
100	45688	Nutmeg	7.85	8 oz.	Jar	Spice	Order
265	46532	Oregano	10.19	8 oz.	Jar	Herb	OK
73	49652	Rojo Taco	4.09	2 oz.	Foil Packet	Seasoning	Order
185	52164	Cloves, Whole	18.70	8 oz.	Jar	Spice	OK
165	53634	Vanilla, Double Strength	16.75	8 oz.	Bottle	Extract	OK
325	54635	Dill Weed	2.65	4 oz.	Foil Packet	Herb	OK
195	55255	Sea Salt, Pacific	2.55	8 oz.	Tin	Seasoning	OK
312	56853	Peppercorns, Indian	4.59	2 oz.	Jar	Spice	OK
152	64425	Onion Powder	4.85	4 oz.	Jar	Seasoning	OK
215	78655	Garlic Salt	2.58	6 oz.	Jar	Seasoning	OK
540	85655	Peppercorns, Red	3.69	2 oz.	Tin	Spice	OK
225	92258	Vanilla	15.95	4 oz.	Bottle	Extract	OK
368	93157	Almond	7.33	4 oz.	Bottle	Extract	OK
285	93553	Lemon	24.90	6 oz.	Bottle	Extract	OK
126	94236	Cumin	3.55	4 oz.	Foil Packet	Spice	OK
423	96854	Vanilla	31.95	6 oz.	Bottle	Extract	OK
325	98225	Orange	24.19	6 oz.	Bottle	Extract	OK
211	98655	Cloves, Ground	4.55	6 oz.	Jar	Spice	OK

Edited by Frank Barnes
5/2/2010 10:27

Lastname_Firstname_2A_Flavor_Inventory

Figure 2.1
Project 2A Flavor Inventory

Objective 1 | Use the SUM, AVERAGE, MEDIAN, MIN, and MAX Functions

A *function* is a predefined formula—a formula that Excel has already built for you—that performs calculations by using specific values in a particular order or structure. *Statistical functions*, which include the AVERAGE, MEDIAN, MIN, and MAX functions, are useful to analyze a group of measurements.

Activity 2.01 | Using the SUM and AVERAGE Functions

Laura has a worksheet with information about the inventory of flavor product types currently in stock at the Oakland facility. In this activity, you will use the SUM and AVERAGE functions to gather information about the product inventory.

1 **Start** Excel. From **Backstage** view, display the **Open** dialog box, and then from the student files that accompany this textbook, locate and open **e02A_Flavor_Inventory**. Click the **File tab** to redisplay **Backstage** view, and then click **Save As**. In the **Save As** dialog box, navigate to the location where you are storing your projects for this chapter.

2 Create a new folder named **Excel Chapter 2** open the new folder, and then in the **File name** box, type **Lastname_Firstname_2A_Flavor_Inventory** Click **Save** or press Enter.

3 Scroll down. Notice that the worksheet contains data related to types of flavor products in inventory, including information about the *Quantity in Stock*, *Item #*, *Product Name*, *Retail Price*, *Size*, *Packaging*, and *Category*.

4 Leave row 3 blank, and then in cell **A4**, type **Total Items in Stock** In cell **A5**, type **Average Price** In cell **A6**, type **Median Price**

5 Click cell **B4**. Click the **Formulas tab**, and then in the **Function Library group**, click the **AutoSum** button. Compare your screen with Figure 2.2.

The *SUM function* that you have used is a predefined formula that adds all the numbers in a selected range of cells. Because it is frequently used, there are several ways to insert the function.

For example, you can insert the function from the Home tab's Editing group, by using the keyboard shortcut Alt + =, from the Function Library group on the Formulas tab, and also from the Math & Trig button in that group.

Figure 2.2

AutoSum button

Formulas tab

Function Library group

Row 3 blank

Row titles entered

SUM function in cell B4

Excel | Chapter 2

6 With the insertion point blinking in the function, select the range **A11:A65**, dragging down as necessary, and then press Enter. Scroll up to view the top of your worksheet, and notice your result in cell **B4**, *11015*.

7 Click cell **B4** and look at the **Formula Bar**: Compare your screen with Figure 2.3.

> *SUM* is the name of the function. The values in parentheses are the ***arguments***—the values that an Excel function uses to perform calculations or operations. In this instance, the argument consists of the values in the range A11:A65.

Figure 2.3

Function and arguments display in Formula Bar

Result of SUM function displays in B4

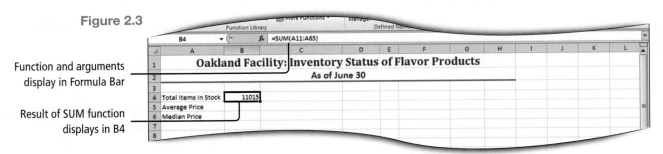

8 Click cell **B5**. In the **Function Library group**, click the **More Functions** button, point to **Statistical**, point to **AVERAGE**, and notice the ScreenTip. Compare your screen with Figure 2.4.

> The ScreenTip describes how the AVERAGE function will compute the calculation.

Figure 2.4

More Functions button

Statistical functions

ScreenTip describes function

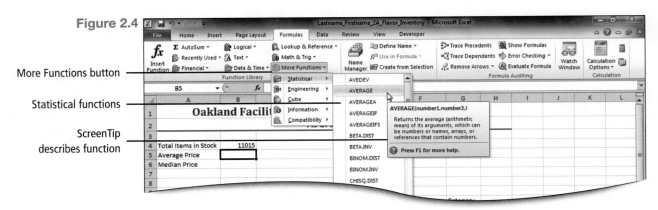

9 Click **AVERAGE**, and then if necessary, drag the title bar of the **Function Arguments** dialog box down and to the right so you can view the **Formula Bar** and cell **B5**.

> The ***AVERAGE function*** adds a group of values, and then divides the result by the number of values in the group.

> In the cell, the Formula Bar, and the dialog box, Excel proposes to average the value in cell B4. Recall that Excel functions will propose a range if data is above or to the left of a selected cell.

Another Way

Alternatively, with the existing text selected, select the range D11:D65 and press Enter.

10 In the **Function Arguments** dialog box, notice that *B4* is highlighted. Press Del to delete the existing text, type **d11:d65** and then compare your screen with Figure 2.5.

> Because you want to average the values in the range D11:D65—and not cell B4—you must edit the proposed range in this manner.

Figure 2.5

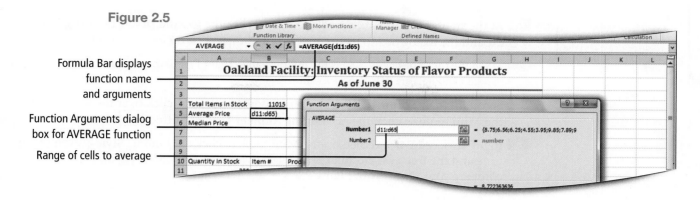

Formula Bar displays function name and arguments

Function Arguments dialog box for AVERAGE function

Range of cells to average

11 In the **Function Arguments** dialog box, click **OK**, and then **Save** 💾.

The result indicates that the average Retail Price of all products is *8.72*.

Activity 2.02 │ Using the MEDIAN Function

The *MEDIAN function* is a statistical function that describes a group of data—you may have seen it used to describe the price of houses in a particular geographical area. The MEDIAN function finds the middle value that has as many values above it in the group as are below it. It differs from AVERAGE in that the result is not affected as much by a single value that is greatly different from the others.

1 Click cell **B6**. In the **Function Library group**, click the **More Functions** button, display the list of **Statistical** functions, scroll down as necessary, and then click **MEDIAN**.

2 In the **Function Arguments** dialog box, to the right of the **Number 1** box, click the **Collapse Dialog** button 📧.

The dialog box collapses to a small size with space only for the first argument so you can see more of your data.

3 Select the range **D11:D65**, and then compare your screen with Figure 2.6.

When indicating which cells you want to use in the function's calculation—known as *defining the arguments*—you can either select the values with your mouse or type the range of values, whichever you prefer.

Figure 2.6

Formula Bar displays function and argument

Collapsed dialog box displays selected range

Selected range surrounded by moving border

40	95	43625 Orange Peel	8.19 4 oz.	Tin	Seasoning
41	211	43633 Peppermint	5.65 4 oz.	Bottle	Extract
42	244	43813 Marjoram	4.45 4 oz.	Jar	Herb
43	168	44482 Garlic Powder	5.89 6 oz.	Jar	Seasoning
44	75	44587 Tand Function Arguments			
45	235	44589 Garli D11:D65			
46	160	44879 Ging			
47	165	45265 Pickling Spice	6.49 2 oz.	Jar	Spice
48	100	45688 Nutmeg	7.85 8 oz.	Jar	Spice
49	265	46532 Oregano	10.19 8 oz.	Jar	Herb
50	73	49652 Rojo Taco	5.29 4 oz.	Paper Envelope	Seasoning
51	185	52164 Cloves, Whole	18.70 8 oz.	Jar	Spice
52	165	53634 Vanilla, Double Strength	16.75 8 oz.	Bottle	Extract
53	325	54635 Dill Weed	2.65 4 oz.	Paper Envelope	Herb
54	195	55255 Sea Salt, Pacific	2.55 8 oz.	Tin	Seasoning
55	312	56853 Peppercorns, Indian	4.59 2 oz.	Jar	Spice
56	152	64525 Onion Powder	4.85 4 oz.	Jar	Seasoning
57	215	78655 Garlic Salt	2.58 6 oz.	Jar	Seasoning
58	540	85655 Peppercorns, Red	3.69 2 oz.	Tin	Spice
59	225	92258 Vanilla	15.95 4 oz.	Bottle	Extract
60	368	93157 Almond	7.33 4 oz.	Bottle	Extract
61	285	93553 Lemon	24.90 6 oz.	Bottle	Extract
62	126	94236 Cumin	3.55 4 oz.	Paper Envelope	Spice
63	423	96854 Vanilla	31.95 6 oz.	Bottle	Extract
64	325	98225 Orange	24.19 6 oz.	Bottle	Extract
65	211	98655 Cloves, Ground	4.55 6 oz.	Jar	Spice
66					

Another Way
Press Enter to expand the dialog box.

4 At the right end of the collapsed dialog box, click the **Expand Dialog** button to expand the dialog box to its original size, and then click **OK** to display *7.85*.

> In the range of prices, 7.85 is the middle value. Half of all flavor products are priced *above* 7.85 and half are priced *below* 7.85.

5 Scroll up to view **row 1**. Select the range **B5:B6** and right-click over the selection. On the Mini toolbar, click the **Accounting Number Format** button.

6 Right-click cell **B4**, and then on the Mini toolbar, click the **Comma Style** button one time and the **Decrease Decimal** button two times. Click **Save** and compare your screen with Figure 2.7.

Figure 2.7

Comma Style applied
with no decimal places

Accounting Number
Format applied

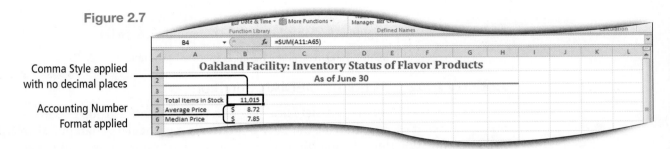

Activity 2.03 | Using the MIN and MAX Functions

The statistical *MIN function* determines the smallest value in a selected range of values. The statistical *MAX function* determines the largest value in a selected range of values.

1 In cell **A7**, type **Lowest Price** and then in cell **A8**, type **Highest Price**

2 Click cell **B7**. On the **Formulas tab**, in the **Function Library group**, click the **More Functions** button, display the list of **Statistical** functions, scroll as necessary, and then click **MIN**.

3 At the right end of the **Number1** box, click the **Collapse Dialog** button, select the range **D11:D65**, and then click the **Expand Dialog** button. Click **OK**.

> The lowest Retail Price is *2.55*.

4 Click cell **B8**, and then by using a similar technique, insert the **MAX** function to determine the highest **Retail Price**—*31.95*.

5 Select the range **B7:B8** and apply the **Accounting Number Format**, click **Save**, and then compare your screen with Figure 2.8.

Figure 2.8

MIN function calculates
lowest price

MAX function calculates
highest price

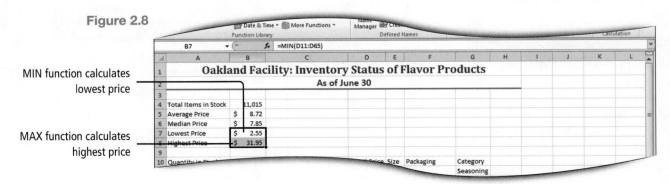

Objective 2 | Move Data, Resolve Error Messages, and Rotate Text

When you move a formula, the cell references within the formula do not change, no matter what type of cell reference you use.

If you move cells into a column that is not wide enough to display number values, Excel will display a message so that you can adjust as necessary.

You can reposition data within a cell at an angle by rotating the text.

Activity 2.04 | Moving Data and Resolving a # # # # # Error Message

1 Select the range **A4:B8**. Point to the right edge of the selected range to display the ⌖ pointer, and then compare your screen with Figure 2.9.

Figure 2.9

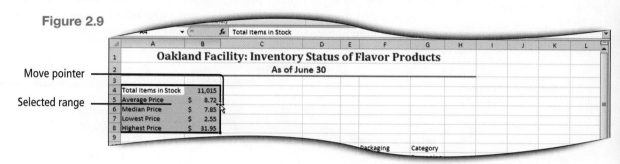

2 Drag the selected range to the right until the ScreenTip displays *D4:E8*, release the mouse button, and then notice that a series of # symbols displays in **column E**. Point to any of the cells that display # symbols, and then compare your screen with Figure 2.10.

Using this technique, cell contents can be moved from one location to another; this is referred to as *drag and drop*.

If a cell width is too narrow to display the entire number, Excel displays the ##### error, because displaying only a portion of a number would be misleading. The underlying values remain unchanged and are displayed in the Formula Bar for the selected cell. An underlying value also displays in the ScreenTip if you point to a cell containing # symbols.

Figure 2.10

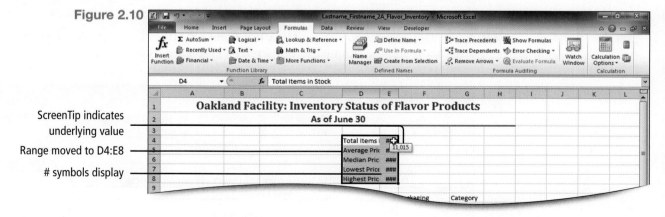

3 Select **column E** and widen it to **50** pixels, and notice that two cells are still not wide enough to display the cell contents.

4 In the **column heading area**, point to the right boundary of **column E** to display the ✛ pointer. Double-click to AutoFit the column to accommodate the widest entry.

5 Using the same technique, AutoFit **column D** to accommodate the widest text entry.

6 Select the range **D4:E8**. On the **Home tab**, in the **Styles group**, display the **Cell Styles** gallery. Under **Themed Cell Styles**, click **20%-Accent1**. Click **Save** 🖫.

Activity 2.05 │ Rotating Text

Rotated text is useful to draw attention to data on your worksheet.

> **Another Way**
> Type the number of degrees directly into the Degrees box or use the spin box arrows to set the number.

1 In cell **C6**, type **Flavor Statistics** Select the range **C4:C8**, right-click over the selection, and then on the shortcut menu, click **Format Cells**. In the **Format Cells** dialog box, click the **Alignment tab**. Under **Text control**, select the **Merge cells** check box.

2 In the upper right portion of the dialog box, under **Orientation**, point to the **red diamond**, and then drag the diamond upward until the **Degrees** box indicates **30**. Compare your screen with Figure 2.11.

Figure 2.11

Range of cells moved and formatted

Format Cells dialog box

Orientation set to 30 degrees

Merge cells selected

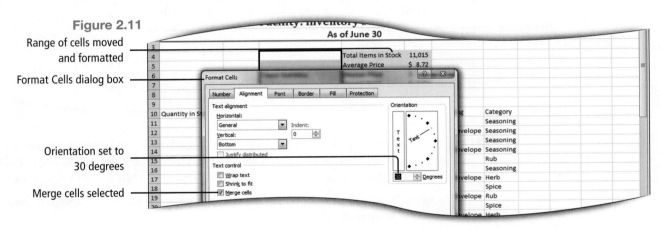

3 In the lower right corner of the **Format Cells** dialog box, click **OK**.

4 With the merged cell still selected, on the **Home tab**, in the **Font group**, change the **Font Size** 11 ▾ to **14**, and then apply **Bold** **B** and **Italic** *I*. Click the **Font Color arrow** **A** ▾, and then in the fourth column, click the first color—**Dark Blue, Text 2**.

5 In the **Alignment group**, apply **Align Text Right** ☰. Click cell **A1**, **Save** 🖫 your workbook, and then compare your screen with Figure 2.12.

Figure 2.12

Text rotated and formatted

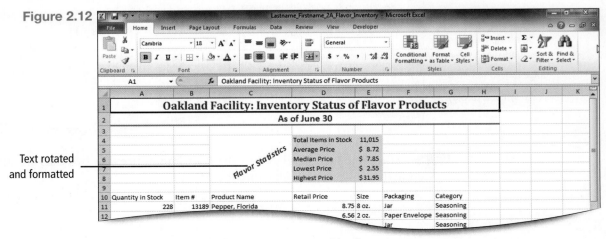

Objective 3 | Use COUNTIF and IF Functions and Apply Conditional Formatting

Recall that statistical functions analyze a group of measurements. Another group of Excel functions, referred to as *logical functions*, test for specific conditions. Logical functions typically use conditional tests to determine whether specified conditions—called *criteria*—are true or false.

Activity 2.06 | Using the COUNTIF Function

The *COUNTIF function* is a statistical function that counts the number of cells within a range that meet the given condition—the criteria that you provide. The COUNTIF function has two arguments—the range of cells to check and the criteria.

The seasonings of Laurales Herbs and Spices will be featured on an upcoming segment of a TV shopping channel. In this activity, you will use the COUNTIF function to determine the number of *seasoning* products currently available in inventory.

1 In the **row heading area**, point to **row 9** and right-click to select the row and display the shortcut menu. Click **Insert**, and then press F4 two times to repeat the last action and thus insert three blank rows.

> F4 is useful to repeat commands in Microsoft Office programs. Most commands can be repeated in this manner.

2 From the **row heading area**, select **rows 9:11**. On the **Home tab**, in the **Editing group**, click the **Clear** button 🖉, and then click **Clear Formats** to remove the blue accent color in columns D and E from the new rows.

> When you insert rows or columns, formatting from adjacent rows or columns repeats in the new cells.

3 Click cell **E4**, look at the **Formula Bar**, and then notice that the arguments of the **SUM** function adjusted and refer to the appropriate cells in rows 14:68.

> The referenced range updates to *A14:A68* after you insert the three new rows. In this manner, Excel adjusts the cell references in a formula relative to their new locations.

4 In cell **A10**, type **Seasoning Types:** and then press Tab.

5 With cell **B10** as the active cell, on the **Formulas tab**, in the **Function Library group**, click the **More Functions** button, and then display the list of **Statistical** functions. Click **COUNTIF**.

> Recall that the COUNTIF function counts the number of cells within a range that meet the given condition.

6 In the **Range** box, click the **Collapse Dialog** button ▦, select the range **G14:G68**, and then at the right end of the collapsed dialog box, click the **Expand Dialog** button ▣. Click in the **Criteria** box, type **Seasoning** and then compare your screen with Figure 2.13.

Figure 2.13

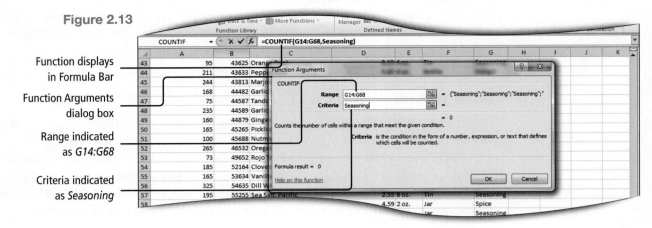

Function displays in Formula Bar

Function Arguments dialog box

Range indicated as *G14:G68*

Criteria indicated as *Seasoning*

7 In the lower right corner of the **Function Arguments** dialog box, click **OK**.

There are *20* different *Seasoning* products available to feature on the TV show.

8 On the **Home tab**, in the **Alignment group**, click **Align Text Left** ▤ to place the result closer to the row title. **Save** 🖫 your workbook.

Activity 2.07 | Using the IF Function

A *logical test* is any value or expression that you can evaluate as being true or false. The *IF function* uses a logical test to check whether a condition is met, and then returns one value if true, and another value if false.

For example, *C14=228* is an expression that can be evaluated as true or false. If the value in cell C14 is equal to 228, the expression is true. If the value in cell C14 is not 228, the expression is false.

In this activity, you will use the IF function to determine the inventory levels and determine if more products should be ordered.

1 Click cell **H13**, type **Stock Level** and then press Enter.

2 In cell **H14**, on the **Formulas tab**, in the **Function Library group**, click the **Logical** button, and then in the list, click **IF**. Drag the title bar of the **Function Arguments** dialog box up or down to view **row 14** on your screen.

3 With the insertion point in the **Logical_test** box, click cell **A14**, and then type **<125**

This logical test will look at the value in cell A14, which is *228*, and then determine if the number is less than 125. The expression *<125* includes the < *comparison operator*, which means *less than*. Comparison operators compare values.

4 Examine the table in Figure 2.14 for a list of comparison operator symbols and their definitions.

Comparison Operators

Comparison Operator	Symbol Definition
=	Equal to
>	Greater than
<	Less than
>=	Greater than or equal to
<=	Less than or equal to
<>	Not equal to

Figure 2.14

5 Press Tab to move the insertion point to the **Value_if_true** box, and then type **Order**

If the result of the logical test is true—the Quantity in Stock is less than 125—cell H14 will display the text *Order* indicating that additional product must be ordered.

6 Click in the **Value_if_false** box, type **OK** and then compare your dialog box with Figure 2.15.

If the result of the logical test is false—the Quantity in Stock is *not* less than 125—then Excel will display *OK* in the cell.

Figure 2.15

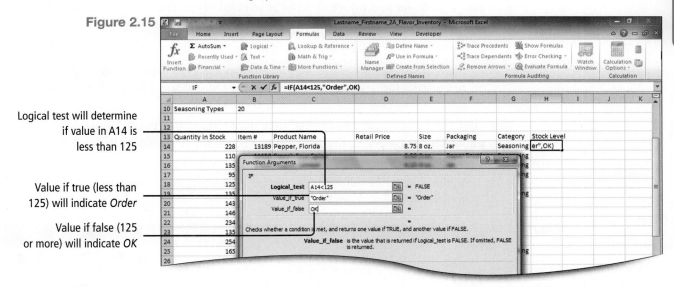

Logical test will determine if value in A14 is less than 125

Value if true (less than 125) will indicate *Order*

Value if false (125 or more) will indicate *OK*

7 Click **OK** to display the result *OK* in cell **H14**.

8 Using the fill handle, copy the function in cell **H14** down through cell **H68**. Then scroll as necessary to view cell **A18**, which indicates *125*. Look at cell **H18** and notice that the **Stock Level** is indicated as *OK*. **Save** your workbook. Compare your screen with Figure 2.16.

The comparison operator indicated <125 (less than 125) and thus a value of *exactly* 125 is indicated as OK.

Figure 2.16

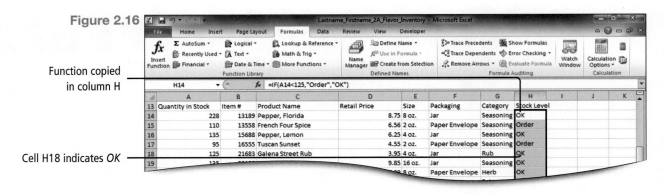

Function copied in column H

Cell H18 indicates *OK*

Activity 2.08 | Applying Conditional Formatting by Using Highlight Cells Rules and Data Bars

A ***conditional format*** changes the appearance of a cell based on a condition—a criteria. If the condition is true, the cell is formatted based on that condition; if the condition is false, the cell is *not* formatted. In this activity, you will use conditional formatting as another way to draw attention to the Stock Level of products.

1 Be sure the range **H14:H68** is selected. On the **Home tab**, in the **Styles group**, click the **Conditional Formatting** button. In the list, point to **Highlight Cells Rules**, and then click **Text that Contains**.

2 In the **Text That Contains** dialog box, with the insertion point blinking in the first box, type **Order** and notice that in the selected range, the text *Order* displays with the default format—Light Red Fill with Dark Red Text.

3 In the second box, click the **arrow**, and then in the list, click **Custom Format**.

> Here, in the Format Cells dialog box, you can select any combination of formats to apply to the cell if the condition is true. The custom format you specify will be applied to any cell in the selected range if it contains the text *Order*.

4 On the **Font tab**, under **Font style**, click **Bold Italic**. Click the **Color arrow**, and then under **Theme Colors**, in the sixth column, click the first color—**Red, Accent 2**. Click **OK**. Compare your screen with Figure 2.17.

> In the range, if the cell meets the condition of containing *Order*, the font color will change to Bold Italic, Red, Accent 2.

Figure 2.17

Custom Format indicated

Text That Contains dialog box

Only cells with the text *Order* will be formatted

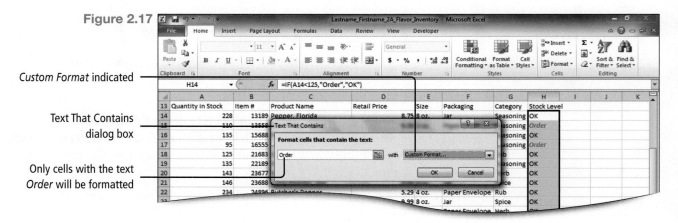

5 In the **Text That Contains** dialog box, click **OK**.

6 Select the range **A14:A68**. In the **Styles group**, click the **Conditional Formatting** button. Point to **Data Bars**, and then under **Gradient Fill**, click **Orange Data Bar**. Click anywhere to cancel the selection; click 🔲. Compare your screen with Figure 2.18.

A ***data bar*** provides a visual cue to the reader about the value of a cell relative to other cells. The length of the data bar represents the value in the cell. A longer bar represents a higher value and a shorter bar represents a lower value. Data bars are useful for identifying higher and lower numbers quickly within a large group of data, such as very high or very low levels of inventory.

Figure 2.18

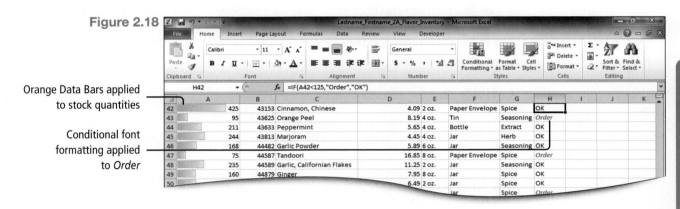

Orange Data Bars applied to stock quantities

Conditional font formatting applied to *Order*

Activity 2.09 │ Using Find and Replace

The ***Find and Replace*** feature searches the cells in a worksheet—or in a selected range—for matches, and then replaces each match with a replacement value of your choice.

Comments from customers on the company's blog indicate that, for dried herbs and seasonings, customers prefer a sealable foil packet rather than a paper envelope. Thus, all products of this type have been repackaged. In this activity, you will replace all occurrences of *Paper Envelope* with *Foil Packet*.

1 Select the range **F14:F68**.

Restrict the find and replace operation to a specific range in this manner, especially if there is a possibility that the name occurs elsewhere.

2 On the **Home tab**, in the **Editing group**, click the **Find & Select** button, and then click **Replace**.

3 Type **Paper Envelope** to fill in the **Find what** box. In the **Replace with** box, type **Foil Packet** and then compare your screen with Figure 2.19.

Figure 2.19

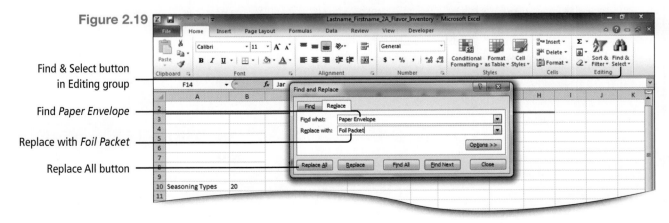

Find & Select button in Editing group

Find *Paper Envelope*

Replace with *Foil Packet*

Replace All button

Excel │ Chapter 2

4 Click the **Replace All** button. In the message box, notice that 19 replacements were made, and then click **OK**. In the lower right corner of the **Find and Replace** dialog box, click the **Close** button. Click **Save** 🔲.

Objective 4 | Use Date & Time Functions and Freeze Panes

Excel can obtain the date and time from your computer's calendar and clock and display this information on your worksheet.

By freezing or splitting panes, you can view two areas of a worksheet and lock rows and columns in one area. When you freeze panes, you select the specific rows or columns that you want to remain visible when scrolling in your worksheet.

Activity 2.10 | Using the NOW Function to Display a System Date

The ***NOW function*** retrieves the date and time from your computer's calendar and clock and inserts the information into the selected cell. The result is formatted as a date and time.

1 Scroll down as necessary, and then click cell **A70**. Type **Edited by Frank Barnes** and then press Enter.

2 With cell **A71** as the active cell, on the **Formulas tab**, in the **Function Library group**, click the **Date & Time** button. In the list of functions, click **NOW**. Compare your screen with Figure 2.20.

Figure 2.20

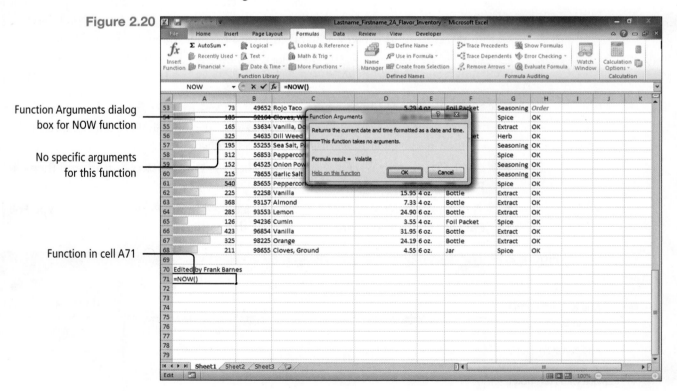

Function Arguments dialog box for NOW function

No specific arguments for this function

Function in cell A71

3 Read the description in the **Function Arguments** dialog box, and notice that this result is *Volatile*.

> The Function Arguments dialog box displays a message indicating that this function does not require an argument. It also states that this function is *volatile*, meaning the date and time will not remain as entered, but rather the date and time will automatically update each time you open this workbook.

4 In the **Function Arguments** dialog box, click **OK** to close the dialog box to display the current date and time in cell **A71. Save** 🖫 your workbook.

More Knowledge | NOW Function Recalculates Each Time a Workbook Opens

The NOW function updates each time the workbook is opened. With the workbook open, you can force the NOW function to update by pressing F9, for example, to update the time.

Activity 2.11 | Freezing and Unfreezing Panes

In a large worksheet, if you scroll down more than 25 rows or scroll beyond column O (the exact row number and column letter varies, depending on your screen resolution), you will no longer see the top rows or first column of your worksheet where identifying information about the data is usually placed. You will find it easier to work with your data if you can always view the identifying row or column titles.

The *Freeze Panes* command enables you to select one or more rows or columns and then freeze (lock) them into place. The locked rows and columns become separate panes. A *pane* is a portion of a worksheet window bounded by and separated from other portions by vertical or horizontal bars.

1 Press Ctrl + Home to make cell **A1** the active cell. Scroll down until **row 40** displays at the top of your Excel window, and notice that all of the identifying information in the column titles is out of view.

2 Press Ctrl + Home again, and then from the **row heading area**, select **row 14**. Click the **View tab**, and then in the **Window group**, click the **Freeze Panes** button. In the list, click **Freeze Panes**. Click any cell to deselect the row, and then notice that a line displays along the upper border of **row 14**.

> By selecting row 14, the rows above—rows 1 - 13—are frozen in place and will not move as you scroll down.

3 Watch the row numbers below **row 13**, and then begin to scroll down to bring **row 40** into view again. Notice that rows 1:13 are frozen in place. Compare your screen with Figure 2.21.

> The remaining rows of data continue to scroll. Use this feature when you have long or wide worksheets.

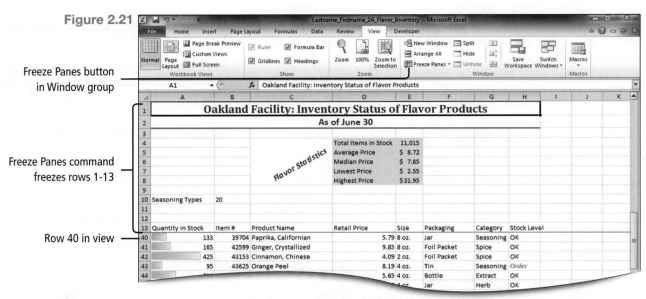

Figure 2.21

Freeze Panes button in Window group

Freeze Panes command freezes rows 1-13

Row 40 in view

4 In the **Window group**, click the **Freeze Panes** button, and then click **Unfreeze Panes** to unlock all rows and columns. **Save** 💾 your workbook.

More Knowledge | **Freeze Columns or Freeze both Rows and Columns**

You can freeze columns that you want to remain in view on the left. Select the column to the right of the column(s) that you want to remain in view while scrolling to the right, and then click the Freeze Panes command. You can also use the command to freeze both rows and columns; click a *cell* to freeze the rows *above* the cell and the columns to the *left* of the cell.

Objective 5 | Create, Sort, and Filter an Excel Table

To analyze a group of related data, you can convert a range of cells to an *Excel table*. An Excel table is a series of rows and columns that contains related data that is managed independently from the data in other rows and columns in the worksheet.

Activity 2.12 | Creating an Excel Table

1 Be sure that you have applied the Unfreeze Panes command—no rows on your worksheet are locked. Then, click any cell in the data below row 13.

> **Another Way**
>
> Select the range of cells that make up the table, including the header row, and then click the Table button.

2 Click the **Insert tab**. In the **Tables group**, click the **Table** button. In the **Create Table** dialog box, if necessary, click to select the **My table has headers** check box, and then compare your screen with Figure 2.22.

The column titles in row 13 will form the table headers. By clicking in a range of contiguous data, Excel will suggest the range as the data for the table. You can adjust the range if necessary.

Figure 2.22

Moving border surrounds range

Column titles will form table headers

Create Table dialog box

Range of data selected

Check box selected

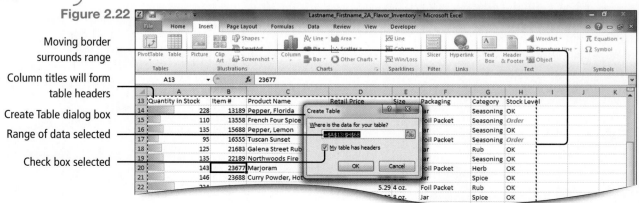

3 Click **OK**. With the range still selected, on the Ribbon notice that the **Table Tools** are active.

4 On the **Design tab**, in the **Table Styles group**, click the **More** button ⊡, and then under **Light**, locate and click **Table Style Light 16**.

5 Press Ctrl + Home. Click **Save** 🖫, and then compare your screen with Figure 2.23.

Sorting and filtering arrows display in the table's header row.

Figure 2.23

Sorting and filtering arrow in header row

Table style with alternating shaded rows applied

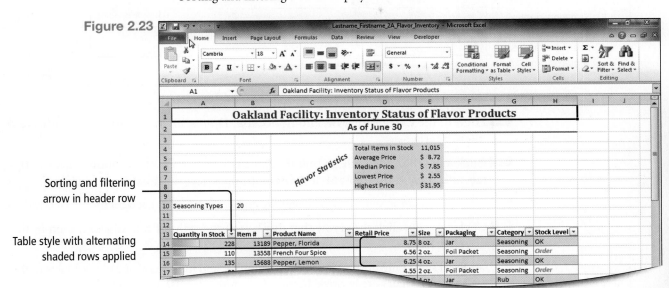

Activity 2.13 | Sorting and Filtering an Excel Table

You can *sort* tables—arrange all the data in a specific order—in ascending or descending order. You can *filter* tables—display only a portion of the data based on matching a specific value—to show only the data that meets the criteria that you specify.

1 In the header row of the table, click the **Retail Price arrow**, and then on the menu, click **Sort Smallest to Largest**. Next to the arrow, notice the small **up arrow** indicating an ascending (smallest to largest) sort.

The rows in the table are sorted from the lowest retail price to highest retail price.

2 In the table's header row, click the **Category arrow**. On the menu, click **Sort A to Z**. Next to the arrow, notice the small **up arrow** indicating an ascending (A to Z) sort.

The rows in the table are sorted alphabetically by Category.

3 Click the **Category arrow** again, and then sort from **Z to A**.

The rows in the table are sorted in reverse alphabetic order by Category name, and the small arrow points downward, indicating a descending (Z to A) sort.

4 Click the **Category arrow** again. On the menu, click the **(Select All)** check box to clear all the check boxes. Click to select only the **Extract** check box, and then click **OK**. Compare your screen with Figure 2.24.

Only the rows containing *Extract* in the Category column display—the remaining rows are hidden from view. A small funnel—the filter icon—indicates that a filter is applied to the data in the table. Additionally, the row numbers display in blue to indicate that some rows are hidden from view. A filter hides entire rows in the worksheet.

Figure 2.24

Funnel indicates filter applied

Blue row numbers indicate some rows hidden

Only products in *Extract* category display

ScreenTip indicates *Equals "Extract"*

	Quantity in Stock	Item #	Product Name	Retail Price	Size	Packaging	Category	Stock Level
9								
10	Seasoning Types	20						
11								
12								
13								
61	211	43633	Peppermint	5.65	4 oz.	Bottle	Extract	
62	368	93157	Almond	7.33	4 oz.	Bottle	Extract	
63	225	92258	Vanilla	15.95	4 oz.	Bottle	Extract	OK
64	165	53634	Vanilla, Double Strength	16.75	8 oz.	Bottle	Extract	OK
65	188	37845	Coffee	17.29	8 oz.	Bottle	Extract	OK
66	325	98225	Orange	24.19	6 oz.	Bottle	Extract	OK
67	285	93553	Lemon	24.90	6 oz.	Bottle	Extract	OK
68	423	96854	Vanilla	31.95	6 oz.	Bottle	Extract	OK
69								
70	Edited by Frank Barnes							
71	5/2/2010 10:07							
72								
73								

(Lowest Price, Highest Price, Category: Equals "Extract")

5 Point to the **Category arrow**, and notice that *Equals "Extract"* displays to indicate the filter criteria.

6 Click any cell in the table so that the table is selected. On the Ribbon, click the **Design tab**, and then in the **Table Style Options group**, select the **Total Row** check box.

> *Total* displays in cell A69. In cell H69, the number *8* indicates that eight rows currently display.

7 Click cell **A69**, click the **arrow** that displays to the right of cell **A69**, and then in the list, click **Sum**.

> Excel sums only the visible rows in Column A, and indicates that 2190 products in the Extract category are in stock. In this manner, you can use an Excel table to quickly find information about a group of data.

8 Click cell **A11**, type **Extract Types:** and press Tab. In cell **B11**, type **8 (2,190 total items in stock)** and then press Enter.

9 In the table header row, click the **Category arrow**, and then on the menu, click **Clear Filter From "Category"**.

> All the rows in the table redisplay. The Z to A sort on Category remains in effect.

10 Click the **Packaging arrow**, click the **(Select All)** check box to clear all the check boxes, and then click to select the **Foil Packet** check box. Click **OK**.

11 Click the **Category arrow**, click the **(Select All)** check box to clear all the check boxes, and then click the **Herb** check box. Click **OK**, and then compare your screen with Figure 2.25.

> By applying multiple filters, Laura can quickly determine that seven items in the Herb category are packaged in foil packets with a total of 1,346 such items in stock.

Figure 2.25

Seven items in *Herb* category are packaged in *Foil Packets*

	Quantity in Stock	Item #	Product Name	Retail Price	Size	Packaging	Category	Stock Level	
10	Seasoning Types	20							
11	Extract Types:	8 (2,190 total items in stock)							
12									
13									
52	325	54635	Dill Weed	2.65	4 oz.	Foil Packet	Herb	OK	
54	143	23677	Marjoram	7.89	8 oz.	Foil Packet	Herb	OK	
55	156	34266	Basil, French	10.19	8 oz.	Foil Packet	Herb	OK	
57	254	25844	Herbes De Provence	10.25	4 oz.	Foil Packet	Herb	OK	
58	156	32544	Mint, Spearmint	10.29	8 oz.	Foil Packet	Herb	OK	
59	167	36820	Mint, Peppermint	10.39	8 oz.	Foil Packet	Herb	OK	
60	145	35988	Basil, California	11.95	8 oz.	Foil Packet	Herb	OK	
69	1346								7
70	Edited by Frank Barnes								
71	5/2/2010 10:12								
72									
73									

(Highest Price)

12 Click the **Category arrow**, and then click **Clear Filter From "Category"**. Use the same technique to remove the filter from the **Packaging** column.

13 In the table header row, click the **Item# arrow**, and then click **Sort Smallest to Largest**, which will apply an ascending sort to the data using the *Item#* column. **Save** 💾 your workbook.

Activity 2.14 | Converting a Table to a Range of Data

When you are finished answering questions about the data in a table by sorting, filtering, and totaling, you can convert the table into a normal range. Doing so is useful if you want to use the feature only to apply an attractive Table Style to a range of cells. For example, you can insert a table, apply a Table Style, and then convert the table to a normal range of data but keep the formatting.

> **Another Way**
>
> With any table cell selected, right-click, point to Table, and then click Convert to Range.

1 Click anywhere in the table to activate the table and display the **Table Tools** on the Ribbon. On the **Design tab**, in the **Table Style Options group**, click the **Total Row** check box to clear the check mark and remove the Total row from the table.

2 On the **Design tab**, in the **Tools group**, click the **Convert to Range** button. In the message box, click **Yes**. Click **Save** 💾, and then compare your screen with Figure 2.26.

Figure 2.26

Table converted to a normal range, color and shading formats remain

	Quantity in Stock	Item #	Product Name	Retail Price	Size	Packaging	Category	Stock Level	
12	...tract Types:	8 (2,190 total items in stock)							
13	Quantity in Stock	Item #	Product Name	Retail Price	Size	Packaging	Category	Stock Level	
14	228	13189	Pepper, Florida	8.75	8 oz.	Jar	Seasoning	OK	
15	110	13558	French Four Spice	6.56	2 oz.	Foil Packet	Seasoning	Order	
16	135	15688	Pepper, Lemon	6.25	4 oz.	Jar	Seasoning	OK	
17	95	16555	Tuscan Sunset	4.55	2 oz.	Foil Packet	Seasoning	Order	
18	125	21683	Galena Street Rub	3.95	4 oz.	Jar	Rub	OK	
19	135	22189	Northwoods Fire	9.85	16 oz.	Jar	Seasoning	OK	
20	143	23677	Marjoram	7.89	8 oz.	Foil Packet	Herb	OK	
21	146	23688	Curry Powder, Hot	9.99	8 oz.	Jar	Spice	OK	
22	234	24896	Butcher's Pepper	5.29	4 oz.	Foil Packet	Rub	OK	
23				9.99	8 oz.	Jar	Spice	OK	
					4 oz.	Foil Packet	Herb	OK	

Objective 6 | Format and Print a Large Worksheet

A worksheet might be too wide, too long—or both—to print on a single page. Use Excel's *Print Titles* and *Scale to Fit* commands to create pages that are attractive and easy to read.

The Print Titles command enables you to specify rows and columns to repeat on each printed page. Scale to Fit commands enable you to stretch or shrink the width, height, or both, of printed output to fit a maximum number of pages.

Activity 2.15 | Printing Titles and Scaling to Fit

1 Press Ctrl + Home to display the top of your worksheet. Select the range **A13:H13**. On the **Home tab**, from the **Styles group**, apply the **Heading 4** cell style, and then apply **Center** ≣.

2 On the **Insert tab**, in the **Text group**, click **Header & Footer**. In the **Navigation group**, click the **Go to Footer** button, and then click just above the word *Footer*.

3 In the **Header & Footer Elements group**, click the **File Name** button to add the name of your file to the footer—*&[File]* displays. Then, click in a cell just above the footer to exit the Footer and view your file name.

4 Delete the unused sheets **Sheet2** and **Sheet3**. On the right edge of the status bar, click the **Normal** button ⊞, and then press Ctrl + Home to display the top of your worksheet.

> Dotted lines indicate where the pages would break if printed as currently formatted; these dotted lines display when you switch from Page Layout view to Normal view.

5 On the **Page Layout tab**, in the **Themes group**, click the **Themes** button, and then click **Concourse**.

6 In the **Page Setup group**, click **Margins**, and then at the bottom, click **Custom Margins**. In the **Page Setup** dialog box, under **Center on page**, select the **Horizontally** check box, and then click **OK**.

7 In the **Page Setup group**, click **Orientation**, and then click **Landscape**. Press Ctrl + F2 to display the **Print Preview**. At the bottom of the **Print Preview**, click the **Next Page** button ▶. Compare your screen with Figure 2.27.

> As currently formatted, the worksheet will print on five pages, and the columns will span multiple pages. Additionally, after Page 1, no column titles are visible to identify the data in the columns.

Figure 2.27

No identifying column titles at top of page

Additional columns not visible on this page

Page 2 indicated

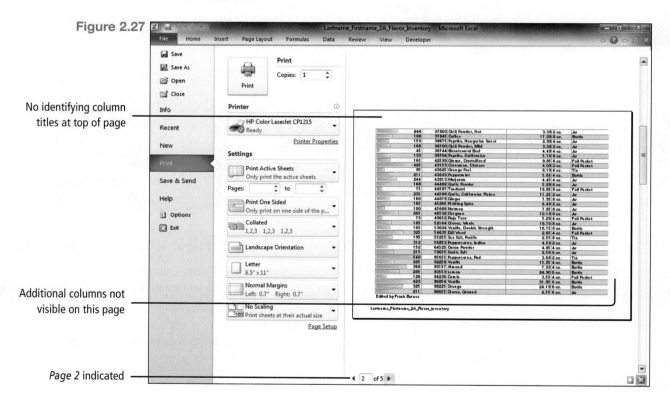

8 Click **Next Page** ▶ two times to display **Page 4**, and notice that two columns move to an additional page.

9 On the Ribbon, click **Page Layout** to redisplay the worksheet. In the **Page Setup group**, click the **Print Titles** button. Under **Print titles**, click in the **Rows to repeat at top** box, and then at the right, click the **Collapse Dialog** button 🔲.

10 From the **row heading area**, select **row 13**, and then click the **Expand Dialog** button 🔲. Click **OK** to print the column titles in row 13 at the top of every page.

Adding the titles on each page increases the number of pages to 6.

Another Way

With the worksheet displayed, on the Page Layout tab, in the Scale to Fit group, click the Width button arrow, and then click 1 page.

11 Press Ctrl + F2 to display the **Print Preview**. In the center panel, at the bottom of the **Settings group**, click the **Scaling** button, and then on the displayed list, point to **Fit All Columns on One Page**. Compare your screen with Figure 2.28.

This action will shrink the width of the printed output to fit all the columns on one page. You can make adjustments like this on the Page Layout tab, or here, in the Print Preview.

Figure 2.28

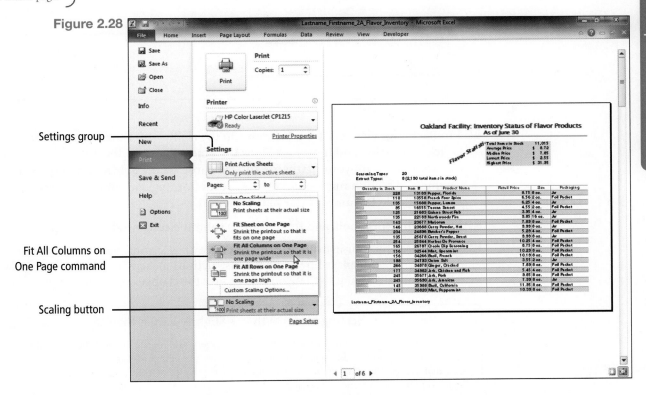

Settings group

Fit All Columns on One Page command

Scaling button

12 Click **Fit All Columns on One Page**. Notice in the **Print Preview** that all the columns display on one page.

13 At the bottom of the **Print Preview**, click the **Next Page** button ▶ one time. Notice that the output will now print on two pages and that the column titles display at the top of **Page 2**. Compare your screen with Figure 2.29.

Figure 2.29

Column titles display
on Page 2

Page 2 of 2 indicated

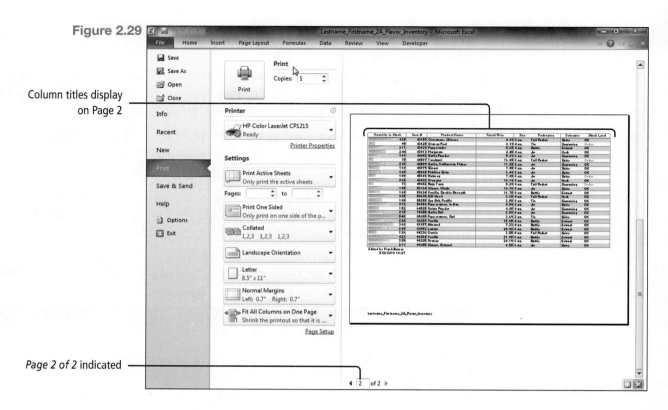

14 In **Backstage** view, click the **Info tab**. On the right, under the document thumbnail, click **Properties**, and then click **Show Document Panel**. In the **Author** box, replace the existing text with your firstname and lastname. In the **Subject** box, type your course name and section number. In the **Keywords** box, type **inventory, Oakland** and then **Close** ☒ the **Document Information Panel**.

15 **Save** your workbook, and then print or submit electronically as directed.

16 If required by your instructor, print or create an electronic version of your worksheets with formulas displayed by using the instructions in Activity 1.16, and then **Close** ☒ Excel without saving so that you do not save the changes you made to print formulas.

More Knowledge | Scaling for Data that is Slightly Larger than the Printed Page

If your data is just a little too large to fit on a printed page, you can scale the worksheet to make it fit. Scaling reduces both the width and height of the printed data to a percentage of its original size or by the number of pages that you specify. To adjust the printed output to a percentage of its actual size, for example to 80%, on the Page Layout tab, in the Scale to Fit group, click the Scale arrows to select a percentage.

End **You have completed Project 2A**

Project 2B Weekly Sales Summary

Project Activities

In Activities 2.16 through 2.26, you will edit an existing workbook for Laura Morales. The workbook summarizes the online and in-store sales of products during a one-week period in July. The worksheets of your completed workbook will look similar to Figure 2.30.

Project Files

For Project 2B, you will need the following file:

e02B_Weekly_Sales

You will save your workbook as:

Lastname_Firstname_2B_Weekly_Sales

Project Results

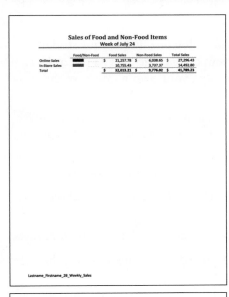

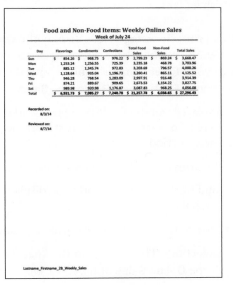

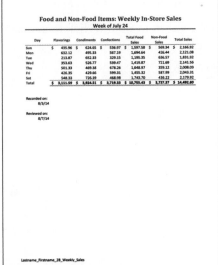

Figure 2.30

Project 2B Weekly Sales

Excel | Chapter 2

Objective 7 | Navigate a Workbook and Rename Worksheets

Use multiple worksheets in a workbook to organize data in a logical arrangement. When you have more than one worksheet in a workbook, you can **navigate** (move) among worksheets by clicking the **sheet tabs**. Sheet tabs identify each worksheet in a workbook and are located along the lower left edge of the workbook window. When you have more worksheets in the workbook than can be displayed in the sheet tab area, use the four sheet tab scrolling buttons to move sheet tabs into and out of view.

Activity 2.16 | Navigating Among Worksheets, Renaming Worksheets, and Changing the Tab Color of Worksheets

Excel names the first worksheet in a workbook *Sheet1* and each additional worksheet in order—*Sheet2*, *Sheet3*, and so on. Most Excel users rename the worksheets with meaningful names. In this activity, you will navigate among worksheets, rename worksheets, and change the tab color of sheet tabs.

> **Another Way**
>
> Press Ctrl + F12 to display the Open dialog box. Press F12 to display the Save As dialog box.

1 **Start** Excel. From **Backstage** view, display the **Open** dialog box. From your student files, open **e02B_Weekly_Sales**. From **Backstage** view, display the **Save As** dialog box, navigate to your **Excel Chapter 2** folder, and then using your own name, save the file as **Lastname_Firstname_2B_Weekly_Sales**

In the displayed workbook, there are two worksheets into which some data has already been entered. For example, on the first worksheet, the days of the week and sales data for the one-week period displays.

2 Along the bottom of the Excel window, point to and then click the **Sheet2 tab**.

The second worksheet in the workbook displays and becomes the active worksheet. *Sheet2* displays in bold.

3 In cell **A1**, notice the text *In-Store*—this worksheet will contain data for in-store sales.

4 Click the **Sheet1 tab**. Then, point to the **Sheet1 tab**, and double-click to select the sheet tab name. Type **Online Sales** and press Enter.

The first worksheet becomes the active worksheet, and the sheet tab displays *Online Sales*.

5 Point to the **Sheet2 tab**, right-click, and then from the shortcut menu, click **Rename**. Type **In-Store Sales** and press Enter. Compare your screen with Figure 2.31.

You can use either of these methods to rename a sheet tab.

Figure 2.31

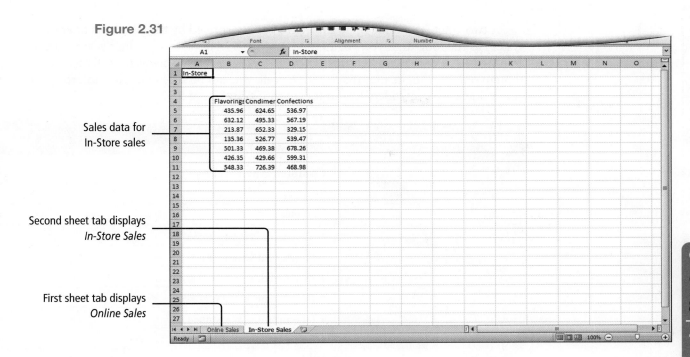

Sales data for
In-Store sales

Second sheet tab displays
In-Store Sales

First sheet tab displays
Online Sales

Another Way

Alternatively, on the
Home tab, in the Cells
group, click the Format
button, and then on the
displayed list, point to
Tab Color.

6 Point to the **In-Store Sales sheet tab** and right-click. On the shortcut menu, point to **Tab Color**, and then in the last column, click the first color—**Orange, Accent 6**.

7 Using the technique you just practiced, change the tab color of the **Online Sales sheet tab** to **Aqua, Accent 5**—in the next to last column, the first color. **Save** your workbook.

Objective 8 | Enter Dates, Clear Contents, and Clear Formats

Dates represent a type of value that you can enter in a cell. When you enter a date, Excel assigns a serial value—a number—to the date. This makes it possible to treat dates like other numbers. For example, if two cells contain dates, you can find the number of days between the two dates by subtracting the older date from the more recent date.

Activity 2.17 | Entering and Formatting Dates

In this activity, you will examine the various ways that Excel can format dates in a cell. Date values entered in any of the following formats will be recognized by Excel as a date:

Format	Example
m/d/yy	7/4/12
d-mmm	4-Jul
d-mmm-yy	4-Jul-12
mmm-yy	Jul-12

On your keyboard, - (the hyphen key) and / (the forward slash key) function identically in any of these formats and can be used interchangeably. You can abbreviate the month name to three characters or spell it out. You can enter the year as two digits, four digits, or even leave it off. When left off, the current year is assumed but does not display in the cell.

A two-digit year value of 30 through 99 is interpreted by the Windows operating system as the four-digit years of 1930 through 1999. All other two-digit year values are assumed to be in the 21st century. If you always type year values as four digits, even though only two digits may display in the cell, you can be sure that Excel interprets the year value as you intended. Examples are shown in Figure 2.32.

How Excel Interprets Dates

Date Typed As:	Completed by Excel As:
7/4/12	7/4/2012
7-4-98	7/4/1998
7/4	4-Jul (current year assumed)
7-4	4-Jul (current year assumed)
July 4	4-Jul (current year assumed)
Jul 4	4-Jul (current year assumed)
Jul/4	4-Jul (current year assumed)
Jul-4	4-Jul (current year assumed)
July 4, 1998	4-Jul-98
July 2012	Jul-12 (first day of month assumed)
July 1998	Jul-98 (first day of month assumed)

Figure 2.32

1 On the **Online Sales** sheet, click cell **A16** and notice that the cell indicates *8/3* (August 3). In the **Formula Bar**, notice that the full date of August 3, 2014 displays in the format *8/3/2014*.

2 With cell **A16** selected, on the **Home tab**, in the **Number group**, click the **Number Format arrow**. At the bottom of the menu, click **More Number Formats** to display the **Number tab** of the **Format Cells** dialog box.

Under Category, *Date* is selected, and under Type, *3/14* is selected. Cell A16 uses this format type; that is, only the month and day display in the cell.

3 In the displayed dialog box, under **Type**, click several other date types and watch the **Sample** area to see how applying the selected date format would format your cell. When you are finished, click the **3/14/01** type, and then compare your screen with Figure 2.33.

Figure 2.33

Format Cells dialog box

Number tab active

8/3/14 displays in Sample box

Date category selected

3/14/01 indicated as Type

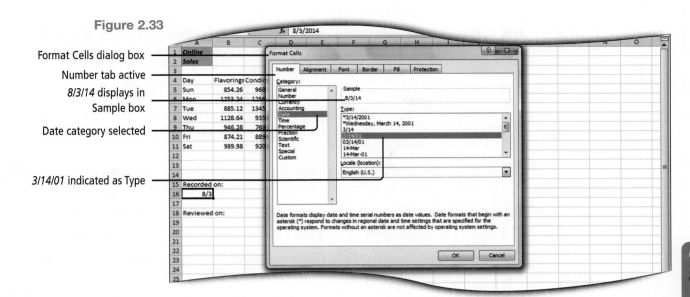

4 At the bottom of the dialog box, click **OK**. Click cell **A19**, type **8-7-14** and then press Enter.

Cell A19 has no special date formatting applied, and thus displays in the default date format *8/7/2014*.

> **Alert!** | **The Date Does Not Display as 8/7/2014?**
>
> Settings in your Windows operating system determine the default format for dates. If your result is different, it is likely that the formatting of the default date was adjusted on the computer at which you are working.

5 Click cell **A19** again. Hold down Ctrl and press ; (semicolon) on your keyboard. Press Enter to confirm the entry.

Excel enters the current date, obtained from your computer's internal calendar, in the selected cell using the default date format. Ctrl + ; is a quick method to enter the current date.

6 Click cell **A19** again, type **8/7/14** and then press Enter.

Because the year *14* is less than 30, Excel assumes a 21st century date and changes *14* to *2014* to complete the four-digit year. Typing *98* would result in *1998*. For two-digit years that you type that are between 30 and 99, Excel assumes a 20th century date.

7 Click cell **A16**, and then on the **Home tab**, in the **Clipboard group**, click the **Format Painter** button. Click cell **A19**, and notice that the date format from cell **A16** is copied to cell **A19**. **Save** your workbook.

Activity 2.18 | Clearing Cell Contents and Formats

A cell has *contents*—a value or a formula—and a cell may also have one or more *formats* applied, for example bold and italic font styles, fill color, font color, and so on. You can choose to clear—delete—the *contents* of a cell, the *formatting* of a cell, or both.

Clearing the contents of a cell deletes the value or formula typed there, but it does *not* clear formatting applied to a cell. In this activity, you will clear the contents of a cell and then clear the formatting of a cell that contains a date to see its underlying content.

1 In the **Online Sales** worksheet, click cell **A1**. In the **Editing group**, click the **Clear** button. On the displayed list, click **Clear Contents** and notice that the text is cleared, but the orange formatting remains.

2 Click cell **A2**, and then press Del.

You can use either of these two methods to delete the *contents* of a cell. Deleting the contents does not, however, delete the formatting of the cell; you can see that the orange fill color format applied to the two cells still displays.

3 In cell **A1**, type **Online Sales** and then on the **Formula Bar**, click the **Enter** button ✓ so that cell **A1** remains the active cell.

In addition to the orange fill color, the bold italic text formatting remains with the cell.

4 In the **Editing group**, click the **Clear** button, and then click **Clear Formats**.

Clearing the formats deletes formatting from the cell—the orange fill color and the bold and italic font styles—but does not delete the cell's contents.

5 Use the same technique to clear the orange fill color from cell **A2**. Click cell **A16**, click the **Clear** button, and then click **Clear Formats**. In the **Number group**, notice that *General* displays as the number format of the cell.

The box in the Number group indicates the current Number format of the selected cell. Clearing the date formatting from the cell displays the date's serial number. The date, August 3, 2014, is stored as a serial number that indicates the number of days since January 1, 1900. This date is the 41,854th day since the reference date of January 1, 1900.

6 On the Quick Access Toolbar, click the **Undo** button to restore the date format. **Save** your workbook, and then compare your screen with Figure 2.34.

Figure 2.34

Date indicated as the Number format

Date in Formula Bar

Orange fill color and bold italic font style cleared from cell A1

Cell A2 contents deleted and formats cleared

A16 reformatted as a date

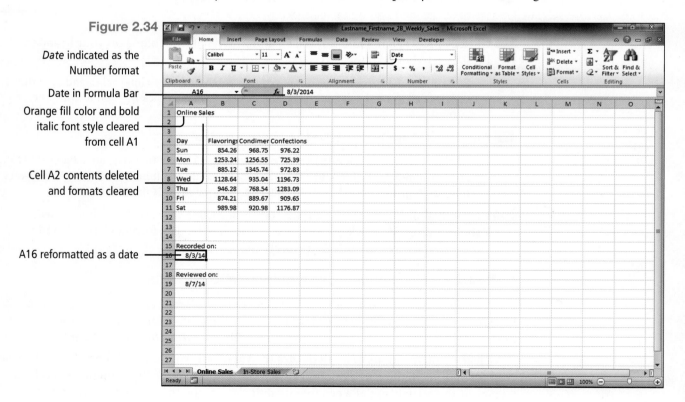

Objective 9 | Copy and Paste by Using the Paste Options Gallery

Data in cells can be copied to other cells in the same worksheet, to other sheets in the same workbook, or to sheets in another workbook. The action of placing cell contents that have been copied or moved to the Office Clipboard into another location is called *paste*.

Activity 2.19 | Copying and Pasting by Using the Paste Options Gallery

Recall that the Office Clipboard is a temporary storage area maintained by your Windows operating system. When you select one or more cells, and then perform the Copy command or the Cut command, the selected data is placed on the Office Clipboard. From the Office Clipboard storage area, the data is available for pasting into other cells, other worksheets, other workbooks, and even into other Office programs. When you paste, the *Paste Options gallery* displays, which includes Live Preview to preview the Paste formatting that you want.

1 With the **Online Sales** worksheet active, select the range **A4:A19**.

A range of cells identical to this one is required for the *In-Store Sales* worksheet.

Another Way

Use the keyboard short-cut for Copy, which is Ctrl + C; or click the Copy button in the Clipboard group on the Home tab.

2 Right-click over the selection, and then click **Copy** to place a copy of the cells on the Office Clipboard. Notice that the copied cells display a moving border.

3 At the bottom of the workbook window, click the **In-Store Sales sheet tab** to make it the active worksheet. Point to cell **A4**, right-click, and then on the shortcut menu, under **Paste Options**, *point* to the first button—**Paste**. Compare your screen with Figure 2.35.

Live Preview displays how the copied cells will be placed in the worksheet if you click the Paste button. In this manner, you can experiment with different paste options, and then be sure you are selecting the paste operation that you want. When pasting a range of cells, you need only point to or select the cell in the upper left corner of the *paste area*—the target destination for data that has been cut or copied using the Office Clipboard.

Figure 2.35

Paste Options (6 option buttons)

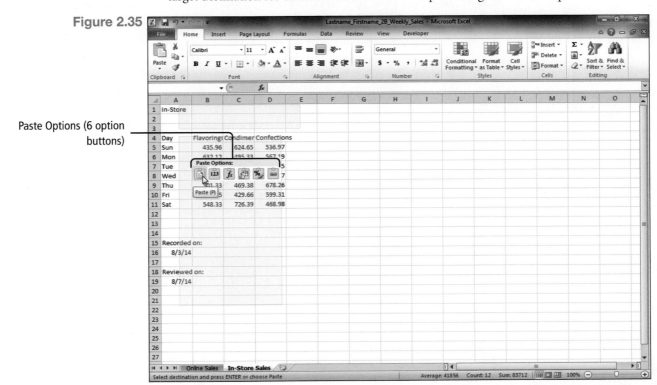

4 Click the first button, **Paste**. In the status bar, notice that the message still displays, indicating that your selected range remains available on the Office Clipboard.

5 Display the **Online Sales** worksheet. Press Esc to cancel the moving border. **Save** 💾 your workbook.

> The status bar no longer displays the message.

Note | Pressing Enter to Complete a Paste Action

If you want to paste the same text more than one time, click the Paste button so that the copied text remains available on the Office Clipboard. Otherwise, you can press Enter to complete the Paste command.

Objective 10 | Edit and Format Multiple Worksheets at the Same Time

You can enter or edit data on several worksheets at the same time by selecting and grouping multiple worksheets. Data that you enter or edit on the active sheet is reflected in all selected sheets. If you apply color to the sheet tabs, the name of the sheet tab will be underlined in the color you selected. If the sheet tab displays with a background color, you know the sheet is not selected.

Activity 2.20 | Grouping Worksheets for Editing

In this activity, you will group the two worksheets, and then format both worksheets at the same time.

1 With the **Online Sales** sheet active, press Ctrl + Home to make cell **A1** the active cell. Point to the **Online Sales sheet tab**, right-click, and then from the shortcut menu, click **Select All Sheets**.

2 At the top of your screen, notice that *[Group]* displays in the title bar. Compare your screen with Figure 2.36.

> Both worksheets are selected, as indicated by *[Group]* in the title bar and the sheet tab names underlined in the selected tab color. Data that you enter or edit on the active sheet will also be entered or edited in the same manner on all the selected sheets in the same cells.

Figure 2.36

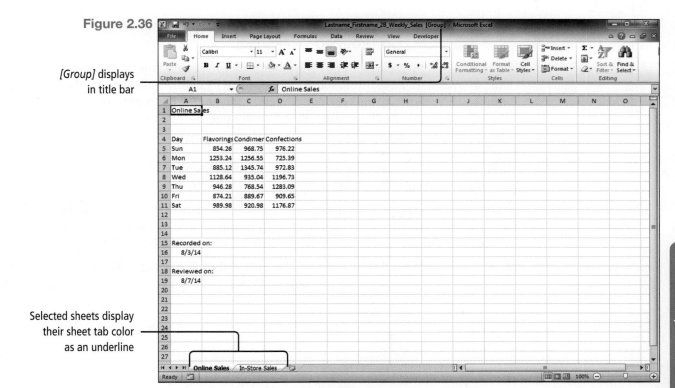

[Group] displays in title bar

Selected sheets display their sheet tab color as an underline

3 Select **columns A:G**, and then set their width to **85 pixels**.

4 Click cell **A2**, type **Week of July 24** and then on the **Formula Bar**, click the **Enter** button ☑ to keep cell **A2** as the active cell. **Merge & Center** 🔳 the text across the range **A2:G2**, and then apply the **Heading 1** cell style.

5 Click cell **E4**, type **Total Food Sales** and then press Tab. In cell **F4**, type **Non-Food Sales** and then press Tab. In cell **G4**, type **Total Sales** and then press Enter.

6 Select the range **A4:G4**, and then apply the **Heading 3** cell style. In the **Alignment group**, click the **Center** 🔳, **Middle Align** 🔳, and **Wrap Text** 🔳 buttons. **Save** 🔳 your workbook.

Another Way
Right-click any sheet tab, and then click Ungroup Sheets.

7 Display the **In-Store Sales** worksheet to cancel the grouping, and then compare your screen with Figure 2.37.

As soon as you select a single sheet, the grouping of the sheets is canceled and [Group] no longer displays in the title bar. Because the sheets were grouped, the same new text and formatting was applied to both sheets. In this manner, you can make the same changes to all the sheets in a workbook at one time.

Figure 2.37

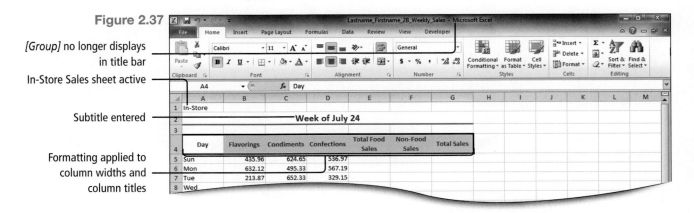

[Group] no longer displays in title bar

In-Store Sales sheet active

Subtitle entered

Formatting applied to column widths and column titles

Excel | Chapter 2

Activity 2.21 | Formatting and Constructing Formulas on Grouped Worksheets

Recall that formulas are equations that perform calculations on values in your worksheet and that a formula starts with an equal sign (=). Operators are the symbols with which you specify the type of calculation that you want to perform on the elements of a formula. In this activity, you will enter sales figures for Non-Food items from both Online and In-Store sales, and then calculate the total sales.

1 Display the **Online Sales** worksheet. Verify that the sheets are not grouped—*[Group]* does *not* display in the title bar.

2 Click cell **A1**, type **Food and Non-Food Items: Weekly Online Sales** and then on the **Formula Bar**, click the **Enter** button ✓ to keep cell **A1** as the active cell. **Merge & Center** 🔳 the text across the range **A1:G1**, and then apply the **Title** cell style.

3 In the column titled *Non-Food Sales*, click cell **F5**, in the range **F5:F11**, type the following data for Non-Food Sales, and then compare your screen with Figure 2.38.

	Non-Food Sales
Sun	**869.24**
Mon	**468.78**
Tue	**796.57**
Wed	**865.11**
Thu	**916.48**
Fri	**1154.22**
Sat	**968.25**

Figure 2.38

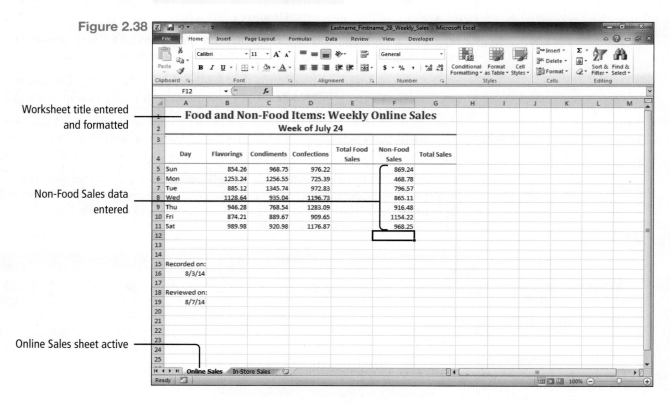

Worksheet title entered and formatted

Non-Food Sales data entered

Online Sales sheet active

4 Display the **In-Store Sales** sheet. In cell **A1**, replace *In-Store* by typing **Food and Non-Food Items: Weekly In-Store Sales** and then on the **Formula Bar**, click the **Enter** button ☑ to keep cell **A1** as the active cell. **Merge & Center** 🔳 the text across the range **A1:G1**, and then apply the **Title** cell style.

5 In the column titled *Non-Food Sales*, click cell **F5**, in the range **F5:F11**, type the following data for Non-Food Sales, and then compare your screen with Figure 2.39.

	Non-Food Sales
Sun	**569.34**
Mon	**426.44**
Tue	**636.57**
Wed	**721.69**
Thu	**359.12**
Fri	**587.99**
Sat	**436.22**

Figure 2.39

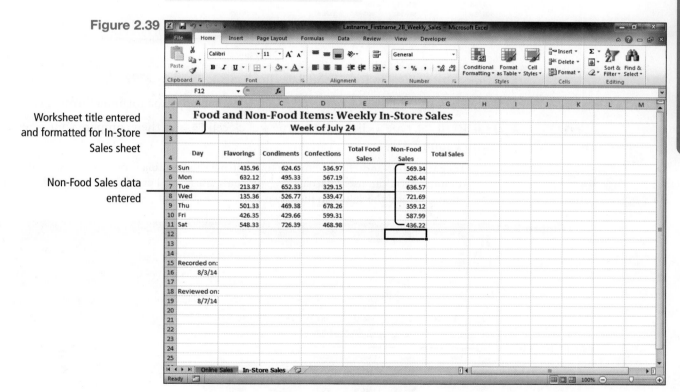

Worksheet title entered and formatted for In-Store Sales sheet

Non-Food Sales data entered

6 **Save** 💾 your workbook. Right-click the **Online Sales sheet tab**, and then from the shortcut menu, click **Select All Sheets**.

The first worksheet becomes the active sheet, and the worksheets are grouped. *[Group]* displays in the title bar, and the sheet tabs are underlined in the tab color to indicate they are selected as part of the group. Recall that when grouped, any action that you perform on the active worksheet is *also* performed on any other selected worksheets.

7 With the sheets *grouped* and the **Online Sales** sheet active, click cell **E5**. On the **Home tab**, in the **Editing group**, click the **Sum** button Σ. Compare your screen with Figure 2.40.

Recall that when you enter the SUM function, Excel looks first above and then left for a proposed range of cells to sum.

Figure 2.40

[Group] indicates the worksheets are grouped

SUM function in cell

Proposed range of cells to sum surrounded by moving border

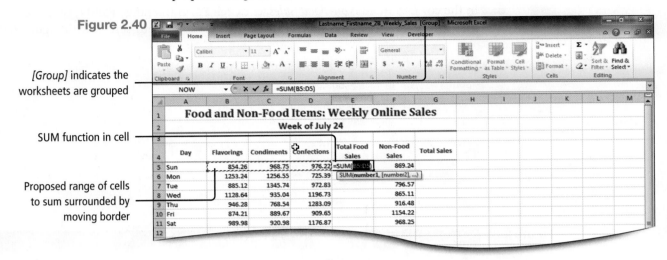

8 Press [Enter] to display Total Food Sales for Sunday, which is *2799.23*.

9 Click cell **E5**, and then drag the fill handle down to copy the formula through cell **E11**.

10 Click cell **G5**, type **=** click cell **E5**, type **+** click cell **F5**, and then compare your screen with Figure 2.41.

Using the point-and-click technique to construct this formula is only one of several techniques you can use. Alternatively, you could use any other method to enter the SUM function to add the values in these two cells.

Figure 2.41

Formula in cell G5

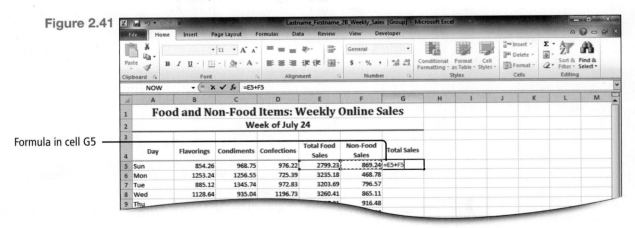

11 Press [Enter] to display the result *3668.47*, and then copy the formula down through cell **G11**.

12 In cell **A12**, type **Total** and then select the range **B5:G12**, which is all of the sales data and the empty cells at the bottom of each column of sales data.

13 With the range **B5:G12** selected, hold down [Alt] and press [=] to enter the **SUM** function in each empty cell.

Selecting a range in this manner will place the Sum function in the empty cells at the bottom of each column.

14 Select the range **A5:A12**, and then apply the **Heading 4** cell style.

15 To apply financial formatting to the worksheets, select the range **B5:G5**, hold down Ctrl, and then select the range **B12:G12**. With the nonadjacent ranges selected, apply the **Accounting Number Format** $ ▾ .

16 Select the range **B6:G11** and apply **Comma Style** , . Select the range **B12:G12** and apply the **Total** cell style.

17 Press Ctrl + Home to move to the top of the worksheet; compare your screen with Figure 2.42.

Figure 2.42

Total sales for each day

Row titles formatted

Columns totaled; financial formatting applied

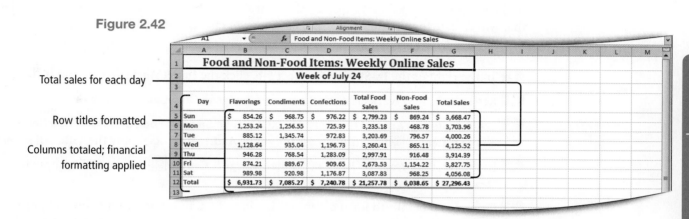

18 Click the **In-Store Sales sheet tab** to cancel the grouping and display the second worksheet. Click **Save** 🖫 , and then compare your screen with Figure 2.43.

> With your worksheets grouped, the calculations on the first worksheet were also performed on the second worksheet.

Figure 2.43

Total sales for each day

Row titles formatted

Columns totaled; financial formatting applied

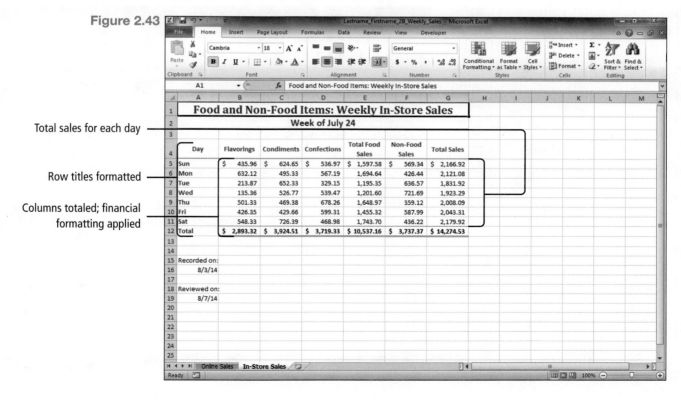

Objective 11 | Create a Summary Sheet with Column Sparklines

A **summary sheet** is a worksheet where totals from other worksheets are displayed and summarized. Recall that sparklines are tiny charts within a single cell that show a data trend.

Activity 2.22 | Constructing Formulas that Refer to Cells in Another Worksheet

In this activity, you will insert a new worksheet in which you will place the totals from the Online Sales worksheet and the In-Store Sales worksheet. You will construct formulas in the Summary worksheet to display the total sales for both online sales and in-store sales that will update the Summary worksheet whenever changes are made to the other worksheet totals.

1 To the right of the **In-Store Sales** sheet tab, click the **Insert Worksheet** button.

2 Rename the new worksheet tab **Summary** Change the **Tab Color** to **Olive Green, Accent 3**.

3 Widen **columns A:E** to **110** pixels. In cell **A1**, type **Sales of Food and Non-Food Items** Merge & Center the title across the range **A1:E1**, and then apply the **Title** cell style.

4 In cell **A2**, type **Week of July 24** and then **Merge & Center** across **A2:E2**; apply the **Heading 1** cell style.

5 Leave **row 3** blank. To form column titles, in cell **B4**, type **Food/Non-Food** and press Tab. In cell **C4**, type **Food Sales** and press Tab. In cell **D4**, type **Non-Food Sales** and press Tab. In cell **E4**, type **Total Sales** Press Enter. Select the range **B4:E4**. Apply the **Heading 3** cell style and **Center**.

6 To form row titles, in cell **A5**, type **Online Sales** In cell **A6**, type **In-Store Sales** and then compare your screen with Figure 2.44.

Figure 2.44

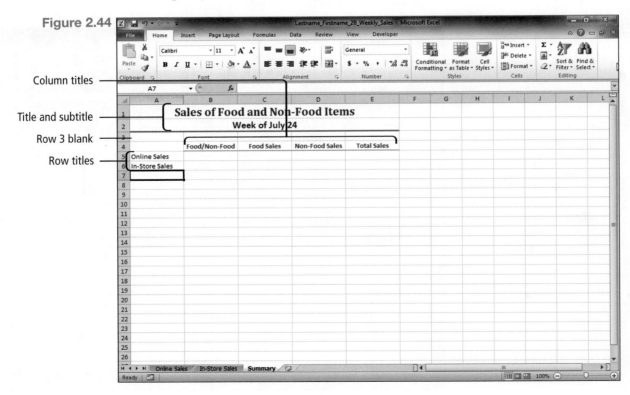

Column titles

Title and subtitle

Row 3 blank

Row titles

7 Click cell **C5**. Type **=** Click the **Online Sales sheet tab**. On the **Online Sales** worksheet, click cell **E12**, and then press [Enter] to redisplay the **Summary** worksheet and insert the total **Food Sales** amount of *$21,257.78*.

8 Click cell **C5** to select it again. Look at the **Formula Bar**, and notice that instead of a value, the cell contains a formula that is equal to the value in another cell in another worksheet. Compare your screen with Figure 2.45.

> The value in this cell is equal to the value in cell E12 of the *Online Sales* worksheet. The Accounting Number Format applied to the referenced cell is carried over. By using a formula of this type, changes in cell E12 on the *Online Sales* worksheet will be automatically updated in this *Summary* worksheet.

Figure 2.45

Formula Bar indicates formula referring to cell in another worksheet

Total Food Sales from Online Sales worksheet

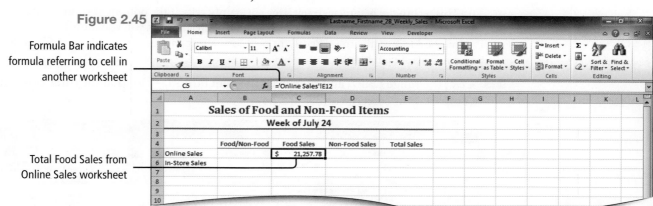

9 Click cell **D5**. Type **=** and then click the **Online Sales sheet tab**. Click cell **F12**, and then press [Enter] to redisplay the **Summary** worksheet and insert the total **Non-Food Sales** amount of *$6,038.65*.

10 By using the techniques you just practiced, in cells **C6** and **D6** insert the total **Food Sales** and **Non-Food Sales** data from the **In-Store Sales** worksheet. Click **Save** 🖫, and then compare your screen with Figure 2.46.

Figure 2.46

Totals from other worksheets

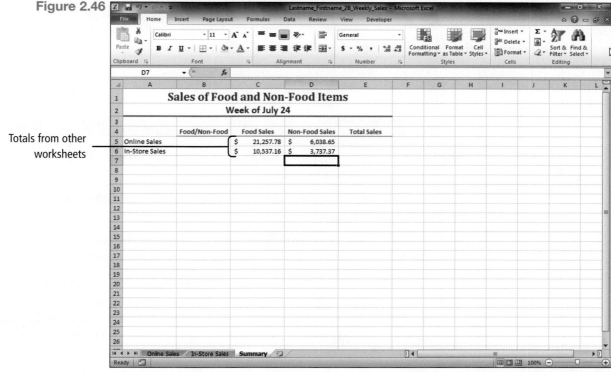

Activity 2.23 | Changing Values in a Detail Worksheet to Update a Summary Worksheet

The formulas in cells C5:D6 display the totals from the other two worksheets. Changes made to any of the other two worksheets—sometimes referred to as *detail sheets* because the details of the information are contained there—that affect their totals will display on this Summary worksheet. In this manner, the Summary worksheet accurately displays the current totals from the other worksheets.

1 In cell **A7**, type **Total** Select the range **C5:E6**, and then click the **Sum** button Σ to total the two rows.

> This technique is similar to selecting the empty cells at the bottom of columns and then inserting the SUM function for each column. Alternatively, you could use any other method to sum the rows. Recall that cell formatting carries over to adjacent cells unless two cells are left blank.

2 Select the range **C5:E7**, and then click the **Sum** button Σ to total the three columns. Compare your screen with Figure 2.47.

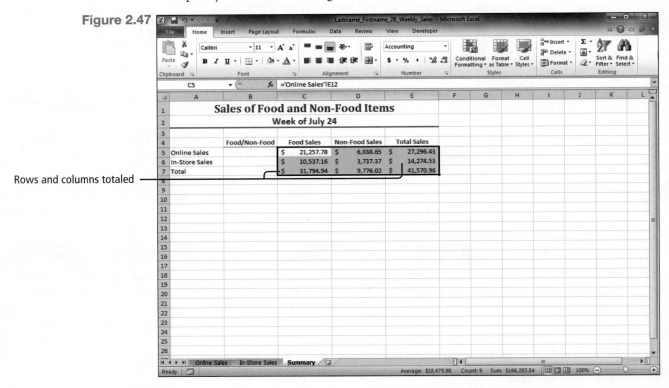

Figure 2.47

Rows and columns totaled

3 In cell **C6**, notice that total **Food Sales** for **In-Store** Sales is *$10,537.16*, and in cell **C7**, notice the total of *$31,794.94*.

4 Display the **In-Store Sales** worksheet, click cell **B8**, type **353.63** and then press Enter. Notice that the formulas in the worksheet recalculate.

5 Display the **Summary** worksheet, and notice that in the **Food Sales** column, both the total for the *In-Store Sales* location and the *Total* also recalculated.

> In this manner, a Summary sheet recalculates any changes made in the other worksheets.

6 Select the range **C6:E6** and change the format to **Comma Style**. Select the range **C7:E7**, and then apply the **Total** cell style. Select the range **A5:A7** and apply the **Heading 4** cell style. **Save** your workbook. Click cell **A1**, and then compare your screen with Figure 2.48.

Figure 2.48

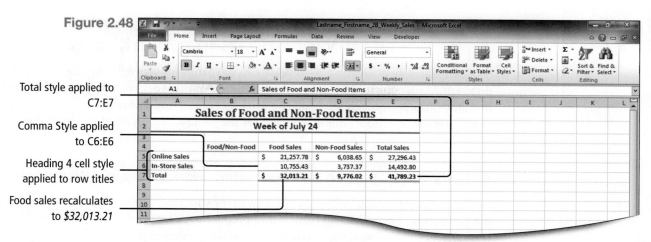

Total style applied to C7:E7

Comma Style applied to C6:E6

Heading 4 cell style applied to row titles

Food sales recalculates to *$32,013.21*

Activity 2.24 | Inserting Sparklines

In this activity, you will insert column sparklines to visualize the ratio of Food to Non-Food sales for both Online and In-Store.

1 Click cell **B5**. On the **Insert tab**, in the **Sparklines group**, click **Column**. In the **Create Sparklines** dialog box, with the insertion point blinking in the **Data Range** box, select the range **C5:D5**. Compare your screen with Figure 2.49.

Figure 2.49

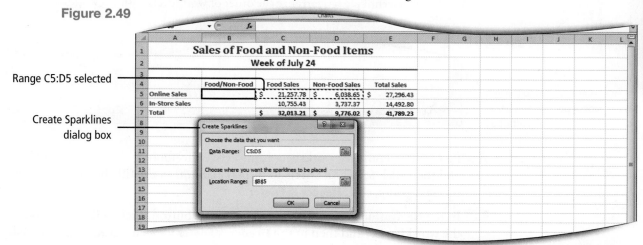

Range C5:D5 selected

Create Sparklines dialog box

2 Click **OK**. Click cell **B6**, and then **Insert** a **Column Sparkline** for the range **C6:D6**. In the **Style group**, apply **Sparkline Style Accent 2, Darker 25%**—in the second row, the second style. Press [Ctrl] + [Home], click **Save** 🖫, and then compare your screen with Figure 2.50.

You can see, at a glance, that for both Online and In-Store sales, Food sales are much greater than Non-Food sales.

Figure 2.50

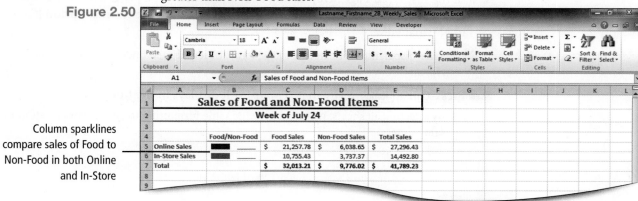

Column sparklines compare sales of Food to Non-Food in both Online and In-Store

Objective 12 | Format and Print Multiple Worksheets in a Workbook

Each worksheet within a workbook can have different formatting, for example different headers or footers. If all the worksheets in the workbook will have the same header or footer, you can select all the worksheets and apply formatting common to all of the worksheets; for example, you can set the same footer in all of the worksheets.

Activity 2.25 | Moving and Formatting Worksheets in a Workbook

In this activity, you will move the Summary sheet to become the first worksheet in the workbook. Then you will format and prepare your workbook for printing. The three worksheets containing data can be formatted simultaneously.

1 Point to the **Summary sheet tab**, hold down the left mouse button to display a small black triangle—a caret—and then notice that a small paper icon attaches to the mouse pointer.

2 Drag to the left until the caret and mouse pointer are to the left of the **Online Sales sheet tab**, as shown in Figure 2.51, and then release the left mouse button.

Use this technique to rearrange the order of worksheets within a workbook.

Figure 2.51

Caret moved to the left; mouse pointer with paper icon attached

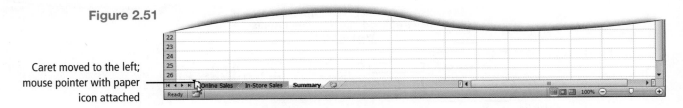

3 Be sure the **Summary** worksheet is the active sheet, point to its sheet tab, right-click, and then click **Select All Sheets** to display *[Group]* in the title bar. On the **Insert tab**, in the **Text group**, click **Header & Footer**.

4 In the **Navigation group**, click the **Go to Footer** button, click in the **left section** above the word *Footer*, and then in the **Header & Footer Elements group**, click the **File Name** button.

5 Click in a cell above the footer to deselect the **Footer area**. On the **Page Layout tab**, in the **Page Setup group**, click the **Margins** button, and then at the bottom of the **Margins** gallery, click **Custom Margins**.

6 In the displayed **Page Setup** dialog box, under **Center on page**, select the **Horizontally** check box. Click **OK**, and then on the status bar, click the **Normal** button ▦ to return to Normal view.

After displaying worksheets in Page Layout View, dotted lines indicate the page breaks in Normal view.

7 Press [Ctrl] + [Home]; verify that *[Group]* still displays in the title bar.

By selecting all sheets, you can apply the same formatting to all the worksheets at the same time.

8 Display **Backstage** view, show the **Document Panel**, type your firstname and lastname in the Author box, and then type your course name and section number in the **Subject** box. As the **Keywords** type **weekly sales, online, in-store** and then **Close** ✕ the **Document Information Panel**.

9 Press Ctrl + F2; compare your screen with Figure 2.52.

> By grouping, you can view all sheets in Print Preview. If you do not see *1 of 3* at the bottom of the Preview, click the Home tab, select all the sheets again, and then redisplay Print Preview.

Figure 2.52

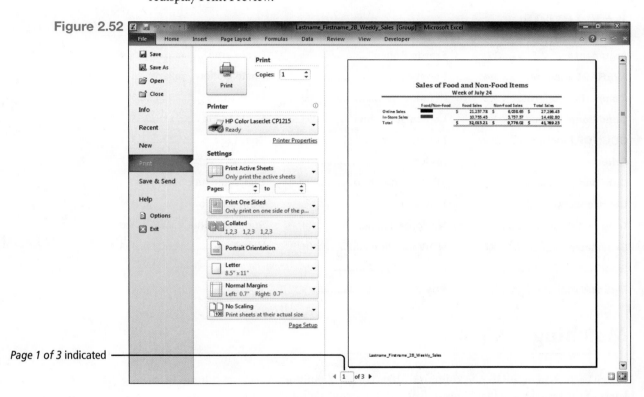

Page 1 of 3 indicated

10 At the bottom of the **Print Preview**, click the **Next Page** ▶ button as necessary and take a moment to view each page of your workbook.

Activity 2.26 | Printing All the Worksheets in a Workbook

1 In **Backstage** view, click the **Save** button to save your workbook before printing. To submit your workbook electronically, follow the instructions provided by your instructor. To print your workbook, continue to Step 2.

2 Display **Backstage** view, click the **Print tab**, verify that the worksheets in your workbook are still grouped—*[Group]* displays in the title bar—and then in the center panel, in the **Print group**, click the **Print** button.

3 If required, print or create an electronic version of your worksheets with formulas displayed by using the instructions in Activity 1.16, and then **Close** ✕ Excel without saving so that you do not save the changes you made to print formulas.

End **You have completed Project 2B**

Content-Based Assessments

Summary

In this chapter, you used the Statistical, Logical, and Date & Time functions from the Function Library. You created a table and analyzed the table's data by sorting and filtering. You also created a workbook with multiple worksheets, and then summarized all the worksheets on a summary worksheet.

Key Terms

Matching

Match each term in the second column with its correct definition in the first column by writing the letter of the term on the blank line in front of the correct definition.

_____ 1. A predefined formula that performs calculations by using specific values in a particular order or structure.

_____ 2. Excel functions such as AVERAGE that are useful to analyze a group of measurements.

_____ 3. A predefined formula that adds all the numbers in a selected range.

_____ 4. A function that adds a group of values, and then divides the result by the number of values in the group.

_____ 5. A function that finds the middle value that has as many values above it in the group as are below it.

_____ 6. A function that determines the smallest value in a range.

_____ 7. A function that determines the largest value in a range.

_____ 8. The action of moving a selection by dragging it to a new location.

_____ 9. A group of functions that tests for specific conditions, and which typically use conditional tests to determine whether specified conditions are true or false.

_____ 10. Conditions that you specify in a logical function.

_____ 11. A statistical function that counts the number of cells within a range that meet the given condition and which has two arguments—the range of cells to check and the criteria.

_____ 12. Any value or expression that can be evaluated as being true or false.

A AVERAGE function

B Comparison operators

C Conditional format

D COUNTIF function

E Criteria

F Drag and drop

G Function

H IF function

I Logical functions

J Logical test

K MAX function

L MEDIAN function

M MIN function

N Statistical functions

O SUM function

Content-Based Assessments

_____ 13. A function that uses a logical test to check whether a condition is met, and then returns one value if true, and another value if false.

_____ 14. Symbols that evaluate each value to determine if it is the same (=), greater than (>), less than (<), or in between a range of values as specified by the criteria.

_____ 15. A format that changes the appearance of a cell based on a condition.

Multiple Choice

Circle the correct answer.

1. A shaded bar that provides a visual cue about the value of a cell relative to other cells is a:
   A. data bar   B. detail bar   C. filter

2. The function that retrieves and then displays the date and time from your computer is the:
   A. DATE function   B. NOW function   C. CALENDAR function

3. The command that enables you to select one or more rows or columns and lock them into place is:
   A. drag and drop   B. scale to fit   C. freeze panes

4. A series of rows and columns with related data that is managed independently from other data is a:
   A. table   B. pane   C. detail sheet

5. The process of arranging data in a specific order based on the value in each field is called:
   A. filtering   B. sorting   C. scaling

6. The process of displaying only a portion of the data based on matching a specific value to show only the data that meets the criteria that you specify is called:
   A. filtering   B. sorting   C. scaling

7. The Excel command that enables you to specify rows and columns to repeat on each printed page is:
   A. navigate   B. print titles   C. conditional format

8. The labels along the lower border of the workbook window that identify each worksheet are the:
   A. data bars   B. sheet tabs   C. detail sheets

9. A worksheet where totals from other worksheets are displayed and summarized is a:
   A. summary sheet   B. detail sheet   C. table

10. The worksheets that contain the details of the information summarized on a summary sheet are called:
    A. summary sheets   B. detail sheets   C. tables

Content-Based Assessments

Apply **2A** skills from these Objectives:

- 1 Use the SUM, AVERAGE, MEDIAN, MIN, and MAX Functions
- 2 Move Data, Resolve Error Messages, and Rotate Text
- 3 Use COUNTIF and IF Functions and Apply Conditional Formatting
- 4 Use Date & Time Functions and Freeze Panes
- 5 Create, Sort, and Filter an Excel Table
- 6 Format and Print a Large Worksheet

Skills Review | Project **2C** Sauces Inventory

In the following Skills Review, you will edit a worksheet for Laura Morales, President, detailing the current inventory of sauces at the Portland facility. Your completed workbook will look similar to Figure 2.53.

Project Files

For Project 2C, you will need the following file:

e02C_Sauces_Inventory

You will save your workbook as:

Lastname_Firstname_2C_Sauces_Inventory

Project Results

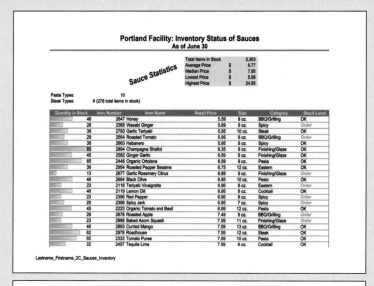

Figure 2.53

(Project 2C Sauces Inventory continues on the next page)

Content-Based Assessments

Skills Review | Project 2C Sauces Inventory (continued)

1 **Start** Excel. From your student files, locate and open **e02C_Sauces_Inventory**. From **Backstage** view, display the **Save As** dialog box, navigate to your **Excel Chapter 2** folder, and then save the workbook as **Lastname_Firstname_2C_Sauces_Inventory**

a. Click cell **B4**. Click the **Formulas tab**, and then in the **Function Library group**, click the **AutoSum** button. Select the range **A14:A68**, and then press Enter.

b. With cell **B5** active, in the **Function Library group**, click the **More Functions** button. Point to **Statistical**, click **AVERAGE**, and then in the **Number1** box, type **d14:d68** Click **OK**.

c. Click cell **B6**. In the **Function Library group**, click the **More Functions** button, point to **Statistical**, and then click **MEDIAN**. In the **Function Arguments** dialog box, to the right of the **Number1** box, click the **Collapse Dialog** button. Select the range **D14:D68**, click the **Expand Dialog** button, and then click **OK**.

d. Click cell **B7**, and then by using a similar technique to insert a statistical function, insert the **MIN** function to determine the lowest **Retail Price**. Click cell **B8**, and then insert the **MAX** function to determine the highest **Retail Price**.

2 Right-click cell **B4**. On the Mini toolbar, click the **Comma Style** button, and then click the **Decrease Decimal** button two times. Select the range **B5:B8**, and apply the **Accounting Number Format**.

a. Select the range **A4:B8**. Point to the right edge of the selected range to display the pointer. Drag the selected range to the right until the ScreenTip displays *D4:E8*, and then release the mouse button.

b. With the range **D4:E8** selected, on the **Home tab**, in the **Styles group**, display the **Cell Styles** gallery, and then under **Themed Cell Styles**, click **20% - Accent1**.

c. In cell **C6**, type **Sauce Statistics** Select the range **C4:C8**, right-click over the selection, and then click **Format Cells**. In the **Format Cells** dialog box, click the **Alignment tab**. Under **Text control**, select the **Merge cells** check box.

d. In the upper right portion of the dialog box, under **Orientation**, point to the **red diamond**, and then drag the diamond upward until the **Degrees** box indicates *20*. Click **OK**.

e. With the merged cell still selected, on the **Home tab**, in the **Font group**, change the **Font Size** to **18**, and then apply **Bold** and **Italic**. Click the **Font Color**

button arrow, and then in the fourth column, click the first color—**Dark Blue, Text 2**.

3 Click cell **B10**. On the **Formulas tab**, in the **Function Library group**, click the **More Functions** button, and then display the list of **Statistical** functions. Click **COUNTIF**.

a. At the right edge of the **Range** box, click the **Collapse Dialog** button, select the range **F14:F68**, and then press Enter. Click in the **Criteria** box, type **Pasta** and then click **OK** to calculate the number of *Pasta* types.

b. Click cell **G14**. On the **Formulas tab**, in the **Function Library group**, click the **Logical** button, and then in the list, click **IF**. If necessary, drag the title bar of the **Function Arguments** dialog box up so that you can view **row 14** on your screen.

c. With the insertion point in the **Logical_test** box, click cell **A14**, and then type **<30** Press Tab to move the insertion point to the **Value_if_true** box, and then type **Order** Press Tab to move the insertion point to the **Value_if_false** box, type **OK** and then click **OK**. Using the fill handle, copy the function in cell **G14** down through cell **G68**.

4 With the range **G14:G68** selected, on the **Home tab**, in the **Styles group**, click the **Conditional Formatting** button. In the list, point to **Highlight Cells Rules**, and then click **Text that Contains**.

a. In the **Text That Contains** dialog box, with the insertion point blinking in the first box, type **Order** and then in the second box, click the **arrow**. In the list, click **Custom Format**.

b. In the **Format Cells** dialog box, on the **Font tab**, under **Font style**, click **Bold Italic**. Click the **Color arrow**, and then under **Theme Colors**, in the sixth column, click the first color—**Red, Accent 2**. In the lower right corner of the **Format Cells** dialog box, click **OK**. In the **Text That Contains** dialog box, click **OK** to apply the font color, bold, and italic to the cells that contain the word *Order*.

c. Select the range **A14:A68**. In the **Styles group**, click the **Conditional Formatting** button. In the list, point to **Data Bars**, and then under **Gradient Fill**, click **Orange Data Bar**. Click anywhere to cancel the selection.

d. Select the range **F14:F68**. On the **Home tab**, in the **Editing group**, click the **Find & Select** button, and then click **Replace**. In the **Find and Replace** dialog box, in the **Find what** box, type **Hot** and then in the

(Project 2C Sauces Inventory continues on the next page)

Replace with box type **Spicy** Click the **Replace All** button and then click **OK**. In the lower right corner of the **Find and Replace** dialog box, click the **Close** button.

e. Scroll down as necessary, and then click cell **A70**. Type **Edited by Michelle Albright** and then press Enter. With cell **A71** as the active cell, on the **Formulas tab**, in the **Function Library group**, click the **Date & Time** button. In the list of functions, click **NOW**, and then click **OK** to enter the current date and time.

5 Select the range **A13:G68**. Click the **Insert tab**, and then in the **Tables group**, click the **Table** button. In the **Create Table** dialog box, if necessary, select the My table has headers check box, and then click **OK**. On the **Design tab**, in the **Table Styles group**, click the **More** button, and then under **Light**, locate and click **Table Style Light 9**.

a. In the header row of the table, click the **Retail Price arrow**, and then from the menu, click **Sort Smallest to Largest**. Click the **Category arrow**. On the menu, click the **(Select All)** check box to clear all the check boxes. Scroll as necessary and then click to select only the **Steak** check box. Click **OK**.

b. On the **Design tab**, in the **Table Style Options group**, select the **Total Row** check box. Click cell **A69**, click the **arrow** that displays to the right of cell **A69**, and then in the list, click **Sum**. In cell **B11**, type the result **6 (278 total items in stock)** and then press Enter.

c. In the header row of the table, click the **Category arrow** and then click **Clear Filter From "Category"** to redisplay all of the data. Click anywhere in the table. Click the **Design tab**, in the **Table Style Options group**, clear the **Total Row** check box, and

then in the **Tools group**, click the **Convert to Range** button. Click **Yes**.

d. On the **Page Layout tab**, in the **Themes group**, click the **Themes** button, and then click **Horizon**.

6 On the **Page Layout tab**, click the **Margins** button, and then click **Custom Margins**. On the **Margins tab**, under **Center on page**, select the **Horizontally** check box. Click **OK**. On the **Page Layout tab**, in the **Scale to Fit group**, click the **Width button arrow**, and then click **1 page**.

a. In the **Page Setup group**, click the **Print Titles** button. Under **Print titles**, click in the **Rows to repeat at top** box, and then to the right, click the **Collapse Dialog** button. From the **row heading area**, select **row 13**, and then click the **Expand Dialog** button. Click **OK**.

b. On the **Insert tab**, in the **Text group**, click the **Header & Footer** button. Insert the **File Name** in the **left section** of the footer. Return to **Normal** view, make cell **A1** the active cell, and then delete the unused sheets.

c. Display the **Document Panel**, and then add your name, your course name and section, and the keywords **inventory, Portland Close** the **Document Information Panel**.

d. **Save** your workbook. Print or submit electronically as directed by your instructor. If required by your instructor, print or create an electronic version of your worksheets with formulas displayed by using the instructions in Activity 1.16, and then **Close** Excel without saving so that you do not save the changes you made to print formulas.

End You have completed Project 2C ————————————————

Content-Based Assessments

- **7** Navigate a Workbook and Rename Worksheets
- **8** Enter Dates, Clear Contents, and Clear Formats
- **9** Copy and Paste by Using the Paste Options Gallery
- **10** Edit and Format Multiple Worksheets at the Same Time
- **11** Create a Summary Sheet with Column Sparklines
- **12** Format and Print Multiple Worksheets in a Workbook

Skills Review | Project **2D** February Sales

In the following Skills Review, you will edit a workbook that summarizes in-store and online sales in the California and Oregon retail locations. Your completed workbook will look similar to Figure 2.54.

Project Files

For Project 2D, you will need the following file:

e02D_February_Sales

You will save your workbook as:

Lastname_Firstname_2D_February_Sales

Project Results

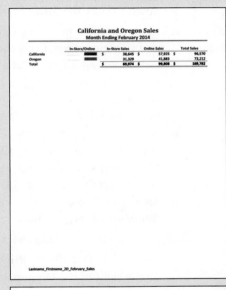

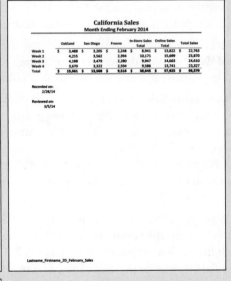

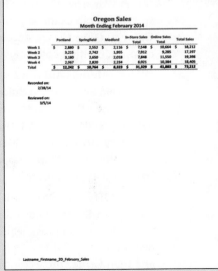

Figure 2.54

(Project 2D February Sales continues on the next page)

Skills Review | Project **2D** February Sales (continued)

1 **Start** Excel. From your student files, locate and open **e02D_February_Sales**. Click the **File tab**, click **Save As**, navigate to your **Excel Chapter 2** folder, and then using your own name, save the file as **Lastname_Firstname_ 2D_February_Sales**

a. Point to the **Sheet1 tab**, and then double-click to select the sheet tab name. Type **California Sales** and then press Enter.

b. Point to the **Sheet2 tab**, right-click, and then from the shortcut menu, click **Rename**. Type **Oregon Sales** and press Enter.

c. Point to the **California Sales sheet tab** and right-click. On the shortcut menu, point to **Tab Color**, and then in the last column, click the first color—**Orange, Accent 6**.

d. Using the technique you just practiced, change the tab color of the **Oregon Sales sheet tab** to **Aqua, Accent 5**—in the next to last column, the first color.

e. Click the **California Sales sheet tab**, and then click cell **A13**. On the **Home tab**, in the **Number group**, click the **Number Format arrow**. From the bottom of the displayed menu, click **More Number Formats** to display the **Number tab** of the **Format Cells** dialog box. Click the **3/14/01** type, and then at the bottom of the dialog box, click **OK**.

f. Click cell **A16**, type **3/5/14** and then press Enter. Click cell **A13**, and then on the **Home tab**, in the **Clipboard group**, click the **Format Painter** button. Click cell **A16** to copy the date format from cell **A13** to cell **A16**.

g. Click cell **A1**. In the **Editing group**, click the **Clear** button. From the displayed list, click **Clear Formats**.

h. Select the range **A4:A16**. On the **Home tab**, in the **Clipboard group**, click the **Copy** button. At the bottom of the workbook window, click the **Oregon Sales sheet tab** to make it the active worksheet. Right-click cell **A4**, and then under **Paste Options**, click the first button—**Paste**. Display the **California Sales** sheet. Press Esc to cancel the moving border.

2 With the **California Sales** sheet active, press Ctrl + Home to make cell **A1** the active cell. Point to the sheet tab, right-click, and then on the shortcut menu, click **Select All Sheets**. Verify that *[Group]* displays in the title bar.

a. **Merge & Center** the text in cell A1 across the range **A1:G1**, and then apply the **Title** cell style. Select **columns A:G**, and then set their widths to **85 pixels**.

b. Click cell **A2**, type **Month Ending February 2014** and then on the **Formula Bar**, click the **Enter** button to keep cell **A2** as the active cell. **Merge & Center** the text across the range **A2:G2**, and then apply the **Heading 1** cell style.

c. Select the range **B4:G4**, and then apply the **Heading 3** cell style. In the **Alignment group**, click the **Center**, **Middle Align**, and **Wrap Text** buttons.

d. With the sheets still *grouped* and the **California Sales** sheet active, click cell **E5**. On the **Home tab**, in the **Editing group**, click the **Sum** button, and then press Enter. Click cell **E5**, and then drag the fill handle down to copy the formula through cell **E8**.

e. Click cell **G5**, type **=** click cell **E5**, type **+** click cell **F5**, and then press Enter. Copy the formula down through cell **G8**. In cell **A9**, type **Total** Select the range **B5:G9**, and then press Alt + = to enter the SUM function for all the columns. Select the range **A5:A9**, and then apply the **Heading 4** cell style.

f. Select the range **B5:G5**, hold down Ctrl, and then select the range **B9:G9**. Apply the **Accounting Number Format** and decrease the decimal places to zero. Select the range **B6:G8**, and then apply **Comma Style** with zero decimal places. Select the range **B9:G9** and apply the **Total** cell style.

3 Click the **Oregon Sales sheet tab** to cancel the grouping and display the second worksheet.

a. To the right of the **Oregon Sales** sheet tab, click the **Insert Worksheet** button. Rename the new worksheet tab **Summary** and then change the **Tab Color** to **Olive Green, Accent 3**—in the seventh column, the first color.

b. Widen **columns A:E** to **125** pixels. In cell **A1**, type **California and Oregon Sales** and then **Merge & Center** the title across the range **A1:E1**. Apply the **Title** cell style. In cell **A2**, type **Month Ending February 2014** and then **Merge & Center** the text across the range **A2:E2**. Apply the **Heading 1** cell style. In cell **A5**, type **California** and in cell **A6**, type **Oregon**

c. In cell **B4**, type **In-Store/Online** and press Tab. In cell **C4**, type **In-Store Sales** and press Tab. In cell **D4**, type **Online Sales** and press Tab. In cell **E4**, type **Total Sales** Select the range **B4:E4**, apply the **Heading 3** cell style, and then **Center** these column titles.

(Project 2D February Sales continues on the next page)

Content-Based Assessments

Skills Review | Project **2D** February Sales (continued)

d. Click cell **C5**. Type **=** and then click the **California Sales sheet tab**. In the **California Sales** worksheet, click cell **E9**, and then press [Enter]. Click cell **D5**. Type **=** and then click the **California Sales sheet tab**. Click cell **F9**, and then press [Enter].

e. By using the techniques you just practiced, in cells **C6** and **D6**, insert the total **In-Store Sales** and **Online Sales** data from the **Oregon Sales** worksheet.

f. Select the range **C5:E6**, and then click the **Sum** button to total the two rows. In cell **A7**, type **Total** and then select the range **C5:E7**. Click the **Sum** button to total the three columns. Select the nonadjacent ranges **C5:E5** and **C7:E7**, and then apply **Accounting Number Format** with zero decimal places. Select the range **C6:E6**, and then apply **Comma Style** with zero decimal places. Select the range **C7:E7**, and then apply the **Total** cell style. Select the range **A5:A7** and apply the **Heading 4** cell style.

g. Click cell **B5**. On the **Insert tab**, in the **Sparklines group**, click **Column**. In the **Create Sparklines** dialog box, with the insertion point blinking in the **Data Range** box, select the range **C5:D5** and then click **OK**.

h. Click cell **B6**, and then **Insert** a **Column Sparkline** for the range **C6:D6**. In the **Style group**, apply the second style in the second row—**Sparkline Style Accent 2, Darker 25%** to this sparkline.

4 Point to the **Summary sheet tab**, hold down the left mouse button to display a small black triangle, and drag to the left until the triangle and mouse pointer are

to the left of the **California Sales sheet tab**, and then release the left mouse button.

a. Be sure the **Summary** worksheet is the active sheet, point to its sheet tab, right-click, and then click **Select All Sheets** to display *[Group]* in the title bar. On the **Insert tab**, in the **Text group**, click the **Header & Footer** button. Display the **Footer** area, and then in the **left section**, insert the **File Name**. Center the worksheets **Horizontally** on the page, return to **Normal** view, and make cell **A1** active.

b. Display the **Document Panel**, and then add your name, your course name and section, and the keywords **February sales Close** the **Document Information Panel**.

c. **Save** your workbook. To submit your workbook electronically, follow the instructions provided by your instructor. To print your workbook, continue to Step d.

d. Display **Backstage** view, verify that the worksheets in your workbook are still grouped—*[Group]* displays in the title bar—and then on the left click **Print**. Under **Settings**, verify that **Print Active Sheets** displays. At the top of the screen, verify that the **Number of Copies** is **1**. Click the **Print** button.

e. If required by your instructor, print or create an electronic version of your worksheets with formulas displayed by using the instructions in Activity 1.16, and then **Close** Excel without saving so that you do not save the changes you made to print formulas.

End **You have completed Project 2D** ———————————

Content-Based Assessments

Apply **2A** skills from these Objectives:

- 1 Use the SUM, AVERAGE, MEDIAN, MIN, and MAX Functions
- 2 Move Data, Resolve Error Messages, and Rotate Text
- 3 Use COUNTIF and IF Functions and Apply Conditional Formatting
- 4 Use Date & Time Functions and Freeze Panes
- 5 Create, Sort, and Filter an Excel Table
- 6 Format and Print a Large Worksheet

Mastering Excel | Project **2E** Desserts

In the following Mastery project, you will edit a worksheet for Laura Morales, President, detailing the current inventory of desserts produced at the San Diego facility. Your completed worksheet will look similar to Figure 2.55.

Project Files

For Project 2E, you will need the following file:

e02E_Desserts

You will save your workbook as:

Lastname_Firstname_2E_Desserts

Project Results

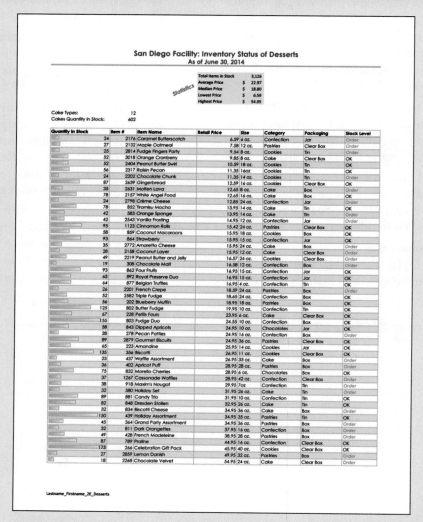

Figure 2.55

(Project 2E Desserts continues on the next page)

Mastering Excel | Project **2E** Desserts (continued)

1 **Start** Excel, from your student files, locate and open **e02E_Desserts**, and then **Save** the file in your **Excel Chapter 2** folder as **Lastname_Firstname_2E_Desserts**

2 In cell **B4**, calculate the **Total Items in Stock** by summing the **Quantity in Stock** data, and then apply **Comma Style** with zero decimal places to the result. In each cell in the range **B5:B8**, insert formulas to calculate the Average, Median, Lowest, and Highest retail prices, and then apply the **Accounting Number Format** to each result.

3 Move the range **A4:B8** to the range **D4:E8**, and then apply the **20% - Accent1** cell style. Widen **column D** to **130 pixels**. In cell **C6**, type **Statistics** select the range **C4:C8**, and then from the **Format Cells** dialog box, merge the selected cells. Change the text **Orientation** to **25 Degrees**, and then apply **Bold** and **Italic**. Change the **Font Size** to **14** and the **Font Color** to **Pink, Accent 1, Darker 25%**. Apply **Middle Align** and **Align Text Right**.

4 In cell **B10**, use the **COUNTIF** function to count the number of **Cake** items. In the **Packaging** column, **Replace All** occurrences of **Cellophane** with **Clear Box**

5 In cell **H14**, enter an **IF** function to determine the items that must be ordered. If the **Quantity in Stock** is less than **50** the **Value_if_true** is **Order** Otherwise the **Value_if_false** is **OK** Fill the formula down through cell **H65**. Apply **Conditional Formatting** to the **Stock Level** column so that cells that contain the text *Order* are formatted with **Bold Italic** and with a **Color** of **Blue, Accent 5**. Apply conditional formatting

to the **Quantity in Stock** column by applying a **Gradient Fill Orange Data Bar**.

6 Format the range **A13:H65** as a **Table** with headers, and apply the **Table Style Light 16** style. Sort the table from smallest to largest by **Retail Price**, and then filter on the **Category** column to display the **Cake** types. Display a **Total Row** in the table and then in cell **A66**, **Sum** the **Quantity in Stock** for the **Cake** items. Type the result in cell **B11**, and apply appropriate number formatting. Click in the table, and then on the **Design tab**, remove the total row from the table. Clear the **Category** filter and convert the table to a range.

7 Change the theme to **Composite**. Display the footer area, and insert the **File Name** in the **left section**. Center the worksheet **Horizontally**, and then use the **Scale to Fit** option to change the **Width** to **1 page**. Return to **Normal** view and make cell **A1** the active cell. In **Backstage** view, display the **Print Preview**, and then make any necessary corrections.

8 Add your name, your course name and section, and the keywords **desserts inventory, San Diego** to the Document Panel. **Save**, and then print or submit electronically as directed. If required by your instructor, print or create an electronic version of your worksheets with formulas displayed by using the instructions in Activity 1.16, and then **Close** Excel without saving so that you do not save the changes you made to print formulas.

End **You have completed Project 2E** ————————————————

Apply 2B skills from these Objectives:

7 Navigate a Workbook and Rename Worksheets

8 Enter Dates, Clear Contents, and Clear Formats

9 Copy and Paste by Using the Paste Options Gallery

10 Edit and Format Multiple Worksheets at the Same Time

11 Create a Summary Sheet with Column Sparklines

12 Format and Print Multiple Worksheets in a Workbook

Mastering Excel | Project 2F Compensation

In the following Mastery project, you will edit a workbook that summarizes the Laurales Herb and Spices salesperson compensation for the month of November. Your completed worksheet will look similar to Figure 2.56.

Project Files

For Project 2F, you will need the following file:

e02F_Compensation

You will save your workbook as:

Lastname_Firstname_2F_Compensation

Project Results

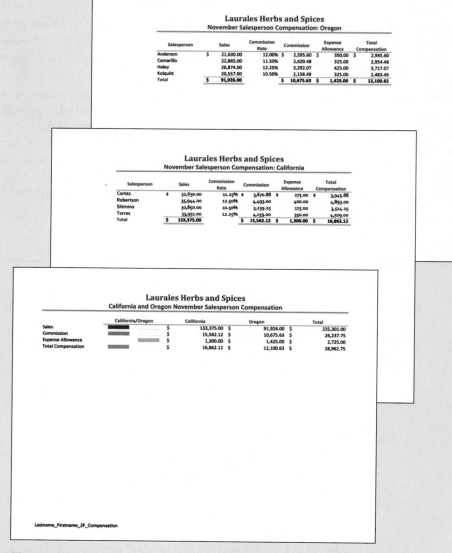

Figure 2.56

(Project 2F Compensation continues on the next page)

Content-Based Assessments

Mastering Excel | Project 2F Compensation (continued)

1 **Start** Excel, from your student files, open **e02F_Compensation**, and then save the file in your **Excel Chapter 2** folder as **Lastname_Firstname_2F_Compensation**

2 Rename **Sheet1** as **California** and change the **Tab Color** to **Green, Accent 1**. Rename **Sheet2** as **Oregon** and change the **Tab Color** to **Gold, Accent 3**.

3 Click the **California sheet tab** to make it the active sheet, and then group the worksheets. In cell **A1**, type **Laurales Herbs and Spices** and then **Merge & Center** the text across the range **A1:F1**. Apply the **Title** cell style. **Merge & Center** the text in cell **A2** across the range **A2:F2**, and then apply the **Heading 1** cell style.

4 With the sheets still grouped, in cell **D5** calculate **Commission** for *Cortez* by multiplying the **Sales** by the **Commission Rate**. Copy the formula down through cell **D8**. In cell **F5**, calculate **Total Compensation** by summing the **Commission** and **Expense Allowance** for *Cortez*. Copy the formula down through the cell **F8**.

5 In **row 9**, sum the **Sales, Commission, Expense Allowance**, and **Total Compensation** columns. Apply the **Accounting Number Format** with two decimal places to the appropriate cells in **row 5** and **row 9** (do not include the percentages). Apply the **Comma Style** with two decimal places to the appropriate cells in **rows 6:8** (do not include the percentages). Apply the **Total** cell style to the appropriate cells in the Total row.

6 Insert a new worksheet. Change the sheet name to **Summary** and then change the **Tab Color** to **Periwinkle, Accent 5**. Widen **columns A:E** to **165** pixels, and then move the **Summary** sheet so that it is the first sheet in the workbook. In cell **A1**, type **Laurales Herbs and Spices** **Merge & Center** the title across the range **A1:E1**, and then apply the **Title** cell style. In cell **A2**, type **California and Oregon November Salesperson Compensation** and then **Merge & Center** the text across the range **A2:E2**. Apply the **Heading 1** cell style.

7 In the range **A5:A8**, type the following row titles and then apply the **Heading 4** cell style:

Sales

Commission

Expense Allowance

Total Compensation

8 In the range **B4:E4**, type the following column titles, and then **Center** and apply the **Heading 3** cell style.

California/Oregon

California

Oregon

Total

9 In cell **C5**, enter a formula that references cell **B9** in the **California** worksheet so that the total sales for California displays in **C5**. Create similar formulas to enter the total **Commission, Expense Allowance** and **Total Compensation** for California in the range **C6:C8**. Using the same technique, enter formulas in the range **D5:D8** so that the **Oregon** totals display.

10 Sum the **Sales, Commission, Expense Allowance**, and **Total Compensation** rows.

11 In cell **B5**, insert a **Column Sparkline** for the range **C5:D5**. In cells **B6, B7**, and **B8**, insert **Column** sparklines for the appropriate ranges to compare California totals with Oregon totals. To the sparkline in **B6**, apply the second style in the third row—**Sparkline Style Accent 2, (no dark or light)**. In **B7** apply the third style in the third row—**Sparkline Style Accent 3, (no dark or light)**. In **B8** apply the fourth style in the third row—**Sparkline Style Accent 4, (no dark or light)**.

12 **Group** the three worksheets, and then insert a footer in the left section with the **File Name**. Center the worksheets **Horizontally** on the page, and then change the **Orientation** to **Landscape**. Return the document to **Normal** view.

13 Display the **Document Panel**. Add your name, your course name and section, and the keywords **November sales Save** your workbook, and then print or submit electronically as directed. If required by your instructor, print or create an electronic version of your worksheets with formulas displayed by using the instructions in Activity 1.16, and then **Close** Excel without saving so that you do not save the changes you made to print formulas.

End **You have completed Project 2F** ⎯⎯⎯⎯⎯⎯⎯⎯⎯⎯⎯⎯⎯⎯⎯

Apply **2A** and **2B** skills from these Objectives:

1. Use the SUM, AVERAGE, MEDIAN, MIN, and MAX Functions

2. Move Data, Resolve Error Messages, and Rotate Text

3. Use COUNTIF and IF Functions and Apply Conditional Formatting

4. Use Date & Time Functions and Freeze Panes

5. Create, Sort, and Filter an Excel Table

6. Format and Print a Large Worksheet

7. Navigate a Workbook and Rename Worksheets

8. Enter Dates, Clear Contents, and Clear Formats

9. Copy and Paste by Using the Paste Options Gallery

10. Edit and Format Multiple Worksheets at the Same Time

11. Create a Summary Sheet with Column Sparklines

12. Format and Print Multiple Worksheets in a Workbook

Mastering Excel | Project **2G** Inventory Summary

In the following Mastery project, you will edit a worksheet that summarizes the inventory status at the Petaluma production facility. Your completed workbook will look similar to Figure 2.57.

Project Files

For Project 2G, you will need the following file:

e02G_Inventory_Summary

You will save your workbook as:

Lastname_Firstname_2G_Inventory_Summary

Project Results

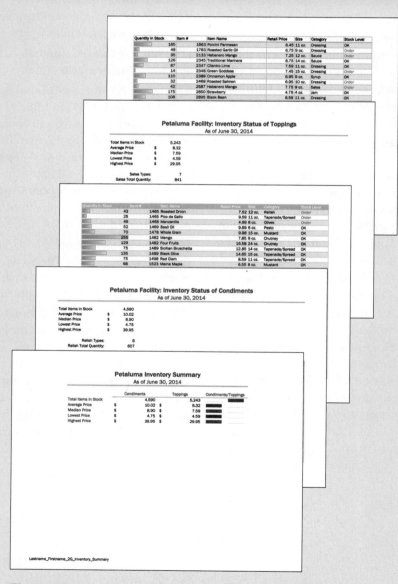

Figure 2.57

(Project 2G Inventory Summary continues on the next page)

Content-Based Assessments

Mastering Excel | Project 2G Inventory Summary (continued)

1 **Start** Excel. From your student files, open **e02G_Inventory_Summary**. Save the file in your **Excel Chapter 2** folder as **Lastname_Firstname_2G_Inventory_Summary**

2 Rename **Sheet1** as **Condiments** and **Sheet2** as **Toppings** Make the following calculations in each of the two worksheets *without* grouping the sheets:

- In cell **B4**, enter a formula to sum the **Quantity in Stock** data, and then apply **Comma Style** with zero decimal places to the result.

- In cells **B5:B8**, enter formulas to calculate the Average, Median, Lowest, and Highest retail prices, and then apply the **Accounting Number Format**.

3 In each of the two worksheets, make the following calculations *without* grouping the sheets:

- In cell **B10**, enter a COUNTIF function to determine how many different types of **Relish** products are in stock on the **Condiments** sheet and how many different types of **Salsa** products are in stock on the **Toppings** worksheet.

- In cell **G15**, enter an **IF** function to determine the items that must be ordered. If the **Quantity in Stock** is less than **50** the **Value_if_true** is **Order** Otherwise the **Value_if_false** is **OK** Fill the formula down through all the rows.

- Apply **Conditional Formatting** to the **Stock Level** column so that cells that contain the text *Order* are formatted with **Bold Italic** with a **Font Color** of **Gold, Accent 1, Darker 25%**. Apply **Gradient Fill Green Data Bars** to the **Quantity in Stock** column.

4 In the **Condiments** sheet, format the range **A14:G64** as a table with headers and apply **Table Style Medium 2**. Insert a **Total Row**, filter by **Category** for **Relish**, and then **Sum** the **Quantity in Stock** column. Record the result in cell **B11**.

5 Select the table, clear the filter, **Sort** the table on the **Item #** column from **Smallest to Largest**, remove the **Total Row**, and then convert the table to a range. On the **Page Layout tab**, set **Print Titles** so that **row 14** repeats at the top of each page.

6 In the **Toppings** sheet, format the range **A14:G61** as a table with headers and apply **Table Style Light 16**. Insert a **Total Row**, filter by **Category** for **Salsa**, and then **Sum** the **Quantity in Stock** column. Record the result in cell **B11**.

7 Select the table, clear the filter, **Sort** the table on the **Item #** column from **Smallest to Largest**, remove the **Total Row**, and then convert the table to a range.

8 On the **Page Layout tab**, set **Print Titles** so that **row 14** repeats at the top of each page, and then **Save** your workbook. **Group** the two worksheets. **Center** the worksheets **Horizontally**, and then use the **Scale to Fit** option to change the **Width** to **1 page**.

9 Insert a new worksheet. Change the sheet name to **Summary** and then widen **columns A:D** to **170** pixels. Move the **Summary** sheet so that it is the first sheet in the workbook. In cell **A1**, type **Petaluma Inventory Summary** **Merge & Center** the title across the range **A1:D1**, and then apply the **Title** cell style. In cell **A2**, type **As of June 30, 2014** and then **Merge & Center** the text across the range **A2:D2**. Apply the **Heading 1** cell style.

10 On the **Condiments sheet**, **Copy** the range **A4:A8**. Display the **Summary sheet** and **Paste** the selection to cell **A5**. Apply the **Heading 4** cell style to the selection. In the **Summary sheet**, in cell **B4**, type **Condiments** In cell **C4**, type **Toppings** and in cell **D4**, type **Condiments/Toppings Center** the column titles, and then apply the **Heading 3** cell style.

11 In cell **B5**, enter a formula that references cell **B4** in the **Condiments sheet** so that the **Condiments Total Items in Stock** displays in **B5**. Create similar formulas to enter the **Average Price**, **Median Price**, **Lowest Price**, and **Highest Price** from the **Condiments sheet** into the **Summary** sheet in the range **B6:B9**.

12 Enter formulas in the range **C5:C9** that reference the appropriate cells in the **Toppings** worksheet. To the range **B5:C5**, apply **Comma Style** with zero decimal places. In cells **D5**, **D6**, **D7**, **D8**, and **D9**, insert **Column** sparklines using the values in the *Condiments* and *Toppings* columns. Format each sparkline using the first five Sparkline styles in the first row.

13 Center the **Summary** worksheet **Horizontally** and change the **Orientation** to **Landscape**. **Group** the worksheets and insert a footer in the left section with the **File Name**. In **Normal** view, make cell **A1** the active cell. Display the **Document Panel**. Add your name, your course name and section, and the keywords **Petaluma inventory**

14 **Save** your workbook, and then print or submit electronically as directed. If required by your instructor, print or create an electronic version of your worksheets with formulas displayed by using the instructions in Activity 1.16, and then **Close** Excel without saving so that you do not save the changes you made to print formulas.

End **You have completed Project 2G**

GO! Fix It | Project 2H Confections

Project Files

For Project 2H, you will need the following file:

e02H_Confections

You will save your workbook as:

Lastname_Firstname_2H_Confections

In this project, you will correct a worksheet that contains the confection inventory for the month of June at the Laurales Herb and Spices Petaluma production facility. From the student files that accompany this textbook, open the file e02H_Confections, and then save the file in your chapter folder as **Lastname_Firstname_2H_Confections**

To complete the project, you must find and correct errors in formulas and formatting. View each formula in cells B4:B8 and edit as necessary. In addition to errors that you find, you should know:

- The table should be sorted smallest to largest by Item #.
- New stock should be ordered when the Quantity in Stock is less than 50, and the word *Order* should be formatted with bold, italic, in font color Red, Accent 3.
- The table should be converted to a range.
- Gradient fill red data bars should be applied to the Quantity in Stock column.

Insert the file name in the left section of the footer, center the worksheet horizontally, and repeat the table column titles on each page. Edit the document properties with your name, course and section, and the keywords **Petaluma, confections** Save your file, and then print or submit your worksheet electronically as directed by your instructor. If required by your instructor, print or create an electronic version of your worksheets with formulas displayed by using the instructions in Activity 1.16, and then Close Excel without saving so that you do not save the changes you made to print formulas.

End **You have completed Project 2H** _____

Content-Based Assessments

GO! Make It | Project 2I Salary Summary

Project Files

For Project 2I, you will need the following file:

    e02I_Salary_Summary

You will save your workbook as:

    Lastname_Firstname_2I_Salary_Summary

Open e02I_Salary_Summary and save the file in your Excel Chapter 2 folder as **Lastname_Firstname_2I_Salary_Summary** Edit the worksheet as shown in Figure 2.58. To calculate Commission for each salesperson, multiply the Sales by the Commission Rate, using absolute cell references as necessary. To determine the Bonus, construct an IF function where the Logical Test determines if Sales are greater than 21,500, the Value_if_true is 500, and the Value_if_false is 0. Calculate Total Compensation by adding the Commission and the Bonus for each salesperson. Determine the Sales and Compensation totals, averages, medians, and highest and lowest amounts. Insert a table, apply Table Medium Style 16, sort the table as shown in Figure 2.58, apply cell styles and number formatting as indicated, and convert the table to a range. Insert a footer with the file name in the left section, center the worksheet horizontally, and add your name, your course name and section, and the keywords **commission, sales** to the document properties. Print or submit electronically as directed by your instructor.

Project Results

Laurales Herbs and Spices
January Sales and Compensation

	Sales	Compensation
Total	$ 394,393.00	$ 64,658.95
Average	$ 23,199.59	$ 3,803.47
Median	$ 22,924.00	$ 3,938.60
Highest	$ 33,909.00	$ 5,586.35
Lowest	$ 12,320.00	$ 1,848.00

Commission Rate 15%

Name	Sales	Commission	Bonus	Total Compensation
Anderson	12,320	1,848	-	1,848
Antonetti	22,299	3,345	500	3,845
Belitti	12,523	1,878	-	1,878
Caprio	12,932	1,940	-	1,940
Chiu	33,909	5,086	500	5,586
Cloutier	30,550	4,583	500	5,083
Fernandez	21,345	3,202	-	3,202
Hernandez	22,045	3,307	500	3,807
Hutchins	31,309	4,696	500	5,196
Jackson	29,505	4,426	500	4,926
Johnson	25,340	3,801	500	4,301
Lee	13,500	2,025	-	2,025
Lin	32,950	4,943	500	5,443
Maya	23,950	3,593	500	4,093
Nguyen	22,924	3,439	500	3,939
Ochoa	25,900	3,885	500	4,385
Patel	21,092	3,164	-	3,164

Lastname_Firstname_2I_Salary Summary

Figure 2.58

End You have completed Project 2I

Content-Based Assessments

GO! Solve It | Project **2J** Toppings

Project Files

For Project 2J, you will need the following file:

e02J_Toppings

You will save your workbook as:

Lastname_Firstname_2J_Toppings

Open the file e02J_Toppings and save it as **Lastname_Firstname_2J_Toppings** Complete the worksheet by entering appropriate formulas in cells B5 and B6. In the Stock Level column, enter an IF function that determines whether the quantity in stock is greater than 65. If the Quantity in Stock is greater than 65, then the Stock Level should display the text **OK** Otherwise the Stock Level should display the text **Order** Insert a Table with a total row and apply an attractive table style. Sort the table by Item #, calculate the values for B7 and B8, and then clear all filters and remove the total row from the table. Convert the table to a range. Format the worksheet attractively, and apply appropriate Data Bars to the Quantity in Stock column and conditional formatting to the Stock Level column so that items that need to be ordered are easily identified. Include the file name in the footer, add appropriate properties, and submit as directed.

		Performance Level	
	Exemplary: You consistently applied the relevant skills	**Proficient:** You sometimes, but not always, applied the relevant skills	**Developing:** You rarely or never applied the relevant skills
Create formulas	All formulas are correct and are efficiently constructed.	Formulas are correct but not always constructed in the most efficient manner.	One or more formulas are missing or incorrect; or only numbers were entered.
Insert and format a table	Table was created and formatted properly.	Table was created but incorrect data was selected or the table was not formatted.	No table was created.
Format worksheet data attractively and appropriately	Formatting is attractive and appropriate.	Adequately formatted but difficult to read or unattractive.	Inadequate or no formatting.

Performance Element (vertical label)

End **You have completed Project 2J**

Content-Based Assessments

Apply a combination of the 2A and 2B skills.

GO! Solve It | Project 2K First Quarter Summary

Project Files

For Project 2K, you will need the following file:

e02K_First_Quarter

You will save your workbook as:

Lastname_Firstname_2K_First_Quarter

Open the file e02K_First_Quarter and save it as **Lastname_Firstname_2K_First_Quarter** This workbook contains two worksheets; one that includes California sales data by product and one that includes Oregon sales data by product. Complete the two worksheets by calculating totals by product and by month. Then calculate the Percent of Total by dividing the Product Total by the Monthly Total, using absolute cell references as necessary. Format the worksheets attractively with a title and subtitle, and apply appropriate financial formatting. Insert a new worksheet that summarizes the monthly totals by state. Enter the months as the column titles and the states as the row titles. Include a Product Total column and a column for sparklines titled **Jan./Feb./March** Format the Summary worksheet attractively with a title and subtitle, insert column sparklines that compare the months, and apply appropriate financial formatting. Include the file name in the footer, add appropriate document properties, and submit as directed.

Performance Level			
	Exemplary: You consistently applied the relevant skills	**Proficient:** You sometimes, but not always, applied the relevant skills	**Developing:** You rarely or never applied the relevant skills
Create formulas	All formulas are correct and are efficiently constructed.	Formulas are correct but not always constructed in the most efficient manner.	One or more formulas are missing or incorrect; or only numbers were entered.
Create Summary worksheet	Summary worksheet created properly.	Summary worksheet was created but the data, sparklines, or formulas were incorrect.	No Summary worksheet was created.
Format attractively and appropriately	Formatting is attractive and appropriate.	Adequately formatted but difficult to read or unattractive.	Inadequate or no formatting.

(Performance Element)

End You have completed Project 2K

Outcomes-Based Assessments

Rubric

The following outcomes-based assessments are *open-ended assessments*. That is, there is no specific correct result; your result will depend on your approach to the information provided. Make *Professional Quality* your goal. Use the following scoring rubric to guide you in *how* to approach the problem, and then to evaluate *how well* your approach solves the problem.

The *criteria*—Software Mastery, Content, Format and Layout, and Process—represent the knowledge and skills you have gained that you can apply to solving the problem. The *levels of performance*—Professional Quality, Approaching Professional Quality, or Needs Quality Improvements—help you and your instructor evaluate your result.

	Your completed project is of Professional Quality if you:	Your completed project is Approaching Professional Quality if you:	Your completed project Needs Quality Improvements if you:
1-Software Mastery	Choose and apply the most appropriate skills, tools, and features and identify efficient methods to solve the problem.	Choose and apply some appropriate skills, tools, and features, but not in the most efficient manner.	Choose inappropriate skills, tools, or features, or are inefficient in solving the problem.
2-Content	Construct a solution that is clear and well organized, contains content that is accurate, appropriate to the audience and purpose, and is complete. Provide a solution that contains no errors in spelling, grammar, or style.	Construct a solution in which some components are unclear, poorly organized, inconsistent, or incomplete. Misjudge the needs of the audience. Have some errors in spelling, grammar, or style, but the errors do not detract from comprehension.	Construct a solution that is unclear, incomplete, or poorly organized; contains some inaccurate or inappropriate content; and contains many errors in spelling, grammar, or style. Do not solve the problem.
3-Format and Layout	Format and arrange all elements to communicate information and ideas, clarify function, illustrate relationships, and indicate relative importance.	Apply appropriate format and layout features to some elements, but not others. Overuse features, causing minor distraction.	Apply format and layout that does not communicate information or ideas clearly. Do not use format and layout features to clarify function, illustrate relationships, or indicate relative importance. Use available features excessively, causing distraction.
4-Process	Use an organized approach that integrates planning, development, self-assessment, revision, and reflection.	Demonstrate an organized approach in some areas, but not others; or, use an insufficient process of organization throughout.	Do not use an organized approach to solve the problem.

Outcomes-Based Assessments

Apply a combination of the **2A** and **2B** skills.

GO! Think | Project **2L** Seasonings

Project Files

For Project 2L, you will need the following file:

> e02L_Seasonings

You will save your workbook as:

> Lastname_Firstname_2L_Seasonings

Laura Morales, President of Laurales Herbs and Spices, has requested a worksheet that summarizes the seasonings inventory data for the month of March. Laura would like the worksheet to include the total Quantity in Stock and Number of Items for each category of items and she would like the items to be sorted from lowest to highest retail price.

Edit the workbook to provide Laura with the information requested. Format the worksheet titles and data and include an appropriately formatted table so that the worksheet is professional and easy to read and understand. Insert a footer with the file name and add appropriate document properties. Save the file as **Lastname_Firstname_2L_Seasonings** and print or submit as directed by your instructor.

End You have completed Project 2L ————————————————

Apply a combination of the **2A** and **2B** skills.

GO! Think | Project **2M** Expense Summary

Project Files

For Project 2M, you will need the following file:

> e02M_Expense_Summary

You will save your workbook as:

> Lastname_Firstname_2M_Expense_Summary

Sara Lopez, Director of the San Diego production facility, has requested a summary analysis of the administrative expenses the facility incurred in the last fiscal year. Open e02M_Expense_Summary and then complete the calculation in the four worksheets containing the quarterly data. Summarize the information in a new worksheet that includes formulas referencing the totals for each expense category for each quarter. Sum the expenses to display the yearly expense by quarter and expense category. Format the worksheets in a manner that is professional and easy to read and understand. Insert a footer with the file name and add appropriate document properties. Save the file as **Lastname_Firstname_2M_Expense_Summary** and print or submit as directed by your instructor.

End You have completed Project 2M ————————————————

Outcomes-Based Assessments

Apply a combination of the 2A and 2B skills.

You and GO! | Project **2N** Annual Expenses

Project Files

For Project 2N, you will need the following file:

New blank Excel workbook

You will save your workbook as:

Lastname_Firstname_2N_Annual_Expenses

Develop a workbook that details the expenses you expect to incur during the current year. Create four worksheets, one for each quarter of the year and enter your expenses by month. For example, the Quarter 1 sheet will contain expense information for January, February, and March. Some of these expenses might include, but are not limited to, Mortgage, Rent, Utilities, Phone, Food, Entertainment, Tuition, Childcare, Clothing, and Insurance. Include monthly and quarterly totals for each category of expense. Insert a worksheet that summarizes the total expenses for each quarter. Format the worksheet by adjusting column width and wrapping text, and by applying appropriate financial number formatting and cell styles. Insert a footer with the file name and center the worksheet horizontally on the page. Save your file as **Lastname_Firstname_2N_ Annual_Expenses** and submit as directed.

End **You have completed Project 2N** ————————————————

Apply a combination of the 2A and 2B skills.

GO! Collaborate | Project **2O** Bell Orchid Hotels Group Running Case

This project relates to the Bell Orchid Hotels. Your instructor may assign this group case project to your class. If your instructor assigns this project, he or she will provide you with information and instructions to work as part of a group. The group will apply the skills gained thus far to help the Bell Orchid Hotels achieve their business goals.

End **You have completed Project 2O** ————————————————

Analyzing Data with Pie Charts, Line Charts, and What-If Analysis Tools

OUTCOMES

At the end of this chapter you will be able to:

OBJECTIVES

Mastering these objectives will enable you to:

PROJECT 3A
Present budget data in a pie chart.

1. Chart Data with a Pie Chart (p. 355)
2. Format a Pie Chart (p. 358)
3. Edit a Workbook and Update a Chart (p. 364)
4. Use Goal Seek to Perform What-If Analysis (p. 365)

PROJECT 3B
Make projections using what-if analysis and present projections in a line chart.

5. Design a Worksheet for What-If Analysis (p. 371)
6. Answer What-If Questions by Changing Values in a Worksheet (p. 378)
7. Chart Data with a Line Chart (p. 381)

Shutterstock

In This Chapter

In this chapter, you will work with two different types of commonly used charts that make it easy to visualize data. You will create a pie chart in a separate chart sheet to show how the parts of a budget contribute to a total budget. You will also practice using parentheses in a formula, calculate the percentage rate of an increase, answer what-if questions, and then chart data in a line chart to show the flow of data over time. In this chapter you will also practice formatting the axes in a line chart.

The projects in this chapter relate to **The City of Orange Blossom Beach**, a coastal city located between Fort Lauderdale and Miami. The city's access to major transportation provides both residents and businesses an opportunity to compete in the global marketplace. Each year the city welcomes a large number of tourists who enjoy the warm climate and beautiful beaches, and who embark on cruises from this major cruise port. The city encourages best environmental practices and partners with cities in other countries to promote sound government at the local level.

Project 3A Budget Pie Chart

Project Activities

In Activities 3.01 through 3.11, you will edit a worksheet for Lila Darius, City Manager, that projects expenses from the city's general fund for the next fiscal year, and then present the data in a pie chart. Your completed worksheet will look similar to Figure 3.1.

Project Files

For Project 3A, you will need the following file:

e03A_Fund_Expenses

You will save your workbook as:

Lastname_Firstname_3A_Fund_Expenses

Project Results

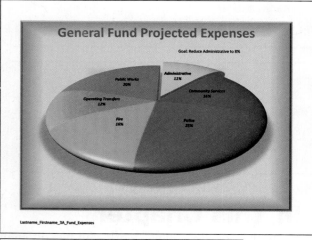

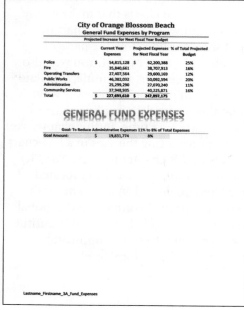

Figure 3.1
Project 3A Fund Expenses

Objective 1 | Chart Data with a Pie Chart

A *pie chart* shows the relationship of each part to a whole. The size of each pie slice is equal to its value compared to the total value of all the slices. The pie chart style charts data that is arranged in a single column or single row, and shows the size of items in a single data series proportional to the sum of the items. Whereas a column or bar chart can have two or more data series in the chart, a pie chart can have only one data series.

Consider using a pie chart when you have only one data series to plot, you do not have more than seven categories, and the categories represent parts of a total value.

Activity 3.01 | Creating a Pie Chart and a Chart Sheet

A *fund* is a sum of money set aside for a specific purpose. In a municipal government like the City of Orange Blossom Beach, the *general fund* is money set aside for the normal operating activities of the city, such as police, fire, and administering the everyday functions of the city.

1 **Start** Excel. From the student files that accompany this textbook, open **e03A_Fund_Expenses**. From **Backstage view**, display the **Save As** dialog box. Navigate to the location where you are storing projects for this chapter.

2 Create a new folder named **Excel Chapter 3** and open the new folder. In the **File name** box, type **Lastname_Firstname_3A_Fund_Expenses** Click **Save** or press Enter.

> The worksheet indicates the expenses for the current year and the projected expenses for the next fiscal year.

3 Click cell **D5**, and then type = to begin a formula.

4 Click cell **C5**, which is the first value that is part of the total Projected Expenses, to insert it into the formula. Type **/** to indicate division, and then click cell **C11**, which is the total Projected Expenses.

> Recall that to determine the percentage by which a value makes up a total, you must divide the value by the total. The result will be a percentage expressed as a decimal.

5 Press F4 to make the reference to the value in cell **C11** absolute, which will enable you to copy the formula. Compare your screen with Figure 3.2.

> Recall that an *absolute cell reference* refers to a cell by its fixed position in the worksheet. The reference to cell C5 is a *relative cell reference*, because when you copy the formula, you want the reference to change *relative* to its row.

> Recall also that dollar signs display to indicate that a cell reference is absolute.

Figure 3.2

Formula Bar displays formula

Cell C5 bordered in blue indicating it is part of an active formula

Reference to cell C11 with $ signs to indicate an absolute cell reference

Cell C11 selected as part of active formula

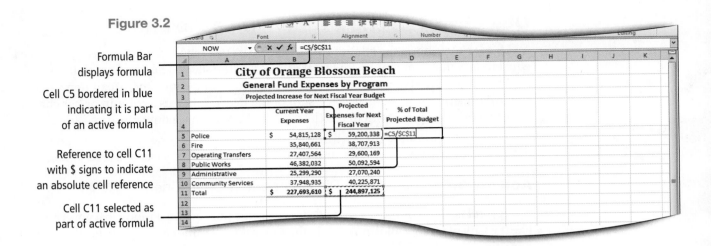

6 On the **Formula Bar**, click the **Enter** button ✔ to confirm the entry and to keep cell **D5** the active cell. Copy the formula down through cell **D10**, and then compare your screen with Figure 3.3.

Figure 3.3

Auto Fill Options button displays

Percentages, expressed as decimals

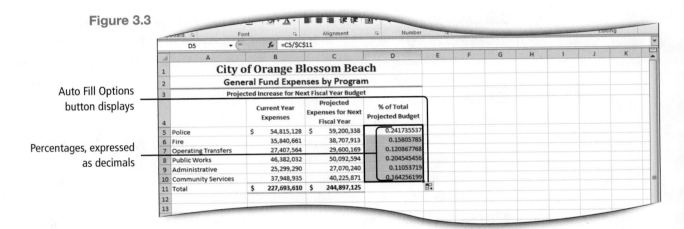

7 With the range **D5:D10** still selected, right-click over the selection, and then on the Mini toolbar, click the **Percent Style** button % and the **Center** button. Click cell **A1** to cancel the selection, and then **Save** your workbook. Compare your screen with Figure 3.4.

Figure 3.4

Percent of Total for each program calculated, expressed as percentages

8 Select the range **A5:A10**, hold down Ctrl, and then select the range **C5:C10** to select the nonadjacent ranges with the program names and the projected expense for each program.

> To create a pie chart, you must select two ranges. One range contains the labels for each slice of the pie chart, and the other range contains the values that add up to a total. The two ranges must have the same number of cells and the range with the values should *not* include the cell with the total.

> The program names (Police, Fire, and so on) are the category names and will identify the slices of the pie chart. Each projected expense is a ***data point***—a value that originates in a worksheet cell and that is represented in a chart by a ***data marker***. In a pie chart, each pie slice is a data marker. Together, the data points form the ***data series***—related data points represented by data markers—and determine the size of each pie slice.

9 With the nonadjacent ranges selected, click the **Insert tab**, and then in the **Charts group**, click **Pie**. Under **3-D Pie**, click the first chart—**Pie in 3-D**—to create the chart on your worksheet.

10 On the **Design tab**, at the right end of the Ribbon in the **Location group**, click the **Move Chart** button. In the **Move Chart** dialog box, click the **New sheet** option button.

11 In the **New sheet** box, replace the highlighted text *Chart1* by typing **Projected Expenses Chart** and then click **OK** to display the chart on a separate worksheet in your workbook. Compare your screen with Figure 3.5.

> The pie chart displays on a separate new sheet in your workbook, and a ***legend*** identifies the pie slices. Recall that a legend is a chart element that identifies the patterns or colors assigned to the categories in the chart.

> A ***chart sheet*** is a workbook sheet that contains only a chart; it is useful when you want to view a chart separately from the worksheet data. The sheet tab indicates *Projected Expenses Chart*.

Figure 3.5

Chart Tools active

Move Chart button on Design tab

Chart displays on a separate new worksheet

Legend identifies pie slices

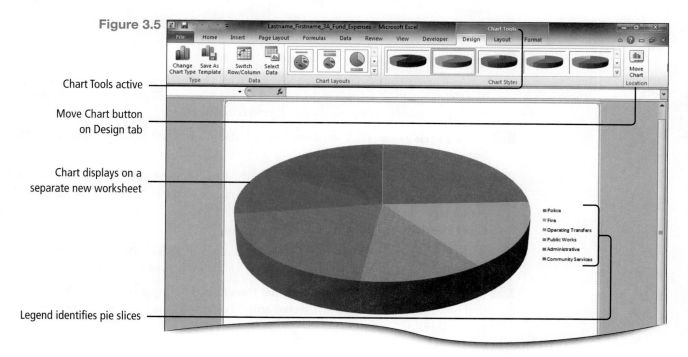

Objective 2 | Format a Pie Chart

Activity 3.02 | Applying Percentages to Labels in a Pie Chart

In your worksheet, for each expense, you calculated the percent of the total in column D. These percentages can also be calculated by the Chart feature and added to the pie slices as labels.

1 On the Ribbon under **Chart Tools**, click the **Layout tab**, and then in the **Labels group**, click the **Chart Title** button. On the displayed list, click **Above Chart**.

2 With the **Chart Title** box selected, watch the **Formula Bar** as you type **General Fund Projected Expenses** and then press [Enter] to create the new chart title in the box.

3 Point to the chart title text, right-click to display the Mini toolbar, and then change the **Font Size** to **36** and change the **Font Color** **A ▾** to **Olive Green, Accent 1, Darker 25%**—in the fifth column, the fifth color. Compare your screen with Figure 3.6.

Figure 3.6

Text displays in Formula Bar as you type

New chart title text entered and formatted

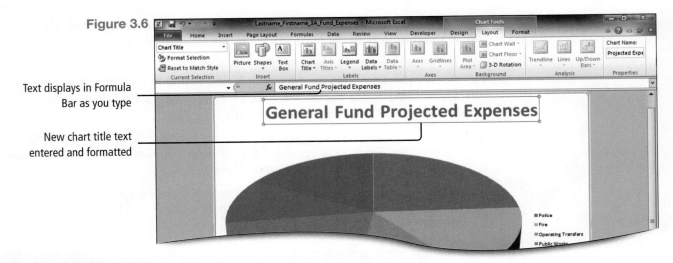

4 In the **Labels group**, click the **Legend** button, and then click **None**.

> The chart expands to fill the new space. In a pie chart, it is usually more effective to place the labels within, or close to, each pie slice. Because you will place the program names (the categories) on the pie slices, a legend is unnecessary.

5 In the **Labels group**, click the **Data Labels** button, and then at the bottom, click **More Data Label Options**.

6 In the **Format Data Labels** dialog box, on the left, be sure **Label Options** is selected. On the right, under **Label Contains**, click as necessary to select the **Category Name** and **Percentage** check boxes. *Clear* any other check boxes in this group. Under **Label Position**, click the **Center** option button.

> In the worksheet, you calculated the percent of the total in column D. Here, the percentage will be calculated by the Chart feature and added to the chart as a label.

7 In the lower right corner of the **Format Data Labels** dialog box, click **Close**, and notice that all of the data labels are selected and display both the category name and the percentage.

8 Point to any of the selected labels, right-click to display the Mini toolbar, and then change the **Font Size** to **11**, apply **Bold** [**B**], and apply **Italic** [*I*].

9 **Save** [💾] your workbook. Press [Esc] to deselect the labels, and then compare your screen with Figure 3.7.

Figure 3.7

Data labels on pie slices
replace legend; labels
include category name
and percentage; data
labels centered in slice,
11 pt font, bold and italic

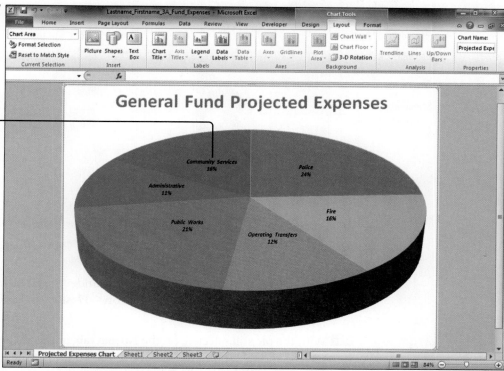

Activity 3.03 | Formatting a Pie Chart with 3-D

3-D, which is short for *three-dimensional*, refers to an image that appears to have all three spatial dimensions—length, width, and depth.

1 Click in any pie slice outside of the label to select the entire pie; notice that selection handles display on the outside corners of each slice.

2 Click the **Format tab**. In the **Shape Styles group**, click the **Shape Effects** button, point to **Bevel**, and then at the bottom of the gallery, click **3-D Options**.

3 In the **Format Data Series** dialog box, on the right, under **Bevel**, click the **Top** button. In the displayed gallery, under **Bevel**, point to the first button to display the ScreenTip *Circle*. Click the **Circle** button. Then click the **Bottom** button, and apply the **Circle** bevel.

> *Bevel* is a shape effect that uses shading and shadows to make the edges of a shape appear to be curved or angled.

4 In the four **Width** and **Height** spin boxes, type **512 pt** and then compare your screen with Figure 3.8.

Figure 3.8

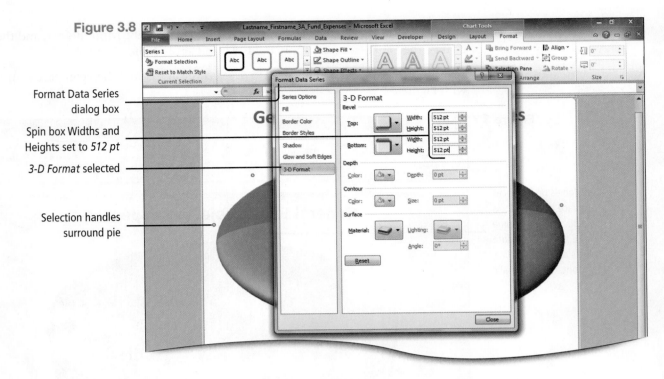

Format Data Series dialog box

Spin box Widths and Heights set to *512 pt*

3-D Format selected

Selection handles surround pie

5 In the lower portion of the dialog box, under **Surface**, click the **Material** button. Under **Standard**, click the third button—**Plastic**. In the lower right corner, click **Close**.

6 With the pie still selected, on the **Format tab**, in the **Shape Styles group**, click **Shape Effects**, and then point to **Shadow**. At the bottom of the displayed gallery, scroll if necessary, and then under **Perspective**, click the third button, which displays the ScreenTip *Below* to display a shadow below the pie chart. Click **Save** 🖫.

Activity 3.04 | Rotating a Pie Chart

The order in which the data series in pie charts are plotted in Excel is determined by the order of the data on the worksheet. To gain a different view of the chart, you can rotate the chart within the 360 degrees of the circle of the pie shape to present a different visual perspective of the chart.

1 Notice the position of the **Fire** and **Police** slices in the chart. Then, with the pie chart still selected—sizing handles surround the pie—point anywhere in the pie and right-click. On the displayed shortcut menu, click **Format Data Series**.

Another Way
Drag the slider to 100.

2 In the **Format Data Series** dialog box, on the left, be sure **Series Options** is selected. On the right, under **Angle of first slice**, click in the box and type **100** to rotate the chart 100 degrees to the right.

3 Close the **Format Data Series** dialog box. Click **Save** 🖫, and then compare your screen with Figure 3.9.

Rotating the chart can provide a better perspective to the chart. Here, rotating the chart in this manner emphasizes that the Fire and Police programs represent a significant portion of the total expenses.

Figure 3.9

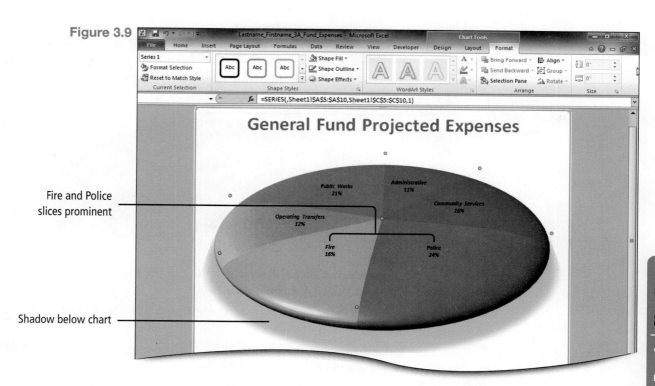

Fire and Police
slices prominent

Shadow below chart

Activity 3.05 | Exploding and Coloring a Pie Slice

You can pull out—***explode***—one or more slices of a pie chart to emphasize a specific slice or slices. Additionally, there is a different chart type you can select if you want *all* the slices to explode and emphasize all the individual slices of a pie chart—the exploded pie or exploded pie in 3-D chart type. The exploded pie chart type displays the contribution of *each* value to the total, while at the same time emphasizing individual values.

1 Press [Esc] to deselect all chart elements. Click any slice to select the entire pie, and then click the **Administrative** slice to select only that slice. Compare your screen with Figure 3.10.

Figure 3.10

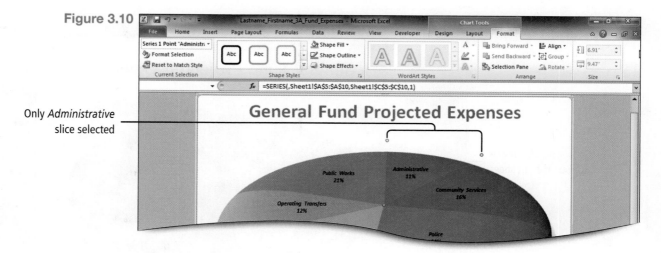

Only *Administrative*
slice selected

2 Point to the **Administrative** slice to display the [⬚] pointer, and then drag the slice slightly upward and away from the center of the pie, as shown in Figure 3.11, and then release the mouse button.

Figure 3.11

Move pointer

Dotted lines indicate
position of slice as
you move it

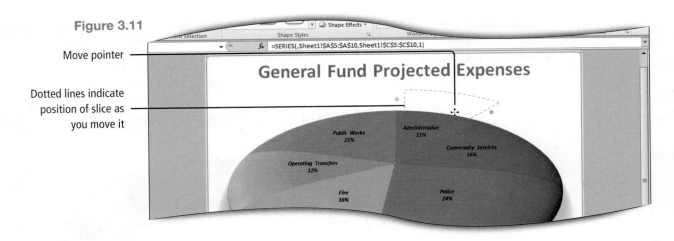

3 With the **Administrative** slice still selected, point to the slice and right-click, and then on the shortcut menu, click **Format Data Point**.

4 In the **Format Data Point** dialog box, on the left, click **Fill**. On the right, under **Fill**, click the **Solid fill** option button.

5 Click the **Color arrow**, and then under **Theme Colors**, in the seventh column, click the fourth color—**Gold, Accent 3, Lighter 40%**.

6 In the lower right corner of the **Format Data Point** dialog box, click the **Close** button.

Activity 3.06 │ Formatting the Chart Area

The entire chart and all of its elements comprise the *chart area*.

1 Point to the white area just inside the border of the chart to display the ScreenTip *Chart Area*. Click one time.

2 On the **Format tab**, in the **Shape Styles group**, click the **Shape Effects** button, point to **Bevel**, and then under **Bevel**, in the second row, click the third bevel—**Convex**.

3 Press Esc to deselect the chart element and view this effect—a convex beveled frame around your entire chart—and then compare your screen with Figure 3.12.

Figure 3.12

Convex beveled frame
surrounds chart sheet

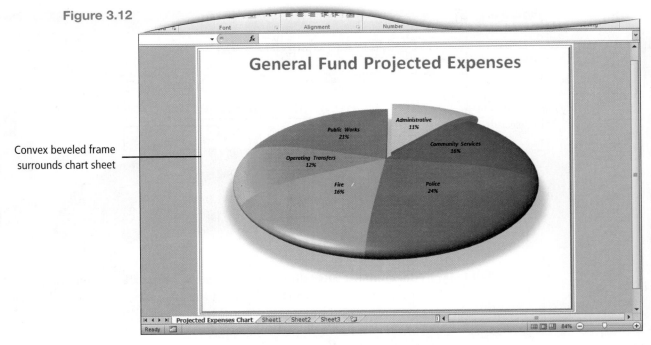

4 Point slightly inside the border of the chart to display the ScreenTip *Chart Area*, right-click, and then on the shortcut menu, click **Format Chart Area**.

5 In the **Format Chart Area** dialog box, on the left, be sure that **Fill** is selected. On the right, under **Fill**, click the **Gradient fill** option button.

6 Click the **Preset colors** arrow, and then in the second row, click the last preset, **Fog**. Click the **Type arrow**, and then click **Path**. Click the **Close** button.

7 Compare your screen with Figure 3.13, and then **Save** 🖫 your workbook.

Figure 3.13

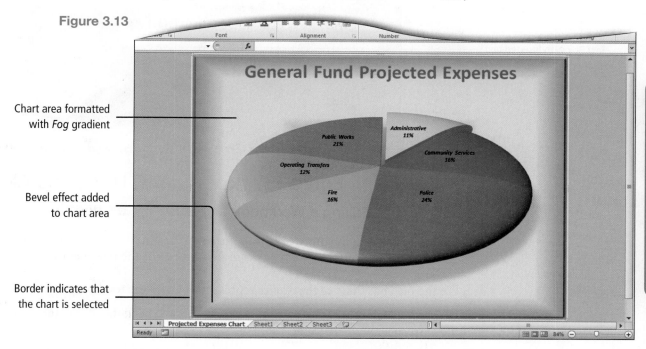

Chart area formatted with *Fog* gradient

Bevel effect added to chart area

Border indicates that the chart is selected

Activity 3.07 | Inserting a Text Box in a Chart

A *text box* is a movable, resizable container for text or graphics.

1 With the Chart Area still selected, click the **Layout tab**, and then in the **Insert group**, click the **Text Box** button, and then move the pointer into the chart area.

2 Position the displayed 🖳 pointer under the *c* in *Projected* and about midway between the title and the pie—above the *Administrative* slice. Hold down the left mouse button, and then drag down and to the right approximately as shown in Figure 3.14; your text box need not be precise.

Figure 3.14

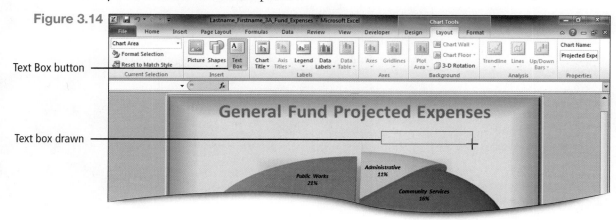

Text Box button

Text box drawn

3 With the insertion point blinking inside the text box, type **Goal: Reduce Administrative to 8%** Press Esc or click outside the chart area to deselect the chart element, and then compare your screen with Figure 3.15.

Figure 3.15

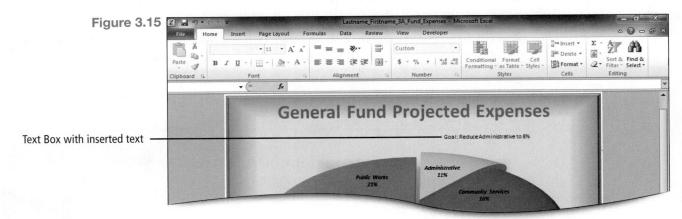

Text Box with inserted text

4 If necessary, select and then adjust or move your text box. **Save** 💾 your workbook.

Objective 3 | Edit a Workbook and Update a Chart

Activity 3.08 | Editing a Workbook and Updating a Chart

If you edit the data in your worksheet, the chart data markers—in this instance the pie slices—will adjust automatically to accurately represent the new values.

1 On the pie chart, notice that *Police* represents 24% of the total projected expenses.

2 In the sheet tab area at the bottom of the workbook, click the **Sheet1 tab** to redisplay the worksheet.

> **Another Way**
> Double-click the cell to position the insertion point in the cell and edit.

3 Click cell **C5**, and then in **Formula Bar**, change *59,200,338* to **62,200,388**

4 Press Enter, and notice that the total in cell **C11** recalculates to *$247,897,175* and the percentages in **column D** also recalculate.

5 Display the **Projected Expenses Chart** sheet. Notice that the pie slices adjust to show the recalculation—*Police* is now *25%* of the projected expenses. Click **Save** 💾, and then compare your screen with Figure 3.16.

Figure 3.16

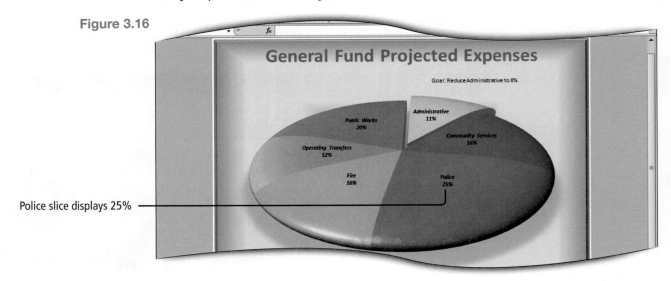

Police slice displays 25%

Activity 3.09 | Inserting WordArt in a Worksheet

WordArt is a gallery of text styles with which you can create decorative effects, such as shadowed or mirrored text. In an Excel worksheet, WordArt can be effective if you plan to display your worksheet in a PowerPoint presentation, or if readers will be viewing the worksheet data online.

1 In the sheet tab area at the bottom of the workbook, click the **Sheet1 tab** to redisplay the worksheet. Click the **Insert tab**, and then in the **Text group**, click the **WordArt** button.

2 In the WordArt gallery, in the last row, click the last style—**Fill – Olive Green, Accent 1, Metal Bevel, Reflection**.

The WordArt indicating *YOUR TEXT HERE* displays in the worksheet.

3 With the WordArt selected, type **general fund expenses** and then point anywhere on the dashed border surrounding the WordArt object. Click the dashed border one time to change it to a solid border, indicating that all of the text is selected.

4 On the **Home tab**, in the **Font group**, change the **Font Size** to **28**.

5 Point to the WordArt border to display the 🔲 pointer, and then drag to position the upper left corner of the WordArt approximately as shown in Figure 3.17. If necessary, hold down Ctrl and press any of the arrow keys on your keyboard to move the WordArt object into position in small increments. Click any cell to deselect the WordArt, and then click **Save** 🔲.

Figure 3.17

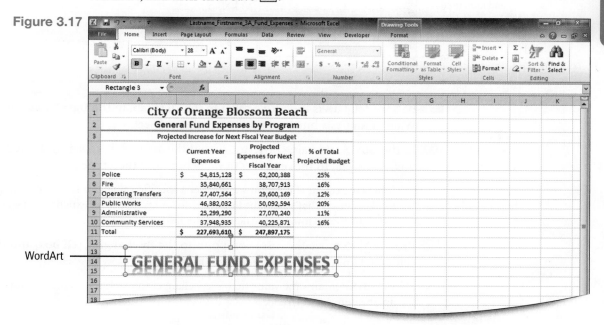

WordArt

Objective 4 | Use Goal Seek to Perform What-If Analysis

Activity 3.10 | Using Goal Seek to Perform What-If Analysis

The process of changing the values in cells to see how those changes affect the outcome of formulas in your worksheet is referred to as *what-if analysis*. A what-if analysis tool that is included with Excel is *Goal Seek*, which finds the input needed in one cell to arrive at the desired result in another cell.

1 In cell **A17**, type **Goal: To Reduce Administrative Expenses from 11% to 8% of Total Expenses** Merge and center the text across the range **A17:D17**, and then apply the **Heading 3** Cell Style.

2 In cell **A18**, type **Goal Amount:** and press Enter.

3 Select the range **C9:D9**, right-click over the selection, and then click **Copy**. Point to cell **B18**, right-click, and then under **Paste Options**, click the **Paste** button.

4 Press Esc to cancel the moving border, click cell **C18**, and then compare your screen with Figure 3.18.

Figure 3.18

Formula Bar indicates formula in C18

Cell C18 active

Heading entered and formatted

Row title entered

Pasted data

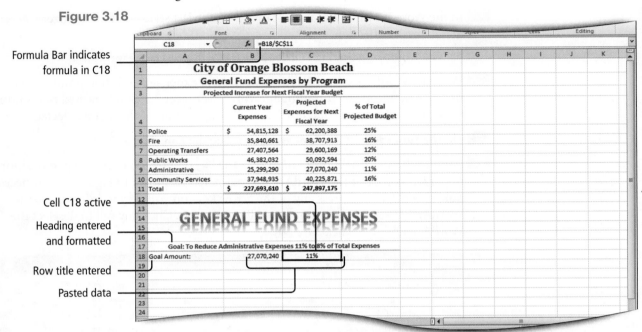

5 Be sure cell **C18** is the active cell. On the **Data tab**, in the **Data Tools group**, click the **What-If Analysis** button, and then click **Goal Seek**.

6 In the **Goal Seek** dialog box, notice that the active cell, **C18**, is indicated in the **Set cell** box. Press Tab to move to the **To value** box, and then type **8%**

C18 is the cell in which you want to set a specific value; 8% is the percentage of the total expenses that you want to budget for Administrative expenses. The Set cell box contains the formula that calculates the information you seek.

7 Press Tab to move the insertion point to the **By changing cell** box, and then click cell **B18**. Compare your screen with Figure 3.19.

Cell B18 contains the value that Excel changes to reach the goal. Excel formats this cell as an absolute cell reference.

Figure 3.19

Goal Seek dialog box

To value indicates 8%

By changing cell formatted as absolute cell reference

Set cell references a cell with a formula

Public Works	46,382,032	50,092,594	20%
9 Administrative	25,299,290		
10 Community Services	37,948,935		
11 Total	$ 227,693,610	$	

Goal Seek
Set cell: C18
To value: 8%
By changing cell: $B$18
OK   Cancel

GENERAL FUND

17 Goal: To Reduce Administrative Expenses 11% to 8% of Total Expenses
18 Goal Amount: 27,070,240   11%

8 Click **OK**. In the displayed **Goal Seek Status** dialog box, click **OK**.

9 Select the range **A18:C18**. From the **Home tab**, display the **Cell Styles** gallery. Under **Themed Cell Styles**, apply **20% - Accent3**. Click cell **B18**, and then from the **Cell Styles** gallery, at the bottom of the gallery under **Number Format**, apply the **Currency [0]** cell style.

10 Press `Ctrl` + `Home`, click **Save** 🖫, and then compare your screen with Figure 3.20.

> Excel calculates that the City must budget for *$19,831,774* in Administrative expenses in order for this item to become 8% of the total projected budget.

Figure 3.20

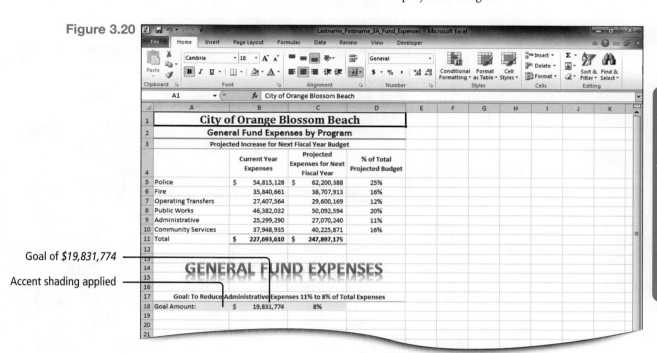

Goal of *$19,831,774*

Accent shading applied

Activity 3.11 | Preparing and Printing a Workbook with a Chart Sheet

Another Way

Right-click the sheet tab, click Rename, type, and press `Enter`.

1 With your worksheet displayed, in the sheet tab area, double-click *Sheet1* to select the text, and then type **Projected Expenses Data** and press `Enter`.

2 Select **Sheet2** and **Sheet3**, right-click over the selected tabs, and then click **Delete** to delete the unused sheets.

3 On the **Insert tab**, click **Header & Footer**. In the **Navigation group**, click the **Go to Footer** button, click in the **left section** above the word *Footer*, and then in the **Header & Footer Elements group**, click the **File Name** button.

4 Click in a cell above the footer to deselect the **Footer area** and view your file name. On the **Page Layout tab**, in the **Page Setup group**, click the **Margins** button, and then at the bottom click **Custom Margins**.

5 In the displayed **Page Setup** dialog box, under **Center on page**, select the **Horizontally** check box. Click **OK**, and then on the status bar, click the **Normal** button 🖿 to return to Normal view.

> Recall that after displaying worksheets in Page Layout View, dotted lines display to indicate the page breaks when you return to Normal view.

6 Press `Ctrl` + `Home` to move to the top of the worksheet.

7 Click the **Projected Expenses Chart** sheet tab to display the chart sheet. On the **Insert tab**, in the **Text group**, click **Header & Footer** to display the **Header/Footer tab** of the **Page Setup** dialog box.

8 In the center of the **Page Setup** dialog box, click **Custom Footer**. With the insertion point blinking in the **Left section**, in the row of buttons in the middle of the dialog box, locate and click the **Insert File Name** button 🗐. Compare your screen with Figure 3.21.

> Use the Page Setup dialog box in this manner to insert a footer on a chart sheet, which has no Page Layout view in which you can see the Header and Footer areas.

Figure 3.21

Page Setup dialog box —
Footer dialog box —
Insert File Name button —
Left section displays *&[File]* —

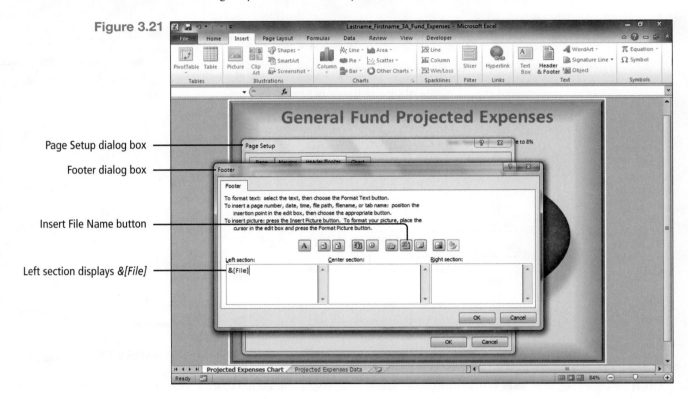

9 Click **OK** two times. Display **Backstage** view, on the right under the thumbnail, click **Properties**, and then click **Show Document Panel**. In the **Author** box, replace the existing text with your firstname and lastname. In the **Subject** box, type your course name and section number. In the **Keywords** box type **general fund, expenses, pie chart** and then **Close** ✕ the **Document Information Panel**.

10 Right-click either of the sheet tabs, and then click **Select All Sheets**. Verify that *[Group]* displays in the title bar.

> Recall that by selecting all sheets, you can view all of the workbook pages in Print Preview.

11 Press Ctrl + F2 to display the **Print Preview**. Examine the first page, and then at the bottom of the **Print Preview**, click the **Next Page** ▶ button to view the second page of your workbook.

> **Note** | Printing a Chart Sheet Uses More Toner
>
> Printing a chart that displays on a chart sheet will use more toner or ink than a small chart that is part of a worksheet. If you are printing your work, check with your instructor to verify whether or not you should print the chart sheet.

12 Click **Save** to redisplay the workbook. Print or submit electronically as directed by your instructor.

13 If you are directed to submit printed formulas, refer to Activity 1.16 in Project 1A to do so.

14 If you printed your formulas, be sure to redisplay the worksheet by clicking the Show Formulas button to turn it off. **Close** the workbook. If you are prompted to save changes, click **No** so that you do not save the changes to the worksheet that you used for printing formulas. **Close** Excel.

> **More Knowledge** | Setting the Default Number of Sheets in a New Workbook
>
> By default, the number of new worksheets in a new workbook is three, but you can change this default number. From Backstage view, display the Excel Options dialog box, click the General tab, and then under When creating new workbooks, change the number in the Include this many sheets box.

End **You have completed Project 3A** ————————————

Project 3B Growth Projection with Line Chart

Project Activities

In Activities 3.12 through 3.19, you will assist Lila Darius, City Manager, in creating a worksheet to estimate future population growth based on three possible growth rates. You will also create a line chart to display past population growth. Your resulting worksheet and chart will look similar to Figure 3.22.

Project Files

For Project 3B, you will need the following files:

e03B_Population_Growth
e03B_Beach

You will save your workbook as:

Lastname_Firstname_3B_Population_Growth

Project Results

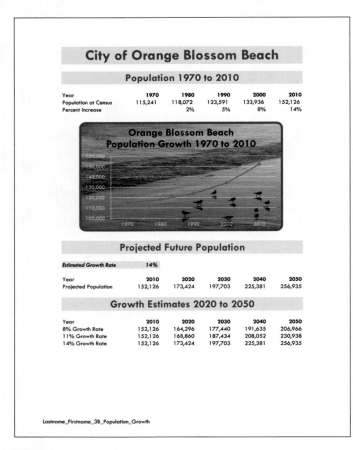

Figure 3.22
Project 3B Population Growth

Objective 5 | Design a Worksheet for What-If Analysis

Excel recalculates; if you change the value in a cell referenced in a formula, Excel automatically recalculates the result of the formula. Thus, you can change cell values to see *what* would happen *if* you tried different values. Recall that this process of changing the values in cells to see how those changes affect the outcome of formulas in your worksheet is referred to as what-if analysis.

Activity 3.12 | Using Parentheses in a Formula to Calculate a Percentage Rate of Increase

Ms. Darius has the city's population figures for the past five 10-year census periods. In each 10-year census period, the population has increased. In this activity, you will construct a formula to calculate the ***percentage rate of increase***—the percent by which one number increases over another number—for each 10-year census period since 1970. From this information, future population growth can be estimated.

1 **Start** Excel. From your student files, open the file **e03B_Population_Growth**. From **Backstage** view, display the **Save As** dialog box. Navigate to your **Excel Chapter 3** folder, in the **File name** box, name the file **Lastname_Firstname_3B_Population_Growth** and then click **Save** or press Enter.

2 Leave **row 4** blank, and then click cell **A5**. Type **Year** and then press Tab. In cell **B5**, type **1970** and then press Tab.

3 In cell **C5**, type **1980** and then press Tab. Select the range **B5:C5**, and then drag the fill handle to the right through cell **F5** to extend the series to 2010.

> By establishing a pattern of 10-year intervals with the first two cells, you can use the fill handle to continue the series. The AutoFill feature will do this for any pattern that you establish with two or more cells.

4 With the range **B5:F5** still selected, right-click over the selection, and then on the Mini toolbar, click **Bold** B . Compare your screen with Figure 3.23.

Figure 3.23

AutoFill used to fill 10-year periods to create column titles

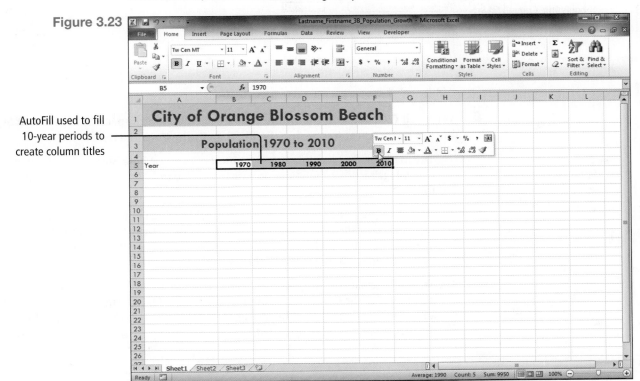

5 In cell **A6**, type **Population at Census** and press `Enter`. In cell **A7**, type **Percent Increase** and press `Enter`.

6 Click cell **B6**, and then beginning in cell **B6**, and pressing `Tab` to move across the row, enter the following values for the population in the years listed:

1970	1980	1990	2000	2010
115241	**118072**	**123591**	**133936**	**152126**

7 Select the range **B6:F6**, right-click, on the Mini toolbar, click **Comma Style** `,`, and then click **Decrease Decimal** two times.

8 Click cell **C7**. Being sure to include the parentheses, type **=(c6-b6)/b6** and then on the **Formula Bar**, click the **Enter** button ✓ to keep cell **C7** active; your result is *0.02456591* (or *0.02*). Compare your screen with Figure 3.24.

> Recall that as you type, a list of Excel functions that begin with the letter *C* and *B* may briefly display. This is **Formula AutoComplete**, an Excel feature which, after typing an = (equal sign) and the beginning letter or letters of a function name, displays a list of function names that match the typed letter(s). In this instance, the letters represent cell references, *not* the beginning of a function name.

Figure 3.24

Formula Bar displays formula

Formula result in cell C7 (yours may display *0.02*)

Values entered for population, Comma Style with no decimals applied

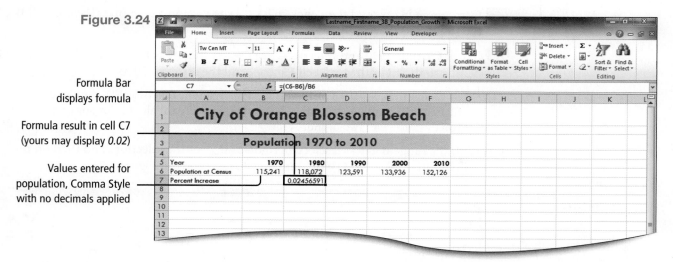

9 With cell **C7** active, on the **Home tab**, in the **Number group**, click the **Percent Style** button `%`, and then examine the formula in the **Formula Bar**.

> The mathematical formula *rate = amount of increase/base* is used to calculated the percentage rate of population increase from 1970 to 1980. The formula is applied as follows:

> First, determine the *amount of increase* by subtracting the *base*—the starting point represented by the 1970 population—from the 1980 population. Thus, the *amount of increase* = 118,072 – 115,241 or 2,831. Between 1970 and 1980, the population increased by 2,831 people. In the formula, this calculation is represented by *C6-B6*.

> Second, calculate the *rate*—what the amount of increase (2,831) represents as a percentage of the base (1970's population of 115,241). Determine this by dividing the amount of increase (2,831) by the base (115,241). Thus, 2,831 divided by 115,241 is equal to 0.02456591 or, when formatted as a percent, 2%.

10 In the **Formula Bar**, locate the parentheses enclosing *C6-B6*.

Excel follows a set of mathematical rules called the ***order of operations***, which has four basic parts:

- Expressions within parentheses are processed first.
- Exponentiation, if present, is performed before multiplication and division.
- Multiplication and division are performed before addition and subtraction.
- Consecutive operators with the same level of precedence are calculated from left to right.

11 Click cell **D7**, type = and then by typing, or using a combination of typing and clicking cells to reference them, construct a formula similar to the one in cell **C7** to calculate the rate of increase in population from 1980 to 1990. Compare your screen with Figure 3.25.

Recall that the first step is to determine the *amount of increase*—1990 population minus 1980 population—and then to write the calculation so that Excel performs this operation first; that is, place it in parentheses.

The second step is to divide the result of the calculation in parentheses by the *base*—the population for 1980.

Figure 3.25

Formula to calculate percent increase from 1980 to 1990

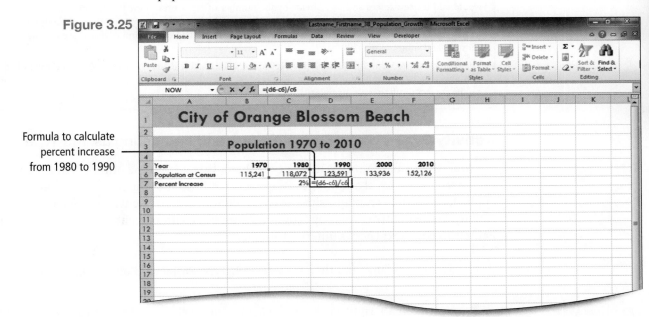

12 Press Enter; your result is *0.04674267* (or *0.05*). Format cell **D7** with the **Percent Style** %.

Your result is *5%*; Excel rounds up or down to format percentages.

13 With cell **D7** selected, drag the fill handle to the right through cell **F7**. Click any empty cell to cancel the selection, **Save** 🖫 your workbook, and then compare your screen with Figure 3.26.

Because this formula uses relative cell references—that is, for each year, the formula is the same but the values used are relative to the formula's location—you can copy the formula in this manner. For example, the result for 1990 uses the 1980 population as the base, the result for 2000 uses the 1990 population as the base, and the result for 2010 uses the 2000 population as the base.

The formula results show the percent of increase for each 10-year period between 1970 and 2010. You can see that in each 10-year period, the population has grown as much as 14%—from 2000 to 2010—and as little as 2%—from 1970 to 1980.

Figure 3.26

Auto Fill Options button displays

Percent increase calculated for the past 10-year census periods

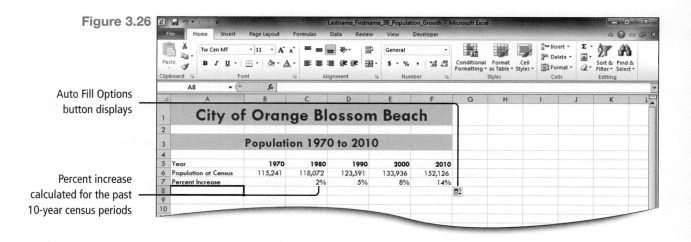

> **More Knowledge** | Use of Parentheses in a Formula
>
> When writing a formula in Excel, use parentheses to communicate the order in which the operations should occur. For example, to average three test scores of 100, 50, and 90 that you scored on three different tests, you would add the test scores and then divide by the number of test scores in the list. If you write this formula as =100+50+90/3, the result would be 180, because Excel would first divide 90 by 3 and then add 100+50+30. Excel would do so because the order of operations states that multiplication and division are calculated *before* addition and subtraction.
>
> The correct way to write this formula is =(100+50+90)/3. Excel will add the three values, and then divide the result by 3, or 240/3 resulting in a correct average of 80. Parentheses play an important role in ensuring that you get the correct result in your formulas.

Activity 3.13 | Using Format Painter and Formatting as You Type

You can format numbers as you type them. When you type numbers in a format that Excel recognizes, Excel automatically applies that format to the cell. Recall that once applied, cell formats remain with the cell, even if the cell contents are deleted. In this activity, you will format cells by typing the numbers with percent signs and use Format Painter to copy text (non-numeric) formats.

1 Leave **row 8** blank, and then click cell **A9**. Type **Projected Future Population** and then press Enter.

Another Way

On the Home tab, in the Clipboard group, click the Format Painter button.

2 Point to cell **A3**, right-click, on the Mini toolbar click the **Format Painter** button 🖌, and then click cell **A9**.

> The format of cell A3 is *painted*—applied to—cell A9, including the merging and centering of the text across the range A9:F9.

3 Leave **row 10** blank, and then click cell **A11**, type **Estimated Growth Rate** and then press Enter.

4 Leave **row 12** blank, and then click cell **A13**. Type **Year** and then in cell **A14**, type **Projected Population**

5 In cell **B13**, type **2010** and then press Tab. In cell **C13**, type **2020** and then press Tab.

6 Select the range **B13:C13**, and then drag the fill handle through cell **F13** to extend the pattern of years to *2050*. Apply **Bold** **B** to the selected range. Compare your screen with Figure 3.27.

Figure 3.27

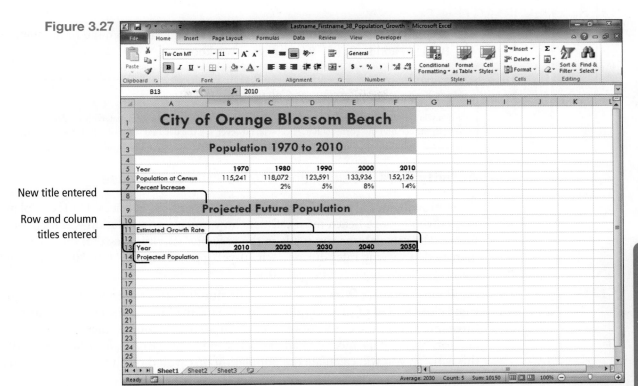

New title entered

Row and column titles entered

7 Click cell **B14**, and then on the **Home tab**, in the **Number group**, notice that the **Number Format** box indicates *General*. Then, being sure to type the comma, type **152,126**

8 On the **Formula Bar**, click the **Enter** button ✔ to keep the cell active, and then in the **Number group**, notice that the format changed to *Number*.

9 Press [Del], and then in the **Number group**, notice that the *Number* format is still indicated.

> Recall that deleting the contents of a cell does not delete the cell's formatting.

10 *Without* typing a comma, in cell **B14**, type **152126** and then press [Enter].

> The comma displays even though you did not type it. When you type a number and include a formatting symbol such as a comma or dollar sign, Excel applies the format to the cell. Thus, if you delete the contents of the cell and type in the cell again, the format you established remains applied to the cell. This is referred to as *format as you type*.

11 Examine the format of the value in cell **B14**, and then compare it to the format in cell **B6** where you used the **Comma Style** button to format the cell. Notice that the number in cell **B14** is flush with the right edge of the cell, but the number in cell **B6** leaves a small amount of space on the right edge.

> When you type commas as you enter numbers, Excel applies the *Number* format, which does *not* leave a space at the right of the number for a closing parenthesis in the event of a negative number. This is different from the format that is applied when you use the *Comma Style* button on the Ribbon or Mini toolbar, as you did for the numbers entered in row 6. Recall that the Comma Style format applied from either the Ribbon or the Mini toolbar leaves space on the right for a closing parenthesis in the event of a negative number.

12 In cell **B11**, type **8%** Select the range **A11:B11**, and then from the Mini toolbar, apply **Bold** `B` and **Italic** `I`. **Save** `💾` your workbook.

> **More Knowledge | Percentage Calculations**
>
> When you type a percentage into a cell—for example *8%*—the percentage format, without decimal points, displays in both the cell and the Formula Bar. Excel will, however, use the decimal value of *0.08* for actual calculations.

Activity 3.14 | Calculating a Value After an Increase

A growing population results in increased use of city services. Thus, city planners in Orange Blossom Beach must estimate how much the population will increase in the future. The calculations you made in the previous activity show that the population has increased at varying rates during each 10-year period from 1970 to 2010, ranging from a low of 2% to a high of 14% per 10-year census period.

Population data from the state and surrounding areas suggests that future growth will trend close to that of the recent past. To plan for the future, Ms. Darius wants to prepare three forecasts of the city's population based on the percentage increases in 2000, in 2010, and for a percentage increase halfway between the two; that is, for 8%, 11%, and 14%. In this activity, you will calculate the population that would result from an 8% increase.

1 Click cell **C14**. Type **=b14*(100%+b11)** and then on the **Formula Bar**, click the **Enter** `✔` button to display a result of *164296.08*. Compare your screen with Figure 3.28.

This formula calculates what the population will be in the year 2020 assuming an increase of 8% over 2010's population. Use the mathematical formula *value after increase = base × percent for new value* to calculate a value after an increase as follows:

First, establish the *percent for new value*. The **percent for new value = base percent + percent of increase**. The *base percent* of 100% represents the base population and the *percent of increase* in this instance is 8%. Thus, the population will equal 100% of the base year plus 8% of the base year. This can be expressed as 108% or 1.08. In this formula, you will use 100% + the rate in cell B11, which is 8%, to equal 108%.

Second, enter a reference to the cell that contains the *base*—the population in 2010. The base value resides in cell B14—*152,126*.

Third, calculate the *value after increase*. Because in each future 10-year period the increase will be based on 8%—an absolute value located in cell B11—this cell reference can be formatted as absolute by typing dollar signs.

Figure 3.28

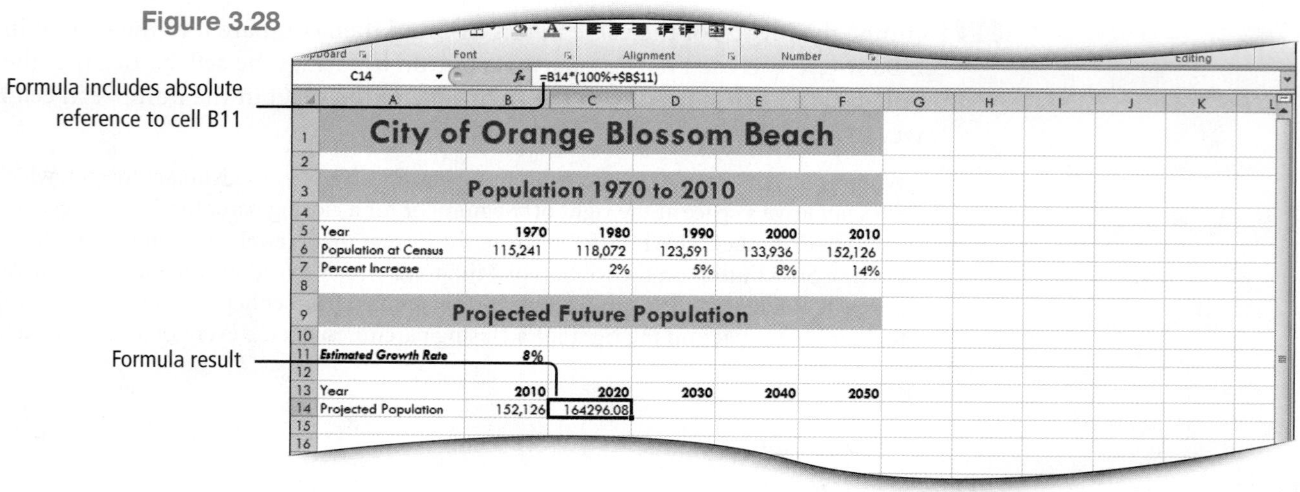

Formula includes absolute reference to cell B11

Formula result

C14		*fx*	=B14*(100%+$B$11)								
	A	B	C	D	E	F	G	H	I	J	K
1	**City of Orange Blossom Beach**										
2											
3	**Population 1970 to 2010**										
4											
5	Year	1970	1980	1990	2000	2010					
6	Population at Census	115,241	118,072	123,591	133,936	152,126					
7	Percent Increase		2%	5%	8%	14%					
8											
9	**Projected Future Population**										
10											
11	*Estimated Growth Rate*	*8%*									
12											
13	Year	2010	2020	2030	2040	2050					
14	Projected Population	152,126	164296.08								
15											
16											

2 With cell **C14** as the active cell, drag the fill handle to copy the formula to the range **D14:F14**.

3 Point to cell **B14**, right-click, click the **Format Painter** 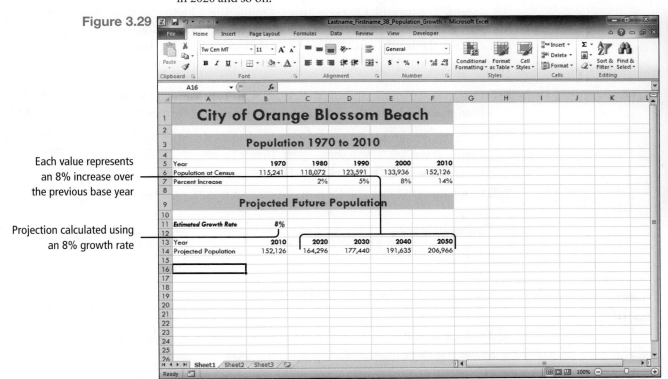 button, and then select the range **C14:F14**. Click an empty cell to cancel the selection, click **Save** 🖫 and then compare your screen with Figure 3.29.

> This formula uses a relative cell address—B14—for the *base*; the population in the previous 10-year period is used in each of the formulas in cells D14:F14 as the *base* value. Because the reference to the *percent of increase* in cell B11 is an absolute reference, each *value after increase* is calculated with the value from cell B11.
>
> The population projected for 2020—*164,296*—is an increase of 8% over the population in 2010. The projected population in 2030—*177,440*—is an increase of 8% over the population in 2020 and so on.

Figure 3.29

Each value represents an 8% increase over the previous base year

Projection calculated using an 8% growth rate

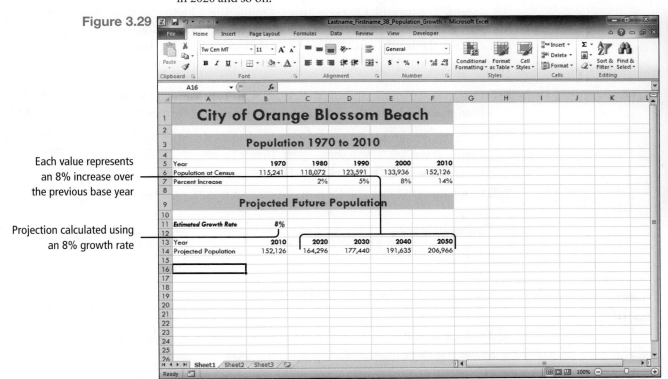

More Knowledge | Percent Increase or Decrease

The basic formula for calculating an increase or decrease can be done in two parts. First determine the percent by which the base value will be increased or decreased, and then add or subtract the results to the base. The formula can be simplified by using (1+amount of increase) or (1–amount of decrease), where 1, rather than 100%, represents the whole. Thus, the formula used in Step 1 of Activity 3.14 could also be written =b14*(1+b11), or =(b14*b11)+b14.

Objective 6 | Answer What-If Questions by Changing Values in a Worksheet

If a formula depends on the value in a cell, you can see what effect it will have if you change the value in that cell. Then, you can copy the value computed by the formula and paste it into another part of the worksheet where you can be compare it to other values.

Activity 3.15 | Answering What-If Questions and Using Paste Special

A growth rate of 8% in each 10-year period will result in a population of almost 207,000 people by 2050. The city planners will likely ask: *What if* the population grows at the highest rate (14%)? *What if* the population grows at a rate that is halfway between the 2000 and 2010 rates (11%)?

Because the formulas are constructed to use the growth rate displayed in cell B11, Ms. Darius can answer these questions quickly by entering different percentages into that cell. To keep the results of each set of calculations so they can be compared, you will paste the results of each what-if question into another area of the worksheet.

1 Leave **row 15** blank, and then click cell **A16**. Type **Growth Estimates 2020 to 2050** and then press Enter. Use **Format Painter** 🖌 to copy the format from cell **A9** to cell **A16**.

2 Select the range **A11:B11**, right-click to display the Mini toolbar, click the **Fill Color button arrow** 🎨▾, and then under **Theme Colors**, in the first column, click the third color—**White, Background 1, Darker 15%**.

3 Leave **row 17** blank, and then in the range **A18:A21**, type the following row titles:

Year

8% Growth Rate

11% Growth Rate

14% Growth Rate

Another Way

Press Ctrl + C; or, on the Home tab, in the Clipboard group, click the Copy button.

4 Select the range **B13:F13**, right-click over the selection, and then on the shortcut menu, click **Copy**.

5 Point to cell **B18,** right-click, and then on the shortcut menu, under **Paste Options**, click the **Paste** button 📋.

Recall that when pasting a group of copied cells to a target range, you need only point to or select the first cell of the range.

6 Select and **Copy** the range **B14:F14**, and then **Paste** it beginning in cell **B19**.

7 Click cell **C19**. On the **Formula Bar**, notice that the *formula* was pasted into the cell, as shown in Figure 3.30.

> This is *not* the desired result. The actual *calculated values*—not the formulas—are needed in the range.

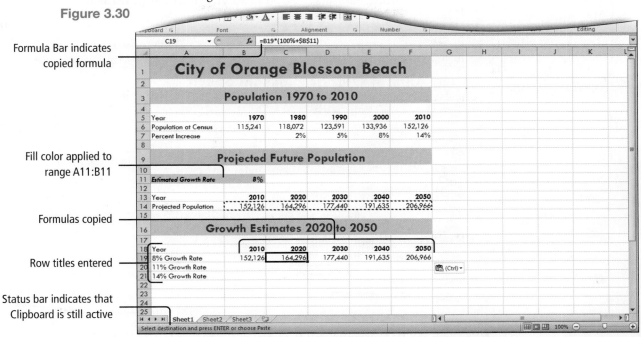

Figure 3.30

Formula Bar indicates copied formula

Fill color applied to range A11:B11

Formulas copied

Row titles entered

Status bar indicates that Clipboard is still active

8 On the Quick Access Toolbar, click the **Undo** button. With the range **B14:F14** still copied to the Clipboard—as indicated by the message in the status bar and the moving border—point to cell **B19**, and then right-click to display the shortcut menu.

9 Under **Paste Options**, point to **Paste Special** to display another gallery, and then under **Paste Values**, point to the **Values & Number Formatting** button to display the ScreenTip as shown in Figure 3.31.

> The ScreenTip *Values & Number Formatting (A)* indicates that you can paste the *calculated values* that result from the calculation of formulas along with the formatting applied to the copied cells. *(A)* is the keyboard shortcut for this command.

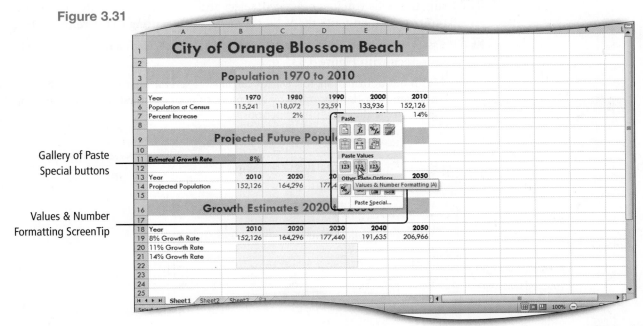

Figure 3.31

Gallery of Paste Special buttons

Values & Number Formatting ScreenTip

10 Click the **Values & Number Formatting** button 📋, click cell **C19** and notice on the **Formula Bar** that the cell contains a *value*, not a formula. Press Esc to cancel the moving border. Compare your screen with Figure 3.32.

> The calculated estimates based on an 8% growth rate are pasted along with their formatting.

Figure 3.32

Formula Bar indicates the value

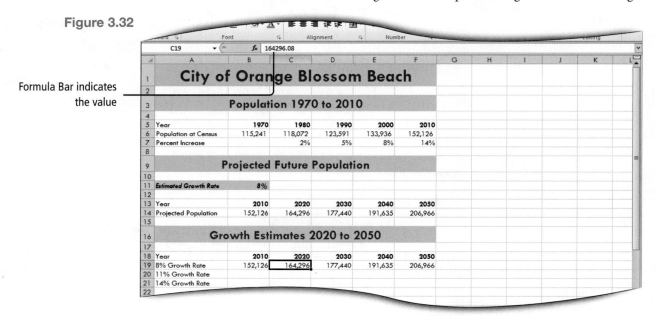

11 Click cell **B11**. Type **11** and then watch the values in **C14:F14** *recalculate* as, on the **Formula Bar**, you click the **Enter** button ✓.

> The value *11%* is halfway between 8% and 14%—the growth rates from the two most recent 10-year periods.

12 Select and **Copy** the new values in the range **B14:F14**. Point to cell **B20**, right-click, and then on the shortcut menu, point to **Paste Special**. Under **Paste Values**, click the **Values & Number Formatting** button 📋.

13 In cell **B11**, change the percentage by typing **14** and then press Enter. Notice that the projected values in **C14:F14** recalculate.

14 Using the skills you just practiced, select and copy the recalculated values in the range **B14:F14**, and then paste the **Values & Number Formatting** to the range **B21:F21**.

15 Press Esc to cancel the moving border, click cell **A1**, click **Save** 💾, and then compare your screen with Figure 3.33.

> With this information, Ms. Darius can answer several what-if questions about the future population of the city and provide a range of population estimates based on the rates of growth over the past 10-year periods.

Figure 3.33

Values copied for each what-if question

Objective 7 | Chart Data with a Line Chart

A *line chart* displays trends over time. Time is displayed along the bottom axis and the data point values connect with a line. The curve and direction of the line makes trends obvious to the reader.

Whereas the columns in a column chart and the pie slices in a pie chart emphasize the distinct values of each data point, the line in a line chart emphasizes the flow from one data point value to the next.

Activity 3.16 | Inserting Multiple Rows and Creating a Line Chart

So that city council members can see how the population has increased over the past five census periods, in this activity, you will chart the actual population figures from 1970 to 2010 in a line chart.

1 In the **row header area**, point to **row 8** to display the ➡ pointer, and then drag down to select **rows 8:24**. Right-click over the selection, and then click **Insert** to insert the same number of blank rows as you selected. Compare your screen with Figure 3.34.

Use this technique to insert multiple rows quickly.

Figure 3.34

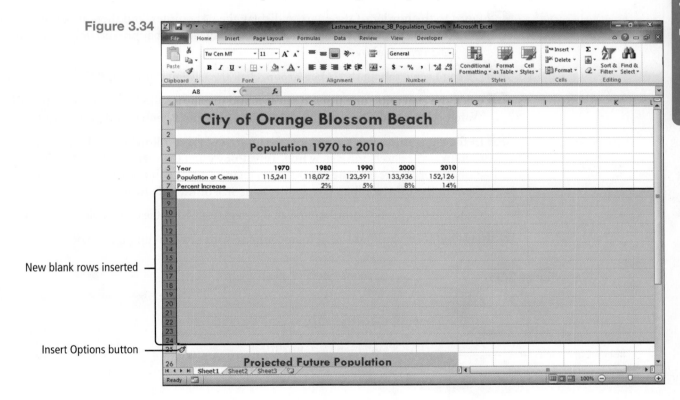

New blank rows inserted

Insert Options button

2 Near **row 25**, click the **Insert Options** button, and then click the **Clear Formatting** option button to clear any formatting from these rows.

You will use this blank area in which to position your line chart.

3 Select the range **A6:F6**. On the **Insert tab**, in the **Charts group**, click the **Line** button.

4 In the displayed gallery of line charts, in the second row, point to the first chart type to display the ScreenTip *Line with Markers*. Compare your screen with Figure 3.35.

Figure 3.35

Line button in Charts group

Line with Markers chart type

Data selected for charting

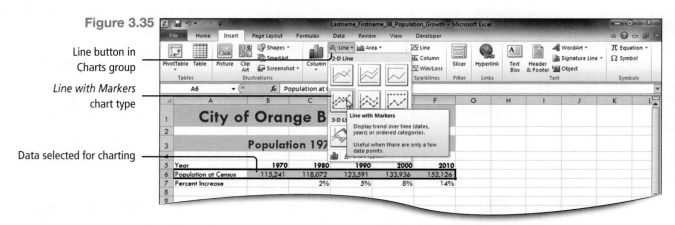

5 Click the **Line with Markers** chart type to create the chart as an embedded chart in the worksheet.

6 Point to the border of the chart to display the 🕇 pointer, and then drag the chart so that its upper left corner is positioned in cell **A9**, aligned approximately under the *t* in the word *Percent* above.

7 On the **Layout tab**, in the **Labels group**, click the **Legend** button, and then click **None**.

8 Click the chart title one time to select it and display a solid border around the title. Watch the **Formula Bar** as you type **Orange Blossom Beach** and then press Enter.

9 In the chart title, click to position the insertion point following the *h* in *Beach*, and then press Enter to begin a new line. Type **Population Growth 1970 to 2010** Click the dashed border around the chart title to change it to a solid border, right-click, and then on the Mini toolbar, change the **Font Size** of the title to **20**.

Recall that a solid border around an object indicates that the entire object is selected.

10 **Save** 💾 your workbook, and then compare your screen with Figure 3.36.

Figure 3.36

Line with Markers chart inserted, upper left corner aligned in cell A9

Chart title on two lines, 20 pt font size

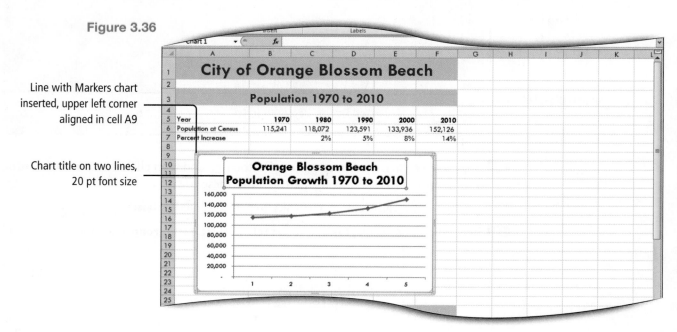

Activity 3.17 | Formatting Axes in a Line Chart

An *axis* is a line that serves as a frame of reference for measurement; it borders the chart *plot area*. The plot area is the area bounded by the axes, including all the data series. Recall that the area along the bottom of a chart that identifies the categories of data is referred to as the *category axis* or the *x-axis*. Recall also that the area along the left side of a chart that shows the range of numbers for the data points is referred to as the *value axis* or the *y-axis*.

In this activity, you will change the category axis to include the names of the 10-year census periods and adjust the numeric scale of the value axis.

> **Another Way**
>
> At the bottom of the chart, point to any of the numbers 1 through 5 to display the ScreenTip *Horizontal (Category) Axis*. Right-click, and then from the shortcut menu, click Select Data.

1 Be sure the chart is still selected—a pale frame surrounds the chart area. Click the **Design tab**, and then in the **Data group**, click the **Select Data** button.

2 On the right side of the displayed **Select Data Source** dialog box, under **Horizontal (Category) Axis Labels**, locate the **Edit** button, as shown in Figure 3.37.

Figure 3.37

Select Data Source dialog box

Edit button to edit labels on the category axis

Category axis requires labels to identify each 10-year period

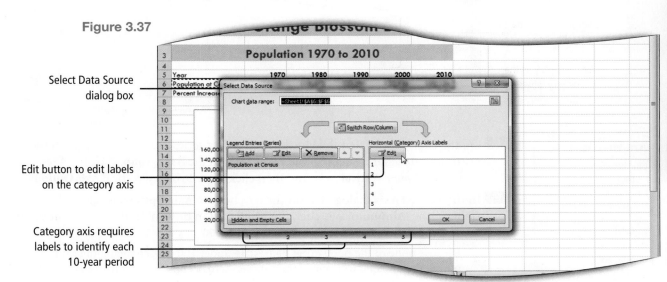

3 In the right column, click the **Edit** button. If necessary, drag the title bar of the **Axis Labels** dialog box to the right of the chart so that it is not blocking your view of the data, and then select the years in the range **B5:F5**. Compare your screen with Figure 3.38.

Figure 3.38

Range of years surrounded by moving border

Axis Labels dialog box

Range indicated with absolute references

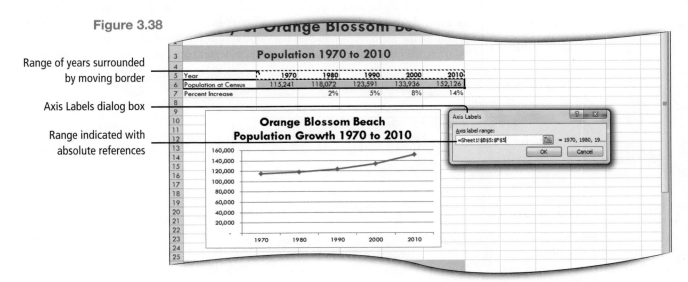

4 In the **Axis Labels** dialog box, click **OK**, and notice that in the right column of the **Select Data Source** dialog box, the years display as the category labels. Click **OK** to close the **Select Data Source** dialog box. Compare your screen with Figure 3.39.

Figure 3.39

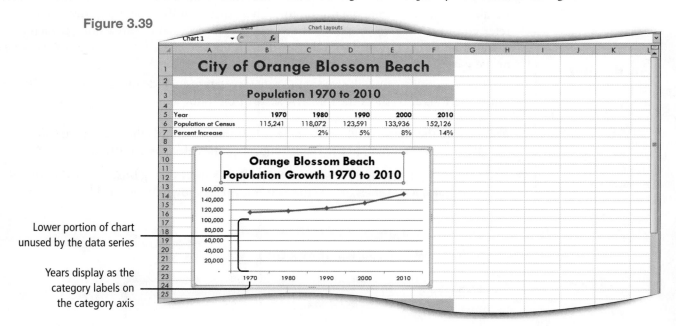

Lower portion of chart unused by the data series

Years display as the category labels on the category axis

Another Way

On the left side of the chart, point to any of the numbers to display the ScreenTip *Vertical (Value) Axis*, and then right-click. From the shortcut menu, click Format Axis.

5 On the chart, notice that the blue line—the data series—does not display in the lower portion of the chart. Then, on the **Layout tab**, in the **Axes group**, click the **Axes** button. Point to **Primary Vertical Axis**, and then click **More Primary Vertical Axis Options**.

6 In the **Format Axis** dialog box, on the left, be sure **Axis Options** is selected. On the right, in the **Minimum** row, click the **Fixed** option button. In the box to the right, select the existing text *0.0*, and then type **100000**

> Because none of the population figures are under 100,000, changing the Minimum number to 100,000 will enable the data series to occupy more of the plot area.

7 In the **Major unit** row, click the **Fixed** option button, select the text in the box to the right *20000.0*, and then type **10000** In the lower right corner, click **Close**. **Save** 🔲 your workbook, and then compare your screen with Figure 3.40.

> The *Major unit* value determines the spacing between *tick marks* and thus between the gridlines in the plot area. Tick marks are the short lines that display on an axis at regular intervals. By default, Excel started the values at zero and increased in increments of 20,000. By setting the Minimum value on the value axis to 100,000 and changing the Major unit from 20,000 to 10,000, the line chart shows a clearer trend in the population growth.

Figure 3.40

Gridlines

Value axis still selected

Tick marks on value axis

Values increase in increments of 10,000 (Major unit)

Values begin with 100,000 (Minimum)

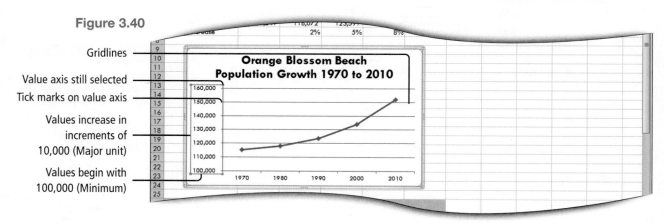

Activity 3.18 | Formatting the Chart and Plot Areas

An Excel chart has two background elements—the plot area and the chart area—which, by default display a single fill color. To add visual appeal to a chart, you can insert a graphic image as the background.

When formatting chart elements, there are several ways to display the dialog boxes that you need. You can right-click the area you want to format and choose a command on the shortcut menu. In this activity, you will use the Chart Elements box in the Current Selection group on the Format tab of the Ribbon, which is convenient if you are changing the format of a variety of chart elements.

1 Click the **Format tab**, and then in the **Current Selection group**, point to the small arrow to the right of the first item in the group to display the ScreenTip *Chart Elements*. Compare your screen with Figure 3.41.

From the ***Chart Elements box***, you can select a chart element so that you can format it.

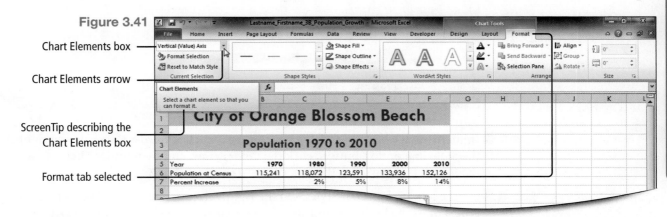

Figure 3.41

- Chart Elements box
- Chart Elements arrow
- ScreenTip describing the Chart Elements box
- Format tab selected

2 Click the **Chart Elements arrow**, and then from the displayed list, click **Chart Area**. Directly below the **Chart Elements** box, click the **Format Selection** button.

The Format Chart Area dialog box displays. Use this technique to select the chart element that you want to format, and then click the Format Selection button to display the appropriate dialog box.

3 In the **Format Chart Area** dialog box, on the left, be sure that **Fill** is selected.

4 On the right, under **Fill**, click the **Picture or texture fill** option button, and then under **Insert from**, click the **File** button. In the **Insert Picture** dialog box, navigate to your student files, and then insert the picture **e03B_Beach**. Leave the dialog box open, and then compare your screen with Figure 3.42.

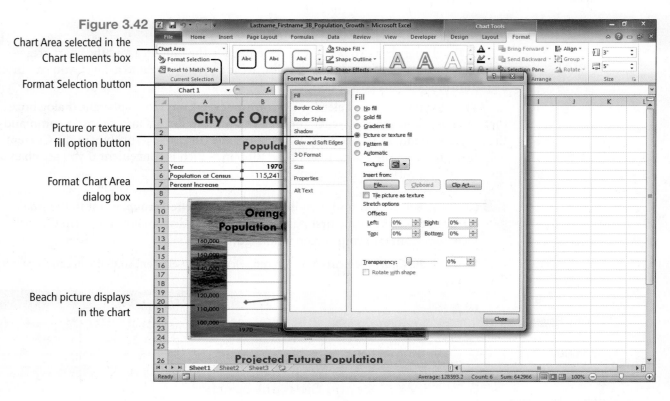

Figure 3.42

Chart Area selected in the Chart Elements box

Format Selection button

Picture or texture fill option button

Format Chart Area dialog box

Beach picture displays in the chart

---

5 In the **Format Chart Area** dialog box, on the left, click **Border Color**, on the right click the **Solid line** option button, click the **Color arrow**, and then under **Theme Colors**, in the fourth column, click the first color—**Dark Teal, Text 2**.

6 On the left, click **Border Styles**. On the right, select the text in the **Width** box and type **4 pt** At the bottom select the **Rounded corners** check box, and then **Close** the dialog box.

A 4 pt teal border with rounded corners frames the chart.

7 In the **Current Selection group**, click the **Chart Elements arrow**, on the list click **Plot Area**, and then click the **Format Selection** button.

8 In the **Format Plot Area** dialog box, on the left, be sure that **Fill** is selected, and then on the right, click the **No fill** option button. **Close** the dialog box.

The fill is removed from the plot area so that the picture is visible as the background.

9 Click the **Chart Elements arrow**, on the list click **Vertical (Value) Axis**, and then click the **Format Selection** button.

10 In the **Format Axis** dialog box, on the left click **Line Color**, on the right click the **Solid line** option button, click the **Color arrow**, and then click the first color—**White, Background 1**. Compare your screen with Figure 3.43.

The vertical line with tick marks displays in white.

Figure 3.43

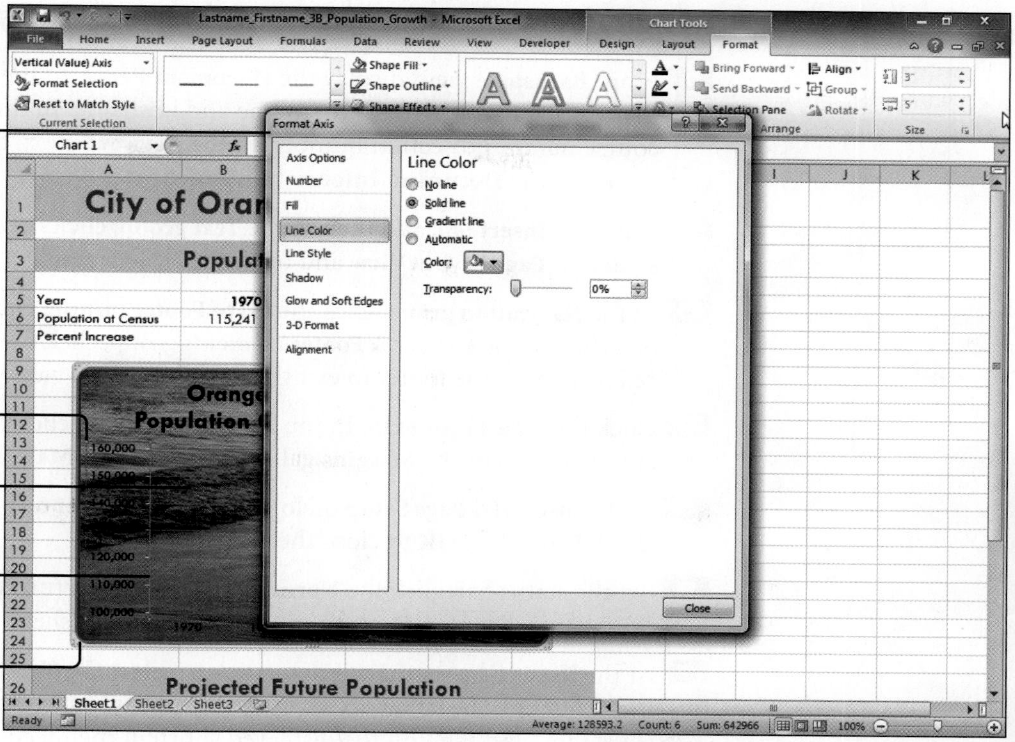

Format Axis dialog box
Value axis selected
Picture visible behind the plot area
Vertical line with tick marks displays in white
4 pt rounded teal border surrounds chart

11 **Close** the dialog box. From the **Chart Elements** box, select the **Vertical (Value) Axis Major Gridlines**, and then click **Format Selection**. Change the **Line Color** to a **Solid line**, and then apply the **White, Background 1** color. **Close** the dialog box.

12 From the **Chart Elements** list, select the **Horizontal (Category) Axis**, and then click **Format Selection**. In the **Format Axis** dialog box, change the **Line Color** to a **Solid line**, and then apply the **White, Background 1** color. **Close** the dialog box.

13 Point to any of the numbers on the vertical value axis, right-click, and then on the Mini toolbar, change the **Font Color** [A] to **White, Background 1**. Point to any of the years on the horizontal category axis, right-click, and then change the **Font Color** [A] to **White, Background 1**.

For basic text-formatting changes—for example changing the size, font, style, or font color—you must leave the Chart Tools on the Ribbon and use commands from the Home tab or the Mini toolbar.

14 Click any cell to deselect the chart, press Ctrl + Home to move to the top of your worksheet, click **Save**, and then compare your screen with Figure 3.44.

Figure 3.44

Values display in white
Gridlines display in white
Years display in white
Orange Blossom Beach
Population Growth 1970 to 2010

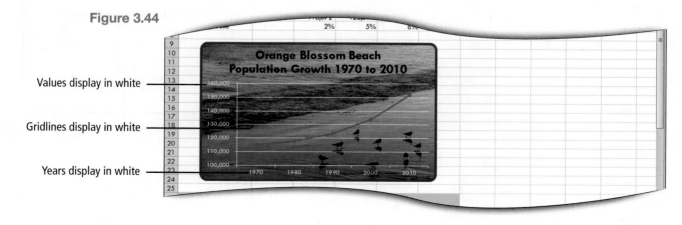

Activity 3.19 | Preparing and Printing Your Worksheet

1 From **Backstage** view, display the **Document Panel**. In the **Author** box, replace the existing text with your firstname and lastname. In the **Subject** box, type your course name and section number. In the **Keywords** box, type **population** and then **Close** ☒ the **Document Information Panel**.

2 Click the **Insert tab**, and then in the **Text group**, click the **Header & Footer** button to switch to **Page Layout View** and open the **Header area**.

3 In the **Navigation group**, click the **Go to Footer** button, click just above the word *Footer*, and then in the **Header & Footer Elements group**, click the **File Name** button. Click in a cell just above the footer to exit the **Footer area** and view your file name.

4 Click the **Page Layout tab**. In the **Page Setup group**, click the **Margins** button, and then at the bottom of the **Margins** gallery, click **Custom Margins**.

5 In the displayed **Page Setup** dialog box, under **Center on page**, select the **Horizontally** check box. Click **OK** to close the dialog box.

6 On the status bar, click the **Normal** button ▦ to return to Normal view, and then press [Ctrl] + [Home] to move to the top of your worksheet.

7 At the lower edge of the window, click to select the **Sheet2 tab**, hold down [Ctrl], and then click the **Sheet3 tab** to select the two unused sheets. Right-click over the selected sheet tabs, and then on the displayed shortcut menu, click **Delete**.

8 **Save** ▦ your workbook before printing or submitting. Press [Ctrl] + [F2] to display the **Print Preview** to check your worksheet. Compare your screen with Figure 3.45.

Figure 3.45

Completed worksheet
in Print Preview

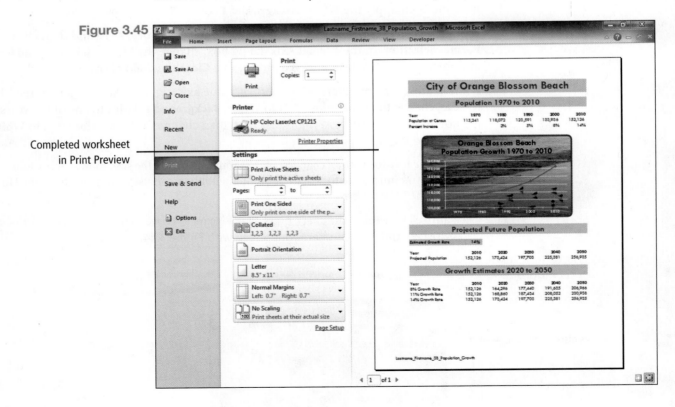

9 If necessary, return to the worksheet to make any necessary adjustments or corrections, and then **Save**.

10 Print or submit electronically as directed. If you are directed to submit printed formulas, refer to Activity 1.16 to do so.

11 If you printed your formulas, be sure to redisplay the worksheet by clicking the Show Formulas button to turn it off. From **Backstage** view, click **Close**. If the dialog box displays asking if you want to save changes, click **No** so that you do *not* save the changes you made for printing formulas. **Close** Excel.

End **You have completed Project 3B**

Content-Based Assessments

Summary

In this chapter, you created a pie chart to show how the parts of a budget contribute to a total budget. Then you formatted the pie chart attractively and used Goal Seek. You also practiced using parentheses in a formula, calculating the percentage rate of an increase, answering what-if questions, and charting data in a line chart to show the flow of data over time.

Key Terms

Matching

Match each term in the second column with its correct definition in the first column by writing the letter of the term on the blank line in front of the correct definition.

_____ 1.   A chart that shows the relationship of each part to a whole.

_____ 2.   The term used to describe money set aside for the normal operating activities of a government entity such as a city.

_____ 3.   In a formula, the address of a cell based on the relative position of the cell that contains the formula and the cell referred to.

_____ 4.   A column, bar, area, dot, pie slice, or other symbol in a chart that represents a single data point.

_____ 5.   A workbook sheet that contains only a chart.

_____ 6.   A shape effect that uses shading and shadows to make the edges of a shape appear to be curved or angled.

_____ 7.   The entire chart and all of its elements.

_____ 8.   The process of changing the values in cells to see how those changes affect the outcome of formulas in a worksheet.

_____ 9.   The mathematical formula to calculate a rate of increase.

A Axis

B Bevel

C Category axis

D Chart area

E Chart sheet

F Data marker

G Format as you type

H General Fund

I Order of operations

J Pie chart

K Rate=amount of increase/base

L Relative cell reference

M Tick marks

N Value axis

O What-if analysis

Content-Based Assessments

_____ 10. The mathematical rules for performing multiple calculations within a formula.

_____ 11. The Excel feature by which a cell takes on the formatting of the number typed into the cell.

_____ 12. A line that serves as a frame of reference for measurement and that borders the chart plot area.

_____ 13. The area along the bottom of a chart that identifies the categories of data; also referred to as the x-axis.

_____ 14. A numerical scale on the left side of a chart that shows the range of numbers for the data points; also referred to as the y-axis.

_____ 15. The short lines that display on an axis at regular intervals.

Multiple Choice

Circle the correct answer.

1. A sum of money set aside for a specific purpose is a:
    A. value axis   **B.** fund   **C.** rate

2. A cell reference that refers to a cell by its fixed position in a worksheet is referred to as being:
    A. absolute   **B.** relative   **C.** mixed

3. A value that originates in a worksheet cell and that is represented in a chart by a data marker is a data:
    A. point   **B.** cell   **C.** axis

4. Related data points represented by data markers are referred to as the data:
    A. slices   **B.** set   **C.** series

5. The action of pulling out a pie slice from a pie chart is called:
    A. extract   **B.** explode   **C.** plot

6. A gallery of text styles with which you can create decorative effects, such as shadowed or mirrored text is:
    A. WordArt   **B.** shape effects   **C.** text fill

7. The percent by which one number increases over another number is the percentage rate of:
    A. decrease   **B.** change   **C.** increase

8. A chart type that displays trends over time is a:
    A. pie chart   **B.** line chart   **C.** column chart

9. The area bounded by the axes of a chart, including all the data series, is the:
    A. chart area   **B.** plot area   **C.** axis area

10. The x-axis is also known as the:
    A. category axis   **B.** value axis   **C.** data axis

1. Chart Data with a Pie Chart
2. Format a Pie Chart
3. Edit a Workbook and Update a Chart
4. Use Goal Seek to Perform What-If Analysis

Skills Review | Project **3C** Fund Revenue

In the following Skills Review, you will edit a worksheet for Jennifer Carson, City Finance Manager, which details the City general fund revenue. Your completed worksheets will look similar to Figure 3.46.

Project Files

For Project 3C, you will need the following file:

e03C_Fund_Revenue

You will save your workbook as:

Lastname_Firstname_3C_Fund_Revenue

Project Results

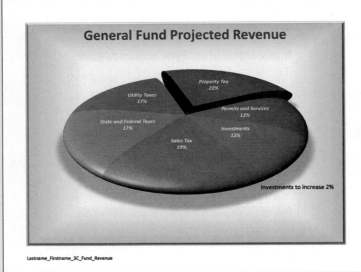

Figure 3.46

(Project 3C Fund Revenue continues on the next page)

Content-Based Assessments

1 **Start** Excel. From your student files, open the file **e03C_Fund_Revenue**. **Save** the file in your **Excel Chapter 3** folder as **Lastname_Firstname_3C_Fund_Revenue**

  a. Click cell **D5**, and then type = to begin a formula. Click cell **C5**, type **/** and then click cell **C11**. Press F4 to make the reference to the value in cell **C11** absolute. On the **Formula Bar**, click the **Enter** button, and then fill the formula down through cell **D10**.

  b. With the range **D5:D10** selected, right-click over the selection, and then on Mini toolbar, click the **Percent Style** button and the **Center** button.

2 Select the nonadjacent ranges **A5:A10** and **C5:C10** to select the revenue names and the projected revenue. Click the **Insert tab**, and then in the **Charts group**, click **Pie**. Under 3-D Pie, click the first chart—**Pie in 3-D**.

  a. On the **Design tab**, in the **Location group**, click the **Move Chart** button. In the **Move Chart** dialog box, click the **New sheet** option button. In the **New sheet** box, replace the highlighted text *Chart1* by typing **Projected Revenue Chart** and then click **OK**.

  b. On the **Layout tab**, in the **Labels group**, click the **Chart Title** button, and then click **Above Chart**. With the **Chart Title** box selected, type **General Fund Projected Revenue** and then press Enter to create the new chart title.

  c. Point to the chart title text, and then right-click to display the Mini toolbar. Change the **Font Size** to **32** and change the **Font Color** to **Blue-Gray, Text 2**— in the fourth column, the first color.

  d. Click in a white area of the chart to deselect the chart title. On the **Layout tab**, in the **Labels group**, click the **Legend** button, and then click **None**.

  e. In the **Labels group**, click the **Data Labels** button, and then click **More Data Label Options**. In the **Format Data Labels** dialog box, on the left, be sure **Label Options** is selected. On the right, under **Label Contains**, click as necessary to select the **Category Name** and **Percentage** check boxes. *Clear* any other check boxes in this group. Under **Label Position**, click the **Center** option button. Click **Close**.

  f. Point to any of the selected labels, right-click to display the Mini toolbar, and then change the **Font Size** to **12**, the **Font Color** to **White, Background 1, Darker 5%**, and then apply **Bold** and *Italic*.

3 3. Click in any pie slice outside of the label to select the entire pie. Click the **Format tab**, and then in the **Shape**

Styles group, click the **Shape Effects** button. Point to **Bevel**, and then at the bottom of the gallery, click **3-D Options**.

  a. In the **Format Data Series** dialog box, on the right, under **Bevel**, click the **Top** button. In the gallery, under **Bevel**, in the first row, click the first button— **Circle**. Then click the **Bottom** button, and apply the **Circle** bevel. In the four **Width** and **Height** spin boxes, type **512**

  b. In the lower portion of the dialog box, under **Surface**, click the **Material** button. Under **Standard**, click the third button—**Plastic**. In the lower right corner, click the **Close** button.

  c. On the **Format tab**, in the **Shape Styles group**, click **Shape Effects**, and then point to **Shadow**. Under **Perspective**, click the third button—**Below**.

  d. With the pie chart still selected, point anywhere in the pie and right-click. On the displayed shortcut menu, click **Format Data Series**. In the **Format Data Series** dialog box, on the left, be sure **Series Options** is selected. On the right, click in the box under **Angle of first slice**, change *0* to type **150** to move the largest slice—*Property Tax*—to the top of the pie. Click **Close**.

  e. Click in the area outside of the chart sheet to deselect all chart elements. Then, on the pie chart, click the outer edge of the **Property Tax** slice one time to select the pie chart, and then click the **Property Tax** slice again to select only that slice.

  f. Point to the **Property Tax** slice, and then explode the slice by dragging it slightly away from the center of the pie.

  g. With the **Property Tax** slice still selected, point to the slice and right-click. On the shortcut menu, click **Format Data Point**. In the displayed **Format Data Point** dialog box, on the left, click **Fill**. On the right, under **Fill**, click the **Solid fill** option button. Click the **Color arrow**, and then under **Theme Colors**, in the sixth column, click the fifth color—**Dark Yellow, Accent 2, Darker 25%**. Click **Close**.

4 Point to the white area just inside the border of the chart to display the ScreenTip **Chart Area**, and then click one time.

  a. On the **Format tab**, in the **Shape Styles group**, click the **Shape Effects** button, point to **Bevel**, and then under **Bevel**, in the second row, click the third bevel—**Convex**.

  b. With the chart area still selected, right-click in a white area at the outer edge of the chart, and then

(Project 3C Fund Revenue continues on the next page)

Excel | Chapter 3

on the shortcut menu, click **Format Chart Area**. In the **Format Chart Area** dialog box, on the left, be sure that **Fill** is selected. On the right, under **Fill**, click the **Gradient fill** option button. Click the **Preset colors** arrow, and then in the third row, click the fourth preset, **Parchment**. Click the **Type arrow**, and then click **Path**. Click the **Close** button.

c. Click the **Layout tab**, and then in the **Insert group**, click the **Text Box** button. Position the pointer near the lower corner of the *Investments* slice. Hold down the left mouse button, and then drag down and to the right so that the text box extends to the end of the chart area and is approximately one-half inch high. With the insertion point blinking inside the text box, type **Investments to increase 2%** Select the text and then on the Mini toolbar, change the **Font Size** to **12**. If necessary, use the sizing handles to widen the text box so that the text displays on one line.

5 In the sheet tab area at the bottom of the workbook, click the **Sheet1 tab** to redisplay the worksheet.

a. Click the **Insert tab**, and then in the **Text group**, click the **WordArt** button.

b. In the **WordArt** gallery, in the last row, click the last style—**Fill – Red, Accent 1, Metal Bevel, Reflection**. Type **general fund revenue** and then point anywhere on the dashed border surrounding the WordArt object. Click the dashed border one time to change it to a solid border, indicating that all of the text is selected. Right-click the border to display the Mini toolbar, and then change the **Font Size** to **28**.

c. Drag to position the upper left corner of the WordArt in cell **A13**, centered below the worksheet.

6 In cell **A17**, type **Projection: Investments to Increase from 13% to 15%** and then **Merge & Center** the text across the range **A17:D17**. Apply the **Heading 3** cell style.

a. In cell **A18**, type **Projected Amount:** and press Enter. Select the range **C10:D10**, right-click over the selection, and then click **Copy**. Point to cell **B18**, right-click, and then under **Paste Options**, click the **Paste** button. Press Esc to cancel the moving border.

b. Click cell **C18**. On the **Data tab**, in the **Data Tools group**, click the **What-If Analysis** button, and then click **Goal Seek**. In the **Goal Seek** dialog box, press Tab to move to the **To value** box, and then type **15%**

c. Press Tab to move the insertion point to the **By changing cell** box, and then click cell **B18**. Click

OK. In the displayed **Goal Seek Status** dialog box, click **OK**.

d. Select the range **A18:C18**. From the **Home tab**, display the **Cell Styles** gallery. Under **Themed Cell Styles**, apply **40% - Accent3**. Click cell **B18**, and then from the **Cell Styles** gallery, apply the **Currency [0]** cell style.

7 With your worksheet displayed, in the sheet tab area, double-click *Sheet1* to select the text, and then type **Projected Revenue Data** and press Enter.

a. On the **Insert tab**, in the **Text group**, click **Header & Footer**. In the **Navigation group**, click the **Go to Footer** button, click in the **left section** above the word *Footer*, and then in the **Header & Footer Elements group**, click the **File Name** button. Click in a cell above the footer to deselect the **Footer area** and view your file name.

b. On the **Page Layout tab**, in the **Page Setup group**, click the **Margins** button, and then at the bottom of the **Margins gallery**, click **Custom Margins**. In the **Page Setup** dialog box, under **Center on page**, select the **Horizontally** check box. Click **OK**, and then on the status bar, click the **Normal** button. Press Ctrl + Home to move to the top of your worksheet.

c. Click the **Projected Revenue Chart** sheet tab to display the chart sheet. On the **Insert tab**, click **Header & Footer**. In the center of the **Page Setup** dialog box, click **Custom Footer**. With the insertion point blinking in the **Left section**, in the row of buttons in the middle of the dialog box, locate and click the **Insert File Name** button. Click **OK** two times.

d. Right-click either of the sheet tabs, and then click **Select All Sheets**. From **Backstage** view, show the **Document Panel**. In the **Author** box, replace the existing text with your firstname and lastname. In the **Subject** box, type your course name and section number. In the **Keywords** box type **general fund, projected revenue** **Close** the **Document Information Panel**.

e. With the two sheets still grouped, press Ctrl + F2 to display the **Print Preview**, and then view the two pages of your workbook.

f. **Save** your workbook. Print or submit electronically as directed by your instructor. If required by your instructor, print or create an electronic version of your worksheets with formulas displayed by using the instructions in Activity 1.16, and then **Close** Excel without saving so that you do not save the changes you made to print formulas.

End **You have completed Project 3C** ———————

Content-Based Assessments

Apply 3B skills from these Objectives:

- 5 Design a Worksheet for What-If Analysis
- 6 Answer What-If Questions by Changing Values in a Worksheet
- 7 Chart Data with a Line Chart

Skills Review | Project 3D Revenue Projection

In the following Skills Review, you will edit a worksheet for Jennifer Carson, City Finance Manager, which forecasts the permit revenue that the City of Orange Blossom Beach expects to collect in the next five years. Your completed worksheet will look similar to Figure 3.47.

Project Files

For Project 3D, you will need the following files:

    e03D_Revenue_Projection
    e03D_Shoreline

You will save your workbook as:

    Lastname_Firstname_3D_Revenue_Projection

Project Results

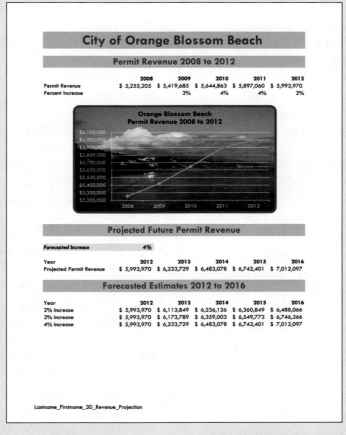

Figure 3.47

(Project 3D Revenue Projection continues on the next page)

1 **Start** Excel. From your student files, open the file **e03D_Revenue_Projection**. **Save** the file in your **Excel Chapter 3** folder with the file name **Lastname_Firstname_ 3D_Revenue_Projection**

a. Click cell **C7**. Being sure to include the parentheses, type **=(c6-b6)/b6** and then on the **Formula Bar**, click the **Enter** button. In the **Number group**, click the **Percent Style** button.

b. Click cell **D7**, type **=** and then by typing, or using a combination of typing and clicking cells to reference them, construct a formula similar to the one in cell **C7** to calculate the rate of increase in population from 2009 to 2010. Format cell **D7** with the **Percent Style**. With cell **D7** selected, drag the fill handle to the right through cell **F7**.

c. In cell **A9**, type **Projected Future Permit Revenue** and then press Enter. Point to cell **A3**, and then right-click. On the Mini toolbar, click the **Format Painter** button, and then click cell **A9**. In cell **A11**, type **Forecasted Increase** and then in cell **A13**, type **Year**

d. In cell **A14**, type **Projected Permit Revenue** and then in cell **B13**, type **2012** and press Tab. In cell **C13**, type **2013** and then press Tab. Select the range **B13:C13**, and then drag the fill handle through cell **F13** to extend the pattern of years to *2016*. Apply **Bold** to the selection.

e. Click cell **B14**, type **5993970** and then from the **Cell Styles** gallery, apply the **Currency [0]** style.

f. In cell **B11**, type **2%** which is the percent of increase from 2011 to 2012, and then on the **Formula Bar**, click **Enter**. Select the range **A11:B11**, and then from the Mini toolbar, apply **Bold** and **Italic**.

2 Click cell **C14**. Type **=b14*(100%+b11)** and then on the **Formula Bar**, click the **Enter** button. With cell **C14** as the active cell, drag the fill handle to copy the formula to the range **D14:F14**.

a. Point to cell **B14**, right-click, click the **Format Painter** button, and then select the range **C14:F14**.

b. Click cell **A16**. Type **Forecasted Estimates 2012 to 2016** and then press Enter. Use **Format Painter** to copy the format from cell **A9** to cell **A16**.

c. Select the range **A11:B11**, right-click to display the Mini toolbar, click the **Fill Color button arrow**, and then under **Theme Colors**, in the first column, click the third color—**White, Background 1, Darker 15%**.

d. In the range **A18:A21**, type the following row titles:

Year

2% Increase

3% Increase

4% Increase

3 Select the range **B13:F13**, right-click over the selection, and then on the shortcut menu, click **Copy**. **Paste** the selection to the range **B18:F18**.

a. Select the range **B14:F14**, right-click over the selection, and then on the shortcut menu, click **Copy**. Point to **B19**, right-click, and then from the shortcut menu, point to **Paste Special**. Under **Paste Values**, click the second button—**Values & Number Formatting**. Press Esc to cancel the moving border,

b. Click cell **B11**. Type **3** and then press Enter. **Copy** the new values in the range **B14:F14**. Point to cell **B20** and right-click, and then point to **Paste Special**. Under **Paste Values**, click the **Values & Number Formatting** button.

c. In cell **B11**, type **4** and then press Enter. Select and copy the range **B14:F14**, and then paste the values and number formats to the range **B21:F21**. Press Esc to cancel the moving border.

4 In the **row header area**, point to **row 8** to display the ➡ pointer, and then drag down to select **rows 8:24**. Right-click over the selection, and then click **Insert** to insert the same number of blank rows as you selected. Under the selection area near cell **A25**, click the **Insert Options** button, and then click the **Clear Formatting** option button to clear any formatting from these rows.

a. Select the range **A6:F6**. On the **Insert tab**, in the **Charts group**, click the **Line** button. In the displayed gallery of line charts, in the second row, click the **Line with Markers** chart type to create the chart as an embedded chart in the worksheet.

b. Point to the border of the chart to display the 🔭 pointer, and then drag the chart so that its upper left corner is positioned in cell **A9**, aligned approximately under the *r* in the word *Increase* above.

c. On the **Layout tab**, in the **Labels group**, click the **Legend** button, and then click **None**. Click the chart title one time to select it. Type **Orange Blossom Beach** and then press Enter.

(Project 3D Revenue Projection continues on the next page)

Skills Review | Project **3D** Revenue Projection (continued)

d. In the chart title, click to position the insertion point following the *h* in *Beach*, and then press Enter to begin a new line. Type **Permit Revenue 2008 to 2012** Click the dashed border around the chart title to change it to a solid border, right-click the solid border, and then on the Mini toolbar, change the **Font Size** of the title to **14**.

5 With the chart selected, click the **Design tab**, and then in the **Data group**, click the **Select Data** button. On the right side of the **Select Data Source** dialog box, under **Horizontal (Category) Axis Labels**, in the right column, click the **Edit** button. If necessary, drag the title bar of the Axis Labels dialog box to the right of the chart so that it is not blocking your view of the data, and then select the years in the range **B5:F5**. Click **OK** two times to enter the years as the category labels.

a. On the **Layout tab**, in the **Axes group**, click the **Axes** button. Point to **Primary Vertical Axis**, and then click **More Primary Vertical Axis Options**. In the **Format Axis** dialog box, on the left, be sure **Axis Options** is selected. On the right, in the **Minimum** row, click the **Fixed** option button. In the box to the right, select the existing text, and then type **5200000**

b. In the **Major unit** row, click the **Fixed** option button, select the value *200000.0* in the box to the right, and then type **100000** In the lower right corner, click **Close**.

c. Click the **Format tab**, and then in the **Current Selection group**, click the **Chart Elements arrow**. From the displayed list, click **Chart Area**. Directly below the **Chart Elements** box, click the **Format Selection** button.

d. In the **Format Chart Area** dialog box, on the left, be sure that **Fill** is selected. On the right, under **Fill**, click the **Picture or texture fill** option button, and then under **Insert from**, click the **File** button. In the **Insert Picture** dialog box, navigate to your student files, and then insert the picture **e03D_Shoreline**. In the **Format Chart Area** dialog box, on the left, click **Border Color**. On the right click the **Solid line** option button, and then click the **Color arrow**. Under **Theme Colors**, in the fourth column, click the first color—**Brown, Text 2**.

e. On the left, click **Border Styles**. On the right, select the text in the **Width** box and type **4** Select the **Rounded corners** check box, and then **Close** the dialog box.

6 In the **Current Selection group**, click the **Chart Elements arrow**, on the list click **Plot Area**, and then click the **Format Selection** button. In the **Format Plot Area** dialog box, on the left, be sure that **Fill** is selected, and then on the right, click the **No fill** option button. **Close** the dialog box.

a. Click the **Chart Elements arrow**, on the list click **Vertical (Value) Axis**, and then click the **Format Selection** button. In the **Format Axis** dialog box, on the left, click **Line Color**. On the right, click the **Solid line** option button, click the **Color arrow**, and then click the first color—**White, Background 1**. **Close** the dialog box.

b. From the **Chart Elements** box, select the **Vertical (Value) Axis Major Gridlines**, and then click **Format Selection**. Change the **Line Color** to a **Solid line**, and then apply the **White, Background 1** color. **Close** the dialog box.

c. From the **Chart Elements** box, select the **Horizontal (Category) Axis**, and then click **Format Selection**. Change the **Line Color** to a **Solid line**, and then apply the **White, Background 1** color. **Close** the dialog box.

d. Point to any of the numbers on the **vertical value axis**, right-click, and then on the Mini toolbar, change the **Font Color** to **White, Background 1**. Point to any of the years on the **horizontal category axis**, right-click, and then change the **Font Color** to **White, Background 1**.

e. Click any cell to deselect the chart. Insert a **Header & Footer** with the **file name** in the **left section** of the footer, and then center the worksheet **Horizontally** on the page. Return to **Normal** view, and press Ctrl + Home. From **Backstage** view, show the **Document Panel**. In the **Author** box, replace the existing text with your firstname and lastname. In the **Subject** box, type your course name and section number. In the **Keywords** box type **permit revenue, forecast Close** the **Document Information Panel**.

f. **Save** your workbook. Print or submit electronically as directed by your instructor. If required by your instructor, print or create an electronic version of your worksheet with formulas displayed by using the instructions in Activity 1.16, and then **Close** Excel without saving so that you do not save the changes you made to print formulas.

End You have completed Project **3D**

Content-Based Assessments

Apply 3A skills from these Objectives:

1️⃣ Chart Data with a Pie Chart

2️⃣ Format a Pie Chart

3️⃣ Edit a Workbook and Update a Chart

4️⃣ Use Goal Seek to Perform What-If Analysis

Mastering Excel | Project **3E** Investments

In the following project, you will you will edit a worksheet for Jennifer Carson, City Finance Manager, that summarizes the investment portfolio of the City of Orange Blossom Beach. Your completed worksheets will look similar to Figure 3.48.

Project Files

For Project 3E, you will need the following file:

e03E_Investments

You will save your workbook as:

Lastname_Firstname_3E_Investments

Project Results

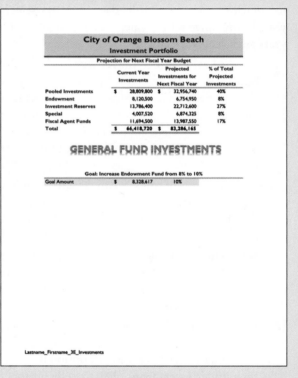

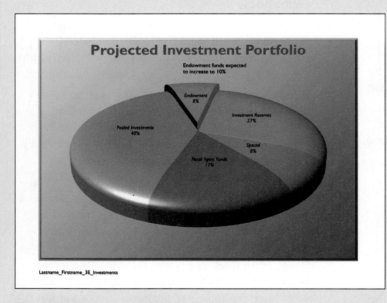

Figure 3.48

(Project 3E Investments continues on the next page)

Content-Based Assessments

Mastering Excel | Project 3E Investments (continued)

1 **Start** Excel. From your student files, locate and open **e03E_Investments**. **Save** the file in your **Excel Chapter 3** folder as **Lastname_Firstname_3E_Investments**

2 In cells **B10** and **C10**, enter formulas to calculate totals for each column. Then, in cell **D5**, enter a formula to calculate the % of Total Projected Investments for Pooled Investments by dividing the **Projected Investments for Next Fiscal Year** for the **Pooled Investments** by the **Total Projected Investments for Next Fiscal Year**. Use absolute cell references as necessary, format the result in **Percent Style**, and **Center** the percentage. Fill the formula down through cell **D9**.

3 Select the nonadjacent ranges **A5:A9** and **C5:C9**, and then insert a **Pie in 3-D** chart. Move the chart to a **New sheet** named **Projected Investment Chart** Insert a **Chart Title** above the chart with the text **Projected Investment Portfolio** Change the chart title **Font Size** to **32** and change the **Font Color** to **Brown, Accent 6**—in the last column, the first color.

4 Remove the **Legend** from the chart, and then add **Data Labels** formatted so that only the **Category Name** and **Percentage** display positioned in the **Center**. Change the data labels **Font Size** to **11**, and then apply **Italic**.

5 Select the entire pie, display the **Shape Effects** gallery, point to **Bevel**, and then at the bottom of the gallery, click **3-D Options**. Change the **Top** and **Bottom** options to the last **Bevel** type—**Art Deco**. Set the **Top Width** and **Height** boxes to **256** and then set the **Bottom Width** and **Height** boxes to **0** Change the **Material** to the third **Standard** type—**Plastic**.

6 With the pie chart selected, display the shortcut menu, and then click **Format Data Series**. Change the **Angle of first slice** to **200** to move the *Endowment* slice to the top of the pie. Select the **Endowment** slice, and then explode the slice slightly.

7 Change the **Fill Color** of the **Pooled Investments** slice to **Gray-50%, Accent 1, Lighter 40%**. Format the **Chart Area** by applying a **Convex Bevel**. To the **Chart Area**, apply the **Moss, Preset Gradient fill**. In the **Angle** box, type **45** and then **Close** the **Format Chart Area** dialog box.

8 **Insert** a **Text Box** positioned approximately halfway between the *Endowment* pie slice and the *v* in the word *Investment* in the title. In the text box, type **Endowment funds expected to increase to 10%** Select the text and then on the Mini toolbar, change the **Font Size** to **12**. Size the text box as necessary so that the text displays on two lines as shown in Figure 3.48.

9 Display **Sheet1** and rename the sheet as **Projected Investment Data** Insert a **WordArt**—in the fifth row, insert the last WordArt style—**Fill – Gray-50%, Accent 1, Plastic Bevel, Reflection**. Type **General Fund Investments** and then change the **Font Size** to **20**. Drag to position the upper left corner of the WordArt in cell **A12**, centered below the worksheet.

10 In cell **A16**, type **Goal: Increase Endowment Fund from 8% to 10%** and then **Merge & Center** the text across the range **A16:D16**. Apply the **Heading 3** cell style. In cell **A17**, type **Goal Amount**

11 **Copy** the range **C6:D6** to cell **B17**. Click cell **C17**, and then use **Goal Seek** to determine the projected amount of endowment funds in cell **B17** if the value in **C17** is **10%**.

12 Select the range **A17:C17**, and then apply the **20% - Accent2** cell style. In **B17**, from the **Cell Styles** gallery, apply the **Currency [0]** cell style.

13 Insert a **Header & Footer** with the file name in the **left section** of the footer. In Page Layout view, check that the WordArt is centered under the worksheet data. Center the worksheet **Horizontally** on the page, and then return to **Normal** view. Display the **Projected Investment Chart** sheet and insert a **Custom Footer** with the file name in the **Left section**.

14 Group the sheets, and then display the **Document Panel**. Add your name, your course name and section, and the keywords **investment portfolio**

15 **Save** your workbook. Print or submit electronically as directed by your instructor. If required by your instructor, print or create an electronic version of your worksheets with formulas displayed by using the instructions in Activity 1.16, and then **Close** Excel without saving so that you do not save the changes you made to print formulas.

End **You have completed Project 3E**

Apply **3B** skills from
these Objectives:

5 Design a Worksheet
for What-If Analysis

6 Answer What-If
Questions by
Changing Values in
a Worksheet

7 Chart Data with a
Line Chart

Mastering Excel | Project **3F** Benefit Analysis

In the following project, you will edit a worksheet that Jeffrey Lovins, Human Resources Director,
will use to prepare a five-year forecast of the annual cost of city employee benefits per employee.
Your completed worksheet will look similar to Figure 3.49.

Project Files

For Project 3F, you will need the following file:

e03F_Benefit_Analysis

You will save your workbook as:

Lastname_Firstname_3F_Benefit_Analysis

Project Results

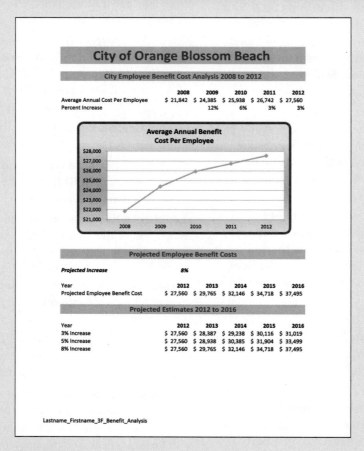

Figure 3.49

(Project 3F Benefit Analysis continues on the next page)

Content-Based Assessments

Mastering Excel | Project 3F Benefit Analysis (continued)

1 **Start** Excel. From your student files, open the file **e03F_Benefit_Analysis. Save** the file in your **Excel Chapter 3** folder as **Lastname_Firstname_3F_Benefit_Analysis**

2 In cell **C7**, construct a formula to calculate the percent of increase in employee annual benefit costs from 2008 to 2009. Format the result with the **Percent Style** and then fill the formula through cell **F7**.

3 In cell **A9**, type **Projected Employee Benefit Costs** and then use **Format Painter** to copy the formatting from cell **A3** to cell **A9**. In cell **A11**, type **Projected Increase** and then in cell **A13**, type **Year** In cell **A14**, type **Projected Employee Benefit Cost** and then in the range **B13:F13**, use the fill handle to enter the years 2012 through 2016. Apply **Bold** to the years. In cell **B14**, type **27560** and then from the **Cell Styles** gallery, apply the **Currency [0]** format. In cell **B11**, type **3%** which is the percent of increase from 2011 to 2012. To the range **A11:B11**, apply **Bold** and **Italic**.

4 In cell **C14**, construct a formula to calculate the annual cost of employee benefits for the year 2013 after the projected increase of 3% is applied. Fill the formula through cell **F14**, and then use **Format Painter** to copy the formatting from cell **B14** to the range **C14:F14**.

5 In cell **A16**, type **Projected Estimates 2012 to 2016** and then use **Format Painter** to copy the format from cell **A9** to cell **A16**. In cells **A18:A21**, type the following row titles:

> Year
> 3% Increase
> 5% Increase
> 8% Increase

6 **Copy** the range **B13:F13**, and then **Paste** the selection to **B18:F18**. Copy the range **B14:F14** and then paste the

Values & Number Formatting to the range **B19:F19**. Complete the Projected Estimates section of the worksheet by changing the *Projected Increase* in **B11** to **5%** and then to **8%** copying and pasting the **Values & Number Formatting** to the appropriate ranges in the worksheet.

7 Select **rows 8:24**, and then **Insert** the same number of blank rows as you selected. **Clear Formatting** from the inserted rows. By using the data in **A5:F6**, insert a **Line with Markers** chart in the worksheet. Move the chart so that its upper left corner is positioned in cell **A9** and centered under the data above. Remove the **Legend**, and then replace the existing chart title with the two-line title **Average Annual Benefit Cost Per Employee** The text *Cost per Employee* should display on the second line. Change the title **Font Size** to **14**.

8 Format the **Primary Vertical Axis** so that the **Minimum** is **21000** and the **Major unit** is **1000** Format the **Chart Area** with a **Gradient fill** by applying the third **Preset color** in the third row—**Wheat**. Change the **Border Color** by applying a **Solid line—Orange, Accent 1, Darker 50%**. Change the **Width** of the border to **4** and apply the **Rounded corners** option.

9 Deselect the chart, and then insert a **Header & Footer** with the file name in the **left section** of the footer; center the worksheet **Horizontally** on the page. In the **Document Panel**, add your name, your course name and section, and the keywords **employee benefits, forecast**

10 **Save** your workbook. Print or submit electronically as directed by your instructor. If required by your instructor, print or create an electronic version of your worksheets with formulas displayed by using the instructions in Activity 1.16, and then **Close** Excel without saving so that you do not save the changes you made to print formulas.

End You have completed Project 3F ————————————

Content-Based Assessments

Apply **3A** and **3B** skills from these Objectives:

1 Chart Data with a Pie Chart

2 Format a Pie Chart

3 Edit a Workbook and Update a Chart

4 Use Goal Seek to Perform What-If Analysis

5 Design a Worksheet for What-If Analysis

6 Answer What-If Questions by Changing Values in a Worksheet

7 Chart Data with a Line Chart

Mastering Excel | Project **3G** Operations Analysis

In the following project, you will you will edit a workbook for Jennifer Carson, City Finance Manager, that summarizes the operations costs for the Public Works Department. Your completed worksheets will look similar to Figure 3.50.

Project Files

For Project 3G, you will need the following file:

> e03G_Operations_Analysis

You will save your workbook as:

> Lastname_Firstname_3G_Operations_Analysis

Project Results

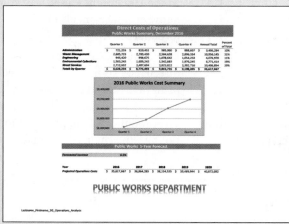

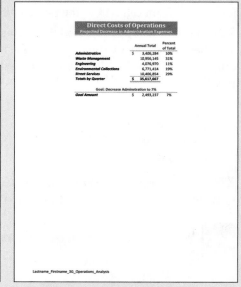

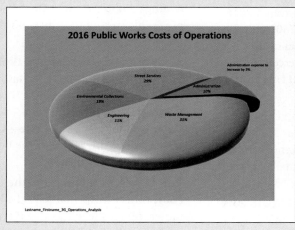

Figure 3.50

(Project 3G Operations Analysis continues on the next page)

Content-Based Assessments

Mastering Excel | Project **3G** Operations Analysis (continued)

1 **Start** Excel. From your student files, open **e03G_Operations_Analysis**. **Save** the file as in your **Excel Chapter 3** folder as **Lastname_Firstname_3G_Operations_Analysis**

2 In the **Public Works** sheet, calculate totals in the ranges **F5:F9** and **B10:F10**. In cell **G5**, construct a formula to calculate the **Percent of Total** by dividing the **Annual Total** for **Administration** in cell **F5** by the **Annual Total** for all quarters in cell **F10**. Use absolute cell references as necessary, format the result in **Percent Style**, and then **Center**. Fill the formula down through cell **G9**.

3 Select the nonadjacent ranges **A5:A9** and **F5:F9**, and then insert a **Pie in 3-D** chart. Move the chart to a **New sheet** with the name **Public Works Summary Chart** Insert a **Chart Title** above the chart with the text **2016 Public Works Costs of Operations** and then change the **Font Size** to **28**.

4 Remove the **Legend** from the chart and then add **Data Labels** formatted so that only the **Category Name** and **Percentage** displays positioned in the **Center**. Change the data labels **Font Size** to **12**, and apply **Bold** and **Italic**.

5 Select the chart, and then modify the pie chart **Shape Effects** by changing the **Bevel, 3-D Options**. Change the **Top** and **Bottom** options to the first **Bevel** type—**Circle**. Set the **Top Width** and **Height** boxes to **256 pt** and then set the **Bottom Width** and **Height** boxes to **50 pt** Change the **Material** to the fourth **Standard Effect** type—**Metal**.

6 In the displayed **Format Data Series** dialog box, on the left, click **Series Options**, and then change the **Angle of first** slice to **50** Explode the **Administration** slice slightly away from the pie. Format the **Chart Area** with a **Solid fill**— **Aqua, Accent 2**—in the sixth column, the first color.

7 Insert a **Text Box** positioned outside the upper corner of the **Administration** pie slice extending to the edge of the chart area and that is about one-half inch in height. In the text box, type **Administration expense to increase by 3%** Change the **Font Size** to **10.5**. Size the text box so that the text displays on two lines. On this chart sheet, insert a **Custom Footer** with the file name in the **left section**.

8 In the **Public Works** sheet, using the data in the nonadjacent ranges **B4:E4** and **B10:E10**, insert a **Line with Markers** chart in the worksheet. Move the chart so that its upper left corner is positioned in cell **A12**, aligned approximately under the *t* in the word *Collections* above.

Remove the **Legend** and then add a **Chart Title** above the chart with the text **2016 Public Works Cost Summary** Edit the **Primary Vertical Axis** so that the **Minimum** is **Fixed** at **8600000** and the **Major unit** is **Fixed** at **200000** Format the **Chart Area** with a **Solid fill** by applying **Aqua, Accent 2, Lighter 40%**—in the sixth column, the fourth color.

9 In cell **B35**, type **35617667** and then apply the **Currency [0]** cell style. In cell **C35**, construct a formula to calculate the **Projected Operations Costs** after the forecasted increase is applied. Fill the formula through cell **F35**, and then use **Format Painter** to copy the formatting from cell **B35** to the range **C35:F35**.

10 Insert a **WordArt** using the last style—**Fill - Brown, Accent 1, Metal Bevel, Reflection** Type **Public Works Department** and then change the **Font Size** to **32**. Drag to position the WordArt in cell **A38**, centered below the worksheet.

11 Change the **Orientation** to **Landscape**, and then use the **Scale to Fit** options to fit the **Height** to **1 page**. Insert a **Header & Footer** with the **file name** in the left area of the footer. In **Page Layout** view, check and adjust if necessary the visual centering of the chart and the WordArt. Center the worksheet **Horizontally** on the page, and then return to **Normal** view.

12 Display the **Projected Decrease sheet**. In cell **C5**, calculate the **Percent of Total** by dividing the *Administration Annual Total* by the *Totals by Quarter*, using absolute cell references as necessary. Apply **Percent Style** and then fill the formula from **C5:C9**.

13 **Copy** cell **B5**, and then use **Paste Special** to paste the **Values & Number Formatting** to cell **B13**. **Copy** and **Paste** cell **C5** to **13**. With cell **C13** selected, use **Goal Seek** to determine the goal amount of administration expenses in cell **B13** if the value in **C13** is set to **7%**

14 On the **Projected Decrease** sheet, insert a **Header & Footer** with the file name in the **left section** of the footer, and then center the worksheet **Horizontally** on the page. Show the **Document Panel**. Add your name, your course name and section, and the keywords **public works**

15 **Save** your workbook. Print or submit electronically as directed by your instructor. If required by your instructor, print or create an electronic version of your worksheets with formulas displayed by using the instructions in Activity 1.16, and then **Close** Excel without saving so that you do not save the changes you made to print formulas.

End **You have completed Project 3G**

Content-Based Assessments

GO! Fix It | Project **3H** Recreation

Project Files

For Project 3H, you will need the following file:

e03H_Recreation

You will save your workbook as:

Lastname_Firstname_3H_Recreation

In this project, you will correct a worksheet that contains the annual enrollment of residents in city-sponsored recreation programs. From the student files that accompany this textbook, open the file e03H_Recreation, and then save the file in your chapter folder as **Lastname_Firstname_ 3H_Recreation**

To complete the project, you must find and correct errors in formulas and formatting. View each formula in the worksheet and edit as necessary. Review the format and title of the pie chart and make corrections and formatting changes as necessary. In addition to errors that you find, you should know:

- The pie chart data should include the Age Group and the Total columns.
- The Chart Area should include a blue solid fill background and the title font color should be white.
- The pie chart should be in a separate worksheet named **Enrollment Analysis Chart**

Add a footer to both sheets, and add your name, your course name and section, and the keywords **Parks and Recreation, enrollment** to the document properties. Save your file and then print or submit your worksheet electronically as directed by your instructor. If required by your instructor, print or create an electronic version of your worksheets with formulas displayed by using the instructions in Activity 1.16, and then close Excel without saving so that you do not save the changes you made to print formulas.

End **You have completed Project 3H** —————————

Content-Based Assessments

Apply a combination of the **3A** and **3B** skills.

GO! Make It | Project 3I Tax Projection

Project Files

For Project 3I, you will need the following file:

New blank Excel workbook

You will save your workbook as:

Lastname_Firstname_3I_Tax_Projection

Start a new blank Excel workbook and create the worksheet shown in Figure 3.51. In the range C7:F7, calculate the rate of increase from the previous year. In the range C31:F31, calculate the projected property tax for each year based on the forecasted increase. Complete the worksheet by entering in the range B36:F38, the projected property tax revenue for each year based on 2%, 3%, and 4% increases. Insert the chart as shown, using the 2010 through 2014 Property Tax Revenue data. Fill the chart area with the Daybreak gradient fill and change the chart title font size to 14. Scale the width to fit to one page, and then add your name, your course name and section, and the keywords **property tax** to the document properties. Save the file in your Excel Chapter 3 folder as **Lastname_Firstname_3I_Tax_Projection** and then print or submit electronically as directed by your instructor.

Project Results

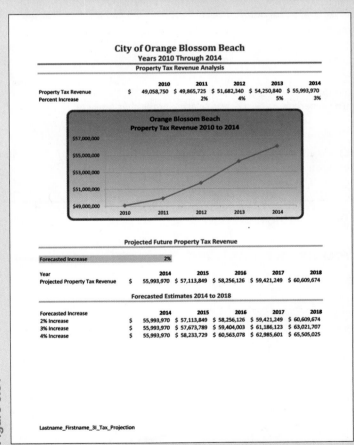

Figure 3.51

End You have completed Project 3I

Content-Based Assessments

GO! Solve It | Project **3J** Staffing

Project Files

For Project 3J, you will need the following file:

e03J_Staffing

You will save your workbook as:

Lastname_Firstname_3J_Staffing

Open the file e03J_Staffing and save it as **Lastname_Firstname_3J_Staffing** Complete the worksheet by calculating totals and the % of Total Employees. Format the worksheet attractively including appropriate number formatting. Insert a pie chart in a separate sheet that illustrates the Two-Year Projection staffing levels by department and use the techniques that you practiced in this chapter to format the chart so that it is attractive and easy to understand. Change the angle of the first slice so that the Public Safety slice displays below the title. Then, insert a text box that indicates that the increase in Public Safety staffing is contingent upon City Council approval. Include the file name in the footer, add appropriate properties, save and submit as directed.

Performance Criteria		**Performance Level**		
		Exemplary: You consistently applied the relevant skills	**Proficient:** You sometimes, but not always, applied the relevant skills	**Developing:** You rarely or never applied the relevant skills
	Create formulas	All formulas are correct and are efficiently constructed.	Formulas are correct but not always constructed in the most efficient manner.	One or more formulas are missing or incorrect; or only numbers were entered.
	Chart inserted and formatted	Chart was inserted and formatted properly.	Chart was inserted but incorrect data was selected or the chart was not formatted.	No chart was inserted.
	Format attractively and appropriately	Formatting is attractive and appropriate.	Adequately formatted but difficult to read or unattractive.	Inadequate or no formatting.

End You have completed Project 3J

Content-Based Assessments

GO! Solve It | Project **3K** Water Usage

Project Files

For Project 3K, you will need the following file:

New blank Excel workbook
e03K_Beach

You will save your workbook as:

Lastname_Firstname_3K_Water_Usage

The City of Orange Blossom Beach is a growing community and the City Council has requested an analysis of future resource needs. In this project, you will create a worksheet for the Department of Water and Power that lists residential water usage over the past ten years and that forecasts the amount of water that city residents will use in the next ten years. Create a worksheet with the following data:

	2008	2010	2012	2014	2016
Water Use in Acre Feet	62500	68903	73905	76044	80342

Calculate the percent increase for the years 2010 to 2016. Below the Percent Increase, insert a line chart that illustrates the city's water usage from 2008 to 2016. Below the chart, add a section to the worksheet to calculate the projected water usage for the years 2016 to 2024 in two-year increments based on a 4% annual increase. The 2016 amount is 80,342. Format the chart and worksheet attractively with a title and subtitle, and apply appropriate formatting. If you choose to format the chart area with a picture, you can use e03K_Beach located with your student files. Include the file name in the footer and enter appropriate document properties. Save the workbook as **Lastname_Firstname_3K_Water_Usage** and submit it as directed.

Performance Criteria	Performance Level		
	Exemplary: You consistently applied the relevant skills	Proficient: You sometimes, but not always, applied the relevant skills	Developing: You rarely or never applied the relevant skills
Create formulas	All formulas are correct and are efficiently constructed.	Formulas are correct but not always constructed in the most efficient manner.	One or more formulas are missing or incorrect or only numbers were entered.
Insert and format line chart	Line chart created correctly and is attractively formatted.	Line chart was created but the data was incorrect or the chart was not appropriately formatted.	No line chart was created.
Format attractively and appropriately	Formatting is attractive and appropriate.	Adequately formatted but difficult to read or unattractive.	Inadequate or no formatting.

End You have completed Project 3K

Outcomes-Based Assessments

Rubric

The following outcomes-based assessments are *open-ended assessments*. That is, there is no specific correct result; your result will depend on your approach to the information provided. Make *Professional Quality* your goal. Use the following scoring rubric to guide you in *how* to approach the problem, and then to evaluate *how well* your approach solves the problem.

The *criteria*—Software Mastery, Content, Format and Layout, and Process—represent the knowledge and skills you have gained that you can apply to solving the problem. The *levels of performance*—Professional Quality, Approaching Professional Quality, or Needs Quality Improvements—help you and your instructor evaluate your result.

	Your completed project is of Professional Quality if you:	Your completed project is Approaching Professional Quality if you:	Your completed project Needs Quality Improvements if you:
1-Software Mastery	Choose and apply the most appropriate skills, tools, and features and identify efficient methods to solve the problem.	Choose and apply some appropriate skills, tools, and features, but not in the most efficient manner.	Choose inappropriate skills, tools, or features, or are inefficient in solving the problem.
2-Content	Construct a solution that is clear and well organized, contains content that is accurate, appropriate to the audience and purpose, and is complete. Provide a solution that contains no errors in spelling, grammar, or style.	Construct a solution in which some components are unclear, poorly organized, inconsistent, or incomplete. Misjudge the needs of the audience. Have some errors in spelling, grammar, or style, but the errors do not detract from comprehension.	Construct a solution that is unclear, incomplete, or poorly organized; contains some inaccurate or inappropriate content; and contains many errors in spelling, grammar, or style. Do not solve the problem.
3-Format and Layout	Format and arrange all elements to communicate information and ideas, clarify function, illustrate relationships, and indicate relative importance.	Apply appropriate format and layout features to some elements, but not others. Overuse features, causing minor distraction.	Apply format and layout that does not communicate information or ideas clearly. Do not use format and layout features to clarify function, illustrate relationships, or indicate relative importance. Use available features excessively, causing distraction.
4-Process	Use an organized approach that integrates planning, development, self-assessment, revision, and reflection.	Demonstrate an organized approach in some areas, but not others; or, use an insufficient process of organization throughout.	Do not use an organized approach to solve the problem.

Outcomes-Based Assessments

GO! Think | Project **3L** School Enrollment

Project Files

For Project 3L, you will need the following file:

New blank Excel workbook

You will save your workbook as:

Lastname_Firstname_3L_School_Enrollment

Marcus Chavez, the Superintendent of Schools for the City of Orange Blossom Beach, has requested an enrollment analysis of students in the city public elementary schools in order to plan school boundary modifications resulting in more balanced enrollments. Enrollments in district elementary schools for the past two years are as follows:

School	2014 Enrollment	2015 Enrollment
Orange Blossom	795	824
Kittridge	832	952
Glenmeade	524	480
Hidden Trails	961	953
Beach Side	477	495
Sunnyvale	515	502

Create a workbook to provide Marcus with the enrollment information for each school and the total district enrollment. Insert a column to calculate the percent change from 2014 to 2015. Note that some of the results will be negative numbers. Format the percentages with two decimal places. Insert a pie chart in its own sheet that illustrates the 2015 enrollment figures for each school and format the chart attractively. Format the worksheet so that it is professional and easy to read and understand. Insert a footer with the file name and add appropriate document properties. Save the file as **Lastname_Firstname_3L_School_Enrollment** and print or submit as directed by your instructor.

End You have completed Project 3L ⎯⎯⎯⎯⎯⎯⎯⎯

Outcomes-Based Assessments

GO! Think | Project **3M** Park Acreage

Project Files

For Project 3M, you will need the following files:

> New blank Excel workbook
> e03M_Park

You will save your workbook as:

> Lastname_Firstname_3M_Park_Acreage

The City of Orange Blossom Beach wants to maintain a high ratio of parkland to residents and has established a goal of maintaining a minimum of 50 parkland acres per 1,000 residents. The following table contains the park acreage and the population, in thousands, since 1980. Start a new blank Excel workbook and then enter appropriate titles. Then, enter the following data in the worksheet and calculate the *Acres per 1,000 residents* by dividing the Park acreage by the Population in thousands.

	1980	1990	2000	2010
Population in thousands	118.4	123.9	133.5	152.6
Park acreage	5,800	6,340	8,490	9,200
Acres per 1,000 residents				

Create a line chart that displays the Park Acres Per 1,000 Residents for each year. Format the chart professionally and insert the picture e03M_Park from your student files in the chart fill area. Below the chart, create a new section titled **Park Acreage Analysis** and then copy and paste the Years and the Park acreage values to the new section. Calculate the *Percent increase* from the previous ten years for the 1990, 2000, and 2010 years. Below the Park Acreage Analysis section, create a new worksheet section titled **Park Acreage Forecast** and then enter the following values.

	2010	2020	2030	2040
Population in thousands	152.6	173.2	197.7	225.3
Park acreage necessary				
Percent increase				

Calculate the *Park acreage necessary* to reach the city's goal by multiplying the Population in thousands by 50. Then calculate the *Percent increase* from the previous ten years for the 2020, 2030, and 2040 years. Use techniques that you practiced in this chapter to format the worksheet professionally. Insert a footer with the file name and add appropriate document properties. Save the file as **Lastname_Firstname_3M_Park_Acreage** and print or submit as directed by your instructor.

End **You have completed Project 3M** ————————————————

Outcomes-Based Assessments

Apply a combination of the 3A and 3B skills.

You and GO! | Project **3N** Expense Analysis

Project Files

For Project 3N, you will need the following file:

New blank Excel workbook

You will save your workbook as:

Lastname_Firstname_3N_Expense_Analysis

Develop a worksheet that details the expenses you have incurred during the past two months and list the expenses for each month in separate columns. Calculate totals for each column and then add a column in which you can calculate the percent change from one month to the next. Insert and format a pie chart that illustrates the expenses that you incurred in the most recent month. After reviewing the pie chart, determine a category of expense in which you might be overspending, and then pull that slice out of the pie and insert a text box indicating how you might save money on that expense. Insert a footer with the file name and center the worksheet horizontally on the page. Save your file as **Lastname_Firstname_3N_Expense_Analysis** and submit as directed.

 You have completed Project 3N ⎯⎯⎯⎯⎯⎯⎯⎯⎯⎯

Apply a combination of the 3A and 3B skills.

GO! Collaborate | Project **3O** Bell Orchid Hotels Group Running Case

This project relates to the **Bell Orchid Hotels**. Your instructor may assign this group case project to your class. If your instructor assigns this project, he or she will provide you with information and instructions to work as part of a group. The group will apply the skills gained thus far to help the Bell Orchid Hotels achieve their business goals.

 You have completed Project 3O ⎯⎯⎯⎯⎯⎯⎯⎯⎯⎯

Business Running Case

Razvan CHIRNOAGA/Shutterstock

This project relates to **Front Range Action Sports**, which is one of the country's largest retailers of sports gear and outdoor recreation merchandise. The company has large retail stores in Colorado, Washington, Oregon, California, and New Mexico, in addition to a growing online business. Major merchandise categories include fishing, camping, rock climbing, winter sports, action sports, water sports, team sports, racquet sports, fitness, golf, apparel, and footwear.

In this project, you will apply the skills you practiced from the Objectives in Excel Chapters 1 through 3. You will develop a workbook for Frank Osei, the Vice President of Finance, that contains year-end sales and inventory summary information. In the first two worksheets, you will summarize and chart net sales. In the next three worksheets, you will detail the ending inventory of the two largest company-owned production facilities in Seattle and Denver. Mr. Osei is particularly interested in data regarding the new line of ski equipment stocked at these two locations. In the last worksheet, you will summarize and chart annual expenses. Your completed worksheets will look similar to Figure 1.1.

Project Files

For Project BRC1, you will need the following files:

> eBRC1_Annual_Report
> eBRC1_Skiing

You will save your workbook as:

Lastname_Firstname_BRC1_Annual_Report

Project Results

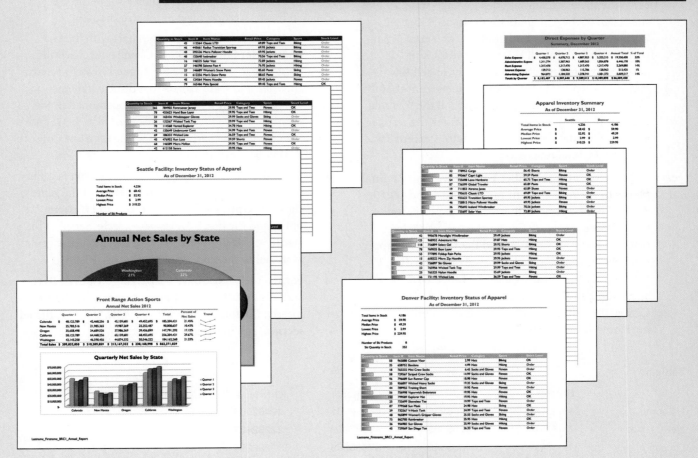

Figure 1.1

Business Running Case

Front Range Action Sports

1 **Start** Excel. From the student files that accompany this textbook, locate and open **eBRC1_Annual_Report**. In the location where you are storing your projects, create a new folder named **Front_Range_Action_Sports** or navigate to this folder if you have already created it. **Save** the new workbook as **Lastname_Firstname_BRC1_Annual_Report**

a. Familiarize yourself with the workbook by clicking each sheet tab, and then display the **Net Sales** worksheet. Click cell **B3**, and then use the fill handle to enter *Quarter 2*, *Quarter 3*, and *Quarter 4* in the range **C3:E3**. In the range **C4:E8**, enter the sales data for Quarter 2, Quarter 3, and Quarter 4 shown in **Table 1** at the bottom of the page.

b. Adjust the width of columns **B:F** to **125** pixels. Adjust the width of columns **G:H** to **100** pixels. In cell **F3**, type **Total** and then in the range **F4:F8**, calculate the annual total sales for each state. In the range **B9:F9**, calculate totals. In cell **G3**, type **Percent of Net Sales** and apply **Wrap Text** formatting to this cell. In cell **H3**, type **Trend** Using absolute cell references as necessary, in cell **G4**, construct a formula to calculate the percent that the *Colorado Total* is of the *Total Sales*. Fill the formula down through the range **G5:G8**. **Center** the results and then format the percentages with **Percent Style** and **two decimal places**.

c. Apply **Accounting Number Format** with **no decimal places** to the nonadjacent ranges **B4:F4** and **B9:F9**. Apply **Comma Style** with **no decimal** places to the range **B5:F8**. **Merge & Center** the two worksheet titles across columns **A:H**, and then to cell **A1**, apply the **Title** style and to cell **A2**, apply the **Heading 1** style. Apply the **Total** style to the range **B9:F9** and apply the **Heading 4** style to the range **B3:H3**. **Center** the column headings in **B3:H3** both horizontally and vertically.

d. In the range **H4:H8**, insert **Line** sparklines to represent the trend of each state across the four quarters. Add **Markers** and apply **Sparkline Style Accent 2 (no dark or light)**.

e. Select the range **A3:E8**, and then insert a **3-D Clustered Column** chart. Align the upper left corner of the chart inside the upper left corner of cell **A11**, and then size the chart so that its lower right corner is slightly inside cell **H24**. Apply chart **Style 26** and chart **Layout 1**. Replace the chart title text with **Quarterly Net Sales by State** Insert the file name in the **left section** of the footer, set the orientation to **Landscape**, and center the worksheet horizontally. Return to **Normal** view.

2 To show the percent that each state contributes to the total sales, select the nonadjacent ranges that represent the state names and state totals. Insert a **Pie in 3-D** chart and move the chart to a **New sheet**. Name the sheet **Net Sales by State** and then move the sheet so that it is the second sheet in the workbook.

a. Insert a **Chart Title** above the chart with the text **Annual Net Sales by State** Change the chart title **Font Size** to **36**. Remove the **Legend** from the chart, and then add **Data Labels** that display only the **Category Name** and **Percentage** positioned in the **Center**. Change the data labels **Font Size** to **14**, and then apply **Bold** and **Italic**. Change the **Font Color** to **White, Background 1**.

b. Select the entire pie, display the **Shape Effects** gallery, point to **Bevel**, and then at the bottom of the gallery, click **3-D Options**. Change the **Top** and **Bottom** options to the first **Bevel** type—**Circle**. Set all of the **Width** and **Height** boxes to **512** and then change the **Material** to the third **Standard** type—**Plastic**.

c. Format the **Chart Area** by applying a **Convex Bevel** and a **Solid fill—Dark Green, Accent 4, Lighter 60%**. Insert a **Custom Footer** with the **File Name** in the **left section**, and then **Save** the workbook.

Table 1

	Quarter 1	Quarter 2	Quarter 3	Quarter 4
Colorado	48123789	42468256	45159681	49452695
New Mexico	25783516	21985365	19987269	22252487
Oregon	35658498	34689526	37986369	39456899
California	58123789	64468256	65159681	68452695
Washington	42143258	46598456	44874332	50546222

- - - → (Return to Step 1-b)

(Business Running Case: Front Range Action Sports continues on the next page)

Front Range Action Sports (continued)

3 Display the **Seattle Inventory** worksheet, and then in cell **B4**, construct a formula to calculate the *Total Items in Stock* by summing the **Quantity in Stock** column. Format the result with **Comma Style** and **no decimal places**.

a. In cell **B5**, construct a formula to calculate the average of the **Retail Price** column. In the range **B6:B8**, construct similar formulas to calculate the median, lowest, and highest retail prices. Format the results in **B5:B8** with **Accounting Number Format**. In cell **B10**, use the **COUNTIF** function to count the number of **Skiing** items that the Seattle location stocks.

b. In cell **G14**, enter an **IF** function to determine the items that must be ordered. If the **Quantity in Stock** is less than **50** then **Value_if_true** is **Order** Otherwise the **Value_if_false** is **OK** Fill the formula down through cell **G87**. Apply **Conditional Formatting** to the **Stock Level** column so that cells that contain the text *Order* are formatted with **Bold Italic** and with a **Font Color** of **Orange, Accent 1**. Apply **Orange Gradient Fill Data Bars** to the **Quantity in Stock** column.

c. Insert a table with headers using the range **A13:G87**. Apply **Table Style Light 11**. **Sort** the table from smallest to largest on the **Retail Price** column, and then filter the table on the **Sport** column to display the **Skiing** types. Display a **Total Row** in the table, and then in cell **A88**, **Sum** the **Quantity in Stock** for the **Skiing** items. Type the result in cell **B11**. Remove the total row from the table, clear the **Sport** filter so that all of the data displays, and then convert the table to a range.

d. Change the **Print Titles** option so that **row 13** prints at the top of each page. Insert the file name in the **left section** of the footer, set the orientation to **Landscape**, and center the worksheet horizontally. Return to **Normal** view.

4 Display the **Denver Inventory** worksheet, and then in cell **B4**, construct a formula to calculate the *Total Items in Stock* by summing the **Quantity in Stock** column. Format the result with **Comma Style** and **no decimal places**.

a. In the range **B5:B8**, use the appropriate statistical functions to calculate the price data. Format the results with **Accounting Number Format**. In cell **B10**, use the **COUNTIF** function to count the number of **Skiing** items that the Denver location stocks.

b. In cell **G14**, enter an **IF** function to determine the items that must be ordered. If the **Quantity in Stock** is less than **50 Value_if_true** is **Order** Otherwise the **Value_if_false** is **OK** Fill the formula down through cell **G87**. Apply **Conditional Formatting** to the **Stock Level** column so that cells that contain the text *Order* are formatted with **Bold Italic** and with a **Font Color** of **Dark Blue, Accent 3**. Apply **Light Blue Gradient Fill Data Bars** to the **Quantity in Stock** column.

c. Create a table with headers using the range **A13:G87**. Apply **Table Style Light 9**. **Sort** the table from smallest to largest on the **Retail Price** column, and then filter the table on the **Sport** column to display the **Skiing** types. Display a **Total Row** in the table and then in cell **A88**, **Sum** the **Quantity in Stock** for the **Skiing** items. Type the result in cell **B11**. Remove the total row from the table, clear the **Sport** filter so that all of the data displays, and then convert the table to a range.

d. Change the **Print Titles** option so that **row 13** prints at the top of each page. Insert the file name in the **left section** of the footer, set the orientation to **Landscape**, and center the worksheet horizontally. Return to **Normal** view.

e. Display the **Inventory Summary** sheet. In cell **B5**, enter a formula that references cell **B4** in the **Seattle Inventory** sheet so that the Seattle *Total Items in Stock* displays in **B5**. Create similar formulas to enter the **Average Price**, **Median Price, Lowest Price,** and **Highest Price** in the range **B6:B9**. Enter similar formulas in the range **C5:C9** so that the **Denver** totals display. Be sure the range **B6:C9** is formatted with **Accounting Number Format**. Insert the file name in the **left section** of the footer, set the orientation to **Portrait**, and center the worksheet horizontally. Return to **Normal** view. **Save** the workbook.

5 Display the **Annual Expenses** worksheet. Construct formulas to calculate the *Totals by Quarter* in the range **B10:E10** and the *Annual Totals* in the range **F5:F10**.

a. Using absolute cell references as necessary, in cell **G5**, construct a formula to calculate the *% of Total* by dividing the **Sales Expense Annual Total** by the **Annual Totals by Quarter**. Apply **Percent Style**, fill the formula down through the range **G6:G9**, and **Center** the percentages.

(Business Running Case: Front Range Action Sports continues on the next page)

Business Running Case

Front Range Action Sports (continued)

b. Apply appropriate financial formatting to the data using no decimal places, and apply the **Total** cell style to the *Totals by Quarter*. **Center** the column headings and apply the **Heading 4** cell style.

c. **Merge & Center** the worksheet title and subtitle across columns **A:G**, and then to cell **A1**, apply the **Title** style and to cell **A2**, apply the **Heading 1** style. To the range **A1:A2**, apply a **Fill Color** using **Dark Blue, Accent 3, Lighter 60%**.

d. Using the data in the nonadjacent ranges **B4:E4** and **B10:E10**, insert a **Line with Markers** chart. Position the upper left corner of the chart slightly inside cell **B12** and resize the chart so that the lower right corner is inside cell **F25**. Remove the **Legend** and then add a **Chart Title** above the chart with the text **2012 Direct Expenses**

e. Apply chart **Style 13**, and then format the **Chart Area** with the picture **eBRC1_Skiing** from your student files. Format the **Plot Area** by changing the **Fill** option to **No fill**. Edit the **Vertical (Value) Axis** so that the **Minimum** is **8000000** and the **Major unit** is **1000000**

6 Use **Format Painter** to copy the formatting from cell **A2** to **A27**. In cell **B32**, enter a formula that references the value in cell **F10**.

a. Using absolute cell references as necessary, in cell **C32**, construct a formula to calculate the projected expenses for 2013 after the *Forecasted increase* in cell **B29** is applied. Fill the formula through cell **F32**. If necessary, use Format Painter to copy the format in cell B32 to the remaining cells in the row.

b. On the **Page Layout tab**, in the **Scale to Fit group**, set both the **Width** and **Height** to scale to **1 page**. Insert the file name in the **left section** of the footer, set the orientation to **Landscape**, and center the worksheet horizontally. Return to **Normal** view. Display the **Document Properties**. Add your name, your course name and section, and the keywords **annual report**

c. **Save** your workbook. Select all the sheets, and then display and check the Print Preview. There are a total of 10 pages. Print or submit electronically as directed. If required by your instructor, print or create an electronic version of your worksheets with formulas displayed by using the instructions in Activity 1.16, and then **Close** Excel without saving so that you do not save the changes you made to print formulas.

End **You have completed Business Running Case 1** ————————————

Getting Started with Access Databases

OUTCOMES

At the end of this chapter you will be able to:

OBJECTIVES

Mastering these objectives will enable you to:

PROJECT 1A
Create a new database.

1. Identify Good Database Design (p. 419)
2. Create a Table and Define Fields in a New Database (p. 420)
3. Change the Structure of Tables and Add a Second Table (p. 432)
4. Create and Use a Query, Form, and Report (p. 442)
5. Save and Close a Database (p. 448)

PROJECT 1B
Create a database from a template.

6. Create a Database Using a Template (p. 450)
7. Organize Objects in the Navigation Pane (p. 454)
8. Create a New Table in a Database Created with a Template (p. 456)
9. Print a Report and a Table in a Database Created with a Template (p. 458)

Joy Brown/Shutterstock

In This Chapter

In this chapter, you will use Microsoft Access 2010 to organize a collection of related information. Access is a powerful program that enables you to organize, search, sort, retrieve, and present information in a professional-looking manner. You will create new databases, enter data into Access tables, and create a query, form, and report—all of which are Access objects that make a database useful. In this chapter, you will also create a database from a template provided with the Access program. The template creates a complete database that you can use as provided, or you can modify it to suit your needs. Additional templates are available from the Microsoft Online Web site. For your first attempt at a database, consider using a template.

The projects in this chapter relate to **Capital Cities Community College**, which is located in the Washington D. C. metropolitan area. The college provides high-quality education and professional training to residents in the cities surrounding the nation's capital. Its four campuses serve over 50,000 students and offer more than 140 certificate programs and degrees at the associate's level. CapCCC has a highly acclaimed Distance Education program and an extensive Workforce Development program. The college makes positive contributions to the community through cultural and athletic programs and partnerships with businesses and non-profit organizations.

Project 1A Contact Information Database with Two Tables

Project Activities

In Activities 1.01 through 1.17, you will assist Dr. Justin Mitrani, Vice President of Instruction at Capital Cities Community College, in creating a new database for tracking the contact information for students and faculty members. Your completed database objects will look similar to Figure 1.1.

Project Files

For Project 1A, you will need the following files:

New blank Access database
a01A_Students (Excel workbook)
a01A_Faculty (Excel workbook)

You will save your database as:

Lastname_Firstname_1A_Contacts

Project Results

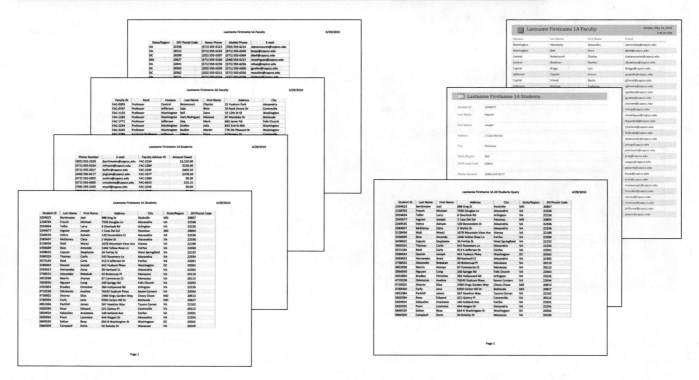

Figure 1.1
Project 1A Contacts

Objective 1 | Identify Good Database Design

A **database** is an organized collection of **data**—facts about people, events, things, or ideas—related to a specific topic or purpose. **Information** is data that is organized in a useful manner. Your personal address book is a type of database, because it is a collection of data about one topic—the people with whom you communicate. A simple database of this type is called a **flat database** because it is not related or linked to any other collection of data. Another example of a simple database is a list of movie DVDs. You do not keep information about your DVDs in your address book because the data is not related to your addresses.

A more sophisticated type of database is a **relational database**, because multiple collections of data in the database are related to one another; for example, data about the students, the courses, and the faculty members at a college. Microsoft Access 2010 is a relational **database management system**—also referred to as a **DBMS**—which is software that controls how related collections of data are stored, organized, retrieved, and secured.

Activity 1.01 | Using Good Design Techniques to Plan a Database

The first step in creating a new database is to determine the information you want to keep track of, and then ask yourself, *What questions should this database be able to answer for me?* The purpose of a database is to store the data in a manner that makes it easy for you to get the information you need by asking questions. For example, in the Contacts database for Capital Cities Community College, the questions to be answered might include:

How many students are enrolled at Capital Cities Community College?

How many faculty members teach in the Accounting Department?

Which and how many students live in Arlington, Virginia?

Which and how many students have a balance owed?

Which and how many students are majoring in Information Systems Technology?

Tables are the foundation of an Access database because all of the data is stored in one or more tables. A table is similar in structure to an Excel worksheet; that is, data is organized into rows and columns. Each table row is a **record**—all of the categories of data pertaining to one person, place, thing, event, or idea. Each table column is a **field**—a single piece of information for every record. For example, in a table storing student contact information, each row forms a record for only one student. Each column forms a field for a single piece of information for every record; for example, the student ID number for all students.

Access | Chapter 1

When organizing the fields of information in your database, break each piece of information into its smallest useful part. For example, create three fields for the name of a student—one field for the last name, one field for the first name, and one field for the middle name or initial.

The *first principle of good database design* is to organize data in the tables so that *redundant*—duplicate—data does not occur. For example, record the contact information for students in only *one* table, because if the address for a student changes, the change can be made in just one place. This conserves space, reduces the likelihood of errors when recording the new data, and does not require remembering all of the different places where the address is stored.

The *second principle of good database design* is to use techniques that ensure the accuracy of data when it is entered into the table. Typically, many different people enter data into a database—think of all the people who enter data at your college. When entering a state in a contacts database, one person might enter the state as *Virginia* and another might enter the state as *VA*. Use design techniques to help those who enter data into a database do so in a consistent and accurate manner.

Normalization is the process of applying design rules and principles to ensure that your database performs as expected. Taking the time to plan and create a database that is well designed will ensure that you can retrieve meaningful information from the database.

The tables of information in a relational database are linked or joined to one another by a *common field*—a field in one or more tables that stores the same data. For example, the Student Contacts table includes the Student ID, name, and address of every student. The Student Activities table includes the name of each club, and the Student ID—but not the name or address—of each student in each club. Because the two tables share a common field—Student ID—you can create a list of names and addresses of all the students in the Photography Club. The names and addresses are stored in the Student Contacts table, and the Student IDs of the Photography Club members are stored in the Student Activities table.

Objective 2 | Create a Table and Define Fields in a New Blank Database

There are two methods to create a new Access database: create a new database using a *database template*—a preformatted database designed for a specific purpose—or create a new database from a blank database. A blank database has no data and has no database tools; you create the data and the tools as you need them.

Regardless of the method you use, you must name and save the database before you can create any *objects* in it. Objects are the basic parts of a database; you create objects to store your data and to work with your data. The most common database objects are tables, forms, and reports. Think of an Access database as a container for the objects that you will create.

Activity 1.02 | Starting with a New Database

1 **Start** Access. Take a moment to compare your screen with Figure 1.2 and study the parts of the Microsoft Access window described in the table in Figure 1.3.

From this Access starting point in Backstage view, you can open an existing database, create a new blank database, or create a new database from a template.

Figure 1.2

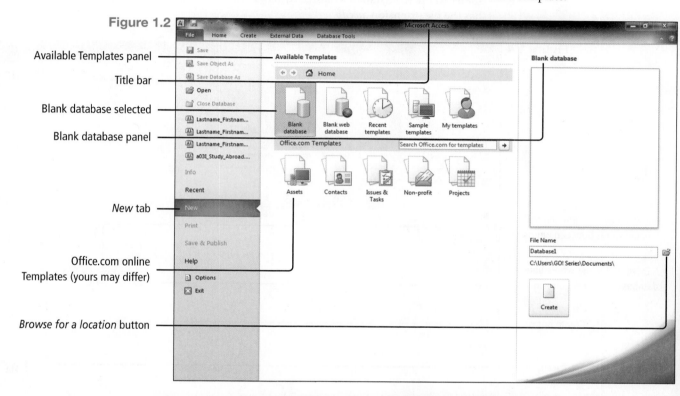

Available Templates panel
Title bar
Blank database selected
Blank database panel

New tab

Office.com online Templates (yours may differ)

Browse for a location button

Access | Chapter 1

Microsoft Access Opening Window

Window Part	Description
Available Templates panel	Displays alternative methods of creating a database.
Blank database	Starts a new blank database.
Blank database panel	Displays when *Blank database* button is selected under Available Templates.
Browse for location button	Enables you to select a storage location for the database.
New tab	Displays, when active in Backstage view, the various methods by which you can create a new database.
Office.com Templates	Displays template categories available from the Office.com Web site.
Title bar	Displays the Quick Access Toolbar, program name, and program-level buttons.

Figure 1.3

2 On the right, under **Blank database**, to the right of the **File Name** box, click the **Browse** button 📁. In the **File New Database** dialog box, navigate to the location where you are saving your databases for this chapter, create a new folder named **Access Chapter 1** and then notice that *Database1* displays as the default file name—the number at the end of your file name might differ if you have saved a database previously with the default name. In the **File New Database** dialog box, click **Open**.

3 In the **File name** box, replace the existing text with **Lastname_Firstname_1A_Contacts** Press Enter, and then compare your screen with Figure 1.4.

On the right, the name of your database displays in the File Name box, and the drive and folder where the database is stored displays under the File Name box. An Access database has the file extension *.accdb*.

Figure 1.4

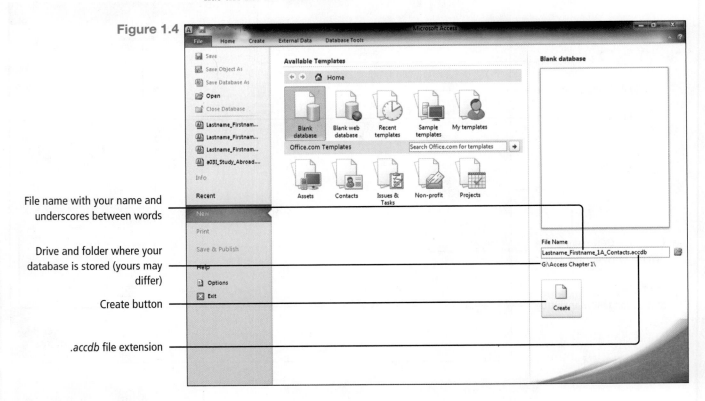

File name with your name and underscores between words

Drive and folder where your database is stored (yours may differ)

Create button

.accdb file extension

4 Under the **File Name** box, click the **Create** button, compare your screen with Figure 1.5, and then take a moment to study the screen elements described in the table in Figure 1.6.

Access creates the new database and opens *Table1*. Recall that a **table** is an Access object that stores your data in columns and rows, similar to the format of an Excel worksheet. Table objects are the foundation of a database because tables store the actual data.

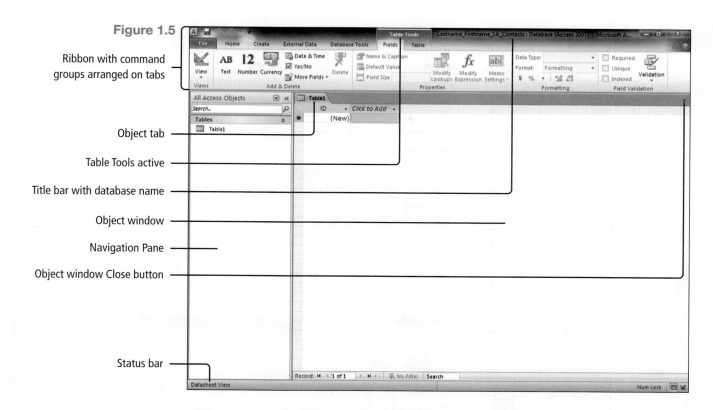

Figure 1.5

Ribbon with command groups arranged on tabs

Object tab

Table Tools active

Title bar with database name

Object window

Navigation Pane

Object window Close button

Status bar

Parts of the Access Database Window

Window Part	Description
Navigation Pane	Displays the database objects; from here you open the database objects to display in the object window at the right.
Object tab	Identifies and enables you to select the open object.
Object window	Displays the active or open object (table, query, or other object).
Object window Close button	Closes the active object (table, query, or other object).
Ribbon with command groups arranged on tabs	Groups the commands for performing related database tasks on tabs.
Status bar	Indicates the active view and the status of actions occurring within the database on the left; provides buttons to switch between Datasheet view and Design view on the right.
Table Tools	Provides tools for working with a table object; Table Tools are available only when a table is displayed.
Title bar	Displays the name of your database.

Figure 1.6

Activity 1.03 | Assigning the Data Type and Name to Fields

After you have saved and named your database, the next step is to consult your database plan, and then create the tables in which to enter your data. Limit the data in each table to *one* subject. For example, in this project, your database will have two tables— one for student contact information and one for faculty contact information.

Access | Chapter 1

Recall that each column in a table is a field and that field names display at the top of each column of the table. Recall also that each row in a table is a record—all of the data pertaining to one person, place, thing, event, or idea. Each record is broken up into its smallest usable parts—the fields. Use meaningful names to name fields; for example, *Last Name*.

1 Notice the new blank table that displays in Datasheet view, and then take a moment to study the elements of the table's object window. Compare your screen with Figure 1.7.

The table displays in *Datasheet view*, which displays the data as columns and rows similar to the format of an Excel worksheet. Another way to view a table is in *Design view*, which displays the underlying design—the *structure*—of the table's fields. The *object window* displays the open object—in this instance, the table object.

In a new blank database, there is only one object—a new blank table. Because you have not yet named this table, the object tab displays a default name of *Table1*. Access creates the first field and names it *ID*. In the ID field, Access assigns a unique sequential number—each number incremented by one—to each record as it is entered into the table.

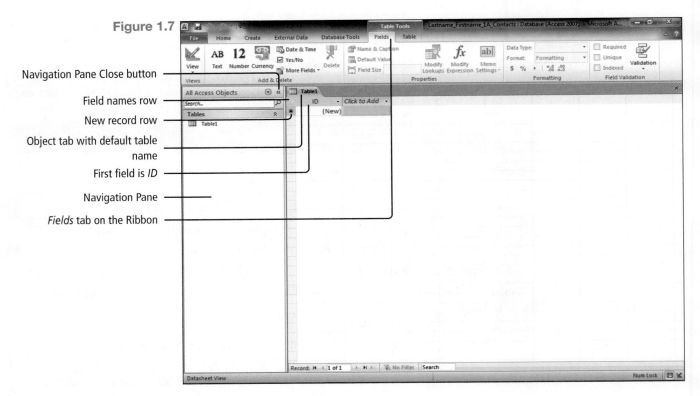

Figure 1.7

- Navigation Pane Close button
- Field names row
- New record row
- Object tab with default table name
- First field is *ID*
- Navigation Pane
- *Fields* tab on the Ribbon

2 In the **Navigation Pane**, click the **Open/Close** button to collapse the **Navigation Pane** to a narrow bar on the left and to display more of the table.

The *Navigation Pane* is an area of the Access window that displays and organizes the names of the objects in a database. From the Navigation Pane, you can open objects for use.

Another Way

To the right of *Click to Add*, click the arrow.

3 In the field names row, click anywhere in the text *Click to Add* to display a list of data types. Compare your screen with Figure 1.8.

Data type is the characteristic that defines the kind of data that you can type in a field, such as numbers, text, or dates. A field in a table can have only one data type. Part of your database design should include deciding on the data type of each field. After you have selected the data type, you can name the field.

Figure 1.8

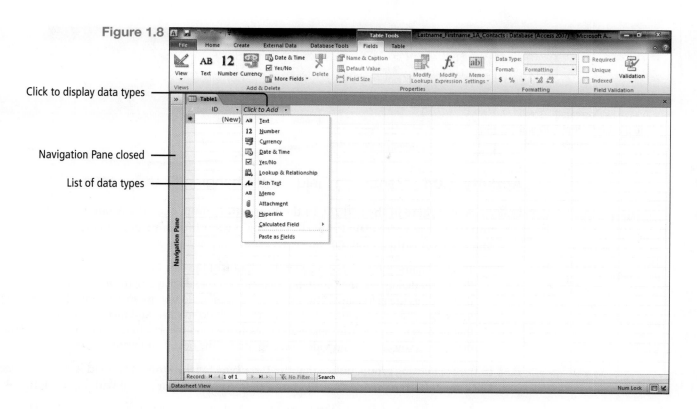

Click to display data types

Navigation Pane closed

List of data types

4 In the list of data types, click **Text**, and notice that in the second column, *Click to Add* changes to *Field1*, which is selected. Type **Last Name** and then press Enter.

> The second column displays *Last Name* as the field name, and the data type list displays in the third column. The ***Text data type*** describes text, a combination of text and numbers, or numbers that are not used in calculations, such as a ZIP code.

Another Way

With the list of data types displayed, type *T* to select Text.

5 In the third field name box, click **Text**, type **First Name** and then press Enter. In the fourth field name box, click **Text**, type **Middle Initial** and then press Enter.

6 Using the technique you just practiced, create the remaining fields as follows by first selecting the data type, then typing the field name, and then pressing Enter. The field names in the table will display on one line.

> The ZIP/Postal Code field is assigned a data type of Text because the number is never used in a calculation. The Amount Owed field is assigned a data type of Currency; the ***Currency data type*** describes monetary values and numeric data used in mathematical calculations involving data with one to four decimal places. Access automatically adds a U.S. dollar sign ($) and two decimal places to all of the numbers in the fields with a data type of *Currency*.

Data Type		Text	Text	Text	**Text**	**Text**	**Text**	**Text**	**Text**	**Text**	**Text**	**Currency**
Field Name	ID	Last Name	First Name	Middle Initial	**Address**	**City**	**State/Region**	**ZIP/Postal Code**	**Phone Number**	**E-mail**	**Faculty Advisor ID**	**Amount Owed**

7 If necessary, by using the horizontal scroll bar at the bottom of the screen, scroll to the left to bring the first column into view. Compare your screen with Figure 1.9.

> Access automatically created the ID field, and you created 11 additional fields in the table. The horizontal scroll bar indicates that there are additional fields that are not displayed on the screen—your screen width may vary.

Access | Chapter 1

Figure 1.9

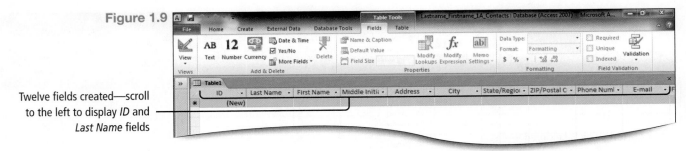

Twelve fields created—scroll
to the left to display *ID* and
Last Name fields

Activity 1.04 | Renaming Fields and Changing Data Types in a Table

Another Way

Right-click the field
name, and then on the
shortcut menu, click
Rename Field.

1 Click anywhere in the text *ID*. In the **Properties group**, click the **Name & Caption** button. In the **Enter Field Properties** dialog box, in the **Name** box, change *ID* to **Student ID** and then click **OK**.

The field name *Student ID* is a better description of the data in this field. In the Enter Field Properties dialog box, the **Caption** property is used to display a name for a field other than that listed as the field name. Many database designers do not use spaces in field names; instead, they might name a field LastName—with no spaces—and then create a caption for that field so it displays with spaces in tables, forms, and reports. In the Enter Field Properties dialog box, you also provide a description for the field if you want to do so.

2 In the **Formatting group**, notice that the **Data Type** for the **Student ID** field is *AutoNumber*. Click the **Data Type arrow**, click **Text**, and then compare your screen with Figure 1.10.

In the new record row, the Student ID field is selected. By default, Access creates an ID field for all new tables and sets the data type for the field to AutoNumber. The **AutoNumber data type** describes a unique sequential or random number assigned by Access as each record is entered. By changing the data type of this field from *AutoNumber* to *Text,* you can enter a custom student ID number.

When records in a database have *no* unique value, for example the names in your address book, the AutoNumber data type is a useful way to automatically create a unique number so that you have a way to ensure that every record is different from the others.

Figure 1.10

Field renamed

New record row—indicated
by asterisk

Selected field

Data type indicates *Text*

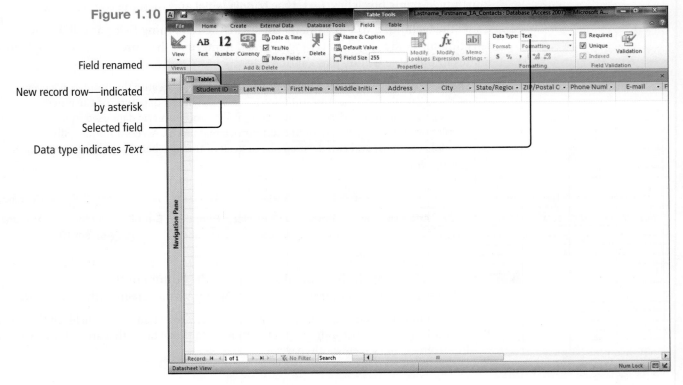

Activity 1.05 | Adding a Record to a Table

A new address book is not useful until you fill it with names, addresses, and phone numbers. Likewise, a new database is not useful until you ***populate*** it—fill one or more tables with data. You can populate a table with records by typing data directly into the table.

Another Way

Press [Tab] to move to the next field.

1 In the new record row, click in the **Student ID** field to display the insertion point, type **1238765** and then press [Enter]. Compare your screen with Figure 1.11.

The pencil icon 🖉 in the ***record selector box***—the small box at the left of a record in Datasheet view that, when clicked, selects the entire record—indicates that a record is being entered or edited.

Figure 1.11

Pencil icon indicates record being entered or edited

Record selector box

First student ID is *1238765*

Insertion point in Last Name field

2 With the insertion point positioned in the **Last Name** field, type **Fresch** and then press [Enter].

> **Note | Correct Typing Errors**
>
> Correct typing errors by using the techniques you have practiced in other Office applications. For example, use [Backspace] to remove characters to the left, [Del] to remove characters to the right, or select the text you want to replace and type the correct information. Press [Esc] to exit out of a record that has not been completely entered.

3 In the **First Name** field, type **Michael** and then press [Enter].

4 In the **Middle Initial** field, type **B** and then press [Enter].

5 In the **Address** field, type **7550 Douglas Ln** and then press [Enter].

Do not be concerned if the data does not completely display in the column. As you progress in your study of Access, you will adjust the column widths so that you can view all of the data.

6 Continue entering data in the fields as indicated below, pressing [Enter] to move to the next field.

City	State/Region	ZIP/Postal Code	Phone Number	E-mail	Faculty Advisor ID
Alexandria	**VA**	**22336**	**(571) 555-0234**	**mfresch@capccc.edu**	**FAC-2289**

> **Note | Format for Typing Telephone Numbers in Access**
>
> Access does not require any specific format for typing telephone numbers in a database. The examples in this project use the format of Microsoft Outlook. Using such a format facilitates easy transfer of Outlook information to and from Access.

7 In the **Amount Owed** field, type **150** and then press [Enter]. Compare your screen with Figure 1.12.

> Pressing [Enter] or [Tab] in the last field moves the insertion point to the next row to begin a new record. As soon as you move to the next row, Access saves the record—you do not have to take any specific action to save a record.

Figure 1.12

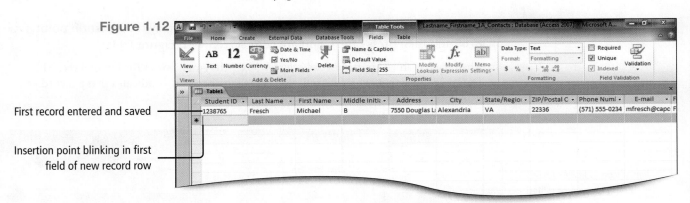

First record entered and saved

Insertion point blinking in first field of new record row

8 To give your table a meaningful name, on the Quick Access Toolbar, click the **Save** button. In the **Save As** dialog box, in the **Table Name** box, using your own name, replace the highlighted text by typing **Lastname Firstname 1A Students**

> Save each database object with a name that identifies the data that it contains. When you save objects within a database, it is not necessary to use underscores. Your name is included as part of the object name so that you and your instructor can identify your printouts or electronic files.

9 In the **Save As** dialog box, click **OK**, and then notice that the object tab displays the new table name you just typed.

More Knowledge | Renaming a Table

To change the name of a table, close the table, display the Navigation Pane, right-click the table name, and then on the shortcut menu, click Rename. Type the new name or edit as you would any selected text.

Activity 1.06 | Adding Additional Records to a Table

1 In the new record row, click in the **Student ID** field, and then enter the contact information for the following two additional students, pressing [Enter] or [Tab] to move from field to field. The data in each field will display on one line in the table.

Student ID	Last Name	First Name	Middle Initial	Address	City	State/ Region	ZIP/ Postal Code	Phone Number	E-mail	Faculty Advisor ID	Amount Owed
2345677	Ingram	Joseph	S	1 Casa Del Sol	Potomac	MD	20854	(240) 555-0177	jingram@ capccc.edu	FAC-2377	378.5
3456689	Bass	Amanda	J	1446 Yellow Rose Ln	Fairfax	VA	22030	(703) 555-0192	abass@ capccc.edu	FAC-9005	0

2 Compare your screen with Figure 1.13.

Figure 1.13

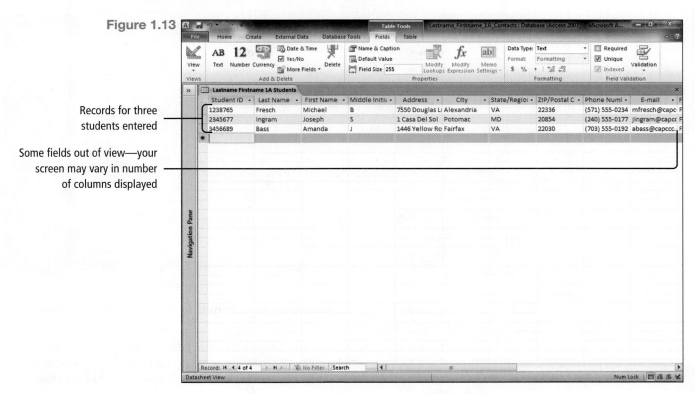

Records for three students entered

Some fields out of view—your screen may vary in number of columns displayed

Activity 1.07 | Importing Data from an Excel Workbook into an Existing Access Table

When you create a database table, you can type the records directly into a table. You can also *import* data from a variety of sources. Importing is the process of copying data from one source or application to another application. For example, you can import data from a Word table or an Excel worksheet into an Access database because the data is arranged in columns and rows, similar to a table in Datasheet view.

In this activity, you will *append*—add on—data from an Excel spreadsheet to your *1A Students* table. To append data, the table must already be created, and it must be closed.

1 In the upper right corner of the table, below the Ribbon, click the **Object Close** ☒ button to close your **1A Students** table. Notice that no objects are open.

2 On the Ribbon, click the **External Data tab**. In the **Import & Link group**, click the **Excel** button. In the **Get External Data - Excel Spreadsheet** dialog box, click the **Browse** button.

Another Way

Select the file name, and in the lower right area of the dialog box, click Open.

3 In the **File Open** dialog box, navigate to your student files, locate and double-click the Excel file **a01A_Students**, and then compare your screen with Figure 1.14.

The path to the *source file*—the file being imported—displays in the File name box. There are three options for importing data from an Excel workbook—import the data into a *new* table in the current database, append a copy of the records to an existing table, or link the data from Excel to a linked table. A *link* is a connection to data in another file. When linking, Access creates a table that maintains a link to the source data.

Figure 1.14

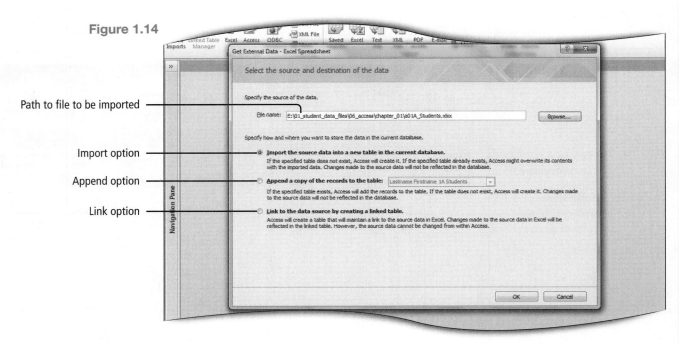

Path to file to be imported

Import option

Append option

Link option

---

4 Click the **Append a copy of the records to the table** option button, and then in the box to its right, click the **arrow**.

> Currently your database has only one table, so no other tables display on the list. However, when a database has multiple tables, here you can select the table to which you want to append records. The table into which you import or append data is referred to as the *destination table*.

5 Press Esc to cancel the list, and then in the lower right corner of the dialog box, click **OK**. Compare your screen with Figure 1.15.

> The first screen of the Import Spreadsheet Wizard displays, and the presence of scroll bars indicates that records and fields are out of view in this window. To append records from an Excel worksheet to an existing database table, the field names in the Excel worksheet must be identical to the field names in the table, and that is true in this table.

Figure 1.15

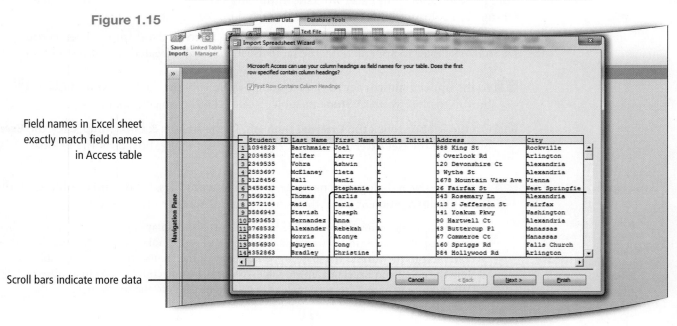

Field names in Excel sheet exactly match field names in Access table

Scroll bars indicate more data

---

6 In the lower right corner, click **Next**. Notice that the name of your table displays under **Import to Table**. In the lower right corner, click **Finish**.

7 In the **Get External Data - Excel Spreadsheet** dialog box, click **Close**, and then **Open** ⟫ the **Navigation Pane**.

8 Point to the right edge of the **Navigation Pane** to display the ⟷ pointer. Drag to the right to widen the pane to display the entire table name, and then compare your screen with Figure 1.16.

Figure 1.16

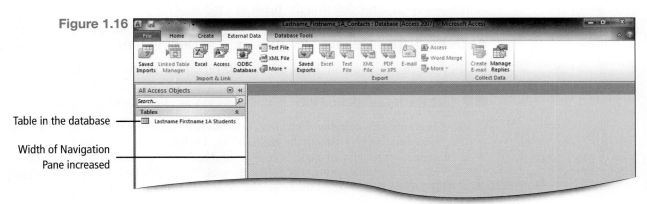

Table in the database

Width of Navigation Pane increased

Another Way

To open an object from the Navigation Pane, right-click the object name, and then on the shortcut menu, click Open.

9 In the **Navigation Pane**, double-click your **1A Students** table to open the table in Datasheet view, and then **Close** ⟪ the **Navigation Pane**.

10 At the bottom left corner of your screen, locate the navigation area, and notice that there are a total of **26** records in the table—you created three records and imported 23 additional records. Compare your screen with Figure 1.17.

The records from the Excel worksheet display in your table, and the first record is selected. The *navigation area* indicates the number of records in the table and contains controls (arrows) with which you can navigate among the records.

Figure 1.17

Three records you entered

26 total records

Navigation area

Current view indicated

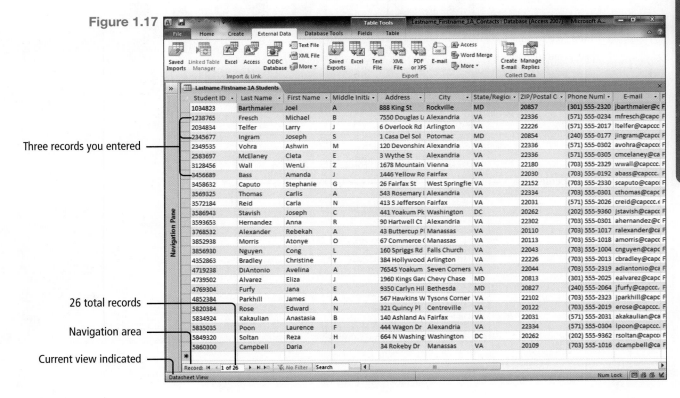

Access | Chapter 1

Objective 3 | Change the Structure of Tables and Add a Second Table

Recall that the structure of a table is the underlying design, including field names and data types. You can create a table or modify a table in Datasheet view. To define and modify fields, many database experts prefer to work in Design view, where you have many additional options for defining the fields in a table.

Activity 1.08 | Deleting a Table Field in Design View

In this activity, you will delete the *Middle Initial* field from the table.

1 Click the **Home tab**, and then in the **Views group**, click the **View button arrow**.

There are four common views in Access, but two that you will use often are Datasheet view and Design view. On the displayed list, Design view is represented by a picture of a pencil, a ruler, and an angle. When one of these four icons is displayed on the View button, clicking the View button will display the table in the view represented by the icon. Datasheet view displays the table data in rows and columns.

2 On the list, click **Design View**, and then compare your screen with Figure 1.18.

Design view displays the underlying design—the structure—of the table and its fields. In Design view, you cannot view the data; you can view only the information about each field's characteristics. Each field name is listed, along with its data type. A column to add a Description—information about the data in the field—is provided.

In the Field Properties area, you can make additional decisions about how each individual field looks and behaves. For example, you can set a specific field size.

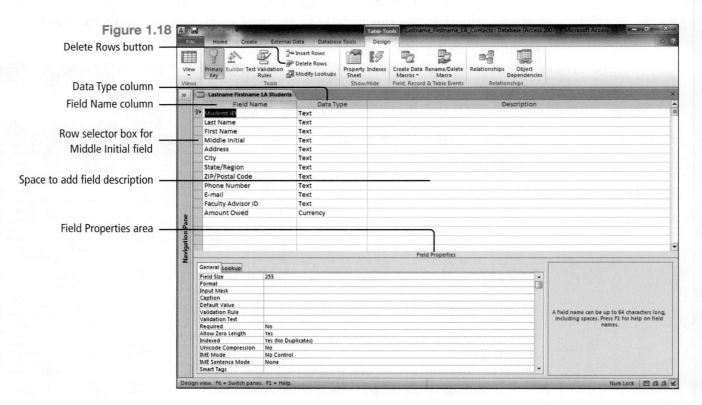

Figure 1.18

Delete Rows button

Data Type column

Field Name column

Row selector box for Middle Initial field

Space to add field description

Field Properties area

3 In the **Field Name** column, to the left of **Middle Initial**, point to the row selector box to display the → pointer, and then click one time to select the entire row.

Another Way

Right-click the selected row and click Delete Rows.

4 On the **Design tab**, in the **Tools group**, click the **Delete Rows** button, read the message in the message box, and then click **Yes**.

Deleting a field deletes both the field and its data; you cannot undo this action. Thus, Access prompts you to be sure you want to proceed. If you change your mind after deleting a field, you must add the field back into the table and then reenter the data in that field for every record.

Activity 1.09 | Modifying a Field Size and Adding a Description

Typically, many individuals enter data into a table. For example, at your college many Registration Assistants enter and modify student and course information daily. Two ways to help reduce errors are to restrict what can be typed in a field and to add descriptive information.

1 With your table still displayed in **Design** view, in the **Field Name** column, click anywhere in the **State/Region** field name.

2 In the lower portion of the screen, under **Field Properties**, click **Field Size** to select the text *255*, type **2** and then compare your screen with Figure 1.19.

This action limits the size of the State/Region field to no more than two characters—the size of the two-letter state abbreviations provided by the United States Postal Service. *Field properties* control how the field displays and how data can be entered in the field. You can define properties for every field in the Field Properties area.

The default field size for a text field is 255. Limiting the field size property to 2 ensures that only two characters can be entered for each state. However, this does not prevent someone from entering two characters that are incorrect. Setting the proper data type for the field and limiting the field size are two ways to *help* to reduce errors.

Figure 1.19

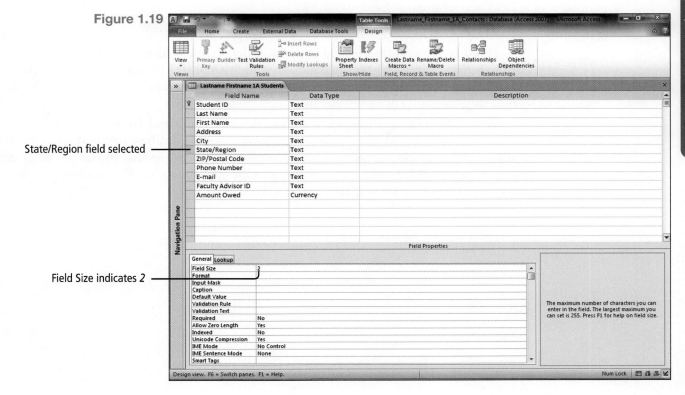

State/Region field selected

Field Size indicates *2*

3 In the **State/Region** row, click in the **Description** box, type **Two-character state abbreviation** and then press Enter.

> Descriptions for fields in a table are optional. Include a description if the field name does not provide an obvious explanation of the field. Information typed in the description area displays on the left side of the status bar in Datasheet view when the field is active, providing additional information to individuals who are entering data.

> When you enter a description for a field, a Property Update Options button displays below the text you typed, which enables you to copy the description for the field to all other database objects that use this table as an underlying source.

4 Click in the **Student ID** field name box. Using the technique you practiced, in the **Field Properties** area, change the **Field Size** to **7**

> By limiting the field size to seven characters, which is the maximum number of characters in a Student ID, you help to ensure the accuracy of the data.

5 In the **Student ID** row, click in the **Description** box, and then type **Seven-digit Student ID number**

6 Click in the **Faculty Advisor ID** field name box. In the **Field Properties** area, change the **Field Size** to **8** In the **Description** box for this field, type **Eight-character ID of faculty member assigned as advisor** and then press Enter.

7 On the Quick Access Toolbar, click the **Save** button 🖫 to save the design changes to your table, and then notice the message.

> The message indicates that the field size property of one or more fields has changed to a shorter size. If more characters are currently present in the Student ID, State/Region, or Faculty Advisor ID than you have allowed, the data could be *truncated*—cut off or shortened—because the fields were not previously restricted to a specific number of characters.

8 In the message box, click **Yes**.

Activity 1.10 | Viewing a Primary Key in Design View

Primary key refers to the field in the table that uniquely identifies a record. For example, in a college registration database, your Student ID number uniquely identifies you—no other student at the college has your exact student number. In the 1A Students table, the Student ID uniquely identifies each student.

When you create a table using the Blank database command, by default Access designates the first field as the primary key field. It is good database design practice to establish a primary key for every table, because doing so ensures that you do not enter the same record more than once. You can imagine the confusion if another student at your college had the same Student ID number as you do.

1 With your table still displayed in Design view, in the **Field Name** column, click in the **Student ID** box. To the left of the box, notice the small icon of a key, as shown in Figure 1.20.

> Access automatically designates the first field as the primary key field, but you can set any field as the primary key by clicking in the box to the left of the field name, and then clicking the Primary Key button.

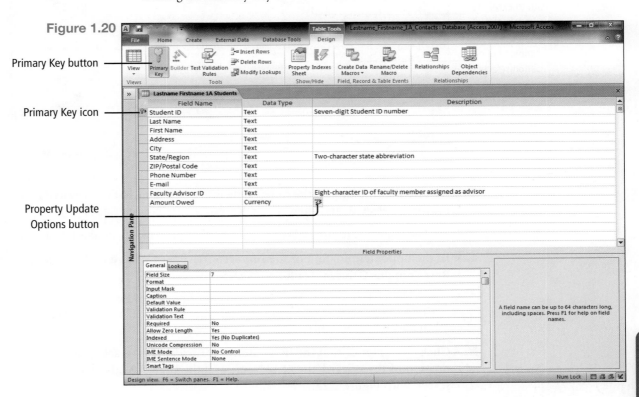

Figure 1.20

Primary Key button

Primary Key icon

Property Update Options button

2 On the **Design tab**, in the **Views group**, notice that the **View** button contains a picture of a Datasheet, indicating that clicking the button will return you to Datasheet view. Click the **View** button.

Activity 1.11 | Adding a Second Table to a Database by Importing an Excel Spreadsheet

Many Microsoft Office users track data in an Excel spreadsheet. The sorting and filtering capabilities of Excel are useful for a simple database where all the information resides in one large Excel spreadsheet. However, Excel is limited as a database management tool because it cannot *relate* the information in multiple spreadsheets in a way in which you could ask a question and get a meaningful result. Data in an Excel spreadsheet can easily become an Access table by importing the spreadsheet, because Excel's format of columns and rows is similar to that of an Access table.

1 On the Ribbon, click the **External Data tab**, and then in the **Import & Link group**, click the **Excel** button. In the **Get External Data – Excel Spreadsheet** dialog box, to the right of the **File name** box, click **Browse**.

2 In the **File Open** dialog box, navigate to your student files, and then double-click **a01A_Faculty**. Compare your screen with Figure 1.21.

Figure 1.21

Get External Data – Excel Spreadsheet dialog box

Browse button

Path to Excel file (yours may differ)

Import option button selected

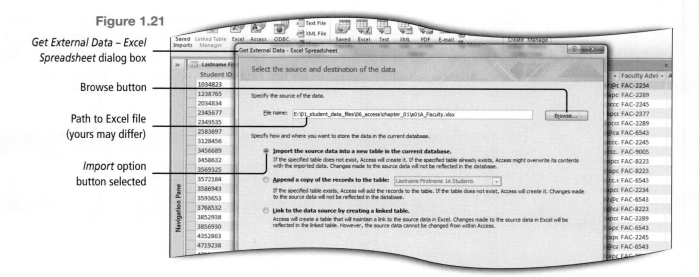

3 Be sure that the **Import the source data into a new table in the current database** option button is selected, and then click **OK**.

The Import Spreadsheet Wizard opens and displays the spreadsheet data.

4 In the upper left portion of the **Import Spreadsheet Wizard** dialog box, select the **First Row Contains Column Headings** check box.

The Excel data is framed, indicating that the first row of Excel column titles will become the Access table field names, and the remaining rows will become the individual records in the new Access table.

5 Click **Next**. Notice that the first column—*Faculty ID*—is selected, and in the upper portion of the Wizard, the **Field Name** and the **Data Type** display. Compare your screen with Figure 1.22.

Here you can review and change the field properties for each field (column). You can also identify fields in the spreadsheet that you do not want to import into the Access table by selecting the Do not import field (Skip) check box.

Figure 1.22

Import Spreadsheet Wizard dialog box

Excel column titles

Spreadsheet data—Excel rows become records

Next button

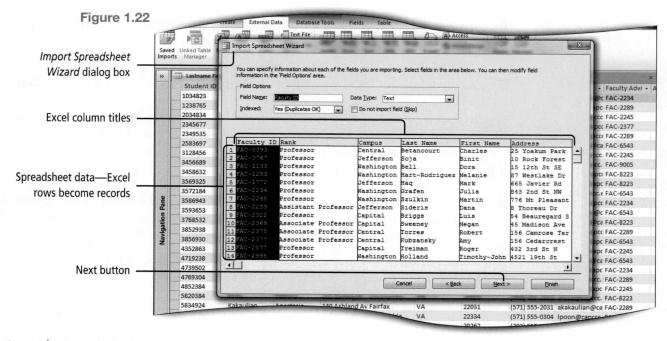

6 Click **Next**. In the upper portion of the Wizard, click the **Choose my own primary key** option button, and then be sure that **Faculty ID** displays.

> In the new table, Faculty ID will be the primary key. No two faculty members have the same Faculty ID. By default, Access selects the first field as the primary key, but you can click the arrow to select a different field.

7 Click **Next**. In the **Import to Table** box, type **Lastname Firstname 1A Faculty** and then click **Finish**.

8 In the **Get External Data – Excel Spreadsheet** dialog box, click **Close**, and then **Open** ≫ the **Navigation Pane**.

9 In the **Navigation Pane**, double-click your **1A Faculty** table to open it in Datasheet view, and then **Close** ≪ the **Navigation Pane**.

10 Click in the **ZIP/Postal Code** field, and then on the Ribbon, click the **Fields tab**. In the **Formatting group**, change the **Data Type** to **Text**. Compare your screen with Figure 1.23.

> The data from the *a01A_Faculty* worksheet displays in your *1A Faculty* table in the database. The navigation area indicates that there are 30 records in the table. Recall that if a field contains numbers that are not used in calculations, the data type should be set to Text. When you import data from an Excel spreadsheet, check the data types of all fields to ensure they are correct.

Figure 1.23

ZIP/Postal Code data type changed to Text

Table created by importing Excel spreadsheet

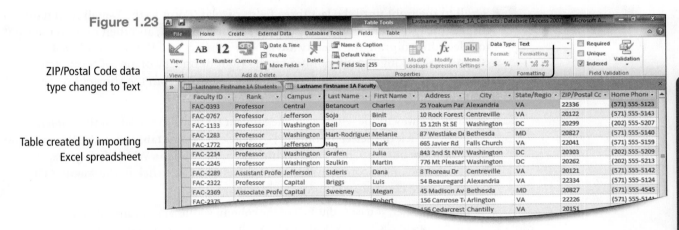

Activity 1.12 | Adjusting Column Widths

By using techniques similar to those you use for Excel worksheets, you can adjust the widths of Access fields that display in Datasheet view.

1 In the object window, click the **object tab** for your **1A Students** table.

> Clicking the object tabs along the top of the object window enables you to display open objects to work with them. All of the columns are the same width regardless of the amount of data in the field, the field size that was set, or the length of the field name. If you print the table as currently displayed, some of the data or field names will not fully print until you adjust the column widths.

Access | Chapter 1

2 In the field names row, point to the right edge of the **Address** field to display the ⊕ pointer, and then compare your screen with Figure 1.24.

Figure 1.24

Pointer positioned on right edge of Address field

3 With your ⊕ pointer positioned as shown in Figure 1.24, double-click the right edge of the **Address** field.

> The column width of the Address field widens to fully display the longest entry in the field. In this manner, the width of a column can be increased or decreased to fit its contents in the same manner as a column in an Excel worksheet. In Access this is referred to as *Best Fit*.

4 Point to the **Phone Number** field name to display the ↓ pointer, right-click to select the entire column and display a shortcut menu, and then click **Field Width**. In the **Column Width** dialog box, click **Best Fit**.

5 Scroll to the right until the last three fields display. Point to the **E-mail** field name to display the ↓ pointer, hold down the left mouse button, and then drag to the right to select this column, the **Faculty Advisor ID** column, and the **Amount Owed** column. By double-clicking the ⊕ pointer on the right boundary of any of the selected columns, or by displaying the Field Width dialog box from the shortcut menu, apply **Best Fit** to the selected columns.

6 Scroll all the way to the left to view the **Student ID** field. To the left of the *Student ID* field name, click the **Select All** button ▣. Click the **Home tab**, and in the **Records group**, click the **More** button. Click **Field Width**, and in the **Column Width** dialog box, click **Best Fit**. In the first record, scroll to the right as necessary, click in the **Amount Owed** field, and then compare your screen with Figure 1.25.

> In this manner, you can adjust all of the column widths at one time. After applying Best Fit, be sure to click in any field to remove the selection from all of the records; otherwise, the layout changes will not be saved with the table. Adjusting the width of columns does not change the data in the table's records; it changes only the *display* of the data.

Figure 1.25

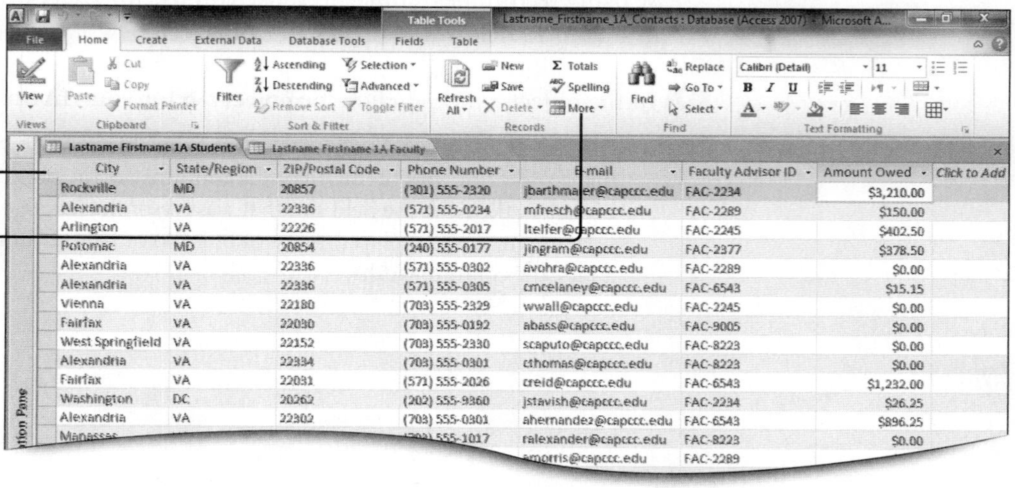

Select All button

More button

> **Note** | Adjusting Column Widths
>
> If you adjust column widths individually, scroll to the right and scroll down to be sure that all of the data displays in all of the fields. Access adjusts the column widths to fit the screen size based on the displayed data. If data is not displayed on the screen when you adjust a column width, the column may not be adjusted adequately to display all of the data in the field. For that reason, select all of the columns and apply Best Fit to be sure that all of the data displays when scrolling or printing. Click in any field after applying Best Fit to remove the selection, and then save the table before performing other tasks.

7 On the Quick Access Toolbar, click the **Save** button 🖫 to save the table design changes—changing the column widths.

> If you do not save the table after making design changes, Access will prompt you to save when you close the table.

Activity 1.13 | Printing a Table

Although a printed table does not look as professional as a printed report, there are times when you will want to print a table. For example, you may need a quick reference or want to proofread the data that has been entered.

1 On the Ribbon, click the **File tab** to display **Backstage** view, click the **Print** tab, click **Print Preview**, and then compare your screen with Figure 1.26.

Figure 1.26

Print Preview window

Navigation Pane

Next Page button

Page 1 displays

Navigation area—used to move from page to page

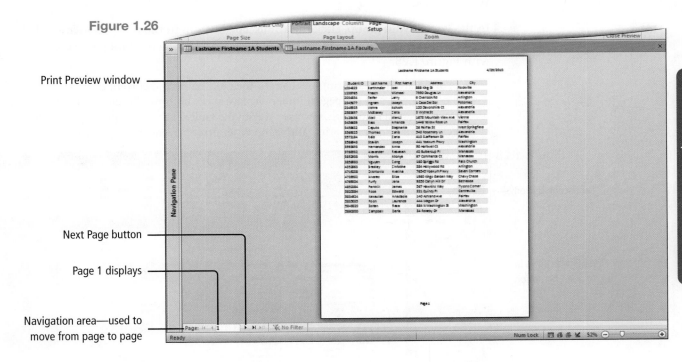

2 In the lower left corner, click the **Next Page** button ▶ two times. Point to the top of the page to display the 🔍 pointer, click one time to zoom in, and then compare your screen with Figure 1.27.

> The display enlarges, and the Zoom Out pointer displays. The third page of the table displays the last two field columns. The Next Page button is dimmed, indicating there are no more pages. The Previous Page button is darker, indicating that pages exist before this page.

Figure 1.27

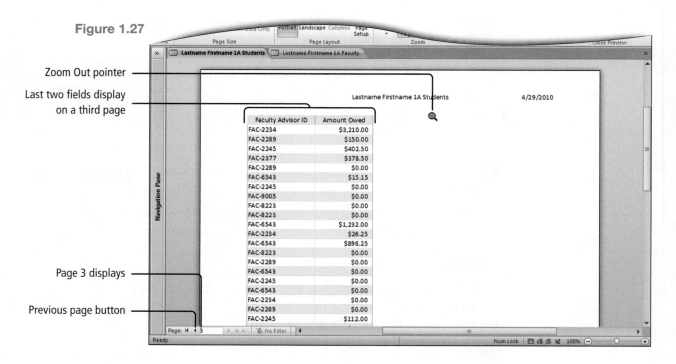

Zoom Out pointer

Last two fields display on a third page

Page 3 displays

Previous page button

Another Way
Click the 🔍 pointer to zoom back to Fit to Window view.

3 On the Ribbon, in the **Zoom group**, click the **Zoom** button to zoom back to Fit to Window view.

4 In the **Page Layout group**, click the **Landscape** button. In the navigation area, click the **Previous Page** button ◀ to display **Page 1**, and then compare your screen with Figure 1.28.

The orientation of the printout changes, the table name and current date display at the top of the page, and the page number displays at the bottom. The change in orientation from portrait to landscape is not saved with the table. Each time you print, you must check the margins, page orientation, and other print parameters to print as you intend.

Figure 1.28

Landscape button

First page displays in landscape orientation

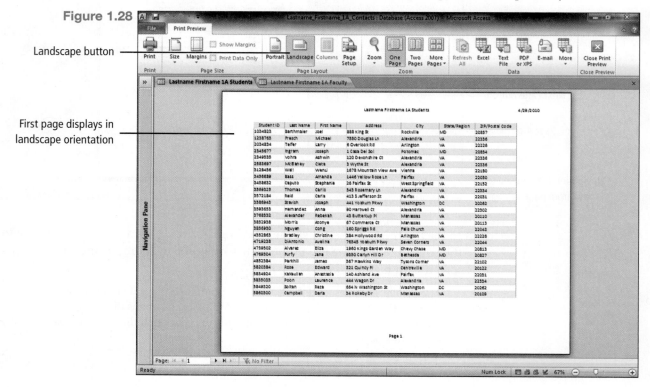

> **Note** | Headers and Footers in Access Objects
>
> The headers and footers in Access tables and queries are controlled by default settings; you cannot add additional information or edit the information. The object name displays in the center of the header area with the date on the right—that is why adding your own name to the object name is helpful to identify your paper or electronic results. The page number displays in the center of the footer area. The headers and footers in Access reports and forms, however, are more flexible; you can add to and edit the information.

5 On the **Print Preview tab**, in the **Print group**, click the **Print** button. In the **Print** dialog box, under **Print Range**, verify that the **All** option button is selected. Under **Copies**, verify that the **Number of Copies** is **1**. Compare your screen with Figure 1.29.

Figure 1.29

Print dialog box

Default printer (yours may differ)

One copy

Print all pages

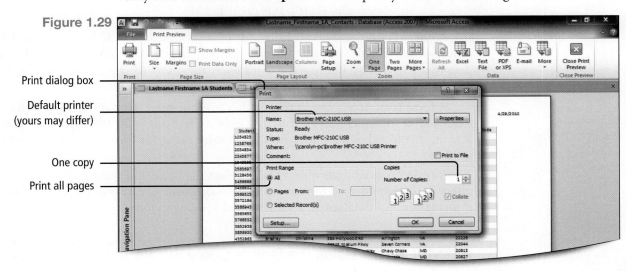

6 Determine how your instructor wants you to submit your work for this project—on paper or electronically. If submitting electronically, determine if, in addition to submitting your Access database, you are to create and submit electronic printouts of individual database objects.

7 To print on paper, in the **Print** dialog box, click **OK**, and then in the **Close Preview group**, click the **Close Print Preview** button. This printout will have two pages. To create an electronic PDF printout of this table object, in the Print dialog box, click Cancel, and then follow the steps in the following Note—or follow the specific directions provided by your instructor.

> **Note** | To Create a PDF Electronic Printout of an Access Object
>
> Display the object (table, report, and so on) in Print Preview and adjust margins and orientation as desired. On the Print Preview tab, in the Data group, click the PDF or XPS button. In the Publish as PDF or XPS dialog box, navigate to your chapter folder. Use the default file name, or follow your instructor's directions to name the object. In the lower right corner, click Publish—the default setting is PDF. If necessary, close the Adobe Acrobat/Reader window and the Export-PDF dialog box. Click the Close Print Preview button; your electronic printout is saved.

8 At the far right edge of the object window, click the **Close Object** button ☒ to close the **1A Students** table.

9 With your **1A Faculty** table displayed, to the left of the **Faculty ID** field name, click the **Select All** button ☐ to select all of the columns. On the **Home tab**, in the **Records group**, click the **More** button. Click **Field Width**, and in the **Column Width** dialog box, click **Best Fit**. Click in any field in the table to remove the selection, and then **Save** 🖫 the table.

Access | Chapter 1

10 Display the table in **Print Preview**. Change the **Orientation** to **Landscape**. If directed to do so by your instructor, create a paper or electronic printout, and then **Close Print Preview**—two pages result.

11 Click the **Close Object** button ⊠.

All of your database objects—the *1A Students* table and the *1A Faculty* table—are closed; the object window is empty.

Objective 4 | Create and Use a Query, Form, and Report

A *query* is a database object that retrieves specific data from one or more database objects—either tables or other queries—and then, in a single datasheet, displays only the data that you specify. Because the word *query* means *to ask a question*, think of a query as a question formed in a manner that Access can answer.

A *form* is an Access object with which you can enter data, edit data, or display data from a table or a query. In a form, the fields are laid out in an attractive format on the screen, which makes working with the database easier for those who must enter and look up data.

A *report* is a database object that displays the fields and records from a table or a query in an easy-to-read format suitable for printing. Create reports to *summarize* information in a database in a professional-looking manner.

Activity 1.14 | Using the Simple Query Wizard to Create a Query

A *select query* is one type of Access query. A select query, also called a *simple select query*, retrieves (selects) data from one or more tables or queries and then displays the selected data in a datasheet. A select query creates subsets of data to answer specific questions; for example, *Which students live in Arlington, VA?*

The objects from which a query selects its data are referred to as the query's *data source*. In this activity, you will create a simple select query using a *wizard*. A wizard is a feature in Microsoft Office programs that walks you step by step through a process. The process involves choosing the data source, and then indicating the fields you want to include in the query result. The query—the question that you want to ask—is *What is the name, complete mailing address, and Student ID of every student?*

1 Click the **Create tab**, and then in the **Queries group**, click the **Query Wizard** button. In the **New Query** dialog box, click **Simple Query Wizard**, and then click **OK**. Compare your screen with Figure 1.30.

Figure 1.30

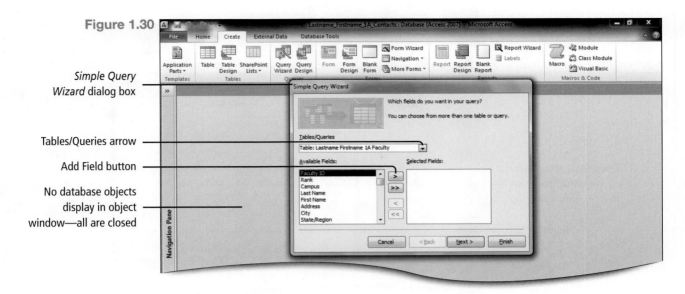

Simple Query Wizard dialog box

Tables/Queries arrow

Add Field button

No database objects
display in object
window—all are closed

2 Click the **Tables/Queries arrow**, and then click your **Table: 1A Students**.

> To create a query, first choose the data source—the object from which to select data. The name and complete mailing address of every student is stored in the 1A Students table, so this table will be your data source.

3 Under **Available Fields**, click **Student ID**, and then click the **Add Field** button [>] to move the field to the **Selected Fields** list on the right. Point to the **Last Name** field, and then double-click to add the field to the **Selected Fields** list.

> Use either method to add fields to the Selected Fields list. Fields can be added in any order.

4 By using the **Add Field** button [>] or by double-clicking the field name, add the following fields to the **Selected Fields** list: **First Name**, **Address**, **City**, **State/Region**, and **ZIP/Postal Code**. Compare your screen with Figure 1.31.

> Choosing these seven fields will answer the question, *What is the Student ID, name, and address of every student?*

Figure 1.31

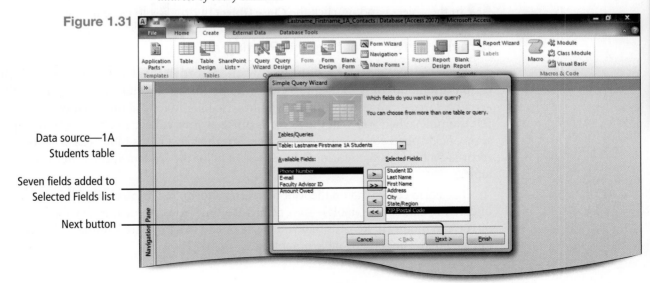

Data source—1A
Students table

Seven fields added to
Selected Fields list

Next button

5 Click **Next**. In the **Simple Query Wizard** dialog box, click in the **What title do you want for your query?** box. Edit as necessary so that the query name, using your own last and first name, is **Lastname Firstname 1A All Students Query** and then compare your screen with Figure 1.32.

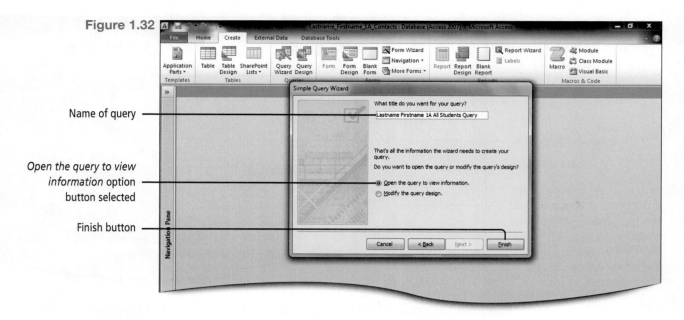

Figure 1.32

Name of query

Open the query to view information option button selected

Finish button

---

6 Click **Finish**.

Access *runs* the query—performs the actions indicated in your query design by searching the records in the data source you selected, and then finding the records that match specified criteria. The records that match the criteria display in a datasheet. A select query *selects*—pulls out and displays—*only* the information from the data source that you requested, including the specified fields.

In the object window, Access displays every student record in Datasheet view, but displays *only* the seven fields that you moved to the Selected Fields list in the Simple Query Wizard dialog box.

7 If necessary, apply Best Fit to the columns and then Save the query. Display the query in **Print Preview**. Change the **Orientation** to **Landscape**, and then create a paper or electronic printout as instructed. **Close** the **Print Preview**.

8 In the object window, click the **Close Object** button ☒ to close the query.

Activity 1.15 | Creating and Printing a Form

One type of Access form displays only one record in the database at a time. Such a form is useful not only to the individual who performs the data entry—typing in the actual records—but also to anyone who has the job of viewing information in a database. For example, when you visit the Records office at your college to obtain a transcript, someone displays your record on a screen. For the viewer, it is much easier to look at one record at a time, using a form, than to look at all of the student records in the database table.

The Form command on the Ribbon creates a form that displays all of the *fields* from the underlying data source (table)—one record at a time. You can use this new form immediately, or you can modify it. Records that you create or edit in a form are automatically added to or updated in the underlying table or tables.

1 **Open** ▸▸ the **Navigation Pane**. Increase the width of the **Navigation Pane** so that all object names display fully. Notice that a table displays a datasheet icon, and a query displays an icon of two overlapping datasheets. Right-click your **1A Students** table to display a menu as shown in Figure 1.33.

Figure 1.33

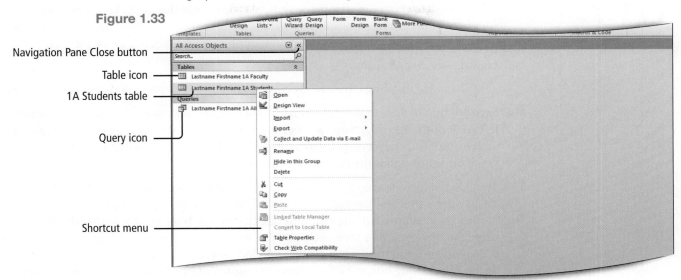

Navigation Pane Close button

Table icon

1A Students table

Query icon

Shortcut menu

2 On the shortcut menu, click **Open** to display the table in the object window, and then **Close** ◂◂ the **Navigation Pane** to maximize your object space.

3 Scroll to the right, and notice that there are 11 fields in the table. On the **Create tab**, in the **Forms group**, click the **Form** button. Compare your screen with Figure 1.34.

Access creates a form based on the currently selected object—the 1A Students table. Access creates the form in a simple top-to-bottom format, with all 11 fields in the record lined up in a single column.

The form displays in *Layout view*—the Access view in which you can make changes to a form or to a report while the object is open. Each field displays the data for the first student record in the table—*Joel Barthmaier*.

Figure 1.34

Form object icon

First record, for *Joel Barthmaier*, displays

Layout View button active

Next record button

Total number of records is 26

Navigation buttons to move among records

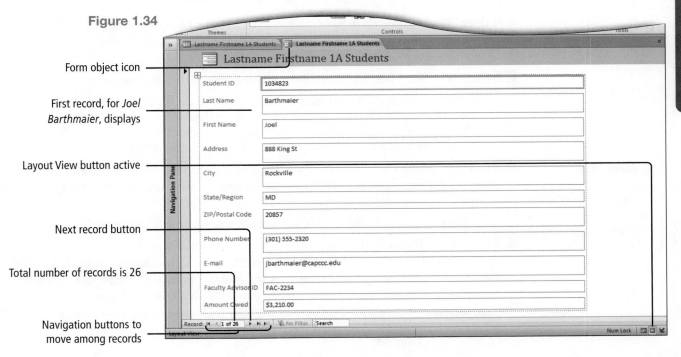

Access | Chapter 1

4 At the right edge of the status bar, notice that the **Layout View** button 🔲 is active, indicating that the form is displayed in Layout view.

Another Way

On the Home tab, in the Views group, click the View button, which displays an icon of a form.

5 At the right edge of the status bar, click the **Form View** button 🔳.

In *Form view*, you can view the records, but you cannot change the layout or design of the form.

6 In the navigation area, click the **Next record** button ▶ three times. The fourth record—for *Joseph Ingram*—displays.

You can use the navigation buttons to scroll among the records to display any single record.

7 **Save** 🔖 the form with the default name—*Lastname Firstname 1A Students*. Along the left edge of the record, under ▶, click anywhere in the narrow gray bar—the *record selector bar*—to select only the record for *Joseph Ingram*. Notice that the bar turns black, indicating that the record is selected.

8 To print the form for *Joseph Ingram* only, click the **File tab**, and then click **Print**—do *not* display Print Preview. Instead, click **Print**. In the **Print** dialog box, in the lower left corner, click **Setup**. Click the **Columns tab**, change the **Width** to **7.5** so that the form prints on one page, and then click **OK**. The maximum column width that you can enter is dependent upon the printer that is installed on your system. In the lower left corner of the **Print** dialog box, click the **Selected Record(s)** option button, and then click **OK**.

> **Note** | To Print a Single Form in PDF
>
> To create a PDF electronic printout of a single record in a form, change the column width to 7.5 as described in step 8 above, and then in the Print dialog box, click Cancel. On the left edge of the form, click the Record Selector bar so that it is black—selected. On the Ribbon click the External Data tab. In the Export group, click the PDF or XPS button. Navigate to your chapter folder, and then in the lower left corner of the dialog box, if necessary, select the Open file after publishing check box. In the lower right corner of the dialog box, click the Options button. In the Options dialog box, under Range, click the Selected records option button, click OK, and then click Publish. Close the Adobe Reader or Acrobat window.

9 **Close** ✖ the form. Notice that your **1A Students** table remains open.

Activity 1.16 | Creating, Modifying, and Printing a Report

1 **Open** ⟫ the **Navigation Pane**, and then open your **1A Faculty** table by double-clicking the table name or by right-clicking and clicking Open from the shortcut menu. **Close** ⟪ the **Navigation Pane**.

2 Click the **Create tab**, and then in the **Reports group**, click the **Report** button.

When you click the Report button, Access generates the report in Layout view and includes all of the fields and all of the records in the table, and does so in a format suitable for printing. Dotted lines indicate how the report would break across pages if you print it. In Layout view, you can make quick changes to the report layout.

Another Way

Right-click the field. From the shortcut menu, click Select Entire Column, and then press Del.

3 Click the **Faculty ID** field name, and then on the Ribbon, click the **Arrange tab**. In the **Rows & Columns group**, click the **Select Column** button, and then press Del. Using the same technique, delete the **Rank** field.

The Faculty ID and Rank fields and data are deleted, and the report readjusts the fields.

4 Click the **Address** field name, and then use the scroll bar at the bottom of the screen to scroll to the right to display the **Mobile Phone** field; be careful not to click in the report. Hold down Shift and then click the **Mobile Phone** field name to select all of the fields from *Address* through *Mobile Phone*. With all the field names selected— surrounded by a colored border—in the **Row & Columns group**, click the **Select Column** button, and then press Del.

Use this technique to select and delete multiple columns in Layout view.

5 Scroll to the left, and notice that you can see all of the remaining fields. In any record, click in the **E-mail** field. Point to the right edge of the field box to display the ⟷ pointer. Drag to the right slightly to increase the width of the field so that all E-mail addresses display on one line.

6 Click the **Last Name** field name. On the Ribbon, click the **Home tab**. In the **Sort & Filter group**, click the **Ascending** button. Compare your screen with Figure 1.35.

> By default, tables are sorted in ascending order by the primary key field, which is the Faculty ID field. You can change the default and sort any field in either ascending order or descending order. The sort order does not change in the underlying table, only in the report.

Figure 1.35

Ascending button selected

Four fields display in report

Report sorted by Last Name field

E-mail addresses display on one line

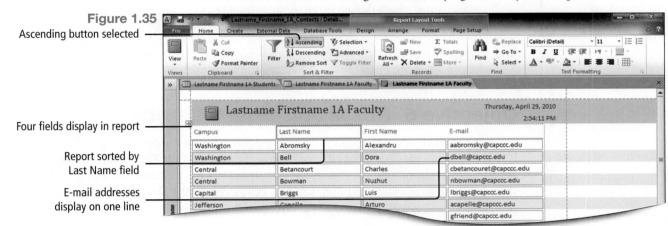

7 Click the **Save** button 🖫. In the **Report Name** box, add **Report** to the end of the suggested name, and then click **OK**.

8 Display the report in **Print Preview**. In the **Zoom group**, click the **Two Pages** button, and then compare your screen with Figure 1.36.

> The report will print on two pages because the page number at the bottom of the report is located beyond the right margin of the report.

Figure 1.36

Two Pages button

Page number at bottom of second page

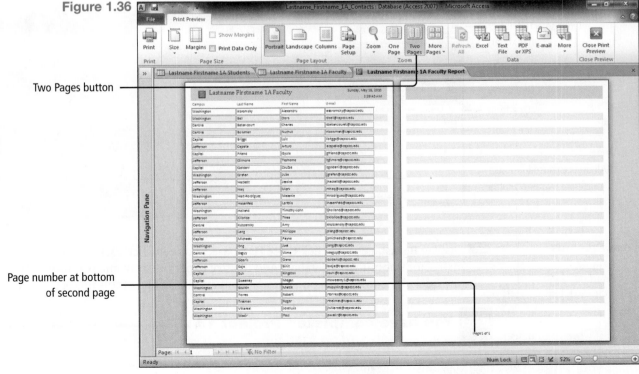

Access | Chapter 1

9 In the **Close Preview group**, click the **Close Print Preview button**. Scroll down to the bottom of the report, and then scroll to the right to display the page number. Click the page number—**Page 1 of 1**—and then press (Del).

10 Display the report in **Print Preview** and notice that the report will print on one page. In the **Zoom group**, click the **One Page** button. **Save** 🖫 the changes to the design of the report, and then create a paper or electronic printout as instructed. At the right end of the Ribbon, click the **Close Print Preview** button.

> The default margins of a report created with the Report tool are 0.25 inch. Some printers require a greater margin so your printed report may result in two pages—you will learn to adjust this later. Also, if a printer is not installed on your system, the report may print on two pages.

11 Along the top of the object window, right-click any object tab, and then click **Close All** to close all of the open objects and leave the object window empty.

Objective 5 | Save and Close a Database

When you close an Access table, any changes made to the records are saved automatically. If you change the design of the table or change the layout of the Datasheet view, such as adjusting the column widths, you will be prompted to save the design changes. At the end of your Access session, close your database and exit Access. If the Navigation Pane is open when you close Access, it will display when you reopen the database.

Activity 1.17 | Closing and Saving a Database

1 **Open** 》 the **Navigation Pane**. Notice that your report object displays with a green report icon. Compare your screen with Figure 1.37.

Figure 1.37

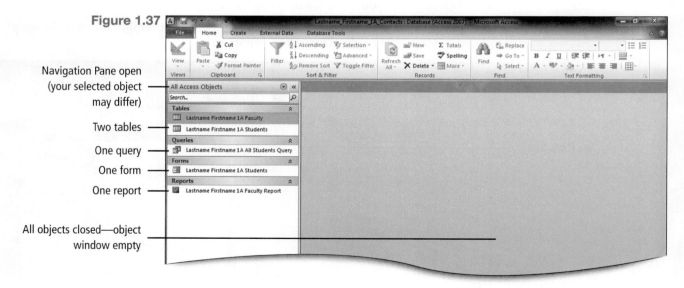

Navigation Pane open (your selected object may differ)

Two tables

One query

One form

One report

All objects closed—object window empty

Another Way

In the upper right corner of the window, click the Close button.

2 Display **Backstage** view, click **Close Database**, and then click **Exit**. As directed by your instructor, submit your database and the five paper or electronic printouts—two tables, one query, one form, and one report—that are the results of this project.

End You have completed Project 1A _____

Project 1B Student Workshops Database

myitlab
Project 1B Training

Project Activities

In Activities 1.18 through 1.23, you will assist Dr. Kirsten McCarty, Vice President of Student Services, by creating a database to store information about student workshops presented by Capital Cities Community College. You will use a database template that tracks event information, add workshop information to the database, and then print the results. Your completed report and table will look similar to Figure 1.38.

Project Files

For Project 1B, you will need the following files:

New Access database using the Events template
a01B_Workshops (Excel workbook)

You will save your database as:

Lastname_Firstname_1B_Student_Workshops

Project Results

Figure 1.38
Project 1B Student Workshops

Access | Chapter 1

Objective 6 | Create a Database Using a Template

A ***database template*** contains pre-built tables, queries, forms, and reports to perform a specific task, such as tracking a large number of events. For example, your college may hold events such as athletic contests, plays, lectures, concerts, and club meetings. Using a predefined template, your college Activities Director can quickly create a database to manage these events. The advantage of using a template to start a new database is that you do not have to create the objects—all you need to do is enter your data and modify the pre-built objects to suit your needs.

The purpose of the database in this project is to track the student workshops offered by Capital Cities Community College. The questions to be answered might include:

What workshops will be offered and when will they be offered?

In what rooms and campus locations will the workshops be held?

Which workshop locations have a computer projector for PowerPoint presentations?

Activity 1.18 | Creating a New Database Using a Template

1 **Start** Access. Under **Available Templates**, click **Sample templates**. If necessary, scroll down to locate and then click **Events**. Compare your screen with Figure 1.39.

Sample templates are stored on your computer; they are included with the Access program.

Figure 1.39

Available Sample templates stored on computer

Events template

2 On the right side of the screen, to the right of the **File Name** box, click the **Browse** button , and then navigate to your **Access Chapter 1** folder.

3 At the bottom of the **File New Database** dialog box, select the text in the **File name** box. Using your own name, type **Lastname_Firstname_1B_Student_Workshops** and then press Enter.

4 In the lower right corner of your screen, click the **Create** button.

> Access creates the *1B Student Workshops* database, and the database name displays in the title bar. A predesigned *form*—Event List—displays in the object window. Although you can enter events for any date, when you open the database in the future, the Event List will display only those events for the current date and future dates.

5 Under the Ribbon, on the **Message Bar**, a Security Warning displays. On the **Message Bar**, click the **Enable Content** button.

> Databases provided by Microsoft are safe to use on your computer.

Activity 1.19 | Building a Table by Entering Records in a Multiple Items Form

The purpose of a form is to simplify the entry of data into a table—either for you or for others who enter data. In Project 1A, you created a simple form that enabled you to display or enter records in a table one record at a time. The Events template creates a *Multiple Items form*, a form that enables you to display or enter *multiple* records in a table, but still with an easier and simplified layout than typing directly into the table itself.

1 Click in the first empty **Title** field. Type **Your Cyber Reputation** and then press Tab. In the **Start Time** field, type **3/9/16 7p** and then press Tab.

> Access formats the date and time. As you enter dates and times, a small calendar displays to the right of the field, which you can click to select a date instead of typing.

2 In the **End Time** field, type **3/9/16 9p** and then press Tab. In the **Description** field, type **Internet Safety** and then press Tab. In the **Location** field, type **Jefferson Campus** and then press Tab three times to move to the **Title** field in the new record row. Compare your screen with Figure 1.40.

> Because the workshops have no unique value, Access uses the AutoNumber data type of the ID field to assign a unique, sequential number to each record. In the navigation area, each record is identified as a task, rather than a record or page.

Figure 1.40

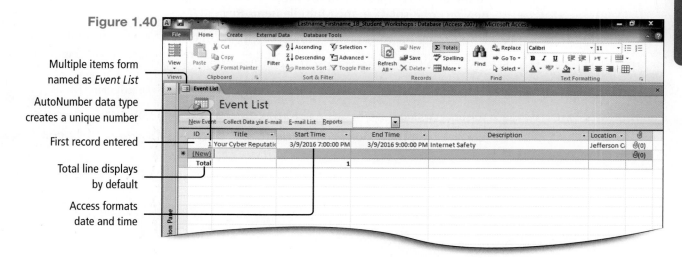

Multiple items form named as *Event List*

AutoNumber data type creates a unique number

First record entered

Total line displays by default

Access formats date and time

3 Directly above the field names row, click **New Event**.

> A *single-record form* displays, similar to the simple form you created in Project 1A. A single-record form enables you to display or enter one record at a time into a table.

4 Using Tab to move from field to field, enter the following record—press Tab three times to move from the **End Time** field to the **Description** field. Compare your screen with Figure 1.41.

Title	Location	Start Time	End Time	Description
Writing a Research Paper	**Washington Campus**	**3/10/16 4p**	**3/10/16 6p**	**Computer Skills**

Figure 1.41

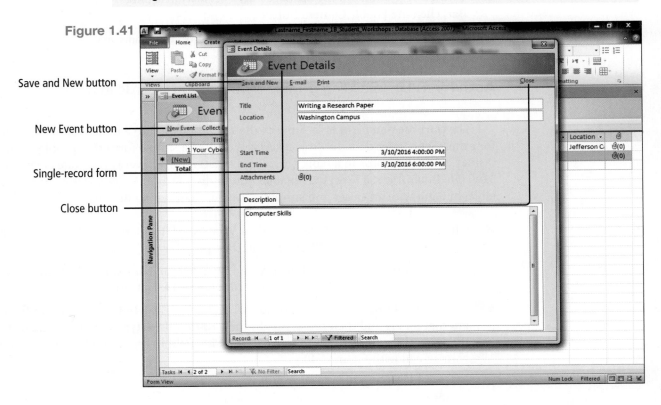

Save and New button

New Event button

Single-record form

Close button

5 In the upper right corner of the single-record form, click **Close**, and notice that the new record displays in the Multiple Items form.

6 Using either the rows on the Multiple Items form or the New Event single-record form, enter the following records, and then compare your screen with Figure 1.42.

ID	Title	Start Time	End Time	Description	Location
3	**Resume Writing**	**3/18/16 2p**	**3/18/16 4p**	**Job Skills**	**Capital Campus**
4	**Careers in the Legal Profession**	**3/19/16 2p**	**3/19/16 4p**	**Careers**	**Central Campus**

Alert! | Does a Single Record Form Open?

In the Multiple Items form, pressing [Enter] three times at the end of a row to begin a new record may display the single-record New Event form. If you prefer to use the Multiple Items form, close the single-record form and continue entering records, using the [Tab] key to move from field to field.

Figure 1.42

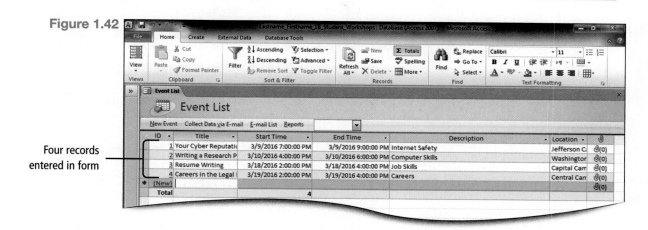

Four records entered in form

---

7 In the upper right corner of the object window, click **Close** ☒ to close the **Event List** form.

8 On the Ribbon, click the **External Data tab**. In the **Import & Link group**, click the **Excel** button.

Recall that you can populate a table by importing data from an Excel workbook.

9 In the **Get External Data – Excel Spreadsheet** dialog box, click the **Browse** button. Navigate to your student files, and then double-click **a01B_Workshops**.

10 Click the second option button—**Append a copy of the records to the table**—and then click **OK**.

11 Click **Next**, click **Finish**, and then **Close** the dialog box.

12 Open ➤➤ the **Navigation Pane**. Double-click **Event List** to open the form that displays data stored in the Events table, and then **Close** ◀◀ the **Navigation Pane**.

13 To the left of the **ID** field name, click the **Select All** button ▱ to select all of the columns.

> **Another Way**
>
> With the columns selected, in the field heading row, point to the right edge of any of the selected columns, and then double-click to apply Best Fit to all of the selected columns.

14 In the field names row, point to any of the selected field names, right-click, and then click **Field Width**. In the **Column Width** dialog box, click **Best Fit**. Notice that the widths of all of the columns are adjusted to accommodate the longest entry in the column.

15 In the first record, click in the **Title** field to deselect the columns. **Save** 🖫 the form, and then compare your screen with Figure 1.43.

Eight additional records display—those imported from the a01B_Workshops Excel workbook.

Access | Chapter 1

Figure 1.43

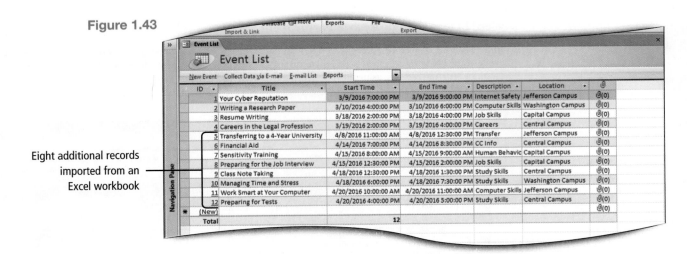

Eight additional records imported from an Excel workbook

Objective 7 | Organize Objects in the Navigation Pane

Use the Navigation Pane to organize database objects, to open them, and to perform common tasks like renaming an object.

Activity 1.20 | Organizing Database Objects in the Navigation Pane

The Navigation Pane groups and displays your database objects and can do so in predefined arrangements. In this activity, you will group your database objects using the *Tables and Related Views* category, which groups objects by the table to which they are related. This grouping is useful because you can easily determine the data source table of queries, forms, and reports.

1 **Open** [»] the **Navigation Pane**. At the top of the **Navigation Pane**, click the **Navigation arrow** [⊙]. In the list, under **Navigate To Category**, click **Tables and Related Views**.

2 Confirm that *Events* displays in the bar under the Search box at the top of the **Navigation Pane**. Compare your screen with Figure 1.44.

The icons to the left of the objects listed in the Navigation Pane indicate that the Events template created a number of objects for you—among them, one table titled *Events*, one query, two forms, and five reports. The Event List Multiple Items form, which is currently displayed in the object window, is included in the Navigation Pane. All of the objects were created using the underlying data source, which is the Events table.

Figure 1.44

One table
One query
Two forms
Five reports

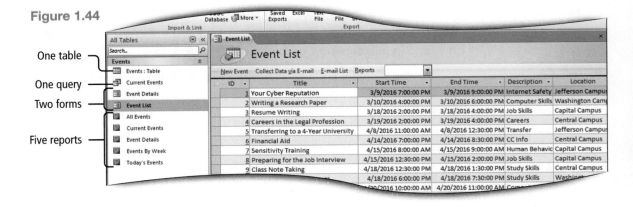

3 In the **Navigation Pane**, point to the **Events** *table*, right-click, and then click **Open**.

The Events table is the active object in the object window. Use the Navigation Pane to open objects for use. The 12 records that you entered using the Multiple Items *form* and by importing from an Excel workbook display in the *table*. Tables are the foundation of your database because your data must be stored in a table. You can enter records directly into a table or you can use a form to enter records.

4 In the object window, click the **Event List tab** to bring the form into view and make it the active object.

Recall that a form presents a more user-friendly screen for entering records into a table.

5 In the **Navigation Pane**, right-click the *report* (green icon) named **Current Events**, and then click **Open**. Compare your screen with Figure 1.45.

An advantage of using a template to begin a database is that many objects, such as attractively formatted reports, are already designed for you.

Figure 1.45

Three open objects

Current Events report preformatted and designed by the template

Current Events report in Navigation Pane

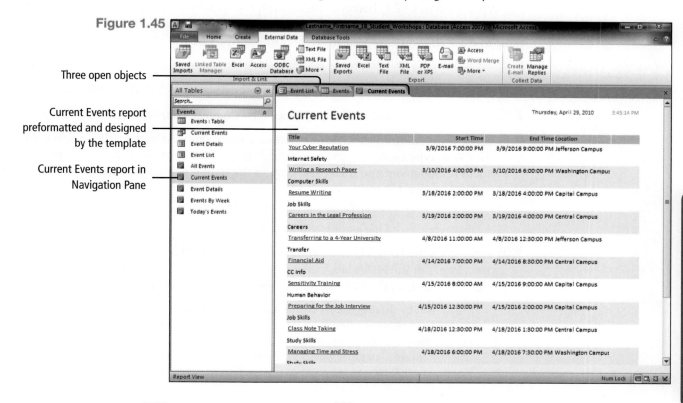

6 In the object window, **Close** ☒ the **Current Events** report.

7 From the **Navigation Pane**, open the **Events By Week** report.

In this predesigned report, the events are displayed by week. After entering records in the form or table, the preformatted reports are updated with the records from the table.

8 **Close** ☒ the **Events By Week** report, and then **Close** ☒ the remaining two open objects. **Close** ☒ the **Navigation Pane**.

Objective 8 | Create a New Table in a Database Created with a Template

The Events database template created only one table—the *Events* table. Although the database was started from a template and contains other objects, you can add additional objects as needed.

Activity 1.21 | Creating a New Table and Changing Its Design

Dr. McCarty has information about the various locations where workshops are held. For example, for the Jefferson campus, she has information about the room, seating arrangements, number of seats, and audio-visual equipment. In the Events table, workshops are scheduled in rooms at each of the four campuses. It would not make sense to store information about the campus rooms multiple times in the same table. It is *not* considered good database design to have duplicate information in a table.

When data in a table becomes redundant, it is usually an indication that you need a new table to contain the information about the topic. In this activity, you will create a table to track the workshop locations and the equipment and seating arrangements in each location.

1 On the Ribbon, click the **Create tab**. In the **Tables group**, click the **Table** button.

2 Click the **Click to Add arrow**, click **Text**, type **Campus/Location** and then press Enter.

3 In the third column, click **Text**, type **Room** and then press Enter. In the fourth column, click **Text**, type **Seats** and then press Enter. In the fifth column, click **Text**, type **Room Arrangement** and then press Enter. In the sixth column, click **Text**, type **Equipment** and then press ↓.

> The table has six fields. Access creates the first field in the table—the ID field—to ensure that every record has a unique value.

4 Right-click the **ID** field name, and then click **Rename Field**. Type **Room ID** and then press Enter. On the **Fields tab**, in the **Formatting group**, click the **Data Type arrow**, and then click **Text**. In the **Field Validation group**, notice that **Unique** is selected.

> Recall that, by default, Access creates the ID field with the AutoNumber data type so that the field can be used as the primary key. Here, this field will store a unique room ID that is a combination of letters, symbols, and numbers, so it is appropriate to change the data type to Text. In Datasheet view, the primary key field is identified by the selection of the Unique check box.

5 In the new record row, click in the **Room ID** field, type **JEFF-01** and then press ⟨Tab⟩. In the **Campus/Location** field, type **Jefferson Campus** and then press ⟨Tab⟩. In the **Room** field, type **J123** and then press ⟨Tab⟩. In the **Seats** field, type **150** and then press ⟨Tab⟩. In the **Room Arrangement** field, type **Theater** and then press ⟨Tab⟩. In the **Equipment** field, type **Computer Projector, Surround Sound, & Microphones** and then press ⟨Tab⟩ to move to the new record row. Compare your screen with Figure 1.46.

> Recall that Access saves the record when you move to another row within the table. You can press either ⟨Tab⟩ or ⟨Enter⟩ to move to another field in a table.

Figure 1.46

New table —
Renamed field —
First record entered —
Room ID field assigned data type of *Text* —
Selected field—Room ID—indicated as primary key field —

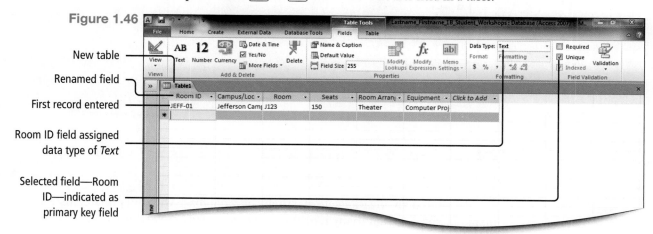

6 In the **Views group**, click the **View** button to switch to **Design** view. In the **Save As** dialog box, save the table as **Lastname Firstname 1B Workshop Locations** and then click **OK**.

7 In the **Field Name** column, to the left of the **Room ID** box, notice the key icon.

> In Design view, the key icon indicates the field—Room ID—that is identified as the primary key.

8 In the **Views group**, click the **View** button to switch to **Datasheet** view.

9 Enter the following records in the table:

Room ID	Campus/Location	Room	Seats	Room Arrangement	Equipment
WASH-01	**Washington Campus**	**A15**	**35**	**Lecture/Classroom**	**Computer Projector**
CAP-01	**Capital Campus**	**C202**	**50**	**Lecture/Classroom**	**Smart Board**
CEN-01	**Central Campus**	**H248**	**20**	**U-shaped**	**White Board**
JEFF-02	**Jefferson Campus**	**A15**	**25**	**U-shaped**	**25 Computers, Projector**

10 To the left of the **Room ID** field name, click the **Select All** button ⬜ to select all of the columns. On the **Home tab**, in the **Records group**, click the **More** button. Click **Field Width**, and in the **Column Width** dialog box, click **Best Fit**. Click in any field to remove the selection, and then **Save** 🖫 the changes to the table. In the object window, **Close** ☒ the **1B Workshop Locations** table.

11 **Open** » the **Navigation Pane**, and then locate the name of your new table. Point to the right edge of the **Navigation Pane** to display the ⟷ pointer. Drag to the right to display the entire table name, and then compare your screen with Figure 1.47.

> Recall that as currently arranged, the Navigation Pane organizes the objects by Tables and Related Views. In Figure 1.47, the Events table is listed first, followed by its related objects, and then the Workshop Locations table is listed. In its current view, the tables are sorted in ascending order by name; therefore, your table may be listed before the Events table depending on your last name.

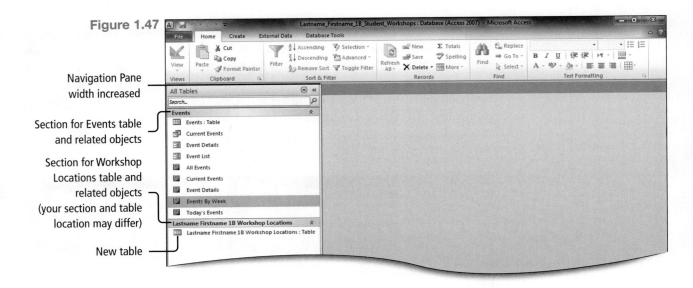

Figure 1.47

Navigation Pane width increased

Section for Events table and related objects

Section for Workshop Locations table and related objects (your section and table location may differ)

New table

Objective 9 | Print a Report and a Table in a Database Created with a Template

Recall that an advantage to starting a new database with a template, instead of from a blank database, is that many report objects are already created for you.

Activity 1.22 | Viewing and Printing a Report

1 From the **Navigation Pane**, open the **Event Details** *report* (not the form).

The pre-built Event Details report displays in an attractively arranged format.

2 **Close** ☒ the **Event Details** report. Open the **All Events** report. In the lower right corner of the status bar, click the **Layout View** button ⊞. At the top of the report, click on the text *All Events* to display a colored border, and then click to the left of the letter *A* to place the insertion point there. Using your own name, type **Lastname Firstname** and then press (Spacebar). Press (Enter), and then **Save** 🖫 the report.

Each report displays the records in the table in different useful formats.

Another Way

Right-click the object tab, and then click Print Preview.

3 Display **Backstage** view, click **Print**, and then click **Print Preview**. In the navigation area, notice that the navigation arrows are dimmed, which indicates that this report will print on one page.

4 Create a paper or electronic printout as instructed, **Close Print Preview**, and then **Close** ☒ the report.

Activity 1.23 | Printing a Table

When printing a table, use the Print Preview command to determine if the table will print on one page or if you need to adjust column widths, margins, or the orientation. Recall that there will be occasions when you want to print a table for a quick reference or for proofreading. For a more professional-looking format, and for more options to format the output, create and print a report.

1 From the **Navigation Pane**, open your **1B Workshop Locations** table. **Close** ⟨«⟩ the **Navigation Pane**. Display **Backstage** view, click **Print**, and then click **Print Preview**.

The table displays in the Print Preview window, showing how it will look when it is printed. The name of the table and the date the table is printed display at the top of the page. The navigation area displays *1* in the Pages box, and the right-pointing arrow—the Next Page arrow—is active. Recall that when a table is in the Print Preview window, the navigation arrows are used to navigate from one page to the next, rather than from one record to the next.

2 In the navigation area, click the **Next Page** button ⟨▸⟩.

The second page of the table displays the last field column. Whenever possible, try to print all of the fields horizontally on one page. Of course, if there are many records, more than one page may be needed to print all of the records.

3 On the **Print Preview tab**, in the **Page Layout group**, click the **Landscape** button, and then compare your screen with Figure 1.48. Notice that the entire table will print on one page.

Figure 1.48

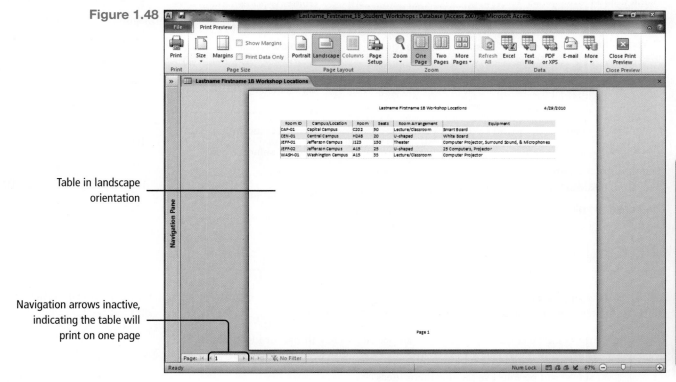

Table in landscape orientation

Navigation arrows inactive, indicating the table will print on one page

4 Create a paper or electronic printout if instructed to do so, and then **Close Print Preview**.

5 **Close** ⟨✕⟩ the **1B Workshop Locations** table. For the convenience of the next person opening the database, **Open** ⟨»⟩ the **Navigation Pane**. In **Backstage** view, click **Close Database**, and then click **Exit** to close the Access program. As directed by your instructor, submit your database and the two paper or electronic printouts—one report and one table—that are the results of this project.

End **You have completed Project 1B** —————————————————

Summary

Microsoft Access 2010 is a database management system that uses various objects—tables, forms, queries, reports—to organize information. Data is stored in tables in which you establish fields, set the data type and field size, and create a primary key. Data from a database can be reported and printed.

Key Terms

Matching

Match each term in the second column with its correct definition in the first column by writing the letter of the term on the blank line in front of the correct definition.

_____ 1. An organized collection of facts about people, events, things, or ideas related to a specific topic.

_____ 2. Facts about people, events, things, or ideas.

_____ 3. Data that is organized in a useful manner.

_____ 4. A simple database file that is not related or linked to any other collection of data.

_____ 5. The database object that stores the data, and which is the foundation of an Access database.

_____ 6. A table row that contains all of the categories of data pertaining to one person, place, thing, event, or idea.

_____ 7. A single piece of information that is stored in every record and represented by a column in a table.

_____ 8. A principle stating that data is organized in tables so that there is no redundant data.

_____ 9. A principle stating that techniques are used to ensure the accuracy of data entered into a table.

A Common field

B Data

C Database

D Field

E First principle of good database design

F Flat database

G Information

H Navigation Pane

I Normalization

J Object window

K Objects

L Populate

M Record

N Second principle of good database design

O Table

_____ 10. The process of applying design rules and principles to ensure that a database performs as expected.

_____ 11. A field in one or more tables that stores the same data.

_____ 12. The basic parts of a database; for example tables, forms, queries, and reports.

_____ 13. The window area that organizes the database objects and from which you open objects.

_____ 14. The window area that displays each open object on its own tab.

_____ 15. The action of filling a database with records.

Multiple Choice

Circle the correct answer.

1. The Access view that displays data in columns and rows like an Excel worksheet is:
   A. Datasheet view　　　　B. Design view　　　　C. Layout view

2. The characteristic that defines the kind of data you can enter into a field is the:
   A. data source　　　　B. data type　　　　C. field property

3. The box at the left of a record in Datasheet view that you click to select an entire record is the:
   A. link　　　　B. navigation area　　　　C. record selector box

4. To add on to the end of an object, such as to add records to the end of an existing table, is to:
   A. append　　　　B. import　　　　C. run

5. Characteristics of a field that control how the field displays and how data is entered are:
   A. data sources　　　　B. data types　　　　C. field properties

6. The field that uniquely identifies a record in a table is known as the:
   A. attachments field　　　　B. common field　　　　C. primary key

7. The underlying design of a table is referred to as the:
   A. caption　　　　B. source file　　　　C. structure

8. The object that retrieves specific data and then displays only the data that you specify is a:
   A. form　　　　B. query　　　　C. report

9. The object that displays fields and records from a table or query in a printable format is a:
   A. form　　　　B. query　　　　C. report

10. Information repeated in a database in a manner that indicates poor design is said to be:
    A. relational　　　　B. redundant　　　　C. truncated

Content-Based Assessments

Apply 1A skills from
these Objectives:

1 Identify Good
Database Design

2 Create a Table and
Define Fields in a
New Database

3 Change the
Structure of Tables
and Add a Second
Table

4 Create and Use a
Query, Form, and
Report

5 Save and Close a
Database

Skills Review | Project 1C Work Study Students Database

In the following Skills Review, you will create a database to store information about the Work Study students and the divisions in which they are employed. Your completed database objects will look similar to Figure 1.49.

Project Files

For Project 1C, you will need the following files:

> New blank Access database
> a01C_Student_Workers (Excel workbook)
> a01C_Divisions (Excel workbook)

You will save your database as:

> Lastname_Firstname_1C_Student_Workers

Project Results

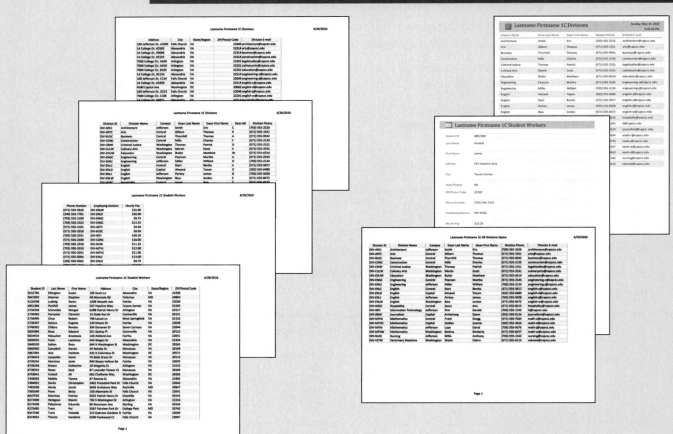

Figure 1.49

(Project 1C Work Study Students Database continues on the next page)

Content-Based Assessments

1 **Start** Access. Click **Blank database**, and then in the lower right corner, click the **Browse** button. In the **File New Database** dialog box, navigate to your **Access Chapter 1** folder, and then in the **File name** box, replace the existing text with **Lastname_Firstname_1C_ Student_Workers** Press Enter, and then in the lower right corner, click **Create**.

a. **Close** the **Navigation Pane**. Click in the text *Click to Add*. Click **Text**, type **Last Name** and then press Enter.

b. In the third field name box, click **Text**, type **First Name** and then press Enter. In the fourth field name box, click **Text**, type **Middle Initial** and then press Enter. Create the remaining fields as shown in **Table 1**, pressing Enter after the last field name.

c. Scroll as necessary to view the first field. Click the **ID** field name. In the **Properties group**, click the **Name & Caption** button. In the **Enter Field Properties** dialog box, in the **Name** box, change *ID* to **Student ID** and then click **OK**. In the **Formatting group**, click the **Data Type arrow**, and then click **Text**.

d. In the first record row, click in the **Student ID** field, type **3512784** and press Enter. In the **Last Name** field, type **Elkington** In the **First Name** field, type **Susan** In the **Middle Initial** field, type **A** In the **Address** field, type **185 Kevin Ln**

e. Continue entering data in the fields as shown in **Table 2**, pressing Enter to move to the next field and to the next row.

f. Click **Save**, and then in the **Table Name** box, using your own name, replace the selected text by typing **Lastname Firstname 1C Student Workers** and then click **OK**.

2 Scroll, if necessary, to view the first field. In the new record row, click in the **Student ID** field, and then enter the information for two additional students as shown in **Table 3**, pressing Enter to move from field to field.

a. **Close** your **1C Student Workers** table. On the **External Data tab**, in the **Import & Link group**, click the **Excel** button. In the **Get External Data - Excel Spreadsheet** dialog box, click the **Browse** button. In the **File Open** dialog box, navigate to your student data files, and then double-click the **a01C_Student_Workers** Excel file.

b. **Append a copy of the records to the table**, and then click **OK**. Click **Next**, click **Finish**, and then click **Close**. **Open** the **Navigation Pane**, and then widen it so that you can view the entire table name. In the **Navigation Pane**, double-click your **1C Student Workers** table to open it, and then **Close** the **Navigation Pane**—30 total records display.

Table 1

Data Type					Text	Text	Text	Text	Text	Text	Currency
Field Name	ID	Last Name	First Name	Middle Initial	Address	City	State/Region	ZIP/Postal Code	Phone Number	Employing Division	Hourly Pay

(Return to Step 1-c)

Table 2

City	State/Region	ZIP/Postal Code	Phone Number	Employing Division	Hourly Pay
Alexandria	VA	22336	(571) 555-5816	DIV-ENLW	15

(Return to Step 1-f)

Table 3

Student ID	Last Name	First Name	Middle Initial	Address	City	State/ Region	ZIP/Postal Code	Phone Number	Employing Division	Hourly Pay
3641892	Monroe	Stephen	D	48 Monrovia Rd	Potomac	MD	20854	(240) 555-7701	DIV-ENLD	10.5
4126598	Ludwig	Karen	E	1508 Moonlit Ave	Fairfax	VA	22030	(703) 555-2109	DIV-ENGC	9.75

(Return to Step 2-a)

(Project 1C Work Study Students Database continues on the next page)

Access | Chapter 1

Skills Review | Project 1C Work Study Students Database (continued)

3 Click the **Home tab**, and then in the **Views group**, click the **View** button to switch to **Design** view.

a. To the left of **Middle Initial**, point to the row selector box, and then click to select the entire row. On the **Design tab**, in the **Tools group**, click the **Delete Rows** button, and then click **Yes**.

b. Click anywhere in the **State/Region** field name, and then under **Field Properties**, set the **Field Size** to **2** In the **State/Region** row, click in the **Description** box, and then type **Two-character state abbreviation**

c. Click in the **Student ID** field name box, set the **Field Size** to **7** and in the **Description** box, type **Seven-digit Student ID** Then **Save** the design of your table; click **Yes**. On the **Design tab**, in the **Views group**, click the **View** button to switch to **Datasheet** view.

4 On the Ribbon, click the **External Data tab**, and then in the **Import & Link group**, click the **Excel** button. In the **Get External Data – Excel Spreadsheet** dialog box, click the **Browse** button. Navigate to your student data files, and then double-click **a01C_Divisions**. Be sure that the **Import the source data into a new table in the current database** option button is selected, and then click **OK**.

a. In the **Import Spreadsheet Wizard** dialog box, click to select the **First Row Contains Column Headings** check box, and then click **Next**.

b. Click **Next** again. Click the **Choose my own primary key** option button, and to the right, be sure that *Division ID* displays. Click **Next**. In the **Import to Table** box, type **Lastname Firstname 1C Divisions** and then click **Finish**. Click **Close**, **Open** the **Navigation Pane**, and then open your **1C Divisions** table. **Close** the **Navigation Pane**—22 records display.

c. At the top of the object window, click the **1C Student Workers tab**. To the left of the **Student ID** field name, click the **Select All** button. Click the **Home tab**, and in the **Records group**, click the **More** button. Click **Field Width**, and in the **Column Width** dialog box, click **Best Fit**. Click in any field, and then **Save** the table.

d. Display **Backstage** view, click **Print**, and then click **Print Preview**. In the **Page Layout group**, click the **Landscape** button. Create a paper or electronic printout as directed by your instructor; two pages result. Click **Close Print Preview**, and then **Close** your **1C Student Workers** table.

e. With your **1C Divisions** table displayed, to the left of the **Division ID** field name, click the **Select All** button, and then apply **Best Fit** to all of the columns. Click in any field, **Save** the table, and then display the table in **Print Preview**. Change the **Orientation** to **Landscape**. Create a paper or electronic printout as directed—two pages result. **Close Print Preview**, and then **Close** your **1C Divisions** table.

5 On the **Create tab**, in the **Queries group**, click the **Query Wizard** button. In the **New Query** dialog box, click **Simple Query Wizard**, and then click **OK**. Click the **Tables/Queries arrow**, and then be sure your **Table: 1C Divisions** is selected.

a. Under **Available Fields**, click **Division ID**, and then click the **Add Field** button to move the field to the **Selected Fields** list on the right. Using either the **Add Field** button or by double-clicking, add the following fields to the **Selected Fields** list: **Division Name, Campus, Dean Last Name, Dean First Name, Division Phone**, and **Division E-mail**. The query will answer the question, *What is the Division ID, Division Name, Campus, Dean's name, Division Phone number, and Division E-mail address of every division?*

b. Click **Next**. In the **Simple Query Wizard** dialog box, change the query title to **Lastname Firstname 1C All Divisions Query** and then click **Finish** to run the query.

c. Display the query in **Print Preview**. Change the **Orientation** to **Landscape**. In the **Page Size group**, click the **Margins** button, and then click **Normal**. Create a paper or electronic printout as directed— one page results. **Close Print Preview**, and then **Close** the query.

d. **Open** the **Navigation Pane**, open your **1C Student Workers** table, and then **Close** the **Navigation Pane**. The table contains 10 fields. On the **Create tab**, in the **Forms group**, click the **Form** button. Click **Save**, and then in the **Save As** dialog box, accept the default name for the form—*Lastname Firstname 1C Student Workers*—by clicking **OK**. In the navigation area, click the **Next record** button three times to display the record for *James Parkhill*. At the left edge of the form, click the gray **record selector bar** to select only this record. By using the instructions in Activity 1.15, print or create an electronic printout of this record as directed. **Close** the form object. Your **1C Student Workers** table object remains open.

(Project 1C Work Study Students Database continues on the next page)

Content-Based Assessments

Skills Review | Project 1C Work Study Students Database (continued)

6 **Open** the **Navigation Pane**, open your **1C Divisions** table, and then **Close** the **Navigation Pane**. On the **Create tab**, in the **Reports group**, click the **Report** button. In the field names row at the top of the report, click the **Division ID** field name. On the Ribbon, click the **Arrange tab**. In the **Rows & Columns group**, click the **Select Column** button, and then press Del. Using the same technique, delete the **Campus** field.

  a. Scroll to position the **Dean MI** field at the left of your screen, and click the field name **Dean MI**. Hold down Ctrl, and then click the field names for **Address**, **City**, **State/Region**, and **ZIP/Postal Code**. On the **Arrange tab**, in the **Rows & Columns group**, click the **Select Column** button, and then press Del.

  b. Scroll to the left, and then click in the **Dean Last Name** field name. By using the ↔ pointer, decrease the width of the field until there is about **0.25 inch** of space between the **Dean Last Name** field and the **Dean First Name** field. Decrease the widths of the **Dean First Name** and **Division Phone** fields in a similar manner. In the **Division E-mail** field, click in the first record—the data in the field displays on two lines. Increase the width of the field slightly so that each record's data in the field displays on one line. Be sure that the width of the report is within the dotted boundaries.

  c. Click the **Division Name** field name. On the Ribbon, click the **Home tab**. In the **Sort & Filter group**, click

the **Ascending** button to sort the report in alphabetic order by Division Name.

  d. **Save** the report as **Lastname Firstname 1C Divisions Report** and then click **OK**. Display the report in **Print Preview**. In the **Zoom group**, click the **Two Pages** button, and notice that the report will print on two pages because the page number is beyond the right margin of the report. **Close Print Preview**. With the report displayed in **Layout** view, scroll down and to the right to display the page number— **Page 1 of 1**. Click the page number, press Del, and then **Save** the changes to the report.

  e. Display the report in **Print Preview**, and notice that the report will print on one page. In the **Zoom group**, click the **One Page** button. Create a paper or electronic printout of the report as directed. Click **Close Print Preview**. Along the top of the object window, right click any **object tab**, and then click **Close All** to close all of the open objects, leaving the object window empty.

  f. **Open** the **Navigation Pane**. If necessary, increase the width of the **Navigation Pane** so that all object names display fully. Display **Backstage** view, click **Close Database**, and then click **Exit**. As directed by your instructor, submit your database and the five paper or electronic printouts—two tables, one query, one form, and one report—that are the results of this project.

End **You have completed Project 1C** ——————————————

Content-Based Assessments

Apply **1B** skills from these Objectives:

- **6** Create a Database Using a Template
- **7** Organize Objects in the Navigation Pane
- **8** Create a New Table in a Database Created with a Template
- **9** Print a Report and a Table in a Database Created with a Template

Skills Review | Project **1D** Benefits Events

In the following Skills Review, you will create a database to store information about Employee Benefit Events at Capital Cities Community College. Your completed report and table will look similar to Figure 1.50.

Project Files

For Project 1D, you will need the following files:

New Access database using the Events template
a01D_Benefits_Events (Excel workbook)

You will save your database as:

Lastname_Firstname_1D_Benefits_Events

Project Results

Figure 1.50

(Project 1D Benefits Events continues on the next page)

Content-Based Assessments

Skills Review | Project **1D** Benefits Events (continued)

1 **Start** Access. Under **Available Templates**, click **Sample templates**, and then click **Events**. On the right, to the right of the **File Name** box, click the **Browse** button, and then navigate to your **Access Chapter 1** folder.

   a. Select the text in the **File name** box, and then using your own information, type **Lastname_Firstname_1D_Benefits_Events** and then press Enter. In the lower right corner of your screen, click the **Create** button. If necessary, click Enable Content.

   b. Click in the first empty **Title** field, type **Medical Plan** and then press Tab. In the **Start Time** field, type **5/2/16 8a** and then press Tab.

   c. In the **End Time** field, type **5/2/16 1p** and then press Tab. In the **Description** field, type **Health Benefits** and then press Tab. In the **Location** field, type **Jefferson Campus** and then press Tab three times to move to the **Title** field in the new record row.

   d. Directly above the field names row, click **New Event**, and then using Tab to move from field to field, enter the record shown in **Table 1** by using the single-record form, which is another way to enter records into a table.

   e. **Close** the single-record form. Using either the rows on the Multiple Items form or the New Event single-record form, enter the records shown in **Table 2**.

   f. **Close** the **Event List** form. On the Ribbon, click the **External Data tab**, and in the **Import & Link group**, click the **Excel** button. In the **Get External Data – Excel Spreadsheet** dialog box, click the **Browse** button. Navigate to your student data files, and then double-click **a01D_Benefits_Events**. Click the second option button—**Append a copy of the records to the table**—and then click **OK**.

   g. Click **Next**, click **Finish**, and then **Close** the dialog box. **Open** the **Navigation Pane**, and then double-click **Event List** to open the form that displays data stored in the Events table—11 total records display.

2 At the top of the **Navigation Pane**, click the **Navigation arrow**. In the list, under **Navigate To Category**, click **Tables and Related Views**.

   a. In the **Navigation Pane**, point to the **Events** *table*, right-click, and then click **Open** to display the records in the underlying table.

   b. In the **Navigation Pane**, double-click the *report* named **Current Events** to view this predesigned report. From the **Navigation Pane**, open the **Events By Week** report to view this predesigned report.

   c. **Close** the **Events By Week** report, and then **Close** the remaining three open objects. **Close** the **Navigation Pane**.

3 On the **Create tab**, in the **Tables group**, click the **Table** button.

   a. Click the **Click to Add arrow**, click **Text**, type **Campus/Location** and then press Enter. In the third column, click **Text**, type **Room** and then press Enter. In the fourth column, click **Text**, type **Seats** and then press Enter. In the fifth column, click **Text**, type **Room Arrangement** and then press Enter. In the sixth column, click **Text**, type **Equipment** and then press ↓.

   b. Right-click the **ID** field name, and then click **Rename Field**. Type **Room ID** and then press Enter. On the **Fields tab**, in the **Formatting group**, click the **Data Type arrow**, and then click **Text**.

   c. In the new record row, click in the **Room ID** field, type **CAP-01** and then press Tab. In the **Campus/Location** field, type **Capital Campus** and then press Tab. In the **Room** field, type **C14** and then press Tab. In the **Seats** field, type **150** and then press Tab. In the **Room Arrangement** field, type **Theater** and then press Tab. In the **Equipment** field, type **Computer Projector, Surround Sound, & Microphones** and then press Tab to move to the new record row.

Table 1

Title	Location	Start Time	End Time	Description	
Eye Care Plan	Washington Campus	5/2/16 2p	5/2/16 4p	Health Benefits	- - - ▶ (Return to Step 1-e)

Table 2

ID	Title	Start Time	End Time	Description	Location	
3	Prescription Plan	5/3/16 8a	5/3/16 10a	Health Benefits	Capital Campus	
4	Pension Plan	5/3/16 2p	5/3/16 4p	Retirement Benefits	Central Campus	- - - ▶ (Return to Step 1-f)

(Project 1D Benefits Events continues on the next page)

Content-Based Assessments

d. In the **Views group**, click the **View** button to switch to **Design** view. In the **Save As** dialog box, save the table as **Lastname Firstname 1D Event Locations** and then click **OK**. Notice that the **Room ID** field is the **Primary Key**.

e. On the **Design tab**, in the **Views group**, click the **View** button to switch to **Datasheet** view. Enter the records in the table as shown in **Table 3**.

f. To the left of the **Room ID** field name, click the **Select All** button to select all of the columns. On the **Home tab**, in the **Records group**, click the **More** button. In the **Column Size** dialog box, click **Best Fit**.

g. Click in any record to cancel the selection of the columns, and then **Save** the table. **Open** the **Navigation Pane**, and then widen the pane to view the full names of all objects.

4 **Open** the **All Events** report, and then **Close** the **Navigation Pane**. In the lower right corner, click the **Layout View** button. At the top of the report, click the text *All Events* to surround the title with a colored border, and then click to the left of the letter *A* to place the insertion

point there. Using your own name, type **Lastname Firstname** and then press Spacebar and Enter. **Save** the report.

a. Display **Backstage** view, click **Print**, and then click **Print Preview**. Notice that the entire report will print on one page in portrait orientation. Create a paper or electronic printout if instructed to do so, and then click **Close Print Preview**. **Close** the **All Events** report.

b. With the **1D Event Locations** table open in **Datasheet** view, display **Backstage** view, click **Print**, and then click **Print Preview**. On the **Print Preview tab**, in the **Page Layout group**, click the **Landscape** button, and then notice that the entire table will print on one page.

c. Create a paper or electronic printout if instructed to do so, and then click **Close Print Preview**. **Close** the **1D Event Locations** table.

d. **Open** the **Navigation Pane**. Display **Backstage** view, click **Close Database**, and then click **Exit**. As directed by your instructor, submit your database and the two paper or electronic printouts—one report and one table—that are the results of this project.

Table 3

Room ID	Campus/Location	Room	Seats	Room Arrangement	Equipment
CEN-01	**Central Campus**	**H212**	**35**	**Lecture/Classroom**	**Computer Projector, 3 screens**
JEFF-01	**Jefferson Campus**	**J520**	**50**	**Lecture/Classroom**	**Smart Board**
WASH-01	**Washington Campus**	**A150**	**40**	**U-shaped**	**White Board & Computer Projector**
CEN-02	**Central Campus**	**C14**	**25**	**Computer Lab**	**25 Computers & Projector**

(Return to Step 3-f)

End **You have completed Project 1D**

Apply 1A skills from these Objectives:

1 Identify Good Database Design

2 Create a Table and Define Fields in a New Database

3 Change the Structure of Tables and Add a Second Table

4 Create and Use a Query, Form, and Report

5 Save and Close a Database

Mastering Access | Project **1E** Kiosk Inventory

In the following Mastering Access project, you will create a database to track information about the inventory of items for sale in the kiosk located on the quad at the Central Campus of Capital Cities Community College. Your completed database objects will look similar to those in Figure 1.51.

Project Files

For Project 1E, you will need the following files:

New blank Access database
a01E_Inventory (Excel workbook)
a01E_Inventory_Storage (Excel workbook)

You will save your database as:

Lastname_Firstname_1E_Inventory

Project Results

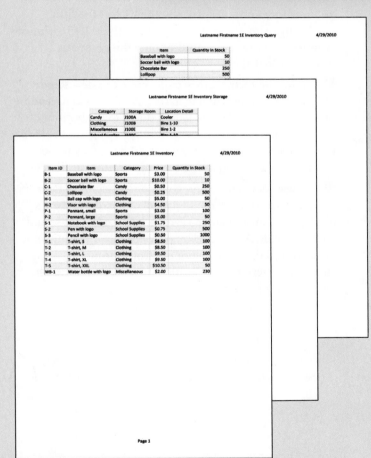

Figure 1.51

(Project 1E Kiosk Inventory continues on the next page)

1 **Start** Access. Create a new **Blank database** in your **Access Chapter 1** folder. Name the database **Lastname_Firstname_1E_Inventory** and then **Close** the **Navigation Pane**. Create additional fields as shown in **Table 1**.

2 Change the **Data Type** of the **ID** field to **Text**, rename the field to **Item ID** and then enter the records as shown in **Table 2**.

3 **Save** the table as **Lastname Firstname 1E Inventory** and then **Close** the table. From your student data files, **Import** and then **Append** the **a01E_Inventory** Excel file to the **1E Inventory** table. Then, from the **Navigation Pane**, open your **1E Inventory** table—17 records display. Widen and then **Close** the **Navigation Pane**.

4 In **Design** view, delete the **Storage Location** field. Click in the **Category** field, change the **Field Size** to **25** and in the **Description** box, type **Enter the category of the Item** Click in the **Item ID** field, and then change the **Field Size** to **10 Save** the changes to the design of your table, click **Yes**, and then switch to **Datasheet** view. Apply **Best Fit** to all of the fields in the table, **Save** the table, and then display the table in **Print Preview**—one page results. Create a paper or electronic printout as directed by your instructor. **Close** the table.

5 From your student data files, **Import** the **a01E_Inventory_Storage** Excel file into the database as a new table; use the first row as the column headings and the **Category** field as the primary key. As the last step in the Wizard, name the table **Lastname Firstname 1E Inventory Storage** and then **Open** the **Navigation Pane**. **Open** your **1E Inventory Storage** table, and then **Close** the **Navigation Pane**. Display the new table in **Design** view, click in the **Location Detail** field, change the **Field Size** to

30 and then as the **Description**, type **Enter room and bin numbers or alternate location of inventory item.** In **Datasheet** view, apply **Best Fit** to all of the fields, **Save** the table, and then display the table in **Print Preview**. Create a paper or electronic printout as directed—one page results. **Close** the table.

6 **Create**, by using the **Query Wizard**, a **Simple Query** based on your **1E Inventory** table. Include only the fields that will answer the question *For all Items, what is the Quantity in Stock?* **Save** the query with the default name. Create a paper or electronic printout as directed and then **Close** the query.

7 Display the **1E Inventory** table, and then **Create** a **Form** for this table. **Save** the form as **Lastname Firstname 1E Inventory Form** Display and then select the fifth record. By using the instructions in Activity 1.15, print or create an electronic printout of only this record as directed. **Close** the form object.

8 With the **1E Inventory** table open, **Create** a **Report**. **Delete** the **Price** field, and then sort the records in **Ascending** order by the **Item ID** field. Scroll down to the bottom of the report and delete the page number—**Page 1 of 1**. **Save** the report as **Lastname Firstname 1E Inventory Report** and then create a paper or electronic printout as directed.

9 **Close All** open objects. **Open** the **Navigation Pane**. If necessary, widen the pane so that all of the object names display fully. In **Backstage** view, click **Close Database** and then click **Exit**. As directed by your instructor, submit your database and the five paper or electronic printouts—two tables, one query, one form, and one report—that are the results of this project.

Table 1

Data Type		Text	Text	Text	Currency	Number	
Field Name	ID	Item	Category	Storage Location	Price	Quantity in Stock	- - - ▶ (Return to Step 2)

Table 2

Item ID	Item	Category	Storage Location	Price	Quantity in Stock	
C-1	Chocolate Bar	Candy	J100A	.5	250	
C-2	Lollipop	Candy	J100A	.25	500	
T-1	T-shirt, S	Clothing	J100B	8.5	100	- - - ▶ (Return to Step 3)

End **You have completed Project 1E** _____

Content-Based Assessments

Apply **1B** skills from these Objectives:

6 Create a Database Using a Template

7 Organize Objects in the Navigation Pane

8 Create a New Table in a Database Created with a Template

9 Print a Report and a Table in a Database Created with a Template

Mastering Access | Project **1F** Recruiting Events

In the following Mastering Access project, you will create a database to store information about the recruiting events that are scheduled to attract new students to Capital Cities Community College. Your completed report and table will look similar to those in Figure 1.52.

Project Files

For Project 1F, you will need the following files:

New Access database using the Events template
a01F_Recruiting_Events (Excel workbook)

You will save your database as:

Lastname_Firstname_1F_Recruiting_Events

Project Results

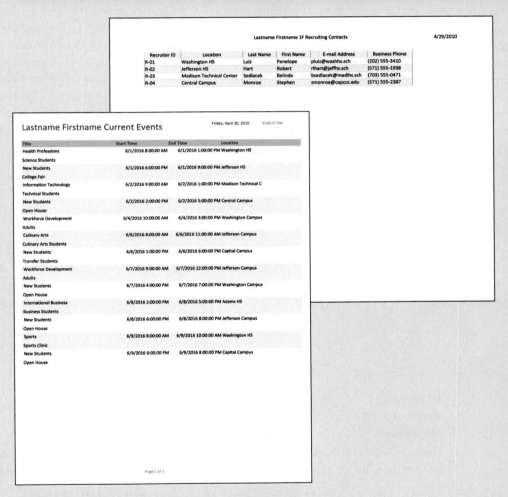

Figure 1.52

(Project 1F Recruiting Events continues on the next page)

Mastering Access | Project **1F** Recruiting Events (continued)

1 **Start** Access, click **Sample templates**, and then click **Events**. In your **Access Chapter 1** folder, save the database as **Lastname_Firstname_1F_Recruiting_Events** If necessary, enable the content.

2 In the Multiple Items form or the New Event single-record form, enter the records shown in **Table 1** into the Events table.

3 **Close** the **Event List** form, and then click the **External Data tab**. **Import** and **Append** the **Excel** file **a01F_Recruiting_Events** to the **Events** table. **Open** the **Navigation Pane**, organize the objects by **Tables and Related Views**, and then **Open** your **Events** table to view 13 records. **Close** the **Navigation Pane**. Apply **Best Fit** to all of the fields, **Save** the table, and then **Close** the table.

4 **Create** a new table using the **Table** button. Click the **Click to Add arrow**, click **Text**, type **Location** and then press Enter. In the third column, click **Text**, type **Last Name** and then press Enter. In the fourth column, click **Text**, type **First Name** and then press Enter. In the fifth column, click **Text**, type **E-mail Address** and then press Enter. In the sixth column, click **Text**, type **Business Phone** and then press ↓.

5 Right-click the **ID** field name, and then **Rename** the field to **Recruiter ID** Change the **Data Type** to **Text**, and then enter the records as shown in **Table 2**.

6 Apply **Best Fit** to all of the columns. **Save** the table as **Lastname Firstname 1F Recruiting Contacts** and then **Close** the table.

7 From the **Navigation Pane**, open the **Current Events Report**. In the lower right corner of the status bar, click the **Layout View** button, click the title *Current Events*, and then click to position your insertion point to the left of *C*. Type your own name in the format **Lastname Firstname** Display the report in **Print Preview**, and then create a paper or electronic printout if instructed to do so. **Close** the **Print Preview**. **Close** the report and save the changes.

8 From the **Navigation Pane**, open your **1F Recruiting Contacts** table. Display the table in **Print Preview**, change to **Landscape** orientation, and then create a paper or electronic printout if instructed to do so. **Close** the **Print Preview**, and then **Close** the table. **Open** the **Navigation Pane** and, if necessary, increase the width of the pane so that your table name displays fully. From **Backstage** view, click **Close Database**, and then click **Exit**. As directed by your instructor, submit your database and the two paper or electronic printouts—one report and one table—that are the results of this project.

Table 1

ID	Title	Start Time	End Time	Description	Location
1	Health Professions	6/1/16 8a	6/1/16 1p	Science Students	Washington HS
2	New Students	6/1/16 6p	6/1/16 9p	College Fair	Jefferson HS
3	Information Technology	6/2/16 9a	6/2/16 1p	Technical Students	Madison Technical Center
4	New Students	6/2/16 2p	6/2/16 5p	Open House	Central Campus

(Return to Step 3)

Table 2

Recruiter ID	Location	Last Name	First Name	E-mail Address	Business Phone
R-01	Washington HS	Luiz	Penelope	pluiz@washhs.sch	(202) 555-3410
R-02	Jefferson HS	Hart	Robert	rlhart@jeffhs.sch	(571) 555-1938
R-03	Madison Technical Center	Sedlacek	Belinda	bsedlacek@madihs.sch	(703) 555-0471
R-04	Central Campus	Monroe	Stephen	smonroe@capccc.edu	(571) 555-2387

(Return to Step 6)

End **You have completed Project 1F** _____

Content-Based Assessments

Apply **1A** and **1B** skills
from these Objectives:

1. Identify Good Database Design
2. Create a Table and Define Fields in a New Database
3. Change the Structure of Tables and Add a Second Table
4. Create and Use a Query, Form, and Report
5. Save and Close a Database
6. Create a Database Using a Template
7. Organize Objects in the Navigation Pane
8. Create a New Table in a Database Created with a Template
9. Print a Report and a Table in a Database Created with a Template

Mastering Access | Project 1G Campus Expansion

In the following Mastering Access project, you will create one database to store information about the campus expansion for Capital Cities Community College and a second database to store information about the public events related to the expansion projects. Your completed database objects will look similar to Figure 1.53.

Project Files

For Project 1G, you will need the following files:

New blank Access database
a01G_Projects (Excel workbook)
a01G_Contractors (Excel workbook)
New Access database using the Events template

You will save your databases as:

Lastname_Firstname_1G_Campus_Expansion
Lastname_Firstname_1G_Public_Events

Project Results

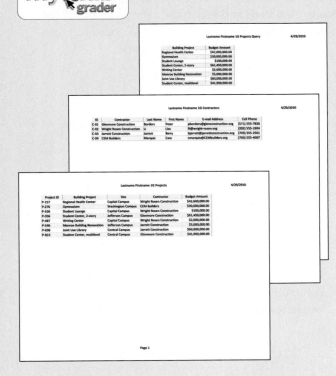

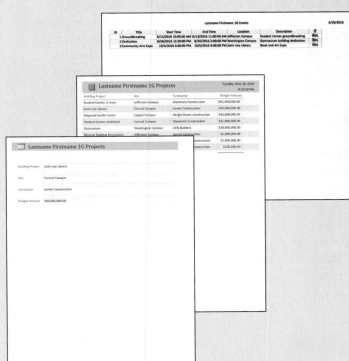

Figure 1.53

(Project 1G Campus Expansion continues on the next page)

1 **Start** Access. Create a new **Blank database** in your **Access Chapter 1** folder. Name the database **Lastname_Firstname_1G_Campus_Expansion** and then **Close** the **Navigation Pane**. Create the additional fields shown in **Table 1**.

2 Change the **ID** field name to **Project ID** and change its **Data Type** to **Text**. Add the three records shown in **Table 2**.

3 **Save** the table as **Lastname Firstname 1G Projects** and then **Close** the table. **Import** and **Append** the **Excel** file **a01G_Projects** to the **1G Projects** table. Then, from the **Navigation Pane**, open your **1G Projects** table—8 total records display. **Close** the **Navigation Pane**.

4 In **Design** view, click in the **Project ID** field, change the **Field Size** to **5** and as the **Description** type **Enter Project ID using the format P-###** Switch to **Datasheet** view, and save by clicking **Yes** two times. Apply **Best Fit** to all of the fields in the table, **Save** the table, and then display it in **Print Preview**. Set the orientation to **Landscape**—one page results. Create a paper or electronic printout as directed by your instructor, and then **Close** the table.

5 From the **External Data tab**, import the **Excel** file **a01G_Contractors** into the database as a new table; use the first row as the column headings and set the **ID** field as the primary key. In the final Wizard dialog box, name the table **Lastname Firstname 1G Contractors** and then **Open** the new table in **Datasheet** view. Apply **Best Fit** to all of the fields, **Save** the table, and then display the table in **Print Preview**. Set the orientation to **Landscape**—one page results. Create a paper or electronic printout as directed, and then **Close** the table.

6 **Create**, by using the **Query Wizard**, a **Simple Query** based on your **1G Projects** table. Include only the appropriate fields to answer the question *For every Building Project, what is the Budget Amount?* Create the query and save it with the default name. Create a paper or electronic printout as directed, and then **Close** the query.

7 Open your **1G Projects** table, and then **Create** a **Form** for this table. Save the form as **Lastname Firstname 1G Projects Form** Display and select the seventh record, and then by using the instructions in Activity 1.15, print or create an electronic printout of this record as directed. **Close** the form object, saving changes to it.

8 With the **1G Projects** table open and active, **Create** a **Report**. **Delete** the **Project ID** field. Sort the records in **Descending** order by the **Budget Amount** field—Access automatically totals this field. Adjust the field widths on the left and right as necessary so that the fields display within the margins of the report. At the bottom of the report, delete the **page number**, and then delete the total that displays in the **Budget Amount** column. **Save** the report as **Lastname Firstname 1G Projects Report** and then create a paper or electronic printout as directed.

9 **Close All** open objects. If necessary, **Open** the **Navigation Pane** and widen the pane so that all object names display fully. Display **Backstage** view, and then click **Close Database**. Do *not* exit Access.

Table 1

Data Type		Text	Text	Text	Currency	
Field Name	ID	**Building Project**	**Site**	**Contractor**	**Budget Amount**	- - - ➤ (**Return to Step 2**)

Table 2

Project ID	Building Project	Site	Contractor	Budget Amount
P-356	**Student Center, 2-story**	**Jefferson Campus**	**Glenmore Construction**	61450000
P-823	**Student Center, multilevel**	**Central Campus**	**Glenmore Construction**	41900000
P-157	**Regional Health Center**	**Capital Campus**	**Wright Rosen Construction**	42600000

(**Return to Step 3**)

(Project 1G Campus Expansion continues on the next page)

Mastering Access | Project **1G** Campus Expansion (continued)

10 From **Sample templates**, create a new database using the **Events** template. **Save** the database in your **Access Chapter 1** folder, and as the file name, type **Lastname_Firstname_1G_Public_Events** If necessary, enable the content. Enter the records in **Table 3** by using the displayed Multiple Items Event List form or the single-record form, which is available by clicking New Event above the field names row.

11 **Close** the **Event List** form. Open the **Navigation Pane**, and then by using the **Navigation Pane arrow**, arrange the database objects by **Tables and Related Views**. Point to the **Events: Table** object, right-click, click **Rename**, and then using your own name, type **Lastname**

Firstname 1G Events Press Enter and then widen the Navigation Pane if necessary.

12 **Open** the **1G Events** table, **Close** the **Navigation Pane**, and then apply **Best Fit** to all of the columns. **Save** the table, display it in **Print Preview**, change the orientation to **Landscape**, set the **Margins** to **Normal**, and then create a paper or electronic printout as directed. **Close** all open objects. **Open** the **Navigation Pane**, display **Backstage** view, click **Close Database**, and then click **Exit**. As directed by your instructor, submit your database and the six paper or electronic printouts—three tables, one query, one form, and one report—that are the results of this project.

Table 3

ID	Title	Start Time	End Time	Description	Location
1	Groundbreaking	6/13/16 10a	6/13/16 11a	Student Center groundbreaking	Jefferson Campus
2	Dedication	8/26/16 12:30p	8/26/16 2p	Gymnasium building dedication	Washington Campus
3	Community Arts Expo	10/5/16 6p	10/5/16 9p	Book and Art Expo	Joint Use Library

(Return to Step 11)

End **You have completed Project 1G** ————————————————

GO! Fix It | Project **1H** Scholarships

Project Files

For Project 1H, you will need the following file:

a01H_Scholarships

You will save your database as:

Lastname_Firstname_1H_Scholarships

In this project, you will make corrections to and update an Access database that will store information about scholarships awarded to students. Start Access. In Backstage view, click Open, navigate to your student files, and then open the file a01H_Scholarships. With the database open, display Backstage view. Click Save Database As, and in the Save As dialog box, navigate to your Access Chapter 1 folder, name the file **Lastname_Firstname_1H_Scholarships** and then click Save. In the message bar, click the Enable Content button.

To complete the project you must find and correct errors in field names, data types, data design, and column widths. You should know:

- The table name should be renamed **Lastname Firstname 1H Scholarships**

- In the table, all of the data in the fields and the field names should display fully.

- Three fields in the table have incorrect data types.

- The field that represents the unique value for each record should be set as the primary key.

- In one of the records, there is a data entry error involving an athlete's name; after correcting the entry, be sure to click in another record so that the record you edit is saved.

- When open, the Navigation Pane should fully display the table name.

- A query should be created for the 1H Scholarships table that answers the question *What is the Amount, Sport, First Name, and Last Name of every athlete receiving a scholarship?* Apply Best Fit to the query results.

- Using the table, a report should be created that includes the Amount, Sport, Award Date, and the last and first name of the athlete. Sort the report in descending order by the amount and then adjust the column widths so that the fields display within the margins of the report. At the bottom of the report, delete the total for the Amount field, and then delete the page number and save with the default name.

If directed to do so, create a paper or electronic printout of the table, the query, and the report. The table should use Landscape orientation, and the query and report should use Portrait orientation. Be sure that the report prints on one page.

End **You have completed Project 1H** ————————————————

Content-Based Assessments

GO! Make It | Project 1I Theater Events

Project Files

For Project 1I, you will need the following file:

New Access database using the Events template

You will save your database as:

Lastname_Firstname_1I_Theater_Events

Using the Events database template, create the table of theater events shown in Figure 1.54 that the Performing Arts department will present or host for April. Name the database **Lastname_Firstname_1I_Theater_Events** Arrange the Navigation Pane by Tables and Related Views, rename the Events table **Lastname Firstname 1I Theater Events** and then widen the Navigation Pane so that all object names display fully. Open the table, apply Best Fit to all the columns, save the table, and then create a paper or electronic printout of the table as directed by your instructor. Use Landscape orientation and Normal margins.

Project Results

Lastname Firstname 1I Theater Events   4/29/2010

ID	Title	Start Time	End Time	Location	Description	📎
1	Symphony Orchestra Concert	4/2/2016 7:30:00 PM	4/2/2016 10:00:00 PM	Jefferson Campus	Opera soprano Barbara Botillini	(0)
2	The Big Band Concert	4/4/2016 7:30:00 PM	4/4/2016 9:00:00 PM	Capital Campus	The Ruth Mystic Big Band Concert	(0)
3	Chaos in the House	4/6/2016 3:00:00 PM	4/6/2016 5:00:00 PM	Central Campus	Gospel Show	(0)
4	Tom Sawyer	4/7/2016 7:00:00 PM	4/7/2016 10:00:00 PM	Washington Campus	CapCCC Players	(0)
5	Tom Sawyer	4/8/2016 3:00:00 PM	4/8/2016 6:00:00 PM	Washington Campus	CapCCC Players	(0)
6	Virginia Arts Festival	4/16/2016 8:00:00 PM	4/16/2016 10:00:00 PM	Jefferson Campus	Anika Shankar	(0)
7	Virginia Arts Festival	4/17/2016 7:00:00 PM	4/17/2016 9:00:00 PM	Central Campus	Music from the Crooked Elbow	(0)
8	College Awards Ceremony	4/22/2016 1:00:00 PM	4/22/2016 4:00:00 PM	Washington Campus	CapCCC Faculty and Staff Awards	(0)
9	Virginia Arts Festival	4/23/2016 7:30:00 PM	4/23/2016 10:00:00 PM	Capital Campus	Russian Folk Dance Spectacular	(0)
10	Music in Motion Dance	4/29/2016 1:00:00 PM	4/29/2016 3:00:00 PM	Central Campus	Dancing to Modern Music	(0)

Page 1

Figure 1.54

End You have completed Project 1I

Content-Based Assessments

GO! Solve It | Project **1J** Student Activities

Project Files

For Project 1J, you will need the following files:

New Access database using the Events template
a01J_Student_Activities (Word document)

You will save your database as:

Lastname_Firstname_1J_Student_Activities

Create a new database from the Events database template and name the database **Lastname_Firstname_1J_Student_Activities** Using the data in the a01J_Student_Activities Word document, enter the data into the Multiple Items form. Each event begins at 7 p.m. and ends at 9 p.m. After entering the records, close the form, arrange the Navigation Pane by Tables and Related Views, rename the table that stores the records as **Lastname Firstname 1J Activities** and then widen the Navigation Pane so that all object names display fully. Open the table, apply Best Fit to the columns, and then save the table. Display the table in Print Preview, and then use the proper commands to be sure that the table prints on one page with the table name at the top of the page. Print the table or submit electronically as directed.

	Performance Level		
	Exemplary: You consistently applied the relevant skills	**Proficient:** You sometimes, but not always, applied the relevant skills	**Developing:** You rarely or never applied the relevant skills
Create database and enter data	Database was created using the correct template and correct name. Data entered correctly.	Some but not all of the data was entered correctly.	Most of the data was entered incorrectly.
Rename table and format table	Table named correctly and Best Fit applied to all columns.	Table named incorrectly and/or Best Fit not properly applied.	Incorrect table name and inadequate formatting applied to all columns.
Create table printout	Printout displays on one page in Landscape orientation and the table name displays at the top.	The printout displays on two pages or the table name does not display at the top.	The printout displays on two pages and the table name does not display at the top of the page.

Performance Elements

End **You have completed Project 1J**

Content-Based Assessments

Apply a combination of the 1A and 1B skills.

GO! Solve It | Project 1K Media Contacts

Project Files

For Project 1K, you will need the following files:

New blank Access database
a01K_Media_Contacts (Excel workbook)

You will save your database as:

Lastname_Firstname_1K_Media_Contacts

Create a new blank database and name the database **Lastname_Firstname_1K_Media_Contacts** Close the default Table1. Create a table by importing the a01K_Media_Contacts Excel workbook, use the first row as the column headings, and use Media ID as the Primary Key. Name the table **Lastname Firstname 1K Media Contacts** Modify the table design by creating separate fields for the Contact's first name and last name, and then adjust the data accordingly. Apply Best Fit to the columns, and then save the table. Display the table in Print Preview, and then use the Page Layout commands to display the table on one page, being sure the table name prints at the top of the page. Print the table or submit electronically as directed.

Create a simple query that answers the following question: *What are the Publication name, first name, last name, and E-mail address for all of the media contacts?* Accept the default name, apply Best Fit to all of the columns, and then create a paper or electronic printout on one page as directed.

Create a report and delete the Media ID column. Adjust the widths of the remaining fields so that all of the data displays within the margins of the report. Sort the report in ascending order by the Publication field. In Layout View, select the report title, and then on the Format tab, in the Font group, change the font of the title of the report to 14. At the bottom of the report, delete the page number. Save the report as **Lastname Firstname 1K Media Contacts Report** and then create a paper or electronic printout as directed. Arrange the Navigation Pane by Tables and Related Views, and then widen the Navigation Pane so that all object names display fully.

	Performance Level		
	Exemplary: You consistently applied the relevant skills	**Proficient:** You sometimes, but not always, applied the relevant skills	**Developing:** You rarely or never applied the relevant skills
Create database, import data to create a table, and then modify the table design	Table created by importing from an Excel workbook, fields correctly modified, and primary key field identified.	Table created by importing from an Excel workbook, but fields are incorrect, or primary key field is incorrect.	Table created by importing from an Excel workbook, but both fields and primary key are incorrect.
Create query	Query created, named correctly, answers the question, formatted correctly.	Query created, but does not completely answer the question or formatted incorrectly.	Query does not answer the question and also includes errors in formatting.
Create report	Report created, Media ID field deleted, field sizes adjusted, sorted by Publication, correctly named, and formatted.	Report created with some errors in fields, report name, sorting, or formatting.	Report created with numerous errors in fields, report name, sorting, or formatting.

End **You have completed Project 1K**

Access | Chapter 1

Outcomes-Based Assessments

Rubric

The following outcomes-based assessments are *open-ended assessments*. That is, there is no specific correct result; your result will depend on your approach to the information provided. Make *Professional Quality* your goal. Use the following scoring rubric to guide you in *how* to approach the problem, and then to evaluate *how well* your approach solves the problem.

The *criteria*—Software Mastery, Content, Format and Layout, and Process—represent the knowledge and skills you have gained that you can apply to solving the problem. The *levels of performance*—Professional Quality, Approaching Professional Quality, or Needs Quality Improvements—help you and your instructor evaluate your result.

	Your completed project is of Professional Quality if you:	Your completed project is Approaching Professional Quality if you:	Your completed project Needs Quality Improvements if you:
1-Software Mastery	Choose and apply the most appropriate skills, tools, and features and identify efficient methods to solve the problem.	Choose and apply some appropriate skills, tools, and features, but not in the most efficient manner.	Choose inappropriate skills, tools, or features, or are inefficient in solving the problem.
2-Content	Construct a solution that is clear and well organized, contains content that is accurate, appropriate to the audience and purpose, and is complete. Provide a solution that contains no errors in spelling, grammar, or style.	Construct a solution in which some components are unclear, poorly organized, inconsistent, or incomplete. Misjudge the needs of the audience. Have some errors in spelling, grammar, or style, but the errors do not detract from comprehension.	Construct a solution that is unclear, incomplete, or poorly organized; contains some inaccurate or inappropriate content; and contains many errors in spelling, grammar, or style. Do not solve the problem.
3-Format and Layout	Format and arrange all elements to communicate information and ideas, clarify function, illustrate relationships, and indicate relative importance.	Apply appropriate format and layout features to some elements, but not others. Overuse features, causing minor distraction.	Apply format and layout that does not communicate information or ideas clearly. Do not use format and layout features to clarify function, illustrate relationships, or indicate relative importance. Use available features excessively, causing distraction.
4-Process	Use an organized approach that integrates planning, development, self-assessment, revision, and reflection.	Demonstrate an organized approach in some areas, but not others; or, use an insufficient process of organization throughout.	Do not use an organized approach to solve the problem.

Outcomes-Based Assessments

Apply a combination of the **1A** and **1B** skills.

GO! Think | Project **1L** Student Clubs

Project Files

For Project 1L, you will need the following files:

> New blank Access database
> a01L_Clubs (Word file)
> a01L_Student_Clubs (Excel file)
> a01L_Club_Presidents (Excel file)

You will save your database as:

> Lastname_Firstname_1L_Student_Clubs

Kirsten McCarty, Vice President of Student Services, needs a database that tracks information about student clubs. The database should contain two tables, one for club information and one for contact information for the club presidents.

Create a new blank database and name it **Lastname_Firstname_1L_Student_Clubs** Using the information provided in the a01L_Clubs Word document, create the first table with two records to store information about the clubs. Then import 23 records from the a01L_Student_Clubs Excel file. Create a second table by importing 25 records from the a0lL_Club_Presidents Excel file. Name the tables appropriately and include your name. Be sure the data types are correct and the records are entered correctly. Apply Best Fit to all of the columns.

Create a simple query based on the Clubs table that answers the following question: *What are the Club Name, Meeting Day, Meeting Time, and Room ID for all of the clubs?* Based on the Clubs table, create a form. Create a report based on the Presidents of the clubs that lists the Last Name (in ascending order), First Name, and Phone number of every president. Print the two tables, the seventh record in Form view, the query, and the report being sure that each object prints on one page, or submit electronically as directed. Group objects on the Navigation Pane by Tables and Related Views. On the Navigation Pane, be sure that all object names display fully.

 You have completed Project 1L ————————————

Apply a combination of the **1A** and **1B** skills.

GO! Think | Project **1M** Faculty Training

Project Files

For Project 1M, you will need the following file:

> New Access database using the Events template
> a01M_Faculty_Training (Word file)

You will save your database as:

> Lastname_Firstname_1M_Faculty_Training

Use the information provided in the a01M_Faculty_Training Word file to create a database using the Events database template. Name the database **Lastname_Firstname_1M_Faculty_ Training** Use the information in the Word file to enter the records. Training times begin at 11:30 a.m. and end at 1 p.m. Arrange the Navigation Pane by Tables and Related Views, and rename the Events table appropriately to include your name. Display the All Events report in Layout View and insert your Lastname Firstname in front of the report title *All Events*. Print the table and the All Events report or submit electronically as directed.

 You have completed Project 1M ————————————

Apply a combination of the 1A and 1B skills.

You and GO! | Project **1N** Personal Contacts

Project Files

For Project 1N, you will need the following file:

New blank Access database

You will save your database as:

Lastname_Firstname_1N_Personal_Contacts

Create a database that stores information about your personal contacts, such as friends and family members. Name the database **Lastname_Firstname_1N_Personal_Contacts** Include a field for a birthday. Enter at least 10 records in the table, and name the table **Lastname Firstname 1N Personal Contacts** Create a query that includes at least three of the fields in the table in the result; for example, a list of names and phone numbers. Create a report that includes the name and address for each contact. Print the table, query, and report, making sure that the data for each object prints on one page, or submit electronically as directed.

 End You have completed Project 1N ——————————————————————

Apply a combination of the 1A and 1B skills.

GO! Collaborate | Project **1O** Bell Orchid Hotels Group Running Case

This project relates to the **Bell Orchid Hotels.** Your instructor may assign this group case project to your class. If your instructor assigns this project, he or she will provide you with information and instructions to work as part of a group. The group will apply the skills gained thus far to help the Bell Orchid Hotels achieve their business goals.

 End You have completed Project 1O ——————————————————————

Sort and Query a Database

OUTCOMES

At the end of this chapter you will be able to:

OBJECTIVES

Mastering these objectives will enable you to:

PROJECT 2A
Sort and query a database.

1. Open an Existing Database (p. 485)
2. Create Table Relationships (p. 486)
3. Sort Records in a Table (p. 491)
4. Create a Query in Design View (p. 494)
5. Create a New Query from an Existing Query (p. 497)
6. Sort Query Results (p. 498)
7. Specify Criteria in a Query (p. 500)

PROJECT 2B
Create complex queries.

8. Specify Numeric Criteria in a Query (p. 506)
9. Use Compound Criteria (p. 511)
10. Create a Query Based on More Than One Table (p. 513)
11. Use Wildcards in a Query (p. 515)
12. Use Calculated Fields in a Query (p. 517)
13. Calculate Statistics and Group Data in a Query (p. 520)
14. Create a Crosstab Query (p. 523)

Brendan Fisher/Shutterstock

In This Chapter

In this chapter, you will sort Access database tables and create and modify queries. To convert data into meaningful information, you must manipulate your data in a way that you can answer questions. One question might be: *Which students have a grade point average of 3.0 or higher?* With such information, you could send information about scholarships or internships to selected students.

Questions can be answered by sorting the data in a table or by creating a query. Queries enable you to isolate specific data in database tables by limiting the fields that display and by setting conditions that limit the records to those that match specified conditions. You can also use a query to create a new field that is calculated by using one or more existing fields.

The projects in this chapter relate to **Capital Cities Community College**, which is located in the Washington D. C. metropolitan area. The college provides high-quality education and professional training to residents in the cities surrounding the nation's capital. Its four campuses serve over 50,000 students and offer more than 140 certificate programs and degrees at the associate's level. CapCCC has a highly acclaimed Distance Education program and an extensive Workforce Development program. The college makes positive contributions to the community through cultural and athletic programs and partnerships with businesses and non-profit organizations.

Project 2A Instructors and Courses Database

Project Activities

In Activities 2.01 through 2.13, you will assist Carolyn Judkins, the Dean of the Business and Information Technology Division at the Jefferson Campus, in locating information about instructors and courses in the Division. Your results will look similar to Figure 2.1.

Project Files

For Project 2A, you will need the following file:

> a02A_Instructors_Courses

You will save your database as:

> Lastname_Firstname_2A_Instructors_Courses

Project Results

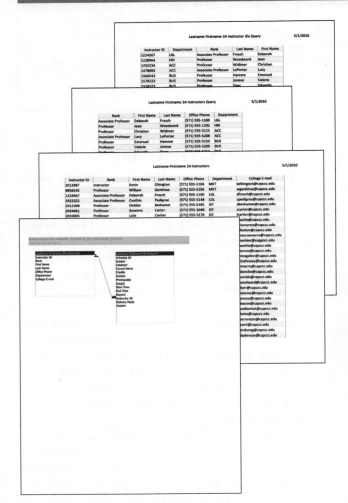
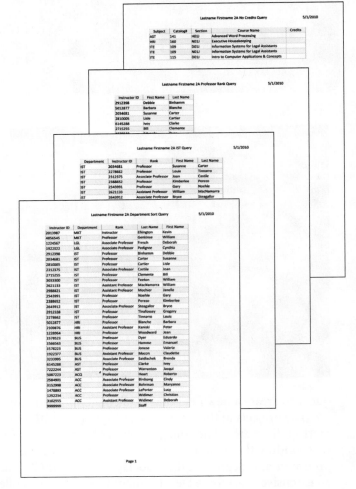

Figure 2.1

Project 2A Instructors and Courses

Objective 1 | Open an Existing Database

There will be instances in which you may want to work with a database and still keep the *original* version of the database. Like the other Microsoft Office 2010 applications, you can open a database file and save it with a new name.

Activity 2.01 | Opening and Renaming an Existing Database

1 Start **Access**. In **Backstage** view, click **Open**. Navigate to the student data files for this textbook, and then open the Access database **a02A_Instructors_Courses**.

2 Click the **File tab** to return to **Backstage** view, and then click **Save Database As.** In the **Save As** dialog box, navigate to the location where you are saving your databases for this chapter. Create a new folder named **Access Chapter 2** and then click **Open**.

3 In the **File name** box, select the file name, to which *1* has been added at the end. Edit as necessary to name the database **Lastname_Firstname_2A_Instructors_Courses** and then press [Enter].

> Use this technique when you want to keep a copy of the original database file.

4 On the **Message Bar**, notice the **Security Warning**. In the **Navigation Pane**, notice that this database contains two table objects. Compare your screen with Figure 2.2.

Figure 2.2

Database name in title bar
Message Bar
2A Instructors table
2A Schedule table
Security Warning message

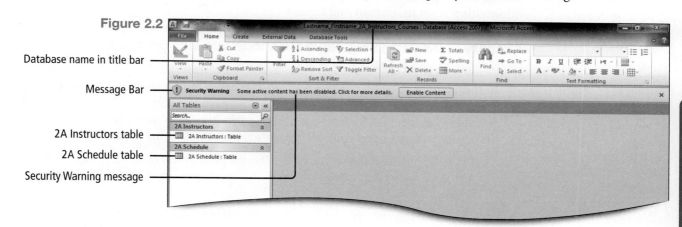

Activity 2.02 | Resolving Security Alerts and Renaming Tables

The *Message Bar* is the area below the Ribbon that displays information such as security alerts when there is potentially unsafe, active content in an Office document that you open. Settings that determine the alerts that display on your Message Bar are set in the Access *Trust Center*, which is an area of Access where you can view the security and privacy settings for your Access installation.

You may or may not be able to change the settings in the Trust Center, depending upon decisions made within your organization's computing environment. You can display the Trust Center from Options, which is available in Backstage view.

1 On the **Message Bar**, click the **Enable Content** button.

> When working with the student files that accompany this textbook, repeat these actions each time you see this security warning. Databases for this textbook are safe to use on your computer.

2 In the **Navigation Pane**, right-click the **2A Instructors** table, and then click **Rename**. With the table name selected and using your own name, type **Lastname Firstname 2A Instructors** and then press Enter to rename the table. Using the same technique, **Rename** the **2A Schedule** table to **Lastname Firstname 2A Schedule**

> Including your name in the table enables you and your instructor to easily identify your work, because Access includes the table name in the header of printed and PDF pages.

3 Point to the right edge of the **Navigation Pane** to display the ⟷ pointer. Drag to the right to widen the pane until both table names display fully.

Objective 2 | Create Table Relationships

Access databases are relational databases because the tables in the database can relate—actually connect—to other tables through common fields. Recall that common fields are fields that contain the same data in more than one table.

After you have a table for each subject in your database, you must provide a way to connect the data in the tables when you need meaningful information. To do this, create common fields in related tables, and then define table relationships. A *relationship* is an association that you establish between two tables based on common fields. After the relationship is established, you can create a query, a form, or a report that displays information from more than one table.

Activity 2.03 | Creating Table Relationships and Enforcing Referential Integrity

In this activity, you will create a relationship between two tables in the database.

1 Double-click your **2A Instructors** table to open it in the object window and examine its contents. Then open your **2A Schedule** table and examine its contents.

> In the 2A Instructors table, *Instructor ID* is the primary key field, which ensures that each instructor will appear in the table only one time. No two instructors have the same Instructor ID.

> In the 2A Schedule table, *Schedule ID* is the primary key field. Every scheduled course section during an academic term has a unique Schedule ID. The 2A Schedule table includes the *Instructor ID* field, which is the common field between the 2A Schedule table and the 2A Instructors table.

2 In the **2A Schedule** table, scroll to the right to display the Instructor ID field, and then compare your screen with Figure 2.3.

> Because *one* instructor can teach *many* different courses, *one* Instructor ID number can be present *many* times in the 2A Schedule table. This relationship between each instructor and the courses is known as a *one-to-many relationship*. This is the most common type of relationship in Access.

Figure 2.3

Two table objects open in the object window; *2A Schedule* table active

Tables renamed

Navigation Pane width increased so that both table names are visible

Instructor teaches more than one course

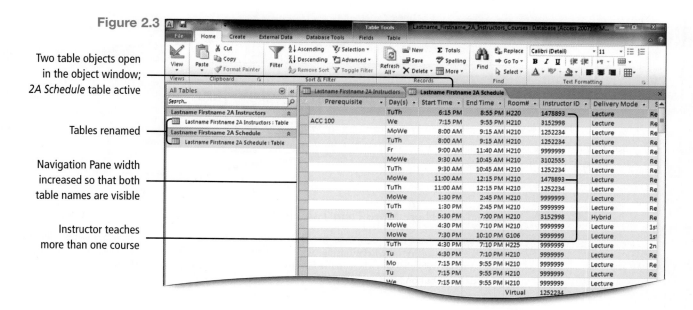

3 In the upper right corner of the object window, click **Close** ⊠ two times to close each table. Click the **Database Tools tab**, and then in the **Relationships group**, click the **Relationships** button. Compare your screen with Figure 2.4.

The Show Table dialog box displays in the Relationships window. In the Show Table dialog box, the Tables tab displays all of the table objects in the database. Your two tables are listed.

Figure 2.4

Relationships window

Two tables in database

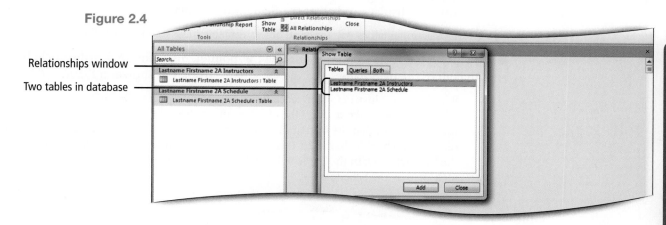

4 Point to the title bar of the **Show Table** dialog box, and then drag down and to the right slightly to move the **Show Table** dialog box away from the top of the **Relationships** window.

Moving the Show Table dialog box enables you to see the tables as they are added to the Relationships window.

5 In the **Show Table** dialog box, click your **2A Instructors** table, and then at the bottom of the dialog box, click **Add**. In the **Show Table** dialog box, double-click your **2A Schedule** table to add the table to the **Relationships** window. In the **Show Table** dialog box, click **Close**, and then compare your screen with Figure 2.5.

You can use either technique to add a table to the Relationships window. A *field list*—a list of the field names in a table—for each of the two table objects displays, and each table's primary key is identified. Although this database currently has only two tables, larger databases can have many tables. Scroll bars in a field list indicate that there are fields that are not currently in view.

Figure 2.5

Field list for 2A
Schedule table

Field list for 2A
Instructors table

Primary keys

Scroll bar indicates there
are fields out of view

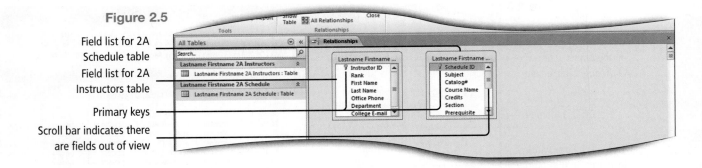

Alert! | **Are There More Than Two Field Lists in the Relationships Window?**

If you double-click a table more than one time, a duplicate field list displays in the Relationships window. To remove a field list from the Relationships window, right-click the title bar of the field list, and then click Hide Table. Alternatively, click anywhere in the field list, and then on the Design tab, in the Relationships group, click the Hide Table button.

---

6 In the **2A Schedule** field list—the field list on the right—point to the title bar to display the pointer. Drag the field list to the right until there is about 2 inches between the field lists.

7 In the **2A Instructors** field list—the field list on the left—point to the lower right corner of the field list to display the pointer, and then drag down and to the right to increase the height and width of the field list until the entire name of the table in the title bar displays and all of the field names display.

> This action enables you to see all of the available fields and removes the vertical scroll bar.

8 By using the same technique and the pointer, resize the **2A Schedule** field list so that all of the field names and the table name display as shown in Figure 2.6.

> Recall that *one* instructor can teach *many* scheduled courses. This arrangement of the tables on your screen displays the *one table* on the left side and the *many table* on the right side. Recall also that the primary key in each table is the field that uniquely identifies the record in each table. In the 2A Instructors table, each instructor is uniquely identified by the Instructor ID. In the 2A Schedule table, each scheduled course section is uniquely identified by the Schedule ID.

Figure 2.6

Table on *many* side
of relationship

Table on *one* side
of relationship

Instructor ID is common
field between the
two tables

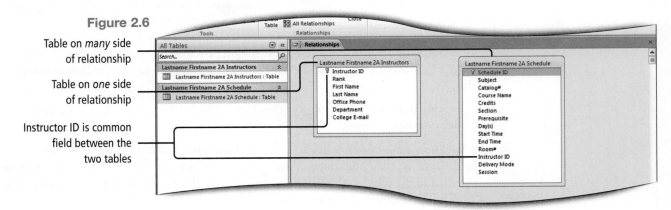

Note | **The Field That Is Highlighted Does Not Matter**

After you rearrange the two field lists in the Relationships window, the highlighted field indicates the active field list, which is the list you moved last. This is of no consequence for completing the activity.

Another Way

On the Design tab, in the Tools group, click the Edit Relationships button. In the Edit Relationships dialog box, click Create New, and then in the Create New dialog box, designate the tables and fields that will create the relationship.

9 In the **2A Instructors** field list, point to **Instructor ID**, hold down the left mouse button, and then drag down and to the right into the **2A Schedule** field list until the ⬚ pointer's arrow is on top of **Instructor ID**. Then release the mouse button to display the **Edit Relationships** dialog box.

As you drag, a small graphic displays to indicate that you are dragging a field from one field list to another. A table relationship works by matching data in two fields—the common field. In these two tables, the common field has the same name—*Instructor ID*. Common fields are not required to have the same names; however, they must have the same data type and field size.

10 Point to the title bar of the **Edit Relationships** dialog box, and then drag the dialog box below the two field lists as shown in Figure 2.7.

Both tables include the Instructor ID field—the common field between the two tables. By dragging, you create the *one-to-many* relationship. In the 2A Instructors table, Instructor ID is the primary key. In the 2A Schedule table, Instructor ID is referred to as the *foreign key* field. The foreign key is the field in the related table used to connect to the primary key in another table. The field on the *one* side of the relationship is typically the primary key.

Figure 2.7

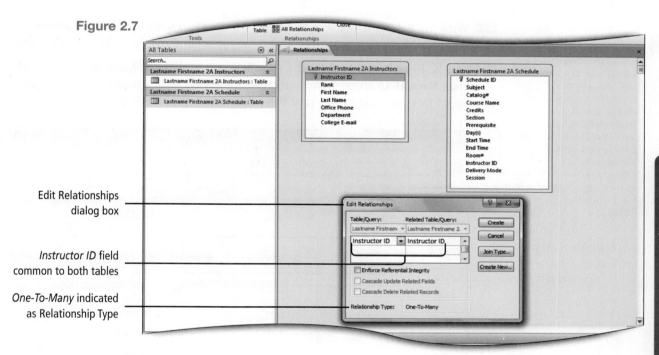

Edit Relationships dialog box

Instructor ID field common to both tables

One-To-Many indicated as Relationship Type

11 In the **Edit Relationships** dialog box, click to select the **Enforce Referential Integrity** check box.

Referential integrity is a set of rules that Access uses to ensure that the data between related tables is valid. Enforcing referential integrity ensures that an instructor cannot be added to the 2A Schedules table if the Instructor ID is *not* included in the 2A Instructors table. Similarly, enforcing referential integrity ensures that you cannot delete an instructor from the 2A Instructors table if there is a course listed in the 2A Schedule table for that instructor.

12 In the **Edit Relationships** dialog box, click the **Create** button, and then compare your screen with Figure 2.8.

A *join line*—the line joining two tables—displays between the two tables. On the join line, *1* indicates the *one* side of the relationship, and the infinity symbol (∞) indicates the *many* side of the relationship. These symbols display when referential integrity is enforced.

Figure 2.8

1 indicates one side of the relationship

Join line connects the two common fields, creating the relationship

∞ indicates many side of the relationship

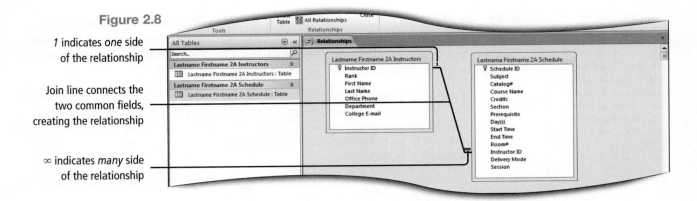

Activity 2.04 | Printing a Relationship Report and Displaying Subdatasheet Records

The Relationships window provides a map of how your database tables are related, and you can print this information as a report.

1 With the **Relationships** window open, on the **Design tab**, in the **Tools group**, click the **Relationship Report** button to create the report and display it in Print Preview.

2 On the **Print Preview tab**, in the **Page Size group**, click the **Margins** button, and then click **Normal**. Compare your screen with Figure 2.9. If instructed to do so, create a paper or electronic printout of this relationship report.

Figure 2.9

Print Preview tab
Margins button

Database name and date (your date will differ)

Field lists with join lines

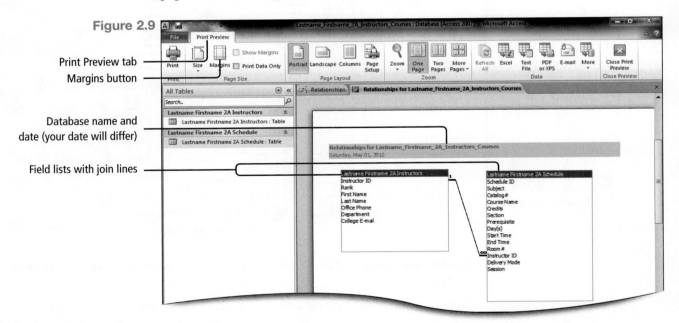

3 On the **Quick Access Toolbar**, click the **Save** button to save the report. In the **Save As** dialog box, click **OK** to accept the default name.

The report name displays in the Navigation Pane under *Unrelated Objects*. Because the report is just a map of the relationships, and not a report containing actual records, it is not associated with any of the tables.

4 In the object window, **Close** the report, and then **Close** the **Relationships** window.

5 From the **Navigation Pane**, open your **2A Instructors** table, and then **Close** ⟪ the **Navigation Pane**. For the first record—*Instructor ID 1224567*—on the left side of the record, click the **plus sign** (+), and then compare your screen with Figure 2.10.

Plus signs to the left of a record in a table indicate that *related* records exist in another table. Clicking the plus sign displays the related records in a ***subdatasheet***. In the first record, for *Deborah Fresch*, you can see that related records exist in the 2A Schedule table—she is teaching five LGL courses that are listed in the schedule. The plus sign displays because you created a relationship between the two tables using the Instructor ID field—the common field.

Figure 2.10

Course sections from the 2A Schedule table for *Associate Professor Deborah Fresch*

Plus sign indicates that related records may exist in another table

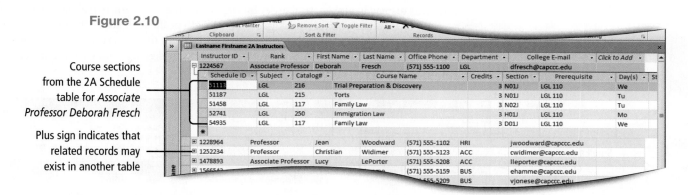

6 For the first record, click the **minus sign** (-) to collapse the subdatasheet.

> **More Knowledge | Other Types of Relationships: One-to-One and Many-to-Many**
>
> There are other relationships you can create using the same process in the Relationships window. The type of relationship is determined by the placement of the primary key field. A one-to-one relationship exists between two tables when a record in one table is related to a single record in a second table. In this case, both tables use the same field as the primary key. This is most often used when data is placed in a separate table because access to the information is restricted.
>
> You can also create a many-to-many relationship between tables, where many records in one table can be related to many records in another table. For example, many students can enroll in many courses. To create a many-to-many relationship, you must create a third table that contains the primary key fields from both tables. These primary key fields are then joined to their related fields in the other tables. In effect, you create multiple one-to-one relationships.

Objective 3 | Sort Records in a Table

Sorting is the process of arranging data in a specific order based on the value in a field. For example, you can sort the names in your address book alphabetically by each person's last name, or you can sort your DVD collection by the date of purchase. Initially, records in an Access table display in the order they are entered into the table. When a primary key is established, the records display in order based on the primary key field.

Activity 2.05 | Sorting Records in a Table in Ascending or Descending Order

In the following activity, you will determine the departments of the faculty in the Business and Information Technology Division by sorting the data. You can sort data in either ***ascending order*** or ***descending order***. Ascending order sorts text alphabetically (A to Z) and sorts numbers from the lowest number to the highest number. Descending order sorts text in reverse alphabetical order (Z to A) and sorts numbers from the highest number to the lowest number.

1 Notice that the records in the **2A Instructors** table are sorted in ascending order by **Instructor ID**, which is the primary key field.

Another Way

On the Home tab, in the Sort & Filter group, click the Ascending button.

2 In the field names row, click the **Department arrow**, click **Sort A to Z**, and then compare your screen with Figure 2.11.

To sort records in a table, click the arrow to the right of the field name in the column on which you want to sort, and then choose the sort order. After a field is sorted, a small arrow in the field name box indicates its sort order. The small arrow in the field name points up, indicating an ascending sort; and in the Ribbon, the Ascending button is selected.

The records display in alphabetical order by Department. Because the department names are now grouped together, you can quickly scroll the length of the table to see the instructors in each department. The first record in the table has no data in the Department field because the Instructor ID number *9999999* is reserved for Staff, a designation that is used until a scheduled course has been assigned to a specific instructor.

Figure 2.11

Ascending button selected

Small arrow indicates order by which the field is sorted

Records sorted alphabetically by Department

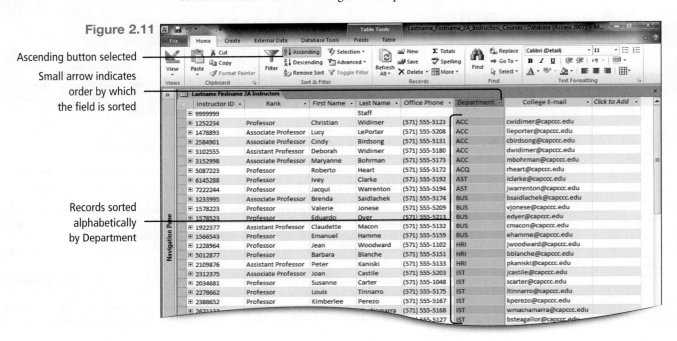

3 On the **Home tab**, in the **Sort & Filter group**, click the **Remove Sort** button to clear the sort and return the records to the default sort order, which is by the primary key field—*Instructor ID*.

4 Click the **Last Name arrow**, and then click **Sort Z to A**.

The records in the table are sorted by last name in reverse alphabetical order. The small arrow in the Field name box points down, indicating a descending sort. On the Ribbon, the Descending button is selected.

5 In the **Sort & Filter group**, click the **Remove Sort** button.

Activity 2.06 | Sorting Records in a Table on Multiple Fields

To sort a table on two or more fields, first identify the fields that will act as the **outermost sort field** and the **innermost sort field**. The outermost sort field is the first level of sorting, and the innermost sort field is the second level of sorting. For example, you might want to sort first by the Last Name field, which would be the outermost sort field, and then by the First Name field, which would be the innermost sort field. After you identify your outermost and innermost sort fields, sort the innermost field first, and then sort the outermost field.

In this activity, you will sort the records in descending order by the department name. Within each department name, you will sort the records in ascending order by last name.

1 In the **Last Name** field, click any record. In the **Sort & Filter group**, click the **Ascending** button.

The records are sorted in ascending alphabetical order by Last Name—the innermost sort field.

2 Point anywhere in the **Department** field, and then right-click. From the shortcut menu, click **Sort Z to A**. Compare your screen with Figure 2.12.

The records are sorted in descending alphabetical order first by Department—the *outermost* sort field—and then within a specific Department grouping, the sort continues in ascending alphabetical order by Last Name—the *innermost* sort field. The records are sorted on multiple fields using both ascending and descending order.

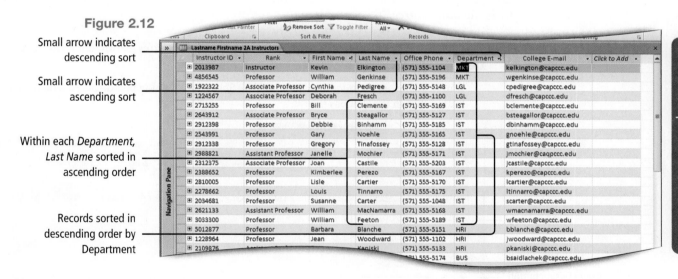

Figure 2.12

Small arrow indicates descending sort

Small arrow indicates ascending sort

Within each *Department*, *Last Name* sorted in ascending order

Records sorted in descending order by Department

3 Display **Backstage** view, click **Print**, and then click **Print Preview**. In the **Page Layout** group, click the **Landscape** button. In the **Zoom group**, click the **Two Pages** button, and notice that the table will print on two pages.

4 On the **Print Preview tab**, in the **Print group**, click the **Print** button. Under **Print Range**, click the **Pages** option button. In the **From** box, type **1** and then in the **To** box, type **1** to print only the first page. If directed to submit a paper copy, click OK or create an electronic copy as instructed. To create a PDF of only the first page, in the Data group, click PDF or XPS, click the Options button, and then indicate *Page 1 to 1*. In the **Close Preview group**, click the **Close Print Preview** button.

5 In the object window, **Close** ☒ the table. In the message box, click **Yes** to save the changes to the sort order.

6 **Open** ⟩⟩ the **Navigation Pane**, and then open the **2A Instructors** table. Notice the table was saved with the sort order you specified.

7 In the **Sort & Filter group**, click the **Remove Sort** button. **Close** ☒ the table, and in the message box, click **Yes** to save the table with the sort removed. **Close** ⟨⟨ the **Navigation Pane**.

> Generally, tables are not stored with the data sorted. Instead, queries are created that sort the data; and then reports are created to display the sorted data.

Objective 4 | Create a Query in Design View

Recall that a **select query** is a database object that retrieves (selects) specific data from one or more tables and then displays the specified data in Datasheet view. A query answers a question such as *Which instructors teach courses in the IST department?* Unless a query has already been set up to ask this question, you must create a new query.

Database users rarely need to see all of the records in all of the tables. That is why a query is so useful; it creates a **subset** of records—a portion of the total records—according to your specifications and then displays only those records.

Activity 2.07 | Creating a New Select Query in Design View

Previously, you created a query using the Query Wizard. To create complex queries, use Query Design view. The table or tables from which a query selects its data is referred to as the **data source**.

1 On the Ribbon, click the **Create tab**, and then in the **Queries group**, click the **Query Design** button. Compare your screen with Figure 2.13.

> A new query opens in Design view and the Show Table dialog box displays, which lists both tables in the database.

Figure 2.13

Query1 tab

Queries group

Query Design button

Show Table dialog box

Available tables

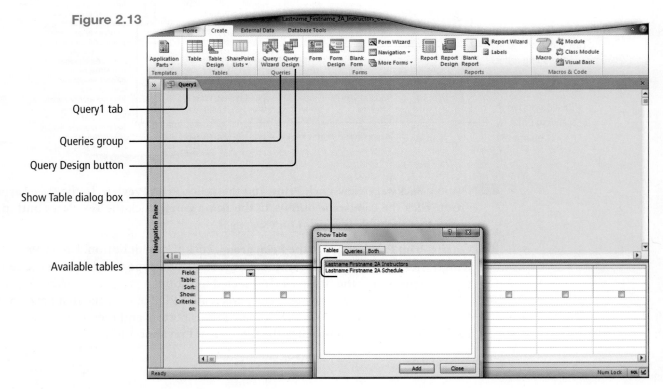

2 In the **Show Table** dialog box, double-click **2A Instructors**, and then **Close** the **Show Table** dialog box.

A field list for the 2A Instructors table displays in the upper area of the Query window. The Instructor ID field is the primary key field in this table. The Query window has two parts: the *table area* (upper area), which displays the field lists for tables that are used in the query, and the *design grid* (lower area), which displays the design of the query.

> **Alert! | Is There More Than One Field List in the Query Window?**
>
> If you double-click a table more than one time, a duplicate field list displays in the Query window. To remove a field list from the Query window, right-click the title bar of the field list, and then click Remove Table.

3 Point to the lower right corner of the field list to display the ⬉ pointer, and then drag down and to the right to expand the field list, displaying all of the field names and the table name. In the **2A Instructors** field list, double-click **Rank**, and then look at the design grid.

The Rank field name displays in the design grid in the Field row. You limit the fields that display when the query is run by placing only the desired field names in the design grid.

4 In the **2A Instructors** field list, point to **First Name**, hold down the left mouse button, and then drag down into the design grid until the ⬇ pointer displays in the **Field** row in the second column. Release the mouse button, and then compare your screen with Figure 2.14.

This is a second way to add field names to the design grid. As you drag the field, a small rectangular shape attaches to the mouse pointer. When you release the mouse button, the field name displays in the Field row.

Figure 2.14

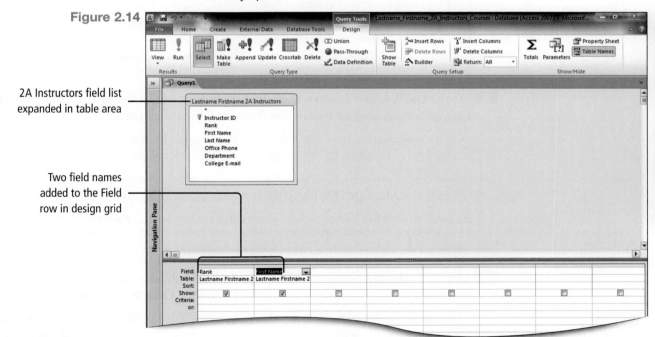

2A Instructors field list expanded in table area

Two field names added to the Field row in design grid

5 In design grid, in the **Field** row, click in the third column, and then click the **arrow** that displays. From the list, click **Last Name** to add the field to the design grid, which is a third way to add a field to the design grid.

6 Using one of the techniques you just practiced, add the **Office Phone** field to the fourth column and the **Department** field to the fifth column in the design grid.

Activity 2.08 | Running, Saving, Printing, and Closing a Query

After you create a query, you **run** it to display the results. When you run a query, Access looks at the records in the table (or tables) you have included in the query, finds the records that match the specified conditions (if any), and displays only those records in a datasheet. Only the fields that you have added to the design grid display in the query results. The query always runs using the current table or tables, presenting the most up-to-date information.

> **Another Way**
>
> On the Design tab, in the Results group, click the View button to automatically start the Run command.

1 On the **Design tab**, in the **Results group**, click the **Run** button, and then compare your screen with Figure 2.15.

This query answers the question, *What is the Rank, First Name, Last Name, Office Phone number, and Department of all of the instructors in the 2A Instructors table?* A query is a subset of the records in one or more tables, arranged in Datasheet view, using the fields and conditions that you specify. The five fields that you specified in the design grid display in columns, and the records from the 2A Instructors table display in rows.

Figure 2.15

Five fields specified in design grid

Records displayed in rows

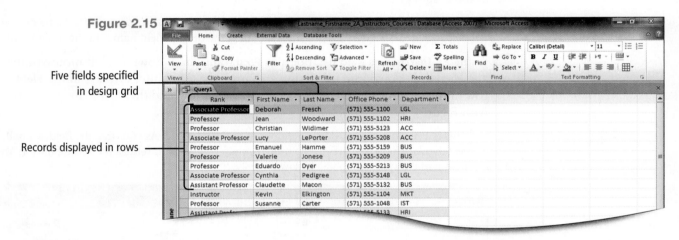

2 On the **Quick Access Toolbar**, click the **Save** button. In the **Save As** dialog box, type **Lastname Firstname 2A Instructors Query** and then click **OK**.

Save your queries if you are likely to ask the same question again; doing so will save you the effort of creating the query again to answer the same question.

> **Alert! | Does a Message Display After Entering a Query Name?**
>
> Query names are limited to 64 characters. For all projects, if you have a long last name or first name that results in your query name exceeding the 64-character limit, ask your instructor how you should abbreviate your name.

3 Display **Backstage** view, click **Print**, and then click **Print Preview**. Create a paper or electronic printout if instructed to do so, and then **Close Print Preview**.

Queries answer questions and gather information from the data in the tables. Queries are typically created as a basis for a report, but query results can be printed like any other table of data.

4 **Close** ☒ the query. **Open** ⟫ the **Navigation Pane**, and then notice that the **2A Instructors Query** object displays under the **2A Instructors** table object.

> The new query name displays in the Navigation Pane under the table with which it is related—the 2A Instructors table. Only the design of the query is saved. The records still reside in the table object. Each time you open the query, Access runs it again and displays the results based on the data stored in the related table(s). Thus, the results of a query always reflect the latest information in the related table(s).

Objective 5 | Create a New Query from an Existing Query

You can create a new query from scratch or you can open an existing query, save it with new name, and modify the design to suit your needs. Using an existing query saves you time if your new query uses all or some of the same fields and conditions in an existing query.

Activity 2.09 | Creating a New Query from an Existing Query

1 From the **Navigation Pane**, open your **2A Instructors Query** by either double-clicking the name or by right-clicking and clicking Open.

> The query runs, opens in Datasheet view, and displays the records from the 2A Instructors table as specified in the query design grid.

2 Display **Backstage** view, and then click **Save Object As**. In the **Save As** dialog box, type **Lastname Firstname 2A Instructor IDs Query** and then click **OK**. Click the **Home tab**, and then in the **Views group**, click the **View** button to switch to **Design** view.

> A new query, based on a copy of the 2A Instructors Query, is created and displays in the object window and in the Navigation Pane under its data source—the 2A Instructors table.

3 **Close** ⟪ the **Navigation Pane**. In the design grid, point to the thin gray selection bar above the **Office Phone** field name until the ↓ pointer displays. Click to select the **Office Phone** column, and then press Del.

> This action deletes the field from the query design only—it has no effect on the field in the underlying 2A Instructors table. The Department field moves to the left. Similarly, you can select multiple fields and delete them at one time.

4 From the gray selection bar, select the **First Name** column. In the selected column, point to the selection bar to display the ▷ pointer, and then drag to the right until a dark vertical line displays on the right side of the **Last Name** column. Release the mouse button to position the **First Name** field in the third column.

> To rearrange fields in the query design, select the field to move, and then drag it to a new position in the design grid.

5 Using the technique you just practiced, move the **Department** field to the left of the **Rank** field.

6 From the field list, drag the **Instructor ID** field down to the first column in the design grid until the ▤ pointer displays, and then release the mouse button. Compare your screen with Figure 2.16.

> The Instructor ID field displays in the first column, and the remaining four fields move to the right. Use this method to insert a field to the left of a field already displayed in the design grid.

Figure 2.16

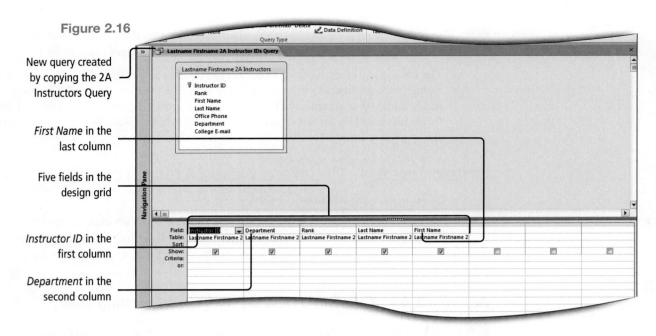

New query created
by copying the 2A
Instructors Query

First Name in the
last column

Five fields in the
design grid

Instructor ID in the
first column

Department in the
second column

7 On the **Design tab**, in the **Results group**, click the **Run** button.

This query answers the question, *What is the Instructor ID, Department, Rank, Last Name, and First Name for every instructor in the 2A Instructors table?* The results of the query are a subset of the records contained in the 2A Instructors table. The records are sorted by the primary key field—Instructor ID.

8 From **Backstage** view, display the query in **Print Preview**. Create a paper or electronic printout if instructed to do so, and then **Close Print Preview**.

9 **Close** ☒ the query, and in the message box, click **Yes** to save the changes to the design—deleting a field, moving two fields, and adding a field. **Open** ⟫ the **Navigation Pane**.

The query is saved and closed. The new query name displays in the Navigation Pane under the related table. Recall that when you save a query, only the *design* of the query is saved; the records reside in the related table object or objects.

Objective 6 | Sort Query Results

You can sort the results of a query in ascending or descending order in either Datasheet view or Design view. Use Design view if your query results should display in a specified sort order, or if you intend to use the sorted results in a report.

Activity 2.10 | Sorting Query Results

In this activity, you will save an existing query with a new name, and then sort the query results by using the Sort row in Design view.

1 On the **Navigation Pane**, click your **2A Instructor IDs Query**. Display **Backstage** view, and then click **Save Object As**. In the **Save As** dialog box, type **Lastname Firstname 2A Department Sort Query** and then click **OK**. Click the **Home tab**, and then drag the right edge of the **Navigation Pane** to the right to increase its width so that the names of the new query and the relationship report display fully.

Access creates a new query, based on a copy of your 2A Instructors ID Query; that is, the new query includes the same fields in the same order as the query on which it is based.

2 In the **Navigation Pane**, right-click your **2A Department Sort Query**, and then click **Design View. Close** the **Navigation Pane**.

3 In the design grid, in the **Sort** row, click in the **Last Name** field to display the insertion point and an arrow. Click the **Sort arrow**, and then in the list, click **Ascending**. Compare your screen with Figure 2.17.

Figure 2.17

Sort row in design grid ──

Ascending sort added to Last Name field ──

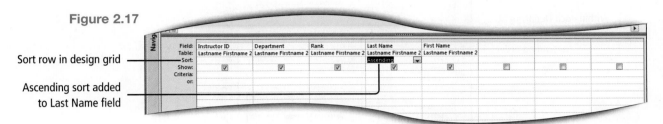

4 On the **Design tab** in the **Results group**, click the **Run** button.

In the query result, the records are sorted in ascending alphabetical order by the Last Name field, and two instructors have the same last name of *Widimer*.

5 On the **Home tab** in the **Views group**, click the **View** button to switch to **Design** view.

6 In the **Sort** row, click in the **First Name** field, click the **Sort arrow**, and then click **Ascending. Run** the query.

In the query result, the records are sorted first by the Last Name field. If instructors have the same last name, then Access sorts those records by the First Name field. The two instructors with the last name of *Widimer* are sorted by their first names.

7 Switch to **Design** view. In the **Sort** row, click in the **Department** field, click the **Sort arrow**, and then click **Descending. Run** the query; if necessary, scroll down to display the last records, and then compare your screen with Figure 2.18.

In Design view, fields with a Sort designation are sorted from left to right. That is, the sorted field on the left becomes the outermost sort field, and the sorted field on the right becomes the innermost sort field.

Thus, the records are sorted first in descending alphabetical order by the Department field—the leftmost sort field. Then, within each same department name field, the Last Names are sorted in ascending alphabetical order. And, finally, within each same last name field, the First Names are sorted in ascending alphabetical order.

If you run a query and the sorted results are not what you intended, be sure that the fields are displayed from left to right according to the groupings that you desire.

Figure 2.18

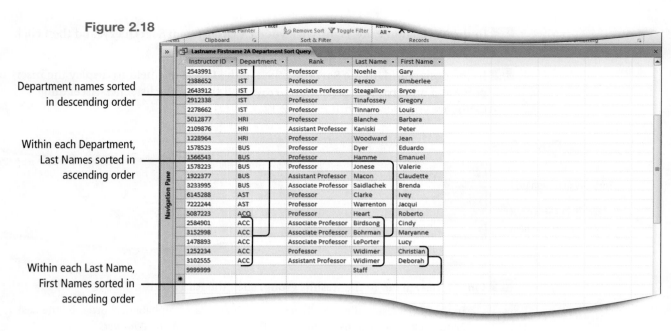

Department names sorted in descending order

Within each Department, Last Names sorted in ascending order

Within each Last Name, First Names sorted in ascending order

8 Display the query in **Print Preview**. Create a paper or electronic printout if instructed to do so, and then **Close Print Preview**. **Close** ☒ the query. In the message box, click **Yes** to save the changes to the query design.

More Knowledge | Sorting

If you add a sort order to the *design* of a query, it remains as a permanent part of the query design. If you use the sort buttons in the Datasheet view, they will override the sort order of the query design, and can be saved as part of the query. A sort order designated in Datasheet view does not display in the Sort row of the query design grid.

Objective 7 | Specify Criteria in a Query

Queries locate information in a database based on *criteria* that you specify as part of the query. Criteria are conditions that identify the specific records for which you are looking.

Criteria enable you to ask a more specific question; therefore, you will get a more specific result. For example, if you want to find out how many instructors are in the IST department, limit the results to that specific department, and then only the records that match the specified department will display.

Activity 2.11 | Specifying Text Criteria in a Query

In this activity, you will assist Dean Judkins by creating a query to answer the question *How many instructors are in the IST Department?*

1 Be sure that all objects are closed and that the **Navigation Pane** is closed. Click the **Create tab**, and then in the **Queries group**, click the **Query Design** button.

2 In the **Show Table** dialog box, **Add** the **2A Instructors** table to the table area, and then **Close** the **Show Table** dialog box.

3 Expand the field list to display all of the fields and the table name. Add the following fields to the design grid in the order given: **Department**, **Instructor ID**, **Rank**, **First Name**, and **Last Name**.

4 In the **Criteria** row of the design grid, click in the **Department** field, type **IST** and then press Enter. Compare your screen with Figure 2.19.

Access places quotation marks around the criteria to indicate that this is a ***text string***—a sequence of characters. Use the Criteria row to specify the criteria that will limit the results of the query to your exact specifications. The criteria is not case sensitive; so you can type *ist* instead of IST.

Figure 2.19

Five fields added to the design grid

Criteria row in design grid

Criteria under Department—Access adds quotation marks

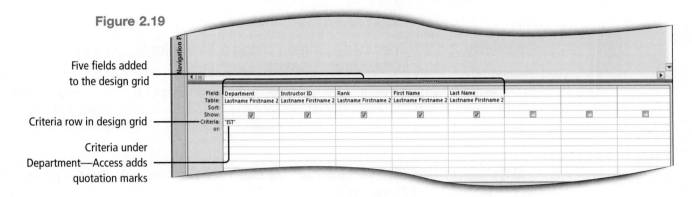

Note | Pressing Enter After Adding Criteria

If you press Enter or click in another column or row in the query design grid after you have added your criteria, you can see how Access alters the criteria so it can interpret what you have typed. Sometimes, there is no change, such as when you add criteria to a number or currency field. Other times, Access may capitalize a letter or add quotation marks or other symbols to clarify the criteria. Whether or not you press Enter after adding criteria has no effect on the query results. It is used here to help you see how the program behaves.

---

5 **Run** the query, and then compare your screen with Figure 2.20.

Thirteen records display that meet the specified criteria—records that have *IST* in the Department field.

Figure 2.20

Thirteen records match Department *IST* criteria

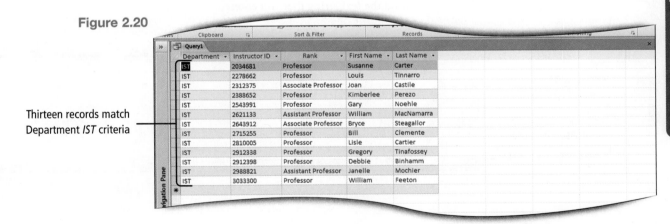

Alert! | Do Your Query Results Differ?

If you mistype the criteria, or enter it under the wrong field, or make some other error, the result will display no records. This indicates that there are no records in the table that match the criteria as you entered it. If this occurs, return to Design view and re-examine the query design. Verify that the criteria is typed in the Criteria row, under the correct field, and without typing errors. Then run the query again.

6 Save 🖫 the query as **Lastname Firstname 2A IST Query** and then display the query in **Print Preview**. Create a paper or electronic printout if instructed to do so, and then **Close Print Preview**.

7 Close ☒ the query, **Open** 》 the **Navigation Pane**, and then notice that the **2A IST Query** object displays under the **2A Instructors** table—its data source.

> Recall that queries in the Navigation Pane display an icon of two overlapping tables.

Activity 2.12 | Specifying Criteria Using a Field Not Displayed in the Query Results

So far, all of the fields that you included in the query design have also been included in the query results. It is not required to have every field in the query display in the results. In this activity, you will create a query to answer the question, *Which instructors have a rank of Professor?*

1 Close ≪ the **Navigation Pane**. Click the **Create tab**, and then in the **Queries group**, click the **Query Design** button.

2 From the **Show Table** dialog box, **Add** the **2A Instructors** table to the table area, and then **Close** the dialog box. Expand the field list.

3 Add the following fields, in the order given, to the design grid: **Instructor ID**, **First Name**, **Last Name**, and **Rank**.

4 In the **Sort** row, in the **Last Name** field, click the **Sort arrow**; click **Ascending**.

5 In the **Criteria** row, click in the **Rank** field, type **professor** and then press ⏎. Compare your screen with Figure 2.21.

> Recall that criteria is not case sensitive. As you start typing *professor*, a list of functions display, from which you can select if including a function in your criteria. When you press ⏎, the insertion point moves to the next criteria box and quotation marks are added around the text string that you entered.

Figure 2.21

Show row; check boxes selected for every field

Last Name field sorted in Ascending order

Criteria for Rank field

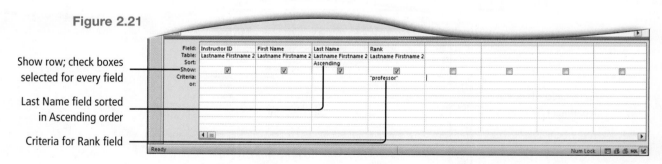

6 In the design grid, in the **Show** row, notice that the check box is selected for every field. **Run** the query to view the query results.

> Nineteen records meet the criteria. In the Rank column each record displays *Professor*, and the records are sorted in ascending alphabetical order by the Last Name field.

7 Switch to **Design** view. In the design grid, under **Rank**, in the **Show** row, click to clear the check box.

> Because it is repetitive and not particularly useful to have *Professor* display for each record in the query results, clear this check box so that the field does not display. However, you should run the query before clearing the Show check box to be sure that the correct records display.

8 **Run** the query, and then notice that the *Rank* field does not display.

> The query results display the same 19 records, but the *Rank* field does not display. Although the Rank field is still included in the query criteria for the purpose of identifying specific records, it is not necessary to display the field in the results. When appropriate, clear the Show check box to avoid cluttering the query results with data that is not useful.

9 **Save** 🔲 the query as **Lastname Firstname 2A Professor Rank Query** and then display the query in **Print Preview**. Create a paper or electronic printout if instructed to do so, and then **Close Print Preview**. **Close** ❌ the query.

Activity 2.13 | Using *Is Null* Criteria to Find Empty Fields

Sometimes you must locate records where data is *missing*. You can locate such records by using *Is Null*—empty—as the criteria in a field. Additionally, you can display only the records where a value *has* been entered in a field by using *Is Not Null* as the criteria, which will exclude records where the specified field is empty. In this activity, you will design a query to find out *Which scheduled courses have no credits listed?*

1 Click the **Create tab**. In the **Queries group**, click the **Query Design** button. Add the **2A Schedule** table to the table area, **Close** the **Show Table** dialog box, and then expand the field list.

2 Add the following fields to the design grid in the order given: **Subject**, **Catalog#**, **Section**, **Course Name**, and **Credits**.

3 In the **Criteria** row, click in the **Credits** field, type **is null** and then press ⏎.

> Access capitalizes *is null*. The criteria *Is Null* examines the field and looks for records that do *not* have any values entered in the Credits field.

4 In the **Sort** row, click in the **Subject** field, click the **Sort arrow**, and then click **Ascending**. **Sort** the **Catalog#** field in **Ascending** order, and then **Sort** the **Section** field in **Ascending** order. Compare your screen with Figure 2.22.

Figure 2.22
Three fields sorted in ascending alphabetical order

Is Null criteria in Credits field

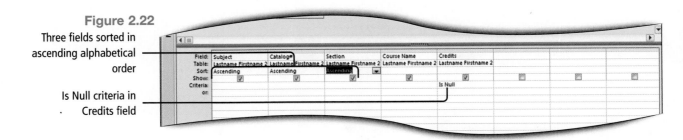

5 **Run** the query, and then compare your screen with Figure 2.23.

> Five scheduled courses do not have credits listed—the Credits field is empty. The records are sorted in ascending order first by the Subject field, then by the Catalog # field, and then by the Section. Using the information displayed in the query results, a course scheduler can more easily locate the records in the table to enter the credits.

Figure 2.23

Credits field empty (null) for five courses

Sorted first by Subject

Within Subject, sorted by Catalog#

Within Catalog#, sorted by Section

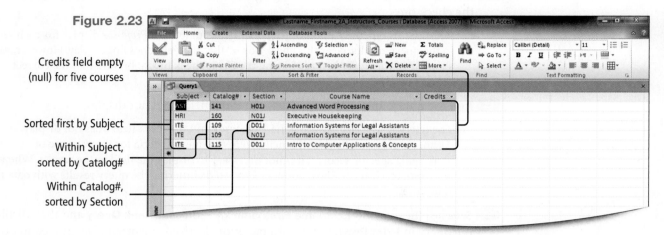

6 **Save** 🖫 the query as **Lastname Firstname 2A No Credits Query** and then display the query in **Print Preview**. Create a paper or electronic printout if instructed to do so, and then **Close Print Preview**.

7 **Close** ❌ the query. **Open** 》 the **Navigation Pane**, and then notice that the **2A No Credits Query** object displays under the **2A Schedule** table object, which is the query's data source.

8 From **Backstage** view, click **Close Database**, and then click **Exit** to close the Access program. As directed by your instructor, submit your database and the eight paper or electronic printouts—relationship report, sorted table, and six queries—that are the results of this project.

End **You have completed Project 2A** ————————————————

Project 2B Athletic Scholarships Database

myitlab
Project 2B Training

Project Activities

In Activities 2.14 through 2.26, you will assist Randy Shavrain, Athletic Director for Capital Cities Community College, in developing and querying his Athletic Scholarships database. Your results will look similar to Figure 2.24.

Project Files

For Project 2B, you will need the following files:

    a02B_Athletes_Scholarships
    a02B_Athletes (Excel file)

You will save your database as:

    Lastname_Firstname_2B_Athletic_Scholarships

Project Results

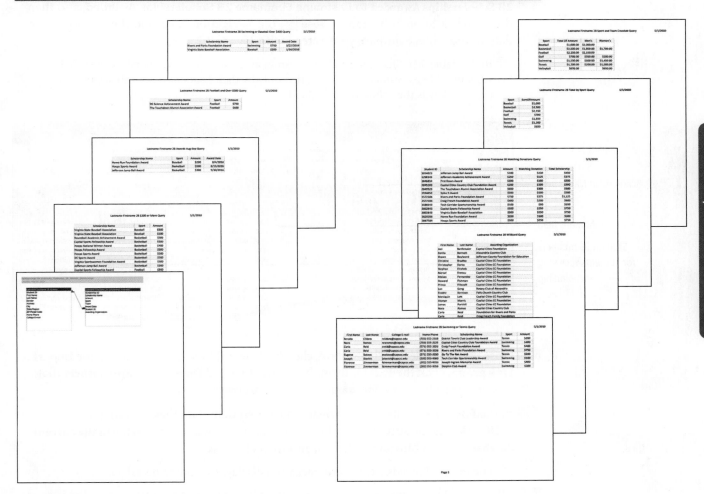

Figure 2.24
Project 2B Athletic Scholarships

Objective 8 | Specify Numeric Criteria in a Query

Criteria can be set for fields containing numeric data. When you design your table, set the appropriate data type for fields that will contain numbers, currency, or dates so that mathematical calculations can be performed.

Activity 2.14 | Opening an Existing Database and Importing a Spreadsheet

In this activity, you will open, rename, and save an existing database, and then import an Excel spreadsheet that Mr. Shavrain wants to bring into Access as a new table.

1 **Start** Access. In **Backstage** view, click **Open**. From your student files, open **a02B_Athletes_Scholarships**.

2 From **Backstage** view, click **Save Database As**. In the **Save As** dialog box, navigate to your **Access Chapter 2** folder, and then in the **File name** box, type **Lastname_Firstname_2B_Athletic_Scholarships** and then press Enter.

3 On the **Message Bar**, click the **Enable Content** button. In the **Navigation Pane**, **Rename 2B Scholarships Awarded** to **Lastname Firstname 2B Scholarships Awarded**, and then double-click to open the table. **Close** « the **Navigation Pane**, and then examine the data in the table. Compare your screen with Figure 2.25.

In this table, Mr. Shavrain tracks the names and amounts of scholarships awarded to student athletes. Students are identified only by their Student ID numbers, and the primary key is the Scholarship ID field.

Figure 2.25

Scholarship Name field

Amount field

Student ID numbers for students receiving scholarship

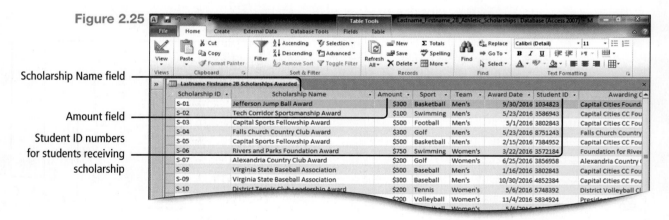

4 **Close** ✕ the table. On the Ribbon, click the **External Data tab**, and then in the **Import & Link group**, click the **Excel** button. In the **Get External Data – Excel Spreadsheet** dialog box, to the right of the **File name** box, click **Browse**.

5 In the **File Open** dialog box, navigate to your student data files, and then double-click **a02B_Athletes**. Be sure that the **Import the source data into a new table in the current database** option button is selected, and then click **OK**.

The Import Spreadsheet Wizard opens and displays the spreadsheet data.

6 Click **Next**. In the upper left portion of the **Import Spreadsheet Wizard** dialog box, select the **First Row Contains Column Headings** check box. Click **Next**, and then click **Next** again.

7 In the upper portion of the Wizard, click the **Choose my own primary key** option button, and then be sure that **Student ID** displays.

> In the new table, Student ID will be the primary key. No two students have the same Student ID.

8 Click **Next**. In the **Import to Table** box, type **Lastname Firstname 2B Athletes** and then click **Finish**. In the **Get External Data – Excel Spreadsheet** Wizard, click **Close**, and then **Open** » the **Navigation Pane**. Widen the **Navigation Pane** so that the table names display fully.

9 **Open** the new **2B Athletes** table, and then on the **Home tab**, switch to **Design View**.

10 For the **Student ID** field, click in the **Data Type** box, click the **arrow**, and then click **Text**. For the **ZIP/Postal Code** field, change the **Data Type** to **Text**, and then set the **Field Size** to **5** Click in the **State/Region** field, set the **Field Size** to **2** and then switch back to **Datasheet View**, saving the changes.

> Recall that numeric data that will not be used in any calculations, such as the Student ID, should have a Data Type of *Text*.

11 In the message box, click **Yes**—no data will be lost. **Close** « the **Navigation Pane**. Take a moment to review the imported data. Using the **Select All** button ☐, apply **Best Fit** to all of the fields. Click in any field to cancel the selection, **Save** 🖫 the table, and then **Close** ✕ the table.

Activity 2.15 │ Creating Table Relationships

In this activity, you will create a one-to-many relationship between the 2B Athletes table and the 2B Scholarships Awarded table by using the common field—*Student ID*.

1 Click the **Database Tools tab**, and then in the **Relationships group**, click the **Relationships** button.

2 In the **Show Table** dialog box, **Add** the **2B Athletes** table, and then **Add** the **2B Scholarships Awarded** table to the table area. **Close** the **Show Table** dialog box.

3 Move and resize the two field lists to display all of the fields and the entire table name, and then position the field lists so that there is approximately one inch of space between the two field lists.

> Resizing and repositioning the field lists is not required, but doing so makes it easier for you to view the field lists and the join line when creating relationships.

4 In the **2B Athletes** field list, point to the **Student ID** field. Hold down the left mouse button, drag into the **2B Scholarships Awarded** field list on top of the **Student ID** field, and then release the mouse button to display the **Edit Relationships** dialog box.

5 Point to the title bar of the **Edit Relationships** dialog box, and then drag it below the two field lists. In the **Edit Relationships** dialog box, be sure that **Student ID** is displayed as the common field for both tables.

> The two tables relate in a *one-to-many* relationship—*one* athlete can have *many* scholarships. The common field between the two tables is the Student ID field. In the 2B Athletes table, Student ID is the primary key. In the 2B Scholarships Awarded table, Student ID is the foreign key.

6 In the **Edit Relationships** dialog box, select the **Enforce Referential Integrity** check box. Click **Create**, and then compare your screen with Figure 2.26.

> The one-to-many relationship is established. The *1* and ∞ indicate that referential integrity is enforced, which ensures that a scholarship cannot be awarded to a student whose Student ID is not in the 2B Athletes table. Similarly, you cannot delete a student athlete from the 2B Athletes table if there is a scholarship listed for that student in the 2B Scholarships Awarded table.

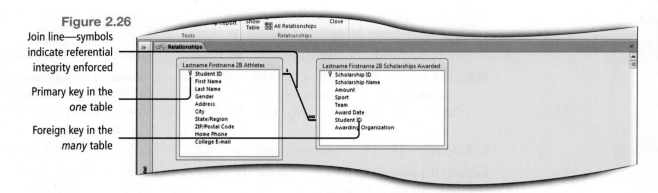

Figure 2.26

Join line—symbols indicate referential integrity enforced

Primary key in the *one* table

Foreign key in the *many* table

7 On the **Design tab**, in the **Tools group**, click the **Relationship Report** button. Create a paper or electronic printout if instructed to do so.

8 **Save** 🖫 the report as **Lastname Firstname 2B Relationships** and then click **OK**. **Close** ✕ the report, and then **Close** ✕ the **Relationships** window.

9 **Open** » the **Navigation Pane**, open the **2B Athletes** table, and then **Close** « the **Navigation Pane**. On the left side of the table, in the first record, click the **plus sign** (+) to display the subdatasheet for the record.

In the first record, for *Joel Barthmaier*, one related record exists in the 2B Scholarships Awarded table. The related record displays because you created a relationship between the two tables using Student ID as the common field.

10 **Close** ✕ the **2B Athletes** table.

Activity 2.16 | Specifying Numeric Criteria in a Query

Mr. Shavrain wants to know *Which scholarships are in the amount of $300, and for which sports?* In this activity, you will specify criteria in the query so that only the records of scholarships in the amount of $300 display.

1 Click the **Create tab**. In the **Queries group**, click the **Query Design** button.

2 In the **Show Table** dialog box, **Add** the **2B Scholarships Awarded** table to the table area, and then **Close** the **Show Table** dialog box. Expand the field list to display all of the fields and the entire table name.

3 Add the following fields to the design grid in the order given: **Scholarship Name**, **Sport**, and **Amount**.

4 In the **Sort** row, click in the **Sport** field. Click the **Sort arrow**, and then click **Ascending**.

5 In the **Criteria** row, click in the **Amount** field, type **300** and then press Enter. Compare your screen with Figure 2.27.

When entering currency values as criteria, do not type the dollar sign. Include a decimal point only if you are looking for a specific amount that includes cents—for example 300.49. Access does not insert quotation marks around the criteria because the field's data type is Number.

Figure 2.27

Numeric criteria—no quotation marks

Sort in ascending order by *Sport*

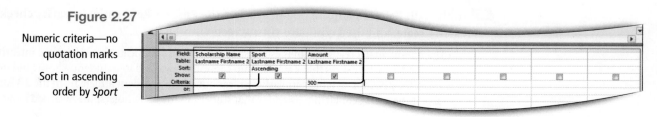

6 On the **Design tab**, in the **Results group**, click the **Run** button to view the results.

Five scholarships were awarded in the exact amount of $300. In the navigation area, *1 of 5* displays to indicate the number of records that match the criteria.

7 On the **Home tab**, in the **Views group**, click the **View** button to switch to **Design** view.

Activity 2.17 | Using Comparison Operators

Comparison operators are symbols that evaluate each field value to determine if it is the same (=), greater than (>), less than (<), or in between a range of values as specified by the criteria.

If no comparison operator is specified, equal (=) is assumed. For example, in the previous activity, you created a query to display only records where the *Amount* is 300. The comparison operator of = was assumed, and Access displayed only records that had values equal to 300.

1 Be sure your query is displayed in **Design** view. In the **Criteria** row, click in the **Amount** field, delete the existing criteria, type **>300** and then press Enter.

2 On the **Design tab**, in the **Results group**, click the **Run** button.

Fourteen records have an Amount that is greater than $300. The results show the records for which the Amount is *greater than* $300, but do not display amounts that are *equal to* $300.

3 Switch to **Design** view. In the **Criteria** row, under **Amount**, delete the existing criteria. Type **<300** and then press Enter. **Run** the query.

Eleven records display and each has an Amount less than $300. The results show the records for which the Amount is *less than* $300, but does not include amounts that are *equal to* $300.

4 Switch to **Design** view. In the **Criteria** row, click in the **Amount** field, delete the existing criteria, type **>=300** and then press Enter.

5 **Run** the query, and then compare your screen with Figure 2.28.

Nineteen records display, including the records for scholarships in the exact amount of $300. The records include scholarships *greater than* or *equal to* $300. In this manner, comparison operators can be combined. This query answers the question, *Which scholarships have been awarded in the amount of $300 or more, and for which sports, with the Sport names in alphabetical order?*

Figure 2.28

Nineteen records with a scholarship amount of $300 or more

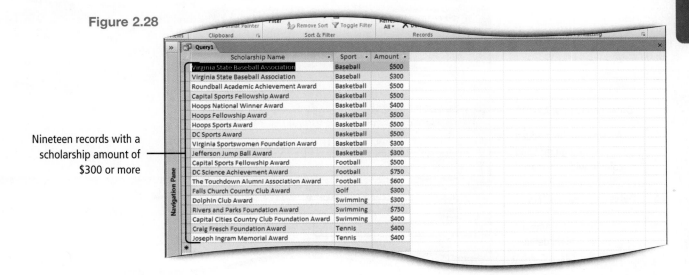

6 Save 🖫 the query as **Lastname Firstname 2B $300 or More Query** and then display the query in **Print Preview**. Create a paper or electronic printout if instructed to do so, and then **Close Print Preview**.

7 Close ✕ the query. **Open** ⟩⟩ the **Navigation Pane**, and notice that the new query displays under the table from which it retrieved the records—*2B Scholarships Awarded*.

Activity 2.18 │ Using the Between … And Comparison Operator

The ***Between … And operator*** is a comparison operator that looks for values within a range. It is useful when you need to locate records that are within a range of dates; for example, scholarships awarded between August 1 and September 30. In this activity, you will create a new query from an existing query, and then add criteria to look for values within a range of dates. The query will answer the question *Which scholarships were awarded between August 1 and September 30?*

1 On the **Navigation Pane**, click the **2B $300 or More Query** object to select it. Display **Backstage** view and click **Save Object As**. In the **Save As** dialog box, type **Lastname Firstname 2B Awards Aug-Sep Query** and then click **OK**.

2 Click the **Home tab**. Open the **2B Awards Aug-Sep Query** object, **Close** ⟨⟨ the **Navigation Pane**, and then switch to **Design** view. From the **2B Scholarships Awarded** field list, add the **Award Date** as the fourth field in the design grid.

3 In the **Criteria** row, click in the **Amount** field, and then delete the existing criteria so that the query is not restricted by amount. In the **Criteria** row, click in the **Award Date** field, type **between 8/1/16 and 9/30/16** and then press Enter.

4 In the selection bar of the design grid, point to the right edge of the **Award Date** column to display the ⊞ pointer, and then double-click. Compare your screen with Figure 2.29.

The width of the Award Date column is increased to fit the longest entry, enabling you to see all of the criteria. Access places pound signs (#) around dates and capitalizes *between* and *and*. This criteria instructs Access to look for values in the Award Date field that begin with 8/1/16 and end with 9/30/16. Both the beginning and ending dates will be included in the query results.

Figure 2.29

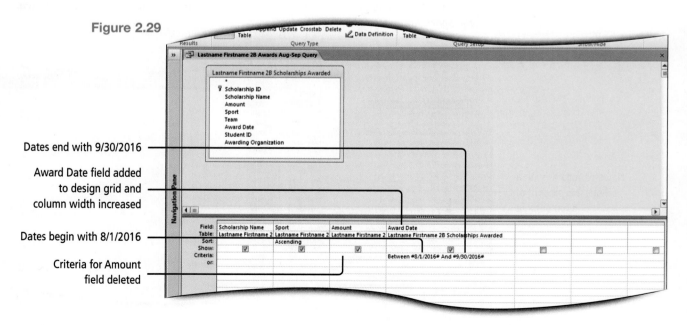

Dates end with 9/30/2016

Award Date field added to design grid and column width increased

Dates begin with 8/1/2016

Criteria for Amount field deleted

5 **Run** the query, and notice that three scholarships were awarded between 08/1/16 and 9/30/16.

6 Display the query in **Print Preview**, create a paper or electronic printout if instructed to do so, and then **Close Print Preview**.

7 **Close** ✕ the query. In the message box, click **Yes** to save the changes to the query design. **Open** » the **Navigation Pane**, and notice that the new query displays under the table that is its data source—*2B Scholarships Awarded*.

Objective 9 | Use Compound Criteria

You can specify more than one condition—criteria—in a query; this is called *compound criteria*. Compound criteria use AND and OR *logical operators*. Logical operators enable you to enter criteria for the same field or different fields.

Activity 2.19 | Using AND Criteria in a Query

Compound criteria use an *AND condition* to display records in the query results that meet all parts of the specified criteria. In this activity, you will help Mr. Shavrain answer the question *Which scholarships over $500 were awarded for Football?*

1 **Close** « the **Navigation Pane**. On the Ribbon, click the **Create tab**. In the **Queries group**, click the **Query Design** button. **Add** the **2B Scholarships Awarded** table to the table area. **Close** the **Show Table** dialog box, and then expand the field list.

2 Add the following fields to the design grid in the order given: **Scholarship Name**, **Sport**, and **Amount**.

3 In the **Criteria** row, click in the **Sport** field, type **football** and then press Enter.

4 In the **Criteria** row, in the **Amount** field, type **>500** and then press Enter. Compare your screen with Figure 2.30.

> You create the AND condition by placing the criteria for both fields on the same line in the Criteria row. The results will display only records that contain *Football* AND an amount greater than *$500*.

Figure 2.30

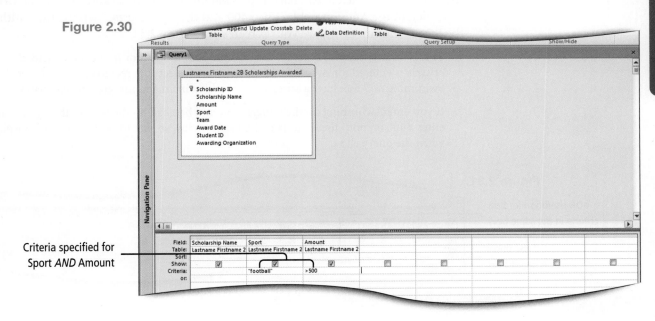

Criteria specified for Sport *AND* Amount

5 On the **Design tab**, in the **Results group**, click the **Run** button.

Two records display that match both conditions—Football in the Sport field *and* greater than $500 in the Amount field.

6 Save 🔲 the query as **Lastname Firstname 2B Football and Over $500 Query** and then click **OK** or press Enter. **Close** ❌ the query.

7 Open 》 the **Navigation Pane**, and then click one time to select the **2B Football and Over $500 Query** object. Display the query in **Print Preview**, create a paper or electronic printout if instructed to do so, and then **Close Print Preview**.

You can print any selected object from the Navigation Pane—the object does not have to be open to print.

8 Close 《 the **Navigation Pane**.

Activity 2.20 | Using OR Criteria in a Query

Use the *OR condition* to specify multiple criteria for a single field, or multiple criteria for different fields when you want to display the records that meet any of the conditions. In this activity, you will help Mr. Shavrain answer the question *Which scholarships over $400 were awarded in the sports of Baseball or Swimming, and what is the award date of each?*

1 Click the **Create tab**. In the **Queries group**, click the **Query Design** button.

2 Add the **2B Scholarships Awarded** table. **Close** the dialog box, expand the field list, and then add the following four fields to the design grid in the order given: **Scholarship Name**, **Sport**, **Amount**, and **Award Date**.

3 In the **Criteria** row, click in the **Sport** field, and then type **baseball**

4 In the design grid, on the **or** row, click in the **Sport** field, type **swimming** and then press Enter. **Run** the query.

The query results display seven scholarship records where the Sport is either Baseball *or* Swimming. Use the OR condition to specify multiple criteria for a single field.

5 Switch to **Design** view. In the **or** row, under **Sport**, delete *swimming*. In the **Criteria** row, under **Sport**, delete *baseball*. Type **swimming or baseball** and then in the **Criteria** row, click in the **Amount** field. Type **>400** and then press Enter. Increase the width of the **Sport** column. Compare your screen with Figure 2.31.

This is an alternative way to use the OR compound operator in the Sport field. Because criteria is entered for two different fields, Access selects the records that are Baseball *or* Swimming *and* that have a scholarship awarded in an amount greater than $400.

If you enter swimming on the Criteria row and baseball on the or row, then you must enter >400 on both the Criteria row and the or row so that the correct records display when the query runs.

Figure 2.31

OR condition for two criteria in the same field

AND condition for Amount field

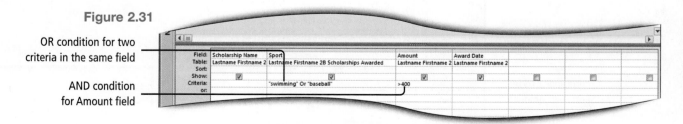

6 **Run** the query to display the two records that match the conditions.

7 **Close** ⊠ the query. In the message box, click **Yes** to save changes to the query. In the **Save As** dialog box, type **Lastname Firstname 2B Swimming or Baseball Over $400 Query** and then click **OK**.

8 **Open** » the **Navigation Pane**, increase the width of the **Navigation Pane** to display the full name of all objects, and then click one time to select the **2B Swimming or Baseball Over $400 Query** object. Display the query in **Print Preview**, create a paper or electronic printout if instructed to do so, and then **Close Print Preview. Close** « the **Navigation Pane**.

Objective 10 | Create a Query Based on More Than One Table

In a relational database, you can retrieve information from more than one table. Recall that a table in a relational database contains all of the records about a single topic. Tables are joined by relating the primary key field in one table to a foreign key field in another table. This common field creates a relationship, so you can include data from more than one table in a query.

For example, the Athletes table contains all of the information about the student athletes—name, address, and so on. The Scholarships Awarded table includes the scholarship name, amount, and so on. When an athlete receives a scholarship, only the Student ID field is included with the scholarship to identify who received the scholarship. It is not necessary to include any other data about the athletes in the Scholarships Awarded table; doing so would result in redundant data.

Activity 2.21 | Creating a Query Based on More Than One Table

In this activity, you will create a query that selects records from two tables. This is possible because a relationship has been created between the two tables in the database. The query will answer the questions *What is the name, e-mail address, and phone number of athletes who have received swimming or tennis scholarships, and what is the name and amount of the scholarship?*

1 Click the **Create tab**. In the **Queries group**, click the **Query Design** button. **Add** the **2B Athletes** table and the **2B Scholarships Awarded** table to the table area, and then **Close** the **Show Table** dialog box. Expand the two field lists, and then drag the **2B Scholarships Awarded** field list to the right so that there is approximately one inch of space between the field lists.

The join line displays because you previously created a relationship between the tables. It indicates a *one-to-many* relationship—*one* athlete can have *many* scholarships.

2 From the **2B Athletes** field list, add the following fields to the design grid in the order given: **First Name**, **Last Name**, **College E-mail**, and **Home Phone**.

3 In the **Sort** row, click in the **Last Name** field. Click the **Sort arrow**, and then click **Ascending** to sort the records in alphabetical order by last name.

4 From the **2B Scholarships Awarded** field list, add the following fields to the design grid in the order given: **Scholarship Name**, **Sport**, and **Amount**.

5 In the **Criteria** row, click in the **Sport** field. Type **swimming or tennis** and then press Enter.

6 In the design grid, increase the width of the **Home Phone** and **Scholarship Name** columns to display the entire table name on the **Table** row. If necessary, scroll to the right to display the *Home Phone* and *Scholarship Name* fields in the design grid, and then compare your screen with Figure 2.32.

> When extracting data from multiple tables, the information on the Table row is helpful, especially when different tables include the same field names, such as address, but different data, such as a student's address or a coach's address.

Figure 2.32

Table row indicates data source

Criteria entered for Sport field

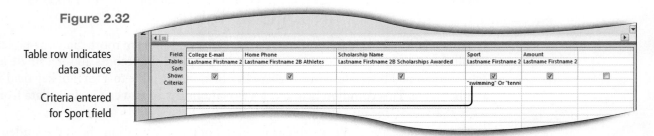

7 **Run** the query, and then compare your screen with Figure 2.33.

> Information for eight student athletes displays. The First Name and Last Name fields are included in the query results even though the common field—*Student ID*—is *not* included in the query design. Because Student ID is included in both tables, and a one-to-many relationship was created between the tables, the Student ID field is used to select the records in both tables by using one query. Two students—*Carla Reid* and *Florence Zimmerman*—received scholarships in both Swimming and Tennis. Recall that *one* student athlete can receive *many* scholarships.

Figure 2.33

Sport of *Tennis* or *Swimming*

Students with scholarships in both sports

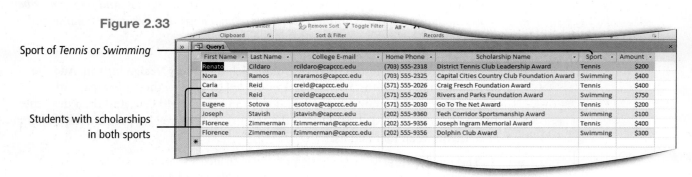

8 Save the query as **Lastname Firstname 2B Swimming or Tennis Query** and then display the query in **Print Preview**. Set the **Margins** to **Normal**, and then change the orientation to **Landscape**. Create a paper or electronic printout if instructed to do so, and then **Close Print Preview**.

9 **Close** ☒ the query, **Open** ≫ the **Navigation Pane**, and then compare your screen with Figure 2.34.

> Your new query—*2B Swimming or Tennis Query*—displays under both tables from which it retrieved records.

Figure 2.34

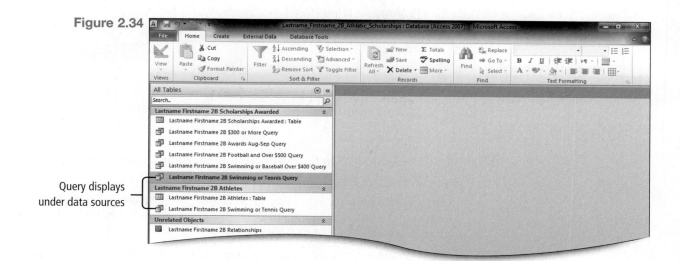

Query displays
under data sources

Objective 11 | Use Wildcards in a Query

Wildcard characters serve as a placeholder for one or more unknown characters in the criteria. When you are unsure of the particular character or set of characters to include in criteria, use wildcard characters in place of the characters.

Activity 2.22 | Using a Wildcard in a Query

Use the asterisk (*) to represent one or more characters. For example, if you use the * wildcard in the criteria Fo*, the results will display Foster, Forrester, Forrest, Fossil, or any word beginning with *Fo*. In this activity, you will use the asterisk (*) wildcard in the criteria row to answer the question *Which athletes received scholarships from local Rotary Clubs, country clubs, or foundations?*

1 **Close** ⌧ the **Navigation Pane**. On the Ribbon, click the **Create tab**. In the **Queries group**, click the **Query Design** button.

2 **Add** both tables to the table area, **Close** the **Show Table** dialog box, and then expand the field lists.

3 Add the following fields to the design grid in the order given: from the **2B Athletes** table, **First Name** and **Last Name**; from the **2B Scholarships Awarded** table, **Awarding Organization**.

4 In the **Sort** row, click in the **Last Name** field. Click the **arrow**, and then click **Ascending**.

5 In the **Criteria** row, under **Awarding Organization**, type **rotary*** and then press Enter.

The wildcard character * is a placeholder to match one or more characters. After pressing Enter, Access adds *Like* to the beginning of the criteria.

6 **Run** the query, and then compare your screen with Figure 2.35.

Three athletes received scholarships from Rotary Clubs. The results are sorted alphabetically by the Last Name field.

Figure 2.35

Awarding Organization
for all records
begins with *Rotary*

First Name	Last Name	Awarding Organization
Lan	Geng	Rotary Club of Alexandria
Eugene	Sotova	Rotary Club of Falls Church
Khrystyna	Tilson	Rotary Club of Arlington

7 Switch to **Design** view. On the **or** row, under **Awarding Organization**, type ***country club** and then press Enter.

The * can be used at the beginning, middle, or end of the criteria. The position of the * wildcard character determines the location of the unknown characters. Here you will search for records that end in *Country Club*.

8 **Run** the query to display six records, and notice that three records begin with *Rotary*, and three records end with *Country Club*—sorted alphabetically by Last Name.

9 Switch to **Design** view. Under **Awarding Organization** and under **Like "*country club"**, type ***foundation*** and then press Enter. Compare your screen with Figure 2.36.

The query will also display records that have the word *Foundation* anywhere—beginning, middle, or end—in the field. Three *OR* criteria have been entered for the Awarding Organization field—the query results will display students who have received scholarships from an organization name that begins with Rotary, *or* that ends in County Club, *or* that has Foundation anywhere in the middle of the name.

Figure 2.36

Three variations of
* wildcard placement

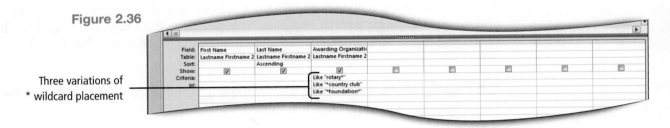

Field:	First Name	Last Name	Awarding Organizatic
Table:	Lastname Firstname 2	Lastname Firstname 2	Lastname Firstname 2
Sort:		Ascending	
Show:	☑	☑	☑
Criteria:			Like "rotary*"
or:			Like "*country club"
			Like "*foundation*"

10 **Run** the query to display 28 records.

Twenty-eight scholarships were from a Country Club, *or* a Rotary Club, *or* a Foundation.

11 **Save** 🖫 the query as **Lastname Firstname 2B Wildcard Query** and then display the results in **Print Preview**. Create a paper or electronic printout if instructed to do so, and then **Close Print Preview**.

12 **Close** ✕ the query, and then **Open** ⟩⟩ the **Navigation Pane**.

Because the 2B Wildcard Query object retrieved data from two tables, it displays below the 2B Scholarships Awarded table *and* the 2B Athletes table—the data sources.

More Knowledge | Search for a Single Unknown Character by Using the ? Wildcard

The question mark (?) is a wildcard that is used to search for unknown single characters. For each question mark included in criteria, any character can be inserted. For example, if you use *b?d* as a criteria, the query might locate bid, bud, bed, or any three-character word beginning with *b* and ending with *d*. If *b??d* is entered as the criteria, the results could include bind, bend, bard, or any four-character word beginning with *b* and ending with *d*.

Objective 12 | Use Calculated Fields in a Query

Queries can create calculated values that are stored in a **calculated field**. A calculated field stores the value of a mathematical operation. For example, you can multiply two fields together, such as Total Credit Hours and Tuition Per Credit Hour to get a Total Tuition Due amount for each student without having to include a specific field for this amount in the table, which reduces the size of the database and provides more flexibility.

There are two steps to produce a calculated field in a query. First, name the field that will store the calculated values. Second, write the **expression**—the formula—that performs the calculation. Each field name used in the calculation must be enclosed within its own pair of square brackets, and the new field name must be followed by a colon (:).

Activity 2.23 | Using Calculated Fields in a Query

For each scholarship received by student athletes, the Capital Cities Community College Alumni Association will donate an amount equal to 50 percent of each scholarship. In this activity, you will create a calculated field to determine the additional amount each scholarship is worth. The query will answer the question *What is the value of each scholarship if the Alumni Association makes a matching 50% donation?*

1 **Close** « the **Navigation Pane**, and then click the **Create tab**. In the **Queries group**, click the **Query Design** button.

2 **Add** the **2B Scholarships Awarded** table to the table area, **Close** the **Show Table** dialog box, and then expand the field list. Add the following fields to the design grid in the order given: **Student ID**, **Scholarship Name**, and **Amount**.

3 In the **Sort** row, click in the **Student ID** field; sort **Ascending**.

4 In the **Field** row, right-click in the first empty column to display a shortcut menu, and then click **Zoom**.

> The Zoom dialog box gives you more working space so that you can see the entire calculation as you type it. The calculation can also be typed directly in the empty Field box in the column.

5 In the **Zoom** dialog box, type **Matching Donation:[Amount]*0.5** and then compare your screen with Figure 2.37.

> The first element, *Matching Donation*, is the new field name where the calculated values will display. Following that is a colon (:), which separates the new field name from the expression. *Amount* is enclosed in square brackets because it is an existing field name in the 2B Scholarships Awarded table; it contains the numeric data on which the calculation will be performed. Following the right square bracket is an asterisk (*), which in math calculations signifies multiplication. Finally, the percentage (0.5 or 50%) displays.

Figure 2.37

Zoom dialog box ——

New field name for calculated value followed by a colon (:) ——

Expression—formula that calculates the value ——

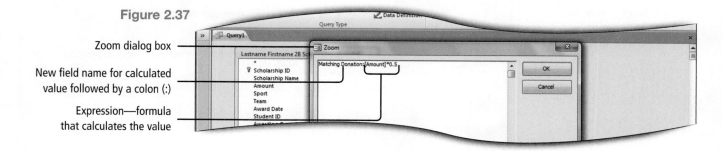

6 In the **Zoom** dialog box, click **OK**, and then **Run** the query. Compare your screen with Figure 2.38.

> The query results display three fields from the 2B Scholarships Awarded table plus a fourth field—*Matching Donation*—in which a calculated value displays. Each calculated value equals the value in the Amount field multiplied by 0.5.

Figure 2.38

New field name

Values calculated (50% of value in Amount field)

Alert! | Does Your Screen Differ?

If your calculations in a query do not work, switch to Design view and carefully check the expression you typed. Spelling or syntax errors prevent calculated fields from working properly.

---

7 Notice the formatting of the **Matching Donation** field—there are no dollar signs, commas, or decimal places; you will adjust this formatting later.

> When using a number, such as 0.5, in an expression, the values in the calculated field may not be formatted the same as in the existing field.

8 Switch to **Design** view. In the **Field** row, in the first empty column, right-click, and then click **Zoom**. In the **Zoom** dialog box, type **Total Scholarship:[Amount]+[Matching Donation]** and then compare your screen with Figure 2.39.

> Each existing field name—*Amount* and *Matching Donation*—must be enclosed in separate pairs of brackets.

Figure 2.39

New field name followed by a colon (:)

Expression with two existing field names in separate pairs of brackets

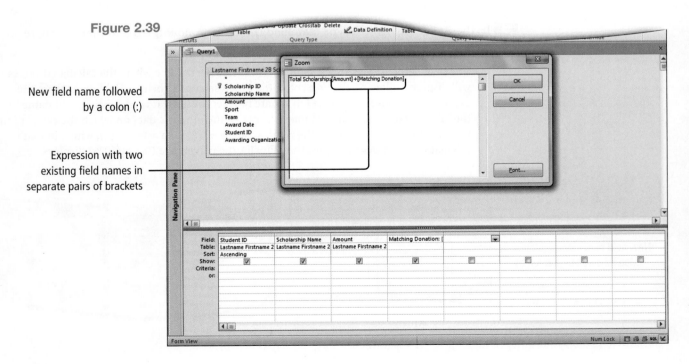

9 In the **Zoom** dialog box, click **OK**, and then **Run** the query to view the results.

> *Total Scholarship* is calculated by adding together the Amount field and the Matching Donation field. The Total Scholarship column includes dollar signs, commas, and decimal points, which carried over from the Currency format in the Amount field.

10 Switch to **Design** view. In the **Field** row, click in the **Matching Donation** field box.

Another Way

Right-click the Matching Donation field name, and then click Properties.

11 On the **Design tab**, in the **Show/Hide group**, click the **Property Sheet** button.

> The *Property Sheet* displays on the right side of your screen. A Property Sheet is a list of characteristics—properties—for fields in which you can make precise changes to each property associated with the field. The left column displays the Property name, for example, Description. To the right of the Property name is the Property setting box.

12 In the **Property Sheet**, on the **General tab**, click in the **Format** property setting box, and then click the **arrow** that displays. Compare your screen with Figure 2.40.

> A list of formats for the Matching Donation field displays.

Figure 2.40

Property Sheet for Matching Donation field

Format arrow

List of formats for numeric field

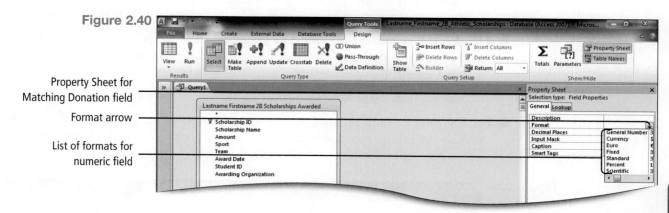

13 In the list, click **Currency**. Click the next property, **Decimal Places**, click the **arrow**, and then click **0**.

14 In the design grid, in the **Field** row, click in the **Total Scholarship** field. On the **Property Sheet**, set the **Format** to **Currency** and the **Decimal Places** to **0**.

15 **Close** ✕ the **Property Sheet**, and then **Run** the query. Select all of the columns and apply **Best Fit**.

> The Matching Donation and Total Scholarship fields are formatted as Currency with 0 decimal places.

16 **Save** 🖫 the query as **Lastname Firstname 2B Matching Donations Query** and then display the query results in **Print Preview**. Change the **Orientation** to **Landscape**. Create a paper or electronic printout if instructed to do so, and then **Close Print Preview**. **Close** ✕ the query.

Access | Chapter 2

Objective 13 | Calculate Statistics and Group Data in a Query

In Access queries, you can perform statistical calculations on a group of records. Calculations that are performed on a group of records are called *aggregate functions*.

Activity 2.24 | Using the MIN, MAX, AVG, and SUM Functions in a Query

In this activity, you will use the minimum, maximum, average, and sum functions in a query to examine the amounts of scholarships awarded. The last query will answer the question *What is the total dollar amount of all scholarships awarded?*

1 On the **Create tab**, in the **Queries group**, click the **Query Design** button.

2 **Add** the **2B Scholarships Awarded** table to the table area, **Close** the **Show Table** dialog box, and then expand the field list. Add the **Amount** field to the design grid.

> Include only the field you want to summarize in the query, so that the aggregate function (minimum, maximum, average, sum, and so forth) is applied to that single field.

3 On the **Design tab**, in the **Show/Hide group**, click the **Totals** button to add a **Total** row as the third row in the design grid. Notice that in the design grid, on the **Total** row, under **Amount**, *Group By* displays.

> Use the Total row to select the aggregate function that you want to use for the field.

4 In the **Total** row, under **Amount**, click in the **Group By** box, and then click the **arrow** to display the list of aggregate functions. Compare your screen with Figure 2.41, and take a moment to review the table in Figure 2.42.

Figure 2.41

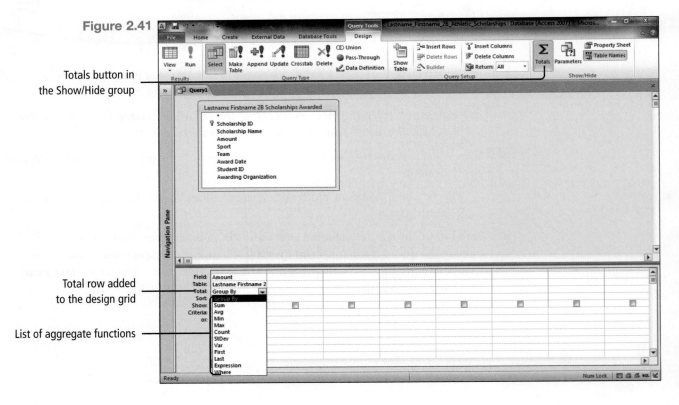

Totals button in the Show/Hide group

Total row added to the design grid

List of aggregate functions

Aggregate Functions

Function Name	What It Does
Sum	Totals the values in a field.
Avg	Averages the values in a field.
Min	Locates the smallest value in a field.
Max	Locates the largest value in a field.
Count	Counts the number of records in a field.
StDev	Calculates the Standard Deviation for the values in a field.
Var	Calculates the Variance for the values in a field.
First	Displays the First value in a field.
Last	Displays the Last value in a field.
Expression	Creates a calculated field that includes an aggregate function.
Where	Limits records to those that match a condition specified in the Criteria row.

Figure 2.42

5 From the list of functions, click **Min**, and then **Run** the query. Double-click the right edge of the column heading to apply Best Fit to the column.

> Access calculates the minimum (smallest) scholarship award—*$100.00*. The field name *MinOfAmount* displays for the calculation. This query answers the question, *What is the minimum (smallest) scholarship amount awarded?*

6 Switch to **Design** view. In the **Amount** field, in the **Total** row, select the **Max** function, and then **Run** the query.

> The maximum (largest) scholarship amount is *$750.00*.

7 Switch to **Design** view, select the **Avg** function, and then **Run** the query.

> The average scholarship amount awarded is *$358.33*.

8 Switch to **Design** view. Select the **Sum** function, and then **Run** the query.

> Access sums the Amount field for all records and displays a result of *$10,750.00*. The field name, SumOfAmount, displays. This query answers the question, *What is the total dollar amount of all the scholarships awarded?*

Activity 2.25 | Grouping Data in a Query

Aggregate functions can also be used to calculate totals by groups of data. For example, to group (summarize) the amount of scholarships awarded to each student, you include the Student ID field, in addition to the Amount field, and then group all of the records for each student together to calculate a total awarded to each student. Similarly, you can calculate how much is awarded for each sport.

1 Switch to **Design** view. Drag the **Student ID** field to the first column of the design grid—**Amount** becomes the second column. On the **Total** row, under **Student ID**, notice that *Group By* displays.

> This query groups—summarizes—the records by StudentID and calculates a total Amount for each student.

2 **Run** the query, and then compare your screen with Figure 2.43.

> The query calculates the total amount of all scholarships for each student.

Figure 2.43

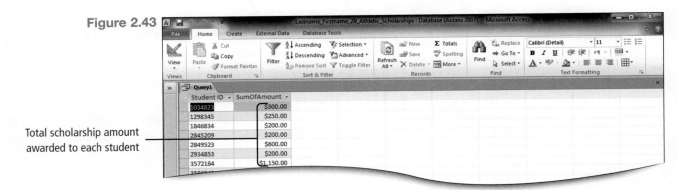

Total scholarship amount awarded to each student

3 Switch to **Design** view. In the design grid, delete the **Student ID** field, and then drag the **Sport** field to the first column—**Amount** becomes the second column.

4 In the design grid, click in the **Amount** field, and then on the **Design tab**, in the **Show/Hide group**, click the **Property Sheet** button.

5 In the **Property Sheet**, set the **Format** to **Currency**, set the **Decimal Places** to **0**, and then **Close** ☒ the **Property Sheet**.

6 **Run** the query, and then compare your screen with Figure 2.44.

> Access summarizes the data by sport. Basketball scholarships are the largest total Amount—*$3,500*.

Figure 2.44

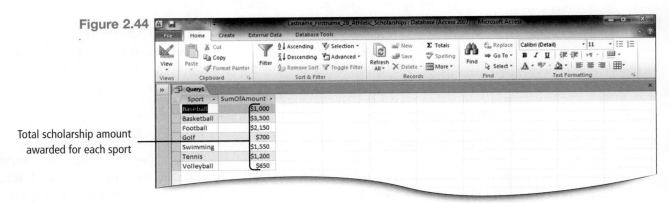

Total scholarship amount awarded for each sport

7 Save 🖫 the query as **Lastname Firstname 2B Total by Sport Query** and then display the query results in **Print Preview**. Create a paper or electronic printout if instructed to do so, and then **Close Print Preview**. **Close** ✕ the query.

Objective 14 | Create a Crosstab Query

A *crosstab query* uses an aggregate function for data that can be grouped by two types of information and displays data in a compact, spreadsheet-like format. A crosstab query always has at least one row heading, one column heading, and one summary field. Use a crosstab query to summarize a large amount of data in a small space that is easy to read.

Activity 2.26 | Creating a Crosstab Query Using One Table

In this activity, you will create a crosstab query that displays the total amount of scholarships awarded for each sport and for each team—women's or men's.

1 On the **Create tab**, in the **Queries group**, click the **Query Wizard** button. In the **New Query** dialog box, click **Crosstab Query Wizard**, and then click **OK**.

2 In the **Crosstab Query Wizard**, click **Table: 2B Scholarships Awarded** and then click **Next**.

3 To select the row headings, under **Available Fields**, double-click **Sport** to sort the scholarship amounts by the different sports. Click **Next**, and then compare your screen with Figure 2.45.

The sports are displayed as *row headings*; here you are prompted to select *column headings*.

Figure 2.45

Crosstab Query Wizard—
select column heading

Sport names display
as row headings

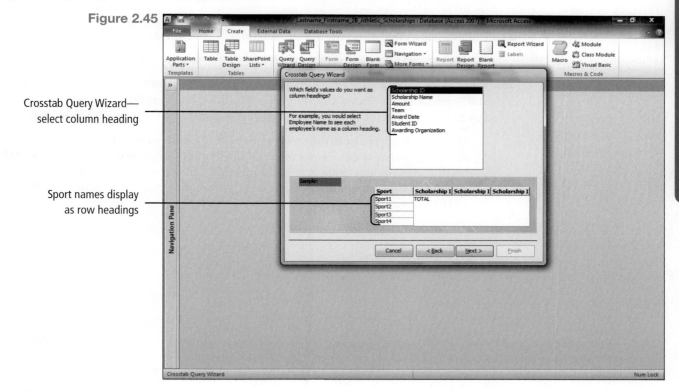

4 To select the column headings, in the field list, click **Team**. Click **Next**, and then compare your screen with Figure 2.46.

The teams will be listed as column headings; here you are prompted to select a field to summarize.

Figure 2.46

Teams display as column headings

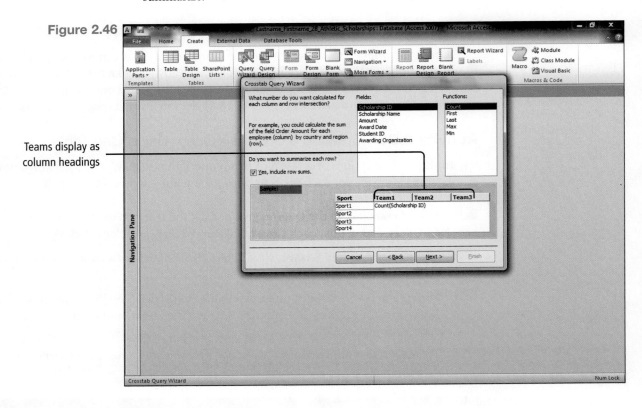

5 Under **Fields**, click **Amount**. Under **Functions**, click **Sum**, and then click **Next**.

The crosstab query will sum the Amount field for each sport and team.

6 In the **What do you want to name your query?** box, type **Lastname Firstname 2B Sport and Team Crosstab Query** and then click **Finish**. Apply **Best Fit** to the columns, click in any field to cancel the selection, and then compare your screen with Figure 2.47.

The crosstab query displays the total amount of scholarships awarded by sport and also by men's or women's teams. For example, for the sport of Golf, a total of $700 was awarded in scholarship money; $500 to men's teams and $200 to women's teams. A crosstab query is useful to display a summary of data based on two different fields—in this case, by sport and by teams.

Figure 2.47

Grouped by Teams

Total amount of
scholarship per Sport

Grouped by Sport

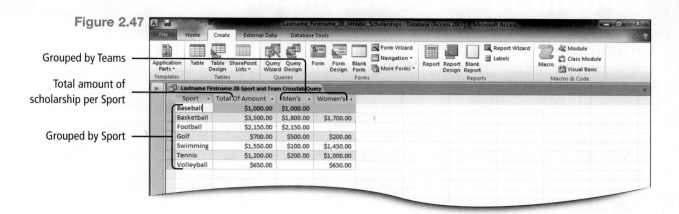

7 Display the query results in **Print Preview**. Create a paper or electronic printout if instructed to do so, and then **Close Print Preview**. **Close** ☒ the query, and click **Yes** to save changes to the query layout.

8 **Open** ☒ the **Navigation Pane**. In **Backstage** view, click **Close Database**, and then click **Exit**. As directed by your instructor, submit your database and the ten paper or electronic printouts—relationship report and nine queries—that are the results of this project.

More Knowledge | Creating a Crosstab Query Using Two Related Tables

To create a crosstab query using fields from more than one table, you must first create a select query with the fields from both tables that will be included in the crosstab query.

End You have completed Project 2B ———————————

Access | Chapter 2

Content-Based Assessments

Summary

Sorting data in a table reorders the records based on one or more fields. Use queries to ask complex questions about the data in a database in a manner that Access can interpret. Save queries so they can be run as needed against current records. Use queries to limit the fields that display, add criteria to restrict the number of records in the query results, create calculated values, include data from more than one table, and to display data grouped by two types of information.

Key Terms

Matching

Match each term in the second column with its correct definition in the first column by writing the letter of the term on the blank line in front of the correct definition.

_____ 1. The area below the Ribbon that displays information such as security alerts.

_____ 2. An area where you can view the security and privacy settings for your Access installation.

_____ 3. An association that you establish between two tables based on common fields.

_____ 4. A relationship between two tables where one record in the first table corresponds to many records in the second table.

_____ 5. A list of field names in a table.

_____ 6. The field that is included in the related table so the field can be joined with the primary key in another table for the purpose of creating a relationship.

_____ 7. A set of rules that ensures that the data between related tables is valid.

_____ 8. The line joining two tables that visually indicates the common fields and the type of relationship.

_____ 9. A format for displaying related records in a datasheet when you click the plus sign (+) next to a record in a table on the one side of a relationship.

_____ 10. The process of arranging data in a specific order based on the value in a field.

A Ascending

B Descending

C Field list

D Foreign key

E Innermost

F Join line

G Message Bar

H One-to-many relationship

I Outermost

J Referential integrity

K Relationship

L Select query

M Sorting

N Subdatasheet

O Trust Center

____ 11. A sorting order that arranges text in alphabetical order (A to Z) or numbers from lowest to highest.

____ 12. A sorting order that arranges text in reverse alphabetical order (Z to A) or numbers from highest to lowest.

____ 13. When sorting on multiple fields in Datasheet view, the field that is used for the first level of sorting.

____ 14. When sorting on multiple fields in Datasheet view, the field that is used for the second level of sorting.

____ 15. A database object that retrieves (selects) specific data from one or more tables and then displays the results in Datasheet view.

Multiple Choice

Circle the correct answer.

1. The lower area of the Query window that displays the design of the query is the:
   A. design grid   **B.** property sheet   **C.** table area

2. The process in which Access searches the records in the table, finds the records that match specified criteria, and then displays the records in a datasheet is:
   A. select   **B.** run   **C.** sort

3. Conditions in a query that identify the specific records for which you are looking are known as:
   A. aggregate functions   **B.** criteria   **C.** expressions

4. A criteria that searches for fields that are empty is:
   A. Is Empty   **B.** Is Not Null   **C.** Is Null

5. The symbols of =, >, and < are known as:
   A. aggregate functions   **B.** comparison operators   **C.** logical operators

6. A comparison operator that looks for values within a range is:
   A. And   **B.** Between ... And   **C.** Or

7. The logical operator that requires all conditions to be met is:
   A. AND   **B.** Is Null   **C.** OR

8. A wildcard character that serves as a placeholder for one or more unknown characters is the:
   A. *   **B.** ?   **C.** /

9. A field that stores the value of a mathematical operation is:
   A. an aggregate field   **B.** a calculated field   **C.** an expression

10. A query that uses an aggregate function for data that can be grouped by two types of information is:
    A. an aggregate query   **B.** a calculated query   **C.** a crosstab query

Content-Based Assessments

- **1** Open an Existing Database
- **2** Create Table Relationships
- **3** Sort Records in a Table
- **4** Create a Query in Design View
- **5** Create a New Query from an Existing Query
- **6** Sort Query Results
- **7** Specify Criteria in a Query

Skills Review | Project **2C** Music Department

In the following Skills Review, you will assist Dr. William Jinkens, the Capital Cities Community College Music Director, in using his database to answer various questions about the instruments in the Music Department's inventory. Your results will look similar to Figure 2.48.

Project Files

For Project 2C, you will need the following file:

a02c_Music_Department

You will save your database as:

Lastname_Firstname_2C_Music_Department

Project Results

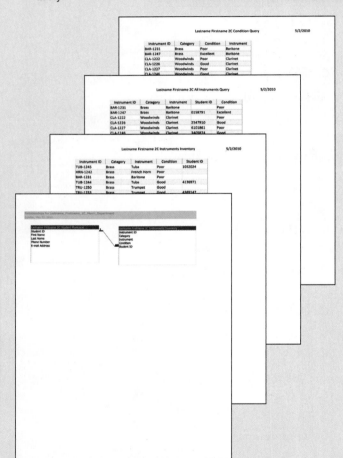

Figure 2.48

(Project 2C Music Department continues on the next page)

Content-Based Assessments

Skills Review | Project 2C Music Department (continued)

1 **Start** Access. In **Backstage** view, click **Open**. Navigate to the student files that accompany this textbook, and then open the **a02C_Music_Department** database.

a. Click the **File tab** to return to **Backstage** view, and then click **Save Database As**. In the **Save As** dialog box, navigate to your **Access Chapter 2** folder. In the **File name** box, select the file name, and then type **Lastname_Firstname_2C_Music_Department** and then press [Enter]. In the **Message Bar**, click **Enable Content**.

b. **Rename** the 2C Student Musicians table to **Lastname Firstname 2C Student Musicians** and then **Rename** the **2C Instruments Inventory** to **Lastname Firstname 2C Instruments Inventory** Widen the **Navigation Pane** to display fully both table names.

2 **Open** both tables to examine the contents of each, **Close** the tables, and then **Close** the **Navigation Pane**.

a. Click the **Database Tools tab**, and in the **Relationships group** click the **Relationships** button. Drag the **Show Table** dialog box down into the lower right portion of your screen.

b. In the **Show Table** dialog box, click your **2C Student Musicians**, and then click **Add**. Double-click your **2C Instruments Inventory** to add the table to the **Relationships** window. In the **Show Table** dialog box, click **Close**.

c. Drag the **2C Instruments Inventory** field list—the field list on the right—to the right about 3 inches. In the **2C Student Musicians** field list—the field list on the left—position your mouse pointer over the lower right corner of the field list to display the ⬊ pointer, and then drag to the right to increase the width of the field list until the entire name of the table in the title bar displays and all of the field names display. Then use the ⬊ pointer to resize the **2C Instruments Inventory** field list so that all of the field names and the table name display.

d. In the **2C Student Musicians** field list, point to **Student ID**, hold down the left mouse button, and then drag down and to the right to the **2C Instruments Inventory** field list until your mouse pointer is on top of **Student ID**. Then release the mouse button. Drag the **Edit Relationships** dialog box to the lower portion of your screen. The relationship between the two tables is a one-to-many relationship; *one* student can play *many* instruments.

e. In the **Edit Relationships** dialog box, click to select the **Enforce Referential Integrity** check box, and then click the **Create** button. On the **Design tab**, in the **Tools group**, click the **Relationship Report** button. On the **Print Preview tab**, in the **Page Size group**, change the **Margins** to **Normal**, and then create a paper or electronic printout as directed.

f. **Save** the relationship report with the default name. **Close** the report, and then **Close** the **Relationships** window. From the **Navigation Pane**, open the **2C Instruments Inventory** table, and then **Close** the **Navigation Pane**.

3 In the **Condition** field, click any record. On the **Home tab**, in the **Sort & Filter group**, click the **Descending** button to sort the records from *Poor* to *Excellent*. In the field names row, click the **Category arrow**, and then click **Sort A to Z** to sort the records first by *Category* and then by *Condition*.

a. Display **Backstage** view, click **Print**, and then click **Print Preview**. Create a paper or electronic copy as directed. **Close Print Preview**, **Close** the table, and then click **No**; you do not need to save the sort changes.

4 Click the **Create tab**, and then in the **Queries group**, click the **Query Design** button. In the **Show Table** dialog box, double-click your **2C Instruments Inventory** table, and then **Close** the **Show Table** dialog box. Expand the field list.

a. Double-click **Instrument ID** to add the field to the design grid. Point to the **Category** field, hold down the left mouse button, and then drag the field down into the design grid until you are pointing to the **Field** row in the second column. Release the mouse button.

b. In design grid, in the **Field** row, click in the third column, and then click the **arrow** that displays. From the list, click **Instrument** to add the field to the design grid. Using the technique of your choice, add the **Student ID** field to the fourth column and the **Condition** field to the fifth column in the design grid.

c. On the **Design tab**, in the **Results group**, click the **Run** button. This query answers the question, *What is the Instrument ID, Category, Instrument, Student ID, and Condition of all of the instruments in the 2C Instruments Inventory table?*

d. **Save** the query as **Lastname Firstname 2C All Instruments Query** and then click **OK**. Display the query in **Print Preview**, and then create a paper or electronic printout as directed. **Close Print Preview**.

(Project 2C Music Department continues on the next page)

5 Display **Backstage** view, click **Save Object As**. In the **Save As** dialog box, type **Lastname Firstname 2C Condition Query** and then click **OK** to create a new query based on an existing query. Click the **Home tab**, and then switch to **Design** view.

a. In the design grid, point to the thin gray selection bar above the **Student ID** field name until the ↓ pointer displays. Click to select the **Student ID** column, and then press [Del].

b. In the gray selection bar, select the **Instrument ID** column. Point to the **selection bar** to display the ↳ pointer, and then drag to the right until a dark vertical line displays on the right side of the **Condition** column. Release the mouse button to position the **Instrument ID** field in the fourth column.

c. **Run** the query. The query results display four fields. This query answers the question, *What is the Category, Instrument, Condition, and Instrument ID for every Instrument in the 2C Instruments Inventory table?*

d. Display the query in **Print Preview**, and then create a paper or electronic printout as directed. **Close Print Preview**, **Close** the query, and in the message box, click **Yes** to save the changes to the design—you moved two fields. **Open** the **Navigation Pane**.

6 **Open** your **2C All Instruments Query**. **Save** the query object as **Lastname Firstname 2C Instrument Sort Query** and then click the **Home tab**. **Close** the **Navigation Pane**. Switch to **Design** view.

a. In the design grid, delete the **Student ID** field. In the **Sort** row, click in the **Category** field. Click the **Sort arrow**, and then in the list, click **Ascending**. In the **Sort** row, click in the **Condition** field, click the **Sort arrow**, and then click **Descending**. **Run** the query. This query answers the question, *For every Instrument ID, within each Category (with Category sorted in ascending order), what Instruments are in the inventory and what is the instrument's Condition (with Condition sorted in descending order)?*

b. Display the query in **Print Preview**. Create a paper or electronic printout if instructed to do so, and then **Close Print Preview**. **Close** the query. In the message box, click **Yes** to save the changes to the query design.

7 Click the **Create tab**, and then in the **Queries group**, click the **Query Design** button. **Add** your **2C Instruments Inventory** table to the table area, and then **Close** the **Show Table** dialog box. Expand the field list. Add the following

fields to the design grid in the order given: **Instrument ID**, **Category**, **Instrument**, and **Condition**.

a. In the design grid, on the **Criteria** row, click in the **Condition** field, type **fair** and then press [Enter]. **Run** the query; three records display that meet the specified criteria—records that have *fair* in the Condition field.

b. **Save** the query as **Lastname Firstname 2C Fair Condition Query** and then create a paper or electronic printout as directed. **Close Print Preview**, and then **Close** the query.

c. **Create** a new query in **Query Design** view. **Add** the **2C Instruments Inventory** table to the table area, and then expand the field list. Add the following fields, in the order given, to the design grid: **Category**, **Instrument**, and **Condition**.

d. In the **Criteria** row, click in the **Category** field, type **woodwinds** and then press [Enter]. Under **Category**, in the **Show** row, click to clear the check box, and then **Run** the query. Ten instruments are categorized as woodwinds. Recall that if all results use the same criteria, such as *woodwinds*, it is not necessary to display the data in the query results.

e. **Save** the query as **Lastname Firstname 2C Woodwinds Query** and then create a paper or electronic printout as directed. **Close Print Preview**. **Close** the query.

f. **Create** a new query in **Query Design** view. **Add** the **2C Student Musicians** table to the table area, and then expand the field list. Add the following fields, in the order given, to the design grid: **First Name**, **Last Name**, **E-mail Address**, and **Phone Number**.

g. In the **Criteria** row, click in the **Phone Number** field, type **is null** and then press [Enter]. In the **Sort** row, click in the **Last Name** field, click the **Sort arrow**, and then click **Ascending**. **Run** the query. Three student musicians do not have a phone number stored in the 2C Student Musicians table.

h. **Save** the query as **Lastname Firstname 2C Missing Phone Numbers Query** and then create a paper or electronic printout as directed. **Close Print Preview**, and then **Close** the query. **Open** the **Navigation Pane**.

i. Display **Backstage** view, click **Close Database**, and then click **Exit** to close the Access program. As directed by your instructor, submit your database and the eight paper or electronic printouts— relationship report, sorted table, and six queries— that are the results of this project.

End **You have completed Project 2C** ————————

Apply 2B skills from these Objectives:

8 Specify Numeric Criteria in a Query

9 Use Compound Criteria

10 Create a Query Based on More Than One Table

11 Use Wildcards in a Query

12 Use Calculated Fields in a Query

13 Calculate Statistics and Group Data in a Query

14 Create a Crosstab Query

Skills Review | Project 2D Concerts and Sponsors

In the following Skills Review, you will assist Dr. William Jinkens, the Capital Cities Community College Music Director, in answering questions about concerts, sponsors, box office receipts, dates, and concert locations. Your results will look similar to Figure 2.49.

Project Files

For Project 2D, you will need the following files:

a02D_Concerts_Sponsors
a02D_Sponsors (Excel file)

You will save your database as:

Lastname_Firstname_2D_Concerts_Sponsors

Project Results

Figure 2.49

(Project 2D Concerts and Sponsors continues on the next page)

Content-Based Assessments

Skills Review | Project 2D Concerts and Sponsors (continued)

1 **Start** Access. In the **Backstage** view, click **Open**. Navigate to the student files that accompany this textbook, and then open the **a02D_Concerts_Sponsors** database.

   a. Click the **File tab** to return to **Backstage** view, and then click **Save Database As**. In the **Save As** dialog box, navigate to your **Access Chapter 2** folder. In the **File name** box, select the file name, and then type **Lastname_Firstname_2D_Concerts_Sponsors** and then press [Enter]. In the **Message Bar**, click **Enable Content**. **Rename** the **2D Concerts** table to **Lastname Firstname 2D Concerts** and then widen the **Navigation Pane** to display the entire table name.

   b. Click the **External Data tab**, and then in the **Import & Link group**, click the **Excel** button. In the **Get External Data – Excel Spreadsheet** dialog box, click **Browse**. Navigate to your student files, and then double-click the Excel file **a02D_Sponsors**. Be sure that the **Import the source data into a new table in the current database** option button is selected, and then click **OK**.

   c. In the **Import Spreadsheet Wizard**, select the **First Row Contains Column Headings** check box, and then click **Next**. Click **Next** again. Click the **Choose my own primary key** option button, and then be sure that **Sponsor ID** displays. Click **Next**. In the **Import to Table** box, type **Lastname Firstname 2D Sponsors** and then click **Finish**. In the Wizard, click **Close**. The imported Excel spreadsheet becomes the second table in the database.

   d. From the **Navigation Pane**, open your **2D Sponsors** table. Apply **Best Fit** to all columns, and then **Close** the table, saving changes to the design. Click the **Database Tools tab**, and in the **Relationships group**, click the **Relationships** button. **Add** the **2D Sponsors** table, and then **Add** the **2D Concerts** table to the table area. **Close** the **Show Table** dialog box. Expand and move the field lists as necessary.

   e. In the **2D Sponsors** field list, point to the **Sponsor ID** field, hold down the left mouse button, drag into the **2D Concerts** field list, position the mouse pointer on top of the **Sponsor ID** field, and then release the mouse button. In the **Edit Relationships** dialog box, select the **Enforce Referential Integrity** check box, and then click the **Create** button. A one-to-many relationship is established; *one* sponsor organization can sponsor *many* concerts.

   f. On the **Design tab**, in the **Tools group**, click the **Relationship Report** button. Create a paper or electronic printout as directed, and then **Close** the report. In the message box, click **Yes**; and then in the **Save As** dialog box, click **OK** to save the report with the default name. **Close** the **Relationships** window, and then **Close** the **Navigation Pane**.

2 Click the **Create tab**, and then in the **Queries group**, click the **Query Design** button. **Add** the **2D Concerts** table to the table area, **Close** the **Show Table** dialog box, and then expand the field list.

   a. Add the following fields to the design grid in the order given: **Concert Name**, **Box Office Receipts**, and **Concert Location**. Click in the **Sort** row under **Concert Location**, click the **Sort arrow**, and then click **Ascending**. In the **Criteria** row, under **Box Office Receipts**, type **>=800** press [Enter], and then **Run** the query. Nine records meet the criteria. This query answers the question, *Which concerts had Box Office Receipts of $800 or more, and where was each concert held in alphabetical order by Concert Location?*

   b. **Save** the query as **Lastname Firstname 2D $800 or More Query** and then create a paper or electronic printout as directed. **Close Print Preview**.

   c. With the query still open, display **Backstage** view, click **Save Object As**, type **Lastname Firstname 2D Concerts Jan-Apr Query** and then click **OK**. Click the **Home tab**, and then switch to **Design** view. From the **2D Concerts** field list, add **Date** as the fourth field in the design grid.

   d. In the **Criteria** row, under **Box Office Receipts**, delete the existing criteria so that the query is not restricted by receipts. Click in the **Sort** row under **Concert Location**, click the **Sort arrow**, and then click **(not sorted)**. Click in the **Sort** row under **Date**, click the **Sort arrow**, and then click **Ascending**.

   e. Click in the **Criteria** row under **Date**, type **between 1/1/16 and 4/30/16** and then press [Enter]. **Run** the query. Five records meet the criteria. This query answers the question, *What is the Concert Name, Box Office Receipts, Concert Location, and Date, in chronological order between January 1, 2016, and April 30, 2016, of concerts held?* **Print** or submit electronically as directed. **Close Print Preview**, **Close** the query, and then click **Yes** to save the changes to the query design.

(Project 2D Concerts and Sponsors continues on the next page)

Skills Review | Project **2D** Concerts and Sponsors (continued)

3 **Create** a query in **Query Design** view. **Add** the **2D Concerts** table to the table area, **Close** the **Show Table** dialog box, and then expand the field list. Add the following fields to the design grid in the order given: **Concert Name**, **Concert Location**, and **Box Office Receipts**.

a. In the **Criteria** row, under **Concert Location**, type **Virginia Community Theater** and then press Enter. In the **Criteria** row, under **Box Office Receipts**, type **<=1000** and then press Enter. In the **Concert Location** field, clear the **Show** check box. **Run** the query; two records display. This query answers the question, *Which concerts that were held at the Virginia Community Theater had Box Office Receipts of $1,000 or less?*

b. **Save** the query as **Lastname Firstname 2D VCT Low Box Office Receipts Query** and then create a paper or electronic printout as directed. **Close** the query.

c. **Create** a query in **Query Design** view. **Add** the **2D Concerts** table to the table area, **Close** the **Show Table** dialog box, and then expand the field list. Add the following fields to the design grid: **Concert Name**, **Concert Location**, **Box Office Receipts**, and **Date**.

d. In the **Criteria** row, under **Concert Location**, type **Virginia Community Theater or DC Events Center** and press Enter. In the **Criteria** row, under **Box Office Receipts**, type **>1000** and then press Enter. In the **Sort** row, under **Date**, click the **Sort arrow**, and then click **Ascending**.

e. **Run** the query. Four records display. This query answers the question, *Which concerts held at either the Virginia Community Theater or the DC Events Center had Box Office Receipts of more than $1,000 and on what dates, in chronological order, were the concerts held?*

f. **Save** the query as **Lastname Firstname 2D VCT or DC Over $1000 Query** and then create a paper or electronic printout as directed. **Close Print Preview**, and then **Close** the query.

4 **Create** a query in **Query Design** view, **Add** both tables to the table area, and then expand the field lists. Reposition the field lists so that **2D Sponsors** is on the left side. From the **2D Sponsors** field list, add the following fields to the design grid in the order given: **Sponsor Name** and **Web Address**. Click in the **Sort** row

under **Sponsor Name**, click the **Sort arrow**, and then click **Ascending**.

a. From the **2D Concerts** field list, add the following fields to the design grid in the order give: **Concert Name**, **Concert Location**, and **Box Office Receipts**.

b. In the **Criteria** row, under **Concert Location**, type **Virginia Community Theater** and then click in the **or** row, under **Concert Location**. Type **DC Events Center** and then press Enter.

c. In the design grid, select the **Box Office Receipts** field, and then drag it to the first field position in the grid. **Run** the query; 12 records display. This query answers the question, *What were the Box Office Receipts, Sponsor Name, sponsor Web Address, Concert Name, and Concert Location of all concerts held at either the Virginia Community Theater or the DC Events Center, sorted alphabetically by Sponsor Name?*

d. **Save** the query as **Lastname Firstname 2D Receipts and Sponsors VCT or DC Query** and then display the query results in **Print Preview**. Change the orientation to **Landscape**, change the **Margins** to **Normal**, and then create a paper or electronic printout as directed. **Close** the query.

5 **Create** a query in **Query Design** view, **Add** both tables to the table area, **Close** the **Show Table** dialog box, and then expand the field lists. Reposition the field lists so that **2D Sponsors** is on the left side.

a. From the **2D Sponsors** field list, add the **Sponsor Name** field to the design grid. From the **2D Concerts** field list, add the **Concert Name** field to the design grid.

b. In the **Criteria** row, under **Sponsor Name**, type ***radio*** and then press Enter. In the **Criteria** row, under **Concert Name**, type ***festival** and then press Enter.

c. **Run** the query; two records have the word *Radio* somewhere in the Sponsor Name and the word *Festival* at the end of the Concert Name. This query answers the question, *Which radio stations are sponsoring Festival-type concerts?* **Save** the query as **Lastname Firstname 2D Radio Festivals Query** and then create a paper or electronic printout as directed. **Close** the query.

6 **Create** a query in **Query Design** view. **Add** both tables to the table area, **Close** the **Show Table** dialog box, and then expand the field lists. If necessary, reposition the

(Project 2D Concerts and Sponsors continues on the next page)

Access | Chapter 2

field lists so that *2D Sponsors* is on the left side. From the field lists, add the following fields to the design grid in the order given: **Concert ID**, **Sponsor Name**, and **Box Office Receipts**. Click in the **Sort** row under **Concert ID**, click the **Sort arrow**, and then click **Ascending**.

a. Sponsors have indicated that they will donate an additional amount to the Music Department based on 50 percent of the Box Office Receipts. On the **Field** row, right-click in the first empty column to display a shortcut menu, and then click **Zoom**. In the **Zoom** dialog box, type **Matching Donation:[Box Office Receipts]*0.5** and then click **OK**.

b. **Run** the query to view the new field—*Matching Donation*. Switch to **Design** view. In the **Field** row, in the first empty column, right-click, and then click **Zoom**. In the **Zoom** dialog box, type **Total Receipts:[Box Office Receipts]+[Matching Donation]** and then click **OK**. **Run** the query to view the results.

c. Switch to **Design** view. In the field row, click in the **Matching Donations** field. In the **Show/Hide group**, click the **Property Sheet** button, and then set the **Format** to **Currency** and the **Decimal Places** to **2**. **Close** the **Property Sheet**.

d. **Run** the query. This query answers the question *In ascending order by Concert ID, assuming each sponsor makes a matching 50 percent donation based on each concert's Box Office Receipts, what is the Sponsor Name, Box Office Receipts, Matching Donation, and Total Receipts for each concert?*

e. Select all of the columns, and then apply **Best Fit**. **Save** the query as **Lastname Firstname 2D Matching Donation Query** and then display the query results in **Print Preview**. Change the orientation to **Landscape**, and then create a paper or electronic printout as directed. **Close** the query.

7 Create a query in **Query Design** view. **Add** the **2D Concerts** table to the table area, **Close** the **Show Table** dialog box, and then expand the field list. Add the **Box Office Receipts** field to the design grid.

a. On the **Design tab**, in the **Show/Hide group**, click the **Totals** button, which adds a *Total* row as the third row in the design grid. On the **Total** row, under **Box Office Receipts**, click in the **Group By** box. Click the **arrow**, and then click the **Sum** function.

b. With the field still selected, display the **Property Sheet**, set the **Decimal Places** to **0**, and then **Close** the **Property Sheet**. **Run** the query. The total Box Office Receipts for all the concerts was *$17,475*. Apply **Best Fit** to the **SumOfBox Office Receipts** column.

c. Switch to **Design** view. In the design grid, add the **Concert Location** field as the first field of the design grid. **Run** the query. This query answers the question *For each Concert Location, what are the total Box Office Receipts?*

d. **Save** the query as **Lastname Firstname 2D Total Receipts by Location Query** and then create a paper or electronic printout as directed. **Close** the query.

8 Create a query using the **Query Wizard**. In the **New Query** dialog box, click **Crosstab Query Wizard**, and then click **OK**. Be sure that **2D Concerts** is selected, and then click **Next**.

a. Under **Available Fields**, double-click **Sponsor ID** so that you can display Box Office Receipts by Sponsor ID, and then click **Next**. In the field list, click **Concert Location** to add the locations as column headings, and then click **Next**.

b. Under **Fields**, click **Box Office Receipts**. Under **Functions**, click **Sum**, and then click **Next**.

c. Name the query **Lastname Firstname 2D Sponsors and Locations Crosstab Query** and then click **Finish**. Click the **Home tab**, switch to **Design** view, click in the **Box Office Receipts** column, display the **Property Sheet**, and then set the **Decimal Places** to **0**. **Close** the **Property Sheet**, **Run** the query, and apply **Best Fit** to all of the columns. This query answers the question *By Sponsor ID, what are the total Box Office Receipts for each Concert Location?*

d. Display the query results in **Print Preview**. Change the orientation to **Landscape**, change the **Margins** to **Normal**, and then create a paper or electronic printout as directed—two pages result. **Close** the query, saving changes to the design.

e. **Open** the **Navigation Pane**. Increase the width of the **Navigation Pane** to display fully all of the object names. Display **Backstage** view, click **Close Database**, and then click **Exit**. As directed by your instructor, submit your database and the ten paper or electronic printouts—relationship report and nine queries—that are the results of this project.

End You have completed Project 2D

Content-Based Assessments

Apply **2A** skills from these Objectives:

1. Open an Existing Database
2. Create Table Relationships
3. Sort Records in a Table
4. Create a Query in Design View
5. Create a New Query from an Existing Query
6. Sort Query Results
7. Specify Criteria in a Query

Mastering Access | Project **2E** Grants and Organizations

In the following Mastering Access project, you will assist Susan Elkington, Director of Grants for the college, in using her database to answer questions about public and private grants awarded to the college departments. Your results will look similar to Figure 2.50.

Project Files

For Project 2E, you will need the following file:

a02E_Grants_Organizations

You will save your database as:

Lastname_Firstname_2E_Grants_Organizations

Project Results

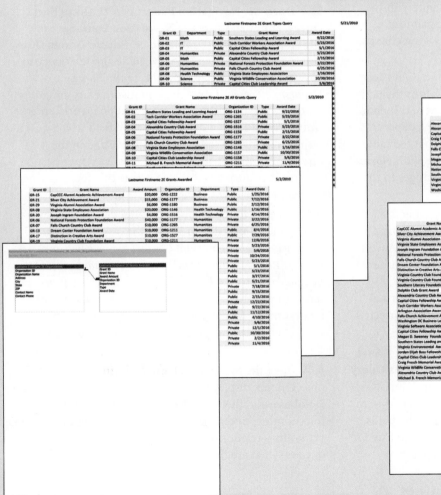

Figure 2.50

(Project 2E Grants and Organizations continues on the next page)

1 **Start** Access. From your student files, open the **a02E_Grants_Organizations** database. Save the database in your **Access Chapter 2** folder as **Lastname_Firstname_2E_Grants_Organizations** and then enable the content. In the **Navigation Pane**, **Rename** the tables by adding **Lastname Firstname** to the beginning of each table name, and then widen the **Navigation Pane** to display fully both table names. **Open** both tables and examine their contents to become familiar with the data. **Close** both tables, and leave the **Navigation Pane** open.

2 Create a *one-to-many* relationship between the **2E Organizations** table and the **2E Grants Awarded** table based on the **Organization ID** field, and then **Enforce Referential Integrity**. *One* organization can award *many* grants. Create a **Relationship Report**, saving it with the default name. Create a paper or electronic printout as directed, and then **Close** all open objects, saving changes if prompted.

3 **Open** the **2E Grants Awarded** table, and then **Close** the **Navigation Pane**. **Sort** so that the records in the table are in alphabetical order by the **Department** and then in descending order by **Award Amount**. Create a paper or electronic printout as directed, being sure that the table prints on only one page by using **Landscape**, with **Normal** margins. **Close** the table, and do *not* save changes to the table.

4 **Create** a query in **Query Design** view, using the **2E Grants Awarded** table to answer the question, *What is the Grant ID, Grant Name, Award Amount, Type, and Award Date for all of the grants?* Display the fields in the order listed in the question. **Save** the query as **Lastname Firstname 2E All Grants Query** and then, with **Normal** margins, create a paper or electronic printout as directed. **Close Print Preview**, and leave the query open.

5 Use **2E All Grants Query** to create a new query. **Save** the **Object As Lastname Firstname 2E Grant Types Query** and then redesign the query to answer the question, *What is the Grant ID, Department, Type, Grant Name, and Award Amount for all grants?* Display the only the fields necessary to answer the question and in the order listed in the question. With **Normal** margins, create a paper or

electronic printout as directed. **Close** the query, saving the design changes.

6 From the **Navigation Pane**, open the **2E All Grants Query**, and then **Close** the **Navigation Pane**. **Save** the **Object As Lastname Firstname 2E Grant Sort Query** and then switch to **Design** view. Redesign the query to answer the question, *What is the Grant Name, Department, Award Amount, and Award Date for grants sorted first in alphabetical order by Department and then in descending order by Amount?* Display only the fields necessary to answer the question and in the order listed in the question. With **Normal** margins, create a paper or electronic printout as directed. **Close** the query, saving changes to the query design.

7 **Open** the **Navigation Pane**, open **2E Grant Sort Query**, and then **Close** the **Navigation Pane**. **Save** the **Object As Lastname Firstname 2E Private Grants Query** and then switch to **Design** view. Redesign the query to answer the question, *What is the Grant Name, Department, Award Amount, and Award Date for grants that have a Type of Private, sorted in alphabetical order by Grant Name?* Do *not* display the **Type** field in the query results; display the fields in the order listed in the question. With **Normal** margins, create a paper or electronic printout as directed. **Close** the query, saving changes to the query design.

8 **Create** a query in **Query Design** view, using the **2E Organizations** table to answer the question, *What is the Organization Name and Contact Name where the Contact Phone number is missing from the table, sorted in alphabetical order by the Organization Name?* Two records meet the criteria. **Save** the query as **Lastname Firstname 2E Missing Phone# Query** and then create a paper or electronic printout as directed. **Close** the query.

9 **Open** the **Navigation Pane** and widen it so that all object names display fully. In **Backstage** view, click **Close Database**, and then click **Exit**. As directed by your instructor, submit your database and the seven paper or electronic printouts—relationship report, sorted table, and five queries—that are the results of this project.

End **You have completed Project 2E**

Content-Based Assessments

Apply 2B skills from these Objectives:

- **8** Specify Numeric Criteria in a Query
- **9** Use Compound Criteria
- **10** Create a Query Based on More Than One Table
- **11** Use Wildcards in a Query
- **12** Use Calculated Fields in a Query
- **13** Calculate Statistics and Group Data in a Query
- **14** Create a Crosstab Query

Mastering Access | Project **2F** Events and Clients

In the following Mastering Access project, you will assist Hank Schwan, the Capital Cities Community College Facilities Manager, in using his database to answer questions about facilities that the college rents to community and private organizations at times when the facilities are not in use for college activities. Your results will look similar to Figure 2.51.

Project Files

For Project 2F, you will need the following files:

> a02F_Events_Clients
> a02F_Rental_Clients (Excel file)

You will save your database as:

> Lastname_Firstname_2F_Events_Clients

Project Results

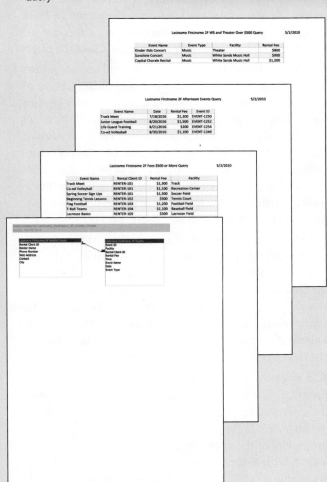
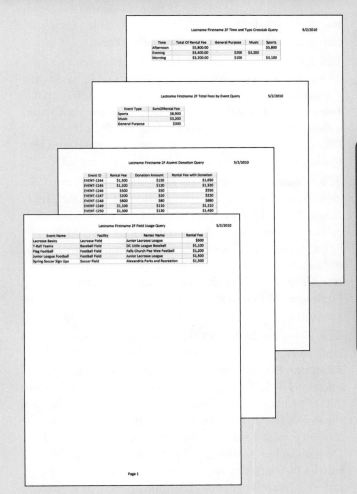

Figure 2.51

(Project 2F Events and Clients continues on the next page)

1 **Start** Access. From your student files, open the **a02F_Events_Clients** database. Save the database in your **Access Chapter 2** folder as **Lastname_Firstname_2F_Events_Clients** and then enable the content. In the **Navigation Pane**, **Rename** the table by adding **Lastname Firstname** to the beginning of the table name.

2 **Import** the **a02F_Rental_Clients** Excel spreadsheet from the student data files that accompany this textbook into the current database as a new table. Designate the first row of the spreadsheet as column headings. Select the **Rental Client ID** field as the primary key. Name the table **Lastname Firstname 2F Rental Clients** and then widen the **Navigation Pane** to display fully the two table names. **Open** both tables and examine their contents to become familiar with the data. In the **2F Rental Clients** table, apply **Best Fit** to all of the columns. **Close** both tables, saving changes, and then **Close** the **Navigation Pane**.

3 Create a *one-to-many* relationship between the **2F Rental Clients** table and the **2F Events** table based on the **Rental Client ID** field, and then **Enforce Referential Integrity**. *One* rental client can have *many* events. Create a **Relationship Report**, saving it with the default name. Create a paper or electronic printout as directed, and then **Close** all open objects, saving changes if prompted.

4 **Create** a query in **Query Design** view using the **2F Events** table to answer the question, *What is the Event Name, Rental Client ID, and Rental Fee for events with fees greater than or equal to $500, in ascending order by Rental Client ID, and in which Facility was the event held?* Display the fields in the order listed in the question. Eleven records meet the criteria. **Save** the query as **Lastname Firstname 2F Fees $500 or More Query** Create a paper or electronic printout as directed. Leave the query open.

5 Using the **2F Fees $500 or More Query** object, create a new query, and save it as **Lastname Firstname 2F Afternoon Events Query** Redesign the query to answer the questions, *Which Events were held in the Afternoon between 7/1/16 and 8/31/16, in chronological order by date, what was the Rental Fee, and what was the Event ID?* (Hint: Open the 2F Events table to see how the Time field data is stored.). Do *not* display the **Time** field in the results, and do *not* restrict the results by **Rental Fee**. Four records meet the criteria. Create a paper or electronic printout as directed, **Close** the query, and save changes to the design.

6 **Create** a query in **Query Design** view using the **2F Events** table to answer the question, *Which Events and Event Types were held in either the White Sands Music Hall or the Theater that had Rental Fees greater than $500?* Display the fields in the order listed in the question. Three records meet the criteria. **Save** the query as **Lastname Firstname 2F WS and Theater Over $500 Query** and then create a paper or electronic printout as directed. **Close** the query.

7 **Create** a query in **Query Design** view using both tables to answer the question, *Which Events were held on one of the sports fields, for which Renter Name, and what was the Rental Fee in order of lowest fee to highest fee?* (Hint: Use a wildcard with the word *Field*.) Display the fields in the order listed in the question. Five records meet the criteria. **Save** the query as **Lastname Firstname 2F Field Usage Query** and then with **Normal** margins, create a paper or electronic printout as directed. **Close** the query.

8 The college Alumni Association will donate money to the Building Fund in an amount based on 10 percent of total facility rental fees. **Create** a query in **Query Design** view to answer the question, *In ascending order by Event ID, what will be the total of each Rental Fee if the Alumni Association donates an additional 10% of each fee?* (Hint: First compute the amount of the donation, name the new field **Donation Amount** and run the query to view the results. Then calculate the new rental fee and name the new field **Rental Fee with Donation**) **Run** the query.

Switch back to **Design** view, change the properties of the new fields to display in **Currency** format with **0** decimal places, and then **Run** the query again. For *EVENT-1244*, the *Donation Amount* is *$150* and the *Rental Fee with Donation* is *$1,650*. Apply **Best Fit** to the columns in the query results. **Save** the query as **Lastname Firstname 2F Alumni Donation Query** and then create a paper or electronic printout as directed. **Close** the query.

9 **Create** a query in **Query Design** view using the **2F Events** table and the **Sum** aggregate function to answer the question, *In descending order by Rental Fee, what are the total Rental Fees for each Event Type?* Change the properties of the appropriate field to display **Currency** format with **0** decimal places, and then **Run** the query. For a *Sports* Event Type, Rental Fees total *$8,900*. Apply **Best Fit** to the columns in the query results. **Save** the query as **Lastname Firstname 2F Total Fees by Event Query** and then create a paper or electronic printout as directed. **Close** the query.

(Project 2F Events and Clients continues on the next page)

Content-Based Assessments

Mastering Access | Project **2F** Events and Clients (continued)

10 By using the **Query Wizard**, create a **Crosstab Query** based on the **2F Events** table. Select **Time** as the **row headings** and **Event Type** as the **column headings**. **Sum** the **Rental Fee** field. Name the query **Lastname Firstname 2F Time and Type Crosstab Query** Change the design to display **Currency** format with **0** decimal places in the appropriate column, and then apply **Best Fit** to all of the columns. This query answers the question *What are the total Rental Fees for each time of the day and for each Event Type?* Create

a paper or electronic printout as directed. **Close** the query, saving changes to the design.

11 **Open** the **Navigation Pane** and widen it so that all object names display fully. In **Backstage** view, click **Close Database**, and then click **Exit**. As directed by your instructor, submit your database and the eight paper or electronic printouts—relationship report and seven queries—that are the results of this project.

End **You have completed Project 2F** ———————————————

Mastering Access | Project **2G** Students and Scholarships

In the following Mastering Access project, you will assist Thao Nguyen, Director of Academic Scholarships, in using her database to answer questions about scholarships awarded to students. Your results will look similar to Figure 2.52.

Project Files

For Project 2G, you will need the following file:

a02G_Students_Scholarships

You will save your database as:

Lastname_Firstname_2G_Students_Scholarships

Project Results

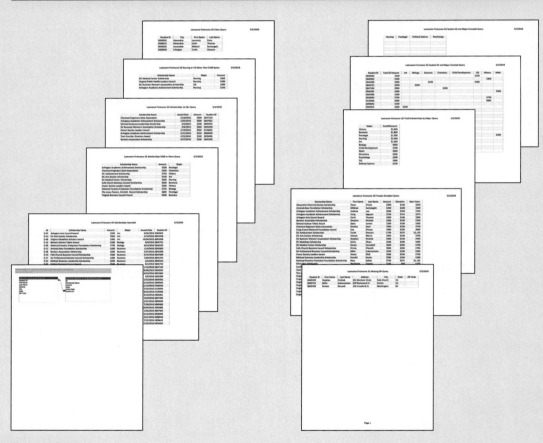

Figure 2.52

(Project 2G Students and Scholarships continues on the next page)

Content-Based Assessments

Mastering Access | Project 2G Students and Scholarships (continued)

1 **Start** Access. From your student files, open the **a02G_Students_Scholarships** database. Save the database in your **Access Chapter 2** folder as **Lastname_Firstname_ 2G_Students_Scholarships** and then enable the content. **Rename** both tables by adding **Lastname Firstname** to the beginning of the table name, and then widen the **Navigation Pane** to display fully the object names.

2 **Open** the two database tables to become familiar with the data. **Close** the tables, and then create a *one-to-many* relationship between the **2G Students** table and the **2G Scholarships Awarded** table based on the **Student ID** field, and then **Enforce Referential Integrity**; *one* student can have *many* scholarships. Create the **Relationship Report**, and create a paper or electronic printout as directed, saving it with the default name. **Close** all open objects.

3 Open the **2G Scholarships Awarded** table, and then **Sort** the appropriate fields in **Ascending** order so that the records are sorted by the **Major** field. Within each Major, the records should be sorted by **Scholarship Name**. Create a paper or electronic printout, being sure to print the results on one page. **Close** the table, and do *not* save changes to the table design. **Close** the **Navigation Pane**.

4 **Create** a query in **Query Design** view using the **2G Scholarships Awarded** table to answer the question, *In alphabetical order by Scholarship Name, what is the Amount and Major for scholarships greater than or equal to $500?* Display the fields in the order listed in the question. Ten records meet the criteria. **Save** the query as **Lastname Firstname 2G Scholarships $500 or More Query** and create a paper or electronic printout as directed. **Close Print Preview**, and leave the query open.

5 Using the **2G Scholarships $500 or More Query**, create a query. **Save** the **Object As Lastname Firstname 2G Scholarships 1st Qtr Query** and then redesign the query to answer the question *Which scholarships were awarded, in chronological order by Award Date, between 1/1/16 and 3/31/16, for what amount, and what was Student ID of the student?* Display the fields in the order listed in the question, display *only* the fields listed in the question, do not restrict the amount, and sort only by date. Eight records meet the criteria. Create a paper or electronic printout as directed. **Close** the query, saving changes.

6 **Create** a query in **Query Design** view using the **2G Scholarships Awarded** table to answer the question, *Which scholarships were awarded for either Nursing or CIS majors for amounts of more than $100, listed in descending*

order by amount? Display the fields in the order listed in the question. Four records meet the criteria. (Hint: If five records display, switch to **Design view** and combine the majors on one criteria line using OR.) **Save** the query as **Lastname Firstname 2G Nursing or CIS More Than $100 Query** and then create a paper or electronic printout as directed. **Close** the query.

7 **Create** a query in **Query Design** view. Use the **2G Students** table and a wildcard to answer the question, *In alphabetical order by City and in alphabetical order by Last Name, what are the Student ID, City, First Name, and Last Name of students from cities that begin with the letter A?* Display the fields in the order listed in the question. Four records meet the criteria. **Save** the query as **Lastname Firstname 2G Cities Query** Create a paper or electronic printout as directed. **Close** the query.

8 **Create** a query in **Query Design** view using the **2G Students** table and all of the table's fields to answer the question *For which students is the ZIP Code missing?* Three students are missing ZIP Codes. **Save** the query as **Lastname Firstname 2G Missing ZIP Query** and then with **Normal** margins, create a paper or electronic printout as directed. **Close** the query. Using the information that displays in the query results, an enrollment clerk can use a reference to look up the ZIP codes for the students and then enter the ZIP codes in the student records in the underlying table.

9 For each scholarship, the Board of Trustees of the college will donate an amount equal to 50 percent of each scholarship. **Create** a query in **Query Design** view. Use both tables and calculated fields to answer the question, *In alphabetical order by scholarship name, and including the first and last name of the scholarship recipient, what will the value of each scholarship be if the Board of Trustees makes a matching 50 percent donation?* (Hint: First compute the amount of the donation, naming the new field **Donation** and then calculate the new scholarship value, naming the new field **New Value**).

Run the query, switch back to **Design** view, and as necessary, change the properties of all the numeric fields to display in **Currency** format with **0** decimal places, and then **Run** the query. For the *Alexandria Historical Society Scholarship*, the *Donation* is *$150* and the *New Value* is *$450*. Apply **Best Fit** to the columns in the query results. **Save** the query as **Lastname Firstname 2G Trustee Donation Query** and then create a paper or electronic printout as directed, being sure to print the results on one page. **Close** the query.

(Project 2G Students and Scholarships continues on the next page)

Mastering Access | Project **2G** Students and Scholarships (continued)

10 **Create** a new query in **Query Design** view. Use the **2G Scholarships Awarded** table and the **Sum** aggregate function to answer the question *For each major, in descending order by amount, what are the total scholarship amounts?* Display the fields in the order listed in the question. Use the **Property Sheet** to display the sums in the **Currency** format with **0** decimal places. *History* majors received *$1,850* in scholarships. Apply **Best Fit** to the columns in the query results. **Save** the query as **Lastname Firstname 2G Total Scholarships by Major Query** and then create a paper or electronic printout as directed. **Close** the query.

11 **Create** a **Crosstab Query** using the **2G Scholarships Awarded** table. Use the **Student ID** field as row headings and the **Major** field as column headings to answer the

question *For each student or major, what is the total scholarship Amount awarded?* Name the query **Lastname Firstname 2G Student ID and Major Crosstab Query** In **Design** view, apply **0** decimal places to the appropriate fields. Apply **Best Fit** to the columns in the query results. **Save** the query, and then as directed, create a paper or electronic printout in **Landscape** orientation—the query results will print on two pages. **Close** the query.

12 **Open** the **Navigation Pane** and widen it to display all of the object names. In **Backstage** view, click **Close Database**, and then click **Exit**. As directed by your instructor, submit your database and the ten paper or electronic printouts—relationship report, sorted table, and eight queries—that are the results of this project.

 You have completed Project 2G ——————————————————————

GO! Fix It | Project **2H** Social Sciences Division

Project Files

For Project 2H, you will need the following file:

a02H_Social_Sciences

You will save your database as:

Lastname_Firstname_2H_Social_Sciences

In this project, you will correct query design errors in a database used by the Dean of Social Sciences. From the student files that accompany this textbook, open the file a02H_Social_Sciences, and then save the database in your Access Chapter 2 folder as **Lastname_Firstname_2H_Social Sciences**

To complete the project you must find and correct errors in relationships, query design, and column widths. In addition to errors that you find, you should know:

- A relationship should be created between the 2H Social Sciences Faculty table and the 2H Anthropology Dept Course Schedule table. A relationship report should be created and named **Lastname Firstname 2H Relationship Report** One faculty member can teach many courses.

- You should add your last name and first name to each query name; do *not* rename the tables.

- Several queries do not accurately reflect the result implied in the query name. Open each query and examine and correct the design of any queries that do not accurately reflect the query name.

- Be sure that all of the object names in the Navigation Pane display fully.

- Create a paper or electronic printout of the relationship report and the four queries as directed by your instructor.

End You have completed Project 2H ——————————————

Apply a combination of the **2A** and **2B** skills.

GO! Make It | Project 2I Faculty Awards

Project Files

For Project 2I, you will need the following file:

a02I_Faculty_Awards

You will save your database as:

Lastname_Firstname_2I_Faculty_Awards

Start Access, navigate to your student files, and then open the a02I_Faculty_Awards database file. Save the database in your Access Chapter 2 folder as **Lastname_Firstname_2I_Faculty Awards** Rename the two tables to include your name, create a relationship and relationship report. Then create two queries as shown in Figure 2.53. Create paper or electronic printouts as directed.

Project Results

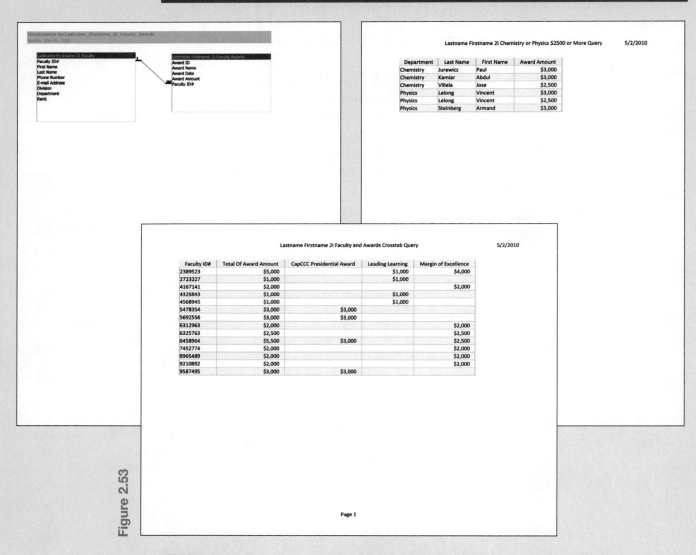

Figure 2.53

End **You have completed Project 2I**

Content-Based Assessments

GO! Solve It | Project **2J** Student Refunds

Project Files

For Project 2J, you will need the following file:

a02J_Student_Refunds

You will save your database as:

Lastname_Firstname_2J_Student_Refunds

Start Access, navigate to your student files and open the a02J_Student_Refunds database file. Save the database in your Access Chapter 2 folder as **Lastname_Firstname_2J_Student Refunds** Rename the tables by adding **Lastname Firstname** to the beginning of each table name. Create a relationship between the tables—one student can have many refunds—and then create a relationship report.

Create and save a query to answer the question, *What is the First Name and Last Name of the students who are eligible for a refund and who live in Alexandria or Falls Church sorted alphabetically by Last Name within City?* Create and save a query to answer the question, *What is the total Refund Amount for Full Time and Part Time Students?* Create and save a query to answer the question, *In ascending order by Refund Eligibility Date, what is the Last Name and First Name of students receiving a Refund of more than $50 between the dates of 8/1/16 and 12/31/16?* Apply Best Fit to all the query results, and then create paper or electronic printouts of the report and queries as directed.

		Performance Level	
	Exemplary: You consistently applied the relevant skills	**Proficient:** You sometimes, but not always, applied the relevant skills	**Developing:** You rarely or never applied the relevant skills
Create relationship and relationship report	Relationship and relationship report created correctly.	Relationship and relationship report created with one error.	Relationship and relationship report created with two or more errors, or missing entirely.
Create City query	Query created with correct name, fields, sorting, and criteria.	Query created with three elements correct and one incorrect.	Query created with two or more elements incorrect, or missing entirely.
Create Refund query	Query created with correct name, fields, and criteria.	Query created with two elements correct and one incorrect.	Query created with two or more elements incorrect, or missing entirely.
Create Refund Eligibility query	Query created with correct name, fields, sorting, and criteria.	Query created with three elements correct and one incorrect.	Query created with two or more two elements incorrect, or missing entirely.

Performance Element

Access | Chapter 2

End You have completed Project 2J

Apply a combination of the **2A** and **2B** skills.

GO! Solve It | Project 2K Leave

Project Files

For Project 2K, you will need the following file:

a02K_Leave

You will save your database as:

Lastname_Firstname_2K_Leave

Start Access, navigate to your student files, and then open the a02K_Leave database file. Save the database in your Access Chapter 2 folder as **Lastname_Firstname_2K_Leave** Rename the tables by adding **Lastname Firstname** to the beginning of each table name. Create a relationship between the tables—one employee can have many leave transactions—and a relationship report.

Create and save a query to answer the question, *Which employees, identified alphabetically by Last Name, have used Personal Leave?* Create and save a query to answer the question, *Which employees, identified alphabetically by Last Name, have no Phone Number?* Create and save a query to answer the question, *How many Leave Transactions were for Vacation leave grouped by the Employee# field?* (Hint: In the Total row of your query, use the Count function.) Create and save a crosstab query to answer the question, *What is the total number of leave transactions for each Employee # (row) by Leave Classification (column)?* Apply Best Fit to all of the query results, and then create paper or electronic printouts of the report and queries as directed by your instructor.

	Performance Level		
Performance Element	**Exemplary:** You consistently applied the relevant skills	**Proficient:** You sometimes, but not always, applied the relevant skills	**Developing:** You rarely or never applied the relevant skills
Create relationship and relationship report	Relationship and relationship report created correctly.	Relationship and relationship report created with one error.	Relationship and relationship report created with two or more errors, or missing entirely.
Create Personal Leave query	Query created with correct name, fields, sorting, and criteria.	Query created with three elements correct and one incorrect.	Query created with two or more elements incorrect, or missing entirely.
Create Phone Number query	Query created with correct name, fields, and criteria.	Query created with two elements correct and one incorrect.	Query created with two or more elements incorrect, or missing entirely.
Create Vacation Leave query	Query created with correct name, fields, grouping, and aggregate function.	Query created with three elements correct and one incorrect.	Query created with two or more elements incorrect, or missing entirely.
Create Crosstab query	Query created with correct name, row headings, column headings, and aggregate function.	Query created with three elements correct and one incorrect.	Query created with two or more elements incorrect, or missing entirely.

End **You have completed Project 2K**

Outcomes-Based Assessments

Rubric

The following outcomes-based assessments are *open-ended assessments*. That is, there is no specific correct result; your result will depend on your approach to the information provided. Make *Professional Quality* your goal. Use the following scoring rubric to guide you in *how* to approach the problem and then to evaluate *how well* your approach solves the problem.

The *criteria*—Software Mastery, Content, Format and Layout, and Process—represent the knowledge and skills you have gained that you can apply to solving the problem. The *levels of performance*—Professional Quality, Approaching Professional Quality, or Needs Quality Improvements—help you and your instructor evaluate your result.

	Your completed project is of Professional Quality if you:	Your completed project is Approaching Professional Quality if you:	Your completed project Needs Quality Improvements if you:
1-Software Mastery	Choose and apply the most appropriate skills, tools, and features and identify efficient methods to solve the problem.	Choose and apply some appropriate skills, tools, and features, but not in the most efficient manner.	Choose inappropriate skills, tools, or features, or are inefficient in solving the problem.
2-Content	Construct a solution that is clear and well organized, contains content that is accurate, appropriate to the audience and purpose, and is complete. Provide a solution that contains no errors in spelling, grammar, or style.	Construct a solution in which some components are unclear, poorly organized, inconsistent, or incomplete. Misjudge the needs of the audience. Have some errors in spelling, grammar, or style, but the errors do not detract from comprehension.	Construct a solution that is unclear, incomplete, or poorly organized; contains some inaccurate or inappropriate content; and contains many errors in spelling, grammar, or style. Do not solve the problem.
3-Format and Layout	Format and arrange all elements to communicate information and ideas, clarify function, illustrate relationships, and indicate relative importance.	Apply appropriate format and layout features to some elements, but not others. Overuse features, causing minor distraction.	Apply format and layout that does not communicate information or ideas clearly. Do not use format and layout features to clarify function, illustrate relationships, or indicate relative importance. Use available features excessively, causing distraction.
4-Process	Use an organized approach that integrates planning, development, self-assessment, revision, and reflection.	Demonstrate an organized approach in some areas, but not others; or, use an insufficient process of organization throughout.	Do not use an organized approach to solve the problem.

Outcomes-Based Assessments

GO! Think | Project **2L** Coaches

Project Files

For Project 2L, you will need the following file:

a02L_Coaches

You will save your database as:

Lastname_Firstname_2L_Coaches

    Use the skills you have practiced in this chapter to assist Randy Shavrain, the Athletic Director, in answering questions about the coaches in your database **Lastname_Firstname_2L_Coaches** Create and save the relationship report with the default name, and save the queries you create with your name in the query title. Create paper or electronic printouts of the report and queries as directed by your instructor.

    Mr. Shavrain needs to determine: 1) *In alphabetical order by Last Name, what is the Last Name and First Name of every coach involved with Dive activities? 2) In alphabetical order by Last Name, what is the Last Name and First Name of every coach involved with Basketball or Football activities? 3) In alphabetical order by Last Name, what is the Last Name and First Name of every coach with a Skill Specialty in Volleyball?*

 You have completed Project 2L ——————————

GO! Think | Project **2M** Club Donations

Project Files

For Project 2M, you will need the following file:

a02M_Club_Donations

You will save your database as:

Lastname_Firstname_2M_Club_Donations

    Use the skills you have practiced in this chapter to assist Dr. Kirsten McCarty, Vice President of Student Services, in answering questions about donations collected by students to support student services in your database **Lastname_Firstname_2M_Club_Donations** Create and save the relationship report with the default name, and save the queries you create with your name in the query title. Create paper or electronic printouts of the report and queries as directed.

    Dr. McCarty needs to determine: 1) *In ascending order by Last Name, what is the Last Name and First Name of donors who gave donations that are $25 or more? 2) What is the total of all donations grouped alphabetically by the Club Affiliation? 3) In alphabetical order by the student Last Name, and including the Donation ID#, what will the value of each donation be if the local sports store makes a matching 10 percent donation? 4) What are the total donations by Club Affiliation and Student ID?*

 You have completed Project 2M ——————————

Outcomes-Based Assessments

Apply a combination of the 2A and 2B skills.

You and GO! | Project **2N** Personal Inventory

Project Files

For Project 2N, you will need the following file:

New blank Access database

You will save your database as:

Lastname_Firstname_2N_Personal_Inventory

Create a personal database containing a household inventory of your possessions. Name the new database **Lastname_Firstname_2N_Personal_Inventory** Create one or more tables with at least 10 records. Include fields such as item, room location, value, date of purchase. Your table should have items stored in several locations. Sort the table in descending order by the value of the item. Create a paper or electronic printout. Clear all sorts, and then close the table. Create at least three queries to answer specific questions about your inventory. Name the queries to reflect the question asked. Create paper or electronic printouts of your queries.

End **You have completed Project 2N** ———————————

Apply a combination of the 2A and 2B skills.

GO! Collaborate | Project **2O** Bell Orchid Hotels Group Running Case

This project relates to the **Bell Orchid Hotels**. Your instructor may assign this group case project to your class. If your instructor assigns this project, he or she will provide you with information and instructions to work as part of a group. The group will apply the skills gained thus far to help the Bell Orchid Hotels achieve their business goals.

End **You have completed Project 2O** ———————————

Forms, Filters, and Reports

OUTCOMES

At the end of this chapter you will be able to:

PROJECT 3A
Create forms to enter and display data in a database.

OBJECTIVES

Mastering these objectives will enable you to:

1. Create and Use a Form to Add and Delete Records (p. 553)
2. Create a Form by Using the Form Wizard (p. 559)
3. Modify a Form in Layout View and in Design View (p. 561)
4. Filter Records (p. 569)

PROJECT 3B
Create reports to display database information.

5. Create a Report by Using the Report Tool (p. 575)
6. Create Reports by Using the Blank Report Tool and the Report Wizard (p. 578)
7. Modify the Design of a Report (p. 585)
8. Print a Report and Keep Data Together (p. 589)

Andresr/Shutterstock

In This Chapter

In this chapter, you will create forms to enter data and view data in database tables. Forms can display one record at a time, with fields placed in the same order to match a paper source document to make it easier to enter the new information or view existing information. Records in a form or table can be filtered to display only a portion of the total records based on matching specific values.

In this chapter, you will create reports that summarize data stored in a query or table in a professional-looking manner suitable for printing. After your report is created, you can modify the design so that the final report is laid out in a format that is useful to the person reading it.

The projects in this chapter relate to **Capital Cities Community College**, which is located in the Washington D. C. metropolitan area. The college provides high-quality education and professional training to residents in the cities surrounding the nation's capital. Its four campuses serve over 50,000 students and offer more than 140 certificate programs and degrees at the associate's level. CapCCC has a highly acclaimed Distance Education program and an extensive Workforce Development program. The college makes positive contributions to the community through cultural and athletic programs and partnerships with businesses and non-profit organizations.

Project 3A Students and Majors

myitlab
Project 3A Training

Project Activities

In Activities 3.01 through 3.11, you will assist Juanita Ramirez, Director of Enrollment Services, in using an Access database to track new students and their major fields of study. Your completed forms will look similar to Figure 3.1.

Project Files

For Project 3A, you will need the following file:

a03A_Students_Majors

You will save your document as:

Lastname_Firstname_3A_Students_Majors

Project Results

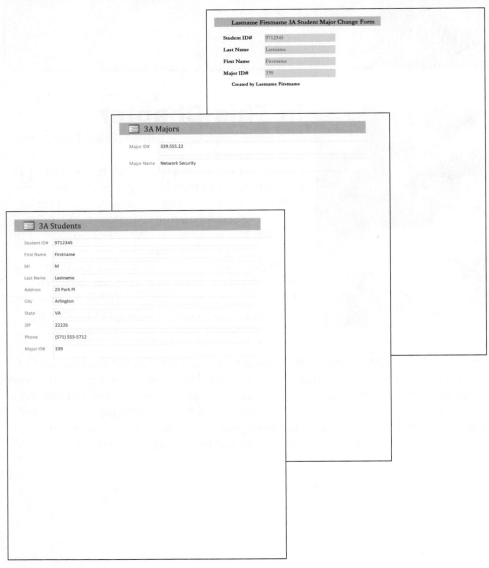

Figure 3.1

Project 3A Students and Majors

Objective 1 | Create and Use a Form to Add and Delete Records

A *form* is an Access object you can use to enter new records into a table, or to edit, delete, or display existing records in a table. A form is useful to control access to the data. For example, you can design a form for college Registration Assistants who can see and enter the courses scheduled and fees paid by an individual student. However, they cannot see or enter grades in the student's record.

Some Access forms display only one record at a time; other forms display multiple records at the same time. A form that displays only one record at a time is useful not only to the individual who performs the *data entry*—typing the actual records—but also to anyone who has the job of viewing information in a database. For example, when you visit the Records Office at your college to obtain a transcript, someone displays your record on a screen. For the viewer, it is much easier to look at one record at a time, using a form, than to look at all of the student records in the database.

Activity 3.01 | Creating a Form

There are several ways to create a form in Access, but the fastest and easiest way is to use the *Form tool*. With a single mouse click, all fields from the underlying data source are placed on the form. You can use the new form immediately, or you can modify it in Layout view or in Design view.

The Form tool incorporates all of the information—both the field names and the individual records—from an existing table or query and then instantly creates the form for you. Records that you edit or create using a form automatically update the underlying table or tables. In this activity, you will create a form and then use it to add new student records to the database.

1 **Start** Access. In **Backstage** view, click **Open**. Navigate to the student data files for this textbook, and then open the **a03A_Students_Majors** database.

2 Display **Backstage** view, click **Save Database As**, and then in the **Save As** dialog box, navigate to the location where you are saving your databases for this chapter. Create a new folder named **Access Chapter 3** and then click **Open**.

3 In the **File name** box, select the file name, and then type **Lastname_Firstname_3A_Students_Majors** and then press Enter. On the **Message Bar**, click the **Enable Content** button. Notice that there are two tables in this database.

4 On the Ribbon, click the **Database Tools tab**. In the **Relationships group**, click the **Relationships** button. Compare your screen with Figure 3.2.

> *One* major is associated with *many* students. Thus, a one-to-many relationship has been established between the 3A Majors table and the 3A Students table using the Major ID# field as the common field.

Figure 3.2

Join line with symbols
indicating one-to-many
relationship and
referential integrity

Major ID# is common field

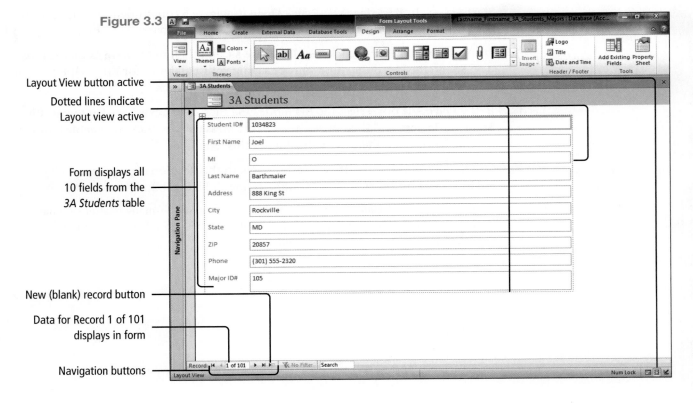

5 **Close** ☒ the **Relationships** window. From the **Navigation Pane**, open the **3A Students**
table. Notice the ten fields—*Student ID#*, *First Name*, *MI*, *Last Name*, *Address*, *City*,
State, *ZIP*, *Phone*, and *Major ID#*. **Close** ☒ the table.

6 In the **Navigation Pane**, be sure the **3A Students** table is selected. Click the **Create tab**,
and then in the **Forms group**, click the **Form** button. **Close** ☒ the **Navigation Pane**,
and then compare your screen with Figure 3.3.

Access creates the form based on the currently selected object—the 3A Students table—
and displays the form in *Layout view*. In Layout view, you can modify the form while it is
displaying data. For example, you can adjust the size of the text boxes to fit the data.

Access creates the form in a simple top-to-bottom layout, with all ten fields in the table
lined up in a single column. The data for the first record in the table displays.

Figure 3.3

Layout View button active

Dotted lines indicate
Layout view active

Form displays all
10 fields from the
3A Students table

New (blank) record button

Data for Record 1 of 101
displays in form

Navigation buttons

7 In the navigation area, click the **Next record** button 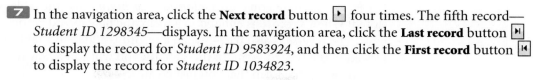 four times. The fifth record—*Student ID 1298345*—displays. In the navigation area, click the **Last record** button to display the record for *Student ID 9583924*, and then click the **First record** button to display the record for *Student ID 1034823*.

> You can use the navigation buttons to scroll among the records to display any single record.

8 **Save** the form as **Lastname Firstname 3A Student Form** and then **Close** the form object.

9 **Open** the **Navigation Pane**, and then, if necessary, increase the width of the **Navigation Pane** to display the entire form name. Notice that your new form displays under the table with which it is related—the **3A Students** table.

10 In the **Navigation Pane**, click to select the **3A Majors** table. Click the **Create tab**, and then in the **Forms group**, click the **Form** button. **Close** the **Navigation Pane**, and then compare your screen with Figure 3.4. Notice that *Major ID 105*, for *Diagnostic Medical Sonography*, has five students selecting this major.

> If a form's record has related records in another table, the related records display in the form because of the established one-to-many relationship between the underlying tables.

Figure 3.4

3A Majors form

Major ID# has related records (students declaring this major)

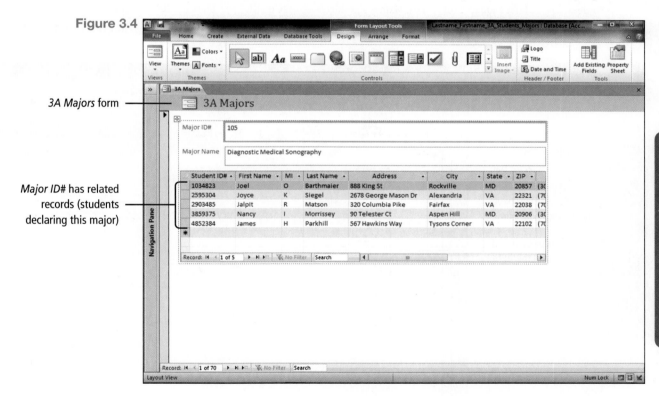

11 **Close** the **3A Majors** form. In the message box, click **Yes**. In the **Save As** dialog box, name the form **Lastname Firstname 3A Major Form** and then click **OK**.

Activity 3.02 | Adding Records to a Table by Using a Form

By using a single-record form to add and delete records, you can reduce the number of data entry errors, because the individual performing the data entry is looking at only one record at a time. Recall that your database is useful only if the information is accurate—just like your personal address book is useful only if it contains accurate addresses and phone numbers.

Forms are based on—also referred to as *bound* to—the table where the records are stored. When a record is entered in a form, the new record is added to the underlying table. The reverse is also true—when a record is added to a table, the new record can be viewed in the related form. In this activity, you will add a new record to the 3A Students table by using the form that you just created.

1 **Open** ▸ the **Navigation Pane**, open your **3A Student Form** object, and then **Close** ◂◂ the **Navigation Pane**. In the navigation area, click the **New (blank) record** button ▸✳ to display a new blank form.

> **Another Way**
>
> Press the Enter key, provided there are no special buttons on the form, such as a link to create a new form or a link to print the form.

2 In the **Student ID#** field, type **9712345** and then press Tab.

Use the Tab key to move from field to field in a form. This is known as *tab order*—the order in which the insertion point moves from one field to the next when you press the Tab key. As you start typing, the pencil icon displays in the *record selector bar* at the left—the bar used to select an entire record. This icon displays when a record is created or edited.

3 Using your own first name and last name, continue entering the data as shown in the following table, and then compare your screen with Figure 3.5.

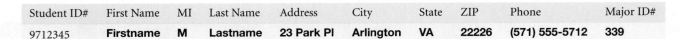

Student ID#	First Name	MI	Last Name	Address	City	State	ZIP	Phone	Major ID#
9712345	**Firstname**	**M**	**Lastname**	**23 Park Pl**	**Arlington**	**VA**	**22226**	**(571) 555-5712**	**339**

Figure 3.5

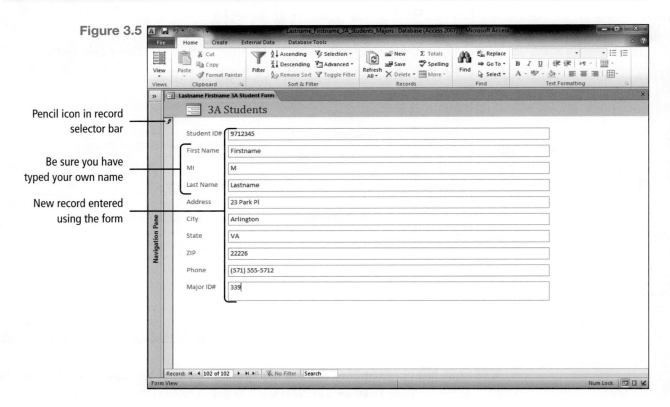

Pencil icon in record selector bar

Be sure you have typed your own name

New record entered using the form

4 With your insertion point in the last field, press Tab to save the record and display a new blank record. **Close** ✕ the **3A Student Form** object.

5 **Open** ▸ the **Navigation Pane**. Open the **3A Students** table. In the navigation area, click the **Last record** button ▸ to verify that the record you entered in the form is stored in the underlying table. **Close** ✕ the **3A Students** table.

6 From the **Navigation Pane**, open the **3A Major Form** object. At the bottom of your screen, in the navigation area for the form—*not* the navigation area for the subdatasheet—click the **New (blank) record** button. In the blank form, enter the information in the following table:

Major ID#	Major Name
339.555.22	**Network Security**

7 **Close** ☒ your **3A Major Form** object. From the **Navigation Pane**, open the **3A Majors** table, and then scroll down to verify that the new record for Major ID# *339.555.22 Network Security* displays in the table—records are sorted by the *Major ID#* field. **Close** ☒ the table.

Activity 3.03 | Deleting Records from a Table by Using a Form

You can delete records from a database table by using a form. In this activity, you will delete Major ID# 800.03 because the program has been discontinued.

> **Another Way**
>
> Press Ctrl + F.

1 From the **Navigation Pane**, open your **3A Major Form** object. On the **Home tab**, in the **Find group**, click the **Find** button to open the **Find and Replace** dialog box.

2 In the **Look In** box, notice that *Current field* displays. In the **Find What** box, type **800.03** and then click **Find Next**. Compare your screen with Figure 3.6, and confirm that the record for **Major ID# 800.03** displays.

Because you clicked in the Major ID# field before opening the dialog box, Access searches for the data in this field.

Figure 3.6

Record for *Major ID#* 800.03 displays

Find and Replace dialog box

Find What box

Look In box indicates that Access will search the Current field—*Major ID#*

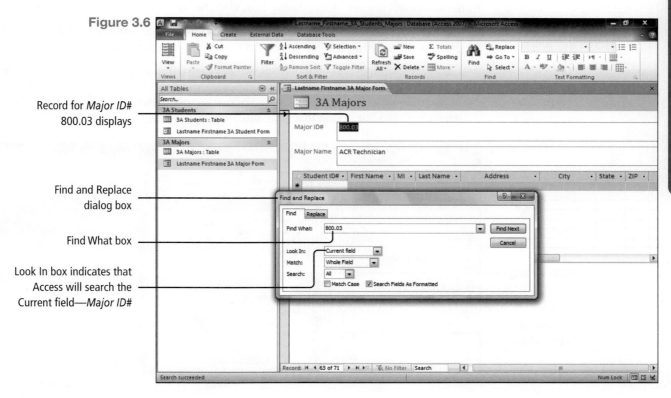

3 **Close** ☒ the **Find and Replace** dialog box. On the **Home tab**, in the **Records group**, click the **Delete button arrow**, and then click **Delete Record** to delete the record for Major ID# 800.03.

> Access removes the record from the screen and displays a message alerting you that you are about to delete *1 record(s)*. If you click Yes to delete the record, you cannot use the Undo button to reverse the action. If you delete a record by mistake, you must re-create the record by reentering the data. Because no students are associated with this major, you can delete it from the table.

4 In the message box, click **Yes** to delete the record. In the navigation area for the form, notice that the number of records in the table is *70*. **Close** ☒ the form.

5 From the **Navigation Pane**, open the **3A Majors** table. Examine the table to verify that the *Major ID# 800.03* record no longer exists, and then **Close** ☒ the table.

> Adding and deleting records in a form updates the records stored in the underlying table.

Activity 3.04 | Printing a Form

Clicking the Print button while a form is displayed causes *all* of the records to print in the form layout. In this activity, you will print only *one* record.

1 From the **Navigation Pane**, open your **3A Student Form** object. Press ⌃Ctrl + F to display the **Find and Replace** dialog box. In the **Find What** box, type **9712345** and then click **Find Next** to display the record with your name. **Close** ☒ the **Find and Replace** dialog box.

2 Display **Backstage** view. Click the **Print tab**, and then in the **Print group**, click **Print**. In the **Print** dialog box, under **Print Range**, click the **Selected Record(s)** option button. In the lower left corner of the dialog box, click **Setup**.

3 In the **Page Setup** dialog box, click the **Columns tab**. Under **Column Size**, in the **Width** box, delete the existing text, and type **7.5** Compare your screen with Figure 3.7.

> Change the width of the column in this manner so that the form prints on one page. Forms are not typically printed, so the width of the column in a form may be greater than the width of the paper on which you are printing. The maximum column width that you can enter is dependent upon the printer that is installed on your system.

Figure 3.7

Column Width set to 7.5

Selected Record(s) option button selected

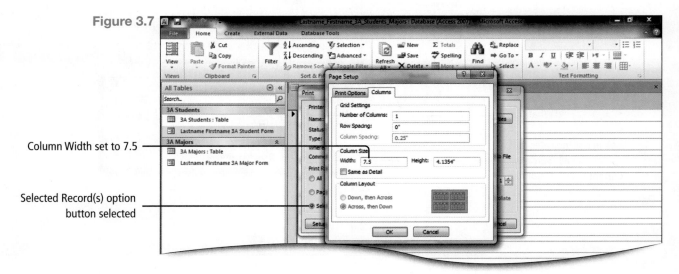

4 Click **OK** to close the **Page Setup** dialog box, and then, to create an electronic printout of this single form, see the instructions in the Note below. To print on paper, click **OK** to close the **Print** dialog box and to print only your record in the form layout.

> **Note | To Print a Single Form in PDF**
>
> To create a PDF electronic printout of a single record in a form, change the column width to 7.5 as described in step 3 above, and then in the Print dialog box, click Cancel. On the left edge of the form, click anywhere in the Record Selector bar so that it is black—selected. On the Ribbon, click the External Data tab. In the Export group, click the PDF or XPS button. In the Publish as PDF or XPS dialog box, navigate to the location where you are storing your files for this project. In the File name box, notice that your form name is automatically entered for you. Then, in the lower left corner of the dialog box, if necessary, select the Open file after publishing check box. In the lower right corner of the dialog box, click the Options button. In the Options dialog box, under Range, click the Selected records option button, click OK, and then click Publish. Close the Adobe Reader or Acrobat window, and then hold this file until you complete the project and submit it as directed by your instructor.

5 **Close** ☒ the **3A Student Form** object. Using the techniques you just practiced, open your **3A Major Form** object, display the record for the **Major ID#** of **339.555.22**, and then print only that record, or create an electronic printout of only that record. Then **Close** ☒ the **3A Major Form** object.

If there are no related records in the subdatasheet, the empty subdatasheet does not display in the printed form.

Objective 2 | Create a Form by Using the Form Wizard

The *Form Wizard* creates a form quickly like the Form tool, but gives you more flexibility in the design, layout, and number of fields. The design of the form should be planned for the individuals who use the form—either for entering new records or viewing records. For example, when your college counselor displays information, it may be easier for the counselor to view the information if the fields are arranged in a layout that differs from the manner in which the Form Tool arranges them.

Activity 3.05 | Creating a Form by Using the Form Wizard

At Capital Cities Community College, when a student changes his or her major, the student fills out a paper form. To make it easier to change the information in the database, you will create an Access form that matches the layout of the paper form. This will make it easier for the individual who changes the data in the database.

1 In the **Navigation Pane**, click to select the **3A Students** table. On the **Create tab**, in the **Forms group**, click the **Form Wizard** button.

The Form Wizard walks you step by step through the process of creating a form by asking questions. In the first Form Wizard dialog box, you select the fields to include on the form. The fields can come from more than one table or query.

2 Under **Tables/Queries**, in the text box, click the **arrow** to display a list of available tables and queries from which you can create the form.

There are two tables in the database from which you can create a new form. Because you selected the 3A Students table on the Navigation Pane, the 3A Students table is the selected table.

3 Click **Table: 3A Students**, and then compare your screen with Figure 3.8.

The field names from the 3A Students table display in the Available Fields list.

Figure 3.8

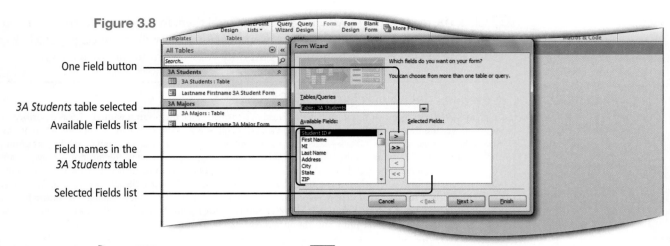

One Field button

3A Students table selected

Available Fields list

Field names in the
3A Students table

Selected Fields list

Another Way
Double-click the field name.

→ **4** Use the **One Field** button **>** to move the following fields to the **Selected Fields** list: **First Name**, **Last Name**, and **Major ID#**. Compare your screen with Figure 3.9.

Three fields from the 3A Students table display in the Selected Fields list.

Figure 3.9

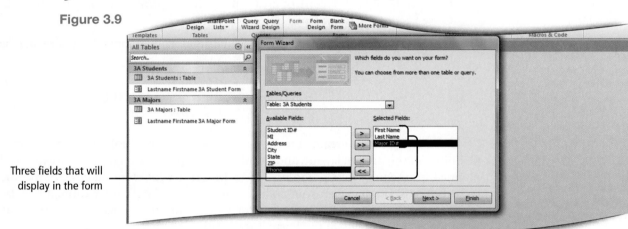

Three fields that will display in the form

5 Click **Next**. Be sure **Columnar** is selected as the layout, and then click **Next**. Under **What title do you want for your form?**, select the existing text, and then type **Lastname Firstname 3A Student Major Change Form** and then click **Finish** to close the wizard and create the form. If necessary, increase the width of the Navigation Pane to display the entire form name, and then compare your screen with Figure 3.10.

The form is saved and added to the Navigation Pane under its data source. The first record in the underlying table displays in *Form view*, which is used to view, add, delete, and modify records stored in a table.

Figure 3.10

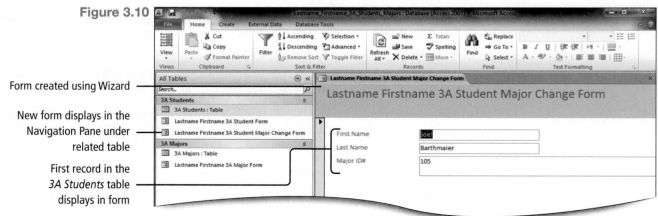

Form created using Wizard

New form displays in the Navigation Pane under related table

First record in the 3A Students table displays in form

Objective 3 | Modify a Form in Layout View and in Design View

After you create a form, you can make changes to it. For example, you can group the fields, resize the fields, and change the style of the form.

Activity 3.06 | Grouping Controls and Applying a Theme to a Form in Layout View

Layout view enables you to make changes to the design of a form while displaying the data from the underlying table. Most changes to a form can be made in Layout view.

Another Way

On the Home tab, in the Views group, click the View button arrow, and then click Layout View; or, right-click the object tab, and then click Layout View.

1 **Close** ⟪ the **Navigation Pane** and be sure your **3A Student Major Change Form** object displays. In the lower right corner of your screen, on the status bar, click the **Layout View** button ⊞, and then compare your screen with Figure 3.11.

The field names and data for the first record display in *controls*—objects on a form that display data, perform actions, and let you view and work with information.

The data in the first record displays in *text box controls*. The most commonly used control is the text box control, which typically displays data from the underlying table. A text box control is a *bound control*—its source data comes from a table or query.

The field names—*First Name*, *Last Name*, and *Major ID#*—display in *label controls*. Access places a label control to the left of a text box control. A label control contains descriptive information that displays on the form, usually the field name. A control that does not have a source of data, for example a label that displays the title of the form, is an *unbound control*.

Figure 3.11

Label control, an unbound control

Label controls—field names

Text box controls—bound to data in table

Form displays in Layout view

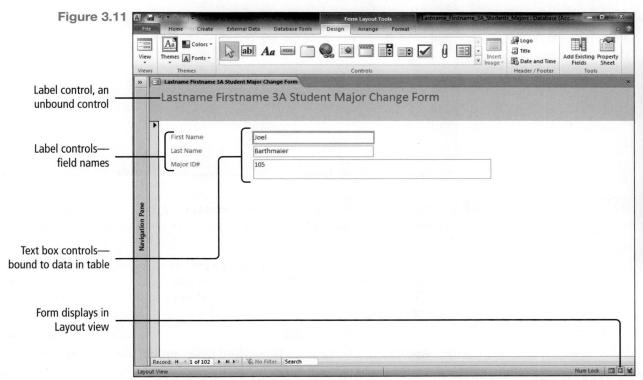

2 Click the **First Name label control**. Hold down Shift, and then click the **Last Name label control**, the **Major ID# label control**, and the **three text box controls** to select all label and text box controls.

Alert! | Do Your Controls Change Order When Selecting?

If, when selecting controls, the controls change order, click Undo and select the controls again. Be careful not to drag the mouse when you are selecting multiple controls.

---

3 With all six controls selected—surrounded by a colored border—on the Ribbon, click the **Arrange tab**. In the **Table group**, click the **Stacked** button. Click the **First Name Label control** to deselect all of the controls and to surround the **First Name label control** with a colored border. Compare your screen with Figure 3.12.

This action groups the controls together in the *Stacked layout* format—a layout similar to a paper form, with labels to the left of each field. Grouping the controls enables you to easily move and edit controls as you redesign your form.

A dotted line forms a border around the field names and data. Above and to the left of the first field name—*First Name*—the *layout selector* displays, with which you can select and move the entire group of controls.

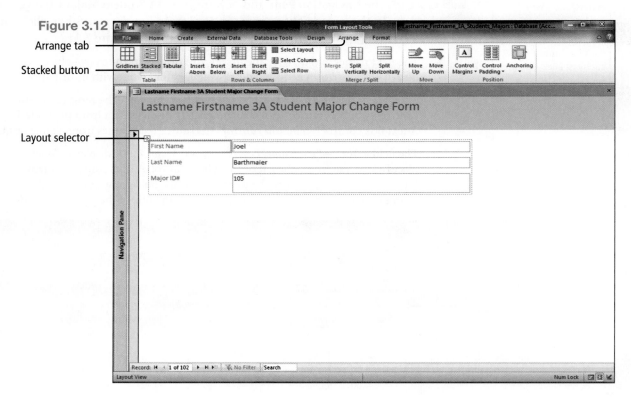

Figure 3.12

Arrange tab

Stacked button

Layout selector

4 Click the **Design tab**, and then in the **Themes group**, click the **Themes** button. In the **Themes** gallery, locate and right-click the **Couture** theme. Click **Apply Theme to This Object Only**.

The *Themes* button enables you to apply a predefined format to all of the database objects or to the current object. Right-click a theme so that you can apply the theme to a single object within the database. Apply a theme before performing other formatting to the text in your form.

> **Note** | Applying a Theme to an Object and Determining the Applied Theme
>
> If you click a theme rather than right-clicking it and selecting an option, the theme is applied to all objects in the database. To determine the applied theme, in the Themes group, point to the Themes button. The ScreenTip displays the current theme.

5 Click anywhere in the title *3A Student Major Change Form* to select it. Click the **Format tab**. In the **Font group**, click the **Font Size arrow**, and then click **14**. Click the **Bold** button **B** to add bold emphasis to the text. Click the **Font Color button arrow**, and then under **Theme Colors**, in the last column, click the last color—**Brown, Accent 6, Darker 50%**.

Activity 3.07 | Modifying a Form in Design View

Design view presents a detailed view of the structure of your form. Because the form is not actually running when displayed in Design view, you cannot view the underlying data. However, some tasks, such as resizing sections, must be completed in Design view.

Another Way

On the Home tab, in the Views group, click the View button arrow, and then click Design View; or, right-click the object tab, and then click Design View.

1 On the status bar, click the **Design View** button ![icon]. Compare your screen with Figure 3.13.

This Design view of a form displays three sections—*Form Header*, *Detail*, and *Form Footer*—each designated by a *section bar* at the top of each section. The form header contains information, such as a form's title, that displays at the top of the screen in Form view and is printed at the top of the first page when records are printed as forms. The detail section displays the records from the underlying table, and the form footer displays at the bottom of the screen in Form view and is printed after the last detail section on the last page of a printout.

Figure 3.13

Form Header section bar
Detail section bar
Form Footer section bar

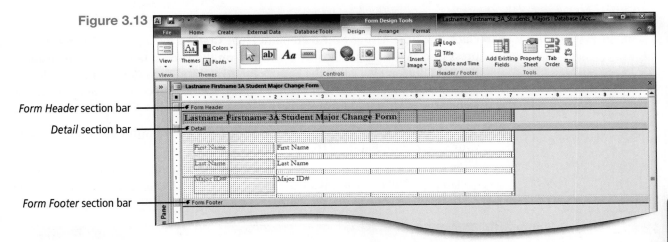

2 At the bottom of the form, point to the *lower* edge of the **Form Footer section bar** to display the ![pointer] pointer, and then drag downward approximately **0.5 inch** to increase the height of the Form Footer section. Compare your screen with Figure 3.14.

Figure 3.14

Form Footer section height increased 0.5 inch

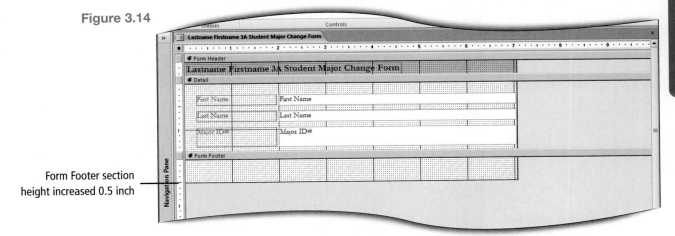

3 On the **Design tab**, in the **Controls group**, click the **Label** button ![Aa]. Move the pointer into the **Form Footer** section, and then position the plus sign of the ![A] pointer in the **Form Footer** section at approximately **0.25 inch on the horizontal ruler** and even with the lower edge of the **Form Footer section bar** as shown in Figure 3.15.

Figure 3.15

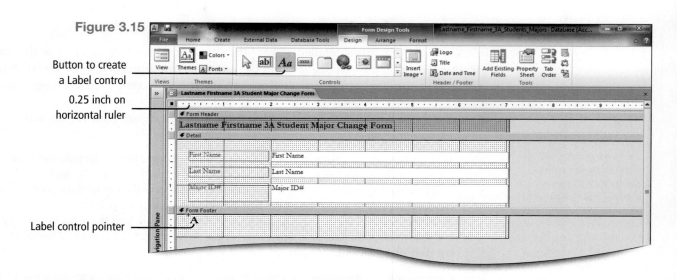

Button to create
a Label control

0.25 inch on
horizontal ruler

Label control pointer

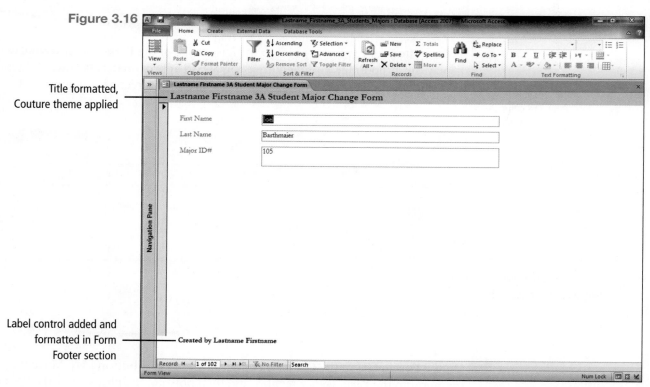

Another Way

On the Home tab, in
the Views group, click
the View button arrow,
and then click Form
View; or, right-click the
object tab, and then
click Form View.

4 Click one time. Using your own name, type **Created by Lastname Firstname** and then press Enter. With the label control selected, on the **Format tab**, in the **Font group**, click the **Bold** button **B**. Click the **Font Color arrow**, and then under **Theme Colors**, in the fourth column, click the first color—**Brown, Text 2**. If necessary, double-click the right edge of the label control to resize the control so that all of the data displays.

5 On the right side of the status bar, click the **Form View** button, and then compare your screen with Figure 3.16.

> Form Footer text displays on the screen at the bottom of the form and prints only on the last page if all of the forms are printed as a group. In the *Form view*, you can add, delete, or modify records stored in a table.

Figure 3.16

Title formatted,
Couture theme applied

Label control added and
formatted in Form
Footer section

6 Save the changes you have made to the design of your form. Leave your **3A Student Major Change Form** open for the next activity.

Activity 3.08 | Adding, Resizing, and Moving Controls in Layout View

In Layout view, you can change the form's *control layout*—the grouped arrangement of controls.

1 At the right side of the status bar, click the **Layout View** button 🔲.

Recall that the layout selector, which displays to the left and above the First Name label control, enables you to select and move the entire group of controls in Layout view.

2 On the **Design tab**, in the **Tools group**, click the **Add Existing Fields** button to display the **Field List** pane, which lists the fields in the underlying table—3A Students. Compare your screen with Figure 3.17.

Figure 3.17

Add Existing Fields button —

Field List pane —

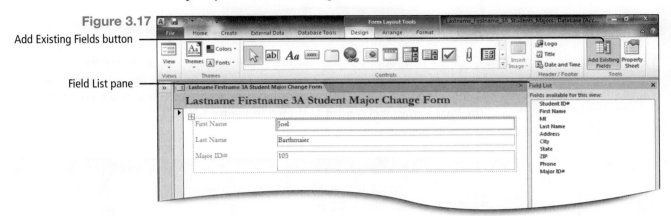

3 In the **Field List** pane, click **Student ID#**, and then drag to the left until the 🔲 pointer displays above the **First Name label control** and a colored line displays above the control. Release the mouse button, and then compare your screen with Figure 3.18. If you are not satisfied with the result, click Undo and begin again.

This action adds the Student ID# label and text box controls to the form above the First Name controls.

Figure 3.18

Student ID# label control —

Text box control for *Student ID#* field —

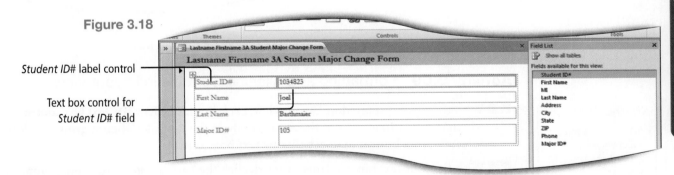

4 **Close** 🗙 the **Field List** pane. Click the **Student ID# text box control**, which currently displays *1034823*, to surround it with a border and to remove the border from the label control.

5 Point to the right edge of the **text box control** until the ↔ pointer displays, and then drag to the left until all of the right edges of the text box controls align under the *C* in *Controls* in the Ribbon's **Controls group** above. Compare your screen with Figure 3.19.

All four text box controls are resized simultaneously. By decreasing the width of the text box controls, you have more space in which to rearrange the form controls. In Layout view, because you can see your data, you can determine visually that the space you have allotted is adequate to display all of the data in every field.

Figure 3.19

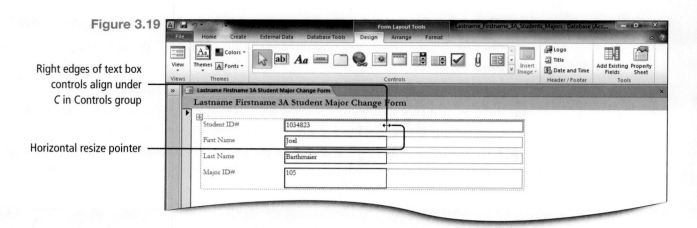

Right edges of text box controls align under *C* in Controls group

Horizontal resize pointer

Another Way

Drag the selected label controls to the desired location and then release the mouse button.

6 Click the **Last Name text box control**, which currently displays *Barthmaier*. Click the **Arrange tab**, and then in the **Rows & Columns group**, click the **Select Row** button. In the **Move group**, click the **Move Up** button one time to move the controls above the **First Name label control** as shown in Figure 3.20.

Figure 3.20

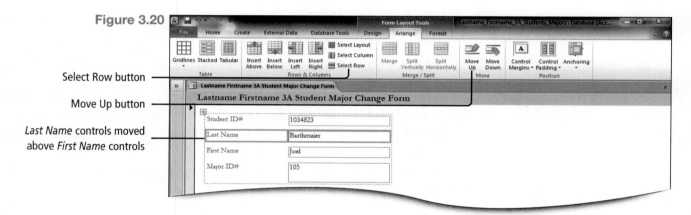

Select Row button

Move Up button

Last Name controls moved above *First Name* controls

7 **Save** 🔲 the changes you have made to the design of your form.

Activity 3.09 | Formatting and Aligning Controls in Layout View

Another Way

Click the first control, hold down Shift, and then click the last control.

1 With the form displayed in Layout view, click in the **Student ID# text box control**, which displays *1034823*. On the **Arrange tab**, in the **Rows & Columns group**, click the **Select Column** button to select all four text box controls.

2 With the four text box controls selected, click the **Format tab**. In the **Font group**, click the **Background Color button arrow** 🎨▾. Under **Theme Colors**, in the fifth column, click the second color—**Brown, Accent 1, Lighter 80%**.

The text box controls display a background color of light brown. This formatting does not affect the label controls on the left.

3 Click the **Student ID# label control**. On the **Arrange tab**, in the **Rows & Columns group**, click the **Select Column** button. Click the **Format tab**, change the **Font Color**—*not* the Background Color—to **Brown, Text 2**—in the fourth column, the first color—and then apply **Bold** **B**. Click in a blank area of the screen to cancel the selection, and then compare your screen with Figure 3.21.

Figure 3.21

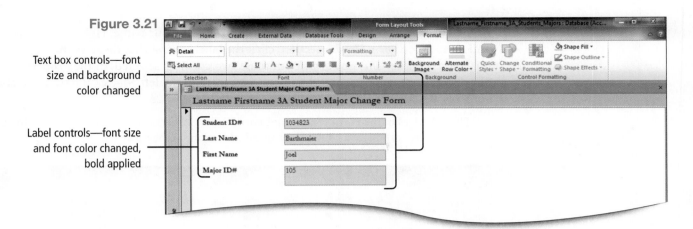

Text box controls—font size and background color changed

Label controls—font size and font color changed, bold applied

---

Another Way

Click any control, and then on the Arrange tab, in the Rows & Columns group, click the Select Layout button.

4 Click any **label control** to display the layout selector, and then click the **layout selector** ⊞ to select all of the controls.

Clicking the layout selector enables you to edit all of the controls at one time.

5 On the **Format tab**, in the **Font group**, click the **Font Size button arrow**, and then click **12** to change the font size of the text in all of the controls.

6 With all of the controls still selected, on the Ribbon, click the **Design tab**. In the **Tools group**, click the **Property Sheet** button. In the **Property Sheet** pane, if necessary, click the **Format tab**, and then compare your screen with Figure 3.22.

The *Property Sheet* for the selected controls displays. Each control has an associated Property Sheet where precise changes to the properties—characteristics—of selected controls can be made. At the top of the Property Sheet, to the right of *Selection type:*, *Multiple selection* displays because you have more than one control selected.

Figure 3.22

Property Sheet button

Selection type

Property Sheet for selected controls

Selected controls

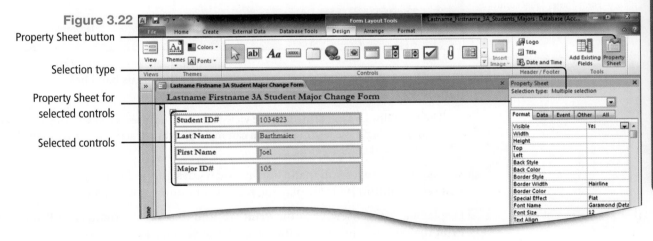

7 In the **Property Sheet**, click the word **Height**, type **0.25** and then press Enter.

The height of each control changes to 0.25 inch.

8 Click the **Student ID# label control** to select only that label control. Click the **Arrange tab**, and then in the **Rows & Columns group**, click the **Select Column** button. In the **Property Sheet**, click **Width** to select its value to the right. Type **1.25** and then press Enter.

The width of each selected label control changes to 1.25 inches.

9 In the **Form Footer section**, click the **label control** with your name. Hold down ⇧Shift, and then in the **Form Header section**, click the **label control** that displays the title *3A Student Major Change Form*. With these two controls selected, in the **Property Sheet**, click **Left**. Type **0.5** and then press Enter to align the left edge of the selected label controls at 0.5 inch. Compare your screen with Figure 3.23.

> The left edges of the Form Header and Form Footer label controls align at 0.5 inch. In this manner, you can place a control in a specific location on the form.

Figure 3.23

Form Header label control left aligned at 0.5 inch

Height of all controls changed to 0.25 inch; width of label controls changed to 1.25 inches

Left property setting

Form Footer label control left aligned at 0.5 inch

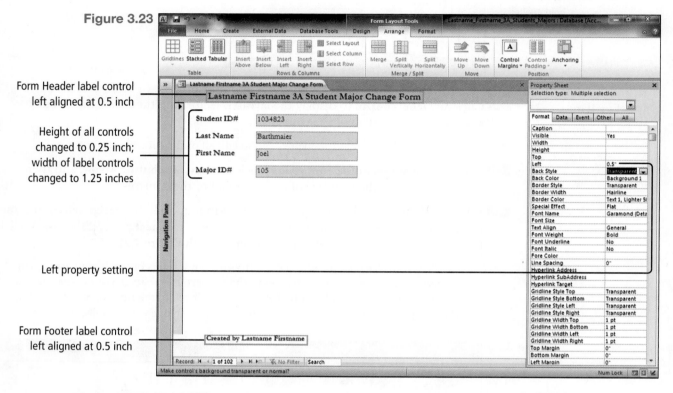

10 **Close** ✕ the **Property Sheet**. On the right side of the status bar, click the **Form View** button 🖩.

> The form displays in Form view, the view an individual uses when entering data in the form. By using these techniques, you can make a form attractive and easy to use for those who view and enter records.

11 **Save** 🖫 the changes you made to your form's design. In the navigation area, click the **Last record** button ▶| to display the record containing your name.

12 Display **Backstage** view, click the **Print tab**, and then on the right, click **Print**. In the **Print** dialog box, under **Print Range**, click the **Selected Record(s)** option button. Create a paper or electronic printout as directed. To create an electronic printout, follow the directions given at the end of Activity 1.04.

> Because you decreased the width of the text box controls, you do *not* have to adjust the Column Size width in the Page Setup dialog box as you did with the form you created using the Form tool.

13 With the **3A Student Major Change Form** object displayed in **Form** view, in the navigation area, click the **First record** button |◀ to prepare for the next activity.

Objective 4 | Filter Records

Filtering records in a form is the process of displaying only a portion of the total records—a *subset*—based on matching specific values. Filters are commonly used to provide a quick answer, and the result is not generally saved for future use. For example, by filtering records in a form, you can quickly display a subset of records for students majoring in Information Systems Technology, which is identified by the Major ID# of 339.

One reason that you create a form is to provide a user interface for the database. For example, the Registration Assistants at your college may not, for security reasons, have access to the entire student database. Rather, by using a form, they can access and edit only some information—the information necessary for their jobs. Filtering records within a form provides individuals who do not have access to the entire database a way to ask questions of the database without constructing a query, and also to save a filter that is used frequently.

Activity 3.10 | Filtering Data by Selection of One Field

The counselor would like to see records for students who are majoring in Information Systems Technology. In a form, you can use the *Filter By Selection* command—which retrieves only the records that contain the value in the selected field and which temporarily removes the records that do *not* contain the value in the selected field.

1 With your **3A Student Major Change Form** object displayed in **Form** view, in the first record, click in the shaded **Major ID# text box control**. On the **Home tab**, in the **Find group**, click the **Find** button. In the **Find and Replace** dialog box, in the **Find What** box, type **339** If necessary, in the Match box, click the arrow, and then click Whole Field. Click **Find Next**, and then compare your screen with Figure 3.24.

This action finds and displays a record with 339—the Major ID# for Information Systems Technology—so that you can filter the records using the selected value.

Figure 3.24

First record with
Major ID# of 339

339 is the *Major ID#*
for Information Systems
Technology

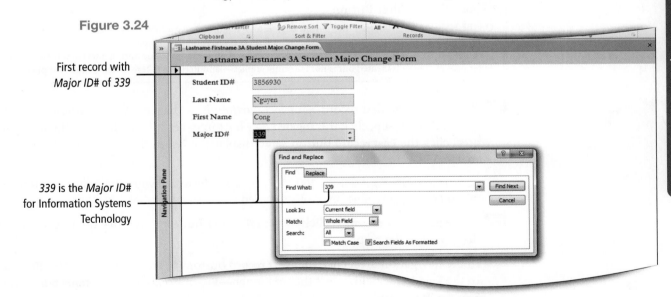

2 **Close** the **Find and Replace** dialog box. In the **Sort & Filter group**, click the **Selection** button, and then click **Equals "339"**. Compare your screen with Figure 3.25.

Seven records match the contents of the selected Student Major ID# field—*339*—the ID# for the Information Systems Technology major. In the navigation area, a *Filtered* button with a funnel icon displays next to the number of records. *Filtered* also displays on the right side of the status bar to indicate that a filter is applied. On the Home tab, in the Sort & Filter group, the Toggle Filter button is active.

Figure 3.25

Toggle Filter button active

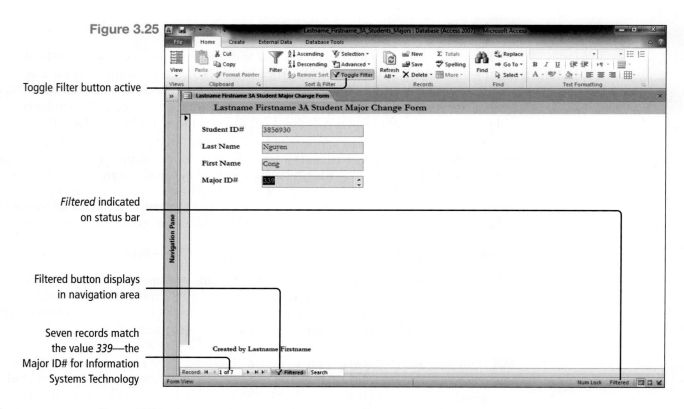

Filtered indicated
on status bar

Filtered button displays
in navigation area

Seven records match
the value *339*—the
Major ID# for Information
Systems Technology

Another Way
Click the Filtered button
in the navigation area.

3 On the **Home tab**, in the **Sort & Filter group**, click the **Toggle Filter** button to remove the filter and display all 102 records. Notice the **Unfiltered** button in the navigation area, which indicates that no filter is active.

> **Note** | Toggle Filter Button
>
> On the Home tab, the Toggle Filter button is used to apply or remove a filter. If no filter has been created, the button is not active—it is not highlighted. After a filter is created, this button becomes active. Because it is a toggle button used to apply or remove filters, the ScreenTip that displays for this button alternates between Apply Filter—when a filter is created but is not currently applied—and Remove Filter—when a filter is applied.

4 Be sure that the first record—for *Joel Barthmaier*—displays. On the **Home tab**, in the **Sort & Filter group**, click the **Toggle Filter** button to reapply the filter. In the navigation area, click the **Last record** button [▶|] to display the last of the seven records that match *339*.

The record for *Student ID# 9712345* displays—the record with your name. In this manner, you can toggle a filter on or off as needed.

5 In the **Sort & Filter group**, click the **Toggle Filter** button to remove the filter and display all of the records.

6 In the navigation area, click the **Next record** button [▶] two times to display **Record 3**. In the **Last Name** field, select the first letter—**E**—of *Eckert*. On the **Home tab**, in the **Sort & Filter group**, click the **Selection** button. Click **Begins with "E"**.

A new filter is applied that displays three records in which the *Last Name* begins with the letter *E*.

7 In the navigation area, click the **Filtered** button to remove the filter and display all of the records.

8 **Save** [💾] the changes to your form, and then **Close** [✕] the form.

The filter is saved with the form even though the filter is not currently applied.

Activity 3.11 | Using Filter By Form and Advanced Filter/Sort

Use the **Filter By Form** command to filter the records in a form based on one or more fields, or based on more than one value in the same field. The Filter By Form command offers greater flexibility than the Filter by Selection command and can be used to answer a question that requires matching multiple values.

In this activity, you will use filtering techniques to help Juanita Ramirez determine how many students live in Alexandria or Arlington. Then you will determine how many students live in Arlington who are majoring in Information Systems Technology.

1 **Open** » the **Navigation Pane**, open your **3A Student Form** object, and then **Close** « the **Navigation Pane**.

2 On the **Home tab**, in the **Sort & Filter group**, click the **Advanced** button, and then click **Filter By Form**. Compare your screen with Figure 3.26.

The Filter by Form window displays all of the field names, but without any data. In the empty text box for each field, you can type a value or choose from a list of available values. The *Look for* and *Or* tabs display at the bottom.

Figure 3.26

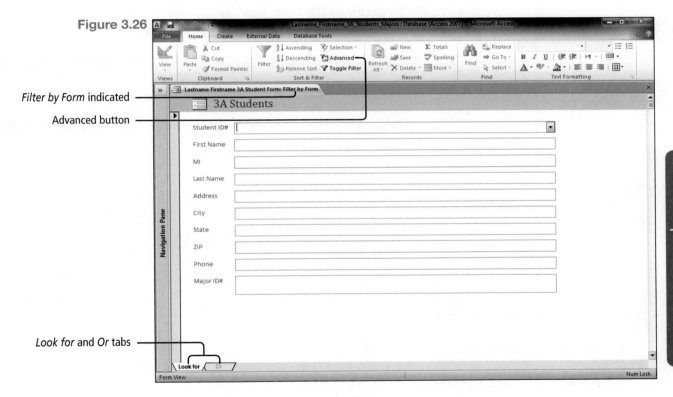

Filter by Form indicated

Advanced button

Look for and *Or* tabs

3 Click in the **City text box control**. At the right edge of the text box control, click the **arrow** that displays. In the list, click **Alexandria**. In the **Sort & Filter group**, click the **Toggle Filter** button.

As displayed in the navigation area, eight student records include *Alexandria* in the City field.

Another Way

Click in the text box control and type the criteria separated by the word *or*. For example, in the City text box control, type *Alexandria or Arlington*.

4 In the **Sort & Filter group**, click the **Advanced** button, and then click **Filter By Form**. At the bottom left of the window, click the **Or tab**. Click the **City text box control arrow**, and then click **Arlington**. In the **Sort & Filter group**, click the **Toggle Filter** button.

> As displayed in the navigation area, eighteen student records include either Alexandria *or* Arlington in the City field. You have created an ***OR condition***; that is, records display where, in this instance, either of two values—Alexandria *or* Arlington—is present in the selected field.

5 In the **Sort & Filter group**, click the **Advanced** button, and then click **Clear All Filters** to display all of the records.

6 Click the **Advanced** button again, and then from the list, click **Advanced Filter/Sort**. Expand the field list.

> The Advanced Filter design grid displays. The design grid is similar to the query design grid.

7 From the **3A Students** field list, add the **City** field and then the **Major ID#** field to the design grid. In the **Criteria** row for the **City** field, type **Arlington** and then click in the **Criteria** row for the **Major ID#** field. Type **339** and then press Enter. Compare your screen with Figure 3.27.

Figure 3.27

Tab indicates *3A Student* Form is being filtered

Field list expanded

Design grid

Criteria for *City* field

Criteria for *Major ID#* field

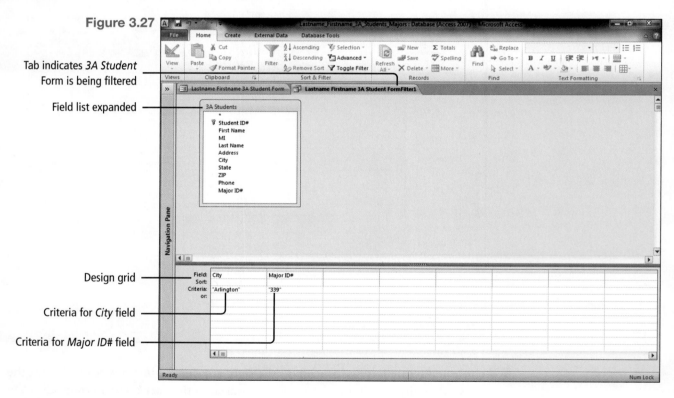

8 In the **Sort & Filter group**, click the **Toggle Filter** button.

> Two records match the criteria. You have created an ***AND condition***; that is, only records display where both values—Arlington *and* 339—are present in the selected fields. There are two Information Systems Technology majors who live in Arlington.

9 In the **Sort & Filter group**, click the **Toggle Filter** button to display all of the records.

In the navigation area, *Unfiltered* displays, which indicates that a filter was created for this form. Unless you Clear All Filters, the filter is saved with the form when the form is closed. When you reopen the form, you can click on the Toggle Filter button or the Unfiltered button to reapply the filter.

10 **Close** ☒ all open objects, and then **Open** ⧸ the **Navigation Pane**. Display **Backstage** view, click **Close Database**, and then click **Exit**. As directed by your instructor, submit your database and the three paper or electronic printouts that are the results of this project.

More Knowledge | Using the Filter Button

You can filter a form in a manner similar to the way you filter records in a table. Click in the text box control of the field you wish to use for the filter. On the Home tab, in the Sort & Filter group, click the Filter button to display a shortcut menu. Select the (Select All) check box to clear the option, and then select the data by which you want to filter by clicking the check boxes preceding the data. To remove the filter, redisplay the menu, and then select the (Select All) check box.

End **You have completed Project 3A** ————————————————

Project 3B Job Openings

my**it**lab
Project 3B Training

Project Activities

In Activities 3.12 through 3.19, you will assist Damon Bass, Career Center Director for Capital Cities Community College, in using an Access database to track the employers and job openings advertised for the annual Career Fair. Your completed reports will look similar to Figure 3.28.

Project Files

For Project 3B, you will need the following file:

a03B_Job_Openings

You will save your database as:

Lastname_Firstname_3B_Job_Openings

Project Results

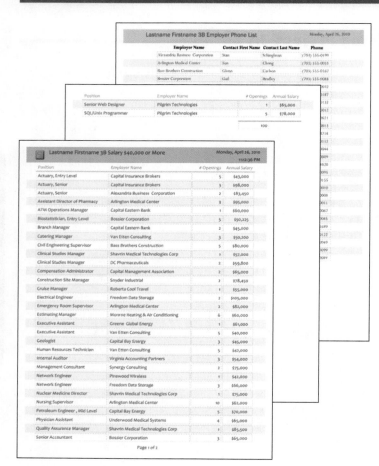

Figure 3.28
Project 3B Job Openings

Objective 5 | Create a Report by Using the Report Tool

A *report* is a database object that summarizes the fields and records from a query or from a table, in an easy-to-read format suitable for printing. A report consists of information extracted from queries or tables and also the report's design items, such as labels, headings, and graphics. The queries or tables that provide the underlying data for a report are referred to as the report's *record source*.

Activity 3.12 | Creating a Report by Using the Report Tool

The *Report tool* is the fastest way to create a report. This tool displays all of the fields and records from the record source that you select. You can use the Report tool to look at the underlying data quickly in an easy-to-read format, after which you can save the report and modify it in Layout view or in Design view. In this activity, you will use the Report tool to create a report from a query that lists all of the job openings with an annual salary of at least $40,000.

1 **Start** Access. In **Backstage** view, click **Open**. Navigate to the student data files for this textbook, and then open the **a03B_Job_Openings** database.

2 In **Backstage** view, click **Save Database As**. In the **Save As** dialog box, navigate to your **Access Chapter 3** folder. In the **File name** box, type **Lastname_Firstname_3B_Job_ Openings** and then press Enter. On the **Message Bar**, click **Enable Content**. Notice that in this database, there are two tables and one query that uses both tables as its record source.

3 On the Ribbon, click the **Database Tools tab**. In the **Relationships group**, click the **Relationships** button. Compare your screen with Figure 3.29. If your relationships do not display, in the Relationships group, click the All Relationships button.

> *One* employer is associated with *many* job openings. Thus, a one-to-many relationship has been established between the 3B Employers table and the 3B Job Openings table by using the Employer ID# field as the common field.

Figure 3.29

Employer ID# is common field

Join line indicating a one-to-many relationship and referential integrity

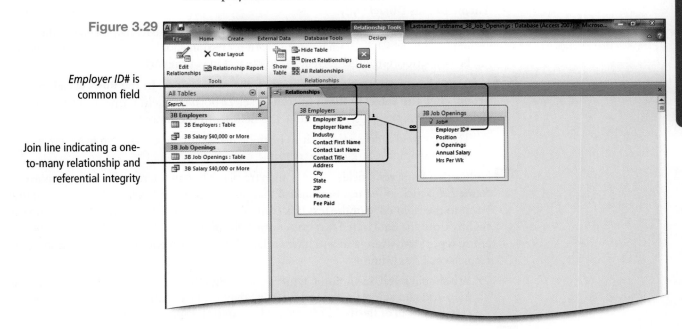

4 **Close** ☒ the **Relationships** window. Open both tables, and look at the fields and data in each table. Open the query to examine the data, and then switch to **Design** view to examine the design grid. When you are finished, **Close** ☒ all objects.

> The query answers the question *What is the Job#, Position, Employer Name, and # of Openings for jobs that have an Annual Salary of $40,000 or more?*

5 In the **Navigation Pane**, click to select the **3B Salary $40,000 or More** query. Click the **Create tab**, and then in the **Reports group**, click the **Report** button. **Close** ☒ the **Navigation Pane**, and then compare your screen with Figure 3.30.

> Access creates the 3B Job Openings report and displays it in Layout view. The report includes all of the fields and all of the records in the query. In Layout view, you can see the margins and page breaks in the report.

Figure 3.30

Dotted lines indicate margins

All fields from query display in report

All records from query display in report

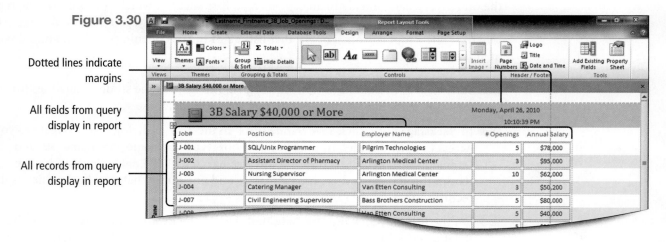

Activity 3.13 | Modifying a Report in Layout View and Printing a Report

1 On the **Design tab**, in the **Themes group**, click the **Themes** button. From the gallery of themes, scroll down, locate, and then right-click the **Waveform** theme. Click **Apply Theme to This Object Only**.

> Recall that right-clicking a theme enables you to apply a predefined format to the active object only, which is another way to give a professional look to a report. Apply a theme before performing other formatting to the text in your report.

2 Click the **Job#** field name, and then click the **Arrange tab**. In the **Rows & Columns group**, click the **Select Column** button to select both the field name and the data in the field, and then press ⌈Del⌉ to remove the field from the report.

> The Job# field is deleted, and the remaining fields move to the left. No fields extend beyond the right margin of the report.

3 Notice that for several fields, there is an extra blank line in the record. In the **Employer Name** field, click in the **text box control** that displays *Monroe Heating & Air Conditioning*. Point to the right edge of the text box control to display the ↔ pointer. Drag to the right slightly until the data in the text box control displays on one line. Scroll down to view the entire report to be sure that you have widened the column enough to accommodate all records on a single line.

> You should scroll down through the report to find the text box control that displays the most text and adjust the field width using that text box control. In this manner, you can be certain that all of the data in every text box control displays on one line.

4 Click the **Position** field name, and then click the **Home tab**. In the **Sort & Filter group**, click the **Ascending** button to sort the records in the report alphabetically by Position.

5 Scroll down to the bottom of the report, and then click the **Annual Salary calculated control**, which displays a total that is truncated at the bottom. Press Del to remove this total.

> Access automatically adds a calculated control to sum any field that is formatted as currency. Here, the total is not a useful number and this can be deleted.

6 At the top of the report, click the **# Openings** field name. Click the **Design tab**. In the **Grouping & Totals group**, click the **Totals** button, and then click **Sum**.

7 Scroll down to display the last line of the report. Click in the **# Openings calculated control**, point to the bottom edge of the control to display the ↕ pointer, and then double-click to resize the control. Compare your screen with Figure 3.31.

> The total number of job openings for positions with a salary equal to or greater than $40,000 is 100. Use Layout view to make quick changes to a report created with the Report tool. The Report tool is not intended to create a perfectly formatted formal report, but it is a way to summarize the data in a table or query quickly in an easy-to-read format suitable for printing and reading.

Figure 3.31

Waveform theme applied

Position field sorted in ascending order

Openings field summed

Calculated control removed from *Annual Salary* field

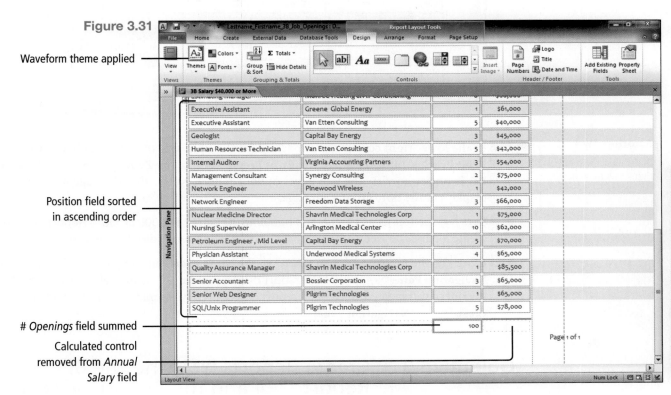

8 At the bottom of the report, notice that the **Page Number control** does not fit entirely within the margins. Click the **Page Number control** that displays *Page 1 of 1*, and then drag the ⤢ pointer to the left until the page number control is visually centered between the margins of the report.

> Always look at the headers and footers to determine if the data will print on one page.

9 Scroll up to display the top of the report. In the **Report Header** section, click the label control that displays *3B Salary $40,000 or More*. Click the **Format tab**, and then in the **Font group**, change the **Font Size** to **14**. Click the **label control** again so that you can edit the title. Using your own name, add **Lastname Firstname** to the beginning of the title, and then press Enter. If necessary, point to the right edge of the label control to display the ↔ pointer, and then double-click to fit the width of the text in the control.

Access | Chapter 3

10 Click any field in the report. In the upper left corner of the report, click the **layout selector** ⊞, and then drag it slightly downward and to the right until the columns are visually centered between the margins of the report. If your columns rearrange, on the Quick Access Toolbar, click Undo and begin again. Compare your screen with Figure 3.32.

> Using the layout selector, you can move the entire layout of the label controls and text box controls to horizontally center the records on the page. It is easier to control this movement if you drag downward slightly while moving the selector to the right.

Figure 3.32

Fields visually centered within margins

Your name displays in Report Header; Font Size of 14

Layout selector

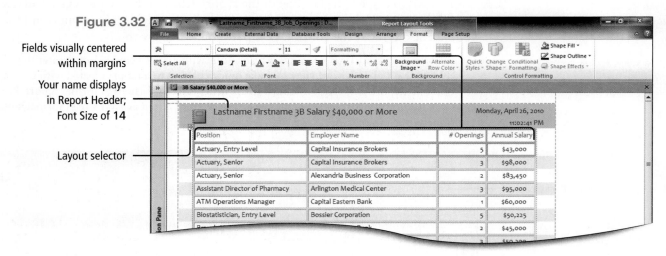

Another Way

In the object window, right-click the object tab, and then click Print Preview.

11 In the lower right corner of your screen, at the right side of the status bar, click the **Print Preview** button 🔍. On the **Print Preview tab**, in the **Zoom group**, click the **Two Pages** button to view the two pages of your report. Notice that the page number displays at the bottom of each page.

12 Save 💾 the report as **Lastname Firstname 3B Salary $40,000 or More Report** and then create a paper or electronic printout as directed. Then **Close Print Preview**.

13 Close ✕ the report, and then **Open** » the **Navigation Pane**. Expand the width of the **Navigation Pane**. Notice that the report displays under the source tables from which the query was created, and that a report object displays a small green notebook icon. **Close** « the **Navigation Pane**.

Objective 6 | Create Reports by Using the Blank Report Tool and the Report Wizard

Use the *Blank Report tool* to create a report without predefined labels and fields. This is an efficient way to create a report, especially if you plan to include only a few fields in your report.

Activity 3.14 | Creating a Report by Using the Blank Report Tool

In this activity, you will build a report that lists only the Employer Name, Contact First Name, Contact Last Name, and Phone fields, which Mr. Bass will use as a quick reference for phoning the employers to verify the details of their Career Fair participation.

1 On the **Create tab**, in the **Reports group**, click the **Blank Report** button.

> A blank report displays in Layout view, and the Field List pane displays.

2 In the **Field List** pane, click **Show all tables**, and then click the **plus sign** (+) next to **3B Employers** to display the field names in the table. Compare your screen with Figure 3.33.

Figure 3.33

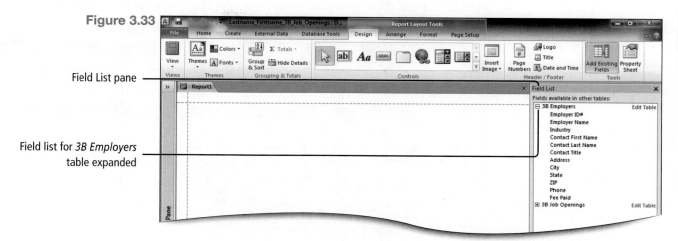

Field List pane

Field list for *3B Employers*
table expanded

3 In the **Field List** pane, point to the **Employer Name** field, right-click, and then click **Add Field to View**.

The Employer Name field and its data display as the first column of the report. Using the Report tool, you build the report field by field in the order that you want the fields to display.

4 From the **Field List** pane, drag the **Contact First Name** field into the blank report—anywhere to the right of *Employer Name*. Double-click the **Contact Last Name** field to add it as the third field in the report. Use any technique that you just practiced to add the **Phone** field as the fourth field in the report, and then compare your screen with Figure 3.34.

Figure 3.34

Four fields added
to the report

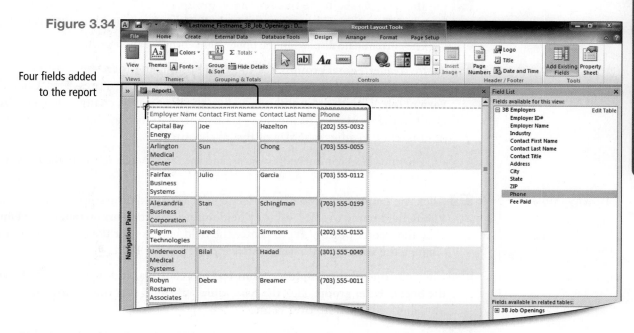

5 **Close** ☒ the **Field List** pane. On the **Design tab**, in the **Themes group**, click the **Themes** button. Right-click the **Equity** theme, and then click **Apply Theme to This Object Only**.

Recall that you should select a theme before making other formatting changes.

6 Under **Employer Name**, click in the **text box control** that displays *Monroe Heating & Air Conditioning*. Point to the right edge of the text box control to display the ↔ pointer, and then drag to the right until the data in the text box control displays on one line and there is a small amount of space between the name and the next column. Compare your screen with Figure 3.35.

Figure 3.35

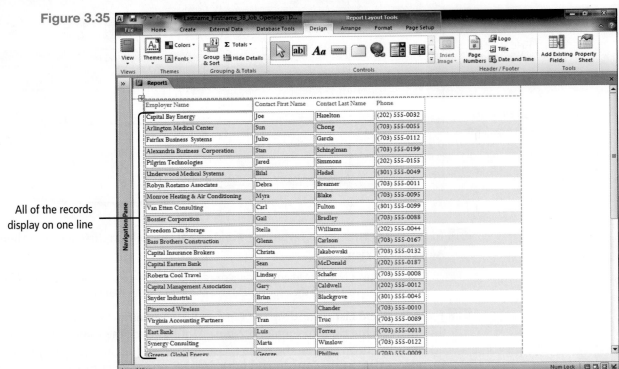

All of the records display on one line

7 On the **Design tab**, in the **Header/Footer group**, click the **Date and Time** button. In the **Date and Time** dialog box, clear the **Include Time** check box, and then click **OK**.

The current date displays in the upper right corner of the report.

8 In the **Header/Footer group**, click the **Title** button, and then using your own name, type **Lastname Firstname 3B Employer Phone List** and then press Enter. Click the **Format tab**. With the title still selected, in the **Font group**, change the **Font Size** to **14**. Point to the right edge of the title's label control to display the ↔ pointer, and then double-click to adjust the size of the label control.

The title's label control width adjusts, and the Date control moves to the left within the margin.

Another Way

Click the first field name, and then click the Arrange tab. In the Rows & Columns group, click the Select Row button.

9 Click the **Employer Name** field name to select it. Hold down Shift, and then click the **Phone** field name to select all four field names. On the **Format tab**, in the **Font group**, click the **Center** button ▤ to center the field names over the data in the columns. Change the **Font Color** to **Automatic**, and then apply **Bold** **B**.

10 Click any one of the **Employer Name text box controls**, and then click the **Home tab**. In the **Sort & Filter group**, click the **Ascending** button to sort the records in the report alphabetically by Employer Name.

11 In the upper left corner of the report, click the **layout selector** ⊞, and then drag it downward slightly and to the right to visually center the fields between the margins. Compare your screen with Figure 3.36.

Recall that it is easier to control this movement if you drag down slightly while moving the layout selector.

Figure 3.36

Field names formatted and centered over data

Report title added and formatted

Layout visually centered between the margins

Equity Theme applied

Date added (yours will vary)

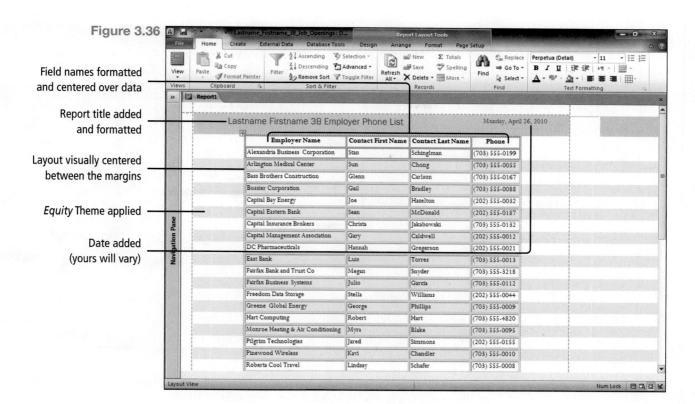

Employer Name	Contact First Name	Contact Last Name	Phone
Alexandria Business Corporation	Stan	Schinglman	(703) 555-0199
Arlington Medical Center	Sun	Chong	(703) 555-0055
Bass Brothers Construction	Glenn	Carlson	(703) 555-0167
Bossier Corporation	Gail	Bradley	(703) 555-0088
Capital Bay Energy	Joe	Hazelton	(202) 555-0032
Capital Eastern Bank	Sean	McDonald	(202) 555-0187
Capital Insurance Brokers	Christa	Jakabowski	(703) 555-0132
Capital Management Association	Gary	Caldwell	(202) 555-0012
DC Pharmaceuticals	Hannah	Gregerson	(202) 555-0021
East Bank	Luis	Torres	(703) 555-0013
Fairfax Bank and Trust Co	Megan	Snyder	(703) 555-3218
Fairfax Business Systems	Julio	Garcia	(703) 555-0112
Freedom Data Storage	Stella	Williams	(202) 555-0044
Greene Global Energy	George	Phillips	(703) 555-0009
Hart Computing	Robert	Hart	(703) 555-4820
Monroe Heating & Air Conditioning	Myra	Blake	(703) 555-0095
Pilgrim Technologies	Jared	Simmons	(202) 555-0155
Pinewood Wireless	Kavi	Chandler	(703) 555-0010
Roberta Cool Travel	Lindsay	Schafer	(703) 555-0008

Report title: Lastname Firstname 3B Employer Phone List — Monday, April 26, 2010

12 Save the report as **Lastname Firstname 3B Employer Phone List** and then on the status bar, click the **Print Preview** button. Create a paper or electronic printout as directed.

13 **Close Print Preview**, and then **Close** the report. **Open** the **Navigation Pane**, and notice that the report displays below the *3B Employers* table—the underlying data source. **Close** the **Navigation Pane**.

Activity 3.15 | Creating a Report by Using the Report Wizard

Use the ***Report Wizard*** when you need flexibility and want to control the report content and design. The Report Wizard enables you to specify how the data is grouped and sorted. You can use fields from more than one table or query, assuming you have created the appropriate relationships between the tables. The Report Wizard is similar to the Form Wizard; it creates a report by asking you a series of questions and then designs the report based on your answers.

In this activity, you will prepare a report for Mr. Bass that displays the employers, grouped by industry, and the total fees paid by employers for renting a booth at the Career Fair.

1 Click the **Create tab**, and then in the **Reports group**, click the **Report Wizard** button.

> Here you select the tables or queries from which you want to extract information, and then select the fields to include in the report. You can also select more than one table or query.

2 Click the **Tables/Queries arrow**, and then click **Table: 3B Employers**. Move the following fields to the **Selected Fields** list in the order given: **Industry**, **Employer Name**, and **Fee Paid** (scroll down as necessary to locate the *Fee Paid* field). Compare your screen with Figure 3.37.

Access | Chapter 3

Figure 3.37

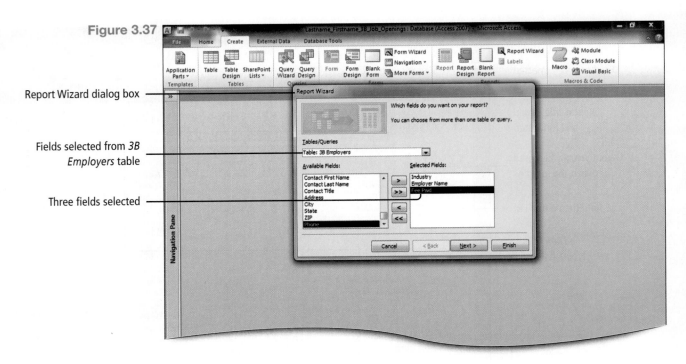

Report Wizard dialog box

Fields selected from *3B Employers* table

Three fields selected

3 Click **Next**, and notice that in this dialog box, you can add grouping levels. A preview of the grouping level displays on the right side of the dialog box.

Grouping data helps to organize and summarize the data in your report.

4 With **Industry** selected, click the **One Field** button ![>], and then compare your screen with Figure 3.38.

The preview window displays how the data will be grouped in the report. Grouping data in a report places all of the records that have the same data in a field together as a group—in this instance, each *Industry* will display as a group.

Figure 3.38

Report will be grouped by *Industry* names

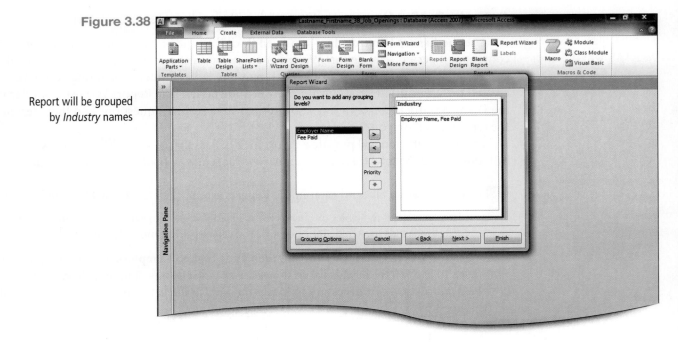

5 Click **Next**, and then click the **1** box **arrow**. Click **Employer Name**, and then compare your screen with Figure 3.39.

> Here you indicate how you want to sort and summarize the information. You can sort on up to four fields. The Summary Options button displays because the data is grouped and contains numerical or currency data. The records in the report will sort alphabetically by Employer Name within Industry. Sorting records in a report presents a more organized report.

Figure 3.39

Sort order

Field that will be sorted

Summary options button displays because report contains numeric or currency fields

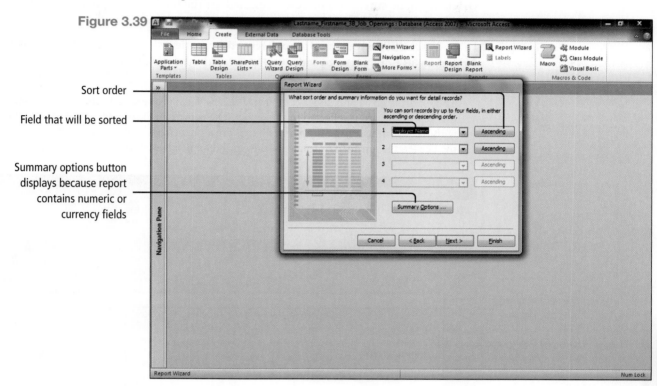

6 In the **Report Wizard** dialog box, click the **Summary Options** button, and then compare your screen with Figure 3.40.

> The Summary Options dialog box displays. The Fee Paid field can be summarized by selecting one of four options—Sum, Avg, Min, or Max. You can also choose to display only summary information or to display both details—each record—and the summary information.

Figure 3.40

Aggregate functions for *Fee Paid* field

Show options

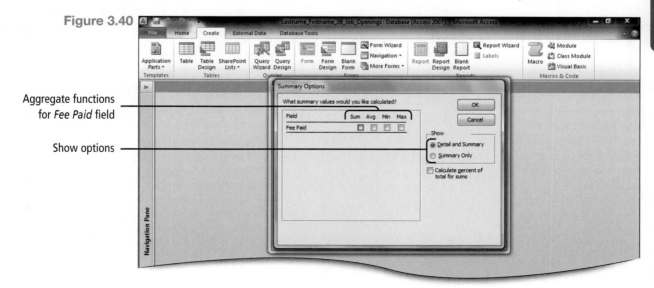

7 To the right of **Fee Paid**, select the **Sum** check box. Under **Show**, be sure that the **Detail and Summary** option button is selected, click **OK**, and then click **Next**.

> Here you select the layout and the page orientation. A preview of the layout displays on the left.

8 Click each **Layout** option button, noticing the changes in the preview box, and then click the **Stepped** option button to select it as the layout for your report. Under **Orientation**, be sure that **Portrait** is selected. At the bottom, be sure that the **Adjust the field width so all fields fit on a page** check box is selected, and then click **Next**.

9 In the **What title do you want for your report?** box, select the existing text, type **Lastname Firstname 3B Booth Fees by Industry Report** and then click **Finish**. Compare your screen with Figure 3.41.

> The report is saved and displays in Print Preview. Each of the specifications you defined in the Report Wizard is reflected in the report. The records are grouped by Industry, and then within each Industry, the Employer Names are alphabetized. Within each Industry grouping, the Fee Paid is summed or totaled—the word *Sum* displays at the end of each grouping.

Figure 3.41

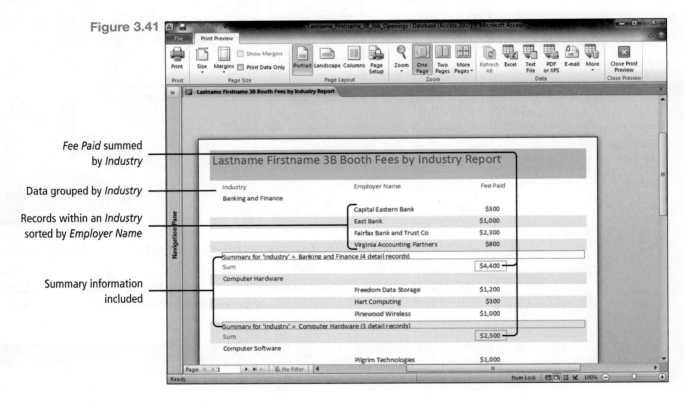

Fee Paid summed by *Industry*

Data grouped by *Industry*

Records within an *Industry* sorted by *Employer Name*

Summary information included

10 **Close Print Preview**. On the status bar, click the **Layout View** button.

Objective 7 | Modify the Design of a Report

After you create your report, you can modify its design by using tools and techniques similar to those you used to modify the design of a form. You can change the format of controls, add controls, remove controls, or change the placement of controls in the report. Most report modifications can be made in Layout view.

Activity 3.16 | Formatting and Deleting Controls in Layout View

1 With your **3B Booth Fees by Industry** report in **Layout** view, on the **Design tab**, in the **Themes group**, click the **Themes** button. In the **Themes gallery**, scroll down, and right-click the **Opulent** theme. Click **Apply Theme to This Object Only**.

2 Click the title—**3B Booth Fees by Industry Report**—to display a border around the label control, and then click the **Format tab**. In the **Font group**, change the **Font Size** to **14**, and then apply **Bold** **B**.

3 Within each *Industry* grouping, notice the **Summary for 'Industry'** information.

Access includes a summary line that details what is being summarized (in this case, summed) and the number of records that are included in the summary total. Now that Mr. Bass has viewed the report, he has decided this information is not necessary and can be removed.

4 Click any one of the **Summary for 'Industry' controls**.

> **Another Way**
>
> Right-click any of the selected controls, and then click Delete.

The control that you clicked is surrounded by a dark border, and all of the related controls are surrounded by paler borders to indicate that all are selected.

5 Press Del to remove the controls from the report. Compare your screen to Figure 3.42.

Figure 3.42

Title formatted; Opulent Theme applied

Summary for 'Industry' label controls deleted

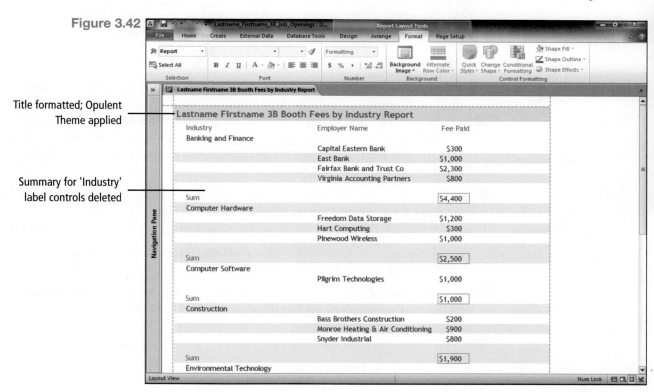

6 **Save** the changes you have made to the report.

Activity 3.17 | Modifying Controls in Layout View

In this activity, you will modify the text in controls, move controls, resize controls, and add a control to the report, all of which is easily accomplished in Layout view.

1 On the left side of the report, click one of the **Sum label controls** to select all of the controls, and then double-click to select the text. Type **Total Fees by Industry** and then press Enter. Compare your screen with Figure 3.43.

The new text more clearly states what is being summed.

Figure 3.43

Text changed

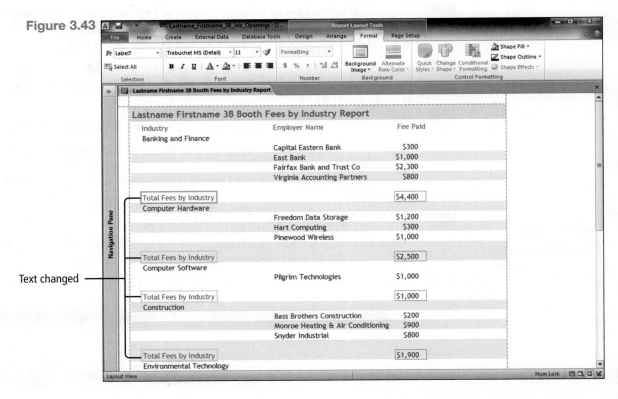

2 At the top of your report, click to select the **Industry label control**. Hold down Shift, click the **Employer Name label control**, and then click the **Fee Paid label control** to select all three field names. On the **Format tab**, in the **Font group**, click the **Bold** button **B**.

3 Scroll down to view the end of the report. Click to select the **calculated control** for the **Grand Total**, which displays *20,400*. Point to the left edge of the control to display the ↔ pointer. Drag to the left slightly and release the mouse to display **$20,400**.

This control is an example of a *calculated control*—a control that contains an expression, often a formula—that uses one or more fields from the underlying table or query.

4 On the left side of the report, increase the width of the right edge of the **Grand Total label control** so that all of the text displays, and then **Save** 🖫 the report.

Activity 3.18 | Aligning Controls in Design View

Design view gives you a more detailed view of the structure of your report. You can see the header and footer sections for the report, for the page, and for groups. In Design view, your report is not actually running, so you cannot see the underlying data while you are working. In the same manner as forms, you can add labels to the Page Footer section or increase the height of sections. Some tasks, such as aligning controls, can also be completed in Design view.

1 On the status bar, click the **Design View** button 🖉, and then compare your screen with Figure 3.44.

The Design view for a report is similar to the Design view for a form. You can modify the layout of the report in this view, and use the dotted grid pattern to align controls. This report contains a *Report Header*, a *Page Header*, a *Group Header*, which in this instance is the *Industry* grouping, a Detail section that displays the data, a *Group Footer* (*Industry*), a *Page Footer*, and a *Report Footer*.

The Report Header displays information at the top of the *first page* of a report. The Page Header displays information at the top of *every page* of a report. The Group Header and Group Footer display the field label by which the data has been grouped—*Industry* in this instance. If you do not group data in a report, the Group Header does not display. Similarly, if you do not summarize data, the Group Footer does not display.

Figure 3.44

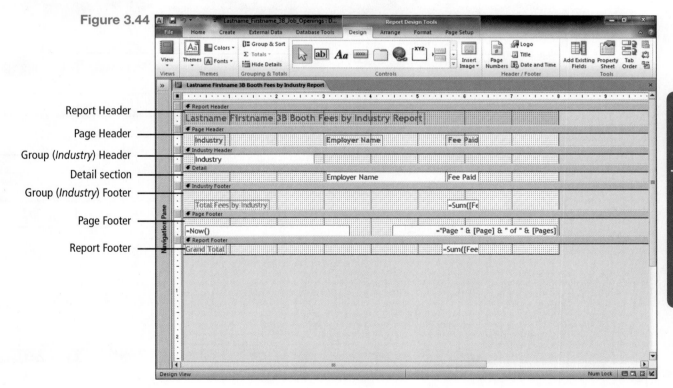

Report Header
Page Header
Group (*Industry*) Header
Detail section
Group (*Industry*) Footer
Page Footer
Report Footer

2 In the **Page Footer** section of the report, examine the two controls in this section.

The Page Footer displays information at the bottom of *every page* in the report, including the page number and the current date inserted by those controls.

The *date control* on the left side, displayed as =*Now( )*, inserts the current date each time the report is opened. The *page number control* on the right side, displayed as =*"Page " & [Page] & " of " & [Pages]*, inserts the page number, for example Page 1 of 2, in the report when the report is displayed in Print Preview or when printed. Both of these are examples of functions that are used by Access to create controls in a report.

3 In the **Industry Footer** section, click the **Total Fees by Industry label control**. Hold down Shift. In the **Report Footer** section, click the **Grand Total label control** to select both controls.

4 On the **Arrange tab**, in the **Sizing & Ordering group**, click the **Align** button, and then click **Left**. **Save** 🔲 the report, and then compare your screen with Figure 3.45.

The left edge of the Grand Total label control is aligned with the left edge of the Total Fees by Industry label control. When using the Align Left feature, Access aligns the left edges of controls with the control that is farthest to the left in the report. Similarly, when using the Align Right feature, Access aligns the right edges of controls with the control that is farthest to the right in the report.

Figure 3.45

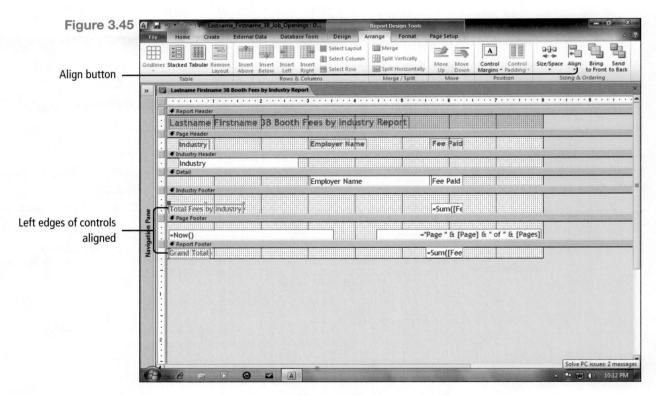

5 Switch to **Layout** view to display the underlying data in the controls. Scroll down, and notice that the **Total Fees by Industry label controls** and the **Grand Total label control** are left aligned.

Objective 8 | Print a Report and Keep Data Together

Before you print a report, examine the preview of the report to ensure that all of the labels and data display fully and to make sure that all of the data is properly grouped. Sometimes a page break occurs in the middle of a group of data, leaving the labels on one page and the data or totals on another page.

Activity 3.19 | Keeping Data Together and Printing a Report

It is possible to keep the data in a group together so it does not break across a page unless, of course, the data itself exceeds the length of a page.

1 On the status bar, click the **Print Preview** button 🖻. If necessary, in the **Zoom group**, click the **Two Pages** button, and then compare your screen with Figure 3.46.

This report will print on two pages. One record and the summary data for the *Hotel and Food Service* group display at the top of page 2, which is separated from the rest of the grouping.

Figure 3.46

Top of second page—one record and summary data

Bottom of first page—*Industry* grouping name and two records

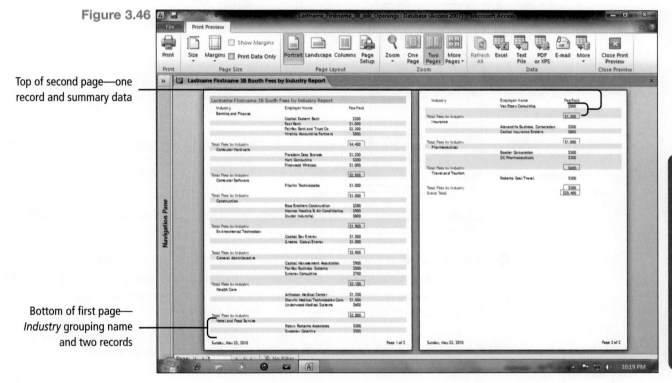

2 Click the **Close Print Preview** button to return to **Layout** view. On the **Design tab**, in the **Grouping & Totals group**, click the **Group & Sort** button.

At the bottom of the screen, the *Group, Sort, and Total pane* displays. Here you can control how information is grouped, sorted, or totaled. Layout view is the preferred view in which to accomplish such tasks, because you can see how the changes affect the display of the data.

3 In the **Group, Sort, and Total** pane, on the **Group on Industry bar**, click **More**. To the right of **do not keep group together on one page**, click the **arrow**, and then compare your screen with Figure 3.47.

The *keep whole group together on one page* command keeps each industry group together, from the name in the group header through the summary in the group footer. Next to *Group on Industry*, with A on top indicates that the industry names display in ascending sort order. The default setting is *do not keep group together on one page*.

Figure 3.47

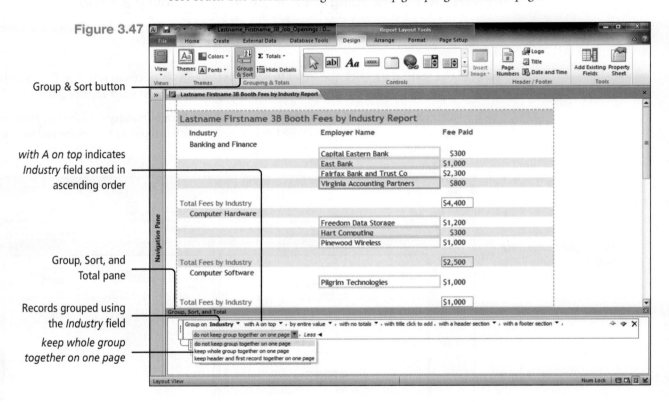

Group & Sort button

with A on top indicates *Industry* field sorted in ascending order

Group, Sort, and Total pane

Records grouped using the *Industry* field

keep whole group together on one page

4 Click **keep whole group together on one page**. In the **Grouping & Totals group**, click the **Group & Sort** button to close the **Group, Sort, and Total** pane. On the status bar, click the **Print Preview** button 🔍. If necessary, in the Zoom group, click the Two Pages button. Compare your screen with Figure 3.48.

All the records in the *Hotel and Food Service* industry group—the group header, the three records, and the summary information—display together at the top of page 2.

Figure 3.48

Entire industry group
displays together

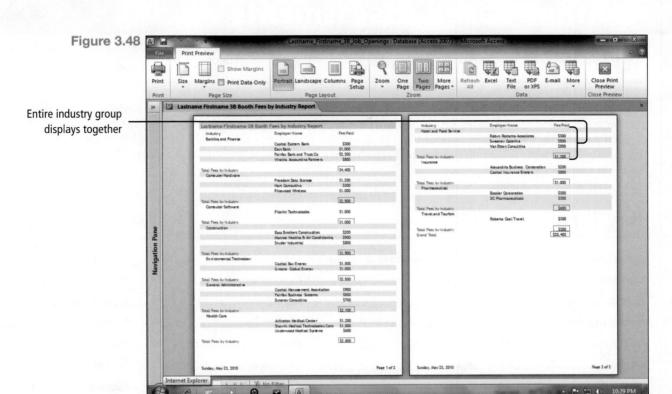

5 **Save** 🖫 the report. Create a paper or electronic copy of the report as directed.

6 **Close Print Preview**, and then **Close** ⊠ the report. **Open** ⟩⟩ the **Navigation Pane**, and, if necessary, increase the width of the pane so that all object names display fully.

7 Display **Backstage** view, click **Close Database**, and then click **Exit**. As directed by your instructor, submit your database and the three paper or electronic printouts that are the results of this project.

End **You have completed Project 3B** ——————

Content-Based Assessments

Summary

A form is an object for either entering or viewing information in a database—it creates a user interface for people using the database. A form is easy to use, because it can display one record at a time. Reports summarize the data in a database in a professional-looking manner suitable for printing. There are several tools for creating forms and reports, and you can modify forms and reports in Layout view or Design view.

Key Terms

Matching

Match each term in the second column with its correct definition in the first column by writing the letter of the term on the blank line in front of the correct definition.

_____ 1. The Access view in which you can make changes to a form or report while viewing the data.

_____ 2. The term used to describe objects and controls that are based on data that is stored in tables.

_____ 3. An Access view that displays the detailed structure of a query, form, or report.

_____ 4. Information, such as a form's title, that displays at the top of the screen in Form view and is printed at the top of the first page when records are printed as forms.

_____ 5. The section of a form or report that displays the records from the underlying table or query.

_____ 6. Information at the bottom of the screen in Form view that prints after the last detail section on the last page.

_____ 7. A gray bar in a form or report that identifies and separates one section from another.

_____ 8. An object on a form or report that displays data, performs actions, and lets you work with information.

_____ 9. The graphical object on a form or report that displays the data from the underlying table or query.

A Bound

B Bound control

C Calculated control

D Control

E Control layout

F Date control

G Design view

H Detail section

I Form footer

J Form header

K Label control

L Layout view

M Section bar

N Text box control

O Unbound control

_____ 10. A control that retrieves its data from an underlying table or query.

_____ 11. A control on a form or report that contains descriptive information, typically a field name.

_____ 12. A control that does not have a source of data, such as a title in a form or report.

_____ 13. The grouped arrangement of controls on a form or report.

_____ 14. A control that contains an expression, often a formula, that uses one or more fields from the underlying table or query.

_____ 15. A control on a form or report that inserts the current date each time the form or report is opened.

Multiple Choice

Circle the correct answer.

1. An Access object to enter new records into a table, edit or delete existing records in a table, or display existing records is a:
   A. bound control B. form C. report

2. The order that the insertion point moves from one field to another in a form when you press Tab is the:
   A. data entry order B. control order C. tab order

3. A small symbol that displays in the upper left corner of a selected control layout in a form or report that is displayed in Layout view and that is used to move an entire group of controls is the:
   A. control layout B. label control C. layout selector

4. A list of characteristics for controls on a form or report in which you can make precise changes to each property associated with the control is the:
   A. bound control B. control layout C. Property Sheet

5. The process of displaying only a portion of the total records (a subset) based on matching a specific value is:
   A. filtering B. reporting C. zooming

6. An Access command that filters the records in a form based on one or more fields, or based on more than one value in the field is Filter by:
   A. Form B. Selection C. Subset

7. A condition in which records that match at least one of the specified values are displayed is:
   A. AND B. BOTH C. OR

8. A database object that summarizes the fields and records from a table or query in an easy-to-read format suitable for printing is a:
   A. control B. form C. report

9. Information printed at the end of each group of records and that is used to display summary information for the group is called a:
   A. group footer B. group header C. Group, Sort, and Total pane

10. A predefined format that can be applied to the entire database or to individual objects in the database is called a:
    A. group header B. subset C. theme

Content-Based Assessments

Apply **3A** skills from these Objectives:

1 Create and Use a Form to Add and Delete Records

2 Create a Form by Using the Form Wizard

3 Modify a Form in Layout View and in Design View

4 Filter Records

Skills Review | Project **3C** Student Advising

In the following Skills Review, you will assist Gerald Finn, the Dean of Information Technology, in using an Access database to track students and their faculty advisors. Your completed forms will look similar to Figure 3.49.

Project Files

For Project 3C, you will need the following file:

a03C_Student_Advising

You will save your database as:

Lastname_Firstname_3C_Student_Advising

Project Results

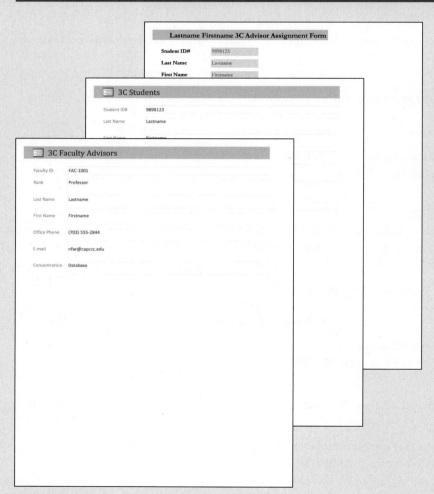

Figure 3.49

(Project 3C Student Advising continues on the next page)

Content-Based Assessments

Skills Review | Project 3C Student Advising (continued)

1 **Start** Access. In **Backstage** view, click **Open**, and then from your student files open the **a03C_Student_Advising** database. In **Backstage** view, click **Save Database As**. Save the database in your **Access Chapter 3** folder as **Lastname_Firstname_3C_Student_Advising** On the **Message Bar**, click the **Enable Content** button.

a. On the **Database Tools tab**, in the **Relationships group**, click the **Relationships** button. Notice the one-to-many relationship between the 3C Faculty Advisors table and the 3C Students table using the Faculty ID and Faculty Advisor ID fields as the common fields. *One* faculty member can advise *many* students. Recall that common fields do not need to have the same name; they must have the same data type. **Close** the **Relationships** window.

b. In the **Navigation Pane**, select the **3C Students** table. Click the **Create tab**, and then in the **Forms group**, click the **Form** button. **Save** the form as **Lastname Firstname 3C Student Form** and then **Close** the form object.

c. In the **Navigation Pane**, select the **3C Faculty Advisors** table. Click the **Create tab**, and then in the **Forms group**, click the **Form** button. **Close** the **Navigation Pane**, and then notice that *Faculty ID FAC-2877*, for *Professor Treiman*, has been assigned one student for advising.

d. **Close** the form, saving it as **Lastname Firstname 3C Faculty Advisor Form**

2 **Open** the **Navigation Pane**, and increase the width to display fully the object names. Open your **3C Student Form** object, and then **Close** the **Navigation Pane**. In the navigation area, click the **New (blank) record** button. In the **Student ID#** field, type **9898123** and then press Tab.

a. Using your own name, continue entering the data as shown in **Table 1**.

b. In the last field, press Tab to save the record and display a new blank record. **Close** the **3C**

Student Form object, and then **Open** the **Navigation Pane**.

c. **Open** your **3C Faculty Advisor Form** object, and then **Close** the **Navigation Pane**. Notice that in the first record, your record displays in the subdatasheet for Professor Treiman. At the bottom of your screen, in the navigation area for the form—not the navigation area for the related records in the form itself—click the **New (blank) record** button. In the blank form, using your own name, enter the information in **Table 2**, being sure to press Tab after entering the data in the last field.

d. In the navigation area, click the **First record** button. Click in the **Last Name** field, and then on the **Home tab**, in the **Find group**, click the **Find** button to open the **Find and Replace** dialog box. In the **Find What** box, type **Holland** and then click **Find Next**. **Close** the **Find and Replace** dialog box.

e. On the **Home tab**, in the **Records group**, click the **Delete button arrow**, and then click **Delete Record** to delete the record for Professor Holland—because Professor Holland has no student advisees assigned, he can be deleted from the table. In the message box, click **Yes** to delete the record. In the navigation area for the form, notice that the number of records in the table is *18*.

f. Use the **Find** button to display the form for the **Faculty ID** of **FAC-1001** Display **Backstage** view. Click the **Print tab**, and then in the right panel, click **Print**. In the **Print** dialog box, under **Print Range**, click the **Selected Record(s)** option button, and then click **Setup**. In the **Page Setup** dialog box, click the **Columns tab**. Under **Column Size**, in the **Width** box, delete the existing text, type **7.5** and then click **OK** two times to print only your record in the form layout, or create an electronic printout. **Close** the **3C Faculty Advisor Form** object, and then **Open** the **Navigation Pane**.

Table 1

Student ID#	Last Name	First Name	Phone Number	E-mail	Concentration	Faculty Advisor ID
9898123	Lastname	Firstname	(703) 555-1257	ns0001@capccc.edu	Network Security	FAC-2877

(Return to Step 2-b)

Table 2

Faculty ID	Rank	Last Name	First Name	Office Phone	E-mail	Concentration
FAC-1001	Professor	Lastname	Firstname	(703) 555-2844	nfac@capccc.edu	Database

(Return to Step 2-d)

(Project 3C Student Advising continues on the next page)

g. Open your **3C Student Form** object, and then **Close** the **Navigation Pane**. Click in the **Last Name** field. Press Ctrl + F to display the **Find and Replace** dialog box. Enter the information to find the record where the **Last Name** field contains your **Lastname** and then **Print** only the selected record, changing the **Column Size Width** to 7.5 or create an electronic printout. **Close** the **3C Student Form** object, and then **Open** the **Navigation Pane**.

3 In the **Navigation Pane**, click to select the **3C Students** table. On the **Create tab**, in the **Forms group** click the **Form Wizard** button.

a. Under **Tables/Queries**, be sure that **Table: 3C Students** displays. Using the **One Field** button or by double-clicking, move the following fields to the **Selected Fields** list in the order specified: **First Name**, **Last Name**, and **Faculty Advisor ID**.

b. Click **Next**. Be sure **Columnar** is selected as the layout, and then click **Next**. In the box **What title do you want for your form?**, select the existing text, and then type **Lastname Firstname 3C Advisor Assignment Form** and then click **Finish** to close the wizard and create the form.

4 **Close** the **Navigation Pane**. Be sure your **3C Advisor Assignment Form** displays. In the lower right corner of your screen, click the **Layout View** button. Click the **First Name label control**. Hold down Shift, and then click the **Last Name label control**, the **Faculty Advisor ID label control**, and the **three text box controls** to select all of the controls. On the Ribbon, click the **Arrange tab**. In the **Table group**, click the **Stacked** button to group the controls. Click the **First Name label control** to deselect all of the controls and to surround the label control with a colored border.

a. On the **Design tab**, in the **Themes group**, click the **Themes** button. Right-click the **Couture** theme, and then click **Apply Theme to This Object Only**.

b. Click anywhere in the title *3C Advisor Assignment Form* to select it. On the **Format tab**, in the **Font group**, click the **Font Size button arrow**, and then click **16**. Click the **Bold** button. Click the **Font Color button arrow**, and then under **Theme Colors**, in the last column, click the last color—**Brown, Accent 6, Darker 50%**.

c. On the status bar, click the **Design View** button. Point to the *lower* edge of the **Form Footer section**

bar to display the ⊞ pointer, and then drag downward approximately **0.5 inch**. On the **Design tab**, in the **Controls group**, click the **Label** button. Position the plus sign of the ⁺A pointer in the **Form Footer** section at **0.25 inch on the horizontal ruler** and even with the lower edge of the Form Footer section bar. Click one time.

d. Using your own name, type **Created by Lastname Firstname** and then press Enter. Click the **Format tab**. With the label control selected, in the **Font group**, click the **Bold** button, and then change the **Font Color** to **Brown, Text 2**—in the fourth column, the first color. Point to a sizing handle to display one of the resize pointers, and then double-click to fit the control to the text you typed.

5 **Save** the form, and then switch to **Layout** view. On the **Design tab**, in the **Tools group**, click the **Add Existing Fields** button. In the **Field List** pane, point to **Student ID#**, and then drag to the left until the pointer is above the *First Name* label control and a thick colored line displays above the control. Release the mouse button to add the Student ID# controls to the form.

a. **Close** the **Field List** pane. Click the **Last Name text box control**, which currently displays *Barthmaier*, to surround it with a border. Point to the right edge of the **text box control** until the ↔ pointer displays, and then drag to the left until there is approximately **1"** of space between *Barthmaier* and the right edge of the text box control.

b. On the **Arrange tab**, in the **Rows & Columns** group, click the **Select Row** button. In the **Move group**, click the **Move Up** button one time to move the **Last Name controls** above the **First Name controls**. **Save** the form.

6 Click the **Student ID# text box control**, which displays *1034823*. In the **Rows & Columns group**, click the **Select Column** button to select all four text box controls. On the **Format tab**, in the **Font group**, click the **Background Color button arrow**. Under **Theme Colors**, in the fifth column, click the second color—**Brown, Accent 1, Lighter 80%**.

a. Click the **Student ID# label control**. On the **Arrange tab**, in the **Rows & Columns group**, click the **Select Column** button to select all four label controls. Click the **Format tab**, change the **Font Color**—*not* the Background Color—to **Brown, Text 2**—in the fourth column, the first color. Then apply **Bold**.

(Project 3C Student Advising continues on the next page)

Content-Based Assessments

b. Click the **layout selector** ⊞ to select all of the controls. Change the **Font Size** to **12**. On the Ribbon, click the **Design tab**, and then in the **Tools group**, click the **Property Sheet** button. In the **Property Sheet**, click the word **Height**, type **0.25** and then press ⏎ to adjust the height of all of the controls.

c. Click the **Student ID# label control** to select only that label. Click the **Arrange tab**, and then in the **Rows & Columns group**, click the **Select Column** button. In the **Property Sheet**, click **Width**, type **1.5** and then press ⏎.

d. In the **Form Footer section**, click the label control with your name. Hold down ⇧Shift, and then in the **Form Header section**, in the **label control** that displays *3C Advisor Assignment Form*, click to select both controls. In the **Property Sheet**, change the **Left** property to **0.5** and then press ⏎. **Save** the form.

e. **Close** the **Property Sheet**, and then switch to **Form** view. In the navigation area, click the **Last record** button to display the record containing your name. Display **Backstage** view, click the **Print tab**, and then click **Print**. In the **Print** dialog box, under **Print Range**, click the **Selected Record(s)** option button. Create a paper or electronic printout as directed, and then **Close Print Preview**.

7 With the form displayed in **Form** view, click the **First record** button, click the **Faculty Advisor ID label control** to select the text in the text box control. On the **Home tab**, in the **Find group**, click the **Find** button. In the **Find and Replace** dialog box, in the **Find What** box, type **FAC-9119** and then click **Find Next** to find and display the record for *Amanda Bass*. **Close** the **Find and Replace** dialog box. In

the **Sort & Filter group**, click the **Selection** button, and then click **Equals "FAC-9119"**. In the navigation area, notice that two students have been assigned to the faculty member with the *FAC-9119* advisor number.

a. In the **Sort & Filter group**, click the **Toggle Filter** button to remove the filter and display all 27 records. **Close** the form, and save changes.

b. **Open** the **Navigation Pane**, open your **3C Student Form** object, and then **Close** the **Navigation Pane**. On the **Home tab**, in the **Sort & Filter group**, click the **Advanced** button, and then click **Filter By Form**. Click in the **Concentration text box control**. At the right edge of the text box control, click the **arrow** that displays. In the list, click Programming. In the **Sort & Filter group**, click the **Toggle Filter** button, and notice that two students have a *Concentration* of *Programming*.

c. In the **Sort & Filter group**, click the **Advanced** button, and then click **Filter By Form**. At the bottom left side of the window, click the **Or tab**. Click the **Concentration text box control arrow**, and then click **Networking**. In the **Sort & Filter group**, click the **Toggle Filter** button. Seven students have a Concentration of *Programming* or *Networking*. In the **Sort & Filter group**, click the **Toggle Filter** button to display all of the records. **Save** and then **Close** the form.

d. **Open** the **Navigation Pane**; be sure all object names display fully. Display **Backstage** view, click **Close Database**, and then click **Exit**. As directed by your instructor, submit your database and the three paper or electronic printouts that are the results of this project.

End **You have completed Project 3C** ——————————

Access | Chapter 3

Content-Based Assessments

Apply 3B skills from these Objectives:

- 5 Create a Report by Using the Report Tool
- 6 Create Reports by Using the Blank Report Tool and the Report Wizard
- 7 Modify the Design of a Report
- 8 Print a Report and Keep Data Together

Skills Review | Project 3D Workshop Rooms

In the following Skills Review, you will assist Michelina Cortez, the Director of Workforce Development, in using an Access database to track the details about workshops offered by community members for the public and for students at the Washington Campus of Capital Cities Community College. Your completed reports will look similar to Figure 3.50.

Project Files

For Project 3D, you will need the following file:

a03D_Workshop_Rooms

You will save your database as:

Lastname_Firstname_3D_Workshop_Rooms

Project Results

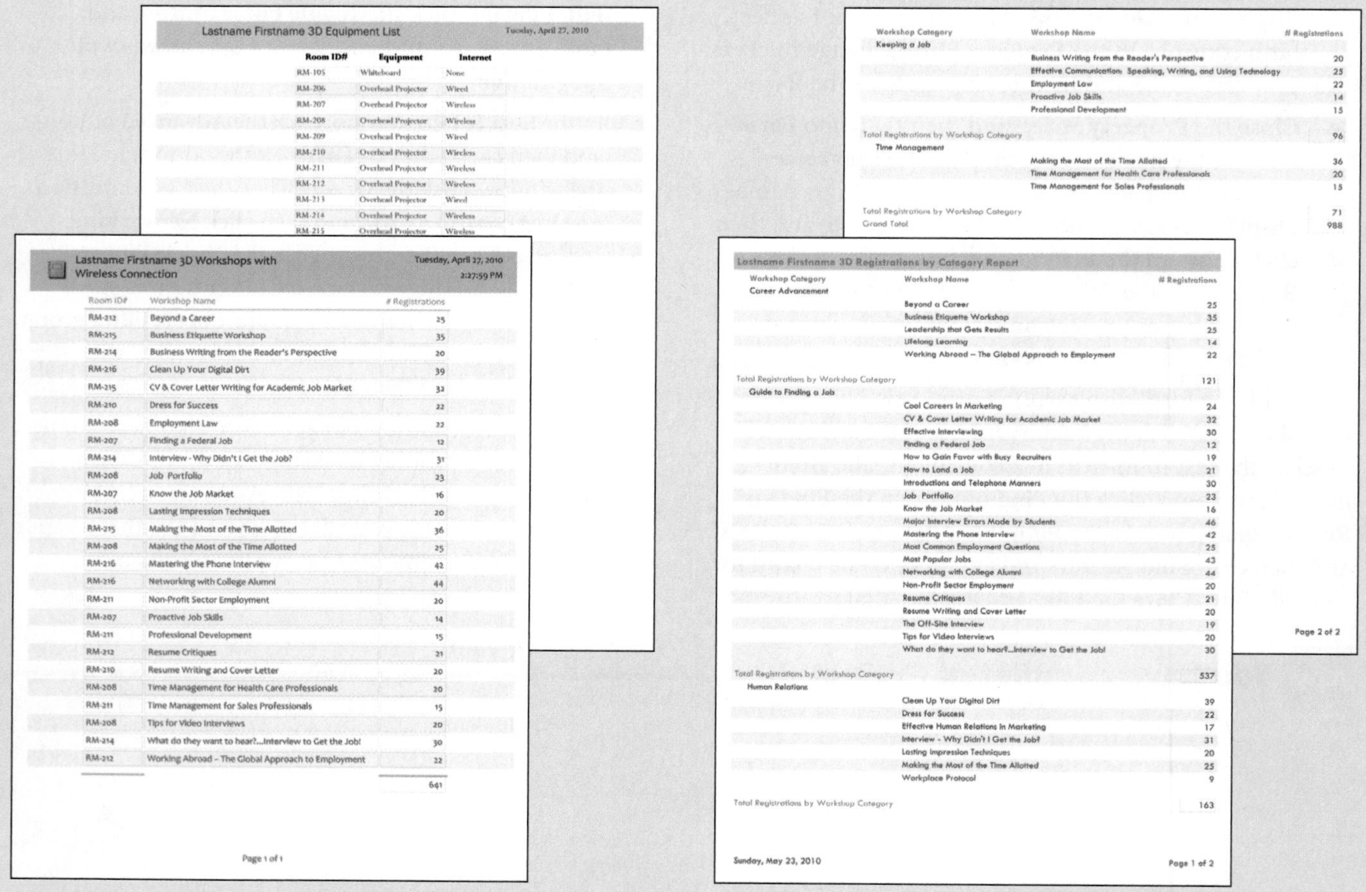

Figure 3.50

(Project 3D Workshop Rooms continues on the next page)

Content-Based Assessments

1 **Start** Access. In **Backstage** view, click **Open**. From your student files, open the **a03D_Workshop_Rooms** database. In **Backstage** view, save the database in your **Access Chapter 3** folder as **Lastname_Firstname_3D_Workshop_Rooms** and then in the **Message Bar**, click the **Enable Content** button. On the Ribbon, click the **Database Tools tab**, and then click the **Relationships** button. If your relationships do not display, in the Relationships group, click the All Relationships button. *One* room is associated with *many* workshops. Thus, a one-to-many relationship has been established between the 3D Rooms table and the 3D Workshops table using Room ID# as the common field. **Close** the **Relationships** window.

a. Open the two tables to examine the data, and then open the query in **Design** view to examine the design grid. This query answers the question *What is the Room ID#, Workshop Name, Workshop Category, and # Registrations for workshops that have wireless Internet connections available?* **Close** all open objects. In the **Navigation Pane**, select the **3D Workshops with Wireless Connection** query. Click the **Create tab**, and then in the **Reports group**, click the **Report** button. **Close** the **Navigation Pane**.

b. On the **Design tab**, in the **Themes group**, click the **Themes** button, right-click the **Waveform** theme, and then click **Apply Theme to This Object Only**.

c. Click the **Workshop Category** field name. Click the **Arrange tab**, and then in the **Rows & Columns group**, click the **Select Column** button. Press ⌦ to remove the field from the report.

d. Click the **Room ID#** field name, and then drag the right edge of the control to the left until there is approximately **0.5** inch of space between the room number and the right edge of the field. Scroll down the report, and then in the **Workshop Name** field—second column—click in the **text box control** that displays *What do they want to hear? . . . Interview to Get the Job!* Drag the right edge of the control to the right until the data in the control displays on one line. With the **Workshop Name** field selected, click the **Home tab**. In the **Sort & Filter group**, click the **Ascending** button.

e. Scroll down to the bottom of the report, and notice that Access counted the number of records in the report—*26* displays under the Room ID# field. Click this **calculated control**, and then press ⌦. At the top of the report, click the **# Registrations** field name. On

the **Design tab**, in the **Grouping & Totals group**, click the **Totals** button, and then click **Sum**. Scroll down to the bottom of the report, and then click the calculated control. Point to the bottom edge of the control to display the ⬍ pointer, and then double-click to resize the control. The total number of registrations for the workshops that have a wireless connection is *641*.

f. Click the **Page number control**, and then drag the control to the left until the control is visually centered between the left and right margins of the report. At the top of the report, in the **Report Header** section, click the text *3D Workshops with Wireless Connection*. On the **Format tab**, in the **Font group**, change the **Font Size** to **14**, and then click the **label control** again to position the insertion point in the title. Using your own name, add **Lastname Firstname** to the beginning of the title. Click any field in the report. Above and to the left of the **Room ID#** field name, click the **layout selector** ⊞, and then drag it down slightly and to the right until the fields are visually centered between the margins of the report. **Save** the report as **Lastname Firstname 3D Workshops with Wireless Connection Report**

g. On the status bar, click the **Print Preview** button. On the **Print Preview tab**, in the **Zoom group**, click the **Two Pages** button, and notice that the report will print on one page. Create a paper or electronic printout as directed, and then **Close Print Preview**.

h. **Close** the report, and then **Open** the **Navigation Pane**. If necessary, increase the width of the **Navigation Pane** to display the entire report name, and then **Close** the **Navigation Pane**.

2 Click the **Create tab**, and then in the **Reports group**, click the **Blank Report** button. If the Field List pane does not display, on the Design tab, in the Tools group, click the Add Existing Fields button. In the **Field List** pane, click **Show all tables**, and then click the **plus sign** (+) next to **3D Rooms**. Point to the **Room ID#** field, right-click, and then click **Add Field to View**. From the **Field List** pane, drag the **Equipment** field into the blank report—anywhere to the right of *Room ID#*. Double-click the **Internet** field to add it as the third field in the report, and then **Close** the **Field List** pane.

a. On the **Design tab**, in the **Themes group**, click the **Themes** button, and then right-click the **Equity** theme. Click **Apply Theme to This Object Only**.

(Project 3D Workshop Rooms continues on the next page)

Access | Chapter 3

Under the **Equipment** field name, click in any **text box control** that displays *Overhead Projector*. Point to the right edge of the control to display the ⟷ pointer, and then drag to the right until the text in the control displays on one line and there is a small amount of space between the text and the next column.

b. On the **Design tab**, in the **Header/Footer group**, click the **Date and Time** button. Clear the **Include Time** check box, and then click **OK**. In the **Header/Footer group**, click the **Title** button. Using your own name, type **Lastname Firstname 3D Equipment List** and then press (Enter).

c. With the title still selected, on the **Format tab**, in the **Font group**, change the **Font Size** to **14**. On the right edge of the **label control** for the title, double-click to resize the title's label control.

d. Click the **Room ID#** field name to select it. Hold down (Shift), and then click the **Internet** field name to select all three field names. On the **Format tab**, in the **Font group**, click the **Center** button to center the field names over the data in the fields. Change the **Font Color** to **Automatic**, and then apply **Bold**. Click the **layout selector** ⊞, and then drag it down slightly and to the right to visually center the fields between the margins. **Save** the report as **Lastname Firstname 3D Equipment List**

e. On the status bar, click the **Print Preview** button. Create a paper or electronic printout as directed, and then **Close Print Preview**. **Close** the report.

3 Click the **Create tab**, and then in the **Reports group**, click the **Report Wizard** button. Click the **Tables/Queries arrow**, and then click **Table: 3D Workshops**. Double-click the following fields in the order given to move them to the **Selected Fields** list: **Workshop Category, Workshop Name**, and **# Registrations**. Click **Next**.

a. With **Workshop Category** selected, click the **One Field** button to group the report by this field, and then click **Next**. Click the **1 box arrow**, and then click **Workshop Name** to sort the records within each Workshop Category by the Workshop Name. Click the **Summary Options** button. To the right of **# Registrations**, select the **Sum** check box. Under **Show**, be sure that the **Detail and Summary** option button is selected, click **OK**, and then click **Next**.

b. Under **Layout**, be sure that the **Stepped** option button is selected. Under **Orientation**, be sure that **Portrait** is selected, and at the bottom of the **Report Wizard** dialog box, be sure that the **Adjust the field width so all fields fit on a page** check box is selected. Click **Next**, In the **What title do you want for your report?** box, select the existing text, type **Lastname Firstname 3D Registrations by Category Report** and then click **Finish**. **Close Print Preview**, and then on the status bar, click the **Layout View** button.

4 On the **Design tab**, in the **Themes group**, click the **Themes** button, right-click the **Median** theme, and then click **Apply Theme to This Object Only**. Click the title of the report. On the **Format tab**, in the **Font group**, change the **Font Size** to **14**, and then apply **Bold**. Click one of the **Summary for 'Workshop Category' controls**, and then press (Del).

a. On the left side of the report, click one of the **Sum label controls**, and then double-click to select the text inside the control. Type **Total Registrations by Workshop Category** and then press (Enter).

b. At the top of your report, click the **Workshop Category label control**. Hold down (Shift), click the **Workshop Name label control**, and then click the **# Registrations label control** to select all three field names. On the **Format tab**, in the **Font group**, click the **Bold** button.

c. On the status bar, click the **Design View** button. In the **Report Footer section**, click the **Grand Total label control**. Hold down (Shift), and in the **Workshop Category Footer section**, click the **Total Registrations by Workshop Category label control** to select both controls. On the **Arrange tab**, in the **Sizing & Ordering group**, click the **Align** button, and then click **Left** to align the left edges of the two controls.

5 On the status bar, click the **Print Preview** button. In the **Zoom group**, click the **Two Pages** button to view how your report is currently laid out. Notice that at the bottom of Page 1 and the top of Page 2, the records in the **Keeping a Job** category are split between the two pages. Click **Close Print Preview**. On the status bar, click the **Layout View** button.

(Project 3D Workshop Rooms continues on the next page)

Content-Based Assessments

Skills Review | Project **3D** Workshop Rooms (continued)

a. On the **Design tab**, in the **Grouping & Totals group**, click the **Group & Sort** button. In the **Group, Sort, and Total** pane, on the **Group on Workshop Category bar**, click **More**. Click the **do not keep group together on one page arrow**, and then click **keep whole group together on one page**. On the **Design tab**, in the **Grouping & Totals group**, click the **Group & Sort** button to close the **Group, Sort, and Total** pane. **Save** the report.

b. On the status bar, click the **Print Preview** button. Notice that the entire **Workshop Category** grouping

of **Keeping a Job** displays together at the top of Page 2. Create a paper or electronic printout as directed, and then **Close Print Preview**. **Save**, and then **Close** the report. **Open** the **Navigation Pane**, and if necessary, increase the width of the Navigation Pane so that all object names display fully. In **Backstage** view, click **Close Database**, and then click **Exit**. As directed by your instructor, submit your database and the three paper or electronic printouts that are the results of this project.

End You have completed Project 3D ————————————————————

Content-Based Assessments

Apply **3A** skills from these Objectives:

1. Create and Use a Form to Add and Delete Records
2. Create a Form by Using the Form Wizard
3. Modify a Form in Layout View and in Design View
4. Filter Records

Mastering Access | Project **3E** Raffle Sponsors

In the following Mastering Access project, you will assist Alina Ngo, Dean of Student Services at the Central Campus of Capital Cities Community College, in using her database to track raffle items and sponsors for the New Student Orientation sessions. Your completed forms will look similar to Figure 3.51.

Project Files

For Project 3E, you will need the following file:

a03E_Raffle_Sponsors

You will save your database as:

Lastname_Firstname_3E_Raffle_Sponsors

Project Results

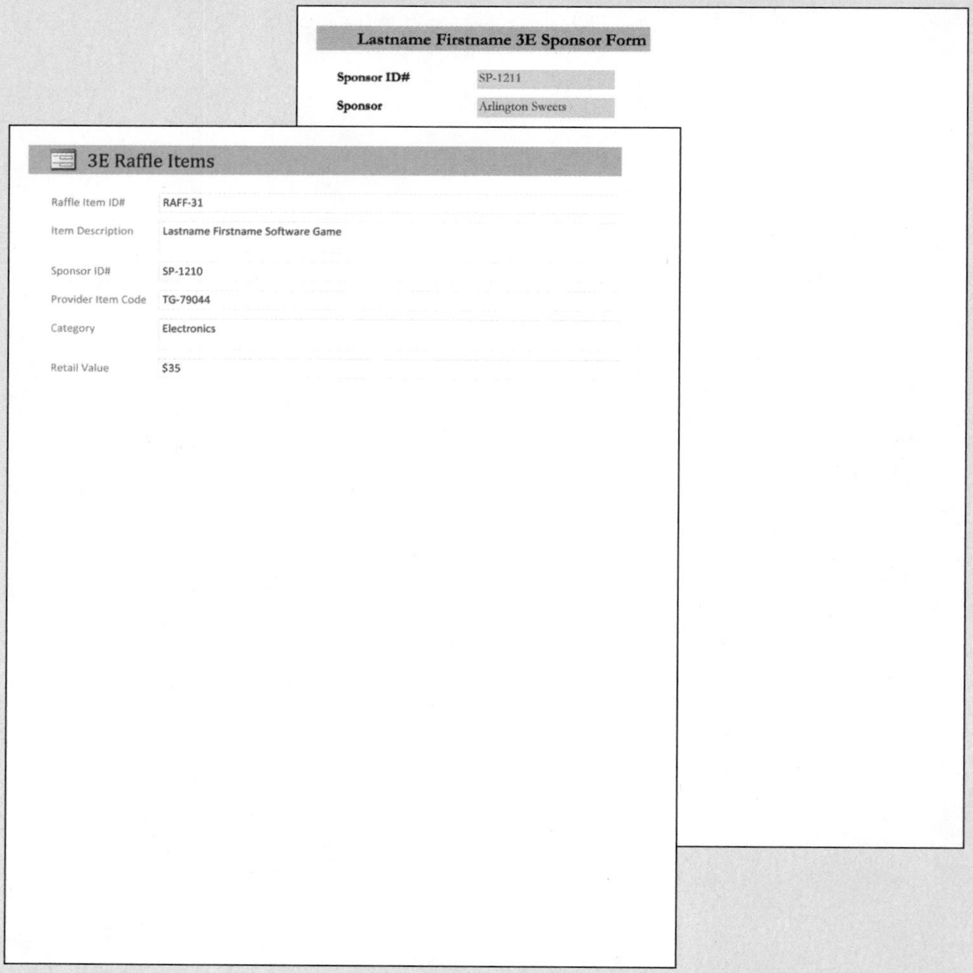

Lastname Firstname 3E Sponsor Form

Sponsor ID#	SP-1211
Sponsor	Arlington Sweets

3E Raffle Items

Raffle Item ID#	RAFF-31
Item Description	Lastname Firstname Software Game
Sponsor ID#	SP-1210
Provider Item Code	TG-79044
Category	Electronics
Retail Value	$35

Figure 3.51

(Project 3E Raffle Sponsors continues on the next page)

Content-Based Assessments

Mastering Access | Project 3E Raffle Sponsors (continued)

1 **Start** Access. From your student data files, **Open** the **a03E_Raffle_Sponsors** database. Save the database in your **Access Chapter 3** folder as **Lastname_Firstname_3E_Raffle_Sponsors** and then enable the content. View the relationship between the 3E Sponsors table and the 3E Raffle Items table. *One* sponsor can provide *many* raffle items for the New Student Orientation sessions.

2 Based on the **3E Raffle Items** table, use the **Form** tool to create a form. **Save** the form as **Lastname Firstname 3E Raffle Item Form** and then switch to **Form** view. Add the new record as shown in **Table 1**, using your own name in the **Item Description** field.

3 Display the first record, and, if necessary, click in the Raffle Item ID# field. Use the **Find** button to display the record for the **Raffle Item ID#** of **RAFF-06**, and then **Delete** the record. Display the record you entered for **RAFF-31**, and then **Print** the **Selected Record**, changing the column width to **7.5"** or create an electronic printout. **Close** the form, saving changes if prompted.

4 Based on the **3E Sponsors** table, use the **Form Wizard** tool to create a form. Include the following fields in the order given: **Sponsor**, **Contact Last Name**, **Contact First Name**, and **Phone Number**. Use a **Columnar** layout, and as the title type **Lastname Firstname 3E Sponsor Form**

5 In **Layout** view, apply the **Stacked** layout to all of the controls, and then apply the **Couture** theme to this object only. For the title of the form, change the **Font Size** to **16**, apply **Bold**, and change the **Font Color** to **Brown, Accent 6, Darker 50%**. In **Design** view, increase the height of the **Form Footer** section to approximately **0.5 inch**. In the **Form Footer** section and using your own name, add a **label control** that displays **Created by Lastname Firstname** For the **label control**, change the **Font Color** to **Brown, Text 2**, apply **Bold**, and then adjust the control to fit the text in the control.

6 **Save** the form, and then switch to **Layout** view. Display the **Field List** pane, and then add the **Sponsor ID#** field to the form above the **Sponsor** field. **Close** the **Field List** pane, and then move the **Contact First Name** controls directly above the **Contact Last Name** controls. Display **Record 5**—this record's Sponsor name is the longest entry of all records. Decrease the width of the **Sponsor text box control** until there is approximately **1 inch** between *Inc* and the right edge of the control. **Save** the form.

7 Select all five **text box controls**, set the **Background Color** to **Brown, Accent 1, Lighter 80%**. Select all of the **label controls**, set the **Font Color** to **Brown, Text 2**, and then apply **Bold**. With the controls selected, display the **Property Sheet**. For the **label controls**, set the **Width** to **1.75** Select all of the **label controls** and **text box controls**, set the **Font Size** to **12**, and the **Height** property to **0.25** In the **Form Header** and **Form Foote**r sections, select the **label controls** with the title and your name. Set the **Left** property to **0.5**

8 **Close** the **Property Sheet**, **Save** the form, and then switch to **Form** view. Using your first name and last name, add the record as shown in **Table 2**, being sure to use the Tab key to move among fields and to save the record.

9 Display the record you just added and then **Print** the **Selected Record**, or create an electronic printout as directed. **Close** the form.

10 Open your **3E Raffle Item Form** object. Using the **Advanced Filter/Sort** tool, create a filter that displays eight records with a **Category** of **Clothing** or **Dining** After verifying that eight records display, use the **Toggle Filter** button to display all 30 records. **Save** the form.

11 **Close** all open objects. **Open** the **Navigation Pane**, and, if necessary, increase the width of the **Navigation Pane** to display fully all of the object names. Display **Backstage** view. Click **Close Database**, and then click **Exit**. As directed by your instructor, submit your database and the two paper or electronic printouts that are the results of this project.

Table 1

Raffle Item ID#	Item Description	Sponsor ID#	Provider Item Code	Category	Retail Value
RAFF-31	**Lastname Firstname Software Game**	**SP-1210**	**TG-79044**	**Electronics**	**35**

(Return to Step 3)

Table 2

Sponsor ID#	Sponsor	Contact First Name	Contact Last Name	Phone Number
SP-1211	**Arlington Sweets**	**Firstname**	**Lastname**	**(703) 555-5355**

- - - ➤ (Return to Step 9)

End **You have completed Project 3E**

Apply **3B** skills from these Objectives:

5 Create a Report by Using the Report Tool

6 Create Reports by Using the Blank Report Tool and the Report Wizard

7 Modify the Design of a Report

8 Print a Report and Keep Data Together

Mastering Access | Project **3F** Contractor Services

In the following Mastering Access project, you will assist Roger Lockheart, Director of Facilities at the Jefferson Campus of Capital Cities Community College, in using a database to track facility and contractor services for an open house for prospective college students. Your completed reports will look similar to Figure 3.52.

Project Files

For Project 3F, you will need the following file:

a03F_Contractor_Services

You will save your database as:

Lastname_Firstname_3F_Contractor_Services

Project Results

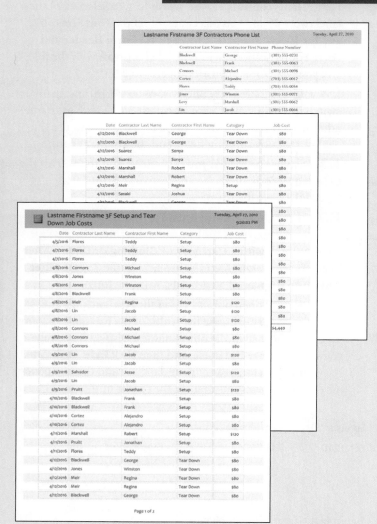
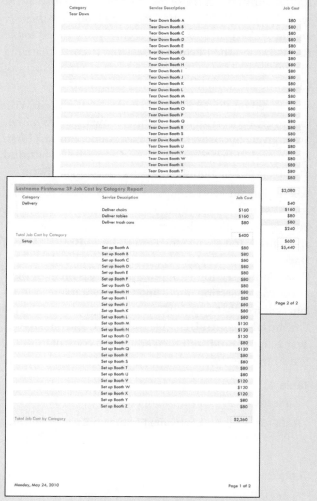

Figure 3.52

(Project 3F Contractor Services continues on the next page)

Content-Based Assessments

Mastering Access | Project **3F** Contractor Services (continued)

1 **Start** Access. From your student files, **Open** the **a03F_Contractor_Services** database. Save the database in your **Access Chapter 3** folder as **Lastname_Firstname_3F_ Contractor_Services** and then enable the content. View the relationship between the 3F Contractors table and the 3F Facility Services table. *One* contractor can provide *many* facility services. **Close** the **Relationships** window. Based on the **3F Setup and Tear Down Job Costs** query, use the **Report** tool to create a report, and then **Close** the **Navigation Pane.** This query answers the question *What is the Date, Job ID, Contractor ID, Contractor Last Name, Contractor First Name, Category, and Job Cost of setup and tear down jobs?*

2 Apply the **Waveform** theme to this object only. **Delete** the **Job ID** and **Contractor ID** fields from the report. Decrease the widths of the **Contractor Last Name, Contractor First Name,** and **Category** fields until there is approximately **0.25 to 0.5 inch** of space between the longest entry in each field—including the field name— and the right edge of each control. Be sure that there is enough space for *Tear Down* to display on one line. **Sort** the **Date** field in ascending order.

Scroll down to the bottom of the report, and increase the height of the **calculated control** that displays *$4,440*. Drag the **page number control** to the left to visually center it between the margins of the report. For the title, change the **Font Size** to **16**, and then using your last name and first name, add **Lastname Firstname** to the beginning of the title. Using the **layout selector**, visually center the fields between the left and right margins. **Save** the report as **Lastname Firstname 3F Setup and Tear Down Job Costs Report** and then create a paper or electronic printout as directed—two pages will print. **Close** the report. **Open** the **Navigation Pane,** and increase the width of the **Navigation Pane** to display the entire report name. **Close** the **Navigation Pane.**

3 Use the **Blank Report** tool to create a report based on the **3F Contractors** table. Add the fields to the report in the order given: **Contractor Last Name, Contractor First Name,** and **Phone Number. Close** the **Field List** pane. Apply the **Equity** theme to this object only. Increase the width of the **Contractor Last Name** field so that the field name displays fully. Add the **Date** to the Report Header section—do not include the time. Add a **Title** of **Lastname Firstname 3F Contractors Phone List** to the report, and change the **Font Size** to **14**. Decrease the width of the

title's **label control** to fit the text and to move the date control to the left within the right margin. Apply **Bold** to the three field names. **Sort** the **Contractor Last Name** field in **Ascending** order. Using the **layout selector**, visually center the fields between the report margins. **Save** the report as **Lastname Firstname 3F Contractors Phone List** and then create a paper or electronic printout as directed. **Close Print Preview,** and then **Close** the report.

4 Use the **Report Wizard** to create a report based on the **3F Facility Services** table. Select the following fields in the order given: **Category, Service Description,** and **Job Cost. Group** the report by **Category, Sort** by **Service Description,** and **Sum** the **Job Cost** field. Select the **Stepped** layout and **Portrait** orientation. For the report title, type **Lastname Firstname 3F Job Cost by Category Report** and then switch to **Layout** view.

5 Apply the **Median** theme to this object only. For the title, change the **Font Size** to **14**, and apply **Bold. Delete** the **Summary for 'Category' controls.** Scroll down to the bottom of the report, and click the **text box control** that displays *Wireless network for laptop lane.* Decrease the width of the control until there is approximately **0.25 inch** of space between the end of the word *lane* and the right edge of the label control. At the bottom of the report, for the last record *Wireless network for laptop lane,* to the right, click the **text box control** that displays #—the number or pound sign displays because the text box control is not wide enough to display the entire value. Hold down Shift, and immediately below the selected control, click the **Sum calculated control,** and then under that, click the **Grand Total calculated control.** Drag the left edge of the three selected controls to the left approximately **0.5 inch** to display the amounts fully. **Save** the report.

6 Change the text in the **Sum label control** to **Total Job Cost by Category** and then at the top of the report, select the three **field names,** and apply **Bold. Save** the report.

7 Switch to **Design** view. Click the **label control** that displays *Total Job Cost by Category,* and then align the left edge of the control with the left edge of the **label control** that displays *Grand Total.* **Save** the report.

8 Display the report in **Print Preview** in the **Two Pages** arrangement, examine how the groupings break across pages, **Close Print Preview,** and then switch to **Layout** view. Display the **Group, Sort, and Total** pane, and then select **keep whole group together on one page.** Close the

(Project 3F Contractor Services continues on the next page)

Access | Chapter 3

Mastering Access | Project **3F** Contractor Services (continued)

Group, **Sort, and Total** pane. Display the report in **Print Preview** in the **Two Pages** arrangement, and then notice that the entire **Tear Down** grouping displays on Page 2. **Save** the report.

 Create a paper or electronic printout as directed, **Close Print Preview**, and then **Close** the report. **Open**

the **Navigation Pane**, and then display **Backstage** view. Click **Close Database**, and then click **Exit**. As directed by your instructor, submit your database and the three paper or electronic printouts that are the results of this project.

End **You have completed Project 3F** ⎯⎯⎯⎯⎯⎯⎯⎯⎯⎯⎯⎯⎯⎯⎯⎯⎯⎯

Content-Based Assessments

- **1** Create and Use a Form to Add and Delete Records
- **2** Create a Form by Using the Form Wizard
- **3** Modify a Form in Layout View and in Design View
- **4** Filter Records
- **5** Create a Report by Using the Report Tool
- **6** Create Reports by Using the Blank Report Tool and the Report Wizard
- **7** Modify the Design of a Report
- **8** Print a Report and Keep Data Together

Mastering Access | Project **3G** Career Books

In the following Mastering Access project, you will assist Teresa Johnson, Head Librarian at the Capital Campus of Capital Cities Community College, in using a database to track publishers and book titles to assist students in finding employment. Your completed forms and reports will look similar to Figure 3.53.

Project Files

For Project 3G, you will need the following file:

a03G_Career_Books

You will save your database as:

Lastname_Firstname_3G_Career_Books

Project Results

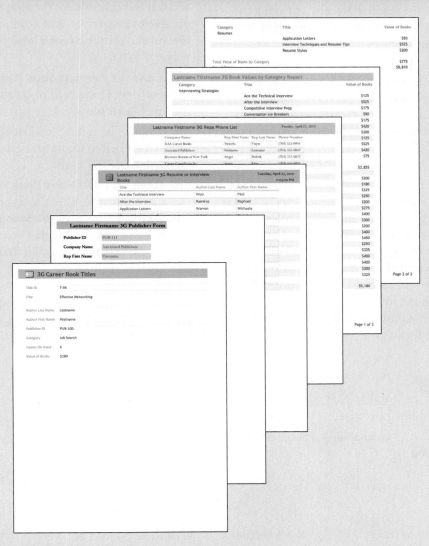

Figure 3.53

(Project 3G Career Books continues on the next page)

Content-Based Assessments

Mastering Access | Project **3G** Career Books (continued)

1 **Start** Access. From your student files, open the **a03G_Career_Books** database. **Save** the database in your **Access Chapter 3** folder as **Lastname_Firstname_3G_Career_Books** and then enable the content. Review the relationship between the 3G Publishers table and the 3G Career Book Titles table. *One* publisher can publish *many* books.

2 Based on the **3G Career Book Titles** table, use the **Form** tool to create a form. Switch to **Form** view, and then using your own name, add the record as shown in **Table 1**.

3 **Save** the form as **Lastname Firstname 3G Career Book Form** and then display the first record. Use the **Find** button to display the record for the **Title ID** of **T-18**, and then **Delete** the record. Display the record you entered for **T-34**, and then **Print** the **Selected Record**, changing the column width to **7.5"** or create an electronic printout. **Close** the form, saving changes if prompted.

4 Use the **Form Wizard** to create a form based on the **3G Publishers** table. Include the following fields: **Company Name**, **Rep Last Name**, **Rep First Name**, **Job Title**, and **Phone Number**. Use a **Columnar** layout, and as the title, type **Lastname Firstname 3G Publisher Form**

5 In **Layout** view, select all of the controls, and then apply the **Stacked** layout. Apply the **Couture** theme to this object only. For the title, change the **Font Size** to **16**, apply **Bold**, and change the **Font Color** to **Brown, Accent 6, Darker 50%**—in the last column, the last color. In **Design** view, increase the height of the **Form Footer** section approximately **0.5 inch**. In the **Form Footer** section, add a **label control** that displays **Created by Lastname Firstname** and then change the **Font Color** to **Brown, Text 2**—in the fourth column, the first color. Apply **Bold**, and then adjust the control to fit the data in the control. **Save** the form.

6 In **Layout** view, display the **Field List** pane, and then add the **Publisher ID** field to the form above the **Company Name** field. **Close** the **Field List** pane. Move the **Rep First Name** field directly above the **Rep Last Name** field. Click the **Job Title text box control**, and then drag the right edge of the control to the left until there is approximately **1 inch** of space between *Representative* and the right edge of the control. **Save** the form.

7 Select all of the **text box controls**, set the **Background Color** to **Brown, Accent 1, Lighter 80%**—in the fifth column, the second color. Select all of the **label controls**. Set the **Font Color** to **Brown, Text 2**, apply **Bold**, and then set the **Width** property to **1.5** Select all of the **label controls** and **text box controls**, set the **Font Size** to **12**, and then set the **Height** property to **0.25** For the **form header label control** and the **form footer label control**, set the **Left** property to **0.5**

8 **Close** the **Property Sheet**, **Save** the form, and switch to **Form** view. Using your own name, add a new record as shown in **Table 2**.

9 Display the record you just added and then **Print** the **Selected Record** or create an electronic printout as directed. **Close** the form.

10 **Open** your **3G Career Book Form** object. Using the **Filter By Form** tool, filter the records to display the **Category** of **Resumes** or **Job Search**. Twenty books meet the criteria. Click the **Toggle Filter** button to display all 31 records. **Save** the form, and then **Close** the form.

11 Use the **Report** tool to create a report based on the **3G Resume or Interview Books** query. Apply the **Waveform** theme to this object only. **Delete** the **Publisher ID**, **Category**, and **Company Name** fields from the report.

Table 1

Title ID	Title	Author Last Name	Author First Name	Publisher ID	Category	Copies On Hand	Value of Books
T-34	**Effective Networking**	**Lastname**	**Firstname**	**PUB-100**	**Job Search**	**6**	**180**

(Return to Step 3)

Table 2

Publisher ID	Company Name	Rep First Name	Rep Last Name	Job Title	Phone Number
PUB-111	**Associated Publishers**	**Firstname**	**Lastname**	**Sales Associate**	**(703) 555-0857**

(Return to Step 9)

(Project 3G Career Books continues on the next page)

Mastering Access | Project **3G** Career Books (continued)

Decrease the widths of the **Author Last Name** and **Author First Name** fields so that there is approximately **0.5 inch** between the word *Name* in the field name and the right edge of the label controls. Increase the width of the **Title** field until each title displays on one line. **Sort** the **Title** field in **Ascending** order.

Click the **Title** field name, and then on the **Design tab**, click the **Totals** button. Add a control that counts the number of records, and then increase the height of the control so that *14* displays fully in the calculated control. Drag the **page number control** to the left to visually center it between the report margins. For the title of the report, change the **Font Size** to **14**, and then using your own name, add **Lastname Firstname** to the beginning of the title. Using the **layout selector** ⊞, visually center the fields between the left and right margins. **Save** the report as **Lastname Firstname 3G Resume or Interview Books Report** and then create a paper or electronic printout as directed. **Close** the report.

12 Use the **Blank Report** tool to create a report based on the **3G Publishers** table. Add the following fields to the report in the order listed: **Company Name**, **Rep First Name**, **Rep Last Name**, and **Phone Number**. **Close** the **Field List** pane, and then apply the **Equity** theme to this object only. Increase the width of the **Company Name** field so that the text in each record displays on one line. Add the **Date** to the report, add a **Title** of **Lastname Firstname 3G Reps Phone List** For the title, change the **Font Size** to **14**, and then adjust the width of the title's label control, being sure that the date displays within the right margin of the report. Apply **Bold** to all of the field names, and then **Center** the field names over the data. **Sort** the **Company Name** field in **Ascending** order. Using the **layout selector**, visually center the fields between the left and right margins. **Save** the report as **Lastname Firstname 3G Reps Phone List** and then create a paper or electronic printout as directed. **Close** the report.

13 Use the **Report Wizard** to create a report based on the **3G Career Book Titles** table, Select the following fields: **Category**, **Title**, and **Value of Books**. **Group** the report by **Category**, **Sort** by **Title**, and **Sum** the **Value of Books** field. Select the **Stepped** layout, and **Portrait** orientation as the report title, type **Lastname Firstname 3G Book Values by Category Report** and then switch to **Layout** view.

14 Apply the **Opulent Theme** to this object only. For the title of the report, change the **Font Size** to **14** and then apply **Bold**. **Delete** the **Summary for 'Category' controls**. Scroll down to the bottom of the report, and in the **Title** field, click the **text box control** that displays *Interview Techniques and Resume Tips*, which is the longest entry in the field. Point to the right edge of the **text box control**, and then drag the pointer to the left until there is approximately **0.25 inch** between *Tips* and the right edge of the text box control. Scroll to the top of the report, and then click in the **Value of Books label control**. Double-click the left edge of the **label control** to increase the width of the label control and to display fully the text in the label control. **Save** the report.

15 Scroll down to the bottom of the report, and then on the right side of the report, increase the width of the **Sum calculated controls** and the **Grand Total calculated control** so that the entire figure, including the dollar sign, displays— the Grand Total is *$8,810*. Change the text in the **Sum label controls** to **Total Value of Books by Category** and then increase the width of the **Grand Total label control** to display fully the text in the control. **Save** the report.

16 At the top of the report, apply **Bold** to the three field names. Select any of the **Title text box controls**. Display the **Property Sheet**, set the **Height to 0.25**. **Close** the **Property Sheet**. In **Design** view, align the left edge of the **label control** that displays *Total Value of Books by Category* with the left edge of the **label control** that displays *Grand Total*. **Save** the report.

17 Display the report in **Print Preview** in the **Two Pages** arrangement, examine how the groupings break across pages, and then **Close Print Preview**. In **Layout** view, display the **Group, Sort, and Total** pane, and then click **keep whole group together on one page**. Close the **Group, Sort, and Total** pane. **Save** the report. Display the report in **Print Preview** in the **Two Pages** arrangement, and then notice that the entire **Resumes** grouping displays on Page 2. Create a paper or electronic printout as directed, and then **Close Print Preview**.

18 **Close** the report, and then **Open** the **Navigation Pane**. If necessary, increase the width of the Navigation Pane to display all of the object names fully. In **Backstage** view, click **Close Database**, and then click **Exit**. As directed by your instructor, submit your database and the five paper or electronic printouts that are the results of this project.

End **You have completed Project 3G**

Access | Chapter 3

Content-Based Assessments

GO! Fix It | Project **3H** Resume Workshops

Project Files

For Project 3H, you will need the following file:

a03H_Resume_Workshops

You will save your database as:

Lastname_Firstname_3H_Resume_Workshops

In this project, you will make corrections to and update an Access database that stores information about resume workshops that are scheduled for students. Start Access, navigate to the student files that accompany this textbook, and then open the a03H_Resume_Workshops database. Save the database in your Access Chapter 3 folder as **Lastname_Firstname_3H_Resume_Workshops** and enable the content.

To complete the project, you should know that:

- In the Participant Form object, all the field heights should be the same, and your name and 3H should display in the title. Create a filter that finds records where the Workshop Fee is $35—five records meet the criteria. Toggle the filter off, and then save the form. In the first record, enter your first name and last name in the appropriate fields. Then, as directed, create a paper or electronic printout of only this record.

- In the Resume Workshop Form object, in the header, change Lastname Firstname to your own last name and first name. Add a label control to the Form Footer section. Using your own name, type **Created by Lastname Firstname** and then bold the text. Save the form. Find the record for Workshop ID# R-002, and then, as directed, create a paper or electronic printout of only this record.

- In the Participant Input Form object, you should adjust the height and width of the controls so that the text in the controls displays on one line. The font sizes for the label controls and text box controls should match. Add your name and 3H to the title, and be sure that the title displays on one line. For the title, change the font size so that the title does not extend to the right of the text box controls beneath it. In the Form Footer section, create a label typing **Created by Lastname Firstname** and then bold the text in the label. Add a light blue background color to the text box controls, and then save the form. Display the record with your name and then, as directed, create a paper or electronic printout of only this record.

- For the Participant Fees Report, apply the Opulent theme to this object only. Add a title to the report that includes your name and 3H. Adjust the font size and the width of the label control, and be sure that the date control displays within the right margin of the report. Center the data in the Workshop ID text box controls. Center the layout between the margins, and add a total for the Workshop Fee column that sums the fees. Sort the Date Fee Received field in ascending order. Save the report, and then create a paper or electronic printout as directed.

- In the Participants by Workshop Name report, apply the Equity theme to this object only. Add your name and 3H to the title, and reduce the Font Size. Adjust controls so that all of the data displays fully. Delete the Summary for 'Workshop ID#' control. Change the text in the Sum label controls so that they reflect what is being summed. Align the left edges of the Sum and Grand Total label controls. Add the date to the Report Header section. Be sure that the groupings are kept together when printed. Create a paper or electronic printout as directed.

End You have completed Project 3H ——————————————

Content-Based Assessments

GO! Make It | Project 3I Study Abroad

Project Files

For Project 3I, you will need the following file:

a03I_Study_Abroad

You will save your database as:

Lastname_Firstname_3I_Study_Abroad

From the student files that accompany this textbook, open the a03I_Study_Abroad database, and then save the database in your Access Chapter 3 folder as **Lastname_Firstname_3I_Study_Abroad** Using the Blank Report tool, create the report shown in Figure 3.54. Apply the Slipstream theme, and then create a paper or electronic printout as directed.

Project Results

Lastname Firstname 3I Trip Dates and Cost Report			
Destination	**Cost of Trip**	**Departure Date**	**Return Date**
Costa Rica	$3,000	2/15/2016	2/25/2016
Egypt	$4,300	2/16/2016	2/26/2016
Great Britain	$6,000	3/22/2016	4/4/2016
Greece	$6,000	5/5/2016	5/15/2016
Ireland	$5,000	5/23/2016	6/2/2016
Italy	$4,500	5/1/2016	5/8/2016
Mexico	$2,000	2/8/2016	2/18/2016
Panama	$2,900	4/30/2016	5/5/2016
Paris	$7,580	5/6/2016	5/17/2016
Rome	$7,250	5/2/2016	5/12/2016
Singapore	$5,000	4/12/2016	4/20/2016
South Africa	$4,780	3/3/2016	3/10/2016
Switzerland	$5,400	2/25/2016	3/3/2016
Tokyo	$4,950	3/4/2016	3/12/2016
Tuscan Valley	$5,600	2/4/2016	2/14/2016

Figure 3.54

End You have completed Project 3I

Access | Chapter 3

Content-Based Assessments

GO! Solve It | Project 3J Job Offers

Project Files

For Project 3J, you will need the following file:

a03J_Job_Offers

You will save your database as:

Lastname_Firstname_3J_Job_Offers

From the student files that accompany this textbook, open the a03J_Job_Offers database file, save the database in your Access Chapter 3 folder as **Lastname_Firstname_3J_Job_Offers** and then enable the content.

Kevin Bodine, coordinator of the Student Employment Office, would like one form and two reports created from the Job Offers database. Using the skills you have practiced in this chapter, create an attractive form that can be used to update student candidate records. Using your own information, add a new record as Student ID# **9091246** with a College Major of **Business** and a Phone Number of **(703) 555-9876** Leave the Internship Completed field blank. Save the form as **Lastname Firstname 3J Candidate Update Form** and then create a paper or electronic printout of only your record.

Mr. Bodine wants an attractive report listing the Organization Name and the Offer Amount of each job offered to a student, grouped by the Student ID#, sorted in ascending order by the Organization Name. The Offer Amount field should display the maximum amount offered. Create and save the report as **Lastname Firstname 3J Job Offers by Student ID# Report** and then create a paper or electronic printout as directed.

Mr. Bodine also wants an attractive report of the names, college majors, and phone numbers of the student candidates, grouped by college majors and then sorted by the Last Name field. Save the report as **Lastname Firstname 3J Student Candidates by Major Report** and then create a paper or electronic printout as directed.

		Performance Level		
		Exemplary You consistently applied the relevant skills	**Proficient** You sometimes, but not always, applied the relevant skills	**Developing** You rarely or never applied the relevant skills
Performance Criteria	Create 3J Candidate Update Form	Form created with correct fields in easy-to-follow format and record entered for student.	Form created with no more than two missing elements.	Form created with more than two missing elements.
	Create 3J Job Offers by Student ID# Report	Report created with correct fields, grouped and sorted correctly, and in an attractive format.	Report created with no more than two missing elements.	Report created with more than two missing elements.
	Create 3J Student Candidates by Major Report	Report created with correct fields, grouped and sorted correctly, and in an attractive format.	Report created with no more than two missing elements.	Report created with more than two missing elements.

End You have completed Project 3J ————————

Content-Based Assessments

GO! Solve It | Project **3K** Financial Aid

Project Files

For Project 3K, you will need the following file:

a03K_Financial_Aid

You will save your database as:

Lastname_Firstname_3K_Financial_Aid

From the student files that accompany this textbook, open the a03K_Financial_Aid database file, and then save the database in your Access Chapter 3 folder as **Lastname_Firstname_3K_Financial_Aid**

Marguerite Simons, the Financial Aid Director, wants an attractive, easy-to-follow form that can be used to update the Financial Aid Students table. Using your first name and last name, add a new record with the following information:

Student ID#	Financial Aid ID	Home Phone#	College E-mail
1472589	FA-07	(703) 555-3874	ns589@capccc.edu

Save the form as **Lastname Firstname 3K FA Student Update Form** and then create a paper or electronic printout of only your record.

Ms. Simons also wants an attractively formatted report listing the Award Name, the Student ID# and the Award Amount for financial aid offered to students, grouped by the Award name and sorted in ascending order by the Student ID# field (Hint: Use data from both tables). The Award Amount should be summed. Save the report as **Lastname Firstname 3K Amount by Award Name Report** and then create a paper or electronic printout of the report.

		Performance Level	
	Exemplary You consistently applied the relevant skills	**Proficient** You sometimes, but not always, applied the relevant skills	**Developing** You rarely or never applied the relevant skills
Create 3K FA Student Update Form	Form created with correct fields in easy-to-follow format and record entered for student.	Form created with no more than two missing elements.	Form created with more than two missing elements.
Create 3K Amount by Award Name Report	Report created with correct fields, grouped and sorted correctly, and in an attractive format.	Report created with no more than two missing elements.	Report created with more than two missing elements.

Performance Criteria

End **You have completed Project 3K** ——————————

Outcomes-Based Assessments

Rubric

The following outcomes-based assessments are *open-ended assessments*. That is, there is no specific correct result; your result will depend on your approach to the information provided. Make *Professional Quality* your goal. Use the following scoring rubric to guide you in *how* to approach the problem, and then to evaluate *how well* your approach solves the problem.

The *criteria*—Software Mastery, Content, Format and Layout, and Process—represent the knowledge and skills you have gained that you can apply to solving the problem. The *levels of performance*—Professional Quality, Approaching Professional Quality, or Needs Quality Improvements—help you and your instructor evaluate your result.

	Your completed project is of Professional Quality if you:	Your completed project is Approaching Professional Quality if you:	Your completed project Needs Quality Improvements if you:
1-Software Mastery	Choose and apply the most appropriate skills, tools, and features and identify efficient methods to solve the problem.	Choose and apply some appropriate skills, tools, and features, but not in the most efficient manner.	Choose inappropriate skills, tools, or features, or are inefficient in solving the problem.
2-Content	Construct a solution that is clear and well organized, contains content that is accurate, appropriate to the audience and purpose, and is complete. Provide a solution that contains no errors in spelling, grammar, or style.	Construct a solution in which some components are unclear, poorly organized, inconsistent, or incomplete. Misjudge the needs of the audience. Have some errors in spelling, grammar, or style, but the errors do not detract from comprehension.	Construct a solution that is unclear, incomplete, or poorly organized; contains some inaccurate or inappropriate content; and contains many errors in spelling, grammar, or style. Do not solve the problem.
3-Format and Layout	Format and arrange all elements to communicate information and ideas, clarify function, illustrate relationships, and indicate relative importance.	Apply appropriate format and layout features to some elements, but not others. Overuse features, causing minor distraction.	Apply format and layout that does not communicate information or ideas clearly. Do not use format and layout features to clarify function, illustrate relationships, or indicate relative importance. Use available features excessively, causing distraction.
4-Process	Use an organized approach that integrates planning, development, self-assessment, revision, and reflection.	Demonstrate an organized approach in some areas, but not others; or, use an insufficient process of organization throughout.	Do not use an organized approach to solve the problem.

Outcomes-Based Assessments

Apply a combination of the 3A and 3B skills.

GO! Think | Project 3L Food Services

Project Files

For Project 3L, you will need the following file:

a03L_Food_Services

You will save your database as:

Lastname_Firstname_3L_Food_Services

Use the skills you have practiced in this chapter to assist Luciano Perez, the Hospitality Director, in creating a form and a report to assist him with the staff scheduling of food services for a two-day student orientation workshop. Create an attractive form that he can use to update the 3L Staff table saving the form as **Lastname Firstname 3L Staff Update Form** Using your own name, add a new record with the following information:

Staff ID: **STAFF-1119** Phone Number: **(703) 555-0845** Title: **Server**

Create a paper or electronic printout of only your record. Create an attractive, easy-to-read report for calling staff members when the schedule changes. Name the report **Lastname Firstname 3L Staff Phone List** and then create a paper or electronic printout of the report as directed.

End You have completed Project 3L ————————————————

Apply a combination of the 3A and 3B skills.

GO! Think | Project 3M Donors and Gifts

Project Files

For Project 3M, you will need the following file:

a03M_Donors_Gifts

You will save your database as:

Lastname_Firstname_3M_Donors_Gifts

Use the skills you have practiced in this chapter to assist the Dean of Information Technology in using her database to create attractive forms and reports. The Dean would like an attractive form that would enable her work study student to enter the information in the Donors table. Create and save a form naming it **Lastname Firstname 3M Donor Update Form** Using your own name, add a new record with the following information:

Donor ID: **DNR-1212** Donor: **Lastname Foundation** Phone Number: **(703) 555-6091**

Create a paper or electronic printout of only your record. Create a donor list with the donor, contact names, and phone numbers so that the Dean can call the donors to thank them for donating gifts that will be distributed during the high school recruitment tours. Save the report as **Lastname Firstname 3M Donor Phone List** and then create a paper or electronic printout as directed.

Create a report grouped by Category and sorted by Item Description that includes the Retail Value totals and a Grand Total of the Retail Value of the gift items. Create a page footer control that displays **Created by Lastname Firstname** and then save the report as **Lastname Firstname 3M Gift Amounts by Category Report** and then create a paper or electronic printout as directed.

End You have completed Project 3M ————————————————

Access | Chapter 3

Outcomes-Based Assessments

Apply a combination of the **3A** and **3B** skills

You and GO! | Project **3N** Personal Inventory

Project Files

For Project 3N, you will need the following file:

Lastname_Firstname_2N_Personal_Inventory (your file from Chapter 2)

You will save your database as:

Lastname_Firstname_3N_Personal_Inventory

If you have your database from Project 2N, save it in your Access Chapter 3 folder as **Lastname_Firstname_3N_Personal_Inventory** If you do not have the database from Project 2N, create a new database, saving it in your Access Chapter 3 folder with the same name given above. In the database, create one table with at least 18 records. Include fields such as item, room location, value, and date of purchase. Your table should have items stored in several locations.

Using the table, create an attractive form, naming it **Lastname Firstname 3N Inventory Update Form** Using the form, enter at least three records and then create a paper or electronic printout of one of the new records. Using the table, create an attractive report including fields for the room location, item name, and value or purchase price of the item—you may add more fields if you desire. Group the report by the room location, and sort by the value or purchase price of the item, summarizing the values. Name the report **Lastname Firstname 3N Room Values Report** and then create a paper or electronic printout as directed.

End **You have completed Project 3N**

Apply a combination of the **1A** and **1B** skills.

GO! Collaborate | Project **3O** Bell Orchid Hotels Group Running Case

This project relates to the **Bell Orchid Hotels**. Your instructor may assign this group case project to your class. If your instructor assigns this project, he or she will provide you with information and instructions to work as part of a group. The group will apply the skills gained thus far to help the Bell Orchid Hotels achieve their business goals.

End **You have completed Project 3O**

Business Running Case

Razvan CHIRNOAGA/Shutterstock

This project relates to **Front Range Action Sports**, which is one of the country's largest retailers of sports gear and outdoor recreation merchandise. The company has large retail stores in Colorado, Washington, Oregon, California, and New Mexico, in addition to a growing online business. Major merchandise categories include fishing, camping, rock climbing, winter sports, action sports, water sports, team sports, racquet sports, fitness, golf, apparel, and footwear.

In this project, you will apply skills you practiced from the Objectives in Access Chapters 1 through 3. You will create a database for Frank Osei, Vice President of Finance, that contains inventory and supplier information. In addition, you will create queries that answer specific questions relating to the inventory items and suppliers, forms for entering and updating information, and reports. Your printed results will look similar to Figure 1.1.

Project Files

For Project BRC1, you will need the following files:

New blank Access database
aBRC1_Inventory (Excel workbook)
aBRC1_Suppliers (Excel workbook)

You will save your database as:

Lastname_Firstname_BRC1_Inventory_Suppliers

Project Results

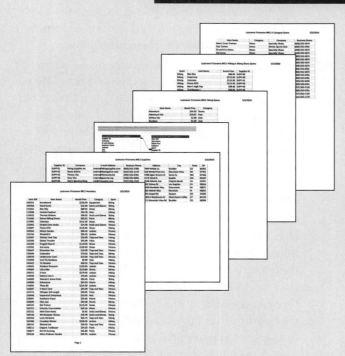

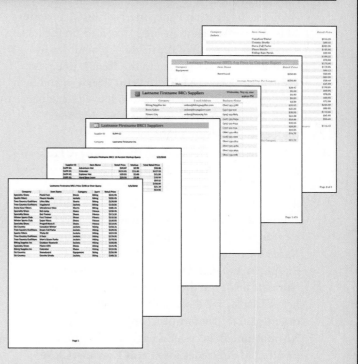

Figure 1.1

Business Running Case 1: Includes Objectives from Access Chapters 1-3

Business Running Case

Front Range Action Sports

1 **Start** Access to create a new **Blank database**. In the location where you are storing your projects, create a new folder named **Front Range Action Sports** or navigate to this folder if you have already created it. **Save** the database as **Lastname_Firstname_BRC1_Inventory_Suppliers**

a. Rename the **ID** field to **Item ID#** and change the **Data Type** to **Text**. Then create the fields as shown in **Table 1**.

b. Enter the two records as shown in **Table 2**.

c. **Close** the table, **Save** it as **Lastname Firstname BRC1 Inventory** and then increase the width of the **Navigation Pane** to display the entire table name. On the **External Data tab**, in the **Import & Link group**, click the **Excel** button. Navigate to your student files, double-click **aBRC1_Inventory**, and then **Append a copy of the records** to the **BRC1 Inventory** table. From the **Navigation Pane**, open the **BRC1 Inventory** table and verify that there are 116 records in the table. Apply **Best Fit** to all of the fields—scroll down to be sure that all of the data in the **Item Name** field displays. Display the table in **Print Preview**, and then create a paper or electronic printout of the first page. **Close Print Preview**, **Close** the table, and **Save** changes to the layout of the table.

d. On the **External Data tab**, in the **Import & Link group**, click the **Excel** button. Navigate to your student files, double-click **aBRC1_Suppliers**, and then **Import the source data into a new table in the current database**. Click **First Row Contains Column Headings** and set the primary key to **Supplier ID**. Name the table **Lastname Firstname BRC1 Suppliers** and then **Open** the table. **Delete** the **Fax Number** field, and then apply **Best Fit** to all of the fields. Display the table in **Print Preview**, change the orientation to **Landscape**, change the **Margins** to **Normal**, and then create a paper or electronic printout as directed. **Close Print Preview**, **Close**

the table, and save changes to the layout of the table. On the **Navigation Pane**, click the **Navigation Pane arrow**, and then click **Tables and Related Views**.

e. Click the **Database Tools tab**, and then in the **Relationships group**, click the **Relationships** button. In the **Show Table** dialog box, double-click **BRC1 Suppliers**, double-click **BRC1 Inventory**, and then **Close** the dialog box. Expand the field lists, and then in the **BRC1 Suppliers** field list, point to **Supplier ID**. Drag to the right into the **BRC1 Inventory** field list on top of the **Supplier ID** field, release the mouse button, click **Enforce Referential Integrity**, and then click **Create**. *One* supplier can supply *many* inventory items. Create a **Relationship Report**, **Save** the report with the default name, and then create a paper or electronic printout as directed. **Close Print Preview**, and then **Close** any open objects. Increase the width of the **Navigation Pane** to display the entire report name, and then **Close** the **Navigation Pane**.

2 Create a query in **Query Design** view, based on the **BRC1 Inventory** table to answer the question, *What is the Item Name (in alphabetical order), Retail Price, and Category for the Sport of Hiking?* Do not display the **Sport** field in the query results. Forty records meet the criteria. **Save** the query as **Lastname Firstname BRC1 Hiking Query** and then create a paper or electronic printout as directed. **Close Print Preview**, and then **Close** the query.

a. Create a copy of the **BRC1 Hiking Query**, saving the object as **Lastname Firstname BRC1 Hiking or Biking Shoes Query** Redesign the query to answer the question, *What is the Sport, Item Name, Retail Price, and Supplier ID for the Category of Shoes where the Sport is Hiking or Biking?* **Sort** the records by the **Sport** field and by the **Item Name** field. Do not display the **Category** field in the query results. Nine records meet the criteria. Create a paper or electronic

Table 1

Data Type	Text	Text	Currency	Text	Text	Text
Field Name	Item ID#	**Item Name**	**Retail Price**	**Category**	**Sport**	**Supplier ID**

Return to Step 1-b

Table 2

Item#	Item Name	Retail Price	Category	Sport	Supplier ID#
106555	**Snowboard**	**256.99**	**Equipment**	**Skiing**	**SUPP-06**
106556	**Wool Socks**	**12.59**	**Socks and Gloves**	**Skiing**	**SUPP-04**

Return to Step 1-c

(Business Running Case: Front Range Action Sports continues on the next page)

printout as directed. **Close Print Preview**, and **Close** the query.

b. Create a query in **Query Design** view, based on the **BRC1 Suppliers** table and the **BRC1 Inventory** table to answer the question, *What is the Item Name, Category, Company, and Business Phone for Categories that begin with the letter S, and sorted by Category, for the Sport of Fitness?* Do not display the **Sport** category in the query results. Eighteen records meet the criteria. **Save** the query as **Lastname Firstname BRC1 S Category Query** and then create a paper or electronic printout as directed. **Close Print Preview**, and **Close** the query.

c. Create a query in **Query Design** view, based on the **BRC1 Suppliers** table and the **BRC1 Inventory** table to answer the question, *What is the Company, Item Name, Category, Sport, and Retail Price for items that have a retail price of $100 or greater sorted in ascending order by Sport and then in descending order by Retail Price?* Twenty records meet the criteria. **Save** the query as **Lastname Firstname BRC1 Price $100 or Over Query** and then create a paper or electronic printout as directed, changing the margins to **Normal**. **Close Print Preview**, and **Close** the query.

d. Create a query in **Query Design** view, based on the **BRC1 Inventory** table to answer the question, *For Supplier ID of SUPP-01, for each Item Name and Retail Price, what is the markup of each item if marked up 10%, and what is the final price?* All numeric fields should be formatted as **Currency**, **2 Decimal** places. Apply **Best Fit** to all of the fields, **Save** the query as **Lastname Firstname BRC1 10 Percent Markup Query** and then create a paper or electronic printout as directed. **Close Print Preview**, and then **Close** the query.

3 Based on the **BRC1 Suppliers** table, use the **Form** tool to create a form. Switch to **Form** view, and then using your own first name and last name for the **Company** field, add a new record as shown in **Table 3**.

a. Save the form as **Lastname Firstname BRC1 Supplier Form** and then create a paper or electronic printout of

only the record you just created in the form, changing the **Column Width** to **7.5"** **Close Print Preview**, and then **Close** the form.

4 Based on the **BRC1 Suppliers** table, use the **Report** tool to create a new report. **Delete** the following fields from the report: **Supplier ID**, **Address**, **City**, **State**, and **ZIP**. Apply the **Paper** theme to this object only. **Sort** the **Company** field in **Ascending** order. Decrease the width of the **Business Phone** field to accommodate the longest entry in the field. **Bold** the field names, and **Center** the **Company** and **E-mail Address** field names over the data. Use the **layout selector** to visually center the layout between the left and right margins, and then visually center the **page number control** between the left and right margins. (Hint: scroll to the right to display the control.) **Save** the report as **Lastname Firstname BRC1 Suppliers Contact List** Display the report in **Print Preview**, and then create a paper or electronic printout as directed. **Close Print Preview**, and then **Close** the report.

5 Using the **Report Wizard**, create a report based on the **BRC1 Inventory** table. Add the following fields to the report: **Category**, **Item Name**, and **Retail Price**. **Group** by **Category**. **Sort** in **Ascending** order by **Item Name**. Find the **Average** of the **Retail Price** field. Select the **Stepped Layout**, and then as the report title, type **Lastname Firstname BRC1 Avg Price by Category Report**

a. In **Print Preview**, display the report by **Two Pages** and notice how the groupings are split between pages, that the **Retail Price** field name displays only *Price*, and that the prices in the text box and calculated controls display **###**. **Close Print Preview**, and then switch to **Layout** view. Apply the **Oriel** theme to the report and no other objects.

b. Click the **Item Name** field name, hold down [Shift], and then click the **text box control** that displays *Snowboard*. Decrease the width of the field until there is approximately **2** inches between **Item Name** and the right edge of the text box control. Scroll down the

Table 3

Supplier ID	Company	E-mail Address	Business Phone	Address	City	State	ZIP
SUPP-12	Lastname Firstname Inc	info@watersports.biz	(305) 555-6543	14 South Beach Rd	Miami	FL	33125

(Business Running Case: Front Range Action Sports continues on the next page)

(Return to Step 3-a)

Front Range Action Sports (continued)

report to be sure that all Item Names display fully. Scroll to the top of the report, and then click the **Retail Price** field name, which displays only a portion of the word *Price*. Hold down [Shift], click the **text box control** below the field name, which displays ###, and then click the **calculated control** that also displays ###. Increase the width of the controls by pointing to the left edge of any one of the selected controls and dragging it to the left until the entire field name— **Retail Price**—displays as the field name.

c. Delete the **Summary for 'Category' label controls**. Change the text in the **Avg label control** from *Avg* to **Average Retail Price Per Category** and then move the **label control** to the right until the right edge of the control is approximately **0.25 inch** from the left edge of its associated calculated control.

d. Click in the **title** of the report, and then change the **Font Size** to **16**. Visually center the title between the left and right margins of the report. Select all of the field names, and then apply **Bold** and **Italic**.

e On the **Design tab**, in the **Grouping & Totals** group, click the **Group & Sort** button. In the **Group, Sort, and Total** pane, click **More**. Click the **do not keep group together on one page arrow**, and then click **keep whole group together on one page**. In the **Grouping & Totals group**, click the **Group & Sort** button to close the **Group, Sort, and Total** pane. **Save** the report.

f. Display the report in **Print Preview** by **Two Pages**, and notice how the groupings are kept together on one page. On the **Print Preview tab**, in the **Print group**, click the **Print** button. In the **Print** dialog box, under **Print Range**, click **Pages**. In the **From** box, type **1** and in the **To** box, type **2** and then click **OK** to create a paper printout—or create an electronic printout as directed. **Close Print Preview**, and then **Close** the report.

6 **Open** the **Navigation Pane**, and if necessary, widen the pane to display fully all object names. Display **Backstage** view, click **Close Database**, and then click **Exit**.

End **You have completed Business Running Case 1** ——————————

Getting Started with PowerPoint

OUTCOMES

At the end of this chapter you will be able to:

OBJECTIVES

Mastering these objectives will enable you to:

PROJECT 1A
Create a new PowerPoint presentation.

1. Create a New Presentation (p. 623)
2. Edit a Presentation in Normal View (p. 627)
3. Add Pictures to a Presentation (p. 634)
4. Print and View a Presentation (p. 637)

PROJECT 1B
Edit and format a PowerPoint presentation.

5. Edit an Existing Presentation (p. 643)
6. Format a Presentation (p. 647)
7. Use Slide Sorter View (p. 650)
8. Apply Slide Transitions (p. 653)

© Steve Murray / Alamy

In This Chapter

In this chapter you will study presentation skills, which are among the most important skills you will learn. Good presentation skills enhance your communications—written, electronic, and interpersonal. In this technology-enhanced world, communicating ideas clearly and concisely is a critical personal skill. Microsoft PowerPoint 2010 is presentation software with which you create electronic slide presentations. Use PowerPoint to present information to your audience effectively. You can start with a new, blank presentation and add content, pictures, and themes, or you can collaborate with colleagues by inserting slides that have been saved in other presentations.

The projects in this chapter relate to **Lehua Hawaiian Adventures**. Named for the small, crescent-shaped island that is noted for its snorkeling and scuba diving, Lehua Hawaiian Adventures offers exciting but affordable adventure tours. Hiking tours go off the beaten path to amazing remote places on the islands. If you prefer to ride into the heart of Hawaii, try the cycling tours. Lehua Hawaiian Adventures also offers Jeep tours. Whatever you prefer—mountain, sea, volcano—our tour guides are experts in the history, geography, culture, and flora and fauna of Hawaii.

Project 1A Company Overview

myitlab
Project 1A Training

Project Activities

In Activities 1.01 through 1.13, you will create the first four slides of a new presentation that Lehua Hawaiian Adventures tour manager Carl Kawaoka is developing to introduce the tour services that the company offers. Your completed presentation will look similar to Figure 1.1.

Project Files

For Project 1A, you will need the following files:

New blank PowerPoint presentation
p01A_Helicopter
p01A_Beach

You will save your presentation as:

Lastname_Firstname_1A_LHA_Overview

Project Results

Figure 1.1
Project 1A LHA Overview

Objective 1 | Create a New Presentation

Microsoft PowerPoint 2010 is software with which you can present information to your audience effectively. You can edit and format a blank presentation by adding text, a presentation theme, and pictures.

Activity 1.01 | Identifying Parts of the PowerPoint Window

In this activity, you will start PowerPoint and identify the parts of the PowerPoint window.

1 **Start** 🌀 PowerPoint to display a new blank presentation in Normal view, and then compare your screen with Figure 1.2.

Normal view is the primary editing view in PowerPoint where you write and design your presentations. Normal view includes the Notes pane, the Slide pane, and the Slides/Outline pane.

Figure 1.2

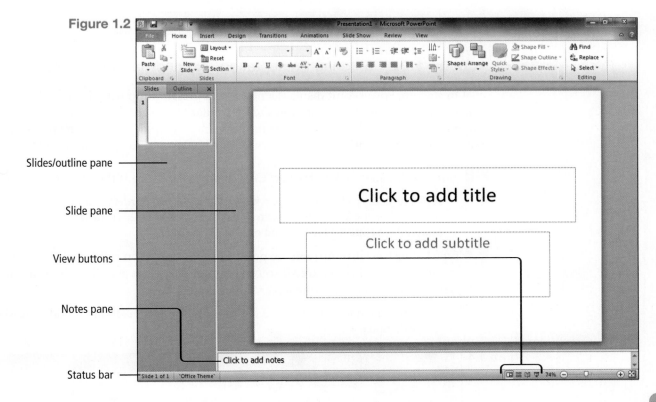

2 Take a moment to study the parts of the PowerPoint window described in the table in Figure 1.3.

PowerPoint | Chapter 1

Microsoft PowerPoint Screen Elements	
Screen Element	**Description**
Notes pane	Displays below the Slide pane and provides space for you to type notes regarding the active slide.
Slide pane	Displays a large image of the active slide.
Slides/Outline pane	Displays either the presentation in the form of miniature images called *thumbnails* (Slides tab) or the presentation outline (Outline tab).
Status bar	Displays, in a horizontal bar at the bottom of the presentation window, the current slide number, number of slides in a presentation, theme, View buttons, Zoom slider, and Fit slide to current window button; you can customize this area to include additional helpful information.
View buttons	Control the look of the presentation window with a set of commands.

Figure 1.3

Activity 1.02 │ Entering Presentation Text and Saving a Presentation

On startup, PowerPoint displays a new blank presentation with a single *slide*—a *title slide* in Normal view. A presentation slide—similar to a page in a document—can contain text, pictures, tables, charts, and other multimedia or graphic objects. The title slide is the first slide in a presentation and provides an introduction to the presentation topic.

1 In the **Slide pane**, click in the text *Click to add title*, which is the title *placeholder*.

A placeholder is a box on a slide with dotted or dashed borders that holds title and body text or other content such as charts, tables, and pictures. This slide contains two placeholders, one for the title and one for the subtitle.

2 Type **Lehua Hawaiian Adventures** point to *Lehua*, and then right-click. On the shortcut menu, click **Ignore All** so *Lehua* is not flagged as a spelling error in this presentation. Compare your screen with Figure 1.4.

Recall that a red wavy underline indicates that the underlined word is not in the Microsoft Office dictionary.

Figure 1.4

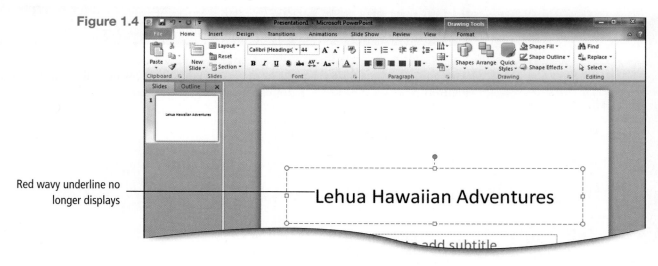

Red wavy underline no longer displays

3 Click in the subtitle placeholder, and then type **Carl Kawaoka**

4 Press [Enter] to create a new line in the subtitle placeholder. Type **Tour Manager**

5 Right-click **Kawaoka**, and then on the shortcut menu, click **Ignore All**. Compare your screen with Figure 1.5.

Figure 1.5

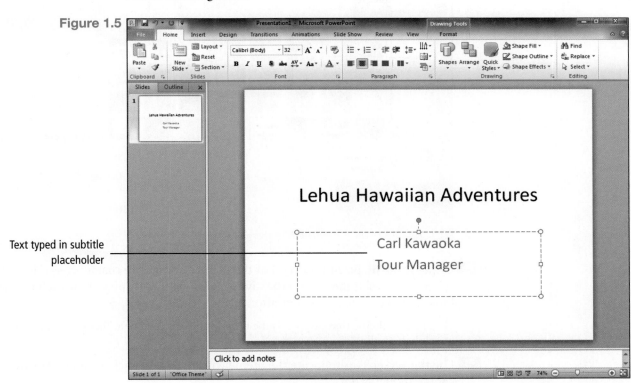

Text typed in subtitle placeholder

6 In the upper left corner of your screen, click the **File tab** to display **Backstage** view, click **Save As**, and then in the **Save As** dialog box, navigate to the location where you will store your files for this chapter. Create a new folder named **PowerPoint Chapter 1** In the **File name** box, replace the existing text with **Lastname_Firstname_1A_LHA_Overview** and then click **Save**.

Activity 1.03 | Applying a Presentation Theme

A **theme** is a set of unified design elements that provides a look for your presentation by applying colors, fonts, and effects.

1 On the Ribbon, click the **Design tab**. In the **Themes group**, click the **More** button ⊡ to display the **Themes** gallery. Compare your screen with Figure 1.6.

Figure 1.6

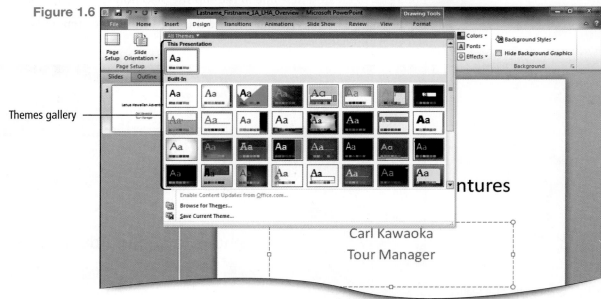

Themes gallery

2 Under **Built-In**, point to several of the themes and notice that a ScreenTip displays the name of each theme and the Live Preview feature displays how each theme would look if applied to your presentation.

> The first theme that displays is the Office theme. Subsequent themes are arranged alphabetically.

3 Use the ScreenTips to locate the theme with the green background—**Austin**—as shown in Figure 1.7.

Figure 1.7

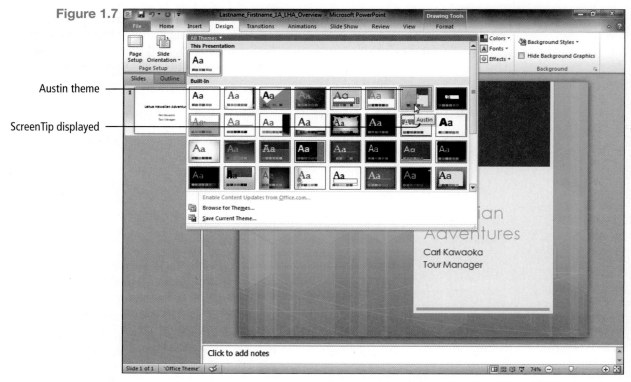

Austin theme

ScreenTip displayed

4 Click the **Austin** theme to change the presentation theme and then **Save** 🖫 your presentation.

Objective 2 | Edit a Presentation in Normal View

Editing is the process of modifying a presentation by adding and deleting slides or by changing the contents of individual slides.

Activity 1.04 | Inserting a New Slide

To insert a new slide in a presentation, display the slide that will precede the slide that you want to insert.

1 On the **Home tab**, in the **Slides group**, point to the **New Slide** button. Compare your screen with Figure 1.8.

The New Slide button is a split button. Recall that clicking the main part of a split button performs a command and clicking the arrow opens a menu, list, or gallery. The upper, main part of the New Slide button, when clicked, inserts a slide without displaying any options. The lower part—the New Slide button arrow—when clicked, displays a gallery of slide *layouts*. A layout is the arrangement of elements, such as title and subtitle text, lists, pictures, tables, charts, shapes, and movies, on a slide.

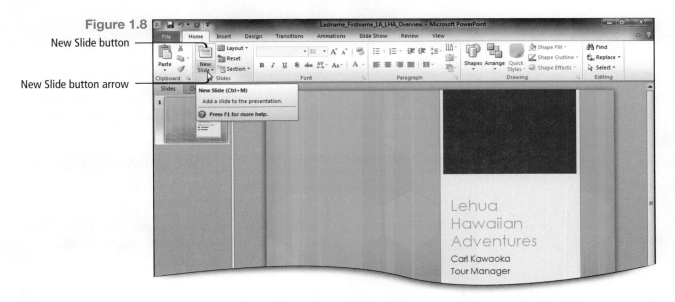

Figure 1.8

New Slide button

New Slide button arrow

2 In the **Slides group**, click the lower portion of the New Slide button—the **New Slide button arrow**—to display the gallery, and then compare your screen with Figure 1.9.

Figure 1.9

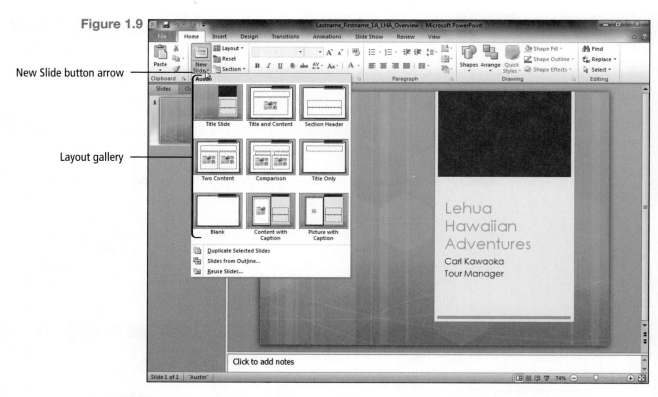

New Slide button arrow

Layout gallery

3 In the gallery, click the **Two Content** layout to insert a new slide. Notice that the new blank slide displays in the **Slide pane** and in the **Slides/Outline pane**. Compare your screen with Figure 1.10.

Figure 1.10

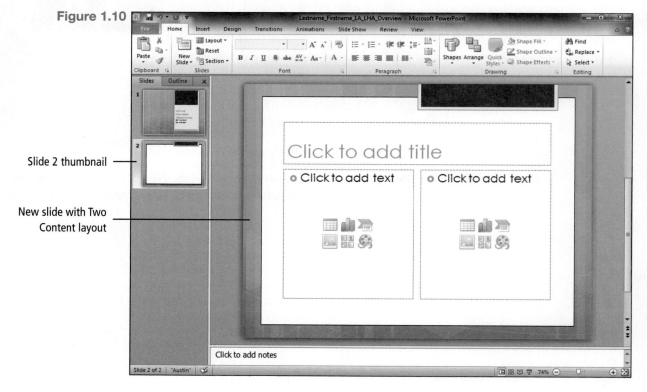

Slide 2 thumbnail

New slide with Two Content layout

4 In the **Slide pane**, click the text *Click to add title*, and then type **Do You Enjoy Adventure?**

5 On the left side of the slide, click anywhere in the content placeholder. Type **Hiking and cycling** and then press Enter.

6 Type **Explore locations** and then compare your screen with Figure 1.11.

Figure 1.11

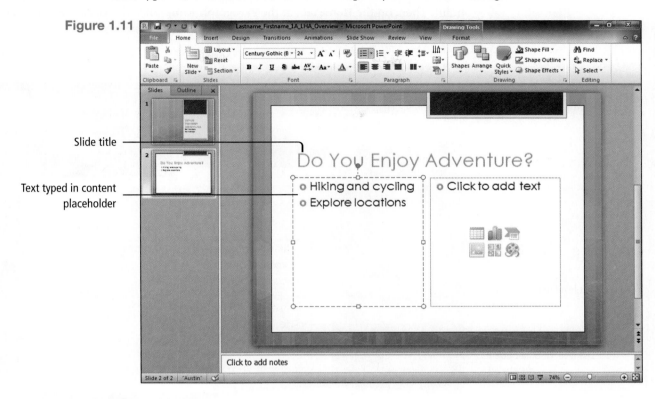

Slide title

Text typed in content placeholder

7 **Save** 🖫 your presentation.

Activity 1.05 | Increasing and Decreasing List Levels

Text in a PowerPoint presentation is organized according to *list levels*. List levels, each represented by a bullet symbol, are similar to outline levels. On a slide, list levels are identified by the bullet style, indentation, and the size of the text.

The first level on an individual slide is the title. Increasing the list level of a bullet point increases its indent and results in a smaller text size. Decreasing the list level of a bullet point decreases its indent and results in a larger text size.

1 On **Slide 2**, if necessary, click at the end of the last bullet point after the word *locations*, and then press Enter to insert a new bullet point.

2 Type **Boating excursions** and then press Enter.

3 Press Tab, and then notice that the green bullet is indented. Type **Exhilarate your senses while at sea**

By pressing Tab at the beginning of a bullet point, you can increase the list level and indent the bullet point.

4 Press Enter. Notice that a new bullet point displays at the same level as the previous bullet point. Then, on the **Home tab**, in the **Paragraph group**, click the **Decrease List Level** button 🔳. Type **Helicopter tours** and then compare your screen with Figure 1.12.

The Decrease List Level button promotes the bullet point. The text size increases and the text is no longer indented.

Figure 1.12

Decrease List Level button

List level of bullet point increased

List level of bullet point decreased

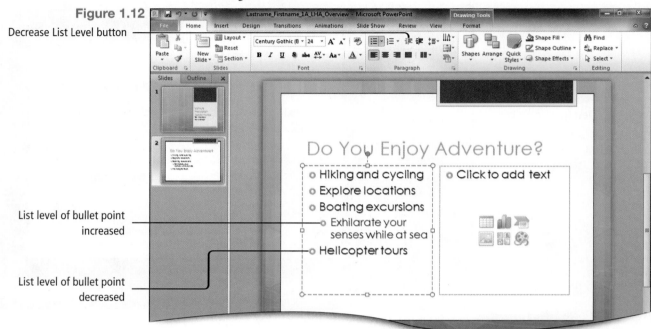

5 Press Enter, and then press Tab to increase the list level. Type **View Hawaii from above**

6 Click anywhere in the second bullet point—*Explore locations*. On the **Home tab**, in the **Paragraph group**, click the **Increase List Level** button 🔳. Compare your screen with Figure 1.13.

The bullet point is indented and the size of the text decreases.

Figure 1.13

Increase List Level button

List level of two bullet points increased

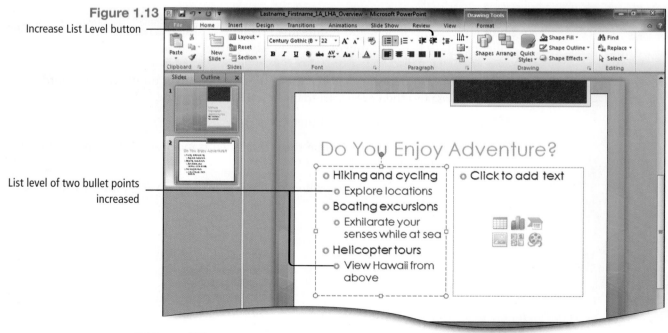

7 **Save** 🔲 your presentation.

Activity 1.06 | Adding Speaker's Notes to a Presentation

Recall that when a presentation is displayed in Normal view, the Notes pane displays below the Slide pane. Use the Notes pane to type speaker's notes that you can print below a picture of each slide. Then, while making your presentation, you can refer to these printouts while making a presentation, thus reminding you of the important points that you want to discuss during the presentation.

1 With **Slide 2** displayed, on the **Home tab**, in the **Slides group**, click the **New Slide button arrow** to display the **Slide Layout** gallery, and then click **Section Header**.

The section header layout changes the look and flow of a presentation by providing text placeholders that do not contain bullet points.

2 Click in the title placeholder, and then type **About Our Company**

3 Click in the content placeholder below the title, and then type **Named for the crescent-shaped island noted for scuba diving, Lehua Hawaiian Adventures offers exciting and affordable tours throughout Hawaii.** Compare your screen with Figure 1.14.

Figure 1.14

Slide title

Text typed in content placeholder

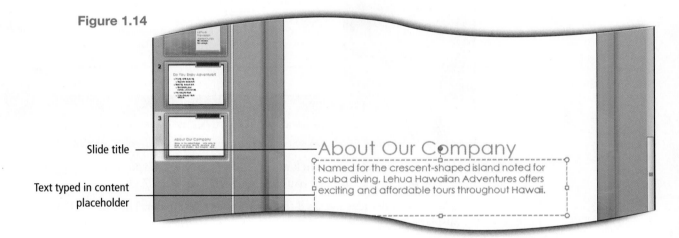

4 Below the slide, click in the **Notes pane**. Type **Lehua Hawaiian Adventures is based in Honolulu but has offices on each of the main Hawaiian islands.** Compare your screen with Figure 1.15, and then **Save** your presentation.

Figure 1.15

Text typed in the Notes pane

Activity 1.07 | Displaying and Editing Slides in the Slide Pane

To edit a presentation slide, display the slide in the Slide pane.

1 Look at the **Slides/Outline pane**, and then notice that the presentation contains three slides. At the right side of the PowerPoint window, in the vertical scroll bar, point to the scroll box, and then hold down the left mouse button to display a ScreenTip indicating the slide number and title.

2 Drag the scroll box up until the ScreenTip displays *Slide: 2 of 3 Do You Enjoy Adventure?* Compare your slide with Figure 1.16, and then release the mouse button to display **Slide 2**.

Figure 1.16

3 In the second bullet point, click at the end of the word *Explore*. Press Spacebar, and then type **amazing** Compare your screen with Figure 1.17.

The placeholder text is resized to fit within the placeholder. The AutoFit Options button displays.

Figure 1.17

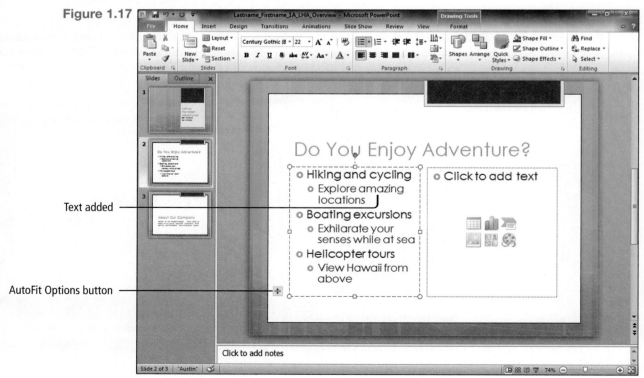

4 Click the **AutoFit Options** button, and then click **AutoFit Text to Placeholder**.

The *AutoFit Text to Placeholder* option keeps the text contained within the placeholder by reducing the size of the text. The *Stop Fitting Text to This Placeholder* option turns off the AutoFit option so that the text can flow beyond the placeholder border; the text size remains unchanged.

5 Below the vertical scroll bar, locate the **Previous Slide** ⏫ and **Next Slide** ⏬ buttons as shown in Figure 1.18.

Figure 1.18

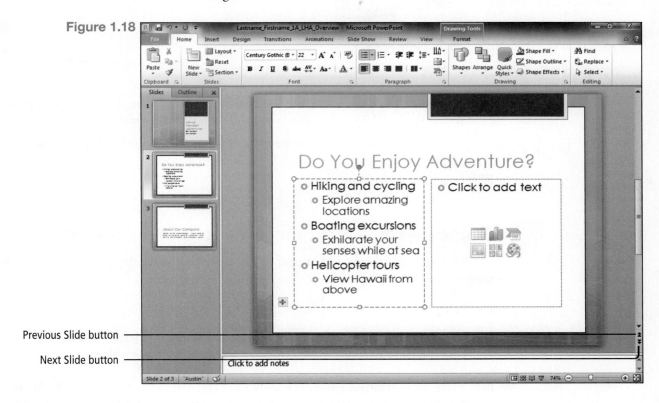

Previous Slide button

Next Slide button

6 In the vertical scroll bar, click the **Previous Slide** button ⏫ so that **Slide 1** displays. Then click the **Next Slide** button ⏬ two times until **Slide 3** displays.

By clicking the Next Slide or the Previous Slide buttons, you can scroll through your presentation one slide at a time.

7 On the left side of the PowerPoint window, in the **Slides/Outline pane**, point to **Slide 1**, and then notice that a ScreenTip displays the slide title. Compare your screen with Figure 1.19.

In the Slides/Outline pane, the slide numbers display to the left of the slide thumbnails.

Figure 1.19

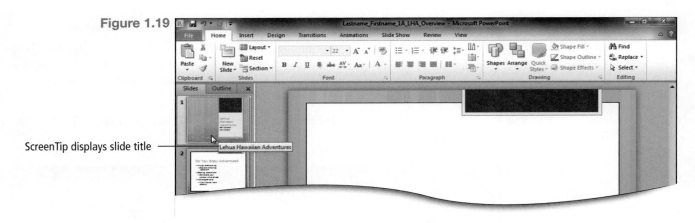

ScreenTip displays slide title

8 Click **Slide 1** to display it in the **Slide pane**, and then in the slide subtitle, click at the end of the word *Tour*. Press [Spacebar], and then type **Operations**

> Clicking a slide thumbnail is the most common method used to display a slide in the Slide pane.

9 **Save** 💾 your presentation.

Objective 3 | Add Pictures to a Presentation

Photographic images add impact to a presentation and help the audience visualize the message you are trying to convey.

Activity 1.08 | Inserting a Picture from a File

Many slide layouts in PowerPoint accommodate digital picture files so that you can easily add pictures you have stored on your system or on a portable storage device.

1 In the **Slides/Outline pane**, click **Slide 2** to display it in the **Slide pane**. On the **Home tab**, in the **Slides group**, click the **New Slide button arrow** to display the **Slide Layout** gallery. Click **Picture with Caption** to insert a new **Slide 3**. Compare your screen with Figure 1.20.

> In the center of the large picture placeholder, the *Insert Picture from File* button displays.

Figure 1.20

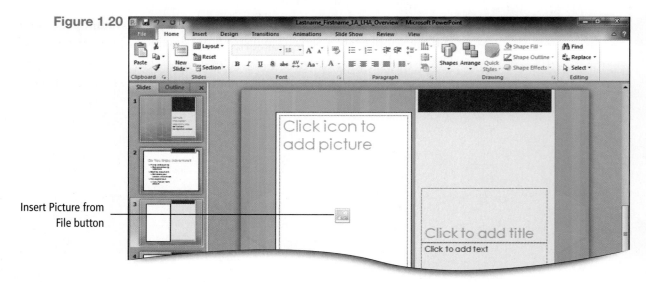

Insert Picture from File button

2 In the picture placeholder, click the **Insert Picture from File** button to open the **Insert Picture** dialog box. Navigate to the location in which your student files are stored, click **p01A_Beach**, then click **Insert** to insert the picture in the placeholder.

3 To the right of the picture, click in the title placeholder. Type **Prepare to be Amazed!**

4 Below the title, click in the caption placeholder, and then type **Mountain, sea, volcano. Our tour guides are experts in the history, geography, culture, and flora and fauna of Hawaii.** Compare your screen with Figure 1.21.

Figure 1.21

Inserted picture

Title

Caption

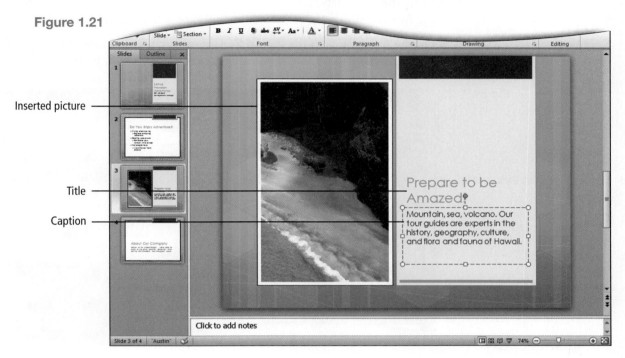

5 Display **Slide 2**. In the placeholder on the right side of the slide, click the **Insert Picture from File** button. Navigate to your student files, and then click **p01A_Helicopter**. Click **Insert**, and then compare your screen with Figure 1.22.

Small circles and squares—**sizing handles**—surround the inserted picture and indicate that the picture is selected and can be modified or formatted. The **rotation handle**—a green circle above the picture—provides a way to rotate a selected image.

Figure 1.22

Rotation handle

Sizing handles

6 Save 🖫 the presentation.

Activity 1.09 | Applying a Style to a Picture

The Picture Tools add the Format tab to the Ribbon, which provides numerous **styles** that you can apply to your pictures. A style is a collection of formatting options that you can apply to a picture, text, or an object.

1 With **Slide 2** displayed, if necessary, click the picture of the helicopter to select it. On the Ribbon, notice that the Picture Tools are active and the Format tab displays.

2 On the **Format tab**, in the **Picture Styles group**, click the **More** button ⤓ to display the **Picture Styles** gallery, and then compare your screen with Figure 1.23.

Figure 1.23

Picture Styles gallery ———

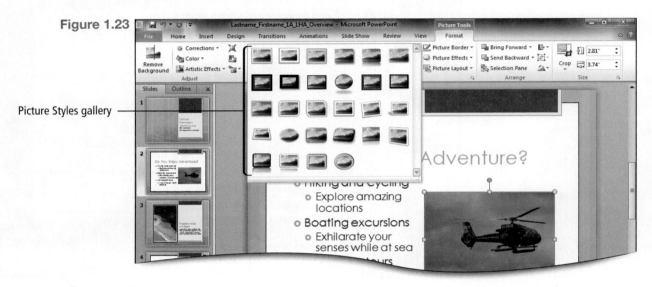

3 In the gallery, point to several of the picture styles to display the ScreenTips and to view the effect on your picture. In the first row, click **Drop Shadow Rectangle**.

4 Click in a blank area of the slide, and then compare your screen with Figure 1.24.

Figure 1.24

Drop Shadow Rectangle
picture style applied to picture

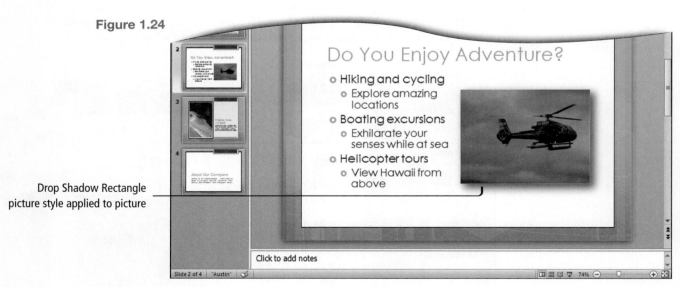

5 Save 🔲 the presentation.

Activity 1.10 | Applying and Removing Picture Artistic Effects

Artistic effects are formats applied to images that make pictures resemble sketches or paintings.

1 With **Slide 2** displayed, select the picture of the helicopter.

2 Click the **Format tab**, and then in the **Adjust group**, click the **Artistic Effects** button to display the **Artistic Effects** gallery. Compare your screen with Figure 1.25.

Figure 1.25

Artistic Effects button

Artistic Effects gallery

3 In the gallery, point to several of the artistic effects to display the ScreenTips and to have Live Preview display the effect on your picture. Then, in the second row, click the **Paint Strokes** effect.

4 With the picture still selected, on the **Format tab**, in the **Adjust group**, click the **Artistic Effects** button to display the gallery. In the first row, click the first effect—**None**—to remove the effect from the picture and restore the previous formatting.

5 Save 🔲 the presentation.

Objective 4 | Print and View a Presentation

Activity 1.11 | Viewing a Slide Show

Another Way

Press F5 to start the slide show from the beginning. Or, display the first slide you want to show and click the Slide Show button on the lower right side of the status bar; or press Shift + F5.

When you view a presentation as an electronic slide show, the entire slide fills the computer screen, and an audience can view your presentation if your computer is connected to a projection system.

1 On the Ribbon, click the **Slide Show tab**. In the **Start Slide Show group**, click the **From Beginning** button.

The first slide fills the screen, displaying the presentation as the audience would see it if your computer was connected to a projection system.

2 Click the left mouse button or press $\boxed{\text{Spacebar}}$ to advance to the second slide.

3 Continue to click or press $\boxed{\text{Spacebar}}$ until the last slide displays, and then click or press $\boxed{\text{Spacebar}}$ one more time to display a black slide.

> After the last slide in a presentation, a ***black slide*** displays, indicating that the presentation is over.

4 With the black slide displayed, click the left mouse button or press $\boxed{\text{Spacebar}}$ to exit the slide show and return to the presentation.

Activity 1.12 | Inserting Headers and Footers

A ***header*** is text that prints at the top of each sheet of ***slide handouts*** or ***notes pages***. Slide handouts are printed images of slides on a sheet of paper. Notes pages are printouts that contain the slide image on the top half of the page and notes that you have created on the Notes pane in the lower half of the page.

In addition to headers, you can insert ***footers***—text that displays at the bottom of every slide or that prints at the bottom of a sheet of slide handouts or notes pages.

1 Click the **Insert tab**, and then in the **Text group**, click the **Header & Footer** button to display the **Header and Footer** dialog box.

2 In the **Header and Footer** dialog box, click the **Notes and Handouts tab**. Under **Include on page**, select the **Date and time** check box, and as you do so, watch the Preview box in the lower right corner of the Header and Footer dialog box.

> The Preview box indicates the placeholders on the printed Notes and Handouts pages. The two narrow rectangular boxes at the top of the Preview box indicate placeholders for the header text and date. When you select the Date and time check box, the placeholder in the upper right corner is outlined, indicating the location in which the date will display.

3 If necessary, click the Update automatically option button so that the current date prints on the notes and handouts each time the presentation is printed.

4 If necessary, *clear* the Header check box to omit this element. Notice that in the **Preview** box, the corresponding placeholder is not selected.

5 Select the **Page number** and **Footer** check boxes, and then notice that the insertion point displays in the **Footer** box. Using your own name, type **Lastname_Firstname_1A_LHA_Overview** so that the file name displays as a footer, and then compare your dialog box with Figure 1.26.

Figure 1.26

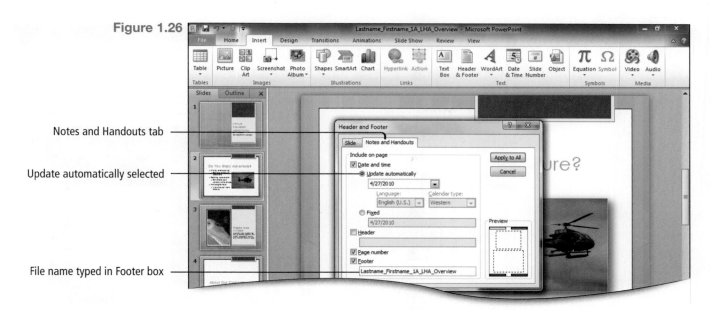

Notes and Handouts tab

Update automatically selected

File name typed in Footer box

6 In the upper right corner of the dialog box, click **Apply to All**. **Save** 🖫 your presentation.

> **More Knowledge | Adding Footers to Slides**
>
> You can also add footers to the actual slides, which will display during your presentation, by using the Slide tab in the Header and Footer dialog box. Headers cannot be added to individual slides.

Activity 1.13 | Printing a Presentation

Use Backstage view to preview the arrangement of slides on the handouts and notes pages.

1 Display **Slide 1**. Click the **File tab** to display **Backstage** view, and then click the **Print tab**.

The Print tab in Backstage view displays the tools you need to select your settings and also to view a preview of your presentation. On the right, Print Preview displays your presentation exactly as it will print.

2 In the **Settings group**, click **Full Page Slides**, and then compare your screen with Figure 1.27.

The gallery displays either the default print setting—Full Page Slides—or the most recently selected print setting. Thus, on your system, this button might indicate the presentation Notes Pages, Outline, or one of several arrangements of slide handouts—depending on the most recently used setting.

Figure 1.27

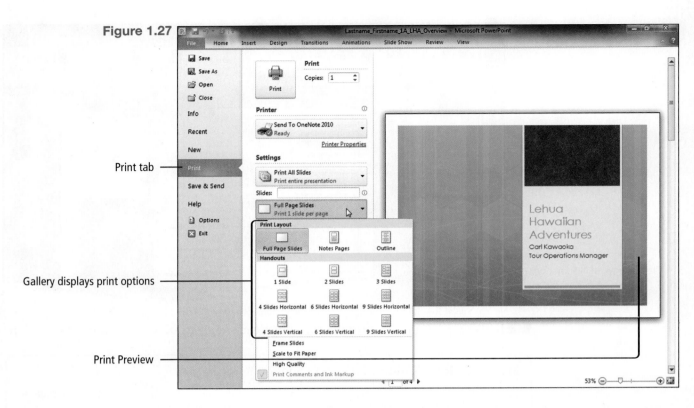

Print tab

Gallery displays print options

Print Preview

3 In the gallery, under **Handouts**, click **4 Slides Horizontal**. Notice that the **Print Preview** on the right displays the slide handout, and that the current date, file name, and page number display in the header and footer.

> In the Settings group, the Portrait Orientation option displays so that you can change the print orientation from Portrait to Landscape. The Portrait Orientation option does not display when Full Page Slides is chosen.

4 To print your handout, be sure your system is connected to a printer, and then in the **Print group**, click the **Print** button.

> The handout will print on your default printer—on a black and white printer, the colors will print in shades of gray. Backstage view closes and your file redisplays in the PowerPoint window.

5 Click the **File tab** to display **Backstage** view, and then click the **Print tab**. In the **Settings group**, click **4 Slides Horizontal**, and then under **Print Layout**, click **Notes Pages** to view the presentation notes for **Slide 1**; recall that you created notes for **Slide 4**.

> Indicated below the Notes page are the current slide number and the number of pages that will print when Notes page is selected. You can use the Next Page and Previous Page arrows to display each Notes page in the presentation.

6 At the bottom of the **Print Preview**, click the **Next Page** button ▶ three times so that **Page 4** displays. Compare your screen with Figure 1.28.

> The notes that you created for Slide 4 display below the image of the slide.

Figure 1.28

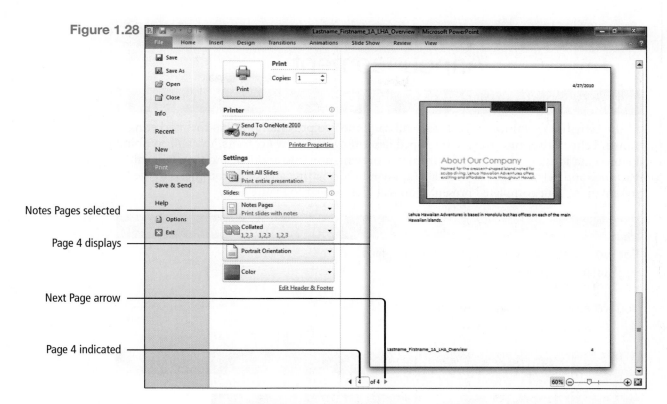

Notes Pages selected

Page 4 displays

Next Page arrow

Page 4 indicated

7 In the **Settings group**, click in the **Slides** box, and then type **4** so that only the Notes pages for **Slide 4** will print. In the **Settings group**, click **Notes Pages**, and then below the gallery, select **Frame Slides**. In the **Print group**, click the **Print** button to print the Notes page.

8 Click the **File tab** to redisplay **Backstage** view, be sure the **Info tab** is active, and then in the third panel, click **Properties**. Click **Show Document Panel**, and then in the **Author** box, delete any text and type your firstname and lastname.

9 In the **Subject** box, type your course name and section number. In the **Keywords** box, type **company overview** and then **Close** ☒ the Document Information Panel.

10 **Save** 🖫 your presentation. On the right end of the title bar, click the **Close** button ☒ to close the presentation and close PowerPoint.

End **You have completed Project 1A**

Project 1B New Product Announcement

Project Activities

In Activities 1.14 through 1.23, you will combine two presentations that the marketing team at Lehua Adventure Travels developed describing their new Ecotours. You will combine the presentations by inserting slides from one presentation into another, and then you will rearrange and delete slides. You will also apply font formatting and slide transitions to the presentation. Your completed presentation will look similar to Figure 1.29.

Project Files

For Project 1B, you will need the following files:

p01B_Ecotours
p01B_Slides

You will save your presentation as:

Lastname_Firstname_1B_Ecotours

Project Results

Figure 1.29
Project 1B—Ecotours

Objective 5 | Edit an Existing Presentation

Recall that editing refers to the process of adding, deleting, and modifying presentation content. You can edit presentation content in either the Slide pane or the Slides/Outline pane.

Activity 1.14 | Displaying and Editing the Presentation Outline

You can display the presentation outline in the Slides/Outline pane and edit the presentation text. Changes that you make in the outline are immediately displayed in the Slide pane.

1 **Start** PowerPoint. From your student files, open **p01B_Ecotours**. On the **File tab**, click **Save As**, navigate to your **PowerPoint Chapter 1** folder, and then using your own name, save the file as **Lastname_Firstname_1B_Ecotours**

2 In the **Slides/Outline pane**, click the **Outline tab** to display the presentation outline. If necessary, below the Slides/Outline pane, drag the scroll box all the way to the left so that the slide numbers display. Compare your screen with Figure 1.30.

The outline tab is wider than the Slides tab so that you have additional space to type your text. Each slide in the outline displays the slide number, slide icon, and the slide title in bold.

Figure 1.30

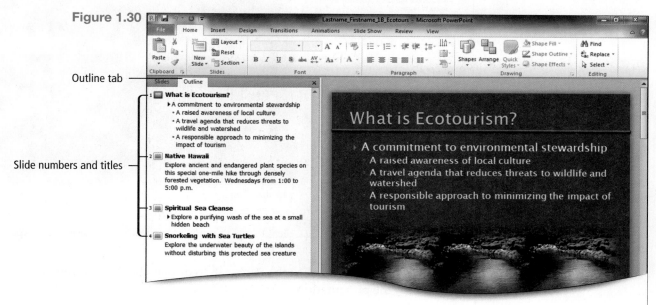

Outline tab

Slide numbers and titles

3 In the **Outline tab**, in **Slide 1**, select the last three bullet points, and then compare your screen with Figure 1.31.

Figure 1.31

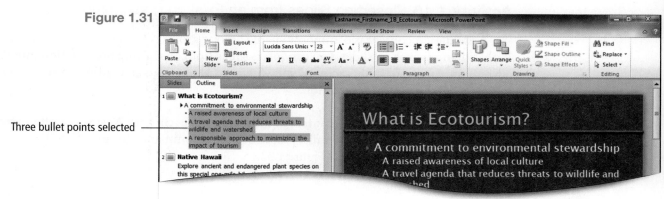

Three bullet points selected

4 On the **Home tab**, in the **Paragraph group**, click the **Decrease List Level** button ▤ one time to decrease the list level of the selected bullet points.

> When you type in the outline or change the list level, the changes also display in the Slide pane.

5 In the **Outline tab**, click anywhere in **Slide 3**, and then click at the end of the last bullet point after the word *beach*. Press ⏎ to create a new bullet point at the same list level as the previous bullet point. Type **Offered Tuesdays and Thursdays one hour before sunset, weather permitting**

6 Press ⏎ to create a new bullet point. Type **Fee: $30** and then compare your screen with Figure 1.32.

Figure 1.32

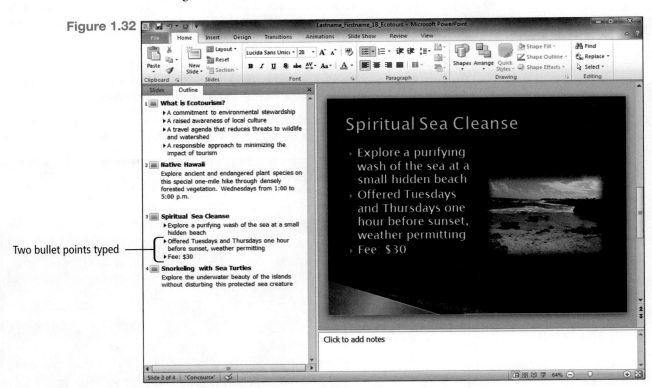

Two bullet points typed

7 In the **Slides/Outline pane**, click the **Slides tab** to display the slide thumbnails, and then **Save** ▤ the presentation.

> You can type text in the Slide tab or in the Outline tab. Displaying the Outline tab enables you to view the entire flow of the presentation.

Activity 1.15 | Inserting Slides from an Existing Presentation

Presentation content is commonly shared among group members in an organization. Rather than re-creating slides, you can insert slides from an existing presentation into the current presentation. In this activity, you will insert slides from an existing presentation into your 1B_Ecotours presentation.

1 Display **Slide 1**. On the **Home tab**, in the **Slides group**, click the **New Slide button arrow** to display the **Slide Layout** gallery and additional commands for inserting slides. Compare your screen with Figure 1.33.

Figure 1.33

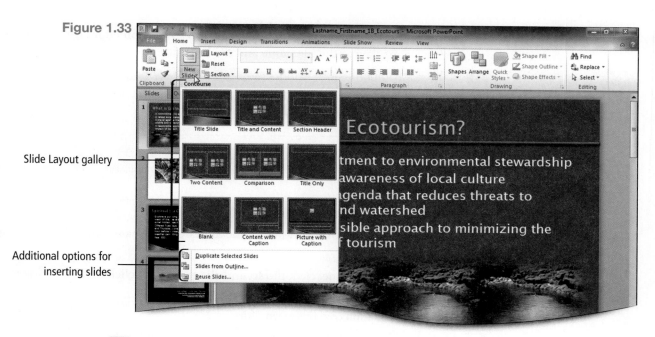

Slide Layout gallery

Additional options for inserting slides

2 Below the gallery, click **Reuse Slides** to open the Reuse Slides pane on the right side of the PowerPoint window.

3 In the **Reuse Slides** pane, click the **Browse** button, and then click **Browse File**. In the **Browse** dialog box, navigate to the location where your student files are stored, and then double-click **p01B_Slides** to display the slides in the Reuse Slides pane.

4 At the bottom of the **Reuse Slides** pane, select the **Keep source formatting** check box, and then compare your screen with Figure 1.34.

By selecting the *Keep source formatting* check box, you retain the formatting applied to the slides when inserted into the existing presentation. When the *Keep source formatting* check box is cleared, the theme formatting of the presentation in which the slides are inserted is applied.

Figure 1.34

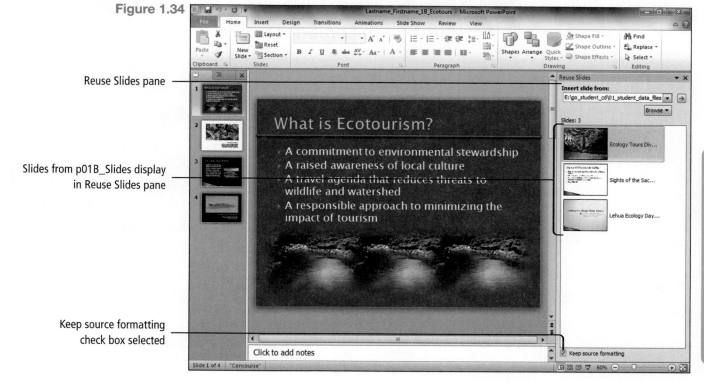

Reuse Slides pane

Slides from p01B_Slides display in Reuse Slides pane

Keep source formatting check box selected

PowerPoint | Chapter 1

5 In the **Reuse Slides** pane, point to each slide to view a zoomed image of the slide and a ScreenTip displaying the file name and the slide title.

6 In the **Reuse Slides** pane, click the first slide—**Ecology Tours Division**—to insert the slide into the current presentation after Slide 1, and then notice that the original slide background formatting is retained.

> **Note** | Inserting Slides
>
> You can insert slides into your presentation in any order; remember to display the slide that will precede the slide that you want to insert.

7 In your **1B_Ecotours** presentation, in the **Slides/Outline pane**, click **Slide 5** to display it in the **Slide pane**.

8 In the **Reuse Slides** pane, click the second slide and then click the third slide to insert both slides after **Slide 5**.

Your presentation contains seven slides.

9 On **Slide 7**, point to *Lehua*, and then right-click to display the shortcut menu. Click **Ignore all**. Use the same technique to ignore the spelling of the word *Ecotour*. Compare your screen with Figure 1.35.

Figure 1.35

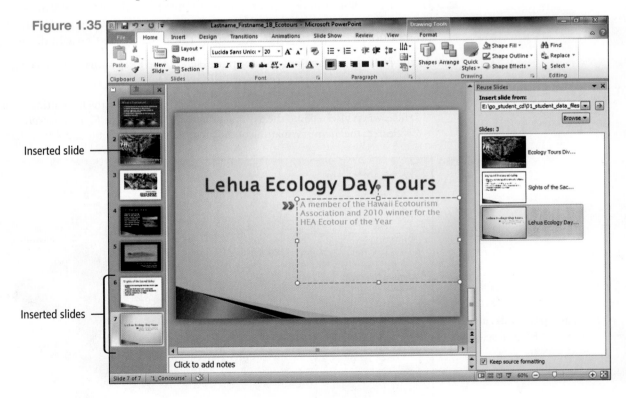

10 Close **X** the **Reuse Slides** pane; click **Save**.

> **More Knowledge** | Inserting All Slides
>
> You can insert all of the slides from an existing presentation into the current presentation at one time. In the Reuse Slides pane, right-click one of the slides that you want to insert, and then click Insert All Slides.

Activity 1.16 | Finding and Replacing Text

The Replace command enables you to locate all occurrences of specified text and replace it with alternative text.

1 Display **Slide 1**. On the **Home tab**, in the **Editing group**, click the **Replace** button. In the **Replace** dialog box, in the **Find what** box, type **Ecology** and then in the **Replace with** box, type **Eco** Compare your screen with Figure 1.36.

Figure 1.36

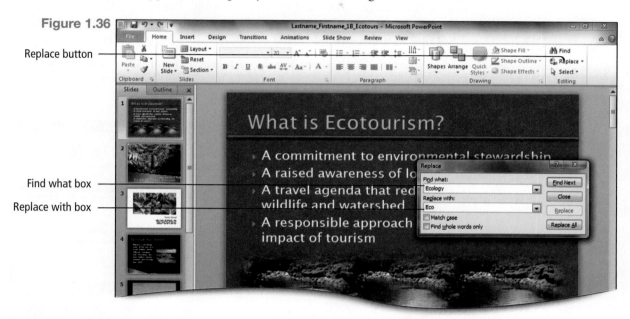

Replace button

Find what box

Replace with box

2 In the **Replace** dialog box, click the **Replace All** button.

A message box displays indicating the number of replacements that were made.

3 In the message box, click **OK**, **Close** ✕ the **Replace** dialog box, and then click **Save** 🖫.

Objective 6 | Format a Presentation

Formatting refers to changing the appearance of the text, layout, and design of a slide. You will find it easiest to do most of your formatting changes in PowerPoint in the Slide pane.

Activity 1.17 | Changing Fonts, Font Sizes, Font Styles, and Font Colors

Recall that a font is a set of characters with the same design and shape and that fonts are measured in points. Font styles include bold, italic, and underline, and you can apply any combination of these styles to presentation text. Font styles and font color are useful to provide emphasis and are a visual cue to draw the reader's eye to important text.

1 On the right side of the **Slides/Outline pane**, drag the scroll box down until **Slide 7** displays, and then click **Slide 7** to display it in the **Slides** pane.

When a presentation contains a large number of slides, a scroll box displays to the right of the slide thumbnails so that you can scroll and then select the thumbnails.

2 Select the title text—*Lehua Eco Day Tours*. Point to the Mini toolbar, and then click the **Font button arrow** to display the available fonts. Click **Arial Black**.

3 Select the light green text in the placeholder below the title, and then on the Mini toolbar, change the **Font** to **Arial Black** and the **Font Size** to **28**. Then, click the **Font Color button arrow** [A ▾], and compare your screen with Figure 1.37.

The colors in the top row of the color gallery are the colors associated with the presentation theme—*Concourse*. The colors in the rows below the first row are light and dark variations of the theme colors.

Figure 1.37

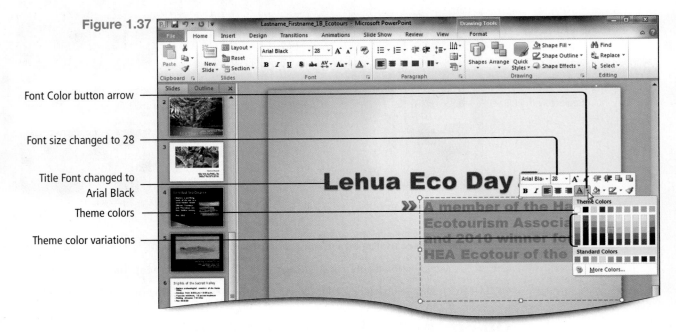

Font Color button arrow

Font size changed to 28

Title Font changed to Arial Black

Theme colors

Theme color variations

4 Point to several of the colors and notice that a ScreenTip displays the color name and Live Preview displays the selected text in the color to which you are pointing.

5 In the second column of colors, click the first color—**Black, Text 1**—to change the font color. Notice that on the Home tab and Mini toolbar, the lower part of the Font Color button displays the most recently applied font color—Black.

When you click the Font Color button instead of the Font Color button arrow, the color displayed in the lower part of the Font Color button is applied to selected text without displaying the color gallery.

6 Display **Slide 2**, and then select the title *Eco Tours Division*. On the Mini toolbar, click the **Font Color button** [A ▾] to apply the font color **Black, Text 1** to the selection. Select the subtitle—*Lehua Adventure Tours*—and then change the **Font Color** to **Black, Text 1**. Compare your screen with Figure 1.38.

Figure 1.38

Font color changed
to black

7 Display **Slide 3**, and then select the title—*Native Hawaii*. From the Mini toolbar, apply **Bold** B and **Italic** I, and then **Save** your presentation.

Activity 1.18 | Aligning Text and Changing Line Spacing

In PowerPoint, *text alignment* refers to the horizontal placement of text within a placeholder. You can align left, centered, right, or justified.

1 Display **Slide 2**. Click anywhere in the title—*Eco Tours Division*.

2 On the **Home tab**, in the **Paragraph group**, click the **Align Text Right** button to right align the text within the placeholder.

3 Display **Slide 7**. Click anywhere in the text below the title. In the **Paragraph group**, click the **Line Spacing** button . In the list, click **1.5** to change from single-spacing between lines to one-and-a-half spacing between lines. **Save** your presentation, and then compare your screen with Figure 1.39.

Figure 1.39

Line Spacing button

Line Spacing
changed to 1.5

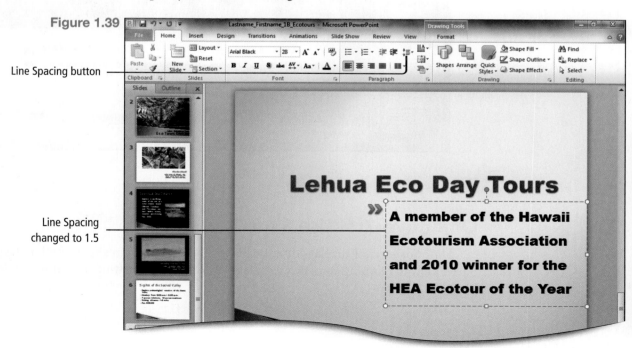

PowerPoint | Chapter 1

Activity 1.19 | Modifying Slide Layout

Recall that the slide layout defines the placement of the content placeholders on a slide. PowerPoint includes predefined layouts that you can apply to your slide for the purpose of arranging slide elements.

For example, a Title Slide contains two placeholder elements—the title and the subtitle. When you design your slides, consider the content that you want to include, and then choose a layout with the elements that will display the message you want to convey in the best way.

1 Display **Slide 3**. On the **Home tab**, in the **Slides group**, click the **Layout** button to display the **Slide Layout** gallery. Notice that *Content with Caption* is selected.

The selection indicates the layout of the current slide.

2 Click **Picture with Caption** to change the slide layout, and then compare your screen with Figure 1.40.

The Picture with Caption layout emphasizes the picture more effectively than the Content with Caption layout.

Figure 1.40

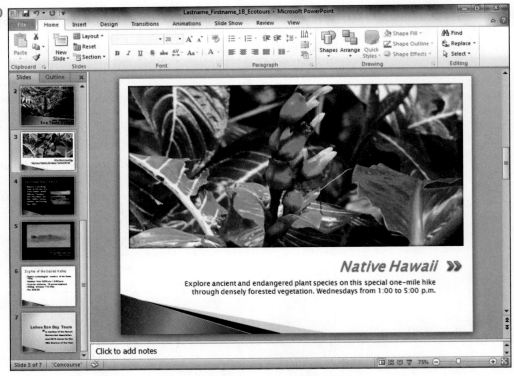

3 **Save** your presentation.

Objective 7 | Use Slide Sorter View

Slide Sorter view displays thumbnails of all of the slides in a presentation. Use Slide Sorter view to rearrange and delete slides and to apply formatting to multiple slides.

Activity 1.20 | Deleting Slides in Slide Sorter View

Another Way

On the Ribbon, click the View tab, and then in the Presentation Views group, click Slide Sorter.

1 In the lower right corner of the PowerPoint window, click the **Slide Sorter** button to display all of the slide thumbnails.

2 Compare your screen with Figure 1.41.

Your slides may display larger or smaller than those shown in Figure 1.41.

Figure 1.41

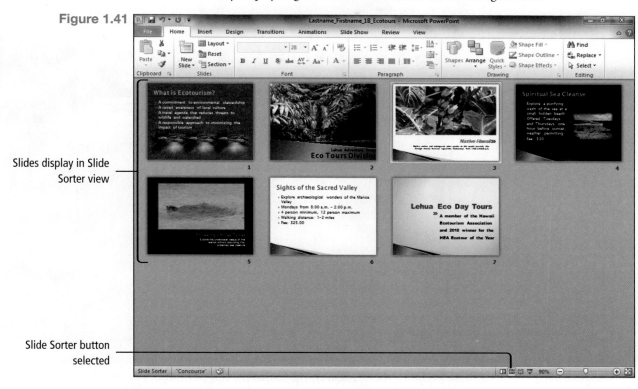

Slides display in Slide Sorter view

Slide Sorter button selected

3 Click **Slide 6**, and notice that a thick outline surrounds the slide, indicating that it is selected. On your keyboard, press Del to delete the slide. Click **Save**.

Activity 1.21 | Moving Slides in Slide Sorter View

1 With the presentation displayed in Slide Sorter view, point to **Slide 2**. Hold down the left mouse button, and then drag the slide to the left until the vertical move bar and pointer indicating the position to which the slide will be moved is positioned to the left of **Slide 1**, as shown in Figure 1.42.

Figure 1.42

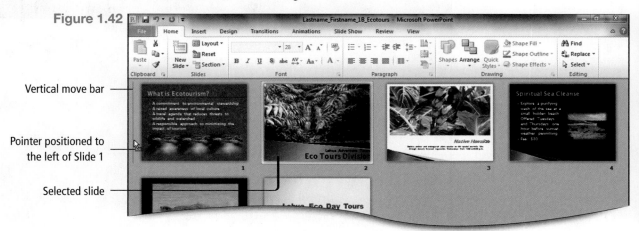

Vertical move bar

Pointer positioned to the left of Slide 1

Selected slide

2 Release the mouse button to move the slide to the Slide 1 position in the presentation.

3 Click **Slide 4**, hold down Ctrl, and then click **Slide 5**. Compare your screen with Figure 1.43.

Both slides are outlined, indicating that both are selected. By holding down Ctrl, you can create a group of selected slides.

Figure 1.43

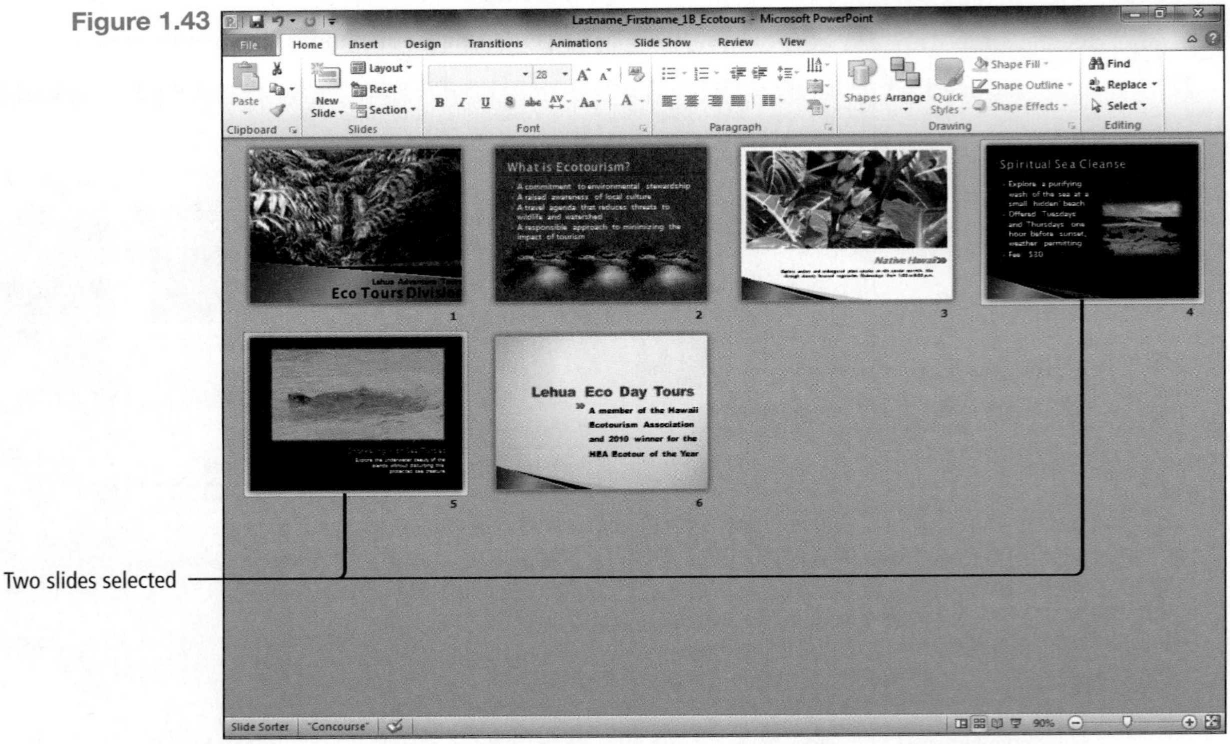

Two slides selected

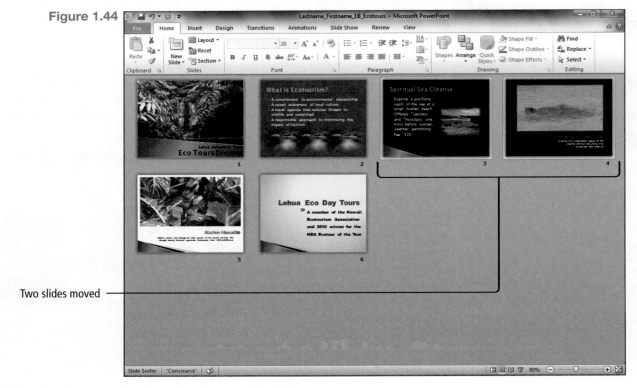

4 Point to either of the selected slides, hold down the left mouse button, and then drag to position the vertical move bar to the left of **Slide 3**. Release the mouse button to move the two slides, and then compare your screen with Figure 1.44.

Figure 1.44

Two slides moved

5 In the status bar, click the **Normal** button 🖳 to return to Normal view. **Save** 🖫 your presentation.

Objective 8 | Apply Slide Transitions

Slide transitions are the motion effects that occur in Slide Show view when you move from one slide to the next during a presentation. You can choose from a variety of transitions, and you can control the speed and method with which the slides advance.

Activity 1.22 | Applying Slide Transitions to a Presentation

1 Display **Slide 1**. On the **Transitions tab**, in the **Transition to This Slide group**, click the **More** button 🔽 to display the **Transitions** gallery. Compare your screen with Figure 1.45.

Figure 1.45

Transitions gallery

2 Under **Exciting**, click **Doors** to apply and view the transition. In the **Transition to This Slide group**, click the **Effect Options** button to display the directions from which the slide enters the screen. Click **Horizontal**.

The Effect Options vary depending upon the selected transition and include the direction from which the slide enters the screen or the shape in which the slide displays during the transition.

3 In the **Timing group**, notice that the **Duration** box displays *01.40*, indicating that the transition lasts 1.40 seconds. Click the **Duration** box **up spin arrow** two times so that *01.75* displays. Under **Advance Slide**, verify that the **On Mouse Click** check box is selected; select it if necessary. Compare your screen with Figure 1.46.

When the On Mouse Click option is selected, the presenter controls when the current slide advances to the next slide by clicking the mouse button or by pressing Spacebar.

Figure 1.46

On Mouse Click check box selected

Doors transition selected

Duration changed to *01.75*

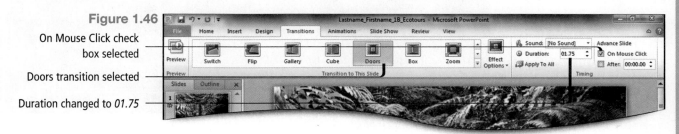

PowerPoint | Chapter 1

4 In the **Timing group**, click the **Apply To All** button so that the Doors, Horizontal with a Duration of 1.75 seconds transition is applied to all of the slides in the presentation. Notice that in the Slides/Outline pane, a star displays below the slide number providing a visual cue that a transition has been applied to the slide.

5 Click the **Slide Show tab**. In the **Start Slide Show group**, click the **From Beginning** button, and then view your presentation, clicking the mouse button to advance through the slides. When the black slide displays, click the mouse button one more time to display the presentation in Normal view. **Save** your presentation 🖫.

> **More Knowledge** | Applying Multiple Slide Transitions
>
> You can apply more than one type of transition in your presentation by displaying the slides one at a time, and then clicking the transition that you want to apply instead of clicking the Apply To All button.

Activity 1.23 | Displaying a Presentation in Reading View

Organizations frequently conduct online meetings when participants are unable to meet in one location. The *Reading view* in PowerPoint displays a presentation in a manner similar to a slide show but the taskbar, title bar, and status bar remain available in the presentation window. Thus, a presenter can easily facilitate an online conference by switching to another window without closing the slide show.

> **Another Way**
> On the View tab, in the Presentation Views group, click Reading View.

1 In the lower right corner of the PowerPoint window, click the **Reading View** button 📖. Compare your screen with Figure 1.47.

In Reading View, the status bar contains the Next and Previous buttons, which are used to navigate in the presentation, and the Menu button which is used to print, copy, and edit slides.

Figure 1.47

Slide displays in Reading View

Reading View button

Next button

Menu button

Previous button

2 In the status bar, click the **Next** button to display **Slide 2**. Press Spacebar to display **Slide 3**. Click the left mouse button to display **Slide 4**. In the status bar, click the **Previous** button to display **Slide 3**.

Another Way

Press Esc to exit Reading view and return to Normal view.

3 In the status bar, click the **Menu** button to display the Reading view menu, and then click **End Show** to return to Normal view.

4 On the **Insert tab**, in the **Text group**, click the **Header & Footer** button, and then click the **Notes and Handouts tab**. Under **Include on page**, select the **Date and time** check box, and if necessary, select **Update automatically**. Clear the **Header** check box, and then select the **Page number** and **Footer** check boxes. In the **Footer** box, using your own name, type **Lastname_Firstname_1B_Ecotours** and then click **Apply to All**.

5 Display **Backstage** view, and then on the right, click **Properties**. Click **Show Document Panel**, and then in the **Author** box, delete any text and type your firstname and lastname. In the **Subject** box, type your course name and section number, and in the **Keywords** box, type **ecotours, ecotourism Close** ☒ the Document Information Panel.

6 Save your presentation 🖫. Submit your presentation electronically or print **Handouts, 6 Slides Horizontal**, as directed by your instructor.

7 Close the presentation and **Exit** PowerPoint.

More Knowledge | Broadcasting a Slide Show

You can broadcast a slide show to remote viewers by using the PowerPoint Broadcast Service or another broadcast service. To broadcast a slide show, on the Slide Show tab, in the Start Slide Show group, click Broadcast Slide Show, and then follow the instructions in the Broadcast Slide Show dialog box to start the broadcast.

End **You have completed Project 1B** ⎯⎯⎯⎯⎯⎯⎯⎯⎯⎯⎯

Content-Based Assessments

Summary

In this chapter, you created a new PowerPoint presentation and edited an existing presentation by reusing slides from another presentation. You entered, edited, and formatted text in Normal view; worked with slides in Slide Sorter view; and viewed the presentation as a slide show. You also added emphasis to your presentations by inserting pictures, applying font formatting, and modifying layout, alignment, and line spacing.

Key Terms

Matching

Match each term in the second column with its correct definition in the first column by writing the letter of the term on the blank line in front of the correct definition.

_____ 1. The PowerPoint view in which the window is divided into three panes—the Slide pane, the Slides/Outline pane, and the Notes pane.

_____ 2. A presentation page that can contain text, pictures, tables, charts, and other multimedia or graphic objects.

_____ 3. The first slide in a presentation, the purpose of which is to provide an introduction to the presentation topic.

_____ 4. A box on a slide with dotted or dashed borders that holds title and body text or other content such as charts, tables, and pictures.

_____ 5. A set of unified design elements that provides a look for your presentation by applying colors, fonts, and effects.

_____ 6. An outline level in a presentation represented by a bullet symbol and identified in a slide by the indentation and the size of the text.

_____ 7. Small circles and squares that indicate that a picture is selected.

_____ 8. A green circle located above a selected picture with which you can rotate the selected image.

_____ 9. A collection of formatting options that can be applied to a picture, text, or object.

_____ 10. A slide that displays at the end of every slide show to indicate that the presentation is over.

_____ 11. Printed images of slides on a sheet of paper.

A Black slide
B Formatting
C List level
D Normal view
E Notes page
F Placeholder
G Rotation handle
H Sizing handles
I Slide
J Slide handouts
K Slide transitions
L Style
M Text alignment
N Theme
O Title slide

_____ 12. A printout that contains the slide image on the top half of the page and notes that you have created in the Notes pane on the lower half of the page.

_____ 13. The process of changing the appearance of the text, layout, and design of a slide.

_____ 14. The term that refers to the horizontal placement of text within a placeholder.

_____ 15. Motion effects that occur in Slide Show view when you move from one slide to the next during a presentation.

Multiple Choice

Circle the correct answer.

1. In Normal view, the pane that displays a large image of the active slide is the:
   A. Slide pane   B. Slides/Outline pane   C. Notes pane

2. In Normal view, the pane that displays below the Slide pane is the:
   A. Slide Sorter pane   B. Slides/Outline pane   C. Notes pane

3. The buttons in the lower right corner that control the look of the presentation window are the:
   A. Normal buttons   B. View buttons   C. Thumbnails buttons

4. The process of modifying a presentation by adding and deleting slides or by changing the contents of individual slides is referred to as:
   A. Editing   B. Formatting   C. Aligning

5. The arrangement of elements, such as title and subtitle text, lists, pictures, tables, charts, shapes, and movies, on a PowerPoint slide is referred to as:
   A. Theme modification   B. Editing   C. Layout

6. Text that prints at the top of a sheet of slide handouts or notes pages is a:
   A. Header   B. Footer   C. Page number

7. Text that displays at the bottom of every slide or that prints at the bottom of a sheet of slide handouts or notes.
   A. Header   B. Footer   C. Page number

8. The command that locates all occurrences of specific text and replaces it with alternative text is:
   A. Replace   B. Find   C. Edit

9. The view in which all of the slides in your presentation display in miniature is:
   A. Slide Sorter view   B. Normal view   C. Reading view

10. A view similar to Slide Show view but that also displays the title bar, status bar, and taskbar is:
    A. Slide Sorter view   B. Normal view   C. Reading view

Apply 1A skills from these Objectives:

1 Create a New Presentation

2 Edit a Presentation in Normal View

3 Add Pictures to a Presentation

4 Print and View a Presentation

Skills Review | Project **1C** Tour Hawaii

In the following Skills Review, you will create a new presentation by inserting content and pictures, adding notes and footers, and applying a presentation theme. Your completed presentation will look similar to Figure 1.48.

Project Files

For Project 1C, you will need the following files:

> New blank PowerPoint presentation
> p01C_Harbor
> p01C_View

You will save your presentation as:

> Lastname_Firstname_1C_Tour_Hawaii

Project Results

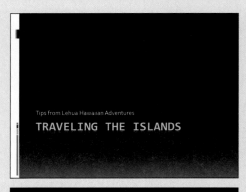

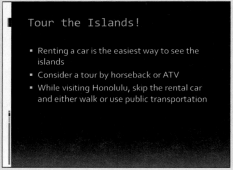

Figure 1.48

(Project 1C Tour Hawaii continues on the next page)

Content-Based Assessments

1 **Start** PowerPoint to display a new blank presentation in Normal view.

a. In the **Slide pane**, click in the title placeholder, which contains the text *Click to add title*. Type **Traveling the Islands**

b. Click in the subtitle placeholder, and then type **Tips from Lehua Hawaiian Adventures**

c. Right-click *Lehua*, and then on the shortcut menu, click **Ignore All**.

d. On the Ribbon, click the **Design tab**. In the **Themes group**, click the **More** button to display the **Themes gallery**. Recall that the themes display alphabetically. Using the ScreenTips, locate and then click **Metro** to apply the Metro theme to the presentation.

e. On the Quick Access Toolbar, click the **Save** button, navigate to your **PowerPoint Chapter 1** folder, and then **Save** the presentation as **Lastname_Firstname_1C_Tour_Hawaii**

2 On the **Home tab**, in the **Slides group**, click the **New Slide button arrow**. In the gallery, click the **Picture with Caption** layout to insert a new slide.

a. In the **Slide pane**, click the text *Click to add title*, and then type **Plan Ahead!**

b. Click in the text placeholder below the title, and then type **A little planning will go a long way toward creating a memorable and trouble-free vacation to the islands.**

c. In the picture placeholder, click the **Insert picture from File** button, and then navigate to your student data files. Click **p01C_View**, and then press Enter to insert the picture.

d. With the picture selected, on the **Format tab**, in the **Picture Styles group**, click the **More** button to display the **Picture Styles** gallery. Use the ScreenTips to locate, and then click the style **Soft Edge Oval**.

e. In the **Adjust group**, click the **Artistic Effects** button, and then in the fourth row, click the second effect—**Texturizer**.

3 On the **Home tab**, in the **Slides group**, click the **New Slide button arrow**. In the gallery, click the **Comparison** layout to insert a new slide. In the title placeholder, type **Destination Hawaii!**

a. Below the title, on the left side of the slide, click in the placeholder containing the pink words *Click to add text*. Type **Arriving by Air**

(Project 1C Tour Hawaii continues on the next page)

b. On the right side of the slide, click in the placeholder containing the pink words *Click to add text*. Type **Arriving by Sea**

c. On the left side of the slide, click in the content placeholder. Type **Western U.S. flight times are approximately 5–7 hours** and then press Enter. Type **Eastern U.S. flight times are approximately 12–14 hours**

d. On the right side of the slide, click in the content placeholder. Type **Embark typically from Western U.S. or Hawaii** and then press Enter. Type **Cruises last from 10 to 14 days**

e. Press Enter, and then on the **Home tab**, in the **Paragraph group**, click the **Increase List Level** button, and then type **Ports of call include Honolulu, Lahaina, Kona, and Hilo**

f. Right-click *Lahaina*, and then on the shortcut menu, click **Ignore All**. **Save** your presentation.

4 On the **Home tab**, in the **Slides group**, click the **New Slide button arrow**. In the gallery, click **Title and Content** to insert a new slide. In the title placeholder, type **Tour the Islands!**

a. In the content placeholder, type the following three bullet points:

Renting a car is the easiest way to see the islands

Consider a tour by horseback or ATV

While visiting Honolulu, skip the rental car and either walk or use public transportation

b. Below the slide, click in the **Notes pane**, and then type **Rental car company offices are located at each major airport.**

5 Insert a **New Slide** using the **Picture with Caption** layout.

a. In the title placeholder, type **Explore!** In the text placeholder, type **Regardless of the mode of transportation that you choose, explore Hawaii for an unforgettable vacation!**

b. In the center of the large picture placeholder, click the **Insert Picture from File** button. Navigate to your student files, and then insert **p01C_Harbor**.

c. With the picture selected, on the **Format tab**, in the **Picture Styles group**, click the **More** button to display the **Picture Styles** gallery. In the first row, click the sixth style—**Soft Edge Rectangle**.

PowerPoint | Chapter 1

6 On the Ribbon, click the **Slide Show tab**. In the **Start Slide Show group**, click the **From Beginning** button.

a. Click the left mouse button or press [Spacebar] to advance to the second slide. Continue to click or press [Spacebar] until the last slide displays, and then click or press [Spacebar] one more time to display a black slide.

b. With the black slide displayed, click the left mouse button or press [Spacebar] to exit the slide show and return to the presentation.

7 Click the **Insert tab**, and then in the **Text group**, click the **Header & Footer** button to display the **Header and Footer** dialog box.

a. In the **Header and Footer** dialog box, click the **Notes and Handouts tab**. Under **Include on page**, select the **Date and time** check box. If necessary, click the Update automatically option button so that the current date prints on the notes and handouts.

b. If necessary, clear the Header check box to omit this element. Select the **Page number** and **Footer** check boxes. In the **Footer** box, type **Lastname_Firstname_1C_Tour_Hawaii** and then click **Apply to All**.

c. Click the **File tab** to display **Backstage** view, and then on the right, click **Properties**. Click **Show Document Panel**, and then in the **Author** box, delete any text and type your firstname and lastname. In the **Subject** box, type your course name and section number, and in the **Keywords** box, type **travel tips, tour tips, trip planning Close** the Document Information Panel.

d. **Save** your presentation. Submit your presentation electronically or print **Handouts, 6 Slides Horizontal** as directed by your instructor. **Close** the presentation.

End **You have completed Project 1C** —————————————————

Skills Review | Project **1D** Luau Information

In the following Skills Review, you will edit an existing presentation by inserting slides from another presentation, applying font and slide formatting, and applying slide transitions. Your completed presentation will look similar to Figure 1.49.

Project Files

For Project 1D, you will need the following files:

p01D_Luau_Information
p01D_History_of_Luaus

You will save your presentation as:

Lastname_Firstname_1D_Luau_Information

Project Results

Figure 1.49

(Project 1D Luau Information continues on the next page)

1 **Start** PowerPoint. From your student files, open **p01D_Luau_Information**. Click the **File tab** to display **Backstage** view, click **Save As**, navigate to your **PowerPoint Chapter 1** folder, and then using your own name, **Save** the file as **Lastname_Firstname_1D_Luau_Information** Take a moment to examine the content of the presentation.

a. In the **Slides/Outline pane**, click the **Outline tab** to display the presentation outline.

b. In the **Outline tab**, in **Slide 2**, click anywhere in the last bullet point, which begins with the text *Luaus were celebrated*.

c. On the **Home tab**, in the **Paragraph group**, click the **Decrease List Level** button one time.

d. In the **Outline tab**, click at the end of the second bullet after the word *journeys*. Press Enter to create a new bullet point at the same list level as the previous bullet point. Type **Today, luaus celebrate events such as weddings, graduations, and first birthdays**

e. In the **Slides/Outline pane**, click the **Slides tab** to display the slide thumbnails.

2 Display **Slide 1**. On the **Home tab**, in the **Slides group**, click the **New Slide button arrow** to display the **Slide Layout** gallery and additional options for inserting slides.

a. Below the gallery, click **Reuse Slides** to open the **Reuse Slides** pane on the right side of the PowerPoint window.

b. In the **Reuse Slides** pane, click the **Browse** button, and then click **Browse File**. In the **Browse** dialog box, navigate to your student files, and then double-click **p01D_History_of_Luaus**.

c. At the bottom of the **Reuse Slides** pane, select the **Keep source formatting** check box.

d. In the **Reuse Slides** pane, click the first slide—*Luau Information*—to insert the slide into the current presentation after **Slide 1**. In the **Reuse Slides** pane, click the second slide—**Celebrating a Luau** to insert it as the third slide in your presentation.

e. In your **1D_Luau_Information** presentation, in the **Slides/Outline pane**, click **Slide 5** to display it in the **Slide pane**.

f. In the **Reuse Slides** pane, click the third slide—*History of the Luau*—and then click the fourth slide—*Luau Delicacies*—to insert both slides after **Slide 5**. In the **Reuse Slides** pane, click the **Close** button.

3 Display **Slide 1**, and then select the title—*Feasting Polynesian Style*.

a. Point to the Mini toolbar, and then click the **Font arrow** to display the available fonts. Click **Arial**, and then click the **Font Size arrow**. Click **44** to change the font size. Use the Mini toolbar to apply **Bold** and **Italic** to the title.

b. Select the subtitle—*A History of the Luau*. Use the Mini toolbar to change the **Font** to **Arial** and the **Font Size** to **28**.

c. On the **Home tab**, in the **Editing group**, click the **Replace** button. In the **Replace** dialog box, click in the **Find what** box. Type **Polynesian** and then in the **Replace with** box, type **Hawaiian**

d. In the **Replace** dialog box, click the **Replace All** button to replace three occurrences of *Polynesian* with *Hawaiian*. Click **OK** to close the message box, and then in the **Replace** dialog box, click the **Close** button.

e. Display **Slide 6**, and then select the second bullet point, which begins *Originally*. On the Mini toolbar, click the **Font Color button arrow**. Under **Theme Colors**, in the sixth column, click the first color—**Teal, Accent 2**.

f. Select the last bullet point, which begins *Taro leaves*. On the Mini toolbar, click the **Font Color button** to apply **Teal, Accent 2** to the selection.

4 With **Slide 6** displayed, click anywhere in the title.

a. On the **Home tab**, in the **Paragraph group**, click the **Center** button to center the text within the placeholder.

b. Display **Slide 7**, and then **Center** the slide title.

c. Display **Slide 5**, and then click anywhere in the text in the lower portion of the slide. In the **Paragraph group**, click the **Line Spacing** button. In the list, click **1.5** to change from single-spacing between lines to one-and-a-half spacing between lines.

d. Display **Slide 3**. On the **Home tab**, in the **Slides group**, click the **Layout** button to display the **Slide Layout** gallery. Click **Title and Content** to change the slide layout.

5 In the lower right corner of the PowerPoint window, in the **View** buttons, click the **Slide Sorter** button to display the slide thumbnails in Slide Sorter view.

(Project 1D Luau Information continues on the next page)

Content-Based Assessments

Skills Review | Project **1D** Luau Information (continued)

a. Click **Slide 2**, and then notice that a thick outline surrounds the slide, indicating that it is selected. Press [Del] to delete the slide.

b. Point to **Slide 5**, hold down the mouse button, and then drag to position the vertical move bar to the left of **Slide 2**. Release the mouse button to move the slide.

c. Point to **Slide 5**, hold down the mouse button, and then drag so that the vertical move bar displays to the right of **Slide 6**. Release the mouse button to move the slide so that it is the last slide in the presentation.

d. Point to **Slide 4**, hold down the mouse button, and then drag so that the vertical move bar displays to the left of **Slide 3**. Release the mouse button to move the slide.

e. In the **View** buttons, click the **Normal** button to return the presentation to Normal view.

6 Display **Slide 1**. On the **Transitions tab**, in the **Transition to This Slide group**, click the **Wipe** button to apply the Wipe transition to the slide.

a. In the **Transition to This Slide group**, click the **Effect Options** button, and then click **From Top**.

b. In the **Timing group**, click the **Duration** box **up spin arrow** twice to change the Duration to *01.50*.

c. In the **Timing group**, under **Advance Slide**, verify that the **On Mouse Click** check box is selected, and select it if necessary.

d. In the **Timing group**, click the **Apply To All** button so that the transition settings are applied to all of the slides in the presentation.

e. Click the **Slide Show tab**. In the **Start Slide Show group**, click the **From Beginning** button, and then view your presentation, clicking the mouse button to advance through the slides. When the black slide displays, click the mouse button one more time to display the presentation in Normal view.

f. On the **Insert tab**, in the **Text group**, click the **Header & Footer** button to display the **Header and Footer** dialog box. Click the **Notes and Handouts tab**. Under **Include on page**, select the **Date and time** check box, and then if necessary, select Update automatically.

g. Clear the **Header** check box if necessary, and then select the **Page number** and **Footer** check boxes. In the **Footer** box, using your own name, type **Lastname_Firstname_1D_Luau_Information** and then click **Apply to All**.

h. Click the **File tab**, and then on the right side of the window, click **Properties**. Click **Show Document Panel**, and then in the **Author** box, delete any text and type your firstname and lastname. In the **Subject** box, type your course name and section number, and in the **Keywords** box, type **luau, Hawaiian history, Hawaiian culture Close** the Document Information Panel.

i. **Save** your presentation. Submit your presentation electronically or print **Handouts, 6 Slides Horizontal** as directed by your instructor. **Close** the presentation.

End **You have completed Project 1D** —————————

Content-Based Assessments

Apply **1A** skills from these Objectives:

1. Create a New Presentation
2. Edit a Presentation in Normal View
3. Add Pictures to a Presentation
4. Print and View a Presentation

Mastering PowerPoint | Project **1E** Boat Tours

In the following Mastering PowerPoint project, you will create a new presentation describing the types of boat tours offered by Lehua Hawaiian Adventures. Your completed presentation will look similar to Figure 1.50.

Project Files

For Project 1E, you will need the following files:

New blank PowerPoint presentation
p01E_Catamaran
p01E_Raft

You will save your presentation as:

Lastname_Firstname_1E_Boat_Tours

Project Results

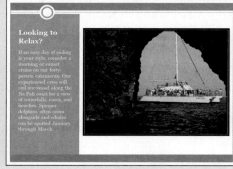
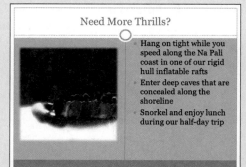

Figure 1.50

(Project 1E Boat Tours continues on the next page)

Content-Based Assessments

Mastering PowerPoint | Project **1E** Boat Tours (continued)

1 **Start** PowerPoint to display a new blank presentation, and then change the **Design** by applying the **Civic** theme. As the title of this presentation type **Viewing Na Pali by Sea** and as the subtitle type **With Lehua Hawaiian Adventures**

2 Correct spelling errors on this slide by choosing the **Ignore All** option for the words *Pali* and *Lehua*. Save the presentation in your **PowerPoint Chapter 1** folder as **Lastname_Firstname_1E_Boat_Tours**

3 Insert a **New Slide** using the **Content with Caption** layout. In the title placeholder, type **Looking to Relax?** In the large content placeholder on the right side of the slide, from your student files, insert the picture **p01E_Catamaran**. Format the picture with the **Compound Frame, Black** picture style and the **Texturizer** artistic effect.

4 In the text placeholder, type **If an easy day of sailing is your style, consider a morning or sunset cruise on our forty-person catamaran. Our experienced crew will sail our vessel along the Na Pali coast for a view of waterfalls, caves, and beaches. Spinner dolphins often swim alongside and whales can be spotted January through March.**

5 Insert a **New Slide** using the **Two Content** layout. In the title placeholder, type **Need More Thrills?** In the content placeholder on the left side of the slide, from your student files, insert the picture **p01E_Raft**. Format the picture with the **Soft Edge Rectangle** picture style and the **Glow Diffused** artistic effect. In the content placeholder on the right side of the slide, type the following three bullet points:

Hang on tight while you speed along the Na Pali coast in one of our rigid hull inflatable rafts

Enter deep caves that are concealed along the shoreline

Snorkel and enjoy lunch during our half-day trip

6 Insert a **New Slide** using the **Comparison** layout. In the title placeholder, type **Which Trip is Right for You?** In the orange placeholder on the left side of the slide, type

Rigid Hull Inflatable Tour and in the orange placeholder on the right side of the slide, type **Catamaran or Sailing Tour**

7 In the content placeholder on the left, type each of the following bullet points, increasing the list level for the last three bullet points as indicated:

Good choice if you are:

> **Interested in adventure**
>
> **Free from recent back injuries**
>
> **Not prone to motion sickness**

8 In the content placeholder on the right, type each of the following bullet points, increasing the list level for the last two bullet points as indicated:

Good choice if you are:

> **Interested in a leisurely cruise**
>
> **Looking forward to an overall smooth ride**

9 On **Slide 4**, type the following notes in the **Notes pane**: **If you need assistance deciding which boat tour is right for you, we'll be happy to help you decide.** Insert a **New Slide** using the **Section Header** layout. In the title placeholder, type **Book Your Trip Today!** In the text placeholder, type **Contact Lehua Hawaiian Adventures**

10 Insert a **Header & Footer** on the **Notes and Handouts**. Include the **Date and time** updated automatically, the **Page number**, and a **Footer**—using your own name—with the text **Lastname_Firstname_1E_Boat_Tours** and apply to all the slides.

11 Display the **Document Information Panel**. Replace the text in the **Author** box with your own firstname and lastname. In the **Subject** box, type your course name and section number, and in the **Keywords** box, type **Na Pali, boat tours, sailing Close** the Document Information Panel.

12 **Save** your presentation, and then view the slide show from the beginning. Submit your presentation electronically or print **Handouts, 6 Slides Horizontal** as directed by your instructor. **Close** the presentation.

End You have completed Project 1E ————

Apply **1B** skills from these Objectives:

5 Edit an Existing Presentation

6 Format a Presentation

7 Use Slide Sorter View

8 Apply Slide Transitions

Mastering PowerPoint | Project **1F** Helicopter Tour

In the following Mastering PowerPoint project, you will edit a presentation describing the helicopter tours offered by Lehua Hawaiian Adventures. Your completed presentation will look similar to Figure 1.51.

Project Files

For Project 1F, you will need the following files:

p01F_Helicopter_Tour
p01F_Aerial_Views

You will save your presentation as:

Lastname_Firstname_1F_Helicopter_Tour

Project Results

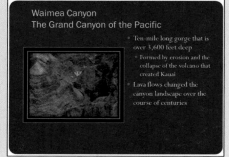
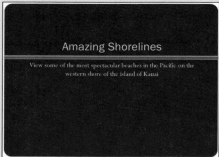

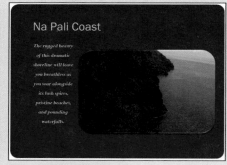

Figure 1.51

(Project 1F Helicopter Tour continues on the next page)

Content-Based Assessments

Mastering PowerPoint | Project **1F** Helicopter Tour (continued)

1 **Start** PowerPoint, and then from your student data files, open the file **p01F_Helicopter_Tour**. In your **PowerPoint Chapter 1** folder, **Save** the file as Lastname_Firstname_1F_Helicopter_Tour

2 Display the presentation **Outline**. In the **Outline tab**, in **Slide 2**, increase the list level of the bullet point that begins *Formed by erosion*. In the **Outline tab**, click at the end of the second bullet point after the word *Kauai*. Press [Enter], and then decrease the list level of the new bullet point. Type **Lava flows changed the canyon landscape over the course of centuries**

3 In the **Slides/Outline pane**, click the **Slides tab** to display the slide thumbnails, and then display **Slide 1**. Display the **Reuse Slides** pane, and then click the **Browse** button. Click **Browse File**, and then in the **Browse** dialog box, from your student files, open **p01F_Aerial_Views**. Select the **Keep source formatting** check box, and then from this group of slides, insert the first and second slides—*Aerial View of Kauai* and *Dramatic Overhead*.

4 In the **Slides/Outline pane**, click **Slide 4** to display it in the **Slide pane**, and then from the **Reuse Slides** pane, insert the third, fourth, fifth, and sixth slides—*Na Pali Coast, Honopu Beach, Amazing Shorelines, Tunnels Beach*. **Close** the **Reuse Slides** pane.

5 Display **Slide 1**, and then select the title—*Maui from the Sky*. Change the **Font** to **Arial**, and the **Font Size** to **44**. Change the **Font Color** to **White, Text 1**. Display the **Replace** dialog box. **Replace All** occurrences of the word **Maui** with **Kauai** and then **Close** the **Replace** dialog box.

6 Display **Slide 5**, and then select the paragraph in the content placeholder. Apply **Bold** and **Italic**, and then **Center** the text. Change the **Line Spacing** to **1.5**. Display **Slide 7**, and then change the **Slide Layout** to **Section Header**. **Center** the text in both placeholders.

7 In **Slide Sorter** view, delete **Slide 2**. Then select **Slides 6** and **7** and move both slides so that they are positioned after **Slide 3**. In **Normal** view, display **Slide 1**. Apply the **Split** transition and change the **Effect Options** to **Horizontal Out**. Apply the transition to all of the slides in the presentation. View the slide show from the beginning.

8 **Insert** a **Header & Footer** on the **Notes and Handouts**. Include the **Date and time** updated automatically, the **Page number**, and a **Footer** with the text **Lastname_Firstname_1F_Helicopter_Tour** Apply to all the slides.

9 Check spelling in the presentation. If necessary, select the Ignore All option if proper names are indicated as misspelled.

10 Display the **Document Information Panel**. Replace the text in the **Author** box with your own firstname and lastname. In the **Subject** box, type your course name and section number, and in the **Keywords** box, type **helicopter, Kauai Close** the Document Information Panel.

11 **Save** your presentation, and then submit your presentation electronically or print **Handouts, 4 Slides Horizontal** as directed by your instructor. **Close** the presentation.

End You have completed Project 1F

Mastering PowerPoint | Project **1G** Volcano Tour

In the following Mastering PowerPoint project, you will edit an existing presentation that describes the tour of Volcanoes National Park offered by Lehua Hawaiian Adventures. Your completed presentation will look similar to Figure 1.52.

Project Files

For Project 1G, you will need the following files:

p01G_Crater_Information
p01G_Lava
p01G_Volcano_Tour

You will save your presentation as:

Lastname_Firstname_1G_Volcano_Tour

Project Results

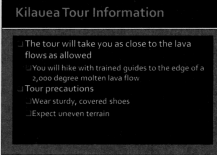

Figure 1.52

(Project 1G Volcano Tour continues on the next page)

Mastering PowerPoint | Project **1G** Volcano Tour (continued)

1 **Start** PowerPoint, and then from your student files, open the file **p01G_Volcano_Tour**. In your **PowerPoint Chapter 1** folder, **Save** the file as **Lastname_Firstname_1G_Volcano_Tour**

2 Replace all occurrences of the text **Diamond Head** with **Kilauea** Display **Slide 3**, open the **Reuse Slides** pane, and then from your student files browse for and display the presentation **p01G_Crater_Information**. If necessary, clear the Keep source formatting check box, and then insert both slides from the **p01G_Crater_Information** file. **Close** the **Reuse Slides** pane.

3 Display the presentation outline, and then in **Slide 3**, increase the list level of the bullet point beginning *You will hike*. In either the **Slide pane** or the **Outline**, click at the end of the last bullet point after the word *flow*, and then insert a new bullet point. Decrease its list level. Type **Tour precautions** and then press ⏎ Enter. Increase the list level, and then type the following two bullet points.

Wear sturdy, covered shoes

Expect uneven terrain

4 Display the slide thumbnails. In **Slide 1**, select the subtitle—*The Big Island's Most Majestic Sight*—and then change the **Font Color** to **White, Text 1** and the **Font Size** to **28**. On **Slide 2**, center the caption text located below the slide title and apply **Bold** and **Italic**. Change the **Line Spacing** to **2.0**. Click in the content placeholder on the right, and then from your student files, insert the picture

p01G_Lava. Format the picture with the **Beveled Oval, Black** picture style and the **Paint Brush** artistic effect.

5 In **Slide Sorter** view, move **Slide 5** between **Slides 3** and **4**. In **Normal** view, on **Slide 5**, change the slide **Layout** to **Title Slide**, and then type the following notes in the **Notes pane: Recent volcanic activity at the national park site may result in changes to the tour itinerary.** Apply the **Uncover** transition and change the **Effect Options** to **From Top**. Change the **Timing** by increasing the **Duration** to **01.50**. Apply the transition effect to all of the slides. View the slide show from the beginning.

6 **Insert** a **Header & Footer** on the **Notes and Handouts**. Include the **Date and time** updated automatically, the **Page number**, and a **Footer**, using your own name, with the text **Lastname_Firstname_1G_Volcano_Tour**

7 Check spelling in the presentation. If necessary, select the Ignore All option if proper names are indicated as misspelled.

8 Display the **Document Information Panel**. Replace the text in the **Author** box with your own firstname and lastname. In the **Subject** box, type your course name and section number, and in the **Keywords** box, type **Kilauea, volcano Close** the Document Information Panel.

9 **Save** your presentation. Submit your presentation electronically or print **Handouts, 6 Slides Horizontal** as directed by your instructor. **Close** the presentation.

End **You have completed Project 1G** ——————————————

Content-Based Assessments

GO! Fix It | Project **1H** Hawaii Guide

Project Files

For Project 1H, you will need the following files:

>   p01H_Hawaii_Guide
>   p01H_Islands

You will save your presentation as:

>   Lastname_Firstname_1H_Hawaii_Guide

In this project, you will edit a presentation prepared by Lehua Hawaiian Adventures that describes some of the activities on each of the Hawaiian Islands. From the student files that accompany this textbook, open the file p01H_Hawaii_Guide, and then save the file in your chapter folder as **Lastname_ Firstname_1H_Hawaii_Guide**

To complete the project, you should know:

- All of the slides in the p01H_Islands presentation should be reused in this presentation and inserted after Slide 2. Correct two spelling errors and ignore all instances of proper names that are indicated as misspelled.

- The Opulent theme should be applied.

- Slides 3 through 8 should be arranged alphabetically according to the name of the island

- On the Maui and Molokai slides, the list level of the second bullet points should decreased.

- The Layout for Slide 2 should be Section Header, the slide should be moved to the end of the presentation, and the Flip transition using the Left effect option should be applied to all of the slides in the presentation.

- Document Properties should include your name, course name and section, and the keywords **guide, islands** A Header & Footer should be inserted on the Notes and Handouts that includes the Date and time updated automatically, the Page number, and a Footer with the text **Lastname_Firstname_1H_Hawaii_Guide**

Save your presentation and submit electronically or print Handouts, 4 Slides Horizontal as directed by your instructor. Close the presentation.

End **You have completed Project 1H** ———————————————————

Content-Based Assessments

Apply a combination of the **1A** and **1B** skills.

GO! Make It | Project 1I Dolphin Encounter

Project Files

For Project 1I, you will need the following files:

p01I_Dolphin_Encounters
p01I_Dolphin

You will save your presentation as:

Lastname_Firstname_1I_Dolphin_Encounters

From your student files, open p01I_Dolphin_Encounters, and then save it in your PowerPoint Chapter 1 folder as **Lastname_Firstname_1I_Dolphin_Encounters**

By using the skills you practiced in this chapter, create the slide shown in Figure 1.53 by inserting a new Slide 2 with the layout and text shown in the figure. The title font size is 36, and the font color is Black, Background 1. The caption text font is Arial, and the font size is 16 with bold and italic applied. To complete the slide, from your student files, insert the picture p01H_Dolphin. Insert the date and time updated automatically, the file name, and a page number in the Notes and Handouts footer. In the Document Information Panel, add your name and course information and the keyword **dolphin** Save your presentation, and then print or submit electronically as directed by your instructor.

Project Results

Figure 1.53

Dolphin Encounters!

Learn about dolphins during our 30-minute training program. Then join the trainers in our pool as you swim and play with our dolphin friends!

End You have completed Project 1I _____

Content-Based Assessments

GO! Solve It | Project **1J** Planning Tips

Project Files

For Project 1J, you will need the following file:

p01J_Planning_Tips

You will save your presentation as:

Lastname_Firstname_1J_Planning_Tips

Open the file p01J_Planning_Tips and save it as **Lastname_Firstname_1J_Planning_Tips** Complete the presentation by applying a theme and by correcting spelling errors. Format the presentation attractively by applying appropriate font formatting and by changing text alignment and line spacing. Change the layout of at least one slide to a layout that will accommodate a picture. Insert a picture that you have taken yourself, or use one of the pictures in your student data files that you inserted in other projects in this chapter. On the last slide, insert an appropriate picture, and then apply picture styles to both pictures. Apply slide transitions to all of the slides in the presentation, and then insert a header and footer that includes the date and time updated automatically, the file name in the footer, and the page number. Add your name, your course name and section number, and the keywords **planning, weather** to the Properties area. Save and print or submit as directed by your instructor.

	Performance Level		
	Exemplary: You consistently applied the relevant skills	**Proficient:** You sometimes, but not always, applied the relevant skills	**Developing:** You rarely or never applied the relevant skills
Apply a theme	An appropriate theme was applied to the presentation.	A theme was applied but was not appropriate for the presentation.	A theme was not applied.
Apply font and slide formatting	Font and slide formatting is attractive and appropriate.	Adequately formatted but difficult to read or unattractive.	Inadequate or no formatting.
Use appropriate pictures and apply styles attractively	Two appropriate pictures are inserted and styles are applied attractively.	Pictures are inserted but styles are not applied or are inappropriately applied.	Pictures are not inserted.

Performance Elements

End **You have completed Project 1J** ——————————————

Content-Based Assessments

GO! Solve It | Project **1K** Hikes

Project Files

For Project 1K, you will need the following file:

p01K_Hikes

You will save your presentation as:

Lastname_Firstname_1K_Hikes

Open the file p01K_Hikes and save it as **Lastname_Firstname_1K_Hikes** Complete the presentation by applying an appropriate theme. Move Slide 2 to the end of the presentation, and then change the layout to one appropriate for the end of the presentation. Format the presentation attractively by applying font formatting and by changing text alignment and line spacing. Review the information on Slide 3, and then increase list levels appropriately on this slide. Apply picture styles to the two pictures in the presentation and an artistic effect to at least one picture. Apply slide transitions to all of the slides. Insert a header and footer that includes the date and time updated automatically, the file name in the footer, and the page number. Add your name, your course name and section number, and the keywords **hiking Akaka Falls, Waimea Canyon** to the Properties area. Save and print or submit as directed by your instructor.

		Performance Level		
		Exemplary: You consistently applied the relevant skills	**Proficient:** You sometimes, but not always, applied the relevant skills	**Developing:** You rarely or never applied the relevant skills
Performance Elements	Apply a theme	An appropriate theme was applied to the presentation.	A theme was applied but was not appropriate for the presentation.	A theme was not applied.
	Apply appropriate formatting	Formatting is attractive and appropriate.	Adequately formatted but difficult to read or unattractive.	Inadequate or no formatting.
	Apply appropriate list levels	List levels are applied appropriately.	Some, but not all, list levels are appropriately applied.	Changes to list levels were not made.

End You have completed Project 1K —————————————————

Outcomes-Based Assessments

Rubric

The following outcomes-based assessments are *open-ended assessments*. That is, there is no specific correct result; your result will depend on your approach to the information provided. Make *Professional Quality* your goal. Use the following scoring rubric to guide you in *how* to approach the problem, and then to evaluate *how well* your approach solves the problem.

The *criteria*—Software Mastery, Content, Format and Layout, and Process—represent the knowledge and skills you have gained that you can apply to solving the problem. The *levels of performance*—Professional Quality, Approaching Professional Quality, or Needs Quality Improvements—help you and your instructor evaluate your result.

	Your completed project is of Professional Quality if you:	Your completed project is Approaching Professional Quality if you:	Your completed project Needs Quality Improvements if you:
1-Software Mastery	Choose and apply the most appropriate skills, tools, and features and identify efficient methods to solve the problem.	Choose and apply some appropriate skills, tools, and features, but not in the most efficient manner.	Choose inappropriate skills, tools, or features, or are inefficient in solving the problem.
2-Content	Construct a solution that is clear and well organized, contains content that is accurate, appropriate to the audience and purpose, and is complete. Provide a solution that contains no errors in spelling, grammar, or style.	Construct a solution in which some components are unclear, poorly organized, inconsistent, or incomplete. Misjudge the needs of the audience. Have some errors in spelling, grammar, or style, but the errors do not detract from comprehension.	Construct a solution that is unclear, incomplete, or poorly organized; contains some inaccurate or inappropriate content; and contains many errors in spelling, grammar, or style. Do not solve the problem.
3-Format and Layout	Format and arrange all elements to communicate information and ideas, clarify function, illustrate relationships, and indicate relative importance.	Apply appropriate format and layout features to some elements, but not others. Overuse features, causing minor distraction.	Apply format and layout that does not communicate information or ideas clearly. Do not use format and layout features to clarify function, illustrate relationships, or indicate relative importance. Use available features excessively, causing distraction.
4-Process	Use an organized approach that integrates planning, development, self-assessment, revision, and reflection.	Demonstrate an organized approach in some areas, but not others; or, use an insufficient process of organization throughout.	Do not use an organized approach to solve the problem.

Outcomes-Based Assessments

GO! Think | Project 1L Big Island

Project Files

For Project 1L, you will need the following files:

New blank PowerPoint presentation
p01L_Fishing
p01L_Monument

You will save your presentation as:

Lastname_Firstname_1L_Big_Island

Carl Kawaoka, Tour Operations Manager for Lehua Hawaiian Adventures, is developing a presentation describing sea tours on the Big Island of Hawaii to be shown at a travel fair on the mainland. In the presentation, Carl will be showcasing the company's two most popular sea excursions: The Captain Cook Monument Snorkeling Tour and the Kona Deep Sea Fishing Tour.

On the Captain Cook Monument Snorkeling Tour, guests meet at 8:00 a.m. at the Lehua Hawaiian Adventures Kona location and then board a 12-passenger rigid hull inflatable raft. Captained by a U.S. Coast Guard licensed crew, the raft is navigated along the Hawaii coastline, exploring sea caves, lava tubes, and waterfalls. Upon arrival at the Monument, guests snorkel in Hawaii's incredible undersea world of colorful fish, sea turtles, and stingrays. Lehua Hawaiian Adventures provides the lunch, snacks, drinks, and snorkeling equipment and asks that guests bring their own towels, sunscreen, swim suits, and sense of adventure. This tour lasts 5 hours and the fee is $85.

On the Kona Deep Sea Fishing Tour, guests meet at 7:00 a.m. at the Lehua Hawaiian Adventures Kona location and then board a 32-foot Blackfin fishing boat. The boat is captained by a U.S. Coast Guard licensed crew of three. A maximum of six guests are allowed on each trip, which sails, weather permitting, every Wednesday, Friday, and Saturday. For deep sea fishing, there is no better place than the Kona coast. On full-day adventures, it is common for guests to catch marlin, sailfish, ahi, ono, and mahi-mahi. This tour lasts 8 hours and the fee is $385.

Using the preceding information, create a presentation that Carl can show at the travel fair. The presentation should include four to six slides describing the two tours. Apply an appropriate theme and use slide layouts that will effectively present the content. From your student files, insert the pictures p01L_Fishing and p01L_Monument on appropriate slides and apply picture styles or artistic effects to enhance the pictures. Apply font formatting and slide transitions, and modify text alignment and line spacing as necessary. Save the file as **Lastname_Firstname_1L_Big_Island** and then insert a header and footer that include the date and time updated automatically, the file name in the footer, and the page number. Add your name, your course name and section number, and the keywords **sea tours, deep sea fishing, snorkeling tours** to the Properties area. Save and print or submit as directed by your instructor.

End You have completed Project 1L ────────────

Outcomes-Based Assessments

Apply a combination of the **1A** and **1B** skills.

GO! Think | Project **1M** Beaches

Project Files

For Project 1M, you will need the following files:

> New blank PowerPoint presentation
> p01M_Black_Sand
> p01M_Kite_Surf
> p01M_Lithified_Cliffs
> p01M_Reef
> p01M_Tide_Pools

You will save your presentation as:

> Lastname_Firstname_1M_Beaches

Katherine Okubo, President of Lehua Hawaiian Adventures, is making a presentation to groups of tourists at a number of hotels on the Hawaiian Islands. She would like to begin the presentation with an introduction to the beaches of Hawaii before discussing the many ways in which her company can assist tourists with selecting the places they would like to visit. The following paragraphs contain some of the information about the shorelines and beaches that Katherine would like to include in the presentation.

The shorelines of Hawaii vary tremendously, from black sand beaches with pounding surf to beaches of pink and white sand with calm waters perfect for snorkeling. Many of the shorelines provide picturesque hiking, shallow tide pools for exploring, beautiful reef where fish and turtles delight snorkelers, and waves that the most adventurous kite and board surfers enjoy. The terrain and the water make it easy for visitors to find a favorite beach in Hawaii.

The northern shore of Oahu is famous for its surfing beaches, while the southern shores of Kauai provide hikers with amazing views of the lithified cliffs formed by the power of the ocean. Black sand beaches are common on Hawaii, formed by the lava flows that created the islands. The reef that buffers many beaches from the open ocean is home to a wide variety of sea life that can be enjoyed while scuba diving and snorkeling.

Using the preceding information, create the first four to six slides of a presentation that Katherine can show during her discussion. Apply an appropriate theme and use slide layouts that will effectively present the content. Several picture files listed at the beginning of this project have been provided that you can insert in your presentation. Apply font formatting, picture styles, and slide transitions, and modify text alignment and line spacing as necessary. Save the file as **Lastname_Firstname_1M_Beaches** and then insert a header and footer that include the date and time updated automatically, the file name in the footer, and the page number. Add your name, your course name and section number, and the keywords **beaches, Black Sands beach, tide pools, lithified cliffs, scuba, snorkeling** to the Properties area. Save and print or submit as directed by your instructor.

End You have completed Project 1M ——————————

Outcomes-Based Assessments

Apply a combination of the **1A** and **1B** skills.

You and GO! | Project **1N** Travel

Choose a place to which you have traveled or would like to travel. Create a presentation with at least six slides that describes the location, the method of travel, the qualities of the location that make it interesting or fun, the places you can visit, and any cultural activities in which you might like to participate. Choose an appropriate theme, slide layouts, and pictures, and then format the presentation attractively. Save your presentation as **Lastname_Firstname_1N_Travel** and submit as directed.

 You have completed Project 1N ——————————————

Apply a combination of the **1A** and **1B** skills.

GO! Collaborate | Project **1O** Bell Orchid Hotels Group Running Case

This project relates to the **Bell Orchid Hotels**. Your instructor may assign this group case project to your class. If your instructor assigns this project, he or she will provide you with information and instructions to work as part of a group. The group will apply the skills gained thus far to help the Bell Orchid Hotels achieve their business goals.

 You have completed Project 1O ——————————————

Formatting PowerPoint Presentations

OUTCOMES

At the end of this chapter you will be able to:

PROJECT 2A
Format a presentation to add visual interest and clarity.

OBJECTIVES

Mastering these objectives will enable you to:

1. Format Numbered and Bulleted Lists (p. 681)
2. Insert Clip Art (p. 685)
3. Insert Text Boxes and Shapes (p. 690)
4. Format Objects (p. 694)

PROJECT 2B
Enhance a presentation with WordArt and diagrams.

5. Remove Picture Backgrounds and Insert WordArt (p. 703)
6. Create and Format a SmartArt Graphic (p. 708)

Nikolay Okhitin/Shutterstock

In This Chapter

A PowerPoint presentation is a visual aid in which well-designed slides help the audience understand complex information while keeping them focused on the message. Color is an important element that enhances your slides and draws the audience's interest by creating focus. When designing the background and element colors for your presentation, be sure that the colors you use provide contrast so that the text is visible on the background

Fascination Entertainment Group operates 15 regional theme parks across the United States, Mexico, and Canada. Park types include traditional theme parks, water parks, and animal parks. This year the company will launch three of its new "Fascination Parks" where attractions combine fun and the discovery of math and science information, and where teens and adults enjoy the free Friday night concerts.

Project 2A Employee Training Presentation

Project Activities

In Activities 2.01 through 2.14, you will format a presentation for Yuki Hiroko, Director of Operations for Fascination Entertainment Group, that describes important safety guidelines for employees. Your completed presentation will look similar to Figure 2.1.

Project Files

For Project 2A, you will need the following file:

> p02A_Safety

You will save your presentation as:

> Lastname_Firstname_2A_Safety

Project Results

Figure 2.1
Project 2A Safety

Objective 1 | Format Numbered and Bulleted Lists

Recall that formatting is the process of changing the appearance of the text, layout, or design of a slide. You can format slide content by changing the bulleted and numbered list styles and colors.

Activity 2.01 | Selecting Placeholder Text

Recall that a placeholder is a box on a slide with dotted or dashed borders that holds title and body text or other content such as charts, tables, and pictures. You can format placeholder contents by selecting text or by selecting the entire placeholder.

1 **Start** PowerPoint. From the student files that accompany this textbook, locate and open **p02A_Safety**. On the **File tab**, click **Save As**, and then navigate to the location where you are storing your projects for this chapter. Create a new folder named **PowerPoint Chapter 2** and then in the **File name** box and using your own name, type **Lastname_Firstname_2A_Safety** Click **Save** or press Enter. Take a moment to view each slide and become familiar with the contents of this presentation.

2 Display **Slide 2**. Click anywhere in the content placeholder with the single bullet point, and then compare your screen with Figure 2.2.

A dashed border displays, indicating that you can make editing changes to the placeholder text.

Figure 2.2

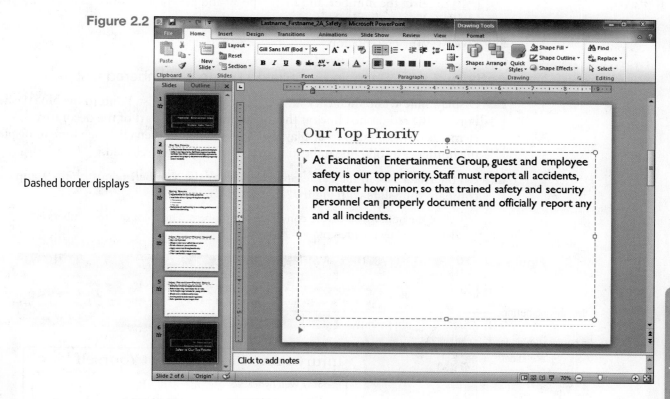

Dashed border displays

3 Point anywhere on the dashed border to display the 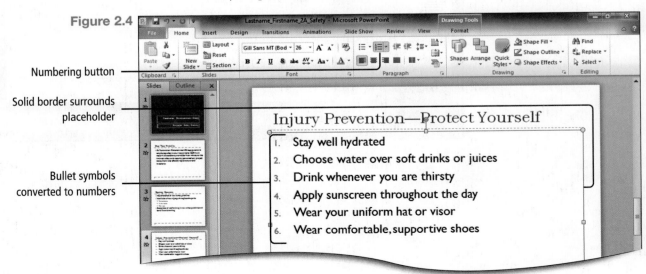 pointer, and then click one time to display the border as a solid line. Compare your screen with Figure 2.3.

> When a placeholder's border displays as a solid line, all of the text in the placeholder is selected, and any formatting changes that you make will be applied to *all* of the text in the placeholder.

Figure 2.3

Solid border indicates that all placeholder text is selected

4 With the border of the placeholder displaying as a solid line, click in the **Font Size** box 44 ▾ to select the number, and then type **30** and press Enter. Notice that the font size of *all* of the placeholder text increases.

5 Save 🖫 your presentation.

Activity 2.02 | Changing a Bulleted List to a Numbered List

1 Display **Slide 4**, and then click anywhere in the bulleted list. Point to the blue dashed border (the red dashed lines at the top and bottom are part of the decorative elements of the theme) to display the 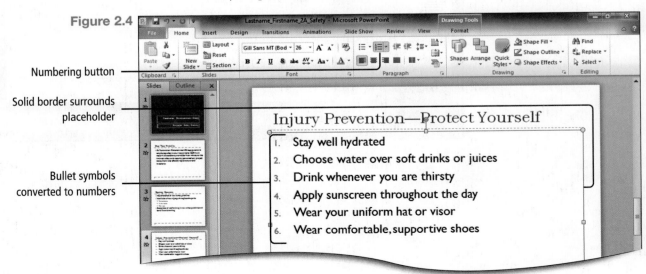 pointer, and then click one time to display the border as a solid line indicating that all of the text is selected.

2 On the **Home tab**, in the **Paragraph group**, click the **Numbering** button ▯▾, and then compare your slide with Figure 2.4.

> All of the bullet symbols are converted to numbers. The color of the numbers is determined by the presentation theme.

Figure 2.4

Numbering button

Solid border surrounds placeholder

Bullet symbols converted to numbers

3 Save 💾 your presentation.

Activity 2.03 | Modifying a Bulleted List Style

The presentation theme includes default styles for the bullet points in content placeholders. You can customize a bullet by changing its style, color, and size.

1 Display **Slide 3**, and then select the three second-level bullet points—*Ride entrances*, *Visitor center*, and *Rest areas*.

2 On the **Home tab**, in the **Paragraph group**, click the **Bullets button arrow** ☰ ▾ to display the **Bullets** gallery, and then compare your screen with Figure 2.5.

The Bullets gallery displays several bullet characters that you can apply to the selection.

Figure 2.5

Bullets button arrow

Bullets gallery

Selected bullet points

3 At the bottom of the **Bullets** gallery, click **Bullets and Numbering**. In the **Bullets and Numbering** dialog box, point to each bullet style to display its ScreenTip. Then, in the second row, click **Star Bullets**. If the Star Bullets are not available, in the second row of bullets, click the second bullet style, and then click the Reset button.

4 Below the gallery, click the **Color** button. Under **Theme Colors**, in the sixth column, click the fifth color—**Red, Accent 2, Darker 25%**. In the **Size** box, select the existing number, type **100** and then compare your dialog box with Figure 2.6.

Figure 2.6

Bullets and Numbering
dialog box

Star Bullets selected

Bullet size changed
to 100% of text

Bullet color changed

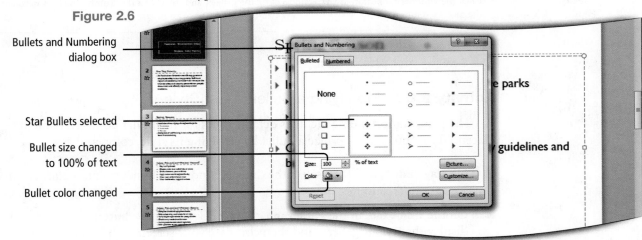

5 Click **OK** to apply the bullet style, and then **Save** 🖫 your presentation.

More Knowledge | Using Other Symbols as Bullet Characters

Many bullets styles are available to insert in your presentation. In the Bullets and Numbering dialog box, click the Customize button to view additional bullet styles.

Activity 2.04 | Removing a Bullet Symbol from a Bullet Point

The Bullet button is a toggle button, enabling you to turn the bullet symbol on and off. A slide that contains a single bullet point can be formatted as a single paragraph *without* a bullet symbol.

1 Display **Slide 2**, and then click in the paragraph. On the **Home tab**, in the **Paragraph group**, click the **Bullets** button 📋▾. Compare your screen with Figure 2.7.

The bullet symbol no longer displays, and the bullet button is no longer selected. Additionally, the indentation associated with the list level is removed.

2 **Center** 📑 the paragraph. On the **Home tab**, in the **Paragraph group**, click the **Line Spacing** button 📑▾, and then click **1.5**.

Figure 2.7

Bullets button

Bullet symbol and
indentation removed
from paragraph

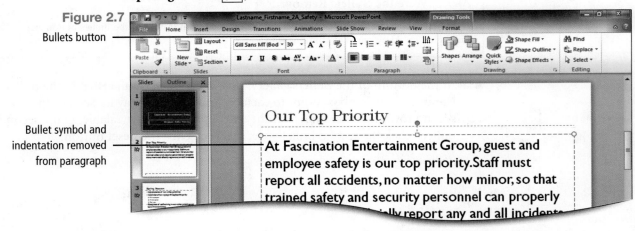

3 Click the dashed border to display the solid border and to select all of the text in the paragraph, and then apply **Bold** 𝐁 and **Italic** 𝐼. Click in the slide title, and then click the **Center** button 📑. **Save** 🖫 your presentation.

Objective 2 | Insert Clip Art

There are many sources from which you can insert images into a presentation. One type of image that you can insert is a **clip**—a single media file such as art, sound, animation, or a movie.

Activity 2.05 | Inserting Clip Art

1 Display **Slide 4**, and then on the **Home tab**, in the **Slides group**, click the **Layout** button. Click **Two Content** to change the slide layout.

2 In the placeholder on the right side of the slide, click the **Clip Art** button 📇 to display the **Clip Art** pane, and then compare your screen with Figure 2.8.

Figure 2.8

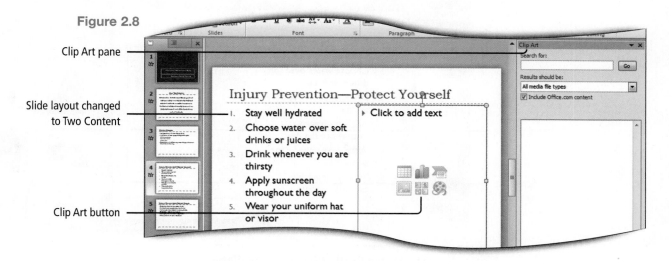

3 In the **Clip Art** pane, click in the **Search for** box, and then replace any existing text with **bottled water** so that PowerPoint can search for images that contain the keyword *bottled water*.

4 Click the **Results should be arrow**, and then click as necessary to *clear* the **Illustrations**, **Videos**, and **Audio** check boxes and to select only the **Photographs** check box. Compare your screen with Figure 2.9.

> With the Photographs check box selected, PowerPoint will search for images that were created with a digital camera or a scanner.

Figure 2.9

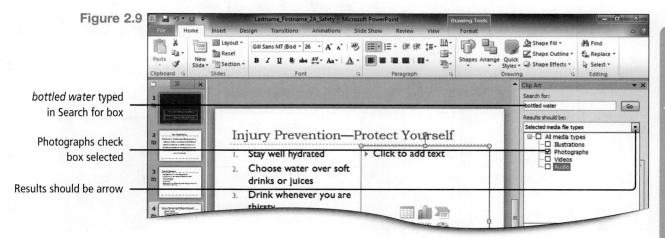

5 In the **Clip Art** pane, click the **Results should be arrow** to close the list. Then, if necessary, select the **Include Office.com content** check box so that images available on Office.com are included in the search.

6 In the **Clip Art** pane, click **Go** to display clips in the Clip Art pane. Scroll through the clips, and then locate and point to the image of the water pouring from a glass water bottle on a blue background. Compare your screen with Figure 2.10.

> When you point to an image in the Clip Art pane, a ScreenTip displays the keywords and information about the size of the image.

Figure 2.10

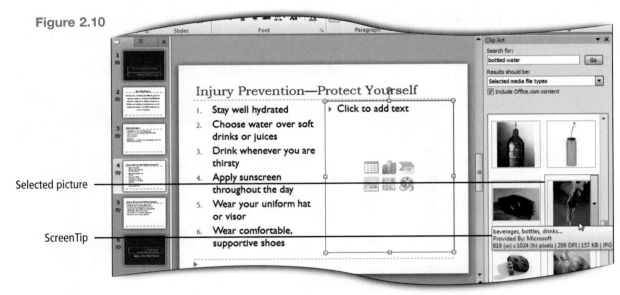

Selected picture

ScreenTip

Alert! | **Is the Water Bottle Picture Unavailable?**

If you are unable to locate the suggested picture, choose another similar image.

---

7 Click the water bottle picture to insert it in the content placeholder on the right side of the slide. **Close** ☒ the **Clip Art** pane, and then compare your slide with Figure 2.11.

> On the Ribbon, the Picture Tools display, and the water bottle image is surrounded by sizing handles, indicating that it is selected.

Figure 2.11

Picture Tools display

Picture inserted and selected

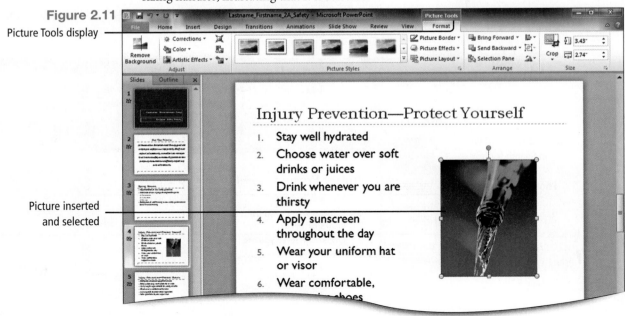

8 Display **Slide 1**. Click the **Insert tab**, and then in the **Images group**, click **Clip Art**.

9 In the **Clip Art** pane, in the **Search for** box, search for **red lights** and then click **Go**. Scroll as necessary to locate the picture of the single red warning light. Point to the picture, and then compare your screen with Figure 2.12.

If you cannot locate the picture, select another appropriate image.

Figure 2.12

red lights typed in Search for box

Selected picture

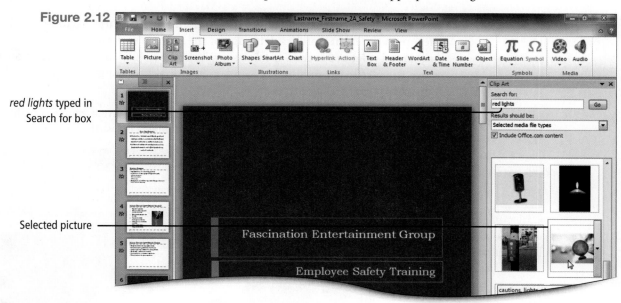

10 Click the **red light** picture to insert it in the center of the slide, and then **Close** ✖ the **Clip Art** pane. **Save** 🖫 your presentation.

When you use the Clip Art command on the Ribbon instead of the Clip Art button in a content placeholder, PowerPoint inserts the image in the center of the slide.

Activity 2.06 | Moving and Sizing Images

Recall that when an image is selected, it is surrounded by sizing handles that you can drag to resize the image. You can also resize an image using the Shape Height and Shape Width boxes on the Format tab. When you point to the image, rather than pointing to a sizing handle, the move pointer—a four-headed arrow—displays, indicating that you can move the image.

> **Another Way**
>
> Alternatively, drag a corner sizing handle to resize an image proportionately.

1 If necessary, select the picture of the red light. On the **Format tab**, in the **Size group**, click in the **Shape Height** box 🔳, and then replace the selected number with **3.5**

2 Press Enter to resize the image. Notice that the picture is resized proportionately, and the **Width** box displays *5.26*. Compare your screen with Figure 2.13.

When a picture is resized in this manner, the width adjusts in proportion to the picture height.

Figure 2.13

3.5 typed in Shape Height box

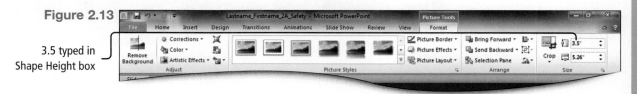

PowerPoint | Chapter 2

3 Display the **View tab**. In the **Show group**, verify that the **Ruler** check box is selected and if necessary, select it. On the horizontal and vertical rulers, notice that *0* displays in the center.

> Horizontally, the PowerPoint ruler indicates measurements from the center *out* to the left and to the right. Vertically, the PowerPoint ruler indicates measurements from the center up and down.

4 Point to the picture to display the 🔧 pointer. Hold down Shift, and then drag the picture to the right until the left edge of the picture is aligned with the **left half of the horizontal ruler at 3 inches**. If necessary, hold down Ctrl and press an arrow key to move the picture in small increments in any direction for a more precise placement. Compare your screen with Figure 2.14.

> Pressing Shift while dragging an object constrains object movement in a straight line either vertically or horizontally. Here, pressing Shift maintains the vertical placement of the picture.

Figure 2.14

Ruler check box selected

Horizontal ruler

Left edge of picture aligns with left half of horizontal ruler at 3 inches

Vertical ruler

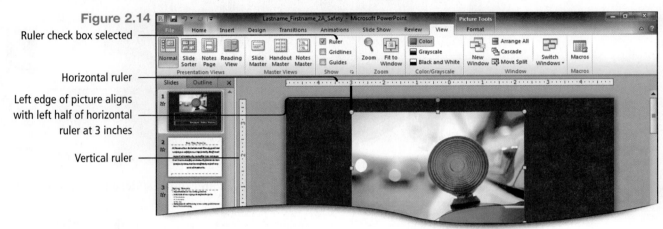

5 Display **Slide 6**. On the **Insert tab**, in the **Images group**, click the **Clip Art** button. In the **Clip Art** pane, search for **amusement park** and then click **Go**. Locate and click any picture of a ferris wheel, and then compare your slide with Figure 2.15.

Figure 2.15

Keyword amusement park typed in Search for box

Your picture may differ

6 **Close** ☒ the **Clip Art** pane, and be sure that the picture is still selected. On the **Format tab**, in the **Size group**, click in the **Shape Height** box 🔢. Replace the displayed number with **2.5** and then press Enter to resize the picture. Compare your screen with Figure 2.16.

Figure 2.16

2.5 typed in
Shape Height box

Picture resized

7 **Save** 🖫 your presentation.

> **More Knowledge | Moving an Object by Using the Arrow Keys**
>
> You can use the directional arrow keys on your keyboard to move a picture, shape, or other object in small increments. Select the object so that its outside border displays as a solid line. Then, on your keyboard, hold down the [Ctrl] key and press the directional arrow keys to move the selected object in precise increments.

Activity 2.07 | Changing the Shape of a Picture

An inserted picture is rectangular in shape; however, you can modify a picture by changing its shape.

1 Display **Slide 1**, and then select the picture.

2 On the **Format tab**, in the **Size group**, *point* to the **Crop button arrow**, and then compare your screen with Figure 2.17.

The Crop button is a split button. The upper section—the Crop button—enables the *crop* feature, which reduces the size of a picture by removing vertical or horizontal edges. The lower section—the Crop arrow—displays cropping options, such as the option to crop a picture to a shape.

Figure 2.17

Crop button arrow

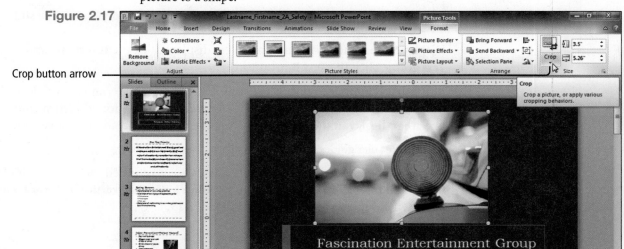

PowerPoint | Chapter 2

3 Click the **Crop button arrow**, and then point to **Crop to Shape** to display a gallery of shapes. Compare your screen with Figure 2.18.

Figure 2.18

Crop to Shape option

Crop button arrow

Selected picture

Shapes gallery

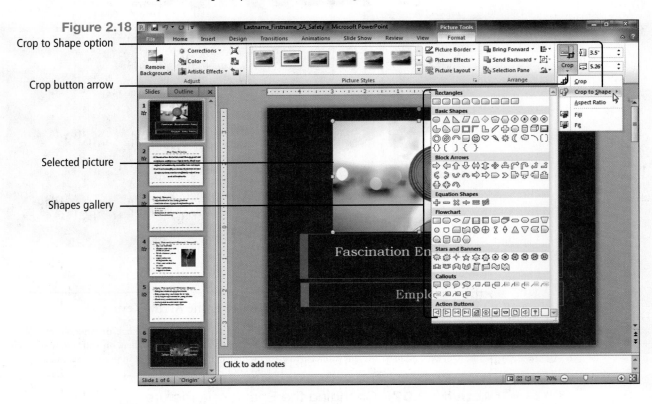

4 Under **Basic Shapes**, in the first row, click the first shape—**Oval**—to change the picture's shape to an oval. **Save** your presentation.

Objective 3 | Insert Text Boxes and Shapes

You can use objects, including text boxes and shapes, to draw attention to important information or to serve as containers for slide text. Many shapes, including lines, arrows, ovals, and rectangles, are available to insert and position anywhere on your slides.

Activity 2.08 | Inserting a Text Box

A *text box* is an object with which you can position text anywhere on a slide.

1 Display **Slide 5** and verify that the rulers display. Click the **Insert tab**, and then in the **Text group**, click the **Text Box** button.

2 Move the ⬇ pointer to several different places on the slide, and as you do so, in the horizontal and vertical rulers, notice that *ruler guides*—dotted vertical and horizontal lines that display in the rulers indicating the pointer's position—move also.

Use the ruler guides to help you position objects on a slide.

3 Position the pointer so that the ruler guides are positioned on the **left half of the horizontal ruler at 4.5 inches** and on the **lower half of the vertical ruler at 1.5 inches**, and then compare your screen with Figure 2.19.

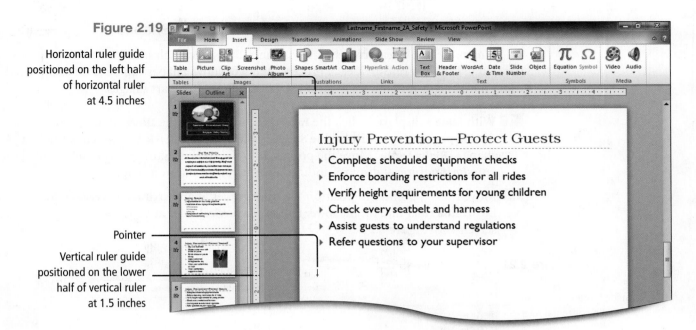

Figure 2.19

Horizontal ruler guide positioned on the left half of horizontal ruler at 4.5 inches

Pointer

Vertical ruler guide positioned on the lower half of vertical ruler at 1.5 inches

4 Click one time to create a narrow rectangular text box. With the insertion point blinking inside the text box, type **If Safety is Questionable** Notice that as you type, the width of the text box expands to accommodate the text. Compare your screen with Figure 2.20.

Do not be concerned if your text box is not positioned exactly as shown in Figure 2.20.

Figure 2.20

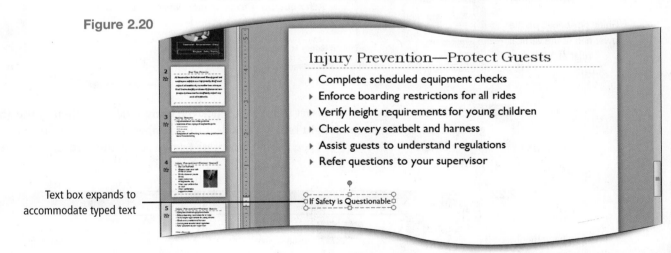

Text box expands to accommodate typed text

Alert! | Does the Text in the Text Box Display Vertically, One Character at a Time?

If you move the pointer when you click to create the text box, PowerPoint sets the width of the text box and does not widen to accommodate the text. If this happened to you, your text may display vertically instead of horizontally or it may display on two lines. Click Undo, and then repeat the steps again, being sure that you do not move the mouse when you click to insert the text box.

5 Select the text that you typed, change the **Font Size** to **24** and then **Save** your presentation.

You can format the text in a text box by using the same techniques that you use to format text in any other placeholder. For example, you can change the font, font style, font size, and font color.

PowerPoint | **Chapter 2**

Activity 2.09 | Inserting, Sizing, and Positioning Shapes

Shapes include lines, arrows, stars, banners, ovals, rectangles, and other basic shapes you can use to illustrate an idea, a process, or a workflow. Shapes can be sized and moved using the same techniques that you use to size and move clip art images.

1 With **Slide 5** displayed, click the **Insert tab**, and then in the **Illustrations group**, click the **Shapes** button to display the **Shapes** gallery. Under **Block Arrows**, click the first shape—**Right Arrow**. Move the pointer into the slide until the ⊞ pointer—called the *crosshair pointer*—displays, indicating that you can draw a shape.

2 Move the ⊞ pointer to position the ruler guides at approximately **zero on the horizontal ruler** and on the **lower half of the vertical ruler at 1.5 inches**. Compare your screen with Figure 2.21.

Figure 2.21

Guide positioned at zero on the horizontal ruler

Crosshair pointer

Guide positioned on the lower half of the vertical ruler at 1.5 inches

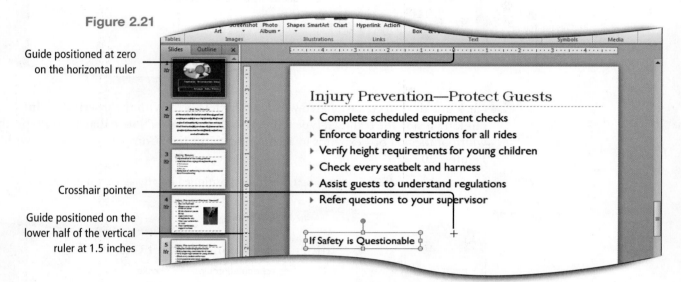

3 Click the mouse button to insert the arrow. Click the **Format tab**, and then in the **Size group**, click in the **Shape Height** box to select the number. Type **.5** and then click in the **Shape Width** box. Type **2** and then press Enter to resize the arrow. Compare your screen with Figure 2.22.

Figure 2.22

Shape Height changed to 0.5″

Shape Width changed to 2″

Arrow resized

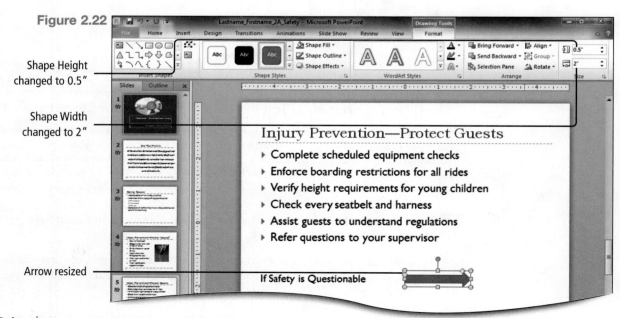

4 On the **Format tab**, in the **Insert Shapes group**, click the **More** button ⏷. In the gallery, under **Basic Shapes**, in the first row, click the second to last shape—**Octagon**.

5 Move the ⊞ pointer to position the ruler guides on the **right half of the horizontal ruler at 2.5 inches** and on the **lower half of the vertical ruler at 1 inch**, and then click one time to insert an octagon.

6 On the **Format tab**, in the **Size group**, click in the **Shape Height** box 🔲 to select the number. Type **2** and then click in the **Shape Width** box 🔲. Type **2** and then press Enter to resize the octagon. Compare your slide with Figure 2.23. Do not be concerned if your shapes are not positioned exactly as shown in the figure.

Figure 2.23

Shape Height and Width each changed to 2″

Octagon inserted and sized

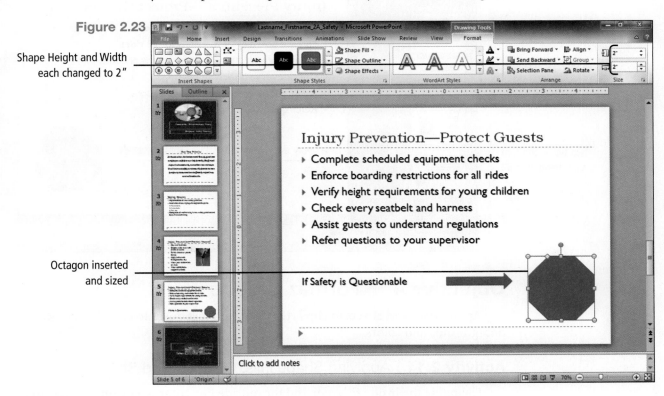

7 **Save** 💾 your presentation.

Activity 2.10 | Adding Text to Shapes

Shapes can serve as a container for text. After you add text to a shape, you can change the font and font size, apply font styles, and change text alignment.

1 On **Slide 5**, if necessary, click the octagon so that it is selected. Type **STOP** and notice that the text is centered within the octagon.

2 Select the text *STOP*, and then on the Mini toolbar, change the **Font Size** to **32**. Compare your screen with Figure 2.24, and then **Save** 🖫 your presentation.

Figure 2.24

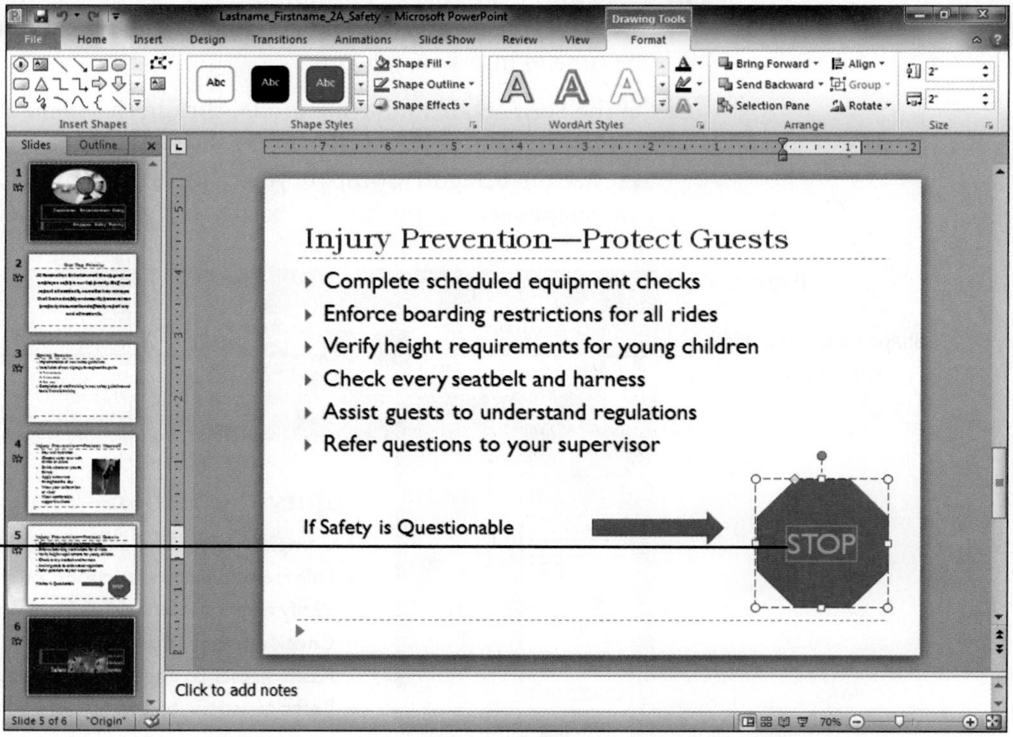

Text typed and font size changed to 32

Objective 4 | Format Objects

Apply styles and effects to clip art, shapes, and text boxes to complement slide backgrounds and colors.

Activity 2.11 | Applying Shape Fills, Outlines, and Styles

Changing the inside *fill color* and the outside line color is a distinctive way to format a shape. A fill color is the inside color of text or of an object. Use the Shape Styles gallery to apply predefined combinations of these fill and line colors and also to apply other effects.

1 On **Slide 5**, click anywhere in the text *If Safety is Questionable* to select the text box. On the **Format tab**, in the **Shape Styles group**, click the **More** button ⤓ to display the **Shape Styles** gallery.

2 In the last row, click the third style—**Intense Effect - Red, Accent 2**. Select the **octagon** shape, and then apply the same style you applied to the text box—**Intense Effect - Red, Accent 2**.

3 Select the **arrow**, and then display the **Shape Styles** gallery. In the last row, click the second style—**Intense Effect - Blue, Accent 1**.

4 Click in a blank part of the slide so that no objects are selected, and then compare your screen with Figure 2.25.

Figure 2.25

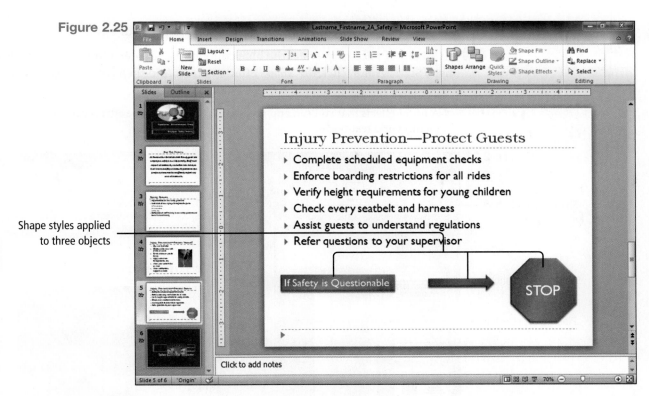

Shape styles applied to three objects

5 Display **Slide 2**, and then click anywhere in the paragraph of text to select the content placeholder.

6 On the **Format tab**, in the **Shape Styles group**, click the **Shape Fill** button, and then point to several of the theme colors and watch as Live Preview changes the inside color of the text box. In the fifth column, click the first color—**Blue, Accent 1**.

7 In the **Shape Styles group**, click the **Shape Outline** button. Point to **Weight**, click **3 pt**, and notice that a thick outline surrounds the text placeholder. Click in a blank area of the slide so that nothing is selected, and then compare your slide with Figure 2.26.

You can use combinations of shape fill, outline colors, and weights to format an object.

Figure 2.26

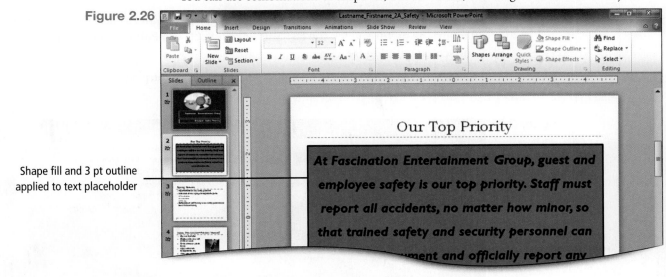

Shape fill and 3 pt outline applied to text placeholder

8 Click in the paragraph, and then press Ctrl + A to select all of the paragraph text, right-click in the selection to display the Mini toolbar, and then click the **Font Color button arrow** A to display the **Theme Colors** gallery. Click the first color—**White, Background 1**. **Save** your presentation.

PowerPoint | Chapter 2

Activity 2.12 | Applying Shape and Picture Effects

1 On **Slide 2**, if necessary, select the blue content placeholder. On the **Format tab**, in the **Shape Styles group**, click the **Shape Effects** button, and then compare your screen with Figure 2.27.

A list of effects that you can apply to shapes displays. These effects can also be applied to pictures and text boxes.

Figure 2.27

Shape Effects button

Shape effects options

Placeholder selected

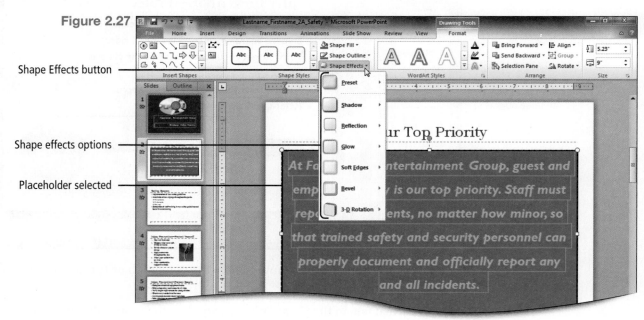

2 Point to **Bevel** to display the **Bevel** gallery. Point to each bevel to view its ScreenTip and to use Live Preview to examine the effect of each bevel on the content placeholder. In the last row, click the last bevel—**Art Deco**.

3 Display **Slide 1**, and then select the picture. On the **Format tab**, in the **Picture Styles group**, click the **Picture Effects** button.

4 Point to **Soft Edges**, and then in the **Soft Edges** gallery, point to each style to view its effect on the picture. Click the last **Soft Edges** effect—**50 Point**, and then compare your screen with Figure 2.28.

The soft edges effect softens and blurs the outer edge of the picture so that it blends into the slide background.

Figure 2.28

Soft edges effect applied to selected picture

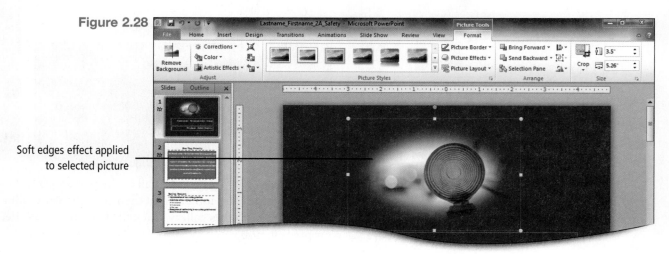

5 Display **Slide 4**, and then select the picture. On the **Format tab**, in the **Picture Styles group**, click the **Picture Effects** button, and then point to **Glow**.

6 Point to several of the effects to view the effect on the picture, and then under **Glow Variations**, in the second row, click the second glow effect—**Red, 8 pt glow, Accent color 2**. Click in a blank area of the slide to deselect the picture. Compare your slide with Figure 2.29, and then **Save** 🖫 your presentation.

The glow effect applies a colored, softly blurred outline to the selected object.

Figure 2.29

Glow effect applied to picture

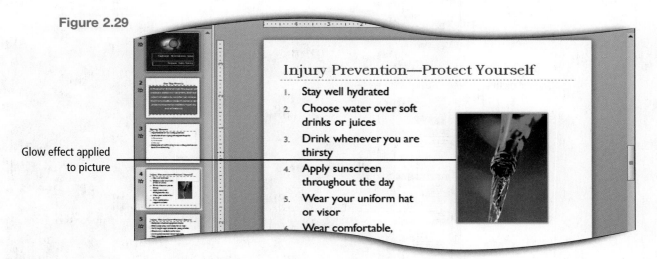

Activity 2.13 │ Duplicating Objects

1 Display **Slide 6**, point to the picture to display the pointer, and then drag up and to the left so that the upper left corner of the picture aligns with the upper left corner of the slide.

2 Press and hold down Ctrl, and then press D one time. Release Ctrl.

A duplicate of the picture overlaps the original picture and the duplicated image is selected.

3 Point to the duplicated picture to display the pointer, and then drag down and to the right approximately 1 inch in both directions so that both pictures are visible. Compare your screen with Figure 2.30. Do not be concerned if your pictures are not positioned exactly as shown in the figure.

Figure 2.30

Original picture moved to upper left corner of slide

Duplicated picture moved so that both pictures are visible

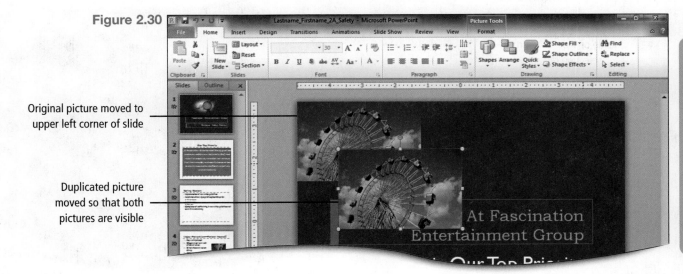

4 With the duplicated image selected, hold down Ctrl, and then press D to insert a third copy of the image.

5 Click anywhere on the slide so that none of the three pictures are selected. **Save** 💾 your presentation, and then compare your screen with Figure 2.31. Do not be concerned if your pictures are not positioned exactly as shown.

Figure 2.31

Original picture

First copy

Second copy

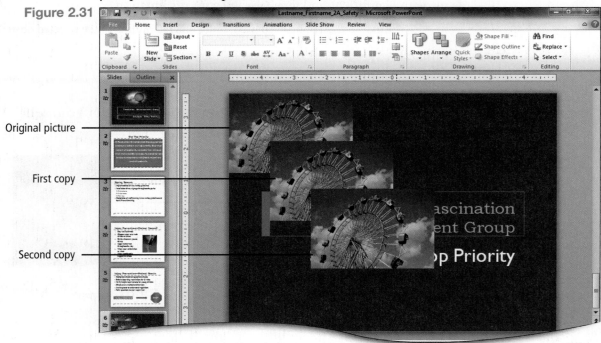

Activity 2.14 | Aligning and Distributing Objects

Another Way

Hold down Shift and click each object that you want to select.

When you insert multiple objects on a slide, you can use commands on the Ribbon to align and distribute the objects precisely.

1 With **Slide 6** displayed, position the pointer in the gray area of the Slide pane just outside the upper left corner of the slide to display the 🔍 pointer. Drag down and to the right to draw a transparent blue rectangle that encloses the three pictures. Compare your slide with Figure 2.32.

Figure 2.32

Pointer initially positioned outside of slide to begin selection rectangle

Transparent, blue selection rectangle encloses three pictures

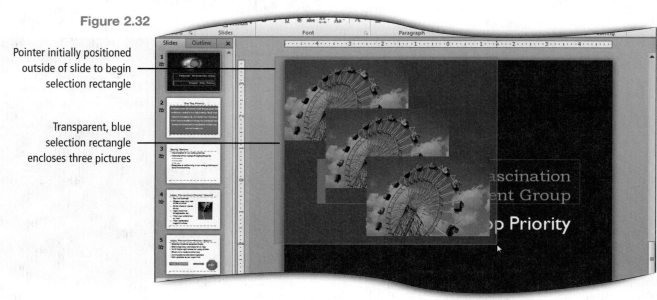

2 Release the mouse button to select the three objects, and then compare your screen with Figure 2.33.

> Objects completely enclosed by a selection rectangle are selected when the mouse button is released.

Figure 2.33

Three pictures selected

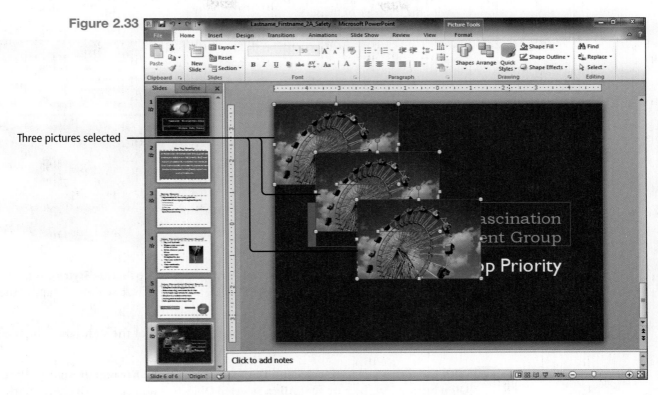

3 Click the **Format tab**, and then in the **Arrange group**, click the **Align** button. Toward the bottom of the menu, click **Align to Slide** to activate this setting.

> When you select an alignment option, this setting will cause the objects to align with the edges of the slide.

4 On the **Format tab**, in the **Arrange group**, click the **Align** button again, and then click **Align Top**.

> The top of each of the three pictures aligns with the top edge of the slide.

5 Click in a blank area of the slide so that nothing is selected. Then, click the third picture. Point to the picture so that the pointer displays, and then drag to the right so that its upper right corner aligns with the upper right corner of the slide.

6 Hold down Shift and click the remaining two pictures so that all three pictures are selected. On the **Format tab**, in the **Arrange group**, click the **Align** button. Click **Align Selected Objects** to activate this setting.

> When you select an alignment option, this setting will cause the objects that you select to align relative to each other.

PowerPoint | Chapter 2

7 With the three pictures still selected, on the **Format tab**, in the **Arrange group**, click the **Align** button 🖹 again, and then click **Distribute Horizontally**. Compare your screen with Figure 2.34.

> The three pictures are spaced and distributed evenly across the top of the slide and aligned with the top edge of the slide.

Figure 2.34

Pictures aligned with top edge of slide and distributed evenly across top edge of slide

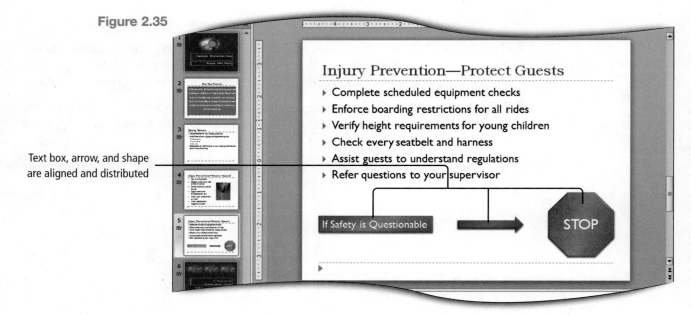

8 With the three pictures selected, on the **Format tab**, in the **Picture Styles group**, click the **Picture Effects** button. Point to **Soft Edges**, and then click **50 Point** to apply the picture effect to all three images.

9 Display **Slide 5**, hold down Shift, and then at the bottom of the slide, click the **text box**, the **arrow**, and the **octagon** to select all three objects.

10 With the three objects selected, on the **Format tab**, in the **Arrange group**, click the **Align** button 🖹. Be sure that **Align Selected Objects** is still active—a check mark displays to its left. Then, click **Align Middle**. Click the **Align** button again, and then click **Distribute Horizontally**.

> The midpoint of each object aligns and the three objects are distributed evenly.

11 Click anywhere on the slide so that none of the objects are selected, and then compare your screen with Figure 2.35.

Figure 2.35

Text box, arrow, and shape are aligned and distributed

12 On the **Slide Show tab**, in the **Start Slide Show group**, click the **From Beginning** button, and then view the slide show. Press Esc when the black slide displays.

13 On the **Insert tab**, in the **Text group**, click the **Header & Footer** button to display the **Header and Footer** dialog box. Click the **Notes and Handouts tab**. Under **Include on page**, select the **Date and time** check box, and then select **Update automatically**. If necessary, clear the Header check box. Select the **Page number** and **Footer** check boxes. In the **Footer** box, using your own name, type **Lastname_Firstname_2A_Safety** and then click **Apply to All**.

14 Display the **Document Properties**. Replace the text in the **Author** box with your own firstname and lastname, in the **Subject** box, type your course name and section number, and in the **Keywords** box, type **safety, injury prevention Close** the **Document Information Panel**.

15 **Save** your presentation ⊟. Print **Handouts 6 Slides Horizontal**, or submit your presentation electronically as directed by your instructor.

16 **Close** the presentation and exit PowerPoint.

End **You have completed Project 2A** ————————————

Project 2B Event Announcement

Project Activities

In Activities 2.15 through 2.24, you will format slides in a presentation for the Fascination Entertainment Group Marketing Director that informs employees about upcoming events at the company's amusement parks. You will enhance the presentation using SmartArt and WordArt graphics. Your completed presentation will look similar to Figure 2.36.

Project Files

For Project 2B, you will need the following files:

p02B_Celebrations
p02B_Canada_Contact
p02B_Mexico_Contact
p02B_US_Contact

You will save your presentation as:

Lastname_Firstname_2B_Celebrations

Project Results

Figure 2.36
Project 2B Celebrations

Objective 5 | Remove Picture Backgrounds and Insert WordArt

To avoid the boxy look that results when you insert an image into a presentation, use **Background Removal** to flow a picture into the content of the presentation. Background Removal removes unwanted portions of a picture so that the picture does not appear as a self-contained rectangle.

WordArt is a gallery of text styles with which you can create decorative effects, such as shadowed or mirrored text. You can choose from the gallery of WordArt styles to insert a new WordArt object or you can customize existing text by applying WordArt formatting.

Activity 2.15 | Removing the Background from a Picture and Applying Soft Edge Options

1 **Start** PowerPoint. From your student files, open **p02B_Celebrations**. On the **View tab**, in the **Show group**, if necessary, select the Ruler check box. In your **PowerPoint Chapter 2** folder, save the file as **Lastname_Firstname_2B_Celebrations**

2 Display **Slide 6**. Notice how the picture is a self-contained rectangle and that it has a much darker black background than the presentation. Click the picture to select it, and then on the **Format tab**, in the **Adjust group**, click the **Remove Background** button. Compare your screen with Figure 2.37.

PowerPoint determines what portion of the picture is the foreground—the portion to keep—and which portion is the background—the portion to remove. The background is overlaid in magenta, leaving the remaining portion of the picture as it will look when the background removal is complete. A rectangular selection area displays that can be moved and sized to select additional areas of the picture. The Background Removal options display in the Refine group on the Ribbon.

Figure 2.37
Background Removal commands
Background Removal tab
Picture background overlaid with magenta color
Area of picture in foreground as determined by PowerPoint
Selection rectangle

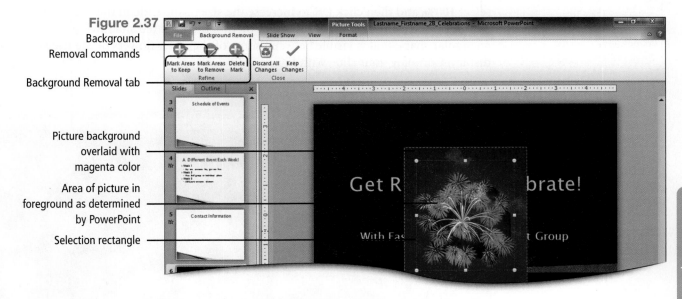

PowerPoint | Chapter 2

3 On the **selection rectangle**, point to the left center sizing handle to display the ↔ pointer, and then drag to the left so that the left edge of the selection area aligns with the dashed border surrounding the picture. Compare your screen with Figure 2.38.

> When you move or size the selection area, the areas outside the selection are treated as background and are removed. Thus, you have control over which portions of the picture that you keep. Here, by resizing the selection area on the left, a larger area of each *flower* in the fireworks is included in the foreground of the picture. On the right side of the fireworks picture, some dark red shadowing is visible as part of the picture.

Figure 2.38

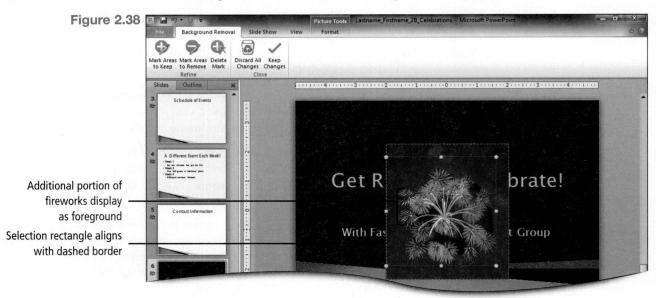

Additional portion of fireworks display as foreground

Selection rectangle aligns with dashed border

Another Way

In the status bar, use the Zoom Slider options to increase the Zoom to 100%.

4 On the **View tab**, in the **Zoom group**, click the **Zoom** button. In the **Zoom** dialog box, select **100%**, and then click **OK** to increase the size of the slide in the Slide pane. Notice on the right side of the fireworks picture the dark red shadowing in a triangular shape that is visible between some of the outer flowers of the fireworks display. Compare your slide with Figure 2.39.

Figure 2.39

Dark red triangle-shaped shadowing between outer flowers

Zoom level set to 100%

5 On the **Background Removal tab**, in the **Refine group**, click the **Mark Areas to Remove** button, and then position the pencil pointer so that the ruler guides align on the **right half of the horizontal ruler at 1 inch** and on the **lower half of the vertical ruler at 0.5 inch**. Click one time to insert a deletion mark, and then compare your screen with Figure 2.40. If your mark is not positioned as shown in the figure, click Undo and begin again.

> You can surround irregular-shaped areas that you want to remove with deletion marks. Here, you can begin to surround the dark red shadow by placing a deletion mark in one corner of the red triangular area.

Figure 2.40

Mark Areas to Remove button

Deletion mark

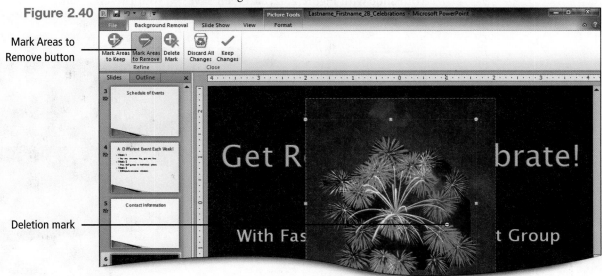

6 With the pencil pointer still active, position the pointer to align the ruler guides on the **right half of the horizontal ruler at approximately 1.5 inches** and on the **lower half of the vertical ruler to 0.75 inch** so that the pointer is aligned on the right edge of the dark red triangle. Click one time to insert another mark. Compare your screen with Figure 2.41.

> The two inserted marks provide PowerPoint sufficient information to remove the triangular-shaped red and black shadowed area. If the area is not removed as shown in the figure, insert additional deletion marks as necessary.

Figure 2.41

Background area removed from picture

Additional deletion mark inserted

7 On the **Background Removal tab**, in the **Close group**, click the **Keep Changes** button to remove the background. On the far right edge of the status bar, click the **Fit slide to current window** button.

PowerPoint | Chapter 2

8 With the picture selected, on the **Format tab**, in the **Picture Styles group**, click the **Picture Effects** button, point to **Soft Edges**, and then click **50 Point**. In the **Adjust group**, click the **Artistic Effects** button, and then in the fourth row, click the third effect—**Crisscross Etching**.

9 In the **Size group**, click in the **Shape Height** box ⬚, replace the number with **3.5** and then press ⏎. In the **Arrange group**, click the **Align** button ⬚, and then click **Align Center**. Click the **Align** button ⬚ again, and then click **Align Middle**. Compare your slide with Figure 2.42, and then **Save** 💾 your presentation.

Figure 2.42

Picture sized, moved, and formatted

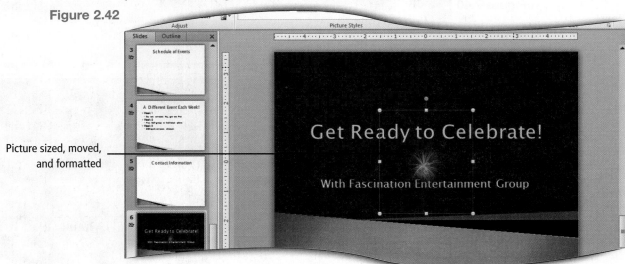

Activity 2.16 | Applying WordArt Styles to Existing Text

1 On **Slide 6**, click anywhere in the word *Get* to activate the title placeholder, and then select the title—*Get Ready to Celebrate*. Click the **Format tab**, and then in the **WordArt Styles group**, click the **More** button ▾.

The WordArt Styles gallery displays in two sections. If you choose a WordArt style in the Applies to Selected Text section, you must first select all of the text to which you want to apply the WordArt. If you choose a WordArt style in the Applies to All Text in the Shape section, the WordArt style is applied to all of the text in the placeholder or shape.

2 Under **Applies to Selected Text**, in the first row, click the fourth style—**Fill – White, Outline – Accent 1**, and then compare your screen with Figure 2.43.

Figure 2.43

WordArt style is applied to selected text

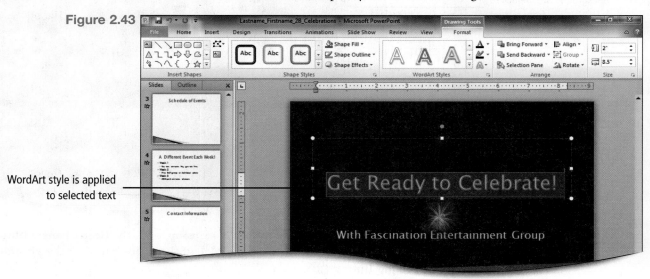

3 With the text still selected, in the **WordArt Styles group**, click the **Text Fill button arrow** ▲. Under **Theme Colors**, in the sixth column, click the fourth color—**Dark Red, Accent 2, Lighter 40%**, and then compare your screen with Figure 2.44.

Figure 2.44

Text Fill button reflects applied color

Text Fill color applied to WordArt

4 Display **Slide 1**, and then click anywhere in the title—*Fascination Entertainment Group*.

5 Click the **Format tab**, and then in the **WordArt Styles group**, click the **More** button ▼ to display the **WordArt Styles** gallery. Under **Applies to All Text in the Shape**, in the first row, click the third style—**Fill – Dark Red, Accent 2, Warm Matte Bevel**, and then compare your screen with Figure 2.45.

Figure 2.45

WordArt style applied to title

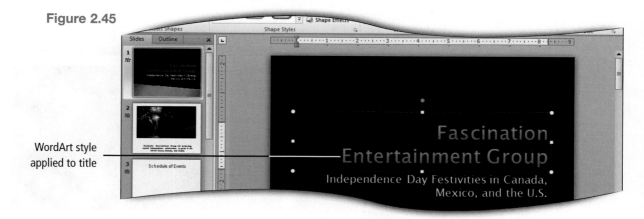

6 Save 🖫 your presentation.

Activity 2.17 | Inserting a WordArt Object

In addition to formatting existing text using WordArt, you can insert a new WordArt object anywhere on a slide.

1 Display **Slide 2**. Click the **Insert tab**, and then in the **Text group**, click the **WordArt** button. In the gallery, in the last row, click the third WordArt style—**Fill – Dark Red, Accent 2, Matte Bevel**.

In the center of your slide, a WordArt placeholder displays *Your text here*. Text that you type will replace this text and the placeholder will expand to accommodate the text. The WordArt is surrounded by sizing handles with which you can adjust its size.

2 Type **Get Ready for 2014!** to replace the WordArt placeholder text. Compare your screen with Figure 2.46.

Figure 2.46

WordArt inserted in the center of slide

3 Point to the WordArt border to display the ⌖ pointer. Hold down ⇧Shift, and then drag down to position the WordArt between the picture and the text at the bottom of the slide and centered between the left and right edge of the slide. Use ⌃Ctrl + any of the arrow keys to move the WordArt in small increments. Compare your slide with Figure 2.47 and move the WordArt again if necessary.

Recall that holding down ⇧Shift when dragging an object constrains the horizontal and vertical movement so that the object is moved in a straight line.

Figure 2.47

WordArt dragged to new location

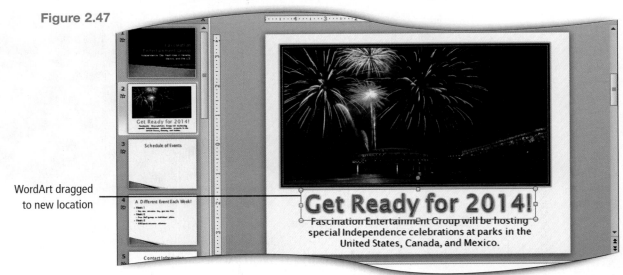

4 **Save** 🖫 your presentation.

Objective 6 | Create and Format a SmartArt Graphic

A **SmartArt graphic** is a visual representation of information that you create by choosing from among various layouts to communicate your message or ideas effectively. SmartArt graphics can illustrate processes, hierarchies, cycles, lists, and relationships. You can include text and pictures in a SmartArt graphic, and you can apply colors, effects, and styles that coordinate with the presentation theme.

Activity 2.18 | Creating a SmartArt Graphic from Bulleted Points

You can convert an existing bulleted list into a SmartArt graphic. When you create a SmartArt graphic, consider the message that you are trying to convey, and then choose an appropriate layout. The table in Figure 2.48 describes types of SmartArt layouts and suggested purposes.

Microsoft PowerPoint SmartArt Graphic Types	
Graphic Type	**Purpose of Graphic**
List	Shows non-sequential information
Process	Shows steps in a process or timeline
Cycle	Shows a continual process
Hierarchy	Shows a decision tree or displays an organization chart
Relationship	Illustrates connections
Matrix	Shows how parts relate to a whole
Pyramid	Shows proportional relationships with the largest component on the top or bottom
Picture	Includes pictures in the layout to communicate messages and ideas

Figure 2.48

> **Another Way**
>
> Right-click on a bulleted list to display the short-cut menu, and then click **Convert to SmartArt**.

1 Display **Slide 4**, and then click anywhere in the bulleted list placeholder. On the **Home tab**, in the **Paragraph group**, click the **Convert to SmartArt** button. Below the gallery, click **More SmartArt Graphics**.

Three sections comprise the Choose a SmartArt Graphic dialog box. The left section lists the SmartArt graphic types. The center section displays the SmartArt graphics according to type. The third section displays the selected SmartArt graphic, its name, and a description of its purpose.

2 On the left side of the **Choose a SmartArt Graphic** dialog box, click **List**. Use the ScreenTips to locate and then click **Vertical Bullet List**. Compare your screen with Figure 2.49.

Figure 2.49

Vertical Bullet List selected

List type selected

SmartArt graphic types

Gallery of SmartArt graphics within each type

Preview, name, and description of selected SmartArt graphic—Vertical Bullet List—displays

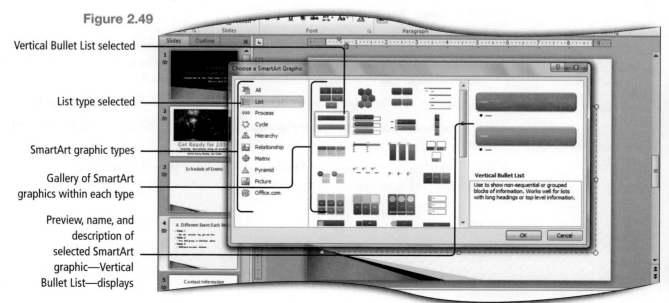

PowerPoint | Chapter 2

3 In the **Choose a SmartArt Graphic** dialog box, click **OK**. If the Text Pane displays to the right of the SmartArt graphic, click its Close button ⊠.Compare your screen with Figure 2.50, and then **Save** 🔲 your presentation.

It is not necessary to select all of the text in the list. By clicking in the list, PowerPoint converts all of the bullet points to the selected SmartArt graphic. On the Ribbon, the SmartArt contextual tools display two tabs—Design and Format. The thick border surrounding the SmartArt graphic indicates that it is selected and displays the area that the object will cover on the slide.

Figure 2.50

Text pane button not selected

SmartArt Tools display Design and Format tabs

Text converted to Vertical Bullet List SmartArt graphic

Border indicates SmartArt selection

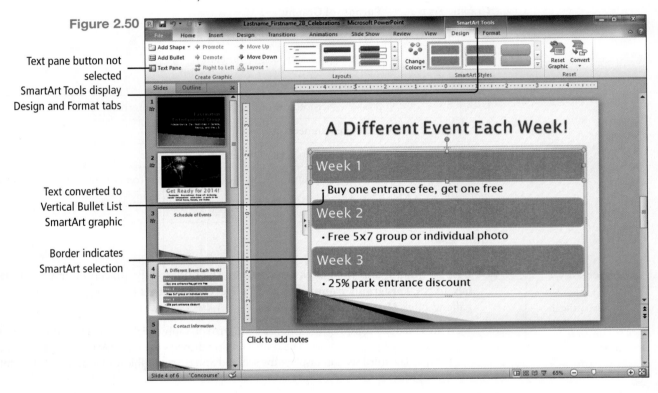

Activity 2.19 | Adding Shapes in a SmartArt Graphic

If a SmartArt graphic does not have enough shapes to illustrate a concept or display the relationships, you can add more shapes.

<table>
<tr><td>

Another Way

Right-click the shape, point to **Add Shape**, and then click **Add Shape After**.

</td><td>

1 Click in the shape that contains the text *Week 3*. In the **SmartArt Tools,** click the **Design tab**. In the **Create Graphic group**, click the **Add Shape arrow**, and then click **Add Shape After** to insert a shape at the same level. Type **Week 4**

The text in each of the SmartArt shapes resizes to accommodate the added shape.

</td></tr>
</table>

2 On the **Design tab**, in the **Create Graphic group**, click the **Add Bullet** button to add a bullet below the *Week 4* shape.

3 Type **25% discount on food and beverages** Compare your slide with Figure 2.51, and then **Save** 🔲 your presentation.

Figure 2.51

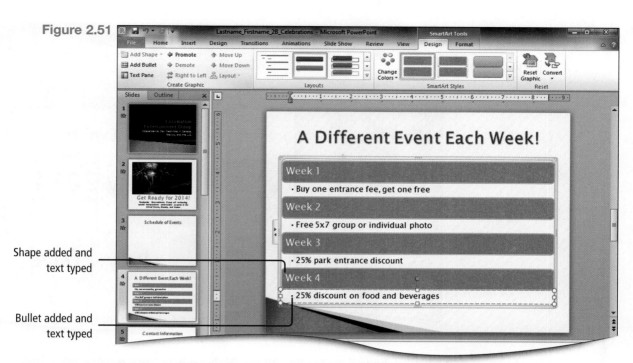

Shape added and text typed

Bullet added and text typed

Activity 2.20 | Creating a SmartArt Graphic Using a Content Layout

1 Display **Slide 3**. In the center of the content placeholder, click the **Insert SmartArt Graphic** button to open the **Choose a SmartArt Graphic** dialog box.

2 On the left, click **Process**, and then scroll as necessary and use the ScreenTips to locate **Vertical Arrow List**. Click **Vertical Arrow List**. Compare your screen with Figure 2.52.

Figure 2.52

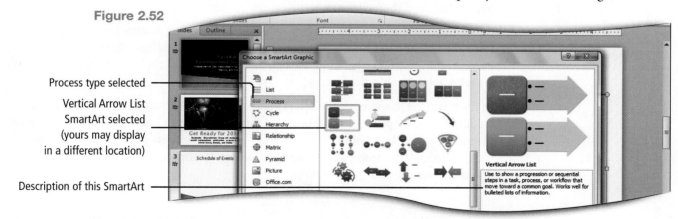

Process type selected

Vertical Arrow List SmartArt selected (yours may display in a different location)

Description of this SmartArt

3 Click **OK** to insert the SmartArt graphic.

The SmartArt graphic displays with two rounded rectangle shapes and two arrow shapes. You can type text directly into the shapes or you can type text in the Text Pane, which may display to the left of your SmartArt graphic. You can display the Text Pane by clicking the Text Pane tab on the left side of the SmartArt graphic border, or by clicking the Text Pane button in the Create Graphic group. Depending on your software settings, the Text Pane may display.

4 In the SmartArt graphic, click in the first orange rectangle, and then type **Canada** In the arrow shape to the immediate right, click in the first bullet point. Type **July 2014** and then press [Del] to remove the second bullet point in the arrow shape.

5 Click in the second orange rectangle, and then type **U.S.** In the arrow shape to the immediate right, click in the first bullet point. Type **July 2014** and then press [Del]. Compare your slide with Figure 2.53.

Figure 2.53

Text Pane button not selected

Text typed in SmartArt Graphic

6 Click in the *U.S.* rectangle. On the **Design tab**, in the **Create Graphic group**, click the **Add Shape arrow**. Click **Add Shape After** to insert a new rectangle and arrow. Type **Mexico** and then in the arrow shape to the right, type **September 2014**

7 Display **Slide 5**. In the center of the content placeholder, click the **Insert SmartArt Graphic** button 🖼. In the **Choose a SmartArt Graphic** dialog box, click **Picture**, and then scroll as necessary to locate **Vertical Picture Accent List**. Click **Vertical Picture Accent List**, and then click **OK** to insert the graphic.

8 In the SmartArt graphic, in the top rectangle shape, type **Rachel Lewis** and then press [Enter]. Type **United States** and then click in the middle rectangle shape. Type **Javier Perez** and then press [Enter]. Type **Mexico** and then click in the last rectangle shape, type **Annette Johnson** and then press [Enter]. Type **Canada**

9 In the top circle shape, click the **Insert Picture from File** button 🖼. Navigate to your student files, click **p02B_US_Contact**, and then press [Enter] to insert the picture. Using the technique you just practiced, in the middle circle shape, insert **p02B_Mexico_Contact**. In the last circle shape, insert **p02B_Canada_Contact**. Compare your screen with Figure 2.54, and then **Save** 💾 your presentation.

Figure 2.54

Vertical Picture Accent List SmartArt graphic inserted

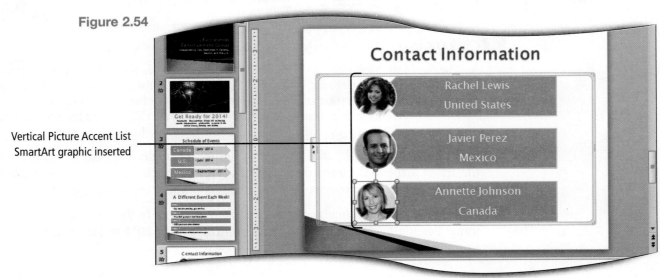

Activity 2.21 | Changing the SmartArt Layout

1 Display **Slide 3**, and then click anywhere in the SmartArt graphic. In the **SmartArt Tools**, click the **Design tab**. In the **Layouts group**, click the **More** button ▼, and then click **More Layouts**. In the **Choose a SmartArt Graphic** dialog box, click **Hierarchy**. Locate and click **Hierarchy List**, and then click **OK**.

2 Compare your slide with Figure 2.55, and then **Save** 🖫 the presentation.

Figure 2.55

Hierarchy List layout applied

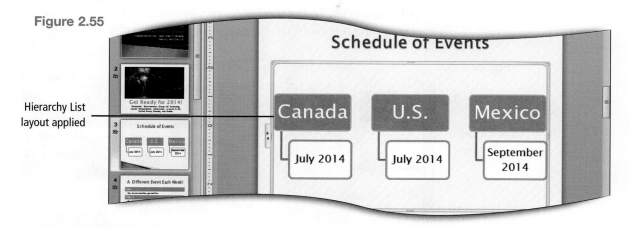

Activity 2.22 | Changing the Color and Style of a SmartArt Graphic

SmartArt Styles are combinations of formatting effects that you can apply to SmartArt graphics.

1 With **Slide 3** displayed and the SmartArt graphic selected, on the **Design tab**, in the **SmartArt Styles group**, click the **Change Colors** button. In the color gallery, under **Colorful**, click the first style—**Colorful - Accent Colors**—to change the color.

2 On the **Design tab**, in the **SmartArt Styles group**, click the **More** button ▼ to display the **SmartArt Styles gallery**. Under **3-D**, click the second style, **Inset**. Compare your slide with Figure 2.56.

Figure 2.56

Color changed and style applied to SmartArt

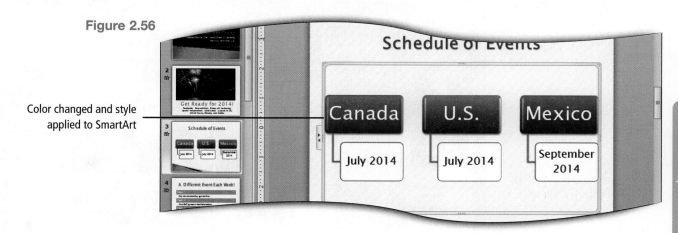

3 Display **Slide 5**, and select the SmartArt. On the **Design tab**, in the **SmartArt Styles group**, click the **Change Colors** button. Under **Accent 2**, click the second style—**Colored Fill - Accent 2**. On the **Design tab**, in the **SmartArt Styles group**, click the **More** button ▼. Under **Best Match for Document**, click the last style, **Intense Effect**. **Save** 🖫 the presentation.

Activity 2.23 | Customizing the Size and Shape of a SmartArt Graphic

You can select individual or groups of shapes in a SmartArt graphic and make them larger or smaller, and you can change selected shapes to another type of shape.

1 With **Slide 5** displayed, click in the upper red shape that contains the text *Rachel Lewis*. Hold down Shift, and then click in each of the two remaining red shapes containing the text *Javier Perez* and *Annette Johnson* so that all three text shapes are selected.

2 On the **Format tab**, in the **Shapes group**, click the **Larger** button two times to increase the size of the three selected shapes. Compare your screen with Figure 2.57.

Figure 2.57

Three shapes selected and resized

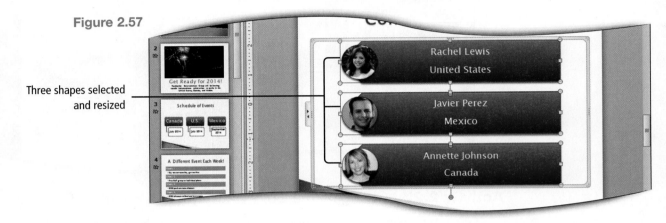

3 With the three shapes selected, on the **Home tab**, in the **Font group**, increase the **Font Size** to **28**.

4 Select the first circle picture, and then hold down Shift and click the remaining two circles so that all three circles are selected. In the **SmartArt Tools**, on the **Format tab**, in the **Shapes group**, click the **Change Shape** button. Under **Rectangles**, click the first shape—**Rectangle**—to change the circles to rectangles. With the three shapes selected, in the **Shapes group**, click the **Larger** button two times. Compare your screen with Figure 2.58, and then **Save** the presentation.

Figure 2.58

Larger button

Change Shape button

Three shapes changed to rectangles and resized

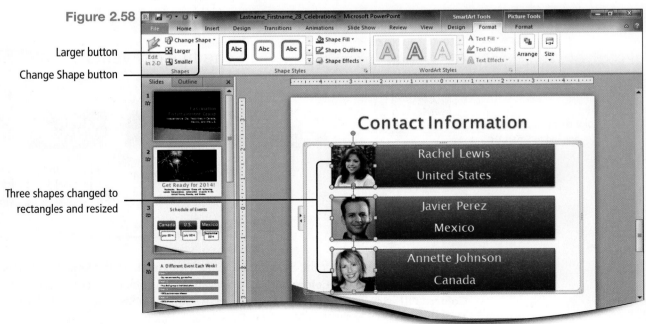

Activity 2.24 | Converting a SmartArt to Text

1 Display **Slide 4**, and then click anywhere in the SmartArt graphic. On the **Design tab**, in the **Reset group**, click the **Convert** button, and then click **Convert to Text** to convert the SmartArt graphic to a bulleted list. Compare your screen with Figure 2.59.

Figure 2.59

SmartArt graphic converted to text

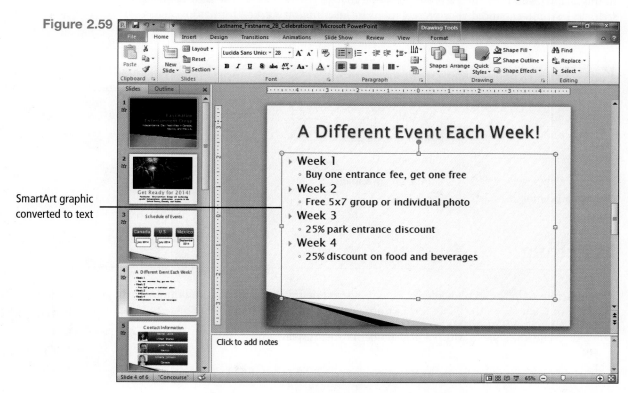

2 Display the **Document Properties**. Replace the text in the **Author** box with your own firstname and lastname, in the **Subject** box, type your course name and section number, and in the **Keywords** box, type **Independence day, celebrations Close** the **Document Information Panel**.

3 Insert a **Header & Footer** on the **Notes and Handouts**. Include the **Date and time updated automatically**, the **Page number**, and a **Footer** with the text **Lastname_Firstname_2B_Celebrations** Apply to all the slides. View the presentation from the beginning, and then make any necessary adjustments.

4 **Save** 🔲 your presentation. Print **Handouts 6 Slides Horizontal**, or submit your presentation electronically as directed by your instructor.

5 **Close** the presentation.

End You have completed Project 2B ——————————

Content-Based Assessments

Summary

In this chapter, you formatted a presentation by changing the bullet style and by applying WordArt styles to text. You enhanced your presentations by inserting, sizing, and formatting shapes, pictures, and SmartArt graphics, resulting in a professional-looking presentation.

Key Terms

Matching

Match each term in the second column with its correct definition in the first column by writing the letter of the term on the blank line in front of the correct definition.

_____ 1. The line style in which a placeholder border displays, indicating that all of the text in the placeholder is selected.

_____ 2. A common format for a slide that contains a single point without a bullet symbol.

_____ 3. A single media file, for example art, sound, animation, or a movie.

_____ 4. A four-headed arrow-shaped pointer that indicates that you can reposition an object or image.

_____ 5. An object within which you can position text anywhere on the slide.

_____ 6. Vertical and horizontal lines that display in the rulers to provide a visual indication of the pointer position so that you can draw a shape.

_____ 7. Lines, arrows, stars, banners, ovals, or rectangles used to illustrate an idea, a process, or a workflow.

_____ 8. The pointer that indicates that you can draw a shape.

_____ 9. The inside color of text or an object.

_____ 10. A style gallery displaying predefined combinations of shape fill and line colors.

_____ 11. A setting used to align selected objects.

_____ 12. The command that reduces the size of a picture by removing vertical or horizontal edges.

_____ 13. A gallery of text styles from which you can create shadowed or mirrored text.

_____ 14. A visual representation of information that you create by choosing from among layouts to communicate your message or ideas.

_____ 15. Combinations of formatting effects that are applied to SmartArt graphics.

A Align to Slide

B Clip

C Crop

D Crosshair pointer

E Fill color

F Move pointer

G Paragraph

H Ruler guides

I Shapes

J Shape Styles

K SmartArt graphic

L SmartArt Styles

M Solid

N Text box

O WordArt

Content-Based Assessments

Multiple Choice

Circle the correct answer.

1. The color of the numbers or bullet symbols in a list is determined by the:
   - **A.** Slide layout
   - **B.** Presentation theme
   - **C.** Gallery

2. When you point to an image in the Clip Art pane, the screen element that displays the keywords and information about the size of the image is the:
   - **A.** ScreenTip
   - **B.** Navigation bar
   - **C.** Menu

3. To horizontally or vertically position selected objects on a slide relative to each other, use the:
   - **A.** Align tools
   - **B.** Distribute tools
   - **C.** Crop tools

4. The command that removes unwanted portions of a picture so that the picture does not appear as a self-contained rectangle is:
   - **A.** Shape height
   - **B.** Picture adjust
   - **C.** Background removal

5. The SmartArt type that shows steps in a process or timeline is:
   - **A.** Radial
   - **B.** Process
   - **C.** List

6. The SmartArt type that shows a continual process is:
   - **A.** Hierarchy
   - **B.** Radial
   - **C.** Cycle

7. The SmartArt type with which you can show a decision tree or create an organization chart is:
   - **A.** Matrix
   - **B.** Pyramid
   - **C.** Hierarchy

8. The SmartArt type that illustrates connections is:
   - **A.** Picture
   - **B.** Radial
   - **C.** Relationship

9. The SmartArt type that shows how parts relate to a whole is:
   - **A.** Matrix
   - **B.** Pyramid
   - **C.** Radial

10. The SmartArt type that shows proportional relationships with the largest component on the top or bottom is:
    - **A.** Matrix
    - **B.** Pyramid
    - **C.** Relationship

Content-Based Assessments

Apply 2A skills from these Objectives:

1 Format Numbered and Bulleted Lists

2 Insert Clip Art

3 Insert Text Boxes and Shapes

4 Format Objects

Skills Review | Project **2C** Concerts

In the following Skills Review, you will format a presentation by inserting and formatting Clip Art, text boxes, and shapes, and by modifying bullets and numbering. Your completed presentation will look similar to Figure 2.60.

Project Files

For Project 2C, you will need the following file:

p02C_Concerts

You will save your presentation as:

Lastname_Firstname_2C_Concerts

Project Results

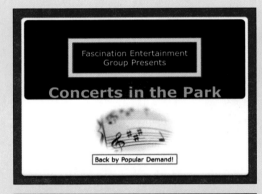

Figure 2.60

(Project 2C Concerts continues on the next page)

Content-Based Assessments

Skills Review | Project 2C Concerts (continued)

1 **Start** PowerPoint. From the student files that accompany this textbook, locate and open **p02C_Concerts**. **Save** the presentation in your **PowerPoint Chapter 2** folder as **Lastname_Firstname_2C_Concerts**

a. If necessary, display the Rulers. With **Slide 1** displayed, on the **Insert tab**, in the **Illustrations group**, click the **Shapes** button, and then under **Basic Shapes**, in the second row, click the fifth shape—**Frame**.

b. Move the pointer to align the ruler guides with the **left half of the horizontal ruler at 3 inches** and with the **upper half of the vertical ruler at 2.5 inches**, and then click to insert the Frame.

c. On the **Format tab**, in the **Size group**, click in the **Shape Height** box to select the number, and then type **1.7** Click in the **Shape Width** box. Replace the selected number with **5.5** and then press [Enter] to resize the shape.

d. With the frame selected, type **Fascination Entertainment Group Presents** and then change the **Font Size** to **24**. On the **Format tab**, in the **Shape Styles group**, click the **Shape Fill** button, and then under **Theme Colors**, in the fourth column, click the first color—**Lavender, Text 2**.

2 On the **Insert tab**, in the **Images group**, click the **Clip Art** button to display the **Clip Art** pane.

a. In the **Clip Art** pane, click in the **Search for** box and replace any existing text with **compositions musical notes** Click the **Results should be arrow**, and then click as necessary to so that only the **Photographs** check box is selected. Include Office.com content. Click **Go** to display the musical notes pictures.

b. Click the black and white picture of the two lines of music on a music sheet, and then **Close** the **Clip Art** pane. With the picture selected, on the **Format tab**, in the **Size group**, click in the **Shape Height** box. Replace the selected number with **2.5** and then press [Enter] to resize the image.

c. Point to the picture and then drag down and to the right so that it is centered just below the title—*Concerts in the Park*—and its top edge aligns with the lower edge of the black rounded rectangle.

d. With the picture selected, on the **Format tab**, in the **Size group**, click the **Crop arrow**, and then point to **Crop to Shape**. Under **Basic Shapes**, click the first shape—**Oval**. In the **Picture Styles group**, click the

(Project 2C Concerts continues on the next page)

Picture Effects button, point to **Soft Edges**, and then click **25 Point**.

e. On the **Insert tab**, in the **Text group**, click the **Text Box** button. Move the pointer to position the ruler guides on the **horizontal ruler at 0 inches** and on the **lower half of the vertical ruler at 2.5 inches**, and then click to insert the text box.

f. On the **Format tab**, in the **Shape Styles group**, click the **More** button. In the first row, click the second style—**Colored Outline - Pink, Accent 1**. Type **Back by Popular Demand!**

g. With the text box selected, hold down [Shift], and then click the frame shape, the title placeholder, and the picture so that all four objects are selected. Under **Drawing Tools**, on the **Format tab**, in the **Arrange group**, click the **Align** button, and then click **Align to Slide**. Click the **Align** button again, and then click **Align Center**. **Save** the presentation.

3 Display **Slide 2**, and then click in the title placeholder containing the text *Every Friday in June and July*.

a. On the **Home tab**, in the **Paragraph group**, click the **Bullets** button to remove the bullet symbol from the title.

b. On the left side of the slide, in the content placeholder, click the **Clip Art** button. In the **Clip Art** pane, in the **Search for** box, search for **cymbals** set the results to **Photographs**, include Office.com content, and then click **Go**. Insert the picture of the drum set on a white background.

c. On the **Format tab**, in the **Picture Styles group**, click the **Picture Effects** button, point to **Soft Edges**, and then click **50 Point**. **Close** the **Clip Art** pane.

4 Display **Slide 3**, and then select the third and fourth bullet points—the two, second-level bullet points.

a. On the **Home tab**, in the **Paragraph group**, click the **Bullets button arrow**, and then click **Bullets and Numbering**. In the first row of bullets, click the last style—**Filled Square Bullets**. Replace the number in the **Size** box with **125** and then click the **Color** button. In the eighth column, click the first color—**Gold, Accent 4**—and then click **OK** to change the bullet style.

b. Display **Slide 4**, and then click the bulleted list placeholder. Click the dashed border so that it displays as a solid line, and then on the **Home tab**, in the **Paragraph group**, click the **Numbering button** to change the bullets to numbers.

PowerPoint | Chapter 2

Content-Based Assessments

5 Display **Slide 5**. On the **Insert tab**, in the **Images group**, click the **Clip Art** button. In the **Clip Art** pane, in the **Search for** box, search for **electric guitar in monochrome** and then click **Go**. Insert the picture of the black electric guitar on the white, blue, and black background.

a. Change the picture **Height** to **4.5** and then drag the picture down and to the left so that its upper left corner aligns with the upper left corner of the black rectangle on the slide background. **Close** the **Clip Art** pane.

b. With the picture selected, on the **Format tab**, in the **Picture Styles group**, click **Picture Effects**, and then point to **Reflection**. Click the first reflection variation—**Tight Reflection, touching**.

c. With the picture selected, hold down Ctrl, and then press D to create a duplicate of the picture. Drag the duplicated picture to the right about 1 inch, and then hold down Ctrl and press D to create another duplicate.

d. Point to the third guitar picture that you inserted, and then drag to the right so that its upper right corner aligns with the upper right corner of the black rectangle on the slide background.

e. Hold down Shift, and then click the first two guitar pictures so that all three pictures are selected. On the **Format tab**, in the **Arrange group**, click the **Align** button, and then click **Align Selected Objects**. Click the **Align** button again, and then click **Align Top**. Click the **Align** button again, and then click **Distribute Horizontally**.

f. **Insert** a **Header & Footer** on the **Notes and Handouts**. Include the **Date and time updated automatically**, the **Page number**, and a **Footer** with the text **Lastname_Firstname_2C_Concerts** Click **Apply to All**.

g. Display the **Document Properties**. Replace the text in the **Author** box with your own firstname and lastname, in the **Subject** box, type your course name and section number, and in the **Keywords** box, type **concerts, summer events Close** the **Document Information Panel**.

h. View your slide show from the beginning, and then **Save** your presentation. Submit your presentation electronically or print **Handouts 6 Slides Horizontal** as directed by your instructor. **Close** the presentation and exit PowerPoint.

End You have completed Project 2C

Content-Based Assessments

Skills Review | Project **2D** Corporate Events

In the following Skills Review, you will format a presentation by inserting and formatting WordArt and SmartArt graphics. Your completed presentation will look similar to Figure 2.61.

Project Files

For Project 2D, you will need the following file:

p02D_Corporate_Events

You will save your presentation as:

Lastname_Firstname_2D_Corporate_Events

Project Results

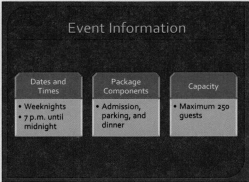

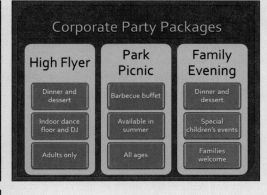

Figure 2.61

(Project 2D Corporate Events continues on the next page)

PowerPoint | Chapter 2

Content-Based Assessments

Skills Review | Project **2D** Corporate Events (continued)

1 **Start** PowerPoint. From the student files that accompany this textbook, locate and open **p02D_Corporate_Events**. **Save** the presentation in your PowerPoint Chapter 2 folder as **Lastname_Firstname_2D_Corporate_Events**

a. With **Slide 1** displayed, select the title—*Fascination Entertainment Group*. On the **Format tab**, in the **WordArt Styles group**, click the **More** button. Under **Applies to All Text in the Shape**, click the first style—**Fill - White, Warm Matte Bevel**. Change the **Font Size** to **40** so that all of the text displays on one line.

b. Display **Slide 2**. On the **Insert tab**, in the **Text group**, click the **WordArt** button. In the **WordArt** gallery, in the second row, click the second style—**Fill - Lime, Accent 6, Outline - Accent 6, Glow - Accent 6**. With the text *Your text here* selected, type **Corporate Events**

c. Point to the dashed, outer edge of the WordArt placeholder, hold down Shift, and drag straight down so that the WordArt is positioned between the picture and the text at the bottom of the slide.

d. With the WordArt selected, on the **Format tab**, in the **Arrange group**, click the **Align** button, and then click **Align Center** so that the WordArt is horizontally centered on the slide. **Save** the presentation.

2 Display **Slide 3**. In the center of the content placeholder, click the **Insert SmartArt Graphic** button to open the **Choose a SmartArt Graphic** dialog box. On the left, click **List**, and then use the ScreenTips to locate and then click **Vertical Bullet List**. Click **OK**.

a. In the SmartArt graphic, click *Text* in the first blue rectangle. Type **Dates and Times** and then click the bullet symbol below the first blue rectangle. Type **Weeknights** and then press Enter to insert a new bullet point. Type **7 p.m. until midnight**

b. Click in the second blue rectangle. Type **Package Components** and then click the bullet symbol below the second blue rectangle. Type **Admission, parking, and dinner**

c. Click in the *Package Components* rectangle, and then on the **SmartArt Tools Design tab**, in the **Create Graphic group**, click the **Add Shape arrow**. Click **Add Shape After** to insert a blue rectangle. Type **Capacity** and then on the **SmartArt Tools Design tab**, in the **Create Graphic group**, click the **Add Bullet** button. Type **Maximum 250 guests**

d. With the SmartArt selected, on the **SmartArt Tools Design tab**, in the **Layouts group**, click the **More** button, and then click **More Layouts**. On the left side of the dialog box, click **List**, and then in the center section of the dialog box, locate and click **Horizontal Bullet List**. Click **OK** to change the SmartArt layout.

e. On the **SmartArt Tools Design tab**, in the **SmartArt Styles group**, click the **More** button. Under **3-D**, in the first row, click the third style—**Cartoon**.

f. Hold down Shift, and then select the **Dates and Times**, **Package Components**, and **Capacity** rectangles. On the **Format tab**, in the **Shapes group**, click the **Change Shape** button, and then under **Rectangles**, click the fourth shape—**Snip Same Side Corner Rectangle**. **Save** the presentation.

3 Display **Slide 4**. In the content placeholder, right-click anywhere in the bulleted list. On the shortcut menu, point to **Convert to SmartArt**, and at the bottom of the gallery, click **More SmartArt Graphics**. On the left side of the **Choose a SmartArt Graphic** dialog box, click **Relationship**. Locate and click **Grouped List**, and then click **OK** to convert the list to a SmartArt graphic.

a. On the **SmartArt Tools Design tab**, in the **SmartArt Styles group**, click the **Change Colors** button. In the **Color** gallery, under **Accent 1**, click the last style—**Transparent Gradient Range - Accent 1**.

b. On the **Design tab**, in the **SmartArt Styles group**, click the **More** button to display the **SmartArt Styles gallery**. Under **3-D**, in the first row, click the third style—**Cartoon**. **Save** the presentation.

4 Display **Slide 5**, and if necessary, display the Rulers. On the **Insert tab**, in the **Text group**, click the **WordArt** button. In the **WordArt** gallery, in the first row, click the fourth style—**Fill - White, Outline - Accent 1**. With the text *Your text here* selected, type **Corporate_events@feg.com**

a. Point to the dashed, outer edge of the WordArt placeholder, and then drag down so that the top edge of the WordArt aligns with the **lower half of the vertical ruler at 1 inch**.

b. With the WordArt selected, on the **Format tab**, in the **Arrange group**, click the **Align** button, and then click **Align Center** so that the WordArt is horizontally centered on the slide.

(Project 2D Corporate Events continues on the next page)

Skills Review | Project **2D** Corporate Events (continued)

c. **Insert** a **Header & Footer** on the **Notes and Handouts**. Include the **Date and time updated automatically**, the **Page number**, and a **Footer** with the text **Lastname_ Firstname_2D_Corporate_Events** and **Apply to All**.

d. Display the **Document Properties**. Replace the text in the **Author** box with your own firstname and lastname, in the **Subject** box, type your course name and section number, and in the **Keywords** box, type **corporate events, group packages Close** the **Document Information Panel**. View the presentation from the beginning.

e. **Save** your presentation. Submit your presentation electronically or print **Handouts 6 Slides Horizontal** as directed by your instructor. **Close** the presentation and exit PowerPoint.

End You have completed Project 2D ——————————————————

Content-Based Assessments

Apply **2A** skills from these Objectives:

1. Format Numbered and Bulleted Lists
2. Insert Clip Art
3. Insert Text Boxes and Shapes
4. Format Objects

Mastering PowerPoint | Project **2E** Roller Coasters

In the following Mastering PowerPoint project, you will format a presentation describing new roller coaster attractions at the Fascination Entertainment Group theme parks. Your completed presentation will look similar to Figure 2.62.

Project Files

For Project 2E, you will need the following file:

p02E_Roller_Coasters

You will save your presentation as:

Lastname_Firstname_2E_Roller_Coasters

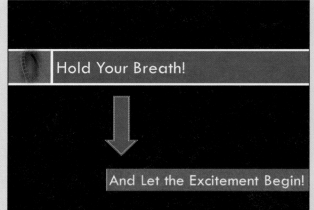

Figure 2.62

(Project 2E Roller Coasters continues on the next page)

Content-Based Assessments

Mastering PowerPoint | Project 2E Roller Coasters (continued)

1 **Start** PowerPoint. From the student files that accompany this textbook, locate and open **p02E_Roller_Coasters**. In your **PowerPoint Chapter 2** folder, **Save** the file as **Lastname_Firstname_2E_Roller_Coasters**

2 On **Slide 2**, remove the bullet symbol from the paragraph. **Center** the paragraph, apply **Bold** and **Italic** to the text, and then set the **Line Spacing** to **2.0**. With the content placeholder selected, display the **Shape Styles** gallery, and then in the fifth row, apply the third style—**Moderate Effect - Red, Accent 2**.

3 On **Slide 3**, apply **Numbering** to the first-level bullet points—*Intensity, Hang Time,* and *Last Chance.* Under each of the numbered items, change all of the hollow circle bullet symbols to **Filled Square Bullets**, and then change the bullet color to **Dark Blue, Text 2**—the first color in the fourth column.

4 In the content placeholder on the right side of the slide, insert a **Clip Art** photograph by searching for **roller coaster** Insert the close-up picture of the roller coaster with the red cars on the blue sky background, as shown in Figure 2.62 at the beginning of this project. Crop the picture shape to **Rounded Rectangle**, and then modify the **Picture Effect** by applying the last **Bevel** style—**Art Deco**.

5 On **Slide 4**, insert the picture of the white looped roller coaster on the lighter blue sky background. Change the picture **Height** to **1.5** and then apply a **25 Point Soft Edges** effect. Drag the picture up and to the left to position it in the center of the red rectangle to the left of the slide title. Deselect the picture.

6 From the **Shapes** gallery, under **Block Arrows**, insert a **Down Arrow** aligned with the **left half of the horizontal ruler at 1 inch** and the **upper half of the vertical ruler at**

0.5 inches. On the **Format tab**, from the **Shape Styles** gallery, in the third row, apply the second style—**Light 1 Outline, Colored Fill - Blue, Accent 1**. Change the **Shape Height** to **2** and the **Shape Width** to **1**

7 Insert a **Text Box** aligned with the **left half of the horizontal ruler at 1.5 inches** and with the **lower half of the vertical ruler at 2 inches**. On the **Format tab**, from the **Shape Styles** gallery, in the last row, apply the third style—**Intense Effect - Red, Accent 2**. In the inserted text box, type **And Let the Excitement Begin!** Change the **Font Size** to **40**, and then if necessary, drag the text box so that its right edge aligns with the right edge of the slide. Select the arrow and the text box, and then apply **Align Left** alignment using the **Align Selected Objects** option.

8 Select the title, the arrow, and the text box. Distribute the objects vertically using the **Align Selected Objects** option. Apply the **Box** transition to all of the slides in the presentation, and then view the slide show from the beginning.

9 **Insert** a **Header & Footer** on the **Notes and Handouts**. Include the **Date and time updated automatically**, the **Page number**, and a **Footer** with the text **Lastname_Firstname_2E_Roller_Coasters** Apply to all.

10 Display the **Document Properties**. Replace the text in the **Author** box with your own firstname and lastname, in the **Subject** box, type your course name and section number, and in the **Keywords** box, type **roller coasters, new attractions Close** the **Document Information Panel**.

11 **Save** your presentation. Submit your presentation electronically or print **Handouts 4 Slides Horizontal** as directed by your instructor. **Close** the presentation and exit PowerPoint.

End **You have completed Project 2E**

PowerPoint | Chapter 2

Content-Based Assessments

Mastering PowerPoint | Project **2F** Coaster Club

In the following Mastering PowerPoint project, you will format a presentation describing an event sponsored by Fascination Entertainment Group for roller coaster club members. Your completed presentation will look similar to Figure 2.63.

Project Files

For Project 2F, you will need the following file:

p02F_Coaster_Club

You will save your presentation as:

Lastname_Firstname_2F_Coaster_Club

Project Results

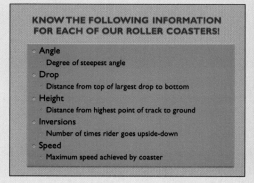

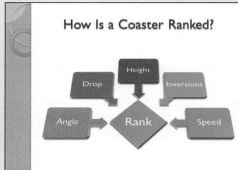

Figure 2.63

(Project 2F Coaster Club continues on the next page)

Content-Based Assessments

Mastering PowerPoint | Project **2F** Coaster Club (continued)

1 **Start** PowerPoint. From the student files that accompany this textbook, open **p02F_Coaster_Club**, and then **Save** the file in your **PowerPoint Chapter 2** folder as **Lastname_Firstname_2F_Coaster_Club**

2 On **Slide 1**, select the title and display the **WordArt** gallery. In the last row, apply the third WordArt style— **Fill - Aqua, Accent 2, Matte Bevel**. On **Slide 2**, convert the bulleted list to a **SmartArt** graphic by applying the **Vertical Bracket List** graphic. Change the SmartArt color to **Colorful Range - Accent Colors 3 to 4**, and then apply the **Inset 3-D** style.

3 On **Slide 4**, in the content placeholder, insert a **Relationship** type **SmartArt** graphic—**Converging Radial**. In the circle shape, type **Rank** In the left rectangle, type **Angle** in the middle rectangle, type **Drop** and in the right rectangle type **Height** Add a shape after the *Height* rectangle, and then type **Inversions** Add a shape after the *Inversions* rectangle, and then type **Speed** so that your SmartArt contains five rectangular shapes pointing to the circle shape.

4 Change the SmartArt color to **Colorful Range - Accent Colors 3 to 4**, and then apply the **3-D Flat Scene** style. Change the circle shape to the **Diamond** basic shape. On the **Format tab**, in the **Shapes group**, click the **Larger** button two times to increase the size of the diamond.

5 On **Slide 5**, select the content placeholder, and then from the **Shape Styles** gallery, in the last row, apply the third style—**Intense Effect - Aqua, Accent 2**. Change the **Font Color** of all the text in the content placeholder to **Black, Text 1**.

6 On **Slide 6**, insert a **WordArt**—the third style in the last row—**Fill - Aqua, Accent 2, Matte Bevel**. Replace the WordArt text with **Mark Your Calendars!** Change the **Font Size** to **48**, and align the right edge of the WordArt placeholder with the right edge of the slide.

7 **Insert** a **Header & Footer** on the **Notes and Handouts**. Include the **Date and time updated automatically**, the **Page number**, and a **Footer** with the text **Lastname_Firstname_ 2F_Coaster_Club** Apply to all.

8 Display the **Document Properties**. Replace the text in the **Author** box with your own firstname and lastname, in the **Subject** box, type your course name and section number, and in the **Keywords** box, type **roller coasters, coaster club, events Close** the **Document Information Panel**.

9 **Save** your presentation, and then view the slide show from the beginning. Submit your presentation electronically or print **Handouts 6 Slides Horizontal** as directed by your instructor. **Close** the presentation and exit PowerPoint.

End **You have completed Project 2F**

Content-Based Assessments

Apply **2A** and **2B** skills from these Objectives:

1 Format Numbered and Bulleted Lists

2 Insert Clip Art

3 Insert Text Boxes and Shapes

4 Format Objects

5 Remove Picture Backgrounds and Insert WordArt

6 Create and Format a SmartArt Graphic

Mastering PowerPoint | Project **2G** Orientation

In the following Mastering PowerPoint project, you will edit an existing presentation that is shown to Fascination Entertainment Group employees on their first day of a three-day orientation. Your completed presentation will look similar to Figure 2.64.

Project Files

For Project 2G, you will need the following files:

> p02G_Orientation
> p02G_Maya_Ruiz
> p02G_David_Jensen
> p02G_Ken_Lee

You will save your presentation as:

> Lastname_Firstname_2G_Orientation

Project Results

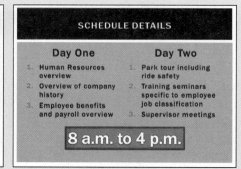

Figure 2.64

(Project 2G Orientation continues on the next page)

Content-Based Assessments

Mastering PowerPoint | Project **2G** Orientation (continued)

1 **Start** PowerPoint, and then from your student data files, open the file **p02G_Orientation**. In your **PowerPoint Chapter 2** folder, **Save** the file as **Lastname_Firstname_2G_Orientation**

2 On **Slide 1**, format the title as a **WordArt** using the fourth style in the first row—**Fill - White, Outline - Accent 1**. Select the five pictures, and then using the **Align to Slide** option, align the pictures using the **Distribute Vertically** and **Align Right** commands. On **Slide 2**, change the **Shape Style** of the content placeholder to the second style in the last row—**Intense Effect - Tan, Accent 1**.

3 On **Slide 3**, convert the bulleted list to the **Picture** type SmartArt graphic—**Title Picture Lineup**. Change the color to **Colorful Range - Accent Colors 5 to 6**, and then apply the **3-D Inset** style. In the three picture placeholders, from your student files insert the following pictures: **p02G_Maya_Ruiz, p02G_David_Jensen**, and **p02G_Ken_Lee**.

4 On **Slide 4**, change the two bulleted lists to **Numbering**. Then, insert a **WordArt** using the **Fill - White, Drop Shadow** style with the text **8 a.m. to 4 p.m.** and position the WordArt centered below the two content placeholders. Apply a **Shape Style** to the WordArt using **Intense Effect - Tan, Accent 1**.

5 On **Slide 5**, change the bullet symbols to **Checkmark Bullets**, and then in the placeholder on the right, insert a **Clip Art** photograph by searching for **first aid kit** Insert the picture of the opened first aid box, and then remove the background from the picture so that only the items in the kit display. Mark areas to keep and remove as necessary. Change the **Shape Height** to **3.25** and then apply the **Brown, 18 pt glow, Accent color 4** picture effect.

6 On **Slide 5**, insert a **Text Box** aligned with the **left half of the horizontal ruler at 4 inches** and with the **lower half of the vertical ruler at 2.5 inches**. In the text box, type **All employees will be tested on park safety procedures!** Apply **Italic**, and then **Align Center** the text box using the **Align to Slide** option.

7 Insert a **New Slide** with the **Blank** layout. From the **Shapes** gallery, under **Basic Shapes**, insert a **Diamond** of any size anywhere on the slide. Then, resize the diamond so that its **Shape Height** is **6** and its **Shape Width** is **8** Using the **Align to Slide** option, apply the **Align Center**, and **Align Middle** alignment commands. Apply the **Moderate Effect - Tan, Accent 1** shape style to the diamond, and then in the diamond, type **Fascination Entertainment Group Welcomes You!** Change the **Font Size** to **40**, and then apply the **Art Deco Bevel** effect to the diamond shape.

8 Insert a **Header & Footer** on the **Notes and Handouts**. Include the **Date and time updated automatically**, the **Page number**, and a **Footer** with the text **Lastname_Firstname_2G_Orientation** Apply to all.

9 Display the **Document Properties**. Replace the text in the **Author** box with your own firstname and lastname, in the **Subject** box, type your course name and section number, and in the **Keywords** box, type **orientation, employee training Close** the **Document Information Panel**.

10 **Save** your presentation, and then view the slide show from the beginning. Submit your presentation electronically or print **Handouts 6 Slides Horizontal** as directed by your instructor. **Close** the presentation and exit PowerPoint.

End **You have completed Project 2G** ——————————

Content-Based Assessments

GO! Fix It | Project **2H** Summer Jobs

Project Files

For Project 2H, you will need the following file:

p02H_Summer_Jobs

You will save your presentation as:

Lastname_Firstname_2H_Summer_Jobs

In this project, you will edit several slides from a presentation prepared by the Human Resources Department at Fascination Entertainment Group regarding summer employment opportunities. From the student files that accompany this textbook, open the file p02H_Summer_Jobs, and then save the file in your chapter folder as **Lastname_Firstname_2H_Summer_Jobs**

To complete the project you should know:

- The Theme should be changed to Module and two spelling errors should be corrected.
- On Slide 1, the pictures should be aligned with the top of the slide and distributed horizontally.
- On Slide 2, the bulleted list should be converted to a Vertical Box List SmartArt and an attractive style should be applied. The colors should be changed to Colorful Range - Accent Colors 5 to 6.
- On Slide 3, the bulleted list should be formatted as a numbered list.
- On Slide 4, insert a Fill - White, Drop Shadow WordArt with the text **Apply Today!** and position the WordArt centered approximately 1 inch below the title placeholder.
- Document Properties should include your name, course name and section, and the keywords **summer jobs, recruitment** A Header & Footer should be inserted on the Notes and Handouts that includes the Date and time updated automatically, the Page number, and a Footer with the text **Lastname_Firstname_2H_Summer_Jobs**

Save and submit your presentation electronically or print Handouts 4 Slides Horizontal as directed by your instructor. Close the presentation.

End You have completed Project 2H ————————————

Content-Based Assessments

Apply a combination of the **2A** and **2B** skills.

GO! Make It | Project **2I** Renovation Plans

Project Files

For Project 2I, you will need the following file:

New blank PowerPoint presentation

You will save your presentation as:

Lastname_Firstname_2I_Renovation_Plans

By using the skills you practiced in this chapter, create the first two slides of the presentation shown in Figure 2.65. Start PowerPoint to begin a new blank presentation, and apply the Urban theme and the Aspect color theme. Type the title and subtitle shown in Figure 2.65, and then change the background style to Style 12 and the title font size to 40. Apply the Fill - Black, Background 1, Metal Bevel WordArt style to the title. Save the file in your PowerPoint Chapter 2 folder as **Lastname_Firstname_2I_Renovation_Plans**

To locate the picture on Slide 1, search for a clip art photograph with the keyword **carnival rides** Resize the picture Height to **2** and then apply soft edges, duplicate, align, and distribute the images as shown in the figure.

Insert a new Slide 2 using the Content with Caption layout. Insert the Basic Matrix SmartArt layout shown in Figure 2.65 and change the color and style as shown. Type the title and caption text, changing the title Font Size to 28 and the caption text Font Size to 18. Modify line spacing and apply formatting to the caption text as shown in Figure 2.65. Insert the date, file name, and page number in the Notes and Handouts footer. In the Document Information Panel, add your name and course information and the Keywords **renovation, goals** Save, and then print or submit electronically as directed by your instructor.

Project Results

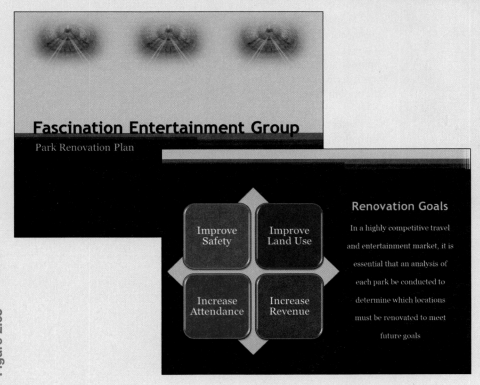

Figure 2.65

End You have completed Project 2I

PowerPoint | Chapter 2

Content-Based Assessments

Apply a combination of the 2A and 2B skills.

GO! Solve It | Project **2J** Business Summary

Project Files

For Project 2J, you will need the following file:

p02J_Business_Summary

You will save your presentation as:

Lastname_Firstname_2J_Business_Summary

Open the file p02J_Business_Summary and save it in your chapter folder as **Lastname_Firstname_2J_Business_Summary** Format the presentation attractively by applying appropriate font formatting and by changing text alignment and line spacing. Insert at least one clip art image and change the picture shape and effect. On Slide 2, align and format the text box and shape attractively and insert a clip art image that can be duplicated, aligned, and distributed across the bottom edge of the slide. On Slide 3, insert an appropriate photo on the right. On Slide 4, convert the bulleted list to an appropriate SmartArt graphic and format the graphic appropriately. Apply slide transitions to all of the slides in the presentation and insert a header and footer that includes the date and time updated automatically, the file name in the footer, and the page number. Add your name, your course name and section number, and the keywords **business summary, revenue** to the Properties area. Save, and then print or submit electronically as directed by your instructor.

Performance Elements	Performance Level		
	Exemplary: You consistently applied the relevant skills	**Proficient:** You sometimes, but not always, applied the relevant skills	**Developing:** You rarely or never applied the relevant skills
Insert and format appropriate clip art	Appropriate clip art was inserted and formatted in the presentation.	Clip art was inserted but was not appropriate for the presentation or was not formatted.	Clip art was not inserted.
Insert and format appropriate SmartArt graphic	Appropriate SmartArt graphic was inserted and formatted in the presentation.	SmartArt graphic was inserted but was not appropriate for the presentation or was not formatted.	SmartArt graphic was not inserted.
Format text boxes and shapes attractively	Text boxes and shapes were formatted attractively.	Text boxes and shapes were formatted but the formatting was inappropriately applied.	Inadequate or no formatting.
Insert transitions	Appropriate transitions were applied to all slides.	Transitions were applied to some, but not all slides.	Transitions were not applied.

End You have completed Project 2J

Content-Based Assessments

Apply a combination of the **2A** and **2B** skills.

GO! Solve It | Project **2K** Hotel

Project Files

For Project 2K, you will need the following file:

p02K_Hotel

You will save your presentation as:

Lastname_Firstname_2K_Hotel

Open the file p02K_Hotel and save it as **Lastname_Firstname_2K_Hotel** Complete the presentation by inserting a clip art image on the first slide and applying appropriate picture effects. On Slide 2, format the bullet point as a single paragraph, and then on Slide 3, convert the bulleted list to an appropriate SmartArt graphic. Change the SmartArt color and apply a style. On Slide 4, insert and attractively position a WordArt with the text **Save the Date!** Apply slide transitions to all of the slides. Insert a header and footer that includes the date and time updated automatically, the file name in the footer, and the page number. Add your name, your course name and section number, and the keywords **hotel, accommodations** to the Properties area. Save your presentation. Print or submit as directed by your instructor.

		Performance Level		
		Exemplary: You consistently applied the relevant skills	**Proficient:** You sometimes, but not always, applied the relevant skills	**Developing:** You rarely or never applied the relevant skills
Performance Elements	Insert and format appropriate clip art	Appropriate clip art was inserted and formatted in the presentation.	Clip art was inserted but was not appropriate for the presentation or was not formatted.	Clip art was not inserted.
	Insert and format appropriate SmartArt graphic	Appropriate SmartArt graphic was inserted and formatted in the presentation.	SmartArt graphic was inserted but was not appropriate for the presentation or was not formatted.	SmartArt graphic was not inserted.
	Insert and format appropriate WordArt	Appropriate WordArt was inserted and formatted in the presentation.	WordArt was inserted but was not appropriate for the presentation or was not formatted.	WordArt was not inserted.
	Insert transitions	Appropriate transitions were applied to all slides.	Transitions were applied to some, but not all slides.	Transitions were not applied.

End You have completed Project 2K

Outcomes-Based Assessments

Rubric

The following outcomes-based assessments are *open-ended assessments*. That is, there is no specific correct result; your result will depend on your approach to the information provided. Make *Professional Quality* your goal. Use the following scoring rubric to guide you in *how* to approach the problem, and then to evaluate *how well* your approach solves the problem.

The *criteria*—Software Mastery, Content, Format and Layout, and Process—represent the knowledge and skills you have gained that you can apply to solving the problem. The *levels of performance*—Professional Quality, Approaching Professional Quality, or Needs Quality Improvements—help you and your instructor evaluate your result.

	Your completed project is of Professional Quality if you:	Your completed project is Approaching Professional Quality if you:	Your completed project Needs Quality Improvements if you:
1-Software Mastery	Choose and apply the most appropriate skills, tools, and features and identify efficient methods to solve the problem.	Choose and apply some appropriate skills, tools, and features, but not in the most efficient manner.	Choose inappropriate skills, tools, or features, or are inefficient in solving the problem.
2-Content	Construct a solution that is clear and well organized, contains content that is accurate, appropriate to the audience and purpose, and is complete. Provide a solution that contains no errors in spelling, grammar, or style.	Construct a solution in which some components are unclear, poorly organized, inconsistent, or incomplete. Misjudge the needs of the audience. Have some errors in spelling, grammar, or style, but the errors do not detract from comprehension.	Construct a solution that is unclear, incomplete, or poorly organized; contains some inaccurate or inappropriate content; and contains many errors in spelling, grammar, or style. Do not solve the problem.
3-Format and Layout	Format and arrange all elements to communicate information and ideas, clarify function, illustrate relationships, and indicate relative importance.	Apply appropriate format and layout features to some elements, but not others. Overuse features, causing minor distraction.	Apply format and layout that does not communicate information or ideas clearly. Do not use format and layout features to clarify function, illustrate relationships, or indicate relative importance. Use available features excessively, causing distraction.
4-Process	Use an organized approach that integrates planning, development, self-assessment, revision, and reflection.	Demonstrate an organized approach in some areas, but not others; or, use an insufficient process of organization throughout.	Do not use an organized approach to solve the problem.

Outcomes-Based Assessments

Apply a combination of the **2A** and **2B** skills.

GO! Think | Project **2L** Interactive Ride

Project Files

For Project 2L, you will need the following file:

New blank PowerPoint presentation

You will save your presentation as:

Lastname_Firstname_2L_Interactive_Ride

As part of its mission to combine fun with the discovery of math and science, Fascination Entertainment Group is opening a new, interactive roller coaster at its South Lake Tahoe location. FEG's newest coaster is designed for maximum thrill and minimum risk. In a special interactive exhibit located next to the coaster, riders can learn about the physics behind this powerful coaster and even try their hand at building a coaster.

Guests will begin by setting the height of the first hill, which determines the coaster's maximum potential energy to complete its journey. Next they will set the exit path, and build additional hills, loops, and corkscrews. When completed, riders can submit their coaster for a safety inspection to find out whether the ride passes or fails.

In either case, riders can also take a virtual tour of the ride they created to see the maximum speed achieved, the amount of negative G-forces applied, the length of the track, and the overall thrill factor. They can also see how their coaster compares with other coasters in the FEG family, and they can e-mail the coaster simulation to their friends.

Using the preceding information, create a presentation that Marketing Director, Annette Chosek, will present at a travel fair describing the new attraction. The presentation should include four to six slides with at least one SmartArt graphic and one clip art image. Apply an appropriate theme and use slide layouts that will effectively present the content, and use text boxes, shapes, and WordArt if appropriate. Apply font formatting and slide transitions, and modify text alignment and line spacing as necessary. Save the file as **Lastname_Firstname_2L_Interactive_Ride** and then insert a header and footer that includes the date and time updated automatically, the file name in the footer, and the page number. Add your name, your course name and section number, and the keywords **roller coaster, new rides** to the Properties area. Print or submit as directed by your instructor.

End **You have completed Project 2L** ────────────────

Outcomes-Based Assessments

GO! Think | Project 2M Research

Project Files

For Project 2M, you will need the following file:

New blank PowerPoint presentation

You will save your presentation as:

Lastname_Firstname_2M_Research

As the number of theme park vacations continues to rise, Fascination Entertainment Group is developing plans to ensure that its top theme parks are a true vacation destination. Fascination Entertainment Group research has verified that visitors use several factors in determining their theme park destinations: top attractions, overall value, and nearby accommodations.

Visitors, regardless of age, look for thrills and entertainment at a good value. Fascination Entertainment Group owns four of North America's top 15 coasters and two of its top 10 water parks, thus making the parks prime attraction destinations. Typical costs for visitors include park entrance fees, food and beverages, souvenirs, transportation, and lodging. Beginning this year, FEG will offer vacation packages. Package pricing will vary depending on number of adults, number of children, length of stay, and number of parks attended (i.e., theme park, water park, and zoo). Each park will continue to offer annual passes at a discount.

Research shows that visitors who travel more than 100 miles one way will consider the need for nearby accommodations. For its top 10 theme parks, Fascination Entertainment Group will open hotels at any parks that do not currently have them within the next two years. Until then, the company will partner with area hotels to provide discounts to theme park visitors.

Using the preceding information, create the first four slides of a presentation that the Fascination Entertainment Group marketing director can show at an upcoming board of directors meeting. Apply an appropriate theme and use slide layouts that will effectively present the content. Include clip art and at least one SmartArt graphic. Apply font and WordArt formatting, picture styles, and slide transitions, and modify text alignment and line spacing as necessary. If appropriate, insert and format a text box or a shape. Save the file as **Lastname_Firstname_2M_Research** and then insert a header and footer that includes the date and time updated automatically, the file name in the footer, and the page number. Add your name, your course name and section number, and the keywords **visitor preferences, research findings** to the Properties area. Print or submit as directed by your instructor.

End You have completed Project 2M ————————————————

Outcomes-Based Assessments

Apply a combination of the **2A** and **2B** skills.

You and GO! | Project **2N** Theme Park

Project Files

For Project 2N, you will need the following file:

New blank PowerPoint presentation

You will save your presentation as:

Lastname_Firstname_2N_Theme_Park

Research your favorite theme park and create a presentation with at least six slides that describes the park, its top attractions, nearby accommodations, and the reasons why you enjoy the park. Choose an appropriate theme, slide layouts, and pictures, and format the presentation attractively, including at least one SmartArt graphic and one WordArt object or shape. Save your presentation as Lastname_Firstname_2N_Theme_Park and submit as directed.

End You have completed Project 2N ———————————————

Apply a combination of the **2A** and **2B** skills.

GO! Collaborate | Project **2O** Bell Orchid Hotels Group Running Case

This project relates to the **Bell Orchid Hotels**. Your instructor may assign this group case project to your class. If your instructor assigns this project, he or she will provide you with information and instructions to work as part of a group. The group will apply the skills gained thus far to help the Bell Orchid Hotels achieve their business goals.

End You have completed Project 2O ———————————————

Enhancing a Presentation with Animation, Video, Tables, and Charts

OUTCOMES

At the end of this chapter you will be able to:

OBJECTIVES

Mastering these objectives will enable you to:

PROJECT 3A
Customize a presentation with animation and video.

1. Customize Slide Backgrounds and Themes (p. 741)
2. Animate a Slide Show (p. 748)
3. Insert a Video (p. 755)

PROJECT 3B
Create a presentation that includes data in tables and charts.

4. Create and Modify Tables (p. 765)
5. Create and Modify Charts (p. 770)

Travis Houston/Shutterstock

In This Chapter

Recall that a presentation theme applies a consistent look to a presentation. You can customize a presentation by modifying the theme and by applying animation to slide elements, and you can enhance your presentations by creating tables and charts that help your audience understand numeric data and trends just as pictures and diagrams help illustrate a concept. The data that you present should determine whether a table or a chart would most appropriately display your information. Styles applied to your tables and charts unify these slide elements by complementing your presentation theme.

The projects in this chapter relate to **Golden Grove**, a growing city located between Los Angeles and San Diego. Just 10 years ago the population was under 100,000; today it has grown to almost 300,000. Community leaders have always focused on quality and economic development in decisions on housing, open space, education, and infrastructure, making the city a model for other communities its size around the United States. The city provides many recreational and cultural opportunities with a large park system, thriving arts, and a friendly business atmosphere.

Project 3A Informational Presentation

myitlab
Project 3A Training

Project Activities

In Activities 3.01 through 3.11, you will edit and format a presentation that Mindy Walker, Director of Golden Grove Parks and Recreation, has created to inform residents about the benefits of using the city's parks and trails. Your completed presentation will look similar to Figure 3.1.

Project Files

For Project 3A, you will need the following files:

    p03A_Park
    p03A_Pets
    p03A_Trails
    p03A_Walking_Trails
    p03A_Trails_Video

You will save your presentation as:

    Lastname_Firstname_3A_Walking_Trails

Project Results

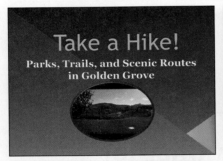

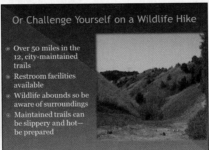

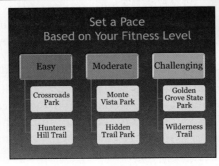
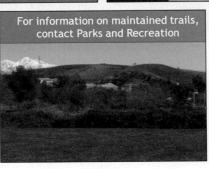

Figure 3.1
Project 3A Walking Trails

Objective 1 | Customize Slide Backgrounds and Themes

You have practiced customizing presentations by applying themes with unified design elements, backgrounds, and colors that provide a consistent look in your presentation. Additional ways to customize a slide include changing theme fonts and colors, applying a background style, modifying the background color, or inserting a picture on the slide background.

Activity 3.01 | Changing the Theme Colors and Theme Fonts

Recall that the presentation theme is a coordinated, predefined set of colors, fonts, lines, and fill effects. In this activity, you will open a presentation in which the Verve theme is applied, and then you will change the **theme colors**—a set of coordinating colors that are applied to the backgrounds, objects, and text in a presentation.

In addition to theme colors, every presentation theme includes **theme fonts** that determine the font to apply to two types of slide text—headings and body. The **Headings font** is applied to slide titles and the **Body font** is applied to all other text. When you apply a new theme font to the presentation, the text on every slide is updated with the new heading and body fonts.

1 From the student files that accompany this textbook, locate and open **p03A_Walking_Trails**. Display **Backstage** view, click **Save As**, and then navigate to the location where you are storing your projects for this chapter. Create a new folder named **PowerPoint Chapter 3** and then in the **File name** box and using your own name, type **Lastname_Firstname_3A_Walking_Trails** Click **Save** or press Enter.

2 Click the **Design tab**, and then in the **Themes group**, click the **Colors** button to display the list of theme colors. Point to several themes and notice the color changes on **Slide 1**. Scroll the **Theme Colors** list, and then click **Metro** to change the theme colors.

Changing the theme colors does not change the overall design of the presentation. In this presentation, the *Verve* presentation theme is still applied to the presentation. By modifying the theme colors, you retain the design of the *Verve* theme. The colors of the *Metro* theme, which coordinate with the pictures in the presentation, are available as text, accent, and background colors.

3 With **Slide 1** displayed, click anywhere in the title placeholder. Click the **Home tab**, and then in the **Font group**, click the **Font button arrow**. Notice that at the top of the **Font** list, under **Theme Fonts**, Century Gothic (Headings) and Century Gothic (Body) display. Compare your screen with Figure 3.2.

Figure 3.2

Theme fonts

4 Click anywhere on the slide to close the Font list. Click the **Design tab**, and then in the **Themes group**, click the **Fonts** button.

> This list displays the name of each theme and the pair of fonts in the theme. The first and larger font in each pair is the Headings font and the second and smaller font in each pair is the Body font.

5 Point to several of the themes and watch as Live Preview changes the title and subtitle text. Then, scroll to the bottom of the **Theme Fonts** list and click **Urban**. Compare your screen with Figure 3.3, and then **Save** 💾 your presentation.

Figure 3.3

Theme Fonts applied to presentation

Theme Colors applied to presentation

Activity 3.02 | Applying a Background Style

1 With **Slide 1** displayed, on the **Design tab**, in the **Background group**, click the **Background Styles** button. Compare your screen with Figure 3.4.

> A *background style* is a slide background fill variation that combines theme colors in different intensities or patterns.

Figure 3.4

Background Styles button

Background Styles gallery

2 Point to each of the background styles to view the style on **Slide 1**. Then, in the first row, *right-click* **Style 2** to display the shortcut menu. Click **Apply to Selected Slides** and then compare your screen with Figure 3.5.

> The background style is applied only to Slide 1.

3 **Save** 🖫 your presentation.

Figure 3.5

Background style applied to slide

More Knowledge | **Applying Background Styles to All Slides in a Presentation**

To change the background style for all of the slides in the presentation, click the background style that you want to apply and the style will be applied to every slide.

Activity 3.03 | Hiding Background Graphics

Many of the PowerPoint 2010 themes contain graphic elements that display on the slide background. In the Verve theme applied to this presentation, the background includes a triangle and lines that intersect near the lower right corner of the slide. Sometimes the background graphics interfere with the slide content. When this happens, you can hide the background graphics.

1 Display **Slide 6**, and notice that on this slide, you can clearly see the triangle and lines on the slide background.

> You cannot delete these objects because they are a part of the slide background; however, you can hide them.

2 Display **Slide 5**, and notice that the background graphics distract from the connecting lines on the diagram. On the **Design tab**, in the **Background group**, select the **Hide Background Graphics** check box, and then compare your slide with Figure 3.6.

> The background objects no longer display behind the SmartArt diagram.

Figure 3.6

Hide Background Graphics
check box selected

Background graphics
do not display on slide

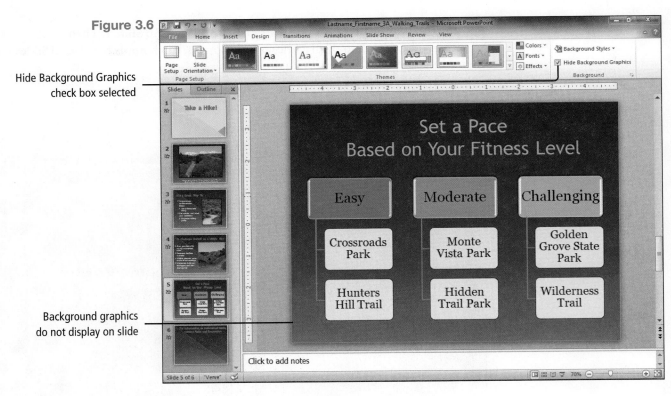

3 Save 🖫 the presentation.

Activity 3.04 | Formatting a Slide Background with a Picture

You can insert a picture on a slide background so the image fills the entire slide.

1 Display **Slide 3**, and then click the **Home tab**. In the **Slides group**, click the **New Slide arrow**, and then click the **Title Only** layout to insert a new slide with the Title Only layout.

2 With the new **Slide 4** displayed, click the **Design tab**. In the **Background group**, select the **Hide Background Graphics** check box, and then click the **Background Styles** button. Below the displayed gallery, click **Format Background**.

In the Format Background dialog box, you can customize a slide background by changing the formatting options.

3 If necessary, on the left side of the dialog box, click Fill. On the right side of the dialog box, under **Fill**, click the **Picture or texture fill** option button, and then notice that on the slide background, a textured fill displays. Compare your screen with Figure 3.7.

Figure 3.7

Format Background
dialog box

Fill selected

Picture or texture fill
option button selected

Textured fill displays
on slide background

Hide Background Graphics
check box selected

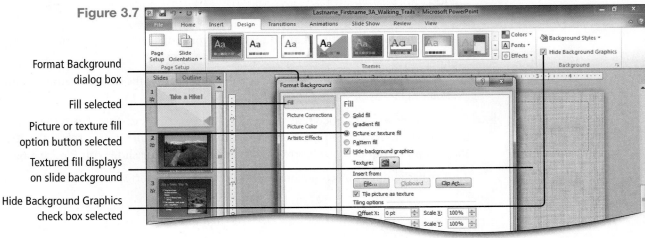

4 Under **Insert from,** click the **File** button to display the **Insert Picture** dialog box. Navigate to your student files, and then click **p03A_Pets.** Click **Insert,** and then at the bottom of the **Format Background** dialog box, click **Close.** Compare your slide with Figure 3.8 and notice that the picture displays as the background of Slide 4.

> When a picture is applied to a slide background using the Format Background option, the picture is not treated as an object. The picture fills the background and you cannot move it or size it.

Figure 3.8

Picture inserted on
slide background

5 Click in the title placeholder, type **Find a Pet Friendly Trail** and then notice that the background picture does not provide sufficient contrast with the text to display the title effectively.

6 With your insertion point still in the title placeholder, click the **Format tab.** In the **Shape Styles group,** click the **Shape Fill button arrow.** In the fifth column, click the last color—**Green, Accent 1, Darker 50%.** Select the title text, and then on the **Format tab,** in the **WordArt Styles group,** in the first row, click the third style—**Fill - White, Drop Shadow. Center** ▤ the text.

> The green fill color and the white WordArt style provide good contrast against the slide background so that the text is readable.

7 Point to the outer edge of the title placeholder to display the 🔁 pointer, and then drag the placeholder up and to the left so that its upper left corner aligns with the upper left corner of the slide. Point to the center right sizing handle and drag to the right so that the placeholder extends to the right edge of the slide. Click outside of the placeholder, and then compare your slide with Figure 3.9.

Figure 3.9

Title placeholder moved and sized, fill color applied

Text centered and WordArt style applied

8 Display **Slide 5**, and then insert a **New Slide** with the **Title Only** layout. On the **Design tab**, in the **Background group**, select the **Hide Background Graphics** check box, and then click the **Background Styles** button. Click **Format Background**.

9 Under **Fill**, click the **Picture or texture fill** option button. Under **Insert from**, click **File**. Navigate to your student files, click **p03A_Trails**, click **Insert**, and then **Close** the dialog box. In the title placeholder, type **Get Outside! Get Fit! Get Walking!** and then **Center** ▤ the text.

10 Select the text, and then change the **Font Size** to **36**. Then, apply the same **Shape Fill** color and **WordArt** style to the title placeholder that you applied to the title on **Slide 4**. Size the placeholder so that it extends from the left edge of the slide to the right edge of the slide, and then drag the placeholder up so that its upper edge aligns with the upper edge of the slide. Click outside of the title so that it is not selected. Compare your slide with Figure 3.10.

The green fill color and white text provide good contrast with the slide background and complement the green color of the grass on the slide.

Figure 3.10

Title placeholder sized and moved, fill color applied

Font size changed, text centered, WordArt style applied

Picture inserted on slide background

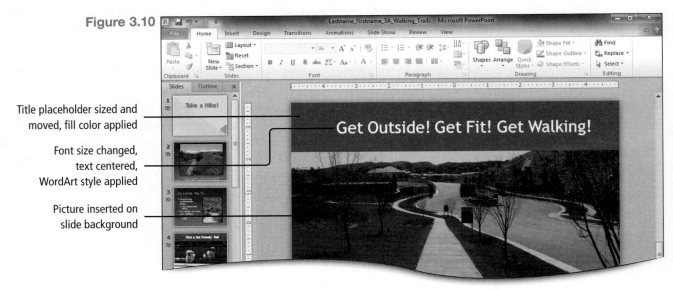

11 Display **Slide 8**, and then format the slide background with a picture from your student files—**p03A_Park**. On the **Design tab**, in the **Background group**, select the **Hide Background Graphics** check box.

12 Select the title placeholder. On the **Format tab**. In the **Shape Styles group**, click the **More** button ⊽. In the **Shape Styles** gallery, in the second row, click the sixth style— **Colored Fill – Periwinkle, Accent 5**.

13 Select the text, and then on the **Format tab**, in the **WordArt Styles group**, click the third style—**Fill - White, Drop Shadow**. Click outside of the placeholder, and then compare your slide with Figure 3.11. **Save** 🖫 the presentation.

Figure 3.11

Title formatted, shape style applied

Picture inserted on slide background

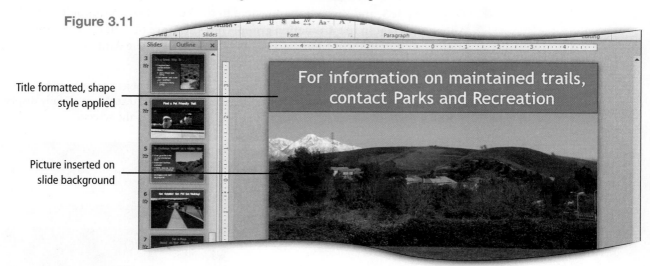

Activity 3.05 | Applying a Background Fill Color and Resetting a Slide Background

1 Display **Slide 1**, and then click the **Design tab**. In the **Background group**, click the **Background Styles** button, and then click **Format Background**.

2 In the **Format Background** dialog box, if necessary, click the Solid fill option button. Under **Fill Color**, click the **Color** button 🖾. Under **Theme Colors**, in the first column, click the last color—**White, Background 1, Darker 50%**. Click **Close**.

The solid fill color is applied to the slide background.

3 On the **Design tab**, in the **Background group**, click the **Background Styles** button. Below the gallery, click **Reset Slide Background**, and then **Save** 🖫 the presentation.

After making many changes to a slide background, you may decide that the original theme formatting is the best choice for displaying the text and graphics on a slide. The Reset Slide Background feature restores the original theme and color theme formatting to a slide.

Objective 2 | Animate a Slide Show

Animation is a visual or sound effect added to an object or text on a slide. Animation can focus the audience's attention, providing the speaker with an opportunity to emphasize important points using the slide element as an effective visual aid.

Activity 3.06 | Applying Animation Entrance Effects and Effect Options

Entrance effects are animations that bring a slide element onto the screen. You can modify an entrance effect by using the animation Effect Options command.

1 Display **Slide 3**, and then click anywhere in the bulleted list placeholder. On the **Animations tab**, in the **Animation group**, click the **More** button ⬇. If necessary, scroll slightly so that the word *Entrance* displays at the top of the Animation gallery, and then compare your screen with Figure 3.12.

> Recall that an entrance effect is animation that brings an object or text onto the screen. An *emphasis effect* is animation that emphasizes an object or text that is already displayed. An *exit effect* is animation that moves an object or text off the screen.

Figure 3.12

Entrance effects

Animation gallery

Emphasis effects

Exit Effects

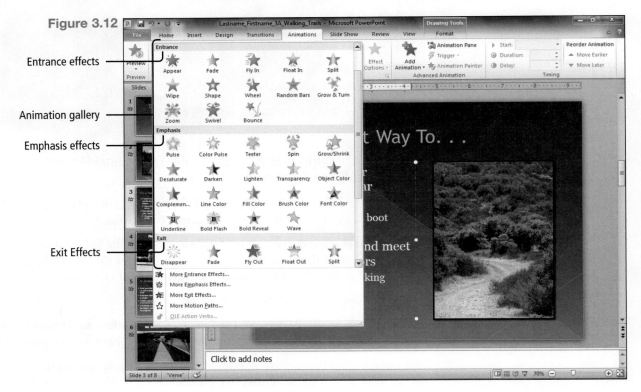

2 Under **Entrance**, click **Split**, and then notice the animation applied to the list. Compare your screen with Figure 3.13.

The numbers *1* and *2* display to the left of the bulleted list placeholder, indicating the order in which the bullet points will be animated during the slide show. For example, the first bullet point and its subordinate bullet are both numbered *1*. Thus, both will display at the same time.

Figure 3.13

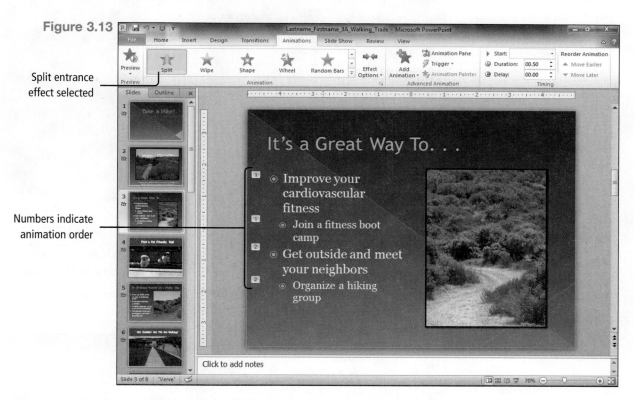

3 Select the bulleted text placeholder. In the **Animation group**, click the **Effect Options** button, and then compare your screen with Figure 3.14.

The Effect Options control the direction and sequence in which the animation displays. Additional options may be available with other entrance effects.

Figure 3.14

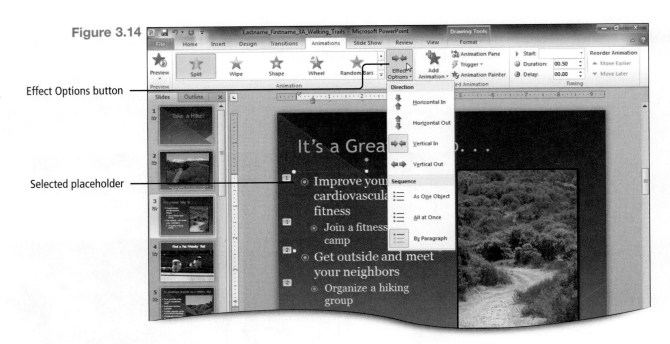

Effect Options button

Selected placeholder

4 Click **Vertical Out** and notice the direction from which the animation is applied.

5 Select the picture. In the **Animation group**, click the **More** button ▾, and then below the gallery, click **More Entrance Effects**. Compare your screen with Figure 3.15.

The Change Entrance Effect dialog box displays additional entrance effects grouped in four categories: Basic, Subtle, Moderate, and Exciting.

Figure 3.15

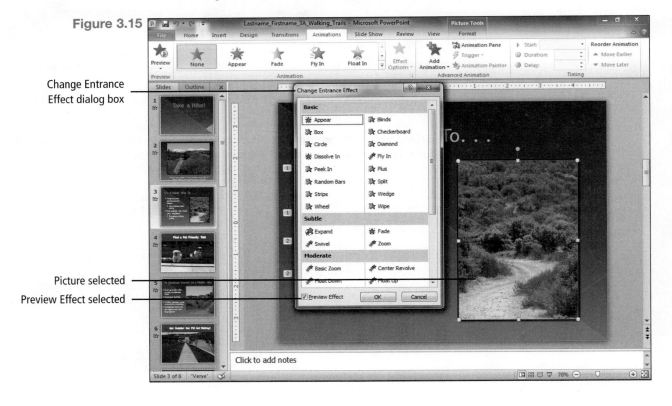

Change Entrance Effect dialog box

Picture selected

Preview Effect selected

6 In the lower right corner of the **Change Entrance Effect** dialog box, verify that the **Preview Effect** check box is selected. Under **Basic**, click **Dissolve In**, and then watch as Live Preview displays the selected entrance effect. Click **OK**.

> The number *3* displays next to the picture, indicating that it is third in the slide animation sequence.

7 Select the title. On the **Animations tab**, in the **Animation group**, click the **More** button ⊽, and then under **Entrance**, click **Split** to apply the animation to the title.

> The number *4* displays next to the title, indicating that it is fourth in the slide animation sequence.

8 **Save** 🖫 the presentation.

Activity 3.07 | Setting Animation Timing Options

Timing options control when animated items display in the animation sequence.

1 With **Slide 3** displayed, on the **Animations tab**, in the **Preview group**, click the **Preview** button.

> The list displays first, followed by the picture, and then the title. The order in which animation is applied is the order in which objects display during the slide show.

2 Select the title. On the **Animations tab**, in the **Timing group**, under **Reorder Animation**, click the **Move Earlier** button two times, and then compare your screen with Figure 3.16.

> To the left of the title placeholder, the number *1* displays. You can use the Reorder Animation buttons to change the order in which text and objects are animated during the slide show.

Figure 3.16

Reorder Animation options

Animation reordered so that title displays first

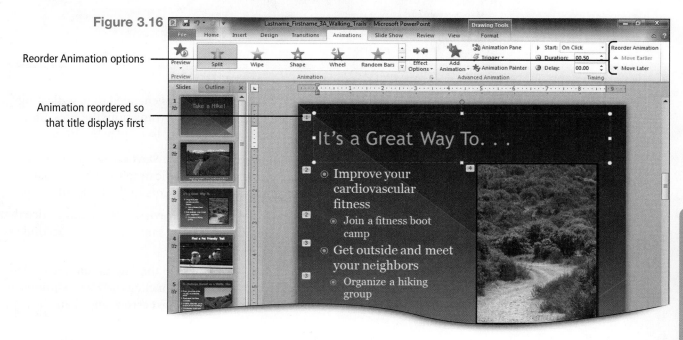

3 With the title selected, on the **Animations tab**, in the **Timing group**, click the **Start button arrow** to display three options—*On Click*, *With Previous*, and *After Previous*. Compare your screen with Figure 3.17.

> The *On Click* option begins the animation sequence for the selected slide element when the mouse button is clicked or the [Spacebar] is pressed. The *With Previous* option begins the animation sequence at the same time as the previous animation or slide transition. The *After Previous* option begins the animation sequence for the selected slide element immediately after the completion of the previous animation or slide transition.

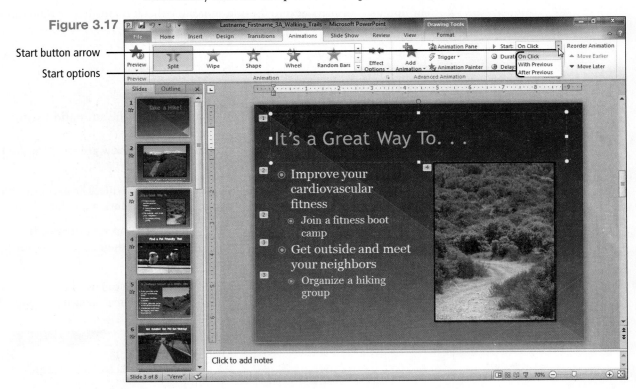

Figure 3.17

Start button arrow

Start options

4 Click **After Previous**, and then notice that the number *1* is changed to *0*, indicating that the animation will begin immediately after the slide transition; the presenter does not need to click the mouse button or press [Spacebar] to display the title.

5 Select the picture, and then in the **Timing group**, click the **Start arrow**. Click **With Previous** and notice that the number is changed to *2*, indicating that the animation will begin at the same time as the second set of bullet points in the bulleted list.

6 On the **Animations tab**, in the **Preview group**, click the **Preview** button and notice that the title displays first, and that the picture displays at the same time as the second set of bullet points.

7 Display **Slide 1**, and then click in the title placeholder. On the **Animations tab**, in the **Animation group**, click the **Entrance** effect **Fly In**, and then click the **Effect Options** button. Click **From Top**. In the **Timing group**, click the **Start arrow**, and then click **After Previous**.

> The number *0* displays to the left of the title indicating that the animation will begin immediately after the slide transition.

8 With the title selected, in the **Timing group**, click the **Duration** down arrow so that *00.25* displays in the **Duration** box. Compare your screen with Figure 3.18.

> Duration controls the speed of the animation. You can set the duration of an animation by typing a value in the Duration box, or you can use the spin box arrows to increase and decrease the duration in 0.25-second increments. When you decrease the duration, the animation speed increases. When you increase the duration, the animation is slowed.

Figure 3.18

Duration set to *00.25*

Fly In animation applied to title

Zero displays to the left of title placeholder

Duration down arrow

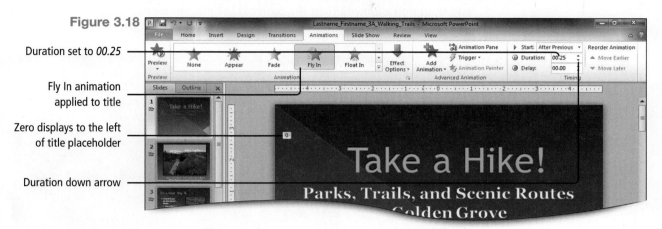

9 Select the subtitle, and then in the **Animation group**, apply the **Fly In** entrance effect. In the **Timing group**, click the **Start arrow**, and then click **After Previous**. In the **Timing group**, select the value in the **Delay** box, type **00.50** and then press Enter. Compare your screen with Figure 3.19.

> You can use Delay to begin a selected animation after a specified amount of time has elapsed. Here, the animation is delayed by one-half of a second after the completion of the previous animation—the title animation. You can type a value in the Delay or Duration boxes, or you can use the up and down arrows to change the timing.

Figure 3.19

Fly In animation applied to subtitle

Delay set to *00.50*

10 View the slide show from the beginning and notice the animation on Slides 1 and 3. When the black slide displays, press Esc to return to Normal view, and then **Save** the presentation.

Activity 3.08 | Using Animation Painter and Removing Animation

Animation Painter is a feature that copies animation settings from one object to another.

1 Display **Slide 3**, and then click anywhere in the bulleted list. On the **Animations tab**, in the **Advanced Animation group**, click the **Animation Painter** button. Display **Slide 5**, and then point anywhere in the bulleted list placeholder to display the Animation Painter pointer ⃕⃕. Compare your screen with Figure 3.20.

Figure 3.20

Animation Painter button

Animation Painter pointer

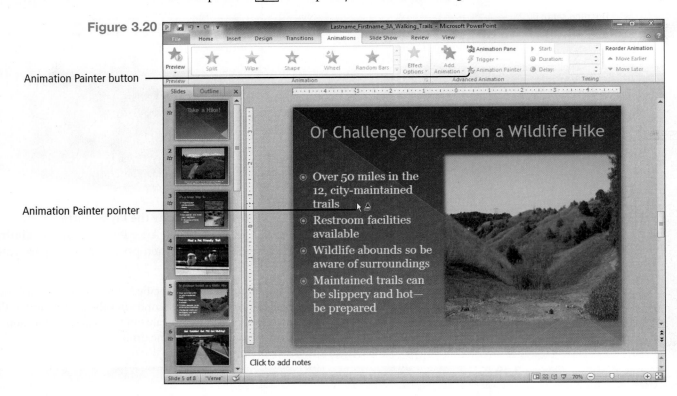

2 Click the bulleted list to copy the animation settings from the list on **Slide 3** to the list on **Slide 5**.

3 Display **Slide 3**, and then select the picture. Using the technique that you just practiced, use **Animation Painter** to copy the animation from the picture on **Slide 3** to the picture on **Slide 5**. With **Slide 5** displayed, compare your screen with Figure 3.21.

The numbers displayed to the left of the bulleted list and the picture indicate that animation is applied to the objects.

Figure 3.21

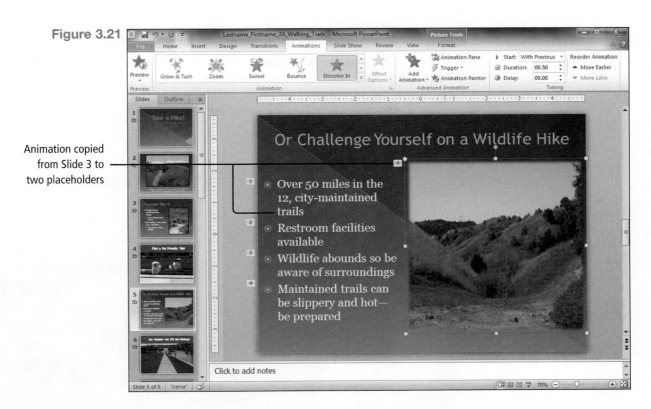

Animation copied from Slide 3 to two placeholders

4 Display **Slide 3**, and then click in the title placeholder. On the **Animations tab**, in the **Animation group**, click the **More** button ⊡. At the top of the gallery, click **None** to remove the animation from the title placeholder. Compare your screen with Figure 3.22, and then **Save** 🖫 the presentation.

Figure 3.22

Animation set to None

Animation removed from title

Objective 3 | Insert a Video

You can insert, size, and move videos in a PowerPoint presentation, and you can format videos by applying styles and effects. Video editing features in PowerPoint 2010 enable you to trim parts of a video and to fade the video in and out during a presentation.

PowerPoint | Chapter 3

Activity 3.09 | Inserting a Video

1 Display **Slide 1**. On the **Insert tab**, in the **Media group**, click the upper part of the **Video** button. In the **Insert Video** dialog box, navigate to your student files, and then click **p03A_Trails_Video**. Click **Insert**, and then compare your screen with Figure 3.23.

The video displays in the center of the slide, and playback and volume controls display in the control panel below the video. Video formatting and editing tools display on the Ribbon.

Figure 3.23

Video Tools display

Video inserted

Control panel

2 Below the video, on the control panel, click the **Play/Pause** button ▶ to view the video and notice that as the video plays, the control panel displays the time that has elapsed since the start of the video.

3 On the **Format tab**, in the **Size group**, click in the **Video Height** box ⬚. Type **3** and then press Enter. Notice that the video width adjusts proportionately.

4 Point to the video to display the ⬚ pointer, and then drag the video down so that the top of the video is aligned at **zero on the vertical ruler**. On the **Format tab**, in the **Arrange group**, click the **Align** button ⬚, and then click **Align Center** to center the video horizontally on the slide. Compare your screen with Figure 3.24.

Figure 3.24

Video height and width changed

Video aligned and moved

5 In the lower right corner of the PowerPoint window, in the **View** buttons, click the **Slide Show** button 🖵 to display **Slide 1** in the slide show.

6 Point to the video to display the 🖑 pointer, and then compare your screen with Figure 3.25.

When you point to the video during the slide show, the control panel displays.

Figure 3.25

Link select pointer

Control panel displays

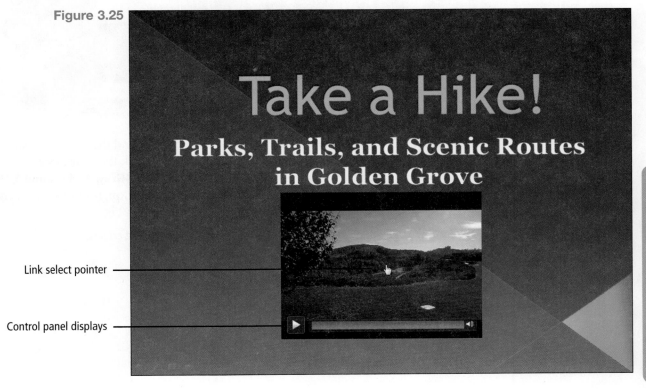

7 With the ⟨🖐⟩ pointer displayed, click the mouse button to view the video. Move the pointer away from the video and notice that the control panel no longer displays. When the video is finished, press ⟨Esc⟩ to exit the slide show.

8 Save ⟨💾⟩ the presentation.

Activity 3.10 | Formatting a Video

You can apply styles and effects to a video and change the video shape and border. You can also recolor a video so that it coordinates with the presentation theme.

1 With **Slide 1** displayed, select the video. On the **Format tab**, in the **Video Styles group**, click the **More** button ⟨▾⟩ to display the **Video Styles** gallery.

2 Using the ScreenTips to view the style name, under **Moderate**, click the first style— **Compound Frame, Black**. Compare your screen with Figure 3.26.

Figure 3.26

Compound Frame, Black style applied to video

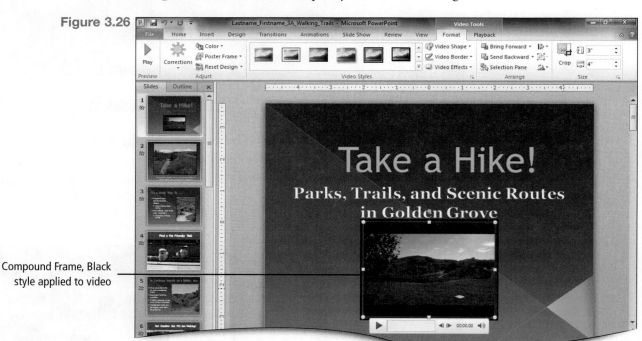

3 In the **Video Styles group**, click the **Video Shape** button, and then under **Basic Shapes**, click the first shape—**Oval**. In the **Video Styles group**, click the **Video Border** button, and then in the third column, click the fifth color—**Blue-Gray, Background 2, Darker 25%**. In the **Video Styles group**, click the **Video Effects** button, point to **Bevel**, and then click the last bevel—**Art Deco**. Compare your screen with Figure 3.27.

You can format a video with any combination of styles and effects.

Figure 3.27

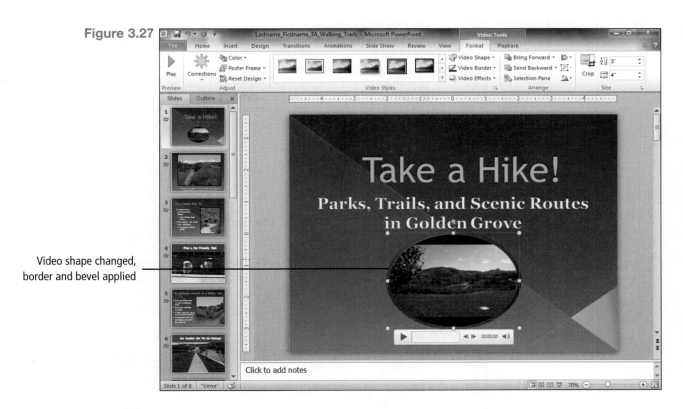

Video shape changed, border and bevel applied

4 If necessary, select the video. On the **Format tab**, in the **Adjust group**, click the **Color** button to display the **Recolor** gallery.

> The first row of the Recolor gallery displays options to recolor the video in grayscale, sepia, washout, or black and white variations. The remaining rows in the gallery display options to recolor the video in the theme colors.

5 In the **Recolor** gallery, in the second row, point to the first style—**Light Blue, Text color 2 Dark** and notice that Live Preview displays the video in the selected color. Compare your screen with Figure 3.28.

Figure 3.28

Color button

Recolor gallery

Selected color

Live Preview displays the video in the selected color

PowerPoint | Chapter 3

6 Click **Light Blue, Text color 2 Dark** to change the color of the video.

7 In the **Adjust group**, click the **Color** button to display the Recolor gallery. In the first row, click the first color—**No Recolor**, and then **Save** 🖫 the presentation.

The No Recolor option restores the video to its original color.

Activity 3.11 | Editing and Compressing a Video

You can *trim*—delete parts of a video to make it shorter—and you can compress a video file to reduce the file size of your PowerPoint presentation.

1 If necessary, select the video. On the **Playback tab**, in the **Editing group**, click the **Trim Video** button, and then compare your screen with Figure 3.29.

At the top of the displayed Trim Video dialog box, the file name and the video duration display. Below the video, a timeline displays with start and end markers indicating the video start and end time. Start Time and End Time boxes display the current start and end of the video. The Previous Frame and Next Frame buttons move the video forward and backward one frame at a time.

Figure 3.29

Duration of video
Video file name
Timeline end marker
End Time box
Timeline start marker
Start Time box

Another Way

Drag the red ending marking until its ScreenTip displays the ending time that you want; or type in the box.

2 Click in the **End Time** box, and then use the spin box arrows to set the End Time to **0:07.040**. Compare your screen with Figure 3.30.

The blue section of the timeline indicates the portion of the video that will play during the slide show. The gray section indicates the portion of the video that is trimmed.

Figure 3.30

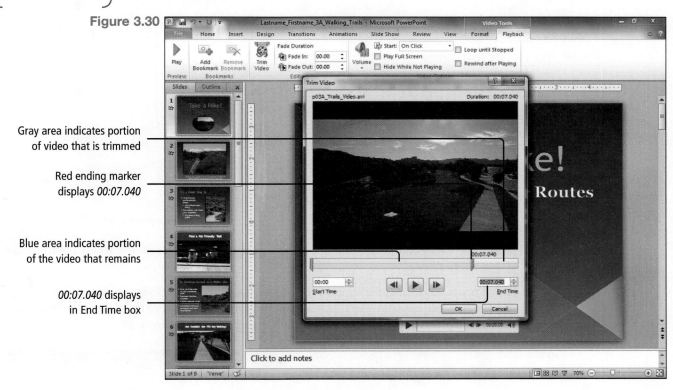

Gray area indicates portion of video that is trimmed

Red ending marker displays *00:07.040*

Blue area indicates portion of the video that remains

00:07.040 displays in End Time box

3 Click **OK** to apply the trim settings.

4 Display **Backstage** view, and then on the **Info tab**, click the **Compress Media** button. Read the description of each video quality option, and then click **Low Quality.** Compare your screen with Figure 3.31.

The Compress Media dialog box displays the slide number on which the selected video is inserted, the video file name, the original size of the video file, and when compression is complete, the amount that the file size was reduced.

Figure 3.31

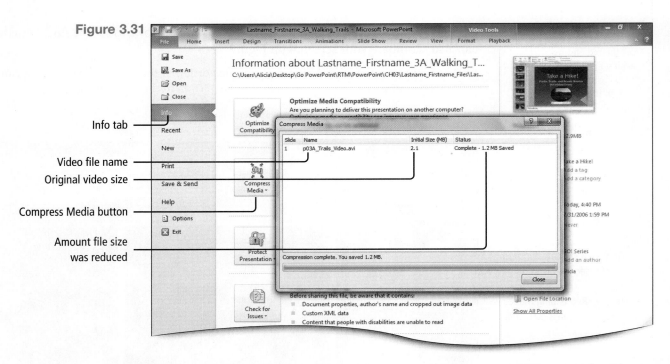

Info tab

Video file name

Original video size

Compress Media button

Amount file size
was reduced

5 In the **Compress Media** dialog box, click **Close**, and then click the **Home tab** to return to **Slide 1**.

6 If necessary, select the video. On the **Playback tab**, in the **Video Options group**, click the **Start arrow**, and then click **Automatically** so that during the slide show, the video will begin automatically. Compare your screen with Figure 3.32.

Figure 3.32

Start option set to *Automatically*

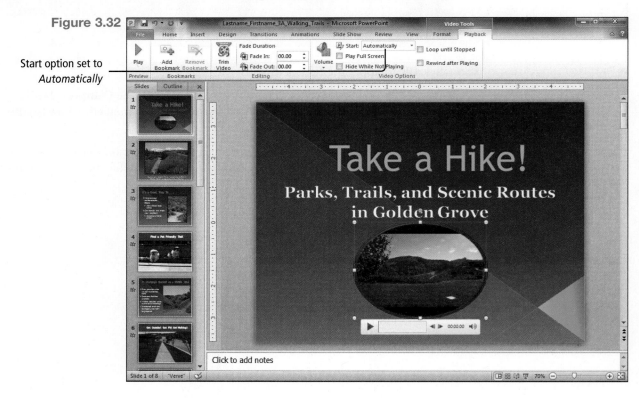

7 Click the **Slide Show tab**, in the **Start Slide Show group**, click the **From Beginning** button, and then view the slide show. Press Esc when the black slide displays.

> **Note** | Your Video May Look Blurry
>
> On playback, a compressed video may look slightly blurry. If you are certain that your presentation file will not be transmitted over the Internet, for example, in an e-mail message or in your learning management system, it is not necessary to compress the video.

8 On the **Insert tab**, in the **Text group**, click the **Header & Footer** button to display the **Header and Footer** dialog box. Click the **Notes and Handouts tab**. Under **Include on page**, select the **Date and time** check box, and then select **Update automatically**. If necessary, clear the **Header** check box, and then select the **Page number** and **Footer** check boxes. In the **Footer** box, using your own name, type **Lastname_Firstname_3A_ Walking_Trails** and then click **Apply to All**.

9 Show the **Document Panel**. Replace the text in the **Author** box with your own firstname and lastname. In the **Subject** box, type your course name and section number, and in the **Keywords** box, type **trails, hiking Close** the **Document Information Panel**.

10 **Save** 🖫 your presentation. Print **Handouts 4 Slides Horizontal**, or submit your presentation electronically as directed by your instructor.

11 **Close** the presentation and exit PowerPoint.

End **You have completed Project 3A**

Project 3B Summary and Analysis Presentation

myitlab
Project 3B Training

Project Activities

In Activities 3.12 through 3.17, you will add a table and two charts to a presentation that Mindy Walker, Director of Parks and Recreation, is creating to inform the City Council about enrollment trends in Golden Grove recreation programs. Your completed presentation will look similar to Figure 3.33.

Project Files

For Project 3B, you will need the following file:

p03B_Recreation_Enrollment

You will save your presentation as:

Lastname_Firstname_3B_Recreation_Enrollment

Project Results

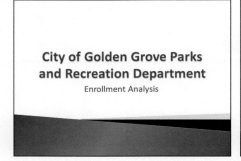

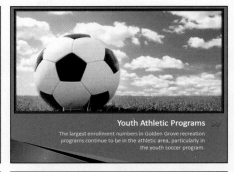

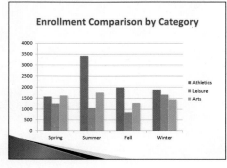

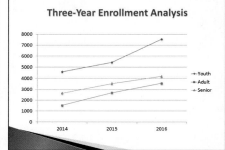

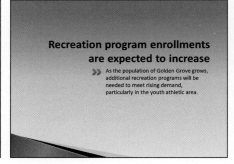

Figure 3.33
Project 3B Recreation Enrollment

Objective 4 | Create and Modify Tables

A *table* is a format for information that organizes and presents text and data in columns and rows. The intersection of a column and row is referred to as a *cell* and is the location in which you type text in a table.

Activity 3.12 | Creating a Table

There are several ways to insert a table in a PowerPoint slide. For example, you can use the Draw Table pointer, which is useful when the rows and columns contain cells of different sizes. Another way is to insert a slide with a Content Layout and then click the Insert Table button. Or, click the Insert tab and then click Table. In this activity, you will use a Content Layout to create a table.

1 **Start** PowerPoint. From your student files, open **p03B_Recreation_Enrollment**, and then **Save** the presentation in your **PowerPoint Chapter 3** folder as **Lastname_Firstname_3B_Recreation_Enrollment**

2 With **Slide 1** displayed, on the **Home tab**, in the **Slides group**, click the **New Slide** button to insert a slide with the **Title and Content** layout. In the title placeholder, type **Recreation Program Summary** and then **Center** the title.

3 In the content placeholder, click the **Insert Table** button to display the **Insert Table** dialog box. In the **Number of columns** box, type **3** and then press Tab. In the **Number of rows** box, type **2** and then compare your screen with Figure 3.34.

Here you enter the number of columns and rows that you want the table to contain.

Figure 3.34

Table set for 3 columns and 2 rows

Insert Table button

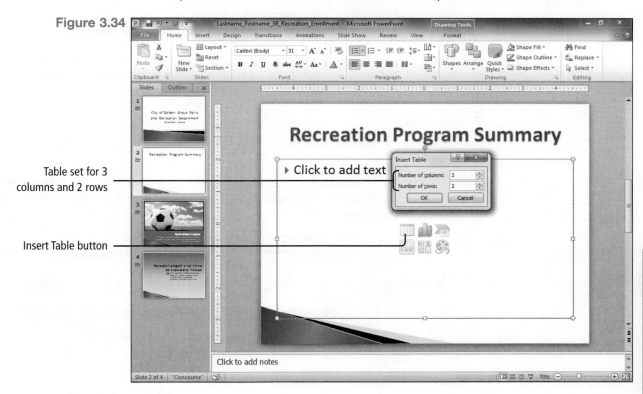

4 Click **OK** to create a table with three columns and two rows. Notice that the insertion point is blinking in the upper left cell of the table.

The table extends from the left side of the content placeholder to the right side, and the three columns are equal in width. By default, a style is applied to the table.

5 With the insertion point positioned in the first cell of the table, type **Athletics** and then press Tab.

> Pressing Tab moves the insertion point to the next cell in the same row. If the insertion point is positioned in the last cell of a row, pressing Tab moves the insertion point to the first cell of the next row.

Alert! | Did You Press Enter Instead of Tab?

In a table, pressing Enter creates another line in the same cell. If you press Enter by mistake, you can remove the extra line by pressing Backspace.

---

6 With the insertion point positioned in the second cell of the first row, type **Leisure** and then press Tab. Type **Arts** and then press Tab to move the insertion point to the first cell in the second row. Compare your table with Figure 3.35.

Figure 3.35

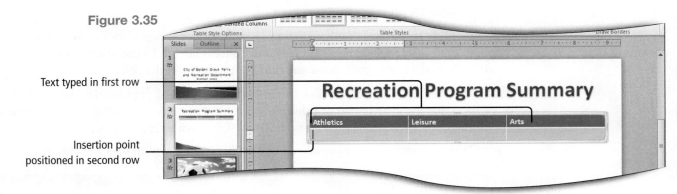

Text typed in first row

Insertion point positioned in second row

7 With the insertion point positioned in the first cell of the second row, type **Team sports** and then press Tab. Type **Personal development classes** and then press Tab. Type **Music and dance classes**

8 Press Tab to insert a new blank row.

> When the insertion point is positioned in the last cell of a table, pressing Tab inserts a new blank row at the bottom of the table.

9 In the first cell of the third row, type **Youth** and then press Tab. Type **Older adults** and then press Tab. Type **Young adults** and then compare your table with Figure 3.36. **Save** your presentation.

Figure 3.36

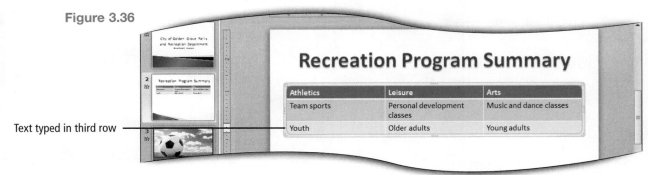

Text typed in third row

Alert! | Did You Add an Extra Row to the Table?

Recall that when the insertion point is positioned in the last cell of the table, pressing Tab inserts a new blank row. If you inadvertently inserted a blank row in the table, on the Quick Access Toolbar, click Undo.

Activity 3.13 | Modifying the Layout of a Table

You can modify the layout of a table by inserting or deleting rows and columns, changing the alignment of the text in a cell, adjusting the height and width of the entire table or selected rows and columns, and by merging multiple cells into one cell.

1 Click in any cell in the first column, and then click the **Layout tab**. In the **Rows & Columns group**, click the **Insert Left** button.

> A new first column is inserted and the width of the columns is adjusted so that all four columns are the same width.

2 In the *second* row, click in the first cell, and then type **Largest Enrollments**

3 In the third row, click in the first cell, and then type **Primary Market** Compare your table with Figure 3.37.

Figure 3.37

Column inserted and text typed

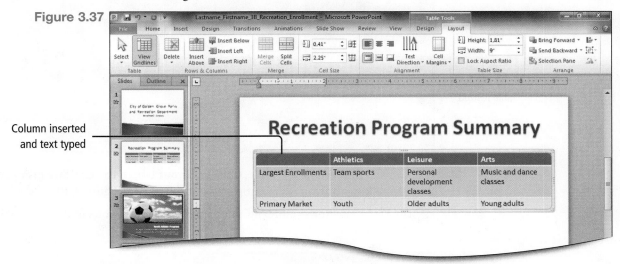

4 With the insertion point positioned in the third row, on the **Layout tab**, in the **Rows & Columns group**, click the **Insert Above** button to insert a new third row. In the first cell, type **Enrollment Capacity** and then press Tab. Type the remaining three entries, pressing Tab to move from cell to cell: **Enrolled at 85% capacity** and **Enrolled at 70% capacity** and **Enrolled at 77% capacity**

5 At the center of the lower border surrounding the table, point to the cluster of four dots—the sizing handle—to display the ↕ pointer. Compare your screen with Figure 3.38.

Figure 3.38

Row inserted and text typed

Vertical resize pointer positioned over sizing handle

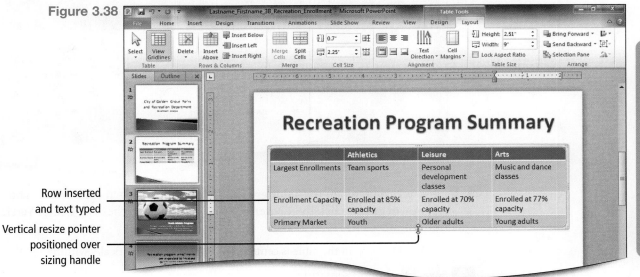

6 Drag down to resize the table until the lower left corner of the table outline is just above the graphic in the lower left corner of the slide. Compare your screen with Figure 3.39.

Figure 3.39

Table resized

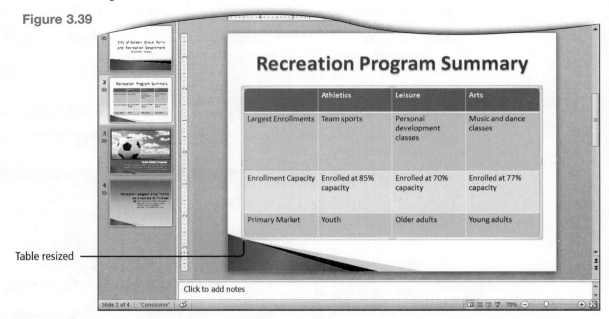

7 Click in the first cell of the table. On the **Layout tab**, in the **Cell Size group**, click the **Distribute Rows** button. Compare your table with Figure 3.40.

The Distribute Rows command adjusts the height of the rows in the table so that they are equal.

Figure 3.40

Distribute Rows button

Table rows equal in height

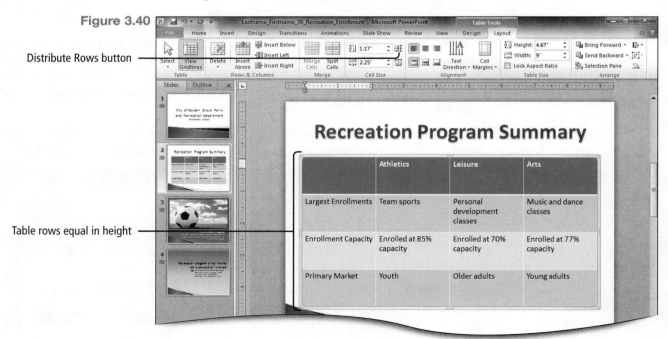

8 On the **Layout tab**, in the **Table group**, click **Select**, and then click **Select Table**. In the **Alignment group**, click the **Center** button, and then click the **Center Vertically** button.

All of the text in the table is centered horizontally and vertically within the cells.

9 **Save** your presentation.

> **More Knowledge** | Deleting Rows and Columns
>
> To delete a row or column from a table, click in the row or column that you want to delete. Click the Layout tab, and then in the Rows & Columns group, click Delete. In the displayed list, click Delete Columns or Delete Rows.

Activity 3.14 | Modifying a Table Design

You can modify the design of a table by applying a *table style*. A table style formats the entire table so that it is consistent with the presentation theme. There are color categories within the table styles—Best Match for Document, Light, Medium, and Dark.

1 Click in any cell in the table. In the **Table Tools**, click the **Design tab**, and then in the **Table Styles group**, click the **More** button ⏷. In the displayed **Table Styles** gallery, point to several of the styles to view the Live Preview of the style.

2 Under **Medium**, scroll as necessary, and then in the third row, click the third button— **Medium Style 3 – Accent 2**—to apply the style to the table.

3 On the **Design tab**, in the **Table Style Options group**, clear the **Banded Rows** check box. Notice that each row except the header row displays in the same color.

> The check boxes in the Table Style Options group control where Table Style formatting is applied.

4 Select the **Banded Rows** check box.

5 Move the pointer outside of the table so that it is positioned to the left of the first row in the table to display the ➡ pointer, as shown in Figure 3.41.

Figure 3.41

Select row pointer →

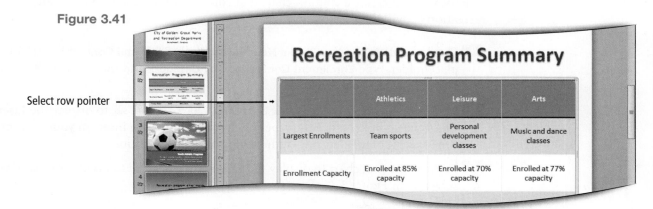

6 With the ➡ pointer pointing to the first row in the table, click the mouse button to select the entire row so that you can apply formatting to the selection. Move the pointer into the selected row, and then right-click to display the Mini toolbar and shortcut menu. On the Mini toolbar, change the **Font Size** to **28**.

7 With the first row still selected, in the **Table Tools**, on the **Design tab**, in the **Table Styles group**, click the **Effects** button 🔲. Point to **Cell Bevel**, and then under **Bevel**, click the first bevel—**Circle**.

8 Position the pointer above the first column to display the ⬇ pointer, and then right-click to select the first column and display the shortcut menu. Click **Bold** **B** and **Italic** **I**.

9 Click in a blank area of the slide, and then compare your slide with Figure 3.42. **Save** 💾 the presentation.

PowerPoint | Chapter 3

Figure 3.42

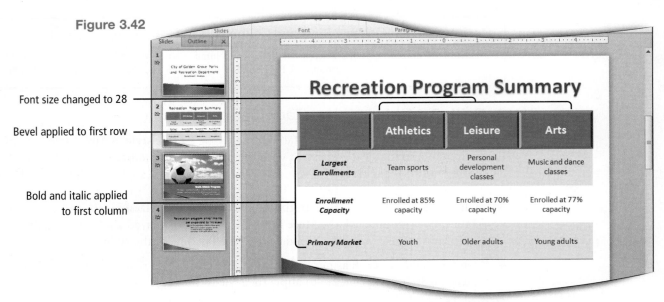

Font size changed to 28

Bevel applied to first row

Bold and italic applied to first column

Objective 5 | Create and Modify Charts

A ***chart*** is a graphic representation of numeric data. Commonly used chart types include bar and column charts, pie charts, and line charts. A chart that you create in PowerPoint is stored in an Excel worksheet that is incorporated into the PowerPoint file.

Activity 3.15 | Creating a Column Chart and Applying a Chart Style

A ***column chart*** is useful for illustrating comparisons among related numbers. In this activity, you will create a column chart that compares enrollment in each category of recreation activities by season.

1 Display **Slide 3**, and then add a **New Slide** with the **Title and Content** layout. In the title placeholder, type **Enrollment Comparison by Category** and then **Center** 🗏 the title and change the **Font Size** to **36**.

2 In the content placeholder, click the **Insert Chart** button 📊 to display the **Insert Chart** dialog box. Notice the types of charts that you can insert in your presentation. If necessary, on the left side of the dialog box, click Column.

3 Point to the first chart to display the ScreenTip *Clustered Column*. Compare your screen with Figure 3.43.

Figure 3.43

Clustered Column chart

Chart types

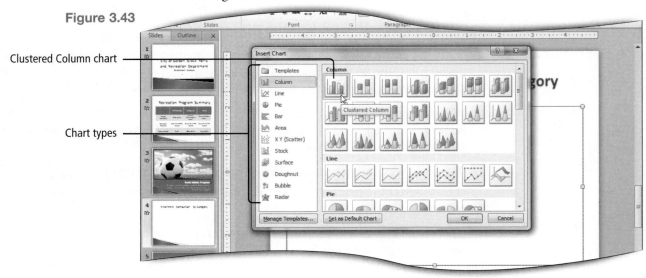

4 Click **Clustered Column**. Click **OK**, and then compare your screen with Figure 3.44.

The PowerPoint window displays a column chart on one side of your screen. On the other side of your screen, an Excel worksheet displays columns and rows. A cell is identified by the intersecting column letter and row number, forming the *cell reference*.

The worksheet contains sample data in a data range outlined in blue, from which the chart in the PowerPoint window is generated. The column headings—*Series 1*, *Series 2*, and *Series 3* display in the chart *legend* and the row headings—*Category 1*, *Category 2*, *Category 3*, and *Category 4*—display as *category labels*. The legend identifies the patterns or colors that are assigned to the data series in the chart. The category labels display along the bottom of the chart to identify the categories of data.

Figure 3.44

Column headings

Row headings

Excel worksheet displays sample data outlined in blue

Column chart displays in PowerPoint window

Legend displays column heading text

Category labels display row heading data

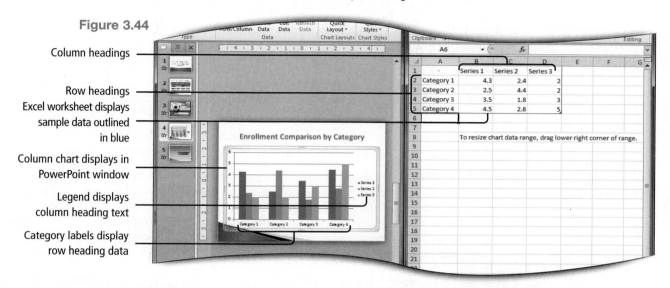

5 In the Excel window, click in cell **B1**, which contains the text *Series 1*. Type **Athletics** and then press Tab to move to cell **C1**.

The chart legend is updated to reflect the change in the Excel worksheet.

6 In cell **C1**, which contains the text *Series 2*, type **Leisure** and then press Tab to move to cell **D1**. Type **Arts** and then press Tab. Notice that cell **A2**, which contains the text *Category 1*, is selected. Compare your screen with Figure 3.45.

The blue box outlining the range of cells defines the area in which you are entering data. When you press Tab in the rightmost cell, the first cell in the next row becomes active.

Figure 3.45

Column headings entered

Cell A2 selected

Legend updated

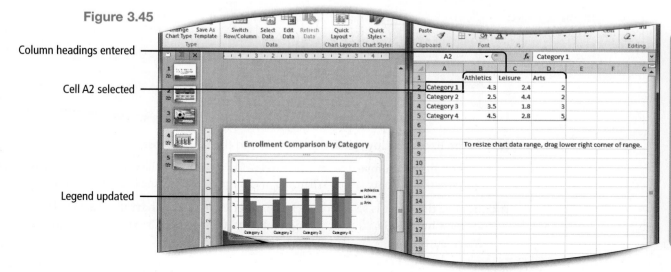

PowerPoint | Chapter 3

7 Beginning in cell **A2**, type the following data, pressing Tab to move from cell to cell.

	Athletics	Leisure	Arts
Spring	1588	1263	1639
Summer	3422	1058	1782
Fall	1987	852	1293
Winter	1889	1674	

8 In cell **D5**, which contains the value 5, type **1453** and then press Enter.

Pressing Enter in the last cell of the blue outlined area maintains the existing data range.

> **Alert!** | **Did You Press Tab After the Last Entry?**
>
> If you pressed Tab after entering the data in cell D5, you expanded the chart range. In the Excel window, click Undo.

9 Compare your worksheet and your chart with Figure 3.46. Correct any typing errors by clicking in the cell that you want to change, and then retype the data.

Each of the 12 cells containing the numeric data that you entered is a ***data point***—a value that originates in a worksheet cell. Each data point is represented in the chart by a ***data marker***—a column, bar, area, dot, pie slice, or other symbol in a chart that represents a single data point. Related data points form a ***data series***; for example, there is a data series for *Athletics*, *Leisure*, and *Arts*. Each data series has a unique color or pattern represented in the chart legend.

Figure 3.46

Worksheet data entered

Chart data markers reflect data in Excel worksheet

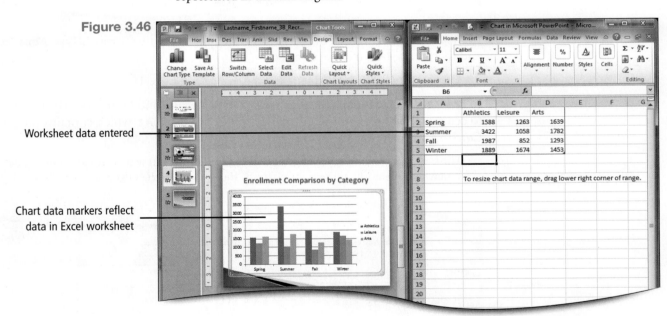

10 In the Excel window, click the **File tab**, and then click **Close**.

You are not prompted to save the Excel worksheet because the worksheet data is a part of the PowerPoint presentation. When you save the presentation, the Excel data is saved with it.

11 Be sure the chart is selected; click the outer edge of the chart if necessary to select it. In the **Chart Tools**, click the **Design tab**, and then in the **Chart Styles group**, click the **More** button ⊡.

12 In the **Chart Styles** gallery, the chart styles are numbered sequentially. Use ScreenTips to display the style numbers. Click **Style 10** to apply the style to the chart.

13 **Save** 🖫 your presentation.

> **More Knowledge** | **Editing the Chart Data After Closing Excel**
>
> You can redisplay the Excel worksheet and make changes to the data after you have closed Excel. To do so, in PowerPoint, click the chart to select it, and then on the Design tab in the Data group, click Edit Data.

Activity 3.16 | Creating a Line Chart and Deleting Chart Data

To analyze and compare annual data over a three-year period, the presentation requires an additional chart. Recall that there are a number of different types of charts that you can insert in a PowerPoint presentation. In this activity, you will create a *line chart*, which is commonly used to illustrate trends over time.

1 With **Slide 4** displayed, add a **New Slide** with the **Title and Content** layout. In the title placeholder, type **Three-Year Enrollment Analysis** and then **Center** ≡ the title and change the **Font Size** to **36**.

2 In the content placeholder, click the **Insert Chart** button 📊. On the left side of the displayed **Insert Chart** dialog box, click **Line**, and then on the right, under **Line**, click the fourth chart—**Line with Markers**. Click **OK**.

3 In the Excel worksheet, click in cell **B1**, which contains the text *Series 1*. Type **Youth** and then press Tab. Type **Adult** and then press Tab. Type **Senior** and then press Tab.

4 Beginning in cell **A2**, type the following data, pressing Tab to move from cell to cell. If you make any typing errors, click in the cell that you want to change, and then retype the data.

	Youth	Adult	Senior
2014	4586	1534	2661
2015	5422	2699	3542
2016	7565	3572	4183

5 In the Excel window, position the pointer over **row heading 5** so that the → pointer displays. Compare your screen with Figure 3.47.

Figure 3.47

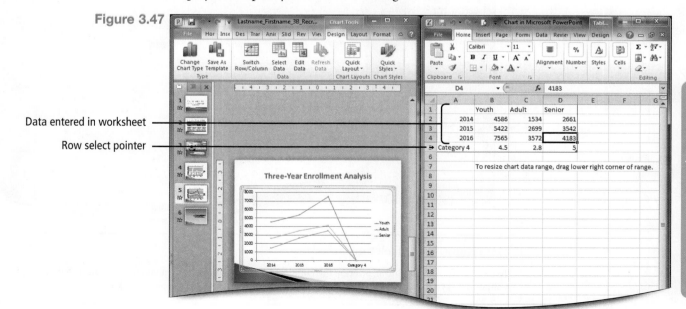

Data entered in worksheet

Row select pointer

6 With the ➜ pointer displayed, *right-click* to select the row and display the shortcut menu. On the shortcut menu, click **Delete** to delete the extra row from the worksheet, and then compare your screen with Figure 3.48.

> The data in the worksheet contains four columns and four rows, and the blue outline defining the chart data range is resized. You must delete columns and rows that you do not want to include in the chart. You can add additional rows and columns by typing column and row headings and then entering additional data. When data is typed in cells adjacent to the chart range, the range is resized to include the new data.

Figure 3.48

Row with sample data deleted

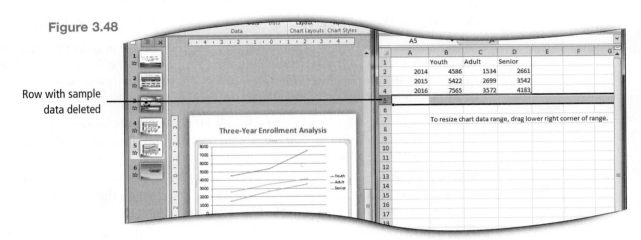

7 **Close** ❎ the Excel window. In the **Chart Styles group**, click the **More** button ▾. In the **Chart Styles** gallery, click **Style 26**, and then compare your slide with Figure 3.49. **Save** 💾 your presentation.

Figure 3.49

Chart Style 26 selected

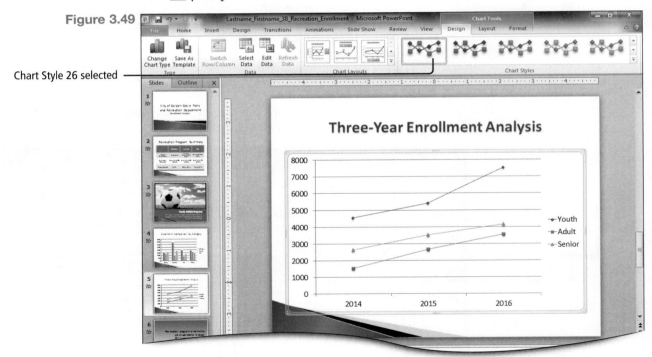

More Knowledge | Deleting Columns

To delete a worksheet column, position the pointer over the column letter that you want to select so that the ⬇ pointer displays. Right-click to select the column and display the shortcut menu. Click Delete.

Activity 3.17 | Animating a Chart

1 Display **Slide 4**, and then click the column chart to select it. On the **Animations tab**, in the **Animation group**, click the **More** button ⏷, and then under **Entrance**, click **Split**.

2 In the **Animation group**, click the **Effect Options** button, and then under **Sequence**, click **By Series**. Compare your screen with Figure 3.50.

The By Series option displays the chart one data series at a time, and the numbers 1, 2, 3, and 4 to the left of the chart indicate the four parts of the chart animation sequence. The chart animation sequence includes the background, followed by the Athletics data series for each season, and then the Leisure series, and then the Arts series.

Figure 3.50

Split animation applied to chart

Numbers indicate animation sequence

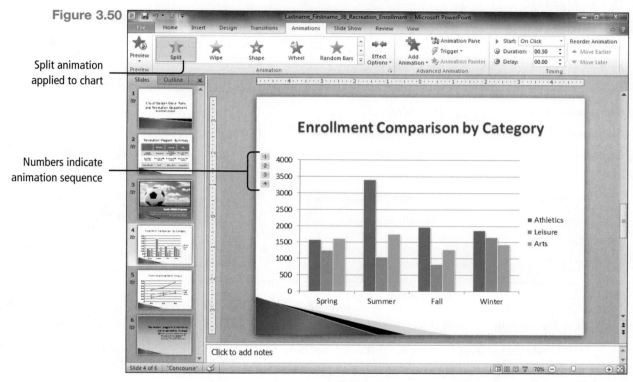

3 Click the **Slide Show tab**. In the **Start Slide Show group**, click **From Current Slide** to view the animation on **Slide 4**. Press Spacebar to display the legend and labels. Press Spacebar again to display the *Athletics* data.

4 Continue to press Spacebar to advance through the remaining animation effects. After the animations for Slide 4 are complete, press Esc to end the slide show and return to the presentation.

5 Insert a **Header & Footer** for the **Notes and Handouts**. Include the **Date and time updated automatically**, the **Page number**, and a **Footer** with the file name **Lastname_Firstname_3B_Recreation_Enrollment**

6 Show the **Document Panel**. Replace the text in the **Author** box with your own firstname and lastname. In the **Subject** box, type your course name and section number, and in the **Keywords** box, type **enrollment, recreation Close** the **Document Information Panel**.

7 **Save** 🖫 your presentation. Print **Handouts 6 Slides Horizontal**, or submit your presentation electronically as directed by your instructor. **Close** the presentation and exit PowerPoint.

End You have completed Project 3B

Summary

In this chapter, you formatted a presentation by applying background styles, inserting pictures on slide backgrounds, and changing the theme fonts. You enhanced your presentation by inserting video, applying animation effects, and by changing effect and timing options. You practiced creating tables to present information in an organized manner, and you used charts to visually represent data.

Key Terms

After Previous 752	**Column chart** 770	**Line chart** 773
Animation 748	**Data marker** 772	**On Click** 752
Animation Painter 754	**Data point** 772	**Table** 765
Background style 742	**Data series** 772	**Table style** 769
Body font 741	**Emphasis effect** 748	**Theme colors** 741
Category label 771	**Entrance effect** 748	**Theme font** 741
Cell 765	**Exit effect** 748	**Timing options** 751
Cell reference 771	**Headings font** 741	**Trim** 760
Chart 770	**Legend** 771	**With Previous** 752

Matching

Match each term in the second column with its correct definition in the first column by writing the letter of the term on the blank line in front of the correct definition.

_____ 1.	A slide background fill variation that combines theme colors in different intensities.	**A** Animation
_____ 2.	A theme that determines the font applied to two types of slide text—headings and body.	**B** Background style
_____ 3.	Of the two types of fonts in the theme font, the type that is applied to slide titles.	**C** Body font
_____ 4.	Of the two types of fonts in the theme font, the type that is applied to all slide text except titles.	**D** Cell
_____ 5.	A visual or sound effect added to an object or text on a slide.	**E** Cell reference
_____ 6.	Animations that bring a slide element onto the screen.	**F** Chart
_____ 7.	Animation that emphasizes an object or text that is already displayed.	**G** Column chart
_____ 8.	Animation that moves an object or text off the screen.	**H** Emphasis effect
_____ 9.	A format for information that organizes and presents text and data in columns and rows.	**I** Entrance effect
_____ 10.	The intersection of a column and row.	**J** Exit effect
_____ 11.	Formatting applied to an entire table so that it is consistent with the presentation theme.	**K** Headings font
_____ 12.	A graphic representation of numeric data.	**L** Legend
_____ 13.	A type of chart used to compare data.	**M** Table
_____ 14.	A combination of the column letter and row number identifying a cell.	**N** Table style
_____ 15.	A chart element that identifies the patterns or colors that are assigned to the each data series in the chart.	**O** Theme font

Multiple Choice

Circle the correct answer.

1. The set of coordinating colors applied to the backgrounds, objects, and text in a presentation is called:

   A. theme colors   **B.** colors set   **C.** coordinating colors

2. The command that is used to prevent background graphics from displaying on a slide is:

   A. Hide Background Styles   **B.** Cover Background Graphics   **C.** Hide Background Graphics

3. Animation options that control when animated items display in the animation sequence are called:

   A. timing options   **B.** effect options   **C.** sequence options

4. A feature that copies animation settings from one object to another is:

   A. copy   **B.** format painter   **C.** animation painter

5. The action of deleting parts of a video to make it shorter is referred to as:

   A. edit   **B.** trim   **C.** crop

6. A chart element that identifies categories of data is a:

   A. data marker   **B.** category label   **C.** category marker

7. A column, bar, area, dot, pie slice, or other symbol in a chart that represents a single data point is a:

   A. data marker   **B.** data point   **C.** data series

8. A chart value that originates in a worksheet cell is a:

   A. data marker   **B.** data point   **C.** data series

9. A group of related data points is called a:

   A. data marker   **B.** data point   **C.** data series

10. A type of chart that shows trends over time is a:

    A. pie chart   **B.** column chart   **C.** line chart

Content-Based Assessments

Apply **3A** skills from these Objectives:

1. Customize Slide Backgrounds and Themes
2. Animate a Slide Show
3. Insert a Video

Skills Review | Project **3C** Lake

In the following Skills Review, you will format a presentation by applying slide background styles, colors, pictures, and animation. Your completed presentation will look similar to Figure 3.51.

Project Files

For Project 3C, you will need the following files:

p03C_Lake
p03C_Scenery
p03C_Lake_Video

You will save your presentation as:

Lastname_Firstname_3C_Lake

Project Results

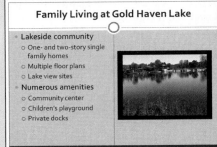

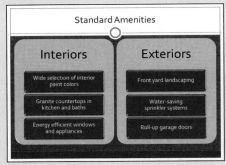

Figure 3.51

(Project 3C Lake continues on the next page)

Content-Based Assessments

Skills Review | Project **3C** Lake (continued)

1 **Start** PowerPoint, from your student files open **p03C_Lake**, and then **Save** the presentation in your **PowerPoint Chapter 3** folder as **Lastname_Firstname_ 3C_Lake**

a. On the **Design tab**, in the **Themes group**, click the **Colors** button, and then click **Aspect** to change the theme colors. On the **Design tab**, in the **Themes group**, click the **Fonts** button, and then click **Module** to change the theme fonts.

b. Display **Slide 2**, and then on the **Home tab,** in the **Slides group**, click the **New Slide arrow**. Click **Title Only** to insert a new slide with the Title Only layout. On the **Design tab**, in the **Background group**, select the **Hide Background Graphics** check box. Click in the title placeholder, and then type **Enjoy the Lakeside Scenery**

c. On the **Design tab**, in the **Background group**, click the **Background Styles** button. Below the gallery, click **Format Background**, and then in the **Format Background** dialog box, verify that on the left side, **Fill** is selected. On the right side of the dialog box, under **Fill**, click the **Picture or texture fill** option button. Under **Insert from**, click the **File** button, and then navigate to your student data files. Click **p03C_Scenery**, and then click **Insert**. In the **Format Background** dialog box, click **Close** to format the slide background with the picture.

d. Click in the title placeholder. On the **Format tab**, in the **Shape Styles group**, click the **More** button, and then in the second row, click the fourth style— **Colored Fill - Dark Blue, Accent 3**.

e. Point to the outer edge of the title placeholder to display the ⊕ pointer, and then drag the placeholder up and to the left so that its top left corner aligns with the top left corner of the slide. Point to the center right sizing handle and drag to the right so that placeholder extends to the right edge of the slide.

2 Display **Slide 4**. On the **Design tab**, in the **Background group**, click the **Background Styles** button. In the second row, point to the third button—**Style 7**. *Right-click* to display the shortcut menu, and then click **Apply to Selected Slides** to apply the dark gray, patterned background to Slide 4.

a. Display **Slide 5**. On the **Design tab**, in the **Background group**, click the **Background Styles** button. Below the gallery, click **Format Background**.

b. In the **Format Background** dialog box, verify that on the left side, **Fill** is selected. On the right side, under **Fill**, click the **Solid Fill** option button, and then under **Fill Color**, click the **Color** button. In the seventh column, click the first color—**Dark Blue, Accent 3**, and then click **Close** to apply the background fill color to the slide.

3 Display **Slide 2**, and then on the **Insert tab**, in the **Media group**, click the **Video** button. Navigate to your student files, and then click **p03_Lake_Video**. Click **Insert** to insert the video.

a. With the video selected, on the **Format tab**, in the **Size group**, replace the value in the **Video Height** box with **3.25** and then press ⏎.

b. Point to the video, and then hold down ⇧ and drag to the right so that its right edge aligns at **4.5 inches on the right side of the horizontal ruler**.

c. With the video selected, on the **Format tab**, in the **Video Styles group**, click the **Video Border** button, and then in the seventh column, click the first color—**Dark Blue, Accent 3**. Click the **Video Effects** button, point to **Bevel**, and then click the last style— **Art Deco**.

d. With the video selected, on the **Playback tab**, in the **Video Options group**, click the **Start arrow**, and then click **Automatically**. In the **Editing group**, click the **Trim Video** button. In the **Trim Video** dialog box, in the **End Time** box, use the spin box arrows to set the end time to **00:6.520** Click **OK**.

e. Display **Backstage** view. On the **Info page**, in the center panel, click the **Compress Media** button, and then click **Low Quality**. Recall that compressing in this manner facilitates sending your file over the Internet in an e-mail or in a learning management system, although it may make the video less clear when played. When the compression is complete, **Close** the **Compress Media** dialog box, and then click the **Home tab** to return to the presentation.

4 On **Slide 2**, click anywhere in the bulleted list placeholder. On the **Animations tab**, in the **Animation group**, click the **More** button, and then under **Entrance**, click **Split**.

a. In the **Animation group**, click the **Effect Options** button, and then click **Vertical Out**.

(Project 3C Lake continues on the next page)

Content-Based Assessments

b. In the **Timing group**, click the **Start arrow**, and then click **With Previous** so that the list displays at the same time as the video begins to play.

c. In the **Timing group**, click the **Duration up arrow** two times so that *01.00* displays in the **Duration** box. Click the **Delay up arrow** one time so that *00.25* displays in the **Delay** box.

5 Display **Slide 5**, and then click in the title placeholder. On the **Animations tab**, in the **Animation group**, click the **More** button, and then under **Entrance**, click **Wipe**. In the **Timing group**, click the **Start arrow**, and then click **After Previous**.

a. Select the title, and then in the **Advanced Animation group**, click the **Animation Painter** button. Click the subtitle to apply the title animation effects to the subtitle.

b. Display **Slide 1**, and then select the title. On the **Animations tab**, in the **Animation group**, click the **More** button, and then click **None** to remove the animation from the title.

c. On the **Slide Show tab**, in the **Start Slide Show group**, click **From Beginning**, and then view your presentation, clicking the mouse button to advance through the slides.

d. Insert a **Header & Footer** for the **Notes and Handouts**. Include the **Date and time updated automatically**, the **Page number**, and a **Footer** with the file name **Lastname_Firstname_3C_Lake** Click **Apply to All**.

e. Show the **Document Panel**. Replace the text in the **Author** box with your own firstname and lastname. In the **Subject** box, type your course name and section number, and in the **Keywords** box, type **Gold Haven, lake Close** the **Document Information Panel**.

f. **Save** your presentation. Print **Handouts 6 Slides Horizontal**, or submit your presentation electronically as directed by your instructor. **Close** the presentation.

End **You have completed Project 3C** —————————————————————

Content-Based Assessments

Apply **3B** skills from
these Objectives:

4 Create and Modify
Tables

5 Create and Modify
Charts

Skills Review | Project **3D** School Enrollment

In the following Skills Review, you will format a presentation by inserting and formatting a table,
column chart, and line chart. Your completed presentation will look similar to Figure 3.52.

Project Files

For Project 3D, you will need the following file:

p03D_School_Enrollment

You will save your presentation as:

Lastname_Firstname_3D_School_Enrollment

Project Results

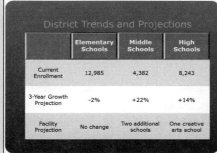

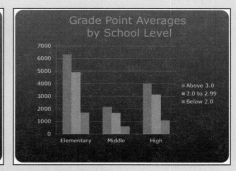

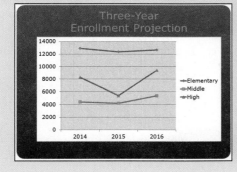

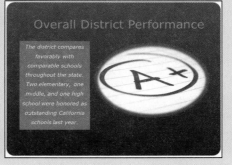

Figure 3.52

(Project 3D School Enrollment continues on the next page)

PowerPoint | Chapter 3

1 **Start** PowerPoint, from your student files open **p03D_School_Enrollment**, and then **Save** the presentation in your **PowerPoint Chapter 3** folder as **Lastname_Firstname_3D_School_Enrollment**

a. Display **Slide 2**. In the content placeholder, click the **Insert Table** button to display the **Insert Table** dialog box. In the **Number of columns** box, type **3** and then press Tab. In the **Number of rows** box, type **2** and then click **OK** to create the table.

b. In the first row of the table, click in the *second* cell. Type **Elementary Schools** and then press Tab. Type **High Schools** and then press Tab to move the insertion point to the first cell in the second row.

c. With the insertion point positioned in the first cell of the second row, type **Current Enrollment** and then press Tab. Type **12,985** and then press Tab. Type **8,243** and then press Tab to insert a new blank row. In the first cell of the third row, type **Facility Projection** and then press Tab. Type **No change** and then press Tab. Type **One creative arts school**

d. With the insertion point positioned in the last column, on the **Layout tab**, in the **Rows & Columns group**, click the **Insert Left** button. Click in the top cell of the inserted column, and then type **Middle Schools** In the second and third rows of the inserted column, type **4,382** and **Two additional schools**

e. With the insertion point positioned in the third row, on the **Layout tab**, in the **Rows & Columns group**, click the **Insert Above** button. Click in the first cell of the row you inserted, type **3-Year Growth Projection** and then press Tab. Type the remaining three entries in the row as follows: **-2%** and **+22%** and **+14%**

2 At the center of the lower border surrounding the table, point to the cluster of four dots—the sizing handle—and make the table larger by dragging down until the lower edge of the table aligns at **3 inches on the lower half of the vertical ruler**.

a. Click in the first cell of the table. On the **Layout tab**, in the **Cell Size group**, click the **Distribute Rows** button.

b. On the **Layout tab**, in the **Table group**, click **Select**, and then click **Select Table**. In the **Alignment group**, click the **Center** button, and then click the **Center Vertically** button.

c. Click in any cell in the table. In the **Table Tools**, click the **Design tab**, and then in the **Table Styles group**, click the **More** button. Under **Medium**, in the third row, click the second style—**Medium Style 3 – Accent 1**—to apply the style to the table.

d. Move the pointer outside of the table so that is positioned to the left of the first row in the table to display the ➡ pointer, click one time to select the entire row. Click the **Design tab**, and then in the **Table Styles group**, click the **Effects** button. Point to **Cell Bevel**, and then under **Bevel**, click the first bevel—**Circle**. Change the **Font Size** of the text in the first row to **20**.

3 Display **Slide 3**. In the content placeholder, click the **Insert Chart** button to display the **Insert Chart** dialog box. Click the first chart—*Clustered Column*—and then click **OK**.

a. In the Excel window, click in cell **B1**, which contains the text *Series 1*. Type **Above 3.0** and then press Tab to move to cell **C1**.

b. In cell **C1**, which contains the text *Series 2*, type **2.0 to 2.99** and then press Tab to move to cell **D1**, which contains the text *Series 3*. Type **Below 2.0** and then press Tab.

c. Beginning in cell **A2**, type the following data, pressing Tab to move from cell to cell.

	Above 3.0	2.0 to 2.99	Below 2.0
Elementary	6318	4900	1676
Middle	2147	1665	596
High	4039	3132	1070

d. In the Excel window, position the pointer over **row heading 5** so that the ➡ pointer displays. Then, *right-click* to select the row and display the shortcut menu. On the shortcut menu, click **Delete**. **Close** the Excel window.

e. If necessary, click the edge of the chart so that it is selected. In the **Chart Tools**, click the **Design tab**, and then in the **Chart Styles group**, click the **More** button. In the **Chart Styles** gallery, click **Style 10** to apply the style to the chart.

f. With the chart selected, click the **Animations tab**, and then in the **Animation group**, click the **More** button. Under **Entrance**, click **Split**. In the

(Project 3D School Enrollment continues on the next page)

Content-Based Assessments

Skills Review | Project **3D** School Enrollment (continued)

Animation group, click the **Effect Options** button, and then under **Sequence**, click **By Series**.

4 Display **Slide 4**. In the content placeholder, click the **Insert Chart** button. On the left side of the displayed **Insert Chart** dialog box, click **Line**, and then under **Line**, click the fourth chart—**Line with Markers**. Click **OK**.

a. In the Excel worksheet, click in cell **B1**, which contains the text *Series 1*. Type **Elementary** and then press Tab. Type **Middle** and then press Tab. Type **High** and then press Tab.

b. Beginning in cell **A2**, type the following data, pressing Tab to move from cell to cell.

	Elementary	Middle	High
2014	12895	4382	8243
2015	12322	4156	5346
2016	12637	5346	9397

c. In the Excel window, position the pointer over **row heading 5** so that the ➡ pointer displays. Then, right-click to select the row and display the shortcut

menu. On the shortcut menu, click **Delete**. **Close** the Excel window.

d. On the **Chart Tools Design tab**, in the **Chart Styles group**, click the **More** button. In the **Chart Styles** gallery, click **Style 34**.

e. Insert a **Header & Footer** for the **Notes and Handouts**. Include the **Date and time updated automatically**, the **Page number**, and a **Footer** with the file name **Lastname_Firstname_3D_School_Enrollment** Click **Apply to All**.

f. Show the **Document Panel**. Replace the text in the **Author** box with your own firstname and lastname. In the **Subject** box, type your course name and section number, and in the **Keywords** box, type **enrollment, schools Close** the **Document Information Panel**.

g. View the slide show from the beginning, and then **Save** your presentation. Print **Handouts 6 Slides Horizontal**, or submit your presentation electronically as directed by your instructor. **Close** the presentation and exit PowerPoint.

End You have completed Project 3D —————————————————————

Content-Based Assessments

Mastering PowerPoint | Project **3E** Spotlight Neighborhood

In the following Mastering PowerPoint project, you will format a presentation created by the Golden Grove Public Relations department that announces the winner of the Spotlight Neighborhood award. Your completed presentation will look similar to Figure 3.53.

Project Files

For Project 3E, you will need the following files:

p03E_Spotlight_Neighborhood
p03E_Neighborhood
p03E_Neighborhood_Video

You will save your presentation as:

Lastname_Firstname_3E_Spotlight_Neighborhood

Project Results

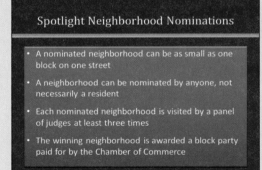

Figure 3.53

(Project 3E Spotlight Neighborhood continues on the next page)

Content-Based Assessments

1 **Start** PowerPoint. From the student files that accompany this textbook, locate and open **p03E_Spotlight_Neighborhood**. Change the **Theme Colors** for the presentation to **Office**, and the **Theme Fonts** to **Adjacency**. **Save** the presentation in your **PowerPoint Chapter 3** folder as **Lastname_Firstname_3E_Spotlight_Neighborhood**

2 On **Slide 1**, hide the background graphics, and then format the slide background by inserting a picture from your student files—**p03E_Neighborhood**. To the title, apply the first **WordArt** style—**Fill - Tan Text 2, Outline - Background 2**.

3 On **Slide 2**, display the **Background Styles** gallery, right-click **Background Style 12**, and then apply the style to this slide only. Select the paragraph on the left side of the slide, and then change the **Font Color** to **White, Text 1**. With the paragraph selected, apply the **Split** entrance effect, and then change the **Effect Options** to **Horizontal Out**. Change the **Start** setting to **After Previous**, and then change the **Duration** to **01.00**. Animate the **SmartArt** graphic by applying the **Fade** entrance effect and so that it starts **With Previous**.

4 On **Slide 3**, format the **Background Style** by applying a **Solid fill—Dark Blue, Text 2**. Change the **Font Color** of the title text to **White, Background 1**. Remove the entrance effect from the title.

5 On **Slide 4**, hide the background graphics, and then apply background **Style 12**. From your student files, insert the video **p03E_Neighborhood_Video**. Change the **Video Height** to **4** and **Align Center** the video. Format the video by applying, from the **Video Styles** gallery, an **Intense** style—**Monitor, Gray**. Change the **Start** setting to **Automatically**.

6 Display **Slide 2**, and then use **Animation Painter** to apply the animation from the paragraph on the left side of the slide to the bulleted list on **Slide 3**.

7 Insert a **Header & Footer** on the **Notes and Handouts**. Include the **Date and time updated automatically**, the **Page** number, and a **Footer** with the text **Lastname_Firstname_3E_Spotlight_Neighborhood**

8 Update the **Document Properties** with your name, course name and section number, and the **Keywords** **spotlight neighborhood Close** the **Document Information Panel**.

9 **Save** your presentation, and then view the slide show from the beginning. Submit your presentation electronically, or print **Handouts 4 Slides Horizontal** as directed by your instructor. **Close** the presentation.

End **You have completed Project 3E** ———————————————————

Content-Based Assessments

Apply 3B skills from these Objectives:

- ◢ Create and Modify Tables
- ◢ Create and Modify Charts

Mastering PowerPoint | Project 3F Water Conservation

In the following Mastering PowerPoint project, you will format a presentation that the Golden Grove Chief Water Engineer will present at a community forum. Your completed presentation will look similar to Figure 3.54.

Project Files

For Project 3F, you will need the following file:

p03F_Water_Conservation

You will save your presentation as:

Lastname_Firstname_3F_Water_Conservation

Project Results

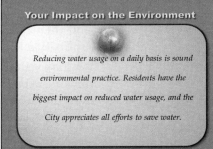
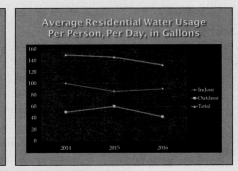
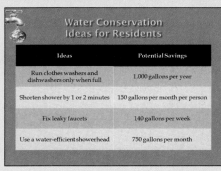
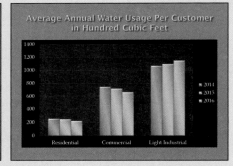

Figure 3.54

(Project 3F Water Conservation continues on the next page)

Mastering PowerPoint | Project **3F** Water Conservation (continued)

1 **Start** PowerPoint. From your student files open **p03F_Water_Conservation**, and then **Save** the presentation in your **PowerPoint Chapter 3** folder as **Lastname_Firstname_3F_Water_Conservation**

2 On **Slide 3**, in the content placeholder, insert a **Line with Markers** chart. In the Excel worksheet, in cell **B1**, type **Indoor** and then enter the following data:

	Indoor	Outdoor	Total
2014	100	50	150
2015	86	60	146
2016	90	42	132

3 In the Excel window, delete **row 5**, and then **Close** the Excel window. Apply **Chart Style 42** to the chart, and then apply the **Wipe** entrance effect to the chart.

4 On **Slide 5**, in the content placeholder, insert a **Clustered Column** chart. In the Excel worksheet, in cell **B1**, type **2014** and then enter the following data:

	2014	2015	2016
Residential	256	249	225
Commercial	746	718	660
Light Industrial	1065	1092	1146

5 In the Excel window, delete **row 5**, and then **Close** the Excel window. Apply **Chart Style 42** to the chart, and then apply the **Wipe** entrance effect to the chart. Change the **Effect Options** so that the animation is applied **By Series**. Change the **Timing** so that the animation starts **After Previous**.

6 On **Slide 6**, in the content placeholder, insert a **Table** with **2 columns** and **5 rows**, and then type the text in **Table 1** at the bottom of the page.

7 Resize the table so that its lower edge extends to **3 inches on the lower half of the vertical ruler**, and then distribute the table rows. Align the table text so that it is centered horizontally and vertically within the cells. Apply table style **Medium Style 2**, and then apply a **Circle Bevel** to the first row. Change the table text **Font Size** to **20**.

8 Insert a **Header & Footer** for the **Notes and Handouts**. Include the **Date and time updated automatically**, the **Page number**, and a **Footer** with the file name **Lastname_Firstname_3F_Water_Conservation** Update the **Document Properties** with your name, course name and section number, and the **Keywords water conservation Close** the **Document Information Panel**.

9 View the slide show from the beginning, and then **Save** your presentation. Print **Handouts 4 Slides Horizontal**, or submit your presentation electronically as directed by your instructor. **Close** the presentation.

Table 1

Ideas	Potential Savings
Run clothes washers and dishwashers only when full	1,000 gallons per year
Shorten shower by 1 or 2 minutes	150 gallons per month per person
Fix leaky faucets	140 gallons per week
Use a water-efficient showerhead	750 gallons per month

- - - ▶ (Return to Step 7)

End **You have completed Project 3F** ————————

Mastering PowerPoint | Project **3G** Restaurants

In the following Mastering PowerPoint project, you will format a presentation that the Golden Grove Public Relations Director will show at a meeting of the National Restaurant Owners Association to encourage new restaurant and catering business in the city. Your completed presentation will look similar to Figure 3.55.

Project Files

For Project 3G, you will need the following files:

> p03G_Restaurants
> p03G_Town_Center
> p03G_Catering

You will save your presentation as:

> Lastname_Firstname_3G_Restaurants

Project Results

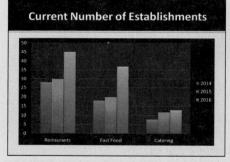

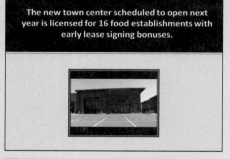

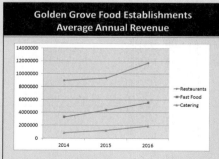

Figure 3.55

(Project 3G Restaurants continues on the next page)

Content-Based Assessments

Mastering PowerPoint | Project **3G** Restaurants (continued)

1 **Start** PowerPoint. From the student files that accompany this textbook, locate and open **p03G_Restaurants**. Change the **Theme Colors** for the presentation to **Apothecary**, and the **Theme Fonts** to **Composite**. **Save** the presentation in your **PowerPoint Chapter 3** folder as **Lastname_Firstname_3G_Restaurants**

2 On **Slide 2**, insert a **Table** with **3 columns** and **4 rows**. Apply table style **Medium Style 3 - Accent 2**, and then type the information in **Table 1**, shown at the bottom of this page, into the inserted table.

3 On the **Design tab**, in the **Table Style Options group**, select *only* the **First Column** and **Banded Rows** check boxes. Resize the table so that its lower edge extends to **3 inches on the lower half of the vertical ruler**, and then distribute the table rows. Align the table text so that it is centered horizontally and vertically within the cells, and then change the **Font Size** of all of the table text to **24**.

4 On **Slide 3**, display the **Background Styles** gallery, right-click **Background Style 3**, and then apply the style to this slide only. Animate the **SmartArt** graphic using the **Wipe** entrance effect starting **After Previous**. Apply the **Split** entrance effect to the bulleted list placeholder, and then change the **Effect Options** to **Vertical Out**.

5 On **Slide 4**, insert a **Clustered Column** chart. In the Excel worksheet, in cell **B1** type **2014** and then enter the following data:

	2014	2015	2016
Restaurants	28	30	45
Fast Food	18	20	37
Catering	8	12	13

6 In the Excel window, delete **row 5**, and then **Close** the Excel window. Apply **Chart Style 42** to the chart, and then apply the **Wipe** entrance effect to the chart.

7 On **Slide 5**, from your student files, insert the video **p03G_Town_Center**. Change the **Video Height** to **3** and then drag the video down so that its top edge aligns at **zero on the vertical ruler**. Apply the **Align Center** alignment option, display the **Video Styles** gallery, and

then apply the first **Moderate** style—**Compound Frame, Black**. Change the **Video Border** to **Gray-50%, Accent 1, Darker 50%**—in the fifth column, the last color.

8 On the **Playback tab**, change the **Video Options** to **Start** the video **Automatically**. **Trim** the video so that the **End Time** is **00:05.560**

9 On **Slide 6**, in the content placeholder, insert a **Line with Markers** chart. In the Excel worksheet, in cell **B1**, type **Restaurants** and then enter the following data:

	Restaurants	Fast Food	Catering
2014	8956231	3284680	856700
2015	9326852	4369571	1235640
2016	11689730	5526895	1894325

10 In the Excel window, delete **row 5**, and then **Close** the Excel window. Apply **Chart Style 34** to the chart, and then use **Animation Painter** to copy the animation from the column chart on **Slide 4** to the line chart on **Slide 6**.

11 On **Slide 7**, hide the background graphics. Format the slide background by inserting a picture from your student files—**p03G_Catering**. Change the title placeholder **Shape Fill** color to **Black, Text 1**, and then change the **Font Color** to **Red, Accent 2**. Size the placeholder so that it extends from the left edge of the slide to the right edge of the slide, and then position it so that its lower edge aligns with the lower edge of the slide. **Center** the text.

12 Insert a **Header & Footer** for the **Notes and Handouts**. Include the **Date and time updated automatically**, the **Page number**, and a **Footer** with the file name **Lastname_Firstname_3G_Restaurants** Update the **Properties** with your name, course name and section number, and the **Keywords catering, restaurants Close** the **Document Information Panel**.

13 View the slide show from the beginning, and then **Save** your presentation. Print **Handouts 4 Slides Horizontal**, or submit your presentation electronically as directed by your instructor. **Close** the presentation.

Table 1

Population	218,381	Expected 5-year increase: 12%
Households	62,394	Expected 5-year increase: 3%
Average years in residence	6.8	62% families with children
Owner occupied	75%	Expected to increase with new construction

- - - ► (Return to Step 3)

End **You have completed Project 3G** ————————

PowerPoint | Chapter 3

Content-Based Assessments

GO! Fix It | Project **3H** Housing Developments

Project Files

For Project 3H, you will need the following file:

    p03H_Housing_Developments

You will save your presentation as:

    Lastname_Firstname_3H_Housing_Developments

In this project, you will edit several slides from a presentation prepared by the Golden Grove Planning Department regarding real estate developments in the city. From the student files that accompany this textbook, open the file p03H_Housing_Developments, and then save the file in your chapter folder as **Lastname_Firstname_3H_Housing_Developments**

To complete the project, you should know:

- The Theme Colors should be changed to Module and the Theme Fonts should be changed to Apex.

- The titles on Slides 2 and 3 should be centered.

- On Slide 2, the table style Light Style 2 - Accent 2 should be applied and a column should be added to right of the last column in the table. In the inserted column, the following text should be entered in the three cells: **Bering** and **37%** and **August 2016**

- On Slides 3 and 4, the charts should be animated with the Wipe entrance effect.

- Document Properties should include your name, course name and section, and the keywords **property tax, housing** A Header & Footer should be inserted on the Notes and Handouts that includes the Date and time updated automatically, the Page number and a Footer with the text **Lastname_Firstname_3H_Housing_Developments**

Save and submit your presentation electronically or print Handouts 4 Slides Horizontal as directed by your instructor. Close the presentation.

End You have completed Project 3H ————————

Content-Based Assessments

GO! Make It | Project **3I** Arboretum

Project Files

For Project 3I, you will need the following files:

> New blank PowerPoint presentation
> p03I_Flowers

You will save your presentation as:

> Lastname_Firstname_3I_Arboretum

Start PowerPoint to begin a new blank presentation, and apply the Opulent theme. Save the file in your PowerPoint Chapter 3 folder as **Lastname_Firstname_3I_Arboretum**

By using the skills you practiced in this chapter, create the first two slides of the presentation shown in Figure 3.56. The layout for Slide 1 is Title Only, and the background is formatted with the picture from your student data file— p03I_Flowers. The title Shape Fill color is Purple, Accent 2, Darker 50%. On Slide 2, insert and format the table as shown. Change the Font Size of the text in the first row to 32. Insert the file name, date, and page number in the Notes and Handouts footer. In the Document Information Panel, add your name and course information and the Keywords **arboretum, events** Save, and then print or submit electronically as directed by your instructor.

Project Results

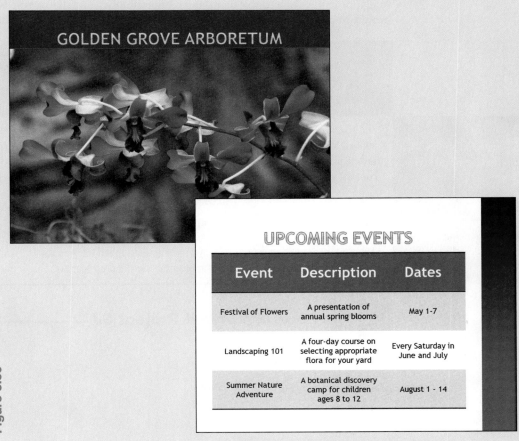

Figure 3.56

End **You have completed Project 3I**

Content-Based Assessments

Apply a combination of the 3A and 3B skills.

GO! Solve It | Project 3J Aquatic Center

Project Files

For Project 3J, you will need the following file:

 p03J_Aquatic_Center

You will save your presentation as:

 Lastname_Firstname_3J_Aquatic_Center

Open the file p03J_Aquatic_Center and save it as **Lastname_Firstname_3J_Aquatic_Center** Complete the presentation by changing the Theme Fonts and then formatting the slide background of at least one of the slides using a Background Style or Solid Fill color. On Slide 4, insert and format a table with the following information regarding the fee schedule for swim passes.

Membership	Monthly	Seasonal
Youth	$10	$25
Adult	$25	$50
Senior	$15	$30

Apply appropriate animation and slide transitions to the slides. Insert a header and footer that includes the date and time updated automatically, the file name in the footer, and the page number. Add your name, your course name and section number, and the keywords **aquatic center, swim program** to the Properties area. Save and then print, or submit it as directed by your instructor.

	Performance Level		
	Exemplary: You consistently applied the relevant skills	**Proficient:** You sometimes, but not always, applied the relevant skills	**Developing:** You rarely or never applied the relevant skills
Format slide with a background style	Slide background style was applied to at least one slide and text displayed with good contrast against the background.	Slide background was formatted but text did not display well against the chosen background.	Slide background was not formatted with a background style.
Insert and format appropriate table	Appropriate table was inserted and formatted.	A table was inserted but was not appropriately formatted.	Table was not inserted.
Apply appropriate animation	Appropriate animation was applied to the presentation.	Animation was applied but was not appropriate for the presentation.	Animation was not applied.

(Performance Elements)

End You have completed Project 3J

Content-Based Assessments

GO! Solve It | Project **3K** Power

Project Files

For Project 3K, you will need the following files:

> p03K_Power
> p03K_Tower

You will save your presentation as:

> Lastname_Firstname_3K_Power

Open the file p03K_Power and save it as **Lastname_Firstname_3K_Power** Complete the presentation by applying a theme and then formatting the slide background of one of the slides with the picture found in your student files—p03K_Tower. Adjust the size, position, fill color, and font color of the slide titles as necessary so that the title text displays attractively against the background picture. Format the background of at least one other slide using a Background Style or Solid Fill color. Insert a new Slide 3 that includes an appropriate title and a table with the following information regarding the power sources that the City uses.

Power Sources	Percent Used by City
Natural gas	32%
Hydroelectric	17%
Renewables	18%
Coal	23%
Nuclear	10%

On Slide 4, insert and format an appropriate chart to demonstrate the revenue collected from residential power sales over the past three years. Revenue in 2014 was 35.5 million dollars, in 2015 revenue was 42.6 million dollars, and in 2016 revenue was 48.2 million dollars. Apply appropriate animation and slide transitions to the slides. Insert a header and footer that includes the date and time updated automatically, the file name in the footer, and the page number. Add your name, your course name and section number, and the keywords **power sources, revenue** to the Properties area. Save and then print or submit the presentation as directed by your instructor.

	Performance Level		
	Exemplary: You consistently applied the relevant skills	**Proficient:** You sometimes, but not always, applied the relevant skills	**Developing:** You rarely or never applied the relevant skills
Format two slide backgrounds with pictures and styles	Two slide backgrounds were formatted attractively and text displayed with good contrast against backgrounds.	Slide backgrounds were formatted but text did not display well against the chosen background, or only one slide background was formatted.	Slide backgrounds were not formatted with pictures or styles.
Insert and format appropriate table and chart	Appropriate table and chart were inserted and formatted and the entered data was accurate.	A table and a chart were inserted but were not appropriate for the presentation or either a table or a chart was omitted.	Table and chart were not inserted.
Apply appropriate animation	Appropriate animation was applied to the presentation.	Animation was applied but was not appropriate for the presentation.	Animation was not applied.

Performance Elements

End You have completed Project 3K

Outcomes-Based Assessments

Rubric

The following outcomes-based assessments are *open-ended assessments*. That is, there is no specific correct result; your result will depend on your approach to the information provided. Make *Professional Quality* your goal. Use the following scoring rubric to guide you in *how* to approach the problem, and then to evaluate *how well* your approach solves the problem.

The *criteria*—Software Mastery, Content, Format and Layout, and Process—represent the knowledge and skills you have gained that you can apply to solving the problem. The *levels of performance*—Professional Quality, Approaching Professional Quality, or Needs Quality Improvements—help you and your instructor evaluate your result.

	Your completed project is of Professional Quality if you:	Your completed project is Approaching Professional Quality if you:	Your completed project Needs Quality Improvements if you:
1-Software Mastery	Choose and apply the most appropriate skills, tools, and features and identify efficient methods to solve the problem.	Choose and apply some appropriate skills, tools, and features, but not in the most efficient manner.	Choose inappropriate skills, tools, or features, or are inefficient in solving the problem.
2-Content	Construct a solution that is clear and well organized, contains content that is accurate, appropriate to the audience and purpose, and is complete. Provide a solution that contains no errors in spelling, grammar, or style.	Construct a solution in which some components are unclear, poorly organized, inconsistent, or incomplete. Misjudge the needs of the audience. Have some errors in spelling, grammar, or style, but the errors do not detract from comprehension.	Construct a solution that is unclear, incomplete, or poorly organized; contains some inaccurate or inappropriate content; and contains many errors in spelling, grammar, or style. Do not solve the problem.
3-Format and Layout	Format and arrange all elements to communicate information and ideas, clarify function, illustrate relationships, and indicate relative importance.	Apply appropriate format and layout features to some elements, but not others. Overuse features, causing minor distraction.	Apply format and layout that does not communicate information or ideas clearly. Do not use format and layout features to clarify function, illustrate relationships, or indicate relative importance. Use available features excessively, causing distraction.
4-Process	Use an organized approach that integrates planning, development, self-assessment, revision, and reflection.	Demonstrate an organized approach in some areas, but not others; or, use an insufficient process of organization throughout.	Do not use an organized approach to solve the problem.

Outcomes-Based Assessments

GO! Think | Project **3L** Animal Sanctuary

Project Files

For Project 3L, you will need the following file:

New blank PowerPoint presentation

You will save your presentation as:

Lastname_Firstname_3L_Animal Sanctuary

The Golden Grove Animal Sanctuary, a non-profit organization, provides shelter and care for animals in need, including dogs, cats, hamsters, and guinea pigs. The Sanctuary, which celebrates its tenth anniversary in July, has cared for more than 12,000 animals since it opened and is a state-of-the-art facility. Funding for the Sanctuary comes in the form of business sponsorships, individual donations, and pet adoption fees. The following table indicates revenue generated by the Sanctuary during the past three years.

	Fees	Donations	Sponsorships
2014	125,085	215,380	175,684
2015	110,680	256,785	156,842
2016	132,455	314,682	212,648

In addition to shelter services, the Sanctuary offers community service and training programs, veterinarian services, and vaccine clinics. Examples of these services include Canine Obedience classes, microchipping ($25 fee), and the Healthy Pet Hotline (free). Canine Obedience classes are for puppies and adult dogs to improve obedience, socialization, and behavior. Classes last two, three, or four months and cost $150 to $250.

Using the preceding information, create the first five slides of a presentation that the director of the Golden Grove Animal Sanctuary will show at an upcoming pet fair. Apply an appropriate theme and use slide layouts that will effectively present the content. Include a line chart with the revenue data, a table with the community service programs information, and at least one slide formatted with a dog or cat on the slide background. Apply styles to the table and chart, and apply animation and slide transitions to the slides. Use the techniques that you practiced in this chapter so that your presentation is professional and attractive. Save the file as **Lastname_Firstname_3L_ Animal_Sanctuary** and then insert a header and footer that includes the date and time updated automatically, the file name in the footer, and the page number. Add your name, your course name and section number, and the keywords **animals, pets** to the Properties area. Save and then print or submit the presentation as directed by your instructor.

End You have completed Project 3L ————————————————

Outcomes-Based Assessments

GO! Think | Project **3M** Water Sources

Project Files

For Project 3M, you will need the following file:

New blank PowerPoint presentation

You will save your presentation as:

Lastname_Firstname_3M_Water_Sources

The Golden Grove Department of Water and Power operations are financed solely through sales of water and electric services. A portion of capital expenditures are funded through the sale of municipal bonds. The city's water supply is generated from a number of sources, with 35% from the Sierra Nevada aqueduct system, 42% from water districts, 18% from groundwater, and 5% from recycled sources. This supply provides water for the City's residents and commercial and industrial customers.

In the past three years, the Department has renovated several reservoirs and pump stations, resulting in better reserves and emergency preparedness capacity. The following table details the in-city reservoir capacities over the past three years. Water capacity is measured in acre feet, in which one acre foot is equal to approximately 325,000 gallons. Years in which zero or low capacity is specified indicates years in which the reservoir was undergoing renovation.

	2014	2015	2016
Elkhart Reservoir	350	1250	2243
Gold Lake Reservoir	3685	865	2865
Diamond Canyon Reservoir	2650	3850	4635

Using the preceding information, create a title slide and four additional slides of a presentation that the Golden Grove Chief Water Engineer can show at an upcoming City Council meeting. Apply an appropriate theme and use slide layouts that will effectively present the content. Include a table that details the water supply sources, and a column chart with the reservoir information. Apply animation and slide transitions and use the techniques that you practiced in this chapter so that your presentation is professional and attractive. Save the file as **Lastname_Firstname_3M_Water_Sources** and then insert a header and footer that includes the date and time updated automatically, the file name in the footer, and the page number. Add your name, your course name and section number, and the keywords **reservoirs, water capacity** to the Properties area. Save, and then print or submit the presentation as directed by your instructor.

End You have completed Project 3M ————————————

Outcomes-Based Assessments

Apply a combination of the **3A** and **3B** skills.

You and GO! | Project **3N** Recreation Programs

Project Files

For Project 3N, you will need the following file:

New blank PowerPoint presentation

You will save your presentation as:

Lastname_Firstname_3N_Recreation_Programs

Research the recreation programs available in the city in which you live, and then create a presentation about the program. Include a table that describes some of the activities, the location in which they are held, and the fees. Choose an appropriate theme, slide layouts, and pictures, and format the presentation attractively, including at least one slide with a picture on the slide background. Save your presentation as **Lastname_Firstname_3N_Recreation_Programs** and submit as directed.

End You have completed Project 3N ——————

Apply a combination of the **3A** and **3B** skills.

GO! Collaborate | Project **3O** Bell Orchid Hotels Group Running Case

This project relates to the **Bell Orchid Hotels**. Your instructor may assign this group case project to your class. If your instructor assigns this project, he or she will provide you with information and instructions to work as part of a group. The group will apply the skills gained thus far to help the Bell Orchid Hotels achieve their business goals.

End You have completed Project 3O ——————

Business Running Case

Razvan CHIRNOAGA/Shutterstock

This project relates to **Front Range Action Sports**, which is one of the country's largest retailers of sports gear and outdoor recreation merchandise. The company has large retail stores in Colorado, Washington, Oregon, California, and New Mexico, in addition to a growing online business. Major merchandise categories include fishing, camping, rock climbing, winter sports, action sports, water sports, team sports, racquet sports, fitness, golf, apparel, and footwear.

In this project, you will apply skills you practiced from the Objectives in PowerPoint Chapters 1 through 3. You will develop a presentation that Irene Shviktar, Vice President of Marketing, will show at a corporate marketing retreat that summarizes the company's plans to expand the winter sports product line. Your completed presentation will look similar to Figure 1.1.

Project Files

For Project BRC1, you will need the following files:

You will save your presentation as:

Lastname_Firstname_BRC1_Winter_Products

pBRC1_Company_Overview
pBRC1_Heights
pBRC1_Lake
pBRC1_Mountain
pBRC1_Skiing
pBRC1_Winter_Products

Project Results

Figure 1.1

Front Range Action Sports (continued)

1 **Start** PowerPoint. From the student files that accompany this textbook, locate and open **pBRC1_Winter_Products**. In the location where you are storing your projects, create a new folder named **Front Range Action Sports** or navigate to this folder if you have already created it. **Save** the presentation as **Lastname_Firstname_BRC1_Winter_Products**

a. Display **Slide 1**. Change the presentation theme to **Concourse**, and then change the **Theme Colors** to **Office**. Change the **Theme Fonts** to **Elemental**. On **Slide 1**, format the background with a picture from your student files—**pBRC1_Skiing**.

b. Display the **Reuse Slides** pane. Browse your student files, and display in the **Reuse Slides** pane **pBRC1_Company_Overview**. Insert the second slide—**Mission**—as **Slide 2**, and then **Close** the **Reuse Slides** pane. Remove the bullet symbol from the paragraph, **Center** the text, and then apply **Bold** and **Italic**.

c. With **Slide 2** displayed, change the **Line Spacing** of the content placeholder text to **2.0**. Change the **Shape Fill** to the first color in the fourth column—**Dark Blue, Text 2**, and then change the **Font Color** to **White, Background 1**. Format the placeholder with the first **Bevel** shape effect—**Circle**—and then hide the background graphics on the slide.

d. Display **Slide 3**, and then in the picture placeholder, from your student files insert **pBRC1_Heights**. Apply the first **Glow** picture effect—**Blue, 5 pt glow, Accent color 1**. Format the slide background by applying **Style 12**, being sure to apply the background only to **Slide 3**.

2 Display **Slide 4**, and then in the content placeholder, insert the **Process** SmartArt graphic **Alternating Flow**. Change the color to **Colorful - Accent Colors**, and then apply **3-D Cartoon** style.

a. In the **red shape**, type **Washington and California Resorts** and then click in the first bullet point in the rounded rectangle above the red shape. Type **Mammoth Mountain and Lake Tahoe in California** Click in the second bullet point, and then type **Mission Ridge and Crystal Mountain in Washington**

b. In the **green shape**, type **Our Market Position** and then click in the first bullet point in the rounded rectangle below the green shape. Type **Trusted brand name in the sporting world** In the second bullet point, type **Winter sports product line not fully marketed in the Western United States**

c. In the **purple shape**, type **Poised for Growth** and then click in the first bullet point in the rounded rectangle above the purple shape. Type **New warehouses in Washington** In the second bullet point, type **Proposed retail division in Northern California**

d. Animate the SmartArt by applying the **Wipe** entrance effect. Change the **Start** option so that the SmartArt animation begins **After Previous**.

3 Display **Slide 5**, and then apply background **Style 3** to the slide. In both content placeholders, change the bullet symbol to **Star Bullets**, and then change the bullet **Color** to **Olive Green, Accent 3**. In the **blue shapes** at the bottom of the slide, change the **Font Color** to **White, Text 1**.

a. Insert a **Down Arrow** shape by clicking on the slide with the guides aligned with the **left half of the horizontal ruler at 3 inches** and with the **lower half of the vertical ruler at 1 inch**.

b. Change the arrow **Shape Height** to **1** and the **Shape Width** to **0.5** and then apply the fourth **Shape Style** in the first row—**Colored Outline - Olive Green, Accent 3**. Select the arrow, the content placeholder on the left, and the *Skiing* shape, and then on the **Format tab**, in the **Arrange group**, click the **Align** button. Click **Align Selected Objects**. Click the **Align** button again, and then click **Align Center**.

c. Duplicate the arrow shape, and then drag the duplicated arrow so that its left edge aligns with the **right half of the horizontal ruler at 2 inches** and its top edge aligns with the **lower half of the vertical ruler at 1 inch**. Select the arrow, the content placeholder on the right, and the *Snowboarding* shape, and then using the **Align Selected Objects** option apply **Align Center**. Select the two arrows, and then using the **Align Selected Objects** option, apply **Align Top** to the two arrow shapes.

4 With **Slide 5** displayed, insert a **New Slide** with the **Two Content** layout and then apply background **Style 3** to the inserted slide. Type the slide title **Our Most Popular Winter Products** Change the **Font Size** to **32** and then **Center** the title.

(Business Running Case: Front Range Action Sports continues on the next page)

a. In the content placeholder on the left, type the following six bullet points:

Snowboards

Boots

Goggles

Bindings

Skis

Jackets

b. Change the bulleted list to **Numbering**, and then change the number **Color** to **White, Text 1**.

c. In the placeholder on the right, insert a **Clip Art** by searching for a **Photograph** with the keyword **snowboard** Insert the black and white silhouette picture of the person holding a snowboard behind his back. If you cannot locate the picture, choose another image, and then **Close** the Clip Art pane.

d. Change the **Height** of the picture to **5** and then move the picture so that its upper left corner aligns with **zero on the horizontal ruler** and with the **upper half of the vertical ruler at 2.5 inches**. Apply a **Soft Edges** picture effect of **25 Point**.

e. Display **Slide 7**, and then in the content placeholder, insert a **Clustered Column** chart. In the **Excel** worksheet, enter the following data.

	Oregon	Colorado	British Columbia
2012	12.2	17.5	6.5
2013	14.5	19.2	8.7
2014	11.9	18.6	10.6
2015	17.6	22.4	11.3

f. **Close** the Excel worksheet. Apply **Chart Style 26**, and then animate the chart by applying the **Wipe** entrance effect.

5 Display **Slide 8**, and then hide the background graphics on the slide. Format the background with a picture from your student files—**pBRC1_Lake**.

a. Select the title placeholder, and then using the **Align to Slide** option, align the title using the **Align Top** and **Align Center** options.

b. Display **Slide 9**, and then in the content placeholder, insert a **Table** with **3** columns and **3** rows. Type the following text in the table.

Targeted Retail Expansion	2013 Goal	2016 Goal
Northern California	Three new franchises with rental services	Four new franchises
Central and Eastern Washington	Four new franchises with rental services and lessons	Eight new franchises with rental services

c. Apply the **Light Style 2 - Accent 1** table style, and then resize the table so that its lower left corner touches the graphic in the lower left corner of the slide. Distribute the table rows.

d. To the first row, apply the first **Cell Bevel** effect—**Circle**, and then change the **Font Size** to **24**. Center all of the text in the table horizontally and vertically, and then apply the **Wipe** entrance effect to the table.

6 Display **Slide 10**. Apply background **Style 3** to the slide, and then hide the background graphics. To the title, apply the fourth **WordArt** style in the first row **Fill - White, Outline -Accent 1**.

a. With **Slide 10** displayed, from your student files, insert the picture **pBRC1_Mountain**. Change the picture **Height** to **2.5** and then apply a **Soft Edges** picture effect of **25 Point**. Use the **Crop to Shape** option to change the picture shape to the tenth **Basic Shape** in the third row—**Cloud**. **Align Center** and **Align Middle** the picture using the **Align to Slide** option.

b. On **Slide 10**, insert a **WordArt** using the fourth **WordArt** style in the first row **Fill - White, Outline - Accent 1**. Type **Moving to the Top of the Winter Sports Action** and then change the **Font Size** to **28**. Drag the WordArt down so that its top edge aligns with the **lower half of the vertical ruler at 1 inch**. Select the title placeholder, picture, and WordArt, and then using the **Align to Slide** option, apply **Align Center**.

c. To all of the slides in the presentation, apply the **Box** transition, and then change the **Effect Options** to **From Top**. Display **Slide 6**, and then apply the **Split** entrance effect to the numbered list.

d. Display **Slide 3**. In the **Notes pane**, type **The key elements necessary to achieve our 2016 goals are the expansion of the winter sports product line, an aggressive marketing campaign, and new retail locations in California and Washington.**

(Business Running Case: Front Range Action Sports continues on the next page)

Business Running Case 1: Includes Objectives from PowerPoint Chapters 1-3

Business Running Case

Front Range Action Sports (continued)

e. Insert a **Header & Footer** for the **Notes and Handouts**. Include the **Date and time** updated automatically, the **Page number**, and a **Footer** with the file name **Lastname_Firstname_BRC1_Winter_Products**

f. Display the **Document Properties**. Add your name, your course name and section, and the keywords winter products, goals **Close** the **Document Information Panel**.

g. View the slide show from the beginning, and then **Save** your presentation. Print **Handouts 6 Slides Horizontal**, or submit your presentation electronically as directed by your instructor. **Close** the presentation.

End **You have completed Business Running Case 1** ————————————

Integrating Word, Excel, Access, and PowerPoint

OUTCOMES

At the end of this chapter you will be able to:

OBJECTIVES

Mastering these objectives will enable you to:

PROJECT 1A

Create an Excel workbook that includes data exported from Access and data copied from Word.

1. Export Access Data to Excel (p. 805)
2. Create an Excel Worksheet from a Word Table (p. 808)
3. Copy and Paste an Excel Chart into Other Programs (p. 812)
4. Copy and Paste an Object from PowerPoint into Excel (p. 817)

PROJECT 1B

Link Excel data to a Word document and complete a mail merge in Word using Access data.

5. Link Excel Data to a Word Document (p. 821)
6. Modify Linked Data and Update Links (p. 823)
7. Create a Table in Word from Access Data (p. 824)
8. Use Access Data to Complete a Mail Merge in Word (p. 826)

Razvan CHIRNOAGA/Shutterstock

In This Chapter

One of the advantages of using the applications in a software suite is that all the applications work well with one another. By using the best application to complete the work with the data you have, you can create graphics or input data in one application and then export the data to another application without having to take the time to re-create or retype the graphic or data. You do need to identify the most appropriate software to produce solutions and to best utilize the functions of the various software.

In this chapter, you will copy and paste data and objects between software. You will practice linking the data in the destination file and then modify and update the link.

The projects in this chapter relate to **Front Range Action Sports**, one of the country's largest retailers of sports gear and outdoor recreation merchandise. The company has large retail stores in Colorado, Washington, Oregon, and New Mexico, in addition to a growing online business. Major merchandise categories include fishing, camping, rock climbing, winter sports, action sports, water sports, team sports, racquet sports, fitness, golf, apparel, and footwear.

Project 1A State Sales

Project Activities

In Activities 1.01 through 1.11, you will export Access data into an Excel workbook, and then you will copy and paste Word data into the Excel workbook. In Excel, you will create a chart based on the data, and then copy the chart into a PowerPoint presentation. Your completed documents will look similar to Figure 1.1.

Project Files

For Project 1A, you will need the following files:

> New blank Excel workbook
> i01A_Store_Locations.accdb
> i01A_State_Sales.docx
> i01A_Sales_Presentation.pptx

You will save your files as:

> Lastname_Firstname_1A_Sales_Chart.xlsx
> Lastname_Firstname_1A_Store_Locations.accdb
> Lastname_Firstname_1A_State_Sales.docx
> Lastname_Firstname_1A_Sales_Presentation.pptx

Project Results

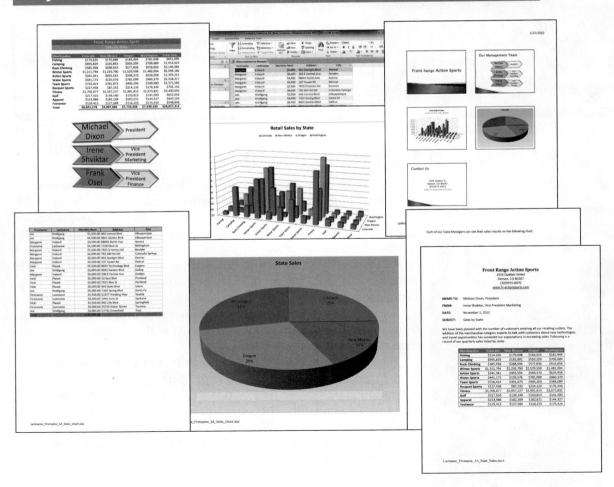

Figure 1.1
Project 1A State Sales

Objective 1 | Export Access Data to Excel

Access includes a tool to export data from an Access database into an Excel workbook. When you export Access data, you create a copy of the data in Excel.

Activity 1.01 | Exporting Access Data to Excel

In the following activity, you will export Access data into an Excel workbook.

1 Click **Start** 🏵. Click **Control Panel**, and then click **Appearance and Personalization**. Under **Folder Options**, click **Show hidden files and folders**. Under **Advanced settings**, clear the **Hide extensions for known file types** checkbox. Click **OK**, and then click **Close**. **Start** Access. Navigate to the student data files and then open the Access database **i01A_Store_Locations**. Click the **File tab** to display **Backstage** view, and then click **Save Database As**.

2 In the **Save As** dialog box, navigate to the location where you are saving your files. Click **New folder**, type **Integrated Projects** and then press Enter. In the **File name** box, name the file **Lastname_Firstname_1A_Store_Locations** and then press Enter. If the Security Warning message displays, click the Enable Content button.

3 In the **navigation pane**, double-click the **Managers** table. At the bottom of the table, replace *Firstname* with your **Firstname** and replace *Lastname* with your **Lastname** and then press Enter.

4 In the **navigation pane**, double-click the query **Store Locations by Manager**, and verify that your name displays. Compare your screen with Figure 1.2.

Figure 1.2

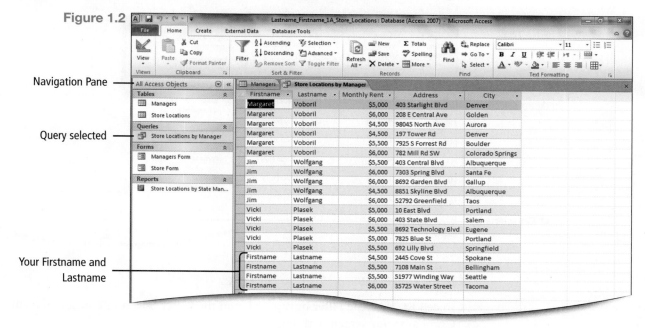

5 On the **External Data tab**, in the **Export group**, click the **Excel** button. In the **Export - Excel Spreadsheet** dialog box, click the **Browse** button. Navigate to your **Integrated Projects** folder, type the file name **Lastname_Firstname_1A_Sales_Chart** and then click **Save**.

6 In the **Export - Excel Spreadsheet** dialog box, verify that the **File format** is **Excel Workbook (*.xlsx)**. Select the **Export data with formatting and layout** check box, and then click **OK**. In the dialog box, verify that the **Save export steps** check box is not selected, and then click **Close**.

7 Click the **File tab** to display **Backstage** view, and then click **Exit**.

8 **Start** Excel. Navigate to your **Integrated Projects** folder, and then open the Excel workbook **Lastname_Firstname_1A_Sales_Chart**.

Notice the exported Access query name—*Store Locations by Manager*—becomes the Excel worksheet name.

Activity 1.02 | Creating and Sorting an Excel Table

To make managing and analyzing a group of related data easier, you can turn a range of cells into an Excel table. An Excel table typically contains data in a series of rows and columns, and the Excel table can be managed independently from the data in other rows and columns in the worksheet. In the following activity, you will change a range of data into an Excel table, and then sort the data.

1 Click cell **A1**. On the **Insert tab**, in the **Tables group**, click the **Table** button. In the **Create Table** dialog box, under **Where is the data for your table?**, verify that the range is =**$A$1:$E$21**, verify that the **My table has headers** check box is selected, and then compare your screen with Figure 1.3.

Figure 1.3

Create Table dialog box

My table has headers check box selected

A1:E21 selected

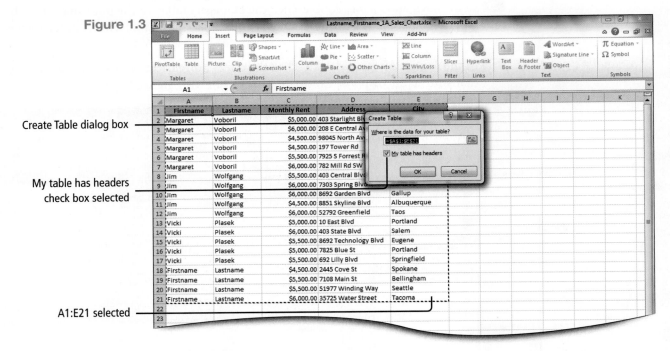

2 In the **Create Table** dialog box, click **OK**.

3 In cell **E1**, click the **Filter** button ▾, and then click **Sort A to Z** to sort the entire table. Compare your screen with Figure 1.4.

The rows in column E—the City column—are sorted in ascending order.

After a column is sorted in ascending or descending order, a small arrow displays on the Filter button to indicate its sort order.

Figure 1.4

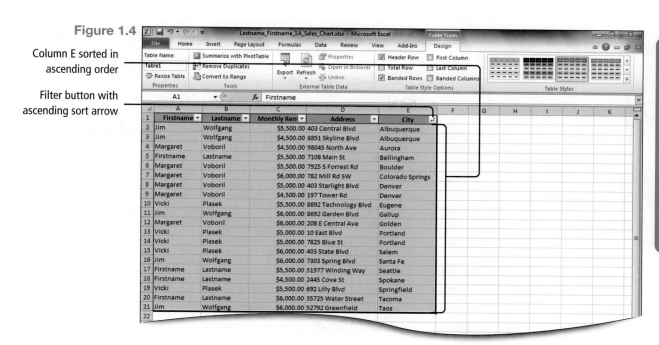

4 **Save** 💾 the Excel workbook.

Activity 1.03 | Inserting a Total Row in an Excel Table

An Excel table can help manage and analyze data. You can quickly total the data in an Excel table by displaying a Totals Row at the end of the table, and then by using the functions that are provided in drop-down lists for each totals row cell. In the following activity, you will insert a total row and sum a column using the total row.

1 On the **Design tab**, in the **Table Style Options group**, select the **Total Row** check box. Click cell **E22**, and then compare your screen with Figure 1.5.

Cell E22 displays the number 20. The Total Row counts the number of cells containing text in column E. The header row is not included in the Total Row calculations.

Figure 1.5

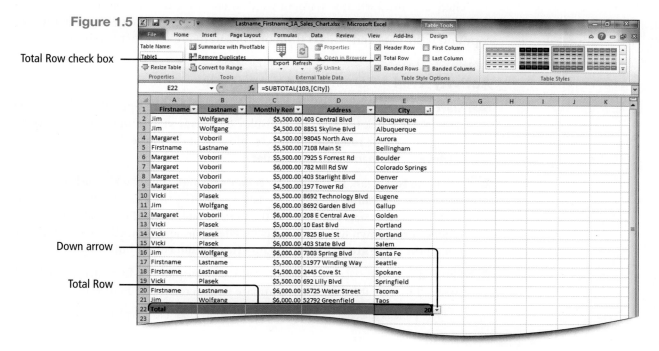

2 On the Total Row, in cell **E22**, click the **down arrow**, and then click **None**.

3 Click cell **C22**. Click the **down arrow** next to the active cell **C22**, and then click **Sum**. Compare your screen with Figure 1.6.

The Total Monthly Rent for all locations displays in cell C22.

Figure 1.6

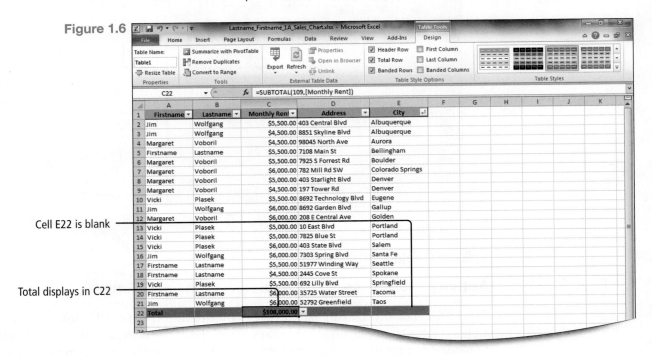

4 Save 💾 the Excel workbook.

Objective 2 | Create an Excel Worksheet from a Word Table

There are times when you might want to use some of the data from one file in a different program without having to retype the data. In the following activities, you will copy and paste data and objects from one program into another program.

Activity 1.04 | Formatting a Word Table

1 **Start** Word. Navigate to the student data files, and then open the document **i01A_ State_Sales**. Click the **File tab** to display **Backstage** view, and then click **Save As**. Navigate to your **Integrated Projects** folder, and then **Save** the document as **Lastname_Firstname_1A_State_Sales**

2 Click the **Insert tab**. In the **Header & Footer group**, click the **Footer** button. At the bottom of the **Footer** gallery, click **Edit Footer**. On the **Design tab**, in the **Insert group**, click the **Quick Parts** button, and then click **Field**. In the **Field** dialog box, under **Field names**, scroll down to locate and click **FileName**, and then click **OK**. On the **Design tab**, in the **Close group**, click the **Close Header and Footer** button.

3 Scroll down to display the table. If necessary, display the formatting marks. Click the first cell in the table, and then compare your screen with Figure 1.7.

The table is selected and the Table Tools contextual tabs display.

Figure 1.7

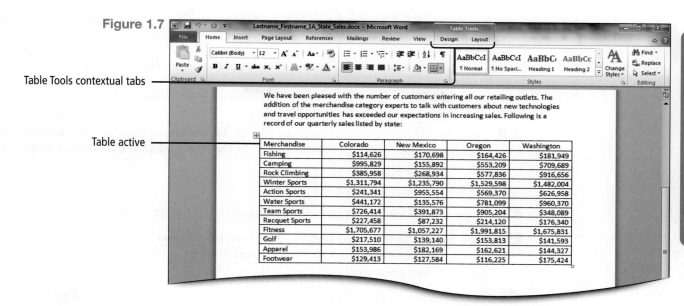

Table Tools contextual tabs

Table active

We have been pleased with the number of customers entering all our retailing outlets. The addition of the merchandise category experts to talk with customers about new technologies and travel opportunities has exceeded our expectations in increasing sales. Following is a record of our quarterly sales listed by state:

Merchandise	Colorado	New Mexico	Oregon	Washington
Fishing	$114,626	$170,698	$164,426	$181,949
Camping	$995,829	$155,892	$553,209	$709,689
Rock Climbing	$385,958	$268,934	$577,836	$916,656
Winter Sports	$1,311,794	$1,235,790	$1,529,598	$1,482,004
Action Sports	$241,341	$955,554	$569,370	$626,958
Water Sports	$441,172	$135,576	$781,099	$960,370
Team Sports	$726,414	$391,873	$905,204	$348,089
Racquet Sports	$227,458	$87,232	$214,120	$176,340
Fitness	$1,705,677	$1,057,227	$1,991,815	$1,675,831
Golf	$217,510	$139,140	$153,813	$141,593
Apparel	$153,986	$182,169	$162,621	$144,327
Footwear	$129,413	$127,584	$116,225	$175,424

4 Click the **Design tab**, and then in the **Table Styles group**, click the **More** button ⬇ . In the **Table Styles** gallery, under **Built-In**, click the **Light List - Accent 1** button.

5 On the **Layout tab**, in the **Cell Size group**, click the **AutoFit** button, and then click **AutoFit Contents**. In the **Table group**, click the **Properties** button. In the **Table Properties** dialog box, under **Alignment**, click the **Center** button. Compare your screen with Figure 1.8.

Figure 1.8

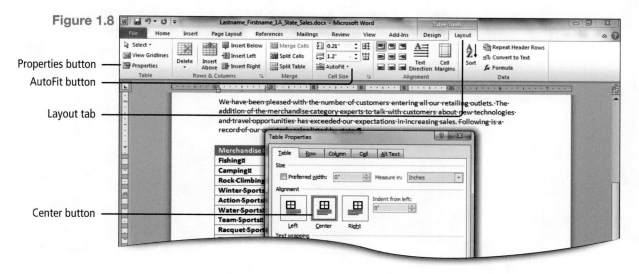

Properties button
AutoFit button
Layout tab

Center button

6 In the **Table Properties** dialog box, click **OK** to center the table horizontally on the page.

7 Save 💾 the Word document.

Activity 1.05 │ Copying and Pasting a Word Table into an Excel Workbook

After you have started a Word document, you may realize that you can manipulate the data better in another program, such as Excel. Instead of starting over and retyping all of the data, you can copy the data from Word and paste the data into Excel.

> **Note | Multiple Open Windows Notice**
>
> In this chapter, you will work with a number of different files and will have a number of different windows open. When you have completed the work in one file, save the file and minimize the window. When you need to use the file again, click the program icon on the taskbar to maximize that window.

1 Verify that Word is the active window. On the **Layout tab**, in the **Table group**, click the **Select** button, and then click **Select Table**. On the **Home tab** in the **Clipboard group**, click the **Copy** button.

> The entire table is selected and copied.

2 On the taskbar, click the **Excel** icon to make the Excel window active.

3 At the bottom of the worksheet, click the **Insert Worksheet** button to insert a new blank worksheet. Right-click the **Sheet1** worksheet tab, and then click **Rename**. Type **Sales** and then press Enter.

4 Click cell **A4** to make it the active cell. On the **Home tab**, in the **Clipboard group**, click the **Paste** button. Compare your screen with Figure 1.9.

> The Word data is pasted into the Excel worksheet, starting in cell A4—the active cell.
>
> The pound sign (#) will display if a column is not wide enough to display an entire number.

Figure 1.9

Pasted data in Excel —

indicates columns are too narrow to display entire number

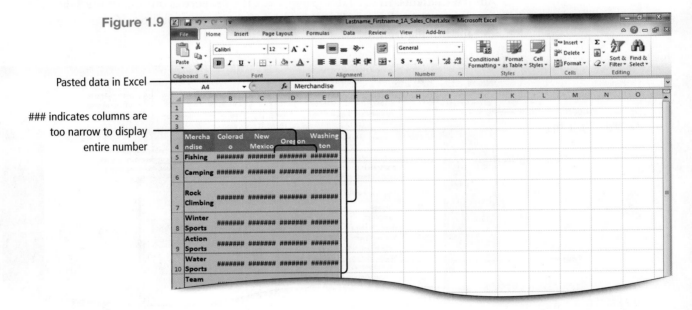

5 Select cell **A4**. On the **Home tab**, in the **Cells group**, click the **Format** button, and then click **Column Width**. In the **Column Width** dialog box, type **16** and then press **OK**.

6 Select the range **B4:E4**. In the **Cells group**, click the **Format** button, and then click **Column Width**. In the **Column Width** dialog box, type **12** and then click **OK**.

> All columns are wide enough to display all data.

7 Select the range **A4:A16**. In the **Cells group**, click the **Format** button, and then click **Row Height**. In the **Row Height** dialog box, type **17** and then click **OK**.

8 In cell **A1**, type **Front Range Action Sports** and then press Enter. In cell **A2**, type **Sales by State** and then press Enter. Select the range **A1:F1**, and then on the **Home tab**, in the **Alignment group**, click the **Merge & Center** button . In the **Styles group**, click the **Cell Styles** button, and then click **Accent1**. In the **Font group**, click the **Font Size** button , and then click **16**.

9 Select the range **A2:F2**. Using the same technique you just practiced, **Merge & Center** the range, apply the cell style **60% - Accent1**, and then change the **Font Size** to **14**. Compare your screen with Figure 1.10.

Figure 1.10

Column widths adjusted

Titles in rows 1 and 2

Row heights adjusted

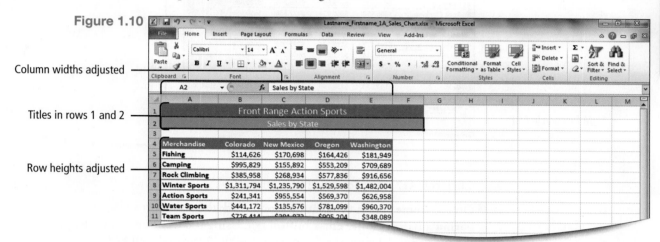

10 Save the Excel workbook.

Activity 1.06 | Using the SUM Function and Fill Handle in Excel

One of Excel's most powerful features is the capability to perform mathematical calculations. In the following activity, you will use the SUM function to add numbers.

1 Click cell **F4**, type **Total Sales** and then press Enter.

2 Verify that **F5** is the active cell. On the **Home tab**, in the **Editing group**, click the **Sum** button Σ and then on the **Formula Bar**, click the **Enter** button ✓ to confirm the entry while keeping cell **F5** the active cell. Using the technique you previously practiced, widen column **F** to **13**

3 In cell **F5**, point to the fill handle to display the + pointer, hold down the left mouse button, and then drag down to cell **F16**. Release the mouse button. In the **Font group**, click the **Increase Font Size** button A, and then compare your screen with Figure 1.11.

Figure 1.11

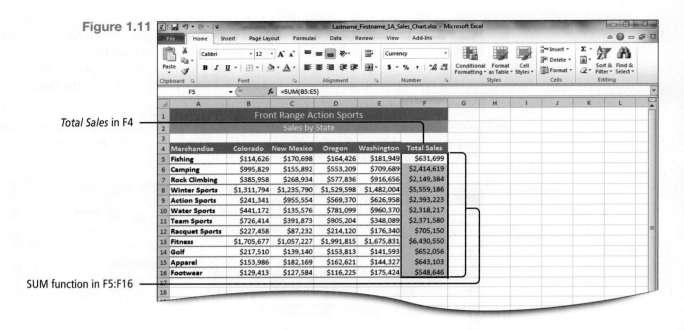

Total Sales in F4

SUM function in F5:F16

4 Click cell **A17**, type **Total** and then press ⟨Tab⟩.

5 On the **Home tab**, in the **Editing group**, click the **Sum** button **Σ** and then on the **Formula Bar**, click the **Enter** button ✓. Using the technique you just practiced, use the fill handle to copy the formula to the right through cell **F17**.

6 Select the range **A5:E16**. In the **Font group**, click the **Border button arrow**, and then click **No Border**. Select the range **B17:F17**, in the **Styles group**, click the **Cell Styles** button, and then under **Titles and Headings**, click **Total**. In the **Font group**, click the **Increase Font Size** button **A**.

7 **Save** 🖫 the Excel workbook.

Objective 3 | Copy and Paste an Excel Chart into Other Programs

When reviewing numbers in an Excel worksheet, sometimes it takes a minute to compare one number to another number. A chart is a visual way to illustrate the Excel data in an understandable manner. After a chart is created in Excel, it can be copied and pasted to other programs.

Activity 1.07 | Creating and Formatting Charts in Excel

In this activity you will create a column chart and a pie chart in Excel.

1 Select the range **A4:E16**. On the **Insert tab**, in the **Charts group**, click the **Column** button. Under **3-D Column**, click the fourth chart—**3-D Column**. On the **Design tab**, in the **Location group**, click the **Move Chart** button. In the **Move Chart** dialog box, click the **New sheet** option button, type **Merchandise Chart** and then click **OK**.

A 3-D column chart is created and moved to a new chart sheet named Merchandise Chart.

2 Click the **Layout tab**. In the **Labels group**, click the **Chart Title** button, and then click **Above Chart**. Type **Retail Sales by State** and then press ⟨Enter⟩.

3 In the **Labels group**, click the **Legend** button, and then click **Show Legend at Top**. Compare your screen with Figure 1.12.

Figure 1.12

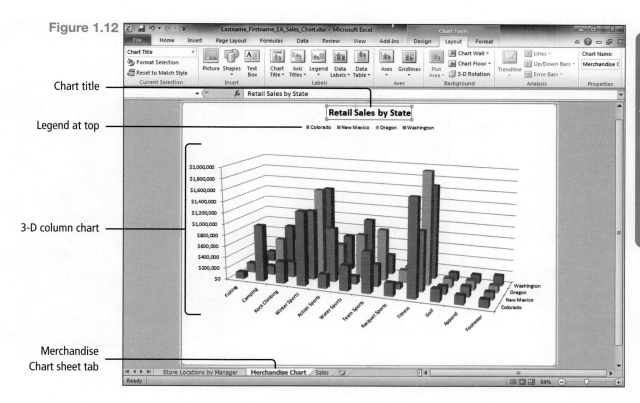

Chart title

Legend at top

3-D column chart

Merchandise
Chart sheet tab

4 Click the **Sales** worksheet tab. Select the range **B4:E4**, hold down Ctrl, and then select the range **B17:E17**.

The range B4:E4 and the range B17:E17 are selected. Recall that holding down Ctrl enables you to select nonadjacent cells.

5 On the **Insert tab**, in the **Charts group**, click the **Pie** button, and then under **3-D Pie**, click **Pie in 3-D**. On the **Design tab**, in the **Location group**, click the **Move Chart** button. In the **Move Chart** dialog box, click the **New sheet** option button, type **State Sales Chart** and then click **OK**.

6 On the **Design tab**, in the **Chart Layouts group**, click the **More** button ⊡ , and then click **Layout 5**. On the chart, click the **Chart Title**, type **State Sales** and then click outside of the title.

7 On the **Layout tab**, in the **Labels group**, click the **Data Labels** button, and then click **More Data Label Options**. In the **Format Data Labels** dialog box, under **Label Contains**, verify the **Category Name** check box is selected, select the **Percentage** check box, and clear any other check boxes. Under **Label Position**, verify that the **Best Fit** option button is selected and then click **Close**. With the data labels still selected, on the **Home tab**, in the **Font group**, click the **Font Size** button ⊡ , and then click **14**.

8 On the **Layout tab**, in the **Current Selection group**, click the **Chart Elements arrow**, and then from the displayed list, click **Chart Area**. In the **Current Selection group**, click the **Format Selection** button. In the **Format Chart Area** dialog box, click the **Gradient fill** option button. Click **Close**, and then compare your screen with Figure 1.13.

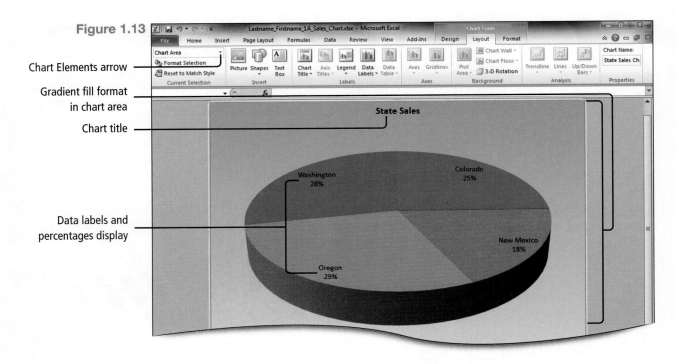

Figure 1.13

Chart Elements arrow

Gradient fill format in chart area

Chart title

Data labels and percentages display

9 Press Ctrl, and then click the **Merchandise Chart** sheet tab.

With both chart sheets selected, the footer will be inserted on both sheets.

10 On the **Insert tab**, in the **Text group**, click the **Header & Footer** button. In the **Page Setup** dialog box, click the **Custom Footer** button. In the **Footer** dialog box, verify that the insertion point is in the *Left section*, and then click the **Insert File Name** button 📖. In the **Footer** dialog box, click **OK**, and then in the **Page Setup** dialog box, click **OK**.

11 Click the **Sales** worksheet tab to make it the active worksheet and to deselect the chart sheets. Press Ctrl, and then click the **Store Locations by Manager** worksheet tab.

Footers are inserted differently in worksheets and in chart sheets.

Both worksheets are selected and the footer will be inserted on both worksheets.

12 On the **Insert tab**, in the **Text group**, click the **Header & Footer** button. On the **Design tab**, in the **Navigation group**, click the **Go to Footer** button. In the **Footer** area, click just above the word *Footer*, and then in the **Header & Footer Elements group**, click the **File Name** button. Click any cell in the workbook to exit the footer. On the status bar, click the **Normal** button 🏢 to return to **Normal** view.

13 Press Ctrl + Home to display the top of the worksheet. Right-click a sheet tab, and then click Ungroup Sheets.

14 **Save** 💾 the Excel workbook.

Activity 1.08 | Copying and Pasting an Excel Chart into Word

1 On the **Home tab**, in the **Clipboard group**, click the **Dialog Box Launcher** 🔲 to display the Clipboard. Click the **State Sales Chart** sheet tab, and then click the border of the pie chart to select the chart. On the **Home tab** in the **Clipboard group**, click the **Copy** button 📋.

2 Click the **Merchandise Chart** sheet tab, and then click the border of the column chart to select the chart. In the **Clipboard group**, click the **Copy** button 📋.

3 At the bottom of the screen, on the taskbar, click the **Word** icon. Press Ctrl + End to move the insertion point to the end of the document.

4 On the **Insert tab**, in the **Pages group**, click the **Page Break** button.

A new blank page 2 is inserted.

5 Type **Each of our State Managers can see their sales results on the following chart.** Press Enter two times.

6 On the **Home tab**, in the **Clipboard group**, click the **Dialog Box Launcher** 🖫 to display the Clipboard task pane, as shown in Figure 1.14.

Figure 1.14

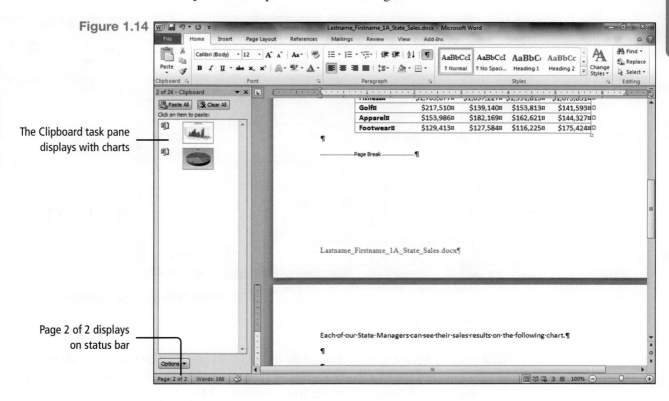

The Clipboard task pane displays with charts

Page 2 of 2 displays on status bar

7 In the **Clipboard** task pane, click the **column chart**.

The column chart is pasted into the Word document.

8 **Close** 🗙 the **Clipboard** task pane.

9 Click the chart and then click the **Layout tab**. In the **Background group**, click the **3-D Rotation** button. In the **Format Chart Area** dialog box, under **Chart Scale**, change the **Depth (% of base)** to **160** and then click **Close**.

All four state names display on the chart.

10 **Save** 🖫 the Word document. **Print** or submit your file electronically as directed by your instructor.

11 **Close** 🗙 the Word document, and then **Exit** Word.

Activity 1.09 | Pasting an Excel Chart in PowerPoint

1 **Start** PowerPoint. Navigate to the student data files and open the presentation **i01A_Sales_Presentation**. Click the **File tab** to display **Backstage** view, and then click **Save As**. Navigate to the **Integrated Projects** folder, and then **Save** the presentation as **Lastname_Firstname_1A_Sales_Presentation**

2 On the **Insert tab**, in the **Text group**, click the **Header & Footer** button. In the displayed **Header and Footer** dialog box, click the **Notes and Handouts** tab. Select the **Footer** check box, type **Lastname_Firstname_1A_Sales_Presentation** and then compare your screen with Figure 1.15.

Figure 1.15

Notes and Handouts tab

Footer checkbox

Footer

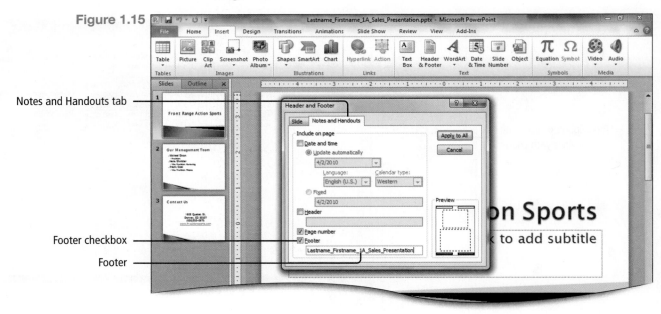

3 Click the **Apply to All** button.

4 Display **Slide 2**. On the **Home tab**, in the **Slides group**, click the **New Slide button arrow**, and then from the displayed gallery, click **Blank**. On the **Design tab**, in the **Background group**, select the **Hide Background Graphics** check box. Compare your screen with Figure 1.16.

A new blank Slide 3 is inserted into the presentation, and the background graphics do not display.

Figure 1.16

Hide Background
Graphics check box

Slide 3

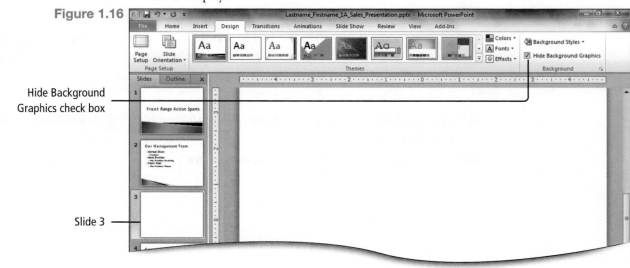

5 On the **Home tab**, in the **Clipboard group**, click the **Dialog Box Launcher** 🔲 . In the **Clipboard** task pane, click the column chart.

The column chart is pasted into Slide 3 of the presentation.

6 Click the chart and then click the **Layout tab**. In the **Background group**, click the **3-D Rotation** button. In the **Format Chart Area** dialog box, under **Chart Scale**, change the **Depth (% of base)** to **160** and then click **Close**.

7 On the **Home tab**, in the **Slides group**, click the **New Slide button arrow**, and from the displayed gallery, click **Blank**. Using the technique you just practiced, select the **Hide Background Graphics** check box. In the **Clipboard** task pane, click the pie chart. Compare your screen with Figure 1.17.

Figure 1.17

Pie chart in Slide 4

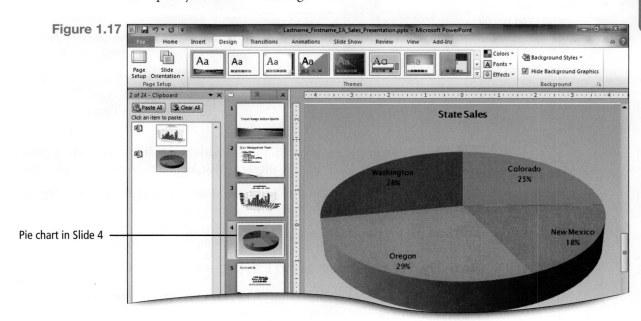

8 **Close** ⊠ the **Clipboard** task pane, and then **Save** 🔲 the presentation.

Objective 4 | Copy and Paste an Object from PowerPoint into Excel

In PowerPoint, bullet points can be converted into a SmartArt graphic to illustrate your message visually. After you have created a SmartArt graphic in PowerPoint, you can copy the graphic and paste it into another program. This saves you the time of recreating the graphic.

Activity 1.10 | Inserting a SmartArt Graphic

1 Make **Slide 2** the active slide. In **Slide 2**, click the placeholder containing the names of the managers. On the **Home tab**, in the **Paragraph group**, click the **Convert to SmartArt** button 📊 . In the displayed gallery, click **Chevron List**.

Notice on the Ribbon that there are now two Design tabs. The active tab is the Design tab to the right—the SmartArt Tools Design contextual tab is used to format the SmartArt graphic.

2 On the **Design tab**, in the **SmartArt Styles group**, click the **More** button 🔽 , and then under **3-D**, click **Metallic Scene**. Click on a blank area of the slide to deselect the SmartArt graphic, and then compare your screen with Figure 1.18.

Figure 1.18

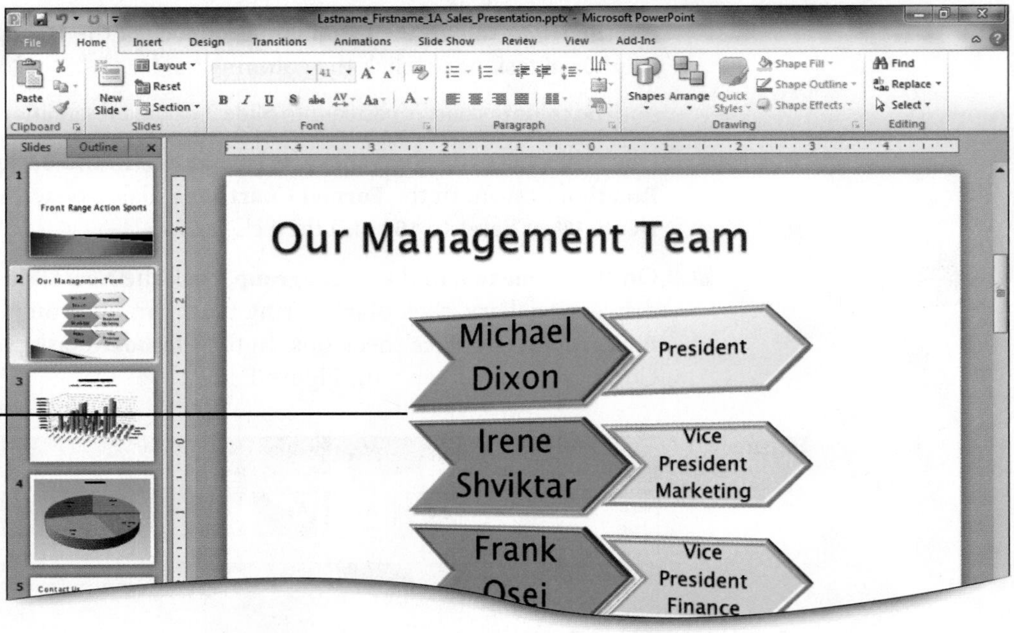

Bullet points converted to SmartArt graphic

3 Click the **SmartArt** graphic. On the **Animations tab**, in the **Animation group**, click the **More** button ▾. From the displayed list, under **Entrance**, click **Float In**.

4 On the **Slide Show tab**, in the **Start Slide Show group**, click the **From Beginning** button to view the presentation. Press Enter to view each slide and to return to **Normal** view.

5 Save ▦ the presentation.

Activity 1.11 | Copying and Pasting a SmartArt Graphic

After you create an object in one program, you can copy and paste the object into a different program. In this activity, you will copy a SmartArt graphic in PowerPoint and paste it into an Excel workbook.

1 Click the border of the SmartArt graphic.

By clicking the border of an object, you select the entire object, not just a part of the object.

2 On the **Home tab**, in the **Clipboard group**, click the **Copy** button ▣.

3 On the taskbar, click the Excel icon. Click the **Sales** worksheet tab, and then click cell **A20**. On the **Home tab**, in the **Clipboard group**, click the **Paste** button.

The SmartArt graphic is pasted into the Sales worksheet. The top left corner of the graphic is in cell A20.

4 Scroll down to view the graphic. On the **Format tab**, click the **Size** button. Click in the **Height** box, type **4** click in the **Width** box, type **5.5** and then press Enter. Compare your screen with Figure 1.19.

Figure 1.19

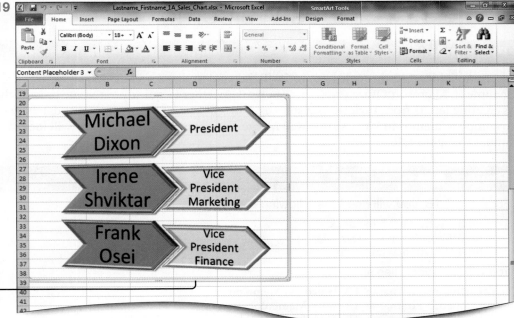

SmartArt graphic pasted
in Sales worksheet

5 **Save** 🔲 the Excel workbook.

6 Click the **File tab** to display **Backstage** view, and then click the **Print tab**. In the **Print** page, under **Settings**, click **Print Active Sheets**, and then click **Print Entire Workbook**. If you are directed by your instructor to print, click the **Print** button. To submit electronically, use the process provided by your instructor.

7 **Close** ❎ the Excel workbook, and then **Exit** Excel.

8 In PowerPoint, click the **File tab** to display **Backstage** view, and then click the **Print tab**. On the **Print** page, under **Settings**, click **Full Page Slides**. Under **Handouts** , click **6 Slides Vertical**. If you are directed by your instructor to print, click the **Print** button. To submit electronically, use the process provided by your instructor.

9 **Close** ❎ the PowerPoint presentation, and then **Exit** PowerPoint.

End **You have completed Project 1A** _____

Project 1B Taos Welcome

In Activities 1.12 through 1.18, you will link and update Excel data in a Word document. Microsoft Office programs can work together to quickly automate tasks such as creating letters from various data sources. You will use data from an Access database to complete memos in Word using Mail Merge. Your completed documents will look similar to Figure 1.20.

For Project 1B, you will need the following files:

> i01B_Welcome_Memo.docx
> i01B_Taos_Inventory.xlsx
> i01B_All_Associates.accdb

You will save your files as:

> Lastname_Firstname_1B_Welcome_Memo.docx
> Lastname_Firstname_1B_Taos_Memo.docx
> Lastname_Firstname_1B_Taos_Inventory.xlsx
> Lastname_Firstname_1B_All_Associates.accdb
> Lastname_Firstname_1B_Store_Location.rtf

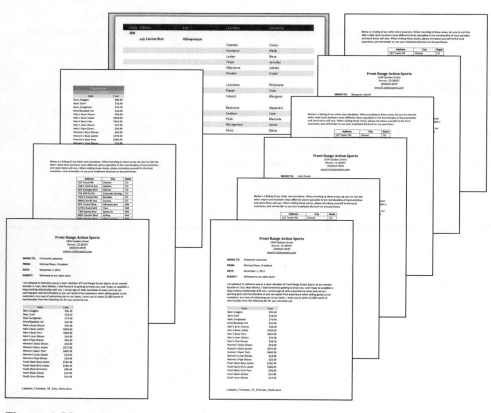

Figure 1.20
Project 1B Taos Welcome

Objective 5 | Link Excel Data to a Word Document

By using the linking tools in Office, you can refer to the contents of an Excel worksheet within a Word document. Changes you make in the Excel data will be updated in the linked Word document. If you link an Excel chart into a Word document, changes made in the Excel workbook will be shown in the chart in the Word document. Information about links is saved with the Word document. By default, when you open the Word document, Word checks the linked files and prompts you to apply any changes.

Activity 1.12 | Accessing Paste Special

In this activity, you will insert Excel data into a Word document. By selecting options in the Paste Special dialog box, you can link your Word document to the Excel data.

1 **Start** Word. Navigate to the student data files and then open the document **i01B_Welcome_Memo**. **Save** the document in your **Integrated Projects** folder as **Lastname_Firstname_1B_Welcome_Memo** If necessary, display the formatting marks.

2 Click the **Insert tab**, and then in the **Header & Footer group**, click the **Footer** button. At the bottom of the **Footer** gallery, click **Edit Footer**. On the **Design tab**, in the **Insert group**, click the **Quick Parts** button, and then click **Field**. In the **Field** dialog box, under **Field names**, locate and click **FileName**, and then click **OK**. In the **Close group**, click the **Close Header and Footer** button.

3 **Start** Excel. Navigate to the student data files, and then open the Excel workbook **i01B_Taos_Inventory**. **Save** the workbook in your **Integrated Projects** folder as **Lastname_Firstname_1B_Taos_Inventory**

4 On the **Insert tab**, in the **Text group**, click the **Header & Footer** button. On the **Design tab**, in the **Navigation group**, click the **Go to Footer** button. In the **Footer** area, click just above the word *Footer*, and then in the **Header & Footer Elements group**, click the **File Name** button. Click any cell in the workbook to exit the footer. On the status bar, click the **Normal** button.

5 Press Ctrl + Home to display the top of the worksheet, and then **Save** the Excel workbook.

6 Select the range **A3:B22**. On the **Home tab** in the **Clipboard group**, click the **Copy** button.

7 On the taskbar, click the **Word** icon. In the Word document, click the blank line below the paragraph that begins *I am pleased to welcome you.*

8 On the **Home tab**, in the **Clipboard group**, click the **Paste button arrow**, and then click **Paste Special**. In the **Paste Special** dialog box, click the **Paste link** option button, and under **As**, click **Microsoft Excel Worksheet Object**, as shown in Figure 1.21.

Figure 1.21

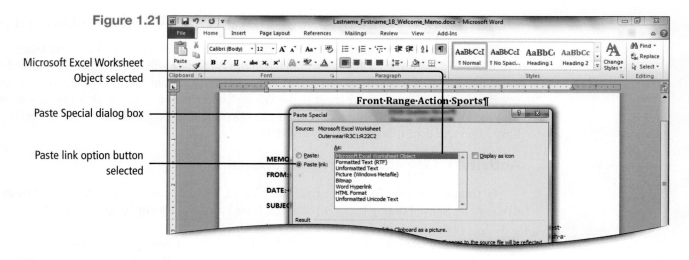

Microsoft Excel Worksheet Object selected

Paste Special dialog box

Paste link option button selected

9 In the **Paste Special** dialog box, click **OK**.

The linked data from Excel is pasted into the Word document.

10 **Save** 🖫, and then **Close** 🗵 the Word document.

Note | Security Notice

From this point forward, when you reopen a Word document that has a link to an external file, a Security Notice will automatically display. The notice will inform you that the file contains links and you have the option of updating the links or not updating them. If you trust the source of the file, you can update links. If you do not know where a file originated, you should cancel the update and investigate where the file came from before continuing.

---

11 In Word, navigate to your **Integrated Projects** folder, and then open the **Lastname_Firstname_1B_Welcome_Memo** document. A message box displays, as shown in Figure 1.22.

The message box informs you that the Word document is linked to another file, and it asks whether you want to update the data in the document.

Figure 1.22

Message box

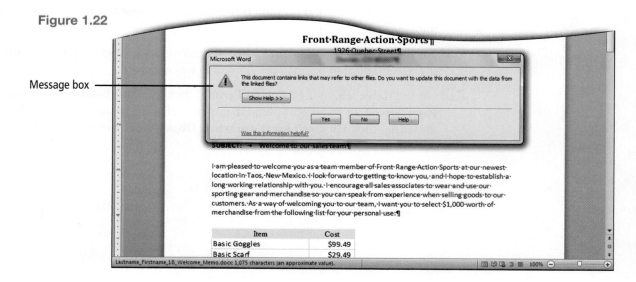

12 In the message box, click **Yes**.

The linked information has been updated.

Objective 6 | Modify Linked Data and Update Links

It is common to make changes to your data after you have completed your documents. You can modify the data in the source file and all linked data to that source file will be updated.

Activity 1.13 | Updating the Linked Data

In the following activity, you will update the Excel data, and then verify that the updated data displays in the Word document.

1 Double-click the pasted data in the Word document to access the Excel source file.

Excel becomes the active window.

2 If necessary, maximize the Excel worksheet, and then press Esc to cancel the copy. Click cell **B9**, type **389.99** and then press Enter. Click cell **B14**, type **379.99** and then press Enter.

3 Save 🔲 the Excel workbook.

4 On the taskbar, click the **Word** icon. Notice the updates made to the Excel data are reflected in the linked Word document, as shown in Figure 1.23.

> **Alert! | What If the Data Is Not Updated?**
>
> If you do not see the new numbers in the Word document, click one time in the data to select it, and then press F9 to update the Excel data.

Figure 1.23

Updated data in the Word document

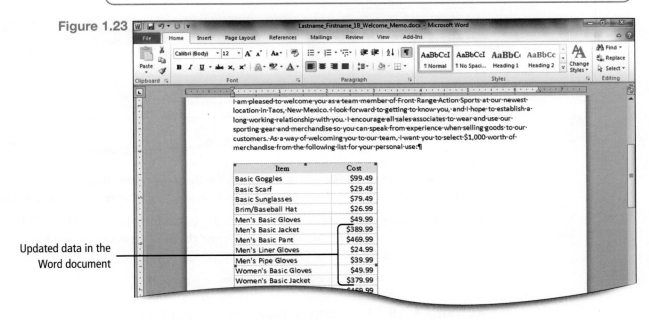

5 Save 🔲 the Word document.

6 On the taskbar, click the **Excel** icon. **Print** or submit the workbook electronically as directed by your instructor.

7 Close ⊠ the Excel workbook, and then **Exit** Excel.

Objective 7 | Create a Table in Word from Access Data

Exporting is a way to output Access data to another database, worksheet, or file format so another database or program can use the data. Exporting is similar to copying and pasting. You can export large amounts of data without having to select the data to copy it. If your data is up-to-date in an Access database, you can export an Access table to Word instead of retyping the information. Exporting saves you time and will reduce the number of errors.

Activity 1.14 | Exporting an Access Table to an RTF File

1 **Start** Access. Navigate to the student data files and then open the Access database **i01B_All_Associates**. Click the **File tab** to display **Backstage** view, and then click **Save Database As**.

2 In the **Save As** dialog box, navigate to your **Integrated Projects** folder, and then **Save** the database as **Lastname_Firstname_1B_All_Associates** If the Security Warning message displays, click the Enable Content button.

3 In the **navigation pane**, click the **Store Location** table to select the table. On the **External Data tab**, in the **Export group**, click the **More** button, and then click **Word**. Compare your screen with Figure 1.24.

> The Export - RTF File dialog box displays. You can click the Browse button to determine the location where the new file will be saved.

Figure 1.24

More button

Export – RTF File dialog box

Browse button

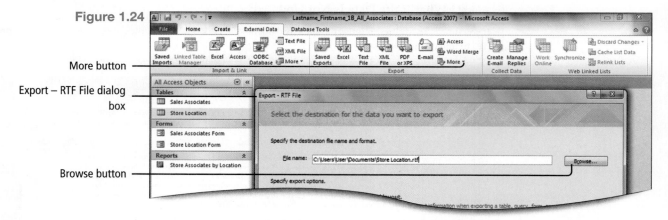

4 In the **Export – RTF File** dialog box, click the **Browse** button, and then navigate to your **Integrated Projects** folder. Save the file as **Lastname_Firstname_1B_Store_Location**

5 In the **Export – RTF File** dialog box, click the **OK** button. In the next dialog box, when asked, *Do you want to save these export steps?* the **Save export steps** check box should not be selected. Click the **Close** button.

> The Access table is saved as a rich text file.

Activity 1.15 | Inserting Access Data into a Word Document

1 On the taskbar, click the **Word** icon. Press [Ctrl]+[End] to move to the end of the document.

2 On the **Insert tab**, in the **Text group**, click the **Object button arrow**, and then click **Text from File**. In the **Insert File** dialog box, navigate to the **Integrated Projects** folder, click the file name **Lastname_Firstname_1B_Store_Location**, and then click **Insert**. Compare your screen with Figure 1.25.

Figure 1.25

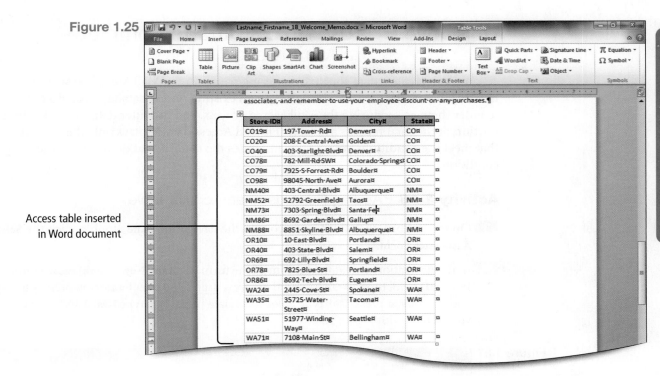

Access table inserted
in Word document

3 In the inserted table, click in the first cell, **Store ID,** to make the cell the active cell. On the **Design tab**, in the **Table Styles group**, click the **More** button ⊽ , and then click **Light List - Accent 4**.

4 On the **Layout tab**, in the **Rows & Columns group**, click the **Delete** button, and then click **Delete Columns** to delete the Store ID column.

5 In the **Cell Size group**, click the **AutoFit** button, and then click **AutoFit Contents**.

The columns are automatically resized to fit the contents of the cells.

6 In the **Table group**, click the **Properties** button, and then click **Center**. Click **OK**, and then compare your screen with Figure 1.26.

The table is centered horizontally on the page.

Figure 1.26

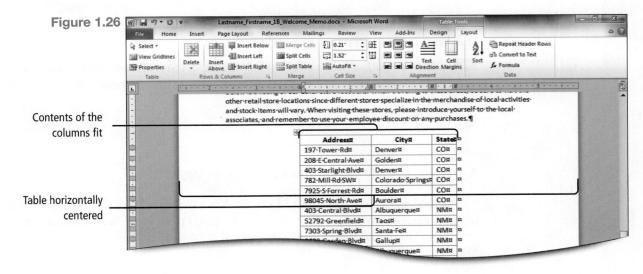

Contents of the
columns fit

Table horizontally
centered

7 **Save** 🖫 the Word document.

Objective 8 | Use Access Data to Complete a Mail Merge in Word

You can create a data source by entering names in the Mail Merge Wizard in Word, however, if you already have the names in an existing Access database, you do not need to enter them again during the Mail Merge process. You can filter data to quickly find a portion of the total records available. Filtered Access data displays only the records that meet the conditions you specify and hides the records that do not meet the conditions.

Activity 1.16 | Adding Records to an Access Table

1 On the taskbar, click the **Access** icon. In the **navigation pane**, double-click the **Sales Associates Form**.

2 In the navigation area at the bottom of the form, click the **New (blank) record** button ▶. In the **ID** field, type **10-60531** and then press Tab. Type your **Firstname** press Tab, type your **Lastname** press Tab, type **Sales Associate** press Tab, type **NM52** and then compare your screen with Figure 1.27.

Figure 1.27

Sales Associates Form

Completed form

3 Press Tab to accept your record.

4 In the **navigation pane**, double-click the report **Store Associates by Location**. Scroll through the report and verify that your name displays under **NM** for the **Taos** location.

5 **Exit** Access.

Activity 1.17 | Starting Mail Merge in Word

Mail Merge can be used to add placeholders for inserting a data field into a document to make each document unique. In the following activity, you will start the mail merge process in Word and filter the Access records.

1 Make the **Word** document active.

2 On the **Mailings tab**, in the **Start Mail Merge group**, click the **Select Recipients** button, and then click **Use Existing List**.

3 In the **Select Data Source** dialog box, navigate to your **Integrated Projects** folder, select the **Lastname_Firstname_1B_All_Associates** database, and then click **Open** to display the **Select Table** dialog box. Compare your screen with Figure 1.28.

> The Access database contains more than one table. You need to select which table will be used for the mail merge.

Figure 1.28

Select Table dialog box

List of Access tables

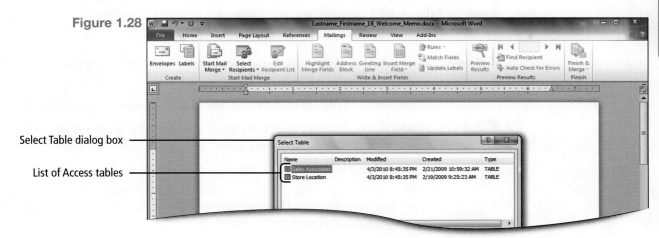

4 In the **Select Table** dialog box, verify that **Sales Associates** is selected, and then click **OK**.

5 In the **Start Mail Merge group**, click the **Edit Recipient List** button.

> You can add or edit fields in the Mail Merge Recipients dialog box.

6 In the **Mail Merge Recipients** dialog box, under **Refine recipient list**, click **Filter**.

7 In the **Filter and Sort** dialog box, click the **Field arrow**, and then click **Store ID**. Under **Comparison**, verify that **Equal to** is selected. In the **Compare to** box, type **NM52** and then compare your screen with Figure 1.29.

> You can filter on any of the fields.

Figure 1.29

NM52

Equal to

Store ID field

Filter and Sort dialog box

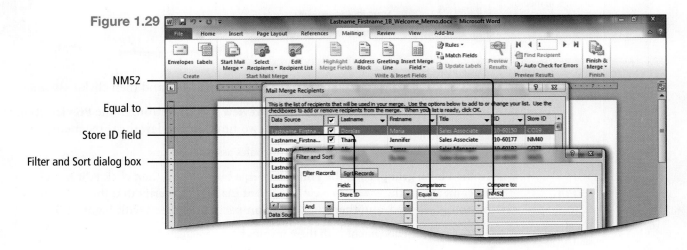

8 At the bottom of the **Filter and Sort** dialog box, click **OK**.

The three Taos records—including your record—display.

9 In the **Mail Merge Recipients** dialog box, click **OK**.

Activity 1.18 | Adding Merge Fields

You will add merge fields as placeholders in the Word document for the information that will be inserted from the Access database. The Mail Merge process includes the data source and the main document, and it will create a new Word document that contains the finished memos.

1 Scroll to the top of the Word document, and then click to place the insertion point after the heading *MEMO TO*.

This is the location in the memo where the sales associate names will be inserted.

2 On the **Mailings tab**, in the **Write & Insert Fields group**, click the **Insert Merge Field button arrow**, and then click **Firstname**. Compare your screen with Figure 1.30.

The Firstname field is inserted in the memo.

When you insert a mail merge field into the main document, the field name is always surrounded by chevrons (« »). These chevrons help distinguish the fields in the main document and will not display on the final document.

Figure 1.30

Insert Merge Field button

Firstname field displays in memo

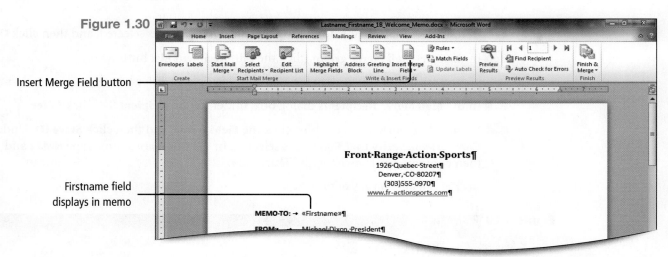

3 Press Spacebar. Click the **Insert Merge Field button arrow**, and then click **Lastname**.

4 In the **Preview Results group**, click the **Preview Results** button. In the **Preview Results group**, click the **Next Record** button ▶ two times to preview the three memos.

The memos are the same except for the sales associate's name.

5 In the **Finish group**, click the **Finish & Merge** button, and then click **Edit Individual Documents**. In the **Merge to New Document** dialog box, verify that the **All** option button is selected, and then click **OK**. Compare your screen with Figure 1.31.

A new Word document with three memos has been created.

Figure 1.31

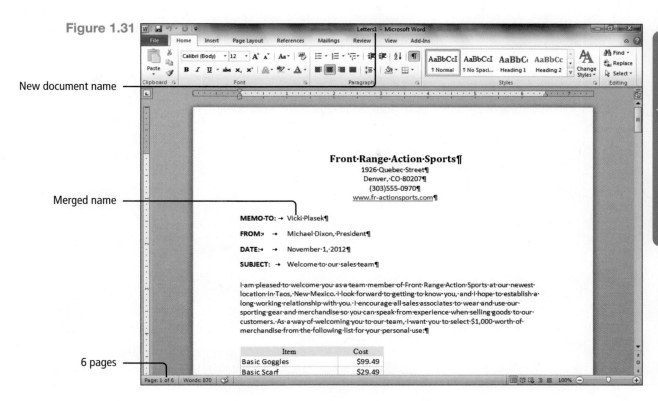

New document name

Merged name

6 pages

6 **Save** the new merged document in the **Integrated Projects** folder with the file name **Lastname_Firstname_1B_Taos_Memo**

7 Click the **Insert tab**. In the **Header & Footer group**, click the **Footer** button, and then click **Remove Footer**. Click the **Footer** button again, and then click **Edit Footer**. On the **Design tab**, in the **Insert group**, click the **Quick Parts** button, and then click **Field**. In the **Field** dialog box, under **Field names**, locate and click **FileName**, and then click **OK**. In the **Close group**, click the **Close Header and Footer** button.

8 **Save** 🖫 the Word document.

9 **Print** or submit your Word documents electronically as directed by your instructor.

10 **Close** ❌ the Word documents, and then **Exit** Word.

End **You have completed Project 1B** _____

Glossary

3-D The shortened term for *three-dimensional*, which refers to an image that appears to have all three spatial dimensions—length, width, and depth.

Absolute cell reference A cell reference that refers to cells by their fixed position in a worksheet; an absolute cell reference remains the same when the formula is copied.

Accounting Number Format The Excel number format that applies a thousand comma separator where appropriate, inserts a fixed U.S. Dollar sign aligned at the left edge of the cell, applies two decimal places, and leaves a small amount of space at the right edge of the cell to accommodate a parenthesis for negative numbers.

Active cell The cell, surrounded by a black border, ready to receive data or be affected by the next Excel command.

Address bar The bar at the top of a folder window with which you can navigate to a different folder or library, or go back to a previous one.

After Previous An animation command that begins the animation sequence for the selected PowerPoint slide element immediately after the completion of the previous animation or slide transition.

Aggregate functions Calculations such as MIN, MAX, AVG, and SUM that are performed on a group of records.

Alignment The placement of paragraph text relative to the left and right margins.

All Programs An area of the Start menu that displays all the available programs on your computer system.

American Psychological Association (APA) One of two commonly used style guides for formatting research papers.

Anchor The symbol that indicates to which paragraph an object is attached.

AND condition A condition in which only records where all of the values are present in the selected fields.

Animation A visual or sound effect added to an object or text on a slide.

Animation Painter A feature that copies animation settings from one object to another.

Append To add on to the end of an object; for example, to add records to the end of an existing table.

Application Another term for a program.

Arguments The values that an Excel function uses to perform calculations or operations.

Arithmetic operators The symbols +, −, *, /, %, and ^ used to denote addition, subtraction (or negation), multiplication, division, percentage, and exponentiation in an Excel formula.

Artistic effects Formats applied to images that make pictures resemble sketches or paintings.

Ascending order A sorting order that arranges text in alphabetical order (A to Z) or numbers from the lowest to highest number.

Auto Fill An Excel feature that generates and extends values into adjacent cells based on the values of selected cells.

AutoComplete (Excel) A feature that speeds your typing and lessens the likelihood of errors; if the first few characters you type in a cell match an existing entry in the column, Excel fills in the remaining characters for you.

AutoCorrect A feature that corrects common spelling errors as you type, for example, changing *teh* to *the*.

AutoFit An Excel feature that adjusts the width of a column to fit the cell content of the widest cell in the column.

AutoNumber data type A data type that describes a unique sequential or random number assigned by Access as each record is entered and that is useful for data that has no distinct field that can be considered unique.

AutoPlay A Windows feature that displays when you insert a CD, a DVD, or other removable device, and which lets you choose which program to use to start different kinds of media, such as music CDs, or CDs and DVDs containing photos.

AutoSum Another name for the *SUM* function.

AVERAGE function An Excel function that adds a group of values, and then divides the result by the number of values in the group.

Axis A line that serves as a frame of reference for measurement and which borders the chart plot area.

Back and Forward buttons Buttons at the top of a folder window that work in conjunction with the address bar to change folders by going backward or forward one folder at a time.

Background Removal A command that removes unwanted portions of a picture so that the picture does not appear as a self-contained rectangle.

Background style A slide background fill variation that combines theme colors in different intensities or patterns.

Backstage tabs The area along the left side of Backstage view with tabs to display various pages of commands.

Backstage view A centralized space for file management tasks; for example, opening, saving, printing, publishing, or sharing a file. A navigation pane displays along the left side with tabs that group file-related tasks together.

Bar tab stop A vertical bar that displays at a tab stop.

Base The starting point; used in calculating the rate of increase, which is the amount of increase divided by the base.

Best Fit An Access command that adjusts the width of a column to accommodate the column's longest entry.

Between ... And operator A comparison operator that looks for values within a range.

Bevel A shape effect that uses shading and shadows to make the edges of a shape appear to be curved or angled.

Bibliography A list of cited works in a report or research paper also referred to as *Works Cited*, *Sources*, or *References*, depending upon the report style.

Black slide A slide that displays at the end of an electronic slide show indicating that the presentation is over.

Blank database A database that has no data and has no database tools—you must create the data and the tools as you need them.

Blank Report tool An Access tool with which you can create a report from scratch by adding the fields you want in the order in which you want them to display.

Body font A font that is applied to all slide text except titles.

Body The text of a letter.

Bound control A control that retrieves its data from an underlying table or query; a text box control is an example of a bound control.

Bound The term used to describe objects and controls that are based on data that is stored in tables.

Bullets Text symbols such as small circles or check marks that precede each item in a bulleted list.

Bulleted list A list of items with each item introduced by a symbol such as a small circle or check mark, and which is useful when the items in the list can be displayed in any order.

Calculated control A control that contains an expression, often a formula, that uses one or more fields from the underlying table or query.

Calculated field A field that stores the value of a mathematical operation.

Caption A property setting that displays a name for a field in a table, query, form, or report other than that listed as the field name.

Category axis The area along the bottom of a chart that identifies the categories of data; also referred to as the *x-axis*.

Category label A chart element that identifies a category of data.

Category labels The labels that display along the bottom of a chart to identify the categories of data; Excel uses the row titles as the category names.

Cell The intersection of a column and a row.

Cell (Word) The box at the intersection of a row and column in a Word table.

Cell address Another name for a *cell reference*.

Cell content Anything typed into a cell.

Cell reference The identification of a specific cell by its intersecting column letter and row number.

Cell style A defined set of formatting characteristics, such as font, font size, font color, cell borders, and cell shading.

Center alignment An arrangement of text in which the text is centered between the left and right margins.

Center alignment The alignment of text or objects that is centered horizontally between the left and right margin.

Center tab stop A tab stop in which the text centers around the tab stop location.

Chart A graphic representation of numeric data.

Chart (Excel) The graphic representation of data in a worksheet; data presented as a chart is usually easier to understand than a table of numbers.

Chart area The entire chart and all of its elements.

Chart Elements box The box in the Chart Tools tabs from which you can select a chart element so that you can format it.

Chart layout The combination of chart elements that can be displayed in a chart such as a title, legend, labels for the columns, and the table of charted cells.

Chart Layouts gallery A group of predesigned chart layouts that you can apply to an Excel chart.

Chart sheet A workbook sheet that contains only a chart.

Chart style The overall visual look of a chart in terms of its graphic effects, colors, and backgrounds; for example, you can have flat or beveled columns, colors that solid or transparent, and backgrounds that are dark or light.

Chart Styles gallery A group of predesigned chart styles that you can apply to an Excel chart.

Chart types Various chart formats used in a way that is meaningful to the reader; common examples are column charts, pie charts, and line charts.

Citation A note inserted into the text of a research paper that refers the reader to a source in the bibliography.

Click The action of pressing the left button on your mouse pointing device one time.

Clip art Predefined graphics included with Microsoft Office or downloaded from the Web.

Clip A single media file, for example art, sound, animation, or a movie.

Column A vertical group of cells in a worksheet.

Column break indicator A single dotted line with the text *Column Break* that indicates where a manual column break was inserted.

Column chart A chart in which the data is arranged in columns and which is useful for showing data changes over a period of time or for illustrating comparisons among items.

Column chart A type of chart used to compare data.

Column heading The letter that displays at the top of a vertical group of cells in a worksheet; beginning with the first letter of the alphabet, a unique letter or combination of letters identifies each column.

Comma Style The Excel number format that inserts thousand comma separators where appropriate and applies two decimal places; Comma Style also leaves space at the right to accommodate a parenthesis when negative numbers are present.

Command An instruction to a computer program that causes an action to be carried out.

Common dialog boxes The set of dialog boxes that includes Open, Save, and Save As, which are provided by the Windows programming interface, and which display and operate in all of the Office programs in the same manner.

Common field A field in one or more tables that stores the same data.

Comparison operator Symbols that evaluate each value to determine if it is the same (=), greater than (>), less than (<), or in between a range of values as specified by the criteria.

Complimentary closing A parting farewell in a business letter.

Compound criteria Multiple conditions in a query or filter.

Compressed file A file that has been reduced in size and thus takes up less storage space and can be transferred to other computers quickly.

Conditional format A format that changes the appearance of a cell—for example, by adding cell shading or font color—based on a condition; if the condition is true, the cell is formatted based on that condition, and if the condition is false, the cell is *not* formatted.

Constant value Numbers, text, dates, or times of day that you type into a cell.

Content control In a template, an area indicated by placeholder text that can be used to add text, pictures, dates, or lists.

Context sensitive A command associated with activities in which you are engaged; often activated by right-clicking a screen item.

Context sensitive command A command associated with activities in which you are engaged.

Contextual tabs Tabs that are added to the Ribbon automatically when a specific object, such as a picture, is selected, and that contain commands relevant to the selected object.

Control An object on a form or report that displays data, performs actions, and lets you view and work with information.

Control layout The grouped arrangement of controls on a form or report.

Copy A command that duplicates a selection and places it on the Clipboard.

COUNTIF function A statistical function that counts the number of cells within a range that meet the given condition and that has two arguments—the range of cells to check and the criteria.

Criteria (Access) Conditions in a query that identify the specific records for which you are looking.

Criteria (Excel) Conditions that you specify in a logical function.

Crop A command that reduces the size of a picture by removing vertical or horizontal edges.

Crosshair pointer A pointer that indicates that you can draw a shape.

Crosstab query A query that uses an aggregate function for data that can be grouped by two types of information and displays the data in a compact, spreadsheet-like format.

Currency data type An Access data type that describes monetary values and numeric data that can be used in mathematical calculations involving data with one to four decimal places.

Cut A command that removes a selection and places it on the Clipboard.

Data Facts about people, events, things, or ideas.

Data (Excel) Text or numbers in a cell.

Data bar A cell format consisting of a shaded bar that provides a visual cue to the reader about the value of a cell relative to other cells; the length of the bar represents the value in the cell—a longer bar represents a higher value and a shorter bar represents s lower value.

Data entry The action of typing the record data into a database form or table.

Data marker A column, bar, area, dot, pie slice, or other symbol in a chart that represents a single data point; related data points form a data series.

Data point A value that originates in a worksheet cell and that is represented in a chart by a data marker.

Data series Related data points represented by data markers; each data series has a unique color or pattern represented in the chart legend.

Data source (Access) The table or tables from which a form, query, or report retrieves its data.

Data source (Word) A list of variable information, such as names and addresses, that is merged with a main document to create customized form letters or labels.

Data type The characteristic that defines the kind of data that can be entered into a field, such as numbers, text, or dates.

Database management system Database software that controls how related collections of data are stored, organized, retrieved, and secured; also known as a *DBMS*.

Database template A preformatted database designed for a specific purpose.

Database An organized collection of facts about people, events, things, or ideas related to a specific topic or purpose.

Datasheet view The Access view that displays data organized in columns and rows similar to an Excel worksheet.

Date control A control on a form or report that inserts the current date each time the form or report is opened.

Date line The first line in a business letter that contains the current date and that is positioned just below the letterhead if a letterhead is used.

DBMS An acronym for *database management system*.

Decimal tab stop A tab stop in which the text aligns with the decimal point at the tab stop location.

Default The term that refers to the current selection or setting that is automatically used by a computer program unless you specify otherwise.

Descending order A sorting order that arranges text in reverse alphabetical order (Z to A) or numbers from the highest to lowest number.

Deselect The action of canceling the selection of an object or block of text by clicking outside of the selection.

Design grid The lower area of the Query window that displays the design of the query.

Design view An Access view that displays the detailed structure of a query, form, or report; for forms and reports, may be the view in which some tasks must be performed, and only the controls, and not the data, display in this view.

Desktop In Windows, the opening screen that simulates your work area.

Destination table (Access) The table to which you import or append data.

Detail section The section of a form or report that displays the records from the underlying table or query.

Detail sheets The worksheets that contain the details of the information summarized on a summary sheet.

Details pane The area at the bottom of a folder window that displays the most common file properties.

Dialog Box Launcher A small icon that displays to the right of some group names on the Ribbon, and which opens a related dialog box or task pane providing additional options and commands related to that group.

Dialog box A small window that contains options for completing a task.

Displayed value The data that displays in a cell.

Document properties Details about a file that describe or identify it, including the title, author name, subject, and keywords that identify the document's topic or contents; also known as *metadata*.

Dot leader A series of dots preceding a tab that guides the eye across the line.

Double-click The action of clicking the left mouse button two times in rapid succession.

Drag The action of holding down the left mouse button while moving your mouse.

Drag and drop The action of moving a selection by dragging it to a new location.

Drawing objects Graphic objects, such as shapes, diagrams, lines, or circles.

Edit The actions of making changes to text or graphics in an Office file.

Editing The process of modifying a presentation by adding and deleting slides or by changing the contents of individual slides.

Ellipsis A set of three dots indicating incompleteness; when following a command name, indicates that a dialog box will display.

Emphasis effect Animation that emphasizes an object or text that is already displayed.

Enclosures Additional documents included with a business letter.

Endnote In a research paper, a note placed at the end of a document or chapter.

Enhanced ScreenTip A ScreenTip that displays more descriptive text than a normal ScreenTip.

Entrance effect Animation that brings a slide element onto the screen.

Excel table A series of rows and columns that contains related data that is managed independently from the data in other rows and columns in the worksheet.

Exit effect Animation that moves an object or text off the screen.

Expand Formula Bar button An Excel window element with which you can increase the height of the Formula Bar to display lengthy cell content.

Expand horizontal scroll bar button An Excel window element with which you can increase the width of the horizontal scroll bar.

Explode The action of pulling out one or more pie slices from a pie chart for emphasis.

Expression A formula.

Extract To decompress, or pull out, files from a compressed form.

Field A single piece of information that is stored in every record and formatted as a column in a database table.

Field (Word) A placeholder that displays preset content, such as the current date, the file name, a page number, or other stored information.

Field list A list of the field names in a table.

Field properties Characteristics of a field that control how the field displays and how data can be entered in the field.

Fields In a mail merge, the column headings in the data source.

File A collection of information stored on a computer under a single name, for example a Word document or a PowerPoint presentation.

File list In a folder window, the area on the right that displays the contents of the current folder or library.

Fill The inside color of an object.

Fill color The inside color of text or of an object.

Fill handle The small black square in the lower right corner of a selected cell.

Filter The process of displaying only a portion of the data based on matching a specific value to show only the data that meets the criteria that you specify.

Filter by Form An Access command that filters the records in a form based on one or more fields, or based on more than one value in the field.

Filter by Selection An Access command that retrieves only the records that contain the value in the selected field.

Filtering The process of displaying only a portion of the total records (a subset) based on matching a specific value.

Find and replace (Excel) A command that searches the cells in a worksheet—or in a selected range—for matches and then replaces each match with a replacement value of your choice.

First principle of good database design A principle of good database design stating that data is organized in tables so that there is no redundant data.

Flat database A simple database file that is not related or linked to any other collection of data.

Floating object A graphic that can be moved independently of the surrounding text characters.

Folder window In Windows, a window that displays the contents of the current folder, library, or device, and contains helpful parts so that you can navigate.

Folder A container in which you store files.

Font A set of characters with the same design and shape.

Font styles Formatting emphasis such as bold, italic, and underline.

Footer (PowerPoint) Text that displays at the bottom of every slide or that prints at the bottom of a sheet of slide handouts or notes pages.

Footer A reserved area for text or graphics that displays at the bottom of each page in a document.

Footnote In a research paper, a note placed at the bottom of the page.

Foreign key The field that is included in the related table so the field can be joined with the primary key in another table for the purpose of creating a relationship.

Form A database object used to enter data, edit data, or display data from a table or query.

Form (Access) An Access object you can use to enter new records into a table, edit or delete existing records in a table, or display existing records.

Form footer Information at the bottom of the screen in Form view that is printed after the last detail section on the last page.

Form header Information, such as a form's title, that displays at the top of the screen in Form view and is printed at the top of the first page when records are printed as forms.

Form tool The Access tool that creates a form with a single mouse click, which includes all of the fields from the underlying data source (table or query).

Form view The Access view in which you can view the records, but you cannot change the layout or design of the form.

Form Wizard The Access tool that creates a form by asking a series of questions.

Format (Excel) Changing the appearance of cells and worksheet elements to make a worksheet attractive and easy to read.

Format as you type The Excel feature by which a cell takes on the formatting of the number typed into the cell.

Format Painter An Office feature that copies formatting from one selection of text to another.

Formatting The process of establishing the overall appearance of text, graphics, and pages in an Office file—for example, in a Word document.

Formatting (PowerPoint) The process of changing the appearance of the text, layout, and design of a slide.

Formatting marks Characters that display on the screen, but do not print, indicating where the Enter key, the Spacebar, and the Tab key were pressed; also called *nonprinting characters*.

Formula AutoComplete An Excel feature which, after typing an = (equal sign) and the beginning letter or letters of a function name, displays a list of function names that match the typed letter(s).

Formula An equation that performs mathematical calculations on values in a worksheet.

Formula Bar An element in the Excel window that displays the value or formula contained in the active cell; here you can also enter or edit values or formulas.

Freeze Panes A command that enables you to select one or more rows or columns and freeze (lock) them into place; the locked rows and columns become separate panes.

Function A predefined formula—a formula that Excel has already built for you—that performs calculations by using specific values in a particular order or structure.

Fund A sum of money set aside for a specific purpose.

Gallery An Office feature that displays a list of potential results instead of just the command name.

General format The default format that Excel applies to numbers; this format has no specific characteristics—whatever you type in the cell will display, with the exception that trailing zeros to the right of a decimal point will not display.

General fund The term used to describe money set aside for the normal operating activities of a government entity such as a city.

Goal Seek A what-if analysis tool that finds the input needed in one cell to arrive at the desired result in another cell.

Graphics Pictures, clip art images, charts, or drawing objects.

Group footer Information printed at the end of each group of records; used to display summary information for the group.

Group header Information printed at the beginning of each new group of records, for example, the group name.

Group, Sort, and Total pane A pane that displays at the bottom of the screen in which you can control how information is sorted and grouped in a report; provides the most flexibility for adding or modifying groups, sort orders, or totals options on a report.

Groups On the Office Ribbon, the sets of related commands that you might need for a specific type of task.

Hanging indent An indent style in which the first line of a paragraph extends to the left of the remaining lines, and that is commonly used for bibliographic entries.

Header (PowerPoint) Text that prints at the top of each sheet of slide handouts or notes pages.

Header A reserved area for text or graphics that displays at the top of each page in a document.

Headings font The font that is applied to slide titles.

Horizontal window split box (Excel) An Excel window element with which you can split the worksheet into two horizontal views of the same worksheet.

HTML See Hypertext Markup Language (HTML).

Hypertext Markup Language (HTML) The language used to format documents that can be opened using any Web browser.

Icons Pictures that represent a program, a file, a folder, or some other object.

IF function A function that uses a logical test to check whether a condition is met, and then returns one value if true, and another value if false.

Import The process of copying data from another file, such as a Word table or an Excel workbook, into a separate file, such as an Access database.

Info tab The tab in Backstage view that displays information about the current file.

Information Data that is organized in a useful manner.

Inline object An object or graphic inserted in a document that acts like a character in a sentence.

Innermost sort field When sorting on multiple fields in Datasheet view, the field that will be used for the second level of sorting.

Insert Worksheet button Located on the row of sheet tabs, a sheet tab that, when clicked, inserts an additional worksheet into the workbook.

Insertion point A blinking vertical line that indicates where text or graphics will be inserted.

Inside address The name and address of the person receiving the letter; positioned below the date line.

Is Not Null A criteria that searches for fields that are not empty.

Is Null A criteria that searches for fields that are empty.

Join line In the Relationships window, the line joining two tables that visually indicates the related field and the type of relationship.

Justified alignment An arrangement of text in which the text aligns evenly on both the left and right margins.

Keyboard shortcut A combination of two or more keyboard keys, used to perform a task that would otherwise require a mouse.

KeyTips The letter that displays on a command in the Ribbon and that indicates the key you can press to activate the command when keyboard control of the Ribbon is activated.

Label control A control on a form or report that contains descriptive information, typically a field name.

Labels Another name for a text value, and which usually provides information about number values.

Landscape orientation A page orientation in which the paper is wider than it is tall.

Layout The arrangement of elements, such as title and subtitle text, lists, pictures, tables, charts, shapes, and movies, on a PowerPoint slide.

Layout selector A small symbol that displays in the upper left corner of a selected control layout in a form or report that is displayed in Layout view or Design view; used to move an entire group of controls.

Layout view The Access view in which you can make changes to a form or report while the object is running—the data from the underlying data source displays.

Leader characters Characters that form a solid, dotted, or dashed line that fills the space preceding a tab stop.

Left alignment An arrangement of text in which the text aligns at the left margin, leaving the right margin uneven.

Left alignment (Excel) The cell format in which characters align at the left edge of the cell; this is the default for text entries and is an example of formatting information stored in a cell.

Left tab stop A tab stop in which the text is left aligned at the tab stop and extends to the right.

Legend A chart element that identifies the patterns or colors that are assigned to the categories in the chart.

Lettered column headings The area along the top edge of a worksheet that identifies each column with a unique letter or combination of letters.

Letterhead The personal or company information that displays at the top of a letter.

Library In Windows, a collection of items, such as files and folders, assembled from various locations that might be on your computer, an external hard drive, removable media, or someone else's computer.

Line break indicator A small nonprinting bent arrow that displays where a manual line break was inserted.

Line chart A chart type that is useful to display trends over time; time displays along the bottom axis and the data point values are connected with a line.

Line spacing The distance between lines of text in a paragraph.

Link A connection to data in another file.

List level An outline level in a presentation represented by a bullet symbol and identified in a slide by the indentation and the size of the text.

Live Preview A technology that shows the result of applying an editing or formatting change as you point to possible results—*before* you actually apply it.

Location Any disk drive, folder, or other place in which you can store files and folders.

Logical functions A group of functions that test for specific conditions and that typically use conditional tests to determine whether specified conditions are true or false.

Logical operators Operators that combine criteria using AND and OR. With two criteria, AND requires that both conditions be met and OR requires that either condition be met.

Logical test Any value or expression that can be evaluated as being true or false.

Mail merge A Microsoft Word feature that joins a main document and a data source to create customized letters or labels.

Main document In a mail merge, the document that contains the text or formatting that remains constant.

Major unit The value in a chart's value axis that determines the spacing between tick marks and between the gridlines in the plot area.

Manual column break An artificial end to a column to balance columns or to provide space for the insertion of other objects.

Manual line break The action of ending a line, before the normal end of the line, without creating a new paragraph.

Manual page break The action of forcing a page to end and placing subsequent text at the top of the next page.

Margins The space between the text and the top, bottom, left, and right edges of the paper.

MAX function An Excel function that determines the largest value in a selected range of values.

MEDIAN function An Excel function that finds the middle value that has as many values above it in the group as are below it; it differs from AVERAGE in that the result is not affected as much by a single value that is greatly different from the others.

Merge & Center A command that joins selected cells in an Excel worksheet into one larger cell and centers the contents in the new cell.

Message Bar The area directly below the Ribbon that displays information such as security alerts when there is potentially unsafe, active content in an Office 2010 document that you open.

Metadata Details about a file that describe or identify it, including the title, author name, subject, and keywords that identify the document's topic or contents; also known as *document properties*.

Microsoft Access A database program, with which you can collect, track, and report data.

Microsoft Excel A spreadsheet program, with which you calculate and analyze numbers and create charts.

Microsoft InfoPath An Office program that enables you to create forms and gather data.

Microsoft Office 2010 A Microsoft suite of products that includes programs, servers, and services for individuals, small organizations, and large enterprises to perform specific tasks.

Microsoft OneNote An Office program with which you can manage notes that you make at meetings or in classes.

Microsoft Outlook An Office program with which you can manage e-mail and organizational activities.

Microsoft PowerPoint A presentation program, with which you can communicate information with high-impact graphics.

Microsoft Publisher An Office program with which you can create desktop publishing documents such as brochures.

Microsoft SharePoint Workspace An Office program that enables you to share information with others in a team environment.

Microsoft Word A word processing program, also referred to as an authoring program, with which you create and share documents by using its writing tools.

MIN function An Excel function that determines the smallest value in a selected range of values.

Mini toolbar A small toolbar containing frequently used formatting commands that displays as a result of selecting text or objects.

Modern Language Association (MLA) One of two commonly used style guides for formatting research papers.

Multiple Items form A form that enables you to display or enter multiple records in a table.

Name Box An element of the Excel window that displays the name of the selected cell, table, chart, or object.

Nameplate The banner on the front page of a newsletter that identifies the publication; also referred to as a *banner, flag,* or *masthead.*

Navigate The process of exploring within the organizing structure of Windows.

Navigate (Excel) The process of moving within a worksheet or workbook.

Navigation area An area at the bottom of the Access window that indicates the number of records in the table and contains controls (arrows) with which you can navigate among the records.

Navigation Pane (Access) An area of the Access window that displays and organizes the names of the objects in a database; from here, you open objects for use.

Navigation pane (Windows) In a folder window, the area on the left in which you can navigate to, open, and display favorites, libraries, folders, saved searches, and an expandable list of drives.

New from existing The Word command that opens an existing document as a new unnamed document, so that you can use it as a starting point for a new document.

No Spacing style The Word style that inserts *no* extra space following a paragraph and uses single spacing.

Nonprinting characters Characters that display on the screen, but do not print, indicating where the Enter key, the Spacebar, and the Tab key were pressed; also called *formatting marks.*

Normal template The template that serves as a basis for all new Word documents.

Normal view (Excel) A screen view that maximizes the number of cells visible on your screen and keeps the column letters and row numbers close to the columns and rows.

Normal view (PowerPoint) The primary editing view in PowerPoint in which you write and design your presentations; consists of the Notes pane, Slide pane, and the Slides/Outline pane.

Normalization The process of applying design rules and principles to ensure that your database performs as expected.

Note In a research paper, information that expands on the topic, but that does not fit well in the document text.

Notes page A printout that contains the slide image on the top half of the page and notes that you have created on the Notes pane in the lower half of the page.

Notes pane The PowerPoint screen element that displays below the Slide pane with space to type notes regarding the active slide.

NOW function An Excel function that retrieves the date and time from your computer's calendar and clock and inserts the information into the selected cell.

Nudge The action of moving an object on the page in small precise increments.

Number format A specific way in which Excel displays numbers in a cell.

Number values Constant values consisting of only numbers.

Numbered list A list of items in which each item is introduced by a consecutive number to indicate definite steps, a sequence of actions, or chronological order.

Numbered row headings The area along the left edge of a worksheet that identifies each row with a unique number.

Object window An area of the Access window that displays open objects, such as tables, forms, queries, or reports; by default, each object displays on its own tab.

Objects The basic parts of a database that you create to store your data and to work with your data; for example, tables, forms, queries, and reports.

Office Clipboard A temporary storage area that holds text or graphics that you select and then cut or copy.

On Click An animation command that begins the animation sequence for the selected PowerPoint slide element when the mouse button is clicked or the spacebar is pressed.

One-to-many relationship A relationship between two tables where one record in the first table corresponds to many records in the second table—the most common type of relationship in Access.

Open dialog box A dialog box from which you can navigate to, and then open on your screen, an existing file that was created in that same program.

Operators The symbols with which you can specify the type of calculation you want to perform in an Excel formula.

Option button A round button that allows you to make one choice among two or more options.

Options dialog box A dialog box within each Office application where you can select program settings and other options and preferences.

OR condition A condition in which records that match at least one of the specified values are displayed.

Order of operations The mathematical rules for performing multiple calculations within a formula.

Outermost sort field When sorting on multiple fields in Datasheet view, the field that will be used for the first level of sorting.

Page break indicator A dotted line with the text *Page Break* that indicates where a manual page break was inserted.

Page footer Information printed at the end of every page in a report; used to print page numbers or other information that you want to display at the bottom of every report page.

Page header (Access) Information printed at the top of every page of a report.

Page Layout view A screen view in which you can use the rulers to measure the width and height of data, set margins for printing, hide or display the numbered row headings and the lettered column headings, and change the page orientation; this view is useful for preparing your worksheet for printing.

Page number control A control on a form or report that inserts the page numbers when displayed in Print Preview or when printed.

Pane (Excel) A portion of a worksheet window bounded by and separated from other portions by vertical and horizontal bars.

Paragraph symbol The symbol ¶ that represents a paragraph.

Parenthetical citation In the MLA style, a citation that refers to items on the *Works Cited* page, and which is placed in parentheses; the citation includes the last name of the author or authors, and the page number in the referenced source.

Paste The action of placing text or objects that have been copied or moved from one location to another location.

Paste area The target destination for data that has been cut or copied using the Office Clipboard.

Paste Options Icons that provide a Live Preview of the various options for changing the format of a pasted item with a single click.

Paste Options gallery (Excel) A gallery of buttons that provides a Live Preview of all the Paste options available in the current context.

PDF (Portable Document Format) file A file format that creates an image that preserves the look of your file, but that cannot be easily changed; a popular format for sending documents electronically, because the document will display on most computers.

Percent for new value = base percent + percent of increase The formula for calculating a percentage by which a value increases by adding the base percentage—usually 100%—to the percent increase.

Percentage rate of increase The percent by which one number increases over another number.

Picture element A point of light measured in dots per square inch on a screen; 64 pixels equals 8.43 characters, which is the average number of digits that will fit in a cell in an Excel worksheet using the default font.

Picture styles Frames, shapes, shadows, borders, and other special effects that can be added to an image to create an overall visual style for the image.

Pie chart A chart that shows the relationship of each part to a whole.

Pixel The abbreviated name for a *picture element*.

Placeholder text Text in a content control that indicates the type of information to be entered in a specific location.

Placeholder A box on a slide with dotted or dashed borders that holds title and body text or other content such as charts, tables, and pictures.

Plot area The area bounded by the axes of a chart, including all the data series.

Point The action of moving your mouse pointer over something on your screen.

Point and click method The technique of constructing a formula by pointing to and then clicking cells; this method is convenient when the referenced cells are not adjacent to one another.

Pointer Any symbol that displays on your screen in response to moving your mouse.

Points A measurement of the size of a font; there are 72 points in an inch, with 10-12 points being the most commonly used font size.

Populate The action of filling a database table with records.

Portrait orientation A page orientation in which the paper is taller than it is wide.

Preview pane button In a folder window, the button on the toolbar with which you can display a preview of the contents of a file without opening it in a program.

Primary key The field that uniquely identifies a record in a table; for example, a Student ID number at a college.

Print Preview A view of a document as it will appear when you print it.

Print Titles An Excel command that enables you to specify rows and columns to repeat on each printed page.

Program A set of instructions that a computer uses to perform a specific task, such as word processing, accounting, or data management; also called an *application*.

Program-level control buttons In an Office program, the buttons on the right edge of the title bar that minimize, restore, or close the program.

Property Sheet A list of characteristics—properties—for fields or controls on a form or report in which you can make precise changes to each property associated with the field or control.

Protected view A security feature in Office 2010 that protects your computer from malicious files by opening them in a restricted environment until you enable them; you might encounter this feature if you open a file from an e-mail or download files from the Internet.

Pt. The abbreviation for *point*; for example when referring to a font size.

Query A database object that retrieves specific data from one or more database objects—either tables or other queries—and then, in a single datasheet, displays only the data you specify.

Quick Access Toolbar In an Office program, the small row of buttons in the upper left corner of the screen from which you can perform frequently used commands.

Quick Commands The commands Save, Save As, Open, and Close that display at the top of the navigation pane in Backstage view.

Range Two or more selected cells on a worksheet that are adjacent or nonadjacent; because the range is treated as a single unit, you can make the same changes or combination of changes to more than one cell at a time.

Range finder An Excel feature that outlines cells in color to indicate which cells are used in a formula; useful for verifying which cells are referenced in a formula.

Range finder An Excel feature that outlines cells in color to indicate which cells are used in a formula; useful for verifying which cells are referenced in a formula.

Rate = amount of increase/base The mathematical formula to calculate a rate of increase.

Read-Only A property assigned to a file that prevents the file from being modified or deleted; it indicates that you cannot save any changes to the displayed document unless you first save it with a new name.

Reading view A view in PowerPoint that displays a presentation in a manner similar to a slide show but in which the taskbar, title bar, and status bar remain available in the presentation window.

Record selector bar The bar at the left edge of a record when it is displayed in a form, and which is used to select an entire record.

Record All of the categories of data pertaining to one person, place, thing, event, or idea, and which is formatted as a row in a database table.

Record In a mail merge, a row of information that contains data for one person.

Record selector box The small box at the left of a record in Datasheet view that, when clicked, selects the entire record.

Record source The tables or queries that provide the underlying data for a form or report.

Redundant In a database, information that is repeated in a manner that indicates poor database design.

Referential integrity A set of rules that Access uses to ensure that the data between related tables is valid.

Relational database A sophisticated type of database that has multiple collections of data within the file that are related to one another.

Relationship An association that you establish between two tables based on common fields.

Relative cell reference In a formula, the address of a cell based on the relative position of the cell that contains the formula and the cell referred to.

Report A database object that summarizes the fields and records from a table or query in an easy-to-read format suitable for printing.

Report footer Information printed once at the end of a report; used to print report totals or other summary information for the entire report.

Report header Information printed once at the beginning of a report; used for logos, titles, and dates.

Report tool The Access tool that creates a report with one mouse click, which displays all of the fields and records from the record source that you select—a quick way to look at the underlying data.

Report Wizard An Access feature with which you can create a report by answering a series of questions; Access designs the report based on your answers.

Ribbon The user interface in Office 2010 that groups the commands for performing related tasks on tabs across the upper portion of the program window.

Ribbon tabs The tabs on the Office Ribbon that display the names of the task-oriented groups of commands.

Right alignment An arrangement of text in which the text aligns at the right margin, leaving the left margin uneven.

Right tab stop A tab stop in which the text is right aligned at the tab stop and extends to the left.

Right-click The action of clicking the right mouse button one time.

Rotation handle A green circle that provides a way to rotate a selected image.

Rounding A procedure in which you determine which digit at the right of the number will be the last digit displayed and then increase it by one if the next digit to its right is 5, 6, 7, 8, or 9.

Row A horizontal group of cells in a worksheet.

Row heading The numbers along the left side of an Excel worksheet that designate the row numbers.

Ruler guides Dotted vertical and horizontal lines that display in the rulers indicating the pointer's position.

Run The process in which Access searches the records in the table(s) included in the query design, finds the records that match the specified criteria, and then displays the records in a datasheet; only the fields that have been included in the query design display.

Salutation The greeting line of a business letter.

Sans serif A font design with no lines or extensions on the ends of characters.

Scale to Fit Excel commands that enable you to stretch or shrink the width, height, or both, of printed output to fit a maximum number of pages.

Scaling (Excel) The process of shrinking the width and/or height of printed output to fit a maximum number of pages.

Screenshot An image of an active window on your computer that you can paste into a document.

ScreenTip A small box that that displays useful information when you perform various mouse actions such as pointing to screen elements or dragging.

Scroll bar A vertical or horizontal bar in a window or a pane to assist in bringing an area into view, and which contains a scroll box and scroll arrows.

Scroll box The box in the vertical and horizontal scroll bars that can be dragged to reposition the contents of a window or pane on the screen.

Search box In a folder window, the box in which you can type a word or a phrase to look for an item in the current folder or library.

Second principle of good database design A principle stating that appropriate database techniques are used to ensure the accuracy of data entered into a table.

Section A portion of a document that can be formatted differently from the rest of the document.

Section bar A gray bar in a form or report that identifies and separates one section from another; used to select the section and to change the size of the adjacent section.

Section break A double dotted line that indicates the end of one section and the beginning of another section.

Select To highlight, by dragging with your mouse, areas of text or data or graphics, so that the selection can be edited, formatted, copied, or moved.

Select All box A box in the upper left corner of the worksheet grid that, when clicked, selects all the cells in a worksheet.

Select query A type of Access query that retrieves (selects) data from one or more tables or queries, displaying the selected data in a datasheet; also known as a *simple select query*.

Series A group of things that come one after another in succession; for example, January, February, March, and so on.

Serif font A font design that includes small line extensions on the ends of the letters to guide the eye in reading from left to right.

Shapes Lines, arrows, stars, banners, ovals, rectangles, and other basic shapes with which you can illustrate an idea, a process, or a workflow.

Sheet tab scrolling buttons Buttons to the left of the sheet tabs used to display Excel sheet tabs that are not in view; used when there are more sheet tabs than will display in the space provided.

Sheet tabs The labels along the lower border of the Excel window that identify each worksheet.

Shortcut menu A menu that displays commands and options relevant to the selected text or object.

Simple select query Another name for a select query.

Single File Web Page A document saved using HTML and that opens using a Web browser.

Single-record form A form that enables you to display or enter one record at a time in a table.

Sizing handles Small circles and squares that indicate that a picture is selected.

Slide A presentation page that can contain text, pictures, tables, charts, and other multimedia or graphic objects.

Slide handouts Printed images of slides on a sheet of paper.

Slide pane A PowerPoint screen element that displays a large image of the active slide.

Slide Sorter view A presentation view that displays thumbnails of all of the slides in a presentation.

Slide transitions The motion effects that occur in Slide Show view when you move from one slide to the next during a presentation.

Slides/Outline pane A PowerPoint screen element that displays the presentation either in the form of thumbnails (Slides tab) or in outline format (Outline tab).

Small caps A font effect, usually used in titles, that changes lowercase text into capital (uppercase) letters using a reduced font size.

SmartArt graphic A visual representation of information that you can create by choosing from among many different layouts to communicate your message or ideas effectively.

SmartArt Styles Combinations of formatting effects that you can apply to SmartArt graphics.

SmartArt A designer-quality visual representation of your information that you can create by choosing from among many different layouts to effectively communicate your message or ideas.

Sort The process of arranging data in a specific order based on the value in each field.

Source file When importing a file, refers to the file being imported.

Sparkline A tiny chart in the background of a cell that gives a visual trend summary alongside your data; makes a pattern more obvious.

Spin box A small box with an upward- and downward-pointing arrow that lets you move rapidly through a set of values by clicking.

Split button A button divided into two parts and in which clicking the main part of the button performs a command and clicking the arrow opens a menu with choices.

Spreadsheet Another name for a *worksheet*.

Stacked layout A control layout format that is similar to a paper form, with label controls placed to the left of each textbox control. The controls are grouped together for easy editing.

Start button The button on the Windows taskbar that displays the Start menu.

Start menu The Windows menu that provides a list of choices and is the main gateway to your computer's programs, folders, and settings.

Statistical functions Excel functions, including the AVERAGE, MEDIAN, MIN, and MAX functions, which are useful to analyze a group of measurements.

Status bar (Excel) The area along the lower edge of the Excel window that displays, on the left side, the current cell mode, page number, and worksheet information; on the right side, when numerical data is selected, common calculations such as Sum and Average display.

Status bar The area along the lower edge of an Office program window that displays file information on the left and buttons to control how the window looks on the right.

Structure In Access, the underlying design of a table, including field names, data types, descriptions, and field properties.

Style A group of formatting commands, such as font, font size, font color, paragraph alignment, and line spacing that can be applied to a paragraph with one command.

Style (PowerPoint) A collection of formatting options that can be applied to a picture, text, or an object.

Style guide A manual that contains standards for the design and writing of documents.

Subdatasheet A format for displaying related records when you click the plus sign (+) next to a record in a table on the *one* side of a relationship.

Subfolder A folder within a folder.

Subject line The optional line following the inside address in a business letter that states the purpose of the letter.

Subpoints Secondary-level information in a SmartArt graphic.

Subset A portion of the total records available.

SUM function A predefined formula that adds all the numbers in a selected range of cells.

Summary sheet A worksheet where totals from other worksheets are displayed and summarized.

Synonyms Words with the same or similar meaning.

Tab order The order in which the insertion point moves from one field to another in a form when you press the Tab key.

Tab stop Specific locations on a line of text, marked on the Word ruler, to which you can move the insertion point by pressing the Tab key, and which is used to align and indent text.

Table A format for information that organizes and presents text and data in columns and rows.

Table (Access) The database object that stores data organized in an arrangement of columns and rows, and which is the foundation of an Access database.

Table (Word) An arrangement of information organized into rows and columns.

Table area The upper area of the Query window that displays field lists for the tables that are used in the query.

Table style Formatting applied to an entire table so that it is consistent with the presentation theme.

Tables and Related Views An arrangement in the Navigation Pane that groups objects by the table to which they are related.

Tabs On the Office Ribbon, the name of each activity area in the Office Ribbon.

Tags Custom file properties that you create to help find and organize your own files.

Task pane A window within a Microsoft Office application in which you can enter options for completing a command.

Template An existing document that you use as a starting point for a new document; it opens a copy of itself, unnamed, and then you use the structure—and possibly some content, such as headings—as the starting point for the new document.

Text alignment (PowerPoint) The horizontal placement of text within a placeholder.

Text box A movable resizable container for text or graphics.

Text box (PowerPoint) An object within which you can position text anywhere on a slide.

Text box control The graphical object on a form or report that displays the data from the underlying table or query; a text box control is known as a bound control.

Text control A content control that accepts only a text entry.

Text data type An Access data type that describes text, a combination of text and numbers, or numbers that are not used in calculations, such as a number that is an identifier like a Student ID.

Text effects Decorative formats, such as shadowed or mirrored text, text glow, 3-D effects, and colors that make text stand out.

Text string A sequence of characters.

Text values Constant values consisting of only text, and which usually provides information about number values; also referred to as *labels*.

Text wrapping The manner in which text displays around an object.

Theme A predefined format that can be applied to the entire database or to individual objects in the database.

Theme A predesigned set of colors, fonts, lines, and fill effects that look good together and that can be applied to your entire document or to specific items.

Theme (PowerPoint) A set of unified design elements that provides a look for your presentation by applying colors, fonts, and effects.

Theme colors A set of coordinating colors that are applied to the backgrounds, objects, and text in a presentation.

Theme font A theme that determines the font applied to two types of slide text—headings and body.

Thesaurus A research tool that provides a list of synonyms.

Thumbnails (PowerPoint) Miniature images of presentation slides.

Tick marks The short lines that display on an axis at regular intervals.

Timing options Animation options that control when animated items display in the animation sequence.

Title bar The bar at the top edge of the program window that indicates the name of the current file and the program name.

Title slide The first slide in a presentation the purpose of which is to provide an introduction to the presentation topic.

Toggle button A button that can be turned on by clicking it once, and then turned off by clicking it again.

Toolbar In a folder window, a row of buttons with which you can perform common tasks, such as changing the view of your files and folders or burning files to a CD.

Top-level points The main text points in a SmartArt graphic.

Trim The action of deleting parts of a video to make it shorter.

Triple-click The action of clicking the left mouse button three times in rapid succession.

Truncated Refers to data that is cut off or shortened.

Trust Center An area of the Access program where you can view the security and privacy settings for your Access installation.

Trusted Documents A security feature in Office 2010 that remembers which files you have already enabled; you might encounter this feature if you open a file from an e-mail or download files from the Internet.

Unbound control A control that does not have a source of data, such as a title in a form or report.

Underlying formula The formula entered in a cell and visible only on the Formula Bar.

Underlying value The data that displays in the Formula Bar.

USB flash drive A small data storage device that plugs into a computer USB port.

Value Another name for a *constant value*.

Value after increase = base x percent for new value The formula for calculating the value after an increase by multiplying the original value—the base—by the percent for new value (see the *Percent for new value* formula).

Value axis A numerical scale on the left side of a chart that shows the range of numbers for the data points; also referred to as the *y-axis*.

Vertical window split box (Excel) A small box on the vertical scroll bar with which you can split the window into two vertical views of the same worksheet.

Views button In a folder window, a toolbar button with which you can choose how to view the contents of the current location.

Volatile A term used to describe an Excel function that is subject to change each time the workbook is reopened; for example the NOW function updates itself to the current date and time each time the workbook is opened.

What-if analysis The process of changing the values in cells to see how those changes affect the outcome of formulas in a worksheet.

Wildcard character In a query, a character that serves as a placeholder for one or more unknown characters in your criteria; an asterisk (*) represents one or more unknown characters, and a question mark (?) represents a single unknown character.

Window A rectangular area on a computer screen in which programs and content appear, and which can be moved, resized, minimized, or closed.

Windows Explorer The program that displays the files and folders on your computer, and which is at work anytime you are viewing the contents of files and folders in a window.

Windows taskbar The area along the lower edge of the Windows desktop that contains the Start button and an area to display buttons for open programs.

With Previous An animation command that begins the animation sequence on a PowerPoint slide at the same time as the previous animation or slide transition.

Wizard A feature in Microsoft Office that walks you step by step through a process.

WordArt A gallery of text styles with which you can create decorative effects, such as shadowed or mirrored text.

Wordwrap The feature that moves text from the right edge of a paragraph to the beginning of the next line as necessary to fit within the margins.

Workbook An Excel file that contains one or more worksheets.

Workbook-level buttons Buttons at the far right of the Ribbon tabs that minimize or restore a displayed workbook.

Workbook-level buttons Buttons at the far right of the Ribbon tabs that minimize or restore a displayed workbook.

Works Cited In the MLA style, a list of cited works placed at the end of a research paper or report.

Worksheet The primary document that you use in Excel to work with and store data, and which is formatted as a pattern of uniformly spaced horizontal and vertical lines.

Writer's identification The name and title of the author of a letter, placed near the bottom of the letter under the complimentary closing—also referred to as the *writer's signature block*.

Writer's signature block The name and title of the author of a letter, placed near the bottom of the letter, under the complimentary closing—also referred to as the *writer's identification*.

x-axis Another name for the *category axis*.

x-axis Another name for the horizontal *(category) axis*.

y-axis Another name for the *value axis*.

y-axis Another name for the vertical *(value) axis*.

Zoom The action of increasing or decreasing the viewing area on the screen.

Index

H

Hanging Indent tab alignment option, 78
hanging indents, 177
headers, 33
   objects (Access), 441
   presentations
     adding, 638–639
     definition, 638
headings
   column headings (worksheets), 229
   research papers, 166
Headings font, 741
height
   sizing images in presentations, 687–689
   video (presentations), 757
Help, 43–44
hiding
   background graphics, slides, 743–744
   formulas, worksheets, 250–251
Hierarchy SmartArt graphic, 709
Highlight Cells Rules, conditional formatting, 302–303
horizontal rulers (PowerPoint 2010), 688
Horizontal window split box, 229
HTML (Hypertext Markup Language), 139
Hypertext Markup Language (HTML), 139

I

icons, definition, 5
IF function, 300–302
images (presentations). *See also* clip art; graphics; pictures
   moving, 687–689
   sizing, 687–689
importing
   definition, 429
   workbook data into Access tables, 429–431
   worksheets, 435–437
     specifying numeric criteria in a query, 506–507
Increase List Level button, 630
increasing list levels (presentations), 629–630
increasing values, calculating values after increases, 376–377
indentation
   hanging indents, 177
   page breaks, 176
   text in documents, 71–73, 167
Info tab, 14
InfoPath, 7
information, definition, 419
inline objects, 54
innermost sort field, definition, 493
Insert Picture from File button, 634
Insert Worksheet button, 228
inserting
   clip art into newsletters, 184–185
   column breaks into newsletters, 183–184
   columns into worksheets, 262–264
   controls into forms, 565–566
   data by ranges into worksheets, 255–256
   data into worksheets, Auto Fill, 232–233
   dates into worksheets, 315–317
   descriptions into table fields, 433–434
   file names into footers, documents, 62–64
   footers into presentations, 638–639
   footnotes into research papers, 167–169

headers into presentations, 638–639
numbers into worksheets, 234–235
page breaks into documents, 175–176
pictures
   into documents, 54–55
   into presentations from files, 634–636
records into database tables, 427–429, 555–557
rows
   into charts, 381–382
   into tables (presentations), 766
   into tables (documents), 112–113
   into worksheets, 262–264
screenshots into newsletters, 186
shapes
   into documents, 58–59
   into presentations, 692–693
slides into presentations, 627–629, 644–646
SmartArt graphics, 80–81, 817–818
sparklines, 329
speaker notes into presentations, 631
tables
   into databases, 432–442
   into documents, 130
text, 9–11
   into documents, 51–53
   into tables (documents), 108–110
   into worksheets, 230–231
text boxes
   into documents, 58–59
   into presentations, 690–691
text into presentations, 624–625
Total Rows, into tables (worksheets), 807–808
video into presentations, 755–758
WordArt into worksheets, 365
WordArt objects into slides, 707–708
insertion point, 9
inside addresses
   definition, 123
   spacing, 124
Is Not Null criteria (fields), 503–504
Is Null criteria (fields), 503–504

J

join line, definition, 489
justification (text alignment), 68, 183

K

Keep source formatting check box, 645
keyboard keys
   controlling Ribbon, 31–32
   nudging, 57
keyboard shortcuts, 10
   inserting data into worksheets, 230–231
   navigating documents, 38
   navigating worksheets, 233
KeyTips, 31–32

L

labels
   category labels, 243
   charts, presentations, 771
   controls, definition, 561